OFFICIAL BASEBALL GUIDE for 1980

•

PUBLISHER
J. MICHAEL HADLEY

EDITORS
LARRY WIGGE
CARL CLARK
CRAIG CARTER
JOE MARCIN

•

PUBLISHED BY

The Sporting News

1212 North Lindbergh Boulevard
P. O. Box 56
St. Louis, Missouri 63166

Copyright © 1980
The Sporting News Publishing Company
a Times Mirror company

ISBN 0-89204-057-2
ISSN 0078-3838

51

Directory of Organized Baseball

MAJOR LEAGUES

COMMISSIONER—Bowie K. Kuhn
SECRETARY-TREASURER—Alexander H. Hadden
HEADQUARTERS—75 Rockefeller Plaza
New York, N. Y. 10019
Telephone—586-7400 (area code 212)
Teletype—710-581-4279

EXECUTIVE COUNCIL—Bowie K. Kuhn, Commissioner; Leland S. Mac-Phail, Jr., President of American League; Charles S. Feeney, President of National League; John E. Fetzer, Edmund B. Fitzgerald, Ewing Kauffman and Haywood C. Sullivan, representatives of American League, and Robert L. Howsam, Robert A. Lurie, John J. McHale and Peter F. O'Malley, representatives of National League.

EXECUTIVE DIRECTOR OF MARKETING AND BROADCASTING—
C. J. (Tom) Villante
SPECIAL ASSISTANTS TO THE COMMISSIONER—
Joseph L. Reichler, Monte Irvin
DIRECTOR OF INFORMATION—Robert A. Wirz
DIRECTOR OF SECURITY—Henry A. Fitzgibbon
CONTROLLER—Donald C. Marr, Jr.
CO-ORDINATOR OF INTER-AMERICAN BASEBALL
(acting co-ordinator)—Pedro Arias
ASSISTANT TO ADMINISTRATIVE OFFICER—George E. Pfister
ADMINISTRATIVE ASSISTANTS—Harry Simmons, Rick Cunningham
ASSISTANT COUNSEL—Edwin M. Durso
ASSOCIATE DIRECTOR OF INFORMATION, MEDIA—Martin Appel
ASSOCIATE DIRECTOR OF INFORMATION, PUBLICATIONS—Vince Nauss
ASSISTANT DIRECTOR OF SECURITY—Art Fuss
OFFICE MANAGER—Mary Ann Burns
BOOKKEEPER—Rita Datz

NATIONAL ASSOCIATION REPRESENTATIVES—John Johnson, President of the National Association, and members of National Association Executive Committee.

NATIONAL ASSOCIATION
OF PROFESSIONAL BASEBALL LEAGUES

PRESIDENT-TREASURER—John H. Johnson
VICE-PRESIDENT—Joe Ryan
ADMINISTRATOR OF ASSOCIATION TRANSACTION—Don Avery
FIELD REPRESENTATIVES—Robert L. Freitas, Jim Mills
HEADQUARTERS—201 Bayshore Dr. S.E., P. O. Box A
St. Petersburg, Fla. 33731
Telephone—822-6937 (area code 813)
Teletype—810-863-0361

EXECUTIVE COMMITTEE—Joe Ryan, Chairman, President of the American Association, John Moss, President of the South Atlantic League, Carl Sawatski, President of the Texas League.

TABLE OF CONTENTS

For Index to Contents See Page 592

(Index to Minor League Cities on Page 587)

ON THE COVER: Top left, Mike Flanagan, Baltimore—THE SPORTING NEWS AL Pitcher of the Year, 1979; top right, Keith Hernandez, St. Louis—THE SPORTING NEWS NL Player of the Year, 1979; bottom left, Joe Niekro, Houston—THE SPORTING NEWS NL PItcher of the Year, 1979; bottom right, Don Baylor, California—THE SPORTING NEWS AL Player of the Year, 1979.

CHARLES S. FEENEY
President of the National League

NATIONAL LEAGUE

Including

Club Directories

Club Reviews of 1979 Season

Club Day-by-Day Scores

NL Team Pictures

1979 League Leaders

1979 Official NL Averages

All-Time NL Player Performance Tables

WILLIE STARGELL, top center, is hugged by teammates after the Pirates defeated the Baltimore Orioles in the final game of the World Series.

National League

Organized 1876

CHARLES S. FEENEY
President and Treasurer

JOHN J. McHALE
Vice-President

PHYLLIS B. COLLINS
Secretary

BLAKE CULLEN
Administrator and Public Relations Director

KATY FEENEY
Assistant Public Relations Director

LOUIS H. KREMS
Business Manager

ROSE TROTTA
Computer Manager

JOSEPHINE TROY
Administrative Assistant

Headquarters—1 Rockefeller Plaza, New York, N. Y. 10020

Telephone—582-4213 (area code 212)

UMPIRES—Fred Brocklander, Nick Colosi, Jerry Crawford, Jerry Dale, David Davidson, Robert Engel, Steve Fields, Bruce Froemming, Eric Gregg, Lanny Harris, H. Douglas Harvey, John Kibler, John McSherry, Ed Montague, Andy Olsen, Dave Pallone, Paul Pryor, Frank Pulli, Jim Quick, Lawrence (Dutch) Rennert, Paul Runge, Dick Stello, Terry Tata, Ed Vargo, Harry Wendelstedt, Joe West, Lee Weyer, William G. Williams.

OFFICIAL STATISTICIANS—Elias Sports Bureau, Inc., 500 5th Ave., Suite 2114, New York, N. Y. 10036. Telephone (212) 869-1530.

Players cannot be transferred from one major league club to another after June 15 to the close of the championship season except through regular waiver channels.

WAIVER PRICE, $20,000. Interleague waivers, $20,000, except for selected players and draft-excluded players.

ATLANTA BRAVES

Chairman of the Board—William C. Bartholomay

President—R. E. (Ted) Turner III
Executive Vice-President—Allison Thornwell
General Manager—John Mullen
Vice-President, Player Development—Hank Aaron
Minor League Administrator—Paul Snyder
Manager of Broadcast Sales—Wayne Long
Director of Broadcasting—Ernie Johnson
Vice-President & Controller—Charles Sanders
Chief Accountant—Michael Warren
Ticket Distribution Manager—Ed Newman
Director Public Relations, Promotions—Wayne Minshew
Ticket Sales Manager—Kris Krebs
Group Sales Manager—Andre DeLorenzo
Director of Stadium Operations—Joe Shirley
Manager—Bobby Cox
Club Physician—Dr. David T. Watson
Executive Offices—P. O. Box 4064, Atlanta, Ga. 30302
Telephone—522-7630 (area code 404)

SCOUTS—Sam Berry, Ted Cabrall, Pedro Gonzales, Phil Holmes, Burney R. (Dickey) Martin, Tom Morgan, Pat Nugent, Bob Turzilli, William R. Wright, H. F. (Red) Wooten, Wesley Westrum.

PARK LOCATION—Atlanta-Fulton County Stadium, on Capitol Avenue at the junction of Interstate Highways 20, 75 and 85.

Seating capacity—52,532

FIELD DIMENSIONS—Home plate to left field at foul line, 330 feet; to center field, 402 feet; to right field at foul line, 330 feet.

CHICAGO CUBS

Chairman of the Executive Committee—William Wrigley

President, Chief Executive Officer & Treasurer—Wm. J. Hagenah, Jr.
Executive Vice-President—Robert D. Kennedy
Assistant to Executive Vice-President—John Cox
Vice-President—Park Operations & Secretary—E. R. Saltwell
Honorary Vice-President—Charles Grimm
Assistant Secretary—Claude Brooks
Assistant Director of Park Operations—Dennis Beyreuther
Chief Accounting Officer—Joseph Kirchen
Director of Player Development—C. V. Davis
Director of Scouting—Vedie Himsl
Traveling Secretary & Statistician—Jim Davidovich
Assistant Traveling Secretary—G. A. Settergren
Home Secretary—Howard Roberts
Director of Information & Services—Buck Peden
Community Relations—Ernie Banks
Director of Ticket Services—Jerome Foran
Manager of Group Sales—Ernie Banks
Manager of Group Services—Dave Lamont
Grounds Superintendent—Roy Bogren
Manager—Preston Gomez
Club Physician—Dr. Jacob Suker
Executive Offices—Wrigley Field, N. Clark and Addison Streets,
Chicago, Ill. 60613
Telephone—281-5050 (area code 312)

SCOUTS—Dave Bartosch, William Capps, Frank DeMoss, Walt Dixon, Eugene Handley, Herman Hannah, Bob Hartsfield, John Hennessy, Roy Johnson, Bill Jurges, Robert D. Kennedy, Jr., Eddie Lyons, Julio Navarro, John (Buck) O'Neil, Evo Pusich, Pete Reiser, Barney Schultz, Fred J. Shaffer, George Silvey, Gene Thompson, Joaquin Velilla, Harrison Wickel, H. D. (Rube) Wilson, Pedrin Zorilla.

PARK LOCATION—Wrigley Field, Addison Street, N. Clark Street, Waveland Avenue and Sheffield Avenue.

Seating capacity—37,741

FIELD DIMENSIONS—Home plate to left field at foul line, 355 feet; to center field, 400 feet; to right field at foul line, 353 feet.

CINCINNATI REDS

Chairman of the Board—Louis Nippert
Vice-Chairman of the Board—Robert L. Howsam
President & Chief Executive Officer—Richard Wagner
Vice-President—William J. Williams
Vice-President/Marketing—Roger Ruhl
Vice-President/Player Personnel—Sheldon Bender
Vice-President/Scouting—Joe Bowen
Business Manager—Don Tecklenburg
Treasurer—James R. Williams
Secretary—Andrew Hopple
Assistant Secretary—Henry W. Hobson Jr.
Special Assignment Scout—Ray Shore
Director of Publicity—Jim Ferguson
Controller—D. L. Porco
Business Coordinator, Player Development—Sal Artiaga
Traveling Secretary—Doug Bureman
Director of Speakers Bureau—Gordy Coleman
Director of Stadium Operations—Doug Duennes
Director of Group Sales—Charlie Taylor
Director of Special Projects—Bob Kruetzkamp
Director of Season Tickets & Customer Relations—Janet Wendel
Director of Publications—John Olberding
Director of Ticket Department—Bill Stewart
Director of Broadcasting—Jim Winters
Manager—John McNamara
Club Physician—Dr. George Ballou
Executive Offices—100 Riverfront Stadium, Cincinnati, O. 45202
Telephone—421-4510 (area code 513)

SCOUTS—Larry Barton, Jr., Gene Bennett, Porter Blinn, David Calaway, Joseph Caputo, Bill Clark, Larry D'Amato, Reno DeBenedetti, Larry Doughty, Elmer Gray, Edwin Howsam, Chester Montgomery, Johnny Sierra, Neil Summers, Fred Uhlman, George Zuraw.

PARK LOCATION—Riverfront Stadium, downtown Cincinnati, bounded by Second Street to Ohio River and from Walnut Street to Broadway.

Seating capacity—52,392

FIELD DIMENSIONS—Home plate to left field at foul line, 330 feet; to center field, 404 feet; to right field at foul line, 330 feet.

HOUSTON ASTROS

General Partner—John J. McMullen

Limited Partners—Carl Allen, Peter J. Allen, Richard L. Allen, Thomas E. Allen Jr., J. Evans Atwell, Audrey Jones Beck, Briarwood Management Trust, Stephen C. Cook, John H. Duncan, James A. Elkins Jr., A. J. Foyt, Stuart Hellmann, Gerald D. Hines, Jeffrey C. Hines, William S. Kilroy, Allan C. King, David E. LeFevre, James A. Lovell, Robert J. Marco, Catherine J. McMullen, Jacqueline J. McMullen, Mary Mochary, Edward Randall III, Don A. Sanders, Mrs. R. E. Smith, R. John Stanton Jr., Jack T. Trotter, Jack N. Warren, Donn R. Wilson.

President & General Manager—Talbot M. Smith

Administrative Asst. to the President & Traveling Secretary—
Donald Davidson

Asst. to General Manager, Player Personnel—Anthony G. Siegle

Administrative Asst., Major League Operations—Judy Vieno

Director of Minor League Operations—William J. Wood

Administrative Asst., Minor League Operations—Lorie M. Thomas

Director of Scouting—Lynwood Stallings

Coordinator of Minor League Instruction—Bob Cluck

Clerk, Scouting & Player Development—John Jackson

Director of Publicity—Edward A. Wade

Assistant Director of Publicity—Rick Rivers

Director of Broadcasting & Promotions—Art Elliott

Promotions, Scoreboard Operations—Paul Darst

Broadcast & Promotions Sales—Hugh Pickett

Manager, Promotions-Director of Ticket Sales—Larry Dierker

Manager, Season Ticket Sales—M. M. "Buddy" Hancken

Manager, Group Sales—Larry Serota

Club Physicians—Drs. Harold H. Brelsford, Hatch Cummings

Director of Physical Conditions—Dr. A. Eugene Coleman

Field Manager—Bill Virdon

Executive Offices—Astrodome, P.O. Box 288
Houston, Tex. 77001

Telephone—749-9500 (area code 713)

Teletype—910 881-1740

HOUSTON SPORTS ASSOCIATION, INC.

President & Chief Operating Officer—Robert G. Harter

Vice-President, Administration—E. Michael Crowley

Vice-President, Engineering—W. Gary Keller

Vice-President, Public Relations & Advertising—James H. Weidler

Exec. V.P., Astrodome-Astrohall Stadium Corp.—Jimmie D. Fore

Director, Event Coordination—Jordy Tollett

SCOUTS—Clary Anderson, Stan Benjamin, Paul Florence, Stan Hollmig, Jerry Hunsicker, David Lakey, Gordon Lakey, Walter Matthews, John Miller, Tony Pacheco, Carlos Alfonso, Diogenes Cedeno, Julio Linares, William Melendez, Domingo Mercedes, Fernando Tatis.

PARK LOCATION—Astrodome, Kirby and Interstate Loop 610

Seating capacity—45,000

FIELD DIMENSIONS—Home plate to left field at foul line, 340 feet; to center field, 406 feet; to right field at foul line, 340 feet.

LOS ANGELES DODGERS

BOARD OF DIRECTORS

Peter O'Malley, President; Harry M. Bardt, Treasurer;
Roland Seidler, Jr., Secretary; Mrs. Roland (Terry) Seidler

President—Peter O'Malley
Vice-President, Player Personnel—Al Campanis
Vice-President, Public Relations and Promotions—Fred Claire
Vice-President, Minor League Operations—William P. Schweppe
Vice-President, Marketing—Merritt Willey
Special Consultant—Walter Alston
Controller and Assistant Treasurer—Ken Hasemann
Assistant Secretary—Irene Tanji
Director, Advertising, Novelties and Souvenirs—Danny Goodman
Director, Dodgertown—Charles Blaney
Director, Stadium Operations—Bob Smith
Director, Ticket Department—Walter Nash
Director, Stadium Club and Transportation—Bob Schenz
Director, Dodger Network—David Van de Walker
Director, Scouting—Ben Wade
Director, Publicity—Steve Brener
Director, Community Relations—Don Newcombe
Community Relations—Roy Campanella
Director, Ticket Marketing—Barry Stockhamer
Director, Speakers' Bureau—Bill Shumard
Director, 1980 All-Star Game—Willie Sanchez
Executive Pilot, Dodger 720-B Fan Jet—Captain Lewis G. Carlisle
Administrative Assistant—Ike Ikuhara
Traveling Secretary—Billy DeLury
Auditor—Michael Strange
Manager—Tom Lasorda
Club Physicians—Dr. Frank Jobe, Dr. Robert Woods
Executive Offices—Dodger Stadium, 1000 Elysian Park Avenue,
Los Angeles, Calif. 90012.
Telephone—224-1500 (area code 213)

SCOUTS—Rafael Avila, Boyd Bartley, Gib Bodet, Mike Brito, Rex
Carr, Jim Garland, Dick Hager, Dennis Haren, Gail Henley, Goldie Holt,
Elvio Jimenez, Tony John, Dale Jones, John Keenan, Ron King, Ed Li-
beratore, Dale McReynolds, Charlie Metro, Tommy Mixon, John O'Neil,
Regie Otero, Medardo Perez, Bill Pleis, Ed Roebuck, Jerry Stephenson,
Dick Teed, Corito Varona, Guy Wellman.

PARK LOCATION—Dodger Stadium, 1000 Elysian Park Avenue.

Seating capacity—56,000

FIELD DIMENSIONS—Home plate to left field at foul line, 330 feet;
to center field, 395 feet; to right field at foul line, 330 feet.

MONTREAL EXPOS

Board of Directors—Charles R. Bronfman, Lorne C. Webster,
John J. McHale, Sydney Maislin, Paul Beaudry, Hugh Hallward,
Charlemagne Beaudry, E. Leo Kolber, Melvin W. Griffin,
Louis R. Desmarais, Arnold Ludwick, Honorary Secretary

Chairman of the Board—Charles R. Bronfman
President and Chief Executive Officer—John J. McHale
Vice-President, Player Development—James Fanning
Vice-President, Secretary-Treasurer—Harry J. Renaud
Vice-President, Marketing & Public Affairs—Roger D. Landry
Assistant to the President—Danny Menendez
Administrative Assistant, Player Relations—Gene Kirby
Director, Team Travel—Peter Durso
Head Scout, Canada—Ronald Piche
Publicists—Monique Giroux, Richard Griffin
Administrative Coordinator, Minor League & Scouting—Pat McDermott
Director, Business Operations—Gerry Trudeau
Concession Manager—Joseph Boire
Manager, Game Services—Gilles Rochefort
Manager, Marketing & Business Development—Normand Martin
Manager, Special Events & Community Relations—Rodger Brulotte
Box Office Manager—Guy Paradis
Manager, Group Business Development—Roger Savard
Manager, Group Sales—Suzanne Lemoignan
Manager—Dick Williams
Club Physician—Dr. Robert Brodrick
Mailing Address—P. O. Box 500, Station M, Montreal, Quebec,
Canada H1V 3P2
Telephone—253-3434 (area code 514)

SCOUTS—(special assignment)—Charlie Fox, Carroll (Whitey)
Lockman, Ed Lopat; (regular)—Bill Adair, Terry Boyle, Harry Bright, Al
Harper, Mercer Harris, Dick Lemay, Walter Millies, John (Red) Murff,
Herb Newberry, Bob Oldis, Jack Paepke, Harry Postove, Jack Warner;
(Canadian)—Wayne Norton, Andre Pratte.

PARK LOCATION—Olympic Stadium, 4545 Pierre de Coubertin,
Montreal, Quebec, Canada H1V 3N7.

Seating capacity—59,984

FIELD DIMENSIONS—Home plate to left field at foul line, 325 feet;
to center field, 404 feet; to right field at foul line, 325.

NEW YORK METS

Chairman of the Board—Nelson Doubleday

President—Fred Wilpon
Executive Vice-President & Chief Operating Officer—J. Frank Cashen
Vice-President-Business Manager—James Nagourney
Vice-President & Treasurer—William A. Murray
Directors—Nelson Doubleday, Fred Wilpon, James McGreth,
John O'Donnell, Steve O'Neil, John Sargent
Vice-President & GM—Joseph A. McDonald
Director of Scouting & Asst. to GM—Pete Gebrian
Director of Player Development—Dick Gernert
Special Consultant—Robert B. Scheffing
Ticket Manager—Bob Mandt
Director of Minor Leagues—Chris Kager
Director of Public Relations & Traveling Secretary—Arthur Richman
Manager—Joe Torre
Club Physician—Dr. James C. Parkes II
Executive Offices—William A. Shea Stadium, Roosevelt
Avenue and 126th Street, Flushing, N. Y. 11368
Telephone—672-2000 (area code 212)

SCOUTS—Bob Bishop, Ed Charles, Jocko Collins, Nino Escalera, Joe
Frazier, Denny Galehouse, Jim Hughes, Roger Jongewaard, Hank Kelly,
Buddy Kerr, Dave Madison, Harry Minor, Julian Morgan, Roy Partee,
Marvin Scott, Ollie Vanek, Len Zanke.

PARK LOCATION—William A. Shea Stadium, Roosevelt Avenue and
126th Street, Flushing, N. Y. 11368

Ticket Information—672-3000 (area code 212)

Seating capacity—55,300

FIELD DIMENSIONS—Home plate to left field at foul line, 341 feet;
to center field, 410 feet; to right field at foul line, 341 feet.

PHILADELPHIA PHILLIES

Chairman of Board—R. R. M. (Bob) Carpenter, Jr.

President—R. R. M. (Ruly) Carpenter III
Executive Vice-President—William Y. Giles
Vice-President-Director of Player Personnel—Paul Owens
Vice-President-Director of Finance—George F. H. Harrison
Secretary-Treasurer—G. Theodore Harrison
Director of Minor Leagues—Howie Bedell
Director of Scouting—Jack Pastore
Administrative Assistant—Keith Carpenter
Director of Sales—David P. Montgomery
Director of Publicity and Public Relations—Larry Shenk
Ticket Manager—Raymond B. Krise
Director of Advertising—Thomas T. Hudson
Director of Promotions—Frank H. Sullivan
Director of Stadium Operations—Patrick J. Cassidy
Traveling Secretary—Eddie Ferenz
Director of Group Sales—Richard Deats
Director of Season Ticket Sales—Ray Krise, Jr.
Executive Secretary, Minor Leagues—William V. Gargano
Assistant Director of Stadium Operations—Andrew J. Clarke
Assistant Director of Publicity and Public Relations—
Chris Wheeler
Public Relations Assistant-Director of Radio Network—
Dennis Lehman
National Scouting Supervisor—Brandy Davis
Special Scouting Assistant—Hugh Alexander
Manager—Dallas Green
Club Physician—Dr. Phillip Marone
Executive Offices—Philadelphia Veterans Stadium
Mailing Address—P. O. Box 7575, Philadelphia, Pa. 19101
Telephone—463-6000 (area code 215)

SCOUTS—Hugh Alexander, Ruben Amaro, Edward Bockman, George Bradley, Keith Carpenter, Paul Duval, Doug Gassaway, Charles Gault, Gordon Goldsberry, Carl Greene, Bill Harper, Wilbur Johnson, John Jorgensen, Lou Kahn, Dick Lawlor, Carl Loewenstine, Anthony Lucadello, Ben Marmo, Gene Martin, Gary Nickels, Tom Oliver, Scott Reid, Joe Reilly, Andy Seminick, Billy Tracy, Elmer Valo, Randy Waddill, Don Williams.

PARK LOCATION—Philadelphia Veterans Stadium, Broad Street and Pattison Avenue.

Seating capacity—64,976

FIELD DIMENSIONS—Home plate to left field at foul line, 330 feet; to center field, 408 feet; to right field at foul line, 330 feet.

PITTSBURGH PIRATES

President—Daniel M. Galbreath

Chairman of the Board—John W. Galbreath
Executive Vice-President—Harding Peterson
Vice-President/Administration—Joseph M. O'Toole
Vice-President/Public Relations and Marketing—Jack Schrom
Assistant to the Vice-Presidents—Milt Graff
Director of Publicity—Joseph Safety
Administrative Assistant/Publicity—Sally O'Leary
Director of Minor League Clubs and Scouting—Murray Cook
Assistant Director of Minor League Clubs and Scouting—
Branch B. Rickey III
Assistant Farm Director—William G. Turner
Assistant Director of Scouting—Jon Neiderer
Director of Sales and Advertising—Olin J. Depolo
Assistant Director of Group and Season Sales—Jack H. Berger
Assistant Director of Group and Season Sales—Steve Greenberg
Director of Promotions—Steve Schanwald
Treasurer/Assistant Secretary—Douglas G. McCormick
Assistant to the Treasurer—Kenneth C. Curcio
Ticket Manager—Richard C. Holland
Manager—Chuck Tanner
Traveling Secretary—Charles Muse
Club Physician—Dr. Joseph Coroso
Executive Offices—Three Rivers Stadium, 600 Stadium Circle
Pittsburgh, Pa. 15212
Telephone—323-5000 (area code 412)

SPECIAL ASSIGNMENT SCOUTS—Gene Baker, Babe Barberis, Joe L. Brown, Pablo Cruz, George Detore, Jerry Gardner, Fred Goodman, Howie Haak, Carlton Keller, Jim Maxwell, Mike Mulleady, Lenny Yochim.

SCOUTING ASSISTANTS—Ed Bakale, Bud Baurle, Calvin Biron, Willie Bojos, Paul Bordi, Bill Bryan, Dave Buccolo, Joe Buccolo, F. "Kid" Carr, Bill Cayavec, Frank Coimbre, Cecil Cole, Nick Creola, Bob Dawson, Pal Eldridge, Ed Farnum, Charles Fletcher, Jim Frail, Pete Grasso, Fred Hannum, Leroy Hill, Bud Hoff, Tom Holliday, Myron Hunt, Bob Johnson, Jim Lehman, Jose Luna, Roy Marks, Andy Moynihan, Tom Myers, Boyd Odom, Steve Oleschuk, Ed Olivares, Elmo Plaskett, Dick Probola, Ron Rahr, Harold Ray, Doug Robbins, Ken Saybel, George Schmidt, Jesse Smith, Lloyd Sorrells, Les Stewart, Cloy Sykes, Joe Tuley, Tom Urich, Roy Velasco, Tom Venditelli, Bill White, Bill Wigle, Jack Zduriencik, Ed Zeidler.

PARK LOCATION—Three Rivers Stadium, 600 Stadium Circle.

Seating capacity—50,364

FIELD DIMENSIONS—Home plate to left field at foul line, 335 feet; to center field, 400 feet; to right field at foul line, 335 feet.

ST. LOUIS CARDINALS

Chairman of the Board, President and Chief Executive Officer–
August A Busch, Jr.

Vice-President–August A. Busch, III
Vice-President–Fred L. Kuhlmann
Vice-President–Margaret M. Snyder
Secretary and Treasurer–John L. Hayward
Assistant Secretary–Richard Schwartz
Assistant Treasurer–H. F. Suellentrop
Senior Executive Vice-President and Chief Operating Officer–
John W. Claiborne III
Executive Vice-President, Business Affairs–Joe McShane
Senior Vice-President–Stan Musial
Vice-President-Public Relations–Jim Toomey
Director of Operations and Controller–Gary Blase
Traveling Secretary–Lee Thomas
Director of Player Development & Scouting–Jim Bayens
Ticket Director–Mike Bertani
Director of Promotions–Marty Hendin
Director of Sales–Joe Cunningham
Assistant Director of Player Development–Paul Fauks
Assistant Director of Public Relations–C. J. Cherre
Manager–Ken Boyer
Club Physician–Dr. Stan London
Executive Offices–Busch Memorial Stadium, 250 Stadium
Plaza, St. Louis, Mo. 63102
Telephone–421-3060 (area code 314)

SCOUTS–Jose Arias, Ted Baker, James Belz, Lee Blackfield, Cameron Bonifay, Red Brown, Eddie Collins, Walker Cress, Roberto Diaz, Cecil Espy, Angel Figueroa, Gary Gilmore, Ray Goodman, George Hasser, Don Hennelly, James Holden, Bob Holmes, Fred Jiminez, Roland Johnson, James Johnston, Earl Jones, Marty Keough, Henry Krause, Thornton Lee, Fred McAlister, Tom McCormick, Ben McLure, Martin Maier, Virgil Melvin, Mo Mozzali, Carlos Negron, Jerry Oswald, Jim Rivers, Mike Roberts, James Robinson, John Rotman, William Sayles, Bart Shelly, Danny Simons, John Skurski, Hal Smith, Marvin Stendel, John Tatum, Eddie Taylor, Charles (Tim) Thompson, Charles Thompson, Jr., Bill Warren.

PARK LOCATION–Busch Memorial Stadium, Broadway, Walnut Street, Stadium Plaza and Spruce Street.

Seating capacity–50,100

FIELD DIMENSIONS–Home plate to left field at foul line, 330 feet; to center field, 414 feet; to right field at foul line, 330 feet.

SAN DIEGO PADRES

Owner & Chairman Board of Directors—Ray Kroc
Director—Joan Kroc

President & Director—Ballard Smith
Vice-President-General Manager—Bob Fontaine
Vice-President-Business Manager—Elten Schiller
Controller—Roberto Martinez
Director, Minor League Operations—Jim Weigel
Assistant to General Manager—Jack McKeon
Director of Public Relations & Broadcasting—Bob Chandler
Director of Promotions—Andy Strasberg
Director of Group Sales—Tom Mulcahy
Director of Merchandising—Kathie Redlinger
Traveling Secretary—John Mattei
Trainer—Dick Dent
Manager—Jerry Coleman
Club Physician—Dr. Paul Bauer
Executive Offices—P. O. Box 2000, San Diego, Calif. 92120
Telephone—283-4494 (area code 714)

SCOUTS—Ken Bracey, Bill Bryk, Manny Crespo, Joe Cusick, Curt
Daniels, Cliff Ditto, Bobby Etheridge, Bobby Fontaine, Rich Hacker,
Jack Hays, John Herbold, Frank Lane, Jim Marshall, Jethro McIntyre,
Jim McLaughlin, Bob Miller, Luis Rosa, Ed Stevens, Gary Sutherland,
Paul Weaver, Hank Zacharias, Jim Zerilla.

PARK LOCATION—San Diego Stadium, 9949 Friars Road

Seating capacity—51,362

FIELD DIMENSIONS—Home plate to left field at foul line, 330 feet;
to center field, 420 feet; to right field at foul line, 330 feet.

SAN FRANCISCO GIANTS

President—Bob Lurie

Executive Assistant to the President—Corey Busch
General Manager—H. B. "Spec" Richardson
Director or Marketing and Business Affairs—Pat Gallagher
Director of Scouting and Minor League Operations—
Jack Schwarz
Field Director of Player Development—Tom Haller
Baseball Consultant—Jerry Donovan
Director of Travel—Frank Bergonzi
Traveling Secretary/Statistician—Ralph Nelson
Director of Publicity—Stu Smith
Ticket Manager—Arthur Schulze
Director of Promotions—Charles S. Feeney Jr.
Speakers Bureau—Joe Orengo
Accouting Manager—Ron Mosher
Director of Stadium Operations—Don Foreman
Director of Group Sales—Ben Oakes
Manager—Dave Bristol
Executive Offices—Candlestick Park, San Francisco, Calif. 94124
Telephone—468-3700 (area code 415)

SCOUTS—John D. (Dutch) Anderson, Larry DeHaven, Morris A. (Dutch) Deutsch, Frank (Chick) Genovese, Grady Hatton, Joseph W. Henderson, Carl Hubbell, Richard G. (Richie) Klaus, Bob Knoerlein, Jim Lyke, Horacio Martinez, Marty Miller, Edward F. (Eddie) Montague, Hugh Poland, Del Rice, Jack Shafer, Hank Sauer (also batting instructor), Richard (Dick) Wilson.

PARK LOCATION—Candlestick Point, Bayshore Freeway.

Seating capacity—58,000

FIELD DIMENSIONS—Home plate to left field at foul line, 335 feet; to center field, 410 feet; to right field at foul line, 335 feet.

Pittsburgh catcher Ed Ott reaches the mound to congratulate Bert Blyleven after the righthander had beaten the Cincinnati Reds, 7-1, October 5 to give the Pirates the National League pennant.

EAST DIVISION
Madlock, Foli Acquisitions Boosted Bucs
By CHARLEY FEENEY

When a team wins the division title on the last day of the season and goes on to sweep the playoffs and make a dramatic comeback to win the World Series, it is impossible to pinpoint one game or one player that made the difference.

The Pittsburgh Pirates were World Champions in 1979 because of the basics. Good pitching. Timely hitting. Improved defense.

The Pirates won by being consistent from May through October. The team that opened the season in April was not the same team that drove to a 98-64 record and pennant in September and October.

When the season opened, shortstop Tim Foli was riding the bench in New York with the last-place Mets. When the season opened, Bill Madlock, a third baseman by trade, was playing out of position at second base in San Francisco.

Foli became a Pirate on April 20 and more than two months later, on June 28, Madlock and relief pitcher Dave Roberts became Pirates. Roberts proved valuable as a spot starter and reliever.

When Foli joined the Pirates, they were going through a typical Pittsburgh April. The club lost more than it won and on May 1, the Pirates were 7-11.

"I was the only player who was concerned," Foli recalled. "The rest of the guys told me, 'Don't worry, we'll be there in the end.'"

Nice talk. The Pirates in the three previous seasons didn't back it up. They fell behind the Phillies in 1975, '76 and '77 and couldn't make up the ground despite making big moves during the last two months of the season.

But the 1979 Pirates were different. They were different because Foli, taking over for departed Frank Taveras at short, steadied the infield. They were different because when Madlock arrived, he moved to third base, paving the way for Phil Garner to play second base, his natural position.

Rennie Stennett, the second base regular who broke his right ankle in August 1977 and never fully recovered, rode the bench.

The Pirates expected to be chasing the Phillies after their sub-.500 April. Instead, they chased the Montreal Expos and the chase didn't end until the Pirates, on the last day of the season, defeated the Chicago Cubs and the Expos lost to Steve Carlton and the Phillies.

The Pirates were six and one-half games back in June. In late July, they took first place—for one day. The Expos regained it and in the long run for the top, there were six games between the two contenders in September. The Pirates won five of them.

Manager Chuck Tanner did a marvelous job maneuvering his pitching staff. During one stretch, because of injuries, Tanner used seven starters.

Kent Tekulve, Grant Jackson and Enrique Romo were the heart of the bullpen. Tekulve, after a slow start, won 10 games and saved 31 in a club-record 94 games. Jackson, the 36-year-old lefthanded craftsman, was outstanding, winning eight games and saving 14. And Romo, acquired from Seattle over the winter, gave the bullpen a big lift with seven straight wins in July and August.

PITTSBURGH PIRATES—1979

Front row—Whitson, Bartirome, trainer; Monchak, coach; Haddix, coach; Tanner, manager; Skinner, coach; Lonnett, coach; Rooker, Romo. Second row—Jackson, Stennett, Alexander, Sanguillen, Foli, Milner, Easler, Berra, Lacy, Rhoden, Muse, traveling secretary. Third row—B. Robinson, Blyleven, Moreno, Parker, Candelaria, Bibby, Tekulve, Stargell, Kison, D. Robinson. Seated in front—Nicosia, Hallahan, batboy; Graff, batboy; Garner, Ott.

The staff was without a 15-game winner. John Candelaria (14-9 and eight complete games) was top man among the starters. Bruce Kison, 4-0 in September, was 13-7, and Jim Bibby and Bert Blyleven were 12-game winners. Bibby lost four, Blyleven five.

Dave Parker was the only Bucs' regular to bat .300 and his 94 RBIs led the club.

At age 38, Willie Stargell led the team with 32 homers and had 82 RBIs. The oldest man ever to win the MVP (shared with Keith Hernandez of St. Louis), Willie was also a postseason hero. He was named MVP in both the Championship Series and World Series. His two homers and six RBIs knocked out the Reds in three games and his three homers, seven RBIs and all-time record 25 total bases keyed the comeback against Baltimore.

Bill Robinson (.264, 24 homers, 75 RBIs) and John Milner (.276, 16 homers, 60 RBIs) gave the club steady production from the left field position. Both men also filled in at first base for Stargell.

Omar Moreno's improvement at bat was fantastic. A .235 batter in 1978, Moreno, after instruction from Harry Walker, hit .282 and had 69 RBIs, a high total for a leadoff man. He swiped a club-record 77 bases, tops in the league, and his defense in center field was consistently good.

Ed Ott and Steve Nicosia were not All-Star catchers, but they were big contributors in the Pirates' drive. Ott, who had a sore arm most of the 1978 season, threw out runners with more regularity and Nicosia was a solid backup.

It was a year of injuries for second-year pitcher Don Robinson, but in the playoffs, he came through in relief, winning one game and saving another.

"It was," Tanner said, "a team that needed every player to win."

Players like Lee Lacy, who was disappointed in his .247 average. Players like Dale Berra, who opened the season as a backup infielder, returned to the minors in July and August, and returned to help in September. Players like Matt Alexander, who stole 13 bases in 14 attempts. Players like veteran Manny Sanguillen whose triple beat the Phillies in a big game in September when the Pirates were battling off a losing streak. Players like pitcher Jim Rooker, who was on the disabled list twice and came back to win two games in September.

"An amazing bunch of people," is the way Willie Stargell, an amazing man, described his Pirate teammates.

SCORES OF PITTSBURGH PIRATES' 1979 GAMES

APRIL			Winner	Loser	MAY			Winner	Loser
6—Montreal	L	2-3*	Sosa	Tekulve	1—Atlanta	L	2-5	Niekro	Tekulve
7—Montreal	W	7-6	Jackson	Sosa	2—Atlanta	W	10-2	Candelaria	M. Mahler
8—Montreal	L	4-5	May	Romo	4—At St.L.	L	3-4	Sykes	Robinson
10—At Phila.	L	3-7	Ruthven	Romo	5—At St.L.	W	6-5	Jackson	Vuckovich
11—At Phila.	L	4-5	Carlton	Blyleven	6—At St.L.	L	2-4	Martinez	Kison
12—St. Louis	W	3-1	Robinson	Denny	7—At Atl.	W	4-2	Candelaria	M. Mahler
13—St. Louis	W	7-6	Bibby	Schultz	8—At Atl.	L	1-4	Solomon	Rhoden
14—St. Louis	W	7-4	Whitson	Forsch	9—At Atl.	W	17-9	Bibby	Garber
15—St. Louis	L	4-9*	Littell	Tekulve	11—Cinn.	L	4-8	Tomlin	Whitson
17—Phila.	L	2-13	Carlton	Blyleven	12—Cinn.	W	3-2	Bibby	Pastore
18—Phila.	L	2-3	Lerch	Robinson	13—Cinn.	L	3-7	LaCoss	Candelaria
20—At Hous.	L	4-5*	Sambito	Bibby	15—N. York	L	0-3	Swan	Robinson
21—At Hous.	L	4-5*	Andujar	Tekulve	16—N. York	W	4-3§	Romo	Lockwood
22—At Hous.	L	2-3	Andujar	Candelaria	17—N. York	W	6-5	Tekulve	Orosco
24—At Cinn.	W	9-2	Robinson	Pastore	18—At Chi.	W	9-5	Candelaria	Holtzman
25—At Cinn.	W	3-2†	Tekulve	Tomlin	19—At Chi.	W	3-0	Rooker	Krukow
27—Houston	L	8-9†	Riccelli	Whitson	20—At Chi.	W	6-5	Robinson	McGlothen
29—Houston	W	10-5	Kison	Niekro	21—At Mon.	W	4-2	Blyleven	Sanderson
		Won 7, Lost 11			22—At Mon.	L	3-6	Grimsley	Whitson

MAY			Winner	Loser
23–At Mon.	L	0-3	Rogers	Candelaria
25–At N.Y.	T	3-3a	....	....
26–At N.Y.	L	8-10	Lockwood	Tekulve
27–At N.Y.	W	2-1	Jackson	Murray
28–At N.Y.	W	6-1	Candelaria	Falcone
29–Chicago	W	8-0	Robinson	Holtzman
30–Chicago	W	9-2	Rooker	McGlothen
31–Chicago	W	4-3*	Kison	Sutter
		Won 16, Lost 10		

JUNE				
1–S. Diego	W	9-8	Tekulve	Shirley
2–S. Diego	L	1-3	Perry	Candelaria
3–S. Diego	W	7-0	Kison	Owchinko
4–Los Ang.	L	2-4	Sutcliffe	Rooker
5–Los Ang.	W	3-1	Blyleven	Sutton
6–Los Ang.	W	5-4	Romo	Welch
8–S. Fran.	W	3-2	Romo	Curtis
9–S. Fran.	L	2-6	Blue	Kison
10–S. Fran.	L	4-7	Lavelle	Romo
12–At S.D.	L	3-6	Perry	Candelaria
13–At S.D.	L	2-3	Owchinko	Kison
14–At S.D.	L	1-2x	D'Acquisto	Candelaria
15–At L.A.	W	6-2	Blyleven	Sutton
16–At L.A.	W	6-3	Robinson	Welch
17–At L.A.	W	5-1	Whitson	Reuss
19–At S.F.	W	9-4	Candelaria	Montefusco
20–At S.F.	W	8-5	Jackson	Lavelle
22–Chicago	W	7-2	Blyleven	Holtzman
23–Chicago	L	3-4	Krukow	Robinson
24–Chicago	L	0-5	Reuschel	Kison
25–At N.Y.	W	8-1	Candelaria	Swan
25–At N.Y.	L	0-4	Falcone	Rooker
26–At N.Y.	W	2-1	Blyleven	Hausman
27–N. York	L	9-12	Twitchell	Jackson
28–N. York	L	2-3	Allen	Bibby
29–Montreal	W	6-5	Kison	Lee
30–Montreal	L	3-5	Sanderson	Blyleven
		Won 14, Lost 13		

JULY				
2–At St.L.	W	5-4	Romo	Knowles
3–At St.L.	W	4-1	Candelaria	Forsch
4–At St.L.	W	6-4	Blyleven	Vuckovich
5–At St.L.	L	0-2	Fulgham	Rooker
6–At Cinn.	L	1-2	Bair	Jackson
7–At Cinn.	L	2-6	Moskau	Robinson
8–At Cinn.	L	2-4	Norman	Candelaria
8–At Cinn.	W	2-1	Jackson	Tomlin
10–At Hous.	W	4-3	Bibby	Andujar
11–At Hous.	W	5-1	Kison	Richard
12–At Hous.	W	5-3	Blyleven	Niekro
13–At Atl.	L	4-13	Niekro	Rooker
14–At Atl.	W	5-1	Candelaria	Matula
15–At Atl.	W	7-3	Bibby	Solomon
19–Houston	W	9-5	Roberts	Forsch
19–Houston	W	4-2	Kison	Niekro
20–Houston	W	9-3	Candelaria	Richard
21–Houston	W	6-5	Romo	Sambito
22–Atlanta	W	5-4	Robinson	Solomon
22–Atlanta	W	3-2	Bibby	M. Mahler
23–Atlanta	W	7-1	Blyleven	Hanna
23–Atlanta	L	0-8	Niekro	Rooker
24–Cinn.	L	5-6	Norman	Kison
25–Cinn.	L	5-6*	Bair	Tekulve
26–Cinn.	L	7-9	Soto	Roberts
27–At Mon.	W	5-4	Tekulve	Sosa
27–At Mon.	W	9-1	Blyleven	Sanderson
28–At Mon.	W	5-3	Bibby	Schatzeder

JULY			Winner	Loser
29–At Mon.	L	3-5	Rogers	Kison
30–N. York	W	8-5	Jackson	Bernard
31–N. York	L	1-2	Twitchell	Blyleven
		Won 20, Lost 11		

AUGUST				
1–St. Louis	W	4-3	Romo	Forsch
2–St. Louis	L	4-5	Frazier	Jackson
3–Phila.	W	6-3	Romo	McGraw
3–Phila.	W	5-1	Bibby	Christenson
4–Phila.	W	4-0	Candelaria	Espinosa
5–Phila.	W	12-8	Tekulve	Eastwick
5–Phila.	W	5-2	Romo	Noles
7–At Chi.	L	2-15	Reuschel	Rooker
8–At Chi.	W	5-2*	Tekulve	Tidrow
9–At Chi.	L	3-11	Lamp	Candelaria
10–At Phila.	L	3-4‡	Eastwick	Jackson
10–At Phila.	W	3-2	Kison	Lerch
11–At Phila.	W	14-11	Romo	Eastwick
13–At Phila.	W	9-1	Bibby	Christenson
14–S. Diego	W	7-1	Candelaria	D'Acquisto
15–S. Diego	W	5-1	Blyleven	Jones
16–S. Diego	W	5-4	Kison	Perry
17–Los Ang.	L	6-7	Patterson	Bibby
18–Los Ang.	L	1-5	Reuss	Robinson
19–Los Ang.	W	2-0	Tekulve	Hooton
20–S. Fran.	W	6-5	Romo	Lavelle
21–S. Fran.	L	1-6	Knepper	Kison
22–S. Fran.	W	8-6	Tekulve	Lavelle
24–At S.D.	L	2-3	Jones	Romo
25–At S.D.	W	4-3z	Roberts	D'Acquisto
26–At S.D.	W	9-2	Kison	Shirley
27–At L.A.	L	2-4	Brett	Tekulve
28–At L.A.	W	4-1	Candelaria	Hough
29–At L.A.	W	4-1	Blyleven	Reuss
31–At S.F.	W	6-4	Robinson	Curtis
		Won 21, Lost 9		

SEPTEMBER				
1–At S.F.	W	5-3	Kison	Montefusco
1–At S.F.	W	7-2	Bibby	Knepper
2–At S.F.	W	5-3	Candelaria	Blue
3–Phila.	L	0-2	Carlton	Blyleven
3–Phila.	W	7-3	Rooker	Lerch
5–At St.L.	W	7-5†	Roberts	Thomas
6–At St.L.	L	6-8	Martinez	Bibby
7–At N.Y.	W	6-4x	Jackson	Allen
8–At N.Y.	L	2-3y	Ellis	Rooker
9–At N.Y.	W	6-5	Tekulve	Glynn
11–St. Louis	W	7-3	Roberts	Denny
12–St. Louis	W	2-0	Candelaria	Forsch
15–N. York	W	5-4	Roberts	Glynn
16–N. York	L	0-3	Falcone	Candelaria
17–At Mon.	W	2-1	Robinson	Rogers
18–At Mon.	W	5-3†	Jackson	Murray
19–At Phila.	W	9-6	Tekulve	Eastwick
19–At Phila.	L	5-6	Kucek	Romo
20–At Phila.	L	1-2	Lerch	Tekulve
21–At Chi.	L	0-2	McGlothen	Robinson
22–At Chi.	W	4-1	Kison	Riley
23–At Chi.	W	6-0	Bibby	Reuschel
24–Montreal	W	5-2	Blyleven	Schatzeder
24–Montreal	L	6-7	Grimsley	Jackson
25–Montreal	W	10-4	Rooker	Sanderson
26–Montreal	W	10-1	Kison	Rogers
27–St. Louis	L	5-9	Forsch	Roberts
28–Chicago	W	6-1	Bibby	Reuschel
29–Chicago	L	6-7§	Caudill	Robinson
30–Chicago	W	5-3	Kison	McGlothen
		Won 20, Lost 10		

*10 innings. †11 innings. ‡12 innings. §13 innings. x14 innings. y15 innings. z19 innings. a11-inning tie game.

Expos Eliminated on Final Day

By IAN MacDONALD

The Montreal Expos' most successful season ever was a total team effort.

With only one regular hitting better than .283 and one pitcher winning more than 13 games, the Expos nevertheless won 30 games more than they lost with a 95-65 season.

Their chances for a possible National League East crown were very much alive on the final day of the schedule. However, they lost 2-0 to Steve Carlton and the Phillies and their most glorious season by far had fallen just short.

Even had they won that final game, the Expos weren't home free. They would have had to flip down to Atlanta for a makeup doubleheader with the Braves on the next day. Had they won those two, then the NL playoffs would have been delayed while the Expos and the Pirates played sudden death in Montreal.

Few would have bet against the Expos at that stage because they had fought gamely through a torturous September schedule as it was. More than anything else, it was that hectic September which saw them play eight doubleheaders that finally took its toll.

By winning 16 more games than any Expos' club had ever managed before, they had a finishing record which would have given them the division title in five of the seasons that the Expos have been in existence since 1969.

Montreal fans, accustomed to excellence and championship performances from their hockey Canadiens, turned out in record numbers and patented some of the most rousing standing ovations ever recorded on a regular basis. All told, more than 2.1 million fans flocked to the Olympic Stadium where the Expos forged a tremendous 56-25 record.

While lefthander Bill Lee was the team's big winner at 16-10, there were six pitchers with 10 wins or more. The staff as a whole led the majors with an ERA of 3.14 and nine members of the staff had ERAs of 3.43 or better.

Lee finished the season with six straight wins but took a back seat in that department to 21-year-old David Palmer who won his last eight decisions and finished with a 10-2 record.

Palmer typifies what this team, which fielded six 25-year-olds among their starting eight, was all about.

The only rookie to head north with the team, Palmer made the Expos as a short man because he threw strikes. It was July 13 when Manager Dick Williams gave Palmer his first start and 17 days later he was made a member of the rotation.

Lefthander Dan Schatzeder and the bullet-throwing Scott Sanderson, with 10 and nine wins respectively, figured to become huge winners before many seasons had passed.

Steve Rogers, the six-year ace of the staff, and Ross Grimsley, the team's '78 player of the year, fell something short of expectations. They barely finished above .500, Rogers at 13-12 and Grimsley at 10-9.

Coming off elbow surgery, Rogers posted an ERA of 3.00 in 249 innings and, as one of four Montreal representatives on the NL All-Star team, threw two shutout innings at the American League in the classic. Grimsley, after

MONTREAL EXPOS—1979

Front row—Perez, Rapp, coach; Alou, coach; Sherry, coach; Williams, manager; Virgil, coach; Brewer, coach; Mullin, coach; Staub. Second row—Kirby, traveling secretary; Stone, equipment manager; Sosa, Rogers, Carter, Lee, Macha, Cash, Fryman, Lavigueur, assistant trainer; Belanger, trainer. Third row—Speier, Cromartie, White, Palmer, Atkinson, Hutton, Bernazard, Raines, Tamargo, Schatzeder. Fourth row—Bahnsen, Dyer, Bass, Grimsley, Dawson, Sanderson, Murray, Parrish, Pate, May. Seated in front—Albertson, ballboy; Scott, Trubiano, batboy.

becoming the Expos' first ever 20-game winner in '78, was off and on from the start and eventually was bounced from the rotation.

It says something for the Expos, though, that with their two big men coming up shy they still managed to have such a wonderful season.

Elias Sosa, the third free agent in as many years to give the Expos a superb first season, led a dogged bullpen corps. Though his record was only 8-7, Sosa saved 18 and his ERA in 62 appearances covering 97 innings was a sparkling 1.95.

The highlight for the pitching staff as a unit was undoubtedly a late May performance which saw Rogers, Lee and Sanderson throw consecutive shutouts at the defending East Division champions, the Phillies.

Third baseman Larry Parrish, the unanimous choice among media followers of the team as the Expos' player of the year, sparked an offense which, bereft of super stars, left the fewest runners on base in the league, scored the most runs in Expos' history (701), and finished third behind the Dodgers and Pirates in home runs (143).

Parrish, who finished fourth in the NL MVP voting, had the second-best average (.307) and second-highest home run total (30) in club history.

So much had been expected of the '78 Expos that their 76-86 record that year was probably the most disappointing ever. Williams vowed that '79, his third year at the helm, would see him return to the hard-nosed leadership which produced winners at Boston and Oakland.

"This isn't a personality contest," Williams pointed out. "I can't take time to worry about what my players think of me. I want them to think of winning. That's all that I'm thinking about and concerned with."

To parlay that attitude into success, President John McHale assumed the role of general manager as well and got Williams some help.

As the Expos lost 36 one-run decisions in '78, the bullpen and bench had to assume much of the responsibility. By wheeling and dealing, McHale rebuilt those areas of the team.

One move in that direction became particularly important. McHale traded Sam Mejias to the Cubs in exchange for Jerry White and Rodney Scott to give the Expos more speed and versatility on their bench.

Then, late in spring training, Williams made a bold move. He turned over veteran Dave Cash's second base job to Scott on the merits of what transpired at the training camp and the Expos were on their way.

Scott helped shore up an infield defense behind a mound staff that featured ground ball pitchers. In his own way and with his whirlwind speed, Scott turned his "little" bat into an offensive asset which sparked many of the Expos' tight wins.

Veteran Tommy Hutton united the bench players into the BUS Squad—broke, underrated superstars—and they all played key roles in the remarkable season.

SCORES OF MONTREAL EXPOS' 1979 GAMES

APRIL			Winner	Loser
6—At Pitts.	W	3-2*	Sosa	Tekulve
7—At Pitts.	L	6-7	Jackson	Sosa
8—At Pitts.	W	5-4	May	Romo
10—At N.Y.	W	3-2x	Palmer	Murray
11—At N.Y.	W	3-2†	Sosa	Lockwood
14—Chicago	W	2-0	Grimsley	Reuschel
15—Chicago	L	1-5	McGlothen	Rogers
16—Chicago	W	2-0	Lee	Krukow

APRIL			Winner	Loser
17—N. York	W	5-4‡	Fryman	Lockwood
18—N. York	W	6-5	Palmer	Murray
20—At Chi.	L	5-8	McGlothen	Fryman
21—At Chi.	L	3-4	Moore	Palmer
22—At Chi.	L	1-4	Reuschel	Sanderson
24—S. Diego	W	5-1	Grimsley	Jones
25—S. Diego	W	9-6	Rogers	Shirley
27—S. Fran.	W	14-8	Lee	Knepper

OFFICIAL BASEBALL GUIDE

			Winner	Loser
APRIL				
28—S. Fran.	W	6-4	Sanderson	Halicki
29—S. Fran.	W	7-5	Schatzeder	Blue
30—Los Ang.	W	8-4	Rogers	Rau
		Won 14, Lost 5		

			Winner	Loser
MAY				
1—Los Ang.	W	7-3	Lee	Welch
3—At S.D.	L	2-10	Jones	Sanderson
4—At S.D.	W	12-1	Grimsley	D'Acquisto
5—At S.D.	L	3-6	Mura	Fryman
6—At S.D.	W	7-5	Lee	Perry
8—At S.F.	W	4-0	Sanderson	Halicki
9—At S.F.	L	2-9	Blue	Grimsley
10—At S.F.	W	3-0	Rogers	Nastu
11—At L.A.	L	0-7	Rau	Lee
12—At L.A.	W	3-4†	Welch	Bahnsen
13—At L.A.	L	2-8	Sutcliffe	Grimsley
15—At St.L.	L	0-1	Denny	Rogers
16—At St.L.	L	0-2	Forsch	Lee
17—At St.L.	W	3-2y	Sosa	Schultz
18—At Phila.	W	5-3	Bahnsen	Ruthven
19—At Phila.	W	10-5	May	Eastwick
20—At Phila.	W	10-6	Bahnsen	Espinosa
21—Pitts.	L	2-4	Blyleven	Sanderson
22—Pitts.	W	6-3	Grimsley	Whitson
23—Pitts.	W	3-0	Rogers	Candelaria
27—St. Louis	W	8-3	Sanderson	Denny
27—St. Louis	L	3-11	Forsch	Grimsley
29—Phila.	W	9-0	Rogers	Ruthven
30—Phila.	W	2-0	Lee	Espinosa
31—Phila.	W	1-0	Sanderson	Christenson
		Won 15, Lost 10		

			Winner	Loser
JUNE				
1—At Hous.	L	2-3	Richard	Grimsley
2—At Hous.	L	1-2	Andujar	Sosa
3—At Hous.	L	4-5	Niekro	Rogers
4—At Atl.	W	8-1	Lee	Brizzolara
5—At Atl.	L	1-4	Matula	Sanderson
6—At Atl.	W	12-2	Grimsley	Niekro
8—At Cinn.	L	2-3	LaCoss	Schatzeder
9—At Cinn.	L	1-7	Seaver	Lee
10—At Cinn.	L	2-3	Hume	Sosa
11—Atlanta	W	6-5†	Fryman	Skok
13—Atlanta	W	4-1	Rogers	Matula
14—Atlanta	W	4-3	Sosa	Garber
15—Houston	L	1-2	Andujar	Sosa
16—Houston	W	4-2	Grimsley	Richard
17—Houston	W	19-3	Schatzeder	Niekro
18—Cinn.	L	2-5	Bonham	Rogers
19—Cinn.	W	3-2	Lee	LaCoss
20—Cinn.	W	5-4†	Sosa	Hume
22—Phila.	W	6-5	Grimsley	Lerch
23—Phila.	W	3-0	Rogers	Espinosa
24—Phila.	L	2-5	Christenson	Lee
25—At St.L.	W	8-2	Schatzeder	Fulgham
26—At St.L.	W	5-3	Grimsley	Denny
27—St.L.	L	0-5	Martinez	Rogers
29—At Pitts.	L	5-6	Kison	Lee
30—At Pitts.	W	5-3	Sanderson	Blyleven
		Won 14, Lost 12		

			Winner	Loser
JULY				
2—At Chi.	W	5-0	Rogers	Lamp
3—At Chi.	L	2-3	Sutter	Fryman
4—At Chi.	W	2-1	Lee	Caudill
5—At Chi.	L	1-3	Reuschel	Sanderson
6—Los Ang.	W	6-4	Schatzeder	Reuss
7—Los Ang.	W	2-1	Rogers	Hooton
8—Los Ang.	L	6-8	Sutcliffe	Grimsley
9—Los Ang.	W	3-0	Lee	Sutton
10—S. Fran.	L	7-11§	Griffin	Fryman
11—S. Fran.	L	0-1	Curtis	Schatzeder
12—S. Fran.	L	3-5	Montefusco	Rogers
13—S. Diego	L	5-7	Owchinko	Sosa

			Winner	Loser
JULY				
13—S. Diego	W	10-7	May	Owchinko
14—S. Diego	L	1-5	Jones	Lee
15—S. Diego	W	4-0	Sanderson	D'Acquisto
19—At L.A.	L	3-7	Hooton	Schatzeder
20—At L.A.	L	5-6†	Patterson	Fryman
21—At L.A.	W	7-2	Lee	Sutton
22—At S.F.	L	6-8	Blue	Grimsley
22—At S.F.	W	15-5	May	Whitson
23—At S.F.	W	8-3	Schatzeder	Curtis
24—At S.D.	L	3-4x	Mura	Palmer
25—At S.D.	W	6-5	May	Owchinko
27—At Pitts.	L	4-5	Tekulve	Sosa
27—At Pitts.	L	1-9	Blyleven	Sanderson
28—At Pitts.	L	3-5	Bibby	Schatzeder
29—At Pitts.	W	5-3	Rogers	Kison
30—St. Louis	L	2-7	Denny	Lee
30—St. Louis	W	5-1	Palmer	Thomas
31—St. Louis	W	5-0	May	Martinez
		Won 14, Lost 16		

			Winner	Loser
AUGUST				
1—Chicago	W	7-5‡	Sanderson	Hernandez
2—Chicago	W	6-4	Schatzeder	Caudill
3—N. York	W	10-6	Bahnsen	Murray
4—N. York	L	2-3	Swan	Lee
5—N. York	L	2-4	Ellis	Grimsley
5—N. York	W	7-3	May	Twitchell
7—At Phila.	L	2-4	Christenson	Sanderson
8—At Phila.	L	3-4	Reed	Sosa
9—At Phila.	L	4-6	Espinosa	Lee
10—At N.Y.	L	1-7	Swan	Grimsley
10—At N.Y.	W	6-5	Palmer	Bernard
11—At N.Y.	W	5-2	Schatzeder	Falcone
13—At Hous.	L	1-4	Richard	Rogers
14—At Hous.	L	1-2	Andujar	Lee
15—At Hous.	W	3-0	Schatzeder	Niekro
17—Atlanta	W	1-0	Palmer	Solomon
18—Atlanta	W	2-1	Rogers	J. McL'ghlin
19—Atlanta	W	5-1	Lee	Brizzolara
20—Atlanta	W	5-2	Schatzeder	Norman
21—At Cinn.	L	2-3	Seaver	May
22—At Cinn.	L	2-7	LaCoss	Rogers
24—At Atl.	W	2-0	Lee	Niekro
27—Houston	L	0-3	Richard	May
28—Houston	W	7-6	Palmer	Ladd
29—Houston	W	5-3	Lee	Niekro
31—Cinn.	W	8-7*	Fryman	Hume
		Won 15, Lost 11		

			Winner	Loser
SEPTEMBER				
1—Cinn.	W	7-2	Palmer	Seaver
2—Cinn.	W	13-1	Rogers	LaCoss
3—N. York	W	7-2	Lee	Burris
3—N. York	W	6-5*	Atkinson	Allen
4—N. York	W	5-1	May	Ellis
5—At Chi.	W	4-3	Sosa	Reuschel
6—At Chi.	W	1-0	Palmer	McGlothen
7—At St.L.	L	4-5	Forsch	Rogers
8—At St.L.	W	7-2	Lee	Fulgham
9—At St.L.	W	4-1	May	Vuckovich
11—Chicago	W	8-6	Palmer	McGlothen
11—Chicago	W	3-2	Schatzeder	Caudill
12—Chicago	W	6-3	Rogers	Sutter
13—Chicago	W	4-3	Atkinson	Reuschel
15—St. Louis	W	2-1†	Sosa	McEnaney
15—St. Louis	L	1-4	Fulgham	May
16—St. Louis	L	3-4	Martinez	Grimsley
16—St. Louis	W	5-1*	Sanderson	Thomas
17—Pitts.	L	1-2	Robinson	Rogers
18—Pitts.	L	3-5†	Jackson	Murray
19—At N.Y.	W	3-1	Grimsley	Swan
19—At N.Y.	W	4-1	May	Hausman
20—At N.Y.	W	6-3	Murray	Reardon
20—At N.Y.	W	2-0	Sanderson	Scott

SEPTEMBER			Winner	Loser
22—At Phila.	L	8-9*	Reed	Murray
22—At Phila.	W	8-2	Palmer	Noles
23—At Phila.	W	7-4	Lee	Espinosa
24—At Pitts.	L	2-5	Blyleven	Schatzeder
24—At Pitts.	W	7-6	Grimsley	Jackson
25—At Pitts.	L	4-10	Rooker	Sanderson

SEPTEMBER			Winner	Loser
26—At Pitts.	L	1-10	Kison	Rogers
28—Phila.	L	2-3†	Reed	Fryman
29—Phila.	W	3-2	Sosa	Eastwick
30—Phila.	L	0-2	Carlton	Rogers
			Won 23, Lost 11	

*10 innings. †11 innings. ‡12 innings. §13 innings. x14 innings. y11-inning suspended game, completed June 25.

Brock Comeback Revitalized Redbirds

By RICK HUMMEL

The comeback of the Cardinals in 1979 was best reflected by the comeback of Lou Brock.

In 1978, St. Louis posted its worst record in 54 years, 69-93, and was spared the basement in the National League East only through the grace of the New York Mets. Meanwhile, Brock was having his worst season ever at .221.

Brock, 100 hits shy of 3,000 after the season and 39 years old, decided he would give it one more try although Manager Ken Boyer was skeptical that the left fielder had anything more to offer. "I thought he had had it," said Boyer, who told Brock in spring training that he would have 30 days—no more—to prove himself.

Proof positive came early as Brock almost immediately leaped into the National League batting lead, a lead he was to hold into mid-July. He completed his last season as a major leaguer with a .304 batting average and 123 hits. The 100th of the season and 3,000th of his career was a line drive off the pitching hand of Chicago's Dennis Lamp on August 13.

"I wanted to orchestrate my own exodus," said Brock of his season. "I wanted to go out in a blaze of glory."

After Brock had passed the 3,000 milestone, he found still another challenge for himself in the stolen-base mark of 937 held by Sliding Billy Hamilton. Never mind that Hamilton's pre-modern era mark had included stolen bases given him for going from first to third on singles. Brock, who was generally accepted as the record-holder, wanted to "close the book, with Sliding Billy in it."

A week before the season ended, Brock closed that book, stealing the last of 938 bases he swiped in a career which began in 1962.

The Cardinals rebounded to have their best season since 1974. Despite four season-ending losses to the Mets, they finished 10 games above .500 at 86-76 and stayed on the periphery of the pennant race until mid-September.

The individual highlight was first baseman Keith Hernandez' five-star season. His .344 average (the majors' best) gave the Cardinals their first batting champ since Joe Torre in 1971 and was the main reason that he was selected the NL Player of the Year by THE SPORTING NEWS in a vote of the players and shared the BBWAA MVP crown with Pittsburgh's Willie Stargell. It was the first time that the balloting ever had resulted in a tie.

Hernandez improved his average 89 points from 1978, drove in 105 runs despite hitting only 11 homers, and led the majors in doubles with 48.

Shortstop Garry Templeton became the first player in recorded history to achieve 100 hits from both sides of the plate. The switch-hitting Templeton

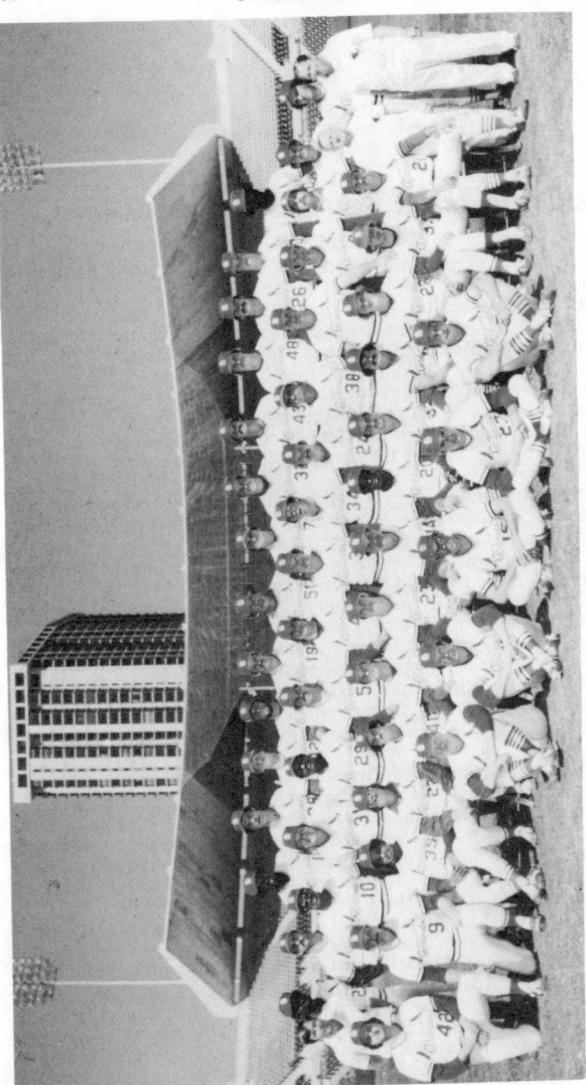

ST. LOUIS CARDINALS—1979

Front row—Sykes, Swisher, Martinez, Schultz, Edelen, Fulgham, Simmons, Boyer, manager; Brock, Hernandez, Reitz, Herr, Ramsey, Lentine, Yatkeman, equipment manager; Bauman, trainer. Second row—Gieselmann, trainer; Hendrick, Bruno, Durham, Forsch, Mumphrey, Siebert, Vuckovich, Willoughby, O'Brien, Oberkfell, Urrea, Kennedy, Grieve, Tyson, Phillips, Carbo. Third row—Templeton, Denny, Penniall, McEnaney, Iorg, Knowles, Freed, Littell, Frazier, Seaman, Dressler, Murphy, Scott. Seated in front—coaches Schoendienst, Osteen, Ricketts, Maxvill and Krol.

was given permission by Boyer to bat strictly righthanded for the last 10 days of the season and he got the nine hits he needed. He led the league with 211 hits.

Before the season, Templeton had demanded to be traded if he wasn't going to be appreciated more. Salary and criticism of his style were among his complaints. Then, he refused to go to the All-Star Game when selected as a reserve because he was miffed at not being the starter ("If I ain't startin', I ain't departin' ") and because he said he wanted to spend the three days at home with his family.

But there were few complaints about Templeton at year's end. He finished with a .314 average, better than any other shortstop in baseball, and led the league in triples (19) for the third straight year, something no one had ever done before. He did make 34 errors, but even that total was down from 40 and was somewhat mitigated by dozens of brilliant plays.

The Cardinals, raising their team batting average from .249 to a league-leading .278, had five regulars at .300 or above. In addition to Brock, Hernandez and Templeton, right fielder George Hendrick hit .300 and second baseman Ken Oberkfell, one of the surprises of the season, ended at .301. Hendrick's year, however, was a disappointment. He drove in only 75 runs and hit only 16 homers.

Inasmuch as Oberkfell had hit only .120 in limited duty the year before, little was expected of him, but he moved into a platoon arrangement with incumbent Mike Tyson early in the season and took over the job fulltime in August when Tyson suffered a knee injury. Oberkfell also made only nine errors in 134 games.

All this hitting and a strong staff of righthanded starters might have been sufficient for a division title had catcher Ted Simmons not been hurt and had the Cardinals had a decent bullpen.

Simmons, off to the best start of his career, suffered a broken bone in his left wrist on June 24 and missed the next month—a span in which the Cardinals were 11-17. When he came back in late July, he was not at full strength although he wound up with 26 homers and 87 RBIs in only 123 games.

Other than Mark Littell, who parlayed a strong second half into a final showing of 9-4, 13 saves and a 2.20 ERA, the Cardinal bullpen was a guessing game. The Redbirds were to finish with the lowest save total in the league (25, tied with San Diego) and lost 26 games in the opposition's last time at bat.

John Denny fought with himself in an 8-11 season in which he walked 100 batters and struck out 99. But he was picked up by second-year man Silvio Martinez, who tied for the staff victory lead at 15, and by rookie John Fulgham, who won 10 games in just 3½ months.

Fulgham was called up from Springfield as a temporary replacement when lefthander Bob Sykes went on the disabled list with a circulatory problem in his shoulder. Fulgham pitched a complete game in his first start, allowing no earned runs, and became a permanent part of the rotation.

Pete Vuckovich, though not quite as sharp as he had been in his first year with the Cardinals, tied Martinez at 15 victories and Bob Forsch won seven of his last eight decisions to even his record at 11-11.

At the beginning of the season, Cardinal management had promised nothing more than a .500 season. The Cardinals went five victories above that and fans in St. Louis were pleased. Attendance was up 349,000 to 1,627,256.

SCORES OF ST. LOUIS CARDINALS' 1979 GAMES

APRIL

Date		Score	Winner	Loser
6–Phila.	W	8-1	Denny	Carlton
7–Phila.	W	3-2	Vuckovich	Reed
8–Phila.	T	2-2*	....	....
10–Chicago	W	7-0	Sykes	McGlothen
12–At Pitts.	L	1-3	Robinson	Denny
13–At Pitts.	L	6-7	Bibby	Schultz
14–At Pitts.	L	4-7	Whitson	Forsch
15–At Pitts.	W	9-4†	Littell	Tekulve
17–At Chi.	L	3-5	Holtzman	Denny
18–At Chi.	W	3-2y	Bruno	Moore
19–At Chi.	L	2-3	Lamp	Forsch
20–Cinn.	L	3-10	Norman	Sykes
21–Cinn.	L	1-4	LaCoss	Martinez
22–Cinn.	W	4-3	Schultz	Hume
23–At Atl.	W	3-2†	Littell	Niekro
24–At Atl.	W	6-5†	Littell	Garber
27–At Cinn.	L	3-4	Pastore	Littell
28–At Cinn.	W	12-1	Vuckovich	Hume
29–At Cinn.	L	1-5	Moskau	Sykes
30–Houston	L	5-6	Sambito	Bruno

Won 9, Lost 10

MAY

Date		Score	Winner	Loser
1–Houston	W	7-6‡	Knowles	Sambito
2–Houston	W	5-2	Denny	K. Forsch
3–Houston	L	1-4	Niekro	Vuckovich
4–Pitts.	W	4-3	Sykes	Robinson
5–Pitts.	L	5-6	Jackson	Vuckovich
6–Pitts.	W	4-2	Martinez	Kison
8–At Hous.	W	4-1	McLaughlin	K. Forsch
9–At Hous.	L	4-5a	McLaughlin	Bruno
10–At Hous.	W	3-1	Sykes	Richard
11–Atlanta	L	0-3	Devine	Forsch
12–Atlanta	W	7-6	Schultz	Garber
13–Atlanta	W	7-3	Vuckovich	Niekro
15–Montreal	W	1-0	Denny	Rogers
16–Montreal	W	2-0	Forsch	Lee
17–Montreal	L	2-3b	Sosa	Schultz
19–At N.Y.	W	9-4§	Knowles	Bernard
20–At N.Y.	L	7-8‡	Allen	Knowles
21–At Phila.	L	3-5	Carlton	Denny
22–At Phila.	L	1-3	McGraw	Forsch
23–At Phila.	W	3-1	Martinez	Ruthven
27–At Mon.	L	3-8	Sanderson	Denny
27–At Mon.	W	11-3	Forsch	Grimsley
29–N. York	L	2-6	Zachry	Vuckovich
30–N. York	W	7-3	Martinez	Swan
31–N. York	W	9-6	Sykes	Scott

Won 15, Lost 10

JUNE

Date		Score	Winner	Loser
1–Los Ang.	W	8-7‡	Schultz	Welch
2–Los Ang.	W	12-5	Forsch	Rau
3–Los Ang.	W	6-4	Vuckovich	Hooton
5–S. Fran.	W	5-4	Littell	Moffitt
6–S. Fran.	W	6-5	Schultz	Moffitt
7–S. Fran.	L	7-8†	Griffin	Littell
8–S. Diego	L	10-12	Fingers	Knowles
9–S. Diego	W	7-4	Vuckovich	Rasmussen
10–S. Diego	W	3-2	Martinez	Jones
11–At L.A.	W	9-7	Bruno	LaGrow
12–At L.A.	L	3-9	Hooton	Denny
13–At L.A.	L	8-9	Sutcliffe	Forsch
15–At S.F.	L	6-9x	Lavelle	Knowles
16–At S.F.	L	1-6	Curtis	Martinez
17–At S.F.	L	4-7	Moffitt	Schultz
18–At S.D.	L	2-3	Jones	Forsch
19–At S.D.	W	7-2	Fulgham	Rasmussen
20–At S.D.	L	1-3	Perry	Vuckovich
22–N. York	W	4-2	Martinez	Kobel
24–N. York	L	2-6	Hassler	Forsch
25–Montreal	L	2-8	Schatzeder	Fulgham

JUNE

Date		Score	Winner	Loser
26–Montreal	L	3-5	Grimsley	Denny
27–Montreal	W	5-0	Martinez	Rogers
29–Phila.	L	7-8	Saucier	Forsch
29–Phila.	W	7-1	Vuckovich	Christenson
30–Phila.	L	4-6†	Reed	Frazier

Won 12, Lost 14

JULY

Date		Score	Winner	Loser
1–Phila.	W	13-7	Littell	McGraw
1–Phila.	W	2-1	Litteli	Lerch
2–Pitts.	L	4-5	Romo	Knowles
3–Pitts.	L	1-4	Candelaria	Forsch
4–Pitts.	L	4-6	Blyleven	Vuckovich
5–Pitts.	W	2-0	Fulgham	Rooker
6–At Atl.	W	9-5	Denny	Solomon
6–At Atl.	W	5-4†	Frazier	Skok
7–At Atl.	L	2-10	Brizzolara	Martinez
8–At Atl.	L	5-6	Garber	Littell
9–At Cinn.	W	6-3	Vuckovich	Bonham
10–At Cinn.	L	2-4	Seaver	Fulgham
11–At Cinn.	L	1-6	LaCoss	Denny
13–At Hous.	W	1-0	Martinez	K. Forsch
14–At Hous.	L	2-3	Andujar	Vuckovich
15–At Hous.	W	3-1	Fulgham	Richard
19–Cinn.	L	4-16	Norman	Vuckovich
20–Cinn.	L	0-3	Seaver	Denny
21–Cinn.	W	12-3	Martinez	LaCoss
22–Houston	L	6-7	Sambito	McEnaney
23–Houston	L	2-3	Niekro	Fulgham
24–Atlanta	W	7-3	Vuckovich	Brizzolara
25–Atlanta	L	4-13	J. McL'ghlin	Frazier
26–Atlanta	L	6-2	Martinez	Solomon
27–At Phila.	W	5-0	Forsch	Espinosa
28–At Phila.	W	5-4	Littell	Reed
29–At Phila.	W	6-5	Vuckovich	Lerch
30–At Mon.	W	7-2	Denny	Lee
30–At Mon.	L	1-5	Palmer	Thomas
31–At Mon.	L	0-5	May	Martinez

Won 15, Lost 15

AUGUST

Date		Score	Winner	Loser
1–At Pitts.	L	3-4	Romo	Forsch
2–At Pitts.	W	5-4	Frazier	Jackson
3–At Chi.	L	2-4	Reuschel	Vuckovich
4–At Chi.	L	6-8	Krukow	Denny
5–At Chi.	L	2-3	Hernandez	Martinez
5–At Chi.	W	5-4	Forsch	Holtzman
7–At N.Y.	W	9-2	Fulgham	Kobel
8–At N.Y.	W	2-1	Thomas	Falcone
8–At N.Y.	W	8-4	Vuckovich	Hassler
9–At N.Y.	W	4-0	Denny	Ellis
10–Chicago	W	13-8	Martinez	Krukow
10–Chicago	W	5-3	Forsch	Caudill
11–Chicago	L	3-7	Reuschel	Thomas
12–Chicago	L	3-5	Hernandez	Fulgham
13–Chicago	W	3-2	Littell	Hernandez
14–Los Ang.	L	0-9	Hooton	Denny
15–Los Ang.	L	5-6	Sutcliffe	Martinez
16–Los Ang.	L	2-4z	Castillo	Frazier
17–S. Fran.	W	3-0	Fulgham	Whitson
18–S. Fran.	W	5-4	Thomas	Blue
19–S. Fran.	W	4-0	Denny	Curtis
20–S. Diego	W	6-3	Martinez	Perry
21–S. Diego	L	2-3‡	Shirley	McEnaney
22–S. Diego	W	8-5	Fulgham	Owchinko
24–At L.A.	W	12-5	Vuckovich	Reuss
25–At L.A.	L	1-4	Thomas	Brett
26–At L.A.	L	1-4	Sutcliffe	Martinez
28–At S.F.	W	2-1	Forsch	Knepper
29–At S.F.	W	5-1	Fulgham	Blue
30–At S.F.	L	2-3	Whitson	Vuckovich
31–At S.D.	W	8-7z	O'Brien	Owchinko

Won 19, Lost 12

SEPTEMBER			Winner	Loser
1—At S.D.	W	5-3	Martinez	Jones
2—At S.D.	W	2-1	Forsch	Lee
3—At Chi.	W	2-1	Fulgham	Lamp
4—At Chi.	W	6-4	Vuckovich	Hernandez
5—Pitts.	L	5-7‡	Roberts	Thomas
6—Pitts.	W	8-6	Martinez	Bibby
7—Montreal	W	5-4	Forsch	Rogers
8—Montreal	L	2-7	Lee	Fulgham
9—Montreal	L	1-4	May	Vuckovich
11—At Pitts.	L	3-7	Roberts	Denny
12—At Pitts.	L	0-2	Candelaria	Forsch
15—At Mon.	L	1-2‡	Sosa	McEnaney
15—At Mon.	W	4-1	Fulgham	May
16—At Mon.	W	4-3	Martinez	Grimsley
16—At Mon.	L	1-5†	Sanderson	Thomas
17—Phila.	L	5-7	Carlton	Knowles

SEPTEMBER			Winner	Loser
18—Phila.	L	3-5†	McGraw	O'Brien
19—Chicago	W	6-3	Vuckovich	Capilla
19—Chicago	L	2-3†	Sutter	Fulgham
20—Chicago	W	2-1	Martinez	Lamp
22—At N.Y.	W	6-3	Denny	Pacella
22—At N.Y.	W	3-2	Forsch	Falcone
23—At N.Y.	W	7-4†	Littell	Hassler
24—At Phila.	W	7-2	Vuckovich	Lerch
25—At Phila.	W	4-1	Fulgham	Larson
26—At Phila.	L	5-11	Carlton	Martinez
27—At Pitts.	W	9-5	Forsch	Roberts
28—N. York	L	2-6	Berenguer	Bruno
28—N. York	L	6-7‡	Allen	Frazier
29—N. York	L	7-8	Swan	Sykes
30—N. York	L	2-4	Jackson	Littell

Won 16, Lost 15

*5-inning tie game. †10 innings. ‡11 innings. §12 innings. x13 innings. y14 innings. z15 innings a16 innings. b11-inning suspended game, completed June 25.

Phils Flopped in Second-Division Finish

By HAL BODLEY

Injuries, disappointment and a fourth-place finish summarized the Philadelphia Phillies' 1979 season.

After winning the National League East Division championship for three straight years, the Phils went out and signed celebrated free-agent Pete Rose for $3.2 million. That acquisition, they thought, would lead them to the World Series, in which they had not played since 1950. But an 84-78 record resulted.

Those thoughts were fueled when they obtained second baseman Manny Trillo, outfielder Greg Gross and catcher Dave Rader from the Chicago Cubs. And to bolster the pitching staff, Nino Espinosa was obtained from the New York Mets and Doug Bird from Kansas City.

But the pattern for 1979 was established in February and continued through September. During a benefit bicycle caravan, righthanded pitcher Larry Christenson fell and fractured his collarbone. That was the first of 22 injuries. The pitching staff, suspect even when healthy, was hit hardest. The injuries and an ineffective bullpen contributed to the team's 4.16 ERA.

Rookie Jim Wright fractured his arm and was lost for the season. Reliever Warren Brusstar, an integral part of the bullpen, had a back problem and was lost for most of the year. Righthanded ace Dick Ruthven came up with bone chips in spring training and even though he sprinted out to a 6-0 record, became ineffective because of the problem, eventually went on the 21-day disabled list, and finally decided to have surgery.

On July 4th, the Phils lost three starting pitchers. Ruthven went on the disabled list, Christenson pulled a groin muscle and joined Ruthven, while lefthander Randy Lerch fractured a thumb during a brawl when he was jumped by some teenagers outside a Philadelphia restaurant the night before.

In addition, shortstop Larry Bowa and Trillo both were lost earlier in the season with broken bones—Bowa a thumb, Trillo a hand.

The final serious injury happened in mid-September when All-Star catcher Bob Boone tore ligaments in his knee and underwent surgery. Every member of the starting lineup and starting pitching corps missed time because of injuries with the exception of Rose, who played in every game.

PHILADELPHIA PHILLIES—1979

Front row—Unser, Aviles, Tiefenauer, coach; Starrette, coach; Wine, coach; Ozark, manager; DeMars, coach; Taylor, coach; Meoli, Gross. Second row—Seger, trainer; Lerch, Ferenz, traveling secretary; Cera, assistant clubhouse manager; Trillo, Cardenal, Rose, Rader, McBride, Schmidt, McCarver, Luzinski, McGraw, Boone, Hoefling, flexibility instructor; Cooper, assistant trainer; Ruthven, Bush, clubhouse manager. Third row—Espinosa, Brusstar, Carlton, Anderson, Lonborg, Maddox, Bird, Reed, Christenson, Eastwick, Bowa. Seated in front—batboys Murphy, Andersen and Watts.

The Phils vaulted out to a 24-10 record, climaxing a 10-4 road trip by winning a record-breaking, 10-inning, 23-22 marathon over the Cubs at Wrigley Field on May 17. That left the Phils atop the East by four games. They were able to win only 11 of their next 34 games and fell out of the race.

They struggled most of the year and on August 31, the dean of NL managers, Danny Ozark, was fired. He had been the pilot since 1973. Minor League Director Dallas Green took over. The Phils were 19-11 under him and he was rewarded with a contract for 1980.

On the plus side, the Phils set a club record in attendance at 2,775,011, second best in the majors. They averaged 36,039 for 77 dates, also a club record. It was their fourth straight season over 2-million spectators.

Rose did not disappoint. He led the majors with a 23-game hitting streak. He batted safely in 26 of his last 27 games, and in that span was 49-for-111 (.441). He became the first player in major league history to collect 200 or more hits in 10 different seasons, surpassing Ty Cobb's record. On August 5 in Pittsburgh, he became the all-time singles hitter in National League history, breaking Honus Wagner's record with single No. 2,427. It came off Bert Blyleven. His .331 average was second to NL champ Keith Hernandez.

Mike Schmidt set a Phillies' season record with 45 home runs, second to the 48 slugged by the Cubs' Dave Kingman. Schmidt hit 13 home runs in July, including seven in five games. His 20 game-winning RBIs and 120 walks led the league.

Shortstop Larry Bowa committed just six errors, all on the road.

Bowa failed to break the major-league record of seven errors held by Eddie Brinkman because he did not play the required 150 games.

In the final breakdown, the Phils had a winning record against the West (40-32) but a losing record against the East (44-46). They were only 43-38 at Veterans Stadium and 41-40 on the road.

SCORES OF PHILADELPHIA PHILLIES' 1979 GAMES

APRIL			Winner	Loser
6—At St.L.	L	1-8	Denny	Carlton
7—At St.L.	L	2-3	Vuckovich	Reed
8—At St.L.	T	2-2*	....	....
10—Pitts.	W	7-3	Ruthven	Romo
11—Pitts.	W	5-4	Carlton	Blyleven
12—At N.Y.	L	2-3	Zachry	Lerch
15—At N.Y.	W	3-2	Ruthven	Swan
15—At N.Y.	W	6-3	Espinosa	Allen
17—At Pitts.	W	13-2	Carlton	Blyleven
18—At Pitts.	W	3-2	Lerch	Robinson
20—N. York	W	8-0	Ruthven	Swan
21—N. York	W	3-0	Espinosa	Allen
22—N. York	L	2-4	Orosco	Carlton
23—Los Ang.	W	4-3‡	McGraw	Rautzhan
24—Los Ang.	W	7-6‡	Reed	Reuss
25—Los Ang.	W	5-4	Reed	Sutcliffe
27—S. Diego	W	2-0	Espinosa	Perry
28—S. Diego	L	0-5	D'Acquisto	Carlton
29—S. Diego	W	4-3	Reed	Fingers
30—S. Fran.	W	4-1	Ruthven	Nastu

Won 14, Lost 5

MAY				
1—S. Fran.	L	0-7	Knepper	Espinosa
3—At L.A.	L	2-5	Sutcliffe	Carlton
4—At L.A.	W	5-2	Lerch	Sutton
5—At L.A.	W	11-0	Ruthven	Messersmith
6—At L.A.	W	4-0	Espinosa	Rau
7—At S.D.	W	11-6	Carlton	Owchinko

MAY			Winner	Loser
8—At S.D.	W	9-8x	Kaat	D'Acquisto
9—At S.D.	W	2-0	Ruthven	Rasmussen
10—At S.D.	W	3-2	Espinosa	Perry
11—At S.F.	L	1-2	Knepper	Carlton
12—At S.F.	L	1-4	Halicki	Lerch
13—At S.F.	W	12-3	Reed	Blue
15—At Chi.	L	1-7	McGlothen	Espinosa
16—At Chi.	W	13-0	Carlton	Reuschel
17—At Chi.	W	23-22‡	Eastwick	Sutter
18—Montreal	L	3-5	Bahnsen	Ruthven
19—Montreal	L	5-10	May	Eastwick
20—Montreal	L	6-10	Bahnsen	Espinosa
21—St. Louis	W	5-3	Carlton	Denny
22—St. Louis	W	3-1	McGraw	Forsch
23—St. Louis	L	1-3	Martinez	Ruthven
25—Chicago	L	0-3	McGlothen	Espinosa
26—Chicago	L	1-4	Lamp	Christenson
27—Chicago	W	6-4	Carlton	Caudill
28—Chicago	L	1-4	Tidrow	Lerch
29—At Mon.	L	0-9	Rogers	Ruthven
30—At Mon.	L	0-2	Lee	Espinosa
31—At Mon.	L	0-1	Sanderson	Christenson

Won 13, Lost 15

JUNE				
1—At Cinn.	L	2-4	Bair	Carlton
2—At Cinn.	L	2-4	LaCoss	Lerch
3—At Cinn.	W	6-4	Reed	Borbon
3—At Cinn.	L	2-12	Hume	Lonborg

JUNE			Winner	Loser
4–At Hous.	L	0-3	Niemann	Christenson
5–At Hous.	W	8-0	Carlton	Williams
6–At Hous.	L	3-4	Sambito	Reed
8–Atlanta	L	5-11‡	Garber	Reed
9–Atlanta	W	9-3	Christenson	M. Mahler
10–Atlanta	L	3-10	Niekro	Carlton
11–Houston	W	4-2	Lerch	Richard
12–Houston	W	4-0	Espinosa	Williams
13–Houston	L	3-4	Niekro	Ruthven
15–Cinn.	L	3-6	Seaver	Christenson
16–Cinn.	W	4-3	McGraw	Bair
17–Cinn.	W	9-3	Lerch	Bair
18–At Atl.	L	5-10	Matula	Espinosa
19–At Atl.	L	4-10	Niekro	Christenson
20–At Atl.	W	10-4	Carlton	Solomon
22–At Mon.	L	5-6	Grimsley	Lerch
23–At Mon.	L	0-3	Rogers	Espinosa
24–At Mon.	W	5-2	Christenson	Lee
25–At Chi.	L	2-8	McGlothen	Carlton
26–At Chi.	W	5-3	Ruthven	Moore
27–At Chi.	L	4-11	Krukow	Lerch
29–At St.L.	W	8-7	Saucier	Forsch
29–At St.L.	L	1-7	Vuckovich	Christenson
30–At St.L.	W	6-4‡	Reed	Frazier
Won 12, Lost 16				

JULY				
1–At St.L.	L	7-13	Littell	McGraw
1–At St.L.	L	1-2	Littell	Lerch
2–N. York	W	6-2	Espinosa	Ellis
3–N. York	W	4-2	Brusstar	Twitchell
4–N. York	W	1-0	Carlton	Hassler
5–N. York	L	2-3	Swan	Noles
6–S. Fran.	W	6-1	Espinosa	Curtis
7–S. Fran.	L	6-8	Borbon	Reed
8–S. Fran.	W	5-3	Carlton	Knepper
9–S. Fran.	W	4-2	Noles	Blue
10–S. Diego	W	6-5	Bird	Fingers
11–S. Diego	L	3-7	D'Acquisto	Lerch
12–S. Diego	W	4-3	Carlton	Fingers
13–Los Ang.	W	3-2	Noles	Sutcliffe
14–Los Ang.	W	10-7	Espinosa	Sutton
15–Los Ang.	W	10-3	Lerch	Welch
19–At S.F.	L	0-1	Curtis	Noles
20–At S.F.	W	6-4	Lerch	Griffin
21–At S.F.	L	1-4	Knepper	Carlton
22–At S.D.	W	5-2	Espinosa	D'Acquisto
23–At S.D.	L	3-6	Fingers	Reed
24–At L.A.	L	3-15	Hooton	Lerch
25–At L.A.	L	8-16	Sutcliffe	Ruthven
27–St. Louis	L	0-5	Forsch	Espinosa
28–St. Louis	L	4-5	Littell	Reed
29–St. Louis	L	5-6	Vuckovich	Lerch
30–Chicago	W	5-4‡	Reed	Sutter
31–Chicago	W	4-1	Espinosa	Krukow
Won 15, Lost 13				

AUGUST				
1–At N.Y.	W	9-6	Noles	Ellis
2–At N.Y.	W	7-4	Reed	Hassler

AUGUST			Winner	Loser
2–At N.Y.	L	1-2	Falcone	Saucier
3–At Pitts.	L	3-6	Romo	McGraw
3–At Pitts.	L	1-5	Bibby	Christenson
4–At Pitts.	L	0-4	Candelaria	Espinosa
5–At Pitts.	L	8-12	Tekulve	Eastwick
5–At Pitts.	L	2-5	Romo	Noles
7–Montreal	W	4-2	Christenson	Sanderson
8–Montreal	W	4-3	Reed	Sosa
9–Montreal	W	6-4	Espinosa	Lee
10–Pitts.	W	4-3x	Eastwick	Jackson
10–Pitts.	L	2-3	Kison	Lerch
11–Pitts.	L	11-14	Romo	Eastwick
13–Pitts.	L	1-9	Bibby	Christenson
14–At Cinn.	L	1-2‡	Hume	Carlton
15–At Cinn.	W	3-2	Espinosa	Norman
17–At Hous.	W	5-2	Lerch	LaCorte
18–At Hous.	W	1-0	Christenson	Richard
19–At Hous.	W	3-2	Carlton	Andujar
20–Atlanta	L	2-5	Niekro	Reed
21–Atlanta	L	4-5	Bradford	Eastwick
22–Atlanta	L	3-4	Solomon	Christenson
24–Houston	W	5-3	Carlton	Andujar
25–Houston	L	1-3	Niekro	Espinosa
26–Houston	L	1-4	Ladd	Saucier
27–Cinn.	L	2-4	Hume	Christenton
28–Cinn.	L	2-5	Pastore	Carlton
29–Cinn.	W	6-7	Soto	Saucier
31–At Atl.	W	6-2†	Bird	Brizzolara
Won 12, Lost 18				

SEPTEMBER				
1–At Atl.	W	6-4	Christenson	Niekro
2–At Atl.	W	2-1‡	Reed	J. McL'ghlin
3–At Pitts.	W	2-0	Carlton	Blyleven
3–At Pitts.	L	3-7	Rooker	Lerch
6–N. York	L	3-5	Glynn	Espinosa
6–N. York	W	2-1	Lerch	Falcone
7–At Chi.	L	3-4	Lamp	McGraw
8–At Chi.	W	9-8	Eastwick	Sutter
9–At Chi.	L	2-15	Reuschel	Saucier
11–At N.Y.	W	5-2	Espinosa	Falcone
12–At N.Y.	W	4-0	Lerch	Swan
13–At N.Y.	W	2-1	Carlton	Berenguer
14–Chicago	L	0-2‡	Sutter	Reed
15–Chicago	W	8-1	Larson	McGlothen
16–Chicago	W	4-3	Reed	Tidrow
17–At St.L.	W	7-5	Carlton	Knowles
18–At St.L.	W	5-3‡	McGraw	O'Brien
19–Pitts.	L	6-9	Tekulve	Eastwick
19–Pitts.	W	6-5	Kucek	Romo
20–Pitts.	W	2-1	Lerch	Tekulve
22–Montreal	W	9-8‡	Reed	Murray
22–Montreal	L	2-8	Palmer	Noles
23–Montreal	L	4-7	Lee	Espinosa
24–St. Louis	L	2-7	Vuckovich	Lerch
25–St. Louis	L	1-4	Fulgham	Larson
26–St. Louis	W	11-5	Carlton	Martinez
28–At Mon.	W	3-2§	Reed	Fryman
29–At Mon.	L	2-3	Sosa	Eastwick
30–At Mon.	W	2-0	Carlton	Rogers
Won 18, Lost 11				

* 5-inning tie game.　† 5½ innings.　‡ 10 innings.　§ 11 innings.　x 12 innings.

"Crazy" Cubs Collapsed Like Skylab

By JOE GODDARD

The Cubs came down from the pennant race like Skylab came down from the heavens—in pieces. No one knew when or where either would fall, but the descent of each was a certainty.

By finishing in fifth place, a drop of two spots from the previous season, the Cubs tied a National League record for futility—34 years in a row without a championship. The Cubs won their last world title in 1908.

To make matters worse, the season ended bitterly. Manager Herman Franks, who began collecting Social Security in January of '79, rode into the West with both guns blazing. He called today's players "whiners" and singled out Bill Buckner, Ted Sizemore, Barry Foote and Mike Vail as his problem children.

"I've had it right up to here. Some of these players actually are crazy," said Franks, who had come out of 10-year retirement in 1977 to finish fourth, third and fifth.

Coach Joey Amalfitano was interim manager the final week, watching the team finish 80-82 after being 67-54 on August 20. A week after the season had ended, General Manager Bob Kennedy hired Dodger coach Preston Gomez as 1980 skipper.

Once again, the Cubs provided excitement at Wrigley Field where 1,648,587 fans, third largest home attendance in club history, spun the freshly painted turnstiles.

One of the most exciting games ever was May 17 when the Cubs lost to the Phillies, 23-22, after coming back from a 17-6 deficit.

Dave Kingman and Bruce Sutter kept the fans interested to the end, Kingman for his chase of 50 home runs and Sutter for his pursuit of a league record for saves.

Kingman fell two homers short, but still led the major leagues with his 48 round-trippers. He also topped the NL with a .613 slugging percentage, was second in runs batted in with 115 and scored 97 runs. More remarkable was his average. By widening his stance and moving closer to the plate, Kingman increased his average to .288. He had entered the season with a .232 lifetime mark.

Sutter with his exasperating split-fingered fastball saved 37 games, tying Clay Carroll (1972) and Rollie Fingers (1978). However, his teammates gave him few opportunities to reach the major league standard of 38 (Detroit's John Hiller in 1973), winning only nine games in September. In the stretch, Sutter saved just two, both in a doubleheader sweep of the Mets.

His 2.23 ERA was lowest in the league among those with 100 or more innings. He yielded just 67 hits in 101 innings and struck out 110.

"I owe half of my saves to Dick Tidrow," Sutter said.

Obtained from the Yankees for Ray Burris in early May, Tidrow had an 11-5 record and a 2.71 ERA. His presence in the bullpen allowed Franks to preserve Sutter until the late innings when the Cubs either were ahead or tied.

Rick Reuschel rebounded from a 14-15 record in 1978 to 18-12. He was prevented from reaching 20 by a shoulder problem in May. He was 7-0 in August, earning the Pitcher of the Month award. Tidrow won it in July, when he was 5-0.

Lynn McGlothen, a spot starter until injuries gave him more opportunities, won 13 games and Dennis Lamp 11, but the rest of the staff was disappointing, particularly Willie Hernandez, who in one year went from 8-2 to 4-4, and Donnie Moore, 9-7 to 1-4.

Jerry Martin (19 homers) and Barry Foote (16) made Kennedy's eight-player trade with the Phillies for Manny Trillo look good, but Ted Sizemore was traded to the Red Sox after the infamous wine incident in Montreal.

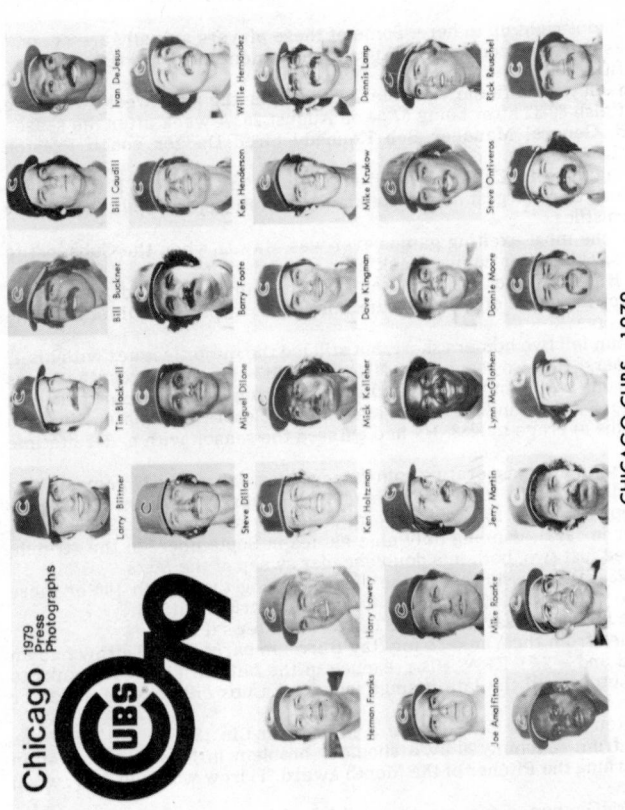

CHICAGO CUBS—1979

Top row—Biittner, Blackwell, Buckner, Caudill, DeJesus. Second row—Dillard, Dilone, Foote, Henderson, Hernandez. Third row—Franks, manager; Lowery, coach; Holtzman, Kelleher, Kingman, Krukow, Lamp. Fourth row—Amalfitano, coach; Roarke, coach; Martin, McGlothen, Moore, Ontiveros, Reuschel. Bottom row—Clines, Rojas, coach; Sizemore, Sutter, Thompson, Tidrow, Vail.

Many linked the decline of the Cubs to the end of a mid-season trip when Sizemore and Tidrow left a posh Montreal restaurant because the Cubs had placed a two-bottle limit of wine per table. The Cubs were treating the team after a rain-delayed defeat.

Sizemore complained loudly on both the bus ride to the airport and on the flight to Chicago, even though it was not Franks who had ordered the limit. But because Franks did not call Sizemore and other complainers onto the carpet, he lost credibility with the rest of the team.

Rookie Scot Thompson hit .289, Steve Ontiveros .285 in his comeback from a .243, injury-riddled 1978, Buckner .284 and Ivan DeJesus .283 as the Cubs hit .269 as a team to rank third in the league.

However, everyone stopped hitting in a nightmarish, late-season spin. In 20 straight games, the Cubs failed to score more than four runs, hitting just .238.

Said McGlothen in late September, "That feeling we had in July is gone. The spark is gone. I don't want to hear the excuse that day ball killed the Cubs again this year. The Cubs killed the Cubs."

SCORES OF CHICAGO CUBS' 1979 GAMES

APRIL			Winner	Loser
5—N. York	L	6-10	Swan	Reuschel
7—N. York	L	4-9	Zachry	Holtzman
10—At St.L.	L	0-7	Sykes	McGlothen
14—At Mon.	L	0-2	Grimsley	Reuschel
15—At Mon.	W	5-1	McGlothen	Rogers
16—At Mon.	L	0-2	Lee	Krukow
17—St. Louis	W	5-3	Holtzman	Denny
18—St. Louis	L	2-3z	Bruno	Moore
19—St. Louis	W	3-2	Lamp	Forsch
20—Montreal	W	8-5	McGlothen	Fryman
21—Montreal	W	4-3	Moore	Palmer
22—Montreal	W	4-1	Reuschel	Sanderson
25—Houston	W	4-0	Lamp	Ruhle
26—Houston	L	2-6	Richard	McGlothen
27—At Atl.	L	2-3	Niekro	Moore
28—At Atl.	L	2-7	Matula	Reuschel
29—At Atl.	W	6-5	McGlothen	Garber

Won 8, Lost 9

MAY				
1—At Cinn.	W	5-1	Holtzman	Norman
2—At Cinn.	L	1-4	LaCoss	Reuschel
4—Atlanta	W	6-2	Krukow	Matula
5—Atlanta	W	9-3	Lamp	Niekro
6—Atlanta	W	14-13	Sutter	Garber
8—Cinn.	L	7-8	LaCoss	Holtzman
9—Cinn.	L	4-7	Moskau	McGlothen
10—Cinn.	W	9-8a	McGlothen	Sarmiento
11—At Hous.	W	5-3	Reuschel	Riccelli
12—At Hous.	L	3-11	Forsch	McGlothen
12—At Hous.	W	2-0	Holtzman	Williams
13—At Hous.	L	0-3	Niekro	Krukow
15—Phila.	W	7-1	McGlothen	Espinosa
16—Phila.	L	0-13	Carlton	Reuschel
17—Phila.	L	22-23‡	Eastwick	Sutter
18—Pitts.	L	5-9	Candelaria	Holtzman
19—Pitts.	L	0-3	Rooker	Krukow
20—Pitts.	L	5-6	Robinson	McGlothen
22—At N.Y.	L	2-4	Kobel	Lamp
24—At N.Y.	W	9-7	Holtzman	Falcone
24—At N.Y.	L	2-4	Zachry	Krukow
25—At Phila.	W	3-0	McGlothen	Espinosa
26—At Phila.	W	4-1	Lamp	Christenson
27—At Phila.	W	4-6	Carlton	Caudill
28—At Phila.	W	4-1	Tidrow	Lerch
29—At Pitts.	L	0-8	Robinson	Holtzman

MAY			Winner	Loser
30—At Pitts.	L	2-9	Rooker	McGlothen
31—At Pitts.	L	3-4‡	Kison	Sutter

Won 12, Lost 16

JUNE				
1—S. Fran.	W	8-2	Reuschel	Nastu
2—S. Fran.	L	6-8	Moffitt	Tidrow
3—S. Fran.	W	2-1	Krukow	Curtis
5—S. Diego	L	3-11	Rasmussen	Lamp
6—S. Diego	W	3-0	Reuschel	Jones
7—S. Diego	W	4-3	McGlothen	Shirley
8—Los Ang.	W	4-11*	Hooton	Krukow
9—Los Ang.	W	5-3	Lamp	Sutcliffe
10—Los Ang.	W	10-3	Reuschel	Sutton
12—At S.F.	L	2-7	Knepper	Holtzman
13—At S.F.	W	3-2‡	Sutter	Moffitt
14—At S.F.	W	8-6	Tidrow	Lavelle
15—At S.D.	W	3-2	Hernandez	D'Acquisto
16—At S.D.	W	5-2	Holtzman	Perry
17—At S.D.	W	8-5	Krukow	Owchinko
18—At L.A.	L	3-7	Hooton	Lamp
19—At L.A.	W	7-4	Tidrow	Sutcliffe
22—At Pitts.	L	2-7	Blyleven	Holtzman
23—At Pitts.	W	4-3	Krukow	Robinson
24—At Pitts.	W	5-0	Reuschel	Kison
25—Phila.	W	8-2	McGlothen	Carlton
26—Phila.	L	3-5	Ruthven	Moore
27—Phila.	W	11-4	Krukow	Lerch
30—N. York	L	8-9§	Twitchell	Tidrow

Won 16, Lost 8

JULY				
1—N. York	W	5-4	Tidrow	Twitchell
1—N. York	W	8-2	McGlothen	Falcone
2—Montreal	L	0-5	Rogers	Lamp
3—Montreal	W	3-2	Sutter	Fryman
4—Montreal	L	1-2	Lee	Caudill
5—Montreal	W	3-1	Reuschel	Sanderson
6—Houston	L	2-4	Niekro	McGlothen
7—Houston	W	6-0	Holtzman	Williams
7—Houston	W	8-3	Lamp	Niemann
8—Houston	W	10-0	Krukow	Forsch
9—At Atl.	W	7-4	Tidrow	Niekro
10—At Atl.	W	7-3	Reuschel	Solomon
11—At Atl.	L	5-6	Brizzolara	McGlothen
12—At Cinn.	W	10-8	Sutter	Bair

JULY			Winner	Loser
13–At Cinn.	W	3-1	Lamp	Norman
14–At Cinn.	W	1-0	Krukow	Bonham
15–At Cinn.	L	1-7	Seaver	Reuschel
19–Atlanta	L	2-8	Niekro	Lamp
20–Atlanta	W	10-2	Reuschel	Brizzolara
21–Atlanta	W	3-2	Tidrow	Garber
22–Cinn.	L	1-12	Bonham	Holtzman
22–Cinn.	W	8-4	Tidrow	Soto
23–Cinn.	W	2-1	Hernandez	Hume
24–At Hous.	L	1-6	Forsch	Lamp
25–At Hous.	L	4-6	Richard	Reuschel
26–At N.Y.	W	9-2	Krukow	Hausman
27–At N.Y.	W	4-2	Tidrow	Ellis
28–At N.Y.	L	4-5	Falcone	Holtzman
29–At N.Y.	L	0-4†	Kobel	Lamp
30–At Phila.	L	4-5‡	Reed	Sutter
31–At Phila.	L	1-4	Espinosa	Krukow
Won 18, Lost 13				

AUGUST				
1–At Mon.	L	5-7x	Sanderson	Hernandez
2–At Mon.	L	4-6	Schatzeder	Caudill
3–St. Louis	W	4-2	Reuschel	Vuckovich
4–St. Louis	W	8-6	Krukow	Denny
5–St. Louis	W	3-2	Hernandez	Martinez
5–St. Louis	L	4-5	Forsch	Holtzman
7–Pitts.	W	15-2	Reuschel	Rooker
8–Pitts.	L	2-5‡	Tekulve	Tidrow
9–Pitts.	W	11-3	Lamp	Candelaria
10–At St.L.	W	8-13	Martinez	Krukow
10–At St.L.	L	3-5	Forsch	Caudill
11–At St.L.	W	7-3	Reuschel	Thomas
12–At St.L.	W	5-3	Hernandez	Fulgham
13–At St.L.	L	2-3	Littell	Hernandez
14–S. Fran.	L	2-8	Curtis	Krukow
15–S. Fran.	W	6-5	Reuschel	Borbon
16–S. Fran.	W	14-4	McGlothen	Knepper
17–S. Diego	W	9-6	Tidrow	D'Acquisto
18–S. Diego	W	3-2	Tidrow	Fingers
19–S. Diego	W	3-1	Reuschel	Jones
20–Los Ang.	W	2-1	McGlothen	Sutcliffe
21–Los Ang.	L	2-4	Sutton	Caudill
22–Los Ang.	L	2-7	Hough	Krukow

AUGUST			Winner	Loser
24–At S.F.	W	4-1	Reuschel	Blue
25–At S.F.	L	2-5	Curtis	McGlothen
26–At S.F.	W	4-1	Lamp	Montefusco
27–At S.D.	L	4-5‡	D'Acquisto	Hernandez
28–At S.D.	W	3-1	Reuschel	Jones
29–At S.D.	L	1-3	Perry	McGlothen
30–At L.A.	W	4-1	Lamp	Hooton
31–At L.A.	L	4-6	Sutcliffe	Caudill
Won 17, Lost 14				

SEPTEMBER				
1–At L.A.	L	4-5	Sutton	Reuschel
2–At L.A.	L	2-6	LaGrow	Sutter
3–St. Louis	L	1-2	Fulgham	Lamp
4–St. Louis	L	4-6	Vuckovich	Hernandez
5–Montreal	L	3-4	Sosa	Reuschel
6–Montreal	L	0-1	Palmer	McGlothen
7–Phila.	W	4-3	Lamp	McGraw
8–Phila.	L	8-9	Eastwick	Sutter
9–Phila.	W	15-2	Reuschel	Saucier
11–At Mon.	L	6-8	Palmer	McGlothen
11–At Mon.	L	2-3	Schatzeder	Caudill
12–At Mon.	L	3-6	Rogers	Sutter
13–At Mon.	L	3-4	Atkinson	Reuschel
14–At Phila.	W	2-0‡	Sutter	Reed
15–At Phila.	L	1-8	Larson	McGlothen
16–At Phila.	L	3-4	Reed	Tidrow
18–At N.Y.	W	2-0	Reuschel	Pacella
18–At N.Y.	W	2-1§	Tidrow	Allen
19–At St.L.	L	3-6	Vuckovich	Capilla
19–At St.L.	W	3-2‡	Sutter	Fulgham
20–At St.L.	L	1-2	Martinez	Lamp
21–Pitts.	W	2-0	McGlothen	Robinson
22–Pitts.	L	1-4	Kison	Riley
23–Pitts.	L	0-6	Bibby	Reuschel
24–N. York	L	2-8	Swan	Lamp
25–N. York	W	11-3	McGlothen	Scott
25–N. York	L	3-4‡	Allen	Tidrow
26–N. York	L	3-8	Hausman	Moore
28–At Pitts.	L	1-6	Bibby	Reuschel
29–At Pitts.	W	7-6y	Caudill	Robinson
30–At Pitts.	L	3-5	Kison	McGlothen
Won 9, Lost 22				

*6½ innings. †7 innings. ‡10 innings. §11 innings. x12 innings. y13 innings. z14 innings. a18-inning suspended game, completed July 23.

Fans Departed Less-Than-Amazing Mets

By JACK LANG

In many ways, the 1979 season was the worst in the 18-year history of the Mets franchise. It's true the team did not lose 120 games the way the first-year Mets did in 1962, but only six straight victories in the final week staved off a 100th defeat and at the box office they were a total disaster.

New York's baseball-wise fans, cognizant of the club's do-nothing approach in the matter of free agents, bonuses, long-term contracts, etc., expressed their disapproval in the best way they could. They stayed away from the ball park. They refused to buy tickets and at season's end the 63-99 Mets had drawn only 788,905 paying customers in the nation's largest city. It was the lowest attendance in club history.

The Mets never attracted as many as 30,000 fans on any one day. They managed to bring in 20,000-plus on promotional days, but the largest crowd on any non-promotional day was the one Cincinnati's Tom Seaver attracted on August 26 when he lured 20,619 sentimentalists into the park to watch him shut out his former mates, 8-0.

There was some indication of what was to come right at the start of the season when Joe Torre was forced to take three rookie pitchers north—Jesse Orosco, Mike Scott and Neil Allen. The Mets didn't have the bats to support a strong pitching staff; they were flirting with danger trying to operate with two of the three freshmen as regular starters.

A couple of months into the season, the Mets recognized their error and sought to pick up any veteran with experience that became available to them. Consequently, they added journeymen like Dock Ellis, Andy Hassler and Ray Burris. It didn't help.

The Mets seemed to be a team in turmoil most of the season with constant rumors of the club's sale circulating around Shea Stadium. Hardly a week went by that there was not some new report of a sale. The fact that the team was not drawing and not winning did not help. Eventually everyone focused in on the remark of Charles Payson, the club's principal stockholder, who said in spring training: "When the season is over, we will sit down and evaluate things. There are a lot of people interested in buying this club."

In January of 1980, the sale of the Mets was finally completed to publishing magnate Nelson Doubleday, the great grand nephew of Abner Doubleday. The sale price was $21.1 million.

If the front office was in a state of chaos, so were things on the field. The Mets were without a home run hitter of note and about the only winning pitcher Torre had was Craig Swan, who was 14-13.

Torre, who had the support of the front office all season, managed to keep his head despite several severe setbacks.

In June, Pat Zachry was placed on the disabled list for the balance of the season before eventually undergoing elbow surgery. He was Torre's most dependable starter for the first two months, winning five of six decisions.

Also in June, Torre lost the services of his top fireman, Skip Lockwood. Having won two and saved nine up to that point, Lockwood never threw another pitch because of a sore shoulder. Allen, rescued from shipment to the minors in June, went on to become the most dependable reliever. Winless as a starter, Allen was 6-6 in relief with eight saves.

There were other problems for Torre. Willie Montanez, his leading RBI man in 1978, never emerged from a slump that began the first day of spring training. Willie was hitting .234 in August when the Mets dealt him to Texas.

It was a bitter reminder of another in a series of bad deals. Only two years earlier the Mets had traded away Jon Matlack and John Milner to obtain Montanez.

Another deal that did not turn out well for the Mets was the Nino Espinosa-for-Richie Hebner swap in spring training. Hebner filled a void at third base for the Mets and drove in 50 runs by the All-Star Game. But he knocked in only 29 the last half of the season and a third of those came in the final week.

Although no teammate had more RBIs, Hebner's dismal second half mirrored—and induced—one of the worst records in club history.

After the All-Star Game, the Mets played 38 games at home and won only six.

There were a couple of significant moves made during the season. For the first time in their history, the Mets handed out three five-year contracts. Recipients, in order, were John Stearns, Frank Taveras (obtained in one of their better deals) and Lee Mazzilli.

NEW YORK METS—1979

Front row—D. Norman, Stearns, Kranepool, Hebner, Torre, manager; Montanez, Mazzilli, Maddox, Flynn, Ferrer. Second row—McKenna, trainer; Falcone, Flores, Lockwood, Henderson, Swan, Youngblood, Ellis, Hodges, Apodaca, Niss, traveling secretary; Mayol, trainer. Third row—H. Norman, equipment manager; Trevino, Kobel, Hassler, Murray, Zachry, Hausman, Twitchell, Glynn, Allen, Samuels, clubhouse attendant. Seated in front—DeLuca, batboy; coaches Cottier, Walker, Pignatano and Sisler; Bradley, batboy.

Mazzilli received a pact for more than $2 million, which made him the highest-paid player in club history.

One week after the season, the Mets also renewed Torre's contract in a strange arrangement. The manager had been seeking two years. The club was offering on year. In announcing Joe's retention, Mrs. Lorinda de Roulet said the club would review the situation "around the All-Star Game next year and decide then whether to sign Joe for another year."

SCORES OF NEW YORK METS' 1979 GAMES

APRIL

Date		Score	Winner	Loser
5-At Chi.	W	10-6		
7-At Chi.	W	9-4	Swan	Reuschel
10-Montreal	L	2-3y	Zachry	Holtzman
11-Montreal	L	2-3‡	Palmer	Murray
12-Phila.	W	3-2	Sosa	Lockwood
15-Phila.	L	2-3	Zachry	Lerch
15-Phila.	L	3-6	Ruthven	Swan
17-At Mon.	L	4-5§	Espinosa	Allen
18-At Mon.	L	5-6	Fryman	Lockwood
20-At Phila.	L	0-8	Palmer	Murray
21-At Phila.	L	0-3	Ruthven	Swan
22-At Phila.	W	4-2	Espinosa	Allen
24-S. Fran.	W	10-3	Orosco	Carlton
25-S. Fran.	W	2-0	Scott	Blue
28-Los Ang.	L	1-3	Swan	Griffin
29-Los Ang.	L	3-8	Hooton	Falcone
29-Los Ang.	W	6-3	Sutton	Allen
30-S. Diego	W	4-3	Murray	Sutcliffe
			Swan	Shirley
			Won 8, Lost 10	

MAY

Date		Score	Winner	Loser
1-S. Diego	L	5-10	Perry	Murray
3-At S.F.	L	5-7	Halicki	Falcone
4-At S.F.	L	3-4	Blue	Lockwood
5-At S.F.	L	4-6	Lavelle	Orosco
6-At S.F.	W	5-4	Murray	Moffitt
7-At L.A.	L	2-5	Hooton	Falcone
8-At L.A.	L	2-3	Sutcliffe	Murray
9-At L.A.	L	2-7	Sutton	Allen
10-At L.A.	L	1-14	Messersmith	Swan
11-At S.D.	W	4-0	Kobel	Mura
12-At S.D.	L	1-2	Owchinko	Allen
13-At S.D.	L	4-5†	Shirley	Lockwood
15-At Pitts.	W	3-0	Swan	Robinson
16-At Pitts.	L	3-4x	Romo	Lockwood
17-At Pitts.	L	5-6	Tekulve	Orosco
19-St. Louis	L	4-9§	Knowles	Bernard
20-St. Louis	W	8-7§	Allen	Knowles
22-Chicago	W	4-2	Kobel	Lamp
24-Chicago	L	7-9	Holtzman	Falcone
24-Chicago	W	4-2	Zachry	Krukow
25-Pitts.	T	3-3b		
26-Pitts.	W	10-8	Lockwood	Tekulve
27-Pitts.	L	1-2	G. Jackson	Murray
28-Pitts.	L	1-6	Candelaria	Falcone
29-At St.L.	W	6-2	Zachry	Vuckovich
30-At St.L.	L	3-7	Martinez	Swan
31-At St.L.	L	6-9	Sykes	Scott
			Won 8, Lost 18	

JUNE

Date		Score	Winner	Loser
1-At Atl.	W	5-4‡	Lockwood	Devine
2-At Atl.	L	6-7	Niekro	Glynn
3-At Atl.	W	9-4	Zachry	M. Mahler
4-At Cinn.	W	6-2	Swan	Seaver
5-At Cinn.	L	1-6	Norman	Kobel
6-At Cinn.	W	5-3	Murray	Sarmiento
8-Houston	L	0-5	Niekro	Zachry
9-Houston	W	4-0	Swan	Andujar
10-Houston	L	3-5	Throop	Kobel
11-Cinn.	W	3-2	Twitchell	Norman
12-Cinn.	W	12-6	Murray	Sarmiento
13-Cinn.	L	1-4	LaCoss	Hausman
15-Atlanta	W	2-1	Swan	J. McL'ghlin
16-Atlanta	W	2-0	Kobel	M. Mahler
17-Atlanta	W	2-1d	Reardon	Garber
18-At Hous.	L	2-3a	Roberge	Hausman
19-At Hous.	L	1-3	Andujar	Hassler
20-At Hous.	L	4-5	Sambito	Swan
22-At St.L.	L	2-4	Martinez	Kobel
24-At St.L.	W	6-2	Hassler	Forsch
25-Pitts.	L	1-8	Candelaria	Swan
25-Pitts.	W	4-0	Falcone	Rooker
26-Pitts.	L	1-2	Blyleven	Hausman
27-At Pitts.	W	12-9	Twitchell	Jackson
28-At Pitts.	W	3-2	Allen	Bibby
30-At Chi.	L	9-8‡	Twitchell	Tidrow
			Won 15, Lost 11	

JULY

Date		Score	Winner	Loser
1-At Chi.	L	4-5	Tidrow	Twitchell
1-At Chi.	L	2-8	McGlothen	Falcone
2-At Phila.	L	2-6	Espinosa	Ellis
3-At Phila.	L	2-4	Brusstar	Twitchell
4-At Phila.	L	0-1	Carlton	Hassler
5-At Phila.	W	3-2	Swan	Noles
6-S. Diego	L	5-6§	Lee	Hausman
7-S. Diego	L	3-11	D'Acquisto	Ellis
8-S. Diego	L	3-5	Perry	Kobel
8-S. Diego	W	4-1	Hassler	Shirley
10-Los Ang.	L	4-7	Hough	Swan
11-Los Ang.	W	4-3†	Allen	Lewallyn
12-Los Ang.	W	12-5	Ellis	Hooton
13-S. Fran.	L	7-6	Kobel	Knepper
13-S. Fran.	W	5-2	Hassler	Halicki
14-S. Fran.	W	3-2	Hausman	Blue
15-S. Fran.	L	0-4	Whitson	Swan
19-At S.D.	L	1-3	Jones	Kobel
20-At S.D.	L	1-2	Perry	Swan
21-At S.D.	W	2-1	Allen	Shirley
22-At L.A.	L	3-4	LaGrow	Glynn
23-At L.A.	L	1-3	Reuss	Falcone
24-At S.F.	L	6-5§	Twitchell	Borbon
25-At S.F.	W	3-0	Swan	Knepper
26-Chicago	L	2-9	Krukow	Hausman
27-Chicago	L	2-4	Tidrow	Ellis
28-Chicago	W	6-4	Falcone	Holtzman
29-Chicago	W	4-0*	Kobel	Lamp
30-At Pitts.	L	5-8	G. Jackson	Bernard
31-At Pitts.	W	2-1	Twitchell	Blyleven
			Won 13, Lost 17	

AUGUST

Date		Score	Winner	Loser
1-Phila.	L	6-9	Noles	Ellis
2-Phila.	L	4-7	Reed	Hassler
2-Phila.	W	2-1	Falcone	Saucier
3-At Mon.	L	6-10	Bahnsen	Murray
4-At Mon.	W	3-2	Swan	Lee
5-At Mon.	W	4-2	Ellis	Grimsley
5-At Mon.	L	3-7	May	Twitchell
7-St. Louis	L	2-9	Fulgham	Kobel
7-St. Louis	L	1-2	Thomas	Falcone

AUGUST			Winner	Loser
8—St. Louis	L	4-8	Vuckovich	Hassler
9—St. Louis	L	0-4	Denny	Ellis
10—Montreal	W	7-1	Swan	Grimsley
10—Montreal	L	5-6	Palmer	Bernard
11—Montreal	L	2-5	Schatzeder	Falcone
14—At Atl.	W	18-5	Hassler	Brizzolara
15—At Atl.	W	6-3	Swan	M. Mahler
16—At Atl.	W	6-3	Falcone	Niekro
17—At Cinn.	L	3-4	Hume	Murray
18—At Cinn.	L	3-4	LaCoss	Allen
19—At Cinn.	L	5-6	Bair	Murray
20—Houston	L	1-8	Niekro	Swan
21—Houston	W	5-0c	Falcone	LaCorte
22—Houston	L	1-3	Richard	Kobel
24—Cinn.	L	0-1	Bonham	Allen
25—Cinn.	L	4-8	Bair	Reardon
26—Cinn.	L	0-8	Seaver	Falcone
27—Atlanta	L	1-5	Solomon	Kobel
28—Atlanta	L	4-6	Niekro	Ellis
29—Atlanta	L	4-5	Matula	Burris
31—At Hous.	L	0-2	Forsch	Swan
			Won 8, Lost 22	

SEPTEMBER				
1—At Hous.	L	1-3	Richard	Falcone
2—At Hous.	W	5-4	Kobel	Niemann
3—At Mon.	L	2-7	Lee	Burris
3—At Mon.	L	5-6†	Atkinson	Allen

SEPTEMBER			Winner	Loser
4—At Mon.	L	1-5	May	Ellis
6—At Phila.	W	5-3	Glynn	Espinosa
6—At Phila.	L	1-2	Lerch	Falcone
7—Pitts.	L	4-6y	G. Jackson	Allen
8—Pitts.	W	3-2z	Ellis	Rooker
9—Pitts.	L	5-6	Tekulve	Glynn
11—Phila.	L	2-5	Espinosa	Falcone
12—Phila.	L	0-4	Lerch	Swan
13—Phila.	L	1-2	Carlton	Berenguer
15—At Pitts.	L	4-5	Roberts	Glynn
16—At Pitts.	W	3-0	Falcone	Candelaria
18—Chicago	L	0-2	Reuschel	Pacella
18—Chicago	L	1-2‡	Tidrow	Allen
19—Montreal	L	1-3	Grimsley	Swan
19—Montreal	L	1-4	May	Hausman
20—Montreal	L	3-6	Murray	Reardon
20—Montreal	L	0-2	Sanderson	Scott
22—St. Louis	L	3-6	Denny	Pacella
22—St. Louis	L	2-3	Forsch	Falcone
23—St. Louis	L	4-7†	Littell	Hassler
24—At Chi.	W	3-1	Swan	Lamp
25—At Chi.	L	3-11	McGlothen	Scott
25—At Chi.	W	4-3†	Allen	Tidrow
26—At Chi.	W	8-3	Hausman	Moore
28—At St.L.	W	6-2	Berenguer	Bruno
28—At St.L.	W	7-6‡	Allen	Frazier
29—At St.L.	W	8-7	Swan	Sykes
30—At St.L.	W	4-2	Jackson	Littell
			Won 11, Lost 21	

*7 innings. †10 innings. ‡11 innings. §12 innings. x13 innings. y14 innings. z15 innings. a18 innings. b11-innings tie games. cProtested game, completed August 22. dSuspended game, completed August 27.

WEST DIVISION

Wagner's "New Direction" Quieted Critics

By EARL LAWSON

They hanged Reds' President and General Manager Dick Wagner in effigy when he fired popular Sparky Anderson late in November of 1978 and replaced him with John McNamara.

And Wagner did nothing to improve his image among Reds' fans a few days later when he refused to open the club's bank vault and prevent Pete Rose from defecting to the Philadelphia Phillies.

"The change in managers is designed to take the Reds in a new direction," Wagner said in announcing the firing of Anderson, who had guided the Reds to five division titles, four pennants and two world championships during his 10-year reign.

"What new direction—down?" asked snickering skeptics, predicting a slide in the standings would be accompanied by a significant dip in attendance at Riverfront Stadium.

It was Wagner who wound up with the last laugh. The Reds, defying injuries and inexperienced pitching, not only wound up reclaiming the title in the National League West with a 90-71 record, lost to the Dodgers three years before, but also drew more than two million fans for a seventh straight year.

The Reds of 1979 were reminiscent of the club of 1961, a collection of castoffs who banded together for one last stand and wound up hoisting a pennant above Crosley Field.

The '79 edition displayed the same dedication, determination and character in beating out the surprising Houston Astros in a down-to-the-wire battle for the title.

That the Reds lost their bid for a fifth pennant in the last 10 years by bowing to Pittsburgh in the playoffs took little luster from their performance.

Tom Seaver, a three-time Cy Young winner, and Fredie Norman, a 36-year-old lefthander with a lifetime record of 89-86, formed the nucleus of the pitching staff when spring training began.

There also was Bill Bonham, who had compiled an 11-5 record in '78, but elbow surgery put a big question mark behind his name.

Mike LaCoss, Tom Hume and Paul Moskau were the top candidates for other berths in the starting rotation. Potential they had. Experience, they didn't.

At season's end, the pitching of the youngsters had exceeded all expectations. LaCoss won a berth on the All-Star squad, finished with a 14-8 record and for almost half of the season led the league in ERA.

Hume became one of the league's most effective relievers, compiling a 10-9 record, 17 saves and a 2.76 ERA, second only to J. R. Richard. During one stretch when the Reds closed a 10-game lead opened by the Astros in early July, the bespectacled righthander reeled off 23 scoreless innings.

Seaver, who finished 16-6, had 11 straight victories from June 9 to August 26. He tied for the league lead in shutouts with five and boosted his lifetime total to 52, tops among active pitchers.

He was aided in the stretch run by the right arm of 22-year-old rookie Frank Pastore. Clobbered for five homers in less than two innings one May night in Los Angeles, Pastore was demoted to Indianapolis. Upon his return, he won five of his last seven decisions, including his first major league shutout, a 3-0 blanking of Atlanta that clinched the title, September 28.

Because of injuries McNamara rarely had his starting lineup intact. But the bench, suspect at season's start, proved a savior.

Junior Kennedy, batting .273, did an admirable job of filling in for Joe Morgan at second base when a sprained ankle and bruised thigh sidelined the two-time MVP.

Twice during the season George Foster was out with injuries, first a sprained ankle and then a torn adductor muscle. Despite missing 40 games, he slammed 30 homers and drove home 98 runs.

One of the pleasant surprises was Dave Collins. Subbing first for Foster and then for Ken Griffey, who underwent knee surgery with almost two months of the season remaining, Collins finished with a .318 batting average, tying him with Ray Knight for the club lead.

Yes, the same Knight who had the unenviable chore of replacing Rose at third base. The gutty, exuberant 26-year-old worked particularly diligently over the winter and turned all the question marks after his name into exclamation points. Even though he took the field most of the time taped like a mummy because of numerous injuries, he finished fifth in the MVP voting.

Not to be overlooked were the performances of Johnny Bench and Dave Concepcion.

Concepcion batted .281, set career highs in homers (16) and RBIs (84), and won his fifth Gold Glove.

Bench, who became the team's all-time home run king, shook off aches

CINCINNATI REDS—1979

Front row—Seaver, Morgan, Concepcion, Nixon, coach; Fischer, coach; McNamara, manager; Dunlop, coach; Plaza, coach; Norman, Bench, Soto. Second row—Bureman, traveling secretary; Stowe, equipment manager; Geronimo, Tomlin, Pastore, Bonham, LaCoss, Foster, Sarmiento, Cruz, Doyle, batboy; Starr, trainer. Third row—Collins, Blair, Auerbach, Hume, Knight, Bair, Driessen, Spilman, Kennedy, Correll. Missing from picture—Griffey.

and pains to hit .276 with 22 homers and 80 RBIs. Moreover, he caught more than 100 games for the 12th straight season, one shy of Bill Dickey's major league record.

Pete was in Philadelphia and Sparky in Detroit, but the Reds were in the money and the hanging of Dick Wagner was incogitable.

SCORES OF CINCINNATI REDS' 1979 GAMES

APRIL

			Winner	Loser
4–S. Fran.	L	5-11	Blue	Seaver
6–S. Fran.	L	2-7	Montefusco	Hume
7–S. Fran.	L	2-4	Griffin	Pastore
8–S. Fran.	W	7-6*	Bair	Curtis
9–At Atl.	W	9-4	Seaver	M. Mahler
10–At Atl.	L	4-6	Niekro	Norman
11–At Atl.	W	9-5	Hume	Solomon
13–At S.D.	W	4-2	Bonham	Shirley
14–At S.D.	L	2-3	Perry	Seaver
15–At S.D.	L	3-6	Jones	Norman
15–At S.D.	W	7-5	Capilla	Lee
17–Atlanta	W	7-4	Hume	McWilliams
19–Atlanta	W	2-0	Seaver	Niekro
20–At St.L.	L	10-3	Norman	Sykes
21–At St.L.	W	4-1	LaCoss	Martinez
22–At St.L.	L	3-4	Schultz	Hume
24–Pitts.	L	2-9	Robinson	Pastore
25–Pitts.	L	2-3‡	Tekulve	Tomlin
27–St. Louis	W	4-3	Pastore	Littell
28–St. Louis	L	1-12	Vuckovich	Hume
29–St. Louis	W	5-1	Moskau	Sykes

Won 11, Lost 10

MAY

			Winner	Loser
1–Chicago	L	1-5	Holtzman	Norman
2–Chicago	W	4-1	LaCoss	Reuschel
4–Houston	W	6-5*	Bair	Riccelli
5–Houston	W	6-2	Hume	Andujar
6–Houston	W	17-5	Borbon	Richard
6–Houston	L	2-8	Riccelli	Norman
8–At Chi.	W	8-7	LaCoss	Holtzman
9–At Chi.	W	7-4	Moskau	McGlothen
10–At Chi.	L	8-9§	McGlothen	Sarmien'o
11–At Pitts.	W	8-4	Tomlin	Whitson
12–At Pitts.	L	2-3	Bibby	Pastore
13–At Pitts.	W	7-3	LaCoss	Candelaria
14–S. Diego	W	7-4	Moskau	Rasmussen
15–S. Diego	L	1-2	Fingers	Pastore
16–S. Diego	W	7-0	Bonham	Mura
18–Los Ang.	W	7-6	Borbon	Reuss
19–Los Ang.	W	5-4	Moskau	Sutcliffe
20–Los Ang.	L	4-6	Sutton	Hume
22–At S.F.	L	2-12	Halicki	Bonham
23–At S.F.	W	5-0	LaCoss	Blue
24–At S.F.	L	1-2	Nastu	Moskau
25–At L.A.	L	6-17	Sutcliffe	Seaver
26–At L.A.	W	3-1	Norman	Sutton
27–At L.A.	L	7-8	LaGrow	Borbon
28–At L.A.	W	3-2‡	Tomlin	Hough
29–At Hous.	L	1-2	Niemann	Moskau
30–At Hous.	L	3-6	Niekro	Seaver
31–At Hous.	L	0-3	Williams	Norman

Won 15, Lost 13

JUNE

			Winner	Loser
1–Phila.	W	4-2	Bair	Carlton
2–Phila.	W	4-2	LaCoss	Lerch
3–Phila.	L	4-6	Reed	Borbon
3–Phila.	W	12-2	Hume	Lonborg
4–N. York	L	2-6	Swan	Seaver
5–N. York	W	6-1	Norman	Kobel
6–N. York	L	3-5	Murray	Sarmiento
8–Montreal	W	3-2	LaCoss	Schatzeder
9–Montreal	W	7-1	Seaver	Lee
10–Montreal	W	3-2	Hume	Sosa

JUNE

			Winner	Loser
11–At N.Y.	L	2-3	Twitchell	Norman
12–At N.Y.	L	6-12	Murray	Sarmiento
13–At N.Y.	W	4-1	LaCoss	Hausman
15–At Phila.	W	6-3	Seaver	Christenson
16–At Phila.	L	3-4	McGraw	Bair
17–At Phila.	L	3-9	Lerch	Bair
18–At Mon.	W	3-2	Bonham	Rogers
19–At Mon.	L	2-3	Lee	LaCoss
20–At Mon.	W	4-5†	Sosa	Hume
22–S. Fran.	L	2-3	Nastu	Moskau
23–S. Fran.	L	2-5	Curtis	Norman
24–S. Fran.	W	8-7	Bair	Roberts
25–At Hous.	W	2-1	Seaver	Richard
25–At Hous.	L	0-4	Niemann	LaCoss
26–At Hous.	L	5-6	Roberge	Bair
27–At L.A.	W	9-1	Norman	Reuss
28–At L.A.	W	2-1	Hume	Hooton
29–At S.F.	L	4-6	Borbon	Sarmiento
30–At S.F.	W	2-0	Seaver	Whitson

Won 15, Lost 14

JULY

			Winner	Loser
1–At S.F.	L	1-2	Curtis	LaCoss
1–At S.F.	L	3-7	Lavelle	Soto
3–Houston	L	2-3	Forsch	Bair
4–Houston	L	2-3	Andujar	Bonham
5–Houston	W	5-4	Seaver	Richard
6–Pitts.	W	2-1	Bair	Jackson
7–Pitts.	W	6-2	Moskau	Robinson
8–Pitts.	W	4-2	Norman	Candelaria
8–Pitts.	L	1-2	Jackson	Tomlin
9–St. Louis	L	3-6	Vuckovich	Bonham
10–St. Louis	W	4-2	Seaver	Fulgham
11–St. Louis	W	6-1	LaCoss	Denny
12–Chicago	L	8-10	Sutter	Bair
13–Chicago	L	1-3	Lamp	Norman
14–Chicago	L	0-1	Krukow	Bonham
15–Chicago	W	7-1	Seaver	Reuschel
19–At St. L.	W	16-4	Norman	Vuckovich
20–At St. L.	W	3-0	Seaver	Denny
21–At St. L.	L	3-12	Martinez	LaCoss
22–At Chi.	W	12-1	Bonham	Holtzman
22–At Chi.	L	4-8	Tidrow	Soto
23–At Chi.	L	1-2	Hernandez	Hume
24–At Pitts.	W	6-5	Norman	Kison
25–At Pitts.	W	6-5*	Bair	Tekulve
26–At Pitts.	W	9-7	Soto	Roberts
27–At Atl.	W	2-0	LaCoss	Niekro
28–At Atl.	W	8-6	Bonham	Brizzolara
28–At Atl.	L	5-8	M. Mahler	Pastore
29–At Atl.	W	9-4	Norman	Matula
30–Los Ang.	W	9-4	Bair	Brett
31–Los Ang.	L	6-7	Sutton	Moskau

Won 17, Lost 14

AUGUST

			Winner	Loser
1–Los Ang.	W	10-5	LaCoss	Hough
3–S. Diego	L	4-6	Shirley	Bonham
4–S. Diego	W	7-1	Norman	D'Acquisto
5–S. Diego	W	9-1	Pastore	Jones
6–Atlanta	W	3-1	LaCoss	M. Mahler
7–Atlanta	L	2-3†	Garber	Bair
8–Atlanta	W	3-1	Bonham	Niekro
9–Atlanta	W	5-2	Norman	Garber
10–At S.D.	L	2-3	Jones	Pastore

AUGUST			Winner	Loser		SEPTEMBER			Winner	Loser
12—At S.D.	W	9-2	Seaver	Perry		4—At Atl.	L	6-7	J. McL'ghlin	Bair
12—At S.D.	L	4-5	Lee	LaCoss		5—S. Fran.	W	6-5	Norman	Montefusco
14—Phila.	W	2-1*	Hume	Carlton		6—S. Fran.	W	12-3	Seaver	Knepper
15—Phila.	L	2-3	Espinosa	Norman		7—Los Ang.	L	5-6	Castillo	Hume
17—N. York	W	4-3	Hume	Murray		8—Los Ang.	W	4-1	Bonham	Reuss
18—N. York	W	4-3	LaCoss	Allen		9—Los Ang.	L	1-3	Sutcliffe	Norman
19—N. York	W	6-5	Bair	Murray		11—Houston	W	9-8	Hume	Sambito
20—Montreal	L	2-5	Schatzeder	Norman		12—Houston	W	7-4	Pastore	Niekro
21—Montreal	W	3-2	Seaver	May		14—At L.A.	L	0-2	Sutcliffe	Bonham
22—Montreal	W	7-2	LaCoss	Rogers		15—At L.A.	W	2-1	Soto	Beckwith
24—At N.Y.	W	1-0	Bonham	Allen		16—At L.A.	W	2-0	Seaver	Sutton
25—At N.Y.	W	8-4	Bair	Reardon		17—At S.F.	L	4-7	Blue	LaCoss
26—At N.Y.	W	8-0	Seaver	Falcone		18—At S.F.	L	1-3	Whitson	Pastore
27—At Phila.	W	4-2	Hume	Christenson		19—At S.D.	W	3-2	Bonham	Shirley
28—At Phila.	W	5-2	Pastore	Carlton		20—At S.D.	W	8-5	Bair	Mura
29—At Phila.	W	7-6	Soto	Saucier		21—At Hous.	L	2-5‡	Sambito	Hume
31—At Mon.	L	7-8*	Fryman	Hume		22—At Hous.	L	1-4	Niekro	LaCoss
		Won 19, Lost 7				23—At Hous.	W	7-1	Pastore	Ruhle
						25—S. Diego	L	2-8	Shirley	Norman
						26—S. Diego	W	4-3	Seaver	Jones
SEPTEMBER						28—Atlanta	W	3-0	Pastore	Solomon
1—At Mon.	L	2-7	Palmer	Seaver		29—Atlanta	L	0-2	McWilliams	Norman
2—At Mon.	L	1-13	Rogers	LaCoss		30—Atlanta	L	2-7	Niekro	Bonham
3—At Atl.	W	6-5	Bair	Garber				**Won 13, Lost 13**		

*10 innings.   †11 innings.   ‡13 innings.   §18-inning suspended game, completed July 23.

Batting-Light Astros Soared With Pitching, Pitching and More Pitching

By HARRY SHATTUCK

For years, the Astros had hinted at becoming a contender and when they failed season after season, Houston baseball fans would be bitterly disappointed.

So 1979, at the outset, loomed as a relaxed, no-pressure year. The Astros seemingly weren't hinting at anything except a second straight fifth-place finish in the National League West Division.

But when least expected, the Astros put their act together. Bolstered by General Manager Tal Smith's key trades for shortstop Craig Reynolds, catcher Alan Ashby, outfielder Jeff Leonard and second baseman Rafael Landestoy and led by a record-setting pitching staff, Houston almost pulled the shocker of the summer.

Almost. Not quite. The Astros finished 89-73, 1½ games behind winner Cincinnati in the National League West, the closest of all second-place teams in divisional races. They built an early 10-game lead and didn't succumb to the more experienced Reds until the season's final weekend.

Houston compiled its most wins ever despite one of the least powerful offenses in recent baseball history. The Astros hit only 49 homers, one more than the Cubs' Dave Kingman. After July 6, only two regulars hit a homer with anybody on base.

In fact, in the spacious Astrodome, Denny Walling led all Houston batters in home runs with three. The Reds' George Foster hit four in his three visits to Houston in 1979.

There was no mystery as to the reason for Houston's success: pitching, pitching and more pitching. The trend began the opening weekend against Atlanta. J. R. Richard and Joaquin Andujar combined to shackle the Braves, 2-1. Ken Forsch then tossed a no-hitter and Joe Niekro wound up the series with a shutout. Two days later, Richard beat the Dodgers, 2-1, despite throwing six wild pitches, a major league record.

Once the season ended, Niekro owned a 21-11 record and was a close second to Chicago's Bruce Sutter in the Cy Young voting. Richard had an 18-13 record, led the league in ERA (2.71), the majors in strikeouts (313), and was right behind Niekro in the balloting.

The Astros became the first team ever to boast four different National League Pitchers of the Month. Forsch won it for April, Niekro for May, Andujar for June and Richard for September.

Niekro, Andujar and Joe Sambito (22 saves) were named to the All-Star team, giving Houston the only team with three pitchers in the midsummer classic at Seattle.

Reynolds also made the All-Star team and that was appropriate because if pitching was Houston's prime asset, defense and speed were big parts of the club's improved showing. And Reynolds, acquired from Seattle for pitcher Floyd Bannister in the offseason, played a solid shortstop and was one of seven Astros to steal 10 or more bases.

The mercurial Astros led the league with a club-record 190 steals. Four players had 30—Enos Cabell (37), Jose Cruz (36), and Terry Puhl and Cesar Cedeno (30 apiece).

Ashby was another key addition. Acquired from Toronto, the veteran catcher steadied Houston's pitching staff. Unfortunately for the Astros, his season ended August 29 when a Niekro knuckleball broke a finger on Ashby's right hand.

Injuries hurt the Astros considerably. At one point, five pitchers were on the disabled list. Regulars Cedeno, Cabell and Art Howe all missed time with illness, injury or both.

Cedeno did come back from knee surgery to give the Astros a solid performance at first base, moving there from his customary center field spot to make room for Leonard, until serious illness sent him to the hospital and caused him to lose 25 pounds.

The Astros' top hitter was Leonard at .290, followed by Cruz at .289 and Puhl at .287. Walling was a big force with a .378 pinch-hitting average.

Manager Bill Virdon was named NL Manager of the Year in one poll and signed a new contract through 1980.

Off the field, the Astros got a new owner. John J. McMullen, a New York businessman, purchased the Astrodomain empire from Ford Motor Credit Company.

Attendance improved more than 750,000, reaching 1.9 million, but most of all the season gave Houstonians hope that a contending team may be a regular treat rather than a mere dream—especially when the team maintained its record of never losing anyone to free agency by awarding multi-year deals to Richard and Cruz.

SCORES OF HOUSTON ASTROS' 1979 GAMES

APRIL			Winner	Loser	APRIL			Winner	Loser
6—Atlanta	W	2-1	Richard	P. Niekro	15—At S.F.	W	4-3	Richard	Montefusco
7—Atlanta	W	6-0	Forsch	McWilliams	15—At S.F.	W	9-1	Andujar	Griffin
8—Atlanta	W	2-0	Niekro	Matula	16—At L.A.	W	4-0	Forsch	Sutton
9—Los Ang.	L	1-2	Welch	Ruhle	17—At L.A.	L	6-10	Reuss	Dixon
10—Los Ang.	W	2-1	Richard	Hooton	18—At L.A.	W	4-0	Ruhle	Rau
11—Los Ang.	W	10-3	Forsch	Sutton	20—Pitts.	W	5-4*	Sambito	Bibby
13—At S.F.	L	7-8	Halicki	Niekro	21—Pitts.	W	5-4*	Andujar	Tekulve
14—At S.F.	L	1-2	Blue	Ruhle	22—Pitts.	W	3-2	Andujar	Candelaria

HOUSTON ASTROS—1979

Front row—Cabell, Niekro, Virdon, manager; Cedeno, Puhl, Sambito, Davidson, traveling secretary. Second row—Coleman, director of physical conditioning; Andujar, Walling, Riccelli, Suba, bullpen assistant; Williams, Cruz, Forsch, Alou, player-coach; Lillis, coach; Wright, coach; Jones, coach; Landestoy, Gonzalez, Ashby, Richard, Dixon, Leonard, Baldwin, Galban, equipment manager; Sexton, Hunter, clubhouse attendant. Third row—Reynolds, Niemann, Throop, Howe, Bochy, Roberge. Seated on Astroturf—Ruhle, Kiger, trainer; Tigerino and Greenlee; batboys Heiser, Tigerino and Greenlee; LaCorte, Ewell, trainer emeritus.

APRIL

			Winner	Loser
25—At Chi.	L	0-4	Lamp	Ruhle
26—At Chi.	W	6-2	Richard	McGlothen
27—At Pitts.	W	9-8†	Riccelli	Whitson
29—At Pitts.	L	5-10	Kison	Niekro
30—At St.L.	W	6-5	Sambito	Bruno
			Won 15, Lost 6	

MAY

1—At St.L.	L	6-7†	Knowles	Sambito
2—At St.L.	L	2-5	Denny	Forsch
3—At St.L.	W	4-1	Niekro	Vuckovich
4—At Cinn.	L	5-6*	Bair	Riccelli
5—At Cinn.	L	2-6	Hume	Andujar
6—At Cinn.	L	5-17	Borbon	Richard
6—At Cinn.	W	8-2	Riccelli	Norman
8—St. Louis	L	1-4	Vuckovich	Forsch
9—St. Louis	W	5-4§	McLaughlin	Bruno
10—St. Louis	L	1-3	Sykes	Richard
11—Chicago	L	3-5	Reuschel	Riccelli
12—Chicago	W	11-3	Forsch	McGlothen
12—Chicago	L	0-2	Holtzman	Williams
13—Chicago	W	3-0	Niekro	Krukow
15—S. Fran.	L	1-8	Nastu	Richard
16—S. Fran.	W	4-8*	Lavelle	McLaughlin
17—S. Fran.	L	0-3	Halicki	Forsch
18—S. Diego	W	3-2	Niekro	Fingers
19—S. Diego	L	2-4†	Fingers	Richard
20—S. Diego	W	1-0	Williams	Perry
20—S. Diego	W	6-3	Andujar	D'Acquisto
21—At Atl.	L	5-7	P. Niekro	McLaughlin
22—At Atl.	W	4-1	Niekro	M. Mahler
23—At Atl.	L	5-6	Brizzolara	Andujar
25—At S.D.	L	1-2*	Fingers	Sambito
26—At S.D.	W	9-0	Niekro	Lolich
27—At S.D.	W	4-2	Richard	Rasmussen
28—At S.D.	L	4-5	Jones	Andujar
29—Cinn.	W	2-1	Niemann	Moskau
30—Cinn.	W	6-3	Niekro	Seaver
31—Cinn.	W	3-0	Williams	Norman
			Won 14, Lost 17	

JUNE

1—Montreal	W	3-2	Richard	Grimsley
2—Montreal	W	2-1	Andujar	Sosa
3—Montreal	W	5-4	Niekro	Rogers
4—Phila.	W	3-0	Niemann	Christenson
5—Phila.	L	0-8	Carlton	Williams
6—Phila.	W	4-3	Sambito	Reed
8—At N.Y.	W	5-0	Niekro	Zachry
9—At N.Y.	L	0-4	Swan	Andujar
10—At N.Y.	W	5-3	Throop	Kobel
11—At Phila.	L	2-4	Lerch	Richard
12—At Phila.	L	0-4	Espinosa	Williams
13—At Phila.	W	4-3	Niekro	Ruthven
15—At Mon.	W	2-1	Andujar	Sosa
16—At Mon.	L	2-4	Grimsley	Richard
17—At Mon.	L	3-19	Schatzeder	Niekro
18—N. York	W	3-2x	Roberge	Hausman
19—N. York	W	3-1	Andujar	Hassler
20—N. York	W	5-4	Sambito	Swan
22—S. Diego	W	2-1	Niekro	Shirley
23—S. Diego	W	3-2	Dixon	Fingers
24—S. Diego	W	4-1	Andujar	Rasmussen
25—Cinn.	L	1-2	Seaver	Richard
25—Cinn.	W	4-0	Niemann	LaCoss
26—Cinn.	W	6-5	Roberge	Bair
27—At S.F.	L	3-6	Minton	Dixon
28—At S.F.	W	6-5	Williams	Curtis
29—At S.D.	W	4-1	Andujar	Perry
30—At S.D.	W	3-0	Richard	Shirley
			Won 20, Lost 8	

JULY

1—At S.D.	W	4-1	Niekro	Jones
3—At Cinn.	W	3-2	Forsch	Bair

JULY

			Winner	Loser
4—At Cinn.	W	3-2	Andujar	Bonham
5—At Cinn.	L	4-5	Seaver	Richard
6—At Chi.	W	4-2	Niekro	McGlothen
7—At Chi.	L	0-6	Holtzman	Williams
7—At Chi.	L	3-8	Lamp	Niemann
8—At Chi.	L	0-10	Krukow	Forsch
10—Pitts.	L	3-4	Bibby	Andujar
11—Pitts.	L	1-5	Kison	Richard
12—Pitts.	L	3-5	Blyleven	Niekro
13—St. Louis	L	0-1	Martinez	Forsch
14—St. Louis	W	3-2	Andujar	Vuckovich
15—St. Louis	L	1-3	Fulgham	Richard
19—At Pitts.	L	5-9	Roberts	Forsch
19—At Pitts.	L	2-4	Kison	Niekro
20—At Pitts.	L	3-9	Candelaria	Richard
21—At Pitts.	L	5-6	Romo	Sambito
22—At St.L.	W	7-6	Sambito	McEnaney
23—At St.L.	W	3-2	Niekro	Fulgham
24—Chicago	W	6-1	Forsch	Lamp
25—Chicago	W	6-4	Richard	Reuschel
26—Los Ang.	L	5-6	Beckwith	Andujar
27—Los Ang.	L	7-11	Hough	Niekro
28—Los Ang.	W	5-2	Forsch	Reuss
29—Los Ang.	W	4-3	Richard	Forster
30—S. Fran.	L	0-8	Knepper	Andujar
31—S. Fran.	W	6-4	Niekro	Whitson
			Won 12, Lost 16	

AUGUST

1—S. Fran.	W	5-4	Forsch	Blue
3—Atlanta	W	4-1	Richard	Matula
4—Atlanta	W	4-3	Sambito	Garber
4—Atlanta	W	6-2	LaCorte	P. Niekro
5—Atlanta	W	3-2	Roberge	Garber
7—At L.A.	L	8-10	Brett	Sambito
8—At L.A.	W	4-1	Richard	Hooton
9—At L.A.	L	3-4	Sutcliffe	Andujar
10—At Atl.	W	2-1	Niekro	Solomon
12—At Atl.	L	2-3	P. Niekro	Williams
13—Montreal	W	4-1	Richard	Rogers
14—Montreal	W	2-1	Andujar	Lee
15—Montreal	L	0-3	Schatzeder	Niekro
17—Phila.	L	2-5	Lerch	LaCorte
18—Phila.	L	0-1	Christenson	Richard
19—Phila.	L	2-3	Carlton	Andujar
20—At N.Y.	W	8-1	Niekro	Swan
21—At N.Y.	L	0-5y	Falcone	LaCorte
22—At N.Y.	W	3-1	Richard	Kobel
24—At Phila.	L	3-5	Carlton	Andujar
25—At Phila.	W	3-1	Niekro	Espinosa
26—At Phila.	W	4-1	Ladd	Saucier
27—At Mon.	W	3-0	Richard	May
28—At Mon.	L	6-7	Palmer	Ladd
29—At Mon.	L	3-5	Lee	Niekro
31—N. York	W	2-0	Forsch	Swan
			Won 15, Lost 11	

SEPTEMBER

1—N. York	W	3-1	Richard	Falcone
2—N. York	L	4-5	Kobel	Niemann
3—Los Ang.	L	0-1	Reuss	Niekro
4—Los Ang.	W	9-4	Williams	Beckwith
5—S. Diego	W	4-3*	Sambito	D'Acquisto
6—S. Diego	W	2-0	Richard	Owchinko
7—S. Fran.	L	2-9	Blue	Andujar
8—S. Fran.	L	1-2	Minton	Sambito
9—S. Fran.	W	4-1	Forsch	Minton
11—At Cinn.	L	8-9	Hume	Sambito
12—At Cinn.	L	4-7	Pastore	Niekro
14—At S.F.	W	7-0	Ruhle	Halicki
15—At S.F.	L	3-5	Borbon	Andujar
16—At S.F.	L	1-2	Minton	Richard
17—At S.D.	W	1-0	Niekro	Owchinko
18—At S.D.	L	0-4	Rasmussen	Williams
19—Atlanta	L	5-6	B. McL'ghlin	Ruhle

SEPTEMBER			Winner	Loser
20 — Atlanta	W	7-1	Forsch	Boggs
21 — Cinn.	W	3-2‡	Sambito	Hume
22 — Cinn.	W	4-1	Niekro	LaCoss
23 — Cinn.	L	1-7	Pastore	Ruhle
24 — At Atl.	L	4-5	M. Mahler	Sambito
24 — At Atl.	L	1-8	Solomon	Williams
25 — At Atl.	W	8-0	Richard	Boggs

SEPTEMBER			Winner	Loser
26 — At Atl.	L	4-9	P. Niekro	J. Niekro
28 — At L.A.	L	5-6	Hough	Ruhle
29 — At L.A.	W	3-0	Richard	Reuss
30 — At L.A.	W	3-2	Niekro	Sutcliffe
Won 13, Lost 15				

*10 innings.   †11 innings.   ‡13 innings.   §16 innings.   x18 innings.   yProtested game, completed August 22.

First-Half Disaster Doomed Dodgers

By GORDON VERRELL

Fittingly, perhaps, the Dodgers lost the first game of the 1979 season on a wild pitch. By a relief pitcher.

It was to be the absence of an adequate bullpen, even a mediocre one, that would lead to the Dodgers' poorest first half (36-57) in the club's 22-year Los Angeles history.

And not even a 43-26 record following the All-Star Game could resurrect the corpse of the first half.

The Dodgers at least rallied to escape the basement of the National League West, where they had spent a fretful three weeks, to finish 79-83 in third place, 11½ games back of the division-winning Reds.

It was a consolation, of sorts, but as onetime captain Dave Lopes noted during the Dodgers' late-season struggle to get back to .500—which they failed to do, for the first time since 1968: "This is embarrassing . . . a club with this much talent, struggling to reach .500."

After winning two successive National League pennants, the Dodgers were favored in most circles to win a third.

It was not to be, partly because of management decisions made over the previous winter, partly because of injuries, partly because of a midseason clubhouse furor and partly because, frankly, they simply weren't good enough.

It began with the loss, through free agency, of Tommy John, who had won 20 and 17 games during the Dodgers' pennant-winning seasons of 1977 and 1978.

Then, too, there was the offseason surgery on the left elbow of relief ace Terry Forster whose 22 saves and five wins were instrumental in the pennant of 1978.

The Dodgers were hopeful that Charlie Hough and Lance Rautzhan would be sufficient in the bullpen until Forster returned sometime in midseason. And that Andy Messersmith—yes, the same Andy Messersmith whose contract squabble with the Dodgers in 1975 led to the sweeping changes in baseball's reserve system and who was back now as a free agent —would be a proper replacement for John.

Neither decision proved sound.

It was Rautzhan's wild pitch on opening day that cost the Dodgers a game against the Padres. Soon, Rautzhan would be gone, the start of several major realignments in the bullpen.

And Messersmith would win only two of 11 starts and, finally, end his season in June, on an operating table. He was one of four Dodgers to undergo surgery during an injury-filled season, prompting the manager, Tom Lasorda, to utter, "Our guys are either walking around with ice bags on their arms or they're flying home to see a doctor."

Doug Rau, a consistent worker—more than that, a consistent winner—in his previous five years, had shoulder surgery. Veteran outfielder Rick Monday had an operation on his heel. And Forster, who pitched in only 17 games —and in pain most of those—was operated on for the second time in less than a year.

At one point, the Dodgers had five players on the disabled list.

Worse yet, the Dodgers' performance afield was dismal. They lost a staggering 31 of 41 games in the six weeks prior to the All-Star Game, including 20 of 27 in the club's worst June in Los Angeles.

It was on July 15, in Philadelphia, that several Dodgers, anonymously, pointed the finger at Reggie Smith, accusing him of "quitting on us." "They should get rid of him even if they have to buy him off," one said.

Smith reacted angrily. He called a team meeting the day following the All-Star break—"One of the best meetings this club has ever had," said Lasorda—and it was following that meeting that Lopes resigned his captainship, explaining, "Now, nothing more will be expected of me than any other player on this team."

There was an immediate, positive response. The Dodgers, 21 games under .500 at the All-Star break, won eight of the first nine games following the break.

Smith, though, injured a leg the second game after the All-Star break and did not start another game, finishing with only 32 RBIs, the fewest of his big league career.

The bullpen finally became a contributing factor late in the year, primarily because of rookies Bobby Castillo, Joe Beckwith and Dave Patterson, and a wily veteran, Ken Brett.

Jerry Reuss, obtained from Pittsburgh the first week of the season for pitcher Rick Rhoden, won three of his final five decisions after losing 10 of his first 13. Burt Hooton produced a 2.97 ERA, though he had an 11-10 record. And veteran Don Sutton, who topped several of Don Drysdale's club records during the year, finished at only 12-15.

NL Rookie of the Year Rick Sutcliffe turned in the most satisfying pitching performance of the year. He won 9 of his last 11 decisions to finish 17-10 with a 3.46 ERA.

The Dodgers led the league in home runs with 183, with Lopes, Ron Cey and Steve Garvey sharing the club lead with 28 apiece. Cey's total left him with 163 for his career, making him the all-time Los Angeles home run leader.

Through all the turmoil, Garvey maintained his remarkable consistency, hitting .315, collecting 204 hits, driving in 110 runs and playing in all the Dodgers' 162 games for the fourth year in a row.

And though they fell nearly 500,000 from their record 3.3 million attendance of the year before, the Dodgers still played to a major-league high 2,860,954 fans in 1979—which isn't bad for a third-place club that finished under .500.

LOS ANGELES DODGERS—1979

Front row—Yeager, Oates, Sutton, Adams, coach; Lasorda, manager; Lefebvre, coach; Basgall, coach; Baker, Garvey, Ferguson. Second row—Delury, traveling secretary; Woods, team physician; Rau, Welch, Rautzhan, Hough, Monday, Reuss, Sutcliffe, Russell, Thomasson, Smith, Vike, trainer; Buhler, trainer. Third row—Forster, Hooton, Messersmith, Joshua, Thomas, Mota, Cey, Lopes, Martinez, Davalillo. Seated in front—batboys Duretto and Waters.

SCORES OF LOS ANGELES DODGERS' 1979 GAMES

APRIL				Winner	Loser
5–S. Diego	L	3-4		Perry	Rautzhan
6–S. Diego	W	10-1		Sutton	Jones
7–S. Diego	W	5-2		Messersmith	Rasmussen
8–S. Diego	W	6-5§		Sutcliffe	Shirley
9–At Hous.	W	2-1		Welch	Ruhle
10–At Hous.	L	1-2		Richard	Hooton
11–At Hous.	L	3-10		Forsch	Sutton
12–Atlanta	L	2-10		McWilliams	Messersmith
13–Atlanta	L	1-2		Matula	Rau
14–Atlanta	W	6-5		Welch	Niekro
15–Atlanta	L	4-11		Solomon	Hooton
16–Houston	L	0-4		Forsch	Sutton
17–Houston	W	10-6		Reuss	Dixon
18–Houston	L	0-4		Ruhle	Rau
20–At S.F.	L	2-3		Lavelle	Reuss
21–At S.F.	W	2-1†		Hooton	Griffin
22–At S.F.	W	9-2		Sutton	Halicki
23–At Phila.	L	3-4†		McGraw	Rautzhan
24–At Phila.	L	6-7†		Reed	Reuss
25–At Phila.	L	4-5		Reed	Sutcliffe
28–At N.Y.	W	3-1		Hooton	Falcone
29–At N.Y.	W	8-3		Sutton	Allen
29–At N.Y.	L	3-6		Murray	Sutcliffe
30–At Mon.	L	4-8		Rogers	Rau
		Won 10, Lost 14			

MAY					
1–At Mon.	L	3-7		Lee	Welch
3–Phila.	W	5-2		Sutcliffe	Carlton
4–Phila.	L	2-5		Lerch	Sutton
5–Phila.	L	0-11		Ruthven	Messersmith
6–Phila.	L	0-4		Espinosa	Rau
7–N. York	W	5-2		Hooton	Falcone
8–N. York	W	3-2		Sutcliffe	Murray
9–N. York	W	7-2		Sutton	Allen
10–N. York	W	14-1		Messersmith	Swan
11–Montreal	W	7-0		Rau	Lee
12–Montreal	W	4-3‡		Welch	Bahnsen
13–Montreal	W	8-2		Sutcliffe	Grimsley
15–At Atl.	W	5-4†		Welch	Devine
16–At Atl.	L	2-3		Solomon	Messersmith
17–At Atl.	L	3-6		Niekro	Hough
18–At Cinn.	L	6-7		Borbon	Reuss
19–At Cinn.	L	4-5		Moskau	Sutcliffe
20–At Cinn.	W	6-4		Sutton	Hume
21–At S.D.	L	2-3		Rasmussen	Messersmith
22–At S.D.	L	6-7†		Fingers	Reuss
23–At S.D.	W	4-2		Hooton	Jones
25–Cinn.	W	17-6		Sutcliffe	Seaver
26–Cinn.	L	1-3		Norman	Sutton
27–Cinn.	W	8-7		LaGrow	Borbon
28–Cinn.	L	2-3x		Tomlin	Hough
29–S. Fran.	W	6-5		Forster	Lavelle
30–S. Fran.	W	6-5		Reuss	Lavelle
31–S. Fran.	W	12-10		Sutton	Blue
		Won 16, Lost 12			

JUNE					
1–At St.L.	L	7-8‡		Schultz	Welch
2–At St.L.	L	5-12		Forsch	Rau
3–At St.L.	L	4-6		Vuckovich	Hooton
4–At Pitts.	W	4-2		Sutcliffe	Rooker
5–At Pitts.	L	1-3		Blyleven	Sutton
6–At Pitts.	L	4-5		Romo	Welch
8–At Chi.	W	11-4*		Hooton	Krukow
9–At Chi.	L	3-5		Lamp	Sutcliffe
10–At Chi.	L	3-10		Reuschel	Sutton
11–St. Louis	L	7-9		Bruno	LaGrow
12–St. Louis	W	9-3		Hooton	Denny
13–St. Louis	W	9-8		Sutcliffe	Forsch
15–Pitts.	L	2-6		Blyleven	Sutton
16–Pitts.	L	3-6		Robinson	Welch
17–Pitts.	L	1-5		Whitson	Reuss
18–Chicago	W	7-3		Hooton	Lamp

JUNE				Winner	Loser
19–Chicago	L	4-7		Tidrow	Sutcliffe
21–At Atl.	W	6-4		Sutton	M. Mahler
22–At Atl.	L	2-3		Brizzolara	Welch
23–At Atl.	L	3-7		Niekro	Reuss
24–At Atl.	L	2-4		Matula	Hooton
25–S. Diego	W	4-3		Brett	Fingers
26–S. Diego	L	1-5		Shirley	Sutton
27–Cinn.	L	1-9		Norman	Reuss
28–Cinn.	L	1-2		Hume	Hooton
29–Atlanta	L	2-5		Matula	Sutcliffe
30–Atlanta	L	4-7†		Garber	Forster
		Won 7, Lost 20			

JULY					
1–Atlanta	L	1-2		Niekro	Brett
2–At S.D.	W	6-3§		Brett	Owchinko
3–At S.D.	L	2-3		Perry	Sutcliffe
4–At S.D.	L	0-6		Shirley	Sutton
6–At Mon.	L	4-6		Schatzeder	Reuss
7–At Mon.	L	1-2		Rogers	Hooton
8–At Mon.	W	8-6		Sutcliffe	Grimsley
9–At Mon.	L	0-3		Lee	Sutton
10–At N.Y.	W	7-4		Hough	Swan
11–At N.Y.	L	3-4†		Allen	Lewallyn
12–At N.Y.	L	5-12		Ellis	Hooton
13–At Phila.	L	2-3		Noles	Sutcliffe
14–At Phila.	L	7-10		Espinosa	Sutton
15–At Phila.	L	3-10		Lerch	Welch
19–Montreal	W	7-3		Hooton	Schatzeder
20–Montreal	W	6-5‡		Patterson	Fryman
21–Montreal	L	2-7		Lee	Sutton
22–N. York	W	4-3		LaGrow	Glynn
23–N. York	W	3-1		Reuss	Falcone
24–Phila.	W	15-3		Hooton	Lerch
25–Phila.	W	16-8		Sutcliffe	Ruthven
26–At Hous.	W	6-5		Beckwith	Andujar
27–At Hous.	W	11-7		Hough	Niekro
28–At Hous.	L	2-5		Forsch	Reuss
29–At Hous.	L	3-4		Richard	Forster
30–At Cinn.	L	4-9		Bair	Brett
31–At Cinn.	W	7-6		Sutton	Moskau
		Won 12, Lost 15			

AUGUST					
1–At Cinn.	L	5-10		LaCoss	Hough
3–S. Fran.	W	11-3		Hooton	Curtis
4–S. Fran.	W	4-3‡		Patterson	Lavelle
5–S. Fran.	W	8-1		Sutton	Knepper
6–S. Fran.	L	1-7		Whitson	Hough
7–Houston	W	10-8		Brett	Sambito
8–Houston	L	1-4		Richard	Hooton
9–Houston	W	4-3		Sutcliffe	Andujar
10–At S.F.	W	9-0		Sutton	Knepper
11–At S.F.	W	7-4		Hough	Whitson
12–At S.F.	L	1-4		Blue	Reuss
14–At St.L.	W	9-0		Hooton	Denny
15–At St.L.	W	6-5		Sutcliffe	Martinez
16–At St.L.	W	4-2y		Castillo	Frazier
17–At Pitts.	W	7-6		Patterson	Bibby
18–At Pitts.	W	5-1		Reuss	Robinson
19–At Pitts.	L	0-2		Tekulve	Hooton
20–At Chi.	L	1-2		McGlothen	Sutcliffe
21–At Chi.	W	4-2		Sutton	Caudill
22–At Chi.	W	7-2		Hough	Krukow
24–St. Louis	L	5-12		Vuckovich	Reuss
25–St. Louis	L	4-5		Thomas	Brett
26–St. Louis	W	4-1		Sutcliffe	Martinez
27–Pitts.	W	4-2		Brett	Tekulve
28–Pitts.	L	1-4		Candelaria	Hough
29–Pitts.	L	1-4		Blyleven	Reuss
30–Chicago	L	1-4		Lamp	Hooton
31–Chicago	W	6-4		Sutcliffe	Caudill
		Won 17, Lost 11			

SEPTEMBER			Winner	Loser		SEPTEMBER			Winner	Loser
1—Chicago	W	5-4	Sutton	Reuschel		17—Atlanta	W	9-4	Hough	Niekro
2—Chicago	W	6-2	LaGrow	Sutter		18—Atlanta	W	6-1	Reuss	Solomon
3—At Hous.	W	1-0	Reuss	Niekro		19—S. Fran.	W	7-2	Sutcliffe	Halicki
4—At Hous.	L	4-9	Williams	Beckwith		20—S. Fran.	W	3-0	Welch	Knepper
5—At Atl.	W	5-3†	LaGrow	Garber		21—At S.D.	L	1-3	Eichelberger	Hannahs
6—At Atl.	L	2-6	Hanna	Sutton		22—At S.D.	L	8-10	Mura	Patterson
7—At Cinn.	W	6-5	Castillo	Hume		23—At S.D.	W	5-2	LaGrow	Mura
8—At Cinn.	L	1-4	Bonham	Reuss		25—At S.F.	W	11-2	Sutcliffe	Halicki
9—At Cinn.	W	3-1	Sutcliffe	Norman		26—At S.F.	W	8-4	Patterson	Griffin
11—S. Diego	L	1-3	Owchinko	Sutton		27—At S.F.	L	3-5	Blue	Hannahs
12—S. Diego	L	5-2	Hough	Rasmussen		28—Houston	W	6-5	Hough	Ruhle
13—S. Diego	W	8-6	Reuss	Shirley		29—Houston	L	0-3	Richard	Reuss
14—Cinn.	W	2-0	Sutcliffe	Bonham		30—Houston	L	2-3	Niekro	Sutcliffe
15—Cinn.	L	1-2	Soto	Beckwith				**Won 17, Lost 11**		
16—Cinn.	L	0-2	Seaver	Sutton						

*6½ innings.   †10 innings.   ‡11 innings.   §12 innings.   x13 innings.   y15 innings.

Giants' Big Four Spoiled Pennant Pitch

By NICK PETERS

It doesn't take much of an explanation for one to understand the kind of season the San Francisco Giants endured in 1979.

Entering the season, the club was full of hope. Why not? The 1978 version stunned the National League West by leading the division most of the way, finishing a strong third with an 89-73 record.

General Manager Spec Richardson was THE SPORTING NEWS Executive of the Year, Vida Blue was TSN's Pitcher of the Year in the NL and Joe Altobelli won several Manager of the Year awards.

An improvement was a natural expectation. Visions of a pennant danced in the Giants' heads. A Big Four of Blue, Bob Knepper, John Montefusco and Ed Halicki combined for 55 victories in '78, so there were predictions of 70 wins from the group in '79. Instant pennant.

But high hopes preface abject depression once goals are not realized. When the Giants struggled through April with a 9-14 record, after being lulled into false security with a 3-0 start at Cincinnati, it was a portent of things to come. A 71-91 record and fourth place finish.

There were signs of life during a 16-12 May, Willie McCovey's torrid month giving false hope, but the club then settled into a .500 groove and stayed there until 24 losses in 32 games set the stage for Altobelli's ouster in Cincinnati on September 5.

Even when the team was leading the league in runs scored during the first half of the season, wins were hard to come by. Shoddy fielding and baserunning blunders were detrimental, but the blame for the club's demise fell squarely on pitching problems.

Righthanders Montefusco and Halicki were struck down by illness and injury. The Count won his first start at Cincy, but posted only two more wins in a 3-8 disaster. Halicki jumped off to a good start, hurling back-to-back two-hitters at one stage, but illness prevented him from winning after May 22 in a 5-8 campaign.

Young southpaw Knepper, troubled by problems encountered by his infant at birth, slumped to 9-12. And Blue was as ineffective as his 5.04 ERA suggests though he finished strong for a 14-14 standoff.

The Big Four talked of 70 wins, but totaled only 31 while losing 42. Big

Bust. The collapse of a potentially strong rotation enabled lefthander John Curtis (10-9) to recapture some lost magic. It also paved the way for a controversial June 28 trade which helped the Pirates win a pennant.

Bill Madlock, struggling at .261 and at odds with Altobelli, was deemed expendable. Desperate for pitching, the Giants obtained righthander Ed Whitson and two minor leaguers for the two-time NL batting champ.

"I'm glad they made the deal, but they should have waited till the end of the season," offered Madlock, who was a .328 batter for the Bucs while the Giants' run production tailed off sharply without him.

"Some panic buttons were pushed," opined reliever Gary Lavelle, whose club-record 20 saves and 2.51 ERA belied the fact he was ineffectual for much of the season.

"The problem," added Jack Clark, "was that we came to spring training thinking it would be easy. We thought we'd get on top and stay there because of our pitching. It just didn't turn out that way."

Clark's campaign mirrored the team's frustration. After setting club records with 46 doubles and a 26-game batting streak in '78, Jack was expected to blossom into stardom. He had a good year (26 homers, 86 RBIs), but it wasn't up to expectations.

The same could be said of most of the Giants, who regressed following their surprise of '78. Unable to handle the disappointment, many of the players resorted to rationalization and complaints.

Bickering led to dissension among the ranks and Altobelli proved a convenient scapegoat, losing his job with the club in a 61-79 fog. New skipper Dave Bristol revived enthusiasm, but his 10-12 record reflected little improvement of the status quo.

But there were flickering signs of hope.

On the bright side, Mike Ivie sealed the first base assignment by whacking 27 homers in only 402 at-bats and batting .286. Bill North played a steady center field and set a San Francisco record with 58 steals despite a late-season injury.

And the venerable McCovey belted 11 home runs from May 15 to June 16, passing Mel Ott, Ernie Banks and Ed Mathews on the all-time list. He finished with 15 for a career total of 520, making him the most prolific lefthanded home run hitter in NL history.

SCORES OF SAN FRANCISCO GIANTS' 1979 GAMES

APRIL			Winner	Loser		APRIL			Winner	Loser
4—At Cinn.	W	11-5	Blue	Seaver		27—At Mon.	L	8-14	Lee	Knepper
6—At Cinn.	W	7-2	Montefusco	Hume		28—At Mon.	L	4-6	Sanderson	Halicki
7—At Cinn.	W	4-2	Griffin	Pastore		29—At Mon.	L	5-7	Schatzeder	Blue
8—At Cinn.	L	6-7*	Bair	Curtis		30—At Phila.	L	1-4	Ruthven	Nastu
10—S. Diego	W	4-2	Blue	D'Acquisto			**Won 9, Lost 14**			
11—S. Diego	L	1-4	Jones	Montefusco						
12—S. Diego	W	4-3	Knepper	Rasmussen		**MAY**				
13—Houston	W	8-7	Halicki	Niekro		1—At Phila.	W	7-0	Knepper	Espinosa
14—Houston	W	2-1	Blue	Ruhle		3—N. York	W	7-5	Halicki	Falcone
15—Houston	L	3-4	Richard	Montefusco		4—N. York	W	4-3	Blue	Lockwood
15—Houston	L	1-9	Andujar	Griffin		5—N. York	W	6-4	Lavelle	Orosco
17—At S.D.	L	3-4	Fingers	Knepper		6—N. York	L	4-5	Murray	Moffitt
18—At S.D.	L	6-7	Mura	Griffin		8—Montreal	L	0-4	Sanderson	Halicki
19—At S.D.	W	14-10	Blue	Lolich		9—Montreal	W	9-2	Blue	Grimsley
20—Los Ang.	W	3-2	Lavelle	Reuss		10—Montreal	L	0-3	Rogers	Nastu
21—Los Ang.	L	1-2*	Hooton	Griffin		11—Phila.	W	2-1	Knepper	Carlton
22—Los Ang.	L	2-9	Sutton	Halicki		12—Phila.	W	4-1	Halicki	Lerch
24—At N.Y.	L	3-10	Scott	Blue		13—Phila.	L	3-12	Reed	Blue
25—At N.Y.	L	0-2	Swan	Griffin		15—At Hous.	W	8-1	Nastu	Richard

SAN FRANCISCO GIANTS—1979

Front row—Alioto, batboy; Dougherty, batboy; North, Moffitt, Davenport, coach; Bristol, coach; Altobelli, manager; Shepard, coach; Haller, coach; Minton, Knepper, McCormick, batboy; Quinlan, batboy; Brinson, assistant equipment manager; Logan, equipment manager. Second row—Liscio, trainer; Murphy, assistant equipment manager; Hill, Curtis, Griffin, Lavelle, Halicki, Blue, Roberts, McCovey, Nastu, Herndon, Whitfield, Evans, Cruz. Kneeling in front—LeMaster, Madlock, Venable, Sadek, Ivie, Metzger, Andrews, Clark. Missing from picture—Montefusco.

MAY

			Winner	Loser
16—At Hous.	W	8-4*	Lavelle	McLaughlin
17—At Hous.	W	3-0	Halicki	Forsch
18—At Atl.	L	4-6	M. Mahler	Blue
19—At Atl.	W	4-2	Griffin	Skok
19—At Atl.	W	7-6†	Curtis	Garber
20—At Atl.	W	8-1	Knepper	Solomon
22—Cinn.	W	12-2	Halicki	Bonham
23—Cinn.	L	0-5	LaCoss	Blue
24—Cinn.	W	2-1	Nastu	Moskau
25—Atlanta	W	6-4	Knepper	Niekro
26—Atlanta	L	4-5	Garber	Roberts
27—Atlanta	L	8-10	Skok	Moffitt
28—Atlanta	L	1-4	M. Mahler	Nastu
29—At L.A.	L	5-6	Forster	Lavelle
30—At L.A.	L	5-6	Reuss	Lavelle
31—At L.A.	L	10-12	Sutton	Blue

Won 16, Lost 12

JUNE

			Winner	Loser
1—At Chi.	L	2-8	Reuschel	Nastu
2—At Chi.	W	8-6	Moffitt	Tidrow
3—At Chi.	L	1-2	Krukow	Curtis
5—At St.L.	L	4-5	Littell	Moffitt
6—At St.L.	L	5-6	Schultz	Moffitt
7—At St.L.	W	12-10	Griffin	Littell
8—At Pitts.	L	2-3	Romo	Curtis
9—At Pitts.	W	6-2	Blue	Kison
10—At Pitts.	W	7-4	Lavelle	Romo
12—Chicago	W	7-2	Knepper	Holtzman
13—Chicago	L	2-3*	Sutter	Moffitt
14—Chicago	L	6-8	Tidrow	Lavelle
15—St. Louis	W	9-6§	Lavelle	Knowles
16—St. Louis	W	6-1	Curtis	Martinez
17—St. Louis	W	7-4	Moffitt	Schultz
19—Pitts.	L	4-9	Candelaria	Montefusco
20—Pitts	L	5-8	Jackson	Lavelle
22—At Cinn.	W	3-2	Nastu	Moskau
23—At Cinn.	W	5-2	Curtis	Norman
24—At Cinn.	L	7-8	Bair	Roberts
25—Atlanta	L	1-6	Solomon	Montefusco
26—Atlanta	W	6-5	Lavelle	Garber
27—Houston	W	6-3	Minton	Dixon
28—Houston	L	5-6	Williams	Curtis
29—Cinn.	W	6-4	Borbon	Sarmiento
30—Cinn.	L	0-2	Seaver	Whitson

Won 13, Lost 13

JULY

			Winner	Loser
1—Cinn.	W	2-1	Curtis	LaCoss
1—Cinn.	W	7-3	Lavelle	Soto
3—At Atl.	L	2-5	Brizzolara	Halicki
4—At Atl.	L	6-7	J. McL'ghlin	Lavelle
5—At Atl.	L	4-5	Niekro	Minton
6—At Phila.	L	1-6	Espinosa	Curtis
7—At Phila.	W	8-6	Borbon	Reed
8—At Phila.	L	3-5	Carlton	Knepper
9—At Phila.	L	2-4	Noles	Blue
10—At Mon.	W	11-7§	Griffin	Fryman
11—At Mon.	W	1-0	Curtis	Schatzeder
12—At Mon.	W	5-3	Montefusco	Rogers
13—At N.Y.	L	6-7	Kobel	Knepper
13—At N.Y.	L	2-5	Hassler	Halicki
14—At N.Y.	L	2-3	Hausman	Blue
15—At N.Y.	W	4-0	Whitson	Swan
19—Phila.	L	1-0	Curtis	Noles
20—Phila.	L	4-6	Lerch	Griffin
21—Phila.	W	4-1	Knepper	Carlton
22—At Montreal	W	8-6	Blue	Grimsley
22—Montreal	L	5-15	May	Whitson
23—Montreal	L	3-8	Schatzeder	Curtis

JULY

			Winner	Loser
24—N. York	L	5-6‡	Twitchell	Borbon
25—N. York	L	0-3	Swan	Knepper
26—At S.D.	W	6-2	Whitson	D'Acquisto
27—At S.D.	W	4-3†	Borbon	Lee
28—At S.D.	L	3-4	Fingers	Borbon
29—At S.D.	W	4-2	Montefusco	Shirley
30—At Hous.	W	8-0	Knepper	Andujar
31—At Hous.	L	4-6	Niekro	Whitson

Won 14, Lost 16

AUGUST

			Winner	Loser
1—At Hous.	L	4-5	Forsch	Blue
3—At L.A.	L	3-11	Hooton	Curtis
4—At L.A.	L	3-4†	Patterson	Lavelle
5—At L.A.	L	1-8	Sutton	Knepper
6—At L.A.	W	7-1	Whitson	Hough
7—S. Diego	W	3-2	Blue	Perry
8—S. Diego	W	10-7	Curtis	Shirley
9—S. Diego	L	0-4	D'Acquisto	Minton
10—Los Ang.	L	0-9	Sutton	Knepper
11—Los Ang.	L	4-7	Hough	Whitson
12—Los Ang.	W	4-1	Blue	Reuss
14—At Chi.	W	8-2	Curtis	Krukow
15—At Chi.	L	5-6	Reuschel	Borbon
16—At Chi.	L	4-14	McGlothen	Knepper
17—At St.L.	L	0-3	Fulgham	Whitson
18—At St.L.	L	4-5	Thomas	Blue
19—At St.L.	L	0-4	Denny	Curtis
20—At Pitts.	L	5-6	Romo	Lavelle
21—At Pitts.	W	6-1	Knepper	Kison
22—At Pitts.	L	6-8	Tekulve	Lavelle
24—Chicago	L	1-4	Reuschel	Blue
25—Chicago	W	5-2	Curtis	McGlothen
26—Chicago	L	1-4	Lamp	Montefusco
28—St. Louis	L	1-2	Forsch	Knepper
29—St. Louis	L	1-5	Fulgham	Blue
30—St. Louis	W	3-2	Whitson	Vuckovich
31—Pitts.	L	4-6	Robinson	Curtis

Won 8, Lost 19

SEPTEMBER

			Winner	Loser
1—Pitts.	L	3-5	Kison	Montefusco
1—Pitts.	L	2-7	Bibby	Knepper
2—Pitts.	L	3-5	Candelaria	Blue
3—At S.D.	L	0-3	Perry	Whitson
4—At S.D.	W	3-1	Curtis	Shirley
5—At Cinn.	L	5-6	Norman	Montefusco
6—At Cinn.	L	3-12	Seaver	Knepper
7—At Hous.	W	9-2	Blue	Andujar
8—At Hous.	W	2-1	Minton	Sambito
9—At Hous.	L	1-4	Forsch	Minton
11—Atlanta	L	1-2	McWilliams	Montefusco
12—Atlanta	W	4-3	Blue	Solomon
13—Atlanta	L	1-4	Niekro	Whitson
14—Houston	L	0-7	Ruhle	Halicki
15—Houston	W	5-3	Borbon	Andujar
16—Houston	L	1-2	Minton	Richard
17—Cinn.	W	7-4	Blue	LaCoss
18—Cinn.	L	3-1	Whitson	Pastore
19—At L.A.	L	2-7	Sutcliffe	Halicki
20—At L.A.	L	0-3	Welch	Knepper
22—At Atl.	L	2-10	Niekro	Blue
23—At Atl.	W	2-1	Minton	Matula
25—Los Ang.	L	2-11	Sutcliffe	Halicki
26—Los Ang.	L	4-8	Patterson	Griffin
27—Los Ang.	W	5-3	Blue	Hannahs
28—S. Diego	L	0-2	Rasmussen	Whitson
29—S. Diego	W	6-5	Griffin	Owchinko
30—S. Diego	L	3-5*	Owchinko	Lavelle

Won 11, Lost 17

*10 innings.   †11 innings.   ‡12 innings.   §13 innings.

Padres Perplexed by Pitching Paradox
By PHIL COLLIER

The 1979 season was the most disappointing in the San Diego Padres' 11-year history because they fell 16 victories short of their record 84 triumphs in 1978.

They went into 1979 believing they were capable of challenging Cincinnati, Los Angeles and San Francisco for the National League's West Division championship, something no San Diego team had ever done.

Instead, the Padres dropped from fourth to fifth in the standings, interest declined and, as is customary with the organization, another managerial change was made.

Roger Craig was sacked the final day of the season after a 68-93 record and was replaced, to everyone's surprise, by broadcaster Jerry Coleman, the former Yankee second baseman who had never managed before.

Craig, who had replaced Alvin Dark in spring training of 1978, lacked many of the tools he had to work with the previous season. The most noticeable missing link was the relief pitching that had helped the San Diego staff rank second in NL ERA tables in 1978.

In '79, the staff ERA rose from 3.28 to 3.69, fifth in the league. The Padre bullpen tied for last with a mere 25 saves. One year earlier, the Padres had 55 saves.

Thirty-seven of those saves had gone to Rollie Fingers, but the two-time NL Fireman of the Year developed elbow problems in 1979. He was out of action for two weeks in midseason, did not pitch after August 25 and finished with only 13 saves.

The rest of the bullpen collapsed with him. John D'Acquisto, 4-3 with 10 saves and a 2.13 ERA in 1978, dropped off to two saves, lost 13 of his 22 decisions and saw his ERA balloon to 4.90.

Sophomore Mark Lee went from 5-1 with two saves to 2-4 with five saves. Bob Shirley, a starter-reliever who had five saves in 1978, had none in 24 relief appearances in '79. Mickey Lolich, who had been counted on for relief help, pitched in 27 games without a victory or a save and announced his retirement.

Lack of bullpen support sorely affected starters Gaylord Perry (12-11), Randy Jones (11-12), Bob Owchinko (6-12), Eric Rasmussen (6-9) and Shirley (8-16).

San Diego pitchers also were handicapped by lack of offensive support. As so frequently happens, the Padres were last in the league with their .242 team batting average.

They were 10th in runs scored (603), 10th in homers (93), 11th in slugging (.348) and ninth in stolen bases (100). A year earlier, they had batted .252 and had stolen 152 bases.

Everything considered, it's a wonder captain and right fielder Dave Winfield was able to make this his finest season. The 27-year-old righthanded power hitter batted .308 for the second year in a row, stole 15 bases and set personal highs with his 34 homers and league-leading 118 RBIs.

"He did it on his own, we had no one to hit behind him and the pitchers consistently pitched around him," Craig said of Winfield, who also led the league in intentional walks (24).

Problems at a number of positions forced Craig to juggle his lineup, an act some of his players deplored.

Newcomer Mike Hargrove, acquired in a trade with Texas, proved a disappointment at first base. He batted only .192 in 52 games and was traded to Cleveland for Paul Dade.

Rookie third baseman Barry Evans (.216) sat out the rest of the season rather than accept a demotion to the minors in mid-June.

Shortstop Ozzie Smith, who had batted .258 as a rookie, began the season without a hit in his first 32 at-bats and struggled to end the year at .211.

Bill Almon, who was to have been a regular at second, was benched after a miserable exhibition game against the Angels and batted only .227. That was 10 points higher than Fernando Gonzalez, who replaced him.

Gene Richards was a disappointment when he moved from left field to center to make room in the lineup for Jerry Turner. Richards dropped from a .308 average in 1978 to .279 in 1979 and went from 37 stolen bases to 24. Turner was erratic in the field, batted only .248 and knocked in 61 runs.

However, newcomer Bill Fahey, another Texas castoff, batted .287 and took over behind the plate. Gene Tenace, who committed only one error in the 94 games he caught, moved to first base, hit 20 homers, drove in 67 runs and lifted his average from .224 to .263.

Another nice surprise was rookie righthander Steve Mura, who was 4-4 with a 3.08 ERA, working mostly in relief. He had two saves and struck out 59 batters in 73 innings.

Owner Ray Kroc turned over the team presidency to his son-in-law, Ballard Smith, after being fined a record $100,000 for tampering. Kroc had said that he would "go after" Graig Nettles and Joe Morgan if they were available in the reentry draft.

The Padres finished the season with a home attendance of 1,456,967, a drop of 213,140 from '78. It was the sixth year in a row that they had exceeded the one million mark, all since Kroc purchased the team in 1974.

SCORES OF SAN DIEGO PADRES' 1979 GAMES

APRIL

			Winner	Loser
5—At L.A.	W	4-3	Perry	Rautzhan
6—At L.A.	L	1-10	Sutton	Jones
7—At L.A.	L	2-5	Messersmith	Rasmussen
8—At L.A.	L	5-6‡	Sutcliffe	Shirley
10—At S.F.	L	2-4	Blue	D'Acquisto
11—At S.F.	W	4-1	Jones	Montefusco
12—At S.F.	L	3-4	Knepper	Rasmussen
13—Cinn.	L	2-4	Bonham	Shirley
14—Cinn.	W	3-2	Perry	Seaver
15—Cinn.	W	6-3	Jones	Norman
15—Cinn.	L	5-7	Capilla	Lee
17—S. Fran.	W	4-3	Fingers	Knepper
18—S. Fran.	W	7-6	Mura	Griffin
19—S. Fran.	L	10-14	Blue	Lolich
20—At Atl.	W	7-4	Jones	Matula
21—At Atl.	W	9-5	D'Acquisto	Garber
22—At Atl.	L	7-8	Garber	Fingers
24—At Mon.	L	1-5	Grimsley	Jones
25—At Mon.	L	6-9	Rogers	Shirley
27—At Phila.	L	0-2	Espinosa	Perry
28—At Phila.	W	5-0	D'Acquisto	Carlton
29—At Phila.	L	3-4	Reed	Fingers
30—At N.Y.	L	3-4	Swan	Shirley
		Won 9, Lost 14		

MAY

1—At N.Y.	W	10-5	Perry	Murray
3—Montreal	W	10-2	Jones	Sanderson
4—Montreal	L	1-12	Grimsley	D'Acquisto

MAY

			Winner	Loser
5—Montreal	W	6-3	Mura	Fryman
6—Montreal	L	5-7	Lee	Perry
7—Phila.	L	6-11	Carlton	Owchinko
8—Phila.	L	8-9‡	Kaat	D'Acquisto
9—Phila.	L	0-2	Ruthven	Rasmussen
10—Phila.	L	2-3	Espinosa	Perry
11—N. York	L	0-4	Kobel	Mura
12—N. York	W	2-1	Owchinko	Allen
13—N. York	W	5-4*	Shirley	Lockwood
14—At Cinn.	L	4-7	Moskau	Rasmussen
15—At Cinn.	W	2-1	Fingers	Pastore
16—At Cinn.	L	0-7	Bonham	Mura
18—At Hous.	L	2-3	Niekro	Fingers
19—At Hous.	W	4-2†	Fingers	Richard
20—At Hous.	L	0-1	Williams	Perry
20—At Hous.	L	3-6	Andujar	D'Acquisto
21—Los Ang.	W	3-2	Rasmussen	Messersmith
22—Los Ang.	W	7-6*	Fingers	Reuss
23—Los Ang.	L	2-4	Hooton	Jones
25—Houston	W	2-1*	Fingers	Sambito
26—Houston	L	0-9	Niekro	Lolich
27—Houston	L	2-4	Richard	Rasmussen
28—Houston	W	5-4	Jones	Andujar
29—Atlanta	W	6-3	Perry	Brizzolara
29—Atlanta	W	3-2	Owchinko	Niekro
30—Atlanta	W	10-2	Shirley	B. McL'ghlin
31—Atlanta	W	3-1	Rasmussen	Matula
		Won 15, Lost 15		

SAN DIEGO PADRES—1979

Front row—Kendall, Gonzalez, Jones, Williams, coach; Herman, coach; Wietelmann, coach; Craig, manager; Estrada, coach; Rader, coach; Shirley, Dade. Second row—V. Peralta, clubhouse assistant; Dent, trainer; Tolan, Wilhelm, Smith, Mura, Fahey, Owchinko, Mattei, traveling secretary; R. Peralta, equipment manager. Third row—Perry, Lolich, Turner, Richards, Lee, Winfield, Fingers, Almon, Tenace, Johnstone, Briggs, D'Acquisto, Rasmussen, Bevacqua. Seated in front—batboys Weatherford, Heye, Piotrowski and Nelson.

JUNE			Winner	Loser
1-At Pitts.	L	8-9	Tekulve	Shirley
2-At Pitts.	W	3-1	Perry	Candelaria
3-At Pitts.	L	0-7	Kison	Owchinko
5-At Chi.	W	11-3	Rasmussen	Lamp
6-At Chi.	L	0-3	Reuschel	Jones
7-At Chi.	L	3-4	McGlothen	Shirley
8-At St.L.	W	8-7*	Fingers	Knowles
9-At St.L.	L	4-7	Vuckovich	Rasmussen
10-At St.L.	L	2-3	Martinez	Jones
12-Pitts.	W	6-3	Perry	Candelaria
13-Pitts.	W	3-2	Owchinko	Kison
14-Pitts.	W	2-1§	D'Acquisto	Candelaria
15-Chicago	L	2-3	Hernandez	D'Acquisto
16-Chicago	L	2-5	Holtzman	Perry
17-Chicago	L	5-8	Krukow	Owchinko
18-St. Louis	W	3-2	Jones	Forsch
19-St. Louis	L	2-7	Fulgham	Rasmussen
20-St. Louis	W	3-1	Perry	Vuckovich
22-At Hous.	L	1-2	Niekro	Shirley
23-At Hous.	L	2-3	Dixon	Fingers
24-At Hous.	L	1-4	Andujar	Rasmussen
25-At L.A.	L	3-4	Brett	Fingers
26-At L.A.	W	5-1	Shirley	Sutton
27-Atlanta	W	2-1	Fingers	Niekro
27-Atlanta	L	2-5	J. McL'ghlin	Owchinko
28-Atlanta	W	6-5	D'Acquisto	Brizzolara
29-Houston	L	1-4	Andujar	Perry
30-Houston	L	0-3	Richard	Shirley
Won 11, Lost 17				

JULY				
1-Houston	L	1-4	Niekro	Jones
2-Los Ang.	L	3-6‡	Brett	Owchinko
3-Los Ang.	W	3-2	Perry	Sutcliffe
4-Los Ang.	W	6-0	Shirley	Sutton
6-At N.Y.	W	6-5‡	Lee	Hausman
7-At N.Y.	L	11-3	D'Acquisto	Ellis
8-At N.Y.	W	5-3	Perry	Kobel
8-At N.Y.	L	1-4	Hassler	Shirley
10-At Phila.	L	5-6	Bird	Fingers
11-At Phila.	W	7-3	D'Acquisto	Lerch
12-At Phila.	L	3-4	Carlton	Fingers
13-At Mon.	W	7-5	Owchinko	Sosa
13-At Mon.	L	7-10	May	Owchinko
14-At Mon.	W	5-1	Jones	Lee
15-At Mon.	L	0-4	Sanderson	D'Acquisto
19-N. York	L	3-1	Jones	Kobel
20-N. York	W	2-1	Perry	Swan
21-N. York	L	1-2	Allen	Shirley
22-Phila.	L	2-5	Espinosa	D'Acquisto
23-Phila.	W	6-5	Fingers	Reed
24-Montreal	W	4-3§	Mura	Palmer
25-Montreal	L	5-6	May	Owchinko
26-S. Fran.	L	2-6	Whitson	D'Acquisto
27-S. Fran.	L	3-4†	Borbon	Lee
28-S. Fran.	W	4-3	Fingers	Borbon
29-S. Fran.	L	2-4	Montefusco	Shirley
31-At Atl.	W	10-3	D'Acquisto	Niekro
Won 14, Lost 13				

AUGUST			Winner	Loser
1-At Atl.	L	4-5	J. McL'ghlin	Fingers
2-At Atl.	L	2-7	Brizzolara	Perry
3-At Cinn.	W	6-4	Shirley	Bonham
4-At Cinn.	L	1-7	Norman	D'Acquisto
5-At Cinn.	L	1-9	Pastore	Jones
7-At S.F.	L	2-3	Blue	Perry
8-At S.F.	L	7-10	Curtis	Shirley
9-At S.F.	W	4-0	D'Acquisto	Minton
10-Cinn.	W	3-2	Jones	Pastore
12-Cinn.	L	2-9	Seaver	Perry
12-Cinn.	W	5-4	Lee	LaCoss
14-At Pitts.	L	1-7	Candelaria	D'Acquisto
15-At Pitts.	L	1-5	Blyleven	Jones
16-At Pitts.	L	4-5	Kison	Perry
17-At Chi.	L	6-9	Tidrow	D'Acquisto
18-At Chi.	L	2-3	Tidrow	Fingers
19-At Chi.	L	1-3	Reuschel	Jones
20-At St.L.	L	3-6	Martinez	Perry
21-At St.L.	W	3-2†	Shirley	McEnaney
22-At St.L.	L	5-8	Fulgham	Owchinko
24-Pitts.	W	3-2	Jones	Romo
25-Pitts.	L	3-4y	Roberts	D'Acquisto
26-Pitts.	L	2-9	Kison	Shirley
27-Chicago	W	5-4*	D'Acquisto	Hernandez
28-Chicago	L	1-3	Reuschel	Jones
29-Chicago	W	3-1	Perry	McGlothen
31-St. Louis	L	7-8x	O'Brien	Owchinko
Won 8, Lost 19				

SEPTEMBER				
1-St. Louis	L	3-5	Martinez	Jones
2-St. Louis	L	1-2	Forsch	Lee
3-S. Fran.	W	3-0	Perry	Whitson
4-S. Fran.	L	1-3	Curtis	Shirley
5-At Hous.	L	3-4*	Sambito	D'Acquisto
6-At Hous.	L	0-2	Richard	Owchinko
7-At Atl.	W	8-0	Rasmussen	Solomon
8-At Atl.	W	9-2	Shirley	Matula
9-At Atl.	W	4-1	Jones	Niekro
11-At L.A.	W	3-1	Owchinko	Sutton
12-At L.A.	L	2-5	Hough	Rasmussen
13-At L.A.	L	6-8	Reuss	Shirley
14-Atlanta	L	7-10	M. Mahler	Lee
15-Atlanta	L	1-6	Matula	Eichelberger
17-Houston	L	0-1	Niekro	Owchinko
18-Houston	W	4-0	Rasmussen	Williams
19-Cinn.	L	2-3	Bonham	Shirley
20-Cinn.	L	5-8	Bair	Mura
21-Los Ang.	W	3-1	Eichelberger	Hannahs
22-Los Ang.	W	10-8	Mura	Patterson
23-Los Ang.	L	2-5	LaGrow	Mura
25-At Cinn.	W	8-2	Shirley	Norman
26-At Cinn.	L	3-4	Seaver	Jones
28-At S.F.	W	2-0	Rasmussen	Whitson
29-At S.F.	L	5-6	Griffin	Owchinko
30-At S.F.	W	5-3*	Owchinko	Lavelle
Won 11, Lost 15				

*10 innings.   †11 innings.   ‡12 innings.   §14 innings.   x15 innings.   y19 innings.

Braves Mourned Loss of GM

By KEN PICKING

In 1979, the Atlanta Braves lost more than 90 games for the fifth year in a row and finished last in the National League West Division for the fourth straight year. All of these defeats, however, were not as devastating as the one they suffered May 2. They lost Bill Lucas.

The night Phil Niekro won his 200th career game, the 43-year-old Lucas,

ATLANTA BRAVES—1979

Front row—Niekro, Royster, Frias, Horner, Aaron, coach; Boyer, coach; Cox, manager; Dews, coach; Grammas, coach; Beall, Nolan, Skok, Hanna. Second row—Acree, equipment manager; Van Wieren, traveling secretary; Chaney, R. Mahler, M. Mahler, Brizzolara, McWilliams, Bonnell, Burroughs, Office, Holland, assistant equipment manager; Pursley, trainer. Third row—Spikes, Matula, Devine, B. McLaughlin, Solomon, Cowans, batboy; Matthews. Seated in front—Warner, batboy; Hubbard, Pocoroba, Easterly, Asselstine, Garber, Lum, Benedict, Hall, batboy. Missing from picture—Murphy.

the Braves' enormously popular general manager and the highest-ranking black in baseball, collapsed in his Atlanta home. He died the next day.

"Losing Bill, especially as suddenly as we did, was something we couldn't just put out of our minds," second baseman Jerry Royster said. "He was special, almost a father, to all of us. It hurts me inside to know I'll never see him again."

The 66-94 Braves' starting lineup did not come together until days before the season began. Third baseman Bob Horner, the 1978 NL Rookie of the Year, held out and went to arbitration, seeking free agency. Although he later lost that claim, he became the highest-paid player in the club's history when he signed a three-year, $1.2 million contract shortly after the season ended.

Horner injured his ankle on opening night and missed the next 32 games. He came back and had a marvelous sophomore season. In 121 games, the 22-year-old led the Braves in average (.314), home runs (33) and RBIs (98).

In Horner's absence, Royster played third base and after the All-Star break took over at second base. Royster completed his best season in the majors. The 26-year-old set career highs in virtually every department and led the Braves in runs (103) and tied the club record for stolen bases with 35.

The acquisition of shortstop Pepe Frias from Montreal for pitcher Dave Campbell was the last trade Lucas made. Though he led the team in errors with 32, Frias hit as he never had before. A lifetime .220 hitter, Pepe was averaging nearly .300 midway through the season and finished at .259.

Dale Murphy moved from first base to catcher to get free agent Mike Lum's bat into the lineup; however, it was the 23-year-old Murphy himself who supplied the firepower. One of baseball's hottest hitters in the early going, Murphy had 13 homers and 36 RBIs when the strains of catching took their toll. Knee surgery disabled the cleanup hitter May 23.

Murphy returned two months later at the first base position. He was unable to regain his stroke and finished with 21 homers and 57 RBIs.

With Murphy at first and Biff Pocoroba out with a torn shoulder, Bruce Benedict and Joe Nolan shared the catching duties. Neither was able to supply any punch—Nolan batted .248 and rookie Benedict .225.

Gary Matthews was a consistent offensive force, especially batting second in front of Horner and Murphy, and was the Braves' lone All-Star. The 29-year-old right fielder set career highs in average (.304), runs (97), hits (192), doubles (34), home runs (27) and RBIs (90).

Rowland Office hit a disappointing .249 before opting for free agency, but his center field replacement Eddie Miller gave the Braves some excitement. Miller, who led the International League with 76 stolen bases at Richmond, brought the club to life in September with his speed (15-for-17 in stolen base attempts) and .310 average from the leadoff spot.

Phil Niekro, at age 40, continued to be among the league's most successful pitchers. The only Brave hurler to win 10 games, his 21 victories were equaled in the NL only by his brother Joe in Houston. Though he lost 20 games, Phil's 342 innings pitched and 23 complete games were tops in the majors.

Rookie Rick Matula (8-10) and Eddie Solomon (7-14) deserved better fate and defense at times, but the Braves' 4.18 ERA was still the league's worst.

Gene Garber, second-year Manager Bobby Cox's ace reliever, saved 25 games, but his ERA went up to 4.33 and he set an all-time record for most losses by a relief pitcher with 16.

Rookie Joey McLaughlin did a good job in middle relief, finishing 5-3 with five saves and a 2.48 ERA.

The season's biggest disappointments were pitcher Larry McWilliams and left fielder Jeff Burroughs. A nine-game winner as a rookie in 1978, McWilliams was hampered by an elbow injury and was not effective until September. Burroughs, the Braves' leading hitter in past years, slumped to a career-low .224 with only 11 homers and 47 RBIs.

SCORES OF ATLANTA BRAVES' 1979 GAMES

APRIL			Winner	Loser
6—At Hous.	L	1-2	Richard	Niekro
7—At Hous.	L	0-6	Forsch	McWilliams
8—At Hous.	L	0-2	J. Niekro	Matula
9—Cinn.	L	4-9	Seaver	M. Mahler
10—Cinn.	W	8-4	Niekro	Norman
11—Cinn.	L	5-9	Hume	Solomon
12—At L.A.	W	10-2	McWilliams	Messersmith
13—At L.A.	W	2-1	Matula	Rau
14—At L.A.	L	5-6	Welch	Niekro
15—At L.A.	W	11-4	Solomon	Hooton
17—At Cinn.	L	4-7	Hume	McWilliams
19—At Cinn.	L	0-2	Seaver	Niekro
20—S. Diego	L	4-7	Jones	Matula
21—S. Diego	L	5-9	D'Acquisto	Garber
22—S. Diego	W	8-7	Garber	Fingers
23—St. Louis	L	2-3†	Littell	Niekro
24—St. Louis	L	5-6†	Littell	Garber
27—Chicago	W	3-2	Niekro	Moore
28—Chicago	W	7-2	Matula	Reuschel
29—Chicago	L	5-6	McGlothen	Garber
		Won 7, Lost 13		
MAY				
1—At Pitts.	W	5-2	Niekro	Tekulve
2—At Pitts.	L	2-10	Candelaria	M. Mahler
4—At Chi.	L	2-6	Krukow	Matula
5—At Chi.	L	3-9	Lamp	Niekro
6—At Chi.	L	13-14	Sutter	Garber
7—Pitts.	L	2-4	Candelaria	M. Mahler
8—Pitts.	W	4-1	Solomon	Rhoden
9—Pitts.	L	9-17	Bibby	Garber
11—At St.L.	W	3-0	Devine	Forsch
12—At St.L.	L	6-7	Schultz	Garber
13—At St.L.	L	2-7	Vuckovich	Niekro
15—Los Ang.	L	4-5†	Welch	Devine
16—Los Ang.	W	3-2	Solomon	Messersmith
17—Los Ang.	W	6-3	Niekro	Hough
18—S. Fran.	W	6-4	M. Mahler	Blue
19—S. Fran.	L	2-4	Griffin	Skok
19—S. Fran.	L	6-7‡	Curtis	Garber
20—S. Fran.	W	1-8	Knepper	Solomon
21—Houston	W	7-5	Niekro	B. McL'ghlin
22—Houston	L	1-4	J. Niekro	M. Mahler
23—Houston	W	6-5	Brizzolara	Andujar
25—At S.F.	L	4-6	Knepper	Niekro
26—At S.F.	W	5-4	Garber	Roberts
27—At S.F.	L	10-8	Skok	Moffitt
28—At S.F.	W	4-1	M. Mahler	Nastu
29—At S.D.	L	3-6	Perry	Brizzolara
29—At S.D.	L	2-3	Owchinko	Niekro
30—At S.D.	L	2-10	Shirley	B. McL'ghlin
31—At S.D.	L	1-3	Rasmussen	Matula
		Won 11, Lost 18		
JUNE				
1—N. York	L	4-5‡	Lockwood	Devine
2—N. York	W	7-6	Niekro	Glynn
3—N. York	L	4-9	Zachry	M. Mahler
4—Montreal	L	1-8	Lee	Brizzolara
5—Montreal	W	4-1	Matula	Sanderson
6—Montreal	L	2-12	Grimsley	Niekro

JUNE			Winner	Loser
8—At Phila.	W	11-5†	Garber	Reed
9—At Phila.	L	3-9	Christenson	M. Mahler
10—At Phila.	W	10-3	Niekro	Carlton
11—At Mon.	L	5-6‡	Fryman	Skok
13—At Mon.	L	1-4	Rogers	Matula
14—At Mon.	L	3-4	Sosa	Garber
15—At N.Y.	L	1-2	Swan	J. McL'ghlin
16—At N.Y.	L	0-2	Kobel	M. Mahler
17—At N.Y.	L	1-2§	Reardon	Garber
18—Phila.	W	10-5	Matula	Espinosa
19—Phila.	W	10-4	Niekro	Christenson
20—Phila.	L	4-10	Carlton	Solomon
21—Los Ang.	L	4-6	Sutton	M. Mahler
22—Los Ang.	W	3-2	Brizzolara	Welch
23—Los Ang.	W	7-3	Niekro	Reuss
24—Los Ang.	W	4-2	Matula	Hooton
25—At S.F.	W	6-1	Solomon	Montefusco
26—At S.F.	L	5-6	Lavelle	Garber
27—At S.D.	L	1-2	Fingers	Niekro
27—At S.D.	W	5-2	J. McL'ghlin	Owchinko
28—At S.D.	L	5-6	D'Acquisto	Brizzolara
29—At L.A.	W	5-2	Matula	Sutcliffe
30—At L.A.	L	4-7‡	Garber	Forster
		Won 13, Lost 16		
JULY				
1—At L.A.	W	2-1	Niekro	Brett
3—S. Fran.	W	5-2	Brizzolara	Halicki
4—S. Fran.	W	7-6	J. McL'ghlin	Lavelle
5—S. Fran.	W	5-4	Niekro	Minton
6—St. Louis	L	5-9	Denny	Solomon
6—St. Louis	L	4-5†	Frazier	Skok
7—St. Louis	W	10-2	Brizzolara	Martinez
8—St. Louis	L	6-5	Garber	Littell
9—Chicago	L	4-7	Tidrow	Niekro
10—Chicago	L	3-7	Reuschel	Solomon
11—Chicago	L	6-5	Brizzolara	McGlothen
13—Pitts.	W	13-4	Niekro	Rooker
14—Pitts.	L	1-5	Candelaria	Matula
15—Pitts.	L	3-8	Bibby	Solomon
19—At Chi.	W	8-2	Niekro	Lamp
20—At Chi.	L	2-10	Reuschel	Brizzolara
21—At Chi.	L	2-3	Tidrow	Garber
22—At Pitts.	L	4-5	Robinson	Solomon
22—At Pitts.	L	2-3	Bibby	M. Mahler
23—At Pitts.	L	1-7	Blyleven	Hanna
23—At Pitts.	W	8-0	Niekro	Rooker
24—At St. L.	L	3-7	Vuckovich	Brizzolara
25—At St. L.	W	13-4	J. McL'ghlin	Frazier
26—At St. L.	L	2-6	Martinez	Solomon
27—Cinn.	L	0-2	LaCoss	Niekro
28—Cinn.	L	6-8	Bonham	Brizzolara
28—Cinn.	W	8-5	M. Mahler	Pastore
29—Cinn.	L	4-9	Norman	Matula
31—S. Diego	L	3-10	D'Acquisto	Niekro
		Won 12, Lost 17		
AUGUST				
1—S. Diego	W	5-4	J. McL'ghlin	Fingers
2—S. Diego	W	7-2	Brizzolara	Perry
3—At Hous.	L	1-4	Richard	Matula

AUGUST			Winner	Loser
4—At Hous.	L	3-4	Sambito	Garber
4—At Hous.	L	2-6	LaCorte	Niekro
5—At Hous.	L	2-3	Roberge	Garber
6—At Cinn.	L	1-3	LaCoss	M. Mahler
7—At Cinn.	W	3-2‡	Garber	Bair
8—At Cinn.	L	1-3	Bonham	Niekro
9—At Cinn.	L	2-5	Norman	Garber
10—Houston	L	1-2	J. Niekro	Solomon
12—Houston	W	3-2	Niekro	Williams
14—N. York	L	5-18	Hassler	Brizzolara
15—N. York	L	3-6	Swan	M. Mahler
16—N. York	L	3-6	Falcone	Niekro
17—At Mon.	L	0-1	Palmer	Solomon
18—At Mon.	L	1-2	Rogers	J. McL'ghlin
19—At Mon.	L	1-5	Lee	Brizzolara
20—At Phila.	W	5-2	Niekro	Reed
21—At Phila.	W	5-4	Bradford	Eastwick
22—At Phila.	W	4-3	Solomon	Christenson
24—Montreal	W	0-2	Lee	Niekro
27—At N.Y.	W	5-1	Solomon	Kobel
28—At N.Y.	W	6-4	Niekro	Ellis
29—At N.Y.	W	5-4	Matula	Burris
31—Phila.	L	2-6*	Bird	Brizzolara
		Won 10, Lost 16		

SEPTEMBER				
1—Phila.	L	4-6	Christenson	Niekro

SEPTEMBER			Winner	Loser
2—Phila.	L	1-2†	Reed	J. McL'ghlin
3—Cinn.	L	5-6	Bair	Garber
4—Cinn.	W	7-6	J. McL'ghlin	Bair
5—Los Ang.	L	3-5†	LaGrow	Garber
6—Los Ang.	W	6-2	Hanna	Sutton
7—S. Diego	L	0-8	Rasmussen	Solomon
8—S. Diego	L	2-9	Shirley	Matula
9—S. Diego	L	1-4	Jones	Niekro
11—At S.F.	W	2-1	McWilliams	Montefusco
12—At S.F.	L	3-4	Blue	Solomon
13—At S.F.	W	4-1	Niekro	Whitson
14—At S.D.	W	10-7	M. Mahler	Lee
15—At S.D.	W	6-1	Matula	Eichelberger
17—At L.A.	L	4-9	Hough	Niekro
18—At L.A.	L	1-6	Reuss	Solomon
19—At Hous.	W	6-5	B. McL'ghlin	Ruhle
20—At Hous.	L	1-7	Forsch	Boggs
22—S. Fran.	W	10-2	Niekro	Blue
23—S. Fran.	L	1-2	Minton	Matula
24—Houston	W	5-4	M. Mahler	Sambito
24—Houston	W	8-1	Solomon	Williams
25—Houston	L	0-8	Richard	Boggs
26—Houston	W	9-4	P. Niekro	J. Niekro
28—At Cinn.	L	0-3	Pastore	Solomon
29—At Cinn.	W	2-0	McWilliams	Norman
30—At Cinn.	W	7-2	Niekro	Bonham
		Won 13, Lost 14		

*5½ innings.   †10 innings.   ‡11 innings.   §Suspended game, completed August 27.

Braves young slugger Bob Horner and the late Atlanta GM Bill Lucas. Horner won salary arbitration during season and later signed as highest-paid Braves player ever.

DAVE KINGMAN
• CUBS •
HOMERS (48)
SLUGGING PCT. (.613)

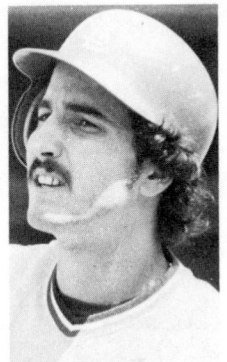

KEITH HERNANDEZ
• CARDINALS •
BATTING CHAMPION (.344)
DOUBLES (48)
RUNS (116)

DAVE WINFIELD
• PADRES •
TOTAL BASES (333)
RUNS BATTED IN (118)

1979 NATIONAL LEAGUE LEADERS

BRUCE SUTTER
• CUBS •
SAVES (37)

PHIL NIEKRO
• BRAVES •
COMPLETE GAMES (23)
INNINGS (342)

J. R. RICHARD
• ASTROS •
STRIKEOUTS (313)
EARNED-RUN AVERAGE (2.71)

National League Averages for 1979

CHAMPIONSHIP WINNERS IN PREVIOUS YEARS

1876—Chicago .788	1911—New York .647	1945—Chicago .636
1877—Boston .646	1912—New York .682	1946—St. Louis* .628
1878—Boston .683	1913—New York .664	1947—Brooklyn .610
1879—Providence .705	1914—Boston .614	1948—Boston .595
1880—Chicago .798	1915—Philadelphia .592	1949—Brooklyn .630
1881—Chicago .667	1916—Brooklyn .610	1950—Philadelphia .591
1882—Chicago .655	1917—New York .636	1951—New York† .624
1883—Boston .643	1918—Chicago .651	1952—Brooklyn .627
1884—Providence .750	1919—Cincinnati .686	1953—Brooklyn .682
1885—Chicago .777	1920—Brooklyn .604	1954—New York .630
1886—Chicago .726	1921—New York .614	1955—Brooklyn .641
1887—Detroit .637	1922—New York .604	1956—Brooklyn .604
1888—New York .641	1923—New York .621	1957—Milwaukee .617
1889—New York .659	1924—New York .608	1958—Milwaukee .597
1890—Brooklyn .667	1925—Pittsburgh .621	1959—Los Angeles‡ .564
1891—Boston .630	1926—St. Louis .578	1960—Pittsburgh .617
1892—Boston .680	1927—Pittsburgh .610	1961—Cincinnati .604
1893—Boston .662	1928—St. Louis .617	1962—San Francisco§ .624
1894—Baltimore .695	1929—Chicago .645	1963—Los Angeles .611
1895—Baltimore .669	1930—St. Louis .597	1964—St. Louis .574
1896—Baltimore .698	1931—St. Louis .656	1965—Los Angeles .599
1897—Boston .705	1932—Chicago .584	1966—Los Angeles .586
1898—Boston .685	1933—New York .599	1967—St. Louis .627
1899—Brooklyn .677	1934—St. Louis .621	1968—St. Louis .599
1900—Brooklyn .603	1935—Chicago .649	1969—New York (East)a .617
1901—Pittsburgh .647	1936—New York .597	1970—Cincinnati (West)b .630
1902—Pittsburgh .741	1937—New York .625	1971—Pittsburgh (East)c .599
1903—Pittsburgh .650	1938—Chicago .586	1972—Cincinnati (West)b .617
1904—New York .693	1939—Cincinnati .630	1973—New York (East)d .509
1905—New York .686	1940—Cincinnati .654	1974—Los Angeles (West)b .630
1906—Chicago .763	1941—Brooklyn .649	1975—Cincinnati (West)b .667
1907—Chicago .704	1942—St. Louis .688	1976—Cincinnati (West)e .630
1908—Chicago .643	1943—St. Louis .682	1977—Los Angeles (West)e .605
1909—Pittsburgh .724	1944—St. Louis .682	1978—Los Angeles (West)e .586
1910—Chicago .675		

*Defeated Brooklyn, two games to none, in playoff for pennant. †Defeated Brooklyn, two games to one, in playoff for pennant. ‡Defeated Milwaukee, two games to none, in playoff for pennant. §Defeated Los Angeles, two games to one, in playoff for pennant. aDefeated Atlanta (West) in Championship Series. bDefeated Pittsburgh (East) in Championship Series. cDefeated San Francisco (West) in Championship Series. dDefeated Cincinnati (West) in Championship Series. eDefeated Philadelphia (East) in Championship Series.

STANDING OF CLUBS AT CLOSE OF SEASON

EAST DIVISION

Club	Pitt.	Mon.	St.L.	Phil.	Chi.	N.Y.	Atl.	Cin.	Hou.	L.A.	S.D.	S.F.	W.	L.	Pct.	G.B.
Pittsburgh	..	11	11	10	12	10	8	4	8	8	7	9	98	64	.605	......
Montreal	7	..	10	11	12	15	9	6	5	6	7	7	95	65	.594	2
St. Louis	7	8	..	11	10	11	8	4	6	6	8	7	86	76	.531	12
Philadelphia	8	7	7	..	9	13	5	4	7	9	9	6	84	78	.519	14
Chicago	6	6	8	9	..	8	8	7	6	5	9	8	80	82	.494	18
New York	8	3	7	5	10	..	8	4	3	3	4	8	63	99	.389	35

WEST DIVISION

Club	Cin.	Hou.	L.A.	S.F.	S.D.	Atl.	Chi.	Mon.	N.Y.	Phil.	Pitt.	St.L.	W.	L.	Pct.	G.B.
Cincinnati	..	8	11	6	10	12	5	6	8	8	8	8	90	71	.559	......
Houston	10	..	10	7	14	11	6	7	9	5	4	6	89	73	.549	1½
Los Angeles	7	8	..	14	9	6	7	6	9	3	4	6	79	83	.488	11½
San Francisco	12	11	4	..	10	7	4	5	4	6	3	5	71	91	.438	19½
San Diego	7	4	9	8	..	12	3	5	8	3	5	4	68	93	.422	22
Atlanta	6	7	12	11	6	..	4	1	4	7	4	4	66	94	.413	23½

Tie Games—Philadelphia vs. St. Louis and Pittsburgh vs. New York.
Cancelled Games—Montreal at Atlanta (2); San Diego at Cincinnati.
Championship Series—Pittsburgh defeated Cincinnati, three games to none.

RECORD AT HOME

EAST DIVISION

Club	Mon.	Pitt.	Chi.	Phil.	St.L.	N.Y.	Hou.	Cin.	L.A.	S.D.	S.F.	Atl.	W.	L.	Pct.
Montreal	.....	3-6	8-1	6-3	5-4	7-2	4-2	5-1	5-1	4-2	3-3	6-0	56	25	.691
Pittsburgh	5-4	.....	6-3	6-3	6-3	4-5	5-1	1-5	3-3	5-1	3-3	4-2	48	33	.593
Chicago	5-4	3-6	.....	5-4	5-4	3-6	4-2	3-3	3-3	5-1	4-2	5-1	45	36	.556
Philadelphia	4-5	5-4	5-4	.....	3-6	6-3	3-3	2-4	6-0	4-2	4-2	1-5	43	38	.531
St. Louis	4-5	4-5	6-3	5-4	.....	3-6	2-4	2-4	3-3	4-2	5-1	4-2	42	39	.519
New York	1-8	3-6	4-5	2-7	1-8	.....	2-4	2-4	3-3	2-4	5-1	3-3	28	53	.346

WEST DIVISION

Club	Hou.	Cin.	L.A.	S.D.	S.F.	Atl.	Mon.	Pitt.	Chi.	Phil.	St.L.	N.Y.	W.	L.	Pct.
Houston	.....	7-2	5-4	8-1	3-6	6-3	5-1	3-3	4-2	2-4	2-4	5-1	52	29	.642
Cincinnati	6-3	.....	5-4	5-3	4-5	6-3	5-1	3-3	2-4	4-2	4-2	4-2	48	32	.600
Los Angeles	4-5	3-6	.....	6-3	8-1	3-6	5-1	4-5	4-2	3-3	3-3	6-0	46	35	.568
San Diego	3-6	4-5	6-3	.....	4-5	3-6	3-3	4-2	2-4	1-5	2-4	4-2	39	42	.481
San Francisco	5-4	7-2	3-6	5-4	.....	3-6	2-4	0-6	2-4	4-2	4-2	3-3	38	43	.469
Atlanta	6-3	3-6	6-3	3-6	5-4	.....	1-3	2-4	3-3	2-4	2-4	1-5	34	45	.460

RECORD ABROAD

EAST DIVISION

Club	Pitt.	St.L.	Phil.	Mon.	Chi.	N.Y.	Cin.	Hou.	L.A.	S.F.	Atl.	S.D.	W.	L.	Pct.
Pittsburgh	.....	5-4	4-5	6-3	6-3	6-3	3-3	3-3	5-1	6-0	4-2	2-4	50	31	.617
St. Louis	3-6	.....	6-3	4-5	4-5	8-1	2-4	4-2	3-3	2-4	4-2	4-2	44	37	.543
Philadelphia	3-6	4-5	.....	3-6	4-5	7-2	2-4	4-2	3-3	2-4	4-2	5-1	39	40	.506
Montreal	4-5	5-4	5-4	.....	4-5	8-1	1-5	1-5	1-5	4-2	3-1	3-3	39	40	.494
Chicago	3-6	3-6	4-5	1-8	.....	5-4	4-2	2-4	2-4	4-2	3-3	4-2	35	46	.432
New York	5-4	6-3	3-6	2-7	6-3	.....	2-4	1-5	0-6	3-3	5-1	2-4	35	46	.432

WEST DIVISION

Club	Cin.	Hou.	L.A.	S.F.	Atl.	S.D.	Pitt.	St.L.	Phil.	Mon.	Chi.	N.Y.	W.	L.	Pct.
Cincinnati	.....	2-7	6-3	2-7	6-3	5-4	5-1	4-2	4-2	1-5	3-3	4-2	39	39	.519
Houston	3-6	.....	5-4	4-5	3-6	6-3	1-5	4-2	3-3	2-4	4-2	4-2	37	44	.457
Los Angeles	4-5	4-5	.....	6-3	3-6	3-6	3-3	3-3	0-6	1-5	3-3	3-3	33	48	.407
San Francisco	5-4	6-3	1-8	.....	4-5	5-4	3-3	1-5	2-4	3-3	2-4	1-5	33	48	.407
Atlanta	3-6	1-8	6-3	6-3	.....	3-6	2-4	2-4	5-1	0-6	1-5	3-3	32	49	.395
San Diego	3-5	1-8	3-6	4-5	6-3	.....	1-5	2-4	2-4	2-4	1-5	4-2	29	51	.363

SHUTOUT GAMES

Club	Mon.	Cin.	St.L.	Hou.	Phil.	Chi.	N.Y.	Pitt.	L.A.	S.D.	S.F.	Atl.	W.	L.	Pct.
Montreal	..	0	1	1	4	4	1	1	1	1	2	2	18	7	.720
Cincinnati	0	..	1	0	0	0	2	0	1	1	2	3	10	5	.667
St. Louis	3	0	..	1	1	1	1	1	0	0	2	0	10	5	.667
Houston	1	2	0	..	1	1	2	0	3	5	1	3	19	15	.559
Philadelphia	1	0	0	3	..	1	4	1	2	2	0	0	14	12	.538
Chicago	0	1	0	4	2	..	1	2	0	1	0	0	11	11	.500
New York	0	0	0	2	0	1	..	3	0	1	2	1	10	12	.455
Pittsburgh	0	0	1	0	1	3	0	..	1	1	0	0	7	9	.438
Los Angeles	1	1	1	1	0	0	0	0	..	0	2	0	6	9	.400
San Diego	0	0	0	1	1	0	0	0	1	..	3	1	7	12	.368
San Francisco	1	0	0	2	2	0	0	1	0	0	..	0	6	14	.300
Atlanta	0	1	1	0	0	0	0	0	1	0	0	..	3	10	.231

OFFICIAL NATIONAL LEAGUE BATTING AVERAGES

Compiled by Elias Sports Bureau, New York, N. Y.

CLUB BATTING

Club	Pct.	G.	AB.	R.	OR.	H.	TB.	2B.	3B.	HR.	RBI.	SH.	SF.	SB.	CS.	LOB.
St. Louis	.278	163	5734	731	693	1594	2299	279	63	100	685	63	63	116	69	1170
Pittsb'gh	.272	163	5661	775	643	1541	2353	264	52	148	710	98	56	180	66	1128
Chicago.	.269	162	5550	706	707	1494	2235	250	43	135	663	77	42	73	52	1140
Phila....	.266	163	5463	683	718	1453	2166	250	53	119	641	60	57	128	76	1216
Montreal	.264	160	5465	701	581	1445	2231	273	42	143	651	67	38	121	56	1026
Cinci.	.264	161	5477	731	644	1445	2169	266	31	132	686	62	46	99	47	1192
Los Ang.	.263	162	5490	739	717	1443	2260	220	24	183	713	83	36	106	46	1111
Houston	.256	162	5394	583	582	1382	1857	224	52	49	542	109	43	190	95	1120
Atlanta .	.256	160	5422	669	763	1389	2043	220	28	126	626	62	38	98	50	1109
N. York.	.250	163	5591	593	706	1399	1958	255	41	74	558	66	40	135	79	1143
S. Fran.	.246	162	5395	672	751	1328	1967	192	36	125	616	89	47	140	73	1131
S. Diego	.242	161	5446	603	681	1316	1894	193	53	93	559	113	43	100	58	1164
Totals	.261	971	66088	8186	8186	17229	25432	2886	518	1427	7650	949	549	1486	767	13650

INDIVIDUAL BATTING

(Top Fifteen Qualifiers for Batting Championship—502 or More Plate Appearances)

*Bats lefthanded.   †Switch-hitter.

Player and Club	Pct.	G.	AB.	R.	H.	TB.	2B.	3B.	HR.	RBI.	SH.	SF.	SB.	CS.
Hernandez, Keith, St. Louis*	.344	161	610	116	210	313	48	11	11	105	0	7	11	6
Rose, Peter, Philadelphia†	.331	163	628	90	208	270	40	5	4	59	0	5	20	11
Knight, C. Ray, Cincinnati	.318	150	551	64	175	250	37	4	10	79	4	8	4	4
Garvey, Steven, Los Angeles	.315	162	648	92	204	322	32	1	28	110	4	6	3	6
Horner, J. Robert, Atlanta	.314	121	487	66	153	269	15	1	33	98	0	3	0	2
Templeton, Garry, St. Louis†	.314	154	672	105	211	308	32	19	9	62	2	3	26	10
Parker, David, Pittsburgh*	.310	158	622	109	193	327	45	7	25	94	0	9	20	4
Winfield, David, San Diego	.308	159	597	97	184	333	27	10	34	118	0	2	15	9
Parrish, Larry, Montreal	.307	153	544	83	167	300	39	2	30	82	7	1	5	1
Matthews, Gary, Atlanta	.304	156	631	97	192	317	34	5	27	90	1	3	18	6
Mazzilli, Lee, New York†	.303	158	597	78	181	268	34	4	15	79	0	3	34	12
Foster, George, Cincinnati	.302	121	440	68	133	247	18	3	30	98	0	3	0	2
Hendrick, George, St. Louis	.300	140	493	67	148	225	27	1	16	75	0	6	2	3
Madlock, Bill, SF-Pitt	.298	154	560	85	167	245	26	5	14	85	3	7	32	11
Garner, Phillip, Pittsburgh	.293	150	549	76	161	242	32	8	11	59	2	3	17	8

DEPARTMENTAL LEADERS: G—Taveras, 164; AB—Moreno, 695; R—K. Hernandez, 116; H—Templeton, 211; TB—Winfield, 333; 2B—K. Hernandez, 48; 3B—Templeton, 19; HR—Kingman, 48; RBI—Winfield, 118; SH—C. Reynolds, 34; SF—Cedeno, Parker, Schmidt, 9; SB—Moreno, 77; CS—North, 24.

(All Players—Listed Alphabetically)

Player and Club	Pct.	G.	AB.	R.	H.	TB.	2B.	3B.	HR.	RBI.	SH.	SF.	SB.	CS.
Alexander, Matthew, Pittsburgh†	.538	44	13	16	7	9	0	1	0	1	0	0	13	1
Allen, Neil, New York	.000	50	14	0	0	0	0	0	0	0	0	0	0	0
Almon, William, San Diego	.227	100	198	20	45	51	3	0	1	8	5	2	6	5
Alou, Jesus, Houston	.256	42	43	3	11	15	4	0	0	10	0	0	0	0
Anderson, Michael, Philadelphia	.231	79	78	12	18	25	4	0	1	2	0	0	1	2
Andrews, Robert, San Francisco	.260	75	154	22	40	49	3	0	2	13	4	4	4	1
Andujar, Joaquin, Houston†	.088	46	57	3	5	12	1	0	2	7	5	1	0	0
Ashby, Alan, Houston*†	.202	108	336	25	68	93	15	2	2	35	3	3	0	0
Asselstine, Brian, Atlanta*	.100	8	10	1	1	1	0	0	0	0	0	0	0	0
Atkinson, William, Montreal*	.000	10	1	0	0	0	0	0	0	0	0	0	0	0
Auerbach, Frederick, Cincinnati	.210	62	100	17	21	34	8	1	1	12	1	1	0	1
Aviles, Ramon, Philadelphia	.279	27	61	7	17	19	2	0	0	12	3	0	0	0
Bahnsen, Stanley, Montreal	.071	55	14	2	1	4	0	0	1	2	0	0	0	0
Bair, C. Douglas, Cincinnati	.000	65	8	0	0	0	0	0	0	0	0	0	0	0
Baker, Johnnie, Los Angeles	.274	151	554	86	152	252	29	1	23	88	2	3	11	4
Baldwin, Reginald, Houston	.200	14	20	0	4	5	1	0	0	1	0	0	0	0
Bass, Randy, Montreal*	.000	2	1	0	0	0	0	0	0	0	0	0	0	0
Beall, Robert, Atlanta†	.133	17	15	1	2	4	2	0	0	1	0	1	0	0
Beckwith, T. Joseph, Los Angeles*..	.000	17	5	1	0	0	0	0	0	0	1	0	0	0
Bench, Johnny, Cincinnati	.276	130	464	73	128	213	19	0	22	80	3	4	4	2
Benedict, Bruce, Atlanta	.225	76	204	14	46	57	11	0	0	15	2	2	1	3
Berenguer, Juan, New York	.143	5	7	0	1	1	0	0	0	0	1	0	0	0

Player and Club	Pct.	G.	AB.	R.	H.	TB.	2B.	3B.	HR.	RBI.	SH.	SF.	SB.	CS.
Bergman, David, Houston*	.400	13	15	4	6	9	0	0	1	2	0	0	0	0
Bernard, Dwight, New York	.000	32	0	0	0	0	0	0	0	0	2	0	0	0
Bernazard, Antonio, Montreal†	.300	22	40	11	12	17	2	0	1	8	2	0	1	2
Berra, Dale, Pittsburgh	.211	44	123	11	26	40	5	0	3	15	2	2	0	0
Bevacqua, Kurt, San Diego	.253	114	297	23	75	98	12	4	1	34	5	6	2	5
Bibby, James, Pittsburgh	.178	34	45	3	8	15	1	0	2	5	6	0	0	0
Biittner, Larry, Chicago*	.290	111	272	35	79	107	13	3	3	50	0	2	1	1
Bird, J. Douglas, Philadelphia	.167	32	6	1	1	1	0	0	0	0	0	0	0	0
Blackwell, Timothy, Chicago†	.164	63	122	8	20	25	3	1	0	12	2	2	0	0
Blair, Paul, Cincinnati	.150	75	140	7	21	33	4	1	2	15	2	2	0	0
Blue, Vida, San Francisco*	.120	37	83	7	10	14	1	0	1	3	8	0	0	0
Blyleven, Rikalbert, Pittsburgh	.129	38	70	1	9	10	1	0	0	3	15	0	0	0
Bochy, Bruce, Houston	.217	56	129	11	28	35	4	0	1	6	0	0	0	0
Boggs, Thomas, Atlanta	.250	3	4	1	1	1	0	0	0	0	0	0	0	0
Boisclair, Bruce, New York*	.184	59	98	7	18	25	5	1	0	4	1	3	0	2
Bonham, William, Cincinnati	.140	29	57	3	8	10	2	0	0	2	6	0	0	0
Bonnell, R. Barry, Atlanta	.259	127	375	47	97	159	20	3	12	45	7	1	8	7
Boone, Robert, Philadelphia	.286	119	375	38	114	168	21	3	9	58	4	1	1	4
Borbon, Pedro, Cin-SF*	.333	60	9	2	3	3	0	0	0	0	0	0	0	0
Bowa, Lawrence, Philadelphia†	.241	147	539	74	130	169	17	11	0	31	12	6	20	9
Boyland, Dorian, Pittsburgh*	.000	4	3	0	0	0	0	0	0	0	0	0	0	0
Bradford, Larry, Atlanta	.000	21	1	0	0	0	0	0	0	0	0	0	0	0
Brett, Kenneth, Los Angeles*	.273	30	11	0	3	3	0	0	0	2	0	0	0	0
Briggs, Daniel, San Diego*	.207	104	227	34	47	81	4	3	8	30	1	3	2	1
Brizzolara, Anthony, Atlanta	.029	20	35	1	1	1	0	0	0	1	1	1	0	0
Brock, Louis, St. Louis*	.304	120	405	56	123	161	15	4	5	38	0	5	21	12
Bruno, Thomas, St. Louis	.200	27	5	0	1	1	0	0	0	1	0	0	0	0
Brusstar, Warren, Philadelphia	.000	13	0	0	0	0	0	0	0	0	0	0	0	0
Buckner, William, Chicago*	.284	149	591	72	168	258	34	7	14	66	1	4	9	4
Burris, B. Ray, Chi-NY	.143	18	7	1	1	1	0	0	0	0	1	0	0	0
Burroughs, Jeffrey, Atlanta	.224	116	397	49	89	138	14	1	11	47	0	2	2	2
Cabell, Enos, Houston	.272	155	603	60	164	222	30	5	6	67	2	1	37	18
Candelaria, John, Pittsburgh*	.132	33	68	0	9	13	4	0	0	6	8	0	0	0
Capilla, Douglas, Cin-Chi*	1.000	18	1	0	1	1	0	0	0	0	0	0	0	0
Carbo, Bernardo, St. Louis*	.281	52	64	6	18	28	1	0	3	12	0	2	1	0
Cardenal, Jose, Phil-NY	.247	40	85	12	21	34	7	0	2	13	0	0	2	0
Carlton, Steven, Philadelphia*	.223	36	94	9	21	24	3	0	0	10	2	1	1	0
Carter, Gary, Montreal	.283	141	505	74	143	245	26	5	22	75	2	7	3	2
Cash, David, Montreal	.321	76	187	24	60	79	11	1	2	19	2	2	7	4
Castillo, Robert, Los Angeles	.000	19	3	0	0	0	0	0	0	0	0	0	0	0
Caudill, William, Chicago	.059	29	17	0	1	1	0	0	0	0	4	0	0	0
Cedeno, Cesar, Houston	.262	132	470	57	123	176	27	4	6	54	3	9	30	13
Cey, Ronald, Los Angeles	.281	150	487	77	137	243	20	1	28	81	0	4	3	3
Chaney, Darrel, Atlanta†	.162	63	117	15	19	24	5	0	0	10	0	1	2	1
Chapman, Kelvin, New York	.150	35	80	7	12	17	1	2	0	4	1	1	0	0
Christenson, Larry, Philadelphia	.290	19	31	4	9	17	3	1	1	3	0	1	0	0
Clark, Jack, San Francisco	.273	143	527	84	144	251	25	2	26	86	1	6	11	8
Clines, Eugene, Chicago	.200	10	10	0	2	2	0	0	0	0	0	0	0	0
Coleman, Joseph, SF-Pitt	.200	15	5	0	1	2	1	0	0	0	0	0	0	0
Collins, David, Cincinnati†	.318	122	396	59	126	159	16	4	3	35	3	1	16	9
Concepcion, David, Cincinnati	.281	149	590	91	166	245	25	3	16	84	6	6	19	7
Correll, Victor, Cincinnati	.233	48	133	14	31	46	12	0	1	15	1	1	0	0
Cromartie, Warren, Montreal*	.275	158	659	84	181	261	46	5	8	46	6	6	8	7
Cruz, Hector, SF-Cin	.227	90	207	26	47	73	10	2	4	28	1	1	0	1
Cruz, Jose, Houston*	.289	157	558	73	161	235	33	7	9	72	1	5	36	14
Curtis, John, San Francisco*	.147	29	34	3	5	6	1	0	0	3	6	0	0	0
D'Acquisto, John, San Diego	.129	51	31	0	4	6	2	0	0	3	3	0	0	0
Dade, L. Paul, San Diego	.276	76	283	38	78	104	19	2	1	19	7	3	13	5
Davalillo, Victor, Los Angeles*	.259	29	27	2	7	8	1	0	0	2	0	0	2	0
Davis, Steven, Chicago	.000	3	4	0	0	0	0	0	0	0	1	0	0	0
Dawson, Andre, Montreal	.275	155	639	90	176	299	24	12	25	92	8	4	35	10
DeFreites, Arturo, Cincinnati	.206	23	34	2	7	9	2	0	0	4	0	1	0	0
DeJesus, Ivan, Chicago	.283	160	636	92	180	241	26	10	5	52	17	2	24	20
Denny, John, St. Louis	.129	31	70	5	9	13	2	1	0	3	8	1	1	2
Devine, P. Adrian, Atlanta	.000	40	7	0	0	0	0	0	0	0	0	0	0	0
Dillard, Stephen, Chicago*	.283	89	166	31	47	70	6	1	5	24	5	1	1	0
Dilone, Miguel, Chicago†	.306	43	36	14	11	11	0	0	0	1	0	0	15	5
Dimmel, Michael, St. Louis	.333	6	3	1	1	1	0	0	0	0	0	0	0	1
Dixon, Thomas, Houston	1.000	19	1	0	1	1	0	0	0	0	0	0	0	0

Player and Club	Pct.	G.	AB.	R.	H.	TB.	2B.	3B.	HR.	RBI.	SH.	SF.	SB.	CS.
Driessen, Daniel, Cincinnati*	.250	150	515	72	129	213	24	3	18	75	2	7	11	5
Dyer, Donald, Montreal	.243	28	74	4	18	27	6	0	1	8	0	0	0	0
Easler, Michael, Pittsburgh*	.278	55	54	8	15	24	1	1	2	11	0	0	0	1
Easterly, James, Atlanta*	.000	4	0	0	0	0	0	0	0	0	0	0	0	0
Eastwick, Rawlins, Philadelphia	.000	51	7	0	0	0	0	0	0	0	0	0	0	0
Eichelberger, Juan, San Diego	.400	3	5	1	2	3	1	0	0	1	1	0	0	0
Ellis, Dock, NY-Pitt†	.074	20	27	2	2	2	0	0	0	0	1	0	0	0
Espinosa, Arnulfo, Philadelphia	.194	36	72	3	14	16	2	0	0	6	4	0	1	0
Evans, Barry, San Diego	.216	56	162	9	35	43	5	0	1	14	5	2	0	2
Evans, Darrell, San Francisco*	.253	160	562	68	142	220	23	2	17	70	1	5	6	7
Fahey, William, San Diego*	.287	73	209	14	60	79	8	1	3	19	3	3	1	1
Falcone, Peter, New York*	.173	33	52	1	9	9	0	0	0	2	5	0	0	0
Ferguson, Joseph, Los Angeles	.262	122	363	54	95	169	14	0	20	69	2	5	1	0
Ferrer, Sergio, New York†	.000	32	7	7	0	0	0	0	0	0	0	0	0	0
Fingers, Roland, San Diego	.083	54	12	1	1	1	0	0	0	2	1	0	0	0
Flannery, Timothy, San Diego	.154	22	65	2	10	12	0	1	0	4	1	1	0	0
Flores, Gilberto, New York	.194	70	93	9	18	24	1	1	1	10	3	1	2	0
Flynn, R. Douglas, New York	.243	157	555	35	135	176	19	5	4	61	6	2	0	3
Foli, Timothy, NY-Pitt	.288	136	532	70	153	181	23	1	1	65	19	6	6	5
Foote, Barry, Chicago	.254	132	429	47	109	183	26	0	16	56	0	1	5	2
Forsch, Kenneth, Houston	.138	26	58	4	8	9	1	0	0	3	6	0	0	0
Forsch, Robert, St. Louis	.110	33	73	7	8	14	2	2	0	5	4	2	0	0
Forster, Terry, Los Angeles*	.000	17	0	0	0	0	0	0	0	0	0	0	0	0
Foster, George, Cincinnati	.302	121	440	68	133	247	18	3	30	98	0	3	0	2
Frazier, George, St. Louis	.000	25	1	0	0	0	0	0	0	0	0	0	0	0
Freed, Roger, St. Louis	.258	34	31	2	8	16	2	0	2	8	0	0	0	0
Frias, Jesus, Atlanta	.259	140	475	41	123	152	18	4	1	44	10	3	3	2
Fryman, Woodrow, Montreal	.000	44	7	0	0	0	0	0	0	0	0	0	0	0
Fulgham, John, St. Louis	.143	22	42	3	6	8	2	0	0	0	0	0	0	0
Garber, H. Eugene, Atlanta	.300	68	10	0	3	3	0	0	0	1	2	0	0	0
Garner, Philip, Pittsburgh	.293	150	549	76	161	242	32	8	11	59	2	3	17	8
Garvey, Steven, Los Angeles	.315	162	648	92	204	322	32	1	28	110	4	6	3	6
Geisel, J. David, Chicago*	.000	7	1	0	0	0	0	0	0	0	0	0	0	0
Geronimo, Cesar, Cincinnati*	.239	123	356	38	85	122	17	4	4	38	3	2	1	1
Glynn, Edward, New York	.000	46	4	0	0	0	0	0	0	0	0	0	0	0
Gonzalez, J. Fernando, San Diego	.217	114	323	22	70	116	13	3	9	34	0	1	0	0
Gonzalez, Julio, Houston	.249	68	181	16	45	54	5	2	0	10	6	0	2	1
Greer, Brian, San Diego	.000	4	3	0	0	0	0	0	0	0	0	0	0	0
Grieve, Thomas, St. Louis	.200	9	15	1	3	4	1	0	0	0	0	0	0	0
Griffey, G. Kenneth, Cincinnati*	.316	95	380	62	120	179	27	4	8	32	0	3	12	5
Griffin, Thomas, San Francisco*	.071	59	14	1	1	1	0	0	0	0	0	0	0	0
Grimsley, Ross, Montreal*	.200	32	55	4	11	13	2	0	0	8	3	0	0	0
Gross, Gregory, Philadelphia*	.333	111	174	21	58	70	6	3	0	15	0	3	5	2
Guerrero, Pedro, Los Angeles	.242	25	62	7	15	23	2	0	2	9	0	1	2	0
Gullickson, William, Montreal	.000	1	0	0	0	0	0	0	0	0	0	0	0	0
Halicki, Edward, San Francisco	.206	33	34	3	7	8	1	0	0	1	2	0	0	0
Hanna, Preston, Atlanta	.000	6	6	1	0	0	0	0	0	0	0	0	0	0
Hannahs, Gerald, Los Angeles*	.250	4	4	1	1	1	0	0	0	0	0	0	0	0
Hargis, Gary, Pittsburgh	.000	1	0	0	0	0	0	0	0	0	0	0	0	0
Hargrove, D. Michael, San Diego*	.192	52	125	15	24	29	5	0	0	8	0	1	0	2
Harrelson, Derrel, Philadelphia†	.282	53	71	7	20	26	6	0	0	7	1	1	3	3
Hassler, Andrew, New York*	.000	29	22	0	0	0	0	0	0	0	0	0	0	0
Hatcher, Michael, Los Angeles	.269	33	93	9	25	34	4	1	1	5	1	0	1	3
Hausman, Thomas, New York	.115	19	26	0	3	3	0	0	0	1	1	0	0	0
Hebner, Richard, New York*	.268	136	473	54	127	186	25	2	10	79	1	8	3	1
Heep, Daniel, Houston*	.143	14	14	0	2	2	0	0	0	2	0	0	2	0
Henderson, Kenneth, Cin-Chi†	.234	72	94	12	22	31	3	0	2	10	0	0	0	0
Henderson, Stephen, New York	.306	98	350	42	107	154	16	8	5	39	1	0	13	5
Hendrick, George, St. Louis	.300	140	493	67	148	225	27	1	16	75	0	6	2	3
Hernandez, Guillermo, Chicago*	.250	52	8	0	2	3	1	0	0	1	1	0	0	0
Hernandez, Keith, St. Louis*	.344	161	610	116	210	313	48	11	11	105	0	7	11	6
Herndon, Larry, San Francisco	.257	132	354	35	91	136	14	5	7	36	3	2	8	6
Herr, Thomas, St. Louis†	.200	14	10	4	2	2	0	0	0	0	0	1	0	0
Hill, Marc, San Francisco	.207	63	169	20	35	47	3	0	3	15	2	3	0	1
Hodges, Ronald, New York*	.163	59	86	4	14	18	4	0	0	5	0	1	0	0
Holland, Alfred, San Francisco*	.000	3	0	0	0	0	0	0	0	0	0	0	0	0
Holtzman, Kenneth, Chicago	.233	24	43	2	10	13	3	0	0	1	0	0	0	0
Hooton, Burt, Los Angeles	.147	30	75	5	11	14	3	0	0	5	8	0	0	0
Horner, J. Robert, Atlanta	.314	121	487	66	153	269	15	1	33	98	0	3	0	2

Player and Club	Pct.	G.	AB.	R.	H.	TB.	2B.	3B.	HR.	RBI.	SH.	SF.	SB.	CS.
Hough, Charles, Los Angeles	.158	42	38	1	6	7	1	0	0	2	5	0	0	0
Howe, Arthur, Houston	.248	118	355	32	88	125	15	2	6	33	2	4	3	1
Hubbard, Glenn, Atlanta	.231	97	325	34	75	96	12	0	3	29	2	2	0	6
Hume, Thomas, Cincinnati	.174	57	46	1	8	9	1	0	0	4	1	0	0	0
Hutton, Thomas, Montreal*	.253	86	83	14	21	28	2	1	1	13	0	0	0	0
Iorg, Dane, St. Louis*	.291	79	179	12	52	68	11	1	1	21	2	1	1	2
Ivie, Michael, San Francisco	.286	133	402	58	115	220	18	3	27	89	0	4	5	1
Jackson, Grant, Pittsburgh*	.000	72	9	0	0	0	0	0	0	1	0	0	0	0
Jackson, Roy, New York	1.000	8	1	0	1	1	0	0	0	0	0	0	0	0
James, Robert, Montreal	.000	2	0	0	0	0	0	0	0	0	0	0	0	0
Johnston, Gregory, San Francisco* ..	.203	42	74	5	15	20	2	0	1	7	0	0	0	0
Johnstone, John, San Diego*	.294	75	201	10	59	71	8	2	0	32	4	2	1	3
Jones, Randall, San Diego*	.174	41	86	8	15	17	2	0	0	5	7	1	1	0
Joshua, Von, Los Angeles*	.282	94	142	22	40	58	7	1	3	14	0	0	1	1
Kaat, James, Philadelphia*	.000	3	1	0	0	0	0	0	0	0	0	0	0	0
Kearney, Robert, San Francisco	.000	2	0	0	0	0	0	0	0	0	0	0	0	0
Kelleher, Michael, Chicago	.254	73	142	14	36	42	4	1	0	10	8	1	2	0
Kendall, Fred, San Diego	.167	46	102	8	17	22	2	0	1	6	1	0	0	0
Kennedy, Junior, Cincinnati	.273	83	220	29	60	70	7	0	1	17	2	0	4	3
Kennedy, Terrence, St. Louis*	.284	33	109	11	31	44	7	0	2	17	0	1	0	0
Kimm, Bruce, Chicago	.091	9	11	0	1	1	0	0	0	0	0	0	0	1
Kingman, David, Chicago	.288	145	532	97	153	326	19	5	48	115	0	8	4	2
Kinney, Dennis, San Diego*	.000	13	1	0	0	0	0	0	0	0	0	0	0	0
Kison, Bruce, Pittsburgh	.145	37	55	6	8	13	2	0	1	6	7	0	0	0
Knepper, Robert, San Francisco*	.182	35	66	6	12	19	4	0	1	9	9	1	0	0
Knicely, Alan, Houston	.000	7	6	0	0	0	0	0	0	0	0	0	0	0
Knight, C. Ray, Cincinnati	.318	150	551	64	175	250	37	4	10	79	4	8	4	4
Knowles, Darold, St. Louis*	.000	48	2	0	0	0	0	0	0	0	0	0	0	0
Kobel, Kevin, New York	.196	30	46	1	9	10	1	0	0	2	9	0	0	0
Kranepool, Edward, New York*	.232	82	155	7	36	47	5	0	2	17	0	5	0	1
Krukow, Michael, Chicago	.314	28	51	4	16	21	2	0	1	8	7	2	0	0
Kucek, John, Philadelphia	.000	4	0	0	0	0	0	0	0	0	0	0	0	0
LaCorte, Frank, Atlanta-Houston	.000	18	4	0	0	0	0	0	0	0	0	0	0	0
LaCoss, Michael, Cincinnati	.129	35	70	3	9	10	1	0	0	5	0	0	0	0
Lacy, Leondaus, Pittsburgh	.247	84	182	17	45	75	9	3	5	15	0	3	6	1
Ladd, Peter, Houston	.000	10	1	0	0	0	0	0	0	0	0	0	0	0
LaGrow, Lerrin, Los Angeles	.333	31	3	0	1	1	0	0	0	0	0	0	0	0
Lamp, Dennis, Chicago	.155	38	58	2	9	10	1	0	0	1	7	0	0	0
Landestoy, Rafael, Houston†	.270	129	282	33	76	97	9	6	0	30	5	2	13	4
Larson, Daniel, Philadelphia	.000	3	5	0	0	0	0	0	0	0	0	0	0	0
Lavelle, Gary, San Francisco†	.250	70	4	2	1	1	0	0	0	0	2	0	0	0
Lee, Mark, San Diego	.333	46	6	0	2	2	0	0	0	0	1	0	0	0
Lee, William, Montreal*	.216	33	74	5	16	18	2	0	0	6	7	0	0	0
Leibrandt, Charles, Cincinnati	.000	3	0	0	0	0	0	0	0	0	0	0	0	0
LeMaster, Johnnie, San Francisco	.254	108	343	42	87	111	11	2	3	29	3	1	9	5
Lentine, James, St. Louis	.391	11	23	2	9	10	1	0	0	1	0	0	0	1
Leonard, Jeffrey, Houston	.290	134	411	47	119	144	15	5	0	47	3	5	23	10
Lerch, Randy, Philadelphia*	.153	38	72	6	11	18	2	1	1	5	3	1	0	1
Lewallyn, Dennis, Los Angeles	.500	7	2	0	1	1	0	0	0	0	1	0	0	0
Littell, Mark, St. Louis*	.000	63	14	1	0	0	0	0	0	0	1	0	0	0
Littlejohn, Dennis, San Francisco	.197	63	193	15	38	49	6	1	1	13	5	3	0	0
Lockwood, Claude, New York	.000	28	2	0	0	0	0	0	0	0	1	0	0	0
Lois, Alberto, Pittsburgh	.000	11	0	6	0	0	0	0	0	0	0	0	1	1
Lolich, Michael, San Diego	.000	27	6	0	0	0	0	0	0	0	1	0	0	0
Lonborg, James, Philadelphia	.000	4	1	0	0	0	0	0	0	0	0	0	0	0
Lopes, David, Los Angeles	.265	153	582	109	154	270	20	6	28	73	6	3	44	4
Lum, Michael, Atlanta*	.249	111	217	29	54	78	6	0	6	27	5	2	0	2
Luzinski, Gregory, Philadelphia	.252	137	452	47	114	193	23	1	18	81	0	7	3	3
Macha, Kenneth, Montreal	.278	25	36	8	10	15	3	1	0	4	1	0	0	0
Macha, Michael, Atlanta	.154	6	13	2	2	2	0	0	0	1	0	0	0	0
Mackanin, Peter, Philadelphia	.111	13	9	2	1	4	0	0	1	2	0	0	0	0
Macko, Steven, Chicago*	.225	19	40	2	9	10	1	0	0	3	0	0	0	0
Maddox, Elliott, New York	.268	86	224	21	60	76	13	0	1	12	1	1	3	2
Maddox, Garry, Philadelphia	.281	148	548	70	154	233	28	6	13	61	1	7	26	13
Madlock, Bill, San F-Pitt.	.298	154	560	85	167	245	26	5	14	85	3	7	32	11
Mahler, Michael, Atlanta†	.111	26	27	0	3	4	1	0	0	3	1	0	0	0
Mahler, Richard, Atlanta	.500	15	2	0	1	1	0	0	0	0	0	0	0	0
Martin, Jerry, Chicago	.272	150	534	74	145	242	34	3	19	73	0	4	2	4
Martinez, Silvio, St. Louis	.129	33	62	5	8	9	1	0	0	4	10	1	0	0

Player and Club	Pct.	G.	AB.	R.	H.	TB.	2B.	3B.	HR.	RBI.	SH.	SF.	SB.	CS.
Martinez, Teodoro, Los Angeles	.268	81	112	19	30	37	5	1	0	2	1	0	3	2
Mason, James, Montreal*	.183	40	71	3	13	20	5	1	0	6	0	0	0	2
Matthews, Gary, Atlanta	.304	156	631	97	192	317	34	5	27	90	1	3	18	6
Matula, Richard, Atlanta	.094	28	53	1	5	5	0	0	0	0	6	0	0	0
May, Rudolph, Montreal*	.143	33	21	2	3	3	0	0	0	3	1	0	0	0
Mazzilli, Lee, New York†	.303	158	597	78	181	268	34	4	15	79	0	3	34	12
McBride, Arnold, Philadelphia*	.280	151	582	82	163	239	16	12	12	60	3	7	25	14
McCarver, J. Timothy, Philadelphia*	.241	79	137	13	33	43	5	1	1	12	2	2	2	0
McCovey, Willie, San Francisco*	.249	117	353	34	88	142	9	0	15	57	0	2	3	0
McEnaney, William, St. Louis*	.000	45	3	0	0	0	0	0	0	0	0	0	0	0
McGlothen, Lynn, Chicago*	.225	42	71	6	16	19	3	0	0	3	4	0	0	0
McGraw, Frank, Philadelphia	.167	65	6	0	1	1	0	0	0	0	1	0	0	0
McLaughlin, Joey, Atlanta	.182	37	11	0	2	3	1	0	0	0	0	0	0	0
McLaughlin, Michael, Hous–Atl	.000	49	6	0	0	0	0	0	0	0	1	0	0	0
McWilliams, Larry, Atlanta*	.208	13	24	4	5	7	2	0	0	1	2	1	0	0
Mejias, Samuel, Chi–Cincinnati	.231	38	13	5	3	3	0	0	0	0	1	0	0	0
Mendoza, Michael, Houston	.000	2	0	0	0	0	0	0	0	0	0	0	0	0
Meoli, Rudolph, Philadelphia*	.178	30	73	2	13	19	4	1	0	6	2	0	2	0
Messersmith, J. Alexander, LA	.091	11	22	1	2	3	1	0	0	2	1	0	0	0
Metzger, Roger, San Francisco†	.251	94	259	24	65	88	7	8	0	31	5	1	11	3
Miller, Edward, Atlanta†	.310	27	113	12	35	36	1	0	0	5	3	0	15	2
Milner, John, Pittsburgh*	.276	128	326	52	90	155	9	4	16	60	0	6	3	5
Minton, Gregory, San Francisco†	.000	46	4	0	0	0	0	0	0	0	1	0	0	0
Moffitt, Randall, San Francisco	.000	29	4	0	0	0	0	0	0	0	1	0	0	0
Monday, Robert, Los Angeles*	.303	12	33	2	10	10	0	0	0	2	0	0	0	0
Montanez, Guillermo, New York*	.234	109	410	36	96	130	19	0	5	47	1	5	0	1
Montefusco, John, San Francisco	.167	24	42	3	7	12	3	1	0	3	2	0	0	1
Moore, Donnie, Chicago*	.154	39	13	0	2	4	0	1	0	1	0	0	0	0
Moreland, B. Keith, Philadelphia	.375	14	48	3	18	25	3	2	0	8	0	0	0	0
Moreno, Omar, Pittsburgh*	.282	162	695	110	196	265	21	12	8	69	6	2	77	21
Morgan, Joe, Cincinnati*	.250	127	436	70	109	164	26	1	9	32	3	5	28	6
Moskau, Paul, Cincinnati	.081	21	37	3	3	4	1	0	0	3	6	1	0	0
Mota, Manuel, Los Angeles	.357	47	42	1	15	15	0	0	0	3	2	0	0	0
Mumphrey, Jerry, St. Louis†	.295	124	339	53	100	125	10	3	3	32	6	4	8	11
Mura, Stephen, San Diego	.000	38	10	1	0	0	0	0	0	0	3	0	0	0
Murcer, Bobby, Chicago*	.258	58	190	22	49	76	4	1	7	22	1	3	2	3
Murphy, Dale, Atlanta	.276	104	384	53	106	180	7	2	21	57	0	5	6	1
Murray, Dale, New York–Montreal	.000	67	8	0	0	0	0	0	0	2	2	0	0	0
Nastu, Philip, San Francisco*	.042	25	24	1	1	1	0	0	0	1	4	0	0	0
Nicosia, Steven, Pittsburgh	.288	70	191	22	55	83	16	0	4	13	1	0	0	2
Niekro, Joseph, Houston	.120	38	83	1	10	12	2	0	0	4	13	1	0	0
Niekro, Philip, Atlanta	.195	44	123	10	24	30	6	0	0	12	7	1	0	0
Niemann, Randy, Houston	.133	26	15	0	2	2	0	0	0	0	1	0	0	0
Nolan, Joseph, Atlanta*	.248	89	230	28	57	84	9	3	4	21	0	1	1	3
Noles, Dickie, Philadelphia†	.100	14	30	1	3	4	1	0	0	1	1	0	0	0
Norman, Daniel, New York	.245	44	110	9	27	41	3	1	3	11	0	1	2	0
Norman, Fredie, Cincinnati†	.153	34	59	2	9	9	0	0	0	6	6	0	0	2
North, William, San Francisco†	.259	142	460	87	119	157	15	4	5	30	1	3	58	24
Oates, Johnny, Los Angeles*	.130	26	46	4	6	8	2	0	0	2	1	0	0	1
Oberkfell, Kenneth, St. Louis*	.301	135	369	53	111	143	19	5	1	35	1	4	4	1
O'Brien, Daniel, St. Louis	.000	6	2	0	0	0	0	0	0	0	1	0	0	0
Oester, Ronald, Cincinnati†	.000	6	3	0	0	0	0	0	0	0	0	0	0	0
Office, Rowland, Atlanta*	.249	124	277	35	69	93	14	2	2	37	1	0	5	4
Ontiveros, Steven, Chicago†	.285	152	519	58	148	192	28	2	4	57	1	5	0	1
Orosco, Jesse, New York	.000	18	6	0	0	0	0	0	0	0	1	0	0	0
Ott, N. Edward, Pittsburgh*	.273	117	403	49	110	155	20	2	7	51	6	4	0	1
Owchinko, Robert, San Diego*	.121	42	33	1	4	4	0	0	0	0	7	0	0	0
Pacella, John, New York	.000	4	4	0	0	0	0	0	0	0	0	0	0	0
Pagel, Karl, Chicago*	.000	1	1	0	0	0	0	0	0	0	0	0	0	0
Palmer, David, Montreal	.032	36	31	1	1	1	0	0	0	0	4	0	0	0
Parker, David, Pittsburgh*	.310	158	622	109	193	327	45	7	25	94	0	9	20	4
Parrish, Larry, Montreal	.307	153	544	83	167	300	39	2	30	82	7	1	5	1
Pastore, Frank, Cincinnati	.160	30	25	2	4	4	0	0	0	1	2	0	0	0
Patterson, David, Los Angeles	.143	37	7	0	1	1	0	0	0	0	2	0	0	1
Perez, Atanasio, Montreal	.270	132	489	58	132	208	29	4	13	73	0	7	2	1
Perkins, Broderick, San Diego*	.264	57	87	8	23	23	0	0	0	8	1	1	0	0
Perlozzo, Samuel, San Diego	.000	2	2	0	0	0	0	0	0	0	0	0	0	0
Perry, Gaylord, San Diego	.085	32	71	2	6	11	2	0	1	2	11	0	0	0

Player and Club	Pct.	G.	AB.	R.	H.	TB.	2B.	3B.	HR.	RBI.	SH.	SF.	SB.	CS.
Phillips, Michael, St. Louis*	.227	44	97	10	22	30	3	1	1	6	1	0	0	0
Pladson, Gordon, Houston	.000	4	0	0	0	0	0	0	0	0	0	0	0	0
Plank, Edward, San Francisco	.000	4	0	0	0	0	0	0	0	0	0	0	0	0
Pocoroba, Biff, Atlanta†	.316	28	38	6	12	16	4	0	0	4	1	0	1	1
Poff, John, Philadelphia*	.105	12	19	2	2	3	1	0	0	1	0	0	0	0
Puhl, Terry, Houston*	.287	157	600	87	172	226	22	4	8	49	8	2	30	22
Pujols, Luis, Houston	.227	26	75	7	17	21	2	1	0	8	1	0	0	0
Rader, David, Philadelphia*	.204	31	54	3	11	17	1	1	1	5	2	0	0	0
Raines, Timothy, Montreal†	.000	6	0	3	0	0	0	0	0	0	0	0	2	0
Rasmussen, Eric, San Diego	.056	46	36	1	2	2	0	0	0	0	6	0	0	0
Rau, Douglas, Los Angeles*	.143	11	14	1	2	3	1	0	0	0	1	0	0	0
Rautzhan, Clarence, Los Angeles	.000	12	0	0	0	0	0	0	0	0	0	0	0	0
Reardon, Jeffrey, New York	.000	18	0	0	0	0	0	0	0	0	0	0	0	0
Reed, Ronald, Philadelphia	.300	61	10	1	3	4	1	0	0	0	2	0	0	0
Reitz, Kenneth, St. Louis	.268	159	605	42	162	231	41	2	8	73	4	5	1	0
Reuschel, Ricky, Chicago	.165	38	79	8	13	17	2	1	0	6	5	0	0	1
Reuss, Jerry, Los Angeles*	.167	39	42	4	7	8	1	0	0	1	3	0	0	0
Reynolds, Donald, San Diego	.222	30	45	6	10	15	1	2	0	6	0	1	0	1
Reynolds, G. Craig, Houston*	.265	146	555	63	147	185	20	9	0	39	34	4	12	6
Rhoden, Richard, Pittsburgh	1.000	1	1	0	1	1	0	0	0	0	0	0	0	0
Riccelli, Frank, Houston*	.333	11	6	1	2	3	1	0	0	3	0	0	0	0
Richard, James, Houston	.126	38	95	6	12	21	1	1	2	6	11	1	0	1
Richards, Eugene, San Diego*	.279	150	545	77	152	199	17	9	4	41	3	3	24	8
Riley, George, Chicago*	.000	4	2	0	0	0	0	0	0	0	1	0	0	0
Roberge, Bertrand, Houston	.000	26	2	0	0	0	0	0	0	0	0	0	0	0
Roberts, David A., SF-Pitt*	.000	47	10	0	0	0	0	0	0	1	0	1	0	0
Robinson, Don, Pittsburgh	.204	29	49	4	10	10	0	0	0	3	4	0	0	0
Robinson, William, Pittsburgh	.264	148	421	59	111	212	17	6	24	75	4	5	13	2
Rogers, Stephen, Montreal	.156	40	77	8	12	14	2	0	0	2	2	0	0	0
Romo, Enrique, Pittsburgh	.167	84	12	0	2	2	0	0	0	1	4	0	0	0
Rooker, James, Pittsburgh	.121	19	33	1	4	4	0	0	0	0	2	0	0	0
Rose, Peter, Philadelphia†	.331	163	628	90	208	270	40	5	4	59	0	5	20	11
Royster, Jeron, Atlanta	.273	154	601	103	164	210	25	6	3	51	6	7	35	8
Ruhle, Vernon, Houston	.053	13	19	3	1	2	1	0	0	0	2	0	0	0
Russell, William, Los Angeles	.271	153	627	72	170	225	26	4	7	56	14	4	6	9
Ruthven, Richard, Philadelphia	.146	21	41	2	6	6	0	0	0	2	2	0	0	0
Sadek, Michael, San Francisco	.238	63	126	14	30	38	5	0	1	11	4	1	1	0
Sambito, Joseph, Houston*	.286	63	7	1	2	3	1	0	0	2	0	0	0	0
Sanderson, Scott, Montreal	.160	34	50	0	8	10	2	0	0	1	7	0	0	0
Sanguillen, Manuel, Pittsburgh	.230	56	74	8	17	26	5	2	0	4	3	1	0	0
Santo Domingo, Rafael, Cincinnati†	.167	7	6	0	1	1	0	0	0	0	0	0	0	0
Sarmiento, Manuel, Cincinnati	.000	23	6	0	0	0	0	0	0	0	1	0	0	0
Saucier, Kevin, Philadelphia	.100	29	10	0	1	1	0	0	0	0	1	0	0	0
Schatzeder, Daniel, Montreal*	.216	32	51	6	11	15	1	0	1	8	1	1	0	0
Schmidt, Michael, Philadelphia	.253	160	541	109	137	305	25	4	45	114	2	9	9	5
Schultz, C. Budd, St. Louis	.000	31	4	0	0	0	0	0	0	0	0	0	0	0
Scott, Anthony, St. Louis†	.259	153	587	69	152	212	22	10	6	68	0	8	37	17
Scott, Michael, New York	.000	18	12	1	0	0	0	0	0	0	1	0	0	0
Scott, Rodney, Montreal†	.238	151	562	69	134	165	12	5	3	42	12	3	39	12
Seaman, Kim, St. Louis*	.000	1	0	0	0	0	0	0	0	0	0	0	0	0
Seaver, G. Thomas, Cincinnati	.158	33	76	3	12	21	3	0	2	8	4	0	0	0
Seibert, Kurt, Chicago†	.000	7	2	2	0	0	0	0	0	0	1	0	0	0
Sexton, Jimmy, Houston	.209	52	43	8	9	9	0	0	0	1	0	0	1	3
Shirley, Robert, San Diego	.091	49	55	2	5	6	1	0	0	0	5	0	0	0
Simmons, Ted, St. Louis†	.283	123	448	68	127	227	22	0	26	87	0	8	0	1
Sizemore, Ted, Chicago	.248	98	330	36	82	105	17	0	2	24	7	2	3	3
Skok, Craig, Atlanta	.000	44	3	0	0	0	0	0	0	0	0	0	0	0
Smith, C. Reginald, Los Angeles†	.274	68	234	41	64	109	13	1	10	32	0	3	6	5
Smith, Keith, St. Louis	.231	6	13	1	3	3	0	0	0	0	0	0	0	1
Smith, Lonnie, Philadelphia	.167	17	30	4	5	7	2	0	0	3	0	0	2	1
Smith, Osborne, San Diego†	.211	156	587	77	124	154	18	6	0	27	22	1	28	7
Solaita, Tolia, Montreal*	.286	29	42	5	12	19	4	0	1	7	0	0	0	0
Solomon, Eddie, Atlanta	.203	32	64	3	13	16	3	0	0	4	3	0	0	0
Sosa, Elias, Montreal	.154	62	13	0	2	3	1	0	0	1	1	0	0	2
Soto, Mario, Cincinnati	.571	25	7	2	4	4	0	0	0	1	0	0	0	0
Speier, Chris, Montreal	.227	113	344	31	78	114	13	1	7	26	0	1	0	0
Spikes, L. Charles, Atlanta	.280	66	93	12	26	43	8	0	3	21	0	2	0	0
Spilman, W. Harry, Cincinnati*	.214	43	56	7	12	15	3	0	0	5	0	0	0	0
Sprowl, Robert, Houston*	.000	3	0	0	0	0	0	0	0	0	0	0	0	0

Player and Club	Pct.	G.	AB.	R.	H.	TB.	2B.	3B.	HR.	RBI.	SH.	SF.	SB.	CS.
Stargell, Wilver, Pittsburgh*	.281	126	424	60	119	234	19	0	32	82	0	6	0	1
Staub, Daniel, Montreal*	.267	38	86	9	23	35	3	0	3	14	0	1	0	0
Stearns, John, New York	.243	155	538	58	131	191	29	2	9	66	3	5	15	15
Stennett, Renaldo, Pittsburgh	.238	108	319	31	76	93	13	2	0	24	2	3	1	4
Strain, Joseph, San Francisco	.241	67	257	27	62	75	8	1	1	12	11	1	8	4
Summers, John, Cincinnati*	.200	27	60	10	12	19	2	1	1	11	0	0	1	0
Sutcliffe, Richard, Los Angeles*	.247	40	85	6	21	27	3	0	1	17	6	1	0	0
Sutter, H. Bruce, Chicago	.250	62	12	0	3	3	0	0	0	3	2	0	1	0
Sutton, Donald, Los Angeles	.143	33	77	2	11	11	0	0	0	3	8	0	0	0
Swan, Craig, New York	.123	35	81	3	10	12	2	0	0	2	4	0	0	1
Swisher, Steven, St. Louis	.151	38	73	4	11	17	1	1	1	3	0	1	0	0
Sykes, Robert, St. Louis†	.095	13	21	2	2	2	0	0	0	0	2	0	0	0
Tamargo, John, SF-Mtl†	.247	42	81	7	20	31	5	0	2	11	0	4	0	0
Taveras, Franklin, Pitt-NY	.262	164	680	93	178	228	29	9	1	34	10	0	44	20
Tekulve, Kenton, Pittsburgh	.133	94	15	3	2	2	0	0	0	1	1	0	0	0
Tellmann, Thomas, San Diego	.000	1	1	0	0	0	0	0	0	0	0	0	0	0
Templeton, Garry, St. Louis†	.314	154	672	105	211	308	32	19	9	62	2	3	26	10
Tenace, F. Gene, San Diego	.263	151	463	61	122	206	16	4	20	67	1	6	2	6
Thomas, Derrel, Los Angeles†	.256	141	406	47	104	142	15	4	5	44	5	3	18	5
Thomas, Roy, St. Louis	.059	26	17	0	1	2	1	0	0	0	1	0	0	0
Thomasson, Gary, Los Angeles*	.248	115	315	39	78	133	11	1	14	45	2	1	4	2
Thompson, V. Scot, Chicago*	.289	128	346	36	100	129	13	5	2	29	1	3	4	3
Throop, George, Houston	.000	14	3	0	0	0	0	0	0	0	0	0	0	0
Tidrow, Richard, Chicago	.200	63	10	0	2	2	0	0	0	0	2	0	0	0
Tolan, Robert, San Diego*	.190	22	21	2	4	6	0	1	0	1	2	0	0	0
Tomlin, David, Cincinnati*	.500	53	2	1	1	1	0	0	0	0	0	0	0	0
Trevino, Alejandro, New York	.271	79	207	24	56	69	11	1	0	20	4	0	2	2
Trillo, J. Manuel, Philadelphia	.260	118	431	40	112	154	22	1	6	42	8	4	4	7
Turner, John, San Diego*	.248	138	448	55	111	165	23	2	9	61	2	4	4	2
Twitchell, Wayne, New York	.375	33	8	0	3	3	0	0	0	0	1	0	0	0
Tyson, Michael, St. Louis	.221	75	190	18	42	69	8	2	5	20	1	2	2	1
Unser, Delbert, Philadelphia*	.298	95	141	26	42	68	8	0	6	29	1	3	2	0
Urrea, John, St. Louis	.250	3	4	0	1	1	0	0	0	1	0	0	0	0
Vail, Michael, Chicago	.335	87	179	28	60	93	8	2	7	35	0	2	0	2
Valentine, Ellis, Montreal	.276	146	548	73	151	249	29	3	21	82	1	3	11	9
Venable, W. McKinley, San Fran*	.165	55	85	12	14	17	1	1	0	3	1	0	3	3
Vuckovich, Peter, St. Louis	.152	34	79	7	12	12	0	0	0	3	8	0	0	0
Vukovich, John, Philadelphia	.200	10	15	0	3	4	1	0	0	1	0	0	0	0
Walling, Dennis, Houston*	.327	82	147	21	48	73	8	4	3	31	0	1	3	2
Watson, Robert, Houston	.239	49	163	15	39	52	4	0	3	18	1	2	0	0
Welch, Robert, Los Angeles	.158	25	19	1	3	3	0	0	0	3	3	0	0	0
Wessinger, James, Atlanta	.000	10	7	2	0	0	0	0	0	0	0	0	0	0
Whisenton, Larry, Atlanta*	.243	13	37	3	9	13	2	1	0	1	0	0	0	0
White, Jerome, Montreal†	.297	88	138	30	41	59	7	1	3	18	0	1	8	4
Whitfield, Terry, San Francisco*	.287	133	394	52	113	156	20	4	5	44	7	4	5	4
Whitson, Eddie, Pitt-SF	.111	37	45	2	5	5	0	0	0	2	9	0	0	0
Wiedenbauer, Thomas, Houston	.667	4	6	0	4	5	1	0	0	2	0	0	0	0
Wilhelm, James, San Diego	.243	39	103	8	25	35	4	3	0	8	2	1	1	1
Williams, Richard, Houston	.258	31	31	2	8	9	1	0	0	0	2	0	0	0
Wilson, Gary, Houston	.000	6	0	0	0	0	0	0	0	0	0	0	0	0
Winfield, David, San Diego	.308	159	597	97	184	333	27	10	34	118	0	2	15	9
Yeager, Stephen, Los Angeles	.216	105	310	33	67	119	9	2	13	41	5	2	1	0
Youngblood, Joel, New York	.275	158	590	90	162	257	37	5	16	60	4	4	18	13
Zachry, Patrick, New York	.125	7	16	0	2	2	0	0	0	0	0	0	0	0

AWARDED FIRST BASE ON INTERFERENCE—Berra, Pitt. 2 (Carter, Simmons); Rose, Phil. 2 (Pocoroba, Bochy); Benedict, Atl. (Foote); Carlton, Phil. (Simmons); Dade, S.D. (Foote); Hebner, N.Y. (Bochy); Ivie, S.F. (Bench); McCovey, S.F. (Foote).

PLAYERS WITH TWO OR MORE CLUBS
(Alphabetically Arranged With Player's First Club on Top)

Player and Club	Pct.	G.	AB.	R.	H.	TB.	2B.	3B.	HR.	RBI.	SH.	SF.	Tot. BB.	Int. BB.	HP.	SO.	SB.	CS.	GI DP.
Borbon, Cincinnati	.333	30	6	2	2	2	0	0	0	0	0	0	0	0	0	1	0	0	0
Borbon, San Francisco	.333	30	3	0	1	1	0	0	0	0	0	0	0	0	0	1	0	0	0
Burris, Chicago	.000	14	1	1	0	0	0	0	0	0	0	0	1	0	0	0	0	0	0
Burris, New York	.167	4	6	0	1	1	0	0	0	0	1	0	0	0	0	2	0	0	0
Capilla, Cincinnati	1.000	5	1	0	1	1	0	0	0	0	0	0	0	0	0	0	0	0	0
Capilla, Chicago	.000	13	0	0	0	0	0	0	0	0	0	0	0	0	0	0	0	0	0
Cardenal, Philadelphia	.208	29	48	4	10	13	3	0	0	9	0	0	8	1	0	8	1	0	3
Cardenal, New York	.297	11	37	8	11	21	4	0	2	4	0	0	6	0	1	3	1	0	0
Coleman, San Fran.	.000	5	0	0	0	0	0	0	0	0	0	0	0	0	0	0	0	0	0
Coleman, Pittsburgh	.200	10	5	0	1	2	1	0	0	0	0	0	0	0	0	3	0	0	0
Cruz, San Francisco	.120	16	25	2	3	3	0	0	0	1	0	0	3	0	0	7	0	0	2
Cruz, Cincinnati	.242	74	182	24	44	70	10	2	4	27	1	1	31	3	0	39	0	1	8
Ellis, New York	.077	17	26	2	2	2	0	0	0	1	1	0	1	0	0	7	0	0	0
Ellis, Pittsburgh	.000	3	1	0	0	0	0	0	0	0	0	0	0	0	0	0	0	0	0
Foli, New York	.000	3	7	0	0	0	0	0	0	0	0	0	0	0	0	0	0	0	1
Foli, Pittsburgh	.291	133	525	70	153	181	23	1	1	65	19	6	28	0	9	14	6	5	7
Henderson, Cincinnati	.231	10	13	1	3	4	1	0	0	2	0	0	0	0	0	2	0	0	0
Henderson, Chicago	.235	62	81	11	19	27	2	0	2	8	0	0	15	1	1	16	0	0	1
LaCorte, Atlanta	.000	6	1	0	0	0	0	0	0	0	0	0	0	0	0	0	0	0	0
LaCorte, Houston	.000	12	3	0	0	0	0	0	0	0	0	0	0	0	0	2	0	0	0
Madlock, San Fran.	.261	69	249	37	65	99	9	2	7	41	1	2	18	3	0	19	11	3	3
Madlock, Pittsburgh	.328	85	311	48	102	146	17	3	7	44	2	5	34	8	1	22	21	8	14
M. McLaughlin, Hous.	.000	12	1	0	0	0	0	0	0	0	0	0	0	0	0	1	0	0	0
M. McLaughlin, Atlanta	.000	37	5	0	0	0	0	0	0	0	1	0	0	0	0	2	0	0	0
Mejias, Chicago	.182	31	11	4	2	2	0	0	0	0	1	0	2	0	0	5	0	0	0
Mejias, Cincinnati	.500	7	2	1	1	1	0	0	0	0	0	0	0	0	0	0	0	0	0
Murray, New York	.000	58	6	0	0	0	0	0	0	0	2	0	1	0	0	3	0	0	0
Murray, Montreal	.000	9	2	0	0	0	0	0	0	0	0	0	0	0	0	1	0	0	1
Roberts, San Francisco	.000	26	5	0	0	0	0	0	0	0	0	0	0	0	0	2	0	0	0
Roberts, Pittsburgh	.000	21	5	0	0	0	0	0	0	0	1	0	1	0	0	1	0	0	0
Tamargo, San Fran.	.200	30	60	7	12	21	3	0	2	6	0	3	4	0	0	8	0	0	0
Tamargo, Montreal	.381	12	21	0	8	10	2	0	0	5	0	1	3	0	0	3	0	0	0
Taveras, San Fran.	.244	11	45	4	11	14	3	0	0	1	0	0	0	0	0	2	2	1	2
Taveras, New York	.263	153	635	89	167	214	26	9	1	33	10	0	33	1	2	72	42	19	11
Whitson, Pittsburgh	.000	19	13	1	0	0	0	0	0	0	4	0	1	0	0	5	0	0	0
Whitson, San Francisco	.156	18	32	1	5	5	0	0	0	2	5	0	0	0	0	10	0	0	0

EXPLANATION OF ABBREVIATION TERMS

G—Games Played. AB—At Bats. R—Runs. H—Hits. TB—Total Bases. 2B—Two-Base Hits. 3B—Three-Base Hits. HR—Home Runs. RBI—Runs Batted In. SH—Sacrifice Hits. SF—Sacrifice Flies. SB—Stolen Bases. CS—Caught Stealing. BB—Bases on Balls. IBB—Intentional Bases on Balls. HP—Hit by Pitcher. SO—Strikeouts. Pct.—Percentage. GIDP—Grounded Into Double Plays. Slg. Pct.—Slugging Percentage. OR—Opponents' Runs. LOB—Left on Bases. PO—Putouts. A—Assists. E—Errors. TC—Total Chances. DP—Double Plays. TP—Triple Plays. PB—Passed Balls. G—Games Pitched. GS—Games Started. CG—Complete Games. GF—Games Finished in Relief. ShO—Shutouts. W—Games Won. L—Games Lost. IP—Innings Pitched. BFP—Total Batters Facing Pitcher. ER—Earned Runs. HB—Hit Batsmen. WP—Wild Pitches. Bk—Balks. ERA—Earned-Run Average. Sv—Saves.

OFFICIAL MISCELLANEOUS NATIONAL LEAGUE BATTING RECORDS

CLUB MISCELLANEOUS BATTING RECORDS

Club	Slg. Pct.	G.	Tot. BB.	Int. BB.	HP.	SO.	GIDP.	ShO.
Pittsburgh	.416	163	483	102	32	855	113	9
Los Angeles	.412	162	556	62	23	834	145	9
Montreal	.408	160	432	68	27	890	123	7
Chicago	.403	162	478	49	35	762	126	11
St. Louis	.401	163	460	69	27	838	116	5
Cincinnati	.396	161	614	73	19	902	128	5
Philadelphia	.396	163	602	66	37	764	124	12
Atlanta	.377	160	490	47	23	818	112	10
San Francisco	.365	162	580	61	20	925	100	14
New York	.350	163	498	53	35	817	117	12
San Diego	.348	161	534	81	32	770	104	12
Houston	.344	162	461	75	22	745	105	15
Totals	.385	971	6188	806	332	9920	1413	121

INDIVIDUAL MISCELLANEOUS BATTING RECORDS
(Top Fifteen Qualifiers for Slugging Championship—502 or More Plate Appearances)

Player—Club	Slg. Pct.	Tot. BB.	Int. BB.	HP.	SO.	GI DP.		Player—Club	Slg. Pct.	Tot. BB.	Int. BB.	HP.	SO.	GI DP.
Kingman, Chi	.613	45	7	4	131	7		Simmons, StL	.507	61	22	4	34	10
Schmidt, Phila	.564	120	12	3	115	13		Matthews, Atl	.502	60	5	0	75	6
Foster, Cin	.561	59	7	3	105	11		Cey, LA	.499	86	8	2	85	11
Winfield, SD	.558	85	24	2	71	9		Garvey, LA	.497	37	16	2	59	25
Horner, Atl	.552	22	6	3	74	9		Carter, Mtl	.485	40	3	5	62	11
Parrish, Mtl	.551	41	11	2	101	8		Clark, SF	.476	63	6	1	95	9
Parker, Pitt	.526	67	14	9	101	7		Dawson, Mtl	.468	27	5	6	115	10
Hernandez, StL	.513	80	5	1	78	9								

DEPARTMENTAL LEADERS: Tot. BB—Schmidt, 120; Int. BB—Winfield, 24; HP—Luzinski, 10; SO—Kingman, 131; GIDP—Garvey, 25.

(All Players—Listed Alphabetically)

Player—Club	Slg. Pct.	Tot. BB.	Int. BB.	HP.	SO.	GI DP.		Player—Club	Slg. Pct.	Tot. BB.	Int. BB.	HP.	SO.	GI DP.
Alexander, Pitt	.692	0	0	0	0	0		Biittner, Chi	.393	21	1	0	23	10
Allen, NY	.000	0	0	0	6	0		Bird, Phila	.167	1	0	0	4	0
Almon, SD	.258	21	7	0	48	1		Blackwell, Chi	.205	32	1	1	25	3
Alou, Hou	.349	6	1	0	7	4		Blair, Cin	.236	11	3	0	27	4
Anderson, Phila	.321	13	0	0	14	2		Blue, SF	.169	6	0	0	35	0
Andrews, SF	.318	8	0	0	9	5		Blyleven, Pitt	.143	0	0	0	33	2
Andujar, Hou	.211	2	0	0	32	0		Bochy, Hou	.271	13	4	1	25	5
Ashby, Hou	.277	26	10	2	70	8		Boggs, Atl	.250	0	0	0	1	0
Asselstine, Atl	.100	1	1	0	2	1		Boisclair, NY	.255	3	0	1	24	2
Atkinson, Mtl	.000	0	0	0	0	0		Bonham, Cin	.175	0	0	0	18	1
Auerbach, Cin	.340	14	1	0	19	1		Bonnell, Atl	.424	26	2	3	55	10
Aviles, Phila	.311	8	1	1	8	1		Boone, Phila	.422	49	9	2	33	9
Bahnsen, Mtl	.286	0	0	0	5	0		Borbon, Cin-SF	.333	0	0	0	2	0
Bair, Cin	.000	0	0	0	5	0		Bowa, Phila	.314	61	5	1	32	11
Baker, LA	.455	56	0	1	70	16		Boyland, Pitt	.000	0	0	0	0	0
Baldwin, Hou	.250	0	0	0	1	2		Bradford, Atl	.000	0	0	0	2	0
Bass, Mtl	.000	0	0	0	0	0		Brett, LA	.273	0	0	0	2	1
Beall, Atl	.267	3	0	0	4	0		Briggs, SD	.357	18	5	5	45	3
Beckwith, LA	.000	0	0	0	2	0		Brizzolara, Atl	.029	2	0	0	14	0
Bench, Cin	.459	67	8	0	73	11		Brock, StL	.398	23	1	3	43	7
Benedict, Atl	.279	33	3	0	18	4		Bruno, StL	.200	0	0	0	2	0
Berenguer, NY	.143	2	0	0	4	0		Brusstar, Phila	.000	0	0	0	0	0
Bergman, Hou	.600	0	0	0	3	0		Buckner, Chi	.437	36	6	2	28	16
Bernard, NY	.000	1	0	0	0	0		Burris, Chi-NY	.143	1	0	0	2	0
Bernazard, Mtl	.425	15	0	1	12	2		Burroughs, Atl	.348	73	7	3	75	14
Berra, Pitt	.325	11	2	0	17	5		Cabell, Hou	.368	21	7	3	68	18
Bevacqua, SD	.330	38	2	0	25	13		Candelaria, Pitt	.191	1	0	0	18	4
Bibby, Pitt	.333	0	0	1	25	0		Capilla, Cin-Chi	1.000	0	0	0	0	0

Player—Club	Slg. Pct.	Tot. BB.	Int. BB.	HP.	SO.	GI DP.
Carbo, StL	.438	10	0	0	22	0
Cardenal, Phila-NY	.400	14	1	1	11	3
Carlton, Phila	.255	3	0	1	17	4
Carter, Mtl	.485	40	3	5	62	11
Cash, Mtl	.422	12	0	0	12	6
Castillo, LA	.000	0	0	0	1	0
Caudill, Chi	.059	0	0	0	10	0
Cedeno, Hou	.374	64	8	3	52	15
Cey, LA	.499	86	8	2	85	11
Chaney, Atl	.205	19	2	0	34	2
Chapman, NY	.213	5	0	0	15	1
Christenson, Phila.	.548	2	0	0	13	0
Clark, SF	.476	63	6	1	95	9
Clines, Chi	.200	0	0	0	1	0
Coleman, SF-Pitt	.400	0	0	0	3	0
Collins, Cin	.402	27	2	2	48	6
Concepcion, Cin	.415	64	5	0	73	18
Correll, Chi	.346	14	2	1	26	3
Cromartie, Mtl	.396	38	19	1	78	11
Cruz, SF-Cin	.353	34	3	0	46	10
Cruz, Hou	.421	72	16	0	66	5
Curtis, SF	.176	2	0	1	9	0
D'Acquisto, SD	.194	2	0	2	21	0
Dade, StL	.367	14	0	2	48	6
Davalillo, LA	.296	2	0	0	0	0
Davis, Chi	.000	0	0	0	0	0
Dawson, Mtl	.468	27	5	6	115	10
DeFreites, Cin	.265	0	0	0	16	1
DeJesus, Chi	.379	59	1	2	82	9
Denny, StL	.186	1	0	0	21	0
Devine, Atl	.000	0	0	0	5	0
Dillard, Chi	.422	17	4	1	24	4
Dilone, Chi	.306	2	0	0	5	0
Dimmel, StL	.333	0	0	0	0	0
Dixon, Hou	1.000	0	0	0	0	0
Driessen, Cin	.414	62	11	3	77	6
Dyer, Mtl	.365	9	4	0	17	1
Easler, Pitt	.444	8	0	0	13	0
Easterly, Atl	.000	0	0	0	0	0
Eastwick, Phila	.000	0	0	0	5	0
Eichelberger, SD	.600	1	0	0	2	0
Ellis, NY-Pitt	.074	1	0	0	7	0
Espinosa, Phila	.222	4	0	0	15	2
Evans, SD	.265	5	0	0	16	2
Evans, SF	.391	91	14	2	80	6
Fahey, SD	.378	21	5	0	17	4
Falcone, NY	.173	2	0	0	19	2
Ferguson, LA	.466	70	6	2	68	10
Ferrer, NY	.000	2	0	0	3	0
Fingers, SD	.083	0	0	0	2	0
Flannery, SD	.185	4	1	2	5	3
Flores, NY	.258	8	0	1	17	1
Flynn, NY	.317	17	7	0	46	15
Foli, NY-Pitt	.340	28	0	9	14	8
Foote, Chi	.427	34	7	5	49	12
Forsch, Hou	.155	4	0	0	22	1
Forsch, StL	.192	5	0	0	17	1
Forster, LA	.000	1	0	0	0	0
Foster, Cin	.561	59	7	3	105	11
Frazier, StL	.000	0	0	0	0	0
Freed, StL	.516	5	0	0	7	1
Frias, Atl	.320	20	5	2	36	13
Fryman, Mtl	.000	0	0	0	3	0
Fulgham, StL	.190	6	0	0	21	0
Garber, Atl	.300	3	0	0	4	0
Garner, Pitt	.441	55	15	3	74	6
Garvey, LA	.497	37	16	2	59	25
Geisel, Chi	.000	0	0	0	1	0
Geronimo, Cin	.343	37	11	2	56	8
Glynn, NY	.000	0	0	0	1	0
Gonzalez, SD	.359	18	11	0	34	8
Gonzalez, Hou	.298	5	0	3	14	4
Greer, SD	.000	0	0	0	1	0
Grieve, StL	.267	4	1	0	1	0
Griffey, Cin	.471	36	3	1	39	7
Griffin, SF	.071	0	0	0	6	0
Grimsley, Mtl	.236	0	0	0	10	0
Gross, Phila	.402	29	4	0	5	3
Guerrero, LA	.371	1	1	0	14	1
Gullickson, Mtl	.000	0	0	0	0	0
Halicki, SF	.235	1	0	0	9	1
Hanna, Atl	.000	1	0	0	5	0
Hannahs, LA	.250	0	0	0	2	0
Hargis, Pitt	.000	0	0	0	1	0
Hargrove, SD	.232	25	3	0	15	1
Harrelson, Phila	.366	13	0	1	14	1
Hassler, NY	.000	1	0	0	17	1
Hatcher, LA	.366	7	0	1	12	5
Hausman, NY	.115	0	0	0	4	1
Hebner, NY	.393	59	6	8	59	7
Heep, Hou	.143	1	1	0	4	0
Henderson, Cin-Chi	.330	15	1	1	18	1
Henderson, NY	.440	38	6	4	58	7
Hendrick, StL	.456	49	5	0	62	17
Hernandez, Chi	.375	0	0	0	5	0
Hernandez, StL	.513	80	5	1	78	9
Herndon, SF	.384	29	5	1	70	3
Herr, StL	.200	2	0	0	2	0
Hill, SF	.278	26	5	0	25	5
Hodges, NY	.209	19	3	0	16	0
Holland, SF	.000	0	0	0	0	0
Holtzman, Chi	.302	2	0	0	9	0
Hooton, LA	.187	1	0	0	18	0
Horner, Atl	.552	22	6	3	74	9
Hough, LA	.184	0	0	0	9	0
Howe, LA	.352	36	5	1	37	7
Hubbard, Atl	.295	27	2	1	43	3
Hume, Cin	.196	1	0	0	17	0
Hutton, Mtl	.337	10	0	0	7	4
Iorg, StL	.380	12	1	1	28	5
Ivie, SF	.547	47	7	1	80	10
Jackson, Pitt	.000	0	0	0	2	0
Jackson, NY	1.000	0	0	0	0	0
James, Mtl	.000	0	0	0	0	0
Johnston, SF	.270	2	0	0	17	1
Johnstone, SD	.353	18	3	0	21	6
Jones, SD	.198	0	0	0	29	0
Joshua, LA	.408	7	1	0	23	5
Kaat, Phila	.000	0	0	0	1	0
Kearney, SF	.000	1	0	0	0	0
Kelleher, Chi	.296	7	0	2	9	4
Kendall, SD	.216	11	2	0	7	4
Kennedy, Cin	.318	28	0	0	31	4
Kennedy, StL	.404	6	2	0	20	2
Kimm, Chi	.091	0	0	0	2	0
Kingman, Chi	.613	45	7	4	131	7
Kinney, SD	.000	0	0	0	1	0
Kison, Pitt	.236	1	0	0	19	2
Knepper, SF	.288	1	0	1	24	0
Knicely, Hou	.000	2	0	0	3	2
Knight, Cin	.454	38	4	3	57	20
Knowles, StL	.000	0	0	0	0	0
Kobel, NY	.217	0	0	0	18	1
Kranepool, NY	.303	13	2	1	18	6
Krukow, Chi	.412	0	0	2	8	0
Kucek, Phila	.000	0	0	0	0	0

Player—Club	Slg. Pct.	Tot. BB	Int. BB	HP	SO	GI DP
LaCorte, Atl-Hou	.000	0	0	0	2	0
LaCoss, Cin	.143	3	0	0	25	2
Lacy, Pitt	.412	22	2	1	36	1
Ladd, Hou	.000	0	0	0	0	0
LaGrow, LA	.333	0	0	0	1	0
Lamp, Chi	.172	2	0	0	9	0
Landestoy, Hou	.344	29	5	1	24	1
Larson, Phila	.000	0	0	0	2	0
Lavelle, SF	.250	0	0	0	2	0
Lee, SD	.333	0	0	0	2	0
Lee, Mtl	.243	0	0	0	21	0
Leibrandt, Cin	.000	0	0	0	0	0
LeMaster, SF	.324	23	1	2	55	6
Lentine, StL	.435	3	0	0	6	0
Leonard, Hou	.350	46	7	2	68	11
Lerch, Phila	.250	3	0	0	8	2
Lewallyn, LA	.500	0	0	0	1	0
Littell, StL	.000	1	0	0	11	0
Littlejohn, StL	.254	21	4	0	46	4
Lockwood, NY	.000	0	0	0	1	0
Lois, Pitt	.000	0	0	0	0	0
Lolich, SD	.000	1	0	0	3	0
Lonborg, Phila	.000	0	0	0	1	0
Lopes, LA	.464	97	4	4	88	8
Lum, Atl	.359	18	1	0	34	7
Luzinski, Phila	.427	56	5	10	103	10
Macha, Mtl	.417	2	1	1	9	3
Macha, Atl	.154	1	0	0	5	0
Mackanin, Phila	.444	1	0	0	2	0
Macko, Chi	.250	4	0	0	8	0
Maddox, NY	.339	20	0	3	27	3
Maddox, Phila	.425	17	5	4	71	8
Madlock, SF-Pitt	.438	52	11	1	41	17
M. Mahler, Atl	.148	1	0	0	5	1
R. Mahler, Atl	.500	0	0	0	0	0
Martin, Chi	.453	38	3	3	85	13
Martinez, StL	.145	1	0	0	26	0
Martinez, LA	.330	4	1	0	16	3
Mason, Mtl	.282	7	1	0	16	3
Matthews, Atl	.502	60	5	0	75	6
Matula, Atl	.094	1	0	0	23	2
May, Mtl	.143	0	0	1	8	0
Mazzilli, NY	.449	93	5	0	74	6
McBride, Phila	.411	41	3	4	77	6
McCarver, Phila	.314	19	5	1	12	7
McCovey, SF	.402	36	2	1	70	7
McEnaney, StL	.000	0	0	0	2	0
McGlothen, Chi	.268	1	0	0	10	5
McGraw, Phila	.167	0	0	0	2	0
J. McLaughlin, Atl	.273	0	0	0	4	1
M. McLaughlin, Ho-At	.000	0	0	0	3	0
McWilliams, Atl	.292	1	0	0	14	0
Mejias, Chi-Cin	.231	2	0	0	5	0
Mendoza, Hou	.000	0	0	0	0	0
Meoli, Phila	.260	9	1	0	15	2
Messersmith, LA	.136	0	0	0	6	0
Metzger, SF	.340	23	2	0	31	6
Miller, Atl	.319	5	1	2	24	1
Milner, Pitt	.475	53	6	1	37	5
Minton, SF	.000	1	0	0	1	0
Moffitt, SF	.000	0	0	0	2	0
Monday, LA	.303	5	0	0	6	1
Montanez, NY	.317	25	7	1	48	15
Montefusco, SF	.286	1	0	0	11	1
Moore, Chi	.308	0	0	0	5	0
Moreland, Phila	.521	3	0	0	5	1
Moreno, Pitt	.381	51	9	3	104	1
Morgan, Cin	.376	93	11	1	45	8
Moskau, Cin	.108	1	0	0	13	1
Mota, StL	.357	3	0	0	4	2
Mumphrey, StL	.369	26	2	0	39	6
Mura, SD	.000	0	0	0	5	0
Murcer, Chi	.400	36	2	1	20	3
Murphy, Atl	.469	38	5	2	67	12
Murray, NY-Mtl	.000	1	0	0	4	1
Nastu, SF	.042	3	0	0	7	0
Nicosia, Pitt	.435	23	7	0	17	5
Niekro, Hou	.145	2	0	0	21	0
Niekro, Atl	.244	1	0	2	19	1
Niemann, Hou	.133	1	0	0	6	1
Nolan, Atl	.365	27	3	3	28	5
Noles, Phila	.133	2	0	0	15	0
Norman, NY	.373	10	2	1	26	1
Norman, Cin	.153	6	0	0	22	3
North, SF	.341	96	3	1	84	5
Oates, LA	.174	4	1	0	1	0
Oberkfell, StL	.388	57	9	4	35	9
O'Brien, Phila	.000	0	0	0	0	0
Oester, Cin	.000	0	0	0	1	0
Office, Atl	.336	27	2	2	33	5
Ontiveros, Chi	.370	58	7	7	68	19
Orosco, NY	.000	0	0	0	4	0
Ott, Pitt	.385	26	8	0	62	6
Owchinko, SD	.121	3	0	0	14	0
Pacella, NY	.000	0	0	0	1	0
Pagel, Chi	.000	0	0	0	1	0
Palmer, Mtl	.032	1	0	0	15	1
Parker, Pitt	.526	67	14	9	101	7
Parrish, Mtl	.551	41	11	2	101	8
Pastore, Cin	.160	0	0	0	10	1
Patterson, LA	.143	0	0	0	2	0
Perez, Mtl	.425	38	4	3	82	14
Perkins, SD	.264	8	2	0	12	3
Perlozzo, SD	.000	1	0	0	0	0
Perry, SD	.155	2	0	0	19	2
Phillips, StL	.309	10	0	1	9	5
Pladson, Hou	.000	0	0	0	0	0
Plank, SF	.000	0	0	0	0	0
Pocoroba, Atl	.421	7	1	0	0	2
Poff, Phila	.158	1	0	0	0	1
Puhl, Hou	.377	58	8	4	46	7
Pujols, Hou	.280	2	0	0	14	3
Rader, Phila	.315	6	0	0	72	3
Raines, Mtl	.000	0	0	0	0	0
Rasmussen, SD	.056	3	0	0	7	0
Rau, LA	.214	2	0	0	2	0
Rautzhan, LA	.000	0	0	0	0	0
Reardon, NY	.000	0	0	0	0	0
Reed, Phila	.400	1	0	0	4	0
Reitz, StL	.382	25	7	4	85	13
Reuschel, Chi	.215	7	0	0	26	0
Reuss, LA	.190	3	0	1	19	1
Reynolds, SD	.333	7	1	0	6	3
Reynolds, Hou	.333	21	0	2	49	2
Rhoden, Pitt	1.000	0	0	0	0	0
Riccelli, Hou	.500	0	0	0	1	0
Richard, Hou	.221	1	0	0	24	4
Richards, SD	.365	47	6	8	62	7
Riley, Chi	.000	0	0	0	2	0
Roberge, Hou	.000	0	0	0	2	0
Roberts, SF-Pitt	.000	0	0	0	3	0
D. Robinson, Pitt	.204	3	0	0	9	0
W. Robinson, Pitt	.504	24	11	1	81	13
Rogers, Mtl	.182	5	0	0	21	2
Romo, Pitt	.167	0	0	0	2	0
Rooker, Pitt	.121	1	0	0	13	1

Player—Club	Slg. Pct.	Tot. BB	Int. BB	HP	SO	GI DP
Rose, Phila	.430	95	10	1	32	18
Royster, Atl	.349	62	0	0	59	8
Ruhle, Hou	.105	1	0	0	11	0
Russell, LA	.359	24	2	1	43	20
Ruthven, Phila	.146	2	0	0	11	0
Sadek, SF	.302	15	2	1	24	6
Sambito, Hou	.429	5	0	0	0	0
Sanderson, Mtl	.200	0	0	0	23	0
Sanguillen, Pitt	.351	2	2	0	5	3
Santo Domingo, Cin	.167	1	0	0	3	0
Sarmiento, Cin	.000	0	0	0	2	0
Saucier, Phila	.100	0	0	0	7	0
Schatzeder, Mtl	.294	6	0	0	13	1
Schmidt, Phila	.564	120	12	3	115	13
Schultz, StL	.000	0	0	0	1	0
Scott, StL	.361	34	4	5	92	13
Scott, NY	.000	1	0	0	8	0
Scott, Mtl	.294	66	2	2	82	4
Seaman, StL	.000	0	0	0	0	0
Seaver, Cin	.276	1	0	0	29	2
Seibert, Chi	.000	0	0	0	1	0
Sexton, Hou	.209	7	0	0	7	0
Shirley, SD	.109	3	0	0	17	1
Simmons, StL	.507	61	22	4	34	10
Sizemore, Chi	.318	32	7	3	25	8
Skok, Atl	.000	1	0	0	2	0
Smith, LA	.466	31	3	2	50	5
Smith, StL	.231	0	0	0	0	0
Smith, Phila	.233	1	0	0	7	0
Smith, SD	.262	37	5	2	37	11
Solaita, Mtl	.452	11	0	0	16	0
Solomon, Atl	.250	1	0	0	16	1
Sosa, Mtl	.231	1	0	0	6	1
Soto, Cin	.571	0	0	0	2	0
Speier, Mtl	.331	43	10	3	45	13
Spikes, Atl	.462	5	1	0	30	3
Spilman, Cin	.268	7	2	2	5	1
Sprowl, Hou	.000	0	0	0	0	0
Stargell, Pitt	.552	47	12	3	105	10
Staub, Mtl	.407	14	3	0	10	3
Stearns, NY	.355	52	5	4	57	21
Stennett, Pitt	.292	24	6	0	25	11
Strain, SF	.292	13	0	3	21	5
Summers, Cin	.317	13	0	1	15	1
Sutcliffe, LA	.318	1	0	0	20	4
Sutter, Chi	.250	1	0	0	5	0
Sutton, LA	.143	1	0	0	17	1
Swan, NY	.148	6	0	0	38	0
Swisher, StL	.233	6	0	0	17	2
Sykes, StL	.095	1	0	2	11	0
Tamargo, SF-Mtl	.383	7	0	0	11	0
Taveras, Pitt-NY	.335	33	1	2	74	13
Tekulve, Pitt	.133	1	0	0	8	0
Tellmann, SD	.000	0	0	0	0	0
Templeton, StL	.445	105	4	7	106	7
Tenace, SD	.350	41	7	5	49	9
Thomas, LA	.118	0	0	0	11	0
Thomas, StL	.422	43	4	1	70	5
Thomasson, LA	.373	17	1	1	37	8
Thompson, Chi	.000	0	0	0	1	0
Throop, Hou	.200	1	0	0	2	0
Tidrow, Chi	.286	0	0	0	2	2
Tolan, SD	.500	2	0	0	1	0
Tomlin, Cin	.333	20	2	1	27	8
Trevino, NY	.357	20	3	4	59	13
Trillo, Phila	.368	34	0	2	58	8
Turner, SD	.375	0	0	0	5	0
Twitchell, NY	.363	13	6	1	28	5
Tyson, StL	.482	14	2	0	33	4
Unser, Phila	.250	0	0	0	1	0
Urrea, StL	.520	14	1	0	27	4
Vail, Chi	.454	22	3	1	74	23
Valentine, Mtl	.200	10	1	1	18	0
Venable, SF	.152	1	0	0	14	2
Vuckovich, StL	.267	0	0	0	3	0
Vukovich, Phila	.497	17	2	0	21	2
Walling, Hou	.319	16	1	0	23	3
Watson, Hou	.158	1	0	0	6	0
Welch, LA	.000	1	0	0	4	0
Wessinger, Atl	.351	3	0	0	3	1
Whisenton, Atl	.428	21	2	1	23	1
White, Mtl	.396	36	6	4	47	15
Whitfield, SF	.111	1	0	0	15	0
Whitson, Pitt-SF	.833	0	0	0	2	0
Wiedenbauer, Hou	.340	2	0	0	12	0
Wilhelm, SD	.290	3	0	0	18	0
Williams, Hou	.000	0	0	0	0	0
Wilson, Hou	.558	85	24	2	71	9
Winfield, SD	.384	29	8	0	68	12
Yeager, LA	.436	60	7	7	84	7
Youngblood, NY	.125	0	0	0	7	0
Zachry, NY						

OFFICIAL NATIONAL LEAGUE FIELDING AVERAGES

CLUB FIELDING

Club	Pct.	G.	PO.	A.	E.	TC.	DP.	TP.	PB.
Philadelphia	.983	163	4324	1800	106	6230	148	0	5
Los Angeles	.981	162	4332	1669	118	6119	123	0	21
Cincinnati	.980	161	4321	1738	124	6183	152	0	9
St. Louis	.980	163	4460	1932	132	6524	166	0	16
Pittsburgh	.979	163	4480	1752	134	6366	163	1	10
Montreal	.979	160	4342	1717	131	6190	123	0	4
San Diego	.978	161	4359	1943	141	6443	154	0	12
New York	.978	163	4448	1768	140	6356	168	0	15
Houston	.978	162	4343	1707	138	6188	146	0	18
Chicago	.975	162	4340	1902	159	6401	163	0	8
San Francisco	.974	162	4308	1806	163	6277	138	0	17
Atlanta	.970	160	4223	1781	183	6187	139	0	25
Totals	.978	971	52280	21515	1669	75464	1783	1	160

INDIVIDUAL FIELDING

*Throws lefthanded.

FIRST BASEMEN

Leader—Club	Pct.	G.	PO.	A.	E.	DP.
STARGELL, PITT*	.997	113	949	47	3	102

(Listed Alphabetically)

Player—Club	Pct.	G.	PO.	A.	E.	DP.
Alou, Hou	1.000	1	2	0	0	1
Baldwin, Hou	1.000	1	7	1	0	0
Bass, Mtl	1.000	1	1	0	0	0
Beall, Atl*	1.000	3	9	1	0	1
Bench, Cin*	1.000	2	13	1	0	1
Bergman, Hou*	1.000	4	8	0	0	1
Bevacqua, SD	.977	8	38	4	1	4
Biittner, Chi*	.992	32	236	20	2	24
Boisclair, NY*	1.000	1	2	0	0	0
Briggs, SD*	.986	50	326	28	5	20
Buckner, Chi*	.995	140	1258	124	7	118
Cabell, Hou	.997	51	287	21	1	20
Cardenal, Phila-NY	1.000	3	18	0	0	3
Cedeno, Hou	.981	91	832	33	17	79
Collins, Cin*	1.000	10	64	1	0	6
DeFreites, Cin	.974	6	37	0	1	5
Driessen, Cin	.993	143	1289	79	9	112
Freed, StL	.889	1	7	1	1	0
Garvey, LA	.995	162	1402	93	7	101
Guerrero, LA	.972	8	33	2	1	0
Hargrove, SD*	.986	37	323	17	5	24
Hebner, Atl	.966	6	26	2	1	1
Hernandez, StL*	.995	160	1489	146	8	145
Hill, SF	1.000	1	2	0	0	1
Horner, Atl	.984	45	414	24	7	32
Howe, Hou	1.000	3	15	3	0	3
Hutton, Mtl*	1.000	25	78	11	0	4
Iorg, StL	1.000	10	70	5	0	2
Ivie, SF	.995	98	724	40	4	51
Johnstone, SD	.979	22	125	14	3	10

Player—Club	Pct.	G.	PO.	A.	E.	DP.
Kendall, SD	1.000	2	8	1	0	0
Kranepool, NY*	1.000	29	203	19	0	18
Lum, Atl*	.998	51	414	30	1	36
Macha, Mtl	1.000	2	12	0	0	1
Madlock, SF	1.000	5	9	0	0	3
Mazzilli, NY	.993	15	122	12	1	15
McCovey, SF*	.987	89	740	48	10	60
Milner, Pitt*	.989	48	255	18	3	27
Montanez, NY*	.989	108	905	76	11	95
Murphy, Atl	.980	76	685	42	15	61
Ontiveros, Chi	1.000	1	7	1	0	1
Perez, Mtl	.991	129	1114	65	11	81
Perkins, SD*	.982	28	155	10	3	16
Poff, Phil*	1.000	1	1	0	0	0
W. Robinson, Pitt	1.000	28	233	13	0	18
Rose, Phila	.995	159	1424	87	8	124
Sanguillen, Pitt	1.000	5	35	2	0	3
Solaita, Mtl*	.989	13	83	6	1	7
Spilman, Cin	1.000	12	62	2	0	3
Stargell, Pitt*	.997	113	949	47	3	102
Staub, Mtl	.994	22	155	7	1	11
Stearns, NY	1.000	16	114	8	0	16
Summers, Cin	.979	6	41	5	1	4
Tenace, SD	.989	72	582	32	7	55
Thomas, LA	.000	1	0	0	0	0
Thomasson, LA*	1.000	1	2	0	0	0
Tolan, SD*	1.000	5	10	2	0	2
Unser, Phila*	.975	22	74	5	2	6
Watson, Hou	.993	44	371	33	3	23

TRIPLE PLAY: Stargell, Pitt.

FIRST BASEMAN WITH TWO OR MORE CLUBS

Player—Club	Pct.	G.	PO.	A.	E.	DP.
Cardenal, Phila	1.000	1	2	0	0	0
Cardenal, NY	1.000	2	16	0	0	3

SECOND BASEMEN

Leader—Club	Pct.	G.	PO.	A.	E.	DP.
OBERKFELL, STL.	.985	117	213	323	8	65

(Listed Alphabetically)

Player—Club	Pct.	G.	PO.	A.	E.	DP.
Almon, SD	.985	61	116	150	4	37
Andrews, SF	.956	53	96	101	9	21
Auerbach, Cin	.667	3	2	0	1	0
Aviles, Phila	.977	27	40	44	2	8
Bernazard, Mtl	.982	14	22	34	1	4
Bevacqua, SD	.967	16	27	32	2	4
Cash, Mtl	.971	47	88	110	6	18
Chaney, Atl	1.000	5	2	5	0	1
Chapman, NY	.980	22	50	46	2	15
Davis, Chi	1.000	2	0	1	0	0
Dillard, Chi	.988	60	111	132	3	31
Evans, SD	1.000	1	0	1	0	0
Ferrer, NY	1.000	4	1	3	0	1
Flannery, SD	.991	21	45	60	1	16
Flynn, NY	.983	148	369	380	13	98
Garner, Pitt	.981	83	175	234	8	58
Gonzalez, SD	.976	103	217	225	11	52
Gonzalez, Hou	.987	32	59	89	2	16
Harrelson, Phila	.990	25	54	47	1	11
Herr, StL	1.000	6	12	11	0	3

Player—Club	Pct.	G.	PO.	A.	E.	DP.
Howe, Hou	.991	68	126	188	3	33
Hubbard, Atl	.968	91	193	268	15	57
Ivie, SF	.000	1	0	0	0	0
Kelleher, Chi	.978	29	52	84	3	16
Kennedy, Cin	.980	59	95	144	5	28
Lacy, Pitt	.923	5	7	5	1	1
Landestoy, Hou	.971	114	166	234	12	53
Lopes, LA	.981	152	341	384	14	82
Mackanin, Phila	1.000	2	1	3	0	0
Macko, Chi	1.000	10	18	21	0	4
Madlock, SF	.976	63	137	144	7	32
Martinez, LA	1.000	18	25	29	0	2
Meoli, Phila	.981	15	14	37	1	7
Metzger, SF	1.000	10	14	18	0	4
Morgan, Cin	.980	121	259	329	12	74
Oberkfell, StL	.985	117	213	323	8	65
Perlozzo, SD	.500	2	1	0	1	0
Phillips, StL	.981	16	21	30	1	5
Rose, Phila	1.000	1	1	0	0	0
Royster, Atl	.983	77	170	224	7	50
Scott, Mtl	.980	113	301	324	13	71
Seibert, Chi	1.000	2	2	0	0	0
Sexton, Hou	1.000	2	0	1	0	0
Sizemore, Chi	.973	96	230	312	15	68

Player—Club	Pct.	G.	PO.	A.	E.	DP.
Stennett, Pitt	.974	102	172	282	12	63
Strain, SF	.982	67	147	188	6	32
Thomas, LA	1.000	5	5	9	0	1
Trevino, NY	1.000	8	6	3	0	1
Trillo, Phila	.985	118	270	368	10	84
Tyson, StL	.975	71	125	184	8	42
Vukovich, Phila	1.000	3	2	4	0	0
Wessinger, Atl	.833	2	2	3	1	0
Youngblood, NY	.956	13	21	22	2	6

TRIPLE PLAY: Garner, Pitt.

THIRD BASEMEN

Leader—Club	Pct.	G.	PO.	A.	E.	DP.
CEY, LA	.977	150	123	265	9	25

(Listed Alphabetically)

Player—Club	Pct.	G.	PO.	A.	E.	DP.
Andrews, SF	1.000	3	1	1	0	0
Auerbach, Cin	.933	18	2	26	2	2
Berra, Pitt	.879	22	18	33	7	3
Bevacqua, SD	.954	64	45	120	8	13
Bonnell, Atl	1.000	1	1	0	0	0
Boone, Phila	.500	2	0	1	1	0
Cabell, Hou	.957	132	109	178	13	11
Cey, LA	.977	150	123	265	9	25
Chaney, Atl	.929	4	3	10	1	0
Chapman, NY	1.000	1	1	0	0	0
Clark, SF	1.000	2	1	0	0	0
Cruz, SF	.833	2	3	2	1	0
Dade, SD	.949	70	44	162	11	12
Davis, Chi	1.000	1	0	2	0	0
Dillard, Chi	.900	9	3	6	1	1
Evans, SD	.952	53	30	108	7	12
Evans, SF	.943	159	129	369	30	28
Ferrer, NY	.833	12	3	2	1	0
Garner, Pitt	.936	78	47	144	13	16
Gonzalez, SD	1.000	3	1	1	0	0
Gonzalez, Hou	1.000	2	3	0	0	0
Guerrero, LA	1.000	3	1	2	0	1
Harrelson, Phila	1.000	9	0	9	0	1
Hatcher, LA	.895	17	11	23	4	0
Hebner, NY	.940	134	99	246	22	26
Horner, Atl	.930	82	56	143	15	11
Howe, Hou	.967	59	47	70	4	6
Ivie, SF	1.000	4	3	4	0	0
Kelleher, Chi	.966	32	17	40	2	1
Kennedy, Cin	1.000	4	0	2	0	0
Knicely, Hou	.000	1	0	0	0	0
Knight, Cin	.962	149	120	262	15	26
Macha, Mtl	1.000	13	12	18	0	1
Macha, Mtl	.769	3	2	8	3	0
Mackanin, Phila	1.000	2	0	3	0	0
Macko, Chi	1.000	4	3	12	0	0
Maddox, NY	.950	11	2	17	1	0
Madlock, Pitt	.969	85	63	153	7	12
Martinez, LA	.769	23	4	6	3	1
Mason, Mtl	1.000	6	4	9	0	1
Meoli, Phila	1.000	1	0	1	0	0
Metzger, SF	.000	1	0	0	0	0
Oberkfell, StL	.967	17	10	19	1	2
Ontiveros, Chi	.941	142	98	268	23	27
Parrish, Mtl	.947	153	119	290	23	25
Phillips, StL	1.000	1	0	1	0	0
Reitz, StL	.972	158	124	290	12	26
W. Robinson, Pitt	.000	3	0	0	0	0
Rose, Phila	.833	5	4	6	2	0
Royster, Atl	.948	80	91	181	15	12
Schmidt, Phila	.954	157	114	361	23	36
Sexton, Hou	1.000	4	1	0	0	0
Spilman, Cin	1.000	4	2	9	0	0
Stearns, NY	.905	11	5	14	2	2
Strain, SF	1.000	1	0	1	0	0
Thomas, LA	.921	18	20	15	3	3
Trevino, NY	.945	27	15	37	3	6
Vail, Chi	1.000	2	0	1	0	0
Vukovich, Phila	1.000	9	0	9	0	1
Youngblood, NY	.926	12	8	17	2	1

TRIPLE PLAY: Madlock, Pitt.

SHORTSTOPS

Leader—Club	Pct.	G.	PO.	A.	E.	DP.
BOWA, PHILA	.991	146	229	448	6	80

(Listed Alphabetically)

Player—Club	Pct.	G.	PO.	A.	E.	DP.
Alexander, Pitt	.000	1	0	0	0	0
Almon, SD	.958	25	26	43	3	11
Auerbach, Cin	.965	16	27	28	2	5
Berra, Pitt	.940	22	25	53	5	11
Bowa, Phila	.991	146	229	448	6	80
Chaney, Atl	.945	39	40	80	7	15
Concepcion, Cin	.967	148	284	495	27	102
DeJesus, Chi	.959	160	235	507	32	97
Evans, SD	1.000	2	0	1	0	0
Ferrer, NY	1.000	5	4	5	0	2
Flynn, NY	.961	20	33	41	3	9
Foli, NY-Pitt	.978	135	259	410	15	98
Frias, Atl	.954	137	229	432	32	79
Garner, Pitt	.968	14	12	18	1	8
Gonzalez, Hou	.966	21	31	54	3	11
Harrelson, Phila	.889	17	9	15	3	1
Kelleher, Chi	.971	14	9	24	1	4
Kennedy, Cin	1.000	5	10	16	0	2
Landestoy, Hou	1.000	3	2	3	0	1
LeMaster, SF	.959	106	160	303	20	52
Mackanin, Phila	1.000	2	0	3	0	0
Martinez, LA	.962	21	16	34	2	4
Mason, Mtl	.966	33	31	53	3	9
Meoli, Phila	.984	16	23	37	1	5
Metzger, SF	.956	78	108	219	15	34
Oberkfell, StL	1.000	3	0	1	0	0
Oester, Cin	1.000	2	1	2	0	0
Phillips, StL	.973	25	33	76	3	11
Reynolds, Hou	.965	143	208	428	23	88
Russell, LA	.957	150	218	452	30	70
Schmidt, Phila	1.000	2	1	2	0	2
Scott, Mtl	.952	39	61	97	8	11
Sexton, Hou	.943	11	10	23	2	6
Smith, SD	.976	155	256	555	20	86
Speier, Mtl	.970	112	194	355	17	52
Taveras,						
Pitt-NY	.964	164	287	464	28	92
Templeton, StL	.960	150	292	525	34	102
Thomas, LA	.889	3	4	4	1	0

SHORTSTOPS WITH TWO OR MORE CLUBS

Player—Club	Pct.	G.	PO.	A.	E.	DP.
Foli, NY	1.000	3	4	6	0	1
Foli, Pitt	.978	132	255	404	15	97
Taveras, Pitt	.935	11	17	26	3	4
Taveras, NY	.966	153	270	438	25	88

OUTFIELDERS

Leader—Club	Pct.	G.	PO.	A.	E.	DP.
PUHL, Hou	1.000	152	352	7	0	3

(Listed Alphabetically)

Player—Club	Pct.	G.	PO.	A.	E.	DP.
Alexander, Pitt	1.000	11	8	1	0	0
Almon, SD	.000	1	0	0	0	0
Alou, Hou	1.000	6	6	0	0	0
Anderson, Phila	.973	70	68	3	2	1
Asselstine, Atl	1.000	1	1	0	0	0
Baker, LA	.990	150	289	14	3	4
Bevacqua, SD	1.000	8	5	0	0	0
Biittner, Chi*	.925	44	46	3	4	0
Blair, Cin	.992	67	117	3	1	0
Boisclair, NY*	1.000	24	34	2	0	0
Bonnell, Atl	.983	124	220	8	4	2
Briggs, SD*	.972	44	67	3	2	1
Brock, StL*	.958	98	152	7	7	2
Burroughs, Atl	.963	110	175	8	7	1
Carbo, LA	1.000	17	10	0	0	0
Cardenal, Phila-NY	1.000	21	31	0	0	0
Cedeno, Hou	1.000	40	116	2	0	0
Clark, SF	.982	140	261	13	5	7
Collins, Cin*	.976	91	159	2	4	2
Cromartie, Mtl*	.976	158	343	16	9	4
Cruz, SF–Cin	.985	75	124	8	2	4
Cruz, Hou*	.959	156	320	7	14	0
Dade, SD	1.000	4	3	1	0	0
Davalillo, LA*	1.000	3	2	0	0	0
Dawson, Mtl	.988	153	394	7	5	1
DeFreites, Cin	1.000	1	1	0	0	0
Dilone, Chi	1.000	22	27	0	0	0
Dimmel, StL	1.000	5	3	0	0	0
Easler, Pitt	.000	4	0	0	0	0
Ferguson, LA	.978	52	88	2	2	2
Flores, NY	.976	32	39	1	1	0
Foster, Cin	.982	116	214	7	4	1
Geronimo, Cin*	.993	118	291	11	2	2
Greer, SD	1.000	4	4	0	0	0
Grieve, StL	.875	5	7	0	1	0
Griffey, Cin*	.984	93	175	8	3	1
Gross, Phila*	.978	73	82	5	2	2
Guerrero, LA	1.000	12	19	0	0	0
Harrelson, Phila	.000	1	0	0	0	0
Hatcher, LA	.974	19	36	1	1	0
Heep, Hou*	1.000	2	7	0	0	0
Henderson, Cin–Chi	.955	25	21	0	1	0
Henderson, NY	.990	94	201	6	2	3
Hendrick, StL	.993	138	254	20	2	7
Herndon, SF	.963	122	196	10	8	2
Hutton, Mtl*	1.000	9	11	0	0	0
Iorg, StL	.964	39	51	2	2	0
Ivie, SF	1.000	24	25	3	0	0
Johnston, SF*	.966	17	27	1	1	0
Johnstone, SD	.985	45	60	4	1	0
Joshua, LA*	.967	46	56	2	2	0
Kingman, Chi	.954	139	240	11	12	3
Kranepool, NY*	1.000	8	12	0	0	0
Lacy, Pitt	.973	41	70	3	2	0
Lentine, StL	1.000	8	12	1	0	1
Leonard, Hou	.959	123	227	6	10	1
Lum, Atl*	1.000	3	6	0	0	0
Luzinski, Phila	.946	125	156	3	9	1
Macha, Mtl	.000	2	0	0	0	0

Player—Club	Pct.	G.	PO.	A.	E.	DP.
Maddox, Phila	.996	140	433	13	2	2
Maddox, NY	.985	65	129	5	2	1
Martin, Chi	.981	144	297	11	6	4
Matthews, Atl	.974	156	292	12	8	4
Mazzilli, NY	.989	143	358	12	4	1
McBride, Phila	.989	147	341	12	4	3
McCarver, Phila	.000	1	0	0	0	0
Mejias, Chi–Cin	.889	28	8	0	1	0
Miller, Atl	.988	27	79	1	1	0
Milner, Pitt*	.958	64	112	2	5	1
Monday, LA*	.964	10	27	0	1	0
Moreno, Pitt*	.975	162	490	11	13	0
Mota, LA	.000	1	0	0	0	0
Mumphrey, StL	.984	114	180	3	3	0
Murcer, Chi	1.000	54	110	4	0	0
Norman, NY	.967	33	54	4	2	0
North, SF	.987	130	300	8	4	2
Office, Atl*	.988	97	164	4	2	0
Parker, Pitt	.960	158	341	15	15	1
Poff, Phila*	.875	4	7	0	1	0
Puhl, Hou	1.000	152	352	7	0	3
Reynolds, SD	.950	14	17	2	1	1
Richards, SD*	.973	132	320	7	9	2
W. Robinson, Pitt	.982	125	161	6	3	0
Sadek, SF	.000	1	0	0	0	0
Scott, StL	.984	151	427	14	7	5
Smith, LA	.988	62	159	5	2	0
Smith, StL	1.000	5	14	1	0	0
Smith, Phila	1.000	11	19	1	0	0
Spikes, Atl	.842	15	16	0	3	0
Staub, Mtl	1.000	1	1	0	0	0
Stearns, NY	.778	6	7	0	2	0
Summers, Cin	.941	13	15	1	1	0
Tekulve, Pitt	1.000	1	1	0	0	0
Thomas, LA	.996	119	269	10	1	4
Thomasson, LA*	.980	100	194	4	4	1
Thompson, Chi*	.971	100	161	7	5	3
Tolan, SD*	.000	1	0	0	0	0
Turner, SD*	.958	115	197	7	9	2
Unser, Phila*	.978	30	44	0	1	0
Vail, Chi	.964	39	51	3	2	0
Valentine, Mtl	.983	144	281	10	5	2
Venable, SF	.914	25	30	2	3	0
Walling, Hou	.985	42	65	2	1	0
Whisenton, Atl*	1.000	13	28	3	0	0
White, Chi	.983	43	55	2	1	1
Whitfield, SF	.957	106	167	10	8	3
Wiedenbauer, Hou	1.000	3	3	0	0	0
Wilhelm, SD	.985	30	61	4	1	0
Winfield, SD	.986	157	344	14	5	3
Youngblood, NY	.985	147	308	18	5	3

OUTFIELDERS WITH TWO OR MORE CLUBS

Player—Club	Pct.	G.	PO.	A.	E.	DP.
Cardenal, Phila	1.000	12	14	0	0	0
Cardenal, NY	1.000	9	17	0	0	0
Cruz, SF	1.000	6	5	0	0	0
Cruz, Cin	.984	69	119	8	2	4
Henderson, Cin	1.000	2	2	0	0	0
Henderson, Chi	.950	23	19	0	1	0
Mejias, Chi	.875	23	7	0	1	0
Mejias, Cin	1.000	5	1	0	0	0

CATCHERS

Leader—Club	Pct.	G.	PO.	A.	E.	DP.	PB.
TENACE, SD	.998	94	413	51	1	8	10

(Listed Alphabetically)

Player—Club	Pct.	G.	PO.	A.	E.	DP.	PB.
Ashby, Hou	.987	105	548	57	8	9	5
Baldwin, Hou	1.000	3	3	0	0	0	0
Bench, Cin	.986	126	619	68	10	5	11
Benedict, Atl	.984	76	344	35	6	8	3
Blackwell, Chi	.975	63	245	28	7	4	3
Bochy, Hou	.970	55	198	29	7	4	4
Boone, Phila	.988	117	527	65	7	2	8
Carter, Mtl	.989	138	751	88	9	3	12
Chaney, Atl	.000	1	0	0	0	0	0
Correll, Cin	.992	47	221	19	2	4	1
Dyer, Mtl	.993	27	141	10	1	1	1
Fahey, SD	.994	68	277	33	2	3	5
Ferguson, LA	.981	67	326	35	7	8	6
Foote, Chi	.979	129	713	63	17	3	9
Hill, SF	.991	58	283	31	3	2	4
Hodges, NY	.980	22	82	16	2	1	1
Kearney, SF	.000	1	0	0	0	0	0
Kendall, SD	.977	40	154	18	4	1	3
Kennedy, StL	.993	32	135	7	1	2	1
Kimm, Chi	.969	9	30	1	1	1	0
Knicely, Hou	1.000	3	2	0	0	0	0
Littlejohn, SF	.986	63	366	43	6	6	7
Macha, Mtl	.000	1	0	0	0	0	0
McCarver, Phil	.989	31	174	12	2	0	0
Moreland, Phila	1.000	13	71	3	0	2	1
Murphy, Atl	.966	27	127	15	5	11	2
Nicosia, Pitt	.991	65	320	25	3	2	4
Nolan, Atl	.983	74	328	27	6	6	2
Oates, LA	.975	20	64	13	2	4	2
Ott, Pitt	.994	116	612	53	4	7	6
Pocoroba, Atl	.933	7	39	3	3	0	0
Pujols, Hou	.993	26	136	6	1	5	0
Rader, Phila	.932	25	62	6	5	1	1
Sadek, SF	.993	60	246	21	2	9	2
Sanguillen, Pitt	.947	8	32	4	2	1	0
Simmons, StL	.985	122	606	69	10	14	10
Stearns, NY	.983	121	628	85	12	7	11
Swisher, StL	.974	33	105	6	3	0	2
Tamargo, SF-Mtl	.989	21	80	6	1	0	4
Tenace, SD	.998	94	413	51	1	8	10
Trevino, NY	.976	36	208	31	6	7	7
Yeager, LA	.984	103	513	56	9	9	7

CATCHER WITH TWO OR MORE CLUBS

Player—Club	Pct.	G.	PO.	A.	E.	DP.	PB.
Tamargo, SF	.985	17	61	5	1	0	4
Tamargo, Mtl	1.000	4	19	1	0	0	0

PITCHERS

Leader—Club	Pct.	G.	PO.	A.	E.	DP.
NIEKRO, Hou	1.000	38	14	39	0	4

(Listed Alphabetically)

Player—Club	Pct.	G.	PO.	A.	E.	DP.
Allen, NY	.958	50	9	14	1	1
Anderson, Phila	.000	1	0	0	0	0
Andujar, Hou	.930	46	16	50	5	2
Atkinson, Mtl	1.000	10	1	0	0	0
Bahnsen, Mtl	.895	55	4	13	2	0
Bair, Cin	.933	65	5	9	1	1
Beckwith, LA	.833	17	5	5	2	0
Berenguer, NY	.500	5	0	1	1	0
Bernard, NY	1.000	32	2	8	0	1
Bibby, Pitt	1.000	34	5	12	0	1
Bird, Phila	1.000	32	4	2	0	0
Blue, SF	.981	34	10	42	1	5
Blyleven, Pitt	1.000	37	14	20	0	0
Boggs, Atl	1.000	3	0	3	0	0
Bonham, Cin	.909	29	9	31	4	0
Borbon, Cin-SF	.895	60	7	10	2	1
Bradford, Atl	.833	21	0	5	1	0
Brett, LA	1.000	30	7	14	0	1
Brizzolara, Atl	.957	27	7	15	1	1
Bruno, StL	1.000	27	2	5	0	0
Brusstar, Phila	1.000	13	1	2	0	0
Burris, Chi-NY	.933	18	7	7	1	0
Candelaria, Pitt	1.000	33	2	36	0	3
Capilla, Cin-Chi	.875	18	0	7	1	0
Carlton, Phila	.875	35	3	32	5	0
Castillo, LA	1.000	19	1	3	0	0
Caudill, Chi	1.000	29	5	11	0	1
Christenson, Phila	1.000	19	4	15	0	0
Coleman, SF-Pitt	.500	15	1	0	1	0
Curtis, SF	1.000	27	4	13	0	1
D'Acquisto, SD	.923	51	3	9	1	0
Denny, StL	.963	31	16	36	2	4
Devine, Atl	.765	40	1	12	4	1
Dixon, Hou	1.000	19	3	6	0	1
Easterly, Atl	1.000	4	0	1	0	0
Eastwick, Phila	1.000	51	4	4	0	0
Eichelberger, SD	1.000	3	0	2	0	0
Ellis, NY-Pitt	1.000	20	7	14	0	1
Espinosa, Phila	.957	33	11	34	2	2
Falcone, NY	.944	33	3	14	1	1
Fingers, SD	.923	54	3	9	1	0
Forsch, Hou	.979	26	10	37	1	5
Forsch, StL	.982	33	25	31	1	3
Forster, LA	1.000	17	1	5	0	0
Frazier, StL	.889	25	4	4	1	0
Fryman, Mtl	1.000	44	3	11	0	1
Fulgham, StL	.905	20	7	12	2	1
Garber, Atl	.968	68	14	16	1	1
Geisel, Chi	1.000	7	2	0	0	0
Glynn, NY	1.000	46	5	3	0	0
Griffin, SF	.960	59	5	19	1	1
Grimsley, Mtl	.909	32	3	27	3	0
Gullickson, Mtl	.000	1	0	0	0	0
Halicki, SF	.875	33	9	19	4	1
Hanna, Atl	1.000	6	0	3	0	0
Hannahs, LA	1.000	4	0	3	0	0
Hassler, NY	.944	29	1	16	1	0
Hausman, NY	1.000	19	10	11	0	0
Hernandez, Chi	.938	51	4	11	1	0
Holland, SF	.000	3	0	0	0	0
Holtzman, Chi	.950	23	8	11	1	0
Hooton, LA	1.000	29	12	26	0	3
Hough, LA	.969	42	5	26	1	0
Hume, Cin	.943	57	6	27	2	1
Jackson, Pitt	1.000	72	2	9	0	0
Jackson, NY	1.000	8	2	1	0	1
James, Mtl	.000	2	0	0	0	0
Jones, SD	.962	39	15	60	3	2
Kaat, Phila	1.000	3	0	1	0	0

Player—Club	Pct.	G.	PO.	A.	E.	DP.
Kinney, SD*	.667	13	0	2	1	0
Kison, Pitt	.976	33	10	30	1	2
Knepper, SF*	.872	34	8	26	5	1
Knowles, StL*	.692	48	2	7	4	0
Kobel, NY*	.929	30	13	26	3	2
Krukow, Chi	1.000	28	11	12	0	3
Kucek, Phila	.000	4	0	0	0	0
LaCorte, Atl-Hou	.500	18	0	1	1	0
LaCoss, Cin	.961	35	15	34	2	4
Ladd, Hou	1.000	10	3	2	0	0
LaGrow, LA	1.000	31	0	5	0	0
Lamp, Chi	.954	38	17	45	3	3
Larson, Phila	1.000	3	1	4	0	1
Lavelle, SF*	.944	70	4	13	1	0
Lee, SD	.944	46	3	14	1	1
Lee, Mtl*	.981	33	11	41	1	2
Leibrandt, Cin*	1.000	3	1	0	0	1
Lerch, Phila*	.981	37	13	38	1	5
Lewallyn, LA	1.000	7	1	4	0	0
Littell, StL	.929	63	6	7	1	1
Lockwood, NY	.800	27	1	3	1	1
Lolich, SD*	1.000	27	0	9	0	0
Lonborg, Phila	1.000	4	1	0	0	0
M. Mahler, Atl*	.944	26	4	13	1	1
R. Mahler, Atl	.800	15	1	3	1	0
Martinez, StL	.889	32	17	15	4	3
Matula, Atl	1.000	28	15	23	0	6
May, Mtl*	1.000	33	6	15	0	0
McEnaney, StL*	1.000	45	2	19	0	2
McGlothen, Chi	1.000	42	15	15	0	0
McGraw, Phila*	1.000	65	6	4	0	0
J. McLaughlin, Atl.	.857	37	4	8	2	0
M. McLaughlin, Hou-Atl	.875	49	3	4	1	0
McWilliams, Atl*	.950	13	2	17	1	2
Mendoza, NY	.000	1	0	0	0	0
Messersmith, LA	1.000	11	5	9	0	1
Minton, SF	.963	46	3	23	1	2
Moffitt, SF	1.000	28	1	5	0	0
Montefusco, SF	.967	22	9	20	1	2
Moore, Chi	.913	39	6	15	2	0
Moskau, Cin	.917	21	3	19	2	3
Mura, SD	.929	38	5	8	1	0
Murray, NY-Mtl	.960	67	5	19	1	3
Nastu, SF*	.952	25	6	14	1	4
Niekro, Hou	1.000	38	14	39	0	4
Niekro, Atl	.989	44	31	56	1	3
Niemann, Hou*	1.000	26	1	7	0	0
Noles, Phila	.955	14	4	17	1	1
Norman, Cin*	.909	34	4	26	3	1
O'Brien, StL	.000	6	0	0	0	0
Orosco, NY*	1.000	18	2	9	0	1
Owchinko, SD*	.929	42	2	24	2	2
Pacella, NY	1.000	4	2	1	0	0
Palmer, Mtl	.960	36	7	17	1	0
Pastore, Cin	1.000	30	5	13	0	2
Patterson, LA	1.000	36	6	5	0	1
Perry, SD	.963	32	11	41	2	2
Pladson, Hou	.000	4	0	0	0	0
Plank, SF	.500	4	1	0	1	0
Rasmussen, SD	.968	45	6	24	1	1
Rau, LA*	1.000	11	2	10	0	0
Rautzhan, LA*	1.000	12	2	3	0	0
Reardon, NY	1.000	18	1	1	0	1
Reed, Phila	1.000	61	3	13	0	3
Reuschel, Chi	.962	36	27	49	3	9
Reuss, LA*	.925	39	2	35	3	1
Rhoden, Pitt	1.000	1	1	1	0	0

Player—Club	Pct.	G.	PO.	A.	E.	DP.
Riccelli, Hou*	1.000	11	U	6	U	U
Richard, Hou	.902	38	14	32	5	0
Riley, Chi*	1.000	4	1	3	0	0
Roberge, Hou	1.000	26	3	3	0	0
Roberts, SF-Pitt*	.909	47	2	18	2	2
D. Robinson, Pitt	.895	29	7	10	2	1
Rogers, Mtl	.952	37	14	46	3	7
Romo, Pitt	.972	84	10	25	1	3
Rooker, Pitt*	.913	19	8	13	2	1
Ruhle, Hou	1.000	13	3	5	0	0
Ruthven, Phila	.938	20	6	9	1	1
Sambito, Hou*	.905	63	5	14	2	2
Sanderson, Mtl	.957	34	9	13	1	1
Sarmiento, Cin	1.000	23	1	4	0	0
Saucier, Phila*	.933	29	2	12	1	1
Schatzeder, Mtl*	.818	32	5	13	4	0
Schultz, StL*	1.000	31	1	5	0	0
Scott, NY	.833	18	3	7	2	0
Seaman, StL*	.000	1	0	0	0	0
Seaver, Cin	.960	32	22	26	2	2
Shirley, SD*	.977	49	13	30	1	1
Skok, Atl*	1.000	44	0	10	0	1
Solomon, Atl	.895	31	12	22	4	0
Sosa, Mtl	.889	62	8	8	2	0
Soto, Cin	1.000	25	1	2	0	0
Sprowl, Hou*	.000	3	0	0	0	0
Sutcliffe, LA	1.000	39	18	24	0	1
Sutter, Chi	.889	62	9	15	3	0
Sutton, LA	.976	33	16	24	1	2
Swan, NY	1.000	35	17	29	0	3
Sykes, StL*	1.000	13	0	7	0	0
Tekulve, Pitt	.972	94	7	28	1	0
Tellmann, SD	1.000	1	1	1	0	0
Thomas, StL	1.000	26	10	13	0	1
Throop, Hou	1.000	14	1	2	0	0
Tidrow, Chi	1.000	63	7	20	0	1
Tomlin, Cin*	.824	53	4	10	3	1
Twitchell, NY	.909	33	2	8	1	1
Urrea, StL	1.000	3	2	1	0	0
Vuckovich, StL	.894	34	14	28	5	2
Welch, LA	.769	25	2	8	3	3
Whitson, Pitt-SF	.926	37	4	21	2	2
Williams, Hou	.963	31	3	23	1	2
Wilson, Hou	.000	6	0	0	0	0
Zachry, NY	1.000	3	7	0	0	0

PITCHERS WITH TWO OR MORE CLUBS

Player—Club	Pct.	G.	PO.	A.	E.	DP.
Borbon, Cin	.909	30	3	7	1	1
Borbon, SF	.875	30	4	3	1	0
Burris, Chi	1.000	14	3	4	0	0
Burris, NY	.875	4	4	3	1	0
Capilla, Cin*	1.000	5	0	2	0	0
Capilla, Chi*	.833	13	0	5	1	0
Coleman, SF	.000	5	0	0	0	0
Coleman, Pitt	.500	10	1	0	1	0
Ellis, NY	1.000	17	7	13	0	1
Ellis, Pitt	1.000	3	0	1	0	0
LaCorte, Atl	.000	6	0	0	0	0
LaCorte, Hou	1.000	12	0	1	0	0
M. McLaughlin, Hou	1.000	12	1	2	0	0
M. McLaughlin, Atl.	.800	37	2	2	1	0
Murray, NY	.960	58	5	19	1	3
Murray, Mtl	.000	9	0	0	0	0
Roberts, SF*	.909	26	1	9	1	1
Roberts, Pitt*	.909	21	1	9	1	1
Whitson, Pitt	1.000	19	2	6	0	1
Whitson, SF	.895	18	2	15	2	1

OFFICIAL NATIONAL LEAGUE PITCHING AVERAGES

CLUB PITCHING

Club	ERA	G	CG	Sv	ShO	IP	H	BFP	R	ER	HR	SH	SF	Tot. BB	Int. BB	HB	SO	WP	Bk
Montreal	3.14	160	33	39	18	1447⅓	1379	6052	581	505	116	84	34	450	51	23	813	28	7
Houston	3.41	162	55	31	19	1447⅓	1278	6014	582	514	90	65	39	504	44	24	854	52	5
Pittsburgh	3.41	163	24	52	7	1493⅓	1424	6272	643	566	125	74	46	504	77	31	904	52	9
Cincinnati	3.58	161	27	40	10	1440⅓	1415	6083	644	573	103	78	50	485	68	18	773	23	7
San Diego	3.69	161	29	25	7	1453	1438	6160	681	596	108	60	40	513	53	23	788	49	9
St. Louis	3.72	162	38	34	10	1486⅔	1449	6255	693	615	127	73	50	501	54	18	779	44	10
Los Angeles	3.83	163	30	34	6	1444	1425	6197	717	614	101	88	50	555	53	27	811	44	11
New York	3.84	162	16	36	10	1482⅔	1486	6357	706	633	120	88	56	607	87	24	819	41	11
Chicago	3.88	162	20	44	11	1446⅔	1500	6232	707	624	127	74	45	521	65	43	933	40	5
Philadelphia	4.16	162	33	29	14	1441⅓	1455	6086	718	666	135	61	52	477	95	29	787	36	18
San Francisco	4.16	162	25	34	6	1436	1484	6259	751	664	143	82	46	577	95	27	880	50	10
Atlanta	4.18	160	32	34	3	1407⅓	1496	6149	763	654	132	70	44	494	62	45	779	45	9
Totals	3.73	971	362	423	121	17426⅔	17229	74116	8186	7224	1427	949	549	6188	806	332	9920	493	111

(BFP total includes 10 batsmen awarded first base because of interference or obstruction)

NOTE.—Total earned runs for several clubs do not agree with composite total of respective club's pitchers due to provisions of Scoring Rule Section 10.18(i). The following differences are to be noted: Chicago pitchers add to 627; Cincinnati 576; Los Angeles 620; Pittsburgh 568; St. Louis 617; San Diego 598; San Francisco 665.

PITCHERS' RECORDS

(Top Fifteen Qualifiers for Earned-Run Leadership—162 or More Innings)

*Throws lefthanded.

Pitcher and Club	ERA	W.	L.	Pct.	G.	GS.	CG.	GF.	ShO.	Sv.	IP.	H.	BFP.	R.	ER.	HR.	SH.	SF.	Tot. BB.	Int. BB.	HB.	SO.	WP.	Bk.
Richard, James, Houston	2.71	18	13	.581	38	38	19	—	4	—	292⅓	220	1175	98	88	13	14	8	98	0	9	313	19	1
Hume, Thomas, Cincinnati	2.76	10	9	.526	57	12	2	33	1	17	163	162	669	54	50	12	8	9	33	9	3	106	2	0
Schatzeder, Daniel, Montreal*	2.83	10	5	.667	21	21	3	—	1	—	162	136	677	57	51	11	10	3	59	2	2	80	6	1
Hooton, Burt, Los Angeles	2.97	11	10	.524	29	29	9	—	2	—	212	191	874	85	70	11	14	6	63	9	1	129	6	0
Niekro, Joseph, Houston	3.00	21	11	.656	38	38	16	—	5	—	264	221	1095	88	88	17	6	7	107	1	6	119	19	0
Rogers, Stephen, Montreal	3.00	13	12	.520	37	37	13	—	5	—	249	232	1032	102	83	14	21	6	78	4	3	143	10	0
Forsch, Kenneth, Houston	3.03	11	6	.647	26	24	10	1	0	0	178	155	700	60	60	14	5	2	35	10	1	58	3	0
Lee, William, Montreal*	3.04	16	10	.615	33	33	6	—	0	0	222	230	925	79	75	20	12	9	46	5	2	104	6	1
Perry, Gaylord, San Diego	3.05	12	11	.522	32	32	10	—	2	0	233	225	963	90	79	20	14	4	67	10	10	140	11	0
Seaver, G. Thomas, Cincinnati	3.14	16	6	.727	32	32	9	—	5	0	215	187	868	85	75	16	6	7	61	4	4	131	2	0
Kison, Bruce, Pittsburgh	3.19	13	7	.650	34	25	8	3	0	2	172	157	704	70	61	13	4	6	45	6	1	62	7	0
Candelaria, John, Pittsburgh*	3.22	14	9	.609	33	30	8	—	3	0	207	201	850	83	74	25	7	4	41	5	6	105	5	0
Martinez, Silvio, St. Louis	3.26	15	8	.652	33	29	9	—	4	0	207	204	867	75	75	14	6	7	67	7	3	101	7	2
Swan, Craig, New York	3.30	14	13	.519	35	35	10	—	1	0	251	241	1027	92	92	20	5	7	57	5	2	145	9	0
Shirley, Robert, San Diego*	3.38	8	16	.333	49	25	4	13	0	0	205	196	843	89	77	15	9	8	59	8	1	117	8	0

DEPARTMENTAL LEADERS: W—J. Niekro, P. Niekro, 21; L—P. Niekro, 20; Pct.—Seaver, .727; G—Tekulve, 94; CP—P. Niekro, 23; GF—Tekulve, 67; Sv—Sutter, 37; ShO—J. Niekro, Rogers, Seaver, 5; IP—P. Niekro, 342; H—P. Niekro, 311; BFP—P. Niekro, 1436; R—P. Niekro, 160; ER—Blue, 132; HR—P. Niekro, 41; SH—Jones, 23; SF—Carlton, 15; Tot.BB—P. Niekro, 113; Int.BB—Tekulve, 20; HB.—P. Niekro, 11; SO—Richard, 313; WP—J. Niekro, Richard, 19; Bk—Carlton, 11.

(All Pitchers—Listed Alphabetically)

Pitcher and Club	ERA	W.	L.	Pct.	G.	GS.	CG.	GF.	Sv.	ShO.	IP.	H.	BFP.	R.	ER.	HR.	SH.	SF.	Tot. BB.	Int. BB.	HB.	SO.	WP.	Bk.
Allen, Neil, New York	3.55	6	10	.375	50	5	0	27	8	0	99	100	431	46	39	4	5	6	47	13	2	65	6	0
Anderson, Michael, Philadelphia	0.00	0	0	.000	3	0	0	1	0	0	2	1	9	0	0	0	0	0	2	0	0	0	0	0
Andujar, Joaquin, Houston	3.43	12	12	.500	46	23	8	9	1	0	194	168	825	86	74	7	9	6	88	7	0	77	5	0
Atkinson, William, Montreal	1.93	1	0	1.000	10	0	0	9	2	0	14	14	57	4	3	0	3	0	4	1	1	7	0	0
Bahnsen, Stanley, Montreal	3.16	11	7	.611	55	0	0	15	5	0	94	93	388	34	33	10	6	3	42	12	1	71	2	1
Bair, C. Douglas, Cincinnati	4.31	1	2	.333	65	0	0	42	16	0	94	80	430	45	45	4	1	5	42	5	0	86	3	0
Beckwith, T. Joseph, Los Angeles	4.38	1	2	.333	17	0	0	8	0	0	37	42	168	18	18	4	1	1	15	0	0	28	0	0
Berenguer, Juan, New York	2.90	0	3	.000	5	5	0	0	0	0	31	28	126	13	10	2	1	1	12	1	1	25	1	0
Bernard, Dwight, New York	4.70	0	0	.000	34	0	0	8	2	0	44	42	208	26	23	2	2	1	26	3	1	20	1	1
Bibby, James, Pittsburgh	2.80	12	4	.750	32	17	4	0	0	0	138	110	562	51	43	9	3	2	47	6	4	103	5	0
Bird, J. Douglas, Philadelphia	5.16	0	3	.000	34	5	0	10	0	0	61	73	263	35	35	7	2	5	22	3	1	33	0	0
Blue, Vida, San Francisco*	5.01	14	14	.500	34	34	8	0	0	0	237	246	1041	113	132	23	11	4	92	11	8	138	9	0
Blyleven, Rikalbert, Pittsburgh	3.61	12	5	.706	37	37	4	0	0	0	237	238	1018	102	95	21	14	6	92	8	6	172	6	0
Boggs, William, Atlanta	6.23	2	2	.500	3	3	0	0	0	0	13	21	64	11	9	0	0	0	4	1	0	11	0	0
Bonham, William, Cincinnati	3.78	6	5	.545	30	29	4	0	0	2	176	173	741	80	74	14	9	4	60	3	3	78	8	1
Borbon, Pedro, Cincinnati-San Fran.	4.15	0	1	.000	60	0	0	31	3	0	91	104	390	45	42	4	6	3	21	7	1	49	6	1
Bradford, Larry, Atlanta*	0.95	4	3	.571	21	0	0	9	0	0	47	33	202	5	5	0	1	2	10	2	0	11	1	0
Brett, Kenneth, Los Angeles*	3.45	6	6	.500	30	19	2	0	0	0	133	133	487	57	51	6	7	5	33	11	3	64	2	0
Brizzolara, Anthony, Atlanta	5.30	1	3	.250	20	10	0	0	0	0	64	66	283	44	38	6	1	5	37	3	2	27	5	1
Bruno, Thomas, St. Louis	4.26	0	1	.000	21	0	0	8	0	0	23	23	107	14	11	1	1	2	22	2	0	24	0	0
Brusstar, Warren, Philadelphia	4.81	1	0	1.000	29	0	0	14	1	0	43	41	191	25	23	4	4	4	30	5	1	24	1	0
Burris, B. Ray, Chicago-New York	4.81	7	13	.350	33	30	8	0	0	0	204	210	887	116	109	22	9	7	66	4	3	101	6	0
Candelaria, John, Pittsburgh*	3.22	14	9	.609	33	30	8	0	0	0	207	201	850	89	74	25	4	6	41	6	1	101	3	0
Capilla, Douglas, Cincinnati-Chicago*	4.13	1	1	.500	19	0	0	7	0	0	26	23	109	13	12	2	2	2	11	5	0	24	1	0
Carlton, Steven, Philadelphia*	3.62	18	11	.621	35	35	13	0	0	4	251	202	1029	113	101	25	4	4	89	11	1	213	10	0
Castillo, Robert, Los Angeles	1.13	1	1	.500	11	1	0	5	2	0	24	15	110	3	3	0	0	2	21	4	1	27	2	0
Caudill, William, Chicago	4.80	1	7	.125	40	5	0	10	2	0	97	89	402	57	52	16	5	1	41	4	0	104	2	0
Christenson, Larry, Philadelphia	4.50	5	10	.333	19	19	6	0	0	0	122	140	520	63	61	16	4	3	42	6	3	85	5	0
Coleman, Joseph, San Fran.-Pittsburgh	5.25	0	0	.000	15	0	0	6	1	0	24	32	119	14	14	9	2	0	11	1	0	22	3	0
Curtis, John, San Francisco*	4.17	10	9	.526	27	27	2	0	0	0	180	206	810	91	83	15	9	5	86	6	6	97	5	0
D'Acquisto, John, San Diego	4.90	8	11	.421	51	18	3	11	0	0	134	140	610	83	73	15	4	8	100	6	3	99	7	0
Denny, John, St. Louis	4.85	8	11	.421	31	31	6	0	0	2	206	206	900	116	111	24	3	4	86	5	3	97	5	0
Devine, P. Adrian, Atlanta	3.22	1	0	1.000	54	0	0	23	1	0	67	67	302	28	24	8	4	3	25	6	1	22	0	0
Dixon, Thomas, Houston	6.58	0	1	.000	4	1	0	0	0	0	26	39	130	23	19	2	0	0	15	0	0	9	1	0
Easterly, James, Atlanta*	12.00	0	0	.000	4	0	0	6	0	0	6	15	39	11	8	2	0	0	3	0	0	3	0	0
Eastwick, Rawlins, Philadelphia	4.88	3	6	.333	33	0	0	0	1	0	83	90	349	46	45	8	4	0	25	3	0	47	0	0
Eichelberger, Juan, San Diego	3.43	1	2	.333	5	3	0	0	0	0	21	15	83	9	8	0	0	0	12	0	0	12	1	0
Ellis, Dock, New York-Pittsburgh	5.77	4	12	.250	33	24	3	0	0	0	92	119	420	59	59	10	3	10	36	8	10	42	3	0
Espinosa, Arnulfo, Philadelphia	3.65	14	12	.538	31	31	8	0	0	0	212	211	881	91	86	20	15	6	65	10	8	113	3	0
Falcone, Peter, New York*	4.16	6	14	.300	31	31	1	0	0	0	184	194	797	97	85	20	13	5	76	10	1	110	6	0
Fingers, Roland, San Diego	4.50	9	9	.500	54	0	0	41	13	0	84	91	372	47	42	14	5	3	37	10	1	65	2	0
Forsch, Kenneth, Houston	3.03	11	6	.647	33	24	6	0	1	0	212	194	881	91	90	16	10	8	65	10	8	92	3	0
Forsch, Robert, St. Louis	3.82	11	11	.500	32	32	10	0	0	3	219	215	894	102	93	16	13	0	35	11	2	58	6	2
Forster, Terry, Los Angeles*	5.63	1	2	.333	17	0	0	7	2	0	16	18	73	11	10	3	0	0	11	1	0	8	0	0
Frazier, George, St. Louis	4.50	2	4	.333	25	0	0	14	1	0	32	35	143	19	16	4	0	1	22	4	0	14	6	0
Fryman, Woodrow, Montreal*	2.79	3	6	.333	44	0	0	10	0	0	58	52	240	25	18	4	5	0	22	3	3	44	2	0

Pitcher and Club	ERA.	W.	L.	Pct.	G.	GS.	CG.	GF.	Sv.	ShO.	IP.	H.	BFP.	R.	ER.	HR.	SH.	SF.	Tot. BB.	Int. BB.	HB.	SO.	WP.	Bk.
Fulgham, John, St. Louis	2.53	10	6	.625	20	19	10	0	0	2	146	123	576	47	41	10	4	3	26	3	3	75	2	1
Garber, H. Eugene, Atlanta	4.33	6	16	.273	68	0	0	55	25	0	106	121	461	66	51	10	10	0	24	10	5	56	0	0
Geisel, J. David, Chicago*	0.60	0	0	.000	7	0	0	0	0	0	15	10	58	1	1	0	1	0	3	0	0	5	0	0
Glynn, Edward, New York*	3.00	1	0	.200	46	0	0	20	7	0	60	57	269	22	20	3	0	3	40	8	1	32	5	0
Griffin, Thomas, San Francisco	3.93	4	6	.455	59	3	0	13	2	0	94	83	407	46	41	9	5	0	46	4	2	82	2	0
Grimsley, Ross, Montreal*	5.36	10	9	.526	32	27	3	0	0	0	151	199	678	102	90	18	7	0	48	8	4	42	0	1
Gullickson, William, Montreal	0.00	0	0	.000	1	0	0	0	0	0	2	4		0	0	0	0	0	0	0	0	0	0	0
Halicki, Edward, San Francisco	4.57	5	8	.385	33	19	0	1	0	0	126	134	562	82	64	12	5	1	47	8	3	81	2	0
Hanna, Preston, Atlanta	3.00	1	2	.500	6	4	0	2	0	0	24	27	112	11	8	6	2	0	15	1	0	15	0	0
Hannams, Gerald, Los Angeles*	3.38	0	1	.000	4	0	0	2	0	0	10	10	71	12	8	1	1	1	13	0	3	6	1	0
Hassler, Andrew, New York*	3.71	4	5	.444	29	8	0	11	1	0	80	74	343	35	33	2	6	1	42	8	1	53	1	1
Hausman, Thomas, New York	2.73	4	1	.250	9	10	2	0	1	0	79	65	315	35	24	5	6	2	13	1	0	33	1	0
Hernandez, Guillermo, Chicago*	5.01	4	4	.500	51	2	0	19	4	0	79	85	359	50	44	8	7	0	39	12	0	53	2	0
Holland, Alfred, San Francisco*	0.00	0	0	.000	3	0	0	0	0	0	5	5	29	5	0	0	0	0	7	0	0	7	1	0
Holtzman, Kenneth, Chicago	4.58	6	9	.400	23	20	3	0	0	0	118	133	529	75	60	15	14	0	53	4	4	44	0	0
Hooton, Burt, Los Angeles	2.97	11	10	.524	30	29	12	0	0	3	212	191	874	85	70	11	9	6	63	4	2	129	0	0
Hough, Charles, Los Angeles	4.77	7	5	.583	42	14	0	10	2	0	151	152	662	88	80	16	9	5	66	9	8	76	0	0
Hume, Thomas, Cincinnati	2.76	10	9	.526	57	2	0	33	17	0	163	162	669	58	50	12	5	6	33	8	2	80	5	0
Jackson, Grant, Pittsburgh*	2.96	8	5	.615	72	0	0	29	14	0	82	67	339	34	27	9	5	3	35	11	0	39	3	1
Jackson, Roy, New York	2.25	1	0	1.000	8	0	0	2	0	0	16	11	61	4	4	1	0	1	5	1	0	10	1	0
James, Robert, Montreal	13.50	0	0	.000	3	0	0	1	0	0	2	2	11	3	3	0	0	0	3	0	0	1	0	0
Jones, Randall, San Diego*	3.63	11	12	.478	39	39	6	0	0	0	263	257	1088	120	106	17	23	3	64	10	3	112	2	0
Kaat, James, Philadelphia*	4.50	1	0	1.000	3	1	0	2	0	0	8	8	37	4	4	1	0	0	3	0	1	4	0	0
Kinney, Dennis, San Diego	3.50	0	0	.000	13	0	0	4	0	0	18	17	78	8	7	1	8	0	8	5	0	11	0	0
Kison, Bruce, Pittsburgh	3.19	13	7	.650	33	25	3	3	0	0	172	157	704	70	61	13	12	3	45	8	6	105	0	2
Knepper, Robert, San Francisco*	4.65	9	12	.429	34	34	6	0	0	0	207	241	926	117	107	30	10	5	77	7	0	123	4	0
Knowles, Darold, St. Louis*	4.04	2	5	.286	48	0	0	18	1	0	49	54	214	24	22	5	11	1	27	8	0	22	0	1
Kobel, Kevin, New York*	3.50	6	8	.429	30	27	1	0	0	1	162	172	683	74	63	14	12	4	46	12	1	67	0	1
Krukow, Michael, Chicago	4.20	9	9	.500	28	28	2	0	0	0	165	177	722	84	77	13	4	0	81	2	3	119	3	0
Kucek, John, Philadelphia	9.00	0	1	.000	3	0	0	2	0	0	4	6	20	4	4	0	1	0	1	0	0	2	0	0
LaCorte, Frank, Atlanta-Houston	5.66	1	2	.333	18	3	0	5	0	0	35	30	152	23	22	5	1	0	15	1	1	30	1	0
LaCoss, Michael, Cincinnati	3.50	14	8	.636	35	32	6	0	0	0	206	202	868	92	80	13	12	6	79	7	3	73	1	0
Ladd, Peter, Houston	3.00	1	1	.500	12	0	0	4	1	0	12	8	56	8	4	0	3	0	8	0	0	6	0	0
LaGrow, Lerrin, Los Angeles	3.41	5	10	.333	31	0	0	18	1	0	37	38	161	16	14	2	2	0	18	5	0	22	3	0
Lamp, Dennis, Chicago	3.51	11	10	.524	38	32	6	0	0	0	200	223	843	96	78	14	8	4	62	6	6	86	3	0
Larson, Daniel, Philadelphia	4.26	1	1	.500	3	3	0	0	0	0	19	17	81	11	9	5	1	0	9	2	0	9	0	0
Lavelle, Gary, San Francisco*	2.51	7	9	.438	70	0	0	55	20	0	97	86	407	31	27	5	9	5	42	15	2	80	0	0
Lee, Mark, San Diego	4.29	2	4	.333	46	0	0	18	5	0	65	88	302	34	31	5	9	0	25	6	0	25	0	0
Lee, William, Montreal*	3.04	16	10	.615	33	33	6	0	0	1	222	230	925	91	75	20	9	3	46	5	0	59	0	0
LeBrandt, Charles, Cincinnati*	3.74	0	0	.000	3	1	0	1	0	0	12	19	61	9	5	1	0	2	7	0	0	5	0	0
Lerch, Randy, Philadelphia*	3.74	10	13	.435	37	35	6	0	0	0	214	228	899	98	89	20	11	15	60	5	3	92	3	1
Lewallyn, Dennis, Los Angeles	5.25	0	1	.000	10	0	0	5	0	0	12	19	61	8	7	1	3	0	5	1	0	5	0	0
Littell, Mark, St. Louis	2.20	9	4	.692	63	0	0	40	13	0	82	60	342	22	20	2	1	3	39	4	3	67	7	1
Lockwood, Claude, New York	1.50	2	5	.286	27	5	0	22	9	0	42	33	164	13	7	3	5	0	14	5	0	42	2	0
Lolich, Michael, San Diego*	4.78	2	5	.286	27	5	0	7	0	0	49	59	223	30	26	6	4	1	24	4	1	20	2	0
Lonborg, James, Philadelphia	11.57	0	1	.000	4	1	0	2	0	0	7	14	41	13	9	3	5	0	4	0	1		0	0

Pitcher and Club	ERA	W.	L.	Pct.	G.	GS.	CG.	GF.	Sv.	ShO.	IP.	H.	BFP.	R.	ER.	HR.	SH.	SF.	Tot. BB.	Int. BB.	HB.	SO.	WP.	Bk.
Mahler, Michael, Atlanta*	5.85	5	11	.313	26	18	0	1	0	0	100	123	470	72	65	11	7	9	47	7	3	71	4	1
Mahler, Richard, Atlanta	6.14	0	0	.000	15	0	0	5	0	0	22	28	101	16	15	4	0	1	11	2	0	12	1	2
Martinez, Silvio, St. Louis	3.26	15	8	.652	33	29	7	1	0	1	207	204	867	90	75	14	7	6	67	9	0	102	3	1
Matula, Richard, Atlanta	4.16	8	10	.444	33	28	8	2	0	1	171	193	754	90	79	14	6	4	64	8	1	67	1	0
May, Rudolph, Montreal*	2.30	10	3	.769	45	7	1	8	2	0	94	88	393	32	24	6	6	3	31	7	3	67	1	0
McEnaney, William, St. Louis*	2.95	0	0	.000	42	0	0	21	2	0	64	60	267	26	21	2	8	2	16	5	1	15	1	0
McGlothen, Lynn, Chicago	4.12	13	14	.481	42	29	6	6	2	2	212	236	906	113	97	27	7	9	59	8	2	147	3	1
McGraw, Frank, Philadelphia*	5.14	4	3	.571	65	0	0	43	16	0	84	83	357	56	48	4	7	2	54	7	3	57	1	0
McLaughlin, Joey, Atlanta	2.48	5	3	.625	49	1	0	13	5	0	69	54	285	22	19	3	2	2	34	6	2	40	0	0
McLaughlin, Michael, Hou-Atl	5.05	2	3	.400	13	13	0	0	0	0	66	85	306	48	37	4	5	4	22	2	1	32	5	0
McWilliams, Larry, Atlanta	5.59	3	2	.600	11	11	2	0	0	0	66	69	287	41	41	4	4	0	20	0	2	41	3	0
Mendoza, Michael, Houston	0.00	0	0	.000	11	0	0	0	0	0	1	3	3	0	0	0	0	0	0	0	0	0	0	0
Messersmith, J. Alexander, Los Angeles	4.94	2	4	.333	11	11	1	0	0	0	62	55	266	34	34	9	6	0	34	2	0	26	1	0
Minton, Gregory, San Francisco	1.80	4	3	.571	46	0	0	18	4	0	80	59	314	25	16	0	11	7	27	7	2	33	3	0
Moffitt, Randall, San Francisco	7.71	2	5	.286	28	0	0	13	0	0	35	53	170	33	30	5	1	2	14	3	0	16	1	0
Montefusco, John, San Francisco	3.94	3	8	.273	39	22	10	2	1	2	137	145	585	64	60	15	5	1	51	6	2	76	8	1
Moore, Donnie, Chicago	5.18	1	4	.200	15	0	0	12	0	0	73	95	330	46	42	8	4	0	25	1	0	43	6	0
Moskau, Paul, Cincinnati	3.91	5	4	.556	38	15	1	4	0	0	106	97	470	53	46	9	5	5	51	5	1	58	3	0
Mura, Stephen, San Diego	3.08	5	5	.500	67	5	0	27	0	0	110	119	481	50	25	6	8	3	37	1	7	59	2	0
Murray, Dale, New York-Montreal	4.32	3	10	.333	25	0	0	4	2	0	100	105	435	62	48	14	5	2	55	8	1	47	1	0
Nastu, Philip, San Francisco*	3.00	3	4	.429	11	14	0	0	0	0	73	57	309	51	41	4	4	16	41	1	1	19	1	0
Niekro, Joseph, Houston	3.39	21	11	.656	26	38	11	0	0	2	264	221	1095	160	88	1	7	1	107	8	1	119	19	4
Niekro, Philip, Atlanta	3.76	21	20	.512	44	44	23	0	0	4	342	311	1436	160	129	41	14	5	113	11	11	208	18	2
Niemann, Randy, Houston*	3.80	3	2	.600	26	0	0	6	0	0	67	72	287	40	38	1	8	1	22	2	0	18	0	1
Noles, Dickie, Philadelphia	3.65	3	4	.429	14	14	1	2	0	0	90	93	377	48	38	8	7	2	38	0	2	24	0	0
Norman, Fredie, Cincinnati*	8.18	11	13	.458	34	31	4	0	0	1	195	193	817	88	88	17	8	7	57	6	2	95	4	1
O'Brien, Daniel, St. Louis	4.89	1	1	.500	18	0	0	6	0	0	11	13	55	10	10	1	2	0	3	0	1	22	2	0
Orosco, Jesse, New York*	3.74	1	2	.333	18	2	0	7	0	0	35	33	154	20	19	4	2	0	22	7	0	66	1	0
Owchinko, Robert, San Diego	4.50	6	12	.333	42	3	0	0	7	0	149	144	631	73	62	16	7	6	55	7	4	12	3	0
Pacella, John, New York	4.50	0	2	.000	3	2	0	0	0	0	16	16	69	10	9	4	0	0	8	1	0	72	0	0
Palmer, David, Montreal	4.26	10	2	.833	36	14	2	7	4	1	123	110	502	41	36	10	8	7	30	5	7	72	5	1
Pastore, Frank, Cincinnati	2.63	6	7	.462	36	9	0	2	1	0	95	102	407	47	45	8	5	6	23	6	1	63	1	0
Patterson, David, Los Angeles	5.26	4	1	.800	36	0	0	13	6	0	53	62	238	35	31	5	1	0	22	0	0	34	3	0
Perry, Gaylord, San Diego	3.05	12	11	.522	32	32	10	0	0	2	233	225	963	90	79	12	14	10	67	10	4	140	4	0
Pladson, Gordon, Houston	4.50	0	0	.000	4	0	0	3	0	0	10	12	47	7	7	1	0	0	2	0	0	0	0	0
Plank, Edward, San Francisco	6.75	0	0	.000	4	0	0	0	0	0	4	9	22	9	9	0	0	0	9	0	1	6	0	0
Rasmussen, Eric, San Diego	3.27	6	9	.400	45	11	1	11	3	3	157	142	643	59	57	9	12	6	42	6	2	54	5	0
Rau, Douglas, Los Angeles	5.30	1	5	.167	11	11	1	0	0	0	56	73	260	37	33	4	5	1	22	2	0	28	0	0
Rautzhan, Clarence, Los Angeles*	7.20	0	2	.000	12	0	0	10	0	0	10	12	47	8	8	2	2	0	11	1	0	5	3	0
Reardon, Jeffrey, New York	1.71	1	1	.333	18	0	0	10	2	0	21	12	81	9	4	5	2	2	9	9	1	58	1	0
Reed, Ronald, Philadelphia	4.15	13	8	.619	61	0	0	37	9	0	102	101	439	52	47	9	5	9	32	8	2	125	2	0
Reuschel, Ricky, Chicago	3.62	18	12	.600	36	36	5	0	0	5	239	251	1021	104	96	16	13	8	75	7	10	83	3	0
Reuss, Jerry, Los Angeles*	3.54	7	14	.333	39	21	7	3	0	1	160	178	712	88	63	13	14	7	60	10	3	20	8	0
Rhoden, Richard, Pittsburgh	7.09	0	2	.000	11	2	0	0	0	0	5	5	21	4	4	0	0	0	2	0	0	313	2	0
Riccelli, Frank, Houston*	4.09	2	2	.500	11	0	0	3	0	0	22	22	103	11	10	4	3	3	18	3	3	20	0	1
Richard, James, Houston	2.71	18	13	.581	38	38	19	0	0	4	292	220	1175	98	88	13	14	8	98	5	3	313	19	1

Pitcher and Club	ERA.	W.	L.	Pct.	G.	GS.	CG.	GF.	Sv.	ShO.	IP.	H.	BFP.	R.	ER.	HR.	SH.	SF.	Tot. BB.	Int. BB.	HB.	SO.	WP.	Bk.
Riley, George, Chicago*	5.54	0	1	.000	4	1	0	0	0	0	13	16	59	9	8	1	1	1	6	1	2	5	0	0
Roberge, Bertrand, Houston	1.69	3	0	1.000	26	0	0	12	2	0	32	20	120	6	6	0	0	1	17	0	1	13	0	0
Roberts, David A., SF-Pitt.*	2.89	5	4	.556	47	4	0	16	2	0	81	89	352	33	26	4	8	5	30	7	2	38	2	0
Robinson, Don, Pittsburgh	3.86	8	8	.500	29	25	4	1	0	0	161	171	684	97	69	12	21	4	52	9	0	74	6	1
Rogers, Stephen, Montreal	3.00	13	12	.520	37	37	13	0	0	5	249	232	1032	93	83	14	7	5	78	9	2	143	10	1
Romo, Enrique, Pittsburgh	3.00	5	5	.500	84	0	0	25	5	0	129	106	537	58	43	11	3	2	43	5	3	106	4	0
Rooker, James, Pittsburgh*	4.59	4	7	.364	19	17	1	0	0	0	104	122	444	58	53	11	7	4	39	0	2	44	3	0
Ruhle, Vernon, Houston	4.09	2	6	.250	13	9	2	1	0	0	66	64	269	40	30	10	2	0	8	4	2	33	3	0
Ruthven, Richard, Philadelphia	4.28	7	5	.583	20	20	3	0	0	0	122	121	518	69	58	8	4	2	37	2	4	58	2	0
Sambito, Joseph, Houston*	1.78	8	7	.533	63	0	0	51	22	0	91	80	375	23	18	16	6	4	23	7	1	83	3	3
Sanderson, Scott, Montreal	3.43	9	8	.529	23	24	5	0	0	2	168	148	696	69	64	14	5	3	54	4	1	138	0	0
Sarmiento, Manuel, Cincinnati	4.62	0	4	.000	23	1	0	3	1	0	39	47	164	21	20	2	5	1	23	3	0	23	0	0
Saucier, Kevin, Philadelphia*	4.21	4	3	.571	29	2	0	5	0	0	62	68	277	31	29	4	4	1	33	3	1	21	2	0
Schatzeder, Daniel, Montreal*	2.83	10	5	.667	32	21	7	1	0	1	162	136	677	57	51	17	10	3	59	5	0	106	6	1
Schultz, C. Budd, St. Louis*	4.50	1	3	.250	31	0	0	12	2	0	42	40	178	25	21	4	5	3	14	2	0	38	2	0
Scott, Michael, New York*	5.37	1	3	.250	18	0	0	7	0	0	52	59	229	35	31	0	4	1	20	0	0	21	1	0
Seaman, Kim, St. Louis*	0.00	0	0	.000	9	0	0	3	0	0	8	8	14	0	0	0	0	0	5	0	0	3	0	0
Seaver, G. Thomas, Cincinnati	3.14	16	6	.727	32	32	9	0	0	5	215	187	868	85	75	16	10	9	61	6	3	131	6	0
Shirley, Robert, San Diego*	3.38	8	16	.333	49	25	5	13	0	1	205	217	843	89	77	15	9	4	67	8	6	117	9	0
Skok, Craig, Atlanta	4.00	2	4	.333	44	0	0	19	2	0	54	58	232	26	24	7	3	1	17	4	1	30	2	1
Solomon, Eddie, Atlanta	4.00	6	7	.462	34	16	2	7	0	0	186	184	792	98	83	19	9	4	87	11	2	96	8	0
Sosa, Elias, Montreal	1.95	8	7	.533	62	0	0	41	18	0	97	77	396	24	22	7	5	1	34	11	1	59	4	0
Soto, Mario, Cincinnati	5.35	3	0	.600	30	11	1	7	0	0	37	33	169	25	22	7	2	0	22	0	0	32	2	0
Sprowl, Robert, Houston*	0.00	0	0	.000	7	0	0	0	0	0	4	3	14	0	0	0	0	0	0	0	0	3	0	0
Sutcliffe, Richard, Los Angeles	3.46	17	10	.630	39	30	5	2	1	0	242	217	1016	104	93	16	16	5	97	6	1	117	9	0
Sutter, H. Bruce, Chicago	2.23	6	6	.500	62	0	0	56	37	0	101	67	403	29	25	5	6	9	32	11	2	110	1	0
Sutton, Donald, Los Angeles	3.82	12	15	.444	35	32	9	0	0	2	226	201	927	109	96	21	15	5	61	5	2	146	4	1
Swan, Craig, New York	3.30	14	13	.519	35	35	10	0	0	0	251	241	1027	102	92	20	13	11	57	6	2	145	8	0
Sykes, Robert, St. Louis*	6.18	10	8	.556	11	11	0	0	0	0	67	86	310	49	46	11	5	2	34	8	1	35	3	0
Tekulve, Kenton, Pittsburgh	2.75	10	8	.556	94	0	0	67	31	0	134	109	550	46	41	5	17	7	49	20	0	75	4	0
Tellmann, Thomas, San Diego	15.00	0	0	.000	6	1	0	2	0	0	3	7	15	5	5	1	0	0	3	0	0	1	0	0
Thomas, Roy, St. Louis	2.92	3	3	.429	26	0	0	9	2	0	77	66	308	29	25	4	9	1	24	3	3	44	2	0
Throop, George, Houston	3.27	1	0	1.000	14	0	0	6	2	0	22	23	100	10	8	1	2	1	15	0	1	15	3	0
Tidrow, Richard, Chicago	2.71	11	5	.688	63	0	0	27	0	0	103	86	425	35	31	7	6	3	42	11	2	68	7	0
Tomlin, David, Cincinnati*	2.64	2	3	.500	53	2	0	17	1	0	58	59	244	29	17	6	6	2	18	5	4	30	1	0
Twitchell, Wayne, New York	5.20	5	3	.625	34	2	0	9	0	0	64	55	294	44	37	5	3	3	55	4	1	44	6	0
Urrea, John, St. Louis	4.09	3	4	.429	25	7	0	5	0	0	11	13	51	5	5	1	6	0	5	3	0	5	0	0
Vuckovich, Peter, St. Louis	3.59	15	10	.600	37	32	12	1	0	2	233	229	968	108	93	22	14	5	64	3	3	145	9	3
Welch, Robert, Los Angeles	4.00	5	6	.455	31	25	3	1	0	1	81	82	349	42	36	7	10	3	32	4	5	64	9	0
Whitson, Eddie, Pitt.-SF	4.10	7	11	.389	31	24	2	5	0	0	158	151	702	83	72	16	10	2	75	9	2	93	5	1
Williams, Richard, Houston	3.27	4	7	.364	31	16	0	3	0	0	121	122	508	45	44	6	5	0	30	2	0	37	6	1
Wilson, Gary, Houston	12.86	0	0	.000	6	0	0	3	1	0	7	15	42	10	10	2	3	0	6	0	2	6	0	1
Zachry, Patrick, New York	3.56	5	1	.833	7	7	0	0	0	0	43	44	194	19	17	3	6	0	21	2	1	17	1	1

NOTE—Following pitchers combined to pitch shutout games: Atlanta (2)—McWilliams, Devine and Garber; McWilliams and Garber; Chicago (6)—Reuschel and Sutter 2, Krukow, Caudill, Tidrow and Sutter, Krukow and Moore, Krukow, Tidrow and Sutter, McGlothen and Sutter; Cincinnati (3)—Bonham and Borbon, Bonham and Hume, LaCoss and Bair; Houston (2)—Forsch, Niemann and Sambito, Richard and Sambito; Los Angeles (1)—Welch and Beckwith; Montreal (5)—Grimsley and Sosa, Lee and Sosa, Palmer and Fryman, Sanderson and Sosa, Schatzeder and Sanderson; New York (5)—Falcone and Allen, Falcone and Kobel, Kobel and Glynn, Kobel and Lockwood, Swan and Lockwood; Philadelphia (4)—Carlton and McGraw, Christenson, McGraw and Reed, Espinosa and McGraw, Ruthven and Reed; Pittsburgh (5)—Candelaria and Tekulve 3, D. Robinson and Jackson, Rooker, Romo and Jackson; St. Louis (3)—Denny and Littell, Forsch and Littell, Sykes, Bruno and Knowles; San Diego (2)—Jones and D'Acquisto, Perry and Rasmussen; San Francisco (1)—Whitson, Nastu and Borbon.

PITCHERS WITH TWO OR MORE CLUBS
(Alphabetically Arranged With Pitcher's First Club on Top)

Pitcher and Club	ERA.	W.	L.	Pct.	G.	GS.	CG.	GF.	Sv.	ShO.	IP.	H.	BFP.	R.	ER.	HR.	SH.	SF.	Tot. BB.	Int. BB.	HB.	SO.	WP.	Bk.
Borbon, Cincinnati	3.40	2	2	.500	30	0	0	18	2	0	44⅔	48	188	17	17	2	3	1	8		4	23	0	0
Borbon, San Francisco	4.89	4	3	.571	30	0	0	13	3	0	46	56	202	28	25	7	1	1	13		3	26	0	0
Burris, Chicago	6.14	0	2	.000	14	4	0	3	0	0	21⅔	23	98	17	15	0	2	1	15		1	14	0	0
Burris, New York	3.27	0	2	.000	4	4	0	0	0	0	21⅔	21	93	10	8	2	1	1	6		1	10	0	0
Capilla, Cincinnati	9.00	1	0	1.000	5	0	0	0	0	0	6⅓	7	32	6	6	1	0	0	5		0	0	1	0
Capilla, Chicago	2.65	1	0	1.000	13	1	0	7	0	0	17⅓	14	77	6	5	1	1	0	7		0	10	1	0
Coleman, San Francisco	0.00	0	0	.000	5	0	0	1	0	0	3⅔	3	18	2	0	0	1	1	2		0	0	0	0
Coleman, Pittsburgh	6.00	0	0	.000	10	0	0	2	0	0	20⅔	29	101	14	14	1	1	1	7		1	14	0	3
Ellis, New York	6.04	3	7	.300	17	14	1	1	0	0	85	110	391	60	57	9	6	6	34	10	1	41	2	0
Ellis, Pittsburgh	2.57	0	0	.000	3	1	0	0	0	0	7	9	29	2	2	1	0	0	10		0	1	1	1
LaCorte, Atlanta	7.88	0	2	.000	6	0	0	3	0	0	8	9	38	7	7	1	0	2	5		1	6	2	0
LaCorte, Houston	5.00	1	2	.333	12	3	0	3	0	0	27		114	16	15	0	2	1	16		0	24	1	0
M. McLaughlin, Houston	5.63	1	2	.333	12	0	0	3	0	0	16⅓	22	76	15	10	2	1	1	4		0	12	1	0
M. McLaughlin, Atlanta	4.86	1	1	.500	37	1	0	12	0	0	49⅔	63	230	33	27	2	1	3	16	6	2	45	0	0
Murray, New York	4.82	4	8	.333	58	0	0	24	4	0	97	105	428	58	52	6	7	3	52	14	0	37	3	0
Murray, Montreal	2.77	1	2	.333	9	0	0	3	1	0	13⅓	14	53	5	4	1	3	1	18		1	4	0	0
Roberts, San Francisco	2.57	0	2	.000	26	3	0	11	1	0	42	42	182	15	12	3	2	1	18		1	23	1	1
Roberts, Pittsburgh	3.23	5	2	.714	21	9	1	5	1	0	38⅔	47	170	18	14	1	6	3	12		1	15	2	0
Whitson, Pittsburgh	4.34	2	3	.400	19	7	0	4	1	0	57⅔	53	263	36	28	6	3	0	36		1	31	2	1
Whitson, San Francisco	3.96	5	8	.385	18	17	2	1	0	0	100⅓	98	439	47	44	5	9	3	39		4	62	3	1

1979 NL Pitching Against Each Club

ATLANTA—66-94

Pitcher	Chi. W–L	Cin. W–L	Hou. W–L	L.A. W–L	Mtl. W–L	N.Y. W–L	Phil. W–L	Pitt. W–L	St.L. W–L	S.D. W–L	S.F. W–L	Totals W–L
Boggs	0–0	0–0	0–2	0–0	0–0	0–0	0–0	0–0	0–0	0–0	0–0	0– 2
Bradford	0–0	0–0	0–0	0–0	0–0	0–0	1–0	0–0	0–0	0–0	0–0	1– 0
Brizzolara	1–1	0–1	1–0	1–0	0–2	0–1	0–1	0–0	1–1	1–2	1–0	6– 9
Devine	0–0	0–0	0–0	0–1	0–0	0–1	0–0	0–0	0–0	0–0	0–0	1– 2
Garber	0–3	1–2	0–2	1–1	0–1	0–1	1–0	0–1	1–2	1–1	1–2	6–16
Hanna	0–0	0–0	0–0	1–0	0–0	0–0	0–0	0–1	0–0	0–0	0–0	1– 1
M. Mahler	0–0	1–2	1–1	0–1	0–0	0–3	0–1	0–3	0–0	1–0	2–0	5–11
Matula	1–1	0–1	0–2	3–0	1–1	1–0	1–0	0–1	0–0	1–3	0–1	8–10
J. McLaughlin	0–0	1–0	0–0	0–0	0–1	0–1	0–1	0–0	1–0	2–0	1–0	5– 3
M. McLaughlin	0–0	0–0	1–0	0–0	0–0	0–0	0–0	0–0	0–1	0–0	0–0	1– 1
McWilliams	0–0	1–1	0–1	1–0	0–0	0–0	0–0	0–0	0–0	0–0	1–0	3– 2
Niekro	2–2	2–3	3–2	3–2	0–2	2–1	3–1	3–0	0–2	0–4	3–1	21–20
Skok	0–0	0–0	0–0	0–0	0–1	0–0	0–0	0–0	0–1	0–0	1–1	1– 3
Solomon	0–1	0–2	1–1	2–1	0–1	1–0	1–1	1–2	0–2	0–1	1–2	7–14
Totals	4–8	6–12	7–11	12–6	1–9	4–8	7–5	4–8	4–8	6–12	11–7	66–94

No Decisions: LaCorte, Easterly, R. Mahler.

CHICAGO—80-82

Pitcher	Atl. W–L	Cin. W–L	Hou. W–L	L.A. W–L	Mtl. W–L	N.Y. W–L	Phil. W–L	Pitt. W–L	St.L. W–L	S.D. W–L	S.F. W–L	Totals W–L
Capilla	0–0	0–0	0–0	0–0	0–0	0–0	0–0	0–0	0–1	0–0	0–0	0– 1
Caudill	0–0	0–0	0–0	0–2	0–3	0–0	0–1	1–0	0–1	0–0	0–0	1– 7
Hernandez	0–0	1–0	0–0	0–0	0–1	0–0	0–0	2–2	1–1	0–0	0–0	4– 4
Holtzman	0–0	1–2	2–0	0–0	0–0	1–2	0–0	0–3	1–1	1–0	0–1	6– 9
Krukow	1–0	1–0	1–1	0–2	0–1	1–1	1–1	1–1	1–1	1–1	1–0	9– 9
Lamp	1–1	1–1	2–1	2–1	0–1	0–3	2–0	1–0	1–2	0–1	1–0	11–10
McGlothen	1–1	1–1	0–3	1–0	2–2	2–0	3–1	1–3	0–1	1–1	1–1	13–14
Moore	0–1	0–0	0–0	0–0	1–0	0–1	0–1	0–0	0–1	0–0	0–0	1– 4
Reuschel	2–1	0–2	1–1	1–1	2–3	1–1	1–1	2–2	2–0	3–0	3–0	18–12
Riley	0–0	0–0	0–0	0–0	0–0	0–0	0–0	0–1	0–0	0–0	0–0	0– 1
Sutter	1–0	1–0	0–0	0–1	1–1	0–0	1–3	0–1	1–0	0–0	1–0	6– 6
Tidrow	2–0	1–0	0–0	1–0	0–0	3–2	1–1	0–1	0–0	2–0	1–1	11– 5
Totals	8–4	7–5	6–6	5–7	6–12	8–10	9–9	6–12	8–10	9–3	8–4	80–82

No Decisions: Burris, Geisel.

CINCINNATI—90-71

Pitcher	Atl. W–L	Chi. W–L	Hou. W–L	L.A. W–L	Mtl. W–L	N.Y. W–L	Phil. W–L	Pitt. W–L	St.L. W–L	S.D. W–L	S.F. W–L	Totals W–L
Bair	1–2	0–1	1–2	1–0	0–0	2–0	1–2	2–0	0–0	1–0	2–0	11– 7
Bonham	2–1	1–1	0–1	1–1	1–0	1–0	0–0	0–0	0–1	3–1	0–1	9– 7
Borbon	0–0	0–0	1–0	1–1	0–0	0–0	0–1	0–0	0–0	0–0	0–0	2– 2
Capilla	0–0	0–0	0–0	0–0	0–0	0–0	0–0	0–0	1–0	0–0	0–0	1– 0
Hume	2–0	0–1	2–1	1–2	1–2	3–0	0–0	0–2	0–0	0–1	1–0	10– 9
LaCoss	2–0	2–0	0–1	1–0	2–2	2–0	1–0	1–0	2–1	0–1	1–2	14– 8
Moskau	0–0	1–0	0–1	1–1	0–0	0–0	0–0	1–0	1–0	1–0	0–0	5– 4
Norman	2–2	0–2	0–2	2–1	0–1	1–1	0–1	2–0	2–0	1–2	1–1	11–13
Pastore	1–1	0–0	2–0	0–0	0–0	0–0	1–0	0–2	1–0	1–2	0–2	6– 7
Sarmiento	0–0	0–1	0–0	0–0	0–0	0–2	0–0	0–0	0–0	0–0	0–0	0– 4
Seaver	2–0	1–0	2–1	1–1	2–1	1–1	1–1	0–0	2–0	2–1	2–1	16– 6
Soto	0–0	0–1	0–0	1–0	0–0	0–0	1–0	1–0	0–0	0–0	0–0	3– 2
Tomlin	0–0	0–0	0–0	1–0	0–0	0–0	0–0	1–2	0–0	0–0	0–0	2– 2
Totals	12–6	5–7	8–10	11–7	6–6	8–4	8–4	8–4	8–4	10–7	6–12	90–71

No Decisions: Leibrandt.

HOUSTON—89-73

Pitcher	Atl. W–L	Chi. W–L	Cin. W–L	L.A. W–L	Mtl. W–L	N.Y. W–L	Phil. W–L	Pitt. W–L	St.L. W–L	S.D. W–L	S.F. W–L	Totals W–L
Andujar	0–1	0–0	1–1	0–2	3–0	1–1	0–2	2–1	1–0	3–1	1–3	12–12
Dixon	0–0	0–0	0–0	0–1	0–0	0–0	0–0	0–0	0–0	1–0	0–1	1–2
Forsch	2–0	2–1	1–0	3–0	0–0	1–0	0–0	0–1	0–3	0–0	2–1	11–6
LaCorte	1–0	0–0	0–0	0–0	0–0	0–1	0–1	0–0	0–0	0–0	0–0	1–2
Ladd	0–0	0–0	0–0	0–0	0–1	0–0	1–0	0–0	0–0	0–0	0–0	1–1
McLaughlin	0–1	0–0	0–0	0–0	0–0	0–0	0–0	0–0	1–0	0–0	0–1	1–2
Niekro	3–1	2–0	2–1	1–2	1–3	2–0	2–0	0–3	2–0	5–0	1–1	21–11
Niemann	0–0	0–1	2–0	0–0	0–0	0–1	1–0	0–0	0–0	0–0	0–0	3–2
Riccelli	0–0	0–1	1–1	0–0	0–0	0–0	0–0	1–0	0–0	0–0	0–0	2–2
Richard	3–0	2–0	0–3	4–0	3–1	2–0	0–2	0–2	0–2	3–1	1–2	18–13
Roberge	1–0	0–0	0–0	0–0	0–0	1–0	0–0	0–0	0–0	0–0	0–0	3–0
Ruhle	0–1	0–1	0–1	1–2	0–0	0–0	0–0	0–0	0–0	0–0	1–1	2–6
Sambito	1–1	0–0	1–1	0–1	0–0	1–0	1–0	1–1	2–1	1–1	0–1	8–7
Throop	0–0	0–0	0–0	0–0	0–0	1–0	0–0	0–0	0–0	0–0	0–0	1–0
Williams	0–2	0–2	1–0	1–0	0–0	0–0	0–2	0–0	0–0	1–1	1–0	4–7
Totals	11–7	6–6	10–8	10–8	7–5	9–3	5–7	4–8	6–6	14–4	7–11	89–73

No Decisions: Mendoza, Pladson, Sprowl, Wilson.

LOS ANGELES—79-83

Pitcher	Atl. W–L	Chi. W–L	Cin. W–L	Hou. W–L	Mtl. W–L	N.Y. W–L	Phil. W–L	Pitt. W–L	St.L. W–L	S.D. W–L	S.F. W–L	Totals W–L
Beckwith	0–0	0–0	0–1	1–1	0–0	0–0	0–0	0–0	0–0	0–0	0–0	1–2
Brett	0–1	0–0	0–1	1–0	0–0	0–0	0–0	1–0	0–1	2–0	0–0	4–3
Castillo	0–0	0–0	1–0	0–0	0–0	0–0	0–0	0–0	1–0	0–0	0–0	2–0
Forster	0–1	0–0	0–0	0–1	0–0	0–0	0–0	0–0	0–0	1–0	0–0	1–2
Hannahs	0–0	0–0	0–0	0–0	0–0	0–0	0–0	0–0	0–1	0–1	0–0	0–2
Hooton	0–2	2–1	0–1	0–2	1–1	2–1	1–0	0–1	2–1	1–0	2–0	11–10
Hough	1–1	1–0	0–2	2–0	0–0	1–0	0–0	0–1	0–0	1–0	1–1	7–5
LaGrow	1–0	1–0	1–0	0–0	0–0	0–0	0–0	0–0	0–1	1–0	0–0	5–1
Lewallyn	0–0	0–0	0–0	0–0	0–0	0–1	0–0	0–0	0–0	0–0	0–0	0–1
Messersmith	0–2	0–0	0–0	0–0	0–0	1–0	0–1	0–0	0–0	1–1	0–0	2–4
Patterson	0–0	0–0	0–0	0–0	1–0	0–0	0–0	1–0	0–0	0–1	2–0	4–1
Rau	0–1	0–0	0–0	0–1	1–1	0–0	0–1	0–0	0–1	0–0	0–0	1–5
Rautzhan	0–0	0–0	0–0	0–0	0–0	0–0	0–0	0–1	0–0	0–0	0–1	0–2
Reuss	1–1	0–0	0–3	2–2	0–1	1–0	0–1	1–2	0–1	1–1	1–2	7–14
Sutcliffe	0–1	1–3	3–1	1–1	2–0	1–1	2–2	1–0	3–0	1–1	2–0	17–10
Sutton	1–1	2–1	2–2	0–2	0–2	2–0	0–2	0–2	0–0	1–3	4–0	12–15
Welch	2–1	0–0	0–0	1–0	1–1	0–0	0–1	0–2	0–1	0–0	1–0	5–6
Totals	6–12	7–5	7–11	8–10	6–6	9–3	3–9	4–8	6–6	9–9	14–4	79–83

No Decisions: None.

MONTREAL—95-65

Pitcher	Atl. W–L	Chi. W–L	Cin. W–L	Hou. W–L	L.A. W–L	N.Y. W–L	Phil. W–L	Pitt. W–L	St.L. W–L	S.D. W–L	S.F. W–L	Totals W–L
Atkinson	0–0	1–0	0–0	0–0	0–0	1–0	0–0	0–0	0–0	0–0	0–0	2–0
Bahnsen	0–0	0–0	0–0	0–0	0–1	1–0	2–0	0–0	0–0	0–0	0–0	3–1
Fryman	1–0	0–2	1–0	0–0	0–1	0–1	0–1	0–0	0–0	0–1	0–1	3–6
Grimsley	1–0	1–0	0–0	1–1	0–2	1–2	1–0	2–0	1–2	2–0	0–2	10–9
Lee	3–0	2–0	1–1	1–1	3–1	1–1	2–2	0–1	1–2	1–1	1–0	16–10
May	0–0	0–0	0–1	0–1	0–0	3–0	1–0	1–0	2–1	2–0	1–0	10–3
Murray	0–0	0–0	0–0	0–0	0–0	1–0	0–1	0–1	0–0	0–0	0–0	1–2
Palmer	1–0	2–1	1–0	1–0	0–0	3–0	1–0	0–0	1–0	0–0	1–0	10–2
Rogers	2–0	2–1	1–2	0–2	2–0	0–0	2–1	2–2	0–3	1–0	1–1	13–12
Sanderson	0–1	1–2	0–0	0–0	0–0	1–0	1–1	1–3	2–0	1–1	2–0	9–8
Schatzeder	0–0	2–0	1–1	2–0	1–1	1–0	0–0	0–2	1–0	0–0	2–1	10–5
Sosa	1–0	1–0	1–1	0–2	0–0	1–0	1–1	1–2	2–0	0–1	0–0	8–7
Totals	9–1	12–6	6–6	5–7	6–6	15–3	11–7	7–11	10–8	7–5	7–5	95–65

No Decisions: Gullickson, James.

NEW YORK—63-99

Pitcher	Atl. W-L	Chi. W-L	Cin. W-L	Hou. W-L	L.A. W-L	Mtl. W-L	Phil. W-L	Pitt. W-L	St.L. W-L	S.D. W-L	S.F. W-L	Totals W-L
Allen	0-0	1-1	0-2	0-0	1-2	0-1	0-2	1-1	2-0	1-1	0-0	6-10
Berenguer	0-0	0-0	0-0	0-0	0-0	0-0	0-0	1-0	1-0	0-0	0-0	1-1
Bernard	0-0	0-0	0-0	0-0	0-0	0-1	0-0	0-1	0-1	0-0	0-0	0-3
Burris	0-1	0-0	0-0	0-0	0-0	0-1	0-0	0-0	0-0	0-0	0-0	0-2
Ellis	0-1	0-1	0-0	0-0	1-0	1-1	0-2	1-0	0-1	0-1	0-0	3-7
Falcone	1-0	1-2	0-1	1-1	0-3	0-1	1-2	2-1	0-2	0-0	0-1	6-14
Glynn	0-1	0-0	0-0	0-0	0-1	0-0	1-0	0-2	0-0	0-0	0-0	1-4
Hassler	1-0	0-0	0-0	0-1	0-0	0-0	0-2	1-2	1-0	1-0	0-0	4-5
Hausman	0-0	1-1	0-0	0-1	0-0	0-0	0-0	0-1	0-0	0-1	1-0	2-6
Jackson	0-0	0-0	0-0	0-0	0-0	0-0	0-0	0-0	1-0	0-0	0-0	1-0
Kobel	1-1	2-0	0-1	1-2	0-0	0-0	0-0	0-0	0-2	1-2	1-0	6-8
Lockwood	1-0	0-0	0-0	0-0	0-0	0-2	0-0	1-1	0-0	0-1	0-1	2-5
Murray	0-0	0-0	2-2	0-0	0-1	1-0	0-3	0-0	0-1	0-0	0-1	4-8
Orosco	0-0	0-0	0-0	0-0	0-0	0-0	1-0	0-0	0-0	0-0	0-1	1-2
Pacella	0-0	0-1	0-0	0-0	0-0	0-0	0-0	0-0	0-1	0-0	0-0	0-2
Reardon	1-0	0-0	0-1	0-0	0-0	0-1	0-0	0-0	0-0	0-0	0-0	1-2
Scott	0-0	0-1	0-0	0-0	0-0	0-0	0-0	0-0	0-1	0-0	1-0	1-3
Swan	2-0	2-0	1-0	1-3	0-2	2-1	1-3	1-1	1-1	1-1	2-1	14-13
Twitchell	0-0	1-1	1-0	0-0	0-0	0-1	1-0	2-0	0-0	1-0	0-0	5-3
Zachry	1-0	2-0	0-0	0-1	0-0	0-0	1-0	0-0	1-0	0-0	0-0	5-1
Totals	8-4	10-8	4-8	3-9	3-9	3-15	5-13	8-10	7-11	4-8	8-4	63-99

No Decisions: None.

PHILADELPHIA—84-78

Pitcher	Atl. W-L	Chi. W-L	Cin. W-L	Hou. W-L	L.A. W-L	Mtl. W-L	N.Y. W-L	Pitt. W-L	St.L. W-L	S.D. W-L	S.F. W-L	Totals W-L
Bird	1-0	0-0	0-0	0-0	0-0	0-0	0-0	0-0	0-0	1-0	0-0	2-0
Brusstar	0-0	0-0	0-0	0-0	0-0	0-0	1-0	0-0	0-0	0-0	0-0	1-0
Carlton	1-1	2-1	0-3	3-0	0-1	1-0	2-1	3-0	3-1	2-1	1-2	18-11
Christenson	2-2	0-1	0-2	1-1	0-0	2-1	0-0	0-2	0-1	0-0	0-0	5-10
Eastwick	0-1	2-0	0-0	0-0	0-0	0-2	0-0	1-3	0-0	0-0	0-0	3-6
Espinosa	0-1	1-2	1-0	1-1	2-0	1-4	4-1	0-1	3-0	1-1	1-1	14-12
Kaat	0-0	0-0	0-0	0-0	0-0	0-0	0-0	0-0	1-0	0-0	0-0	1-0
Kucek	0-0	0-0	0-0	0-0	0-0	0-0	0-0	1-0	0-0	0-0	0-0	1-0
Larson	0-0	1-0	0-0	0-0	0-0	0-0	0-0	0-0	0-1	0-0	0-0	1-1
Lerch	0-0	0-2	1-1	2-0	2-1	0-1	2-1	2-2	0-3	0-1	1-1	10-13
Lonborg	0-0	0-0	0-1	0-0	0-0	0-0	0-0	0-0	2-1	0-0	0-0	4-3
McGraw	0-0	0-1	1-0	0-0	1-0	0-0	0-0	0-1	0-0	0-0	1-1	3-4
Noles	0-0	0-0	0-0	0-0	1-0	0-1	1-1	0-1	0-0	0-0	0-0	3-4
Reed	1-2	2-1	1-0	0-1	2-0	3-0	1-0	0-0	1-2	1-1	1-1	13-8
Ruthven	0-0	1-0	0-0	0-1	1-1	0-2	2-0	1-0	1-0	1-0	0-0	7-5
Saucier	0-0	0-1	0-1	0-0	0-0	0-0	0-1	0-0	1-0	0-0	0-0	1-4
Totals	5-7	9-9	4-8	7-5	9-3	7-11	13-5	8-10	7-11	9-3	6-6	84-78

No Decisions: Anderson.

PITTSBURGH—98-64

Pitcher	Atl. W-L	Chi. W-L	Cin. W-L	Hou. W-L	L.A. W-L	Mtl. W-L	N.Y. W-L	Phil. W-L	St.L. W-L	S.D. W-L	S.F. W-L	Totals W-L
Bibby	3-0	2-0	1-0	1-1	0-1	1-0	0-1	2-0	1-1	0-0	1-0	12-4
Blyleven	1-0	1-0	0-0	1-0	3-0	3-1	1-1	0-3	1-0	1-0	0-0	12-5
Candelaria	3-0	1-1	0-2	1-1	1-0	0-1	2-1	1-0	2-0	1-3	2-0	14-9
Jackson	0-0	0-0	1-1	0-0	0-0	2-1	3-1	0-1	1-1	0-0	1-0	8-5
Kison	0-0	3-1	0-1	3-0	0-0	2-1	0-0	1-0	0-1	3-1	1-2	13-7
Rhoden	0-1	1-0	0-0	0-0	0-0	0-0	0-0	0-0	0-0	0-0	0-0	0-1
Roberts	0-0	0-0	0-1	1-0	0-0	0-0	1-0	0-0	2-1	1-0	0-0	5-2
D. Robinson	1-0	2-3	1-1	0-0	1-1	1-0	0-1	0-1	1-1	0-0	1-0	8-8
Romo	0-0	0-0	0-0	1-0	0-1	0-1	1-0	3-2	2-0	0-1	2-1	10-5
Rooker	0-2	2-1	0-0	0-0	0-1	1-0	0-2	1-0	0-1	0-0	0-0	4-7
Tekulve	0-1	1-0	1-1	0-1	1-1	1-1	2-1	2-1	0-1	1-0	1-0	10-8
Whitson	0-0	0-0	0-1	0-0	1-0	0-1	0-0	0-0	1-0	0-0	0-0	2-3
Totals	8-4	12-6	4-8	8-4	8-4	11-7	10-8	10-8	11-7	7-5	9-3	98-64

No Decisions: Coleman, Ellis.

ST. LOUIS—86-76

Pitcher	Atl. W-L	Chi. W-L	Cin. W-L	Hou. W-L	L.A. W-L	Mtl. W-L	N.Y. W-L	Phil. W-L	Pitt. W-L	S.D. W-L	S.F. W-L	Totals W-L
Bruno	0-0	1-0	0-0	0-2	1-0	0-0	0-1	0-0	0-0	0-0	0-0	2-3
Denny	1-0	0-2	0-2	1-0	0-2	2-2	2-0	1-1	0-2	0-0	1-0	8-11
Forsch	0-1	2-1	0-0	0-0	1-1	3-0	1-1	1-2	1-4	1-1	1-0	11-11
Frazier	1-1	0-0	0-0	0-0	0-1	0-0	0-1	1-0	0-0	0-0	0-0	2-4
Fulgham	0-0	1-2	0-1	1-1	0-0	1-2	1-0	1-0	1-0	2-0	2-0	10-6
Knowles	0-0	0-0	0-0	1-0	0-0	0-0	1-1	0-1	0-1	0-1	0-1	2-5
Littell	2-1	1-0	0-1	0-0	0-0	0-0	1-1	3-0	1-0	0-0	1-1	9-4
Martinez	1-1	2-1	1-1	1-0	0-2	2-1	2-0	1-1	2-0	3-0	0-1	15-8
McEnaney	0-0	0-0	0-0	0-1	0-0	0-1	0-0	0-0	0-0	0-1	0-0	0-3
O'Brien	0-0	0-0	0-0	0-0	0-0	0-0	0-0	0-0	0-1	1-0	0-0	1-1
Schultz	1-0	0-0	0-0	0-0	1-0	0-1	0-0	0-0	0-1	0-0	1-1	4-3
Sykes	0-0	1-0	0-2	1-0	0-0	0-0	1-1	0-0	1-0	0-0	0-0	4-3
Thomas	0-0	0-1	0-0	0-0	1-0	0-2	1-0	0-0	0-1	0-0	1-0	3-4
Vuckovich	2-0	2-1	2-1	1-2	2-0	0-1	1-1	4-0	0-2	1-1	0-1	15-10
Totals	8-4	10-8	4-8	6-6	6-6	8-10	11-7	11-7	7-11	8-4	7-5	86-76

No Decisions: Seaman, Urrea.

SAN DIEGO—68-93

Pitcher	Atl. W-L	Chi. W-L	Cin. W-L	Hou. W-L	L.A. W-L	Mtl. W-L	N.Y. W-L	Phil. W-L	Pitt. W-L	St.L. W-L	S.F. W-L	Totals W-L
D'Acquisto	3-0	1-2	0-1	0-2	0-0	0-2	1-0	2-2	1-2	0-0	1-2	9-13
Eichelberger	0-1	0-0	0-0	0-0	1-0	0-0	0-0	0-0	0-0	0-0	0-0	1-1
Fingers	1-2	0-1	1-0	2-2	1-1	0-0	0-0	1-3	0-0	1-0	2-0	9-9
Jones	2-0	0-3	2-2	1-1	0-2	2-1	1-0	0-0	1-1	1-2	1-0	11-12
Lee	0-1	0-0	1-1	0-0	0-0	0-0	1-0	0-0	0-0	0-1	0-1	2-4
Lolich	0-0	0-0	0-0	0-1	0-0	0-0	0-0	0-0	0-0	0-0	0-1	0-2
Mura	0-0	0-0	0-2	0-0	1-1	2-0	0-1	0-0	0-0	0-0	1-0	4-4
Owchinko	1-1	0-1	0-0	0-2	1-1	1-2	1-0	0-1	1-1	0-2	1-1	6-12
Perry	1-1	1-1	1-1	0-2	2-0	0-1	3-0	0-2	2-1	1-1	1-1	12-11
Rasmussen	2-0	1-0	0-1	1-2	1-2	0-0	0-0	0-1	0-0	0-2	1-1	6-9
Shirley	2-0	0-1	2-2	0-2	2-2	0-1	1-3	0-0	0-2	1-0	0-3	8-16
Totals	12-6	3-9	7-10	4-14	9-9	5-7	8-4	3-9	5-7	4-8	8-10	68-93

No Decisions: Kinney, Tellmann.

SAN FRANCISCO—71-91

Pitcher	Atl. W-L	Chi. W-L	Cin. W-L	Hou. W-L	L.A. W-L	Mtl. W-L	N.Y. W-L	Phil. W-L	Pitt. W-L	St.L. W-L	S.D. W-L	Totals W-L
Blue	1-2	0-1	2-1	2-1	2-1	2-1	1-2	0-2	1-1	0-2	3-0	14-14
Borbon	0-0	0-1	1-0	1-0	0-0	0-0	1-0	0-0	0-0	0-0	1-1	4-3
Curtis	1-0	2-1	2-1	0-1	0-1	1-1	0-0	1-1	0-2	1-1	2-0	10-9
Griffin	1-0	0-0	1-0	0-1	0-2	1-0	0-1	0-1	0-0	1-0	1-1	5-6
Halicki	0-1	0-0	1-0	2-1	0-3	0-2	1-1	1-0	0-0	0-0	0-0	5-8
Knepper	2-0	1-1	0-1	1-0	0-3	0-1	0-2	3-1	1-1	0-1	1-1	9-12
Lavelle	1-1	0-1	1-0	1-0	1-3	0-0	1-0	0-0	1-3	1-0	0-1	7-9
Minton	1-1	0-0	0-0	3-1	0-0	0-0	0-0	0-0	0-0	0-0	0-1	4-3
Moffitt	0-1	1-1	0-0	0-0	0-0	0-0	0-1	0-0	0-0	1-2	0-0	2-5
Montefusco	0-2	0-1	1-1	0-0	1-0	1-0	0-0	0-0	0-2	0-0	1-1	3-8
Nastu	0-1	0-1	2-0	1-0	0-0	0-1	0-0	0-1	0-0	0-0	0-0	3-4
Roberts	0-1	0-0	0-0	0-0	0-0	0-0	0-0	0-0	0-0	0-0	0-2	0-2
Whitson	0-1	0-0	1-1	0-1	1-1	0-1	1-0	0-0	0-0	1-1	1-2	5-8
Totals	7-11	4-8	12-6	11-7	4-14	5-7	4-8	6-6	3-9	5-7	10-8	71-91

No Decisions: Coleman, Holland, Plank.

NATIONAL LEAGUE

PENNANT WINNERS

Year—Club	Manager	W.	L.	Pct.	*G.A.
1900—Brooklyn	Edward (Ned) Hanlon	82	54	.603	4½
1901—Pittsburgh	Frederick Clarke	90	49	.647	7½
1902—Pittsburgh	Frederick Clarke	103	36	.741	27½
1903—Pittsburgh	Frederick Clarke	91	49	.650	6½
1904—New York	John McGraw	106	47	.693	13
1905—New York	John McGraw	105	48	.686	9
1906—Chicago	Frank Chance	116	36	.763	20
1907—Chicago	Frank Chance	107	45	.704	17
1908—Chicago	Frank Chance	99	55	.643	1
1909—Pittsburgh	Frederick Clarke	110	42	.724	6½
1910—Chicago	Frank Chance	104	50	.675	13
1911—New York	John McGraw	99	54	.647	7½
1912—New York	John McGraw	103	48	.682	10
1913—New York	John McGraw	101	51	.664	12½
1914—Boston	George Stallings	94	59	.614	10½
1915—Philadelphia	Patrick Moran	90	62	.592	7
1916—Brooklyn	Wilbert Robinson	94	60	.610	2½
1917—New York	John McGraw	98	56	.636	10
1918—Chicago	Fred Mitchell	84	45	.651	10½
1919—Cincinnati	Patrick Moran	96	44	.686	9
1920—Brooklyn	Wilbert Robinson	93	61	.604	7
1921—New York	John McGraw	94	59	.614	4
1922—New York	John McGraw	93	61	.604	7
1923—New York	John McGraw	95	58	.621	4½
1924—New York	John McGraw	93	60	.608	1½
1925—Pittsburgh	William McKechnie	95	58	.621	8½
1926—St. Louis	Rogers Hornsby	89	65	.578	2
1927—Pittsburgh	Owen (Donie) Bush	94	60	.610	1½
1928—St. Louis	William McKechnie	95	59	.617	2
1929—Chicago	Joseph McCarthy	98	54	.645	10½
1930—St. Louis	Charles (Gabby) Street	92	62	.597	2
1931—St. Louis	Charles (Gabby) Street	101	53	.656	13
1932—Chicago	Charles Grimm	90	64	.584	4
1933—New York	William Terry	91	61	.599	5
1934—St. Louis	Frank Frisch	95	58	.621	2
1935—Chicago	Charles Grimm	100	54	.649	4
1936—New York	William Terry	92	62	.597	5
1937—New York	William Terry	95	57	.625	3
1938—Chicago	Charles (Gabby) Hartnett	89	63	.586	2
1939—Cincinnati	William McKechnie	97	57	.630	4½
1940—Cincinnati	William McKechnie	100	53	.654	12
1941—Brooklyn	Leo Durocher	100	54	.649	2½
1942—St. Louis	William Southworth	106	48	.688	2
1943—St. Louis	William Southworth	105	49	.682	18
1944—St. Louis	William Southworth	105	49	.682	14½
1945—Chicago	Charles Grimm	98	56	.636	3
1946—St. Louis†	Edwin Dyer	98	58	.628	2
1947—Brooklyn	Burton Shotton	94	60	.610	5
1948—Boston	William Southworth	91	62	.595	6½
1949—Brooklyn	Burton Shotton	97	57	.630	1
1950—Philadelphia	Edwin Sawyer	91	63	.591	2
1951—New York‡	Leo Durocher	98	59	.624	1
1952—Brooklyn	Charles Dressen	96	57	.627	4½
1953—Brooklyn	Charles Dressen	105	49	.682	13
1954—New York	Leo Durocher	97	57	.630	5
1955—Brooklyn	Walter Alston	98	55	.641	13½
1956—Brooklyn	Walter Alston	93	61	.604	1
1957—Milwaukee	Fred Haney	95	59	.617	8
1958—Milwaukee	Fred Haney	92	62	.597	8
1959—Los Angeles§	Walter Alston	88	68	.564	2

PENNANT WINNERS—Continued

Year	Club	Manager	W.	L.	Pct.	*G.A.
1960—Pittsburgh		Daniel Murtaugh	95	59	.617	7
1961—Cincinnati		Frederick Hutchinson	93	61	.604	4
1962—San Francisco x		Alvin Dark	103	62	.624	1
1963—Los Angeles		Walter Alston	99	63	.611	6
1964—St. Louis		John Keane	93	69	.574	1
1965—Los Angeles		Walter Alston	97	65	.599	2
1966—Los Angeles		Walter Alston	95	67	.586	1½
1967—St. Louis		Albert (Red) Schoendienst	101	60	.627	10½
1968—St. Louis		Albert (Red) Schoendienst	97	65	.599	9
1969—New York (E)**		Gilbert Hodges	100	62	.617	8
1970—Cincinnati (W)**		George (Sparky) Anderson	102	60	.630	14½
1971—Pittsburgh (E)**		Daniel Murtaugh	97	65	.599	7
1972—Cincinnati (W)**		George (Sparky) Anderson	95	59	.617	10½
1973—New York (E)**		Lawrence (Yogi) Berra	82	79	.509	1½
1974—Los Angeles (W)**		Walter Alston	102	60	.630	4
1975—Cincinnati (W)**		George (Sparky) Anderson	108	54	.667	20
1976—Cincinnati (W)**		George (Sparky) Anderson	102	60	.630	10
1977—Los Angeles (W)**		Thomas Lasorda	98	64	.605	10
1978—Los Angeles (W)**		Thomas Lasorda	95	67	.586	2½
1979—Pittsburgh (E) **		Charles (Chuck) Tanner	98	64	.605	2

*Games ahead of second-place club. †Defeated Brooklyn, two games to none, in playoff for pennant. ‡Defeated Brooklyn, two games to one, in playoff for pennant. §Defeated Milwaukee, two games to none, in playoff for pennant. xDefeated Los Angeles, two games to one, in playoff for pennant. **Won Championship Series.

YEARLY FINISHES

Year	Atl.	Chi.	Cin.	Hou.	L.A.	N.Y.	Phil.	Pitt.	St.L.	S.F.
1900	*4	x5	7	....	†1	....	3	2	x5	‡8
1901	*5	6	8	....	†3	....	2	1	4	‡7
1902	*3	5	4	....	†2	....	1	6	8	‡8
1903	*6	3	4	....	†5	....	7	1	8	‡2
1904	*7	2	3	....	†6	....	8	4	5	‡1
1905	*7	3	5	....	†8	....	4	2	6	‡1
1906	*8	1	6	....	†5	....	4	3	7	‡2
1907	*7	1	6	....	†5	....	3	2	8	‡4
1908	*6	1	5	....	†7	....	4	x2	8	x‡2
1909	*8	2	4	....	†6	....	5	1	7	‡3
1910	*8	1	5	....	†6	....	4	3	7	‡2
1911	*8	2	6	....	†7	....	4	3	5	‡1
1912	*8	3	4	....	†7	....	5	2	6	‡1
1913	*5	3	7	....	†6	....	2	4	8	‡1
1914	*1	4	8	....	†5	....	6	7	3	‡2
1915	*2	4	7	....	†3	....	1	5	6	‡8
1916	*3	5	x7	....	†1	....	2	6	x7	‡4
1917	*6	5	4	....	†7	....	2	8	3	‡1
1918	*7	1	3	....	†5	....	6	4	8	‡2
1919	*6	3	1	....	†5	....	8	4	7	‡2
1920	*7	x5	3	....	†1	....	8	4	x5	‡2
1921	*4	7	6	....	†5	....	8	2	3	‡1
1922	*8	5	2	....	†6	....	7	x3	x3	‡1
1923	*7	4	2	....	†6	....	8	3	5	‡1
1924	*8	5	4	....	†2	....	7	3	6	‡1
1925	*5	8	3	....	x16	....	x6	1	4	‡2
1926	*7	4	2	....	†6	....	8	3	1	‡5
1927	*7	4	5	....	J6	....	8	1	2	‡3
1928	*7	3	5	....	†6	....	8	4	1	‡2
1929	*8	1	7	....	†6	....	5	2	4	‡3
1930	*6	2	7	....	†4	....	8	5	1	‡3
1931	*7	3	8	....	†4	....	6	5	1	‡2
1932	*5	1	8	....	†3	....	4	2	x6	x16
1933	*4	3	8	....	†6	....	7	2	5	‡1
1934	*4	3	8	....	†6	....	7	5	1	‡2
1935	*8	1	6	....	†5	....	7	4	2	‡3
1936	*6	x2	5	....	†7	....	8	4	x2	‡1
1937	*5	2	8	....	†6	....	7	3	4	‡1

YEARLY FINISHES—Continued

Year	Atl.	Chi.	Cin.	Hous.	L.A.	N.Y.	Phil.	Pitt.	St.L.	S.F.
1938	*5	1	4	....	†7	....	8	2	6	‡3
1939	*7	4	1	....	†3	....	8	6	2	‡5
1940	*7	5	1	....	†2	....	8	4	3	‡6
1941	*7	6	3	....	†1	....	8	4	2	‡5
1942	*7	6	4	....	†2	....	8	5	1	‡3
1943	*6	5	2	....	†3	....	7	4	1	‡8
1944	*6	4	3	....	†7	....	8	2	1	‡5
1945	*6	1	7	....	†3	....	8	4	2	‡5
1946	*4	3	6	....	†2	....	5	7	1	‡8
1947	*3	6	5	....	†1	....	x7	x7	2	‡4
1948	*1	8	7	....	†3	....	6	4	2	‡5
1949	*4	8	7	....	†1	....	3	6	2	‡5
1950	*4	7	6	....	†2	....	1	8	5	‡3
1951	*4	8	6	....	†2	....	5	7	3	‡1
1952	*7	5	6	....	†1	....	4	8	3	‡2
1953	*2	7	6	....	†1	....	x3	8	x3	‡5
1954	*3	7	5	....	†2	....	4	8	6	‡1
1955	*2	6	5	....	†1	....	4	8	7	‡3
1956	*2	8	3	....	†1	....	5	7	4	‡6
1957	*1	x7	4	....	†3	....	5	x7	2	‡6
1958	*1	x5	4	....	7	....	8	2	x5	3
1959	*2	x5	x5	....	1	....	8	4	7	3
1960	*2	7	6	....	4	....	8	1	3	5
1961	*4	7	1	....	2	....	8	6	5	3
1962	*5	9	3	8	2	10	7	4	6	1
1963	*6	7	5	9	1	10	4	8	2	3
1964	*5	8	x2	9	x6	10	x2	x6	1	4
1965	*5	8	4	9	1	10	6	3	7	2
1966	5	10	7	8	1	9	4	3	6	2
1967	7	3	4	9	8	10	5	6	1	2
1968	5	3	4	10	x7	9	x7	6	1	2

		EAST DIVISION						WEST DIVISION			
Year	Chi.	Mon.	N.Y.	Phila.	Pitt.	St.L.	Atl.	Cin.	Hous.	L.A.	S.D.	S.F.
1969	2	6	1	5	3	4	1	3	5	4	6	2
1970	2	6	3	5	1	4	5	1	4	2	6	3
1971	x3	5	x3	6	1	2	3	x4	x4	2	6	1
1972	2	5	3	6	1	4	4	1	2	3	6	5
1973	5	4	1	6	3	2	5	1	4	2	6	3
1974	6	4	5	3	1	2	3	2	4	1	6	5
1975	x5	x5	x3	2	1	x3	5	1	6	2	4	3
1976	4	6	3	1	2	5	6	1	3	2	5	4
1977	4	5	6	1	2	3	6	2	3	1	5	4
1978	3	4	6	1	2	5	6	2	5	1	4	3
1979	5	2	6	4	1	3	6	1	2	3	5	4

*Record of predecessor Boston (1900-1952) and Milwaukee (1953-1965) clubs; †Brooklyn club; ‡New York Giants. xTied for position.

LEADING BATSMEN

Year	Player and Club	G.	AB.	R.	H.	TB.	2B.	3B.	HR.	RBI.	B.A.
1900	John (Honus) Wagner, Pittsburgh	134	528	107	201	302	45	22	4	....	.381
1901	Jesse Burkett, St. Louis	142	597	139	228	313	21	17	10	....	.382
1902	Clarence Beaumont, Pittsburgh	131	544	101	194	227	21	6	0	....	.357
1903	John (Honus) Wagner, Pittsburgh	129	512	97	182	265	30	19	5	....	.355
1904	John (Honus) Wagner, Pittsburgh	132	490	97	171	255	44	14	4	....	.349
1905	J. Bentley Seymour, Cincinnati	149	581	95	219	325	40	21	8	....	.377
1906	John (Honus) Wagner, Pittsburgh	140	516	103	175	237	38	9	2	....	.339
1907	John (Honus) Wagner, Pittsburgh	142	515	98	180	264	38	14	6	91	.350
1908	John (Honus) Wagner, Pittsburgh	151	568	100	201	308	39	19	10	106	.354
1909	John (Honus) Wagner, Pittsburgh	137	495	92	168	242	39	10	5	102	.339
1910	Sherwood Magee, Philadelphia	154	519	110	172	263	39	17	6	116	.331
1911	John (Honus) Wagner, Pittsburgh	130	473	87	158	240	23	16	9	108	.334
1912	Henry Zimmerman, Chicago	145	557	95	207	318	41	14	14	98	.372
1913	Jacob Daubert, Brooklyn	139	508	76	178	215	17	7	2	46	.350

LEADING BATSMEN—Continued

Year	Player and Club	G.	AB.	R.	H.	TB.	2B.	3B.	HR.	RBI.	B.A.
1914—Jacob Daubert, Brooklyn		126	474	89	156ʹ	205	17	7	6	44	.329
1915—Lawrence Doyle, New York		150	591	86	189	261	40	10	4	68	.320
1916—Harold Chase, Cincinnati		142	542	66	184	249	29	12	4	84	.339
1917—Edd Roush, Cincinnati		136	522	82	178	237	19	14	4	62	.341
1918—Zachariah Wheat, Brooklyn		105	409	39	137	158	15	3	0	48	.335
1919—Edd Roush, Cincinnati		133	504	73	162	216	19	13	3	69	.321
1920—Rogers Hornsby, St. Louis		149	589	96	218	329	44	20	9	94	.370
1921—Rogers Hornsby, St. Louis		154	592	131	235	378	44	18	21	126	.397
1922—Rogers Hornsby, St. Louis		154	623	141	250	450	46	14	42	152	.401
1923—Rogers Hornsby, St. Louis		107	424	89	163	266	32	10	17	83	.384
1924—Rogers Hornsby, St. Louis		143	536	121	227	373	43	14	25	94	.424
1925—Rogers Hornsby, St. Louis		138	504	133	203	381	41	10	39	143	.403
1926—Eugene Hargrave, Cincinnati		105	326	42	115	171	22	8	6	62	.353
1927—Paul Waner, Pittsburgh		155	623	113	237	338	40	17	9	131	.380
1928—Rogers Hornsby, Boston		140	486	99	188	307	42	7	21	94	.387
1929—Frank O'Doul, Philadelphia		154	638	152	254	397	35	6	32	122	.398
1930—William Terry, New York		154	633	139	254	392	39	15	23	129	.401
1931—Chas. (Chick) Hafey, St. Louis		122	450	94	157	256	35	8	16	95	.349
1932—Frank O'Doul, Brooklyn		148	595	120	219	330	32	8	21	90	.368
1933—Charles Klein, Philadelphia		152	606	101	223	365	44	7	28	120	.368
1934—Paul Waner, Pittsburgh		146	599	122	217	323	32	16	14	90	.362
1935—J. Floyd (Arky) Vaughan, Pittsburgh		137	499	108	192	303	34	10	19	99	.385
1936—Paul Waner, Pittsburgh		148	585	107	218	304	53	9	5	94	.373
1937—Joseph Medwick, St. Louis		156	633	111	237	406	56	10	31	154	.374
1938—Ernest Lombardi, Cincinnati		129	489	60	167	256	30	1	19	95	.342
1939—John Mize, St. Louis		153	564	104	197	353	44	14	28	108	.349
1940—Debs Garms, Pittsburgh		103	358	76	127	179	23	7	5	57	.355
1941—Harold (Pete) Reiser, Brooklyn		137	536	117	184	299	39	17	14	76	.343
1942—Ernest Lombardi, Boston		105	309	32	102	149	14	0	11	46	.330
1943—Stanley Musial, St. Louis		157	617	108	220	347	48	20	13	81	.357
1944—Fred (Dixie) Walker, Brooklyn		147	535	77	191	283	37	8	13	91	.357
1945—Philip Cavarretta, Chicago		132	498	94	177	249	34	10	6	97	.355
1946—Stanley Musial, St. Louis		156	624	124	228	366	50	20	16	103	.365
1947—Harry Walker, St. Louis-Phila.		140	513	81	186	250	29	16	1	41	.363
1948—Stanley Musial, St. Louis		155	611	135	230	429	46	18	39	131	.376
1949—Jack Robinson, Brooklyn		156	593	122	203	313	38	12	16	124	.342
1950—Stanley Musial, St. Louis		146	555	105	192	331	41	7	28	109	.346
1951—Stanley Musial, St. Louis		152	578	124	205	355	30	12	32	108	.355
1952—Stanley Musial, St. Louis		154	578	105	194	311	42	6	21	91	.336
1953—Carl Furillo, Brooklyn		132	479	82	165	278	38	6	21	92	.344
1954—Willie Mays, New York		151	565	119	195	377	33	13	41	110	.345
1955—Richie Ashburn, Philadelphia		140	533	91	180	239	32	9	3	42	.338
1956—Henry Aaron, Milwaukee		153	609	106	200	340	34	14	26	92	.328
1957—Stanley Musial, St. Louis		134	502	82	176	307	38	3	29	102	.351
1958—Richie Ashburn, Philadelphia		152	615	98	215	271	24	13	2	33	.350
1959—Henry Aaron, Milwaukee		154	629	116	223	400	46	7	39	123	.355
1960—Richard Groat, Pittsburgh		138	573	85	186	226	26	4	2	50	.325
1961—Roberto Clemente, Pittsburgh		146	572	100	201	320	30	10	23	89	.351
1962—H. Thomas Davis, Los Angeles		163	665	120	230	356	27	9	27	153	.346
1963—H. Thomas Davis, Los Angeles		146	556	69	181	254	19	3	16	88	.326
1964—Roberto Clemente, Pittsburgh		155	622	95	211	301	40	7	12	87	.339
1965—Roberto Clemente, Pittsburgh		152	589	91	194	273	21	14	10	65	.329
1966—Mateo Alou, Pittsburgh		141	535	86	183	225	18	9	2	27	.342
1967—Roberto Clemente, Pittsburgh		147	585	103	209	324	26	10	23	110	.357
1968—Peter Rose, Cincinnati		149	626	94	210	294	42	6	10	49	.335
1969—Peter Rose, Cincinnati		156	627	120	218	321	33	11	16	82	.348
1970—Ricardo Carty, Atlanta		136	478	84	175	279	23	3	25	101	.366
1971—Joseph Torre, St. Louis		161	634	97	230	352	34	8	24	137	.363
1972—Billy L. Williams, Chicago		150	574	95	191	348	34	6	37	122	.333
1973—Peter Rose, Cincinnati		160	680	115	230	297	36	8	5	64	.338
1974—Ralph Garr, Atlanta		143	606	87	214	305	24	17	11	54	.353
1975—Bill Madlock, Chicago		130	514	77	182	246	29	7	7	64	.354
1976—Bill Madlock, Chicago		142	514	68	174	257	36	1	15	84	.339
1977—David Parker, Pittsburgh		159	637	107	215	338	44	8	21	88	.338
1978—David Parker, Pittsburgh		148	581	102	194	340	32	12	30	117	.334
1979—Keith Hernandez, St. Louis		161	610	116	210	313	48	11	11	105	.344

LEADERS IN RUNS SCORED

Year	Player and Club	Runs
1900—	Roy Thomas, Philadelphia	131
1901—	Jesse Burkett, St. Louis	139
1902—	John (Honus) Wagner, Pittsburgh	105
1903—	Clarence Beaumont, Pittsburgh	137
1904—	George Browne, New York	99
1905—	Michael Donlin, New York	124
1906—	John (Honus) Wagner, Pittsburgh	103
	Frank Chance, Chicago	103
1907—	W. Porter Shannon, New York	104
1908—	Frederick Tenney, New York	101
1909—	Thomas Leach, Pittsburgh	126
1910—	Sherwood Magee, Philadelphia	110
1911—	James Sheckard, Chicago	121
1912—	Robert Bescher, Cincinnati	120
1913—	Thomas Leach, Chicago	99
	Max Carey, Pittsburgh	99
1914—	George Burns, New York	100
1915—	Cliff. (Gavvy) Cravath, Philadelphia	89
1916—	George Burns, New York	105
1917—	George Burns, New York	103
1918—	Henry Groh, Cincinnati	88
1919—	George Burns, New York	86
1920—	George Burns, New York	115
1921—	Rogers Hornsby, St. Louis	131
1922—	Rogers Hornsby, St. Louis	141
1923—	Ross Youngs, New York	121
1924—	Frank Frisch, New York	121
	Rogers Hornsby, St. Louis	121
1925—	Hazen (Kiki) Cuyler, Pittsburgh	144
1926—	Hazen (Kiki) Cuyler, Pittsburgh	113
1927—	Lloyd Waner, Pittsburgh	133
	Rogers Hornsby, New York	133
1928—	Paul Waner, Pittsburgh	142
1929—	Rogers Hornsby, Chicago	156
1930—	Charles (Chuck) Klein, Philadelphia	158
1931—	Terry, New York-Klein, Philadelphia	121
1932—	Charles (Chuck) Klein, Philadelphia	152
1933—	John (Pepper) Martin, St. Louis	122
1934—	Paul Waner, Pittsburgh	122
1935—	August Galan, Chicago	133
1936—	J. Floyd (Arky) Vaughan, Pittsburgh	122
1937—	Joseph Medwick, St. Louis	111
1938—	Melvin Ott, New York	116

Year	Player and Club	Runs
1939—	William Werber, Cincinnati	115
1940—	J. Floyd (Arky) Vaughan, Pittsburgh	113
1941—	Harold (Pete) Reiser, Brooklyn	117
1942—	Melvin Ott, New York	118
1943—	J. Floyd (Arky) Vaughan, Brooklyn	112
1944—	William Nicholson, Chicago	116
1945—	Edward Stanky, Brooklyn	128
1946—	Stanley Musial, St. Louis	124
1947—	John Mize, New York	137
1948—	Stanley Musial, St. Louis	135
1949—	Harold (Pee Wee) Reese, Brooklyn	132
1950—	C. Earl Torgeson, Boston	120
1951—	Musial, St. Louis-Kiner, Pittsburgh	124
1952—	Musial, St. Louis-Hemus, St. Louis	105
1953—	Edwin (Duke) Snider, Brooklyn	132
1954—	Musial, St. Louis-Snider, Brooklyn	120
1955—	Edwin (Duke) Snider, Brooklyn	126
1956—	Frank Robinson, Cincinnati	122
1957—	Henry Aaron, Milwaukee	118
1958—	Willie Mays, San Francisco	121
1959—	Vada Pinson, Cincinnati	131
1960—	William Bruton, Milwaukee	112
1961—	Willie Mays, San Francisco	129
1962—	Frank Robinson, Cincinnati	134
1963—	Henry Aaron, Milwaukee	121
1964—	Richard Allen, Philadelphia	125
1965—	Tommy Harper, Cincinnati	126
1966—	Felipe Alou, Atlanta	122
1967—	Henry Aaron, Atlanta	113
	Louis Brock, St. Louis	113
1968—	Glenn Beckert, Chicago	98
1969—	Bobby Bonds, San Francisco	120
	Peter Rose, Cincinnati	120
1970—	Billy Williams, Chicago	137
1971—	Louis Brock, St. Louis	126
1972—	Joe Morgan, Cincinnati	122
1973—	Bobby Bonds, San Francisco	131
1974—	Peter Rose, Cincinnati	110
1975—	Peter Rose, Cincinnati	112
1976—	Peter Rose, Cincinnati	130
1977—	George Foster, Cincinnati	124
1978—	Ivan DeJesus, Chicago	104
1979—	Keith Hernandez, St. Louis	116

LEADERS IN HITS

Year	Player and Club	Hits
1900—	William Keeler, Brooklyn	208
1901—	Jesse Burkett, St. Louis	228
1902—	Clarence Beaumont, Pittsburgh	194
1903—	Clarence Beaumont, Pittsburgh	209
1904—	Clarence Beaumont, Pittsburgh	185
1905—	J. Bentley Seymour, Cincinnati	219
1906—	Harry Steinfeldt, Chicago	176
1907—	Clarence Beaumont, Boston	187
1908—	John (Honus) Wagner, Pittsburgh	201
1909—	Lawrence Doyle, New York	172
1910—	John (Honus) Wagner, Pittsburgh	178
	Robert Byrne, Pittsburgh	178
1911—	Roy Miller, Boston	192
1912—	Henry Zimmerman, Chicago	207
1913—	Cliff. (Gavvy) Cravath, Philadelphia	179
1914—	Sherwood Magee, Philadelphia	171
1915—	Lawrence Doyle, New York	189
1916—	Harold Chase, Cincinnati	184
1917—	Henry Groh, Cincinnati	182
1918—	Charles Hollocher, Chicago	161

Year	Player and Club	Hits
1919—	Ivy Olson, Brooklyn	164
1920—	Rogers Hornsby, St. Louis	218
1921—	Rogers Hornsby, St. Louis	235
1922—	Rogers Hornsby, St. Louis	250
1923—	Frank Frisch, New York	223
1924—	Rogers Hornsby, St. Louis	227
1925—	James Bottomley, St. Louis	227
1926—	Edward Brown, Boston	201
1927—	Paul Waner, Pittsburgh	237
1928—	Fred Lindstrom, New York	231
1929—	Frank O'Doul, Philadelphia	254
1930—	William Terry, New York	254
1931—	Lloyd Waner, Pittsburgh	214
1932—	Charles Klein, Philadelphia	226
1933—	Charles Klein, Philadelphia	223
1934—	Paul Waner, Pittsburgh	217
1935—	William Herman, Chicago	227
1936—	Joseph Medwick, St. Louis	223
1937—	Joseph Medwick, St. Louis	237
1938—	Frank McCormick, Cincinnati	209

LEADERS IN HITS—Continued

Year	Player and Club	Hits	Year	Player and Club	Hits
1939	Frank McCormick, Cincinnati	209	1960	Willie Mays, San Francisco	190
1940	Stanley Hack, Chicago	191	1961	Vada Pinson, Cincinnati	208
	Frank McCormick, Cincinnati	191	1962	H. Thomas Davis, Los Angeles	230
1941	Stanley Hack, Chicago	186	1963	Vada Pinson, Cincinnati	204
1942	Enos Slaughter, St. Louis	188	1964	Clemente, Pittsburgh-Flood, St. Louis	211
1943	Stanley Musial, St. Louis	220	1965	Peter Rose, Cincinnati	209
1944	Musial, St. Louis-Cavarretta, Chicago	197	1966	Felipe Alou, Atlanta	218
1945	Thomas Holmes, Boston	224	1967	Roberto Clemente, Pittsburgh	209
1946	Stanley Musial, St. Louis	228	1968	Felipe Alou, Atlanta	210
1947	Thomas Holmes, Boston	191		Peter Rose, Cincinnati	210
1948	Stanley Musial, St. Louis	230	1969	Mateo Alou, Pittsburgh	231
1949	Stanley Musial, St. Louis	207	1970	Peter Rose, Cincinnati	205
1950	Edwin (Duke) Snider, Brooklyn	199		Billy Williams, Chicago	205
1951	Richie Ashburn, Philadelphia	221	1971	Joseph Torre, St. Louis	230
1952	Stanley Musial, St. Louis	194	1972	Peter Rose, Cincinnati	198
1953	Richie Ashburn, Philadelphia	205	1973	Peter Rose, Cincinnati	230
1954	Donald Mueller, New York	212	1974	Ralph Garr, Atlanta	214
1955	Theodore Kluszewski, Cincinnati	192	1975	David Cash, Philadelphia	213
1956	Henry Aaron, Milwaukee	200	1976	Peter Rose, Cincinnati	215
1957	Al (Red) Schoendienst, N.Y.-Mil.	200	1977	David Parker, Pittsburgh	215
1958	Richie Ashburn, Philadelphia	215	1978	Steven Garvey, Los Angeles	202
1959	Henry Aaron, Milwaukee	223	1979	Garry Templeton, St. Louis	211

ONE-BASE HIT LEADERS

Year	Player and Club	1B.	Year	Player and Club	1B.
1900	William H. Keeler, Brooklyn	179	1935	Forrest D. Jensen, Pittsburgh	160
1901	Jesse C. Burkett, St. Louis	180	1936	Joseph G. Moore, New York	160
1902	Clarence H. Beaumont, Pittsburgh	167	1937	Paul G. Waner, Pittsburgh	178
1903	Clarence H. Beaumont, Pittsburgh	166	1938	Frank A. McCormick, Cincinnati	160
1904	Clarence H. Beaumont, Pittsburgh	158	1939	John A. Hassett, Boston	162
1905	Michael J. Donlin, New York	162	1940	Burgess U. Whitehead, New York	141
1906	Miller J. Huggins, Cincinnati	141	1941	Stanley C. Hack, Chicago	141
	William P. Shannon, St. Louis-NY	141	1942	Enos B. Slaughter, St. Louis	127
1907	Clarence H. Beaumont, Pittsburgh	150	1943	Nicholas J. Witek, New York	172
1908	Michael J. Donlin, New York	153	1944	Philip J. Cavarretta, Chicago	142
1909	Edward L. Grant, Philadelphia	147	1945	Stanley C. Hack, Chicago	155
1910	Edward L. Grant, Philadelphia	134	1946	Stanley F. Musial, St. Louis	142
1911	Jacob E. Daubert, Brooklyn	146	1947	Thomas F. Holmes, Boston	146
	Roy O. Miller, Boston	146	1948	Stanley A. Rojek, Pittsburgh	150
1912	William J. Sweeney, Boston	159	1949	Albert F. Schoendienst, St. Louis	160
1913	Jacob E. Daubert, Brooklyn	152	1950	Edward S. Waitkus, Philadelphia	143
1914	Beals Becker, Philadelphia	128	1951	Richie Ashburn, Philadelphia	181
1915	Lawrence H. Doyle, New York	135	1952	Robert H. Adams, Cincinnati	145
1916	David A. Robertson, New York	142	1953	Richie Ashburn, Philadelphia	169
1917	Benjamin M. Kauff, New York	141	1954	Donald F. Mueller, New York	165
	Edd J. Roush, Cincinnati	141	1955	Donald F. Mueller, New York	152
1918	Charles J. Hollocher, Chicago	130	1956	John E. Temple, Cincinnati	157
1919	Ivan M. Olson, Brooklyn	140	1957	Richie Ashburn, Philadelphia	152
1920	Milton J. Stock, St. Louis	170	1958	Richie Ashburn, Philadelphia	176
1921	Carson L. Bigbee, Pittsburgh	161	1959	Don L. Blasingame, St. Louis	144
1922	Carson L. Bigbee, Pittsburgh	166	1960	Richard M. Groat, Pittsburgh	154
1923	Frank F. Frisch, New York	169	1961	Vada E. Pinson, Cincinnati	150
1924	Zachariah Wheat, Brooklyn	149		Maurice M. Wills, Los Angeles	150
1925	Milton J. Stock, Brooklyn	164	1962	Maurice M. Wills, Los Angeles	179
1926	Edward W. Brown, Boston	160	1963	Curtis C. Flood, St. Louis	152
1927	Lloyd J. Waner, Pittsburgh	198	1964	Curtis C. Flood, St. Louis	178
1928	Lloyd J. Waner, Pittsburgh	180	1965	Maurice M. Wills, Los Angeles	165
1929	Frank J. O'Doul, Philadelphia	181	1966	Roland T. Jackson, Houston	160
	Lloyd J. Waner, Pittsburgh	181	1967	Maurice M. Wills, Pittsburgh	162
1930	William H. Terry, New York	177	1968	Curtis C. Flood, St. Louis	160
1931	Lloyd J. Waner, Pittsburgh	172	1969	Mateo R. Alou, Pittsburgh	183
1932	Frank J. O'Doul, Brooklyn	158	1970	Mateo R. Alou, Pittsburgh	171
1933	Charles P. Fullis, Philadelphia	162	1971	Ralph A. Garr, Atlanta	180
1934	William H. Terry, New York	169	1972	Louis C. Brock, St. Louis	156

ONE-BASE HIT LEADERS—Continued

Year	Player and Club	1B.	Year	Player and Club	1B.
1973—	Peter E. Rose, Cincinnati	181	1977—	Garry Templeton, St. Louis	155
1974—	David Cash, Philadelphia	167	1978—	Lawrence Bowa, Philadelphia	153
1975—	David Cash, Philadelphia	166	1979—	Peter Rose, Philadelphia	159
1976—	Guillermo Montanez, San Fran.-Atl.	164			

TWO-BASE HIT LEADERS

Year	Player and Club	2B.	Year	Player and Club	2B.
1900—	John (Honus) Wagner, Pittsburgh	45	1940—	Frank McCormick, Cincinnati	44
1901—	Wagner, Pitts-Beckley, Cinn	39	1941—	Reiser, Brooklyn-Mize, St. Louis	39
1902—	John (Honus) Wagner, Pittsburgh	33	1942—	Martin Marion, St. Louis	38
1903—	Clarke, Pittsburgh-Mertes, New York-Steinfeldt, Cincinnati	32	1943—	Stanley Musial, St. Louis	48
			1944—	Stanley Musial, St. Louis	51
1904—	John (Honus) Wagner, Pittsburgh	44	1945—	Thomas Holmes, Boston	47
1905—	J. Bentley Seymour, Cincinnati	40	1946—	Stanley Musial, St. Louis	50
1906—	John (Honus) Wagner, Pittsburgh	38	1947—	Edward Miller, Cincinnati	38
1907—	John (Honus) Wagner, Pittsburgh	38	1948—	Stanley Musial, St. Louis	46
1908—	John (Honus) Wagner, Pittsburgh	39	1949—	Stanley Musial, St. Louis	41
1909—	John (Honus) Wagner, Pittsburgh	39	1950—	Al (Red) Schoendienst, St. Louis	43
1910—	Robert Byrne, Pittsburgh	43	1951—	Alvin Dark, New York	41
1911—	Edward Konetchy, St. Louis	38	1952—	Stanley Musial, St. Louis	42
1912—	Henry Zimmerman, Chicago	41	1953—	Stanley Musial, St. Louis	53
1913—	J. Carlisle Smith, Brooklyn	40	1954—	Stanley Musial, St. Louis	41
1914—	Sherwood Magee, Philadelphia	39	1955—	Logan, Milwaukee-Aaron, Milwaukee	37
1915—	Lawrence Doyle, New York	40	1956—	Henry Aaron, Milwaukee	34
1916—	O. Albert Niehoff, Philadelphia	42	1957—	Donald Hoak, Cincinnati	39
1917—	Henry Groh, Cincinnati	39	1958—	Orlando Cepeda, San Francisco	38
1918—	Henry Groh, Cincinnati	28	1959—	Vada Pinson, Cincinnati	47
1919—	Ross Youngs, New York	31	1960—	Vada Pinson, Cincinnati	37
1920—	Rogers Hornsby, St. Louis	44	1961—	Henry Aaron, Milwaukee	39
1921—	Rogers Hornsby, St. Louis	44	1962—	Frank Robinson, Cincinnati	51
1922—	Rogers Hornsby, St. Louis	46	1963—	Richard Groat, St. Louis	43
1923—	Edd Roush, Cincinnati	41	1964—	A. Lee Maye, Milwaukee	44
1924—	Rogers Hornsby, St. Louis	43	1965—	Henry Aaron, Milwaukee	40
1925—	James Bottomley, St. Louis	44	1966—	John Callison, Philadelphia	40
1926—	James Bottomley, St. Louis	40	1967—	Daniel Staub, Houston	44
1927—	J. Riggs Stephenson, Chicago	46	1968—	Louis Brock, St. Louis	46
1928—	Paul Waner, Pittsburgh	50	1969—	Mateo Alou, Pittsburgh	41
1929—	John Frederick, Brooklyn	52	1970—	M. Wesley Parker, Los Angeles	47
1930—	Charles Klein, Philadelphia	59	1971—	Cesar Cedeno, Houston	40
1931—	Earl (Sparky) Adams, St. Louis	46	1972—	Cesar Cedeno, Houston	39
1932—	Paul Waner, Pittsburgh	62		Guillermo Montanez, Philadelphia	39
1933—	Charles Klein, Philadelphia	44	1973—	Wilver Stargell, Pittsburgh	43
1934—	Cuyler, Chicago-Allen, Philadelphia	42	1974—	Peter Rose, Cincinnati	45
1935—	William Herman, Chicago	57	1975—	Peter Rose, Cincinnati	47
1936—	Joseph Medwick, St. Louis	64	1976—	Peter Rose, Cincinnati	42
1937—	Joseph Medwick, St. Louis	56	1977—	David Parker, Pittsburgh	44
1938—	Joseph Medwick, St. Louis	47	1978—	Peter Rose, Cincinnati	51
1939—	Enos Slaughter, St. Louis	52	1979—	Keith Hernandez, St. Louis	48

THREE-BASE HIT LEADERS

Year	Player and Club	3B.	Year	Player and Club	3B.
1900—	John (Honus) Wagner, Pittsburgh	22	1910—	Michael Mitchell, Cincinnati	18
1901—	James Sheckard, Brooklyn	21	1911—	Lawrence Doyle, New York	25
1902—	Samuel Crawford, Cincinnati	23	1912—	John (Chief) Wilson, Pittsburgh	36
1903—	John (Honus) Wagner, Pittsburgh	19	1913—	Victor Saier, Chicago	21
1904—	Harry Lumley, Brooklyn	18	1914—	Max Carey, Pittsburgh	17
1905—	J. Bentley Seymour, Cincinnati	21	1915—	Thomas Long, St. Louis	25
1906—	Clarke, Pittsburgh-Schulte, Chicago	13	1916—	William Hinchman, Pittsburgh	16
1907—	Ganzel, Cincinnati-Alperman, Brooklyn	16	1917—	Rogers Hornsby, St. Louis	17
1908—	John (Honus) Wagner, Pittsburgh	19	1918—	Jacob Daubert, Brooklyn	15
1909—	Michael Mitchell, Cincinnati	17	1919—	Hi Myers, Brooklyn-Southworth, Pitt.	14

THREE-BASE HIT LEADERS—Continued

Year	Player and Club	3B.
1920—	Henry (Hi) Myers, Brooklyn	22
1921—	Hornsby, St. Louis-Powell, Boston	18
1922—	Jacob Daubert, Cincinnati	22
1923—	Carey, Pittsburgh-Traynor, Pittsburgh	19
1924—	Edd Roush, Cincinnati	21
1925—	Hazen (Kiki) Cuyler, Pittsburgh	26
1926—	Paul Waner, Pittsburgh	22
1927—	Paul Waner, Pittsburgh	17
1928—	James Bottomley, St. Louis	20
1929—	Lloyd Waner, Pittsburgh	20
1930—	Adam Comorosky, Pittsburgh	23
1931—	William Terry, New York	20
1932—	Floyd (Babe) Herman, Cincinnati	19
1933—	J. Floyd (Arky) Vaughan, Pittsburgh	19
1934—	Joseph Medwick, St. Louis	18
1935—	Ival Goodman, Cincinnati	18
1936—	Ival Goodman, Cincinnati	14
1937—	J. Floyd (Arky) Vaughan, Pittsburgh	17
1938—	John Mize, St. Louis	16
1939—	William Herman, Chicago	18
1940—	J. Floyd (Arky) Vaughan, Pittsburgh	15
1941—	Harold (Pete) Reiser, Brooklyn	17
1942—	Enos Slaughter, St. Louis	17
1943—	Stanley Musial, St. Louis	20
1944—	John Barrett, Pittsburgh	19
1945—	Luis Olmo, Brooklyn	13
1946—	Stanley Musial, St. Louis	20
1947—	Harry Walker, St. Louis-Philadelphia	16
1948—	Stanley Musial, St. Louis	18
1949—	Musial, St. Louis-Slaughter, St. Louis	13
1950—	Richie Ashburn, Philadelphia	14

Year	Player and Club	3B.
1951—	Musial, St. Louis-Bell, Pittsburgh	12
1952—	Robert Thomson, New York	14
1953—	James Gilliam, Brooklyn	17
1954—	Willie Mays, New York	13
1955—	Mays, New York-Long, Pittsburgh	13
1956—	William Bruton, Milwaukee	15
1957—	Willie Mays, New York	20
1958—	Richie Ashburn, Philadelphia	13
1959—	Moon, Los Angeles-Neal, Los Angeles	11
1960—	William Bruton, Milwaukee	13
1961—	George Altman, Chicago	12
1962—	Callison, Philadelphia-Virdon, Pitt.	10
	W. Davis, Wills, Los Angeles	10
1963—	Vada Pinson, Cincinnati	14
1964—	Allen, Philadelphia-Santo, Chicago	13
1965—	John Callison, Philadelphia	16
1966—	J. Timothy McCarver, St. Louis	13
1967—	Vada Pinson, Cincinnati	13
1968—	Louis Brock, St. Louis	14
1969—	Roberto Clemente, Pittsburgh	12
1970—	William Davis, Los Angeles	16
1971—	Joe Morgan, Houston	11
	Roger Metzger, Houston	11
1972—	Lawrence Bowa, Philadelphia	13
1973—	Roger Metzger, Houston	14
1974—	Ralph Garr, Atlanta	17
1975—	Ralph Garr, Atlanta	11
1976—	David Cash, Philadelphia	12
1977—	Garry Templeton, St. Louis	18
1978—	Garry Templeton, St. Louis	13
1979—	Garry Templeton, St. Louis	19

HOME RUN LEADERS

Year	Player and Club	HR.
1900—	Herman Long, Boston	12
1901—	Samuel Crawford, Cincinnati	16
1902—	Thomas Leach, Pittsburgh	6
1903—	James Sheckard, Brooklyn	9
1904—	Harry Lumley, Brooklyn	9
1905—	Fred Odwell, Cincinnati	9
1906—	Timothy Jordan, Brooklyn	12
1907—	David Brain, Boston	10
1908—	Timothy Jordan, Brooklyn	12
1909—	John (Red) Murray, New York	7
1910—	Fred Beck, Bos.-F. Schulte, Chi.	10
1911—	Frank Schulte, Chicago	21
1912—	Henry Zimmerman, Chicago	14
1913—	Cliff. (Gavvy) Cravath, Philadelphia	19
1914—	Cliff. (Gavvy) Cravath, Philadelphia	19
1915—	Cliff. (Gavvy) Cravath, Philadelphia	24
1916—	Robertson, New York-Williams, Chi.	12
1917—	Robertson, New York-Cravath, Phila.	12
1918—	Cliff. (Gavvy) Cravath, Philadelphia	8
1919—	Cliff. (Gavvy) Cravath, Philadelphia	12
1920—	Fred (Cy) Williams, Philadelphia	15
1921—	George Kelly, New York	23
1922—	Rogers Hornsby, St. Louis	42
1923—	Fred (Cy) Williams, Philadelphia	41
1924—	Jacques Fournier, Brooklyn	27
1925—	Rogers Hornsby, St. Louis	39

Year	Player and Club	HR.
1926—	Lewis (Hack) Wilson, Chicago	21
1927—	Wilson, Chicago-Williams, Philadelphia	30
1928—	Wilson, Chicago-Bottomley, St. Louis	31
1929—	Charles Klein, Philadelphia	43
1930—	Lewis (Hack) Wilson, Chicago	56
1931—	Charles Klein, Philadelphia	31
1932—	Klein, Philadelphia-Ott, New York	38
1933—	Charles Klein, Philadelphia	28
1934—	Collins, St. Louis-Ott, New York	35
1935—	Walter Berger, Boston	34
1936—	Melvin Ott, New York	33
1937—	Ott, New York-Medwick, St. Louis	31
1938—	Melvin Ott, New York	36
1939—	John Mize, St. Louis	28
1940—	John Mize, St. Louis	43
1941—	Adolph Camilli, Brooklyn	34
1942—	Melvin Ott, New York	30
1943—	William Nicholson, Chicago	29
1944—	William Nicholson, Chicago	33
1945—	Thomas Holmes, Boston	28
1946—	Ralph Kiner, Pittsburgh	23
1947—	Kiner, Pittsburgh-Mize, New York	51
1948—	Kiner, Pittsburgh-Mize, New York	40
1949—	Ralph Kiner, Pittsburgh	54
1950—	Ralph Kiner, Pittsburgh	47
1951—	Ralph Kiner, Pittsburgh	42

HOME RUN LEADERS—Continued

Year	Player and Club	HR.
1952—	Kiner, Pittsburgh-Sauer, Chicago	37
1953—	Edwin Mathews, Milwaukee	47
1954—	Theodore Kluszewski, Cincinnati	49
1955—	Willie Mays, New York	51
1956—	Edwin (Duke) Snider, Brooklyn	43
1957—	Henry Aaron, Milwaukee	44
1958—	Ernest Banks, Chicago	47
1959—	Edwin Mathews, Milwaukee	46
1960—	Ernest Banks, Chicago	41
1961—	Orlando Cepeda, San Francisco	46
1962—	Willie Mays, San Francisco	49
1963—	H. Aaron, Milw.-McCovey, San Fran.	44
1964—	Willie Mays, San Francisco	47
1965—	Willie Mays. San Francisco	52

Year	Player and Club	HR.
1966—	Henry Aaron, Atlanta	44
1967—	Henry Aaron, Atlanta	39
1968—	Willie McCovey, San Francisco	36
1969—	Willie McCovey, San Francisco	45
1970—	Johnny Bench, Cincinnati	45
1971—	Wilver Stargell, Pittsburgh	48
1972—	Johnny Bench, Cincinnati	40
1973—	Wilver Stargell, Pittsburgh	44
1974—	Michael Schmidt, Philadelphia	36
1975—	Michael Schmidt, Philadelphia	38
1976—	Michael Schmidt, Philadelphia	38
1977—	George Foster, Cincinnati	52
1978—	George Foster, Cincinnati	40
1979—	David Kingman, Chicago	48

LEADERS IN TOTAL BASES

Year	Player and Club	T.B.
1900—	John (Honus) Wagner, Pittsburgh	302
	Elmer Flick, Philadelphia	302
1901—	Jesse Burkett, St. Louis	314
1902—	Samuel Crawford, Cincinnati	256
1903—	Clarence Beaumont, Pittsburgh	272
1904—	John (Honus) Wagner, Pittsburgh	255
1905—	J. Bentley Seymour, Cincinnati	325
1906—	John (Honus) Wagner, Pittsburgh	237
1907—	John (Honus) Wagner, Pittsburgh	264
1908—	John (Honus) Wagner, Pittsburgh	308
1909—	John (Honus) Wagner, Pittsburgh	242
1910—	Sherwood Magee, Philadelphia	263
1911—	Frank Schulte, Chicago	308
1912—	Henry Zimmerman, Chicago	318
1913—	Cliff (Gavvy) Cravath, Philadelphia	298
1914—	Sherwood Magee, Philadelphia	277
1915—	Cliff (Gavvy) Cravath, Philadelphia	266
1916—	Zachariah Wheat, Brooklyn	262
1917—	Rogers Hornsby, St. Louis	253
1918—	Charles Hollocher, Chicago	202
1919—	Henry (Hi) Myers, Brooklyn	223
1920—	Rogers Hornsby, St. Louis	329
1921—	Rogers Hornsby, St. Louis	378
1922—	Rogers Hornsby, St. Louis	450
1923—	Frank Frisch, New York	311
1924—	Rogers Hornsby, St. Louis	373
1925—	Rogers Hornsby, St. Louis	381
1926—	James Bottomley, St. Louis	305
1927—	Paul Waner, Pittsburgh	338
1928—	James Bottomley, St. Louis	362
1929—	Rogers Hornsby, Chicago	409
1930—	Charles Klein, Philadelphia	445
1931—	Charles Klein, Philadelphia	347
1932—	Charles Klein, Philadelphia	420
1933—	Charles Klein, Philadelphia	365
1934—	James (Rip) Collins, St. Louis	369
1935—	Joseph Medwick, St. Louis	365
1936—	Joseph Medwick, St. Louis	367
1937—	Joseph Medwick, St. Louis	406
1938—	John Mize, St. Louis	326
1939—	John Mize. St. Louis	353

Year	Player and Club	T.B.
1940—	John Mize, St. Louis	368
1941—	Harold (Pete) Reiser, Brooklyn	299
1942—	Enos Slaughter, St. Louis	292
1943—	Stanley Musial, St. Louis	347
1944—	William Nicholson, Chicago	317
1945—	Thomas Holmes, Boston	367
1946—	Stanley Musial, St. Louis	366
1947—	Ralph Kiner, Pittsburgh	361
1948—	Stanley Musial, St. Louis	429
1949—	Stanley Musial, St. Louis	382
1950—	Edwin (Duke) Snider, Brooklyn	343
1951—	Stanley Musial, St. Louis	355
1952—	Stanley Musial, St. Louis	311
1953—	Edwin (Duke) Snider, Brooklyn	370
1954—	Edwin (Duke) Snider, Brooklyn	378
1955—	Willie Mays, New York	382
1956—	Henry Aaron, Milwaukee	340
1957—	Henry Aaron, Milwaukee	369
1958—	Ernest Banks, Chicago	379
1959—	Henry Aaron, Milwaukee	400
1960—	Henry Aaron, Milwaukee	334
1961—	Henry Aaron, Milwaukee	358
1962—	Willie Mays, San Francisco	382
1963—	Henry Aaron, Milwaukee	370
1964—	Richard Allen, Philadelphia	352
1965—	Willie Mays, San Francisco	360
1966—	Felipe Alou, Atlanta	355
1967—	Henry Aaron, Atlanta	344
1968—	Billy Williams, Chicago	321
1969—	Henry Aaron, Atlanta	332
1970—	Billy Williams, Chicago	373
1971—	Joseph Torre, St. Louis	352
1972—	Billy Williams, Chicago	348
1973—	Bobby Bonds, San Francisco	341
1974—	Johnny Bench, Cincinnati	315
1975—	Gregory Luzinski, Philadelphia	322
1976—	Michael Schmidt, Philadelphia	306
1977—	George Foster, Cincinnati	388
1978—	David Parker, Pittsburgh	340
1979—	David Winfield, San Diego	333

RUNS BATTED IN LEADERS

Year	Player and Club	RBI	Year	Player and Club	RBI
1907	John (Honus) Wagner, Pittsburgh	91	1943	William Nicholson, Chicago	128
1908	John (Honus) Wagner, Pittsburgh	106	1944	William Nicholson, Chicago	122
1909	John (Honus) Wagner, Pittsburgh	102	1945	Fred (Dixie) Walker, Brooklyn	124
1910	Sherwood Magee, Philadelphia	116	1946	Enos Slaughter, St. Louis	130
1911	Frank Schulte, Chicago	121	1947	John Mize, New York	138
1912	Henry Zimmerman, Chicago	98	1948	Stanley Musial, St. Louis	131
1913	Cliff (Gavvy) Cravath, Philadelphia	118	1949	Ralph Kiner, Pittsburgh	127
1914	Sherwood Magee, Philadelphia	101	1950	Delmer Ennis, Philadelphia	126
1915	Cliff (Gavvy) Cravath, Philadelphia	118	1951	Monford Irvin, New York	121
1916	Harold Chase, Cincinnati	84	1952	Henry Sauer, Chicago	121
1917	Henry Zimmerman, New York	100	1953	Roy Campanella, Brooklyn	142
1918	Frederick Merkle, Chicago	71	1954	Theodore Kluszewski, Cincinnati	141
1919	Henry (Hi) Myers, Brooklyn	72	1955	Edwin (Duke) Snider, Brooklyn	136
1920	George Kelly, New York	94	1956	Stanley Musial, St. Louis	109
	Rogers Hornsby, St. Louis	94	1957	Henry Aaron, Milwaukee	132
1921	Rogers Hornsby, St. Louis	126	1958	Ernest Banks, Chicago	129
1922	Rogers Hornsby, St. Louis	152	1959	Ernest Banks, Chicago	143
1923	Emil Meusel, New York	125	1960	Henry Aaron, Milwaukee	126
1924	George Kelly, New York	136	1961	Orlando Cepeda, San Francisco	142
1925	Rogers Hornsby, St. Louis	143	1962	H. Thomas Davis, Los Angeles	153
1926	James Bottomley, St. Louis	120	1963	Henry Aaron, Milwaukee	130
1927	Paul Waner, Pittsburgh	131	1964	Kenton Boyer, St. Louis	119
1928	James Bottomley, St. Louis	136	1965	Deron Johnson, Cincinnati	130
1929	Lewis (Hack) Wilson, Chicago	159	1966	Henry Aaron, Atlanta	127
1930	Lewis (Hack) Wilson, Chicago	190	1967	Orlando Cepeda, St. Louis	111
1931	Charles Klein, Philadelphia	121	1968	Willie McCovey, San Francisco	105
1932	Frank (Don) Hurst, Philadelphia	143	1969	Willie McCovey, San Francisco	126
1933	Charles Klein, Philadelphia	120	1970	Johnny Bench, Cincinnati	148
1934	Melvin Ott, New York	135	1971	Joseph Torre, St. Louis	137
1935	Walter Berger, Boston	130	1972	Johnny Bench, Cincinnati	125
1936	Joseph Medwick, St. Louis	138	1973	Wilver Stargell, Pittsburgh	119
1937	Joseph Medwick, St. Louis	154	1974	Johnny Bench, Cincinnati	129
1938	Joseph Medwick, St. Louis	122	1975	Gregory Luzinski, Philadelphia	120
1939	Frank McCormick, Cincinnati	128	1976	George Foster, Cincinnati	121
1940	John Mize, St. Louis	137	1977	George Foster, Cincinnati	149
1941	Adolph Camilli, Brooklyn	120	1978	George Foster, Cincinnati	120
1942	John Mize, New York	110	1979	David Winfield, San Diego	118

Note—Runs batted in not compiled prior to 1907; officially adopted in 1920.

BATTERS LEADING IN BASES ON BALLS

Year	Player and Club	BB.	Year	Player and Club	BB.
1910	Miller Huggins, St. Louis	116	1931	Melvin Ott, New York	80
1911	James Sheckard, Chicago	147	1932	Melvin Ott, New York	100
1912	James Sheckard, Chicago	122	1933	Melvin Ott, New York	75
1913	Robert Bescher, Cincinnati	94	1934	J. Floyd (Arky) Vaughan, Pittsburgh	94
1914	Miller Huggins, St. Louis	105	1935	J. Floyd (Arky) Vaughan, Pittsburgh	97
1915	Cliff. (Gavvy) Cravath, Philadelphia	86	1936	J. Floyd (Arky) Vaughan, Pittsburgh	118
1916	Henry Groh, Cincinnati	84	1937	Melvin Ott, New York	102
1917	George Burns, New York	75	1938	Adolph Camilli, Brooklyn	119
1918	Max Carey, Pittsburgh	62	1939	Adolph Camilli, Brooklyn	110
1919	George Burns, New York	82	1940	Elburt Fletcher, Pittsburgh	119
1920	George Burns, New York	76	1941	Elburt Fletcher, Pittsburgh	118
1921	George Burns, New York	80	1942	Melvin Ott, New York	109
1922	Max Carey, Pittsburgh	80	1943	August Galan, Brooklyn	103
1923	George Burns, New York	101	1944	August Galan, Brooklyn	101
1924	Rogers Hornsby, St. Louis	89	1945	Edward Stanky, Brooklyn	148
1925	Jacques Fournier, Brooklyn	86	1946	Edward Stanky, Brooklyn	137
1926	Lewis (Hack) Wilson, Chicago	69	1947	Henry Greenberg, Pittsburgh	104
1927	Rogers Hornsby, New York	86		Harold (Pee Wee) Reese, Brooklyn	104
1928	Rogers Hornsby, Boston	107	1948	Robert Elliott, Boston	131
1929	Melvin Ott, New York	113	1949	Ralph Kiner, Pittsburgh	117
1930	Lewis (Hack) Wilson, Chicago	105	1950	Edward Stanky, New York	144

BATTERS LEADING IN BASES ON BALLS—Continued

Year	Player and Club	BB.	Year	Player and Club	BB.
1951	Ralph Kiner, Pittsburgh	137	1965	Joe Morgan, Houston	97
1952	Ralph Kiner, Pittsburgh	110	1966	Ronald Santo, Chicago	95
1953	Stanley Musial, St. Louis	105	1967	Ronald Santo, Chicago	96
1954	Richie Ashburn, Philadelphia	125	1968	Ronald Santo, Chicago	96
1955	Edwin Mathews, Milwaukee	109	1969	James Wynn, Houston	148
1956	Edwin (Duke) Snider, Brooklyn	99	1970	Willie McCovey, San Francisco	137
1957	Richie Ashburn, Philadelphia	94	1971	Willie Mays, San Francisco	112
	John Temple, Cincinnati	94	1972	Joe Morgan, Cincinnati	115
1958	Richie Ashburn, Philadelphia	97	1973	Darrell Evans, Atlanta	124
1959	James Gilliam, Los Angeles	96	1974	Darrell Evans, Atlanta	126
1960	Richie Ashburn, Chicago	116	1975	Joe Morgan, Cincinnati	132
1961	Edwin Mathews, Milwaukee	93	1976	James Wynn, Atlanta	127
1962	Edwin Mathews, Milwaukee	101	1977	F. Gene Tenace, San Diego	125
1963	Edwin Mathews, Milwaukee	124	1978	Jeffrey Burroughs, Atlanta	117
1964	Ronald Santo, Chicago	86	1979	Michael Schmidt, Philadelphia	120

Note—Bases on balls not included in batting records in National League prior to 1910.

BATTERS LEADING IN STRIKEOUTS

Year	Player and Club	SO.	Year	Player and Club	SO.
1910	John Hummel, Brooklyn	81	1944	Vincent DiMaggio, Pittsburgh	83
1911	Robert Coulson, Brooklyn	78	1945	Vincent DiMaggio, Philadelphia	91
	Robert Bescher, Cincinnati	78	1946	Ralph Kiner, Pittsburgh	109
1912	Edward McDonald, Boston	91	1947	William Nicholson, Chicago	83
1913	George Burns, New York	74	1948	Henry Sauer, Cincinnati	85
1914	Frederick Merkle, New York	80	1949	Edwin (Duke) Snider, Brooklyn	92
1915	H. Douglas Baird, Pittsburgh	88	1950	Roy Smalley, Chicago	114
1916	Cliff. (Gavvy) Cravath, Philadelphia	89	1951	Gilbert Hodges, Brooklyn	99
1917	Fred Williams, Chicago	78	1952	Edwin Mathews, Boston	115
1918	Ross Youngs, New York	49	1953	Stephen Bilko, St. Louis	125
	George Paskert, Chicago	49	1954	Edwin (Duke) Snider, Brooklyn	96
1919	Raymond Powell, Boston	79	1955	Walter Post, Cincinnati	102
1920	George Kelly, New York	92	1956	Walter Post, Cincinnati	124
1921	Raymond Powell, Boston	85	1957	Edwin (Duke) Snider, Brooklyn	104
1922	Frank Parkinson, Philadelphia	93	1958	Harry Anderson, Philadelphia	95
1923	George Grantham, Chicago	92	1959	Walter Post, Philadelphia	101
1924	George Grantham, Chicago	63	1960	J. Francisco Herrera, Philadelphia	136
1925	Chas. (Gabby) Hartnett, Chicago	77	1961	Richard Stuart, Pittsburgh	121
1926	Bernard Friberg, Philadelphia	77	1962	Kenneth Hubbs, Chicago	129
1927	Lewis (Hack) Wilson, Chicago	70	1963	Donn Clendenon, Pittsburgh	136
1928	Lewis (Hack) Wilson, Chicago	94	1964	Richard Allen, Philadelphia	138
1929	Lewis (Hack) Wilson, Chicago	83	1965	Richard Allen, Philadelphia	150
1930	Lewis (Hack) Wilson, Chicago	84	1966	Byron Browne, Chicago	143
1931	H. Nicholas Cullop, Cincinnati	86	1967	James Wynn, Houston	137
1932	Lewis (Hack) Wilson, Brooklyn	85	1968	Donn Clendenon, Pittsburgh	163
1933	Walter Berger, Boston	77	1969	Bobby Bonds, San Francisco	187
1934	Adolph Camilli, Chicago-Philadelphia	94	1970	Bobby Bonds, San Francisco	189
1935	Adolph Camilli, Philadelphia	113	1971	Wilver Stargell, Pittsburgh	154
1936	Wilbur Brubaker, Pittsburgh	96	1972	Lee May, Houston	145
1937	Vincent DiMaggio, Boston	111	1973	Bobby Bonds, San Francisco	148
1938	Vincent DiMaggio, Boston	134	1974	Michael Schmidt, Philadelphia	138
1939	Adolph Camilli, Brooklyn	107	1975	Michael Schmidt, Philadelphia	180
1940	Chester Ross, Boston	128	1976	Michael Schmidt, Philadelphia	149
1941	Adolph Camilli, Brooklyn	115	1977	Gregory Luzinski, Philadelphia	140
1942	Vincent DiMaggio, Pittsburgh	87	1978	Dale Murphy, Atlanta	145
1943	Vincent DiMaggio, Pittsburgh	126	1979	David Kingman, Chicago	131

Note—Strikeouts not included in batting records in National League prior to 1910.

LEADING BASE STEALERS

Year	Player and Club	SB.	Year	Player and Club	SB.
1900	James Barrett, Cincinnati	46	1940	Linus Frey, Cincinnati	22
1901	John (Honus) Wagner, Pittsburgh	48	1941	Daniel Murtaugh, Philadelphia	18
1902	John (Honus) Wagner, Pittsburgh	43	1942	Harold (Pete) Reiser, Brooklyn	20
1903	Sheckard, Brooklyn-Chance, Chicago	67	1943	J. Floyd (Arky) Vaughan, Brooklyn	20
1904	John (Honus) Wagner, Pittsburgh	58	1944	John Barrett, Pittsburgh	28
1905	Maloney, Chicago-Devlin, New York	59	1945	Al. (Red) Schoendienst, St. Louis	26
1906	Frank Chance, Chicago	57	1946	Harold (Pete) Reiser, Brooklyn	34
1907	John (Honus) Wagner, Pittsburgh	61	1947	Jack Robinson, Brooklyn	29
1908	John (Honus) Wagner, Pittsburgh	53	1948	Richie Ashburn, Philadelphia	32
1909	Robert Bescher, Cincinnati	54	1949	Jack Robinson, Brooklyn	37
1910	Robert Bescher, Cincinnati	70	1950	Samuel Jethroe, Boston	35
1911	Robert Bescher, Cincinnati	80	1951	Samuel Jethroe, Boston	35
1912	Robert Bescher, Cincinnati	67	1952	Harold (Pee Wee) Reese, Brooklyn	30
1913	Max Carey, Pittsburgh	61	1953	William Bruton, Milwaukee	26
1914	George Burns, New York	62	1954	William Bruton, Milwaukee	34
1915	Max Carey, Pittsburgh	36	1955	William Bruton, Milwaukee	35
1916	Max Carey, Pittsburgh	63	1956	Willie Mays, New York	40
1917	Max Carey, Pittsburgh	46	1957	Willie Mays, New York	38
1918	Max Carey, Pittsburgh	58	1958	Willie Mays, San Francisco	31
1919	George Burns, New York	40	1959	Willie Mays, San Francisco	27
1920	Max Carey, Pittsburgh	52	1960	Maurice Wills, Los Angeles	50
1921	Frank Frisch, New York	49	1961	Maurice Wills, Los Angeles	35
1922	Max Carey, Pittsburgh	51	1962	Maurice Wills, Los Angeles	104
1923	Max Carey, Pittsburgh	51	1963	Maurice Wills, Los Angeles	40
1924	Max Carey, Pittsburgh	49	1964	Maurice Wills, Los Angeles	53
1925	Max Carey, Pittsburgh	46	1965	Maurice Wills, Los Angeles	94
1926	Hazen (Kiki) Cuyler, Pittsburgh	35	1966	Louis Brock, St. Louis	74
1927	Frank Frisch, St. Louis	48	1967	Louis Brock, St. Louis	52
1928	Hazen (Kiki) Cuyler, Chicago	37	1968	Louis Brock, St. Louis	62
1929	Hazen (Kiki) Cuyler, Chicago	43	1969	Louis Brock, St. Louis	53
1930	Hazen (Kiki) Cuyler, Chicago	37	1970	Robert Tolan, Cincinnati	57
1931	Frank Frisch, St. Louis	28	1971	Louis Brock, St. Louis	64
1932	Charles Klein, Philadelphia	20	1972	Louis Brock, St. Louis	63
1933	John (Pepper) Martin, St. Louis	26	1973	Louis Brock, St. Louis	70
1934	John (Pepper) Martin, St. Louis	23	1974	Louis Brock, St. Louis	118
1935	August Galan, Chicago	22	1975	David Lopes, Los Angeles	77
1936	John (Pepper) Martin, St. Louis	23	1976	David Lopes, Los Angeles	63
1937	August Galan, Chicago	23	1977	Franklin Taveras, Pittsburgh	70
1938	Stanley Hack, Chicago	16	1978	Omar Moreno, Pittsburgh	71
1939	Hack, Chicago-Handley, Pittsburgh	17	1979	Omar Moreno, Pittsburgh	77

SLUGGING LEADERS

Year	Player and Club	Slug. Avg.	Year	Player and Club	Slug. Avg.
1900	John (Honus) Wagner, Pittsburgh	.572	1919	Henry (Hi) Myers, Brooklyn	.436
1901	James Sheckard, Brooklyn	.536	1920	Rogers Hornsby, St. Louis	.559
1902	John (Honus) Wagner, Pittsburgh	.467	1921	Rogers Hornsby, St. Louis	.659
1903	Fred Clarke, Pittsburgh	.532	1922	Rogers Hornsby, St. Louis	.722
1904	John (Honus) Wagner, Pittsburgh	.520	1923	Rogers Hornsby, St. Louis	.627
1905	J. Bentley Seymour, Cincinnati	.559	1924	Rogers Hornsby, St. Louis	.696
1906	Harry Lumley, Brooklyn	.477	1925	Rogers Hornsby, St. Louis	.756
1907	John (Honus) Wagner, Pittsburgh	.513	1926	Fred Williams, Philadelphia	.569
1908	John (Honus) Wagner, Pittsburgh	.542	1927	Charles Hafey, St. Louis	.590
1909	John (Honus) Wagner, Pittsburgh	.489	1928	Rogers Hornsby, Boston	.632
1910	Sherwood Magee, Philadelphia	.507	1929	Rogers Hornsby, Chicago	.679
1911	Frank Schulte, Chicago	.534	1930	Lewis (Hack) Wilson, Chicago	.723
1912	Henry Zimmerman, Chicago	.571	1931	Charles Klein, Philadelphia	.584
1913	Cliff. (Gavvy) Cravath, Philadelphia	.568	1932	Charles Klein, Philadelphia	.646
1914	Sherwood Magee, Philadelphia	.501	1933	Charles Klein, Philadelphia	.602
1915	Cliff. (Gavvy) Cravath, Philadelphia	.510	1934	James (Rip) Collins, Philadelphia	.615
1916	Zachariah Wheat, Brooklyn	.461	1935	J. Floyd (Arky) Vaughan, Pittsburgh	.607
1917	Rogers Hornsby, St. Louis	.484	1936	Melvin Ott, New York	.588
1918	Edd Roush, Cincinnati	.455	1937	Joseph Medwick, St. Louis	.641

SLUGGING LEADERS—Continued

Year Player and Club	Slug. Avg.	Year Player and Club	Slug. Avg.
1938—John Mize, St. Louis	.614	1959—Henry Aaron, Milwaukee	.636
1939—John Mize, St. Louis	.626	1960—Frank Robinson, Cincinnati	.595
1940—John Mize, St. Louis	.636	1961—Frank Robinson, Cincinnati	.611
1941—Harold (Pete) Reiser, Brooklyn	.558	1962—Frank Robinson, Cincinnati	.624
1942—John Mize, New York	.521	1963—Henry Aaron, Milwaukee	.586
1943—Stanley Musial, St. Louis	.562	1964—Willie Mays, San Francisco	.607
1944—Stanley Musial, St. Louis	.549	1965—Willie Mays, San Francisco	.645
1945—Tommy Holmes, Boston	.577	1966—Richard Allen, Philadelphia	.632
1946—Stanley Musial, St. Louis	.587	1967—Henry Aaron, Atlanta	.573
1947—Ralph Kiner, Pittsburgh	.639	1968—Willie McCovey, San Francisco	.545
1948—Stanley Musial, St. Louis	.702	1969—Willie McCovey, San Francisco	.656
1949—Ralph Kiner, Pittsburgh	.658	1970—Willie McCovey, San Francisco	.612
1950—Stanley Musial, St. Louis	.596	1971—Henry Aaron, Atlanta	.669
1951—Ralph Kiner, Pittsburgh	.627	1972—Billy Williams, Chicago	.606
1952—Stanley Musial, St. Louis	.538	1973—Wilver Stargell, Pittsburgh	.646
1953—Edwin (Duke) Snider, Brooklyn	.6271	1974—Michael Schmidt, Philadelphia	.546
1954—Willie Mays, New York	.667	1975—David Parker, Pittsburgh	.541
1955—Willie Mays, New York	.659	1976—Joe Morgan, Cincinnati	.576
1956—Edwin (Duke) Snider, Brooklyn	.598	1977—George Foster, Cincinnati	.631
1957—Willie Mays, New York	.626	1978—David Parker, Pittsburgh	.585
1958—Ernest Banks, Chicago	.614	1979—David Kingman, Chicago	.613

DAVE KINGMAN—Silent Slugger

LEADING PITCHERS IN WINNING PERCENTAGE

(15 OR MORE VICTORIES)

Year	Pitcher	Club	Won	Lost	Pct.
1900—Joseph McGinnity		Brooklyn	29	9	.763
1901—John Chesbro		Pittsburgh	21	9	.700
1902—John Chesbro		Pittsburgh	28	6	.824
1903—Samuel Leever		Pittsburgh	25	7	.781
1904—Joseph McGinnity		New York	35	8	.814
1905—Samuel Leever		Pittsburgh	20	5	.800
1906—Edward Reulbach		Chicago	19	4	.826
1907—Edward Reulbach		Chicago	17	4	.810
1908—Edward Reulbach		Chicago	24	7	.774
1909—Christy Mathewson		New York	25	6	.806
Howard Camnitz		Pittsburgh	25	6	.806
1910—Leonard Cole		Chicago	20	4	.833
1911—Richard (Rube) Marquard		New York	24	7	.774
1912—Claude Hendrix		Pittsburgh	24	9	.727
1913—Albert Humphries		Chicago	16	4	.800
1914—Williams James		Boston	26	7	.788
1915—Grover Alexander		Philadelphia	31	10	.756
1916—Thomas Hughes		Boston	16	3	.842
1917—Ferdinand Schupp		New York	21	7	.750
1918—Claude Hendrix		Chicago	20	7	.741
1919—Walter Ruether		Cincinnati	19	6	.760
1920—Burleigh Grimes		Brooklyn	23	11	.676
1921—William L. Doak		St. Louis	15	6	.714
1922—Peter Donohue		Cincinnati	18	9	.667
1923—Adolfo Luque		Cincinnati	27	8	.771
1924—Emil Yde		Pittsburgh	16	3	.842
1925—William Sherdel		St. Louis	15	6	.714
1926—Ray Kremer		Pittsburgh	20	6	.769
1927—Lawrence Benton		Boston-New York	17	7	.708
1928—Lawrence Benton		New York	25	9	.735
1929—Charles Root		Chicago	19	6	.760
1930—Fred Fitzsimmons		New York	19	7	.731
1931—Paul Derringer		St. Louis	18	8	.692
1932—Lonnie Warneke		Chicago	22	6	.786
1933—Benjamin Cantwell		Boston	20	10	.667
1934—Jerome (Dizzy) Dean		St. Louis	30	7	.811
1935—William Lee		Chicago	20	6	.769
1936—Carl Hubbell		New York	26	6	.813
1937—Carl Hubbell		New York	22	8	.733
1938—William Lee		Chicago	22	9	.710
1939—Paul Derringer		Cincinnati	25	7	.781
1940—Fred Fitzsimmons		Brooklyn	16	2	.889
1941—Elmer Riddle		Cincinnati	19	4	.826
1942—Lawrence French		Brooklyn	15	4	.789
1943—Morton Cooper		St. Louis	21	8	.724
1944—Theodore Wilks		St. Louis	17	4	.810
1945—Harry Breechen		St. Louis	15	4	.789
1946—Murry Dickson		St. Louis	15	6	.714
1947—Lawrence Jansen		New York	21	5	.808
1948—Harry Brecheen		St. Louis	20	7	.741
1949—Elwin (Preacher) Roe		Brooklyn	15	6	.714
1950—Salvatore Maglie		New York	18	4	.818
1951—Elwin (Preacher) Roe		Brooklyn	22	3	.880
1952—J. Hoyt Wilhelm		New York	15	3	.833
1953—Carl Erskine		Brooklyn	20	6	.769
1954—John Antonelli		New York	21	7	.750
1955—Donald Newcombe		Brooklyn	20	5	.800
1956—Donald Newcombe		Brooklyn	27	7	.794
1957—Robert Buhl		Milwaukee	18	7	.720
1958—Warren E. Spahn		Milwaukee	22	11	.667
S. Lewis Burdette		Milwaukee	20	10	.667
1959—ElRoy Face		Pittsburgh	18	1	.947
1960—Ernest Broglio		St. Louis	21	9	.700
1961—John Podres		Los Angeles	18	5	.783

LEADING PITCHERS IN WINNING PERCENTAGE—Continued

(15 or MORE VICTORIES)

Year	Pitcher	Club	Won	Lost	Pct.
1962—	Robert Purkey	Cincinnati	23	5	.821
1963—	Ronald Perranoski	Los Angeles	16	3	.842
1964—	Sanford Koufax	Los Angeles	19	5	.792
1965—	Sanford Koufax	Los Angeles	26	8	.765
1966—	Juan Marichal	San Francisco	25	6	.806
1967—	Richard Hughes	St. Louis	16	6	.727
1968—	Stephen R. Blass	Pittsburgh	18	6	.750
1969—	G. Thomas Seaver	New York	25	7	.781
1970—	Robert Gibson	St. Louis	23	7	.767
1971—	Donald E. Gullett	Cincinnati	16	6	.727
1972—	Gary L. Nolan	Cincinnati	15	5	.750
1973—	Thomas E. John	Los Angeles	16	7	.696
1974—	John (Andy) Messersmith	Los Angeles	20	6	.769
1975—	Donald E. Gullett	Cincinnati	15	4	.789
1976—	Steven N. Carlton	Philadelphia	20	7	.741
1977—	John R. Candelaria	Pittsburgh	20	5	.800
1978—	Gaylord J. Perry	San Diego	21	6	.778
1979—	G. Thomas Seaver	Cincinnati	16	6	.727

LEADING PITCHERS—EARNED-RUN AVERAGE

(Based on Ten Complete Games Through 1950, Then 154 Innings Until N. L. Expanded in 1962, When It Became 162 Innings)

Year	Pitcher and Club	G.	IP.	ERA.	Year	Pitcher and Club	G.	IP.	ERA.
1912—	Tesreau, New York	36	243	1.96	1946—	Pollet, St. Louis	40	266	2.10
1913—	Mathewson, New York	40	306	2.06	1947—	Spahn, Boston	40	290	2.33
1914—	Doak, St. Louis	36	256	1.72	1948—	Brecheen, St. Louis	33	233	2.24
1915—	Alexander, Philadelphia	49	376	1.22	1949—	Koslo, New York	38	212	2.50
1916—	Alexander, Philadelphia	48	390	1.55	1950—	Hearn, St. Louis-New York	22	134	2.49
1917—	Alexander, Philadelphia	45	388	1.83	1951—	Nichols, Boston	33	156	2.88
1918—	Vaughn, Chicago	35	290	1.74	1952—	Wilhelm, New York	71	159	2.43
1919—	Alexander, Chicago	30	235	1.72	1953—	Spahn, Milwaukee	35	266	2.10
1920—	Alexander, Chicago	46	363	1.91	1954—	Antonelli, New York	39	259	2.29
1921—	Doak, St. Louis	32	209	2.58	1955—	Friend, Pittsburgh	44	200	2.84
1922—	Ryan, New York	46	192	3.00	1956—	Burdette, Milwaukee	39	256	2.71
1923—	Luque, Cincinnati	41	322	1.93	1957—	Podres, Brooklyn	31	196	2.66
1924—	Vance, Brooklyn	35	309	2.16	1958—	Miller, San Francisco	41	182	2.47
1925—	Luque, Cincinnati	36	291	2.63	1959—	S. Jones, San Francisco	50	271	2.82
1926—	Kremer, Pittsburgh	37	231	2.61	1960—	McCormick, San Francisco	40	253	2.70
1927—	Kremer, Pittsburgh	35	226	2.47	1961—	Spahn, Milwaukee	38	263	3.01
1928—	Vance, Brooklyn	38	280	2.09	1962—	Koufax, Los Angeles	28	184	2.54
1929—	Walker, New York	29	178	3.08	1963—	Koufax, Los Angeles	40	311	1.88
1930—	Vance, Brooklyn	35	259	2.61	1964—	Koufax, Los Angeles	29	223	1.74
1931—	Walker, New York	37	239	2.26	1965—	Koufax, Los Angeles	43	336	2.04
1932—	Warneke, Chicago	35	277	2.37	1966—	Koufax, Los Angeles	41	323	1.73
1933—	Hubbell, New York	45	309	1.66	1967—	P. Niekro, Atlanta	46	207	1.87
1934—	Hubbell, New York	49	313	2.30	1968—	Gibson, St. Louis	34	305	1.12
1935—	Blanton, Pittsburgh	35	254	2.59	1969—	Marichal, San Francisco	37	300	2.10
1936—	Hubbell, New York	42	304	2.31	1970—	Seaver, New York	37	291	2.81
1937—	Turner, Boston	33	257	2.38	1971—	Seaver, New York	36	286	1.76
1938—	W. Lee, Chicago	44	291	2.66	1972—	Carlton, Philadelphia	41	346	1.98
1939—	Walters, Cincinnati	39	319	2.29	1973—	Seaver, New York	36	290	2.08
1940—	Walters, Cincinnati	36	305	2.48	1974—	Capra, Atlanta	39	217	2.28
1941—	E. Riddle, Cincinnati	33	217	2.24	1975—	Jones, San Diego	37	285	2.24
1942—	M. Cooper, St. Louis	37	279	1.77	1976—	Denny, St. Louis	30	207	2.52
1943—	Pollet, St. Louis	16	118	1.75	1977—	Candelaria, Pittsburgh	33	231	2.34
1944—	Heusser, Cincinnati	30	193	2.38	1978—	Swan, New York	29	207	2.43
1945—	Borowy, Chicago	15	122	2.14	1979—	Richard, Houston	38	292	2.71

Note—Earned-run records not tabulated in National League prior to 1912.

STRIKEOUT LEADERS—PITCHING

Year	Pitcher and Club	SO.
1900	George (Rube) Waddell, Pittsburgh	133
1901	Frank (Noodles) Hahn, Cincinnati	233
1902	Victor Willis, Boston	226
1903	Christopher Mathewson, New York	267
1904	Christopher Mathewson, New York	212
1905	Christopher Mathewson, New York	206
1906	Frederick Beebe, Chicago-St. Louis	171
1907	Christopher Mathewson, New York	178
1908	Christopher Mathewson, New York	259
1909	Orval Overall, Chicago	205
1910	Christopher Mathewson, New York	190
1911	Richard (Rube) Marquard, New York	237
1912	Grover Alexander, Philadelphia	195
1913	Thomas Seaton, Philadelphia	168
1914	Grover Alexander, Philadelphia	214
1915	Grover Alexander, Philadelphia	241
1916	Grover Alexander, Philadelphia	167
1917	Grover Alexander, Philadelphia	200
1918	James (Hippo) Vaughn, Chicago	148
1919	James (Hippo) Vaughn, Chicago	141
1920	Grover Alexander, Chicago	173
1921	Burleigh Grimes, Brooklyn	136
1922	Arthur (Dazzy) Vance, Brooklyn	134
1923	Arthur (Dazzy) Vance, Brooklyn	197
1924	Arthur (Dazzy) Vance, Brooklyn	262
1925	Arthur (Dazzy) Vance, Brooklyn	221
1926	Arthur (Dazzy) Vance, Brooklyn	140
1927	Arthur (Dazzy) Vance, Brooklyn	184
1928	Arthur (Dazzy) Vance, Brooklyn	200
1929	Perce (Pat) Malone, Chicago	166
1930	William Hallahan, St. Louis	177
1931	William Hallahan, St. Louis	159
1932	Jerome (Dizzy) Dean, St. Louis	191
1933	Jerome (Dizzy) Dean, St. Louis	199
1934	Jerome (Dizzy) Dean, St. Louis	195
1935	Jerome (Dizzy) Dean, St. Louis	182
1936	Van Lingle Mungo, Brooklyn	238
1937	Carl Hubbell, New York	159
1938	Claiborne Bryant, Chicago	135
1939	Claude Passeau, Philadelphia-Chicago	137
	William (Bucky) Walters, Cincinnati	137
1940	W. Kirby Higbe, Philadelphia	137
1941	John Vander Meer, Cincinnati	202
1942	John Vander Meer, Cincinnati	186
1943	John Vander Meer, Cincinnati	174
1944	William Voiselle, New York	161
1945	Elwin (Preacher) Roe, Pittsburgh	148
1946	John Schmitz, Chicago	135
1947	Ewell Blackwell, Cincinnati	193
1948	Harry Brecheen, St. Louis	149
1949	Warren Spahn, Boston	151
1950	Warren Spahn, Boston	191
1951	Warren Spahn, Boston	164
	Donald Newcombe, Brooklyn	164
1952	Warren Spahn, Boston	183
1953	Robin Roberts, Philadelphia	198
1954	Robin Roberts, Philadelphia	185
1955	Samuel Jones, Chicago	198
1956	Samuel Jones, Chicago	176
1957	John Sanford, Philadelphia	188
1958	Samuel Jones, St. Louis	225
1959	Donald Drysdale, Los Angeles	242
1960	Donald Drysdale, Los Angeles	246
1961	Sanford Koufax, Los Angeles	269
1962	Donald Drysdale, Los Angeles	232
1963	Sanford Koufax, Los Angeles	306
1964	Robert Veale, Pittsburgh	250
1965	Sanford Koufax, Los Angeles	382
1966	Sanford Koufax, Los Angeles	317
1967	James Bunning, Philadelphia	253
1968	Robert Gibson, St. Louis	268
1969	Ferguson Jenkins, Chicago	273
1970	G. Thomas Seaver, New York	283
1971	G. Thomas Seaver, New York	289
1972	Steven Carlton, Philadelphia	310
1973	G. Thomas Seaver, New York	251
1974	Steven Carlton, Philadelphia	240
1975	G. Thomas Seaver, New York	243
1976	G. Thomas Seaver, New York	235
1977	Philip Niekro, Atlanta	262
1978	James R. Richard, Houston	303
1979	James R. Richard, Houston	313

SHUTOUT LEADERS

Year	Pitcher and Club	ShO.
1900	Clark C. Griffith, Chicago	4
	Frank G. Hahn, Cincinnati	4
	Charles A. Nichols, Boston	4
	Denton T. Young, St. Louis	4
1901	John D. Chesbro, Pittsburgh	6
	Albert L. Orth, Philadelphia	6
	Victor G. Willis, Boston	6
1902	John D. Chesbro, Pittsburgh	8
	Christopher Mathewson, New York	8
1903	Samuel W. Leever, Pittsburgh	7
1904	Joseph J. McGinnity, New York	9
1905	Christopher Mathewson, New York	9
1906	Mordecai P. Brown, Chicago	9
1907	Orval Overall, Chicago	9
	Christopher Mathewson, New York	9
1908	Christopher Mathewson, New York	12
1909	Orval Overall, Chicago	9
1910	Earl L. Moore, Philadelphia	7
1911	Charles B. Adams, Pittsburgh	7
	Grover C. Alexander, Philadelphia	7
1912	George N. Rucker, Brooklyn	6
1913	Grover C. Alexander, Philadelphia	9
1914	Charles M. Tesreau, New York	8
1915	Grover C. Alexander, Philadelphia	12
1916	Grover C. Alexander, Philadelphia	16
1917	Grover C. Alexander, Philadelphia	8
1918	George A. Tyler, Chicago	8
	James L. Vaughn, Chicago	8
1919	Grover C. Alexander, Chicago	9
1920	Charles B. Adams, Pittsburgh	8
1921	Grover C. Alexander, Chicago	3
	Philip B. Douglas, New York	3
	Dana Filligim, Boston	3
	Adolph Luque, Cincinnati	3
	Clarence E. Mitchell, Brooklyn	3
	John D. Morrison, Pittsburgh	3
	Joseph C. Oeschger, Boston	3
	Jesse J. Haines, St. Louis	3
1922	Arthur C. Vance, Brooklyn	6
1923	Adolfo Luque, Cincinnati	6

SHUTOUT LEADERS—Continued

Year	Pitcher and Club	ShO.
1924—	Jesse L. Barnes, Boston	4
	A. Wilbur Cooper, Pittsburgh	4
	Remy P. Kremer, Pittsburgh	4
	Eppa Rixey, Cincinnati	4
	Allen S. Sothoron, St. Louis	4
	Emil O. Yde, Pittsburgh	4
1925—	Harold G. Carlson, Philadelphia	4
	Adolfo Luque, Cincinnati	4
	Arthur C. Vance, Brooklyn	4
1926—	Peter J. Donohue, Cincinnati	5
1927—	Jesse J. Haines, St. Louis	6
1928—	John F. Blake, Chicago	4
	Burleigh A. Grimes, Pittsburgh	4
	Charles F. Lucas, Cincinnati	4
	Douglas L. McWeeney, Brooklyn	4
	Arthur C. Vance, Brooklyn	4
1929—	Perce L. Malone, Chicago	5
1930—	Charles H. Root, Chicago	4
	Arthur C. Vance, Brooklyn	4
1931—	William H. Walker, New York	6
1932—	Lonnie Warneke, Chicago	4
	Jerome H. Dean, St. Louis	4
	Stephen A. Swetonic, Pittsburgh	4
1933—	Carl O. Hubbell, New York	10
1934—	Jerome H. Dean, St. Louis	7
1935—	Darrell E. Blanton, Pittsburgh	4
	Freddie L. Fitzsimmons, New York	4
	Lawrence H. French, Chicago	4
	Van L. Mungo, Brooklyn	4
	James D. Weaver, Pittsburgh	4
1936—	Darrell E. Blanton, Pittsburgh	4
	James O. Carleton, Chicago	4
	Lawrence H. French, Chicago	4
	William C. Lee, Chicago	4
	Alfred J. Smith, New York	4
	Williams H. Walters, Philadelphia	4
	Lonnie Warneke, Chicago	4
1937—	Louis H. Fette, Boston	5
	Lee T. Grissom, Cincinnati	5
	James R. Turner, Boston	5
1938—	William C. Lee, Chicago	9
1939—	Louis H. Fette, Boston	6
1940—	William L. Lohrman, New York	5
	Manuel L. Salvo, Boston	5
	J. Whitlow Wyatt, Brooklyn	5
1941—	J. Whitlow Wyatt, Brooklyn	7
1942—	Morton C. Cooper, St. Louis	10
1943—	Hiram G. Bithorn, Chicago	7
1944—	Morton C. Cooper, St. Louis	7
1945—	Claude W. Passeau, Chicago	5
1946—	Ewell Blackwell, Cincinnati	6
1947—	Warren E. Spahn, Boston	7
1948—	Harry D. Brecheen, St. Louis	7
1949—	Kenneth A. Heintzelman, Philadelphia	5
	Donald Newcombe, Brooklyn	5
	Howard J. Pollet, St. Louis	5
	Kenneth D. Raffensberger, Cincinnati	5

Year	Pitcher and Club	ShO.
1950—	James T. Hearn, New York	5
	Lawrence J. Jansen, New York	5
	Salvatore A. Maglie, New York	5
	Robin E. Roberts, Philadelphia	5
1951—	Warren E. Spahn, Boston	7
1952—	Salvatore A. Maglie, New York	7
	Ken D. Raffensberger, Cincinnati	7
	Curtis T. Simmons, Philadelphia	7
1953—	Harvey Haddix, St. Louis	6
1954—	John A. Antonelli, New York	6
1955—	Joseph H. Nuxhall, Cincinnati	5
1956—	John A. Antonelli, New York	6
	S. Lewis Burdette, Milwaukee	6
1957—	John L. Podres, Brooklyn	6
1958—	Carlton F. Willey, Milwaukee	4
1959—	John A. Antonelli, San Francisco	4
	Robert R. Buhl, Milwaukee	4
	S. Lewis Burdette, Milwaukee	4
	Roger L. Craig, Los Angeles	4
	Donald S. Drysdale, Los Angeles	4
	Sam Jones, San Francisco	4
	Warren E. Spahn, Milwaukee	4
1960—	John S. Sanford, San Francisco	6
1961—	Joseph R. Jay, Cincinnati	4
	Warren E. Spahn, Milwaukee	4
1962—	Robert B. Friend, Pittsburgh	4
	Robert Gibson, St. Louis	5
1963—	Sanford Koufax, Los Angeles	11
1964—	Sanford Koufax, Los Angeles	7
1965—	Juan A. Marichal, San Francisco	10
1966—	James P. Bunning, Philadelphia	5
	Robert Gibson, St. Louis	5
	Lawrence C. Jackson, Philadelphia	5
	Larry E. Jaster, St. Louis	5
	Sanford Koufax, Los Angeles	5
	James W. Maloney, Cincinnati	5
1967—	James P. Bunning, Philadelphia	6
1968—	Robert Gibson, St. Louis	13
1969—	Juan A. Marichal, San Francisco	8
1970—	Gaylord J. Perry, San Francisco	5
1971—	Stephen R. Blass, Pittsburgh	5
	Alphonso E. Downing, Los Angeles	5
	Robert Gibson, St. Louis	5
	Milton S. Pappas, Chicago	5
1972—	Donald H. Sutton, Los Angeles	9
1973—	John E. Billingham, Cincinnati	7
1974—	Jonathan T. Matlack, New York	7
1975—	John A. Messersmith, Los Angeles	7
1976—	Jonathan T. Matlack, New York	6
	John J. Montefusco, San Francisco	6
1977—	G. Thomas Seaver, N. York-Cincinnati	7
1978—	Robert W. Knepper, San Francisco	6
1979—	G. Thomas Seaver, Cincinnati	5
	Joseph Niekro, Houston	5
	Stephen Rogers, Montreal	5

PRE-1900 PENNANT WINNERS

Year	Club	Manager	W.	L.	Pct.
1876—Chicago		Albert Spalding	52	14	.788
1877—Boston		Harry Wright	31	17	.646
1878—Boston		Harry Wright	41	19	.683
1879—Providence		George Wright	55	23	.705
1880—Chicago		Adrian Anson	67	17	.798
1881—Chicago		Adrian Anson	56	28	.667
1882—Chicago		Adrian Anson	55	29	.655
1883—Boston		John Morrill	63	35	.643
1884—Providence		Frank Bancroft	84	28	.750
1885—Chicago		Adrian Anson	87	25	.777
1886—Chicago		Adrian Anson	90	34	.726
1887—Detroit		Wm. Watkins	79	45	.637
1888—New York		James Mutrie	84	47	.641
1889—New York		James Mutrie	83	43	.659
1890—Brooklyn		Wm. McGunnigle	86	43	.667
1891—Boston		Frank Selee	87	51	.630
1892—Boston		Frank Selee	102	48	.680
1893—Boston		Frank Selee	86	44	.662
1894—Baltimore		Edward Hanlon	89	39	.695
1895—Baltimore		Edward Hanlon	87	43	.669
1896—Baltimore		Edward Hanlon	90	39	.698
1897—Boston		Frank Selee	93	39	.705
1898—Boston		Frank Selee	102	47	.685
1899—Brooklyn		Edward Hanlon	88	42	.677

PRE-1900 YEARLY FINISHES

*Tied for position

Year	Bos.	Bkn.	Chi.	Cin.	N.Y.	Phil.	Pitt.	St.L.	Balt.	Buf.	Clev.
1876	4		1	8	6	7		3			
1877	1		5					4			
1878	1		4	2							
1879	2		*3	5						*3	6
1880	6		1	8						7	3
1881	6		1							3	7
1882	*3		1							*3	5
1883	1		2		6	8				5	4
1884	2		*4		*4	6				3	7
1885	5		1		2	3		8		7	
1886	5		1		3	4		6			
1887	5		3		4	2	6				
1888	4		2		1	3	6				
1889	2		3		1	4	5				6
1890	5	1	2	4	6	3	8				7
1891	1	6	2	7	3	4	8				5
1892	1	3	7	5	8	4	6	11	12		2
1893	1	*6	9	*6	5	4	2	10	8		3
1894	3	5	8	10	2	4	7	9	1		6
1895	*5	*5	4	8	9	3	7	11	1		2
1896	4	*9	5	3	7	8	6	11	1		2
1897	1	*6	9	4	3	10	8	12	2		5
1898	1	10	4	3	7	6	8	12	2		5
1899	2	1	8	6	10	3	7	5	4		12

Year	Det.	Hart.	Ind.	K.C.	Lou.	Mil.	Prov.	Syr.	Troy	Wash.	Wor.
1876		2			5						
1877		3			2						
1878			5			6	3				
1879							1	8	7		
1880							2		4		5
1881	4						2		5		8
1882	6						2		7		8
1883	7						3				
1884	8						1				
1885	6						4				
1886	2			7						8	
1887	1		8							7	
1888	5		7							8	
1889			7							8	
1890											
1891											
1892					9					10	
1893					11					12	
1894					12					11	
1895					12					10	
1896					12					*9	
1897					11					*6	
1898					9					11	
1899					9					11	

PRE-1900 LEADERS

LEADING BATSMEN

Year	Player and Club	G.	H.	Pct.
1876	Barnes, Chicago	66	138	.404
1877	White, Boston	48	82	.385
1878	Dalrymple, Milwaukee	60	95	.356
1879	Anson, Chicago	49	90	.407
1880	Gore, Chicago	75	114	.365
1881	Anson, Chicago	84	137	.399
1882	Brouthers, Buffalo	84	129	.367
1883	Brouthers, Buffalo	97	156	.371
1884	O'Rourke, Buffalo	104	157	.350
1885	Connor, New York	110	169	.371
1886	Kelly, Chicago	118	175	.388
1887	Anson, Chicago	122	*224	.421
1888	Anson, Chicago	134	177	.343
1889	Brouthers, Boston	126	181	.373
1890	Glasscock, New York	124	172	.336
1891	Hamilton, Philadelphia	133	179	.338
1892	Brouthers, Brooklyn	152	197	.335
	Childs, Cleveland	144	185	.335
1893	Duffy, Boston	131	203	.378
1894	Duffy, Boston	124	236	.438
1895	Burkett, Cleveland	132	235	.423
1896	Burkett, Cleveland	133	240	.410
1897	Keeler, Baltimore	128	243	.432
1898	Keeler, Baltimore	128	214	.379
1899	Delahanty, Philadelphia	145	234	.408

*Bases on balls counted as hits.

TWO-BASE HIT LEADERS

Year	Player and Club	2B.
1876	Roscoe Barnes, Chicago	23
1877	Adrian (Cap) Anson, Chicago	20
1878	Lewis Brown, Providence	18
1879	Charles Eden, Cleveland	31
1880	Fred Dunlap, Cleveland	27
1881	Michael (King) Kelly, Chicago	28
1882	Michael (King) Kelly, Chicago	36
1883	Edward Williamson, Chicago	50
1884	Paul Hines, Providence	34
1885	Adrian (Cap) Anson, Chicago	35
1886	Dennis (Dan) Brouthers, Detroit	41
1887	Dennis (Dan) Brouthers, Detroit	35
1888	James Ryan, Chicago	37
1889	John Glasscock, Indianapolis	39
1890	Samuel Thompson, Philadelphia	38
1891	Michael Griffin, Brooklyn	36
1892	Brouthers, Bkn.-Delahanty, Phil	33
1893	Oliver (Pat) Tebeau, Cleveland	35
1894	Hugh Duffy, Boston	50
1895	Edward Delahanty, Philadelphia	47
1896	Edward Delahanty, Philadelphia	42
1897	Jacob Stenzel, Baltimore	40
1898	Napoleon Lajoie, Philadelphia	40
1899	Edward Delahanty, Philadelphia	56

THREE-BASE HIT LEADERS

Year	Player and Club	3B.
1876	George Hall, Athletics	12
1877	Brown, Bos.-McVey, Chi.-White, Bos	9
1878	Thomas York, Providence	9
1879	L. Dickerson, Cin.-M. Kelly, Cin	14
1880	Harry Stovey, Worcester	14
1881	John Rowe, Buffalo	11
1882	Roger Connor, Troy	17
1883	Dennis (Dan) Brouthers, Buffalo	17
1884	William (Buck) Ewing, New York	18
1885	R. Connor, N.Y.-J. O'Rourke, N.Y.	15
1886	Roger Connor, New York	19
1887	Samuel Thompson, Detroit	23
1888	R. Connor, N.Y.-R. Johnson, Bos	17
1889	Connor, N.Y.-Fogarty, Ph.-Wilmot, W.	17
1890	John McPhee, Cincinnati	25
1891	Jacob Beckley, Pittsburgh	20
1892	Dennis (Dan) Brouthers, Brooklyn	20
1893	Perry Werden, St. Louis	33
1894	Henry Reitz, Baltimore	29
1895	A. Selbach, Wash.-S. Thompson, Phil	22
1896	McCreery, Lou.-G. Van Haltren, N.Y.	21
1897	Harry Davis, Pittsburgh	28
1898	John Anderson, Bkn.-Wash.	19
1899	James Williams, Pittsburgh	27

HOME RUN LEADERS

Year	Player and Club	HR.
1876	George Hall, Athletics	5
1877	George Shaffer, Louisville	3
1878	Paul Hines, Providence	4
1879	Charles Jones, Boston	9
1880	J. O'Rourke, Bos.-H. Stovey, Wor.	6
1881	Dennis (Dan) Brouthers, Buffalo	8
1882	George Wood, Detroit	7
1883	William (Buck) Ewing, New York	10
1884	Edward Williamson, Chicago	27
1885	Abner Dalrymple, Chicago	11
1886	Harding Richardson, Detroit	11
1887	R. Connor, N.Y.-T. O'Brien, Wash	17
1888	Roger Connor, New York	14
1889	Samuel Thompson, Philadelphia	20
1890	T. Burns, Bkn.-M. Tiernan, N.Y.	13
1891	H. Stovey, Bos.-M. Tiernan, N.Y.	16
1892	James Holliday, Cincinnati	13
1893	Edward Delahanty, Philadelphia	19
1894	H. Duffy, Boston-R. Lowe, Boston	18
1895	William Joyce, Washington	17
1896	Delahanty, Phil.-S. Thompson, Phil	13
1897	Napoleon Lajoie, Philadelphia	10
1896	James Collins, Boston	14
1899	John (Buck) Freeman, Washington	25

PRE-1900 LEADERS—Continued

STOLEN BASE LEADERS

Year	Player and Club	SB.	Year	Player and Club	SB.
1886—	George Andrews, Philadelphia	56	1893—	John M. Ward, New York	72
1887—	John M. Ward, New York	111	1894—	William Hamilton, Philadelphia	99
1888—	William (Dummy) Hoy, Washington	82	1895—	William Hamilton, Philadelphia	95
1889—	James Fogarty, Philadelphia	99	1896—	William Lange, Chicago	100
1890—	William Hamilton, Philadelphia	102	1897—	William Lange, Chicago	83
1891—	William Hamilton, Philadelphia	115	1898—	Frederick Clarke, Louisville	66
1892—	John M. Ward, Brooklyn	94	1899—	James Sheckard, Baltimore	78

LEADING PITCHERS IN WINNING PERCENTAGE

(15 OR MORE VICTORIES)

Year	Pitcher and Club	W.	L.	Pct.	Year	Pitcher and Club	W.	L.	Pct.
1876—	Albert Spalding, Chicago	47	13	.783	1888—	Timothy Keefe, New York	35	12	.745
1877—	Thomas Bond, Boston	31	17	.646	1889—	John Clarkson, Boston	49	19	.721
1878—	Thomas Bond, Boston	40	19	.678	1890—	Thomas Lovett, Brooklyn	32	11	.744
1879—	John M. Ward, Providence	44	18	.710	1891—	John Ewing, New York	22	8	.733
1880—	Fred Goldsmith, Chicago	22	3	.880	1892—	Denton (Cy) Young, Cleve.	36	11	.766
1881—	Chas. Radbourn, Providence	25	11	.694	1893—	Frank Killen, Pittsburgh	34	10	.773
1882—	Lawrence Corcoran, Chicago	27	13	.675	1894—	Jouett Meekin, New York	34	9	.791
1883—	James McCormick, Cleveland	27	13	.675	1895—	William Hoffer, Baltimore	30	7	.811
1884—	Chas. Radbourn, Providence	60	12	.833	1896—	William Hoffer, Baltimore	26	7	.788
1885—	Michael Welch, New York	44	11	.800	1897—	Amos Rusie, New York	29	8	.784
1886—	John Flynn, Chicago	24	6	.800	1898—	Edward Lewis, Boston	25	8	.758
1887—	Charles Getzein, Detroit	29	13	.690	1899—	James Hughes, Brooklyn	28	6	.824

Leonard Went 1-for-3 in One At-Bat

A weird set of events in the ninth inning of a game on August 21 at Shea Stadium resulted in Houston outfielder Jeff Leonard batting three times before he was finally given credit for a hit.

With two out in the ninth against Mets' lefthander Pete Falcone, Leonard lifted a fly ball to Lee Mazzilli in center field for what should have been the final out and a 5-0 New York victory.

But third base umpire Doug Harvey ruled that time had been called by Mets' shortstop Frank Taveras. Leonard had to bat over.

Leonard then singled to left. This time, however, it was discovered that the Mets were without a first baseman. Ed Kranepool went to the clubhouse after he thought Mazzilli's catch had retired Leonard.

Umpires Harvey, Frank Pulli and Andy Olsen decided that since the Mets had only eight men on the field Leonard had to bat again. And this time he flied to left.

The Astros filed a protest and the next morning NL President Chub Feeney ruled that "time was in" and the Mets were at fault for not having nine men on the field.

The game was completed that afternoon prior to the regularly-scheduled game when Kevin Kobel replaced Falcone and induced Jose Cruz to ground out.

Leonard had his hit, the Mets' 5-0 victory finally was official, but Falcone had to settle for a combined shutout with Kobel.

Major League Baseball Players Association

1370 Avenue of the Americas

Suite 2602

New York, N.Y. 10019

Telephone—(212) 581-8484

Marvin J. Miller—Executive Director

Donald Fehr—General Counsel

Peter Rose—Associate Counsel

Secretarial Staff—Marlene Widrow and Francine O'Rourke

EXECUTIVE BOARD

Mike Marshall—American League Representative

Bob Boone—National League Representative

Mark Belanger—Pension Committee

Randy Jones—Pension Committee

Jon Matlack—Pension Committee

Steve Rogers—Pension Committee

Plus all remaining player representatives

NATIONAL LEAGUE PLAYER REPRESENTATIVES

Phil Niekro—Atlanta Braves
Bill Buckner—Chicago Cubs
Ray Knight—Cincinnati Reds
Joe Niekro—Houston Astros
Jerry Reuss—Los Angeles Dodgers
Steve Rogers—Montreal Expos
John Stearns—New York Mets
Larry Bowa—Philadelphia Phillies
Phil Garner—Pittsburgh Pirates
Bob Forsch—St. Louis Cardinals
Randy Jones—San Diego Padres
Gary Lavelle—San Francisco Giants

AMERICAN LEAGUE PLAYER REPRESENTATIVES

Mark Belanger—Baltimore Orioles
Steve Renko—Boston Red Sox
Don Baylor—California Angels
Richard Wortham—Chicago White Sox
Wayne Garland—Cleveland Indians
John Hiller—Detroit Tigers
Jerry Terrell—Kansas City Royals
Buck Martinez—Milwaukee Brewers
Mike Marshall—Minnesota Twins
Reggie Jackson—New York Yankees
Dave Heaverlo—Oakland A's
Bruce Bochte—Seattle Mariners
Jon Matlack—Texas Rangers
Roy Howell—Toronto Blue Jays

AMERICAN LEAGUE

Including

Club Directories

Club Reviews of 1979 Season

Club Day-by-Day Scores

AL Team Pictures

1979 League Leaders

1979 Official AL Averages

All-Time AL Player Performance Tables

LELAND S. MacPHAIL, Jr.
President of the American League

American League

Organized 1900

LELAND S. MacPHAIL, Jr.
President

JOSEPH E. CRONIN
Chairman

CALVIN R. GRIFFITH
Vice-President

ROBERT O. FISHEL
Secretary and
Assistant to the President

DONALD C. MARR, Jr.
Controller

DICK BUTLER
Supervisor of Umpires

ROBERT F. HOLBROOK
Special Assistant

JEANNE COLLINS
Manager, Waiver & Records Department

PHYLLIS MERHIGE
Assistant Public Relations Director

TESS BASTA, PAT FREEMAN, ROBERT GRIM
Staff

Headquarters—280 Park Avenue, New York, N. Y. 10017

Telephone—682-7000 (area code 212)

ASSISTANT SUPERVISORS OF UMPIRES—Nestor Chylak, Henry Soar, John Stevens.

UMPIRES—Lawrence Barnett, Nicholas Bremigan, Joseph Brinkman, Alan Clark, Terrance Cooney, Derryl Cousins, William Deegan, Donald Denkinger, Louis DiMuro, James Evans, Dale Ford, Richard Garcia, Russell Goetz, William Haller, Ted Hendry, Kenneth Kaiser, Greg Kosc, William Kunkel, Ronald Luciano, George Maloney, Larry McCoy, James McKean, Durwood Merrill, Jerome Neudecker, Stephen Palermo, Dallas Parks, David Phillips, Michael Reilly, John Shulock, Fred Spenn, Martin Springstead, Vic Voltaggio.

OFFICIAL STATISTICIANS—Sports Information Center, 1776 Heritage Drive, No. Quincy, Mass. 02171. Telephone—(617) 328-4674.

Players cannot be transferred from one major league to another after June 15 to close of the championship season except through regular waiver channels.

WAIVER PRICE, $20,000. Interleague waivers, $20,000, except for selected players and draft-excluded players.

BALTIMORE ORIOLES

Chairman of the Board—Edward Bennett Williams
President—Jerold C. Hoffberger

Executive Vice-President-General Manager—Henry J. Peters
Treasurer—Gerard T. Gabrys
Vice-President for Stadium Operations—Jack Dunn, III
Vice-President for Finance—Joseph P. Hamper, Jr.
Vice-President for Business Affairs—Alan E. Harazin
Public Relations Director—Robert W. Brown
Traveling Secretary—Philip E. Itzoe
Special Assistant to the General Manager—James J. Russo
Director of Scouting and Player Development—Thomas A. Giordano
Director of Tickets and Sales—Robert R. Aylward
Ticket Office Manager—Timothy A. Geraghty
Assistant Scouting and Player Development Director—John J. McCall
Assistant Ticket Manager—Joseph B. Codd
Assistant Public Relations Director—John C. Blake
Assistant Sales Director—Drew M. Sheinman
Consultant-President, Oriole Foundation—Herbert E. Armstrong
Manager—Earl S. Weaver
Club Physician—Dr. Leonard Wallenstein
Executive Offices—Memorial Stadium, Baltimore, Md. 21218
Telephone—243-9800 (area code 301)

SCOUTS—Jack Baker, Dick Bowie, Joe Bowman, Dan Cressman,
Ray Crone, Joe DeLucca, Jim Freitas, Jim Gilbert, Myron Hayworth,
Len Johnston, Allan Lewis, Ed Lewis, Bill Lohr, Frank McGowan, Earl
McKenzie, Don McShane, Domenic Napolitano, Lamar North, Carlos
Pascual, James Pamlayne, Frank Piet, Jim Russo, Jack Sanford, Caesar
Sinabaldi, John Stokoe, William Teed, Tommy Thompson, Herman
Welsh, Bill Werle.

PARK LOCATION—Memorial Stadium, 33rd Street, Ellerslie Avenue, 36th Street and Ednor Road.

Seating capacity—52,862

FIELD DIMENSIONS—Home plate to left field at foul line, 309 feet;
to center field, 405 feet; to right field at foul line, 309 feet.

BOSTON RED SOX

President—Jean R. Yawkey

Executive Vice-President-General Manager—Haywood C. Sullivan
Executive Vice-President, Administration—Edward G. LeRoux, Jr.
Treasurer—James M. Olivier, Jr.
Secretary—Joseph H. LaCour
V. P., Director Player Development—Edward F. Kenney
Director, Scouting—Edward M. Kasko
Traveling Secretary—John J. Rogers
V. P., Director Public Relations—William C. Crowley
Director, Publicity—Richard L. Bresciani
Director, Marketing—James P. Healey
Assistant Publicity Director—John E. McCarthy
Executive Assistant—Joseph F. McDermott
Assistant Treasurer—John J. Reilly
Administrative Assistant—Mary E. Walsh
Director, Tickets—Arthur J. Moscato
Superintendent, Grounds & Maintenance—Joseph Mooney
Field Manager—Donald W. Zimmer
Club Physicians—Drs. Arthur M. Pappas, William W. Southmayd
Executive Offices—24 Yawkey Way, Boston, Mass. 02215
Telephone—267-9440 (area code 617)

SCOUTS—Milton Bolling, Ray Boone, Wayne Britton, George Digby, Howard (Danny) Doyle, Bill Enos, Earl Johnson, Charles Koney, Wilfrid (Lefty) Lefebvre, Don Lenhardt, Tommy McDonald, Felix Maldonado, Frank Malzone, Sam Mele, Ramon Naranjo, Willie Paffen, Edward Scott, Matt Sczesny, Joe Stephenson, Paul Tavares, Larry Thomas, Charlie Wagner.

PARK LOCATION—Fenway Park, Yawkey Way, Lansdowne Street and Ipswich Street.

Seating capacity—33,536

FIELD DIMENSIONS—Home plate to left field at foul line, 315 feet; to center field, 420 feet; to right field at foul line, 302 feet; average right field distance, 382 feet.

CALIFORNIA ANGELS

BOARD OF DIRECTORS

Gene Autry, Chairman of the Board; E. J. (Buzzie) Bavasi, Arthur E. Patterson, Walton S. Reid, Forrest Shumway, Clair L. Stout

President—Gene Autry

Executive Vice-President—E. J. (Buzzie) Bavasi

Assistant to the Chairman of the Board—Arthur E. Patterson

Vice-President, Treasurer—Francis X. Leary

Secretary—Clair L. Stout

Assistant Secretary & Treasurer—Michael M. Schreter

Director of Player Personnel—Mike Port

Director Public Relations/Team Travel—Tom Seeberg

Director Stadium Operations—Dick Foster

Director Scouting—Richard Cuoco

Special Assignments—Bill Rigney, Nick Kamzic

Administrative Assistant—Rose Anderson

Director Ticket Department—Carl Gordon

Asst. Ticket Director—Bob Terzes

Trainer—Richard Smith

Asst. Trainer—Ned Bergert

Director Group Sales—Lynn Kirchmann

Director Publications—Bobby Kargenian

Promotions/Season Tickets—Al Bine

Film Coordinator/Special Statistics—George Goodale

Manager—Jim Fregosi

Club Physicians—Drs. Robert K. Kerlan, Jules Rasinski. Lewis Yocum

Executive Offices—Anaheim Stadium, 2000 State College Blvd., Anaheim, Calif. 92806

Telephone—634-1002 (area code 714) or 625-1123 (area code 213)

SCOUTS—Special Assignments: Nick Kamzic, Bill Rigney; Supervisors: Larry Himes, Tony Roig; Staff: Ken Califano, Vince Capece, Joe Carpenter, Loyd Christopher, Lou Cohenour, Bill Earnhart, Fred Ferreira, Al Goldis, Harry Hayes, Bob Pomeroy, Vic Power, Chester Reese, Philip Rizzo, Reuben Rodriguez, Ernie Rudolph, Cobby Saatzer, Eddy Toledo, George Zabala

PARK LOCATION—Anaheim Stadium, 2000 State College Boulevard.

Seating capacity—43,250

FIELD DIMENSIONS—Home plate to left field at foul line, 333 feet; to center field, 404 feet; to right field at foul line, 333 feet.

CHICAGO WHITE SOX

Chairman of the Board—Wm. O. DeWitt

President—Bill Veeck
Vice-President—Roland Hemond
Treasurer—Leo Breen
Secretary—Newton P. Frye, Jr.
Business Manager—Rudie Schaffer
Promotions Director-Ass't Bus. Mgr.—Mike Veeck
Publicity—Chuck Shriver
Traveling Secretary—Glen Rosenbaum
Director of Park Operations—David Schaffer
Director of Player Development—Paul Richards
Administrative Assistant—Dave Dombrowski
Groundskeepers—Gene and Roger Bossard
Media Co-ordinator—Judy Shoemaker
Clubhouse Men—John McNamara and Willie Thompson
Manager—Tony LaRussa
Club Physicians—Drs. Edwin Feldman, William Meltzer, Michael Lewis
and Sid J. Shafer
Customer Relations—Millie Johnson
Ticket Manager—Bob Devoy
Public Relations—Aaron Cushman & Associates
Supervisor Accounting—Mickey Yunker
Executive Offices—Comiskey Park, Dan Ryan at 35th Street.
Chicago, Ill. 60616
Telephone—924-1000 (area code 312)

SCOUTS—Orlando Cepeda, Bruce Dal Canton, Roger Ferguson, Sam Hairston, Bennie Huffman, Joseph Ingalls, Gary Johnson, Bill Kimball, Jerry Krause, Leo Labossiere, Dario Lodigiani, Mel F. Nelson, Fern Paredes, Mel Preibisch, Silvano Quezada, George Sobek, Walt Widmayer, Stan Zielinski.

PARK LOCATION—Comiskey Park, Dan Ryan at 35th Street, Chicago, Ill. 60616.

Seating capacity—44,492

FIELD DIMENSIONS—Home plate to left field at foul line, 352 feet; to center field, 445 feet; to right field at foul line, 352 feet.

CLEVELAND INDIANS

President & Chief Executive Officer—Gabe Paul

Chairman of the Board—C. C. Tippit
Directors—C. C. Tippit, F. J. O'Neill, Dudley S. Blossom, III,
Alva T. Bonda, Art Modell, Gabe Paul, Maurice Stonehill
Secretary-Treasurer—Dudley S. Blossom III
Vice-President & General Manager—Phillip D. Seghi
Vice-President—Bruce Fine
Director of Minor League Operations & Scouting—Bob Quinn
Manager—Dave Garcia
Traveling Secretary—Mike Seghi
Assistant to the President-Public Relations Director—Joe Bick
Director of Administration—Rich Rollins
Director of Stadium Operations—Dan Zerbey
Ticket Director—Jerry Waring
Director of Promotions—Rob Pike
Controller—Art Pease
Asst. Director of Public Relations—Bob DiBiascio
Director of Community Affairs—Jim Grant
Special Assignment Scout—Dan Carnevale
Farm Club Administration—Joe Pavia
Minor League Administrator—Phil Thomas
Trainer—Jim Warfield
Club Physicians—Drs. William Wilder, Earl Brightman
Club Dentist—Dr. Marvin Schermer
Club Legal Counsel—Armand D. Arnson
Equipment Manager—Cy Buynak
Groundskeeper—Marshall Bossard
Executive Offices—Cleveland Stadium, Cleveland, Ohio 44114
Telephone—861-1200 (area code 216)

SCOUTS—Jimmy Bragan, Dan Carnevale, Jack Cassini, Merrill
Combs, Mel Didier, Red Gaskill, Leon Hamilton, Luis Isaac, Mark Just,
Bobby Malkmus, Bob Shupala, Jack Vallely, Gene Woodling.

PARK LOCATION—Cleveland Stadium, Boudreau Blvd.

Seating capacity—76,713

FIELD DIMENSIONS—Home plate to left field at foul line, 320 feet;
to center field, 400 feet; to right field at foul line, 320 feet.

DETROIT TIGERS

Owner & Chairman of the Board—John E. Fetzer

President & General Manager—James A. Campbell
Vice-President/Finance & Secretary-Treasurer—Alexander C. Callam
Vice-President/Operations—William E. Haase
Vice-President/Baseball—William R. Lajoie
Director of Public Relations—Dan Ewald
Director of Ticket Sales—William H. Willis
Director of Stadium Operations—Ralph E. Snyder
Field Director/Player Development—Walter A. Evers
Scouting Director—David Miller
Administrative Assistant/Minor Leagues—Dan Elve
Traveling Secretary—Bill Brown
Assistant Director of Public Relations—Bob Miller
Asst. Dir. of Public Relations/Special Events—Lew Matlin
Asst. Dir. of Public Relations/Community Affairs—Vince Desmond
Season and Group Ticket Sales—Fred T. Smith
Executive Secretary/Baseball—Alice Sloane
Executive Secretary/Operations—Hazel McLane
Consultants—Richard B. Ferrell, Ralph G. Houk and
Edward G. Katalinas
Asst. Director of Stadium Operations—Frank Feneck
Manager—Sparky Anderson
Club Physician—Clarence S. Livingood M.D.
Orthopaedic Consultant—Edwin R. Guise Jr. M.D.
Executive Offices—Tiger Stadium, Detroit, Mich. 48216
Telephone—962-4000 (area code 313)

SCOUTS—Ray Bellino, Wayne Blackburn, James Miller, Orlando Pena, William Schudlich, Frank Skaff, Jack Tighe, Richard Wiencek, John Young, Del Wilber.

PARK LOCATION—Tiger Stadium, Michigan Avenue, Cochrane Avenue, Kaline Drive and Trumbull Avenue.

Seating capacity—52,067

FIELD DIMENSIONS—Home plate to left field at foul line, 340 feet; to center field, 440 feet; to right field at foul line, 325 feet.

KANSAS CITY ROYALS

BOARD OF DIRECTORS—Joe Burke, William Deramus III,
Charles Hughes, Ewing Kauffman, Mrs. Ewing Kauffman, Earl Smith.

President & Chairman of the Board—Ewing Kauffman
Executive Vice-President and General Manager—Joe Burke
Vice-President—Spencer "Herk" Robinson
Vice-President—John Schuerholz
Vice-President and Legal Counsel—Phil Koury
Controller—Dale Rohr
Director of Public Relations—Dean Vogelaar
Director of Marketing/Special Events—Bryan Burns
Traveling Secretary—Bill Beck
Director of Publications and Assistant Public Relations Director—
Bruce Carnahan
Director of Ticket Operations—Tom Pfannenstiel
Director of Season Ticket Sales—Joe Grigoli
Assistant Farm Director—Dick Balderson
Manager—Jim Frey
Club Physician—Dr. Paul Meyer
Accountant—Darrel Joseph
Director of Event Personnel—Chris Muehlbach
Stadium Engineer—George Humphrey
Stadium Maintenance Coordinator—Bob Frank
Equipment Manager—Al Zych
Groundskeeper—George Toma
Executive Offices—Royals Stadium, Harry S. Truman Sports Complex
Mailing Address—P. O. Box 1969, Kansas City, Mo. 64141
Telephone—921-8000 (area code 816)

SCOUTS—Jose Arcia, Carl Blando, Gary Blaylock, Al Diez, Tom Fer-
rick, Rosey Gilhousen, Ken Gonzales, Al Kubski, Art Lilly, George Noga,
Earl Rapp, Rich Schlenker, Jerry Stephens, Red Whitsett.

PARK LOCATION—Royals Stadium, Harry S. Truman Sports Complex.

Seating capacity—40,628

FIELD DIMENSIONS—Home plate to left field at foul line, 330 feet;
to center field, 410 feet; to right field at foul line, 330 feet.

MILWAUKEE BREWERS

President, Chief Executive Officer—Allan H. (Bud) Selig

Chairman of the Board—Edmund B. Fitzgerald
Directors—Edmund B. Fitzgerald, Allan H. Selig, Everett
G. Smith, Roswell N. Stearns
Secretaries—Bernard S. Kubale, Carlton Wilson
Executive Vice-President, General Manager—Harry Dalton
Vice-President, Marketing—Richard Hackett
Vice-President, Administration—Thomas J. Ferguson
Vice-President, Finance—Richard Hoffmann
Vice-President, Stadium & Broadcast Operations—Gabe Paul, Jr.
Assistant General Manager—Walter Shannon
Special Assistant to the General Manager—Dee Fondy
Special Assignments Scout—Ray Scarborough
Director of Scouting and Player Development—Ray Poitevint
Administrative Assistant Scouting & Player Development—Bruce Manno
Director of Information and Services—Tom Skibosh
Assistant Director of Stadium Operations—Jack Hutchinson
Group Sales Director—Tim Trovato
Director of the Speakers Bureau—John Counsell
Ticket Office Manager—Alice Boettcher
Manager—George Bamberger
Club Physicians—Dr. Frank Jacobs, Dr. Gary Guten
Executive Offices—Milwaukee Brewers Baseball Club
Milwaukee County Stadium, Milwaukee, Wis. 53214
Telephone—(414) 933-1818

SCOUTS— Julio Blanco-Herrera, Nelson E. Burbrink, Felix Delgado, Roland LeBlanc, Tom Gamboa, Lippy Lipari, Joe McIlvaine, Willie Moore, Harry Smith, Milt Sobel, Paul Tretiak, Walter Youse. Part-time: Dick Ehrig, Charles Fitzgerald, Hy Gomberg, Gene Kerns, Bill Moffitt, Johnny Neun, Sam Suplizio, Jerry Weinstein.

PARK LOCATION—Milwaukee County Stadium, S. 46th St. off Bluemound Rd.

Seating capacity—53,192

FIELD DIMENSIONS—Home plate to left field at foul line, 320 feet; to center field, 402 feet; to right field at foul line, 315 feet.

MINNESOTA TWINS

Chairman of Board, President—Calvin R. Griffith
Vice-President—Mrs. Thelma Griffith Haynes
Executive Vice-President—Clark Griffith
Executive Vice-President—Bruce G. Haynes
Director—H. Gabriel Murphy
Director—Eugene V. Young
Director—Wheelock Whitney
Executive Vice-President—Howard T. Fox, Jr.
Vice-President—William S. Robertson
Vice-President—James K. Robertson
Vice-President-Farm Director—George Brophy
Assistant Farm Director—Jim Rantz
Controller—Jack Alexander
Director of Public Relations—Tom Mee
Director of Sales—Gil Lansdale
Stadium Superintendent—Richard Ericson
Manager—Gene Mauch
club Physicians—Dr. Leonard J. Michienzi and Dr. Harvey O'Phelan
Executive Offices—Metropolitan Stadium, 8001 Cedar Avenue,
Bloomington, Minn. 55420
Telephone—854-4040 (area code 612)

SCOUTS—Floyd Baker, Zinn Beck, Spud Chandler, Edward Dunn, Jesse Flores, Jr., Angelo Giuliani, Tom Hull, Lee Irwin, Hank Izquierdo, William Messmann, Marvin Olson, Spencer (Red) Robbins, Stanley Rogers, Herb Stein.

PARK LOCATION—Metropolitan Stadium, 8001 Cedar Avenue, Bloomington, Minn. 55420.

Seating Capacity—45,919

FIELD DIMENSIONS—Home plate to left field at foul line, 343 feet; to center field, 402 feet; to right field at foul line, 330 feet.

NEW YORK YANKEES

Principal Owner—George M. Steinbrenner III

Limited Partners—Harold Bowman, Michael Burke, Lester Crown, John Z. DeLorean, Michael Friedman, Marvin Goldking, Barry Halper, Harvey Leighton, Daniel McCarthy, Harry Nederlander, Robert Nederlander, William J. O'Neill, William Rose, Albert Rosen, Edward Rosenthal, Jack Satter, Charlotte Witkind.

Executive Vice-President—Cedric Tallis
Vice-President, General Manager—Gene Michael
Manager—Dick Howser
Administrative Vice-President—Eugene J. McHale
Vice-President, Secretary—Bruce Poston
Vice-President, General Counsel—Edwin T Broderick
Vice-President, Baseball Operations—Bill Bergesch
Vice-President—Ed Weaver
Treasurer-Controller—David Weidler
Director of Player Development—Bill Livesey
Director of Scouting—Bobby Hofman
Traveling Secretary—Bill Kane
Administrative Assistant—Gerry Murphy
Director of Publicity—Mickey Morabito
Assistant Director of Publicity—Larry Wahl
Director of Marketing Services—John Fugazy
Stadium Manager—Patrick Kelly
Director of Promotions—Peter Gill
Executive Director of Ticket Operations—Frank Swaine
Ticket Director—Michael Rendine
Assistant Ticket Director—Bobby Overland
Director, Customer Services—Jim Naples
Director of Radio-TV Relations—Adrienne Ruddy
Assistant Director of Player Development—Dale Weeks
Assistant Director of Scouting—Jim Sheridan
Director of Group Sales—Frank McCormick
Director of Speakers Bureau, Publicity Assistant—Joe D'Ambrosio
Director of Accounting—Alan Friedman
Stadium Superintendent—Jimmy Esposito
Director, Yankee Alumni Association—Jim Ogle
Director Emeritus, Speakers Bureau—Jackie Farrell
Club Physician—Dr. John J. Bonamo
Executive Offices—Yankee Stadium, Bronx, N. Y. 10451
Telephone—293-4300 (area code 212)

SCOUTS—Luis Arroyo, Joe Begani, Jack Bloomfield, Wilfredo Calvino, Roy Carter, Howard Cassady, Harry Craft, Al Cuccinello, Tony Cuccinello, Joe DiCarlo, Henry Dotterer, Buck Elliott, Whitey Ford, Art Fowler, Tom Greenwade, Jim Gruzdis, Roy Hamey, Gary Hughes, Clyde King, Don Lindeberg, Jack Llewellyn, Tom Morgan, Jim Naples Sr., Bob Nieman, Frank O'Rourke, Meade Palmer, Gust Poulos, Joe Powell, Jax Robertson, Russ Sehon, Birdie Tebbetts, Mickey Vernon, Jerry Walker.

PARK LOCATION—Yankee Stadium, E. 161st St. and River Ave., Bronx, N. Y. 10451.

Ticket Information—293-6000 (area code 212)

Seating capacity—57,545

FIELD DIMENSIONS—Home plate to left field at foul line, 312 feet; to center field, 417 feet; to right field at foul line, 310 feet.

OAKLAND A's

President—Charles O. Finley

Secretary and Treasurer—Charles O. Finley, Jr.
Controller—Chuck Cottonaro
Executive Vice-President—Carl Finley
Minor League Administrator—Norm Koselke
Traveling Secretary—Frank Ciensczyk
Ticket Manager—Lorraine Paulus
Manager—Billy Martin
Club Physician—Dr. Thomas Richman
Executive Offices—Oakland-Alameda County Coliseum,
Oakland, Calif. 94621
Telephone—638-4900 (area code 415)
PARK LOCATION—Oakland-Alameda County Coliseum, Nimitz
Freeway and Hegenberger Road.

Seating capacity—49,649

FIELD DIMENSIONS—Home plate to left field at foul line, 330 feet;
to center field, 400 feet; to right field at foul line, 330 feet.

SEATTLE MARINERS

Partners—Stanley Golub, Danny Kaye, Walter Schoenfeld,
Lester M. Smith, James Stillwell, James Walsh

President & Chief Executive Officer—Daniel F. O'Brien
Executive Director—Kip Horsburgh
General Manager—Lou Gorman
Consultant—Richard Vertlieb
Director of Player Development—Hal Keller
Director of Business Affairs—Jeff Odenwald
Director of Marketing & Promotions—Jack Carvalho
Director of Team Travel—Lee Pelekoudas
Director of Stadium Operations & Novelty Sales—Mike Combs
Director of Ticket Services—Lamar Vernon
Dirctor of Public Relations—Randy Adamack
Controller—Ed Waite
Assistant Director, Player Development—Steve Schryver
Assistant Director, Business Affairs—Dan O'Brien III
Assistant Director, Ticket Services—Steve Krause
Vault Manager—Doug Hopkins
Administrative Aide—Char Yoritsune
Publicity Assistant—Melody Tucker
Trainer—Gary Nicholson
Club Physicians—Drs. Ernie Burgess, Larry Pedegana,
James Thombold
Club Dentist—Dr. Richard Leshgold
Club Attorney—Irwin Treiger
Home Clubhouse—Henry Genzale
Visiting Clubhouse—Fred Genzale
Mailroom Manager—Colin Tudor

Executive Offices—P.O. Box 4100
Seattle, Washington 98104
Telephone—628-3555 (area code 206)

ADMINISTRATIVE STAFF: Anita Duncan, Ethel LaRue, Marie
Legaz, Jan Manning, Joan Moeller, Ann Repanich, Sandra Zimmerman.

SCOUTS—Bill Hallauer, Willie Harris, Bob Harrison, Bill Kearns,
Jeff Malinoff, Whitey Piurek, Steve Ray, Rip Tutor, Steve Vrablik.

PARK LOCATION—Kingdome, 201 South King Street, Seattle, Washington.

Seating capacity—59,438

FIELD DIMENSIONS—Home plate to left field at foul line, 316 feet;
to center field, 410 feet; to right field at foul line, 316 feet.

TEXAS RANGERS

Chairman of the Board—Bradford G. Corbett

Executive Vice-President—Eddie Robinson
General Counsel, Secretary—Dee J. Kelly
Farm Director—Joseph Klein
Director of Business Affairs—Charles F. Wangner
Public Relations Director—Burton S. Hawkins
Marketing Director, Promotions Director—Dave Fendrick
Stadium Operations Director—John L. Welaj
Administrative Assistant—Bobby Bragan
Special Assignments—Bill Hunter, Connie Ryan, Eddie Mathews,
Don Nichols
Ticket Manager—Mary Ann Bosher
Traveling Secretary—Dan Schimek
Group Sales—Tom Grieve
Equipment and Clubhouse Manager—Joseph Macko
Manager—Pat Corrales
Club Physician—Dr. B. J. Mycoskie
Executive Offices—Arlington Stadium, P. O. Box 1111,
1500 Copeland Road, Arlington, Tex. 76010
Telephone—273-5222 (area code 817)

SCOUTS—Harley Anderson, Lee Anthony, Lee Ballanfant, Joseph
Branzell, Jackie Brathwaite, Paddy Cottrell, Sid Hudson, Pete Kramer,
Joseph Lewis, Joseph Marchese.

PARK LOCATION—Arlington Stadium, 1500 Copeland Road, Arlington, Tex.

Seating capacity—41,097

FIELD DIMENSIONS—Home plate to left field at foul line, 330 feet;
to center field, 400 feet; to right field at foul line, 330 feet.

TORONTO BLUE JAYS

DIRECTORS—N. E. Hardy, D. A. Lewis, J. P. Roberts, R. Howard Webster.

Chairman of the Board—R. Howard Webster
President and Chief Operating Officer—Peter Bavasi
Vice-President, Business Operations—Paul Beeston
Vice-President, Baseball Operations—Pat Gillick
Director, Public Relations—Howard Starkman
Director, Operations—Ken Erskine
Director, Ticket Operations—George Holm
Administrator, Player Personnel—Elliott Wahle
Director, Team Travel—Mike Cannon
Director, Group Sales—Mike Nash
Manager, Promotions—Bruce Poore
Director, Player Development—Billy Smith
Director, Canadian Scouting—Bob Prentice
Assistant Director, Public Relations—David Honderich
Assistant Director, Operations—Gord Ash
Assistant Director, Ticket Operations—Len Frejlich
Equipment Manager—John Silverman
Coordinator, Promotions & Group Services—Sue Palmer
Controller—Sue Sirois
Supervisor, Grounds—Mike Maunder
Manager—Bobby Mattick
Team Physician—Dr. Ron Taylor
Executive Offices—Exhibition Stadium, Exhibition Place, Toronto, Ontario
Mailing Address—Box 7777, Adelaide St. P. O., Toronto, Ont. M5C 2K7
Telephone—595-0077 (area code 416)

SCOUTS—Robert Engle, Ric Fleury, Epy Guerrero, Al LaMacchia (senior scouting supervisor), Larry Maxie, John McLaren, Wayne Morgan, Herb Raybourn, Paul Ricciarini, Don Welke, Tim Wilken, Dave Yoakum, Bob Zuk (senior scouting supervisor).

PARK LOCATION—Exhibition Stadium on the gounds of Exhibition Place. Entrances to Exhibition Place via Lakeshore Boulevard, Queen Elizabeth Way Highway and Dufferin and Bathurst Streets.

Seating capacity—43,737

FIELD DIMENSIONS—Home plate to left field at foul line, 330 feet; to center field, 400 feet; to right field at foul line, 330 feet.

THE SPORTING NEWS Major League Manager of the Year Earl Weaver is doused with champagne by John Lowenstein after the Orioles defeated the California Angels for the AL pennant.

EAST DIVISION

Orioles Flourished With "Deep Depth"

By KEN NIGRO

The Baltimore Orioles let the big one slip away but when future historians gather to pass judgment, the year 1979 may well go down as the most memorable in the history of the franchise.

It was a year of tight pitching, long ball hitting, dramatic comebacks, "deep depth," and a brilliant piece of managing by Earl Weaver. It was a year in which this delicately balanced club without a super star blended together to compile a 102-57 won-lost mark, the best record in baseball.

"We are good players who play great together," said Ken Singleton in accurately explaining how the Orioles dislodged the Yankees as the American League champs.

One of those good players, of course, was Singleton. The switch-hitting rightfielder batted .295 and established career highs in home runs (35) and RBIs (111). Another was 23-year-old first baseman Eddie Murray, who tied Singleton for the batting lead and also knocked in 99 runs and hit 25 homers.

In the pitching department, there was Mike Flanagan who led the majors with 23 victories and was a near unanimous choice for the AL Cy Young Award. And, reliever Don Stanhouse enjoyed his second straight strong season, saving 21 games and anchoring the Baltimore bullpen.

This was a club in which every single member contributed something. It was after a victory in Minnesota when Benny Ayala, Kiko Garcia and Billy Smith led the way that Weaver coined the phrase "deep depth." While it was redundant, it was also true.

"I don't think I've had a team since 1970 with the depth of this one," Weaver said. "If we went into a slump, I was able to throw in a guy like Ayala, (John) Lowenstein or (Terry) Crowley. Everyone has to chip in and share in order to win a lot of games. If some guys carry you, you'll only be a .500 club and if nobody does it, you're lost."

It was because of the productive bench that the Orioles were able to counteract a lack of team speed with what Weaver likes to call instant offense. With the exception of Mark Belanger, every player was capable of hitting the ball over the fence. There were several times during the year when the Orioles managed only six or seven hits but still won because two of them were homers.

The Orioles finished with 181 homers to set a club record.

But this depth was not restricted to hitting. From Flanagan and Stanhouse, right on through to the ninth pitcher, the Baltimore staff didn't have a weak link. All nine hurlers had an ERA under 3.78 and the staff ERA of 3.28 was almost a full run lower than the league average.

"I don't hesitate to say this club has a better staff than the 1969, '70 and '71 teams," said Weaver, referring to those three straight pennant-winning years. "Our pitching can be fantastic for years to come."

The hitting and pitching depth, combined with the always strong Baltimore defense, enabled the Orioles to win 32 one-run games and go 11-5 in extra-inning contests. In addition, Weaver's men were swept only once in 11 doubleheaders.

BALTIMORE ORIOLES—1979

Front row—Tyler, equipment manager; Kelly, Singleton, Hendricks, player-coach; Frey, coach; Weaver, manager; Miller, coach; Ripken, coach; Robinson, coach; Bumbry, Salvon, trainer. Second row—Stoddard, Lowenstein, Belanger, Stewart, Ayala, T. Martinez, Murray, Skaggs, Flanagan, Roenicke, Palmer, Stanhouse. Third row—McGregor, Smith, Garcia, Crowley, Dempsey, May, Dauer, DeCinces, D. Martinez, Stone. Seated in front—Cashen, batboy.

"We came from behind more times than I can ever remember," said Belanger, the veteran shortstop who has been on all four Baltimore pennant winners. "To me, that's a sign of integrity and pride. Sure, we made mistakes but we seemed to make them at the right time when they didn't hurt us as much."

The Orioles played the 1979 season with amazing consistency. They did lose six in a row in April when they got off to that miserable 3-8 start and dropped five straight in the first week of July. But these two little tailspins were more than offset by two nine-game winning streaks, two seven-game streaks and three six-game streaks.

And, as their East Division lead grew, Weaver kept making all the right moves and imploring his men to keep moving.

"I don't want to hear any talk about playing .500 ball," he barked at one point. "That's the worst thing you can say. Don't even think it. That's for .500 people. We're better than that."

That the Orioles were better than that should not have shocked those who follow the bouncing ball in the summertime. Baltimore has fared better than any other club in baseball over the past 23 years. It has won 90 or more games 10 times over the past 12 seasons and six East Division titles since the playoffs were first established in 1969.

"It's good to be back," Weaver said. "They all said we'd fall faster than Skylab, but we're still up there, aren't we?"

SCORES OF BALTIMORE ORIOLES' 1979 GAMES

APRIL

			Winner	Loser
6—Chicago	W	5-3	Palmer	Kravec
7—Chicago	W	6-3	Flanagan	Proly
8—Chicago	L	1-5	Wortham	D. Martinez
10—N. York	L	6-7	Gossage	Stewart
11—N. York	W	6-5†	Stanhouse	Gossage
12—N. York	L	0-5	John	Flanagan
13—At Milw.	L	3-9	Sorensen	Stone
14—At Milw.	L	10-11	McClure	Stoddard
15—At Milw.	L	2-4	Caldwell	Palmer
17—At N.Y.	L	1-5	Guidry	Flanagan
18—At N.Y.	L	1-3	John	D. Martinez
19—At N.Y.	W	6-3	Palmer	Mirabella
20—Milw.	W	6-3	Stone	Caldwell
21—Milw.	W	4-2	Stewart	Travers
22—Milw.	W	6-2	D. Martinez	Haas
22—Milw.	W	7-3	Flanagan	Sorensen
24—At Calif.	W	7-2	Palmer	Aase
25—At Calif.	W	5-2	Stone	Tanana
26—At Calif.	W	4-2	Stoddard	LaRoche
27—At Oak.	W	7-1	Flanagan	Keough
28—At Oak.	L	5-8	Todd	McGregor
29—At Oak.	W	13-1	T. Martinez	Johnson
30—At Sea.	W	8-7†	Stanhouse	Honeycutt
		Won 14, Lost 9		

MAY

1—At Sea.	W	3-1	D. Martinez	McLaughlin
2—At Sea.	W	9-3	Flanagan	Mitchell
5—Calif.	W	9-1	Palmer	Aase
6—Calif.	W	6-0	D. Martinez	Barlow
7—Oakland	L	3-5	Langford	T. Martinez
8—Oakland	W	8-2	Flanagan	Todd
9—Oakland	L	2-4	Norris	Palmer
10—Oakland	W	3-1	D. Martinez	Johnson
11—Seattle	W	8-3	Stone	McLaughlin
12—Seattle	W	4-1	Flanagan	Honeycutt
15—At Bos.	L	2-3†	Eckersley	Stanhouse
16—At Bos.	W	10-6	D. Martinez	Hassler
17—At Bos.	L	2-6	Stanley	Stone

MAY

			Winner	Loser
18—At Tor.	W	7-6‡	Stanhouse	Freisleben
19—At Tor.	W	4-3	Palmer	Underwood
20—At Tor.	W	6-2	D. Martinez	Jefferson
22—Boston	L	5-7	Renko	Flanagan
23—Boston	W	5-2†	T. Martinez	Stanley
24—Boston	W	5-3	D. Martinez	Torrez
26—At Det.	W	7-5y	Stewart	Hiller
27—At Det.	L	1-5	Billingham	McGregor
27—At Det.	L	3-10	Rozema	Stone
28—At K.C.	L	4-5y	Gura	Stewart
29—At K.C.	W	8-1	Palmer	Splittorff
30—At K.C.	L	1-2	Gale	Flanagan
		Won 16, Lost 9		

JUNE

1—At Texas	L	2-4	Comer	Stone
2—At Texas	W	5-4	T. Martinez	Lyle
3—At Texas	L	2-4	Alexander	Palmer
4—Minn.	W	3-2†	Stanhouse	Marshall
5—Minn.	L	1-3	Hartzell	Stone
6—Kan. C.	W	3-0	D. Martinez	Splittorff
7—Kan. C.	W	3-1	Stewart	Martin
8—Texas	W	3-0	Flanagan	Alexander
9—Texas	W	4-3	Stone	Ellis
10—Texas	W	5-4	D. Martinez	Kern
11—At Chi.	W	6-0	McGregor	Wortham
12—At Chi.	L	4-12	Kravec	Flanagan
13—At Chi.	W	8-7†	Stoddard	Trout
15—At Minn.	W	6-5	Stanhouse	Marshall
17—At Minn.	W	8-5	Flanagan	Koosman
18—At Cleve.	W	8-7	Stanhouse	Cruz
19—At Cleve.	W	6-4	Stoddard	Paxton
20—At Cleve.	W	5-3*	D. Martinez	Waits
22—Detroit	W	6-5	D. Martinez	Tobik
23—Detroit	W	8-6	T. Martinez	Hiller
23—Detroit	W	6-5	Stewart	Billingham
24—Detroit	L	4-6	Lopez	D. Martinez
25—Cleve.	W	3-2	Stone	Garland
26—Cleve.	W	4-3	Flanagan	Barker

JUNE			Winner	Loser
27—Cleve.	W	3-1	Palmer	Paxton
28—Cleve.	L	3-6	Wise	D. Martinez
29—Toronto	W	6-1	McGregor	Stieb
29—Toronto	W	4-0	Stone	Huffman
30—Toronto	W	2-0	Flanagan	Underwood
		Won 23, Lost 6		

JULY				
1—Toronto	W	10-7	Stewart	Jefferson
2—At Texas	L	0-2	Comer	D. Martinez
3—At Texas	L	0-4	Jenkins	Stone
4—At Texas	L	5-9	Darwin	Flanagan
6—At Calif.	L	3-7	Barr	Stone
7—At Calif.	L	1-10	Frost	D. Martinez
8—At Calif.	W	3-2	McGregor	Aase
9—At Oak.	W	7-3	Flanagan	Keough
10—At Oak.	L	6-7	Langford	Stewart
11—At Oak.	W	3-1	D. Martinez	McCatty
13—At Sea.	L	3-4	Jones	McGregor
14—At Sea.	W	5-2	Flanagan	Parrott
15—At Sea.	W	6-1	D. Martinez	Honeycutt
19—Calif.	L	3-4‡	LaRoche	D. Martinez
19—Calif.	W	3-0	Flanagan	Frost
20—Calif.	W	2-1	McGregor	Barr
21—Calif.	W	10-2	Stewart	Ryan
22—Oakland	W	4-1	Stone	Langford
23—Oakland	W	7-4	T. Martinez	Keough
24—Oakland	W	7-6	D. Martinez	Bannister
24—Seattle	W	11-3	McGregor	Jones
25—Seattle	L	4-5	Parrott	Stewart
26—Seattle	W	12-1	Stone	Stein
27—At K.C.	W	8-0	Flanagan	Leonard
28—At K.C.	L	3-6	Gale	D. Martinez
29—At K.C.	W	6-4	McGregor	Splittorff
30—At Milw.	W	2-1	Stone	Slaton
31—At Milw.	W	9-5	Stewart	Mitchell
		Won 18, Lost 10		

AUGUST				
1—At Milw.	W	5-2	D. Martinez	Sorensen
3—At N.Y.	W	1-0	McGregor	Tiant
4—At N.Y.	W	5-4	Ford	Kaat
5—At N.Y.	L	2-3	John	Flanagan
6—At N.Y.	L	4-5	Guidry	T. Martinez
7—Milw.	L	5-7	Augustine	Stewart
8—Milw.	L	4-8	Travers	Stanhouse
9—Milw.	W	3-2	Flanagan	Augustine
10—N. York	W	8-6	T. Martinez	Davis
13—Chicago	L	0-7	Trout	McGregor

AUGUST			Winner	Loser
14—Chicago	W	2-1§	T. Martinez	Farmer
15—Chicago	W	2-1§	Flanagan	Hoffman
16—Kan. C.	L	2-4	Splittorff	D. Martinez
17—Kan. C.	L	1-7	Chamberlain	Palmer
18—Kan. C.	W	9-2	McGregor	Gura
19—Kan. C.	L	7-11†	Busby	Stanhouse
20—Texas	W	3-0	Flanagan	Allard
21—Texas	L	1-2	Comer	D. Martinez
23—Texas	W	6-5	McGregor	Jenkins
26—At Chi.	W	12-7	Flanagan	Trout
26—At Chi.	W	4-3x	Stanhouse	Farmer
27—At Minn.	L	3-4	Redfern	D. Martinez
27—At Minn.	W	5-1	Palmer	Goltz
29—At Minn.	W	4-0	McGregor	Erickson
29—At Minn.	W	7-4	Ford	Zahn
30—Minn.	W	5-4	Flanagan	Koosman
31—Minn.	L	1-3	Goltz	D. Martinez
		Won 16, Lost 11		

SEPTEMBER				
1—Minn.	L	2-3	Hartzell	Palmer
2—Minn.	W	3-1	McGregor	Erickson
3—Toronto	W	2-1‡	T. Martinez	Buskey
3—Toronto	W	5-1	Flanagan	Lemanczyk
6—Toronto	W	5-0	D. Martinez	Edge
7—At Bos.	W	2-1	Stewart	Rainey
8—At Bos.	W	3-2	Flanagan	Eckersley
9—At Bos.	W	16-4	Stone	Torrez
10—At Bos.	L	2-3	Stanley	D. Martinez
11—At Tor.	L	1-3	Underwood	McGregor
12—At Tor.	L	2-3	Edge	Palmer
13—At Tor.	W	10-4	Flanagan	Huffman
14—Boston	W	5-3	Stone	Stanley
15—Boston	L	2-10	Renko	D. Martinez
16—Boston	W	13-3	Palmer	Tudor
17—At Det.	W	2-1	McGregor	Wilcox
18—At Det.	L	1-2	Petry	Flanagan
19—At Det.	L	0-5	Morris	D. Martinez
20—At Det.	W	8-7	T. Martinez	Billingham
22—Cleve.	L	3-7	Waits	McGregor
23—Cleve.	L	3-4	Monge	D. Martinez
23—Cleve.	W	3-1	Flanagan	Spillner
25—Detroit	L	2-3	Morris	T. Martinez
26—Detroit	W	13-2	McGregor	Chris
28—At Cleve.	W	14-6	Palmer	Barker
29—At Cleve.	L	1-4	Spillner	Flanagan
30—At Cleve.	L	5-6‡	Monge	Ford
		Won 15, Lost 12		

• 5½ innings.   † 10 innings.   ‡ 11 innings.   § 12 innings.   x 13 innings.   y 16 innings.

Brewers Missed Hisle, Pennant in '79

By TOM FLAHERTY

There were two big things missing in the Brewers' best season in their history—Larry Hisle and a pennant.

Manager George Bamberger thought that one might have had a lot to do with the other.

"We could have been in first place if we'd had Larry," Bamberger said. "You're talking about a super ballplayer. The guy gets so many big hits."

Hisle, the Brewers' most valuable player the year before, injured his right shoulder in Baltimore in April and spent most of the season on the disabled list. Don Money also spent a month and a half on the disabled list with a hamstring injury early in the season and never really got untracked.

But despite missing the big hits from Hisle and Money, the Brewers got plenty of production from almost everybody else in setting a team record with a 95-66 record and finishing second, eight games behind Baltimore.

Gorman Thomas led the American League with 45 home runs, a team record, and also set a team record with 123 RBIs. Sixto Lezcano hit 28 home runs and drove in 101 runs, and Cecil Cooper had 24 homers and 106 RBIs. Ben Oglivie added to the team record of 185 homers with 29.

Lezcano hit .321 and Cooper .308, but the Brewers' leading hitter was Paul Molitor, who showed what he thought of the sophomore jinx by hitting .322, another team record.

Molitor, THE SPORTING NEWS American League Rookie Player of the Year in 1978, improved in every department in 1979. He hit 16 triples and stole 33 bases and excited crowds at County Stadium with his aggressive play.

Despite all the offensive fireworks, however, the Brewers never seriously challenged the Orioles in the East Division race. They tied their team record of 10 straight victories in July then returned home for what was expected to be the biggest homestand in their history.

It turned out to be the most disappointing.

After starting it out by sweeping three games from the New York Yankees to move within 6½ games of the Orioles, the Brewers lost three straight to the Orioles and four of five to the Boston Red Sox to fall 11½ games behind.

Their problems were compounded when Mike Caldwell, a 22-game winner the year before, pulled a muscle in his side in a wrestling match with the Yankees' Reggie Jackson in the first game of that homestand and missed three starts.

Caldwell's record was 16-6 and he set a couple of Brewer records by winning eight straight games from mid-June to late August and recording 25 scoreless innings in April.

Jim Slaton, who returned to the Brewers through the reentry draft, posted a 15-9 record and Moose Haas came back from a '78 elbow injury and posted an 11-11 record. Lary Sorensen finished with a 15-14 record and Bill Travers was 14-8, but both were inconsistent.

The Brewers led the major leagues in complete games for the second straight year with 61, but part of that was due to the inability of the bullpen to produce a consistent stopper.

Jerry Augustine had the best statistics of the relievers with a 9-6 record and five saves. Bill Castro had six saves and a 2.05 ERA but made only 39 appearances and pitched a meager 44 innings. Bob McClure had a 5-2 record and also saved five.

But despite their few shortcomings, the Brewers were pleased with a season that showed that their 93 victories in 1978 wasn't a fluke. And the fans agreed. The Brewers drew 1,918,343 fans to County Stadium, topping their previous high by 316,937.

SCORES OF MILWAUKEE BREWERS' 1979 GAMES

APRIL			Winner	Loser	APRIL			Winner	Loser
5 – At N.Y.	W	5-1	Caldwell	Guidry	18 – At Bos.	W	4-1	Sorensen	Renko
7 – At N.Y.	W	4-3	McClure	Figueroa	19 – At Bos.	L	3-5	Rainey	Slaton
8 – At N.Y.	L	1-2	John	Sorensen	20 – At Balt.	L	3-6	Stone	Caldwell
10 – Boston	W	3-0	Caldwell	Eckersley	21 – At Balt.	L	2-4	Stewart	Travers
12 – Boston	L	10-12	Drago	Cleveland	22 – At Balt.	L	2-6	D. Martinez	Haas
13 – Balt.	W	9-3	Sorensen	Stone	22 – At Balt.	L	3-7	Flanagan	Sorensen
14 – Balt.	W	11-10	McClure	Stoddard	26 – Detroit	W	5-1	Slaton	Billingham
15 – Balt.	W	4-2	Caldwell	Palmer	26 – Detroit	W	7-5	Cleveland	Baker
17 – At Bos.	L	5-6	Burgmeier	Cleveland	27 – At Tor.	W	8-5	Sorensen	Huffman

MILWAUKEE BREWERS—1979

Front row—Sullivan, equipment manager; Howard, coach; Mclish, coach; Kuenn, coach; Bamberger, manager; Haney, coach; Rodgers, coach; McClure, Moore, Ferguson, vice-president; Rayer, trainer. Second row—Oglivie, Ksicinski, clubhouse manager; Lezcano, Castro, Gantner, Wohlford, Bando, Mitchell, Money, Nordbrook, Cooper. Third row—Hisle, Sorensen, Caldwell, Martinez, Haas, Slaton, Augustine, Fosse. Fourth row—Davis, Yount, Thomas, Travers, Cleveland, Molitor. Kneeling in front—batboys Doman, Betthauser, D. Rinn, Migliaccio, Sampson, McCormick and S. Rinn.

APRIL			Winner	Loser
28—At Tor.	W	11-8†	McClure	Willis
29—At Tor.	W	3-0	Caldwell	Clancy
29—At Tor.	L	3-5	Lemanczyk	Travers
30—At Cleve.	W	8-0	Slaton	Wilkins

Won 13, Lost 9

MAY				
1—At Cleve.	L	1-3	Paxton	Sorensen
2—At Cleve.	W	6-1	Haas	Garland
3—Toronto	W	5-4	Travers	Underwood
4—Toronto	L	4-5	Clancy	Caldwell
5—Toronto	W	6-1	Slaton	Lemanczyk
6—Toronto	W	4-0	Sorensen	Lemongello
8—Cleve.	W	9-5	Haas	Garland
9—Cleve.	L	7-8	Waits	Caldwell
10—Cleve.	W	1-8	Wilkins	Slaton
11—At Det.	W	5-1	Sorensen	Fidrych
12—At Det.	W	3-2	Augustine	Taylor
13—At Det.	L	2-6	Morris	Haas
15—At Calif.	L	1-2	Clear	Caldwell
16—At Calif.	L	3-4‡	Clear	Augustine
17—At Calif.	L	5-8	Barr	Sorensen
18—At Oak.	W	8-0	Travers	Norris
19—At Oak.	L	4-12	Johnson	Haas
20—At Oak.	L	6-7	Hamilton	Augustine
20—At Oak.	L	1-2	McCatty	Slaton
22—Calif.	W	7-1	Sorensen	Frost
23—Calif.	W	1-0	Travers	Aase
24—Calif.	W	9-6	Augustine	Knapp
25—Oakland	W	3-2	Caldwell	Lacey
26—Oakland	W	8-4	Slaton	Langford
27—Oakland	L	1-2	McCatty	Sorensen
28—N. York	L	1-2†	Davis	Travers
29—N. York	W	7-3	Haas	Hunter
30—N. York	L	2-5†	Davis	McClure
31—N. York	W	5-4	Augustine	Burris

Won 15, Lost 14

JUNE				
1—At K.C.	W	5-4	Sorensen	Martin
2—At K.C.	L	3-4	Splittorff	Cleveland
3—At K.C.	L	1-6	Pattin	Haas
4—At Chi.	W	6-0	Caldwell	Baumgarten
5—At Chi.	W	5-3	Slaton	Howard
6—Texas	W	4-3	Sorensen	Comer
7—Texas	L	1-7	Jenkins	Haas
9—Chicago	L	2-6	Howard	Caldwell
10—Chicago	L	3-13	Barrios	Mitchell
12—At Texas	L	6-7	Kern	Sorensen
13—At Texas	W	5-4	Haas	Jenkins
14—At Texas	W	6-2	Travers	Alexander
15—Kan. C.	L	11-14	Mingori	Cleveland
16—Kan. C.	W	3-2	Slaton	Busby
17—Kan. C.	W	5-3	Sorensen	Gale
19—Minn.	W	10-9	McClure	Bacsik
20—Minn.	W	8-3	Travers	Hartzell
21—Minn.	W	3-2	Caldwell	Serum
22—At Sea.	W	15-8	Slaton	Abbott
23—At Sea.	L	3-8	Parrott	Sorensen
24—At Sea.	W	7-4§	Castro	Montague
26—At Minn.	L	7-8	Marshall	Augustine
27—At Minn.	W	9-8	Caldwell	Serum
28—At Minn.	W	6-5†	Castro	Marshall
29—Seattle	L	2-3	Abbott	Sorensen
30—Seattle	W	8-1	Haas	Montague

Won 16, Lost 10

JULY				
1—Seattle	W	10-3	Slaton	Bannister
3—At N.Y.	W	7-2	Caldwell	Clay
4—At N.Y.	L	3-4	Tiant	Travers
5—At N.Y.	W	3-0	Sorensen	Guidry
6—Detroit	L	4-7	Morris	Haas
6—Detroit	L	4-5	Wilcox	Slaton
7—Detroit	L	3-6	Underwood	Mitchell

JULY			Winner	Loser
8—Detroit	W	5-4	Caldwell	Hiller
8—Detroit	W	3-1	Travers	Petry
9—At Tor.	L	1-7	Stieb	Sorensen
11—At Tor.	W	2-1†	Slaton	Buskey
12—At Tor.	W	5-3	Haas	Underwood
13—Cleve.	W	4-3x	Galasso	Cruz
14—Cleve.	W	10-3	Travers	Clyde
15—Cleve.	W	10-4	Sorensen	Barker
19—Toronto	W	3-2‡	Castro	Buskey
20—Toronto	W	2-0	Slaton	Underwood
21—At Cleve.	W	5-0	Haas	Barker
22—At Cleve.	W	14-5	Caldwell	Paxton
22—At Cleve.	W	5-3	Mitchell	Clyde
23—At Cleve.	L	4-5	Spillner	Sorensen
24—At Det.	W	5-4	Travers	Underwood
25—At Det.	L	2-11	Morris	Slaton
26—At Det.	L	2-5	Petry	Haas
27—N. York	W	6-5	McClure	Gossage
28—N. York	W	9-2	Sorensen	Tiant
29—N. York	W	5-3	Travers	Hunter
30—Balt.	L	1-2	Stone	Slaton
31—Balt.	L	5-9	Stewart	Mitchell

Won 19, Lost 10

AUGUST				
1—Balt.	L	2-5	D. Martinez	Sorensen
2—Boston	L	1-10	Torrez	Travers
3—Boston	W	5-3	Slaton	Renko
4—Boston	L	6-8	Ripley	Cleveland
5—Boston	L	2-7	Eckersley	Sorensen
5—Boston	L	5-19	Remerswaal	Augustine
7—At Balt.	W	7-5	Augustine	Stewart
8—At Balt.	W	8-4	Travers	Stanhouse
9—At Balt.	L	2-3	Flanagan	Augustine
10—At Bos.	L	4-5	Drago	McClure
11—At Bos.	W	9-6†	Galasso	Torrez
13—Kan. C.	W	5-4	Slaton	Quisenberry
14—Kan. C.	W	5-2	Caldwell	Leonard
15—Kan. C.	W	6-5	Augustine	Quisenberry
16—Texas	W	4-1	Sorensen	Allard
17—Texas	W	5-1	Haas	Comer
18—Texas	L	3-7	Jenkins	Slaton
19—Texas	W	4-3	Caldwell	Lyle
20—Chicago	W	5-3	Travers	Kravec
21—Chicago	W	3-2	Sorensen	Proly
21—Chicago	W	9-5	Mitchell	Howard
22—Chicago	L	3-4	Farmer	Haas
24—At Texas	W	9-6	Galasso	Darwin
25—At Texas	W	5-2	Caldwell	Allard
26—At Texas	W	6-2	Travers	Comer
27—At K.C.	W	9-10†	Hrabosky	Galasso
28—At K.C.	W	11-6	Haas	Chamberlain
29—At K.C.	L	8-18	Leonard	Slaton
30—At Chi.	W	4-3§	Augustine	Hoffman
31—At Chi.	L	1-6	Trout	Travers

Won 18, Lost 12

SEPTEMBER				
1—At Chi.	L	3-4*	Wortham	Sorensen
2—At Chi.	W	7-2	Haas	Kravec
3—At Oak.	W	6-3	Slaton	Norris
5—At Oak.	L	1-6	Keough	Caldwell
7—At Calif.	L	3-6	Ryan	Travers
8—At Calif.	L	2-3	Barr	Augustine
9—At Calif.	L	2-5	Tanana	Haas
11—Oakland	W	5-0	Slaton	Keough
12—Oakland	W	7-0	Caldwell	Morgan
13—Oakland	L	3-8	McCatty	Travers
14—Calif.	L	7-8	LaRoche	Castro
15—Calif.	W	3-2	Haas	Ryan
16—Calif.	W	2-1	Slaton	Tanana
17—At Sea.	W	7-6	Travers	Hinton
18—At Sea.	W	7-6	Augustine	Rawley
19—At Sea.	W	12-1	Sorensen	Bannister
21—Minn.	L	2-3	Koosman	Haas

SEPTEMBER			Winner	Loser	SEPTEMBER			Winner	Loser
22—Minn.	L	3-6	Erickson	Slaton	28—At Minn.	W	10-1	Caldwell	Erickson
23—Minn.	W	8-7	Augustine	Redfern	29—At Minn.	W	11-8	Mitchell	Hartzell
25—Seattle	W	7-6	Augustine	Rawley	30—At Minn.	L	0-5	Koosman	Sorensen
26—Seattle	L	1-8	Parrott	Haas			Won 14, Lost 11		
27—Seattle	W	7-6‡	Travers	McLaughlin					

* 5 innings.   † 10 innings.   ‡ 11 innings.   § 12 innings.   x 17 innings.

Second-Half Collapse Spoiled Yaz' Heroics

By JOE GIULIOTTI

The Red Sox' third-place finish could be attributed directly to crippling injuries and the collapse of a pitching staff.

The fans turned out in record numbers (2.3 million) but only saw the starting nine together for a handful of games. Still, the club was in contention until they collapsed during the final six weeks.

On August 17, the Red Sox had a four-game winning streak halted by the Chicago White Sox. They were to play 30 games before again putting consecutive victories together. By the time they did they had fallen from four games off the pace to 14 and began dusting off the golf clubs and fishing poles for the long winter.

The Red Sox were right in the thick of the fight during the first half of the season despite the absence of catcher Carlton Fisk. The perennial All-Star suffered an elbow injury in spring training and was behind the plate for only 35 games all season—the Sox winning 25.

The pitching of Dennis Eckersley, Bob Stanley, Steve Renko and Mike Torrez with bullpen help from Dick Drago and Tom Burgmeier kept the Sox up there, but things started going bad after the break.

The Sox, backed by a fantastic 32-10 first half in friendly Fenway, were 56-32 at the break, two games behind the Baltimore Orioles. But over the second half the pitching collapsed and the club played under .500 (35-37) to end the season in third place, 11½ back, with a 91-69 slate.

The end's beginning came when second baseman Jerry Remy, the only speedster on the club, tore up his left knee sliding into home plate in New York, July 1. He was hitting .304 at the time and was able to play just seven games the rest of the way.

When the club came out of the gate slowly for the second half, Manager Don Zimmer, who almost was fired in September, decided to drop his five-man starting rotation and go with four. It didn't work.

Renko, 8-3 at the break, didn't win in five starts. Eckersley, after pitching seven straight complete-game victories and winning eight in a row, developed a sore arm and won only one game after August 14.

Torrez won but three games after August 7 while help summoned from the Triple-A club at Pawtucket (International) was helpless. John Tudor, Win Remmerswaal, Joel Finch and Allen Ripley couldn't stem the tide. Only Ripley (3-1 in long relief) contributed.

Carl Yastrzemski, plagued with Achilles tendon problems in both feet over the second half, batted a mere .233 after June with five home runs. However, he did provide the biggest thrill of the season when he became the 15th player in history to get 3,000 hits. It came September 12 in Fenway Park off the Yankees' Jim Beattie.

While pitching and injuries were problems, so was the catching. With both Fisk and veteran Bob Montgomery (also sore elbow) unable to see much action, the job fell to a pair of rookies—Gary Allenson and Mike O'Berry. The former hit .203, the latter .169. Aside from problems at the plate, the opposition ran wild, stealing 116 bases in 156 attempts.

As usual, the Red Sox were at or near the top of the league in virtually every offensive category but with a 4.03 team ERA couldn't compete with the Orioles.

On the bright side, Bob Watson, obtained in a trade with the Houston Astros on June 13, did his part before entering the reentry draft after the season. He batted .337, hit 13 homers, knocked in 53 runs and had 11 game-winning hits.

Fred Lynn had his best season and became the first Red Sox player since Yastrzemski (1968) to win the American League batting title. Lynn hit .333, tied Jim Rice for the club lead in homers with 39, had 122 RBIs and won his third Gold Glove.

Shortstop Rick Burleson again was a steady performer, winning his second Gold Glove. When the pressure was on to fire Zimmer, it was Burleson who came out in his defense. "We didn't win because we weren't good enough, not because of the manager," he said. He was right.

SCORES OF BOSTON RED SOX' 1979 GAMES

APRIL			Winner	Loser	MAY			Winner	Loser
5—Cleve.	W	7-1	Eckersley	Wise	26—At Tor.	L	6-7	Buskey	Campbell
7—At Cleve.	L	0-3	Waits	Torrez	27—At Tor.	W	1-0	Rainey	Jefferson
8—At Cleve.	W	7-6y	Drago	Cruz	28—At Texas	L	2-5	Jenkins	Renko
10—At Milw.	L	0-3	Caldwell	Eckersley	30—At Texas	L	2-3§	Kern	Drago
12—At Milw.	W	12-10	Drago	Cleveland	31—At Texas	W	3-2y	Drago	Lyle
15—Cleve.	W	14-4	Eckersley	Paxton				Won 14, Lost 12	
16—Cleve.	L	3-4	Wise	Stanley					
17—Milw.	W	6-5	Burgmeier	Cleveland	JUNE				
18—Milw.	L	1-4	Sorensen	Renko	1—At Minn.	W	5-2	Stanley	Koosman
19—Milw.	W	5-3	Rainey	Slaton	2—At Minn.	L	2-8	Goltz	Rainey
20—Kan. C.	W	9-2	Hassler	Leonard	3—At Minn.	W	8-2	Renko	Zahn
21—Kan. C.	W	10-4	Stanley	Gura	4—Texas	W	13-5	Torrez	Ellis
22—Kan. C.	W	6-0	Torrez	Gale	5—Texas	W	9-3	Eckersley	Matlack
24—At Sea.	W	4-3y	Drago	Rawley	6—Chicago	L	5-8	Barrios	Stanley
25—At Sea.	W	4-1	Wright	Bannister	7—Chicago	W	9-2	Rainey	Kravec
26—At Sea.	W	2-0	Stanley	Mitchell	8—Minn.	W	2-1	Stanley	Goltz
27—At Calif.	L	6-8	Clear	Hassler	9—Minn.	W	12-6	Torrez	Erickson
28—At Calif.	L	0-5	Frost	Rainey	10—Minn.	W	5-0	Eckersley	Hartzell
29—At Calif.	L	2-0	Renko	Aase	11—At K.C.	W	4-0§	Stanley	Busby
30—At Oak.	L	4-5x	Lacey	Drago	12—At K.C.	L	6-7§	Hrabosky	Drago
			Won 13, Lost 7		13—At K.C.	W	11-3	Renko	Gura
					15—At Chi.	L	5-8	Wortham	Torrez
MAY					16—At Chi.	W	11-5	Eckersley	Scarberry
1—At Oak.	L	5-7	McCatty	Stanley	17—At Chi.	L	1-6	Kravec	Rainey
2—At Oak.	W	2-1	Torrez	Keough	18—Detroit	W	9-8	Drago	Arroyo
4—Seattle	W	5-3	Renko	Abbott	19—Detroit	L	4-10a	Lopez	Stanley
5—Seattle	W	11-4	Eckersley	Jones	20—Detroit	W	13-3	Torrez	Baker
6—Seattle	L	2-3	Montague	Campbell	21—Detroit	W	3-2	Eckersley	Morris
7—Calif.	W	9-4	Torrez	Ryan	22—Toronto	W	12-1	Rainey	Jefferson
8—Calif.	L	2-10	Knapp	Rainey	23—Toronto	W	4-3x	Drago	Buskey
9—Calif.	W	9-8	Campbell	LaRoche	24—Toronto	W	8-4	Torrez	Huffman
10—Calif.	L	3-5	Aase	Eckersley	26—At Det.	L	4-6	Morris	Campbell
11—Oakland	W	11-2	Stanley	Keough	27—At Det.	W	3-1	Stanley	Tobik
12—Oakland	W	8-2	Torrez	Langford	28—At Det.	L	3-6	Billingham	Renko
13—Oakland	W	8-2	Rainey	Norris	29—At N.Y.	W	3-2z	Drago	Kaat
15—Balt.	W	3-2§	Eckersley	Stanhouse	30—At N.Y.	W	3-2	Stanley	Tiant
16—Balt.	L	6-10	D. Martinez	Hassler				Won 20, Lost 8	
17—Balt.	W	6-2	Stanley	Stone					
18—N. York	L	0-10	Beattie	Torrez	JULY				
19—N. York	W	4-3	Campbell	Figueroa	1—At N.Y.	L	5-6	Davis	Eckersley
20—N. York	L	0-2	John	Eckersley	2—At N.Y.	L	2-7	John	Finch
22—At Balt.	W	7-5	Renko	Flanagan	3—Kan. C.	W	10-0	Renko	Busby
23—At Balt.	L	2-5§	T. Martinez	Stanley	4—Kan. C.	W	6-4	Torrez	Hrabosky
24—At Balt.	L	3-5	D. Martinez	Torrez	5—Kan. C.	W	5-4	Stanley	Paschall

BOSTON RED SOX—1979

Front row—Burleson, Rice, Yastrzemski, Pesky, coach; Hriniak, coach; Zimmer, manager; Jackson, coach; Yost, coach; Fisk, Lynn, Remy. Second row—Fitzpatrick, clubhouse attendant; Moss, trainer; Brohamer, Wolfe, Montgomery, Hobson, Watson, Evans, O'Berry, Poquette, Allenson, Papi, Dwyer, Orlando, clubhouse attendant. Third row—Rainey, Finch, Campbell, Renko, Eckersley, Torrez, Stanley, Wright, Drago, Burgmeier.

JULY		Winner	Loser
6—At Sea.	L 3-5	Bannister	Eckersley
7—At Sea.	W 10-8	Burgmeier	Parrott
8—At Sea.	W 8-2	Renko	McLaughlin
9—At Calif.	L 0-6	Ryan	Torrez
10—At Calif.	L 3-4	Barr	Stanley
11—At Calif.	W 9-3	Eckersley	Frost
13—At Oak.	W 2-0	Renko	Morgan
14—At Oak.	W 8-7	Ripley	McCatty
15—At Oak.	W 3-2	Stanley	Langford
19—Seattle	W 7-1	Eckersley	Bannister
20—Seattle	L 0-8	Parrott	Torrez
21—Seattle	L 5-13	Montague	Renko
22—Calif.	W 6-5§	Campbell	Clear
23—Calif.	L 2-9	Frost	Finch
24—Oakland	W 7-3	Eckersley	Morgan
25—Oakland	W 16-4	Torrez	Kingman
26—Oakland	L 6-8	McCatty	Renko
27—At Texas	L 2-11	Comer	Stanley
28—At Texas	W 1-0	Eckersley	Jenkins
29—At Texas	W 3-2	Torrez	Alexander
30—At Cleve.	L 5-6	Cruz	Burgmeier
31—At Cleve.	L 10-11x	Monge	Campbell
31—At Cleve.	L 0-3	Barker	Finch
	Won 15, Lost 13		

AUGUST		Winner	Loser
1—At Cleve.	W 7-4	Eckersley	Clyde
2—At Milw.	W 10-1	Torrez	Travers
3—At Milw.	L 3-5	Slaton	Renko
4—At Milw.	W 8-6	Ripley	Cleveland
5—At Milw.	W 7-2	Eckersley	Sorensen
5—At Milw.	W 19-5	Rem'swaal	Augustine
7—Cleve.	W 12-3	Torrez	Clyde
8—Cleve.	L 4-6	Wise	Stanley
8—Cleve.	L 2-8	Spillner	Renko
9—Cleve.	W 3-2	Eckersley	Waits
10—Milw.	W 5-4	Drago	McClure
11—Milw.	L 6-9§	Galasso	Torrez
13—Minn.	W 6-5	Burgmeier	Marshall
14—Minn.	W 12-1	Eckersley	Redfern
15—Minn.	W 9-5	Drago	Bacsik
16—Chicago	W 7-5	Ripley	Proly
17—Chicago	L 1-4	Baumgarten	Stanley
18—Chicago	W 8-2*	Renko	Trout

AUGUST		Winner	Loser
19—Chicago	L 2-3	Wortham	Eckersley
20—At Minn.	L 5-10	Erickson	Torrez
21—At Minn.	L 2-7	Koosman	Tudor
22—At Minn.	W 9-4‡	Stanley	Goltz
24—At K.C.	L 2-4	Chamberlain	Eckersley
25—At K.C.	L 0-1	Leonard	Torrez
26—At K.C.	L 3-6	Splittorff	Renko
27—At Chi.	W 4-3	Stanley	Kravec
28—At Chi.	L 3-7	Baumgarten	Ripley
30—Texas	L 0-6	Medich	Eckersley
31—Texas	W 9-6	Torrez	Comer
	Won 16, Lost 13		

SEPTEMBER		Winner	Loser
1—Texas	L 4-5	Darwin	Drago
2—Texas	L 6-7x	Kern	Drago
3—At N.Y.	L 6-10	Guidry	Eckersley
4—At N.Y.	L 2-3	Tiant	Torrez
5—At N.Y.	W 5-0	Stanley	John
7—Balt.	L 1-2	Stewart	Rainey
8—Balt.	L 2-3	Flanagan	Eckersley
9—Balt.	L 4-16	Stone	Torrez
10—Balt.	W 3-2	Stanley	D. Martinez
11—N. York	L 3-8	Davis	Burgmeier
12—N. York	W 9-2	Rainey	Hunter
13—N. York	L 3-10	Guidry	Torrez
14—At Balt.	L 3-5	Stone	Stanley
15—At Balt.	W 10-2	Renko	D. Martinez
16—At Balt.	L 3-13	Palmer	Tudor
17—At Tor.	L 4-5	Jefferson	Drago
17—At Tor.	L 5-3	Rainey	Freisleben
18—At Tor.	W 8-3	Torrez	Huffman
19—At Tor.	W 8-0	Stanley	Stieb
20—At Tor.	L 2-6	Moore	Renko
21—Detroit	W 4-1†	Tudor	Rozema
23—Detroit	W 2-1	Eckersley	Wilcox
23—Detroit	L 2-3§	Lopez	Torrez
25—Toronto	L 3-5	Stieb	Stanley
26—Toronto	W 6-4	Rainey	Moore
27—Toronto	W 6-5	Drago	Buskey
28—At Det.	W 7-4	Torrez	Wilcox
29—At Det.	W 8-5	Renko	Lopez
30—At Det.	L 1-5	Morris	Stanley
	Won 13, Lost 16		

*5½ innings.   †6½ innings.   ‡8 innings.   §10 innings.   x11 innings.   y12 innings.   z13 innings.   a14 innings.

Yankees Endured Black Border Season

By PHIL PEPE

The New York Yankees' story for 1979 should be written inside a black border. It was a story of unbelievable tragedy and unspeakable grief.

It will be remembered for all time as the year Thurman Munson was killed. Flying his own Cessna jet, Munson missed the landing strip and plunged to his fiery death near the Canton-Akron Airport on August 2, a tragedy that greatly overshadowed the Yankees' failure to win their third straight World Championship and fourth straight American League pennant and their fall to fourth place in the AL East.

Even with Munson, a potential Hall of Famer, there was no way the Yankees were going to overtake the Orioles, but with his loss, the heart and soul seemed to ooze out of the Yankees. They had lost their captain, their leader, their friend, and things would never be the same.

NEW YORK YANKEES—1979

Front row—Munson, Dent, Doyle, Lau, coach; Martin, manager; Ferraro, coach; Fowler, coach; Berra, coach; Hunter, Guidry, White. Second row—Kane, traveling secretary; Monahan, trainer; Scala, bullpen catcher; Murcer, Narron, Kaat, Gossage, Beattie, Chambliss, Weinberg, trainer; Sheehy, equipment manager. Third row—Stanley, John, Hood, Spencer, Burris, Davis, Clay, Jones, Randolph, Melvin, batting practice pitcher. Seated in front—batboys Toulon, Aybar and Friedel.

Munson was just two months past his 32nd birthday when the tragedy occurred, in the prime of his life, at the top of his game.

It was a year not only of tragedy, but of disappointment, discontent, frustration and injury; a year in which old age suddenly seemed to creep up and clout the Yanks over the head; a year when nothing went right and everything went wrong.

Long before Munson's death, the Yankees had dropped out of the pennant race. It happened, in retrospect, on April 19, only 12 games into the season.

In a clubhouse incident, Rich Gossage and Cliff Johnson tangled. Gossage pushed the lumbering Johnson away and, in so doing, sprained a ligament in his right thumb.

Gossage, who had saved 27 games in 1978, missed 83 games. While he was gone, the Yankees dropped out of the race. When he returned, Gossage pitched like the Goose of old. In 36 appearances, he won five games and saved 18. But it was too late. The championship was gone.

Johnson was traded to Cleveland. Mickey Rivers was traded to Texas. And Munson was gone.

There were other injuries, to Ed Figueroa, who won only four games, 16 less than the previous year; to Graig Nettles, who fell off by seven homers and 20 RBIs; to Jim Beattie, who won only three games; to Reggie Jackson; to Ron Guidry, who won seven fewer games and lost five more than in 1978.

Manager Billy Martin, banished in July of 1978, replaced Bob Lemon in June of 1979, but he could pull off no miracle. And saving fourth place from the rush of the youthful Tigers was no consolation.

Catfish Hunter retired with a final season record of 2-9. And Munson was gone.

Not all of it was negative for the Yankees in 1979, however.

Guidry won his second consecutive AL ERA title and became the first Yankee pitcher in history to strike out 200 batters in two separate seasons.

Tommy John made the Yankees' investment worthwhile with 21 victories, joining a select list of pitchers who have won 20 games in both leagues.

Ron Davis fashioned a spectacular rookie year with a 14-2 record, nine saves and a 2.86 ERA.

Luis Tiant proved that reports of his demise were premature with a 13-8 record, matching his 1978 stats, although he did not win a game until late May.

Willie Randolph had career highs of 61 RBIs and 98 runs.

Nettles hit 20 or more homers for the seventh straight season.

Oscar Gamble, obtained in the Rivers trade, batted .389 with 11 homers and 32 RBIs in 36 games as a born-again Yankee.

Jim Spencer had a career-high 23 homers.

Chris Chambliss had a career-high 18 homers.

And the Yankees played before 2,537,765 paying customers at home (4,762,147 home and away), the second highest home attendance in American League history.

But all those positive things, all those personal accomplishments, all the good faded in a year of discontent, disappointment and tragedy. The Yankees' brief dynasty ended. And Thurman Munson was gone.

SCORES OF NEW YORK YANKEES' 1979 GAMES

Date			Winner	Loser
APRIL				
5–Milw.	L	1-5	Caldwell	Guidry
7–Milw.	L	3-4	McClure	Figueroa
8–Milw.	W	2-1	John	Sorensen
10–At Balt.	W	7-6	Gossage	Stewart
11–At Balt.	L	5-6*	Stanhouse	Gossage
12–At Balt.	W	5-0	John	Flanagan
13–At Chi.	L	2-12	Wortham	Tiant
14–At Chi.	W	8-5	Tidrow	Robinson
15–At Chi.	W	6-5	Figueroa	Proly
17–Balt.	W	5-1	Guidry	Flanagan
18–Balt.	L	3-1	John	D. Martinez
19–Balt.	L	3-6	Palmer	Mirabella
20–Texas	W	5-3	Figueroa	Comer
21–Texas	L	0-5	Jenkins	Hunter
22–Texas	W	5-1	Guidry	Ellis
24–At Oak.	W	3-1	John	Johnson
25–At Oak.	L	0-1	Minetto	Figueroa
27–At Sea.	L	5-6	Parrott	Tidrow
28–At Sea.	L	2-3	Rawley	Hunter
29–At Sea.	L	5-6	Vasquez	Mirabella
30–At Calif.	L	1-2	LaRoche	Figueroa
Won 10, Lost 11				
MAY				
1–At Calif.	W	12-8†	John	LaRoche
2–At Calif.	L	0-1	Ryan	Guidry
4–Oakland	L	5-11	Norris	Beattie
5–Oakland	W	5-4	John	Heaverlo
6–Oakland	W	6-5*	Guidry	Heaverlo
7–Seattle	L	4-12	Honeycutt	Mirabella
8–Seattle	L	5-3	Beattie	Bannister
9–Seattle	W	5-0	Figueroa	Abbott
10–Seattle	W	8-1	John	Jones
11–Calif.	L	1-4	Barr	Hunter
12–Calif.	W	6-5	Tidrow	Frost
13–Calif.	W	12-10	Beattie	Knapp
14–Detroit	L	1-3	Wilcox	Figueroa
15–Detroit	W	11-3	John	Baker
16–Detroit	W	6-2	Guidry	Fidrych
18–At Bos.	W	10-0	Beattie	Torrez
19–At Bos.	L	3-4	Campbell	Figueroa
20–At Bos.	W	2-0	John	Eckersley
21–At Det.	L	1-3	Billingham	Guidry
22–At Det.	W	12-8	Tiant	Fidrych
23–At Det.	L	3-4	Hiller	Clay
26–At Cleve.	L	4-8	Waits	John
27–At Cleve.	L	0-5	Wise	Guidry
27–At Cleve.	W	5-4	Burris	Monge
28–At Milw.	L	2-1*	Davis	Travers
29–At Milw.	L	3-7	Haas	Hunter
30–At Milw.	W	5-2†	Davis	McClure
31–At Milw.	L	4-5	Augustine	Burris
Won 16, Lost 12				
JUNE				
1–Chicago	W	4-0	Guidry	Barrios
2–Chicago	L	0-7	Kravec	Beattie
3–Chicago	W	3-2†	Davis	Scarbery
4–Kan. C.	W	8-3	John	Gale
5–Kan. C.	L	1-3	Gura	Tiant
6–Minn.	W	3-2	Guidry	Koosman
7–Minn.	L	1-4	Zahn	Beattie
8–At K.C.	W	11-10*	Clay	Rodriguez
9–At K.C.	L	8-9§	Pattin	Clay
10–At K.C.	W	10-4	Tiant	Mingori
12–At Minn.	W	4-1	Davis	Koosman
13–At Minn.	L	7-8	Redfern	Burris
14–At Minn.	L	2-4	Zahn	John
15–At Texas	L	5-9	Matlack	Figueroa
16–At Texas	W	3-2*	Davis	Lyle
17–At Texas	L	3-6	Comer	Hunter
19–Toronto	L	4-5	Huffman	John
20–Toronto	W	2-1	Hood	Underwood
20–Toronto	L	2-3	Moore	Burris

Date			Winner	Loser
JUNE				
21–Toronto	W	3-1	Tiant	Lemanczyk
22–Cleve.	W	3-2	Hunter	Wilkins
23–Cleve.	W	6-5*	John	Cruz
24–Cleve.	W	8-2	Kaat	Waits
25–At Tor.	L	1-3	Underwood	Clay
26–At Tor.	W	11-2	Tiant	Lemanczyk
28–At Tor.	W	5-3*	Davis	Lemongello
29–Boston	L	2-3§	Drago	Kaat
30–Boston	L	2-3	Stanley	Tiant
Won 15, Lost 13				
JULY				
1–Boston	W	6-5	Davis	Eckersley
2–Boston	W	7-2	John	Finch
3–Milw.	L	2-7	Caldwell	Clay
4–Milw.	W	4-3	Tiant	Travers
5–Milw.	L	0-3	Sorensen	Guidry
6–At Oak.	W	4-3	Davis	McCatty
6–At Oak.	W	3-0	John	Hamilton
7–At Oak.	W	8-3	Hood	Morgan
8–At Oak.	W	2-0	Tiant	Kingman
10–At Sea.	L	1-5	Honeycutt	Guidry
11–At Sea.	L	1-16	Bannister	John
12–At Sea.	W	14-2	Hunter	Parrott
13–At Calif.	L	1-6	Ryan	Tiant
14–At Calif.	L	7-8†	Clear	Davis
15–At Calif.	L	4-5	Barr	Guidry
19–Oakland	W	10-2	Tiant	Morgan
20–Oakland	L	1-5	Kingman	John
21–Oakland	W	12-4	Guidry	Minetto
22–Seattle	W	4-0	Kaat	Honeycutt
23–Seattle	W	6-2	Figueroa	Abbott
24–Calif.	W	6-5	Davis	LaRoche
25–Calif.	L	5-9	Botting	John
26–Calif.	W	2-0	Guidry	Barr
27–At Milw.	L	5-6	McClure	Gossage
28–At Milw.	L	2-9	Sorensen	Tiant
29–At Milw	L	3-5	Travers	Hunter
30–At Chi.	L	7-2	John	Wortham
31–At Chi.	W	7-3	Guidry	Scarbery
Won 16, Lost 12				
AUGUST				
1–At Chi.	W	9-1	Hood	Kravec
3–Balt.	L	0-1	McGregor	Tiant
4–Balt.	L	4-5	Ford	Kaat
5–Balt.	W	3-2	John	Flanagan
6–Balt.	W	5-4	Guidry	T. Martinez
7–Chicago	L	5-9	Scarbery	Clay
8–Chicago	W	4-3	Tiant	Trout
9–Chicago	L	1-5	Wortham	Hunter
10–At Balt.	L	6-8	T. Martinez	Davis
13–Texas	W	3-2	Guidry	Jenkins
14–Texas	W	6-5	Tiant	Kern
15–Texas	W	4-3	John	Gleaton
16–Minn.	L	1-5	Zahn	Hunter
17–Minn.	L	2-5	Koosman	Beattie
18–Minn.	W	5-3	Davis	Marshall
19–Minn.	W	4-3	Guidry	Jackson
20–At K.C.	W	17-4	Tiant	Gale
21–At K.C.	W	6-2	Gossage	Splittorff
22–At K.C.	L	1-3	Gura	Beattie
24–At Minn.	W	7-5	Guidry	Zahn
25–At Minn.	L	1-4	Koosman	Tiant
27–At Texas	W	7-4	John	Jenkins
28–At Texas	L	2-10	Kern	Clay
29–At Texas	W	7-5	Guidry	Rajsich
30–Kan. C.	L	3-8	Gura	Tiant
31–Kan. C.	W	7-3	John	Splittorff
Won 15, Lost 11				
SEPTEMBER				
1–Kan. C.	L	8-9	Hrabosky	Kaat
2–Kan. C.	W	6-5*	Gossage	Mingori
3–Boston	W	10-6	Guidry	Eckersley
4–Boston	W	3-2	Tiant	Torrez

SEPTEMBER			Winner	Loser	SEPTEMBER			Winner	Loser
5—Boston	L	0-5	Stanley	John	18—At Cleve.	L	3-16	Paxton	Mirabella
6—At Det.	W	3-1*	Gossage	Wilcox	19—At Cleve.	W	2-0	John	Wise
7—At Det.	L	0-6	Billingham	Clay	20—At Minn.	L	1-3	Zahn	Righetti
8—At Det.	W	5-4	Guidry	Morris	21—At Tor.	L	2-3	Underwood	Guidry
9—At Det.	L	1-3	Chris	John	22—At Tor.	W	7-4	Tiant	Edge
11—At Bos.	W	8-3	Davis	Burgmeier	23—At Tor.	W	7-5	John	Huffman
12—At Bos.	L	2-9	Rainey	Hunter	25—Cleve.	W	7-5	Davis	Wise
13—At Bos.	W	10-3	Guidry	Torrez	26—Cleve.	W	6-3	Guidry	Paxton
15—Detroit	L	3-4	Morris	John	27—Cleve.	W	5-2	Gossage	Monge
15—Detroit	W	7-1	Davis	Chris	28—Toronto	W	7-3	Tiant	Edge
16—Detroit	L	4-8‡	Lopez	Gossage	29—Toronto	W	9-4	John	Huffman
17—At Cleve.	L	1-5	Waits	Beattie	30—Toronto	W	9-2	Davis	Stieb
17—At Cleve.	L	5-6	Monge	Hood				Won 17, Lost 12	

*10 innings.   †11 innings.   ‡12 innings.   §13 innings.

Sparky's "Lightning" Failed to Ignite Tigers

By TOM GAGE

The more the Tigers change, the more they stay the same. And the 1979 season was a perfect case in point.

The Tigers changed managers in midstream—firing Les Moss and hiring Sparky Anderson; they traded their highest paid player, Rusty Staub; and they developed two promising pitchers, Jack Morris and Aurelio Lopez.

But for all these moves, Detroit went nowhere in the standings, finishing fifth in the American League East Division for the third time in four years. Between the two managers, the Tigers won one less game than the year before (85-76) and ended up 18 games behind the division-winning Orioles.

Mark Fidrych failed in another comeback attempt, going 0-3 with a 10.20 ERA; Dave Rozema suffered arm problems for the second straight year and won only four games; and first baseman Jason Thompson—supposedly the heart of the Tigers' power—slumped to a .246 batting average, 20 home runs and 79 RBIs.

Yet 1979 could be called a year of promise in Detroit. For every slump, there was a surprise—and by the end of the season, there was even a style. The Tigers became a running club, filching 176 bases—second in the league and their highest total since Ty Cobb's days. Ron LeFlore led the way with 78 thefts but four other players were in double figures.

The hiring of Anderson and Staub's departure were the major Tiger stories the first half of the season. Staub skipped spring training as he held out for an extension of a contract already netting him $200,000 a year.

General Manager Jim Campbell didn't budge. He refused to give in and spring training deteriorated into a guessing game of who was going to break the cold war first, Staub or Campbell.

Spring training came and went without Staub, who had driven in 121 runs for Detroit in 1978 as the league's premier DH. Finally Staub left his restaurant business and reported, joining the Tigers in Chicago on May 1. The impasse was over but not forgotten. Staub got off to a fast start but soon slumped. After playing in 68 games, hitting just .236, he was dealt off to the Expos.

Anderson took over as manager in mid-June. In a stunning move following a successful two-week road trip, Campbell dumped soft-spoken Les Moss even though the Tigers were one game over .500.

DETROIT TIGERS—1979

Front row—Taylor, Trammell, Parrish, G. Brown, coach; Grodzicki, coach; Moss, manager; Tracewski, coach; Brinkman, coach; Day, batting practice pitcher, Morales. Second row—B. Brown, traveling secretary; Schmakel, equipment manager; LeFlore, Whitaker, Baker, Kemp, Thompson, Mankowski, Billingham, Behm, trainer; Livingood, team physician. Third row—Wockenfuss, Young, Machemer, Rodriguez, Jones, Lopez, Fidrych, May. Fourth row—Hiller, Burnside, Wilcox, Rozema, Gonzales, Wagner, Corcoran. Seated in front—batboys Nelson, Dobronski and Bjornholm.

Sparky talked about "catching lightning in a bottle" when he arrived. He stirred up the low-key franchise and spoke enthusiastically of making the Tigers a contender in the years to come.

The Tigers didn't catch lightning; they thundered out of sight instead. Detroit lost three straight and nine of Sparky's first 11 games, slipping from seven to 14½ games out of the lead.

By the time the Tigers righted themselves after a doubleheader defeat at Baltimore on June 23, they were in fifth place to stay.

It turned into a season of experimentation for Anderson and many of his formulas worked. Steve Kemp already was aiming at the best season of his three-year career. The 25-year-old left fielder, who was still over .400 six weeks into the season, finished with a .318 average—eighth in the league—26 home runs and 105 RBIs.

Champ Summers, who sat on the bench for Anderson at Cincinnati, was acquired in May and became an instant favorite in Detroit. He found the short right field dimensions at Tiger Stadium to his liking, socking 20 home runs in 90 games and hitting .313.

LeFlore chalked up another good season, too, becoming the first Tigers player since Hank Greenberg to score 100 runs in three straight seasons.

There were bright spots on the pitching staff as well. Morris spent the first month of the season at Evansville (American Association) but became the ace of the staff when he returned. Morris posted a 17-7 mark to tie Boston's Dennis Eckersley and Texas' Steve Comer for the most victories by a righthander in the American League.

And finally there was the portly Lopez—Senor Smoke—who was acquired with outfielder Jerry Morales from St. Louis in an off-season trade for pitcher Bob Sykes. Lopez was 0-1 with no saves when Anderson took over on June 14, but Sparky's strategy of giving Lopez a lot of work succeeded.

"If he wants to pitch," Sparky said, "he's come to the right place. I can crank a pitcher's arm off."

Lopez cranked his way to a 10-5 record with 21 saves, giving Anderson plenty of reason to look forward to his first full season in Detroit.

SCORES OF DETROIT TIGERS' 1979 GAMES

APRIL				Winner	Loser	MAY				Winner	Loser
7—Texas	L		2-8	Jenkins	Rozema	6—At Minn.	L		6-9	Marshall	Hiller
9—At K.C.	W		7-3	Wilcox	Gale	7—Chicago	W		5-4	Taylor	Trout
11—At K.C.	L	3-10		Rodriguez	Taylor	8—Chicago	W	10-8		Billingham	Scarbery
13—At Texas	L		4-5	Kern	Burnside	9—Chicago	L		4-5	Baumgarten	Wilcox
14—At Texas	L		5-7	Lyle	Baker	11—Milw.	L		1-5	Sorensen	Fidrych
15—At Texas	W	11-6		Burnside	Lyle	12—Milw.	L		2-3	Augustine	Taylor
16—Kan. C.	W	10-4		Billingham	Gura	13—Milw.	W		6-2	Morris	Haas
17—Kan. C.	W		6-3	Hiller	Splittorff	14—At N.Y.	W		3-1	Wilcox	Figueroa
20—Toronto	W		7-2	Wilcox	Lemongello	15—At N.Y.	L		3-11	John	Baker
21—Toronto	L		4-5	Huffman	Billingham	16—At N.Y.	L		2-6	Guidry	Fidrych
22—Toronto	W		4-1	Rozema	T. Underw'd	18—At Cleve.	W		5-3	Hiller	Monge
26—At Milw.	L		1-5	Slaton	Billingham	19—At Cleve.	L		0-6	Waits	Morris
26—At Milw.	L		5-7	Cleveland	Baker	20—At Cleve.	L		7-9	Spillner	Hiller
27—Minn.	L		3-5	Koosman	Rozema	21—N. York	W		3-1	Billingham	Guidry
28—Minn.	W		5-3	Young	Goltz	22—N. York	L		8-12	Tiant	Fidrych
29—Minn.	L		3-5	Zahn	Wilcox	23—N. York	W		4-3	Hiller	Clay
			Won 7, Lost 9			26—Balt.	L		5-7y	Stewart	Hiller
						27—Balt.	W		5-1	Billingham	McGregor
						27—Balt.	W	10-3		Rozema	Stone
MAY						28—At Tor.	W		6-2	Morris	Lemanczyk
1—At Chi.	W		5-2	Baker	Kravec	29—At Tor.	W		9-8	Tobik	Buskey
3—At Minn.	L		6-7	Marshall	Billingham	30—At Tor.	W		8-2	Wilcox	Huffman
4—At Minn.	L		6-7	Marshall	Lopez	31—At Tor.	W		1-0	P. Underw'd	T. Underw'd
5—At Minn.	W		8-4	Billingham	Hartzell				**Won 15, Lost 12**		

JUNE			Winner	Loser
1–At Oak.	L	2-3	McCatty	Hiller
2–At Oak.	W	9-3	Morris	Minetto
3–At Oak.	W	2-0	Rozema	Johnson
4–At Sea.	L	2-11	Honeycutt	Wilcox
5–At Sea.	W	3-1	Billingham	Abbott
6–At Sea.	L	3-4	Bannister	Morris
8–At Calif.	L	4-6	Aase	Wilcox
9–At Calif.	L	1-9	Ryan	Rozema
10–At Calif.	W	10-7	Arroyo	Tanana
11–Oakland	W	3-1	Morris	McCatty
12–Oakland	W	9-2	Underwood	Minetto
13–Seattle	W	7-3	Wilcox	Parrott
14–Seattle	L	2-3	Rawley	Hiller
15–Calif.	L	7-8	Clear	Tobik
16–Calif.	L	2-4	Frost	Morris
17–Calif.	W	8-4	Lopez	Aase
18–At Bos.	L	8-9	Drago	Arroyo
19–At Bos.	W	10-4x	Lopez	Stanley
20–At Bos.	L	3-13	Torrez	Baker
21–At Bos.	L	2-3	Eckersley	Morris
22–At Balt.	L	5-6	T. Martinez	Tobik
23–At Balt.	L	6-8	T. Martinez	Hiller
23–At Balt.	L	5-6	Stewart	Billingham
24–At Balt.	W	6-4	Lopez	D. Martinez
26–Boston	W	6-4	Morris	Campbell
27–Boston	L	1-3	Stanley	Tobik
28–Boston	W	6-3	Billingham	Renko
29–Cleve.	W	8-6	Wilcox	Cruz
30–Cleve.	L	2-4	Clyde	Young
Won 13, Lost 16				

JULY				
1–Cleve.	W	10-2	Morris	Barker
2–Cleve.	L	4-8‡	Cruz	Lopez
3–Toronto	L	1-9	Moore	Billingham
4–Toronto	L	6-7‡	Buskey	Tobik
5–Toronto	W	3-2	Young	Huffman
6–At Milw.	W	7-4	Morris	Haas
6–At Milw.	W	5-4	Wilcox	Slaton
7–At Milw.	W	6-3	Underwood	Mitchell
8–At Milw.	L	4-5	Caldwell	Hiller
8–At Milw.	L	1-3	Travers	Petry
9–Minn.	L	3-5	Koosman	Baker
10–Minn.	W	6-5	Lopez	Marshall
11–Minn.	L	0-3	Jackson	Morris
12–At Chi.	W	4-1	Underwood	Howard
12–At Chi.	W	9-0z	......	......
13–At Chi.	W	3-1	Petry	Kravec
14–At Chi.	L	4-12	Baumgarten	Baker
15–At Chi.	W	14-5	Morris	Wortham
19–At Minn.	W	8-3	Underwood	Koosman
20–At Minn.	L	6-14	Serum	Young
21–Chicago	W	4-2	Petry	Baumgarten
22–Chicago	W	1-0	Wilcox	Scarbery
23–Chicago	L	3-11	Trout	Baker
24–Milw.	W	4-5	Travers	Underwood
25–Milw.	W	11-2	Morris	Slaton
26–Milw.	W	5-2	Petry	Haas
27–At Tor.	W	4-3‡	Lopez	Buskey
28–At Tor.	L	0-3	Lemanczyk	Robbins
29–At Tor.	W	5-4	Underwood	Clancy
30–At Texas	W	6-4	Hiller	Darwin
31–At Texas	L	3-11	Medich	Petry
Won 18, Lost 13				

AUGUST			Winner	Loser
1–At Texas	L	3-4	Comer	Wilcox
3–Kan. C.	L	3-5	Busby	Underwood
3–Kan. C.	W	4-3	Lopez	Mingori
4–Kan. C.	W	5-2	Chris	Gura
5–Kan. C.	L	2-3	Leonard	Petry
7–Texas	W	3-1	Wilcox	Kern
7–Texas	W	8-2	Billingham	Rajsich
8–Texas	L	9-16	Jenkins	Underwood
8–Texas	W	10-4	Robbins	Johnson
9–Texas	W	3-2	Chris	Medich
10–At K.C.	L	6-7	Quisenberry	Lopez
10–At K.C.	L	3-7	Leonard	Underwood
11–At K.C.	L	5-11	Splittorff	Billingham
12–At K.C.	L	1-7	Chamberlain	Wilcox
13–At Calif.	W	5-3	Morris	Ryan
14–At Calif.	W	6-3	Robbins	Aase
15–At Calif.	W	6-1	Petry	Barr
17–At Sea.	W	9-2	Wilcox	Honeycutt
18–At Sea.	W	7-4	Morris	Dressler
19–At Sea.	L	4-8	Bannister	Robbins
20–At Oak.	W	7-3	Petry	Heaverlo
21–At Oak.	L	1-8	Kingman	Chris
22–At Oak.	W	3-1	Wilcox	McCatty
24–Seattle	W	5-2	Morris	Bannister
25–Seattle	L	4-8	Parrott	Petry
26–Seattle	W	4-3†	Lopez	McLaughlin
26–Seattle	W	9-8	Tobik	Stein
27–Calif.	W	3-2	Billingham	Barr
28–Calif.	W	12-2	Robbins	Aase
29–Calif.	L	2-1	Morris	Frost
30–Oakland	W	8-7	Tobik	Minetto
31–Oakland	L	3-5	Kingman	Tobik
Won 20, Lost 12				

SEPTEMBER			Winner	Loser
1–Oakland	L	3-6	McCatty	Lopez
2–Oakland	L	4-5	Langford	Robbins
3–At Cleve.	L	3-4	Wise	Morris
4–At Cleve.	L	3-5	Barker	Petry
5–At Cleve.	W	9-3	Lopez	Cruz
6–N. York	L	1-3†	Gossage	Wilcox
7–N. York	W	6-0	Billingham	Clay
8–N. York	L	4-5	Guidry	Morris
9–N. York	W	3-1	Chris	John
11–Cleve.	W	14-1	Rozema	Spillner
12–Cleve.	W	4-1	Wilcox	Waits
15–At N.Y.	W	4-3	Morris	John
15–At N.Y	L	1-7	Davis	Chris
16–At N.Y	W	8-4§	Lopez	Gossage
17–Balt.	L	1-2	McGregor	Wilcox
18–Balt.	L	2-1	Petry	Flanagan
19–Balt.	W	5-0	Morris	D. Martinez
20–Balt.	L	7-8	T. Martinez	Billingham
21–At Bos.	L	1-4*	Tudor	Rozema
23–At Bos.	L	1-2	Eckersley	Wilcox
23–At Bos.	W	3-2†	Lopez	Torrez
25–At Balt.	W	3-2	Morris	T. Martinez
26–At Balt.	L	2-13	McGregor	Chris
28–Boston	L	4-7	Torrez	Wilcox
29–Boston	L	5-8	Renko	Lopez
30–Boston	W	5-1	Morris	Stanley
Won 12, Lost 14				

*6½ innings. †10 innings. ‡11 innings. §12 innings. x14 innings. y16 innings. zForfeit.

Garcia Brought Tribe Order Out of Chaos

By BOB SUDYK

When Cleveland Indians' President Gabe Paul assumed control of the ball club under the new ownership of F. J. (Steve) O'Neill two seasons ago he eloquently labeled this town "A Sleeping Giant"—a baseball gold mine waiting to be discovered.

The summer of '79 did indeed see the slumbering giant open one eye and flicker the other as born-again baseball interest materialized in a gate of more than a million. It was 200,000 more than the year before and the largest draw in five years. A turnout of 56,969 on July 3 against the Chicago White Sox was the American League's highest of the season.

It was winning baseball that nudged awake The Giant. The Indians finished sixth for the second straight season but exceeded .500 baseball with an 81-80 mark for only the second time in 11 years.

Major trades before the season brought the Tribe Bobby Bonds and Toby Harrah from the Texas Rangers, adding home run punch and speed—a commodity long absent from the offense. The Tribe sped past the previous season's stolen base total of 64 on June 3 and totaled 143, third in the league and their most since the 1918 club. Bonds was top thief with 34. Harrah had 20.

Two other acquisitions at the June trading deadline brought the Indians designated hitter Cliff Johnson from the New York Yankees and first baseman-outfielder Mike Hargrove from the San Diego Padres. Both were blockbuster deals.

In a Cleveland uniform, Johnson batted .271, hit 18 homers and drove in 61 runs in only 72 games. He led the team with nine game-winning hits.

Hargrove, hitting in the leadoff spot, batted .355 after the All-Star Game for a team-leading mark of .325. His on-base percentage for the season was .438 and many old-timers called Hargrove the best leadoff hitter on the club since Dale Mitchell in the 1950s.

With a long ball and speed offense, the Indians hoped to outscore the opposition. The team batting average of .258 ranked 12th in the league. The Tribe hit 32 more homers than 1978; eight of the 138 round-trippers were grand slams—a team record. The home run barrage included six players in double figures led by Andre Thornton's 26 and 93 RBIs and Bonds' 25 and 85 RBIs.

But nothing could solve the club's major weaknesses on the mound. The front office gamble on the return of Wayne Garland after shoulder surgery and the arrival of promising rookie Eric Wilkins did not work out. And the comeback of David Clyde was stopped cold.

That trio had records of 4-10, 2-4 and 3-4, respectively, and Wilkins' ERA was best at 4.37.

Neither did trades which brought to the Indians Len Barker and reliever Victor Cruz prove fruitful, although Barker came on strong after being given a starter's role. He won six in a row and finished the year with a 6-6 record.

Top winners for the Indians were Rick Waits (16-13) and Rick Wise (15-10). Waits opened the season with a one-hitter against Boston, winning nine of his first 13 decisions then dropping five in a row until he regained his touch. Wise did the opposite, losing five of eight and then winning his next eight decisions.

The team as a whole was similarly erratic. After a 10-20 start the Tribe won 22 of 32 to improve their record to 32-30. Then came 10 straight defeats, nine of them to Baltimore and New York.

This sealed the doom of Manager Jeff Torborg. Gabe Paul, expressing misgivings about Torborg, quietly contacted recently fired New York Yankee Manager Bob Lemon about coming to the rescue of Cleveland.

CLEVELAND INDIANS—1979

Front row—Warfield, trainer; Seghi, traveling secretary; Nossek, coach; Duncan, coach; Torborg, manager; Garcia, coach (replaced Torborg as manager, July 23); Hartenstein, coach; Sweeney, batboy; Buynak, equipment manager. Second row—Cruz, Paxton, Diaz, Harrah, Hargrove, Manning, Clyde, Alston, Veryzer, Pruitt, Kuiper, Rosello, Norris. Third row—Bonds, Spillner, Wilkins, Hassey, Alexander, Wise, Waits, Reuschel, Johnson, Barker, Cox, Monge, Garland, Thornton.

Torborg, unhappy about the unexpected turn of events, finally agreed to remain manager when Lemon turned down the job. A few weeks later, however, it was all over; Torborg was fired and coach Dave Garcia stepped in as interim manager, July 23.

Garcia's strong, quiet approach brought order out of the chaos that had arisen during Torborg's lame duck term. The Indians won their first 10 games under Garcia and 38 of their final 66 games (.576). Garcia, the 15th manager in 24 years, was given a new contract for 1980.

While Harrah and Bonds were the club's most consistent hitters all season, reliever Sid Monge anchored the bullpen. The All-Star reliever was 12-10 with 19 saves and a 2.40 ERA. His 76 relief appearances set a club record. He struck out 108 batters in 131 innings.

SCORES OF CLEVELAND INDIANS' 1979 GAMES

APRIL			Winner	Loser	JUNE			Winner	Loser
5—At Bos.	L	1-7	Eckersley	Wise	3—At Calif.	W	5-3	Paxton	Barr
7—Boston	W	3-0	Waits	Torrez	4—At Oak.	W	5-4x	Monge	Lacey
8—Boston	L	6-7§	Drago	Cruz	5—At Oak.	W	12-3	Waits	Langford
10—At Texas	L	0-5	Kern	Wise	6—At Oak.	W	6-4	Wise	Heaverlo
11—At Texas	L	0-4	Comer	Wilkins	8—At Sea.	L	2-6	Parrott	Garland
12—At Texas	L	3-5	Jenkins	Waits	9—At Sea.	W	4-3†	Monge	Rawley
15—At Bos.	L	4-14	Eckersley	Paxton	10—At Sea.	L	2-5	Jones	Waits
16—At Bos.	W	4-3	Wise	Stanley	11—Calif.	L	4-9	Clear	Spillner
17—Texas	L	2-6	Jenkins	Waits	12—Calif.	W	11-10	Hood	Clear
18—Texas	W	6-4	Monge	Medich	13—Oakland	W	6-4	Garland	Lacey
20—Chicago	L	2-4†	Proly	Cruz	14—Oakland	W	2-1	Monge	Todd
21—Chicago	L	5-6	Baumgarten	Garland	15—Seattle	W	13-3	Waits	Jones
22—Chicago	W	8-5	Waits	Barrios	16—Seattle	W	4-3	Monge	Montague
24—Minn.	W	7-2	Wise	Erickson	17—Seattle	L	5-6	Rawley	Monge
25—Minn.	L	2-4	Redfern	Monge	18—Balt.	L	7-8	Stanhouse	Cruz
26—At K.C.	L	4-5	Hrabosky	Spillner	19—Balt.	L	4-6	Stoddard	Paxton
27—At K.C.	L	7-15	Splittorff	Garland	20—Balt.	L	3-5*	D. Martinez	Waits
28—At K.C.	L	2-7	Leonard	Waits	22—At N.Y.	L	2-3	Hunter	Wilkins
29—At K.C.	W	5-4	Wise	Gura	23—At N.Y.	L	5-6†	John	Cruz
30—Milw.	L	0-8	Slaton	Wilkins	24—At N.Y.	L	2-8	Kaat	Waits
					25—At Balt.	L	2-3	Stone	Garland
		Won 6, Lost 14			26—At Balt.	L	3-4	Flanagan	Barker
					27—At Balt.	L	1-3	Palmer	Paxton
MAY					28—At Balt.	W	6-3	Wise	D. Martinez
1—Milw.	W	3-1	Paxton	Sorensen	29—At Det.	L	6-8	Wilcox	Cruz
2—Milw.	L	1-6	Haas	Garland	30—At Det.	W	4-2	Clyde	Young
4—Kan. C.	L	4-5†	Hrabosky	Monge					
5—Kan. C.	L	2-3	Gale	Wise			**Won 13, Lost 15**		
6—Kan. C.	W	5-4	Paxton	Hrabosky					
8—At Milw.	L	5-9	Haas	Garland	**JULY**				
9—At Milw.	W	8-7	Waits	Caldwell	1—At Det.	L	2-10	Morris	Barker
10—At Milw.	W	8-1	Wilkins	Slaton	2—At Det.	W	8-4‡	Cruz	Lopez
11—At Minn.	L	3-4	Marshall	Monge	3—Chicago	W	7-3	Wise	Kravec
12—At Minn.	L	0-4	Koosman	Paxton	4—Chicago	L	4-16	Baumgarten	Waits
13—At Minn.	W	3-2	Garland	Goltz	5—Chicago	L	4-5	Wortham	Cruz
14—Toronto	W	1-0	Waits	Underwood	6—Minn.	W	6-5	Spillner	Hartzell
15—Toronto	W	5-3	Monge	Garvin	7—Minn.	W	9-3	Paxton	Jackson
16—Toronto	L	3-4	Lemanczyk	Wise	8—Minn.	W	5-4	Cruz	Marshall
17—Toronto	W	8-3	Paxton	Lemongello	8—Minn.	L	2-7	Goltz	Waits
18—Detroit	L	3-5	Hiller	Monge	9—Kan. C.	W	8-2	Clyde	Leonard
19—Detroit	W	6-0	Waits	Morris	10—Kan. C.	W	7-4	Spillner	Gale
20—Detroit	W	9-7	Spillner	Hiller	11—Kan. C.	W	9-8	Paxton	Splittorff
21—At Tor.	L	1-8	Lemanczyk	Wise	13—At Milw.	L	3-4y	Galasso	Cruz
22—At Tor.	W	8-6	Wilkins	Lemongello	14—At Milw.	L	3-10	Travers	Clyde
23—At Tor.	W	4-3	Garland	Freisleben	15—At Milw.	L	4-10	Sorensen	Barker
26—N. York	W	8-4	Waits	John	19—At K.C.	W	2-1	Wise	Leonard
27—N. York	W	5-0	Wise	Guidry	20—At K.C.	L	1-9	Gale	Waits
27—N. York	L	4-5	Burris	Monge	21—Milw.	L	0-5	Haas	Barker
28—At Chi.	L	1-6	Kravec	Garland	22—Milw.	L	5-14	Caldwell	Paxton
29—At Chi.	L	2-4	Wortham	Wilkins	22—Milw.	L	3-5	Mitchell	Clyde
30—At Chi.	W	6-4	Waits	Baumgarten	23—Milw.	W	5-4	Spillner	Sorensen
					24—At Minn.	W	4-2	Wise	Koosman
		Won 15, Lost 12			25—At Minn.	W	2-0	Waits	Goltz
					26—At Minn.	W	7-2	Spillner	Redfern
JUNE					27—At Chi.	W	7-2	Clyde	Scarberry
1—At Calif.	W	7-4	Wise	Frost	28—At Chi.	W	10-5	Paxton	Trout
2—At Calif.	L	2-5	Clear	Garland					

JULY

			Winner	Loser
29—At Chi.	W	9-6	Wise	Kravec
30—Boston	W	6-5	Cruz	Burgmeier
31—Boston	W	11-10†	Monge	Campbell
31—Boston	W	3-0	Barker	Finch
		Won 19 Lost 11		

AUGUST

				Winner	Loser
29—Seattle	W	2-1		Waits	Twitchell
30—Calif.	W	7-1		Barker	Ryan
31—Calif.	L	8-9		Clear	Reuschel
			Won 16, Lost 14		

AUGUST

			Winner	Loser
1—Boston	L	4-7	Eckersley	Clyde
3—Texas	L	3-8	Jenkins	Wise
4—Texas	W	12-8	Waits	Johnson
5—Texas	W	6-2	Barker	Medich
5—Texas	L	3-14	Darwin	Paxton
7—At Bos.	L	3-12	Torrez	Clyde
8—At Bos.	W	6-4	Wise	Stanley
8—At Bos.	W	8-2	Spillner	Renko
9—At Bos.	L	2-3	Eckersley	Waits
10—At Texas	W	6-1	Barker	Darwin
11—At Texas	L	2-5	Allard	Paxton
12—At Texas	W	6-3	Spillner	Comer
13—At Sea.	W	6-0	Wise	Bannister
14—At Sea.	W	7-4	Waits	Jones
15—At Sea.	L	2-3	Parrott	Monge
17—At Oak.	L	3-5	McCatty	Spillner
18—At Oak.	L	1-4	Langford	Wise
19—At Oak.	L	2-3	Norris	Waits
20—At Calif.	L	5-6	LaRoche	Monge
21—At Calif.	W	12-7	Reuschel	Frost
22—At Calif.	W	13-3	Spillner	Ryan
23—Oakland	L	6-8	Langford	Monge
24—Oakland	W	5-2	Waits	Norris
25—Oakland	W	5-3	Barker	Morgan
26—Oakland	W	7-5	Garland	Kingman
27—Seattle	L	5-6§	McLaughlin	Cruz
29—Seattle	W	5-4	Monge	Rawley

SEPTEMBER

			Winner	Loser
1—Calif.	L	4-7	LaRoche	Garland
2—Calif.	L	2-5	Frost	Waits
3—Detroit	W	4-3	Wise	Morris
4—Detroit	W	5-3	Barker	Petry
5—Detroit	L	3-9	Lopez	Cruz
7—Toronto	W	9-8	Reuschel	Buskey
8—Toronto	W	5-4	Wise	Stieb
9—Toronto	W	14-10	Monge	Buskey
11—At Det.	L	1-14	Rozema	Spillner
12—At Det.	L	1-4	Wilcox	Waits
14—At Tor.	L	3-4	Stieb	Wise
15—At Tor.	L	2-5	Moore	Barker
16—At Tor.	L	2-8	Underwood	Garland
17—N. York	W	5-1	Waits	Beattie
17—N. York	L	6-5	Monge	Hood
18—N. York	W	16-3	Paxton	Mirabella
19—N. York	L	0-2	John	Wise
22—At Balt.	W	7-3	Waits	McGregor
23—At Balt.	W	4-3	Monge	D. Martinez
23—At Balt.	L	1-3	Flanagan	Spillner
25—At N.Y.	L	5-7	Davis	Wise
26—At N.Y.	L	3-6	Guidry	Paxton
27—At N.Y.	L	2-5	Gossage	Monge
28—Balt.	L	6-14	Palmer	Barker
29—Balt.	W	4-1	Spillner	Flanagan
30—Balt.	W	6-5‡	Monge	Ford
		Won 12, Lost 14		

*5½ innings. †10 innings. ‡11 innings. §12 innings. x14 innings. y17 innings.

Third Time Was No Charm For Blue Jays

By NEIL MacCARL

There were too few peaks and too many valleys for the Blue Jays, who finished with a 53-109 record, the worst showing in their three-year history.

The Jays' fate was determined in the stretch between April 15 and June 5. In 48 games, they won only nine times. They never won two in a row, and every win was followed by at least two losses.

By then, their overall record was 13-42 and their percentage (.236) was even worse than the laughingstock New York Mets of 1962 (.250).

At that stage of the season, the pitching was pathetic, the bullpen was the designated disaster area, and the impotent Jays could not begin to score enough runs to overcome these weaknesses.

Veteran designated hitter Rico Carty was a major disappointment as his home run production dropped from 31 to 12, and his RBIs from 99 to 55. Right fielder Bob Bailor never was able to break out of a prolonged batting slump, and he finished with a .229 average.

Big things were expected from righthander Jim Clancy, a 10-game winner in 1978, but twice he dislocated a tendon in his right ankle, requiring surgery. It was a wasted season as he pitched only 64 innings, finishing with a 2-7 record.

The best thing that happened to the Jays was the trade of Victor Cruz to Cleveland for rookie shortstop Alfredo Griffin. The switch-hitter was hitting

.082 after the first three weeks, but he came on strong to bat .347 in September when he was the American League Player of the Month. He finished with a .287 average, led the team in triples with 10, and had a team-record 21 stolen bases. Griffin tied with Minnesota's John Castino for the AL Rookie of the Year honors.

Part-time outfielder Otto Velez was a pleasant surprise with 15 homers. That matched the combined number hit by outfield mates Rick Bosetti, Al Woods, Bailor and J. J. Cannon.

Danny Ainge, the Brigham Young basketball star, was promoted from Syracuse in May, replacing Dave McKay at second base. Without benefit of spring training, he started fast but slipped to .237 before returning to school.

First baseman John Mayberry boosted his batting average to .274 and set a team record with 74 RBIs before a hand injury sidelined him late in September.

Third baseman Roy Howell had personal highs with 15 homers and 72 RBIs, but his average dipped to .247.

Righthander Dave Lemanczyk rebounded from a disastrous 4-14 1978 season and was 8-8 in August before a nerve inflammation in his lower back affected the feeling in his right leg.

After a 0-9 start, lefthander Tommy Underwood was 9-7 the rest of the way, lowering his ERA from 5.00 to a respectable 3.69.

Rookie Dave Stieb, with less than a year's experience in pro ball, joined the team at the end of June and had a creditable 8-8 record.

Lemanczyk tossed a one-hitter against the Texas Rangers in April, and rookie righthander Phil Huffman had one against the Oakland A's in August.

Reliever Tom Buskey missed the start of the season because of chicken pox and a pulled leg muscle in spring training. By the end of August, he had a 6-5 record, five saves and a nifty 1.97 ERA.

Buskey blew the lid off the Jays' mounting frustrations when he said Manager Roy Hartsfield should be replaced because he did not know how to handle a pitching staff. In September, Buskey's ERA jumped to 3.42 and he finished 6-10; in October, Hartsfield was fired and replaced by 63-year-old Bobby Mattick.

Another major disappointment was righthander Mark Lemongello, acquired from Houston in a trade. He was demoted to Syracuse after his record reached 1-9.

Despite the worst record in baseball, the Jays continued to do well at the gate, drawing 1,431,651 customers to Exhibition Stadium.

SCORES OF TORONTO BLUE JAYS' 1979 GAMES

APRIL			Winner	Loser
5—At K.C.	L	2-11	Leonard	Underwood
7—At K.C.	L	4-7	Gura	Clancy
8—At K.C.	L	3-8	Splittorff	Lemongello
10—At Chi.	W	10-2	Huffman	Kravec
12—At Chi.	W	9-7	Murphy	LaGrow
13—Kan. C.	W	4-1*	Clancy	Splittorff
14—Kan. C.	W	8-6	Freisleben	Leonard
15—Kan. C.	L	10-12	Rodriguez	Murphy
16—Chicago	L	4-8	Scarbery	Murphy
17—Chicago	L	1-6	Barrios	Underwood
18—Chicago	L	5-12	Wortham	Clancy
20—At Det.	L	2-7	Wilcox	Lemongello
21—At Det.	W	5-4	Huffman	Billingham
22—At Det.	L	1-4	Rozema	Underwood

APRIL			Winner	Loser
23—At Texas	L	0-5	Alexander	Clancy
24—At Texas	W	2-0	Lemanczyk	Comer
25—At Texas	L	3-4†	Lyle	Jefferson
27—Milw.	L	5-8	Sorensen	Huffman
28—Milw.	L	8-11†	McClure	Willis
29—Milw.	L	0-3	Caldwell	Clancy
29—Milw.	W	5-3	Lemanczyk	Travers
30—Minn.	L	3-6	Hartzell	Lemongello
			Won 7, Lost 15	

MAY				
1—Minn.	L	2-3	Koosman	Jefferson
2—Minn.	L	5-7	Goltz	Huffman

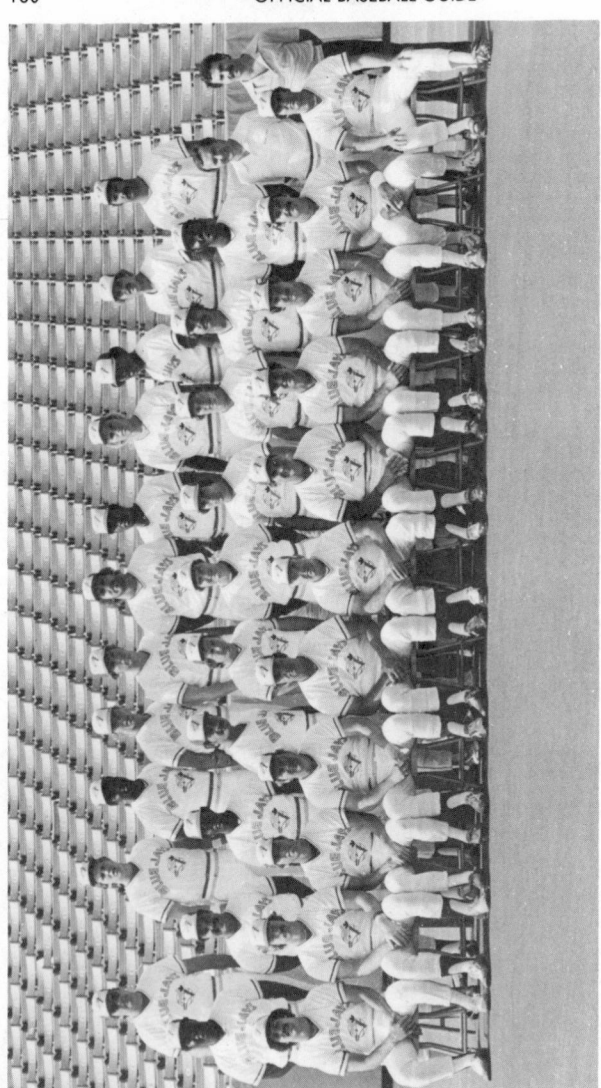

TORONTO BLUE JAYS—1979

Front row—Cerone, Howell, Bailor, Miller, coach; Leppert, coach; Hartsfield, manager; Warner, coach; J. Moore, coach; Underwood, Bosetti, Gomez. Second row—Mayberry, Velez, Griffin, Solaita, Freisleben, Davis, Stieb, Huffman, Johnson, Carty, Carson, trainer; Silverman, equipment manager. Third row—Kusick, Ainge, Woods, B. Moore, Edge, Lemanczyk, Cannon, Garvin, Jefferson, Todd, Buskey. Missing from picture—Clancy, Doerr, coach.

MAY			Winner	Loser
3-At Milw.	L	4-5	Travers	Underwood
4-At Milw.	W	5-4	Clancy	Caldwell
5-At Milw.	L	1-6	Slaton	Lemanczyk
6-At Minn.	L	0-4	Sorensen	Lemongello
7-At Minn.	L	1-6	Goltz	Huffman
8-At Minn.	L	6-16	Bacsik	Willis
11-Texas	L	1-3	Matlack	Clancy
12-Texas	L	1-3	Comer	Lemanczyk
13-Texas	W	3-1	Lemongello	Alexander
13-Texas	L	5-7	Farmer	Huffman
14-At Cleve.	L	0-1	Waits	Underwood
15-At Cleve.	L	3-4	Monge	Garvin
16-At Cleve.	W	4-3	Lemanczyk	Wise
17-At Cleve.	L	3-8	Paxton	Lemongello
18-Balt.	L	6-7‡	Stanhouse	Freisleben
19-Balt.	L	3-4	Palmer	Underwood
20-Balt.	L	2-6	D. Martinez	Jefferson
21-Cleve.	W	8-1	Lemanczyk	Wise
22-Cleve.	L	6-8	Wilkins	Lemongello
23-Cleve.	L	3-4	Garland	Freisleben
26-Boston	W	7-6	Buskey	Campbell
27-Boston	L	0-1	Rainey	Jefferson
28-Detroit	L	2-6	Morris	Lemanczyk
29-Detroit	L	8-9	Tobik	Buskey
30-Detroit	L	2-8	Wilcox	Huffman
31-Detroit	L	0-1	P. Underw'd	T. Underw'd

Won 5, Lost 23

JUNE				
1-At Sea.	L	2-7	Mitchell	Jefferson
2-At Sea.	W	6-2	Lemanczyk	Jones
3-At Sea.	L	5-10	Parrott	Lemongello
4-At Calif.	L	2-4	Barlow	Huffman
5-At Calif.	L	0-3	Tanana	Underwood
6-At Calif.	W	5-4	Jefferson	LaRoche
8-At Oak.	W	2-1	Buskey	Heaverlo
9-At Oak.	W	5-0	Huffman	Keough
10-At Oak.	L	1-12	Hamilton	Underwood
11-Seattle	W	2-0	Lemanczyk	Bannister
12-Seattle	L	1-5	Abbott	Jefferson
13-Calif.	W	9-8	Freisleben	LaRoche
13-Calif.	L	2-10	Aase	Willis
14-Calif.	L	2-10	Ryan	Huffman
15-Oakland	W	6-0	Underwood	Hamilton
16-Oakland	W	3-2	Lemanczyk	McCatty
17-Oakland	W	10-9	Buskey	Heaverlo
19-At N.Y.	W	5-4	Huffman	John
20-At N.Y.	L	1-2	Hood	Underwood
20-At N.Y.	L	3-2	Moore	Burris
21-At N.Y.	L	1-3	Tiant	Lemanczyk
22-At Bos.	L	1-12	Rainey	Jefferson
23-At Bos.	L	3-4‡	Drago	Buskey
24-At Bos.	L	4-8	Torrez	Huffman
25-N.York	W	3-1	Underwood	Clay
26-N.York	L	2-11	Tiant	Lemanczyk
28-N.York	L	3-5†	Davis	Lemongello
29-At Balt.	L	1-6	McGregor	Steib
29-At Balt.	L	0-4	Stone	Huffman
30-At Balt.	L	0-2	Flanagan	Underwood

Won 12, Lost 18

JULY				
1-At Balt.	L	7-10	Stewart	Jefferson
3-At Det.	W	9-1	Moore	Billingham
4-At Det.	W	7-6‡	Buskey	Tobik
5-At Det.	L	2-3	Young	Huffman
6-At Texas	W	5-1	Underwood	Johnson
7-At Texas	L	0-2	Medich	Lemanczyk
8-At Texas	L	3-4	Comer	Moore
9-Milw.	W	7-1	Stieb	Sorensen
11-Milw.	L	1-2†	Slaton	Buskey
12-Milw.	L	3-5	Haas	Underwood
13-Minn.	L	4-6	Goltz	Lemanczyk
14-Minn.	W	4-2	Stieb	Koosman
15-Minn.	L	4-9	Zahn	Clancy
19-At Milw.	L	2-3‡	Castro	Buskey

JULY			Winner	Loser
20-At Milw.	L	0-2	Slaton	Underwood
21-At Minn.	L	4-6	Goltz	Huffman
21-At Minn.	L	3-4	Hartzell	Moore
22-At Minn.	L	1-13	Redfern	Lemanczyk
23-At Minn.	L	6-7	Marshall	Lemongello
25-Texas	W	8-3	Stieb	Johnson
26-Texas	W	8-4	Underwood	Medich
27-Detroit	L	3-4‡	Lopez	Buskey
28-Detroit	W	3-0	Lemanczyk	Robbins
29-Detroit	L	4-5	Underwood	Clancy
30-At K.C.	L	0-9	Gura	Stieb
31-At K.C.	L	5-6	Pattin	Jefferson

Won 8, Lost 18

AUGUST				
1-At K.C.	L	3-4	Gale	Huffman
3-Chicago	L	5-8	Trout	Moore
4-Chicago	W	5-2	Buskey	Wortham
5-Chicago	L	4-5	Kravec	Lemanczyk
6-Kan. C.	L	12-16	Mingori	Stieb
7-Kan. C.	W	3-2	Underwood	Splittorff
9-Kan. C.	L	3-10	Gura	Huffman
11-At Chi.	L	1-6	Kravec	Todd
11-At Chi.	W	6-0	Stieb	Scarbery
12-At Chi.	L	0-7	Baumgarten	Underwood
12-At Chi.	W	7-5	Moore	Proly
13-At Oak.	W	4-2	Edge	Norris
14-At Oak.	W	6-2	Huffman	Minetto
15-At Oak.	L	1-3	Kingman	Jefferson
17-At Calif.	W	6-5	Stieb	Clear
18-At Calif.	L	5-7	Ryan	Underwood
19-At Calif.	L	2-4	Aase	Moore
20-At Sea.	L	4-7	Parrott	Edge
21-At Sea.	L	4-8	Montague	Huffman
22-At Sea.	L	3-6	Honeycutt	Stieb
24-Calif.	W	6-4	Underwood	Knapp
25-Calif.	L	2-24	Frost	Moore
26-Calif.	W	9-3	Edge	Ryan
27-Oakland	W	7-0	Huffman	McCatty
28-Oakland	L	3-6	Langford	Stieb
29-Oakland	L	4-6	Norris	Underwood
30-Seattle	L	2-8	Parrott	Moore
31-Seattle	W	5-4‡	Buskey	McLaughlin

Won 11 Lost 17

SEPTEMBER				
1-Seattle	L	2-3†	Honeycutt	Buskey
2-Seattle	W	8-5	Stieb	Twitchell
3-At Balt.	L	1-2‡	T. Martinez	Buskey
3-At Balt.	L	1-5	Flanagan	Lemanczyk
6-At Balt.	L	0-5	D. Martinez	Edge
7-At Cleve.	L	8-9	Reuschel	Buskey
8-At Cleve.	L	4-5	Wise	Stieb
9-At Cleve.	W	10-14	Monge	Buskey
11-Balt.	W	3-1	Underwood	McGregor
12-Balt.	W	3-2	Edge	Palmer
13-Balt.	L	4-10	Flanagan	Huffman
14-Cleve.	W	4-3	Stieb	Wise
15-Cleve.	W	5-2	Moore	Barker
16-Cleve.	W	8-2	Underwood	Garland
17-Boston	W	5-4	Jefferson	Drago
17-Boston	L	3-5	Rainey	Freisleben
18-Boston	L	3-8	Torrez	Huffman
19-Boston	L	0-8	Stanley	Stieb
20-Boston	W	6-2	Moore	Renko
21-N. York	W	3-2	Underwood	Guidry
22-N. York	L	4-7	Tiant	Edge
23-N. York	L	5-7	John	Huffman
25-At Bos.	W	5-3	Stieb	Stanley
26-At Bos.	L	4-6	Rainey	Moore
27-At Bos.	L	5-6	Drago	Buskey
28-At N.Y.	L	3-7	Tiant	Edge
29-At N.Y.	L	4-9	John	Huffman
30-At N.Y.	L	2-9	Davis	Stieb

Won 10, Lost 18

*5½ innings. †10 innings. ‡11 innings.

WEST DIVISION

Angels Feasted on Free-Agent Slugging

By CARL CLARK

Enough is as good as a feast. The California Angels would attest to that adage after their 1979 season. Although their 88-74 record was only one game better than the year before, it was enough to take the American League West crown away from the Kansas City Royals, champions from 1976-78. The title was the first in the Angels' 19-year history.

It was a close race all the way. Never down by more than four and one-half games and never ahead by more than five, the Angels moved into first place for good with a 9-8 victory at Cleveland on August 31. And when Frank Tanana hurled a 4-1 win over the Royals on September 25, 37-year-old Jim Fregosi had brought home a winner in his first full season as a manager.

It was also a boffo season at the box office. A club-record home attendance of 2,523,575—fourth best in the majors—gave some vindication to 73-year-old Owner Gene Autry's policy of offering generous contracts to free agents.

Appropriately, two such players were most responsible for the club's success. Outfielder and designated hitter Don Baylor made his third season in Anaheim his best one. An easy winner of the league's MVP award, Baylor hit .296 with 36 homers and 22 stolen bases and set club records with his 139 RBIs, 333 total bases and .530 slugging percentage. Bobby Grich treated his third California campaign the same way. He completed his recovery from back surgery by hitting .294 with 30 homers and 101 RBIs and was named second baseman on THE SPORTING NEWS AL All-Star team.

The lineup was stacked with productive bats. No team could match their 866 runs and only a few could surpass other club records they set—1,563 hits, 242 doubles, a .282 batting average and a .429 slugging percentage.

Catcher Brian Downing's .326 average led all righthanded hitters in the majors. A thumb injury hampered Rod Carew's pursuit of another batting title, but he managed to hit .318 in 110 games. His stand-in, Willie Mays Aikens, batted .280 with 21 homers and 81 RBIs.

Aikens broke into the starting cast in April when right fielder Dan Ford's knee injury resulted in Baylor's vacating the DH spot. Ford returned to drive in 101 runs and hit 21 homers with a .290 average.

Carney Lansford, in his second year at the hot corner, hit .287 and cracked 19 homers with 79 RBIs. Rick Miller didn't let a broken wrist keep him from logging a career-high .293 and playing a solid center field.

None of these bat tricks were superfluous because the pitching was perhaps the worst any champion has ever had. The Angels' 4.34 ERA was ninth in the league and higher than the league average of 4.22. The only pennant winner with a higher ERA was the 1930 St. Louis Cardinals; their 4.40 mark, however, came in a season in which the league batting average was .303 and the league ERA 4.97.

Of the starting pitchers only Nolan Ryan and Dave Frost had respectable seasons. In his final year with the Angels, Ryan was 16-14 with a 3.59 ERA and tied for the league lead in shutouts with five. All of those shutouts came before the All-Star break, at which juncture Ryan was 12-6 with a 2.54 ERA.

Frost, the club's most dependable man in the stretch, went 16-10 and his 3.58 ERA led the team.

Don Aase, free-agent Jim Barr, Chris Knapp and Frank Tanana divvied up the other starting assignments. Together they were 31-32 with a 4.57 ERA. Only Tanana posted a winning record at 7-5, but arm problems limited the lefthander to 90 innings.

The bullpen was anchored by rookie Mark Clear, who came to his major league debut with a minor league record of 23-33 but became THE SPORTING NEWS American League Rookie Pitcher of the Year with 11 victories and 14 saves. When he faltered in the final weeks, John Montague came to the rescue. Acquired from Seattle in the last week of August, Montague won two and saved six in 14 games with the Angels.

The ace fireman of seasons past, Dave LaRoche, endured a trying year, going 7-11 with a 5.55 ERA.

Haunted by injuries all season, the Angels went into the playoffs the same way. Aikens was on crutches after a disabling slide at Kansas City, outfielder Joe Rudi (who hit three grand slams for the second year in a row) was sidelined with an Achilles tendon problem, and Barr was nursing the finger he broke in off-the-field horseplay.

In the AL playoffs, Baltimore ousted the Angels in four games, winning the first in extra innings and the second by one run. All the "Yes, We Can" signs were put away until next year when Scott McGregor eliminated California with an 8-0 shutout.

"It's tough to win the division and the pennant all in the first year," said Fregosi. "We'll be back."

It wasn't the World Series, but for the Angels it was enough. This time.

SCORES OF CALIFORNIA ANGELS' 1979 GAMES

APRIL			Winner	Loser
4—At Sea.	L	4-5	Montague	Tanana
6—At Sea.	L	6-14	McLaughlin	Ryan
7—At Sea.	W	5-4	Clear	Honeycutt
8—At Sea.	W	7-5	LaRoche	Rawley
10—Minn.	L	1-8	Koosman	Tanana
11—Minn.	W	11-2	Ryan	Goltz
12—Minn.	W	7-1	Knapp	Erickson
13—At Oak.	W	10-1	Aase	Johnson
14—At Oak.	W	9-3	Frost	Langford
15—At Oak.	W	8-1	Tanana	Keough
17—At Minn.	W	6-0	Ryan	Goltz
18—At Minn.	W	11-6	Miller	Erickson
19—At Minn.	W	6-4	Aase	Marshall
20—Oakland	W	7-4	Tanana	Langford
21—Oakland	W	13-1	Ryan	Keough
22—Oakland	L	6-7	Heaverlo	LaRoche
24—Balt.	L	2-7	Palmer	Aase
25—Balt.	L	2-5	Stone	Tanana
26—Balt.	L	2-4	Stoddard	LaRoche
27—Boston	W	8-6	Clear	Hassler
28—Boston	W	5-0	Frost	Rainey
29—Boston	L	0-2	Renko	Aase
30—N. York	W	2-1	LaRoche	Figueroa
		Won 15, Lost 8		

MAY				
1—N. York	L	8-12†	John	LaRoche
2—N. York	W	1-0	Ryan	Guidry
5—At Balt.	L	1-9	Palmer	Aase
6—At Balt.	L	0-6	D. Martinez	Barlow
7—At Bos.	L	4-9	Torrez	Ryan
8—At Bos.	W	10-2	Knapp	Rainey
9—At Bos.	L	8-9	Campbell	LaRoche

MAY			Winner	Loser
10—At Bos.	W	5-3	Aase	Eckersley
11—At N.Y.	W	4-1	Barr	Hunter
12—At N.Y.	L	5-6	Tidrow	Frost
13—At N.Y.	L	10-12	Beattie	Knapp
15—Milw.	W	2-1	Clear	Caldwell
16—Milw.	W	4-3†	Clear	Augustine
17—Milw.	W	8-5	Barr	Sorensen
18—Chicago	W	7-3	Tanana	Schueler
19—Chicago	W	10-6	Knapp	Wortham
20—Chicago	W	4-0	Ryan	Baumgarten
22—At Milw.	L	1-7	Sorensen	Frost
23—At Milw.	L	0-1	Travers	Aase
24—At Milw.	L	6-9	Augustine	Knapp
25—At Chi.	L	1-6	Baumgarten	Ryan
26—At Chi.	W	8-4	Tanana	Howard
27—At Chi.	W	4-2	Frost	Barrios
27—At Chi.	W	9-1	Aase	Hinton
29—At Sea.	W	6-4	Barr	Parrott
30—At Sea.	W	3-2	Ryan	Rawley
31—At Sea.	L	10-12	McLaughlin	Clear
		Won 15, Lost 12		

JUNE				
1—Cleve.	L	4-7	Wise	Frost
2—Cleve.	W	5-2	Clear	Garland
3—Cleve.	L	3-5	Paxton	Barr
4—Toronto	W	4-2	Barlow	Huffman
5—Toronto	W	3-0	Tanana	Underwood
6—Toronto	L	4-5	Jefferson	LaRoche
8—Detroit	W	6-4	Aase	Wilcox
9—Detroit	W	9-1	Ryan	Rozema
10—Detroit	L	7-10	Arroyo	Tanana
11—At Cleve.	W	9-4	Clear	Spillner

CALIFORNIA ANGELS—1979

Front row—Carew, Reese, coach; Sherry, coach; Johnson, coach; Fregosi, manager; Knoop, coach; B. Clear, coach; Downing, Campaneris. Second row—Yocum, team physician; Seeberg, traveling secretary; Rettenmund, Thon, Anderson, Hampton, Donohue, Rasinski, team physician; Triggs, team physician. Third row—Ryan, LaRoche, Davis, Lansford, Ford, Aikens, Grich, Miller, Botting. Fourth row—Barr, Baylor, Aase, Knapp, Barlow, Frost, M. Clear, Tanana, Eddy, Harlow. Seated in front—Smith, trainer; Bergert, assistant trainer; Kurutz, ballboy; Atlas, ballboy; Buzbee, batboy; Uhlich, assistant equipment manager; Shishido, clubhouse manager. Missing from picture—Rudi.

JUNE		Winner	Loser
12–At Cleve.	L 10-11	Hood	Clear
13–At Tor.	L 8-9	Freisleben	LaRoche
13–At Tor.	W 10-2	Aase	Willis
14–At Tor.	W 10-2	Ryan	Huffman
15–At Det.	W 8-7	Clear	Tobik
16–At Det.	W 4-2	Frost	Morris
17–At Det.	L 4-8	Lopez	Aase
18–Texas	W 5-0	Ryan	Jenkins
19–Texas	L 1-2	Johnson	Barr
20–Texas	W 5-4	Frost	Matlack
21–Texas	L 2-3†	Lyle	LaRoche
22–Kan. C.	L 5-9	Gale	Ryan
23–Kan. C.	W 4-13	Gura	Barr
24–Kan. C.	L 2-5	Leonard	Frost
26–At Texas	L 1-2	Matlack	Aase
27–At Texas	L 2-4	Comer	Ryan
28–At Texas	L 4-14	Jenkins	Barr
29–At K.C.	W 6-5†	Clear	Pattin
30–At K.C.	W 8-5	Aase	Gale
	Won 14, Lost 15		
JULY			
1–At K.C.	W 14-2	Ryan	Splittorff
2–Oakland	W 8-3	Barr	Morgan
3–Oakland	W 3-0	Frost	Kingman
4–Oakland	W 17-6	Clear	Heaverlo
5–Oakland	L 0-3	Langford	Ryan
6–Balt.	W 7-3	Barr	Stone
7–Balt.	W 10-1	Frost	D. Martinez
8–Balt.	L 2-3	McGregor	Aase
9–Boston	W 6-0	Ryan	Torrez
10–Boston	W 4-3	Barr	Stanley
11–Boston	L 3-9	Eckersley	Frost
13–N. York	W 6-1	Ryan	Tiant
14–N. York	W 8-7‡	Clear	Davis
15–N. York	W 5-4	Barr	Guidry
19–At Balt.	W 4-3†	LaRoche	D. Martinez
19–At Balt.	L 0-3	Flanagan	Frost
20–At Balt.	L 1-2	McGregor	Barr
21–At Balt.	L 2-10	Stewart	Ryan
22–At Bos.	L 5-6*	Campbell	Clear
23–At Bos.	W 9-2	Frost	Finch
24–At N.Y.	L 5-6	Davis	LaRoche
25–At N.Y.	W 9-5	Botting	John
26–At N.Y.	L 0-2	Guidry	Barr
27–Minn.	L 1-3	Zahn	Frost
28–Minn.	W 5-0	Aase	Koosman
29–Minn.	W 9-3	Eddy	Jackson
30–Seattle	L 0-8	Parrott	Barr
31–Seattle	W 8-1	Frost	Dressler
	Won 17, Lost 11		
AUGUST			
1–Seattle	L 6-7	Stein	LaRoche
3–At Minn.	L 1-4	Koosman	Barr
4–At Minn.	W 7-1	Frost	Goltz

AUGUST		Winner	Loser
5–At Minn.	W 11-7	LaRoche	Erickson
5–At Minn.	L 1-7	Redfern	Eddy
6–At Oak.	W 5-2	Botting	McCatty
7–At Oak.	L 5-9	Langford	Barr
8–At Oak.	W 8-1	Frost	Keough
10–Seattle	L 6-8§	Stein	LaRoche
11–Seattle	W 8-1	Barr	Honeycutt
12–Seattle	W 4-3	Frost	Stein
13–Detroit	L 3-5	Morris	Ryan
14–Detroit	L 3-6	Robbins	Aase
15–Detroit	L 1-6	Petry	Barr
17–Toronto	L 5-6	Stieb	Clear
18–Toronto	W 7-5	Ryan	Underwood
19–Toronto	W 4-2	Aase	Moore
20–Cleve.	W 6-5	LaRoche	Monge
21–Cleve.	L 7-12	Reuschel	Frost
22–Cleve.	L 3-13	Spillner	Ryan
24–At Tor.	L 4-6	Underwood	Knapp
25–At Tor.	W 24-2	Frost	Moore
26–At Tor.	L 3-9	Edge	Ryan
27–At Det.	L 2-3	Billingham	Barr
28–At Det.	L 2-12	Robbins	Aase
29–At Det.	L 1-2	Morris	Frost
30–At Cleve.	L 1-7	Barker	Ryan
31–At Cleve.	W 9-8	Clear	Reuschel
	Won 11, Lost 17		
SEPTEMBER			
1–At Cleve.	W 7-4	LaRoche	Garland
2–At Cleve.	W 5-2	Frost	Waits
3–Chicago	W 6-5	Ryan	Baumgarten
4–Chicago	L 7-10	Proly	Barr
5–Chicago	W 9-8	Montague	Scarbery
6–Chicago	W 10-9	Montague	Farmer
7–Milw.	W 6-3	Ryan	Travers
8–Milw.	W 3-2	Barr	Augustine
9–Milw.	W 5-2	Tanana	Haas
11–At Chi.	L 7-8	Farmer	Aase
12–At Chi.	L 5-11	Kravec	Knapp
14–At Milw.	W 8-7	LaRoche	Castro
15–At Milw.	L 2-3	Haas	Ryan
16–At Milw.	L 1-2	Slaton	Tanana
17–At K.C.	L 4-16	Leonard	Knapp
18–At K.C.	W 6-4	Frost	Gale
19–At K.C.	L 4-6	Gura	Ryan
20–At K.C.	W 11-6	Barr	Chamberlain
21–Texas	L 1-3	Medich	Clear
22–Texas	W 3-1	Knapp	Comer
23–Texas	W 6-1	Frost	Jenkins
24–Kan. C.	W 4-3	Ryan	Gura
25–Kan. C.	W 4-1	Tanana	Chamberlain
26–Kan. C.	L 0-4	Leonard	LaRoche
28–At Texas	L 0-5	Jenkins	Ryan
29–At Texas	L 3-6	Rajsich	Frost
30–At Texas	W 11-5	Knapp	Comer
	Won 16, Lost 11		

*10 innings.   †11 innings.   ‡12 innings.   §14 innings.

Poor Pitching Knocked Royals From Throne

By SID BORDMAN

With their bats blazing and Willie Wilson's feet flying, the Kansas City Royals had a banner statistical season offensively.

But their once-proud pitching staff fizzled, and the Royals had to settle for second place in the American League West, with an 85-77 record, after notching three straight divisional championships.

Not only did Kansas City lose the pennant, but it lost its manager. Whitey

KANSAS CITY ROYALS—1979

Front row—Otis, Brett, Sullivan, coach; Cisco, coach; Herzog, manager; Boros, coach; Hiller, coach; Patek, McRae. Second row—Zych, equipment manager; Washington, Wathan, Pattin, Wilson, Gura, Cruz, White, Braun, Hrabosky, Paschall, Busby, Terrell, Cobb, trainer. Third row—LaCock, Cowens, Rodriguez, Porter, Scott, Gale, Splittorff, Quirk, Quisenberry, Leonard. Seated in front—Stiegler, batboy; Harrison, ballboy.

Herzog, who had guided the Royals to their three flags, was not rehired by General Manger Joe Burke.

Royals' pitchers combined for a dismal 4.45 ERA. Only three of them won 10 or more games—Dennis Leonard (14-12), Larry Gura (13-12) and Paul Splittorff (15-17). Leonard, a 20-game winner in both 1977 and 1978, needed a sparkling finish to climb above the .500 level.

The strong-armed righthander, who was sidelined with a sore elbow from May 24 to June 19 and missed at least six starts, fashioned four of his five shutouts in his last nine starts.

But the Royals did not lag in the hitting department, even though designated hitter Hal McRae was out of action for almost two months because of a shoulder injury. With a solid finish, McRae managed to lift his average to .288 to go with his 10 homers and 74 RBIs.

George Brett, who missed most of spring training because of thumb surgery, spiced Kansas City's potent attack (a .282 team average and 5.25 runs per game) by swatting away for .329 and leading the AL with 212 hits and 20 triples. The All-Star third baseman slugged 23 home runs, drove in 107 runs and set club records for runs with 119, total bases with 363 and slugging percentage with .563.

By bagging the hit and triples titles in the AL, the colorful 26-year-old joined Ty Cobb with three or more AL championships in each of the two departments. Brett also became only the fifth major league player to join the exclusive 20-20-20 club for doubles, triples and home runs.

All-Star catcher Darrell Porter provided more muscle for the Royals, hitting .291 with 112 RBIs, 101 runs, 20 homers and a league-leading 121 walks. Porter also was tops in the AL with a .429 on-base percentage.

Porter became only the second catcher in AL history to eclipse 100 runs, walks and RBIs in a season. Mickey Cochrane turned the trick for the Philadelphia A's in 1932 with 100 bases on balls, 118 runs and 112 RBIs.

While Brett, Porter, Amos Otis and McRae provided most of the run production for the Royals, Wilson was the detonator.

After struggling to a .217 season as a backup outfielder and pinch-runner in his 1978 rookie season, the swift 24-year-old switch-hitter, took charge as the left fielder.

Not only did Wilson hit a sparkling .315, but he led the AL with 83 stolen bases, jumping from his 46 in 1978. A single or base on balls often meant a double for Wilson, whose speed in the outfield also was felt by Kansas City foes. Wilson, who was caught stealing only 12 times, matched Cobb's 1911 steal total for the third highest in AL history.

Otis and Al Cowens, the other two outfielders, turned in .295 seasons with the former driving in 90 runs and scoring 100.

Cowens and Frank White, the Gold Glove second baseman and third All-Star of the club, were felled by injuries on the same night, May 8, in Texas. Righthanded pitcher Ed Farmer of the Rangers hit Cowens with a pitch, fracturing his left jaw. The rifle-armed right fielder did not return to duty until May 30, missing 21 games. White, hit by a pitch, broke a bone on his right hand and missed 33 games.

White, nevertheless, had a good season with the bat, hitting .266 with career highs in homers (10) and stolen bases (28).

Otis chipped in 30 steals as the Royals rang up a league-leading 207.

All was not sour in pitching for Kansas City, however. Craig Chamberlain, in his first full pro season, came up from Jacksonville of the AA Southern League and won his first three starts, all complete games. Dan Quisenberry, another rookie, came up from Omaha of the American Association and had a 3-2 record and five saves.

Tied with Texas at 42-33 on June 28, the Royals fell 10½ games behind but rallied to take the lead again on August 30 when Larry Gura defeated New York 8-3 on a seven-hitter. But that half-game edge over California was lost the next day.

On September 17 the Royals whipped the Angels 16-4 in the opener of a four-game series in Kansas City to reduce their deficit to two games. But they managed only a split of the series, and they never were able to catch the Angels, finishing three games behind.

SCORES OF KANSAS CITY ROYALS' 1979 GAMES

APRIL			Winner	Loser
5—Toronto	W	11-2	Leonard	Underwood
7—Toronto	W	7-4	Gura	Clancy
8—Toronto	W	8-3	Splittorff	Lemongello
9—Detroit	L	3-7	Wilcox	Gale
11—Detroit	W	10-3	Rodriguez	Taylor
13—At Tor.	L	1-4*	Clancy	Splittorff
14—At Tor.	L	6-8	Freisleben	Leonard
15—At Tor.	W	12-10	Rodriguez	Murphy
16—At Det.	L	4-10	Billingham	Gura
17—At Det.	L	3-6	Hiller	Splittorff
20—At Bos.	L	2-9	Hassler	Leonard
21—At Bos.	L	4-10	Stanley	Gura
22—At Bos.	L	0-6	Torrez	Gale
23—Chicago	W	4-3	Splittorff	Wortham
24—Chicago	W	5-0	Leonard	LaGrow
25—Chicago	W	7-6	Hrabosky	Proly
26—Cleve.	W	5-4	Hrabosky	Spillner
27—Cleve.	W	15-7	Splittorff	Garland
28—Cleve.	W	7-2	Leonard	Waits
29—Cleve.	L	4-5	Wise	Gura
30—Texas	L	7-8	Kern	Busby
Won 11, Lost 10				

MAY				
1—Texas	W	9-3	Splittorff	Matlack
2—Texas	W	2-3	Comer	Leonard
4—At Cleve.	W	5-4†	Hrabosky	Monge
5—At Cleve.	W	3-2	Gale	Wise
6—At Cleve.	L	4-5	Paxton	Hrabosky
7—At Texas	W	10-6	Rodriguez	Medich
8—At Texas	L	7-8	Kern	Gura
9—At Texas	W	4-3	Gale	Jenkins
10—At Chi.	L	2-5	Trout	Splittorff
11—At Chi.	L	3-5	Kravec	Busby
12—At Chi.	W	5-4	Pattin	Hinton
13—At Chi.	L	14-5	Rodriguez	Wortham
14—At Sea.	W	1-0	Gale	Bannister
15—At Sea.	W	7-4	Splittorff	Abbott
15—At Sea.	L	2-6	McLaughlin	Gura
16—At Sea.	W	4-3	Busby	Jones
17—Minn.	L	6-7	Koosman	Leonard
18—Minn.	L	6-10†	Marshall	Martin
20—Minn.	W	5-1	Splittorff	Erickson
21—Sea.	L	7-12	Abbott	Gale
22—Sea.	L	11-12§	Rawley	Hrabosky
24—Sea.	W	5-4	Leonard	Jones
25—At Minn.	W	4-3	Splittorff	Marshall
26—At Minn.	W	7-4	Gale	Hartzell
27—At Minn.	W	2-1	Busby	Koosman
28—Balt.	W	5-4z	Gura	Stewart
29—Balt.	L	1-8	Palmer	Splittorff
30—Balt.	W	2-1	Gale	Flanagan
Won 17, Lost 11				

JUNE			Winner	Loser
1—Milw.	L	4-5	Sorensen	Martin
2—Milw.	W	4-3	Splittorff	Cleveland
3—Milw.	W	6-1	Pattin	Haas
4—At N.Y.	L	3-8	John	Gale
5—At N.Y.	W	3-1	Gura	Tiant
6—At Balt.	L	0-3	D. Martinez	Splittorff
7—At Balt.	L	1-3	Stewart	Martin
8—N. York	L	10-11†	Clay	Rodriguez
9—N. York	W	9-8x	Pattin	Clay
10—N. York	L	4-10	Tiant	Mingori
11—Boston	L	0-4†	Stanley	Busby
12—Boston	W	7-6†	Hrabosky	Drago
13—Boston	L	3-11	Renko	Gura
15—At Milw.	W	14-11	Mingori	Cleveland
16—At Milw.	L	2-3	Slaton	Busby
17—At Milw.	L	3-5	Sorensen	Gale
18—At Oak.	W	3-2	Gura	Norris
19—At Oak.	L	5-6	Heaverlo	Hrabosky
20—At Oak.	W	9-2	Splittorff	Hamilton
21—At Oak.	L	7-10	McCatty	Busby
22—At Calif.	W	9-5	Gale	Ryan
23—At Calif.	W	13-4	Gura	Barr
24—At Calif.	W	5-2	Leonard	Frost
26—Oakland	W	7-6†	Hrabosky	Todd
27—Oakland	W	10-3	Busby	Morgan
28—Oakland	W	7-6	Hrabosky	Heaverlo
29—Calif.	L	5-6‡	Clear	Pattin
30—Calif.	L	5-8	Aase	Gale
Won 14, Lost 14				

JULY				
1—Calif.	L	2-14	Ryan	Splittorff
3—At Bos.	L	0-10	Renko	Busby
4—At Bos.	L	4-6	Torrez	Hrabosky
5—At Bos.	L	4-5	Stanley	Paschall
6—Chicago	L	1-4	Trout	Splittorff
7—Chicago	W	4-3	Busby	Hoffman
8—Chicago	L	2-4	Barrios	Pattin
9—At Cleve.	L	2-8	Clyde	Leonard
10—At Cleve.	L	4-7	Spillner	Gale
11—At Cleve.	L	8-9	Paxton	Splittorff
12—Texas	L	2-6	Medich	Gura
13—Texas	L	4-9	Comer	Leonard
14—Texas	L	3-7	Jenkins	Gale
15—Texas	W	4-3	Splittorff	Johnson
19—Cleve.	L	1-2	Wise	Leonard
20—Cleve.	W	9-1	Gale	Waits
21—At Texas	L	1-4	Medich	Splittorff
22—At Texas	W	7-6	Quisenberry	Lyle
23—At Texas	W	5-4	Leonard	Jenkins
24—At Chi.	W	11-6	Mingori	Hoffman
25—At Chi.	L	2-6	Wortham	Splittorff
26—At Chi.	W	6-1	Gura	Baumgarten

JULY			Winner	Loser
27—Balt.	L	0-8	Flanagan	Leonard
28—Balt.	W	6-3	Gale	D. Martinez
29—Balt.	L	4-6	McGregor	Splittorff
30—Toronto	W	9-0	Gura	Stieb
31—Toronto	W	6-5	Pattin	Jefferson
		Won 10, Lost 17		
AUGUST				
1—Toronto	W	4-3	Gale	Huffman
3—At Det.	W	5-3	Busby	Underwood
3—At Det.	L	3-4	Lopez	Mingori
4—At Det.	L	2-5	Chris	Gura
5—At Det.	W	3-2	Leonard	Petry
6—At Tor.	W	16-12	Mingori	Stieb
7—At Tor.	L	2-3	Underwood	Splittorff
9—At Tor.	W	10-3	Gura	Huffman
10—Detroit	W	7-6	Quisenberry	Lopez
10—Detroit	W	7-3	Leonard	Underwood
11—Detroit	W	11-5	Splittorff	Billingham
12—Detroit	W	7-1	Chamberlain	Wilcox
13—At Milw.	L	4-5	Slaton	Quisenberry
14—At Milw.	L	2-5	Caldwell	Leonard
15—At Milw.	L	5-6	Augustine	Quisenberry
16—At Balt.	W	4-2	Splittorff	D. Martinez
17—At Balt.	W	7-1	Chamberlain	Palmer
18—At Balt.	L	2-9	McGregor	Gura
19—At Balt.	W	11-7†	Busby	Stanhouse
20—N. York	L	4-17	Tiant	Gale
21—N. York	L	2-6	Gossage	Splittorff
22—N. York	W	3-1	Gura	Beattie
24—Boston	W	4-2	Chamberlain	Eckersley
25—Boston	W	1-0	Leonard	Torrez
26—Boston	W	6-3	Splittorff	Renko
27—Milw.	W	10-9†	Hrabosky	Galasso
28—Milw.	L	6-11	Haas	Chamberlain

AUGUST			Winner	Loser
29—Milw.	W	18-8	Leonard	Slaton
30—At N.Y.	W	8-3	Gura	Tiant
31—At N.Y.	L	3-7	John	Splittorff
		Won 19, Lost 11		
SEPTEMBER				
1—At N.Y.	W	9-8	Hrabosky	Kaat
2—At N.Y.	L	5-6†	Gossage	Mingori
3—At Minn.	W	1-0	Leonard	Zahn
4—At Minn.	L	1-5	Koosman	Gura
5—At Minn.	L	3-8	Goltz	Splittorff
7—At Sea.	W	6-2	Chamberlain	Honeycutt
8—At Sea.	L	2-4	Bannister	Leonard
9—At Sea.	W	3-1	Gura	Parrott
10—Minn.	W	6-5y	Quisenberry	Marshall
10—Minn.	L	2-5	Goltz	Splittorff
11—Minn.	L	1-3	Zahn	Chamberlain
12—Minn.	W	4-0	Leonard	Koosman
14—Seattle	L	5-7	Bannister	Gura
15—Seattle	W	5-4‡	Hrabosky	McLaughlin
16—Seattle	L	3-6	Dressler	Splittorff
17—Calif.	W	16-4	Leonard	Knapp
18—Calif.	L	4-6	Frost	Gale
19—Calif.	W	6-4	Gura	Ryan
20—Calif.	L	6-11	Barr	Chamberlain
21—At Oak.	W	13-4	Splittorff	Langford
22—At Oak.	L	0-2	Keough	Leonard
23—At Oak.	W	4-2	Pattin	McCatty
24—At Calif.	L	3-4	Ryan	Gura
25—At Calif.	L	1-4	Tanana	Chamberlain
26—At Calif.	W	4-0	Leonard	LaRoche
28—Oakland	W	13-1	Gurd	McCatty
29—Oakland	W	6-2	Splittorff	Morgan
30—Oakland	L	5-6	Kingman	Leonard
		Won 14, Lost 14		

*5½ innings. †10 innings. ‡11 innings. §12 innings. x13 innings. y14 innings. z16 innings.

Rangers Filed '79 in Cabinet Marked SOS

By RANDY GALLOWAY

It's a familiar story. Season after season the Rangers are regarded as strong pennant contenders. Season after season they fail to live up to those expectations.

File the year of 1979 in the cabinet marked SOS—Same Ol' Stuff.

The Rangers finished at 83-79 and in third place in the American League West.

"It was," sighed Manager Pat Corrales, "one big disappointment."

Yes, it was, but the '79 season had many positive aspects where statistics were concerned.

This team scored 750 runs and drove in more runs (717), hit more home runs (140) and had a higher batting average (.278) than any other Ranger product during the eight years the club had been in Texas.

The staff ERA of 3.86 was inferior only to Batimore and New York and the defense committed 23 fewer errors than the season before.

Jim Kern shared the THE SPORTING NEWS American League Fireman of the Year award with Mike Marshall of Minnesota. Kern was 13-5 with 29 saves. Second-year man Steve Comer won 17 games and his 3.68 ERA was best among Ranger starters.

Third baseman Buddy Bell had 200 hits and 101 RBIs, Al Oliver finished fifth in the league in hitting at .323, rookie first baseman Pat Putnam—chosen

TEXAS RANGERS—1979

Front row—Oliver, Lucchesi, coach; Brown, coach; Ryan, coach; Corrales, manager; Ellis, Koenig, coach; Sundberg, Sample, Blanks. Second row—Zeigler, trainer; Grubb, Zisk, Comer, Johnson, Bell, Jorgensen, Rivers, Lyle, Wills, Putnam, Norman. Third row—Soderholm, Babcock, Jenkins, Medich, Kern, Roberts, Darwin, Rajsich, Gamble, Alexander.

the AL Rookie Player of the Year by THE SPORTING NEWS—hit .277 with 18 homers, and backstop Jim Sundberg received a fourth consecutive Gold Glove.

On top of that, 1.5 million paying customers set a new attendance record at Arlington Stadium.

"We did have so many good things going for us this season," said Corrales, "but I guess the first negative sign happened in the final week of spring training. When Jon Matlack walked off the mound that day in Florida we were in trouble. We knew Jon meant a great deal to our pitching staff but no one realized just how much until we didn't have him."

Matlack was scheduled to make his final spring training start on April 3 in Pompano Beach. He took his warm-up pitches, walked in from the bullpen, stepped on the mound, reached down for the resin bag, picked it up, threw it back down, then grabbed his left elbow.

It was a case of bone chips in the elbow. After much medical attention it was determined that Matlack shouldn't undergo immediate surgery. He waited a month on the disabled list, then made his first start on May 1. It was like spring training for awhile, just a couple of innings each outing to get his conditioning back.

Then he reeled off some impressive wins. Matlack appeared to be on his way and so did the Rangers. But in early July there was a relapse and Matlack was disabled for the remainder of the season. He underwent surgery in September.

"I'm not saying we'd have won the pennant with a healthy Matlack," said Corrales, "but the facts are right there regardless. Jon would have meant 15 more wins, minimum, plus he's our stopper. And man did we ever need a stopper."

The Rangers were playing well through the All-Star break, standing 52-39. Immediately following that three-day rest period, they lost 30 of the next 40 contests and fell out of contention.

"Obviously, those 40 days killed us," said Corrales. "It was one nightmare after another."

Corrales refused to point the finger at one individual player to place in the category of biggest disappointment, but it would have to be Richie Zisk. He hit only .262 with 18 homers and 64 RBIs.

"We need more out of Richie," said Corrales. But the Rangers always seem to need more of something.

SCORES OF TEXAS RANGERS' 1979 GAMES

APRIL			Winner	Loser
7—At Det.	W	8-2	Jenkins	Rozema
10—Cleve.	W	5-0	Kern	Wise
11—Cleve.	W	4-0	Comer	Wilkins
12—Cleve.	W	5-3	Jenkins	Waits
13—Detroit	W	5-4	Kern	Burnside
14—Detroit	W	7-5	Lyle	Baker
15—Detroit	L	6-11	Burnside	Lyle
17—At Cleve.	W	6-2	Jenkins	Waits
18—At Cleve.	L	4-6	Monge	Medich
20—At N.Y.	L	3-5	Figueroa	Comer
21—At N.Y.	W	5-0	Jenkins	Hunter
22—At N.Y.	L	1-5	Guidry	Ellis
23—Toronto	W	5-0	Alexander	Clancy
24—Toronto	L	0-2	Lemanczyk	Comer
25—Toronto	W	4-3*	Lyle	Jefferson
27—At Chi.	L	0-11	Baumgarten	Alexander
28—At Chi.	L	2-3	Barrios	Comer

APRIL			Winner	Loser
29—At Chi.	W	10-0	Ellis	Wortham
30—At K.C.	W	8-7	Kern	Busby
		Won 12, Lost 7		
MAY				
1—At K.C.	L	3-9	Splittorff	Matlack
2—At K.C.	W	3-2	Comer	Leonard
4—Chicago	L	5-7	Barrios	Lyle
4—Chicago	W	7-6	Farmer	LaGrow
5—Chicago	L	6-7	Wortham	Ellis
6—Chicago	L	0-3	Kravec	Matlack
7—Kan. C.	L	6-10	Rodriguez	Medich
8—Kan. C.	W	8-7	Kern	Gura
9—Kan. C.	L	3-4	Gale	Jenkins
11—At Tor.	W	3-1	Matlack	Clancy
12—At Tor.	W	3-1	Comer	Lemanczyk
13—At Tor.	L	1-3	Lemongello	Alexander

MAY				Winner	Loser
13—At Tor.	W	7-5		Farmer	Huffman
14—At Minn.	W	7-5		Kern	Marshall
15—At Minn.	W	9-8		Lyle	Marshall
16—At Minn.	W	8-4		Matlack	Hartzell
18—At Sea.	L	5-13		Montague	Comer
19—At Sea.	L	0-4		Bannister	Jenkins
20—At Sea.	W	6-4		Alexander	Rawley
21—Minn.	L	6-7		Redfern	Lyle
22—Minn.	W	4-3		Kern	Koosman
23—Minn.	W	7-2		Jenkins	Goltz
25—Seattle	L	2-3		Parrott	Alexander
25—Seattle	L	3-5		Honeycutt	Ellis
26—Seattle	W	2-1		Matlack	Abbott
27—Seattle	W	7-3		Comer	Mitchell
28—Boston	W	5-2		Jenkins	Renko
30—Boston	W	3-2*		Kern	Drago
31—Boston	L	2-3‡		Drago	Lyle
		Won 16, Lost 13			
JUNE					
1—Balt.	W	4-2		Comer	Stone
2—Balt.	L	4-5		T. Martinez	Lyle
3—Balt.	W	4-2		Alexander	Palmer
4—At Bos.	L	5-13		Torrez	Ellis
5—At Bos.	L	3-9		Eckersley	Matlack
6—At Milw.	L	3-4		Sorensen	Comer
7—At Milw.	W	7-1		Jenkins	Haas
8—At Balt.	L	0-3		Flanagan	Alexander
9—At Balt.	L	3-4		Stone	Ellis
10—At Balt.	L	4-5		D. Martinez	Kern
12—Milw.	W	7-6		Kern	Sorensen
13—Milw.	L	4-5		Haas	Jenkins
14—Milw.	L	2-6		Travers	Alexander
15—N. York	W	9-5		Matlack	Figueroa
16—N. York	L	2-3*		Davis	Lyle
17—N. York	W	6-3		Comer	Hunter
18—At Calif.	L	0-5		Ryan	Jenkins
19—At Calif.	L	2-1		Johnson	Barr
20—At Calif.	L	4-5		Frost	Matlack
21—At Calif.	W	3-2†		Lyle	LaRoche
22—At Oak.	L	5-6		Langford	Comer
23—At Oak.	W	8-5*		Kern	Lacey
24—At Oak.	W	5-1		Johnson	Keough
24—At Oak.	W	7-2		Medich	Hamilton
26—Calif.	W	2-1		Matlack	Aase
27—Calif.	W	4-2		Comer	Ryan
28—Calif.	W	14-4		Jenkins	Barr
29—Oakland	W	5-3		Darwin	Keough
30—Oakland	W	4-3		Kern	Todd
		Won 16, Lost 13			
JULY					
1—Oakland	L	12-13§		Langford	Medich
2—Balt.	W	2-0		Comer	D. Martinez
3—Balt.	W	4-0		Jenkins	Stone
4—Balt.	W	9-5		Darwin	Flanagan
6—Toronto	L	1-5		Underwood	Johnson
7—Toronto	W	2-0		Medich	Lemanczyk
8—Toronto	W	4-3		Comer	Moore
9—At Chi.	L	4-5		Baumgarten	Jenkins
10—At Chi.	L	3-6		Wortham	Kern
11—At Chi.	L	3-5		Trout	Darwin
12—At K.C.	W	6-2		Medich	Leonard
13—At K.C.	W	9-4		Comer	Leonard
14—At K.C.	W	7-3		Jenkins	Gale
15—At K.C.	L	3-4		Splittorff	Johnson
19—Chicago	L	6-9		Trout	Rajsich
19—Chicago	L	4-5		Kravec	Jenkins
20—Chicago	L	1-2		Wortham	Johnson
21—Kan. C.	W	4-1		Medich	Splittorff
22—Kan. C.	L	6-7		Quisenberry	Lyle
23—Kan. C.	L	4-5		Leonard	Jenkins

JULY				Winner	Loser
25—At Tor.	L	3-8		Stieb	Johnson
26—At Tor.	L	4-8		Underwood	Medich
27—Boston	W	11-2		Comer	Stanley
28—Boston	L	0-1		Eckersley	Jenkins
29—Boston	L	2-3		Torrez	Alexander
30—Detroit	L	4-6		Hiller	Darwin
31—Detroit	W	11-3		Medich	Petry
		Won 11, Lost 16			
AUGUST					
1—Detroit	W	4-3		Comer	Wilcox
3—At Cleve.	W	8-3		Jenkins	Wise
4—At Cleve.	L	8-12		Waits	Johnson
5—At Cleve.	L	2-6		Barker	Medich
5—At Cleve.	W	14-3		Darwin	Paxton
7—At Det.	L	1-3		Wilcox	Kern
7—At Det.	L	2-8		Billingham	Rajsich
8—At Det.	W	16-9		Jenkins	Underwood
8—At Det.	L	4-10		Robbins	Johnson
9—At Det.	L	2-3		Chris	Medich
10—Cleve.	L	1-6		Barker	Darwin
11—Cleve.	W	5-2		Allard	Paxton
12—Cleve.	L	3-6		Spillner	Comer
13—At N.Y.	L	2-3		Guidry	Jenkins
14—At N.Y.	L	5-6		Tiant	Kern
15—At N.Y.	L	3-4		John	Gleaton
16—At Milw.	L	1-4		Sorensen	Allard
17—At Milw.	L	1-5		Haas	Comer
18—At Milw.	W	7-3		Jenkins	Slaton
19—At Milw.	L	3-4		Caldwell	Lyle
20—At Balt.	L	0-3		Flanagan	Allard
21—At Balt.	W	2-1		Comer	D. Martinez
23—At Balt.	L	5-6		McGregor	Jenkins
24—Milw.	L	6-9		Galasso	Darwin
25—Milw.	L	2-5		Caldwell	Allard
26—Milw.	L	2-6		Travers	Comer
27—N. York	L	4-7		John	Jenkins
28—N. York	W	10-2		Kern	Clay
29—N. York	L	5-7		Guidry	Rajsich
30—At Bos.	W	6-0		Medich	Eckersley
31—At Bos.	L	6-9		Torrez	Comer
		Won 9, Lost 22			
SEPTEMBER					
1—At Bos.	W	5-4		Darwin	Drago
2—At Bos.	W	7-6†		Kern	Drago
3—At Sea.	W	4-1		Medich	Bannister
4—At Sea.	W	5-2		Comer	Parrott
5—At Sea.	L	0-1		Dressler	Jenkins
7—At Minn.	W	5-4		Lyle	Marshall
8—At Minn.	W	6-2		Medich	Koosman
9—At Minn.	W	6-5		Comer	Hartzell
10—Seattle	L	2-5		Dressler	Jenkins
11—Seattle	W	5-2		Alexander	Branch
12—Seattle	W	13-3		Medich	Honeycutt
13—Minn.	L	4-7‡		Jackson	Kern
14—Minn.	W	5-3		Jenkins	Goltz
15—Minn.	L	4-13		Zahn	Alexander
16—Minn.	L	2-6		Erickson	Medich
17—At Oak.	W	6-3		Comer	Morgan
18—At Oak.	W	9-5		Jenkins	McCatty
19—At Oak.	W	9-4		Alexander	Kingman
21—At Calif.	W	3-1		Medich	Clear
22—At Calif.	L	1-3		Knapp	Comer
23—At Calif.	L	1-6		Frost	Jenkins
25—Oakland	W	5-3		Kern	Kingman
26—Oakland	W	5-2		Comer	Langford
27—Oakland	W	4-3		McCall	Keough
28—Calif.	W	5-0		Jenkins	Ryan
29—Calif.	W	6-3		Rajsich	Frost
30—Calif.	L	5-11		Knapp	Comer
		Won 19, Lost 8			

*10 innings.   †11 innings.   ‡12 innings.   §15 innings.

Twins Contended Without Pitching, Defense

By BOB FOWLER

It's unlikely reporters covering the Twins in the future will listen to any spring training proclamations. If club officials make predictions, or if managers give evaluations during the exhibition campaign, newsmen probably will scoff and say, "You're not going to burn us like you did in 1979."

During the team's month in Florida that spring, President Calvin Griffith and Manager Gene Mauch constantly talked about the club's pitching staff. With the addition of Jerry Koosman to the starting rotation, they said, Minnesota would have its best mound corps in a decade.

And without Rod Carew, the seven-time American League batting champion traded to California a year before he could become a free agent, the Twins would have to rely on a new game plan to become contenders in the West Division.

Day after day, Mauch talked about pitching and defense in the upcoming campaign.

Well, Minnesota was a contender until the final week, finishing fourth with an 82-80 record, six games behind California. But pitching and defense weren't responsible for the Twins improving on their 73-89 showing in 1978.

The team had a .278 batting average in 1979, compared to its .267 mark the previous year with Carew. Its run production jumped to 764 from 666 and its home run output to 112 from 82.

Pitching? Well, the 1979 staff had a 4.13 ERA compared to the 3.69 ERA of 1978. It had a mere 31 complete games (48 in 1978) and gave up 128 homers (102 in 1978).

The fielding was a little better as indicated by a club-record 203 double plays.

So how did Minnesota remain in contention? It received some outstanding performances from individuals, but it enjoyed a successful season because so many contributed.

Koosman became the American League Comeback Player of the Year (UPI) at age 35. After winning three games with the 1978 Mets, he had a 20-13 record and 3.38 ERA. Geoff Zahn was 13-7 with a 3.57 ERA and Dave Goltz wrapped up 13 years in the organization with a 14-13 record and 4.16 ERA before declaring himself a free agent.

Pete Redfern became an excellent middle reliever, posting a 7-3 mark and 3.50 ERA in 40 games and Mike Marshall, the 36-year-old bullpen ace, set a league record by making 90 appearances and had 32 saves to go with his 10-15 record and 2.64 ERA. Marshall tied Texas righthander Jim Kern as THE SPORTING NEWS Fireman of the Year.

Otherwise, the pitching was disappointing. Roger Erickson, who won 14 games in 1978 as a rookie, was 3-10. Paul Hartzell, obtained in the Carew trade, was 6-10 and Darrell Jackson could manage only a 4-4 showing in 24 games.

Indeed, when the club jumped off to a 22-8 record and was in first place, and in early September when it moved within two games of the top spot, it relied on hitting as it had done in years past.

All-Star shortstop Roy Smalley was hitting .372 on July 4 but hit only .178 after that to finish at .271. But he still led the club with 24 homers and 95 RBIs.

MINNESOTA TWINS—1979

Front row—Rivera, Morales, Castino, Kuehl, coach; Zimmerman, coach; Mauch, manager; Pascual, coach; Goryl, coach; Jackson, Norwood, Marshall. Second row—Dunn, clubhouse attendant; Wiesner, clubhouse attendant; Edwards, Sofield, Wynegar, Zahn, Smalley, Powell, Cubbage, Landreaux, Martin, trainer; Crump, equipment manager. Third row—Borgmann, Wilfong, Redfern, Koosman, Kusick, Holly, Goltz, Hartzell, Erickson, Randall, Serum. Seated in front—batboys O'Hara, Betzold, Stavros and Ericksen.

First baseman Ron Jackson, obtained with Danny Goodwin from the Angels for Dan Ford, had 14 homers and 68 RBIs. Second baseman Rob Wilfong was the team's most improved player, hitting .313 with nine homers and 59 RBIs after batting .266 with one homer and 11 RBIs in 1979. Third baseman John Castino tied Toronto shortstop Alfredo Griffin for the AL Rookie of the Year with a .285 average, 52 RBIs and too many spectacular defensive plays to mention.

Center fielder Ken Landreaux, included in the Carew deal, was the team's best performer with a .305 average, 15 homers and 83 RBIs. Hosken Powell hit .293, Bombo Rivera .281 and rookie Dave Edwards knocked in 35 runs.

Catcher Butch Wynegar improved his average from .229 to .270, lefthanded designated-hitter Glenn Adams hit .301 and Goodwin, after being recalled from the minors, had a .289 mark and 27 RBIs in 58 games.

Why didn't the Twins win?

They lacked a righthanded power hitter, especially in the DH spot. Jose Morales hit .267 with only two homers. And while their pitching was inconsistent, so was their hitting with men in scoring position. They left a whopping 1,201 runners on base (more than any other team in the league) and most of them seemed to be stranded at third.

It was announced that in 1982 the Twins would move into a new domed stadium in downtown Minneapolis. Club officials said something about how the team would have to stress pitching and defense to win in the dome, but few listened.

SCORES OF MINNESOTA TWINS' 1979 GAMES

APRIL			Winner	Loser	MAY			Winner	Loser
6–At Oak.	W	5-3	Goltz	Langford	17–At K.C.	W	7-6	Koosman	Leonard
7–At Oak.	W	3-1§	Marshall	Todd	18–At K.C.	W	10-6†	Marshall	Martin
8–At Oak.	W	3-1	Zahn	Norris	20–At K.C.	L	1-5	Splittorff	Erickson
10–At Calif.	W	8-1	Koosman	Tanana	21–At Texas	W	7-6	Redfern	Lyle
11–At Calif.	L	2-11	Ryan	Goltz	22–At Texas	L	3-4	Kern	Koosman
12–At Calif.	L	1-7	Knapp	Erickson	23–At Texas	L	2-7	Jenkins	Goltz
13–At Sea.	W	8-2	Zahn	Mitchell	25–Kan. C.	W	3-4	Splittorff	Marshall
14–At Sea.	W	6-5	Marshall	Bannister	26–Kan. C.	L	4-7	Gale	Hartzell
15–At Sea.	W	18-6	Koosman	Abbott	27–Kan. C.	L	1-2	Busby	Koosman
17–Calif.	L	0-6	Ryan	Goltz	28–Oakland	W	10-7	Marshall	Heaverlo
18–Calif.	L	6-11	Miller	Erickson	30–Oakland	L	4-5	Johnson	Erickson
19–Calif.	L	4-6	Aase	Marshall	31–Oakland	W	13-2	Hartzell	Langford
21–Seattle	W	6-5	Koosman	Bannister			**Won 14, Lost 12**		
22–Seattle	W	3-1	Goltz	Abbott					
24–At Cleve.	L	2-7	Wise	Erickson	JUNE				
25–At Cleve.	W	4-2	Redfern	Monge	1–Boston	L	2-5	Stanley	Koosman
27–At Det.	W	5-3	Koosman	Rozema	2–Boston	W	8-2	Goltz	Rainey
28–At Det.	L	3-5	Young	Goltz	3–Boston	L	2-8	Renko	Zahn
29–At Det.	W	5-3	Zahn	Wilcox	4–At Balt.	L	2-3†	Stanhouse	Marshall
30–At Tor.	W	6-3	Hartzell	Lemongello	5–At Balt.	W	3-1	Hartzell	Stone
		Won 13, Lost 7			6–At N.Y.	L	2-3	Guidry	Koosman
					7–At N.Y.	W	4-1	Zahn	Beattie
MAY					8–At Bos.	L	1-2	Stanley	Goltz
1–At Tor.	W	3-2	Koosman	Jefferson	9–At Bos.	L	6-12	Torrez	Erickson
2–At Tor.	W	7-5	Goltz	Huffman	10–At Bos.	L	0-5	Eckersley	Hartzell
3–Detroit	W	7-6	Marshall	Billingham	12–N. York	L	1-4	Davis	Koosman
4–Detroit	W	7-6	Marshall	Lopez	13–N. York	W	8-7	Redfern	Burris
5–Detroit	L	4-8	Billingham	Hartzell	14–N. York	W	4-2	Zahn	John
6–Detroit	W	9-6	Marshall	Hiller	15–Balt.	L	5-6	Stanhouse	Marshall
7–Toronto	W	6-1	Goltz	Huffman	17–Balt.	L	5-8	Flanagan	Koosman
8–Toronto	W	16-6	Bacsik	Willis	19–At Milw.	L	9-10	McClure	Bacsik
11–Cleve.	W	4-3	Marshall	Monge	20–At Milw.	L	3-8	Travers	Hartzell
12–Cleve.	W	4-0	Koosman	Paxton	21–At Milw.	L	2-3	Caldwell	Serum
13–Cleve.	W	2-3	Garland	Goltz	22–At Chi.	W	5-3	Zahn	Kravec
14–Texas	L	5-7	Kern	Marshall	23–At Chi.	W	6-1	Goltz	Baumgarten
15–Texas	L	8-9	Lyle	Marshall	24–At Chi.	W	4-3	Bacsik	Wortham
16–Texas	L	4-8	Matlack	Hartzell	24–At Chi.	W	7-1	Koosman	Farmer

JUNE			Winner	Loser
26—Milw.	W	8-7	Marshall	Augustine
27—Milw.	L	8-9	Caldwell	Serum
28—Milw.	L	5-6†	Castro	Marshall
29—Chicago	W	5-2	Koosman	Wortham
30—Chicago	W	16-4	Zahn	Farmer
		Won 12, Lost 15		

JULY				
1—Chicago	W	2-1†	Hartzell	Howard
2—Seattle	W	7-0	Jackson	Jones
3—Seattle	W	12-2	Redfern	Parrott
3—Seattle	L	2-10	McLaughlin	Serum
4—Seattle	W	7-2	Koosman	Abbott
5—Seattle	L	0-4	Honeycutt	Zahn
6—At Cleve.	L	5-6	Spillner	Hartzell
7—At Cleve.	L	3-9	Paxton	Jackson
8—At Cleve.	L	4-5	Cruz	Marshall
8—At Cleve.	W	7-2	Goltz	Waits
9—At Det.	W	5-3	Koosman	Baker
10—At Det.	L	5-6	Lopez	Marshall
11—At Det.	W	3-0	Jackson	Morris
13—At Tor.	W	6-4	Goltz	Lemanczyk
14—At Tor.	L	2-4	Stieb	Koosman
15—At Tor.	W	9-4	Zahn	Clancy
19—Detroit	L	3-8	Underwood	Koosman
20—Detroit	W	14-6	Serum	Young
21—Toronto	W	6-4	Goltz	Huffman
21—Toronto	W	4-3	Hartzell	Moore
22—Toronto	W	13-1	Redfern	Lemanczyk
23—Toronto	W	7-6	Marshall	Lemongello
24—Cleve.	L	2-4	Wise	Koosman
25—Cleve.	L	0-2	Waits	Goltz
26—Cleve.	L	2-7	Spillner	Redfern
27—At Calif.	W	3-1	Zahn	Frost
28—At Calif.	L	0-5	Aase	Koosman
29—At Calif.	L	3-9	Eddy	Jackson
30—At Oak.	W	3-0	Goltz	Kingman
31—At Oak.	L	1-2	McCatty	Zahn
		Won 16, Lost 14		

AUGUST				
1—At Oak.	L	1-7	Langford	Hartzell
3—Calif.	W	4-1	Koosman	Barr
4—Calif.	L	1-7	Frost	Goltz
5—Calif.	L	7-11	LaRoche	Erickson
5—Calif.	W	7-1	Redfern	Eddy
6—At Sea.	L	4-7	Honeycutt	Jackson
7—At Sea.	W	5-2	Koosman	Hinton
8—At Sea.	W	3-1	Goltz	Bannister
10—Oakland	L	5-6‡	Heaverlo	Marshall
10—Oakland	W	3-2§	Jackson	Heaverlo
11—Oakland	W	9-7	Bacsik	McCatty

AUGUST			Winner	Loser
12—Oakland	W	1-0	Koosman	Langford
13—At Bos.	L	5-6	Burgmeier	Marshall
14—At Bos.	L	1-12	Eckersley	Redfern
15—At Bos.	L	5-9	Drago	Bacsik
16—At N.Y.	W	5-1	Zahn	Hunter
17—At N.Y.	W	5-2	Koosman	Beattie
18—At N.Y.	L	3-5	Davis	Marshall
19—At N.Y.	L	3-4	Guidry	Jackson
20—Boston	W	10-5	Erickson	Torrez
21—Boston	W	7-2	Koosman	Tudor
22—Boston	L	4-9*	Stanley	Goltz
24—N. York	L	5-7	Guidry	Zahn
25—N. York	W	4-1	Koosman	Tiant
27—Balt.	W	4-3	Redfern	D. Martinez
27—Balt.	L	1-5	Palmer	Goltz
29—Balt.	L	0-4	McGregor	Erickson
29—Balt.	L	4-7	Ford	Zahn
30—At Balt.	L	4-5	Flanagan	Koosman
31—At Balt.	W	3-1	Goltz	D. Martinez
		Won 14, Lost 16		

SEPTEMBER				
1—At Balt.	W	3-2	Hartzell	Palmer
2—At Balt.	L	1-3	McGregor	Erickson
3—Kan. C.	L	0-1	Leonard	Zahn
4—Kan. C.	W	5-1	Koosman	Gura
5—Kan. C.	W	8-3	Goltz	Splittorff
7—Texas	L	4-5	Lyle	Marshall
8—Texas	L	2-6	Medich	Koosman
9—Texas	L	5-6	Comer	Hartzell
10—At K.C.	L	5-6x	Quisenberry	Marshall
10—At K.C.	W	5-2	Goltz	Splittorff
11—At K.C.	W	3-1	Zahn	Chamberlain
12—At K.C.	L	0-4	Leonard	Koosman
13—At Texas	W	7-4§	Jackson	Kern
14—At Texas	L	3-5	Jenkins	Goltz
15—At Texas	W	11-4	Zahn	Alexander
16—At Texas	W	6-2	Erickson	Medich
17—At Chi.	W	10-3	Bacsik	Wortham
18—At Chi.	L	0-1†	Kravec	Goltz
19—At Chi.	L	0-6	Baumgarten	Hartzell
20—N. York	W	3-1	Zahn	Righetti
21—At Milw.	W	3-2	Koosman	Haas
22—At Milw.	W	6-3	Erickson	Slaton
23—At Milw.	L	7-8	Augustine	Redfern
25—Chicago	L	3-9	Kravec	Zahn
26—Chicago	L	5-6†	Farmer	Marshall
27—Chicago	L	2-4†	Proly	Goltz
28—Milw.	L	1-10	Caldwell	Erickson
29—Milw.	L	8-11	Mitchell	Hartzell
30—Milw.	W	5-0	Koosman	Sorensen
		Won 13, Lost 16		

*8 innings.   †10 innings.   ‡11 innings.   §12 innings.   x14 innings.

ChiSox Drowned by Leaky Defense

By RICHARD DOZER

For the White Sox, 1979 ran from the unusual to the bizarre.

They were low finishers again, running a distant fifth in the less-than-spectacular West Division. Yet they were only one game below .500 on the road while flopping miserably at home; had four lefthanded starters that won in double figures; batted a comfortable .275 as a team, a figure bettered by only six clubs; and posted their best staff ERA (4.10) in four years, trailing only five clubs—all contenders.

It was easy, of course, to determine why the 73-87 White Sox were no factor in the race. Their fielding, which had been the main target for improvement by player-manager Don Kessinger in the spring, was bad again. Their 173 errors led the league.

Kessinger went down the drain with the defense. He resigned as manager on August 2, and both he and management insisted it was his own idea. It's true Kessinger was not pushed. But neither was he grabbed when he went over the precipice toward an announced retirement.

The club was 14 games below .500 when the popular Kessinger stepped aside, and that's exactly the way they finished under Tony LaRussa, who is baseball's only barrister-manager. Things looked up under LaRussa, who led the club to a 27-27 standoff through a stormy August and September during which Owner Bill Veeck's credibility was questioned because of what three rock concerts and horrid weather did to Comiskey Park.

Even the players were upset for a time, some reacting bitterly to field conditions they felt were hazardous.

None suffered more than Owner Veeck and those who try to show him a profit, however. Two cancellations and one postponement that had to be made up as part of a doubleheader cost the White Sox, conservatively, 100,000 at the gate and $200,000 in the treasury. The bad field—not to mention the adverse publicity—contributed heavily to an attendance drop of more than 200,000 from the previous season.

If that weren't enough, a promotion called "Disco Demolition Night" unwittingly became a between-games invitation to thousands of Chicago's young to clutter the field. And the second game of a doubleheader against Detroit was forfeited.

"But we survived," said Veeck, surveying a $75,000 post-season resodding project that left the field with improved drainage and raised certain low spots by as much as 14 inches.

Even though it was a year in which there was more talk about the side attractions—or distractions—the season had some bright spots. The only major injuries, indeed, were to pitchers Francisco Barrios and Mike Proly, and with the future in mind, necessity was the mother of some improvement that otherwise would not have been required.

Ed Farmer, picked up at the trade deadline from Texas for Eric Soderholm after Proly was disabled with a bum elbow, responded with 14 saves and three victories after going to the bullpen in early July. And when Barrios bowed out with shoulder problems, leaving an 8-3 record behind, the Sox had to turn to their young pitchers in earnest. Ken Kravec, the only established member of the young staff, finished 15-13 with five three-hitters and three shutouts. Rookies Ross Baumgarten and Steve Trout won 13 and 11, respectively, and Richard Wortham, barely beyond rookie status, won 14.

The leading White Sox hitter was All-Star Chet Lemon, who rebounded from an emotional flare-up in which he left the club for a day and came on strong the last six weeks to hit .318. It was the highest White Sox batting average since Minnie Minoso batted .320 in 1954. Lemon also shared the league lead in doubles with 44 and led the club with 86 RBIs.

Lamar Johnson, at .309, gave the Sox another .300 hitter, and Claudell Washington had an excellent year despite a six-week slump during which he was six-for-60. Claudell wound up at .280 and stole 19 bases, second only to Alan Bannister's 22.

A big plus was the restructuring of the infield, a project which bore fruit after Jim Morrison was obtained from the Phillies' system as final payment

CHICAGO WHITE SOX—1979

Front row—Morris, clubhouse attendant; Garr, Winkles, coach; Schueler, player-coach; Kessinger, player-manager; Sparks, coach; Hoffman, McNamara, clubhouse attendant. Second row—Fountain, physical fitness coordinator; Rosenbaum, traveling secretary; Bannister, Torres, Squires, Proly, Orta, Tassone, clubhouse attendant; Schneider, trainer. Third row—Washington, Pryor, Bell, Scarbery, Lemon, Wortham, May, Morrison. Fourth row—Nahorodny, Kravec, Nordhagen, Trout, Farmer, Howard, Colbern, Barrios, Johnson, Moore.

for pitcher Jack Kucek. Morrison, playing only the final 10 weeks, belted 14 homers and played superbly at second base. Greg Pryor, a surprise with the bat, hit .275 but had defensive troubles—partly because he played three infield positions before settling at short. Mike Squires came on strong at first base with his slick glove, and Kevin Bell wound up at third.

Catching was improved with the addition of Milt May, but he was hurt in September and Marvis Foley raised eyebrows with his fine work in reserve. May opted for free agency along with Jorge Orta, who played little in the second half but hit 11 homers nonetheless.

SCORES OF CHICAGO WHITE SOX' 1979 GAMES

APRIL			Winner	Loser		JUNE			Winner	Loser
6—At Balt.	L	3-5	Palmer	Kravec		6—At Bos.	W	8-5	Barrios	Stanley
7—At Balt.	L	3-6	Flanagan	Proly		7—At Bos.	L	2-9	Rainey	Kravec
8—At Balt.	W	5-1	Wortham	D. Martinez		9—At Milw.	W	6-2	Howard	Caldwell
10—Toronto	L	2-10	Huffman	Kravec		10—At Milw.	W	13-3	Barrios	Mitchell
12—Toronto	L	7-9	Murphy	LaGrow		11—Balt.	L	0-6	McGregor	Wortham
13—N. York	W	12-2	Wortham	Tiant		12—Balt.	W	12-4	Kravec	Flanagan
14—N. York	L	5-8	Tidrow	Robinson		13—Balt.	L	7-8‡	Stoddard	Trout
15—N. York	W	5-6	Figueroa	Proly		15—Boston	W	8-5	Wortham	Torrez
16—At Tor.	W	8-4	Scarbery	Murphy		16—Boston	L	5-11	Eckersley	Scarbery
17—At Tor.	W	6-1	Barrios	Underwood		17—Boston	W	6-1	Kravec	Rainey
18—At Tor.	W	12-5	Wortham	Clancy		18—Seattle	L	1-5	Parrott	Baumgarten
20—At Cleve.	W	4-2‡	Proly	Cruz		19—Seattle	L	2-7	Honeycutt	Wortham
21—At Cleve.	W	6-5	Baumgarten	Garland		20—Seattle	L	3-5	Jones	Farmer
22—At Cleve.	L	5-8	Waits	Barrios		21—Seattle	W	9-5	Barrios	Decker
23—At K.C.	L	3-4	Splittorff	Wortham		22—Minn.	L	3-5	Zahn	Kravec
24—At K.C.	L	0-5	Leonard	LaGrow		23—Minn.	L	1-6	Goltz	Baumgarten
25—At K.C.	L	6-7	Hrabosky	Proly		24—Minn.	L	3-4	Bacsik	Wortham
27—Texas	W	11-0	Baumgarten	Alexander		24—Minn.	L	1-7	Koosman	Farmer
28—Texas	W	3-2	Barrios	Comer		26—At Sea.	L	2-3	McLaughlin	Trout
29—Texas	L	0-10	Ellis	Wortham		27—At Sea.	L	3-4	Rawley	Kravec
			Won 9, Lost 11			28—At Sea.	W	2-1	Baumgarten	Parrott
						29—At Minn.	L	2-5	Koosman	Wortham
MAY						30—At Minn.	L	4-16	Zahn	Farmer
1—Detroit	L	2-5	Baker	Kravec					**Won 9, Lost 19**	
4—At Texas	W	7-5	Barrios	Lyle						
4—At Texas	L	6-7	Farmer	LaGrow		**JULY**				
5—At Texas	W	7-6	Wortham	Ellis		1—At Minn.	L	1-2‡	Hartzell	Howard
6—At Texas	W	3-0	Kravec	Matlack		3—At Cleve.	L	3-7	Wise	Kravec
7—At Det.	L	4-5	Taylor	Trout		4—At Cleve.	W	16-4	Baumgarten	Waits
8—At Det.	L	8-10	Billingham	Scarbery		5—At Cleve.	W	5-4	Wortham	Cruz
9—At Det.	W	5-4	Baumgarten	Wilcox		6—At K.C.	W	4-1	Trout	Splittorff
10—Kan. C.	W	5-2	Trout	Splittorff		7—At K.C.	L	3-4	Busby	Hoffman
11—Kan. C.	W	5-3	Kravec	Busby		8—At K.C.	W	4-2	Barrios	Pattin
12—Kan. C.	W	4-5	Pattin	Hinton		9—Texas	W	5-4	Baumgarten	Jenkins
13—Kan. C.	L	5-14	Rodriguez	Wortham		10—Texas	W	6-3	Wortham	Kern
15—At Oak.	W	2-1	Baumgarten	Johnson		11—Texas	W	5-3	Trout	Darwin
16—At Oak.	W	3-1	Barrios	Keough		12—Detroit	L	1-4	Underwood	Howard
17—At Oak.	W	5-1	Kravec	Langford		12—Detroit	L	0-9z	......	......
18—At Calif.	L	3-7	Tanana	Schueler		13—Detroit	L	1-3	Petry	Kravec
19—At Calif.	L	6-10	Knapp	Wortham		14—Detroit	W	12-4	Baumgarten	Baker
20—At Calif.	L	0-4	Ryan	Baumgarten		15—Detroit	L	5-14	Morris	Wortham
22—Oakland	W	5-4	Hinton	Heaverlo		19—At Texas	W	9-6	Trout	Rajsich
23—Oakland	W	6-1	Kravec	Johnson		19—At Texas	W	5-4	Kravec	Jenkins
24—Oakland	W	10-1	Wortham	Keough		20—At Texas	W	2-1	Wortham	Johnson
25—Calif.	W	6-1	Baumgarten	Ryan		21—At Det.	L	2-4	Petry	Baumgarten
26—Calif.	L	4-8	Tanana	Howard		22—At Det.	L	0-1	Wilcox	Scarbery
27—Calif.	L	2-4	Frost	Barrios		23—At Det.	W	11-3	Trout	Baker
27—Calif.	L	1-9	Aase	Hinton		24—Kan. C.	L	6-11	Mingori	Hoffman
28—Cleve.	W	6-1	Kravec	Garland		25—Kan. C.	W	6-2	Wortham	Splittorff
29—Cleve.	W	4-2	Wortham	Wilkins		26—Kan. C.	L	1-6	Gura	Baumgarten
30—Cleve.	L	4-6	Waits	Baumgarten		27—Cleve.	L	2-7	Clyde	Scarbery
			Won 15, Lost 13			28—Cleve.	L	5-10	Paxton	Trout
						29—Cleve.	L	6-9	Wise	Kravec
JUNE						30—N. York	W	2-7	John	Wortham
1—At N.Y.	L	0-4	Guidry	Barrios		31—N. York	L	3-7	Guidry	Scarbery
2—At N.Y.	W	7-0	Kravec	Beattie					**Won 13, Lost 16**	
3—At N.Y.	L	2-3§	Davis	Scarbery						
4—Milw.	L	0-6	Caldwell	Baumgarten		**AUGUST**				
5—Milw.	L	3-5	Slaton	Howard		1—N. York	L	1-9	Hood	Kravec

AUGUST			Winner	Loser		SEPTEMBER			Winner	Loser
3–At Tor.	W	8-5	Trout	Moore		1–Milw.	W	4-3*	Wortham	Sorensen
4–At Tor.	L	2-5	Buskey	Wortham		2–Milw.	L	2-7	Haas	Kravec
5–At Tor.	W	5-4	Kravec	Lemanczyk		3–At Calif.	L	5-6	Ryan	Baumgarten
7–At N.Y.	W	9-5	Scarbery	Clay		4–At Calif.	W	10-7	Proly	Barr
8–At N.Y.	L	3-4	Tiant	Trout		5–At Calif.	L	8-9	Montague	Scarbery
9–At N.Y.	W	5-1	Wortham	Hunter		6–At Calif.	L	9-10	Montague	Farmer
11–Toronto	W	6-1	Kravec	Todd		7–At Oak.	L	3-4‡	Langford	Proly
11–Toronto	L	0-6	Stieb	Scarbery		8–At Oak.	L	1-2	McCatty	Proly
12–Toronto	W	7-0	Baumgarten	Underwood		9–At Oak.	L	0-3	Kingman	Trout
12–Toronto	L	5-7	Moore	Proly		9–At Oak.	W	7-0	Dotson	Norris
13–At Balt.	W	7-0	Trout	McGregor		11–Calif.	W	8-7	Farmer	Aase
14–At Balt.	L	1-2x	T. Martinez	Farmer		12–Calif.	W	11-5	Kravec	Knapp
15–At Balt.	L	1-2x	Flanagan	Hoffman		14–Oakland	L	3-8	Kingman	Farmer
16–At Bos.	L	5-7	Ripley	Proly		15–Oakland	W	3-0	Trout	Langford
17–At Bos.	W	4-1	Baumgarten	Stanley		16–Oakland	W	5-2	Dotson	Keough
18–At Bos.	L	2-8†	Renko	Trout		17–Minn.	L	3-10	Bacsik	Wortham
19–At Bos.	W	3-2	Wortham	Eckersley		18–Minn.	W	1-0‡	Kravec	Goltz
20–At Milw.	L	3-5	Travers	Kravec		19–Minn.	W	6-0	Baumgarten	Hartzell
21–At Milw.	L	2-3	Sorensen	Proly		21–At Sea.	W	7-4	Trout	Parrott
21–At Milw.	L	5-9	Mitchell	Howard		22–At Sea.	L	4-6	McLaughlin	Hoffman
22–At Milw.	W	4-3	Farmer	Haas		23–At Sea.	L	3-8	Honeycutt	Wortham
26–Balt.	L	7-12	Flanagan	Trout		25–At Minn.	W	9-3	Kravec	Zahn
26–Balt.	L	3-4y	Stanhouse	Farmer		26–At Minn.	L	6-5‡	Farmer	Marshall
27–Boston	L	3-4	Stanley	Kravec		27–At Minn.	W	4-2‡	Proly	Goltz
28–Boston	W	7-3	Baumgarten	Ripley		28–Seattle	W	3-1	Trout	Honeycutt
30–Milw.	L	3-4x	Augustine	Hoffman		29–Seattle	L	2-9	Bannister	Wortham
31–Milw.	W	6-1	Trout	Travers		30–Seattle	W	6-1	Kravec	Parrott
			Won 12, Lost 16						**Won 15, Lost 12**	

*5 innings.   †5½ innings.   ‡10 innings.   §11 innings.   x12 innings.   y13 innings.   zForfeit.

Mariners Produced First Farm Club Product

By HY ZIMMERMAN

Though the Mariners scored the most victories, 67, of their brief history, their 1979 season was marked more by individual excellence than collective class. Club records fell at the plate and on the mound.

Willie Horton, the 36-year-old designated hitter, established a new home run standard with 29 and an RBI mark of 106. He was selected the AL Comeback Player of the Year by THE SPORTING NEWS. Bruce Bochte's .316 batting average was the highest ever. He also drove in 100 runs. Horton and Bochte were the first two Mariners to reach the century mark in ribbies.

Righthander Mike Parrott had 14 victories and 13 complete games, both Seattle records. For the first time the Mariners had more than one pitcher with 10 wins. Rick Honeycutt recorded 11 victories and Floyd Bannister 10.

Despite that individual production, the M's were hard put to attain their 67-95 mark, only three more victories than in their first season. Early season blahs did them in. In April, they lost 11 straight games.

They snapped back with three straight triumphs over the Yankees in the Kingdome, truly a chamber of horrors for the Bronx Bunch. The Yankees have lost 13 of 17 under the roof.

The respite from defeat was brief. The club dropped 12 of its next 14 games. After that 5-23 stretch, the club impressed many observers, but the lapse precluded the fifth-place finish which had been the goal among the players in spring training.

The M's might have done a bit better than those 67 wins, but injuries to two key performers militated against it. The M's lost Shane Rawley, the precocious southpaw reliever, and Julio Cruz, the grasshopper second baseman—each with thumb injuries, each for two months.

But never mind the M's finish. The season saw the beginnings of a creditable pitching staff. With Parrott, Honeycutt, Bannister and Rob Dressler, who finished with a 3-2 record as a starter, the Mariners had the nucleus of a solid starting crew.

And the bullpen came alive, too. From the right side, Byron McLaughlin compiled a 7-7 record and led with 14 saves. Rawley, despite his enforced idleness, had 11 saves.

The Mariners' last month was marked by the appearance of their first farm product. Switch-hitting, tempermental outfielder Rodney Craig played 16 games and batted .385. He displayed speed and a fairly strong arm.

The M's 67 victories were an increase of 11 over the preceding season, which had been a total loss because of the drop in production by key players, among them Ruppert Jones and Danny Meyer. Both rebounded in 1979, with Jones slamming 21 homers and Meyer 20. Jones also stole 37 bases.

But Cruz remained the most larcenous Mariner. Despite missing 55 games, he swiped 49 bases, only 10 less than his 1978 total. The youngster hit better after his injury than before and finished with a respectable .271.

Despite all the individual attractions, however, the Mariners' attendance dropped for the second straight year. After drawing 1.3 million fans in their first campaign, the M's brought in 877,440 in 1978 and some 30,000 less in 1979.

SCORES OF SEATTLE MARINERS' 1979 GAMES

APRIL			Winner	Loser
4—Calif.	W	5-4	Montague	Tanana
6—Calif.	W	14-6	McLaughlin	Ryan
7—Calif.	L	4-5	Clear	Honeycutt
8—Calif.	L	5-7	LaRoche	Rawley
9—Oakland	W	5-2	Bannister	Johnson
10—Oakland	W	4-1	Abbott	Langford
11—Oakland	L	7-14	Todd	Honeycutt
12—Oakland	W	4-3	Montague	Lacey
13—Minn.	L	2-8	Zahn	Mitchell
14—Minn.	L	5-6	Marshall	Bannister
15—Minn.	L	6-18	Koosman	Abbott
16—At Oak.	L	2-4	Norris	Rawley
17—At Oak.	L	5-6	Heaverlo	Jones
18—At Oak.	L	2-5	Wirth	Honeycutt
21—At Minn.	L	5-6	Koosman	Bannister
22—At Minn.	L	1-3	Goltz	Abbott
24—Boston	L	3-4‡	Drago	Rawley
25—Boston	L	1-4	Wright	Bannister
26—Boston	L	0-2	Stanley	Mitchell
27—N. York	W	6-5	Parrott	Tidrow
28—N. York	W	3-2	Rawley	Hunter
29—N. York	W	6-5	Vasquez	Mirabella
30—Balt.	L	7-8*	Stanhouse	Honeycutt
			Won 8, Lost 15	

MAY				
1—Balt.	L	1-3	D. Martinez	McLaughlin
2—Balt.	L	3-9	Flanagan	Mitchell
4—At Bos.	L	3-5	Renko	Abbott
5—At Bos.	L	4-11	Eckersley	Jones
6—At Bos.	W	3-2	Montague	Campbell
7—At N.Y.	W	12-4	Honeycutt	Mirabella
8—At N.Y.	L	3-5	Beattie	Bannister
9—At N.Y.	L	0-5	Figueroa	Abbott
10—At N.Y.	L	1-8	John	Jones
11—At Balt.	L	3-8	Stone	McLaughlin
12—At Balt.	L	1-4	Flanagan	Honeycutt
14—Kan. C.	L	0-1	Gale	Bannister
15—Kan. C.	L	4-7	Splittorff	Abbott
15—Kan. C.	W	6-2	McLaughlin	Gura
16—Kan. C.	L	3-4	Busby	Jones
18—Texas	W	13-5	Montague	Comer

MAY				
19—Texas	W	4-0	Bannister	Jenkins
20—Texas	L	4-6	Alexander	Rawley
21—At K.C.	W	12-7	Abbott	Gale
22—At K.C.	W	12-11‡	Rawley	Hrabosky
24—At K.C.	L	4-5	Leonard	Jones
25—At Texas	W	3-2	Parrott	Alexander
25—At Texas	W	5-3	Honeycutt	Ellis
26—At Texas	L	1-2	Matlack	Abbott
27—At Texas	L	3-7	Comer	Mitchell
29—Calif.	L	4-6	Barr	Parrott
30—Calif.	L	2-3	Ryan	Rawley
31—Calif.	W	12-10	McLaughlin	Clear
			Won 10, Lost 18	

JUNE				
1—Toronto	W	7-2	Mitchell	Jefferson
2—Toronto	L	2-6	Lemanczyk	Jones
3—Toronto	W	10-5	Parrott	Lemongello
4—Detroit	W	11-2	Honeycutt	Wilcox
5—Detroit	L	1-3	Billingham	Abbott
6—Detroit	W	4-3	Bannister	Morris
8—Cleve.	W	6-2	Parrott	Garland
9—Cleve.	L	3-4*	Monge	Rawley
10—Cleve.	W	5-2	Jones	Waits
11—At Tor.	L	0-2	Lemanczyk	Bannister
12—At Tor.	W	5-1	Abbott	Jefferson
13—At Det.	L	3-7	Wilcox	Parrott
14—At Det.	W	3-2	Rawley	Hiller
15—At Cleve.	L	3-13	Waits	Jones
16—At Cleve.	L	3-4	Monge	Montague
17—At Cleve.	W	6-5	Rawley	Monge
18—At Chi.	W	5-1	Parrott	Baumgarten
19—At Chi.	W	7-2	Honeycutt	Wortham
20—At Chi.	W	5-3	Jones	Farmer
21—At Chi.	L	5-9	Barrios	Decker
22—Milw.	L	8-15	Slaton	Abbott
23—Milw.	W	8-3	Parrott	Sorensen
24—Milw.	L	4-7‡	Castro	Montague
26—Chicago	W	3-2	McLaughlin	Trout
27—Chicago	W	4-3	Rawley	Kravec
28—Chicago	L	1-2	Baumgarten	Parrott
29—At Milw.	W	3-2	Abbott	Sorensen
30—At Milw.	L	1-8	Haas	Montague
			Won 16, Lost 12	

SEATTLE MARINERS—1979

Front row—Valentine, B. Stein, Cox, Beamon, Mazeroski; coach; Pinson, coach; Johnson, manager; Bryant, coach; Stock, coach; Bannister, Meyer, Milbourne. Second row—Genzale, clubhouse manager; Nicholson, trainer; Decker, McLaughlin, Stinson, R. Jones, Horton, Rawley, Honeycutt, Mendoza, Szen, traveling secretary; Reuteman, clubhouse attendant. Third row—Hale, Simpson, Bochte, Roberts, Paciorek, Parrott, Abbott, R. Stein, O. Jones, Dressler, Montague. Seated in front—batboys Green and McGillis.

JULY			Winner	Loser
1—At Milw.	L	3-10	Slaton	Bannister
2—At Minn.	L	0-7	Jackson	Jones
3—At Minn.	L	2-12	Redfern	Parrott
3—At Minn.	W	10-2	McLaughlin	Serum
4—At Minn.	L	2-7	Koosman	Abbott
5—At Minn.	W	4-0	Honeycutt	Zahn
6—Boston	W	5-3	Bannister	Eckersley
7—Boston	L	8-10	Burgmeier	Parrott
8—Boston	L	2-8	Renko	McLaughlin
10—N. York	W	5-1	Honeycutt	Guidry
11—N. York	W	16-1	Bannister	John
12—N. York	L	2-14	Hunter	Parrott
13—Balt.	W	4-3	Jones	McGregor
14—Balt.	L	2-5	Flanagan	Parrott
15—Balt.	L	1-6	D. Martinez	Honeycutt
19—At Bos.	L	1-7	Eckersley	Bannister
20—At Bos.	W	8-0	Parrott	Torrez
21—At Bos.	W	13-5	Montague	Renko
22—At N.Y.	L	0-4	Kaat	Honeycutt
23—At N.Y.	L	2-6	Figueroa	Abbott
24—At Balt.	L	6-7	D. Martinez	Bannister
24—At Balt.	L	3-11	McGregor	Jones
25—At Balt.	W	5-4	Parrott	Stewart
26—At Balt.	L	1-12	Stone	Stein
27—At Oak.	W	1-0	Honeycutt	Langford
28—At Oak.	L	5-6	Hamilton	Jones
29—At Oak.	L	1-2	Morgan	Bannister
30—At Calif.	W	8-0	Parrott	Barr
31—At Calif.	L	1-8	Frost	Dressler
Won 11, Lost 18				

AUGUST			Winner	Loser
1—At Calif.	W	7-6	Stein	LaRoche
3—Oakland	W	1-0	Bannister	Keough
4—Oakland	L	3-5	Morgan	Parrott
5—Oakland	L	8-9	Kingman	Montague
6—Minn.	W	7-4	Honeycutt	Jackson
7—Minn.	L	2-5	Koosman	Hinton
8—Minn.	L	1-3	Goltz	Bannister
10—At Calif.	W	8-6§	Stein	LaRoche
11—At Calif.	L	1-8	Barr	Honeycutt
12—At Calif.	L	3-4	Frost	Stein
13—Cleve.	L	0-6	Wise	Bannister
14—Cleve.	L	4-7	Waits	Jones
15—Cleve.	W	3-2	Parrott	Monge

AUGUST			Winner	Loser
17—Detroit	L	2-9	Wilcox	Honeycutt
18—Detroit	L	4-7	Morris	Dressler
19—Detroit	W	8-4	Bannister	Robbins
20—Toronto	W	7-4	Parrott	Edge
21—Toronto	W	8-4	Montague	Huffman
22—Toronto	W	6-3	Honeycutt	Stieb
23—At Det.	L	2-5	Morris	Bannister
25—At Det.	W	8-4	Parrott	Petry
26—At Det.	L	3-4*	Lopez	McLaughlin
26—At Det.	L	8-9	Tobik	Stein
27—At Cleve.	W	6-5‡	McLaughlin	Cruz
29—At Cleve.	L	4-5	Monge	Rawley
29—At Cleve.	L	1-2	Waits	Twitchell
30—At Tor.	W	8-2	Parrott	Moore
31—At Tor.	L	4-5†	Buskey	McLaughlin
Won 12, Lost 16				

SEPTEMBER			Winner	Loser
1—At Tor.	W	3-2*	Honeycutt	Buskey
2—At Tor.	L	5-8	Stieb	Twitchell
3—Texas	L	1-4	Medich	Bannister
4—Texas	L	2-5	Comer	Parrott
5—Texas	W	1-0	Dressler	Jenkins
7—Kan. C.	L	2-6	Chamberlain	Honeycutt
8—Kan. C.	W	4-2	Bannister	Leonard
9—Kan. C.	L	1-5	Gura	Parrott
10—At Texas	W	5-2	Dressler	Jenkins
11—At Texas	L	2-5	Alexander	Branch
12—At Texas	L	3-13	Medich	Honeycutt
14—At K.C.	W	7-5	Bannister	Gura
15—At K.C.	L	4-5†	Hrabosky	McLaughlin
16—At K.C.	W	6-3	Dressler	Splittorff
17—Milw.	L	6-7	Travers	Hinton
18—Milw	L	6-7	Augustine	Rawley
19—Milw.	L	1-12	Sorensen	Bannister
21—Chicago	L	4-7	Trout	Parrott
22—Chicago	W	6-4	McLaughlin	Hoffman
23—Chicago	W	8-3	Honeycutt	Wortham
25—At Milw.	L	6-7	Augustine	Rawley
26—At Milw.	W	8-1	Parrott	Haas
27—At Milw.	L	6-7†	Travers	McLaughlin
28—At Chi.	L	1-3	Trout	Honeycutt
29—At Chi.	W	9-2	Bannister	Wortham
30—At Chi.	L	1-6	Kravec	Parrott
Won 10, Lost 16				

*10 innings.   †11 innings.   ‡12 innings.   §14 innings.

A's Got Worse—Attendance Reached Bottom

By TOM WEIR

For the Oakland A's, 1979 was a year when they accomplished the seemingly impossible.

Things actually got worse.

The team finished with the league's worst batting and fielding averages, and had the worst home gate in the major leagues, drawing just 306,763 fans.

The problems of Matt Keough symbolized Oakland's 54-108 cellar year. The second-year pitcher, an All-Star in 1978, tied a 73-year-old major league record by losing his first 14 decisions. Coupled with four season-ending losses in '78, Keough dropped 18 consecutive games.

Rick Langford's 10 consecutive complete games broke the team record set by Vida Blue during Blue's Cy Young season of 1971, yet Langford still couldn't register a .500 record. The righthander finished 12-16 but still was the brightest spot on the pitching staff.

OAKLAND A's—1979

Front row—Picciolo, Langford, Stange, coach; Walls, coach; Marshall, manager; Saul, coach; Mitterwald, coach; Norris, Keough. Second row—Hofman, traveling secretary; Chalk, Hamilton, Essian, Revering, Gross, McCatty, Todd, Lacey, Cienczyk, equipment manager; Romo, trainer. Third row—Murray, Murphy, Morgan, Armas, Heaverlo, Page, Wallis, Newman, Bryant, Minetto. Seated in front—Henderson, Guerrero, Edwards, Heath. Missing from picture—Kingman.

Oakland did take some solace in not finishing with the worst winning percentage in all of baseball, but then they only missed that by one game.

The person in charge of this disaster chose not to come and view the rubble. A's Owner Charlie Finley did not attend a single game, even when the A's came to his home town of Chicago.

Had Finley visited his club occasionally, he would have witnessed some strange lineups that were not the fault of Manager Jim Marshall. With virtually no bench because of a steady string of injuries, Marshall often had three catchers on the field. Jeff Newman, Jim Essian and Mike Heath all took regular turns at third base.

The year also was marked by Glenn Burke's walkout and a near brawl between Marshall and Miguel Dilone.

The outfielder's exit never was explained. He simply left the A's chaos behind and refused to talk about it.

Dilone was enraged enough to go after Marshall with a bat simply because the skipper had instituted a rule about all players having to be on the bench during games. Exit another outfielder, this time via sale to the Chicago Cubs.

But even amid the madness that always is part of the A's, there were a few sparkling performances.

Langford and Mike Norris both tossed one-hitters. Then again, Oakland itself was one-hit three times, with two no-hit bids being broken up by rookie Rickey Henderson.

Dave Revering had a sluggish first half because of a separated shoulder that he played with for a month before sitting down to rest. When he healed, Revering managed 14 home runs after the All-Star break and finished as the team leader in RBIs (77) and average (.288).

Newman's 22 home runs more than doubled his previous one-year high. Henderson didn't break in until June, yet still finished with 33 stolen bases.

Dwayne Murphy, Henderson's predecessor in center field, was leading the league in walks when he was sidelined in June for a month with an injury.

If nothing else, this will be remembered as the quietest A's season ever, as far as Finley was concerned. There were only a few of the traditional calls to the manager's office, and practically no trades.

Finley's only trade during the season was to send pitcher John Henry Johnson to the Texas Rangers in exchange for Heath, Dave Chalk and $400,000.

Biggest disappointment for the A's was Mitchell Page, a .307 hitter as a rookie in 1977 who slumped to .285 in '78 and just .247 in '79.

Page was bothered by a sore shoulder that required cortisone shots, but he seemed more troubled by his role as designated hitter. He finished the season by vowing not to work as the DH again.

Still, the A's showed they might gain respectability again because of their promising young pitchers. Besides the 27-year-old Langford, there were Steve McCatty and Brian Kingman.

The 25-year-old Kingman was the club's only .500 pitcher, finishing with an 8-7 mark. McCatty, also 25, was 11-12.

Most of Kingman's and McCatty's wins came during the second half, when Oakland shocked a few people by playing .500 ball for more than a month. There was a bitter end, though, when Revering concluded the season by ripping his teammates, saying only four or five qualified as regular major leaguers.

No one was happy with that statement, but no one could argue too much with it, either.

SCORES OF OAKLAND ATHLETICS' 1979 GAMES

APRIL			Winner	Loser
6—Minn.	L	3-5	Goltz	Langford
7—Minn.	L	1-3‡	Marshall	Todd
8—Minn.	L	1-3	Zahn	Norris
9—At Sea.	L	2-5	Bannister	Johnson
10—At Sea.	L	1-4	Abbott	Langford
11—At Sea.	W	14-7	Todd	Honeycutt
12—At Sea.	L	3-4	Montague	Lacey
13—Calif.	L	1-10	Aase	Johnson
14—Calif.	L	3-9	Frost	Langford
15—Calif.	L	1-8	Tanana	Keough
16—Seattle	W	4-2	Norris	Rawley
17—Seattle	W	6-5	Heaverlo	Jones
18—Seattle	W	5-2	Wirth	Honeycutt
20—At Calif.	L	4-7	Tanana	Langford
21—At Calif.	L	1-13	Ryan	Keough
22—At Calif.	W	7-6	Heaverlo	LaRoche
24—N. York	L	1-3	John	Johnson
25—N. York	L	1-0	Minetto	Figueroa
27—Balt.	L	1-7	Flanagan	Keough
28—Balt.	W	8-5	Todd	McGregor
29—Balt.	L	1-13	T. Martinez	Johnson
30—Boston	W	5-4†	Lacey	Drago
			Won 8, Lost 14	

MAY				
1—Boston	W	7-5	McCatty	Stanley
2—Boston	L	1-2	Torrez	Keough
4—At N.Y.	W	11-5	Norris	Beattie
5—At N.Y.	L	4-5	John	Heaverlo
6—At N.Y.	L	5-6*	Guidry	Heaverlo
7—At Balt.	W	5-3	Langford	T. Martinez
8—At Balt.	L	2-8	Flanagan	Todd
9—At Balt.	W	4-2	Norris	Palmer
10—At Balt.	L	1-3	D. Martinez	Johnson
11—At Bos.	L	2-11	Stanley	Keough
12—At Bos.	L	2-8	Torrez	Langford
13—At Bos.	L	2-8	Rainey	Norris
15—Chicago	L	1-2	Baumgarten	Johnson
16—Chicago	L	1-3	Barrios	Keough
17—Chicago	L	1-5	Kravec	Langford
18—Milw.	L	0-8	Travers	Norris
19—Milw.	W	12-4	Johnson	Haas
20—Milw.	W	7-6	Hamilton	Augustine
20—Milw.	W	2-1	McCatty	Slaton
22—At Chi.	L	4-5	Hinton	Heaverlo
23—At Chi.	L	1-6	Kravec	Johnson
24—At Chi.	L	1-10	Wortham	Keough
25—At Milw.	L	2-3	Caldwell	Lacey
26—At Milw.	L	4-8	Slaton	Langford
27—At Milw.	W	2-1	McCatty	Sorensen
28—At Minn.	L	7-10	Marshall	Heaverlo
30—At Minn.	W	5-4	Johnson	Erickson
31—At Minn.	L	2-13	Hartzell	Langford
			Won 9, Lost 19	

JUNE				
1—Detroit	W	3-2	McCatty	Hiller
2—Detroit	L	3-9	Morris	Minetto
3—Detroit	L	0-2	Rozema	Johnson
4—Cleve.	L	4-5§	Monge	Lacey
5—Cleve.	L	3-12	Waits	Langford
6—Cleve.	L	4-6	Wise	Heaverlo
8—Toronto	L	1-2	Buskey	Heaverlo
9—Toronto	L	0-5	Huffman	Keough
10—Toronto	W	12-1	Hamilton	Underwood
11—At Det.	L	1-3	Morris	McCatty

JUNE			Winner	Loser
12—At Det.	L	2-9	Underwood	Minetto
13—At Cleve.	L	4-6	Garland	Lacey
14—At Cleve.	L	1-2	Monge	Todd
15—At Tor.	L	0-6	Underwood	Hamilton
16—At Tor.	L	2-3	Lemanczyk	McCatty
17—At Tor.	L	9-10	Buskey	Heaverlo
18—Kan. C.	L	2-3	Gura	Norris
19—Kan. C.	W	6-5	Heaverlo	Hrabosky
20—Kan. C.	L	2-9	Splittorff	Hamilton
21—Kan. C.	W	10-7	McCatty	Busby
22—Texas	W	6-5	Langford	Comer
23—Texas	L	5-8*	Kern	Lacey
24—Texas	L	1-5	Johnson	Keough
24—Texas	L	2-7	Medich	Hamilton
26—At K.C.	L	6-7*	Hrabosky	Todd
27—At K.C.	L	3-10	Busby	Morgan
28—At K.C.	L	6-7	Hrabosky	Heaverlo
29—At Texas	L	3-5	Darwin	Keough
30—At Texas	L	2-7	Kern	Todd
			Won 5, Lost 24	

JULY				
1—At Texas	W	13-12x	Langford	Medich
2—At Calif.	L	3-8	Barr	Morgan
3—At Calif.	L	0-3	Frost	Kingman
4—At Calif.	L	6-17	Clear	Heaverlo
5—At Calif.	W	3-0	Langford	Ryan
6—N. York	L	3-4	Davis	McCatty
6—N. York	L	0-3	John	Hamilton
7—N. York	L	3-8	Hood	Morgan
8—N. York	L	0-2	Tiant	Kingman
9—Balt.	L	3-7	Flanagan	Keough
10—Balt.	W	7-6	Langford	Stewart
11—Balt.	L	1-3	D. Martinez	McCatty
13—Boston	L	0-2	Renko	Morgan
14—Boston	L	7-8	Ripley	McCatty
15—Boston	L	2-3	Stanley	Langford
19—At N.Y.	L	2-10	Tiant	Morgan
20—At N.Y.	W	5-1	Kingman	John
21—At N.Y.	L	4-12	Guidry	Minetto
22—At Balt.	L	1-4	Stone	Langford
23—At Balt.	L	4-7	T. Martinez	Keough
24—At Bos.	L	3-7	Eckersley	Morgan
25—At Bos.	L	4-16	Torrez	Kingman
26—At Bos.	W	8-6	McCatty	Renko
27—Seattle	L	0-1	Honeycutt	Langford
28—Seattle	W	6-5	Hamilton	Jones
29—Seattle	W	2-1	Morgan	Bannister
30—Minn.	L	0-3	Goltz	Kingman
31—Minn.	W	2-1	McCatty	Zahn
			Won 8, Lost 20	

AUGUST				
1—Minn.	W	7-1	Langford	Hartzell
3—At Sea.	L	0-1	Bannister	Keough
4—At Sea.	W	5-3	Morgan	Parrott
5—At Sea.	W	9-8	Kingman	Montague
6—Calif.	L	2-5	Botting	McCatty
7—Calif.	W	9-5	Langford	Barr
8—Calif.	L	1-8	Frost	Keough
10—At Minn.	W	6-5†	Heaverlo	Marshall
10—At Minn.	L	2-3‡	Jackson	Heaverlo
11—At Minn.	L	7-9	Bacsik	McCatty
12—At Minn.	L	0-1	Koosman	Langford
13—Toronto	L	2-4	Edge	Norris
14—Toronto	L	2-6	Huffman	Minetto

AUGUST			Winner	Loser
15—Toronto	W	3-1	Kingman	Jefferson
17—Cleve.	W	5-3	McCatty	Spillner
18—Cleve.	W	4-1	Langford	Wise
19—Cleve.	W	3-2	Norris	Waits
20—Detroit	L	3-7	Petry	Heaverlo
21—Detroit	W	8-1	Kingman	Chris
22—Detroit	L	1-3	Wilcox	McCatty
23—At Cleve.	W	8-6	Langford	Monge
24—At Cleve.	L	2-5	Waits	Norris
25—At Cleve.	L	3-5	Barker	Morgan
26—At Cleve.	L	5-7	Garland	Kingman
27—At Tor.	L	0-7	Huffman	McCatty
28—At Tor.	W	6-3	Langford	Stieb
29—At Tor.	W	6-4	Norris	Underwood
30—At Det.	L	7-8	Tobik	Minetto
31—At Det.	W	5-3	Kingman	Tobik
			Won 14, Lost 15	

SEPTEMBER				
1—At Det.	W	6-3*	McCatty	Lopez
2—At Det.	W	5-4	Langford	Robbins
3—Milw.	L	3-6	Slaton	Norris
5—Milw.	W	6-1	Keough	Caldwell

SEPTEMBER			Winner	Loser
7—Chicago	W	4-3*	Langford	Proly
8—Chicago	W	2-1	McCatty	Proly
9—Chicago	W	3-0	Kingman	Trout
9—Chicago	L	0-7	Dotson	Norris
11—At Milw.	L	0-5	Slaton	Keough
12—At Milw.	L	0-7	Caldwell	Morgan
13—At Milw.	W	8-3	McCatty	Travers
14—At Chi.	W	8-3	Kingman	Farmer
15—At Chi.	L	0-3	Trout	Langford
16—At Chi.	L	2-5	Dotson	Keough
17—Texas	L	3-6	Comer	Morgan
18—Texas	L	5-9	Jenkins	McCatty
19—Texas	L	4-9	Alexander	Kingman
21—Kan. C.	L	4-13	Splittorff	Langford
22—Kan. C.	W	2-0	Keough	Leonard
23—Kan. C.	L	2-4	Pattin	McCatty
25—At Texas	L	3-5	Kern	Kingman
26—At Texas	L	2-5	Comer	Langford
27—At Texas	L	3-4	McCall	Keough
28—At K.C.	L	1-13	Gura	McCatty
29—At K.C.	L	2-6	Splittorff	Morgan
30—At K.C.	W	6-5	Kingman	Leonard
			Won 10, Lost 16	

*10 innings.   †11 innings.   ‡12 innings.   §14 innings.   x15 innings.

GEORGE BRETT
• ROYALS •
HITS (212)
TRIPLES (20)

FRED LYNN
• RED SOX •
BATTING CHAMPION (.333)
SLUGGING PCT. (.637)

DON BAYLOR
• ANGELS •
RUNS (120)
RUNS BATTED IN (139)

1979 AMERICAN LEAGUE LEADERS

RON GUIDRY
• YANKEES •
ERA (2.78)

NOLAN RYAN
• ANGELS •
STRIKEOUTS (223)

MIKE FLANAGAN
• ORIOLES •
WINS (23)

American League Averages for 1979

CHAMPIONSHIP WINNERS IN PREVIOUS YEARS

1900—Chicago* .607	1927—New York .714	1954—Cleveland .721
1901—Chicago .610	1928—New York .656	1955—New York .623
1902—Philadelphia .610	1929—Philadelphia .693	1956—New York .630
1903—Boston .659	1930—Philadelphia .662	1957—New York .636
1904—Boston .617	1931—Philadelphia .704	1958—New York .597
1905—Philadelphia .622	1932—New York .695	1959—Chicago .610
1906—Chicago .616	1933—Washington .651	1960—New York .630
1907—Detroit .613	1934—Detroit .656	1961—New York .673
1908—Detroit .588	1935—Detroit .616	1962—New York .593
1909—Detroit .645	1936—New York .667	1963—New York .646
1910—Philadelphia .680	1937—New York .662	1964—New York .611
1911—Philadelphia .669	1938—New York .651	1965—Minnesota .630
1912—Boston .691	1939—New York .702	1966—Baltimore .606
1913—Philadelphia .627	1940—Detroit .584	1967—Boston .568
1914—Philadelphia .651	1941—New York .656	1968—Detroit .636
1915—Boston .669	1942—New York .669	1969—Baltimore (East)‡ .673
1916—Boston .591	1943—New York .636	1970—Baltimore (East)‡ .667
1917—Chicago .649	1944—St. Louis .578	1971—Baltimore (East)§ .639
1918—Boston .595	1945—Detroit .575	1972—Oakland (West)a .600
1919—Chicago .629	1946—Boston .675	1973—Oakland (West)b .580
1920—Cleveland .636	1947—New York .630	1974—Oakland (West)b .556
1921—New York .641	1948—Cleveland† .626	1975—Boston (East)c .594
1922—New York .610	1949—New York .630	1976—New York (East)d .610
1923—New York .645	1950—New York .636	1977—New York (East)d .617
1924—Washington .597	1951—New York .636	1978—New York (East)d .613
1925—Washington .636	1952—New York .617	
1926—New York .591	1953—New York .656	

*Not recognized as major league in 1900. †Defeated Boston in one-game playoff for pennant. ‡Defeated Minnesota (West) in Championship Series. §Defeated Oakland (West) in Championship Series. aDefeated Detroit (East) in Championship Series. bDefeated Baltimore (East) in Championship Series. cDefeated Oakland (West) in Championship Series. dDefeated Kansas City (West) in Championship Series.

STANDING OF CLUBS AT CLOSE OF SEASON

EAST DIVISION

Club	Balt.	Mil.	Bos.	N.Y.	Det.	Clev.	Tor.	Cal.	Chi.	K.C.	Min.	Oak.	Sea.	Tex.	W.	L.	Pct.	G.B.
Baltimore	..	8	8	5	7	8	11	9	8	6	8	8	10	6	102	57	.642	....
Milwaukee	5	..	4	9	7	9	10	5	7	7	8	6	9	9	95	66	.590	8
Boston	5	8	..	5	8	6	9	5	5	8	9	9	8	6	91	69	.569	11½
New York	6	4	8	..	6	8	9	5	8	7	5	9	6	8	89	71	.556	13½
Detroit	6	6	5	7	..	6	9	8	9	5	4	7	7	6	85	76	.528	18
Cleveland	5	4	7	5	6	..	8	6	6	6	8	8	7	5	81	80	.503	22
Toronto	2	3	4	4	4	5	..	5	5	5	3	1	8	4	53	109	.327	50½

WEST DIVISION

Club	Cal.	K.C.	Tex.	Min.	Chi.	Sea.	Oak.	Balt.	Bos.	Clev.	Det.	Mil.	N.Y.	Tor.	W.	L.	Pct.	G.B.
California	..	7	5	9	9	7	10	5	7	6	4	7	7	7	88	74	.543	....
Kansas City	6	..	6	7	8	7	9	6	4	6	7	5	5	9	85	77	.525	3
Texas	8	7	..	9	2	7	11	6	6	7	6	3	4	7	83	79	.512	5
Minnesota	4	6	4	..	8	10	9	4	3	4	8	4	7	11	82	80	.506	6
Chicago	4	5	11	5	..	5	9	3	6	6	3	5	4	7	73	87	.456	14
Seattle	6	6	6	3	8	..	5	2	4	5	5	3	6	8	67	95	.414	21
Oakland	3	4	2	4	4	8	..	4	3	4	3	5	6	8	54	108	.333	34

Forfeited Game—Chicago forfeited second game of doubleheader to Detroit at Chicago, July 12.

Cancelled Games—New York at Baltimore (2); Milwaukee at Boston; Baltimore at Chicago; Boston at Chicago; Cleveland at Detroit.

Championship Series—Baltimore defeated California, three games to one.

RECORD AT HOME

EAST DIVISION

Club	Balt.	Mil.	Bos.	N.Y.	Clev.	Det.	Tor.	Cal.	K.C.	Tex.	Minn.	Sea.	Chi.	Oak.	W.	L.	Pct.
Baltimore..	.....	5-2	4-2	2-2	4-3	4-2	7-0	5-1	3-3	5-1	3-3	5-1	4-2	4-2	55	24	.696
Milwaukee.	3-3	.....	2-5	5-2	4-2	4-3	5-1	5-1	5-1	4-2	4-2	4-2	3-3	4-2	52	29	.642
Boston	3-4	3-2	.....	2-4	4-3	5-2	5-1	3-3	6-0	3-3	6-0	3-3	3-3	5-1	51	29	.638
New York..	4-3	2-4	4-3	.....	6-0	3-3	5-2	4-2	3-3	5-1	3-3	5-1	3-3	4-2	51	30	.630
Cleveland .	2-4	2-5	4-2	5-2	.....	4-2	6-1	2-4	4-2	3-3	4-2	4-2	2-4	5-1	47	34	.580
Detroit	4-3	3-3	3-3	4-3	4-2	.....	3-3	4-2	4-2	4-2	2-4	4-2	4-2	3-3	46	34	.575
Toronto	2-4	2-5	3-4	2-4	4-2	1-6	.....	3-3	3-3	3-3	1-5	3-3	1-5	4-2	32	49	.395

WEST DIVISION

Club	Cal.	K.C.	Tex.	Minn.	Sea.	Chi.	Oak.	Balt.	Mil.	Bos.	N.Y.	Clev.	Det.	Tor.	W.	L.	Pct.
California..	.....	2-4	4-3	4-2	3-3	6-1	5-2	2-4	6-0	4-2	5-1	2-4	2-4	4-2	49	32	.605
Kan. City ..	2-5	.....	2-5	3-4	2-4	4-2	5-1	3-3	4-2	4-2	2-4	4-2	5-1	6-0	46	35	.568
Texas	5-1	2-4	.....	3-4	4-3	1-6	5-1	5-1	1-5	3-3	3-3	4-2	4-2	4-2	44	37	.543
Minnesota .	2-5	2-4	0-6	.....	5-2	3-3	5-2	1-5	2-4	3-3	4-2	4-2	6-0		39	42	.481
Seattle	3-4	2-5	3-3	1-5	.....	4-2	4-3	1-5	1-5	1-5	1-5	3-3	3-3	5-1	36	45	.444
Chicago	3-3	3-4	5-1	2-5	3-4	.....	5-1	1-4	2-4	3-2	1-5	1-5	3-3	2-4	33	46	.418
Oakland	1-5	3-4	1-6	2-4	5-1	3-4	.....	2-4	4-2	2-4	1-5	3-3	2-4	2-4	31	50	.383

RECORD ABROAD

EAST DIVISION

Club	Balt.	Mil.	Bos.	Det.	N.Y.	Clev.	Tor.	Minn.	Chi.	Cal.	K.C.	Tex.	Sea.	Oak.	W.	L.	Pct.
Baltimore..	.....	3-3	4-3	3-4	3-4	4-2	4-2	5-1	4-1	4-2	3-3	1-5	5-1	4-2	47	33	.588
Milwaukee.	2-5	.....	2-3	3-3	4-2	5-2	5-2	4-2	0-6	2-4	2-4	3-3	5-1	2-4	43	37	.538
Boston	2-4	5-2	.....	3-3	2-4	2-4	4-3	3-3	2-3	2-4	2-4	3-3	5-1	4-2	40	40	.500
Detroit	2-4	3-4	2-5	.....	3-3	2-4	6-1	2-4	5-1	4-2	1-5	2-4	3-3	4-2	39	42	.481
New York..	2-2	2-5	4-2	3-4	.....	2-4	2-5	4-2	2-4	5-1	1-5	4-2	3-3	5-1	38	41	.481
Cleveland .	3-4	2-4	3-4	2-4	0-6	.....	2-4	4-2	4-2	4-2	2-4	2-4	3-3	3-3	34	46	.425
Toronto	0-7	1-5	1-5	3-3	2-5	1-6	.....	0-6	4-2	2-4	2-4	0-6	2-4	1-5	21	60	.259

WEST DIVISION

Club	Minn.	Chi.	Cal.	K.C.	Tex.	Sea.	Oak.	Balt.	Mil.	Bos.	Det.	N.Y.	Clev.	Tor.	W.	L.	Pct.
Minnesota.	.....	5-2	2-4	4-3	4-3	5-1	4-2	3-3	2-4	0-6	4-2	3-3	2-4	5-1	43	38	.531
Chicago	3-3	.....	1-6	2-4	6-1	2-4	4-3	2-4	3-3	3-3	2-4	4-2	3-3	3-3	40	41	.494
California..	5-2	3-3	.....	5-2	1-5	4-3	5-1	1-5	1-5	3-3	2-4	3-3	2-4	3-3	39	42	.481
Kan. City..	2-4	4-3	4-2	.....	4-2	5-2	4-3	3-3	5-1	0-6	2-4	3-3	2-4	3-3	39	42	.481
Texas	6-0	1-5	3-4	5-2	.....	3-3	6-1	1-5	2-4	3-3	2-4	1-5	2-4	3-3	39	42	.481
Seattle	2-5	4-3	3-3	4-2	3-4	.....	1-5	1-5	2-4	3-3	2-4	1-5	2-4	1-5	31	50	.383
Oakland	2-5	1-5	2-5	1-5	1-5	3-4	.....	2-4	2-4	1-5	3-3	2-4	1-5	2-4	23	58	.284

SHUTOUT GAMES

Club	Mil.	Balt.	Det.	Clev.	K.C.	N.Y.	Tex.	Bos.	Cal.	Chi.	Sea.	Minn.	Tor.	Oak.	W.	L.	Pct.
Milwaukee..	..	0	0	2	0	1	0	1	1	1	0	0	3	3	12	1	.923
Baltimore..	0	..	0	0	2	1	2	0	2	1	0	1	3	0	12	5	.706
Detroit	0	1	..	0	0	1	0	0	1	0	0	1	1	0	5	3	.625
Cleveland ..	0	0	1	..	0	1	0	2	0	0	1	1	1	0	7	6	.538
Kan. City ..	0	0	0	0	..	0	0	1	1	1	2	1	0	1	7	6	.538
New York..	0	1	0	1	0	..	0	2	1	1	1	0	2	1	10	9	.526
Texas	0	2	0	2	0	1	..	1	1	0	1	1	1	0	10	9	.526
Boston	0	0	0	0	3	1	1	..	1	0	1	2	1	1	11	10	.524
California ..	0	0	0	0	0	1	1	2	..	1	0	2	1	1	9	9	.500
Chicago	0	1	0	0	0	1	2	0	0	..	0	0	2	1	7	7	.500
Seattle	0	0	0	0	0	0	2	1	1	0	..	1	0	1	6	10	.375
Minnesota .	1	0	1	1	0	0	0	0	0	0	1	..	0	3	7	15	.318
Toronto	0	0	1	0	0	0	1	0	0	1	1	0	..	3	7	15	.318
Oakland	0	0	0	0	1	1	0	0	1	1	0	0	0	..	4	17	.190

OFFICIAL AMERICAN LEAGUE BATTING AVERAGES

Compiled by Sports Information Center, No. Quincy, Mass.

CLUB BATTING

Club	Pct.	G.	AB.	R.	OR.	H.	TB.	2B.	3B.	HR.	RBI.	SH.	SF.	SB.	CS.	LOB.
Boston ..	.283	160	5538	841	711	1567	2527	310	34	194	805	42	59	60	43	1087
Kan. C ..	.282	162	5653	851	816	1596	2388	286	79	116	791	57	76	207	76	1168
Calif	.282	162	5550	866	768	1563	2383	242	43	164	808	79	56	100	53	1154
Milw	.280	161	5536	807	722	1552	2480	291	41	185	766	72	50	100	53	1142
Minn	.278	162	5544	764	725	1544	2228	256	46	112	714	142	53	66	45	1201
Texas	.278	162	5562	750	698	1549	2273	252	26	140	718	78	59	75	51	1136
Chicago..	.275	159	5463	730	748	1505	2242	290	33	127	680	58	45	97	62	1085
Detroit ..	.269	160	5375	770	738	1446	2229	221	35	164	729	56	52	176	86	1057
Seattle ..	.269	162	5544	711	820	1490	2240	250	52	132	676	61	54	126	52	1145
N. York .	.266	160	5421	734	672	1443	2199	226	40	150	694	50	63	65	46	1063
Balt	.261	159	5371	757	582	1401	2250	258	24	181	717	42	54	99	49	1099
Cleve	.258	161	5376	760	805	1388	2066	206	29	138	707	70	60	143	90	1149
Toronto .	.251	162	5423	613	862	1362	1968	253	34	95	562	65	38	75	56	1064
Oakland .	.239	162	5348	573	860	1276	1852	188	32	108	541	75	46	104	69	1030
Totals	.270	1127	76704	10527	10527	20682	31325	3529	548	2006	9908	947	765	1497	831	15580

INDIVIDUAL BATTING

(Top Fifteen Qualifiers for Batting Championship—502 or More Plate Appearances)

*Bats lefthanded.   †Switch-hitter.

Player and Club	Pct.	G.	AB.	R.	H.	TB.	2B.	3B.	HR.	RBI.	SH.	SF.	SB.	CS.
Lynn, Fredric, Boston*	.333	147	531	116	177	338	42	1	39	122	0	5	2	2
Brett, George, Kansas City*	.329	154	645	119	212	363	42	20	23	107	1	4	17	10
Downing, Brian, California	.326	148	509	87	166	235	27	3	12	75	3	2	3	3
Rice, James, Boston	.325	158	619	117	201	369	39	6	39	130	0	8	9	4
Oliver, Albert, Texas*	.323	136	492	69	159	231	28	4	12	76	1	7	4	5
Molitor, Paul, Milwaukee	.322	140	584	88	188	274	27	16	9	62	6	5	33	13
Lezcano, Sixto, Milwaukee	.321	138	473	84	152	271	29	3	28	101	6	7	4	3
Kemp, Steven, Detroit*	.318	134	490	88	156	266	26	3	26	105	2	8	5	6
Lemon, Chester, Chicago	.318	148	556	79	177	276	44	2	17	86	3	4	7	11
Bochte, Bruce, Seattle*	.316	150	554	81	175	273	38	6	16	100	3	10	2	2
Wilson, Willie, Kansas City†	.315	154	588	113	185	247	18	13	6	49	13	4	83	12
Johnson, Lamar, Chicago	.309	133	479	60	148	215	29	1	12	74	0	4	8	2
Cooper, Cecil, Milwaukee*	.308	150	590	83	182	300	44	1	24	106	6	8	15	3
Landreaux, Kenneth, Minnesota*	.305	151	564	81	172	254	27	5	15	83	10	8	10	3
LeFlore, Ronald, Detroit	.300	148	600	110	180	249	22	10	9	57	0	2	78	14

DEPARTMENTAL LEADERS: G—Baylor, B. Bell, Bosetti, Horton, R. Jones, Smalley, 162; AB—B. Bell, 670; R—Baylor, 120; H—Brett, 212; TB—Rice, 369; 2B—Cooper, Lemon, 44; 3B—Brett, 20; HR—Thomas, 45; RBI—Baylor, 139; SH—Wilfong, 25; SF—Ford, Porter, 13; SB—Wilson, 83; CS—Bonds, 23.

(All Players—Listed Alphabetically)

Player and Club	Pct.	G.	AB.	R.	H.	TB.	2B.	3B.	HR.	RBI.	SH.	SF.	SB.	CS.
Adams, Glenn, Minnesota*	.301	119	326	34	98	137	13	1	8	50	1	6	2	2
Aikens, Willie, California*	.280	116	379	59	106	187	18	0	21	81	0	6	1	3
Ainge, Daniel, Toronto	.237	87	308	26	73	88	7	1	2	19	7	2	1	0
Alexander, Gary, Cleveland	.229	110	358	54	82	140	9	2	15	54	3	7	4	2
Allenson, Gary, Boston	.203	108	241	27	49	72	10	2	3	22	6	3	1	1
Alston, Wendell, Cleveland*	.290	54	62	10	18	25	0	2	1	12	1	1	4	4
Anderson, James, California	.248	96	234	33	58	82	13	1	3	23	9	3	3	2
Armas, Antonio, Oakland	.248	80	278	29	69	117	9	3	11	34	0	2	1	0
Ayala, Benigno, Baltimore	.256	42	86	15	22	45	5	0	6	13	0	2	0	0
Bailor, Robert, Toronto	.229	130	414	50	95	119	11	5	1	38	4	5	14	8
Bando, Salvatore, Milwaukee	.246	130	476	57	117	164	14	3	9	43	6	1	2	0
Bannister, Alan, Chicago	.285	136	506	71	144	194	28	8	2	55	4	4	22	6
Barranca, German, Kansas City*	.600	5	5	3	3	4	1	0	0	0	0	0	3	1
Baylor, Donald, California	.296	162	628	120	186	333	33	3	36	139	0	3	22	12
Beamon, Charles, Seattle*	.200	27	25	5	5	6	1	0	0	0	0	0	1	0
Belanger, Mark, Baltimore	.167	101	198	28	33	43	6	2	0	9	11	3	5	1
Bell, David, Texas	.299	162	670	89	200	302	42	3	18	101	7	10	5	4
Bell, Kevin, Texas	.245	70	200	20	49	71	8	1	4	22	3	1	2	4
Beniquez, Juan, New York	.254	62	142	19	36	56	6	1	4	17	1	4	3	3
Bernhardt, Juan, Seattle	1.000	1	1	0	1	1	0	0	0	0	0	0	0	0
Blair, Paul, New York	.200	2	5	0	1	1	0	0	0	0	0	0	0	0

Player and Club	Pct.	G.	AB.	R.	H.	TB.	2B.	3B.	HR.	RBI.	SH.	SF.	SB.	CS.
Blanks, Larvell, Texas	.200	68	120	13	24	32	5	0	1	15	3	4	0	0
Bochte, Bruce, Seattle*	.316	150	554	81	175	273	38	6	16	100	3	10	2	2
Bonds, Bobby, Cleveland	.275	146	538	93	148	249	24	1	25	85	4	7	34	23
Borgmann, Glenn, Minnesota	.200	31	70	4	14	17	3	0	0	8	2	0	1	0
Bosetti, Richard, Toronto	.260	162	619	59	161	224	35	2	8	65	6	7	13	12
Bosley, Thaddis, Chicago*	.312	36	77	13	24	30	1	1	1	8	0	0	4	1
Braun, Stephen, Kansas City*	.267	58	116	15	31	45	2	0	4	10	1	0	0	0
Brett, George, Kansas City	.329	154	645	119	212	363	42	20	23	107	1	4	17	10
Brohamer, John, Boston*	.266	64	192	25	51	63	7	1	1	11	1	2	0	3
Brookens, Thomas, Detroit	.263	60	190	23	50	71	5	2	4	21	4	1	10	3
Brown, Rogers, Tor-NY*	.218	34	78	8	17	22	3	1	0	3	1	0	2	1
Bryant, Derek, Oakland	.179	39	106	8	19	23	2	1	0	13	2	2	0	0
Bumbry, Alonza, Baltimore*	.285	148	569	80	162	214	29	1	7	49	2	4	37	12
Burke, Glenn, Oakland	.213	23	89	4	19	23	2	1	0	4	1	0	3	1
Burleson, Richard, Boston	.278	153	627	93	174	231	32	5	5	60	9	8	9	5
Cage, Wayne, Cleveland*	.232	29	56	6	13	18	2	0	1	6	0	0	0	2
Campaneris, Dagoberto, Tex-Calif	.230	93	248	29	57	69	4	4	0	15	11	2	13	4
Cannon, Joseph, Toronto*	.211	61	142	14	30	36	1	1	1	5	3	0	12	2
Carew, Rodney, California*	.318	110	409	78	130	160	15	3	3	44	8	3	18	8
Carty, Ricardo, Toronto	.256	132	461	48	118	180	26	0	12	55	0	4	3	1
Castino, John, Minnesota	.285	148	393	49	112	156	13	8	5	52	22	2	5	2
Cerone, Richard, Toronto	.239	136	469	47	112	168	27	4	7	61	3	4	1	4
Chalk, Dave, Tex-Oak	.223	75	220	15	49	61	6	0	2	13	8	1	2	1
Chambliss, C. Christopher, N. York*.	.280	149	554	61	155	242	27	3	18	63	1	5	3	2
Chappas, Harry, Chicago†	.288	26	59	9	17	21	1	0	1	4	0	0	0	0
Chism, Thomas, Baltimore*	.000	6	3	0	0	0	0	0	0	0	0	0	0	0
Clark, Robert, California	.296	19	54	8	16	25	2	2	1	5	1	0	1	1
Colbern, Michael, Chicago	.241	32	83	5	20	27	5	1	0	8	4	0	0	0
Cooper, Cecil, Milwaukee*	.308	150	590	83	182	300	44	1	24	106	6	8	15	3
Corcoran, Timothy, Detroit*	.227	18	22	4	5	6	1	0	0	6	0	1	1	1
Corey, Mark, Baltimore	.154	13	13	1	2	2	0	0	0	1	0	0	1	0
Cowens, Alfred, Kansas City	.295	136	516	69	152	211	18	7	9	73	2	7	10	8
Cox, Larry, Seattle	.215	100	293	32	63	92	11	3	4	36	3	5	2	1
Cox, W. Ted, Cleveland	.212	78	189	17	40	58	6	0	4	22	2	1	3	4
Craig, Rodney, Seattle†	.385	16	52	9	20	30	8	1	0	6	0	0	1	1
Crowley, Terrence, Baltimore*	.317	61	63	8	20	30	5	1	1	8	0	0	0	0
Cruz, Todd, Kansas City	.203	55	118	9	24	37	7	0	2	15	1	3	0	1
Cruz, Julio, Seattle†	.271	107	414	70	112	135	16	2	1	29	4	3	49	9
Cubbage, Michael, Minnesota*	.276	94	243	26	67	85	10	1	2	23	5	4	1	8
Dade, L. Paul, Cleveland	.282	44	170	22	48	63	4	1	3	18	1	2	12	6
Dauer, Richard, Baltimore	.257	142	479	63	123	170	20	0	9	61	4	8	0	1
Davis, William, California*	.250	43	56	9	14	18	2	1	0	2	1	0	1	0
Davis, Richard, Milwaukee	.266	91	335	51	89	140	13	1	12	41	1	1	3	5
Davis, Ronald, New York	.000	44	1	0	0	0	0	0	0	0	0	0	0	0
Davis, Robert, Toronto	.124	32	89	6	11	16	2	0	1	8	5	0	0	0
DeCinces, Douglas, Baltimore	.230	120	422	67	97	174	27	1	16	61	0	5	5	3
Dempsey, J. Richard, Baltimore	.239	124	368	48	88	129	23	0	6	41	3	4	0	1
Dent, Russell, New York	.230	141	431	47	99	123	14	2	2	32	13	8	0	0
Diaz, Baudilio, Cleveland	.156	15	32	0	5	7	2	0	0	1	1	0	0	0
Dilone, Miguel, Oakland†	.187	30	91	15	17	25	1	2	1	6	2	0	6	5
Donohue, Thomas, California	.224	38	107	13	24	38	3	1	3	14	1	0	2	3
Downing, Brian, California*	.326	148	509	87	166	235	27	3	12	75	3	2	3	3
Doyle, Brian, New York*	.125	20	32	2	4	6	2	0	0	5	1	0	0	0
Duffy, Frank, Boston	.000	6	3	0	0	0	0	0	0	0	0	0	0	0
Dwyer, James, Boston*	.265	76	113	19	30	43	7	0	2	14	0	2	3	1
Edwards, David, Minnesota	.249	96	229	42	57	89	8	0	8	35	3	0	6	3
Edwards, Michael, Oakland	.233	122	400	35	93	112	12	2	1	23	4	1	10	6
Ellis, John, Texas	.285	111	316	33	90	138	12	0	12	61	0	4	2	2
Essian, James, Oakland	.243	98	313	34	76	116	16	0	8	40	3	9	0	1
Evans, Dwight, Boston	.274	152	489	69	134	223	24	1	21	58	3	1	6	9
Finch, Joel, Boston	.000	15	1	0	0	0	0	0	0	0	0	0	0	0
Fisk, Carlton, Boston	.272	91	320	49	87	144	23	2	10	42	1	3	3	0
Foley, Marvis, Chicago*	.247	34	97	6	24	33	3	0	2	10	4	2	0	0
Ford, Darnell, California	.290	142	569	100	165	264	26	5	21	101	3	13	8	5
Fosse, Raymond, Milwaukee	.231	19	52	6	12	17	3	1	0	2	0	0	0	0
Gamble, Oscar, Tex-NY*	.358	100	274	48	98	167	10	1	19	64	0	2	2	1
Gantner, James, Milwaukee*	.284	70	208	29	59	81	10	3	2	22	5	3	3	5
Garcia, Alfonso, Baltimore	.247	126	417	54	103	151	15	9	5	24	5	1	11	9
Garcia, Damaso, New York	.263	11	38	3	10	11	1	0	0	4	0	0	2	0

Player and Club	Pct.	G.	AB.	R.	H.	TB.	2B.	3B.	HR.	RBI.	SH.	SF.	SB.	CS.
Garr, Ralph, Chi-Calif*	.269	108	331	34	89	130	10	2	9	39	2	2	2	4
Gates, Joseph, Chicago*	.063	16	16	5	1	3	0	1	0	1	0	0	1	1
Gaudet, James, Kansas City	.167	3	6	0	1	1	0	0	0	0	0	0	0	0
Gibson, Kirk, Detroit*	.237	12	38	3	9	15	3	0	1	4	0	0	3	3
Gomez, Luis, Toronto	.239	59	163	11	39	46	7	0	0	11	2	0	1	0
Gonzales, Daniel, Detroit*	.222	7	18	1	4	5	1	0	0	2	0	0	1	0
Goodwin, Danny, Minnesota*	.289	58	159	22	46	79	8	5	5	27	2	0	0	0
Graham, Daniel, Minnesota*	.000	2	4	0	0	0	0	0	0	0	0	0	0	0
Gray, Gary, Texas	.238	16	42	4	10	10	0	0	0	1	0	0	1	1
Greene, Altar, Detroit*	.136	29	59	9	8	18	1	0	3	6	0	1	0	1
Grich, Robert, California	.294	153	534	78	157	287	30	5	30	101	12	2	1	0
Griffin, Alfredo, Toronto†	.287	153	624	81	179	227	22	10	2	31	16	4	21	16
Gross, Wayne, Oakland*	.224	138	442	54	99	162	19	1	14	50	3	3	4	3
Grubb, John, Texas*	.273	102	289	42	79	123	14	0	10	37	2	2	2	4
Guerrero, Mario, Oakland	.229	46	166	12	38	43	5	0	0	18	3	2	0	1
Gulden, Bradley, New York*	.163	40	92	10	15	19	4	0	0	6	4	0	0	1
Hale, John, Seattle*	.222	54	63	6	14	23	3	0	2	7	1	1	0	0
Hampton, Isaac, California	.400	4	5	0	2	2	0	0	0	0	0	0	0	0
Hargrove, D. Michael, Cleveland*	.325	100	338	60	110	169	21	4	10	56	2	5	2	3
Harlow, Larry, Balt-Calif*	.240	100	200	27	48	61	9	2	0	15	1	0	2	6
Harper, Brian, California	.000	1	2	0	0	0	0	0	0	0	0	0	0	0
Harrah, Colbert, Cleveland	.279	149	527	99	147	234	25	1	20	77	7	4	20	9
Harris, John, California*	.000	1	2	0	0	0	0	0	0	0	0	0	0	0
Hassey, Ronald, Cleveland*	.287	75	223	20	64	90	14	0	4	32	4	3	1	0
Heath, Michael, Oakland	.256	74	258	19	66	83	8	0	3	27	3	5	1	0
Heaverlo, David, Oakland	.000	62	1	0	0	0	0	0	0	0	0	0	0	0
Henderson, Rickey, Oakland	.274	89	351	49	96	118	13	3	1	26	8	3	33	11
Hendricks, Elrod, Baltimore*	.000	1	1	0	0	0	0	0	0	0	0	0	0	0
Hernandez, Pedro, Toronto	.000	3	0	1	0	0	0	0	0	0	0	0	0	0
Hisle, Larry, Milwaukee	.281	26	96	18	27	43	7	0	3	14	0	1	1	0
Hobson, Clell, Boston	.261	146	528	74	138	262	26	7	28	93	6	6	3	2
Holle, Gary, Texas	.167	5	6	0	1	2	1	0	0	0	0	0	0	0
Horton, Willie, Seattle	.279	162	646	77	180	296	19	5	29	106	2	2	1	1
Howell, Roy, Toronto*	.247	138	511	60	126	207	28	4	15	72	1	3	1	4
Humphrey, Terryal, California	.059	9	17	2	1	1	0	0	0	0	1	0	0	0
Hurdle, Clinton, Kansas City*	.240	59	171	16	41	66	10	3	3	30	0	4	0	1
Jackson, Ronnie, Minnesota	.271	159	583	85	158	250	40	5	14	68	6	4	3	1
Jackson, Reginald, New York*	.297	131	465	78	138	253	24	2	29	89	0	5	9	8
Johnson, Lamar, Chicago	.309	133	479	60	148	215	29	1	12	74	0	4	8	2
Johnson, Cliff, NY-Clev	.270	100	304	48	82	158	16	0	20	67	1	6	2	0
Johnson, Timothy, Toronto*	.186	43	86	6	16	20	2	1	0	6	2	0	0	1
Johnstone, John, New York*	.208	23	48	7	10	14	1	0	1	7	0	0	1	0
Jones, Lynn, Detroit	.296	95	213	33	63	83	8	0	4	26	1	1	9	6
Jones, Darryl, New York	.255	18	47	6	12	19	5	1	0	6	2	0	0	0
Jones, Ruppert, Seattle*	.267	162	622	109	166	276	29	9	21	78	2	4	33	12
Jorgensen, Michael, Texas*	.223	90	157	21	35	60	7	0	6	16	3	1	0	2
Kelly, H. Patrick, Baltimore*	.288	68	153	25	44	82	11	0	9	25	0	3	4	5
Kemp, Steven, Detroit*	.318	134	490	88	156	266	26	3	26	105	2	8	5	6
Kessinger, Donald, Chicago†	.200	56	110	14	22	31	6	0	1	7	3	1	1	0
Klutts, Gene, Oakland	.192	24	73	3	14	21	2	1	1	4	0	0	0	1
Krenchicki, Wayne, Baltimore*	.190	16	21	1	4	5	1	0	0	0	2	0	0	0
Kuiper, Duane, Cleveland*	.255	140	479	46	122	141	9	5	0	39	8	0	4	9
Kuntz, Russell, Chicago	.091	5	11	0	1	1	0	0	0	0	0	0	0	0
Kusick, Craig, Minn-Tor	.222	48	108	11	24	44	5	0	5	13	0	1	0	0
LaCock, R. Pierre, Kansas City	.277	132	408	54	113	155	25	4	3	56	1	6	2	1
Landreaux, Kenneth, Minnesota*	.305	151	564	81	172	254	27	5	15	83	10	8	10	3
Lansford, Carney, California	.287	157	654	114	188	285	30	5	19	79	12	4	20	8
LeFlore, Ronald, Detroit	.300	148	600	110	180	249	22	10	9	57	0	2	78	14
Lemon, Chester, Chicago	.318	148	556	79	177	276	44	2	17	86	3	4	7	11
Lezcano, Sixto, Milwaukee	.321	138	473	84	152	271	29	3	28	101	6	7	4	3
Lowenstein, John, Baltimore*	.254	97	197	33	50	95	8	2	11	34	1	3	16	4
Lynn, Fredric, Boston*	.333	147	531	116	177	338	42	1	39	122	0	5	2	2
Machemer, David, Detroit	.192	19	26	8	5	6	1	0	0	2	1	0	0	3
Mahlberg, Greg, Texas	.118	7	17	2	2	5	0	0	1	1	2	0	0	0
Mankowski, Phillip, Detroit*	.222	42	99	11	22	26	4	0	0	8	1	3	0	0
Manning, Richard, Cleveland*	.259	144	560	67	145	170	12	2	3	51	9	7	30	8
Martinez, John, Milwaukee	.270	69	196	17	53	73	8	0	4	26	8	2	0	1
May, Lee, Baltimore	.254	124	456	59	116	188	15	0	19	69	2	4	3	4
May, Milton, Det-Chi*	.254	71	213	24	54	90	15	0	7	31	2	1	0	0

Player and Club	Pct.	G.	AB.	R.	H.	TB.	2B.	3B.	HR.	RBI.	SH.	SF.	SB.	CS.
Mayberry, John, Toronto*	.274	137	464	61	127	214	22	1	21	74	1	2	1	1
McKay, David, Toronto†	.218	47	156	19	34	43	9	0	0	12	5	0	1	1
McRae, Harold, Kansas City	.288	101	393	55	113	183	32	4	10	74	1	7	5	4
Mendoza, Mario, Seattle	.198	148	373	26	74	93	10	3	1	29	13	5	3	0
Meyer, Daniel, Seattle*	.278	144	525	72	146	241	21	7	20	74	6	6	11	7
Milbourne, Lawrence, Seattle†	.278	123	356	40	99	126	13	4	2	26	2	2	5	3
Miller, Richard, California*	.293	120	427	60	125	156	15	5	2	28	9	1	5	4
Molinaro, Robert, Baltimore*	.000	8	6	0	0	0	0	0	0	0	0	0	1	0
Molitor, Paul, Milwaukee	.322	140	584	88	188	274	27	16	9	62	6	5	33	13
Money, Donald, Milwaukee	.237	92	350	52	83	123	20	1	6	38	6	4	1	0
Montanez, Guillermo, Texas*	.319	38	144	19	46	76	6	0	8	24	0	1	0	1
Montgomery, Robert, Boston	.349	32	86	13	30	36	4	1	0	7	1	1	1	0
Moore, Alvin, Chicago	.264	88	201	24	53	66	6	2	1	23	0	4	0	2
Moore, Charles, Milwaukee	.300	111	337	45	101	136	16	2	5	38	3	2	8	5
Morales, Julio, Detroit	.211	129	440	50	93	160	23	1	14	56	2	8	10	4
Morales, Jose, Minnesota	.267	92	191	21	51	64	5	1	2	27	4	3	0	0
Morris, John, Detroit	.000	28	0	1	0	0	0	0	0	0	0	0	0	0
Morrison, James, Chicago	.275	67	240	38	66	122	14	0	14	35	7	3	11	3
Mulliniks, S. Rance, California*	.147	22	68	7	10	13	0	0	1	8	0	5	0	0
Munson, Thurman, New York	.288	97	382	42	110	143	18	3	3	39	1	4	1	2
Murcer, Bobby, New York*	.273	74	264	42	72	108	12	0	8	33	2	1	1	1
Murphy, Dwayne, Oakland*	.255	121	388	57	99	150	10	4	11	40	13	3	15	11
Murray, Eddie, Baltimore†	.295	159	606	90	179	288	30	2	25	99	1	6	10	2
Murray, Larry, Oakland‡	.186	105	226	25	42	63	11	2	2	20	6	1	6	6
Nahorodny, William, Chicago	.257	65	179	20	46	74	10	0	6	29	0	2	0	1
Narron, Jerry, New York*	.171	61	123	17	21	38	3	1	4	18	3	1	0	0
Nettles, James, Kansas City†	.087	11	23	0	2	2	0	0	0	1	0	0	0	0
Nettles, Graig, New York*	.253	145	521	71	132	209	15	1	20	73	0	8	1	2
Newman, Jeffrey, Oakland	.231	143	516	53	119	206	17	2	22	71	2	6	2	1
Nordbrook, Timothy, Milwaukee	.500	2	2	0	1	1	0	0	0	0	0	0	0	0
Nordhagen, Wayne, Chicago	.280	78	193	20	54	90	15	0	7	25	0	1	0	0
Norman, Nelson, Texas†	.222	147	343	36	76	91	9	3	0	21	18	3	4	1
Norris, James, Cleveland*	.246	124	353	50	87	123	15	6	3	30	6	3	15	10
Norwood, Willie, Minnesota	.248	96	270	32	67	104	13	3	6	30	3	1	9	5
O'Berry, Mike, Boston	.169	43	59	8	10	14	1	0	1	4	2	1	0	0
Oglivie, Benjamin, Milwaukee*	.282	139	514	88	145	270	30	4	29	81	4	4	12	5
Oliver, Albert, Texas*	.323	136	492	69	159	231	28	4	12	76	1	7	4	5
Orta, Jorge, Chicago*	.262	113	325	49	85	142	18	3	11	46	3	4	1	5
Otis, Amos, Kansas City	.295	151	577	100	170	256	28	2	18	90	7	5	30	5
Paciorek, Thomas, Seattle	.287	103	310	38	89	138	23	4	6	42	3	3	6	4
Page, Mitchell, Oakland*	.247	133	478	51	118	160	11	2	9	42	3	3	17	16
Papi, Stanley, Boston	.188	50	117	9	22	33	8	0	1	6	4	0	0	0
Parrish, Lance, Detroit	.276	143	493	65	136	225	26	3	19	65	3	1	6	7
Patek, Fred, Kansas City	.252	106	306	30	77	97	17	0	1	37	10	3	11	12
Peters, Richard, Detroit†	.263	12	19	3	5	5	0	0	0	2	1	0	0	0
Picciolo, Robert, Oakland	.253	115	348	37	88	114	16	2	2	27	11	0	2	1
Piniella, Louis, New York	.297	130	461	49	137	196	22	2	11	69	3	8	3	2
Poquette, Thomas, KC-Bos*	.311	84	180	15	56	71	9	0	2	26	0	6	2	2
Porter, Darrell, Kansas City*	.291	157	533	101	155	258	23	10	20	112	4	13	3	4
Powell, Hosken, Minnesota*	.293	104	338	49	99	128	17	3	2	36	5	1	5	1
Pruitt, Ronald, Cleveland	.283	64	166	23	47	60	7	0	2	21	1	2	0	0
Pryor, Gregory, Chicago	.275	143	476	60	131	169	23	3	3	34	7	5	3	4
Putman, Eddy, Detroit	.231	21	39	4	9	18	3	0	2	4	0	0	0	1
Putnam, Patrick, Texas*	.277	139	426	57	118	195	19	2	18	64	4	6	1	6
Quirk, James, Kansas City*	.304	51	79	8	24	35	6	1	1	11	0	0	0	0
Ramirez, Orlando, California	.000	13	12	1	0	0	0	0	0	0	1	0	1	0
Ramirez, Milton, Oakland	.161	28	62	4	10	13	1	1	0	3	1	0	0	0
Randall, Robert, Minnesota	.246	80	199	25	49	56	7	0	0	14	13	0	2	2
Randle, Leonard, New York†	.179	20	39	2	7	7	0	0	0	3	0	0	0	0
Randolph, William, New York	.270	153	574	98	155	211	15	13	5	61	5	5	33	12
Remy, Gerald, Boston*	.297	80	306	49	91	106	11	2	0	29	6	2	14	9
Rettenmund, Mervin, California	.263	35	76	7	20	25	2	0	1	10	1	1	1	0
Revering, David, Oakland*	.288	125	472	63	136	228	25	5	19	77	1	5	1	4
Rice, James, Boston	.325	158	619	117	201	369	39	6	39	130	0	8	9	4
Rivera, Jesus, Minnesota	.281	112	263	37	74	103	13	5	2	31	13	1	5	5
Rivers, John, N.Y.-Tex.*	.293	132	533	72	156	226	27	8	9	50	5	8	10	9
Roberts, Leon, Seattle	.271	140	450	61	122	203	24	6	15	54	7	3	3	3
Roberts, David, Texas	.262	44	84	12	22	35	2	1	3	14	2	0	1	0
Robertson, Robert, Toronto	.103	15	29	1	3	6	0	0	1	1	0	0	0	0

Player and Club	Pct.	G.	AB.	R.	H.	TB.	2B.	3B.	HR.	RBI.	SH.	SF.	SB.	CS.
Robinson, Bruce, New York*	.167	6	12	0	2	2	0	0	0	2	0	0	0	0
Rodriguez, Aurelio, Detroit	.254	106	343	27	87	120	18	0	5	36	5	3	0	2
Roenicke, Gary, Baltimore	.261	133	376	60	98	191	16	1	25	64	1	3	1	3
Rosello, David, Cleveland	.243	59	107	20	26	43	6	1	3	14	9	3	1	0
Rudi, Joseph, California	.242	90	330	35	80	130	11	3	11	61	4	2	0	0
Sakata, Lenn, Milwaukee	.500	4	14	1	7	9	2	0	0	1	0	0	0	0
Sample, William, Texas	.292	128	325	60	95	135	21	2	5	35	10	3	8	6
Scott, George, Bos.-K.C.-N.Y.	.254	105	346	46	88	134	20	4	6	49	2	3	2	1
Simpson, Joe, Seattle*	.283	120	265	29	75	92	11	0	2	27	5	2	6	3
Singleton, Kenneth, Baltimore†	.295	159	570	93	168	304	29	1	35	111	1	7	3	1
Sizemore, Ted, Boston	.261	26	88	12	23	33	7	0	1	6	0	0	1	0
Skaggs, David, Baltimore	.248	63	137	9	34	45	8	0	1	14	2	0	0	0
Smalley, Roy, Minnesota†	.271	162	621	94	168	274	28	3	24	95	15	9	2	3
Smith, Billy, Baltimore†	.249	68	189	18	47	82	9	4	6	33	7	1	1	0
Soderholm, Eric, Chi.-Tex.	.261	119	357	46	93	141	14	2	10	53	3	4	0	1
Sofield, Richard, Minnesota*	.301	35	93	8	28	33	5	0	0	12	2	0	2	3
Solaita, Tolia, Toronto*	.265	36	102	14	27	43	8	1	2	13	0	2	0	0
Speed, Horace, Cleveland	.143	26	14	6	2	2	0	0	0	1	0	0	2	1
Spencer, James, New York*	.288	106	295	60	85	175	15	3	23	53	1	2	0	2
Squires, Michael, Chicago*	.264	122	295	44	78	96	10	1	2	22	5	2	15	5
Staiger, Roy, New York	.273	4	11	1	3	4	1	0	0	1	0	1	0	0
Stanley, Frederick, New York	.200	57	100	9	20	27	1	0	2	14	4	1	0	1
Staub, Daniel, Detroit*	.236	68	246	32	58	99	12	1	9	40	1	4	1	0
Stegman, David, Detroit	.194	12	31	6	6	15	0	0	3	5	0	0	1	1
Stein, William, Seattle	.248	88	250	28	62	96	9	2	7	27	3	4	1	2
Stinson, G. Robert, Seattle†	.243	95	247	19	60	86	8	0	6	28	6	3	1	2
Summers, John, Detroit*	.313	90	246	47	77	151	12	1	20	51	0	1	7	6
Sundberg, James, Texas	.275	150	495	50	136	182	23	4	5	64	5	5	3	3
Terrell, Jerry, Kansas City	.300	31	40	5	12	18	3	0	1	2	1	0	1	0
Thomas, J. Gorman, Milwaukee	.244	156	557	97	136	300	29	0	45	123	5	6	1	5
Thompson, Jason, Detroit*	.246	145†	492	58	121	199	16	1	20	79	1	5	2	0
Thon, Richard, California	.339	35	56	6	19	22	3	0	0	8	1	0	0	0
Thornton, Andre, Cleveland	.233	143	515	89	120	231	31	1	26	93	1	7	5	4
Torres, Rosendo, Chicago†	.253	90	170	26	43	72	5	0	8	24	8	0	0	0
Trammell, Alan, Detroit	.276	142	460	68	127	164	11	4	6	50	12	5	17	14
Travers, William, Milwaukee*	.000	30	0	0	0	0	0	0	0	0	1	0	0	0
Valentine, Robert, Seattle	.276	62	98	9	27	33	6	0	0	7	1	1	1	2
Vega, Jesus, Minnesota	.000	4	7	0	0	0	0	0	0	0	0	0	0	0
Velez, Otoniel, Toronto	.288	99	274	45	79	145	21	0	15	48	2	0	0	1
Veryzer, Thomas, Cleveland	.220	149	449	41	99	114	9	3	0	34	10	4	2	5
Wagner, Mark, Detroit	.274	75	146	16	40	46	3	0	1	13	7	2	3	2
Wallis, H. Joseph, Oakland†	.141	23	78	6	11	16	2	0	1	3	2	0	1	0
Ward, Gary, Minnesota	.286	10	14	2	4	4	0	0	0	1	0	0	0	1
Washington, Claudell, Chicago*	.280	131	471	79	132	214	33	5	13	66	2	4	19	11
Washington, U.L., Kansas City†	.254	101	268	32	68	96	12	5	2	25	6	6	10	7
Washington, LaRue, Texas	.278	25	18	5	5	5	0	0	0	2	0	0	2	1
Wathan, John, Kansas City	.206	90	199	26	41	60	7	3	2	28	5	5	2	1
Watson, Robert, Boston	.337	84	312	48	105	171	19	4	13	53	0	1	3	2
Werth, Dennis, New York	.250	3	4	1	1	1	0	0	0	0	0	0	0	0
Whitaker, Louis, Detroit*	.286	127	423	75	121	160	14	8	3	42	14	4	20	10
White, Frank, Kansas City	.266	127	467	73	124	188	26	4	10	48	3	7	28	8
White, Roy, New York†	.215	81	205	24	44	59	6	0	3	27	5	3	2	2
Wilborn, Thaddeaus, Toronto†	.000	22	12	3	0	0	0	0	0	0	1	0	0	1
Wilfong, Robert, Minnesota†	.313	140	419	71	131	192	22	6	9	59	25	10	11	4
Wills, Elliott, Texas†	.273	146	543	90	148	190	21	3	5	46	14	3	35	11
Wilson, Willie, Kansas City†	.315	154	588	113	185	247	18	13	6	49	13	4	83	12
Wockenfuss, Johnny, Detroit	.264	87	231	27	61	117	9	1	15	46	1	2	2	2
Wohlford, James, Milwaukee	.263	63	175	19	46	64	13	1	1	17	5	3	6	2
Wolfe, Laurence, Boston	.244	47	78	12	19	32	4	0	3	15	2	2	0	0
Woods, Alvis, Toronto*	.278	132	436	57	121	168	24	4	5	36	7	4	6	4
Wynegar, Harold, Minnesota†	.270	149	504	74	136	177	20	0	7	57	11	4	2	2
Yastrzemski, Carl, Boston*	.270	147	518	69	140	233	28	1	21	87	0	8	3	3
Yount, Robin, Milwaukee	.267	149	577	72	154	214	26	5	8	51	10	3	11	8
Zdeb, Joseph, Kansas City	.174	15	23	3	4	7	1	1	0	0	0	0	1	0
Zisk, Richard, Texas	.262	144	503	69	132	209	21	1	18	64	1	2	1	1

The following pitchers had no plate appearances primarily because of use of designated hitters; they are listed alphabetically by club with number of games, including pinch-running and defensive appearances, in parentheses:

BALTIMORE—Flanagan, Michael (39); Flinn, John (4); Ford, David (9); Martinez, Felix (39); Martinez, J. Dennis (40); McGregor, Scott (27); Palmer, James (23); Rineer, Jeffrey (1); Stanhouse, Donald (52); Stewart, Samuel (31); Stoddard, Timothy (29); Stone, Steven (32).

BOSTON—Burgmeier, Thomas (44); Campbell, William (41); Drago, Richard (53); Eckersley, Dennis (33); Hassler, Andrew (8); Rainey, Charles (20); Remmerswaal, Wilhelmus (8); Renko, Steven (27); Ripley, Allen (16); Stanley, Robert (40); Torrez, Michael (36); Tudor, John (6); Wright, James (11).

CALIFORNIA—Aase, Donald (37); Barlow, Michael (35); Barr, James (36); Botting, Ralph (12); Clear, Mark (52); Eddy, Steven (7); Ferris, Robert (2); Frost, David (36); Knapp, R. Christian (20); LaRoche, David (53); Montague, John (55—includes 41 with Seattle); Ryan, L. Nolan (34); Schuler, David (1); Tanana, Frank (18).

CHICAGO—Barrios, Francisco (15); Baumgarten, Ross (28); Burns, R. Britt (6); Dotson, Richard (5); Esser, Mark (2); Farmer, Edward (53—includes 42 with Texas); Hoffman, Guy (24); Howard, Fred (28); Hoyt, Dewey (2); Kravec, Kenneth (36); Kucek, John (1); LaGrow, Lerrin (11); Proly, Michael (38); Robinson, Dewey (11); Rondon, Gilbert (4); Scarbery, Randy (45); Schueler, Ronald (8); Torrealba, Pablo (39); Trout, Steven (34); Wortham, Richard (34).

CLEVELAND—Andersen, Larry (8); Barker, Leonard (29); Clyde, David (9); Cruz, Victor (61); Garland, M. Wayne (18); Monge, Isidro (76); Paxton, Michael (33); Reuschel, Paul (17); Spillner, Daniel (49); Waits, M. Richard (34); Wihtol, Alexander (5); Wilkins, Eric (16); Wise, Richard (34).

DETROIT—Arroyo, Fernando (6); Baker, Steven (21); Billingham, John (35); Burnside, Sheldon (10); Chris, Michael (13); Fidrych, Mark (4); Hiller, John (43); Lopez, Aurelio (61); Morris, John (28); Petry, Daniel (15); Robbins, Bruce (10); Rozema, David (16); Taylor, Bruce (10); Tobik, David (37); Underwood, Patrick (27); Wilcox, Milton (33); Young, Kip (13).

KANSAS CITY—Busby, Steven (22); Chamberlain, Craig (10); Christenson, Gary (6); Eaton, Craig (5); Gale, Richard (34); Gura, Lawrence (39); Hrabosky, Alan (58); Leonard, Dennis (32); Martin, D. Renie (25); Mingori, Stephen (30); Paschall, William (7); Pattin, Martin (31); Rodriguez, Eduardo (29); Quisenberry, Daniel (32); Splittorff, Paul (36); Throop, George (4).

MILWAUKEE—Augustine, Gerald (43); Boitano, Danny (5); Caldwell, R. Michael (30); Castro, William (39); Cleveland, Reginald (29); Galasso, Robert (31); Haas, Bryan (29); McClure, Robert (36); Mitchell, Paul (28—includes 10 with Seattle); Rautzhan, Clarence (3); Replogle, Andrew (3); Slaton, James (32); Sorensen, Lary (34).

MINNESOTA—Bacsik, Michael (31); Brett, Kenneth (9); Erickson, Roger (24); Felton, Terry (1); Goltz, David (36); Hartzell, Paul (28); Holly, Jeffrey (6); Jackson, Darrell (25); Koosman, Jerry (37); Marshall, Michael (90); Redfern, Peter (41); Serum, Gary (20); Stanfield, Kevin (3); Thormodsgard, Paul (1); Zahn, Geoffrey (26).

NEW YORK—Anderson, Richard (1); Beattie, James (15); Burris, B. Ray (15); Clay, Kenneth (32); Figueroa, Eduardo (16); Griffin, Michael (3); Guidry, Ronald (34); Gossage, Richard (36); Hood, Donald (40—includes 13 with Cleveland); Hunter, James (19); John, Thomas (37); Kaat, James (40); Kammeyer, Robert (1); Mirabella, Paul (10); Righetti, David (3); Slagle, Roger (1); Tiant, Luis (32); Tidrow, Richard (14)

OAKLAND—Hamilton, David (40); Keough, Matthew (30); Kingman, Brian (18); Lacey, Robert (42); Langford, J. Rick (34); McCatty, Steven (31); Minetto, Craig (36); Morgan, Michael (13); Norris, Michael (29); Todd, James (51); Wirth, Alan (5).

SEATTLE—Abbott, W. Glenn (23); Bannister, Floyd (30); Branch, Roy (2); Decker, George (9); Dressler, Robert (21); Hinton, Richard (30—includes 16 with Chicago); Honeycutt, Frederick (33); Jones, Odell (25); Lewis, James (2); McLaughlin, Byron (47); Parrott, Michael (38); Rawley, Shane (49); Stein, W. Randolph (23); Twitchell, Wayne (4); Vasquez, Rafael (9).

TEXAS—Alexander, Doyle (23); Allard, Brian (7); Babcock, Robert (4); Comer, Steven (36); Darwin, Danny (20); Ellis, Dock (10); Gleaton, Jerry (5); Jenkins, Ferguson (37); Johnson, John (31—includes 14 with Oakland); Kern, James (71); Lyle, Albert (67); Matlack, Jonathon (13); McCall, Larry (2); Medich, George (29); Rajsich, David (27).

TORONTO—Buskey, Thomas (44); Clancy, James (12); Edge, Claude (9); Freisleben, David (42); Garvin, T. Jared (8); Grilli, Stephen (1); Huffman, Phillip (31); Jefferson, Jesse (34); Lemanczyk, David (22); Lemongello, Mark (18); Luebber, Stephen (1); Miller, Dyar (24—includes 14 with California); Moore, Balor (34); Murphy, Thomas (10); Stieb, David (20); Todd, Jackson (12); Underwood, Thomas (33); Willis, Michael (17).

AWARDED FIRST BASE ON INTEREFERENCE—Stinson, Sea. 3 (Skaggs 2, Fisk); Adams, Minn. (L. Cox); Cox, Sea. (Davis); Dade, Clev. (M. May); McRae, K.C. (L. Cox); Meyer, Sea. (Essian); Norris, Clev. (L. Cox); Rodriguez, Det. (Dempsey); Soderholm, Tex. (M. May).

PLAYERS WITH TWO OR MORE CLUBS
(Alphabetically Arranged With Player's First Club on Top)

Player and Club	Pct.	G.	AB.	R.	H.	TB.	2B.	3B.	HR.	RBI.	SH.	SF.	Tot. BB.	Int. BB.	HP.	SO.	SB.	CS.	GI DP.
Brown, Toronto	.000	4	10	1	0	0	0	0	0	0	2	0	0	1	0	0	0	0	0
Brown, New York	.250	30	68	7	17	22	3	1	0	3	1	0	2	0	0	17	2	1	0
Campaneris, Texas	.111	8	9	2	1	1	0	0	0	0	0	1	0	0	0	3	1	0	0
Campaneris, California	.234	85	239	27	56	68	4	4	0	15	11	2	19	0	2	32	12	4	8

Player and Club	Pct.	G.	AB.	R.	H.	TB.	2B.	3B.	HR.	RBI.	SH.	SF.	Tot. BB.	Int. BB.	HP.	SO.	SB.	CS.	GI DP.
Chalk, Texas	.250	9	8	0	2	2	0	0	0	0	1	0	0	0	0	0	0	0	1
Chalk, Oakland	.222	66	212	15	47	59	6	0	2	13	7	1	29	0	1	14	2	1	6
Gamble, Texas	.335	64	161	27	54	84	6	0	8	32	0	2	37	11	1	15	2	1	6
Gamble, New York	.389	36	113	21	44	83	4	1	11	32	0	0	13	1	0	13	0	0	1
Garr, Chicago	.280	102	307	34	86	127	10	2	9	39	2	2	17	0	1	19	2	4	5
Garr, California	.125	6	24	0	3	3	0	0	0	0	0	0	0	0	0	3	0	0	0
Harlow, Baltimore	.268	38	41	5	11	12	1	0	0	1	0	0	7	0	0	4	1	3	0
Harlow, California	.233	62	159	22	37	49	8	2	0	14	1	0	25	0	2	34	1	3	2
Johnson, New York	.266	28	64	11	17	29	6	0	2	6	1	1	10	4	0	7	0	0	0
Johnson, Cleveland	.271	72	240	37	65	129	10	0	18	61	0	5	24	1	5	39	2	0	6
Kusick, Minnesota	.241	24	54	8	13	26	4	0	3	6	0	0	3	0	0	11	0	0	1
Kusick, Toronto	.204	24	54	3	11	18	1	0	2	7	0	1	7	0	1	7	0	0	2
May, Detroit	.273	6	11	1	3	5	2	0	0	3	0	0	1	1	0	1	0	0	1
May, Chicago	.252	65	202	23	51	85	13	0	7	28	2	1	14	1	2	27	0	0	3
Poquette, Kansas City	.192	21	26	1	5	5	0	0	0	3	0	1	1	0	0	4	0	0	0
Poquette, Boston	.331	63	154	14	51	66	9	0	2	23	0	5	8	1	3	7	2	2	2
Rivers, New York	.287	74	286	37	82	119	18	5	3	25	2	5	13	2	1	21	3	7	3
Rivers, Texas	.300	58	247	35	74	107	9	3	6	25	3	3	9	0	1	18	7	2	2
Scott, Boston	.224	45	156	18	35	58	9	1	4	23	1	1	17	1	0	22	-0	0	12
Scott, Kansas City	.267	44	146	19	39	54	8	2	1	20	1	1	12	1	2	32	1	1	12
Scott, New York	.318	16	44	9	14	22	3	1	1	6	0	1	2	0	0	7	1	0	0
Soderholm, Chicago	.252	56	210	31	53	83	8	2	6	34	1	1	19	1	0	19	0	1	9
Soderholm, Texas	.272	63	147	15	40	58	6	0	4	19	2	3	12	0	1	9	0	0	5

OFFICIAL MISCELLANEOUS AMERICAN LEAGUE BATTING RECORDS

CLUB MISCELLANEOUS BATTING RECORDS

Club	Slg. Pct.	G.	Tot. BB.	Int. BB.	HP.	SO.	GIDP.	ShO.
Boston	.456	160	512	38	33	708	158	10
Milwaukee	.448	161	549	48	20	745	130	1
California	.429	162	589	42	37	843	136	9
Kansas City	.422	162	528	56	35	675	114	6
Baltimore	.419	159	608	52	31	847	143	5
Detroit	.415	160	575	28	22	814	140	3
Chicago	.410	159	454	29	36	668	151	9
Texas	.409	162	461	49	33	607	135	9
New York	.406	160	509	48	18	590	148	9
Seattle	.404	162	515	45	28	725	158	7
Minnesota	.402	162	526	37	31	693	116	10
Cleveland	.384	161	657	31	42	786	122	6
Toronto	.363	162	448	21	36	663	131	15
Oakland	.346	162	482	36	20	751	131	17
Totals	.408	1127	7413	560	422	10115	1913	116

INDIVIDUAL MISCELLANEOUS BATTING RECORDS
(Top Fifteen Qualifiers for Slugging Championship—502 or More Plate Appearances)

Player—Club	Slg. Pct.	Tot. BB.	Int. BB.	HP.	SO.	GI DP.	Player—Club	Slg. Pct.	Tot. BB.	Int. BB.	HP.	SO.	GI DP.
Lynn, Bos	.637	82	4	4	79	9	Singleton, Balt	.533	109	16	1	118	16
Rice, Bos	.596	57	4	4	97	16	Baylor, Calif	.530	71	6	11	51	10
Lezcano, Milw	.573	77	5	3	74	11	Oglivie, Milw	.525	48	12	2	56	11
Brett, KC	.563	51	14	0	36	8	Cooper, Milw	.508	56	10	0	77	14
Jackson, NY	.544	65	3	2	107	17	Lemon, Chi	.496	56	6	13	68	15
Kemp, Det	.543	68	2	2	70	13	Hobson, Bos	.496	30	2	0	78	23
Thomas, Milw	.539	98	6	2	175	8	Bochte, Sea	.493	67	8	2	64	27
Grich, Calif	.537	59	10	2	84	14							

DEPARTMENTAL LEADERS: Tot. BB—Porter, 121; Int. BB—Singleton, 16; HP—Lemon, 13; SO—Thomas, 175; GIDP—Bochte, 27.

(All Players—Listed Alphabetically)

Player—Club	Slg. Pct.	Tot. BB.	Int. BB.	HP.	SO.	GI DP.	Player—Club	Slg. Pct.	Tot. BB.	Int. BB.	HP.	SO.	GI DP.
Adams, Minn	.420	25	0	3	27	3	Dempsey, Balt	.351	38	1	0	37	12
Aikens, Calif	.493	61	8	1	79	10	Dent, NY	.285	37	1	1	30	5
Ainge, Tor	.286	12	1	2	58	8	Diaz, Clev	.219	2	0	0	6	1
Alexander, Clev	.391	46	3	1	100	7	Dilone, Oak	.275	6	0	0	7	2
Allenson, Bos	.299	20	0	1	42	8	Donohue, Calif	.355	3	0	2	29	1
Alston, Clev	.403	10	1	0	10	0	Downing, Calif	.462	77	4	5	57	17
Anderson, Calif	.350	17	0	1	31	6	Doyle, NY	.188	3	0	0	1	1
Armas, Oak	.421	16	2	1	67	6	Duffy, Bos	.000	0	0	0	1	0
Ayala, Balt	.523	6	1	0	9	2	Dwyer, Bos	.381	17	1	1	9	7
Bailor, Tor	.287	36	2	6	27	6	Edwards, Minn	.389	24	1	1	45	5
Bando, Milw	.345	57	3	3	42	17	Edwards, Oak	.280	15	0	2	37	11
Bannister, Chi	.383	43	1	3	40	9	Ellis, Tex	.437	15	1	2	55	3
Barranca, KC	.800	0	0	0	0	0	Essian, Oak	.371	25	1	2	29	12
Baylor, Calif	.530	71	6	11	51	10	Evans, Bos	.456	69	7	1	76	14
Beamon, Sea	.240	0	0	0	5	1	Finch, Bos	.000	0	0	0	0	0
Belanger, Balt	.217	29	0	1	33	3	Fisk, Bos	.450	10	0	6	38	9
Bell, Chi	.355	15	0	0	43	3	Foley, Chi	.340	7	1	0	5	4
Bell, Tex	.451	30	4	3	45	16	Ford, Calif	.464	40	0	3	86	17
Beniquez, NY	.394	9	0	2	17	5	Fosse, Milw	.327	2	0	2	6	1
Bernhardt, Sea	1.000	0	0	0	0	0	Gamble, Tex-NY	.609	50	12	1	28	7
Blair, NY	.200	0	0	0	1	0	Gantner, Milw	.389	16	1	2	17	3
Blanks, Tex	.267	11	0	0	9	1	Garcia, Balt	.362	32	0	2	87	14
Bochte, Sea	.493	67	8	2	64	27	Garcia, NY	.289	0	0	0	2	1
Bonds, Clev	.463	74	4	8	135	9	Garr, Chi-Calif	.393	17	0	1	22	5
Borgmann, Minn	.243	12	0	0	11	3	Gates, Clev	.188	2	0	0	3	0
Bosetti, Tor	.362	22	0	3	70	17	Gaudet, KC	.167	0	0	0	0	0
Bosley, Chi	.390	9	0	0	14	1	Gibson, Det	.395	1	0	0	3	0
Braun, KC	.388	22	2	0	11	2	Gomez, Tor	.282	6	0	0	17	7
Brett, KC	.563	51	14	0	36	8	Gonzales, Det	.278	0	0	0	2	2
Brohamer, Bos	.328	15	1	0	15	8	Goodwin, Minn	.497	11	1	0	23	5
Brookens, Det	.374	11	0	2	40	3	Graham, Minn	.000	0	0	0	0	0
Brown, Tor-NY	.282	4	0	0	18	0	Gray, Tex	.238	2	0	0	8	2
Bryant, Oak	.217	10	1	0	10	4	Greene, Det	.305	10	1	0	15	1
Bumbry, Balt	.376	43	3	3	74	6	Grich, Calif	.537	59	10	2	84	14
Burke, Oak	.258	4	1	0	10	3	Griffin, Tor	.364	40	0	5	59	10
Burleson, Bos	.368	35	0	3	54	13	Gross, Oak	.367	72	9	1	62	8
Cage, Clev	.321	5	0	0	16	1	Grubb, Tex	.426	34	3	1	44	6
Campaneris, Tex-Calif	.278	20	0	2	35	8	Guerrero, Oak	.259	6	0	0	7	5
Cannon, Tor	.254	1	0	0	34	2	Gulden, NY	.207	9	0	0	16	3
Carew, Calif	.391	73	7	0	46	9	Hale, Sea	.365	12	4	0	26	2
Carty, Tor	.390	46	4	1	45	21	Hampton, Calif	.400	0	0	0	1	0
Castino, Minn	.397	27	0	1	72	9	Hargrove, Clev	.500	63	2	5	40	10
Cerone, NY	.358	37	1	1	40	5	Harlow, Balt-Calif	.305	32	0	2	38	2
Chalk, Tex-Oak	.277	29	0	1	14	7	Harper, Calif	.000	0	0	0	1	0
Chambliss, NY	.437	34	4	5	53	9	Harrah, Clev	.444	89	2	8	60	8
Chappas, Chi	.356	5	0	1	5	2	Harris, Calif	.000	0	0	0	0	0
Chism, Balt	.000	0	0	0	0	1	Hassey, Clev	.404	19	2	0	19	8
Clark, Calif	.463	5	0	0	11	3	Heath, Oak	.322	17	1	3	18	14
Colbern, Chi	.325	4	0	0	25	1	Heaverlo, Oak	.000	0	0	0	0	0
Cooper, Milw	.508	56	10	0	77	14	Henderson, Oak	.336	34	0	2	39	4
Corcoran, Det	.273	4	1	0	2	1	Hendricks, Balt	.000	0	0	0	0	0
Corey, Balt	.154	0	0	0	4	1	Hernandez, Tor	.000	0	0	0	0	0
Cowens, KC	.409	40	4	3	44	12	Hisle, Milw	.448	11	2	0	19	4
Cox, Clev	.307	14	1	2	27	7	Hobson, Bos	.496	30	2	0	78	23
Cox, Sea	.314	22	0	0	39	9	Holle, Tex	.333	1	0	0	0	0
Craig, Sea	.577	1	0	0	5	0	Horton, Sea	.458	42	4	4	112	20
Crowley, Balt	.476	14	2	1	13	2	Howell, Tor	.405	42	4	6	91	12
Cruz, KC	.314	3	0	1	19	2	Humphrey, Calif	.059	1	0	0	2	0
Cruz, Sea	.326	62	0	0	61	7	Hurdle, KC	.386	28	4	1	24	4
Cubbage, Minn	.350	39	2	0	26	2	Jackson, Minn	.429	51	5	9	59	14
Dade, Clev	.371	12	1	0	22	1	Jackson, NY	.544	65	3	2	107	17
Dauer, Balt	.355	36	2	1	36	15	Johnson, Chicago	.449	41	1	2	56	23
Davis, Calif	.321	4	0	0	7	2	Johnson, N.Y.-Cleve.	.520	34	5	5	46	6
Davis, Milw	.418	16	0	0	46	10	Johnson, Toronto	.233	8	0	0	15	2
Davis, NY	.000	0	0	1	0	0	Johnstone, New York	.292	2	0	0	7	0
Davis, Tor	.180	6	0	1	15	7	Jones, Detroit	.390	17	0	1	22	5
DeCinces, Balt	.412	54	5	3	68	11	Jones, New York	.404	2	0	0	7	1

Player—Club	Slg. Pct.	Tot. BB.	Int. BB.	HP.	SO.	GI DP.
R. Jones, Seattle	.444	85	4	3	78	19
Jorgensen, Texas	.382	14	1	2	29	3
Kelly, Baltimore	.536	20	1	1	25	2
Kemp, Detroit	.543	68	2	2	70	13
Kessinger, Chicago	.282	10	1	0	12	5
Klutts, Oakland	.288	7	0	0	20	1
Krenchicki, Baltimore	.238	0	0	0	0	1
Kuiper, Cleveland	.294	37	7	4	27	14
Kuntz, Chicago	.091	2	0	0	6	1
Kusick, Minn.-Toronto	.407	10	0	1	18	3
LaCock, Kansas City	.380	37	7	1	26	16
Landreaux, Minnesota	.450	37	4	4	57	13
Lansford, California	.436	39	2	3	115	16
LeFlore, Detroit	.415	52	2	0	95	16
Lemon, Chicago	.496	56	6	13	68	15
Lezcano, Milwaukee	.573	77	5	3	74	11
Lowenstein, Baltimore	.482	30	3	1	37	2
Lynn, Boston	.637	82	4	4	79	9
Machemer, Detroit	.231	3	0	0	2	0
Mahlberg, Texas	.294	2	0	0	4	2
Mankowski, Detroit	.263	10	4	0	16	3
Manning, Cleveland	.304	55	3	1	48	13
Martinez, Milwaukee	.372	8	0	0	25	3
May, Baltimore	.412	28	4	1	100	18
May, Detroit-Chicago	.423	15	2	2	28	4
Mayberry, Toronto	.461	69	7	5	60	10
McKay, Toronto	.276	7	0	1	19	5
McRae, Kansas City	.466	38	0	4	46	6
Mendoza, Seattle	.249	9	0	1	62	12
Meyer, Seattle	.459	29	10	4	35	13
Milbourne, Seattle	.354	19	2	0	20	7
Miller, California	.365	50	1	1	69	7
Molinaro, Baltimore	.000	1	0	0	3	1
Molitor, Milwaukee	.469	48	5	2	48	9
Money, Milwaukee	.351	40	0	2	47	10
Montanez, Texas	.528	8	1	1	14	4
Montgomery, Boston	.419	4	1	0	24	3
Moore, Chicago	.328	12	0	0	20	8
Moore, Milwaukee	.404	29	1	1	32	11
Morales, Detroit	.364	30	0	2	56	15
Morales, Minnesota	.335	14	5	2	27	10
Morris, Detroit	.000	0	0	0	0	0
Morrison, Chicago	.508	15	0	4	48	2
Mulliniks, California	.191	4	0	1	14	2
Munson, New York	.374	32	2	0	37	15
Murcer, New York	.409	25	2	2	32	10
Murphy, Oakland	.387	84	6	1	80	10
Murray, Baltimore	.475	72	9	2	78	16
Murray, Oakland	.279	28	1	0	34	2
Nahorodny, Baltimore	.413	18	1	0	23	5
Narron, New York	.309	9	0	0	26	2
Nettles, Kansas City	.087	3	0	0	2	0
Nettles, New York	.401	59	6	0	53	14
Newman, Oakland	.349	27	2	1	88	17
Nordbrook, Milwaukee	.500	0	0	0	0	0
Nordhagen, Chicago	.466	13	2	0	22	9
Norman, Texas	.265	19	0	0	41	5
Norris, Cleveland	.348	44	1	0	35	12
Norwood, Minnesota	.385	20	2	0	51	8
O'Berry, Boston	.237	5	0	1	16	3
Oglivie, Milwaukee	.525	48	12	2	56	11
Oliver, Texas	.470	34	8	4	34	14
Orta, Chicago	.437	44	2	1	33	6
Otis, Kansas City	.444	68	8	3	92	12
Paciorek, Seattle	.445	28	1	5	62	6
Page, Oakland	.335	52	5	3	93	9
Papi, Boston	.282	5	0	0	20	0
Parrish, Detroit	.456	49	2	2	105	15
Patek, Kansas City	.317	16	0	3	42	6
Peters, Detroit	.263	5	0	0	3	0
Picciolo, Oakland	.328	3	1	1	45	9
Piniella, New York	.425	17	6	2	31	17
Poquette, K.C.-Boston	.394	9	1	3	11	2
Porter, Kansas City	.484	121	8	8	65	11
Powell, Minnesota	.379	33	1	3	25	9
Pruitt, Cleveland	.361	19	1	0	21	5
Pryor, Chicago	.355	35	1	2	41	16
Putman, Detroit	.462	4	0	0	12	1
Putnam, Texas	.458	23	6	6	50	12
Quirk, Kansas City	.443	5	0	1	13	0
Ramirez, California	.000	1	0	1	6	0
Ramirez, Oakland	.210	3	0	0	8	1
Randall, Minnesota	.281	15	0	0	17	2
Randle, New York	.179	3	0	0	2	1
Randolph, New York	.368	95	5	3	39	23
Remy, Boston	.346	26	1	0	25	2
Rettenmund, California	.329	11	1	1	14	3
Revering, Oakland	.483	34	5	1	65	6
Rice, Boston	.596	57	4	4	97	16
Rivera, Minnesota	.392	17	0	0	40	6
Rivers, N.Y.-Texas	.424	22	2	2	39	5
Roberts, Seattle	.451	56	6	2	64	8
Roberts, Texas	.417	7	0	0	17	3
Robertson, Toronto	.207	3	0	0	9	0
Robinson, New York	.167	1	0	0	0	0
Rodriguez, Detroit	.350	11	0	1	40	9
Roenicke, Baltimore	.508	61	4	12	74	11
Rosello, Cleveland	.402	15	0	0	27	2
Rudi, California	.394	24	3	1	61	7
Sakata, Milwaukee	.643	0	0	0	1	0
Sample, Texas	.415	37	1	2	28	6
Scott, Bos.-K.C.-N.Y.	.387	31	2	2	61	24
Simpson, Seattle	.347	11	1	1	21	5
Singleton, Baltimore	.533	109	16	1	118	16
Sizemore, Boston	.375	4	0	1	5	6
Skaggs, Baltimore	.328	13	0	0	14	8
Smalley, Minnesota	.441	80	8	4	80	9
Smith, Baltimore	.434	15	1	2	33	1
Soderholm, Chi.-Texas	.395	31	1	1	28	14
Sofield, Minnesota	.355	12	0	0	27	2
Solaita, Toronto	.422	17	0	0	16	2
Speed, Cleveland	.143	5	0	0	7	0
Spencer, New York	.593	38	11	0	25	12
Squires, Chicago	.325	22	3	2	9	10
Staiger, New York	.364	1	0	0	0	1
Stanley, New York	.270	5	0	0	17	1
Staub, Detroit	.402	32	1	5	18	9
Stegman, Detroit	.484	2	0	0	3	0
Stein, Seattle	.384	17	1	2	28	11
Stinson, Seattle	.348	33	3	4	38	7
Summers, Detroit	.614	40	4	3	33	4
Sundberg, Texas	.368	51	5	5	51	17
Terrell, Kansas City	.450	1	0	0	1	2
Thomas, Milwaukee	.539	98	6	2	175	8
Thompson, Detroit	.404	70	8	1	90	15
Thon, California	.393	5	0	0	10	2
Thornton, Cleveland	.449	90	2	4	93	8
Torres, Chicago	.424	23	1	2	37	4
Trammell, Detroit	.357	43	0	0	55	6
Travers, Milwaukee	.000	0	0	0	0	0
Valentine, Seattle	.337	22	1	0	5	4
Vega, Minnesota	.000	0	0	0	2	0
Velez, Toronto	.529	46	2	3	45	8
Veryzer, Cleveland	.254	34	0	4	54	10
Wagner, Detroit	.315	16	0	0	25	2
Wallis, Oakland	.205	10	1	1	18	1

Player—Club	Slg. Pct.	Tot. BB.	Int. BB.	HP.	SO.	GI DP.
Ward, Minnesota	.286	3	0	0	3	0
Washington, Chicago	.454	28	7	3	93	10
Washington, Kan. C.	.358	20	1	0	44	1
Washington, Texas	.278	4	0	0	0	0
Wathan, Kansas City	.302	7	1	0	24	7
Watson, Boston	.548	29	7	5	33	10
Werth, New York	.250	0	0	0	0	0
Whitaker, Detroit	.378	78	2	1	66	10
White, Kansas City	.403	25	3	1	54	11
White, New York	.288	23	1	0	21	6
Wilborn, Toronto	.000	1	0	0	7	0
Wilfong, Minnesota	.458	29	3	2	54	2
Wills, Texas	.350	53	4	4	58	12
Wilson, Kansas City	.420	28	3	7	92	1
Wockenfuss, Detroit	.506	18	0	2	40	9
Wohlford, Milwaukee	.366	8	0	0	28	3
Wolfe, Boston	.410	17	0	1	21	1
Woods, Toronto	.385	40	0	1	28	7
Wynegar, Minnesota	.351	74	5	2	36	13
Yastrzemski, Boston	.450	62	8	2	46	12
Yount, Milwaukee	.371	35	3	1	52	15
Zdeb, Kansas City	.304	2	0	0	4	1
Zisk, Texas	.416	57	4	0	75	15

OFFICIAL AMERICAN LEAGUE DESIGNATED HITTING

CLUB DESIGNATED HITTING

Club	Pct.	AB.	R.	H.	TB.	2B.	3B.	HR.	RBI.	SH.	SF.	BB.	HP.	SO.	SB.	CS.	GI DP.
California	.318	616	110	196	340	31	1	37	134	2	7	80	3	82	14	6	10
Boston	.279	614	94	171	295	36	5	26	104	1	6	59	9	74	6	4	22
Seattle	.277	653	81	181	298	20	5	29	106	2	2	42	4	114	1	2	20
Kansas City	.275	628	91	173	264	40	6	13	104	2	12	67	6	68	6	7	13
Cleveland	.269	602	102	162	273	24	0	29	108	6	5	81	8	116	18	7	5
New York	.261	582	92	152	267	31	3	26	86	5	6	57	2	66	2	2	14
Minnesota	.260	620	65	161	216	19	3	10	82	7	8	58	1	84	3	7	17
Toronto	.260	599	71	156	249	37	1	18	82	1	6	66	1	74	3	2	23
Texas	.255	624	76	159	236	27	1	16	74	4	6	49	4	95	4	3	15
Chicago	.249	614	81	153	246	29	2	20	96	2	4	57	1	65	4	4	26
Baltimore	.247	623	84	154	245	25	0	22	85	2	6	54	1	129	6	5	21
Milwaukee	.245	621	88	152	229	23	3	16	75	5	5	57	7	97	7	3	24
Oakland	.245	600	63	147	201	15	3	11	60	4	4	60	3	112	15	16	16
Detroit	.231	597	94	138	239	20	3	25	84	1	8	76	5	82	17	6	19
Totals	.262	8593	1192	2255	3598	377	36	298	1280	44	85	863	55	1258	106	74	245

INDIVIDUAL DESIGNATED HITTING
(Listed According to Number of Official Times at Bat)

Player and Club	Pct.	G.	AB.	R.	H.	TB.	2B.	3B.	HR.	RBI.	SH.	SF.	BB.	HP.	SO.	SB.	CS.	GI DP.
Horton, Seattle	.279	162	646	77	180	296	19	5	29	106	2	2	42	4	112	1	1	20
Page, Oakland	.244	126	463	50	113	151	10	2	8	41	3	3	49	3	91	15	16	9
Carty, Toronto	.255	129	458	48	117	179	26	0	12	53	0	4	46	1	45	3	1	21
May, Baltimore	.253	117	442	58	112	181	15	0	18	68	2	4	27	1	96	3	4	18
McRae, Kansas City	.288	100	392	55	113	183	32	4	10	74	1	7	38	4	46	5	4	6
Johnson, N.Y.-Clev.	.275	84	284	46	78	151	16	0	19	64	1	6	31	5	41	0	0	5
Baylor, California	.349	65	252	57	88	167	11	1	22	73	0	4	35	2	17	9	5	3
Staub, Detroit	.238	66	244	32	58	99	12	1	9	40	1	4	32	5	18	1	0	9
Yastrzemski, Boston	.225	56	200	17	45	72	12	0	5	33	0	3	24	0	17	1	2	9
Ellis, Texas	.241	62	199	20	48	74	8	0	6	34	0	3	8	1	44	2	1	1
Davis, Milwaukee	.273	53	198	32	54	80	6	1	6	25	1	1	11	0	25	1	2	7
Spencer, New York	.280	71	193	42	54	117	7	1	18	37	0	1	26	0	20	0	1	6
Orta, Chicago	.216	62	190	32	41	64	6	1	5	24	2	2	32	1	20	1	3	4
Morales, Minnesota	.270	77	178	20	48	59	3	1	2	26	4	3	12	1	24	0	0	9
Aikens, California	.295	51	173	26	51	90	9	0	10	36	0	2	28	0	33	0	1	3
Fisk, Boston	.279	42	172	29	48	78	14	2	4	21	1	1	6	3	25	0	0	5
Adams, Minnesota	.316	55	158	19	50	71	6	0	5	25	0	3	14	0	12	0	2	1
Johnson, Chicago	.303	37	145	16	44	60	7	0	3	26	0	2	8	0	15	2	0	10
Goodwin, Minnesota	.261	51	138	14	36	56	7	2	3	22	2	0	9	0	23	0	0	5
Nordhagen, Chicago	.265	47	136	18	36	67	10	0	7	23	0	0	10	0	14	0	0	5
LeFlore, Detroit	.229	34	131	22	30	45	4	1	3	11	0	2	17	0	22	12	3	7
Rice, Boston	.310	33	126	28	39	79	6	2	10	29	0	2	15	2	21	4	1	4
Money, Milwaukee	.200	33	120	18	24	32	5	0	1	6	2	1	17	2	18	0	0	5
Bonds, Cleveland	.257	29	113	20	29	45	4	0	4	14	1	0	15	3	29	8	2	0
Gamble, Tex.-N.Y.	.264	43	110	16	29	44	3	0	4	15	0	1	23	0	12	1	0	3
White, New York	.219	29	96	11	21	30	6	0	1	15	2	1	9	0	11	0	1	1
Watson, Boston	.368	26	95	16	35	59	4	1	6	18	0	0	12	3	9	1	1	2
Putnam, Texas	.247	32	93	11	23	37	3	1	3	11	0	0	4	3	16	0	1	4

Player and Club	Pct.	G.	AB.	R.	H.	TB.	2B.	3B.	HR.	RBI.	SH.	SF.	BB.	HP.	SO.	SB.	CS.	GI DP.
Garr, Chi.-Calif.	.207	23	82	8	17	30	1	0	4	11	0	0	5	0	5	0	0	3
Solaita, Toronto	.256	26	82	12	21	33	7	1	1	12	0	2	14	0	15	0	0	0
Bando, Milwaukee	.314	19	70	8	22	27	2	0	1	7	1	0	8	1	5	0	0	6
Montanez, Texas	.328	17	67	8	22	35	4	0	3	10	0	2	0	6	0	0	2
Downing, California	.415	18	65	11	27	41	5	0	3	18	1	0	6	0	7	0	0	2
Revering, Oakland	.234	18	64	8	15	25	2	1	2	10	0	1	8	0	10	0	0	2
Kelly, Baltimore	.226	18	62	9	14	21	4	0	1	4	0	0	5	0	12	3	1	1
Cooper, Milwaukee	.121	15	58	1	7	12	2	0	1	6	0	1	4	0	14	1	0	1
Singleton, Baltimore	.228	16	57	10	13	24	2	0	3	9	0	1	13	0	12	0	0	2
Wockenfuss, Detroit	.228	18	57	9	13	32	1	0	6	11	0	0	5	0	12	1	1	1
Chambliss, New York	.246	16	57	6	14	22	2	0	2	9	0	1	4	2	3	0	0	3
Hisle, Milwaukee	.273	15	55	12	15	20	2	0	1	7	0	1	8	0	16	1	0	2
Porter, Kansas City	.360	15	50	14	18	30	2	2	2	14	0	2	12	2	2	0	0	2
LaCock, Kansas City	.265	16	49	8	13	15	2	0	0	7	0	1	7	0	3	0	1	2
Rettenmund, Calif.	.283	17	46	5	13	18	2	0	1	4	0	1	7	1	10	1	0	2
Oglivie, Milwaukee	.239	13	46	9	11	22	2	0	3	12	1	0	4	1	5	0	1	1
Cubbage, Minnesota	.222	21	45	2	10	11	1	0	0	3	0	2	13	0	4	1	4	0
Jones, New York	.244	15	45	5	11	18	5	1	0	3	2	0	1	0	7	0	0	1
Scott, K.C.-N.Y.	.311	17	45	9	14	22	3	1	1	6	0	1	2	0	7	1	0	0
Thornton, Cleveland	.250	13	44	8	11	25	2	0	4	11	0	0	6	0	8	0	0	0
Soderholm, Texas	.227	14	44	5	10	13	3	0	0	3	1	2	4	0	2	0	0	0
Greene, Detroit	.140	15	43	6	6	12	0	0	2	2	0	0	6	0	10	0	0	1
Piniella, New York	.333	16	42	4	14	18	1	0	1	5	0	1	2	0	1	1	0	2
Alexander, Cleveland	.268	13	41	11	11	16	2	0	1	4	0	0	5	0	14	1	0	0
Bannister, Chicago	.128	9	39	3	5	9	2	1	0	3	0	0	1	0	5	0	0	1
Norris, Cleveland	.282	13	39	4	11	14	3	0	0	3	3	0	8	0	6	3	2	0
Kemp, Detroit	.308	11	39	12	12	22	1	0	3	11	0	2	8	0	6	3	0	0
Gray, Texas	.205	13	39	4	8	8	0	0	0	1	0	0	2	0	7	1	1	2
Pruitt, Cleveland	.278	14	36	4	10	12	2	0	0	6	0	0	5	0	3	0	0	0
Braun, Kansas City	.194	11	36	5	7	8	1	0	0	1	1	0	8	0	3	0	0	1
Kusick, Minn.-Tor.	.143	13	35	2	5	6	1	0	0	3	0	0	2	0	9	0	0	1
Norwood, Minnesota	.219	14	32	1	7	8	1	0	0	1	0	0	5	0	9	2	1	0
Velez, Toronto	.313	9	32	4	10	19	3	0	2	6	0	0	4	0	7	0	0	2
Summers, Detroit	.290	10	31	4	9	16	2	1	1	5	0	0	4	0	5	0	1	0
Harrah, Cleveland	.333	9	30	9	10	16	0	0	2	4	1	0	10	0	3	1	0	0
Oliver, Texas	.233	10	30	0	7	8	1	0	0	0	0	0	1	0	1	0	0	2
Cage, Cleveland	.207	9	29	1	6	6	0	0	0	2	0	0	4	0	11	0	2	0
Crowley, Baltimore	.333	15	27	6	9	12	3	0	0	2	0	0	6	0	4	0	0	0
Quirk, Kansas City	.148	9	27	1	4	4	0	0	0	0	0	0	1	0	4	0	0	0
Molitor, Milwaukee	.222	8	27	2	6	11	1	2	0	4	0	1	3	1	3	3	0	0
Newman, Oakland	.083	7	24	0	2	2	0	0	0	0	0	0	1	0	6	0	0	4
Carew, California	.273	6	22	5	6	11	2	0	1	2	0	0	4	0	3	3	0	0
Wathan, K.C.	.227	11	22	4	5	5	0	0	0	4	0	2	0	0	4	0	0	1
Munson, New York	.273	5	22	3	6	7	1	0	0	1	0	0	2	0	3	0	0	1
Moore, Chicago	.381	10	21	3	8	12	1	0	1	5	0	0	1	0	2	0	0	3
Davis, California	.400	6	20	4	8	10	2	0	0	1	1	0	0	0	4	0	0	0
Morales, Detroit	.053	7	19	0	1	1	0	0	0	1	0	0	1	0	4	0	1	0
Otis, Kansas City	.222	4	18	2	4	5	1	0	0	1	0	0	0	0	1	1	0	1
Sample, Texas	.389	9	18	5	7	10	3	0	0	0	1	0	1	0	1	0	0	0
Howell, Toronto	.389	4	18	3	7	14	1	0	2	10	0	0	1	0	3	0	0	0
Fosse, Milwaukee	.176	5	17	1	3	4	1	0	0	1	0	0	1	2	3	0	0	1
Thomas, Milwaukee	.353	4	17	2	6	13	1	0	2	5	0	0	0	0	4	0	0	0
Ayala, Baltimore	.250	10	16	4	4	4	0	0	0	1	0	0	1	0	1	0	0	0
Hargrove, Cleveland	.313	7	16	4	5	9	1	0	1	3	0	0	4	0	1	0	0	0
Grubb, Texas	.188	6	16	4	3	4	1	0	0	0	0	0	4	0	3	0	0	1
Hurdle, Kansas City	.267	4	15	0	4	4	0	0	0	0	0	0	1	0	1	0	0	0
Essian, Oakland	.400	3	15	2	6	7	1	0	0	1	1	0	0	0	3	0	0	0
Heath, Oakland	.385	3	13	2	5	9	1	0	1	3	0	0	0	0	0	0	0	0
Powell, Minnesota	.083	5	12	1	1	1	0	0	0	0	0	0	1	0	0	1	0	1
Rudi, California	.000	3	11	0	0	0	0	0	0	0	0	0	0	0	3	0	0	0
Nahorodny, Chicago	.182	3	11	0	2	4	2	0	0	2	0	0	0	0	5	0	0	0
Dade, Cleveland	.182	4	11	2	2	2	0	0	0	1	0	0	2	0	2	0	1	0
Peters, Detroit	.364	3	11	1	4	4	0	0	0	2	0	0	1	0	1	0	0	0
Jackson, New York	.091	3	11	1	1	4	0	0	1	2	0	0	0	0	5	0	0	0
Poquette, Boston	.300	4	10	0	3	3	0	0	0	1	0	0	1	1	0	0	0	1
Wohlford, Milwaukee	.250	5	8	2	2	3	1	0	0	0	0	0	0	0	3	1	0	1
Bryant, Oakland	.375	2	8	1	3	4	1	0	0	4	0	0	1	0	1	0	0	0
Lowenstein, Balt.	.143	3	7	0	1	2	1	0	0	0	0	0	1	0	1	0	0	0

Player and Club	Pct.	G.	AB.	R.	H.	TB.	2B.	3B.	HR.	RBI.	SH.	SF.	BB.	HP.	SO.	SB.	CS.	GI. DP.
Murray, Baltimore	.143	2	7	0	1	1	0	0	0	1	0	1	1	0	1	0	0	0
Washington, Chicago	.286	3	7	0	2	2	0	0	0	1	0	0	0	0	1	0	1	0
Thompson, Detroit....	.286	2	7	1	2	5	0	0	1	1	0	0	1	0	0	0	0	0
Wynegar, Minnesota .	.429	2	7	2	3	3	0	0	0	2	0	0	1	0	0	0	0	0
Edwards, Oakland	.286	2	7	0	2	2	0	0	0	0	0	0	0	0	0	0	0	1
Zisk, Texas	.286	3	7	2	2	3	1	0	0	0	0	0	1	0	0	0	0	0
Robertson, Toronto....	.143	4	7	1	1	4	0	0	1	1	0	0	1	0	3	0	0	0
Alston, Cleveland	.333	7	6	2	2	2	0	0	0	1	0	0	0	0	0	2	0	0
Jones, Detroit............	.500	6	6	3	3	3	0	0	0	0	0	0	0	0	0	0	0	0
Vega, Minnesota	.000	3	6	0	0	0	0	0	0	0	0	0	0	0	1	0	0	0
Klutts, Oakland	.167	2	6	0	1	1	0	0	0	1	0	0	1	0	1	0	0	0
Roberts, Texas	.167	4	6	1	1	1	0	0	0	0	0	0	0	0	3	0	0	0
Lemon, Chicago........	.000	1	5	0	0	0	0	0	0	0	0	0	0	0	1	0	0	0
Washington, K.C......	.000	3	5	0	0	0	0	0	0	0	0	0	0	0	2	0	0	0
Lezcano, Milwaukee .	.400	1	5	1	2	5	0	0	1	2	0	0	1	0	1	0	0	0
Ward, Minnesota	.200	3	5	1	1	1	0	0	0	0	0	0	2	0	1	0	0	0
Lynn, Boston	.250	1	4	1	1	4	0	0	1	2	0	0	0	0	1	0	0	0
Hassey, Cleveland	.000	1	4	0	0	0	0	0	0	0	0	0	0	0	3	0	0	0
Corcoran, Detroit	.000	2	4	0	0	0	0	0	0	0	0	0	0	0	1	0	0	0
Brett, Kansas City	.750	1	4	1	3	5	2	0	0	2	0	0	0	0	0	0	0	0
Randle, New York	.250	2	4	0	1	1	0	0	0	0	0	0	0	0	0	0	0	0
Dwyer, Boston..........	.000	4	3	3	0	0	0	0	0	0	0	0	1	0	0	0	0	1
Papi, Boston	.000	1	3	0	0	0	0	0	0	0	0	0	0	0	0	0	0	0
Gonzales, Detroit......	.000	1	3	0	0	0	0	0	0	0	0	0	0	0	1	0	0	0
Cowens, Kansas City.	.667	1	3	1	2	5	0	0	1	1	0	0	0	0	0	0	1	0
Wilson, Kansas City ..	.000	2	3	0	0	0	0	0	0	0	0	0	0	0	1	0	1	0
Graham, Minnesota ..	.000	1	3	0	0	0	0	0	0	0	0	0	0	0	0	0	0	0
Johnstone, New York	.000	3	3	0	0	0	0	0	0	0	0	0	0	0	1	0	0	0
Chalk, Texas............	.000	2	3	0	0	0	0	0	0	0	1	0	0	0	0	0	0	0
Beamon, Seattle........	.000	5	3	2	0	0	0	0	0	0	0	0	0	0	1	0	0	0
Corey, Baltimore	.000	1	2	0	0	0	0	0	0	0	0	0	0	0	2	0	0	0
Roenicke, Baltimore .	.000	2	2	0	0	0	0	0	0	0	0	0	0	0	0	0	0	0
Harper, California	.000	1	2	0	0	0	0	0	0	0	0	0	0	0	1	0	0	0
Brookens, Detroit	.000	1	2	0	0	0	0	0	0	0	0	0	1	0	1	0	0	0
Valentine, Seattle	.500	1	2	0	1	2	1	0	0	0	0	0	0	0	0	0	0	0
Hale, Seattle	.000	2	2	1	0	0	0	0	0	0	0	0	0	0	1	0	0	0
Wolfe, Boston	.000	1	1	0	0	0	0	0	0	0	0	0	0	0	1	0	0	0
Harlow, Baltimore	.000	1	1	0	0	0	0	0	0	0	0	0	0	0	0	0	0	0
Miller, California	.000	2	1	0	0	0	0	0	0	0	0	0	0	0	1	0	0	0
Bosley, Chicago........	1.000	1	1	0	1	1	0	0	0	1	0	0	0	0	0	1	0	0
Gates, Chicago..........	.000	1	1	1	0	0	0	0	0	0	0	0	0	0	0	0	0	0
Cox, Cleveland..........	1.000	1	1	0	1	1	0	0	0	1	0	0	0	0	0	0	0	0
Barranca, K.C...........	.000	1	1	0	0	0	0	0	0	0	0	0	0	0	1	0	0	0
Terrell, Kansas City ..	.000	1	1	0	0	0	0	0	0	0	0	0	0	0	0	0	0	0
Edwards, Minnesota .	.000	3	1	3	0	0	0	0	0	0	0	0	0	0	1	0	0	0
Rivera, Minnesota	.000	2	1	0	0	0	0	0	0	0	1	0	0	0	1	0	0	0
Brown, New York	.000	1	1	1	0	0	0	0	0	0	0	0	0	0	0	0	0	0
Narron, New York	.000	1	1	0	0	0	0	0	0	0	0	0	1	0	1	0	0	0
Blanks, Texas............	.000	1	1	0	0	0	0	0	0	0	0	0	0	0	0	0	0	0
Jorgensen, Texas......	.000	2	1	1	0	0	0	0	0	0	1	0	0	0	1	0	0	0
Rivers, Texas............	.000	1	1	0	0	0	0	0	0	0	0	0	0	0	1	0	0	0
Washington, Texas ...	1.000	1	1	0	1	1	0	0	0	2	0	0	0	0	0	0	0	0
Woods, Toronto........	.000	2	1	0	0	0	0	0	0	0	0	0	0	0	0	0	0	0
Campaneris, Calif	.000	1	0	0	0	0	0	0	0	0	0	0	0	0	0	1	0	0
Ramirez, California....	.000	1	0	0	0	0	0	0	0	0	0	0	0	0	0	0	0	0
Thon, California	.000	1	0	0	0	0	0	0	0	0	0	0	0	0	0	0	0	0
Manning, Cleveland ..	.000	1	0	0	0	0	0	0	0	0	1	0	0	0	0	0	0	0
Speed, Cleveland	.000	4	0	1	0	0	0	0	0	0	0	0	0	0	0	1	0	0
Mankowski, Detroit ..	.000	1	0	1	0	0	0	0	0	0	0	0	0	0	0	0	0	0
Machemer, Detroit ...	.000	1	0	1	0	0	0	0	0	0	0	0	0	0	0	0	0	0
Morris, Detroit..........	.000	1	0	1	0	0	0	0	0	0	0	0	0	0	0	0	0	0
Wagner, Detroit	.000	1	0	1	0	0	0	0	0	0	0	0	0	0	0	0	0	0
Roberts, Seattle	.000	1	0	0	0	0	0	0	0	0	0	0	0	0	0	0	0	0
Rawley, Seattle	.000	1	0	0	0	0	0	0	0	0	0	0	0	0	0	0	0	0
Simpson, Seattle	.000	3	0	1	0	0	0	0	0	0	0	0	0	0	0	0	1	0
Ainge, Toronto	.000	1	0	1	0	0	0	0	0	0	0	0	0	0	0	0	0	0
Bailor, Toronto.........	.000	1	0	1	0	0	0	0	0	0	0	0	0	0	0	0	0	0
Hernandez, Toronto ..	.000	2	0	1	0	0	0	0	0	0	0	0	0	0	0	0	0	0
Wilborn, Toronto	.000	4	0	0	0	0	0	0	0	0	1	0	0	0	0	0	1	0

OFFICIAL AMERICAN LEAGUE FIELDING AVERAGES

CLUB FIELDING

Club	Pct.	G.	PO.	A.	E.	TC.	DP.	TP.	PB.
New York	.9809	160	4297	1970	122	6389	183	0	15
Detroit	.9805	160	4270	1767	120	6157	184	0	24
Milwaukee	.980	161	4319	1905	127	6351	153	1	10
Baltimore	.980	159	4303	1764	125	6192	161	1	10
Texas	.979	162	4311	1862	130	6303	151	0	8
Minnesota	.979	162	4333	2007	134	6474	203	0	5
Cleveland	.978	161	4295	1642	134	6071	149	0	16
Seattle	.978	162	4314	1879	141	6334	170	0	7
California	.978	162	4308	1608	135	6051	172	0	12
Boston	.977	160	4294	1853	142	6289	166	3	20
Kansas City	.977	162	4345	1777	146	6268	160	0	15
Toronto	.975	162	4251	1878	159	6288	187	2	8
Chicago	.972	159	4227	1831	173	6231	142	0	17
Oakland	.972	162	4288	1718	174	6180	137	3	15
Totals	.978	1127	60155	25461	1962	87578	2318	10	182

INDIVIDUAL FIELDING

FIRST BASEMEN

*Throws lefthanded.

Leader—Club	Pct.	G.	PO.	A.	E.	DP.
LaCOCK, KC*	.997	108	829	68	3	79

(Listed Alphabetically)

Player—Club	Pct.	G.	PO.	A.	E.	DP.
Aikens, Calif	.996	55	462	31	2	49
Bochte, Sea*	.991	147	1361	114	14	140
Carew, Calif	.988	103	804	55	10	101
Chambliss, NY	.995	134	1299	95	7	135
Cooper, Milw*	.993	135	1323	78	10	119
Dwyer, Bos*	.981	25	141	15	3	15
Ellis, Tex	.978	30	216	11	5	17
Gross, Oak	.993	18	129	14	1	8
Hargrove, Clev*	.996	28	221	13	1	23
Jackson, Minn	.994	157	1447	137	9	175
Johnson, Chi	.987	94	748	63	11	62
Jorgensen, Tex*	.988	60	287	30	4	28
Kusick, Minn-Tor	.983	28	209	18	4	20
LaCock, KC*	.997	108	829	68	3	79
Mayberry, Tor*	.995	135	1192	74	6	129
Meyer, Sea	1.000	15	73	4	0	5
Money, Milw	1.000	19	196	11	0	20
Montanez, Tex*	.995	19	191	16	1	14
Murray, Balt	.994	157	1456	107	10	135
Newman, Oak	.982	46	350	30	7	29
Paciorek, Sea	.991	15	100	10	1	12
Putnam, Tex	.994	96	832	62	5	65
Revering, Oak	.986	104	828	80	13	77
Scott, Bos-KC-NY	.987	83	737	46	10	67
Spencer, NY*	.992	26	232	17	2	35
Squires, Chi*	.995	110	741	60	4	62
Thompson, Det*	.994	140	1176	91	8	135
Thornton, Clev	.994	130	1089	82	7	100
Wathan, KC	.993	49	264	19	2	30
Watson, Bos	.988	58	525	47	7	58
Wockenfuss, Det	.996	31	205	18	1	22
Yastrzemski, Bos	.996	51	466	55	2	42

(Fewer Than Ten Games)

Player—Club	Pct.	G.	PO.	A.	E.	DP.
Bando, Milw	1.000	4	18	2	0	3
Bannister, Chi	1.000	1	2	0	0	1
Baylor, Calif	1.000	1	5	0	0	1
Beamon, Sea*	1.000	7	14	2	0	0
Brett, KC	.981	8	47	5	1	6
Cage, Clev*	1.000	7	37	4	0	3

Player—Club	Pct.	G.	PO.	A.	E.	DP.
Chism, Balt	1.000	4	6	0	0	0
Corcoran, Det*	1.000	5	35	1	0	2
Crowley, Balt*	1.000	2	5	0	0	1
Cubbage, Minn	1.000	1	4	0	0	0
Duffy, Bos	.000	1	0	0	0	0
Essian, Oak	1.000	4	35	2	0	4
Fosse, Milw	1.000	1	9	0	0	0
Goodwin, Minn	1.000	8	40	2	0	5
Hampton, Calif	1.000	2	10	2	0	0
Harris, Calif*	1.000	1	6	0	0	0
Hassey, Clev	1.000	2	23	0	0	1
Holle, Tex*	1.000	1	11	0	0	1
Johnson, Tex	1.000	7	27	2	0	2
Kessinger, Chi	1.000	1	2	0	0	0
Lowenstein, Balt	1.000	1	4	1	0	1
May, Balt	.913	2	21	0	2	2
Morales, Minn	1.000	1	2	0	0	0
Munson, NY	1.000	3	23	0	0	2
Nettles, KC*	1.000	1	2	0	0	0
Oglivie, Milw*	.986	9	68	3	1	3
Putman, Det	.974	5	35	3	1	5
Roberts, Tex	1.000	6	9	0	0	1
Robertson, Tor	1.000	9	54	7	0	6
Rodriguez, Det	.000	1	0	0	0	0
Rudi, Calif	1.000	5	33	2	0	3
Smalley, Minn	1.000	1	9	0	0	2
Soderholm, Tex	.909	2	9	1	1	0
Solaita, Tor*	1.000	6	39	4	0	8
Stanley, NY	1.000	1	5	0	0	0
Summers, Det	1.000	4	23	1	0	1
Velez, Tor	1.000	6	29	2	0	2
Werth, NY	1.000	1	5	1	0	0
Wolfe, Bos	1.000	1	6	1	0	0

TRIPLE PLAYS: Cooper, Kusick (Tor.), Mayberry, Murray, Revering 2, Scott (Bos.), Watson, Yastrzemski.

FIRST BASEMEN WITH TWO OR MORE CLUBS

Player—Club	Pct.	G.	PO.	A.	E.	DP.
Kusick, Minn	1.000	8	46	3	0	6
Kusick, Tor	.977	20	163	15	4	14
Scott, Bos	.986	41	400	25	6	40
Scott, KC	.989	41	335	21	4	27
Scott, NY	1.000	1	2	0	0	0

SECOND BASEMEN

Leader—Club	Pct.	G.	PO.	A.	E.	DP.
KUIPER, Clev.	.988	140	345	380	9	89

(Listed Alphabetically)

Player—Club	Pct.	G.	PO.	A.	E.	DP.
Ainge, Tor	.977	86	198	261	11	67
Bannister, Chi	.963	65	150	160	12	32
Blanks, Tex	1.000	16	26	25	0	6
Brohamer, Bos	.982	36	65	98	3	21
Brookens, Det	.963	19	37	42	3	10
Chalk, Tex-Oak	.988	38	78	93	2	22
Cruz, Sea	.979	107	258	361	13	87
Dauer, Balt	.979	103	213	260	10	68
Doyle, NY	.944	13	11	23	2	5
Edwards, Oak	.962	113	244	314	22	54
Gantner, Milw	.984	22	50	76	2	16
Garcia, Balt	.933	25	34	49	6	12
Gomez, Tor	.971	20	29	38	2	10
Grich, Calif	.984	153	340	438	13	111
Johnson, Tor	.958	25	62	52	5	21
Kuiper, Clev	.988	140	345	380	9	89
Machemer, Det	.972	11	15	20	1	6
McKay, Tor	.974	46	119	148	7	37
Milbourne, Sea	.967	49	90	141	8	37

Player—Club	Pct.	G.	PO.	A.	E.	DP.
Molitor, Milw	.979	122	289	413	15	81
Money, Milw	.971	16	26	42	2	7
Morrison, Chi	.982	48	104	120	4	33
Orta, Chi	.978	41	57	75	3	17
Papi, Bos	.982	26	37	72	2	16
Pryor, Chi	.989	25	42	48	1	13
Ramirez, Oak	.971	11	14	19	1	5
Randall, Minn	.983	71	130	166	5	48
Randolph, NY	.985	153	355	478	13	128
Remy, Bos	.970	76	147	205	11	43
Rosello, Clev	.976	33	40	84	3	12
Sizemore, Bos	.993	26	53	85	1	24
Smith, Balt	.980	63	107	142	5	33
Stein, Sea	1.000	17	18	42	0	7
Thon, Calif	.923	24	34	38	6	12
Wagner, Det	.960	29	57	63	5	10
Washington, KC	.949	46	112	111	12	37
Whitaker, Det	.986	126	280	369	9	103
White, KC	.982	125	317	332	12	78
Wilfong, Minn	.979	133	287	379	14	92
Wills, Tex	.976	146	337	468	20	95
Wolfe, Bos	.963	27	28	50	3	11

TRIPLE PLAYS: Brohamer, Dauer, Edwards, Gomez, Klutts, McKay, Molitor, Remy.

(Fewer Than Ten Games)

Player—Club	Pct.	G.	PO.	A.	E.	DP.
Anderson, Calif	1.000	6	5	8	0	2
Bando, Milw	1.000	1	1	0	0	0
Barranca, KC	1.000	1	4	7	0	3
Cox, Clev	1.000	4	2	1	0	0
Cubbage, Minn	.000	1	0	0	0	0
Duffy, Bos	1.000	3	3	2	0	0
Gates, Chi	.966	8	12	16	1	3
Hobson, Bos	.000	1	0	0	0	0
Kessinger, Chi	1.000	1	2	6	0	0
Klutts, Oak	.971	8	19	15	1	3
Krenchicki, Balt	1.000	6	3	7	0	1
Moore, Chi	1.000	2	0	2	0	0
Murray, Oak	1.000	3	1	1	0	0

Player—Club	Pct.	G.	PO.	A.	E.	DP.
Norman, Tex	.000	1	0	0	0	0
Peters, Det	1.000	2	1	0	0	0
Picciolo, Oak	1.000	6	11	16	0	4
Roberts, Tex	1.000	8	15	23	0	9
Sakata, Milw	1.000	4	10	13	0	5
Stanley, NY	.960	8	9	15	1	3
Terrell, KC	1.000	7	5	7	0	3
Valentine, Cal	1.000	4	0	2	0	0

SECOND BASEMAN WITH TWO OR MORE CLUBS

Player—Club	Pct.	G.	PO.	A.	E.	DP.
Chalk, Tex	1.000	1	1	0	0	0
Chalk, Oak	.988	37	77	93	2	22

THIRD BASEMEN

Leader—Club	Pct.	G.	PO.	A.	E.	DP.
LANSFORD, CALIF	.983	157	135	263	7	29

(Listed Alphabetically)

Player—Club	Pct.	G.	PO.	A.	E.	DP.
Anderson, Calif	1.000	10	4	8	0	0
Bando, Milw	.963	109	87	222	12	16
Bannister, Chi	.850	12	10	24	6	4
Bell, Chi	.923	68	51	153	17	11
Bell, Tex	.969	147	112	364	15	22
Brett, KC	.944	149	129	373	30	28
Brohamer, Bos	.962	22	9	42	2	6
Brookens, Det	.945	42	39	99	8	11
Castino, Minn	.963	143	85	277	14	31
Chalk, Oak	.930	16	15	25	3	1
Cox, Clev	.964	52	29	78	4	11
Cubbage, Minn	.928	63	34	94	10	9
Dauer, Balt	.943	44	21	95	7	4
DeCinces, Balt	.964	120	99	247	13	21
Essian, Oak	.972	10	15	20	1	2
Gantner, Milw	.952	42	28	71	5	8
Gomez, Tor	1.000	22	21	37	0	9
Gross, Oak	.943	120	120	211	20	19
Harrah, Clev	.940	127	91	160	16	19
Hobson, Bos	.935	142	110	251	25	18

Player—Club	Pct.	G.	PO.	A.	E.	DP.
Howell, Tor	.952	133	108	290	20	28
Lansford, Calif	.983	157	135	263	7	29
Mankowski, Det	.963	36	22	56	3	6
Meyer, Sea	.936	101	76	201	19	22
Milbourne, Sea	.958	11	8	15	1	0
Money, Milw	1.000	26	18	64	0	6
Morrison, Chi	.943	29	17	65	5	5
Nettles, NY	.966	144	110	339	16	30
Pryor, Chi	.929	22	15	37	4	2
Ramirez, Oak	.923	12	4	8	1	0
Rodriguez, Det	.956	106	72	211	13	23
Rosello, Clev	.875	14	2	12	2	3
Soderholm, Chi-Tex	.975	93	75	202	7	17
Stanley, NY	.875	16	5	30	5	2
Stein, Sea	.959	67	45	120	7	13
Terrell, KC	.963	19	5	21	1	1

TRIPLE PLAYS: Bando, DeCinces, Gross 3, Hobson, Howell.

(Fewer Than Ten Games)

Player—Club	Pct.	G.	PO.	A.	E.	DP.
Allenson, Bos	1.000	3	3	2	0	1
Bailor, Tor	1.000	9	7	16	0	0
Barranca, KC	.000	1	0	0	0	0
Beniquez, NY	1.000	3	1	11	0	0

THIRD BASEMEN—Continued

Player—Club	Pct.	G.	PO.	A.	E.	DP.
Braun, Calif	.000	2	0	0	0	0
Cruz, KC	.885	9	7	16	3	3
Dade, Clev	.000	2	0	0	0	0
Doyle, NY	1.000	6	1	4	0	0
Garcia, Balt	.000	2	0	0	0	0
Garcia, NY	.000	1	0	0	0	0
Gates, Chi	1.000	1	0	0	0	0
Heath, Oak	1.000	1	0	1	0	0
Hurdle, KC	1.000	7	1	14	0	0
Jackson, Minn	1.000	1	1	0	0	0
Johnson, Tor	.900	9	2	16	2	1
Klutts, Oak	.913	6	7	14	2	0
Krenchicki, Balt	.875	7	9	5	2	0
Lowenstein, Balt	1.000	1	0	2	0	0
McKay, Tor	1.000	2	0	2	0	0
Newman, Oak	.933	7	2	12	1	2
Peters, Det	.000	3	0	0	2	0
Picciolo, Oak	1.000	4	1	7	0	0

Player—Club	Pct.	G.	PO.	A.	E.	DP.
Pruitt, Clev	1.000	3	1	1	0	0
Quirk, KC	1.000	3	1	4	0	0
Randall, Minn	1.000	7	0	3	0	0
Roberts, Tex	1.000	1	0	1	0	0
Scott, KC	.000	1	0	0	0	0
Staiger, NY	1.000	4	2	7	0	1
Thon, Calif	1.000	1	1	0	0	0
Valentine, Sea	.933	4	4	10	1	2
Wagner, Det	.000	2	0	0	0	0
Washington, KC	1.000	1	0	1	0	0
Washington, Tex	1.000	1	0	1	0	0
Wolfe, Bos	.933	9	10	18	2	3

THIRD BASEMAN WITH TWO OR MORE CLUBS

Player—Club	Pct.	G.	PO.	A.	E.	DP.
Soderholm, Chi	.986	56	55	154	3	12
Soderholm, Tex	.944	37	20	48	4	5

SHORTSTOPS

Leader—Club	Pct.	G.	PO.	A.	E.	DP.
BURLESON, BOS	.980	153	272	523	16	109

(Listed Alphabetically)

Player—Club	Pct.	G.	PO.	A.	E.	DP.
Anderson, Calif	.949	82	126	189	17	42
Belanger, Balt	.990	98	110	195	3	38
Bell, Tex	.980	33	35	65	2	9
Blanks, Tex	.972	49	39	65	3	16
Burleson, Bos	.980	153	272	523	16	109
Campaneris, Tx-Cal	.957	90	148	233	17	74
Chalk, Tex-Oak	.917	19	30	36	6	8
Chappas, Chi	.929	23	28	63	7	13
Cruz, KC	.974	48	47	102	4	13
Dent, NY	.977	141	219	512	17	107
Garcia, Balt	.955	113	173	271	21	66
Garcia, NY	.902	10	9	28	4	4
Gomez, Tor	.984	15	20	41	1	6
Griffin, Tor	.956	153	272	501	36	124
Guerrero, Oak	.952	43	68	129	10	33
Harrah, Clev	.963	33	22	55	3	11
Kessinger, Chi	.988	54	57	103	2	17
Klutts, Oak	.882	10	9	21	4	3
Mendoza, Sea	.968	148	177	422	20	91
Milbourne, Sea	.981	65	46	109	3	20
Molitor, Milw	.979	10	20	27	1	3
Mulliniks, Calif	.957	22	46	43	4	13
Norman, Tex	.952	142	177	302	24	64
Papi, Bos	.986	21	24	46	1	8
Patek, KC	.955	104	153	249	19	54

Player—Club	Pct.	G.	PO.	A.	E.	DP.
Picciolo, Oak	.964	105	191	265	17	51
Pryor, Chi	.961	119	161	362	21	54
Ramirez, Calif	.844	10	7	20	5	3
Rosello, Clev	1.000	11	1	2	0	1
Smalley, Minn	.968	161	296	572	29	144
Stanley, NY	.978	31	23	68	2	18
Trammell, Det	.961	142	245	388	26	99
Valentine, Sea	.971	29	11	23	1	3
Veryzer, Clev	.974	148	238	446	18	90
Wagner, Det	.974	41	31	83	3	18
Washington, KC	.970	50	62	131	6	31
Yount, Milw	.969	149	267	517	25	97

TRIPLE PLAYS: Burleson 2, Chalk (Oak), Griffin.

(Fewer Than Ten Games)

Player—Club	Pct.	G.	PO.	A.	E.	DP.
Bell, Chi	1.000	2	0	1	0	0
Castino, Minn	.938	5	6	9	1	3
Edwards, Oak	1.000	3	2	4	0	0
Gantner, Milw	1.000	3	2	13	0	2
Jackson, Minn	.000	1	0	0	0	0
Nordhook Milw	1.000	2	1	0	0	0
Quirk, KC	1.000	5	0	3	0	0
Ramirez, Oak	.885	8	7	16	3	0
Randall, Minn	.000	1	0	0	0	0
Smith, Balt	.833	5	1	9	2	2
Stein, Sea	1.000	3	1	0	0	0
Terrell, KC	.000	1	0	0	0	0
Thon, Calif	.846	8	3	8	2	1
Wolfe, Bos	1.000	2	2	1	0	1

SHORTSTOPS WITH TWO OR MORE CLUBS

Player—Club	Pct.	G.	PO.	A.	E.	DP.
Campaneris, Tex	.962	8	12	13	1	5
Campaneris, Cal	.957	82	136	220	16	69

Player—Club	Pct.	G.	PO.	A.	E.	DP.
Chalk, Tex	1.000	3	0	3	0	0
Chalk, Oak	.913	16	30	33	6	8

OUTFIELDERS

Leader—Club	Pct.	G.	PO.	A.	E.	DP.
OTIS, KC	.992	146	385	11	3	5

(Listed Alphabetically)

Player—Club	Pct.	G.	PO.	A.	E.	DP.
Adams, Minn	.958	53	66	2	3	0
Alston, Clev	.969	30	29	2	1	0
Armas, Oak	.976	80	194	7	5	2
Ayala, Balt	.974	24	38	0	1	0
Bailor, Tor	.987	118	210	16	3	2

Player—Club	Pct.	G.	PO.	A.	E.	DP.
Bannister, Chi	.968	47	88	3	3	0
Baylor, Calif	.976	97	198	3	5	0
Beniquez, NY	.981	60	99	4	2	0
Bonds, Clev	.979	116	267	9	6	1
Bosetti, Tor	.974	162	466	18	13	4
Bosley, Chi*	.967	28	57	2	2	1
Braun, KC	1.000	18	26	4	0	0
Brown, Tor-NY	.955	31	64	0	3	0
Bryant, Oak	1.000	33	55	2	0	0

OUTFIELDERS—Continued

Player—Club	Pct.	G.	PO.	A.	E.	DP.
Bumbry, Balt	.982	146	367	7	7	1
Burke, Oak	1.000	23	46	2	0	0
Cannon, Tor	1.000	50	81	5	0	1
Clark, Calif	.978	19	41	4	1	0
Corey, Balt	1.000	11	10	0	0	0
Cowens, KC	.986	134	288	3	4	0
Cox, Clev	.933	16	26	2	2	0
Craig, Sea	.923	15	24	0	2	0
Dade, Clev	.963	37	73	4	3	1
Davis, Milw	.973	35	72	1	2	0
Dilone, Oak	.959	25	47	0	2	0
Dwyer, Bos*	.964	19	26	1	1	0
Edwards, Minn	.983	86	165	7	3	0
Evans, Bos	.988	149	307	15	4	5
Ford, Calif	.977	141	332	10	8	2
Gamble, Tex-NY	.969	48	88	5	3	4
Garr, Chi	.951	67	94	3	5	1
Gibson, Det*	1.000	10	15	0	0	0
Grubb, Tex	.986	82	135	8	2	4
Hale, Sea	1.000	42	34	0	0	0
Hargrove, Clev*	.993	65	135	3	1	0
Harlow, Balt-Calif*	.974	89	147	4	4	1
Heath, Oak	.978	46	86	5	2	2
Henderson, Oak*	.973	88	215	5	6	0
Hisle, Milw	1.000	10	17	2	0	0
Hurdle, KC	.968	50	88	2	3	0
Jackson, NY*	.986	125	274	7	4	2
Johnstone, NY	1.000	19	32	0	0	0
Jones, Det	.980	84	142	3	3	1
Jones, Sea*	.989	161	453	13	5	4
Jorgensen, Tex*	1.000	20	33	1	0	0
Kelly, Balt*	1.000	24	36	0	0	0
Kemp, Det*	.976	120	229	12	6	2
Landreaux, Minn	.981	147	292	10	6	1
LeFlore, Det	.990	113	293	6	3	3
Lemon, Chi	.977	147	411	10	10	2
Lezcano, Milw	.986	135	281	10	4	2
Lowenstein, Balt	.992	72	120	4	1	2
Lynn, Bos*	.987	143	381	10	5	4
Manning, Clev	.986	141	417	9	6	2
Meyer, Sea	.942	31	49	0	3	0
Miller, Calif*	.989	117	349	3	4	1
Moore, Chi	.966	61	83	3	3	0
Morales, Det	.986	119	206	6	3	2
Murcer, NY	.983	70	169	4	3	0
Murphy, Oak	.988	118	322	10	4	0
Murray, Oak	.963	90	173	7	7	2
Nordhagen, Chi	1.000	12	19	4	0	0
Norris, Clev*	.982	93	214	2	4	0
Norwood, Minn	.974	71	147	4	4	0
Oglivie, Milw*	.985	120	252	7	4	0
Oliver, Tex*	.975	119	260	9	7	2
Otis, KC	.992	146	385	11	3	5
Paciorek, Sea	1.000	75	137	2	0	0
Piniella, NY	.982	112	204	13	4	1
Poquette, KC-Bos	.954	53	80	3	4	2
Powell, Minn*	.977	93	165	6	4	3
Pruitt, Clev	.957	29	43	1	2	0
Randle, NY	1.000	11	19	2	0	0
Rice, Bos	.984	125	241	8	4	1
Rivera, Minn	.989	105	169	12	2	0
Rivers, NY-Tex*	.978	126	300	8	7	1
Roberts, Sea	.983	136	286	6	5	2
Roberts, Tex	1.000	11	13	1	0	0
Roenicke, Balt	.981	130	246	10	5	1
Rudi, Calif	.989	80	174	5	2	2
Sample, Tex	1.000	103	173	7	0	1
Simpson, Sea°	.966	105	162	10	6	4
Singleton, Balt	.981	143	247	8	5	2
Sofield, Minn	.954	35	61	1	3	1
Speed, Clev	.875	16	14	0	2	0
Stegman, Det	1.000	12	35	0	0	0
Summers, Det	.989	69	87	3	1	0
Thomas, Milw	.991	152	435	4	4	0
Torres, Chi	.976	85	117	4	3	0
Valentine, Sea	1.000	15	17	3	0	0
Velez, Tor	.971	73	130	3	4	1
Wallis, Oak	1.000	23	41	1	0	0
Washington, Chi*	.974	122	256	7	7	3
Washington, Tex	1.000	13	16	0	0	0
White, NY	1.000	27	45	3	0	0
Wilson, KC	.985	152	384	13	6	0
Wohlford, Milw	.969	55	126	0	4	0
Woods, Tor*	.967	127	251	10	9	2
Yastrzemski, Bos*	.970	36	63	1	2	0
Zisk, Tex	.972	134	234	10	7	6

TRIPLE PLAY: Armas.

(Fewer Than Ten Games)

Player—Club	Pct.	G.	PO.	A.	E.	DP.
Alexander, Clev	.000	2	0	0	0	0
Beamon, Sea*	1.000	2	1	0	0	0
Blair, NY	1.000	2	6	0	0	0
Corcoran, Det*	1.000	9	10	1	0	0
Davis, Calif*	1.000	7	8	0	0	0
Essian, Oak	1.000	4	2	0	0	0
Fisk, Bos	.000	1	0	0	0	0
Garcia, Balt	1.000	2	2	1	0	0
Gonzales, Det	1.000	3	3	0	0	0
Greene, Det	1.000	6	14	0	0	0
Gross, Oak	1.000	2	3	0	0	0
Guidry, NY*	1.000	1	0	0	0	0
Jackson, Minn	.000	1	0	0	0	0
Jones, NY	1.000	2	1	0	0	0
Kuntz, Chi	1.000	5	12	1	0	1
Machemer, Det	1.000	1	3	0	0	0
Molinaro, Balt*	1.000	5	7	0	0	0
Nettles, KC*	1.000	8	19	0	0	0
Page, Oak	1.000	4	6	0	0	0
Peters, Det	1.000	1	3	0	0	0
Picciolo, Oak	.000	1	0	0	0	0
Randall, Minn	.000	1	0	0	0	0
Rettenmund, Calif	1.000	1	9	0	0	0
Squires, Chi*	1.000	1	3	0	0	0
Stanley, NY	1.000	1	0	0	0	0
Ward, Minn	1.000	5	8	0	0	0
Wathan, KC	1.000	3	2	0	0	0
Wilborn, Tor	.875	7	7	0	1	0
Wilfong, Minn	.000	3	0	0	0	0
Wockenfuss, Det	1.000	6	4	0	0	0
Zdeb, KC	1.000	9	13	0	0	0

OUTFIELDERS WITH TWO OR MORE CLUBS

Player—Club	Pct.	G.	PO.	A.	E.	DP.
Brown, Tor	1.000	4	8	0	0	0
Brown, NY	.949	27	56	0	3	0
Gamble, Tex	1.000	21	41	2	0	2
Gamble, NY	.949	27	47	3	3	2
Harlow, Balt	.970	31	32	0	1	0
Harlow, Calif	.975	58	115	4	3	1
Poquette, KC	1.000	10	7	1	0	1
Poquette, Bos	.949	43	73	2	4	1
Rivers, NY	.974	69	147	4	4	0
Rivers, Tex	.981	57	153	4	3	1

CATCHERS

Leader—Club	Pct.	G.	PO.	A.	E.	DP.	PB.
SUNDBERG, Tex..	.995	150	754	75	4	13	8

(Listed Alphabetically)

Player—Club	Pct.	G.	PO.	A.	E.	DP.	PB.
Alexander, Clev	.961	91	404	40	18	5	13
Allenson, Bos	.980	104	407	40	9	3	13
Borgmann, Minn..	.993	31	129	11	1	0	0
Cerone, Tor	.980	136	560	68	13	10	6
Colbern, Chi	.971	32	121	12	4	4	1
Cox, Sea	.981	99	408	49	9	6	2
Davis, Tor	.984	32	114	11	2	1	2
Dempsey, Balt	.990	124	615	81	7	13	5
Diaz, Clev	.958	15	63	6	3	1	1
Donohue, Calif ..	.981	38	136	16	3	4	5
Downing, Calif..	.985	129	669	35	11	5	6
Essian, Oak	.981	70	348	57	8	5	7
Fisk, Bos	.982	39	155	8	3	1	3
Foley, Chi.............	.993	33	128	11	1	1	2
Fosse, Milw	1.000	13	32	3	0	1	0
Gulden, NY	.995	40	178	24	1	4	1
Hassey, Clev.........	.992	68	345	29	3	4	2

Player—Club	Pct.	G.	PO.	A.	E.	DP.	PB.
Heath, Oak..........	.969	22	80	13	3	0	4
Martinez, Milw ...	.967	68	198	39	8	2	4
May, Det-Chi	.982	70	296	28	6	1	7
Montgomery, Bos .	.984	31	121	5	2	0	2
Moore, Milw.........	.979	106	414	58	10	7	6
Munson, NY.........	.978	88	405	44	10	5	5
Nahorodny, Chi ...	.973	60	223	25	7	3	6
Narron, NY.........	.973	56	167	15	5	2	8
Newman, Oak......	.977	81	378	53	10	7	4
O'Berry, Bos	.957	43	103	7	5	1	2
Parrish, Det	.989	142	707	79	9	10	21
Porter, KC	.982	141	628	68	13	15	15
Pruitt, Clev.........	1.000	11	22	3	0	1	0
Putman, Det.........	1.000	16	40	4	0	0	1
Roberts, Tex.........	.980	14	45	5	1	0	0
Skaggs, Balt	.984	63	222	24	4	1	5
Stinson, Sea	.978	91	376	29	9	2	5
Sundberg, Tex	.995	150	754	75	4	14	8
Wathan, KC	.987	23	70	5	1	0	0
Wockenfuss, Det...	.983	20	109	8	2	0	2
Wynegar, Minn...	.992	146	653	65	6	10	5

(Fewer Than Ten Games)

Player—Club	Pct.	G.	PO.	A.	E.	DP.	PB.
Anderson, Calif..	1.000	3	6	0	0	0	1
Ellis, Tex	1.000	7	16	1	0	1	0
Gaudet, KC	1.000	3	13	0	0	0	0
Hendricks, Balt	.500	1	1	0	1	0	0
Humphrey, Calif ..	.983	9	55	3	1	1	0
Johnson, NY-Clev.	1.000	5	10	1	0	0	1
Mahlberg, Tex	1.000	7	22	1	0	0	0
Nordhagen, Chi ...	.750	5	9	0	3	0	1
Quirk, KC	.944	9	15	2	1	0	0
Robinson, NY	.943	6	33	0	2	1	0

Player—Club	Pct.	G.	PO.	A.	E.	DP.	PB.
Sizemore, Bos	1.000	2	2	0	0	0	0
Valentine, Sea	.000	2	0	0	0	0	0
Wolfe, Bos	1.000	1	2	0	0	0	0

CATCHERS WITH TWO OR MORE CLUBS

Player—Club	Pct.	G.	PO.	A.	E.	DP.	PB.
May, Det	1.000	5	19	1	0	0	0
May, Chi	.981	65	277	27	6	1	7
Johnson, NY.........	1.000	4	10	1	0	0	1
Johnson, Clev	1.000	1	0	0	0	0	0

PITCHERS

Leader—Club	Pct.	G.	PO.	A.	E.	DP.
PARROTT, Sea	1.000	38	27	39	0	1

(Listed Alphabetically)

Player—Club	Pct.	G.	PO.	A.	E.	DP.
Aase, Calif	.926	37	8	17	2	3
Abbott, Sea..........	1.000	23	6	18	0	2
Alexander, Tex	1.000	23	12	23	0	1
Augustine, Milw*..	1.000	43	3	6	0	1
Bacsik, Minn	1.000	31	4	9	0	0
Baker, Det	1.000	21	3	8	0	1
Bannister, Sea*	1.000	30	10	15	0	0
Barker, Clev	.913	29	8	13	2	1
Barlow, Calif........	1.000	35	4	11	0	2
Barr, Calif.............	1.000	36	6	41	0	5
Barrios, Chi........	.857	15	10	8	3	2
Baumgarten, Chi*..	.977	28	14	28	1	1
Beattie, NY	.962	15	9	16	1	1
Billingham, Det ...	.931	35	6	21	2	3
Botting, Calif*	1.000	12	1	4	0	0
Burgmeier, Bos*....	1.000	44	5	14	0	3
Burnside, Det*......	1.000	10	0	4	0	1
Burris, NY.............	1.000	15	2	3	0	0
Busby, KC	1.000	22	4	24	0	1
Buskey, Tor	.960	44	5	19	1	1
Caldwell, Milw*....	.973	30	7	64	2	3
Campbell, Bos	1.000	41	10	11	0	1
Castro, Milw	.889	39	1	7	1	1
Chamberlain, KC	1.000	10	5	2	0	0

Player—Club	Pct.	G.	PO.	A.	E.	DP.
Chris, Det*	1.000	13	1	8	0	0
Clancy, Tor	1.000	12	1	11	0	0
Clay, NY	.952	32	8	12	1	0
Clear, Calif.............	.875	52	4	10	2	0
Cleveland, Milw ...	.778	29	2	5	2	1
Comer, Tex...........	.934	36	19	38	4	0
Cruz, Clev.............	.714	61	1	4	2	0
Darwin, Tex...........	1.000	20	2	6	0	0
Davis, NY.............	1.000	44	5	15	0	2
Drago, Bos	.941	53	5	11	1	2
Dressler, Sea.........	1.000	21	4	16	0	1
Eckersley, Bos......	.900	33	12	42	6	3
Ellis, Tex...............	.909	10	2	8	1	0
Erickson, Minn	.929	24	9	17	2	1
Farmer, Tex-Chi ...	1.000	53	9	15	0	1
Figueroa, NY	.926	16	9	16	2	1
Finch, Bos	.952	15	10	10	1	1
Flanagan, Balt*	.957	39	4	41	2	2
Freisleben, Tor ...	.941	42	3	13	1	1
Frost, Calif.............	.955	36	8	34	2	2
Galasso, Milw......	1.000	31	0	7	0	0
Gale, KC	.895	34	9	25	4	3
Garland, Clev	.864	18	11	8	3	0
Goltz, Minn	.962	36	16	34	2	3
Gossage, NY.........	1.000	36	1	4	0	0
Guidry, NY*	.976	33	11	29	1	1
Gura, KC*.............	.964	39	15	38	2	5
Haas, Milw.............	.972	29	14	21	1	3

PITCHERS—Continued

Player—Club	Pct.	G.	PO.	A.	E.	DP.
Hamilton, Oak*	1.000	40	3	15	0	0
Hartzell, Minn	.936	28	14	30	3	1
Heaverlo, Oak	.917	62	9	13	2	1
Hiller, Det*	1.000	43	4	10	0	0
Hinton, Chi-Sea*	.941	30	6	10	1	0
Hoffman, Chi*	1.000	24	1	5	0	1
Honeycutt, Sea*	.872	33	6	28	5	2
Hood, Clev.-NY*	1.000	40	5	18	0	2
Howard, Chi	1.000	28	7	4	0	0
Hrabosky, KC*	.750	58	2	4	2	0
Huffman, Tor	1.000	31	7	30	0	0
Hunter, NY	.952	19	10	10	1	0
Jackson, Minn*	.941	24	3	13	1	2
Jefferson, Tor	.889	34	10	22	4	1
Jenkins, Tex	.962	37	25	50	3	5
John, NY*	.957	37	15	51	3	5
Johnson, Oak-Tex*	1.000	31	5	18	0	3
Jones, Sea	.810	25	8	9	4	0
Kaat, NY*	.909	40	5	5	1	0
Keough, Oak	.944	30	23	28	3	5
Kern, Tex	.781	71	9	16	7	1
Kingman, Oak	.889	18	8	8	2	0
Knapp, Calif	.957	20	8	14	1	1
Koosman, Minn*	.923	37	10	50	5	6
Kravec, Chi*	.977	36	8	35	1	1
Lacey, Oak*	1.000	42	3	7	0	0
LaGrow, Chi	.750	11	0	3	1	0
Langford, Oak	1.000	34	26	36	0	3
LaRoche, Calif*	1.000	53	4	17	0	0
Lemanczyk, Tor	.941	22	12	20	2	2
Lemongello, Tor	.920	18	8	15	2	0
Leonard, KC	.981	32	19	32	1	2
Lopez, Det	.960	61	9	15	1	1
Lyle, Tex*	.867	67	2	11	2	0
Marshall, Minn	.977	90	11	31	1	4
Martin, KC	.929	25	5	8	1	0
T. Martinez, Balt*	.944	39	4	13	1	2
D. Martinez, Balt	.944	40	26	59	5	3
Matlack, Tex*	.905	13	3	16	2	1
McCatty, Oak	.914	31	12	20	3	3
McClure, Milw*	.727	36	1	7	3	1
McGregor, Balt*	1.000	27	10	21	0	0
McLaughlin, Sea	.944	47	6	11	1	0
Medich, Tex	.951	29	6	33	2	0
Miller, Calif-Tor	1.000	24	4	10	0	0
Minetto, Oak*	1.000	36	4	10	0	0
Mingori, KC*	.833	30	6	4	2	0
Mirabella, NY*	1.000	10	0	2	0	0
Mitchell, Sea-Milw.	1.000	28	5	13	0	1
Monge, Clev*	.885	76	6	17	3	2
Montague, Se-Cal	.931	55	6	21	2	0
Moore, Tor*	.867	34	4	22	4	1
Morgan, Oak	.960	13	9	15	1	0
Morris, Detroit	.949	27	14	23	2	3
Murphy, Toronto	1.000	10	3	5	0	1
Norris, Oakland	.958	29	6	17	1	0
Palmer, Baltimore	1.000	23	10	23	0	1
Parrott, Seattle	1.000	38	27	39	0	1
Pattin, Kansas City	.944	31	4	13	1	0
Paxton, Cleveland	1.000	33	16	20	0	3
Petry, Detroit	.909	15	9	11	2	0
Proly, Chicago	.957	38	5	17	1	2
Quisenberry, K.C.	.909	32	0	10	1	2
Rainey, Boston	.966	20	10	18	1	2
Rajsich, Texas*	1.000	27	1	13	0	0
Rawley, Seattle*	1.000	48	4	15	0	1
Redfern, Minnesota	.941	40	7	9	1	2
Renko, Boston	.944	27	14	20	2	0
Reuschel, Cleveland	.923	17	2	10	1	2
Ripley, Boston	.875	16	2	5	1	0
Robbins, Detroit*	1.000	10	1	5	0	1
Robinson, Chicago	1.000	11	0	1	0	0
Rodriguez, Kan. City	.889	29	0	8	1	0
Rozema, Detroit	.960	16	7	17	1	1
Ryan, California	.902	34	8	29	4	1
Scarbery, Chicago	.917	45	5	17	2	1
Serum, Minnesota	.938	20	5	10	1	0
Slaton, Milwaukee	.981	32	16	35	1	3
Sorensen, Milw.	.912	34	23	39	6	3
Spillner, Cleveland	1.000	49	9	18	0	0
Splittorff, K.C.*	.933	36	15	27	3	3
Stanhouse, Balt.	.950	52	3	16	1	2
Stanley, Boston	.954	40	19	43	3	2
Stein, Seattle	.800	23	1	3	1	0
Stewart, Baltimore	.974	31	10	27	1	1
Stieb, Toronto	.977	18	12	31	1	1
Stoddard, Baltimore	.933	29	9	5	1	0
Stone, Baltimore	.980	32	21	27	1	3
Tanana, California*	.938	18	3	12	1	1
Taylor, Detroit	.833	10	2	3	1	1
Tiant, New York	.952	30	13	27	2	2
Tidrow, New York	1.000	14	2	8	0	1
Tobik, Detroit	1.000	37	5	5	0	1
Todd, Oakland	1.000	51	5	14	0	2
Todd, Toronto	1.000	12	6	3	0	0
Torrez, Boston	.931	36	19	35	4	3
Travers, Milw.*	.941	30	7	25	2	0
Trout, Chicago*	.929	34	6	33	3	2
Underwood, Det.*	.941	27	1	15	1	0
Underwood, Tor.*	.894	33	6	36	5	2
Waits, Cleveland*	1.000	34	15	43	0	2
Wilcox, Detroit	1.000	33	10	41	0	7
Wilkins, Cleveland	.727	16	4	12	6	2
Willis, Toronto*	1.000	17	1	5	0	0
Wise, Cleveland	.974	34	23	53	2	2
Wortham, Chicago*	.872	34	7	27	5	0
Wright, Boston	1.000	11	2	1	0	0
Young, Detroit	1.000	13	3	10	0	0
Zahn, Minnesota*	.918	26	8	37	4	2

(Fewer Than Ten Games)

Player—Club	Pct.	G.	PO.	A.	E.	DP.
Allard, Texas	1.000	7	3	5	0	0
Anderson, Cleveland	1.000	8	0	4	0	1
Anderson, New York	1.000	1	0	3	0	0
Arroyo, Detroit	1.000	6	1	2	0	0
Babcock, Texas	1.000	4	0	1	0	0
Bando, Milwaukee	.000	1	0	0	0	0
Boitano, Milwaukee	1.000	5	0	1	0	0
Branch, Seattle	.000	2	0	0	0	0
Brett, Minnesota*	1.000	9	3	3	0	0
Burns, Chicago*	.000	6	0	0	0	0
Christenson, K.C.*	1.000	6	2	1	0	1
Clyde, Cleveland*	.889	9	2	6	1	0
Decker, Seattle	.909	9	4	6	1	1
Dotson, Chicago	1.000	5	1	4	0	0
Eaton, Kansas City	1.000	5	1	1	0	1
Eddy, California	.857	7	5	7	2	0
Edge, Toronto	1.000	9	1	7	0	0
Esser, Chicago*	.000	2	0	0	0	0

PITCHERS—Continued

Player—Club	Pct.	G.	PO.	A.	E.	DP.	Player—Club	Pct.	G.	PO.	A.	E.	DP.
Felton, Minnesota...	.000	1	0	0	0	0	Paschall, Kan. City .	1.000	7	0	2	0	0
Ferris, California	1.000	2	0	2	0	0	Rautzhan, Milw.* ...	1.000	3	2	0	0	0
Fidrych, Detroit......	1.000	4	2	1	0	0	Remmerswaal, Bos.	1.000	8	1	1	0	0
Flinn, Baltimore.....	1.000	4	1	0	0	0	Replogle, Milwaukee	1.000	3	0	2	0	0
Ford, Baltimore......	1.000	9	0	7	0	0	Righetti, New York*	1.000	3	1	3	0	1
Gantner, Milwaukee	1.000	1	0	1	0	0	Rineer, Baltimore* .	.000	1	0	0	0	0
Garvin, Toronto*	1.000	8	1	1	0	1	Rondon, Chicago....	1.000	4	0	1	0	0
Gleaton, Texas*	1.000	5	0	4	0	0	Schueler, Chicago...	1.000	8	0	3	0	0
Griffin, New York	.000	3	0	0	0	0	Schuler, California*	.000	1	0	0	0	0
Grilli, Toronto........	.000	1	0	0	0	0	Slagle, New York....	1.000	1	1	0	0	0
Hassler, Boston*	1.000	8	2	0	0	0	Stanfield, Minn.* ...	1.000	3	1	0	0	0
Holly, Minnesota* ..	1.000	6	0	1	0	0	Terrell, Kansas City	.000	1	0	0	0	0
Hoyt, Chicago........	.000	2	0	0	0	0	Thormodsgard, Minn.	.000	1	0	0	0	0
Kammeyer, N.Y......	.000	1	0	0	0	0	Throop, Kansas City	.000	4	0	0	0	0
Kucek, Chicago......	.000	1	0	0	0	0	Torrealba, Chicago*	1.000	3	0	1	0	0
Kusick, Toronto	.000	1	0	0	0	0	Tudor, Boston*	1.000	6	1	7	0	1
Lewis, Seattle	.000	2	0	0	1	0	Twitchell, Seattle ...	1.000	4	0	2	0	0
Luebber, Toronto	1.000	1	0	0	0	0	Vasquez, Seattle	1.000	9	0	1	0	0
Martinez, Milw.......	.000	1	0	0	0	0	Wihtol, Cleveland....	1.000	5	2	2	0	0
McCall, Texas	1.000	2	0	1	0	1	Wirth, Oakland	1.000	5	0	3	0	0
Nordhagen, Chicago	.000	2	0	0	0	0							

PITCHERS WITH TWO OR MORE CLUBS

Player—Club	Pct.	G.	PO.	A.	E.	DP.	Player—Club	Pct.	G.	PO.	A.	E.	DP.
Farmer, Texas	1.000	11	2	4	0	0	Miller, California	1.000	14	2	2	0	0
Farmer, Chicago.....	1.000	42	7	11	0	1	Miller, Toronto	1.000	10	2	1	0	0
Hinton, Chicago.....	.923	16	4	8	1	0	Mitchell, Seattle	1.000	10	2	5	0	0
Hinton, Seattle	1.000	14	2	2	0	0	Mitchell, Milwaukee	1.000	18	3	8	0	1
Hood, Cleveland	1.000	13	3	4	0	0	Montague, Seattle..	.963	41	5	21	1	0
Hood, New York	1.000	27	2	14	0	2	Montague, Calif......	.500	14	1	0	1	0
Johnson, Oakland ...	1.000	14	4	7	0	2							
Johnson, Texas.......	1.000	17	1	11	0	1							

EXPLANATION OF ABBREVIATION TERMS

G—Games Played. AB—At Bats. R—Runs. H—Hits. TB—Total Bases. 2B—Two-Base Hits. 3B—Three-Base Hits. HR—Home Runs. RBI—Runs Batted In. SH—Sacrifice Hits. SF—Sacrifice Flies. SB—Stolen Bases. CS—Caught Stealing. BB—Bases on Balls. IBB—Intentional Bases on Balls. HP—Hit by Pitcher. SO—Strikeouts. Pct.—Percentage. GIDP—Grounded Into Double Plays. Slg. Pct.—Slugging Percentage. OR—Opponents' Runs. LOB—Left on Bases. PO—Putouts. A—Assists. E—Errors. TC—Total Chances. DP—Double Plays. TP—Triple Plays. PB—Passed Balls. G—Games Pitched. GS—Games Started. CG—Complete Games. GF—Games Finished in Relief. ShO—Shut-outs. W—Games Won. L—Games Lost. IP—Innings Pitched. BFP—Total Batters Facing Pitcher. ER—Earned Runs. HB—Hit Batsmen. WP—Wild Pitches. Bk—Balks. ERA—Earned-Run Average. Sv—Saves.

OFFICIAL AMERICAN LEAGUE PITCHING AVERAGES

Compiled by Sports Information Center, No. Quincy, Mass.

CLUB PITCHING

Club	ERA	G.	CG.	Sv.	ShO.	IP.	H.	BFP.	R.	ER.	HR.	SH.	SF.	Tot. BB.	Int. BB.	SO.	WP.	Bk.
Baltimore	3.26	159	52	30	12	1434⅓	1279	5897	582	520	133	59	44	467	20	786	36	5
New York	3.83	160	43	30	10	1432⅓	1446	6001	672	610	123	80	47	455	22	731	45	1
Texas	3.86	162	26	42	10	1437	1371	6092	698	617	135	73	48	532	24	773	37	2
Boston	4.03	162	47	29	11	1431⅓	1487	6120	711	641	141	59	47	463	45	731	31	1
Milwaukee	4.03	161	61	23	5	1439⅔	1563	6106	748	645	162	50	53	381	24	580	48	3
Chicago	4.10	159	28	25	2	1409	1365	6117	748	642	114	65	60	618	37	675	51	1
Minnesota	4.13	162	31	33	9	1444⅓	1590	6157	725	663	128	68	44	452	40	721	39	7
Detroit	4.27	162	25	37	6	1423⅓	1429	6111	738	676	167	72	64	547	21	802	53	7
California	4.34	162	46	33	9	1436	1463	6213	768	692	131	58	63	573	56	820	51	5
Kansas City	4.45	162	42	27	7	1448⅓	1477	6242	816	716	165	81	65	536	33	640	40	4
Cleveland	4.57	161	28	32	7	1431⅔	1502	6236	805	727	138	60	65	570	48	781	44	3
Seattle	4.58	162	37	26	1	1438	1567	6314	820	731	165	62	65	571	32	736	43	7
Oakland	4.75	162	41	20	4	1429⅔	1606	6436	860	754	147	75	70	654	74	726	72	4
Toronto	4.82	162	44	11	7	1417	1537	6220	862	759	165	67	50	594	67	613	64	7
Totals	4.22	1127	551	417	116	20051⅓	20682	86262	10527	9393	2006	947	765	7413	560	10115	653	55

(BFP total includes 11 batsmen awarded first base because of interference or obstruction.)

NOTE—Totals for earned runs for several clubs do not agree with the composite totals for all pitchers of each respective club due to instances in which provisions of Section 10.18 (i) of the Scoring Rules were applied. The following differences are to be noted: Baltimore pitchers add to 522; Cleveland, 729; Detroit, 677; Kansas City, 717; Milwaukee, 646; Minnesota, 667; New York, 613; Oakland, 759; Seattle, 736; Toronto, 763.

PITCHERS' RECORDS

(Top Fifteen Qualifiers for Earned-Run Leadership—162 or More Innings)

Pitcher and Club	ERA	W.	L.	Pct.	G.	GS.	CG.	GF.	Sv.	ShO.	IP.	H.	BFP.	R.	ER.	HR.	SH.	SF.	Tot. BB.	Int. BB.	SO.	WP.	Bk.
Guidry, Ronald, New York*	2.78	18	8	.692	33	33	15	1	0	2	236	203	946	83	73	20	9	5	71	6	201	9	0
John, Thomas, New York*	2.97	21	9	.700	37	36	17	1	0	4	276	268	1116	109	91	29	11	5	65	6	111	11	1
Eckersley, Dennis, Boston	2.99	17	10	.630	33	33	17	0	0	2	247	234	1018	89	82	29	17	6	59	4	150	1	0
Flanagan, Michael, Baltimore*	3.08	23	9	.719	39	38	16	1	0	5	266	245	1085	107	91	23	4	9	70	1	190	6	0
Morris, John, Detroit	3.27	17	7	.708	27	27	9	0	0	1	198	179	806	76	72	18	6	4	59	0	113	9	0
Caldwell, R. Michael, Milwaukee*	3.29	16	6	.727	30	30	16	0	0	3	235	252	967	86	86	18	12	5	39	2	89	5	1
McGregor, Scott, Baltimore*	3.34	13	6	.684	27	23	7	1	0	0	175	165	706	70	65	19	13	7	23	0	81	3	1
Koosman, Jerry, Minnesota*	3.38	20	13	.606	37	36	10	0	0	3	264	268	1101	108	99	19	3	3	83	1	157	2	1
Baumgarten, Ross, Chicago*	3.53	13	8	.619	26	24	4	2	1	1	191	175	818	82	75	18	7	10	83	1	72	6	0
Zahn, Geoffrey, Minnesota*	3.57	13	7	.650	34	34	12	0	0	1	199	181	702	74	79	18	11	6	77	1	58	0	0
Frost, David, California	3.58	16	13	.615	36	33	17	0	0	3	239	226	1001	108	95	17	8	10	114	3	107	0	0
Ryan, L. Nolan, California	3.59	16	14	.533	34	34	5	0	0	5	223	169	937	104	89	15	15	8	114	1	223	9	0
Slaton, James, Milwaukee	3.63	15	9	.625	32	31	12	0	0	1	213	229	894	95	86	15	28	12	78	1	80	5	0
Martinez, J. Dennis, Baltimore	3.67	15	16	.484	40	39	18	0	0	2	292	279	1206	129	119	24	12	3	78	1	132	9	2
Comer, Steven, Texas	3.68	17	12	.586	36	36	6	0	0	1	242	230	1021	114	99	24	1	8	84	4	86	7	0

*Throws lefthanded.

DEPARTMENTAL LEADERS: W—Flanagan, 23; L—Huffman, 18; Pct.—Davis, .875; G—Marshall, 90; GS—J. Dennis Martinez, 39; CG—J. Dennis Martinez, 18; GF—Marshall, 84; Sv—Marshall, 32; ShO—Flanagan, Leonard, Ryan, 5; IP—J. Dennis Martinez, 291; H—Goltz, 282; BFP—J. Dennis Martinez, 1206; R—Torrez, 144; ER—Torrez, 126; HR—Jenkins, 126; SH—McCatty, 14; SF—Kravec, J. Dennis Martinez, 12; Int. BB—Torrez, 12; Tot. BB—Heaverlo, 18; HB—Kravec, 14; SO—Ryan, 223; WP—Langford, 16; Bk—Erickson 4.

(All Pitchers—Listed Alphabetically)

Pitcher and Club	ERA	W	L	Pct.	G	GS	CG	GF	Sv	ShO	IP	H	BFP	R	ER	HR	SH	SF	Tot. BB	Int. BB	HB	SO	WP	Bk
Aase, Donald, California	4.82	9	10	.474	37	28	7	4	2	0	185	200	817	104	99	19	8	8	77	7	1	96	5	0
Abbott, W. Glenn, Seattle	5.15	4	10	.286	23	19	3	1	0	0	117	138	518	78	67	19	8	10	38	2	3	25	1	0
Alexander, Doyle, Texas	4.46	5	7	.417	23	18	4	0	0	0	113	114	508	65	56	6	5	7	69	3	1	50	4	0
Allard, Brian, Texas	4.36	1	3	.250	7	4	0	0	0	0	33	36	141	17	16	3	1	0	14	0	0	14	0	0
Anderson, Larry, Cleveland	7.41	0	0	.000	8	1	0	0	0	0	17	25	77	14	14	4	0	1	7	0	0	7	0	0
Anderson, Richard, New York	4.50	0	0	.000	1	0	0	0	0	0	2	1	10	1	1	0	0	0	4	0	0	0	0	0
Arroyo, Fernando, Detroit.	8.25	1	0	1.000	6	0	0	3	0	0	12	17	57	11	11	1	2	0	4	1	0	7	0	0
Augustine, Gerald, Milwaukee*	3.45	9	6	.600	43	6	2	23	5	0	86	95	375	38	33	6	5	4	30	4	0	41	4	0
Babcock, Robert, Texas	4.36	4	2	.667	31	0	0	13	1	0	66	61	283	39	32	6	9	2	29	4	0	33	1	0
Bacsik, Michael, Minnesota	6.64	1	7	.125	21	12	0	2	0	0	84	97	392	63	62	13	3	6	51	2	6	54	7	0
Baker, Steven, Detroit	6.00	0	2	.000	12	1	0	2	0	0	30	46	146	31	20	6	2	1	15	1	0	22	4	0
Bando, Salvatore, Milwaukee	10.80	0	0	.000	2	0	0	1	0	0	5	10	26	6	6	1	0	0	2	0	0	3	0	0
Bannister, Floyd, Seattle*	4.05	10	15	.400	30	29	6	0	0	0	182	185	792	92	82	25	5	3	68	4	4	115	2	1
Barker, Leonard, Cleveland	4.93	6	6	.500	29	19	3	6	0	1	137	146	609	79	75	8	6	3	70	2	2	93	3	0
Barlow, Michael, California	5.13	1	1	.500	35	0	0	30	15	0	86	106	378	54	49	8	3	5	55	2	0	33	3	1
Barr, James, California	4.20	5	6	.455	36	25	5	0	0	2	197	217	826	100	92	22	8	5	83	5	3	69	1	0
Barrios, Francisco, Chicago	3.60	8	3	.727	28	15	2	2	0	1	95	88	406	42	38	9	5	5	41	1	0	28	1	1
Baumgarten, Ross, Chicago*	3.53	13	8	.619	28	28	5	0	0	0	191	175	818	82	75	18	7	6	83	5	0	72	3	2
Beattie, James, New York	5.21	3	6	.333	17	13	1	0	0	1	76	85	343	45	44	7	5	7	60	3	1	59	0	0
Billingham, John, Detroit	3.30	10	7	.588	35	19	2	11	0	2	158	163	668	74	58	13	9	6	41	10	1	22	7	0
Boitano, Danny, Milwaukee	1.50	0	1	.000	12	0	0	5	0	0	6	6	26	1	1	0	0	2	1	0	0	6	0	0
Botting, Ralph, California*	8.70	1	0	1.000	2	2	0	0	0	0	10	28	52	17	10	6	3	0	15	1	0	3	0	0
Branch, Roy, Seattle	8.18	0	1	.000	6	2	0	2	0	0	13	16	58	13	12	1	0	1	8	0	0	13	0	0
Brett, Kenneth, Minnesota*	4.85	3	2	.600	15	0	0	9	1	0	21	18	96	13	11	7	2	7	16	2	1	19	3	0
Burgmeier, Thomas, Boston*	2.73	8	3	.727	44	0	0	24	0	0	89	78	368	32	27	8	8	1	25	3	0	45	0	0
Burns, R. Britt, Chicago*	5.40	0	2	.000	9	9	0	0	0	0	53	74	239	41	32	10	5	4	64	1	4	44	3	1
Burnside, Sheldon, Detroit*	6.43	1	3	.250	10	0	0	5	0	0	21	40	96	16	15	3	1	2	8	2	0	16	0	0
Burris, B. Ray, New York	6.11	1	1	.500	15	4	1	2	0	0	28	46	132	22	19	4	1	1	10	3	0	19	2	0
Busby, Steven, Kansas City	3.64	3	5	.375	12	9	1	0	0	0	55	68	239	33	22	10	3	7	21	4	0	45	1	1
Buskey, Thomas, Toronto	3.42	5	5	.500	44	0	0	22	0	0	74	74	329	35	28	10	6	0	25	5	0	38	0	0
Caldwell, R. Michael, Milwaukee*	3.29	16	6	.727	41	34	16	0	0	3	235	252	967	96	86	18	12	11	31	3	1	89	7	3
Campbell, William, Boston	4.25	3	4	.429	39	0	0	30	8	0	55	55	239	26	26	5	5	2	25	9	2	25	5	0
Castro, William, Milwaukee	2.05	3	1	.750	41	0	0	17	6	0	44	40	181	14	10	2	2	1	13	6	1	23	2	0
Chamberlain, Craig, Kansas City	3.73	3	3	.500	10	10	2	0	0	1	70	68	287	29	29	7	2	7	21	3	1	30	6	0
Chris, Michael, Detroit*	6.92	0	2	.000	10	10	1	0	0	0	39	46	179	30	30	3	1	0	21	0	0	31	2	0
Christenson, Gary, Kansas City*	3.27	2	7	.222	6	8	1	0	0	0	11	10	43	4	4	1	1	3	10	1	0	4	0	0
Clancy, James, Toronto	5.48	2	7	.222	12	12	0	0	0	0	64	65	278	44	39	12	6	5	31	2	1	33	9	0
Clay, Kenneth, New York	5.42	1	7	.125	15	11	2	0	0	0	78	88	338	47	47	9	8	5	25	3	0	28	7	0
Clear, Mark, California	3.63	11	5	.688	52	0	0	37	14	0	109	87	481	48	44	6	9	4	68	4	1	98	5	1
Cleveland, Reginald, Milwaukee	6.71	1	5	.167	29	5	0	11	1	0	55	77	258	41	41	9	4	5	23	3	0	22	2	0
Clyde, David, Cleveland*	5.87	3	4	.429	9	9	1	0	0	0	46	50	195	33	30	7	1	8	13	0	2	17	4	0

Pitcher and Club	ERA	W.	L.	Pct.	G.	GS.	CG.	GF.	Sv.	ShO.	IP.	H.	BFP.	R.	ER.	HR.	SH.	SF.	Tot. BB.	Int. BB.	HB.	SO.	WP.	Bk.
Comer, Steven, Texas	3.68	17	12	.586	36	36	6	0	0	1	242	230	1021	114	99	24	12	3	84	4	4	86	7	2
Cruz, Victor, Cleveland	4.22	3	9	.250	61	0	0	48	10	0	79	70	343	41	37	10	6	5	44	4	1	63	1	0
Darwin, Danny, Texas	4.04	4	4	.500	20	6	0	4	0	0	78	50	313	36	35	5	3	6	30	2	5	58	0	1
Davis, Ronald, New York	2.86	14	2	.875	44	2	0	21	6	0	85	84	357	29	27	5	0	3	28	2	8	43	2	0
Decker, George, Seattle	4.33	4	0	1.000	9	2	0	2	0	0	27	27	121	14	13	6	4	1	14	0	1	12	2	0
Dotson, Richard, Chicago	3.75	2	0	1.000	5	5	1	0	0	0	24	28	107	13	10	0	4	0	6	0	0	13	0	0
Drago, Richard, Boston	3.03	10	6	.625	53	0	0	37	13	0	89	85	367	33	30	6	5	5	21	6	1	67	1	0
Dressler, Robert, Seattle	4.93	3	2	.600	21	5	0	2	0	0	104	134	458	61	57	11	10	4	22	3	2	36	0	0
Eaton, Craig, Kansas City	2.70	6	4	.630	33	11	0	6	0	0	10	8	41	5	3	0	1	0	59	2	0	150	1	0
Eckersley, Dennis, Boston	2.99	17	10	.630	33	33	17	0	0	2	247	234	1018	89	82	29	5	2	59	2	1	150	1	0
Eddy, Steven, California	4.78	1	1	.500	7	9	0	3	0	0	32	36	152	19	17	1	9	1	20	1	0	7	4	1
Edge, Claude, Toronto	5.19	1	4	.429	10	9	0	0	0	0	52	60	240	32	30	6	2	3	24	0	0	19	1	0
Ellis, Dock, Texas	5.94	3	5	.167	9	10	0	1	0	0	47	64	215	34	31	5	3	1	16	0	0	10	0	0
Erickson, Roger, Minnesota	5.63	3	10	.231	24	21	0	1	0	0	123	154	556	86	77	17	5	5	48	1	0	47	4	0
Esser, Mark, Chicago*	13.50	0	1	.000	2	0	0	0	0	0	2	2	11	3	3	0	0	0	3	0	0	1	0	0
Farmer, Edward, Tex-Chi	3.00	5	7	.417	53	0	0	35	14	0	114	96	491	57	38	4	6	4	53	10	3	73	9	1
Felton, Terry, Minnesota	0.00	0	0	.000	2	0	0	0	0	0	6	6	27	2	0	1	0	0	2	0	0	1	0	0
Ferris, Robert, California	1.50	0	0	.000	4	0	0	1	0	0	15	17	73	17	2	1	3	0	9	1	0	2	0	0
Fidrych, Mark, Detroit	10.20	0	3	.000	4	4	0	0	0	0	15	23	116	49	17	3	3	1	35	0	1	5	0	0
Figueroa, Eduardo, New York	4.11	4	6	.400	16	16	6	0	0	0	105	109	437	48	48	6	1	4	25	0	1	42	0	1
Finch, Joel, Boston	4.89	0	3	.000	15	7	0	5	0	0	57	65	253	31	31	11	0	4	25	5	1	25	0	1
Flanagan, Michael, Baltimore*	3.08	23	9	.719	39	38	16	0	0	5	266	245	1085	107	91	23	9	9	70	1	3	190	6	0
Flinn, John, Baltimore	0.00	2	1	.667	4	0	0	2	0	0	11	11	41	0	0	0	1	0	7	0	0	7	0	0
Ford, David, Baltimore	2.10	2	1	.667	2	2	1	0	0	0	30	23	116	7	7	1	0	0	9	0	0	10	0	0
Freisleben, David, Toronto	4.95	2	3	.400	42	9	2	14	2	0	91	101	407	57	50	9	2	3	53	5	3	35	9	0
Frost, David, California	3.58	16	10	.615	36	33	12	2	0	1	239	226	1001	108	95	17	10	5	77	4	0	107	5	0
Galasso, Robert, Milwaukee	4.41	4	4	.474	34	4	0	14	0	0	51	64	243	33	25	5	9	8	26	4	5	28	3	0
Gale, Richard, Kansas City	5.64	9	10	.750	31	31	0	0	0	0	182	197	830	131	114	19	10	9	99	3	4	103	5	0
Gantner, James, Milwaukee	0.00	0	0	.000	1	0	0	0	0	0	1	1	5	0	0	0	0	0	0	0	0	0	0	0
Garland, M. Wayne, Cleveland	5.21	4	10	.286	18	14	0	2	0	0	95	120	431	70	55	11	8	2	34	3	0	40	3	0
Garvin, T. Jared, Toronto*	6.30	1	0	1.000	8	1	0	4	0	0	23	15	91	9	7	0	1	1	10	0	0	14	0	0
Gleaton, Jerry, Texas*	2.74	1	0	1.000	5	5	0	0	0	0	10	15	45	7	7	0	0	0	8	0	1	2	1	0
Goltz, David, Minnesota	4.16	14	13	.519	36	35	12	0	0	0	251	282	1061	124	116	22	11	2	69	3	4	132	1	0
Gossage, Richard, New York	2.64	5	3	.625	36	0	0	33	18	0	58	48	234	18	17	6	2	1	19	4	0	41	5	3
Griffin, Michael, New York	4.50	0	0	.000	1	0	0	1	0	0	4	1	19	2	2	0	0	1	2	0	0	5	0	0
Grilli, Stephen, Toronto.	0.00	0	0	.000	1	0	0	0	0	0	2	5	8	0	0	0	1	0	0	0	0	1	0	0
Guidry, Ronald, New York*	2.78	18	8	.692	33	30	15	2	0	2	236	203	946	83	73	20	9	5	71	5	3	201	4	0
Gura, Lawrence, Kansas City*	4.46	13	12	.520	39	39	8	0	0	1	234	226	991	137	116	29	7	7	73	4	7	85	9	1
Haas, Bryan, Milwaukee	4.77	11	11	.500	20	28	6	0	0	0	185	198	790	112	98	26	8	8	59	2	2	52	5	0
Hamilton, David, Oakland*	3.69	6	10	.429	40	27	4	4	0	0	163	80	361	42	34	5	6	7	43	2	4	52	2	0
Hartzell, Paul, Minnesota	5.36	3	5	.375	28	8	0	6	2	0	105	193	704	102	98	18	7	8	44	4	1	47	1	0
Hassler, Andrew, Boston*	9.00	0	2	.333	8	0	0	4	0	0	15	23	72	13	15	0	2	1	12	1	0	7	0	0
Heaverlo, David, Oakland	4.19	4	11	.267	62	0	0	42	3	0	86	97	392	42	40	14	7	12	42	18	4	40	4	0
Hiller, John, Detroit*	5.24	4	7	.364	43	3	0	30	9	0	83	83	372	47	46	8	11	3	55	7	3	46	4	0
Hinton, Richard, Chi-Sea*	5.81	1	4	.200	30	3	0	14	2	0	62	80	278	44	40	0	4	1	13	5	1	34	4	3
Hoffman, Guy, Chicago*	5.40	0	5	.000	24	0	0	9	0	0	30	30	142	18	18	0	3	0	23	1	1	18	3	1

Pitcher and Club	ERA	W.	L.	Pct.	G.	GS.	CG.	GF.	Sv.	ShO.	IP.	H.	BFP.	R.	ER.	HR.	SH.	SF.	Tot. BB.	Int. BB.	SO.	HB.	WP.	Bk.
Holly, Jeffrey, Minnesota*	7.50	0	1	.000	6	0	0	2	0	0	6	10	31	5	5	0	2	1	3	0	5	0	1	0
Honeycutt, Frederick, Seattle*	4.04	11	12	.478	33	28	8	2	0	0	194	201	839	103	87	24	11	2	67	7	83	6	0	0
Hood, Donald, Clev-New York*	3.24	4	1	.800	40	6	0	12	2	0	89	75	380	33	32	4	6	2	44	7	63	6	5	1
Howard, Fred, Chicago	3.57	1	5	.167	28	6	0	10	0	0	68	73	302	34	27	5	6	0	32	2	36	3	0	0
Hoyt, Dewey, Chicago	0.00	0	0	.000	2	0	0	1	0	0	2	2	10	0	0	0	0	0	2	0	0	0	0	0
Hrabosky, Alan, Kansas City*	3.74	9	4	.692	58	0	0	37	11	0	65	67	294	27	27	5	5	1	41	10	39	0	0	0
Huffman, Phillip, Toronto	5.77	6	18	.250	31	31	5	0	0	0	173	220	802	130	111	25	4	6	68	0	56	8	7	0
Hunter, James, New York	5.31	2	9	.182	19	19	2	1	0	0	105	128	460	68	62	15	3	4	26	0	34	2	5	0
Jackson, Darrell, Minnesota*	4.30	4	6	.400	24	18	1	7	0	2	69	89	311	53	33	15	4	0	36	0	43	1	2	0
Jefferson, Jesse, Toronto	5.51	2	8	.167	34	34	4	0	0	0	150	150	513	75	71	19	9	2	45	6	43	3	2	0
Jenkins, Ferguson, Texas	4.07	16	14	.533	37	37	10	0	0	1	259	252	1089	127	117	40	10	6	81	2	164	3	4	0
John, Thomas, New York*	2.97	21	9	.700	37	36	17	1	0	3	276	268	1116	109	91	9	11	6	65	1	111	4	1	1
Johnson, John, Oak-Tex*	4.63	4	14	.222	31	25	3	1	0	1	167	168	729	90	86	25	7	2	72	6	96	0	6	0
Jones, Odell, Seattle	6.05	4	14	.222	25	19	2	3	0	0	119	151	553	95	80	16	6	8	58	3	72	2	6	1
Kaat, James, New York*	3.88	2	3	.400	40	1	0	13	2	0	58	64	249	29	25	6	4	0	23	7	23	0	0	0
Kammeyer, Robert, New York		0	0	.000	1	0	0	0	0	0	0	6	8	2	2	0	0	0	2	0	0	0	0	0
Keough, Matthew, Oakland	5.03	2	17	.105	30	28	7	2	0	0	177	220	800	115	99	18	13	2	78	2	95	1	13	0
Kern, James, Texas	1.57	13	5	.722	71	0	0	57	29	0	143	99	578	35	25	5	3	6	62	7	136	2	0	0
Kingman, Brian, Oakland	4.30	8	7	.533	18	17	5	0	0	0	113	113	481	59	54	10	5	1	35	0	58	6	2	0
Knapp, R. Christian, California	5.51	5	5	.500	18	18	4	0	0	0	98	109	440	73	60	8	13	3	43	1	36	1	0	1
Koosman, Jerry, Minnesota	3.38	20	13	.606	37	36	10	0	0	2	264	268	1101	111	99	19	10	3	83	2	157	5	1	1
Kravec, Kenneth, Chicago*	3.74	15	13	.536	36	35	11	0	0	3	250	208	1041	115	104	20	12	4	111	0	132	4	7	0
Kucek, John, Chicago	0.00	0	0	.000	1	0	0	1	0	0	6	6	14	0	0	0	0	0	0	0	6	0	0	0
Kusick, Craig, Toronto	4.50	0	0	.000	1	0	0	1	0	0	2	4	9	1	1	0	0	0	0	0	4	0	0	0
Lacey, Robert, Oakland*	5.81	1	5	.167	42	0	0	20	4	0	48	66	230	34	31	1	8	1	24	6	33	0	4	0
LaGrow, Lerrin, Chicago	9.00	0	2	.000	11	0	0	4	1	0	18	27	95	21	18	2	1	0	16	1	9	0	0	0
Langford, J. Rick, Oakland	4.27	12	16	.429	34	29	14	0	0	0	219	233	934	114	104	22	12	4	57	8	101	4	2	1
LaRoche, David, California*	5.55	2	5	.286	53	0	0	25	10	0	86	107	387	65	53	7	11	4	34	16	59	2	1	0
Lemanczyk, David, Toronto	3.71	8	10	.444	22	20	6	1	0	1	143	137	597	65	59	12	12	6	45	2	63	0	2	0
Lemongello, Mark, Toronto	6.29	1	9	.100	18	10	1	5	0	0	83	97	369	64	58	9	10	3	34	0	40	0	1	0
Leonard, Dennis, Kansas City	4.08	14	12	.538	32	32	10	0	0	3	236	226	966	117	107	33	11	5	56	3	126	2	0	0
Lewis, James, Seattle	18.00	0	0	.000	1	0	0	1	0	0	1	7	17	7	2	1	0	0	4	0	0	0	0	0
Lopez, Aurelio, Detroit	2.41	10	5	.667	61	0	0	49	21	0	127	95	519	37	34	12	8	1	51	3	106	3	0	0
Luebber, Stephen, Toronto	3.13	0	2	.000	6	0	0	2	0	0	23	28	103	14	8	2	2	0	14	0	10	0	2	0
Lyle, Albert, Texas*	3.13	5	8	.385	67	1	0	53	13	0	95	78	384	47	33	8	10	2	28	8	48	0	0	0
Marshall, Michael, Minnesota	2.64	10	15	.400	90	1	0	84	32	0	143	132	586	47	42	9	10	8	48	10	81	1	2	0
Martin, D. Renie, Kansas City	5.14	0	3	.000	25	0	0	11	5	0	35	32	149	20	20	1	5	0	14	0	25	0	0	1
Martinez, John, Milwaukee	9.00	0	0	.000	1	0	0	1	0	0	1	5	5	1	1	0	0	0	0	0	0	0	0	0
Martinez, Felix, Baltimore*	2.88	10	3	.769	39	0	0	23	3	0	78	59	318	29	29	3	0	0	31	1	61	0	0	0
Martinez, J. Dennis, Baltimore	3.67	15	16	.484	40	39	18	0	0	3	292	279	1206	129	119	28	12	7	78	1	132	1	6	0
Matlack, Jonathon, Texas*	4.13	5	4	.556	13	13	2	0	0	0	85	98	355	43	39	9	2	12	15	1	35	1	1	0
McCall, Larry, Texas	2.25	1	0	1.000	3	1	0	1	0	0	8	7	35	2	2	0	1	0	2	0	3	0	0	0
McCatty, Steven, Oakland	4.21	11	12	.478	31	23	4	4	0	1	186	207	841	106	87	17	14	3	80	8	87	3	5	0
McClure, Robert, Milwaukee*	3.88	5	2	.714	36	0	0	16	5	0	51	53	229	22	22	6	9	0	23	2	37	1	1	0
McGregor, Scott, Baltimore*	3.34	13	6	.684	27	23	7	1	0	2	175	165	706	70	65	19	10	6	24	0	81	1	0	0
McLaughlin, Byron, Seattle	4.21	7	7	.500	47	7	1	31	14	0	124	114	529	58	58	13	5	4	60	2	74	7	1	0
Medich, George, Texas	4.17	10	7	.588	29	19	4	1	0	0	149	156	647	78	69	13	9	3	49	4	58	4	0	0

Pitcher and Club	ERA	W	L	Pct.	G	GS	CG	GF	Sv	ShO	IP	H	BFP	R	ER	HR	SH	SF	Tot. BB	Int. BB	HB	SO	WP	Bk.
Miller, Dyar, Cal-Tor	5.47	1	1	.500	24	0	0	13	0	0	51	71	232	32	31	5	0	5	18	2	3	23	3	0
Minetto, Craig, Oakland*	5.57	1	5	.167	36	13	1	12	0	0	118	131	539	85	73	16	6	8	58	1	1	64	2	1
Mingori, Stephen, Kansas City	5.74	3	3	.500	30	1	0	8	1	0	47	69	223	36	30	10	2	1	17	9	1	18	0	0
Mirabella, Paul, New York*	9.00	0	4	.000	14	1	0	1	0	0	14	16	71	16	16	3	7	1	10	0	0	4	3	1
Mitchell, Paul, Sea-Milw	5.30	4	7	.364	26	14	1	5	0	0	112	127	478	76	66	15	1	6	25	8	2	50	1	0
Monge, Isidro, Cleveland*	2.40	12	10	.545	76	0	0	53	19	0	131	96	542	35	35	9	6	11	56	8	1	108	0	2
Montague, John, Sea-Calif	5.51	8	4	.667	51	1	0	25	7	0	77	141	583	85	82	17	10	9	79	13	1	66	5	1
Moore, Balor, Toronto*	4.86	5	7	.417	13	5	0	0	0	0	135	135	614	85	75	17	4	9	85	8	3	51	1	0
Morgan, Michael, Oakland	5.96	0	2	.000	2	0	0	0	0	0	77	102	368	57	51	7	8	0	50	0	0	17	8	2
Morris, John, Detroit	3.27	1	5	.167	29	2	0	24	2	0	198	179	806	76	72	19	4	0	59	9	4	113	5	0
Murphy, Thomas, Toronto	5.50	0	8	.000	38	0	0	21	5	0	18	23	82	11	11	2	0	0	8	0	0	7	0	0
Nordhagen, Wayne, Chicago	9.00	0	2	.333	31	0	0	0	0	0	2	2	8	2	2	0	0	0	0	0	0	2	0	0
Norris, Michael, Oakland	4.81	5	8	.385	33	18	3	2	0	2	146	146	669	87	78	11	3	6	94	9	2	96	10	0
Palmer, James, Baltimore	3.29	10	6	.625	23	22	7	0	0	5	156	144	639	66	57	12	7	1	43	6	4	67	1	1
Parrott, Michael, Seattle	3.77	14	12	.538	38	30	13	1	0	0	229	231	973	104	96	17	11	5	86	16	6	127	1	1
Paschall, William, Kansas City	6.43	1	0	1.000	27	0	0	5	0	0	14	18	68	11	10	2	7	0	10	2	2	3	0	0
Pattin, Martin, Kansas City	4.60	5	2	.714	48	7	1	11	0	0	94	109	403	50	48	11	5	5	21	5	2	41	3	0
Paxton, Michael, Cleveland	5.91	3	3	.500	20	15	1	0	0	0	109	135	543	75	72	14	5	7	52	2	4	40	3	1
Petry, Daniel, Detroit	3.95	6	5	.545	15	24	6	0	0	0	98	90	401	43	43	11	3	3	33	1	1	43	3	1
Proly, Michael, Chicago	3.89	3	8	.273	38	0	0	21	5	0	88	89	387	46	38	6	7	2	40	5	1	32	1	0
Quisenberry, Daniel, Kansas City	3.15	3	2	.600	47	0	0	24	33	0	40	42	163	11	11	2	4	0	7	0	1	32	5	0
Rainey, Charles, Boston	3.81	8	5	.615	17	16	2	5	0	0	104	90	437	47	44	7	5	2	41	1	1	41	1	1
Rajsich, David, Texas*	3.50	0	3	.000	16	2	0	8	0	0	54	56	229	29	21	7	3	0	25	0	0	32	0	0
Rautzhan, Clarence, Milwaukee*	9.06	0	0	.000	29	0	0	8	0	0	3	8	20	4	3	2	1	2	10	1	1	2	0	0
Rawley, Shane, Seattle*	3.86	5	9	.357	48	0	0	30	11	0	84	88	364	45	36	8	3	2	35	1	0	48	2	0
Redfern, Peter, Minnesota	3.50	7	3	.700	10	6	0	4	0	0	108	106	455	45	42	8	1	2	42	1	1	85	2	0
Remmerswaal, Wilhelmus, Boston	7.20	0	1	.000	11	3	0	13	0	0	20	26	97	16	16	2	0	1	16	0	1	16	1	0
Renko, Steven, Boston	4.11	11	9	.550	29	27	5	0	0	2	171	174	730	86	78	22	1	0	53	1	1	99	3	0
Replogle, Andrew, Milwaukee	5.63	0	0	.000	16	1	0	5	0	0	45	73	212	42	40	5	0	0	11	0	0	2	0	0
Reuschel, Paul, Cleveland	8.00	2	1	.667	16	3	0	7	0	0	17	10	36	13	7	1	1	1	11	3	0	22	0	0
Righetti, David, New York*	3.71	1	3	.250	9	3	0	0	0	0	17	10	67	12	7	0	0	0	13	0	0	13	0	1
Rineer, Jeffrey, Baltimore*	0.00	0	1	.000	20	1	0	7	0	0	1	2	2	0	0	0	0	0	0	0	0	7	0	0
Ripley, Allen, Boston	5.12	0	1	.000	32	3	0	0	0	0	65	77	292	42	37	9	2	0	25	2	3	34	3	0
Robbins, Bruce, Detroit*	3.91	3	3	.500	49	3	0	13	0	0	46	45	194	21	20	7	7	2	21	0	3	22	4	0
Robinson, Dewey, Chicago	6.43	0	1	.000	16	16	3	0	0	0	14	19	61	12	10	2	0	0	6	0	0	5	0	0
Rodriguez, Eduardo, Kansas City	4.86	4	1	.800	16	4	0	7	0	0	74	79	330	40	40	9	2	4	34	3	3	26	0	0
Rondon, Gilbert, Chicago	3.60	0	1	.000	45	0	0	0	0	0	10	11	46	5	4	2	3	0	6	3	0	2	0	0
Rozema, David, Detroit	3.53	4	4	.500	16	16	4	0	0	0	97	101	424	52	38	12	8	7	20	3	6	33	3	0
Ryan, L. Nolan, California	3.59	16	14	.533	34	34	4	0	0	5	223	169	937	104	89	15	8	10	114	3	3	223	9	0
Scarbery, Randy, Chicago	4.63	2	8	.200	45	5	0	15	0	0	101	102	436	56	52	10	5	3	34	3	1	45	6	1
Schueler, Ronald, Chicago	7.20	0	3	.000	8	0	0	4	0	0	20	19	90	16	16	0	1	1	13	0	0	6	1	0
Schuler, David, California*	9.00	0	1	.000	1	0	0	1	0	0	2	7	7	2	2	0	0	0	0	0	0	2	0	0
Serum, Gary, Minnesota	6.61	1	3	.250	20	5	0	0	0	0	64	93	287	47	47	10	3	2	20	2	0	31	1	0
Slagle, Roger, New York	0.00	0	0	.000	1	0	0	1	0	0	3	6	6	0	0	0	0	0	2	0	0	2	0	0
Slaton, James, Milwaukee	3.63	15	9	.625	32	31	8	0	0	3	213	229	894	95	86	15	5	8	54	3	1	80	5	0
Sorensen, Lary, Milwaukee	3.98	15	14	.517	34	34	13	0	0	2	235	250	967	104	104	30	8	8	52	1	4	63	5	0
Spillner, Daniel, Cleveland	4.61	9	5	.643	49	13	1	7	1	1	158	153	680	82	81	16	8	8	64	4	3	97	5	0

Pitcher and Club	ERA	W	L	Pct.	G	GS	CG	GF	Sv.	Sho.	IP	H	BFP	R	ER	HR	SH	SF	Tot. BB	Int. BB	HB	SO	WP	Bk.
Splittorff, Paul, Kansas City*	4.24	15	17	.469	36	35	11	0	0	0	240	248	1026	137	113	25	9	8	101	7	5	77	1	0
Stanfield, Kevin, Minnesota*	6.00	0	3	.000	1	0	0	1	0	0	3	10	10	3	2	1	0	1	1	0	0	1	0	0
Stanhouse, Donald, Baltimore	2.84	7	3	.700	52	0	0	46	21	0	73	49	307	24	23	4	11	2	51	7	1	34	2	0
Stanley, Robert, Boston	3.98	16	12	.571	40	30	9	7	1	1	217	250	914	110	96	14	7	2	44	4	5	56	2	1
Stein, W. Randolph, Seattle	5.93	8	12	.400	23	5	1	10	0	0	41	48	197	29	27	4	2	5	27	4	4	39	5	3
Stewart, Samuel, Baltimore	3.51	8	5	.615	31	1	0	12	1	0	118	96	498	47	46	7	5	1	48	3	5	71	3	1
Sieb, David, Toronto	4.33	8	8	.500	18	18	7	0	0	0	129	139	563	70	62	11	4	2	48	1	1	52	5	0
Stoddard, Timothy, Baltimore	3.77	3	1	.750	29	0	0	15	9	0	58	44	228	27	24	3	8	1	19	8	2	47	3	0
Stone, Steven, Baltimore	3.90	11	7	.611	32	17	3	9	0	0	186	173	781	91	78	31	8	1	73	3	1	96	6	0
Tanana, Frank, California*	4.74	7	5	.583	18	17	2	0	0	0	90	93	382	44	39	9	1	4	25	1	0	46	6	0
Taylor, Bruce, Detroit	0.00	0	0	.000	10	0	0	8	0	0	19	16	81	13	0	1	0	2	7	2	0	8	0	0
Terrell, Jerry, Kansas City	9.00	0	1	.000	1	0	0	0	0	0	1	3	6	1	1	0	0	0	0	0	0	0	1	0
Thormodsgard, Paul, Minnesota	12.00	0	2	.000	4	0	0	0	0	0	3	7	20	4	4	1	0	0	5	0	0	1	0	0
Throop, George, Kansas City	3.90	0	0	.000	1	0	0	1	0	0	1	1	6	0	0	0	0	0	0	0	0	1	0	0
Tiant, Luis, New York	3.91	13	8	.619	30	30	5	0	0	1	196	190	819	94	85	22	5	2	53	0	1	104	0	0
Tidrow, Richard, New York	7.83	2	1	.667	14	0	0	6	0	0	23	38	101	24	20	5	4	2	4	1	1	2	4	0
Tobik, David, Detroit	4.30	3	5	.375	37	7	0	9	3	0	81	59	287	34	33	12	7	0	25	0	2	48	4	0
Todd, James, Oakland	6.56	2	5	.286	51	0	0	19	1	0	108	144	391	66	50	9	3	1	51	5	3	26	5	0
Todd, Jackson, Toronto	5.91	0	0	.000	12	0	0	7	0	0	32	40	144	26	21	5	2	0	7	0	1	14	4	1
Torrealba, Pablo, Chicago*	1.50	1	0	1.000	6	0	0	0	0	0	6	5	24	5	1	1	0	0	4	0	0	14	2	0
Torrez, Michael, Boston	4.50	16	13	.552	36	36	12	0	0	2	252	254	1109	144	126	20	11	8	121	3	5	125	6	1
Travers, William, Milwaukee*	3.90	14	8	.636	36	27	9	6	0	1	187	196	785	89	81	33	10	3	45	5	0	76	1	0
Trout, Steven, Chicago*	3.89	11	8	.579	27	24	6	2	0	0	155	165	677	77	67	10	6	3	59	5	3	76	5	1
Tudor, John, Boston*	6.43	1	2	.333	6	4	1	0	0	0	28	34	128	28	20	2	3	0	20	0	2	1	3	0
Twitchell, Wayne, Seattle	5.14	0	4	.000	33	2	0	8	0	0	14	18	64	11	8	1	1	1	10	1	2	5	3	0
Underwood, Patrick, Detroit*	4.57	6	4	.600	27	15	1	4	1	0	122	126	508	64	62	17	5	6	29	2	9	83	3	1
Underwood, Thomas, Toronto*	5.06	9	16	.360	33	32	8	0	0	0	227	213	963	113	93	23	11	6	95	9	1	127	11	0
Vasquez, Rafael, Seattle	3.69	1	0	1.000	5	0	0	2	0	0	16	23	73	9	7	4	1	0	9	1	4	1	0	0
Waits, M. Richard, Cleveland*	5.06	16	13	.552	34	34	8	0	0	3	231	230	982	123	114	26	6	9	91	3	0	91	5	0
Wihtol, Alexander, Detroit	4.44	0	0	.000	5	0	0	4	0	0	11	10	45	4	4	0	0	1	6	0	0	4	0	0
Wilcox, Milton, Detroit	3.27	12	10	.545	33	29	7	0	0	0	196	201	854	105	95	18	10	8	73	8	11	109	6	0
Wilkins, Eric, Cleveland	4.36	2	4	.333	16	14	0	0	0	0	70	77	316	41	34	2	3	1	38	1	1	52	1	0
Willis, Michael, Toronto*	4.37	2	3	.333	17	1	0	7	0	0	12	35	128	27	25	4	1	2	16	2	0	8	0	0
Wirth, Alan, Oakland	8.33	0	3	.000	5	1	0	0	0	0	12	14	58	12	14	1	0	1	18	1	0	7	0	0
Wise, Richard, Cleveland	6.00	2	0	1.000	11	5	0	2	0	0	27	58	58	22	14	8	4	7	68	0	8	108	2	3
Wortham, Richard, Chicago*	3.72	15	10	.600	34	34	9	0	0	2	232	229	979	111	96	24	7	8	100	9	10	119	14	0
Wright, James, Boston	4.90	14	14	.500	11	11	5	0	0	0	23	195	889	126	111	21	10	10	100	3	10	15	3	0
Young, Kip, Detroit	5.09	2	2	.500	11	7	1	3	0	0	23	19	96	19	13	5	3	0	11	1	1	20	0	0
Zahn, Geoffrey, Minnesota*	3.57	13	7	.650	26	24	7	4	1	0	169	181	702	74	67	13	7	6	41	0	1	58	1	1

NOTE—Following pitchers combined to pitch shutout games: Baltimore (2)—Stone and Stanhouse, McGregor and F. Martinez; Boston (2)—Renko, Drago and Campbell, Renko and Campbell; Cleveland (2)—Waits, Hood and Spillner, Barker and Monge; Detroit (3)—Underwood, Tobik and Hiller, Wilcox and Lopez, Robbins and Billingham; Minnesota (3)—Koosman and Marshall, Jackson and Marshall, Jackson and Redfern; New York (2)—Hood and Kaat, John and Davis; Oakland (1)—Minetto and Todd; Seattle (2)—Honeycutt and McLaughlin, Dressler and McLaughlin; Texas (5)—Alexander and Kern 2, Comer and Lyle, Ellis and Kern, Medich and Kern; Toronto (1)—Huffman and Miller.

PITCHERS WITH TWO OR MORE CLUBS
(Alphabetically Arranged With Pitcher's First Club on Top)

Pitcher and Club	ERA.	W.	L.	Pct.	G.	GS.	CG.	GF.	Sv.	ShO.	IP.	H.	BFP.	R.	ER.	HR.	SH.	SF.	Tot. BB.	Int. BB.	HB.	SO.	WP.	Bk.
Farmer, Texas	4.36	2	0	1.000	11	2	0	5	0	0	33	30	144	21	16	2	2	2	19	2	2	25	3	0
Farmer, Chicago	2.44	3	7	.300	42	3	0	30	14	0	81	66	347	36	22	2	9	2	34	8	1	48	6	0
Hinton, Chicago	6.00	1	2	.333	16	2	0	8	2	0	42	57	188	30	28	4	4	3	8	1	2	27	0	0
Hinton, Seattle	5.40	0	2	.000	14	1	0	6	0	0	20	23	90	14	12	4	1	1	5	1	2	7	1	0
Hood, Cleveland	3.68	1	0	1.000	13	0	0	3	1	0	22	13	92	9	9	1	0	1	14	1	1	7	1	0
Hood, New York	3.09	3	1	.750	27	0	0	9	1	0	67	62	288	24	23	3	6	0	30	2	2	22	1	0
Johnson, Oakland	4.34	2	8	.200	14	13	1	0	0	0	85	89	372	45	41	13	2	2	36	0	3	50	1	1
Johnson, Texas	4.94	2	6	.250	17	12	1	0	0	0	82	79	357	50	45	12	5	5	36	1	1	46	3	1
Miller, California	3.34	1	0	1.000	14	1	0	8	0	0	35	44	157	14	13	2	0	1	13	3	0	16	2	0
Miller, Toronto	10.80	0	0	.000	10	0	0	5	0	0	15	27	75	18	18	3	1	0	5	0	0	7	1	0
Mitchell, Seattle	4.38	1	4	.200	10	6	1	1	1	0	37	46	166	26	18	4	1	1	15	0	0	18	1	0
Mitchell, Milwaukee	5.76	3	3	.500	18	8	0	4	0	0	75	81	312	50	48	11	0	6	10	3	0	32	0	0
Montague, Seattle	5.59	6	4	.600	41	1	0	15	1	1	116	125	508	73	72	14	10	0	47	2	0	60	3	0
Montague, California	5.00	2	0	1.000	14	0	0	10	6	0	18	16	75	12	10	3	0	0	9	0	0	6	2	0

1979 AL Pitching Against Each Club

BALTIMORE—102-57

Pitcher	Bos. W-L	Cal. W-L	Chi. W-L	Clev. W-L	Det. W-L	K.C. W-L	Mil. W-L	Min. W-L	N.Y. W-L	Oak. W-L	Sea. W-L	Tex. W-L	Tor. W-L	Totals W-L
Flanagan	1-1	1-0	3-1	2-1	0-1	1-1	2-0	2-0	0-3	3-0	3-0	2-1	3-0	23- 9
Ford	0-0	0-0	0-0	0-1	0-0	0-0	0-0	1-0	1-0	0-0	0-0	0-0	0-0	2- 1
Martinez, D.	2-2	1-2	0-1	1-2	0-2	1-2	2-0	0-2	0-1	2-0	3-0	1-2	2-0	15-16
Martinez, T.	1-0	0-0	1-0	0-0	3-1	0-0	0-0	0-0	1-1	2-1	0-0	1-0	1-0	10- 3
McGregor	0-0	2-0	1-1	0-1	2-1	2-0	0-0	2-0	1-0	0-1	1-1	1-0	1-1	13- 6
Palmer	1-0	2-0	1-0	2-0	0-0	1-1	0-1	1-1	1-0	0-1	0-0	0-1	1-1	10- 6
Stanhouse	0-1	0-0	1-0	1-0	0-0	0-1	1-2	0-1	1-0	0-0	1-0	0-0	1-0	7- 3
Stewart	1-0	1-0	0-0	0-0	2-0	1-1	2-1	0-0	0-1	0-1	0-1	0-0	1-0	8- 5
Stoddard	0-0	1-0	1-0	1-0	0-0	0-0	0-0	1-0	0-0	0-0	0-0	0-0	0-0	3- 1
Stone	2-1	1-1	0-0	1-0	0-1	0-0	2-1	0-1	0-0	1-0	2-0	1-2	1-0	11- 7
Totals	8-5	9-3	8-3	8-5	7-6	6-6	8-5	8-4	5-6	8-4	10-2	6-6	11-2	102-57

No Decisions: Flinn, Rineer.

BOSTON—91-69

Pitcher	Balt. W-L	Cal. W-L	Chi. W-L	Clev. W-L	Det. W-L	K.C. W-L	Mil. W-L	Min. W-L	N.Y. W-L	Oak. W-L	Sea. W-L	Tex. W-L	Tor. W-L	Totals W-L
Burgmeier	0-0	0-0	0-0	0-1	0-0	0-0	1-0	1-0	0-1	0-0	1-0	0-0	0-0	3- 2
Campbell	0-0	2-0	0-0	0-1	0-1	0-0	0-0	0-0	1-0	0-0	0-1	0-0	0-1	3- 4
Drago	0-0	0-0	0-0	1-0	1-0	0-1	2-0	1-0	1-0	0-1	1-0	1-3	2-1	10- 6
Eckersley	1-1	1-1	1-1	4-0	2-0	0-1	1-1	2-0	0-3	1-0	2-1	2-1	0-0	17-10
Finch	0-0	0-1	0-0	0-1	0-0	0-0	0-0	0-0	0-1	0-0	0-0	0-0	0-0	0- 3
Hassler	0-1	0-1	0-0	0-0	0-0	1-0	0-0	0-0	0-0	0-0	0-0	0-0	0-0	1- 2
Rainey	0-1	0-2	1-1	0-0	0-0	0-0	1-0	0-1	1-0	1-0	0-0	0-0	4-0	8- 5
Remmersw'l.	0-0	0-0	0-0	0-0	0-0	0-0	1-0	0-0	0-0	0-0	0-0	0-0	0-0	1- 0
Renko	2-0	1-0	1-0	0-1	1-1	2-1	0-2	1-0	0-0	1-1	2-1	0-1	0-1	11- 9
Ripley	0-0	0-0	1-1	0-0	0-0	0-0	1-0	0-0	0-0	1-0	0-0	0-0	0-0	3- 1
Stanley	2-2	0-1	1-2	0-2	1-2	3-0	0-0	3-0	2-0	2-1	1-0	0-1	1-1	16-12
Torrez	0-2	1-1	0-1	1-1	2-1	2-1	1-1	1-1	0-3	3-0	0-1	3-0	2-0	16-13
Tudor	0-1	0-0	0-0	0-0	1-0	0-0	0-0	0-1	0-0	0-0	0-0	0-0	0-0	1- 2
Wright	0-0	0-0	0-0	0-0	0-0	0-0	0-0	0-0	0-0	0-0	1-0	0-0	0-0	1- 0
Totals	5-8	5-7	5-6	6-7	8-5	8-4	8-4	9-3	5-8	9-3	8-4	6-6	9-4	91-69

No Decisions: None.

CALIFORNIA—88-74

Pitcher	Balt. W-L	Bos. W-L	Chi. W-L	Clev. W-L	Det. W-L	K.C. W-L	Mil. W-L	Min. W-L	N.Y. W-L	Oak. W-L	Sea. W-L	Tex. W-L	Tor. W-L	Totals W-L
Aase	0-3	1-1	1-1	0-0	1-3	1-0	0-1	2-0	0-0	1-0	0-0	0-1	2-0	9-10
Barlow	0-1	0-0	0-0	0-0	0-0	0-0	0-0	0-0	0-0	0-0	0-0	0-0	1-0	1- 1
Barr	1-1	1-0	0-1	0-1	0-2	1-1	0-0	0-1	2-1	1-1	2-1	0-2	0-0	10-12
Botting	0-0	0-0	0-0	0-0	0-0	0-0	0-0	0-0	1-0	1-0	0-0	0-0	0-0	2- 0
Clear	0-0	1-1	0-0	3-1	1-0	1-0	2-0	0-0	1-0	1-0	1-1	0-1	0-1	11- 5
Eddy	0-0	0-0	0-0	0-0	0-0	0-0	0-0	1-1	0-0	0-0	0-0	0-0	0-0	1- 1
Frost	1-1	2-1	1-0	1-2	1-1	1-1	0-1	1-1	0-1	3-0	2-0	2-1	1-0	16-10
Knapp	0-0	1-0	1-1	0-0	0-0	0-1	1-1	1-0	0-1	0-0	0-0	2-0	0-1	5- 5
LaRoche	1-1	0-1	0-0	2-0	0-0	0-1	1-0	1-0	1-2	0-1	1-2	0-1	0-2	7-11
Miller	0-0	0-0	0-0	0-0	0-0	0-0	0-0	1-0	0-0	0-0	0-0	0-0	0-0	1- 0
Montague	0-0	0-0	2-0	0-0	0-0	0-0	0-0	0-0	0-0	0-0	0-0	0-0	0-0	2- 0
Ryan	0-1	1-1	2-1	0-2	1-1	2-2	1-1	2-0	2-0	1-1	1-1	1-2	2-1	16-14
Tanana	0-1	0-0	2-0	0-0	0-1	1-0	1-1	0-1	0-0	2-0	0-1	0-0	1-0	7- 5
Totals	3-9	7-5	9-4	6-6	4-8	7-6	7-5	9-4	7-5	10-3	7-6	5-8	7-5	88-74

No Decisions: Ferris, Schuler.

CHICAGO—73-87

Pitcher	Balt. W-L	Bos. W-L	Cal. W-L	Clev. W-L	Det. W-L	K.C. W-L	Mil. W-L	Min. W-L	N.Y. W-L	Oak. W-L	Sea. W-L	Tex. W-L	Tor. W-L	Totals W-L
Barrios	0-0	1-0	0-1	0-1	0-0	1-0	1-0	0-0	0-1	1-0	1-0	2-0	1-0	8- 3
Baumgarten	0-0	2-0	1-2	2-1	2-1	0-1	0-1	1-1	0-0	1-1	1-1	2-0	1-0	13- 8
Dotson	0-0	0-0	0-0	0-0	0-0	0-0	0-0	0-0	2-0	0-0	0-0	0-0	0-0	2- 0
Farmer	0-2	0-0	1-1	0-0	0-0	0-0	1-0	1-2	0-0	0-1	0-1	0-0	0-0	3- 7
Hinton	0-0	0-0	0-1	0-0	0-0	0-1	0-0	0-0	1-0	0-0	0-0	0-0	0-0	1- 2
Hoffman	0-1	0-0	0-0	0-0	0-0	0-2	0-1	0-0	0-0	0-1	0-0	0-0	0-0	0- 5
Howard	0-0	0-0	0-1	0-0	0-0	1-0	1-2	0-1	0-0	0-0	0-0	0-0	0-0	1- 5
Kravec	1-1	1-2	1-0	1-2	0-2	1-0	0-2	2-1	1-1	2-0	1-1	2-0	2-1	15-13
LaGrow	0-0	0-0	0-0	0-0	0-0	0-1	0-0	0-0	0-0	0-0	0-0	0-1	0-1	0- 3
Proly	0-1	0-1	1-0	1-0	0-0	0-1	0-1	1-0	0-1	0-2	0-0	0-0	0-0	3- 8
Robinson	0-0	0-0	0-0	0-0	0-0	0-0	0-0	0-0	0-1	0-0	0-0	0-0	0-0	0- 1
Scarbery	0-0	0-1	0-0	0-1	0-2	0-0	0-0	0-0	0-0	0-0	0-0	1-1	1-1	2- 8
Schueler	0-0	0-0	0-1	0-0	0-0	0-0	0-0	0-0	0-0	0-0	0-0	0-0	0-0	0- 1
Trout	1-2	0-1	0-0	0-1	1-1	2-0	1-0	0-0	0-1	1-1	2-1	2-0	1-0	11- 8
Wortham	1-1	2-0	0-1	2-0	0-1	1-2	1-0	0-3	2-1	1-0	0-3	3-1	1-1	14-14
(Forfeit)	0-0	0-0	0-0	0-0	0-0	0-1	0-0	0-0	0-0	0-0	0-0	0-0	0-0	0- 1
Totals ...	3-8	6-5	4-9	6-6	3-9	5-8	5-7	5-8	4-8	9-4	5-8	11-2	7-5	73-87

No Decisions: Burns, Esser, Hoyt, Kucek, Nordhagen, Rondon, Torrealba.

CLEVELAND—81-80

Pitcher	Balt. W-L	Bos. W-L	Cal. W-L	Chi. W-L	Det. W-L	K.C. W-L	Mil. W-L	Min. W-L	N.Y. W-L	Oak. W-L	Sea. W-L	Tex. W-L	Tor. W-L	Totals W-L
Barker	0-2	1-0	1-0	0-0	1-1	0-0	0-2	0-0	0-0	1-0	0-0	2-0	0-1	6- 6
Clyde	0-0	0-2	0-0	1-0	1-0	1-0	0-2	0-0	0-1	0-0	0-1	0-0	0-0	3- 4
Cruz	0-1	1-1	0-0	0-2	1-2	0-0	0-1	1-0	0-0	2-0	0-1	0-0	1-1	3- 9
Garland	0-1	0-0	0-2	0-2	0-0	0-1	0-2	1-0	0-0	0-0	0-0	0-0	0-0	4-10
Hood	0-0	0-0	1-0	0-0	0-0	0-0	0-0	0-0	0-0	0-0	0-0	0-0	0-0	1- 0
Monge	2-0	1-0	0-1	1-0	0-1	0-1	0-0	0-2	1-2	2-1	3-2	1-0	2-0	12-10
Paxton	0-2	0-1	1-0	1-0	0-0	2-0	1-1	1-1	1-1	0-0	0-0	0-2	1-0	8- 8
Reuschel	0-0	0-0	1-1	0-0	0-0	0-0	0-0	0-0	0-0	0-0	1-0	0-0	0-0	2- 1
Spillner	1-1	1-0	1-1	0-0	1-1	1-1	1-0	2-0	0-0	0-1	0-0	1-0	0-0	9- 5
Waits	1-1	1-1	1-0	2-1	1-1	0-2	1-0	1-1	2-1	2-1	3-1	1-2	1-0	16-13
Wilkins	0-0	0-0	0-0	0-1	0-0	0-0	1-0	0-0	0-1	0-0	0-0	0-1	1-0	2- 4
Wise	1-0	2-1	1-0	2-0	1-0	2-1	0-0	2-0	1-2	1-1	1-0	0-0	1-3	15-10
Totals ...	5-8	7-6	6-6	6-6	6-6	6-6	4-9	8-4	5-8	8-4	7-5	5-7	8-5	81-80

No Decisions: Andersen, Wihtol.

DETROIT—85-76

Pitcher	Balt. W-L	Bos. W-L	Cal. W-L	Chi. W-L	Clev. W-L	K.C. W-L	Mil. W-L	Min. W-L	N.Y. W-L	Oak. W-L	Sea. W-L	Tex. W-L	Tor. W-L	Totals W-L
Arroyo	0-0	0-1	1-0	0-0	0-0	0-0	0-0	0-0	0-0	0-0	0-0	0-0	0-0	1- 1
Baker	0-0	0-1	0-0	1-2	0-0	0-0	0-1	0-1	0-1	0-0	0-0	0-0	0-0	1- 7
Billingham	1-2	1-0	1-0	1-0	0-0	1-1	0-1	1-1	2-0	0-0	1-0	1-0	0-2	10- 7
Burnside	0-0	0-0	0-0	0-0	0-0	1-0	0-0	0-0	0-1	0-0	0-0	0-0	0-0	1- 1
Chris	0-1	0-0	0-0	0-0	0-0	1-0	0-0	0-0	1-1	0-1	1-0	0-0	0-0	3- 3
Fidrych	0-0	0-0	0-0	0-0	0-0	0-1	0-1	0-1	0-0	0-0	0-0	0-0	0-0	0- 3
Hiller	0-2	0-0	0-0	0-0	1-1	0-1	0-1	0-1	1-0	0-1	1-0	0-0	1-0	4- 7
Lopez	1-0	2-1	2-1	1-0	1-2	0-0	1-0	0-1	1-0	2-1	2-1	1-0	0-1	10- 5
Morris	2-0	2-1	2-1	1-0	1-2	0-0	3-0	0-1	1-1	2-0	2-1	1-0	0-0	17- 7
Petry	1-0	0-0	1-0	1-2	0-1	0-1	1-1	0-0	0-0	1-0	0-1	1-0	0-1	6- 5
Robbins	0-0	0-0	2-0	0-0	0-0	0-0	0-0	0-0	0-0	0-1	0-1	1-0	0-1	3- 3
Rozema	1-0	0-1	0-1	0-0	0-0	1-0	0-1	0-1	0-0	1-0	0-0	1-0	0-0	4- 4
Taylor	0-0	0-0	0-0	1-0	0-0	0-1	0-0	0-1	0-0	0-0	0-0	0-0	0-0	1- 2
Tobik	0-1	0-0	0-0	1-0	0-0	0-0	0-2	1-1	0-0	1-0	0-0	0-0	0-1	3- 5
Underwood	0-0	0-0	0-0	1-0	2-0	1-1	1-0	0-1	0-1	1-1	0-0	0-0	0-0	6- 4
Wilcox	1-1	0-2	0-1	1-1	2-0	1-1	1-0	1-1	0-0	1-1	2-1	1-1	1-0	12-10
Young	0-0	0-0	0-0	1-0	0-1	0-0	0-0	0-0	0-0	1-0	0-0	0-0	0-1	2- 2
(Forfeit)	0-0	0-0	0-0	1-0	0-0	0-0	0-0	0-0	0-0	0-0	0-0	0-0	0-0	1- 0
Totals ...	6-7	5-8	8-4	9-3	6-6	5-7	6-7	4-8	7-6	7-5	7-5	6-6	9-4	85-76

No Decisions: None.

KANSAS CITY—85-77

Pitcher	Balt. W-L	Bos. W-L	Cal. W-L	Chi. W-L	Clev. W-L	Det. W-L	Mil. W-L	Min. W-L	N.Y. W-L	Oak. W-L	Sea. W-L	Tex. W-L	Tor. W-L	Totals W-L
Busby	1-0	0-2	0-0	1-1	0-0	1-0	0-1	1-0	0-0	1-1	1-0	0-1	0-0	6-6
Chamberlain	1-0	1-0	0-2	0-0	0-0	1-0	0-1	0-1	0-0	0-0	1-0	0-0	0-0	4-4
Gale	2-0	0-1	1-2	0-0	2-1	0-1	0-1	1-0	0-2	0-0	1-1	1-1	1-0	9-10
Gura	1-1	0-2	2-1	1-0	0-1	0-2	0-0	0-1	3-0	2-0	1-2	0-2	3-0	13-12
Hrabosky	0-0	1-1	0-0	1-0	2-1	0-0	1-0	0-0	1-0	2-1	1-1	0-0	0-0	9-4
Leonard	0-1	1-1	3-0	1-0	1-2	2-0	1-1	2-1	0-0	0-2	1-1	1-2	1-1	14-12
Martin	0-1	0-0	0-0	0-0	0-0	0-0	0-1	0-1	0-0	0-0	0-0	0-0	0-0	0-3
Mingori	0-0	0-0	0-0	1-0	0-0	0-1	1-0	0-0	0-2	0-0	0-0	0-0	0-0	3-3
Paschall	0-0	0-1	0-0	0-0	0-0	0-0	0-0	0-0	0-0	0-0	0-0	0-0	0-0	0-1
Pattin	0-0	0-0	0-1	1-1	0-0	0-0	1-0	0-0	1-0	1-0	0-0	0-0	1-0	5-2
Quisenberry	0-0	0-0	0-0	0-0	0-0	1-0	0-2	1-0	0-0	0-0	0-0	1-0	0-0	3-2
Rodriguez	0-0	0-0	0-0	1-0	0-0	1-0	0-0	0-0	0-1	0-0	0-0	1-0	1-0	4-1
Splittorff	1-3	1-0	0-1	1-3	1-1	1-1	1-0	2-2	0-2	3-0	1-1	2-1	1-2	15-17
Totals	6-6	4-8	6-7	8-5	6-6	7-5	5-7	7-6	5-7	9-4	7-6	6-7	9-3	85-77

No Decisions: Christenson, Eaton, Terrell, Throop.

MILWAUKEE—95-66

Pitcher	Balt. W-L	Bos. W-L	Cal. W-L	Chi. W-L	Clev. W-L	Det. W-L	K.C. W-L	Min. W-L	N.Y. W-L	Oak. W-L	Sea. W-L	Tex. W-L	Tor. W-L	Totals W-L
Augustine	1-1	0-1	1-2	1-0	0-0	1-0	1-0	1-1	1-0	0-1	2-0	0-0	0-0	9-6
Caldwell	1-1	1-0	0-1	1-1	1-1	1-0	1-0	3-0	2-0	2-1	0-0	2-0	1-1	16-6
Castro	0-0	0-0	0-1	0-0	0-0	0-0	0-0	1-0	0-0	0-0	1-0	0-0	1-0	3-1
Cleveland	0-0	0-3	0-0	0-0	0-0	1-0	0-2	0-0	0-0	0-0	0-0	0-0	0-0	1-5
Galasso	0-0	0-0	0-0	0-0	1-0	0-0	0-1	0-0	0-0	0-0	0-0	1-0	0-0	3-1
Haas	0-1	0-0	1-1	1-1	3-0	0-3	1-1	0-1	1-0	0-1	1-1	2-1	1-0	11-11
McClure	1-0	1-0	0-0	0-0	0-0	0-0	0-0	1-0	2-1	0-0	0-0	0-0	1-0	5-2
Mitchell	0-1	0-0	0-0	1-1	1-0	0-1	0-0	1-0	0-0	0-0	0-0	0-0	0-0	3-3
Slaton	0-1	1-1	1-0	1-0	1-1	1-2	2-1	0-1	0-0	3-1	2-0	0-1	3-0	15-9
Sorensen	1-2	1-1	1-1	1-1	1-2	1-0	2-0	0-1	2-1	0-1	1-2	2-1	2-1	15-14
Travers	1-1	0-1	1-1	1-1	1-0	2-0	0-0	1-0	1-2	1-1	2-0	2-0	1-1	14-8
Totals	5-8	4-8	5-7	7-5	9-4	7-6	7-5	8-4	9-4	6-6	9-3	9-3	10-3	95-66

No Decisions: Bando, Boitano, Gantner, Martinez, Rautzhan, Replogle.

MINNESOTA—82-80

Pitcher	Balt. W-L	Bos. W-L	Cal. W-L	Chi. W-L	Clev. W-L	Det. W-L	K.C. W-L	Mil. W-L	N.Y. W-L	Oak. W-L	Sea. W-L	Tex. W-L	Tor. W-L	Totals W-L
Bacsik	0-0	0-1	0-0	2-0	0-0	0-0	0-0	0-1	0-0	1-0	0-0	0-0	1-0	4-2
Erickson	0-2	1-1	0-3	0-0	0-1	0-0	0-1	1-1	0-0	0-1	0-0	1-0	0-0	3-10
Goltz	1-1	1-2	0-3	1-2	1-2	0-1	2-0	0-0	0-0	2-0	2-0	0-2	4-0	14-13
Hartzell	2-0	0-1	0-0	1-1	0-1	0-1	0-1	0-2	0-0	1-1	0-0	0-2	2-0	6-10
Jackson	0-0	0-0	0-1	0-0	0-1	1-0	0-0	0-0	0-1	1-0	1-1	1-0	0-0	4-4
Koosman	0-2	1-1	2-1	2-0	1-1	2-1	2-2	2-0	2-2	1-0	4-0	0-2	1-1	20-13
Marshall	0-2	0-1	0-1	0-1	1-1	3-1	1-2	1-1	0-1	2-1	1-0	0-3	1-0	10-15
Redfern	1-0	0-1	1-0	0-0	1-1	0-0	0-0	0-1	1-0	0-0	1-0	1-0	0-0	7-3
Serum	0-0	0-0	0-0	0-0	0-0	0-0	0-0	0-2	0-0	0-0	0-1	0-0	0-0	1-3
Zahn	0-1	0-1	1-0	2-1	0-0	1-0	1-1	0-0	4-1	1-1	1-1	1-0	1-0	13-7
Totals	4-8	3-9	4-9	8-5	4-8	8-4	6-7	4-8	7-5	9-4	10-3	4-9	11-1	82-80

No Decisions: Brett, Felton, Holly, Stanfield, Thormodsgard.

NEW YORK—89-71

Pitcher	Balt. W-L	Bos. W-L	Cal. W-L	Chi. W-L	Clev. W-L	Det. W-L	K.C. W-L	Mil. W-L	Min. W-L	Oak. W-L	Sea. W-L	Tex. W-L	Tor. W-L	Totals W-L
Beattie	0-0	1-0	1-0	0-1	0-1	0-0	0-1	0-0	0-2	0-1	1-0	0-0	0-0	3- 6
Burris	0-0	0-0	0-0	0-0	1-0	0-0	0-0	0-1	0-1	0-0	0-0	0-0	0-1	1- 3
Clay	0-0	0-0	0-0	0-1	0-0	0-2	1-1	0-1	0-0	0-0	0-0	0-1	0-1	1- 7
Davis	0-1	2-0	1-1	1-0	1-0	1-0	0-0	2-0	2-0	1-0	0-0	1-0	2-0	14- 2
Figueroa	0-0	0-1	0-1	1-0	0-0	0-1	0-0	0-1	2-0	1-0	0-1	0-0	0-1	4- 6
Guidry	2-0	2-0	1-2	1-0	1-1	2-1	2-0	1-0	0-1	3-1	1-1	2-0	0-1	18- 8
Gossage	1-1	0-0	0-0	0-0	1-0	1-1	2-0	0-1	0-0	0-0	0-0	0-0	0-0	5- 3
Hood	0-0	0-0	0-0	1-0	0-1	0-0	0-0	0-0	1-0	0-0	0-0	1-0	0-0	3- 1
Hunter	0-0	0-1	0-1	0-1	1-0	0-0	0-0	0-2	0-1	0-0	1-1	0-2	0-0	2- 9
John	3-0	2-1	1-1	1-0	2-1	1-2	2-0	1-0	0-1	3-1	1-1	2-0	2-1	21- 9
Kaat	0-1	0-1	0-0	0-0	1-0	0-0	0-1	0-0	0-0	1-0	0-0	0-0	0-0	2- 3
Mirabella	0-1	0-0	0-0	0-0	0-0	0-0	0-0	0-1	0-0	0-0	0-2	0-0	0-0	0- 4
Righetti	0-0	0-0	0-0	0-0	0-0	0-0	0-0	0-0	0-1	0-0	0-0	0-0	0-0	0- 1
Tiant	0-1	1-1	0-1	1-1	0-0	1-0	2-2	1-1	0-1	2-0	0-0	1-0	4-0	13- 8
Tidrow	0-1	0-0	0-0	1-0	0-0	0-0	0-0	0-0	0-0	0-0	1-0	0-0	0-0	2- 1
Totals	6-5	8-5	5-7	8-4	8-5	6-7	7-5	4-9	5-7	9-3	6-6	8-4	9-4	89-71

No Decisions: Anderson, Griffin, Kammeyer, Slagle.

OAKLAND—54-108

Pitcher	Balt. W-L	Bos. W-L	Cal. W-L	Chi. W-L	Clev. W-L	Det. W-L	K.C. W-L	Mil. W-L	Min. W-L	N.Y. W-L	Sea. W-L	Tex. W-L	Tor. W-L	Totals W-L
Hamilton	0-0	0-0	0-0	0-0	0-0	0-0	0-1	1-0	0-0	0-1	1-0	0-0	1-1	3- 4
Heaverlo	0-0	0-1	1-1	0-1	0-1	0-1	1-0	0-0	1-2	0-2	1-0	0-0	0-2	4-11
Johnson	0-2	0-0	0-1	0-2	0-0	0-1	0-0	1-0	1-0	0-1	0-0	0-0	0-1	2- 8
Keough	0-3	0-2	0-1	0-3	0-1	0-1	1-0	1-1	0-0	0-0	0-1	0-3	0-1	2-17
Kingman	0-0	0-1	0-1	2-0	0-1	2-0	1-0	0-0	0-1	1-1	1-0	0-2	1-0	8- 7
Lacey	0-0	1-0	0-0	0-0	0-2	0-0	0-0	0-1	0-0	0-1	0-0	0-1	0-0	1- 5
Langford	2-1	0-2	2-2	1-2	2-1	1-0	0-1	0-1	1-3	0-0	0-2	2-1	1-0	12-16
McCatty	0-1	2-1	0-1	1-0	1-0	2-2	1-2	3-0	1-1	0-1	0-1	0-0	0-2	11-12
Minetto	0-0	0-0	0-0	0-0	0-0	0-3	0-0	0-0	0-0	1-1	0-0	0-0	0-1	1- 5
Morgan	0-0	0-2	0-0	0-0	0-0	1-0	0-2	0-1	0-1	1-1	2-0	0-0	1-1	5- 8
Norris	1-0	0-1	0-0	0-1	1-1	0-0	0-1	0-0	0-1	0-0	0-0	0-0	0-0	2- 5
Todd	1-1	0-0	0-0	0-0	0-1	0-0	0-1	0-0	0-1	0-1	0-0	1-0	0-0	2- 5
Wirth	0-0	0-0	0-0	0-0	0-0	0-0	0-0	0-0	0-0	0-0	1-0	0-0	0-0	1- 0
Totals	4-8	3-9	3-10	4-9	4-8	5-7	4-9	6-6	4-9	3-9	8-5	2-11	4-8	54-108

No Decisions: None.

SEATTLE—67-95

Pitcher	Balt. W-L	Bos. W-L	Cal. W-L	Chi. W-L	Clev. W-L	Det. W-L	K.C. W-L	Mil. W-L	Min. W-L	N.Y. W-L	Oak. W-L	Tex. W-L	Tor. W-L	Totals W-L
Abbott	0-0	0-1	0-0	0-0	0-0	0-1	1-1	1-1	0-3	0-2	1-0	0-1	1-0	4-10
Bannister	0-1	1-2	0-1	1-0	0-1	2-1	2-1	0-2	0-3	1-1	2-1	0-0	1-1	10-15
Branch	0-0	0-0	0-0	0-0	0-0	0-0	0-0	0-0	0-0	0-0	0-0	0-1	0-0	0- 1
Decker	0-0	0-0	0-0	0-1	0-0	0-0	0-0	0-0	0-0	0-0	0-0	0-0	0-0	0- 1
Dressler	0-0	0-0	0-1	0-0	0-0	0-1	1-0	0-0	0-0	0-0	0-0	2-0	0-0	3- 2
Hinton	0-0	0-0	0-0	0-0	0-0	0-0	0-0	0-1	0-1	0-0	0-0	0-0	0-0	0- 2
Honeycutt	0-3	0-0	0-2	2-1	0-0	1-1	0-1	0-1	2-0	2-1	1-2	1-1	2-0	11-12
Jones	1-1	0-1	0-1	1-0	1-2	0-0	0-2	0-0	0-1	0-1	0-1	0-0	0-1	3-11
McLaughlin	0-2	0-1	2-0	2-0	1-0	0-1	1-1	0-1	1-0	0-0	0-0	0-1	0-0	7- 7
Mitchell	0-1	0-0	0-0	0-0	0-0	0-1	0-0	0-1	0-0	0-0	0-0	1-0	0-1	1- 4
Montague	0-0	2-0	1-0	0-0	0-1	0-0	0-0	0-2	0-0	0-0	1-1	1-0	1-0	6- 4
Parrott	1-1	1-1	1-1	1-3	2-0	1-1	0-1	2-0	0-1	1-1	0-1	1-1	3-0	14-12
Rawley	0-0	0-1	0-2	1-0	1-2	1-0	1-0	0-0	0-1	1-0	0-0	0-0	0-3	5- 9
Stein	0-1	0-0	2-1	0-0	0-0	0-1	0-0	0-0	0-0	0-0	0-0	0-0	0-0	2- 3
Twitchell	0-0	0-0	0-0	0-0	0-1	0-0	0-0	0-0	0-0	0-0	0-0	0-0	0-1	0- 2
Vasquez	0-0	0-0	0-0	0-0	0-0	0-0	0-0	0-0	0-0	1-0	0-0	0-0	0-0	1- 0
Totals	2-10	4-8	6-7	8-5	5-7	5-7	6-7	3-9	3-10	6-6	5-8	6-7	8-4	67-95

No Decisions: Lewis.

TEXAS—83-79

Pitcher	Balt. W-L	Bos. W-L	Cal. W-L	Chi. W-L	Clev. W-L	Det. W-L	K.C. W-L	Mil. W-L	Min. W-L	N.Y. W-L	Oak. W-L	Sea. W-L	Tor. W-L	Totals W-L
Alexander.....	1-1	0-1	0-0	0-1	0-0	0-0	0-0	0-1	0-1	0-0	1-0	2-1	1-1	5- 7
Allard	0-1	0-0	0-0	0-0	1-0	0-0	0-0	0-2	0-0	0-0	0-0	0-0	0-0	1- 3
Comer	3-0	1-1	1-2	0-1	1-1	1-0	2-0	0-3	1-0	1-1	2-1	2-1	2-1	17-12
Darwin	1-0	1-0	0-0	0-1	1-1	0-1	0-0	0-1	0-0	0-0	1-0	0-0	0-0	4- 4
Ellis	0-1	0-1	0-0	1-1	0-0	0-0	0-0	0-0	0-0	0-1	0-0	0-1	0-0	1- 5
Farmer	0-0	0-0	0-0	1-0	0-0	0-0	0-0	0-0	0-0	0-0	0-0	1-0	0-0	2- 0
Gleaton	0-0	0-0	0-0	0-0	0-0	0-0	0-0	0-0	0-0	0-1	0-0	0-0	0-0	0- 1
Jenkins	1-1	1-1	2-2	0-2	3-0	2-0	1-2	2-1	2-0	1-2	0-0	0-3	0-0	16-14
Johnson	0-0	0-0	1-0	0-1	0-1	0-1	0-1	0-0	0-0	0-0	1-0	0-0	0-2	2- 6
Kern	0-1	2-0	0-0	0-1	1-0	1-1	2-0	1-0	2-1	1-1	3-0	0-0	0-0	13- 5
Lyle	0-1	0-1	1-0	0-1	0-0	1-1	0-1	0-1	2-1	0-1	0-0	0-0	1-0	5- 8
Matlack	0-0	0-1	1-1	0-1	0-0	0-0	0-0	0-0	1-0	1-0	0-0	1-0	1-0	5- 4
McCall	0-0	0-0	0-0	0-0	0-0	0-0	0-0	0-0	0-0	1-0	0-0	0-0	0-0	1- 0
Medich	0-0	1-0	1-0	0-0	0-2	1-1	2-1	0-0	1-1	0-0	1-1	2-0	1-1	10- 7
Rajsich	0-0	0-0	1-0	0-1	0-0	0-1	0-0	0-0	0-0	0-1	0-0	0-0	0-0	1- 3
Totals ...	6-6	6-6	8-5	2-11	7-5	6-6	7-6	3-9	9-4	4-8	11-2	7-6	7-5	83-79

No Decisions: Babcock.

TORONTO—53-109

Pitcher	Balt. W-L	Bos. W-L	Cal. W-L	Chi. W-L	Clev. W-L	Det. W-L	K.C. W-L	Mil. W-L	Min. W-L	N.Y. W-L	Oak. W-L	Sea. W-L	Tex. W-L	Totals W-L
Buskey	0-1	1-2	0-0	1-0	0-2	1-2	0-0	0-2	0-0	0-0	2-0	1-1	0-0	6-10
Clancy.........	0-0	0-0	0-0	0-1	0-0	0-1	1-1	1-1	0-1	0-0	0-0	0-0	0-2	2- 7
Edge	1-1	0-0	1-0	0-0	0-0	0-0	0-0	0-0	0-0	0-2	1-0	0-1	0-0	3- 4
Freisleben	0-1	0-1	1-0	0-0	0-1	0-0	1-0	0-0	0-0	0-0	0-0	0-0	0-0	2- 3
Garvin	0-0	0-0	0-0	0-0	0-1	0-0	0-0	0-0	0-0	0-0	0-0	0-0	0-0	0- 1
Huffman	0-2	0-2	0-2	1-0	0-0	0-2	0-2	0-1	0-3	1-2	3-0	0-1	0-1	6-18
Jefferson	0-2	1-2	1-0	0-0	0-0	0-0	0-1	0-0	0-1	0-0	0-1	0-2	0-1	2-10
Lemanczyk ...	0-1	0-0	0-0	0-1	2-0	1-1	0-0	1-1	0-2	0-2	1-0	2-0	1-2	8-10
Lemongello...	0-0	0-0	0-0	0-0	0-2	0-1	0-1	0-1	0-2	0-1	0-0	0-1	1-0	1- 9
Moore	0-0	1-1	0-2	1-1	1-0	1-0	0-0	0-0	1-0	0-0	0-0	0-1	0-1	5- 7
Murphy	0-0	0-0	0-0	1-1	0-0	0-0	0-1	0-0	0-0	0-0	0-0	0-0	0-0	1- 2
Stieb	0-1	1-1	1-0	1-0	1-1	0-0	0-2	1-0	1-0	0-1	0-1	1-1	1-0	8- 8
Todd	0-0	0-0	0-0	0-1	0-0	0-0	0-0	0-0	0-0	0-0	0-0	0-0	0-0	0- 1
Underwood ..	1-2	0-0	1-2	0-2	1-1	0-2	1-1	0-3	0-0	2-1	1-2	0-0	2-0	9-16
Willis	0-0	0-0	0-1	0-0	0-0	0-0	0-0	0-1	0-1	0-0	0-0	0-0	0-0	0- 3
Totals ...	2-11	4-9	5-7	5-7	5-8	4-9	3-9	3-10	1-11	4-9	8-4	4-8	5-7	53-109

No Decisions: Grilli, Kusick, Luebber, Miller.

Niekros Matched Perrys

For only the second time in history two brothers won 20 games in the same season when Houston's Joe Niekro posted a 21-11 record and Atlanta's Phil Niekro had a 21-20 mark.

The other brothers to win 20 games in the same season were the Perrys in 1970. Jim Perry was 24-12 for Minnesota, while Gaylord was 23-13 for the Giants.

Thus, the Niekros were the first brother combination to win 20 games in one league in the same year.

AMERICAN LEAGUE

PENNANT WINNERS

Year Club	Manager	W.	L.	Pct.	*G.A.
1901—Chicago	Clark Griffith	83	53	.610	4
1902—Philadelphia	Connie Mack	83	53	.610	5
1903—Boston	James Collins	91	47	.659	14½
1904—Boston	James Collins	95	59	.617	1½
1905—Philadelphia	Connie Mack	92	56	.622	2
1906—Chicago	Fielder Jones	93	58	.616	3
1907—Detroit	Hugh Jennings	92	58	.613	1½
1908—Detroit	Hugh Jennings	90	63	.588	½
1909—Detroit	Hugh Jennings	98	54	.645	3½
1910—Philadelphia	Connie Mack	102	48	.680	14½
1911—Philadelphia	Connie Mack	101	50	.669	13½
1912—Boston	Garland Stahl	105	47	.691	14
1913—Philadelphia	Connie Mack	96	57	.627	6½
1914—Philadelphia	Connie Mack	99	53	.651	8½
1915—Boston	William Carrigan	101	50	.669	2½
1916—Boston	William Carrigan	91	63	.591	2
1917—Chicago	Clarence Rowland	100	54	.649	9
1918—Boston	Edward Barrow	75	51	.595	2½
1919—Chicago	William Gleason	88	52	.629	3½
1920—Cleveland	Tristram Speaker	98	56	.636	2
1921—New York	Miller Huggins	98	55	.641	4½
1922—New York	Miller Huggins	94	60	.610	1
1923—New York	Miller Huggins	98	54	.645	16
1924—Washington	Stanley (Bucky) Harris	92	62	.597	2
1925—Washington	Stanley (Bucky) Harris	96	55	.636	8½
1926—New York	Miller Huggins	91	63	.591	3
1927—New York	Miller Huggins	110	44	.714	19
1928—New York	Miller Huggins	101	53	.656	2½
1929—Philadelphia	Connie Mack	104	46	.693	18
1930—Philadelphia	Connie Mack	102	52	.662	8
1931—Philadelphia	Connie Mack	107	45	.704	13½
1932—New York	Joseph McCarthy	107	47	.695	13
1933—Washington	Joseph Cronin	99	53	.651	7
1934—Detroit	Gordon (Mickey) Cochrane	101	53	.656	7
1935—Detroit	Gordon (Mickey) Cochrane	93	58	.616	3
1936—New York	Joseph McCarthy	102	51	.667	19½
1937—New York	Joseph McCarthy	102	52	.662	13
1938—New York	Joseph McCarthy	99	53	.651	9½
1939—New York	Joseph McCarthy	106	45	.702	17
1940—Detroit	Delmer Baker	90	64	.584	1
1941—New York	Joseph McCarthy	101	53	.656	17
1942—New York	Joseph McCarthy	103	51	.669	9
1943—New York	Joseph McCarthy	98	56	.636	13½
1944—St. Louis	J. Luther Sewell	89	65	.578	1
1945—Detroit	Stephen O'Neill	88	65	.575	1½
1946—Boston	Joseph Cronin	104	50	.675	12
1947—New York	Stanley (Bucky) Harris	97	57	.630	12
1948—Cleveland†	Louis Boudreau	97	58	.626	1
1949—New York	Charles (Casey) Stengel	97	57	.630	1
1950—New York	Charles (Casey) Stengel	98	56	.636	3
1951—New York	Charles (Casey) Stengel	98	56	.636	5
1952—New York	Charles (Casey) Stengel	95	59	.617	2
1953—New York	Charles (Casey) Stengel	99	52	.656	8½
1954—Cleveland	Alfonso Lopez	111	43	.721	8
1955—New York	Charles (Casey) Stengel	96	58	.623	3
1956—New York	Charles (Casey) Stengel	97	57	.630	9
1957—New York	Charles (Casey) Stengel	98	56	.636	8
1958—New York	Charles (Casey) Stengel	92	62	.597	10
1959—Chicago	Alfonso Lopez	94	60	.610	5
1960—New York	Charles (Casey) Stengel	97	57	.630	8

PENNANT WINNERS—Continued

Year Club	Manager	W.	L.	Pct.	*G.A.
1961—New York	Ralph Houk	109	53	.673	8
1962—New York	Ralph Houk	96	66	.593	5
1963—New York	Ralph Houk	104	57	.646	10½
1964—New York	Lawrence (Yogi) Berra	99	63	.611	1
1965—Minnesota	Sabath (Sam) Mele	102	60	.630	7
1966—Baltimore	Henry A. Bauer	97	63	.606	9
1967—Boston	Richard H. Williams	92	70	.568	1
1968—Detroit	E. Mayo Smith	103	59	.636	12
1969—Baltimore (E)**	Earl S. Weaver	109	53	.673	19
1970—Baltimore (E)**	Earl S. Weaver	108	54	.667	15
1971—Baltimore (E)**	Earl S. Weaver	101	57	.639	12
1972—Oakland (W)**	Richard H. Williams	93	62	.600	5½
1973—Oakland (W)**	Richard H. Williams	94	68	.580	6
1974—Oakland (W)**	Alvin Ralph Dark	90	72	.556	5
1975—Boston (E)**	Darrell D. Johnson	95	65	.594	4½
1976—New York (E)**	Alfred M. Martin	97	62	.610	10½
1977—New York (E)**	Alfred M. Martin	100	62	.617	2½
1978—New York (E)†**	Alfred M. Martin, Robert G. Lemon	100	63	.613	1
1979—Baltimore (E)**	Earl S. Weaver	102	57	.642	8

*Games ahead of second-place club. †Defeated Boston in one-game playoff.

**Won Championship Series.

YEARLY FINISHES

Year	Balt.	Bos.	Calif.	Chi.	Cleve.	Det.	Minn.	N.Y.	Oak.	Wash.
1901	a8	2	....	1	7	3	‡6	z5		†4
1902	*2	3	....	4	5	7	‡6	z8		†1
1903	*6	1	....	7	3	5	‡8	4		†2
1904	*6	1	....	3	4	7	‡8	2		†5
1905	*8	4	....	2	5	3	‡7	6		†1
1906	*5	8	....	1	3	6	‡7	2		†4
1907	*6	7	....	3	4	1	‡8	5		†2
1908	*4	5	....	3	2	1	‡7	8		†6
1909	*7	3	....	4	6	1	‡8	5		†2
1910	*8	4	....	6	5	3	‡7	2		†1
1911	*8	5	....	4	3	2	‡7	6		†1
1912	*7	1	....	4	5	6	‡2	8		†3
1913	*8	4	....	5	3	6	‡2	7		†1
1914	*5	2	....	x6	8	4	‡3	x6		†1
1915	*6	1	....	3	7	2	‡4	5		†8
1916	*5	1	....	2	6	3	‡7	4		†8
1917	*7	2	....	1	3	4	‡5	6		†8
1918	*5	1	....	6	2	7	‡3	4		†8
1919	*5	6	....	1	2	4	‡7	3		†8
1920	*4	5	....	2	1	7	‡6	3		†8
1921	*3	5	....	7	2	6	‡4	1		†8
1922	*2	8	....	5	4	3	‡6	1		†7
1923	*5	8	....	7	3	2	‡4	1		†6
1924	*4	7	....	8	6	3	‡1	2		†5
1925	*3	8	....	5	6	4	‡1	7		†2
1926	*7	8	....	5	2	6	‡4	1		†3
1927	*7	8	....	5	6	4	‡3	1		†2
1928	*3	8	....	5	7	6	‡4	2		†1
1929	*4	8	....	7	3	6	‡5	2		†1
1930	*6	8	....	7	4	5	‡2	3		†1
1931	*5	6	....	8	4	7	‡3	2		†1
1932	*6	8	....	7	4	5	‡3	1		†2
1933	*8	7	....	6	4	5	‡1	2		†3
1934	*6	4	....	8	3	1	‡7	2		†5
1935	*7	4	....	5	3	1	‡6	2		†8
1936	*7	6	....	3	5	2	‡4	1		†8
1937	*8	5	....	3	4	2	‡6	1		†7
1938	*7	2	....	6	3	4	‡5	1		†8
1939	*8	2	....	4	3	5	‡6	1		†7
1940	*6	x4	....	x4	2	1	‡7	3		†8
1941	x*6	2	....	3	x4	x4	x‡6	1		†8

YEARLY FINISHES—Continued

Year	Balt.	Bos.	Calif.	Chi.	Cleve.	Det.	Minn.	N.Y.	Oak.	Wash.
1942	*3	2	....	6	4	5	‡7	1	†8	....
1943	*6	7	....	4	3	5	‡2	1	†8	....
1944	*1	4	....	7	x5	2	‡8	3	x†5	....
1945	*3	7	....	6	5	1	‡2	4	†8	....
1946	*7	1	....	5	6	2	‡4	3	†8	....
1947	*8	3	....	6	4	2	‡7	1	†5	....
1948	*6	2	....	8	1	5	‡7	3	†4	....
1949	*7	2	....	6	3	4	‡8	1	†5	....
1950	*7	3	....	6	4	2	‡5	1	†8	....
1951	*8	3	....	4	2	5	‡7	1	†6	....
1952	*7	6	....	3	2	8	‡5	1	†4	....
1953	*8	4	....	3	2	6	‡5	1	†7	....
1954	7	4	....	3	1	5	‡6	2	†8	....
1955	7	4	....	3	2	5	‡8	1	†6	....
1956	6	4	....	3	2	5	‡7	1	†8	....
1957	5	3	....	2	6	4	‡8	1	†7	....
1958	6	3	....	2	4	5	‡8	1	†7	....
1959	6	5	....	1	2	4	‡8	3	†7	....
1960	2	7	....	3	4	6	‡5	1	†8	....
1961	3	6	§8	4	5	2	7	1	x†9	x9
1962	7	8	§3	5	6	4	2	1	†9	10
1963	4	7	§9	2	x5	x5	3	1	†8	10
1964	3	8	§5	2	x6	4	x6	1	†10	9
1965	3	9	§7	2	5	4	1	6	†10	8
1966	1	9	6	4	5	3	2	10	†7	8
1967	x6	1	5	4	8	x2	x2	9	†10	x6
1968	2	4	x8	x8	3	1	7	5	6	10

	EAST DIVISION							WEST DIVISION						
Year	Balt.	Bos.	Cleve.	Det.	N.Y.	Wash.	Mil.	Calif.	Chi.	K.C.	Mil.	Minn.	Oak.	Tex.
1969	1	3	6	2	5	4	....	3	5	4	y6	1	2	....
1970	1	3	5	4	2	6	....	3	6	x4	x4	1	2	....
1971	1	3	6	2	4	5	....	4	3	2	6	5	1	....
1972	3	2	5	1	4	....	6	5	2	4	....	3	1	6
1973	1	2	6	3	4	....	5	4	5	2	....	3	1	6
1974	1	3	4	6	2	....	5	6	4	5	....	3	1	2
1975	2	1	4	6	3	....	5	6	5	2	....	4	1	3
1976	2	3	4	5	1	....	6	x4	6	1	....	3	2	x4

	EAST DIVISION							WEST DIVISION						
Year	Balt.	Bos.	Cleve.	Det.	Mil.	N.Y.	Tor.	Calif.	Chi.	K.C.	Minn.	Oak.	Sea.	Tex.
1977	x2	x2	5	4	6	1	7	5	3	1	4	7	6	2
1978	4	2	6	5	3	1	7	x2	5	1	4	6	7	x2
1979	1	3	6	5	2	4	7	1	5	2	4	7	6	3

*Record of predecessor St. Louis club. †Predecessor Philadelphia (1901-54), Kansas City (1955-67). ‡Predecessor Washington Club. §Known as Los Angeles Angels from 1961 to September 2, 1965. yPredecessor Seattle club. zPredecessor Baltimore club. aPredecessor Milwaukee club. xTied for position.

LEADING BATSMEN

Year	Player and Club	G.	AB.	R.	H.	TB.	2B.	3B.	HR.	RBI.	B.A.
1901—Napoleon Lajoie, Philadelphia		131	543	145	229	345	48	13	14	....	.422
1902—Edward Delahanty, Washington		123	474	103	178	279	41	15	10	....	.376
1903—Napoleon Lajoie, Cleveland		126	488	90	173	260	40	13	7	....	.355
1904—Napoleon Lajoie, Cleveland		140	554	92	211	304	50	14	5	....	.381
1905—Elmer Flick, Cleveland		131	496	71	152	231	29	19	4	....	.306
1906—George Stone, St. Louis		154	581	91	208	288	24	19	6	....	.358
1907—Tyrus Cobb, Detroit		150	605	97	212	286	29	15	5	116	.350
1908—Tyrus Cobb, Detroit		150	581	88	188	276	36	20	4	101	.324
1909—Tyrus Cobb, Detroit		156	573	116	216	296	33	10	9	115	.377
1910—Tyrus Cobb, Detroit		140	509	106	196	282	36	13	8	88	.385
1911—Tyrus Cobb, Detroit		146	591	147	248	367	47	24	8	144	.420
1912—Tyrus Cobb, Detroit		140	553	119	227	324	30	23	7	90	.410
1913—Tyrus Cobb, Detroit		122	428	70	167	229	18	16	4	65	.390

LEADING BATSMEN—Continued

Year	Player and Club	G.	AB.	R.	H.	TB.	2B.	3B.	HR.	RBI.	B.A.
1914	Tyrus Cobb, Detroit	97	345	69	127	177	22	11	2	57	.368
1915	Tyrus Cobb, Detroit	156	563	114	208	274	31	13	3	95	.369
1916	Tristram Speaker, Cleveland	151	546	102	211	274	41	8	2	83	.386
1917	Tyrus Cobb, Detroit	152	588	107	225	336	44	23	7	108	.383
1918	Tyrus Cobb, Detroit	111	421	83	161	217	19	14	3	64	.382
1919	Tyrus Cobb, Detroit	124	497	92	191	256	36	13	1	69	.384
1920	George Sisler, St. Louis	154	631	137	257	399	49	18	19	122	.407
1921	Harry Heilmann, Detroit	149	602	114	237	365	43	14	19	139	.394
1922	George Sisler, St. Louis	142	586	134	246	348	42	18	8	105	.420
1923	Harry Heilmann, Detroit	144	524	121	211	331	44	11	18	115	.403
1924	George (Babe) Ruth, New York	153	529	143	200	391	39	7	46	121	.378
1925	Harry Heilmann, Detroit	150	573	97	225	326	40	11	13	133	.393
1926	Henry Manush, Detroit	136	498	95	188	281	35	8	14	86	.378
1927	Harry Heilmann, Detroit	141	505	106	201	311	50	9	14	120	.398
1928	Leon (Goose) Goslin, Washington	135	456	80	173	280	36	10	17	102	.379
1929	Lew Fonseca, Cleveland	148	566	97	209	301	44	15	6	103	.369
1930	Aloysius Simmons, Philadelphia	138	554	152	211	392	41	16	36	165	.381
1931	Aloysius Simmons, Philadelphia	128	513	105	200	329	37	13	22	128	.390
1932	Dale Alexander, Detroit-Boston	124	392	58	144	201	27	3	8	60	.367
1933	James Foxx, Philadelphia	149	573	125	204	403	37	9	48	163	.356
1934	H. Louis Gehrig, New York	154	579	128	210	409	40	6	49	165	.363
1935	Chas. (Buddy) Myer, Washington	151	616	115	215	288	36	11	5	100	.349
1936	Lucius Appling, Chicago	138	526	111	204	267	31	7	6	128	.388
1937	Charles Gehringer, Detroit	144	564	133	209	293	40	1	14	96	.371
1938	James Foxx, Boston	149	565	139	197	398	33	9	50	175	.349
1939	Joseph DiMaggio, New York	120	462	108	176	310	32	6	30	126	.381
1940	Joseph DiMaggio, New York	132	508	93	179	318	28	9	31	133	.352
1941	Theodore Williams, Boston	143	456	135	185	335	33	3	37	120	.406
1942	Theodore Williams, Boston	150	522	141	186	338	34	5	36	137	.356
1943	Lucius Appling, Chicago	155	585	63	192	238	33	2	3	80	.328
1944	Louis Boudreau, Cleveland	150	584	91	191	255	45	5	3	67	.327
1945	George Stirnweiss, New York	152	632	107	195	301	32	22	10	64	.309
1946	Jas. (Mickey) Vernon, Washington	148	587	88	207	298	51	8	8	85	.353
1947	Theodore Williams, Boston	156	528	125	181	335	40	9	32	114	.343
1948	Theodore Williams, Boston	137	509	124	188	313	44	3	25	127	.369
1949	George Kell, Detroit	134	522	97	179	244	38	9	3	59	.343
1950	William Goodman, Boston	110	424	91	150	193	25	3	4	68	.354
1951	Ferris Fain, Philadelphia	117	425	63	146	200	30	3	6	57	.344
1952	Ferris Fain, Philadelphia	145	538	82	176	231	43	3	2	59	.327
1953	Jas. (Mickey) Vernon, Washington	152	608	101	205	315	43	11	15	115	.337
1954	Roberto Avila, Cleveland	143	555	112	189	265	27	2	15	67	.341
1955	Albert Kaline, Detroit	152	588	121	200	321	24	8	27	102	.340
1956	Mickey Mantle, New York	150	533	132	188	376	22	5	52	130	.353
1957	Theodore Williams, Boston	132	420	96	163	307	28	1	38	87	.388
1958	Theodore Williams, Boston	129	411	81	135	240	23	2	26	85	.328
1959	Harvey Kuenn, Detroit	139	561	99	198	281	42	7	9	71	.353
1960	James (Pete) Runnels, Boston	143	528	80	169	208	29	2	2	35	.320
1961	Norman Cash, Detroit	159	535	119	193	354	22	8	41	132	.361
1962	James (Pete) Runnels, Boston	152	562	80	183	256	33	5	10	60	.326
1963	Carl Yastrzemski, Boston	151	570	91	183	271	40	3	14	68	.321
1964	Pedro (Tony) Oliva, Minnesota	161	672	109	217	374	43	9	32	94	.323
1965	Pedro (Tony) Oliva, Minnesota	149	576	107	185	283	40	5	16	98	.321
1966	Frank Robinson, Baltimore	155	576	122	182	367	34	2	49	122	.316
1967	Carl Yastrzemski, Boston	161	579	112	189	360	31	4	44	121	.326
1968	Carl Yastrzemski, Boston	157	539	90	162	267	32	2	23	74	.301
1969	Rodney Carew, Minnesota	123	458	79	152	214	30	4	8	56	.332
1970	Alexander Johnson, California	156	614	85	202	282	26	6	14	86	.329
1971	Pedro (Tony) Oliva, Minnesota	126	487	73	164	266	30	3	22	81	.337
1972	Rodney Carew, Minnesota	142	535	61	170	203	21	6	0	51	.318
1973	Rodney Carew, Minnesota	149	580	98	203	273	30	11	6	62	.350
1974	Rodney Carew, Minnesota	153	599	86	218	267	30	5	3	55	.364
1975	Rodney Carew, Minnesota	143	535	89	192	266	24	4	14	80	.359
1976	George H. Brett, Kansas City	159	645	94	215	298	34	14	7	67	.333
1977	Rodney Carew, Minnesota	155	616	128	239	351	38	16	14	100	.388
1978	Rodney Carew, Minnesota	152	564	85	188	249	26	10	5	70	.333
1979	Fredric Lynn, Boston	147	531	116	177	338	42	1	39	122	.333

LEADERS IN RUNS SCORED

Year	Player and Club	Runs
1900—	(Not classed as major)	
1901—	Napoleon Lajoie, Philadelphia	145
1902—	David Fultz, Philadelphia	110
1903—	Patrick Dougherty, Boston	108
1904—	Patrick Dougherty, Boston-New York	113
1905—	Harry Davis, Philadelphia	92
1906—	Elmer Flick, Cleveland	98
1907—	Samuel Crawford, Detroit	102
1908—	Matthew McIntyre, Detroit	105
1909—	Tyrus Cobb, Detroit	116
1910—	Tyrus Cobb, Detroit	106
1911—	Tyrus Cobb, Detroit	147
1912—	Edward Collins, Philadelphia	137
1913—	Edward Collins, Philadelphia	125
1914—	Edward Collins, Philadelphia	122
1915—	Tyrus Cobb, Detroit	144
1916—	Tyrus Cobb, Detroit	113
1917—	Owen (Donie) Bush, Detroit	112
1918—	Raymond Chapman, Cleveland	84
1919—	George (Babe) Ruth, Boston	103
1920—	George (Babe) Ruth, New York	158
1921—	George (Babe) Ruth, New York	177
1922—	George Sisler, St. Louis	134
1923—	George (Babe) Ruth, New York	151
1924—	George (Babe) Ruth, New York	143
1925—	John Mostil, Chicago	135
1926—	George (Babe) Ruth, New York	139
1927—	George (Babe) Ruth, New York	158
1928—	George (Babe) Ruth, New York	163
1929—	Charles Gehringer, Detroit	131
1930—	Aloysius Simmons, Philadelphia	152
1931—	H. Louis Gehrig, New York	163
1932—	James Foxx, Philadelphia	151
1933—	H. Louis Gehrig, New York	138
1934—	Charles Gehringer, Detroit	134
1935—	H. Louis Gehrig, New York	125
1936—	H. Louis Gehrig, New York	167
1937—	Joseph DiMaggio, New York	151
1938—	Henry Greenberg, Detroit	144
1939—	Robert (Red) Rolfe, New York	139
1940—	Theodore Williams, Boston	134
1941—	Theodore Williams, Boston	135
1942—	Theodore Williams, Boston	141
1943—	George Case, Washington	102
1944—	George Stirnweiss, New York	125
1945—	George Stirnweiss, New York	107
1946—	Theodore Williams, Boston	142
1947—	Theodore Williams, Boston	125
1948—	Thomas Henrich, New York	138
1949—	Theodore Williams, Boston	150
1950—	Dominic DiMaggio, Boston	131
1951—	Dominic DiMaggio, Boston	113
1952—	Lawrence Doby, Cleveland	104
1953—	Albert Rosen, Cleveland	115
1954—	Mickey Mantle, New York	129
1955—	Alphonse Smith, Cleveland	123
1956—	Mickey Mantle, New York	132
1957—	Mickey Mantle, New York	121
1958—	Mickey Mantle, New York	127
1959—	Edward Yost, Detroit	115
1960—	Mickey Mantle, New York	119
1961—	Mantle, New York–Maris, New York	132
1962—	Albert G. Pearson, Los Angeles	115
1963—	W. Robert Allison, Minnesota	99
1964—	Pedro (Tony) Oliva, Minnesota	109
1965—	Zoilo Versalles, Minnesota	126
1966—	Frank Robinson, Baltimore	122
1967—	Carl Yastrzemski, Boston	112
1968—	Richard McAuliffe, Detroit	95
1969—	Reginald Jackson, Oakland	123
1970—	Carl Yastrzemski, Boston	125
1971—	Donald Buford, Baltimore	99
1972—	Bobby Murcer, New York	102
1973—	Reginald Jackson, Oakland	99
1974—	Carl Yastrzemski, Boston	93
1975—	Fredric Lynn, Boston	103
1976—	Roy White, New York	104
1977—	Rodney Carew, Minnesota	128
1978—	Ronald LeFlore, Detroit	126
1979—	Donald Baylor, California	120

LEADERS IN HITS

Year	Player and Club	Hits
1900—	(Not classed as major)	
1901—	Napoleon Lajoie, Philadelphia	229
1902—	Charles Hickman, Cleveland	194
1903—	Patrick Dougherty, Boston	195
1904—	Napoleon Lajoie, Cleveland	211
1905—	George Stone, St. Louis	187
1906—	Napoleon Lajoie, Cleveland	214
1907—	Tyrus Cobb, Detroit	212
1908—	Tyrus Cobb, Detroit	188
1909—	Tyrus Cobb, Detroit	216
1910—	Napoleon Lajoie, Cleveland	227
1911—	Tyrus Cobb, Detroit	248
1912—	Tyrus Cobb, Detroit	227
1913—	Joseph Jackson, Cleveland	197
1914—	Tristram Speaker, Boston	193
1915—	Tyrus Cobb, Detroit	208
1916—	Tristram Speaker, Cleveland	211
1917—	Tyrus Cobb, Detroit	225
1918—	George Burns, Philadelphia	178
1919—	Cobb, Detroit-Robert Veach, Detroit	191
1920—	George Sisler, St. Louis	257
1921—	Harry Heilmann, Detroit	237
1922—	George Sisler, St. Louis	246
1923—	Charles Jamieson, Cleveland	222
1924—	Edgar (Sam) Rice, Washington	216
1925—	Aloysius Simmons, Philadelphia	253
1926—	George Burns, Cleveland	216
	Edgar (Sam) Rice, Washington	216
1927—	Earle Combs, New York	231
1928—	Henry Manush, St. Louis	241
1929—	Dale Alexander, Detroit	215
	Charles Gehringer, Detroit	215
1930—	U. John Hodapp, Cleveland	225
1931—	H. Louis Gehrig, New York	211
1932—	Aloysius Simmons, Philadelphia	216
1933—	Henry Manush, Washington	221
1934—	Charles Gehringer, Detroit	214
1935—	Joseph Vosmik, Cleveland	216
1936—	H. Earl Averill, Cleveland	232
1937—	Roy (Beau) Bell, St. Louis	218
1938—	Joseph Vosmik, Boston	201
1939—	Robert (Red) Rolfe, New York	213

LEADERS IN HITS—Continued

Year	Player and Club	Hits
1940	Raymond (Rip) Radcliff, St. Louis	200
	W. Barney McCosky, Detroit	200
	Roger (Doc) Cramer, Boston	200
1941	Cecil Travis, Washington	218
1942	John Pesky, Boston	205
1943	Richard Wakefield, Detroit	200
1944	George Stirnweiss, New York	205
1945	George Stirnweiss, New York	195
1946	John Pesky, Boston	208
1947	John Pesky, Boston	207
1948	Robert Dillinger, St. Louis	207
1949	L. Dale Mitchell, Cleveland	203
1950	George Kell, Detroit	218
1951	George Kell, Detroit	191
1952	J. Nelson Fox, Chicago	192
1953	Harvey Kuenn, Detroit	209
1954	Fox, Chicago-Kuenn, Detroit	201
1955	Albert Kaline, Detroit	200
1956	Harvey Kuenn, Detroit	196
1957	J. Nelson Fox, Chicago	196
1958	J. Nelson Fox, Chicago	187

Year	Player and Club	Hits
1959	Harvey Kuenn, Detroit	198
1960	Orestes (Minnie) Minoso, Chicago	184
1961	Norman Cash, Detroit	193
1962	Robert Richardson, New York	209
1963	Carl Yastrzemski, Boston	183
1964	Pedro (Tony) Oliva, Minnesota	217
1965	Pedro (Tony) Oliva, Minnesota	185
1966	Pedro (Tony) Oliva, Minnesota	191
1967	Carl Yastrzemski, Boston	189
1968	Dagoberto Campaneris, Oakland	177
1969	Pedro (Tony) Oliva, Minnesota	197
1970	Pedro (Tony) Oliva, Minnesota	204
1971	Cesar Tovar, Minnesota	204
1972	Joseph Rudi, Oakland	181
1973	Rodney Carew, Minnesota	203
1974	Rodney Carew, Minnesota	218
1975	George Brett, Kansas City	195
1976	George Brett, Kansas City	215
1977	Rodney Carew, Minnesota	239
1978	James Rice, Boston	213
1979	George Brett, Kansas City	212

ONE-BASE HIT LEADERS

Year	Player and Club	1B.
1900	(Not classed as major)	
1901	Napoleon Lajoie, Philadelphia	154
1902	Fielder A. Jones, Chicago	148
1903	Patrick H. Dougherty, Boston	161
1904	William H. Keeler, New York	164
1905	William H. Keeler, New York	147
1906	William H. Keeler, New York	166
1907	Tyrus R. Cobb, Detroit	163
1908	Matthew W. McIntyre, Detroit	131
	George R. Stone, St. Louis	131
1909	Tyrus R. Cobb, Detroit	164
1910	Napoleon Lajoie, Cleveland	165
1911	Tyrus R. Cobb, Detroit	169
1912	Tyrus R. Cobb, Detroit	167
1913	Edward T. Collins, Philadelphia	145
1914	John P. McInnis, Philadelphia	160
1915	Tyrus R. Cobb, Detroit	161
1916	Tristram Speaker, Cleveland	160
1917	Tyrus R. Cobb, Detroit	151
	J. Clyde Milan, Washington	151
1918	George H. Burns, Philadelphia	141
1919	Edgar C. Rice, Washington	144
1920	George H. Sisler, St. Louis	171
1921	John T. Tobin, St. Louis	179
1922	George Sisler, St. Louis	134
1923	Charles D. Jamieson, Cleveland	172
1924	Charles D. Jamieson, Cleveland	168
1925	Edgar C. Rice, Washington	182
1926	Edgar C. Rice, Washington	167
1927	Earle B. Combs, New York	166
1928	Henry E. Manush, St. Louis	161
1929	Earle B. Combs, New York	151
1930	Edgar C. Rice, Washington	158
1931	Oscar D. Melillo, St. Louis	142
	Jonathan T. Stone, Detroit	142
1932	Henry E. Manush, Washington	145
1933	Henry E. Manush, Washington	167
1934	Roger M. Cramer, Philadelphia	158
1935	Roger M. Cramer, Philadelphia	170
1936	Raymond A. Radcliff, Chicago	161
1937	John K. Lewis, Washington	162
1938	Melo B. Almada, Wash.-St. Louis	158

Year	Player and Club	1B.
1939	Roger M. Cramer, Boston	147
1940	Roger M. Cramer, Boston	160
1941	Cecil H. Travis, Washington	153
1942	John M. Pesky, Boston	165
1943	Roger M. Cramer, Detroit	159
1944	George H. Stirnweiss, New York	146
1945	Irvin G. Hall, Philadelphia	139
1946	John M. Pesky, Boston	159
1947	John M. Pesky, Boston	172
1948	L. Dale Mitchell, Cleveland	162
1949	L. Dale Mitchell, Cleveland	161
1950	Philip F. Rizzuto, New York	150
1951	George C. Kell, Detroit	150
1952	J. Nelson Fox, Chicago	157
1953	Harvey E. Kuenn, Detroit	167
1954	J. Nelson Fox, Chicago	167
1955	J. Nelson Fox, Chicago	157
1956	J. Nelson Fox, Chicago	158
1957	J. Nelson Fox, Chicago	155
1958	J. Nelson Fox, Chicago	160
1959	J. Nelson Fox, Chicago	149
1960	J. Nelson Fox, Chicago	139
1961	Robert C. Richardson, New York	148
1962	Robert C. Richardson, New York	158
1963	Albert G. Pearson, Los Angeles	139
1964	Robert C. Richardson, New York	148
1965	Donald A. Buford, Chicago	129
1966	Luis E. Aparicio, Baltimore	143
1967	Horace M. Clarke, New York	140
1968	Dagoberto B. Campaneris, Oakland	139
1969	Horace M. Clarke, New York	146
1970	Alexander Johnson, California	156
1971	Cesar L. Tovar, Minnesota	171
1972	Rodney C. Carew, Minnesota	143
1973	Rodney C. Carew, Minnesota	156
1974	Rodney C. Carew, Minnesota	180
1975	Thurman Munson, New York	151
1976	George Brett, Kansas City	160
1977	Rodney Carew, Minnesota	171
1978	Ronald LeFlore, Detroit	153
1979	Willie Wilson, Kansas City	148

TWO-BASE HIT LEADERS

Year	Player and Club	2B.	Year	Player and Club	2B.
1900—	(Not classed as major)		1942—	Donald Kolloway, Chicago	40
1901—	Napoleon Lajoie, Philadelphia	48	1943—	Richard Wakefield, Detroit	38
1902—	Harry Davis, Philadelphia	43	1944—	Louis Boudreau, Cleveland	45
1903—	Ralph Seybold, Philadelphia	43	1945—	Wallace Moses, Chicago	35
1904—	Napoleon Lajoie, Cleveland	50	1946—	Jas. (Mickey) Vernon, Washington	51
1905—	Harry Davis, Philadelphia	47	1947—	Louis Boudreau, Cleveland	45
1906—	Napoleon Lajoie, Cleveland	49	1948—	Theodore Williams, Boston	44
1907—	Harry Davis, Philadelphia	37	1949—	Theodore Williams, Boston	39
1908—	Tyrus Cobb, Detroit	36	1950—	George Kell, Detroit	56
1909—	Samuel Crawford, Detroit	35	1951—	Kell, Det.-Yost, Wash.-Mele, Wash.	36
1910—	Napoleon Lajoie, Cleveland	51	1952—	Ferris Fain, Philadelphia	43
1911—	Tyrus Cobb, Detroit	47	1953—	Jas. (Mickey) Vernon, Washington	43
1912—	Tristram Speaker, Boston	53	1954—	Jas. (Mickey) Vernon, Washington	33
1913—	Joseph Jackson, Cleveland	39	1955—	Harvey Kuenn, Detroit	38
1914—	Tristram Speaker, Boston	46	1956—	James Piersall, Boston	40
1915—	Robert Veach, Detroit	40	1957—	Minoso, Chicago-Gardner, Baltimore	36
1916—	Graney, Cleveland-Speaker, Cleveland	41	1958—	Harvey Kuenn, Detroit	39
1917—	Tyrus Cobb, Detroit	44	1959—	Harvey Kuenn, Detroit	42
1918—	Tristram Speaker, Cleveland	33	1960—	John (Tito) Francona, Cleveland	36
1919—	Robert Veach, Detroit	45	1961—	Albert Kaline, Detroit	41
1920—	Tristram Speaker, Cleveland	50	1962—	Floyd Robinson, Chicago	45
1921—	Tristram Speaker, Cleveland	52	1963—	Carl Yastrzemski, Boston	40
1922—	Tristram Speaker, Cleveland	48	1964—	Pedro (Tony) Oliva, Minnesota	43
1923—	Tristram Speaker, Cleveland	59	1965—	Zoilo Versalles, Minnesota	45
1924—	J. Sewell, Cleveland-Heilmann, Detroit	45		Carl Yastrzemski, Boston	45
1925—	Martin McManus, St. Louis	44	1966—	Carl Yastrzemski, Boston	39
1926—	George Burns, Cleveland	64	1967—	Pedro (Tony) Oliva, Minnesota	34
1927—	H. Louis Gehrig, New York	52	1968—	C. Reginald Smith, Boston	37
1928—	Manush, St. Louis-Gehrig, New York	47	1969—	Pedro (Tony) Oliva, Minnesota	39
1929—	Manush, St. L.-R. Johnson, Detroit-		1970—	Pedro (Tony) Oliva, Minnesota	36
	Gehringer, Detroit	45		Amos Otis, Kansas City	36
1930—	U. John Hodapp, Cleveland	51		Cesar Tovar, Minnesota	36
1931—	Earl Webb, Boston	67	1971—	C. Reginald Smith, Boston	33
1932—	Eric McNair, Philadelphia	47	1972—	Louis Piniella, Kansas City	33
1933—	Joseph Cronin, Washington	45	1973—	Salvatore Bando, Oakland	32
1934—	Henry Greenberg, Detroit	63		Pedro Garcia, Milwaukee	32
1935—	Joseph Vosmik, Cleveland	47	1974—	Joseph Rudi, Oakland	39
1936—	Charles Gehringer, Detroit	60	1975—	Fredric Lynn, Boston	47
1937—	Roy (Beau) Bell, St. Louis	51	1976—	Amos Otis, Kansas City	40
1938—	Joseph Cronin, Boston	51	1977—	Harold McRae, Kansas City	54
1939—	Robert (Red) Rolfe, New York	46	1978—	George Brett, Kansas City	45
1940—	Henry Greenberg, Detroit	50	1979—	Chester Lemon, Chicago	44
1941—	Louis Boudreau, Cleveland	45		Cecil Cooper, Milwaukee	44

THREE-BASE HIT LEADERS

Year	Player and Club	3B.	Year	Player and Club	3B.
1900—	(Not classed as major)		1919—	Robert Veach, Detroit	17
1901—	James Williams, Baltimore	22	1920—	Joseph Jackson, Chicago	20
1902—	James Williams, Baltimore	23	1921—	Howard Shanks, Washington	19
1903—	Samuel Crawford, Detroit	25	1922—	George Sisler, St. Louis	18
1904—	Charles (Chick) Stahl, Boston	22	1923—	Rice, Washington-Goslin, Washington	18
1905—	Elmer Flick, Cleveland	19	1924—	Walter Pipp, New York	19
1906—	Elmer Flick, Cleveland	22	1925—	Leon (Goose) Goslin, Washington	20
1907—	Elmer Flick, Cleveland	18	1926—	H. Louis Gehrig, New York	20
1908—	Tyrus, Cobb, Detroit	20	1927—	Earle Combs, New York	23
1909—	J. Franklin Baker, Philadelphia	19	1928—	Earle Combs, New York	21
1910—	Samuel Crawford, Detroit	19	1929—	Charles Gehringer, Detroit	19
1911—	Tyrus Cobb, Detroit	24	1930—	Earle Combs, New York	22
1912—	Joseph Jackson, Cleveland	26	1931—	Roy Johnson, Detroit	19
1913—	Samuel Crawford, Detroit	23	1932—	Joseph Cronin, Washington	18
1914—	Samuel Crawford, Detroit	26	1933—	Henry Manush, Washington	17
1915—	Samuel Crawford, Detroit	19	1934—	W. Benjamin Chapman, New York	13
1916—	Joseph Jackson, Chicago	21	1935—	Joseph Vosmik, Cleveland	20
1917—	Tyrus Cobb, Detroit	23	1936—	Averill, Cleveland-J. MiMaggio, N.Y.	15
1918—	Tyrus Cobb, Detroit	14		Rolfe, New York	15

THREE-BASE HIT LEADERS—Continued

Year	Player and Club	3B.
1937—	F. Walker, Chicago-Kreevich, Chicago	16
1938—	J. Geoffrey Heath, Cleveland	18
1939—	John (Buddy) Lewis, Washington	16
1940—	Barney McCosky, Detroit	19
1941—	J. Geoffrey Heath, Cleveland	20
1942—	Stanley Spence, Washington	15
1943—	Lindell, New York-Moses, Chicago	12
1944—	Lindell, N. York-Stirnweiss, N. York	16
1945—	George Stirnweiss, New York	22
1946—	Henry Edwards, Cleveland	16
1947—	Thomas Henrich, New York	13
1948—	Thomas Henrich, New York	14
1949—	L. Dale Mitchell, Cleveland	23
1950—	D. DiMaggio, Doerr, Bos.-Evers, Det.	11
1951—	Orestes (Minnie) Minoso, Clev.-Chi.	14
1952—	Roberto Avila, Cleveland	11
1953—	Manuel (Jim) Rivera, Chicago	16
1954—	Orestes (Minnie) Minoso, Chicago	18
1955—	Mantle, New York-Carey, New York	11
1956—	Minoso, Chicago-Jensen, Boston-Simpson, Kansas City-Lemon, Wash.	11
1957—	McDougald, Bauer, Simpson, New York	9
1958—	Victor Power, Kansas City-Cleveland	10
1959—	W. Robert Allison, Washington	9
1960—	J. Nelson Fox, Chicago	10

Year	Player and Club	3B.
1961—	Jacob Wood, Detroit	14
1962—	Gino Cimoli, Kansas City	15
1963—	Zoilo Versalles, Minnesota	13
1964—	Richard Rollins, Minnesota	10
	Zoilo Versalles, Minnesota	10
1965—	Dagoberto Campaneris, Kansas City	12
	Zoilo Versalles, Minnesota	12
1966—	Robert Knoop, California	11
1967—	Paul L. Blair, Baltimore	12
1968—	James Fregosi, California	13
1969—	Delbert Unser, Washington	8
1970—	Cesar Tovar, Minnesota	13
1971—	Freddie Patek, Kansas City	11
1972—	Carlton Fisk, Boston	9
	Joseph Rudi, Oakland	9
1973—	Alonza Bumbry, Baltimore	11
	Rodney Carew, Minnesota	11
1974—	John (Mickey) Rivers, California	11
1975—	George Brett, Kansas City	13
	John Rivers, California	13
1976—	George Brett, Kansas City	14
1977—	Rodney Carew, Minnesota	16
1978—	James Rice, Boston	15
1979—	George Brett, Kansas City	20

HOME RUN LEADERS

Year	Player and Club	HR.
1900—	(Not classed as major)	
1901—	Napoleon Lajoie, Philadelphia	14
1902—	Ralph (Socks) Seybold, Philadelphia	16
1903—	John (Buck) Freeman, Boston	13
1904—	Harry Davis, Philadelphia	10
1905—	Harry Davis, Philadelphia	8
1906—	Harry Davis, Philadelphia	12
1907—	Harry Davis, Philadelphia	8
1908—	Samuel Crawford, Detroit	7
1909—	Tyrus Cobb, Detroit	9
1910—	J. Garland (Jake) Stahl, Boston	10
1911—	J. Franklin Baker, Philadelphia	9
1912—	J. Franklin Baker, Philadelphia	10
	Tristram Speaker, Boston	10
1913—	J. Franklin Baker, Philadelphia	12
1914—	Baker, Philadelphia-Crawford, Detroit	8
1915—	Robert Roth, Chicago-Cleveland	7
1916—	Walter Pipp, New York	12
1917—	Walter Pipp, New York	9
1918—	Ruth, Boston-Tilly Walker, Phila.	11
1919—	George (Babe) Ruth, Boston	29
1920—	George (Babe) Ruth, New York	54
1921—	George (Babe) Ruth, New York	59
1922—	Kenneth Williams, St. Louis	39
1923—	George (Babe) Ruth, New York	41
1924—	George (Babe) Ruth, New York	46
1925—	Robert Meusel, New York	33
1926—	George (Babe) Ruth, New York	47
1927—	George (Babe) Ruth, New York	60
1928—	George (Babe) Ruth, New York	54
1929—	George (Babe) Ruth, New York	46
1930—	George (Babe) Ruth, New York	49
1931—	Ruth, New York-Gehrig, New York	46
1932—	James Foxx, Philadelphia	58
1933—	James Foxx, Philadelphia	48
1934—	H. Louis Gehrig, New York	49

Year	Player and Club	HR.
1935—	Foxx, Philadelphia-Greenberg, Detroit	36
1936—	H. Louis Gehrig, New York	49
1937—	Joseph DiMaggio, New York	46
1938—	Henry Greenberg, Detroit	58
1939—	James Foxx, Boston	35
1940—	Henry Greenberg, Detroit	41
1941—	Theodore Williams, Boston	37
1942—	Theodore Williams, Boston	36
1943—	Rudolph York, Detroit	34
1944—	Nicholas Etten, New York	22
1945—	Vernon Stephens, St. Louis	24
1946—	Henry Greenberg, Detroit	44
1947—	Theodore Williams, Boston	32
1948—	Joseph DiMaggio, New York	39
1949—	Theodore Williams, Boston	43
1950—	Albert Rosen, Cleveland	37
1951—	Gus Zernial, Chicago-Philadelphia	33
1952—	Lawrence Doby, Cleveland	32
1953—	Albert Rosen, Cleveland	43
1954—	Lawrence Doby, Cleveland	32
1955—	Mickey Mantle, New York	37
1956—	Mickey Mantle, New York	52
1957—	Roy Sievers, Washington	42
1958—	Mickey Mantle, New York	42
1959—	Colavito, Cleveland-Killebrew, Wash.	42
1960—	Mickey Mantle, New York	40
1961—	Roger Maris, New York	61
1962—	Harmon Killebrew, Minnesota	48
1963—	Harmon Killebrew, Minnesota	45
1964—	Harmon Killebrew, Minnesota	49
1965—	Anthony Conigilaro, Boston	32
1966—	Frank Robinson, Baltimore	49
1967—	Harmon Killebrew, Minnesota	44
	Carl Yastrzemski, Boston	44
1968—	Frank Howard, Washington	44
1969—	Harmon Killebrew, Minnesota	49

HOME RUN LEADERS—Continued

Year	Player and Club	HR.	Year	Player and Club	HR.
1970—	Frank Howard, Washington	44	1976—	Graig Nettles, New York	32
1971—	William E. Melton, Chicago	33	1977—	James Rice, Boston	39
1972—	Richard Allen, Chicago	37	1978—	James Rice, Boston	46
1973—	Reginald Jackson, Oakland	32	1979—	J. Gorman Thomas, Milwaukee	45
1974—	Richard Allen, Chicago	32			
1975—	Reginald Jackson, Oakland	36			
	George Scott, Milwaukee	36			

LEADERS IN TOTAL BASES

Year	Player and Club	T.B.	Year	Player and Club	T.B.
1900—	(Not classed as major)		1941—	Joseph DiMaggio, New York	348
1901—	Napoleon Lajoie, Philadelphia	345	1942—	Theodore Williams, Boston	338
1902—	John (Buck) Freeman, Boston	287	1943—	Rudolph York, Detroit	301
1903—	John (Buck) Freeman, Boston	281	1944—	John Lindell, New York	297
1904—	Napoleon Lajoie, Cleveland	304	1945—	George Stirnweiss, New York	301
1905—	George Stone, St. Louis	260	1946—	Theodore Williams, Boston	343
1906—	George Stone, St. Louis	288	1947—	Theodore Williams, Boston	335
1907—	Tyrus Cobb, Detroit	286	1948—	Joseph DiMaggio, New York	355
1908—	Tyrus Cobb, Detroit	276	1949—	Theodore Williams, Boston	368
1909—	Tyrus Cobb, Detroit	296	1950—	Walter Dropo, Boston	326
1910—	Napoleon Lajoie, Cleveland	304	1951—	Theodore Williams, Boston	295
1911—	Tyrus Cobb, Detroit	367	1952—	Albert Rosen, Cleveland	297
1912—	Joseph Jackson, Cleveland	331	1953—	Albert Rosen, Cleveland	367
1913—	Samuel Crawford, Detroit	298	1954—	Orestes (Minnie) Minoso, Chicago	304
1914—	Tristram Speaker, Boston	287	1955—	Albert Kaline, Detroit	321
1915—	Tyrus Cobb, Detroit	274	1956—	Mickey Mantle, New York	376
1916—	Joseph Jackson, Chicago	293	1957—	Roy Sievers, Washington	331
1917—	Tyrus Cobb, Detroit	336	1958—	Mickey Mantle, New York	307
1918—	George Burns, Philadelphia	236	1959—	Rocco Colavito, Cleveland	301
1919—	George (Babe) Ruth, Boston	284	1960—	Mickey Mantle, New York	294
1920—	George Sisler, St. Louis	399	1961—	Roger Maris, New York	366
1921—	George (Babe) Ruth, New York	457	1962—	Rocco Colavito, Detroit	309
1922—	Kenneth Williams, St. Louis	367	1963—	Richard Stuart, Boston	319
1923—	George (Babe) Ruth, New York	399	1964—	Pedro (Tony) Oliva, Minnesota	374
1924—	George (Babe) Ruth, New York	391	1965—	Zoilo Versalles, Minnesota	308
1925—	Aloysius Simmons, Philadelphia	392	1966—	Frank Robinson, Baltimore	367
1926—	George (Babe) Ruth, New York	365	1967—	Carl Yastrzemski, Boston	360
1927—	H. Louis Gehrig, New York	447	1968—	Frank Howard, Washington	330
1928—	George (Babe) Ruth, New York	380	1969—	Frank Howard, Washington	340
1929—	Aloysius Simmons, Philadelphia	373	1970—	Carl Yastrzemski, Boston	335
1930—	H. Louis Gehrig, New York	419	1971—	C. Reginald Smith, Boston	302
1931—	H. Louis Gehrig, New York	410	1972—	Bobby Murcer, New York	314
1932—	James Foxx, Philadelphia	438	1973—	David L. May, Milwaukee	295
1933—	James Foxx, Philadelphia	403		George Scott, Milwaukee	295
1934—	H. Louis Gehrig, New York	409		Salvatore L. Bando, Oakland	295
1935—	Henry Greenberg, Detroit	389	1974—	Joseph Rudi, Oakland	287
1936—	Harold Trosky, Cleveland	405	1975—	George Scott, Milwaukee	318
1937—	Joseph DiMaggio, New York	418	1976—	George Brett, Kansas City	298
1938—	James Foxx, Boston	398	1977—	James Rice, Boston	382
1939—	Theodore Williams, Boston	344	1978—	James Rice, Boston	406
1940—	Henry Greenberg, Detroit	384	1979—	James Rice, Boston	369

RUNS BATTED IN LEADERS

Note--Runs batted in not compiled prior to 1907; officially adopted in 1920.

Year	Player and Club	RBI	Year	Player and Club	RBI
1907—	Tyrus Cobb, Detroit	116	1914—	Samuel Crawford, Detroit	112
1908—	Tyrus Cobb, Detroit	101	1915—	Samuel Crawford, Detroit	116
1909—	Tyrus Cobb, Detroit	115	1916—	Walter Pipp, New York	99
1910—	Samuel Crawford, Detroit	115	1917—	Robert Veach, Detroit	115
1911—	Tyrus Cobb, Detroit	144	1918—	George Burns, Philadelphia	74
1912—	J. Franklin Baker, Philadelphia	133		Robert Veach, Detroit	74
1913—	J. Franklin Baker, Philadelphia	126	1919—	George (Babe) Ruth, Boston	112

RUNS BATTED IN LEADERS—Continued

Year	Player and Club	RBI
1920—	George (Babe) Ruth, New York	137
1921—	George (Babe) Ruth, New York	171
1922—	Kenneth Williams, St. Louis	155
1923—	George (Babe) Ruth, New York	131
1924—	Leon (Goose) Goslin, Washington	129
1925—	Robert Meusel, New York	138
1926—	George (Babe) Ruth, New York	145
1927—	H. Louis Gehrig, New York	175
1928—	George (Babe) Ruth, New York	142
	H. Louis Gehrig, New York	142
1929—	Aloysius Simmons, Philadelphia	157
1930—	H. Louis Gehrig, New York	174
1931—	H. Louis Gehrig, New York	184
1932—	James Foxx, Philadelphia	169
1933—	James Foxx, Philadelphia	163
1934—	H. Louis Gehrig, New York	165
1935—	Henry Greenberg, Detroit	170
1936—	Harold Trosky, Cleveland	162
1937—	Henry Greenberg, Detroit	183
1938—	James Foxx, Boston	175
1939—	Theodore Williams, Boston	145
1940—	Henry Greenberg, Detroit	150
1941—	Joseph DiMaggio, New York	125
1942—	Theodore Williams, Boston	137
1943—	Rudolph York, Detroit	118
1944—	Vernon Stephens, St. Louis	109
1945—	Nicholas Etten, New York	111
1946—	Henry Greenberg, Detroit	127
1947—	Theodore Williams, Boston	114
1948—	Joseph DiMaggio, New York	155
1949—	Theodore Williams, Boston	159
	Vernon Stephens, Boston	159
1950—	Walter Dropo, Boston	144
	Vernon Stephens, Boston	144
1951—	Gus Zernial, Chicago-Philadelphia	129
1952—	Albert Rosen, Cleveland	105
1953—	Albert Rosen, Cleveland	145
1954—	Lawrence Doby, Cleveland	126
1955—	Raymond Boone, Detroit	116
	Jack Jensen, Boston	116
1956—	Mickey Mantle, New York	130
1957—	Roy Sievers, Washington	114
1958—	Jack Jensen, Boston	122
1959—	Jack Jensen, Boston	112
1960—	Roger Maris, New York	112
1961—	Roger Maris, New York	142
1962—	Harmon Killebrew, Minnesota	126
1963—	Richard Stuart, Boston	118
1964—	Brooks Robinson, Baltimore	118
1965—	Rocco Colavito, Cleveland	108
1966—	Frank Robinson, Baltimore	122
1967—	Carl Yastrzemski, Boston	121
1968—	Kenneth Harrelson, Boston	109
1969—	Harmon Killebrew, Minnesota	140
1970—	Frank Howard, Washington	126
1971—	Harmon Killebrew, Minnesota	119
1972—	Richard Allen, Chicago	113
1973—	Reginald Jackson, Oakland	117
1974—	Jeffrey Burroughs, Texas	118
1975—	George Scott, Milwaukee	109
1976—	Lee May, Baltimore	109
1977—	Larry Hisle, Minnesota	119
1978—	James Rice, Boston	139
1979—	Donald Baylor, California	139

BATTERS LEADING IN BASES ON BALLS

Note—Bases on balls not included in batting records in American League prior to 1913.

Year	Player and Club	BB.
1913—	Burton Shotton, St. Louis	102
1914—	Owen (Donie) Bush, Detroit	112
1915—	Edward Collins, Chicago	119
1916—	Burton Shotton, St. Louis	111
1917—	John Graney, Cleveland	94
1918—	Raymond Chapman, Cleveland	84
1919—	John Graney, Cleveland	105
1920—	George (Babe) Ruth, New York	148
1921—	George (Babe) Ruth, New York	144
1922—	L. W. (Whitey) Witt, New York	89
1923—	George (Babe) Ruth, New York	170
1924—	George (Babe) Ruth, New York	142
1925—	William Kamm, Chicago	90
	John Mostil, Chicago	90
1926—	George (Babe) Ruth, New York	144
1927—	George (Babe) Ruth, New York	138
1928—	George (Babe) Ruth, New York	135
1929—	Max Bishop, Philadelphia	128
1930—	George (Babe) Ruth, New York	136
1931—	George (Babe) Ruth, New York	128
1932—	George (Babe) Ruth, New York	130
1933—	George (Babe) Ruth, New York	114
1934—	James Foxx, Philadelphia	111
1935—	H. Louis Gehrig, New York	132
1936—	H. Louis Gehrig, New York	130
1937—	H. Louis Gehrig, New York	127
1938—	James Foxx, Boston	119
	Henry Greenberg, Detroit	119
1939—	Harland Clift, St. Louis	111
1940—	Charles Keller, New York	106
1941—	Theodore Williams, Boston	145
1942—	Theodore Williams, Boston	145
1943—	Charles Keller, New York	106
1944—	Nicholas Etten, New York	97
1945—	Roy Cullenbine, Cleveland-Detroit	112
1946—	Theodore Williams, Boston	156
1947—	Theodore Williams, Boston	162
1948—	Theodore Williams, Boston	126
1949—	Theodore Williams, Boston	162
1950—	Edward Yost, Washington	141
1951—	Theodore Williams, Boston	144
1952—	Edward Yost, Washington	129
1953—	Edward Yost, Washington	123
1954—	Theodore Williams, Boston	136
1955—	Mickey Mantle, New York	113
1956—	Edward Yost, Washington	151
1957—	Mickey Mantle, New York	146
1958—	Mickey Mantle, New York	129
1959—	Edward Yost, Detroit	135
1960—	Edward Yost, Detroit	125
1961—	Mickey Mantle, New York	126
1962—	Mickey Mantle, New York	122

BATTING LEADERS IN BASES ON BALLS—Continued

Year	Player and Club	BB.	Year	Player and Club	BB.
1963—	Carl Yastremski, Boston	95	1972—	Richard Allen, Chicago	99
1964—	Norman Siebern, Baltimore	106		Roy White, New York	99
1965—	Rocco Colavito, Cleveland	93	1973—	John Mayberry, Kansas City	122
1966—	Harmon Killebrew, Minnesota	103	1974—	F. Gene Tenace, Oakland	110
1967—	Harmon Killebrew, Minnesota	131	1975—	John Mayberry, Kansas City	119
1968—	Carl Yastrzemski, Boston	119	1976—	D. Michael Hargrove, Texas	97
1969—	Harmon Killebrew, Minnesota	145	1977—	Colbert (Toby) Harrah, Texas	109
1970—	Frank Howard, Washington	132	1978—	D. Michael Hargrove, Texas	107
1971—	Harmon Killebrew, Minnesota	114	1979—	Darrell Porter, Kansas City	121

BATTERS LEADING IN STRIKEOUTS

Note—Strikeouts not included in batting records in American League prior to 1913.

Year	Player and Club	SO.	Year	Player and Club	SO.
1913—	Daniel Moeller, Washington	106	1947—	Edwin Joost, Philadelphia	110
1914—	August Williams, St. Louis	120	1948—	J. Patrick Seerey, Cleveland-Chicago	102
1915—	John Lavan, St. Louis	83	1949—	Richard Kokos, St. Louis	91
1916—	Walter Pipp, New York	82	1950—	Gus Zernial, Chicago	110
1917—	Robert Roth, Cleveland	73	1951—	Gus Zernial, Chicago-Philadelphia	101
1918—	George (Babe) Ruth, Boston	58	1952—	Lawrence Doby, Cleveland	111
1919—	Maurice Shannon, Philadelphia-Boston	70		Mickey Mantle, New York	111
1920—	Aaron Ward, New York	84	1953—	Lawrence Doby, Cleveland	121
1921—	Robert Meusel, New York	88	1954—	Mickey Mantle, New York	107
1922—	James Dykes, Philadelphia	98	1955—	Norbert Zauchin, Boston	105
1923—	George (Babe) Ruth, New York	93	1956—	James Lemon, Washington	138
1924—	George (Babe) Ruth, New York	81	1957—	James Lemon, Washington	94
1925—	Martin McManus, St. Louis	69	1958—	James Lemon, Washington	120
1926—	Anthony Lazzeri, New York	96		Mickey Mantle, New York	120
1927—	George (Babe) Ruth, New York	89	1959—	Mickey Mantle, New York	126
1928—	George (Babe) Ruth, New York	87	1960—	Mickey Mantle, New York	125
1929—	James Foxx, Philadelphia	70	1961—	Jacob Wood, Detroit	141
1930—	James Foxx, Philadelphia	66	1962—	Harmon Killebrew, Minnesota	142
	Edward Morgan, Cleveland	66	1963—	David Nicholson, Chicago	175
1931—	James Foxx, Philadelphia	84	1964—	Nelson Mathews, Kansas City	143
1932—	Bruce Campbell, Chicago-St. Louis	104	1965—	Zoilo Versalles, Minnesota	122
1933—	James Foxx, Philadelphia	93	1966—	George Scott, Boston	152
1934—	Harlond Cliff, St. Louis	100	1967—	Frank Howard, Washington	155
1935—	James Foxx, Philadelphia	99	1968—	Reginald Jackson, Oakland	171
1936—	James Foxx, Boston	119	1969—	Reginald Jackson, Oakland	142
1937—	Frank Crosetti, New York	105	1970—	Reginald Jackson, Oakland	135
1938—	Frank Crosetti, New York	97	1971—	Reginald Jackson, Oakland	161
1939—	Hank Greenberg, Detroit	95	1972—	A. Bobby Darwin, Minnesota	145
1940—	Samuel Chapman, Philadelphia	96	1973—	A. Bobby Darwin, Minnesota	137
1941—	James Foxx, Boston	103	1974—	A. Bobby Darwin, Minnesota	127
1942—	Joseph Gordon, New York	95	1975—	Jeffrey Burroughs, Texas	155
1943—	Chester Laabs, St. Louis	105	1976—	James Rice, Boston	123
1944—	J. Patrick Seerey, Cleveland	99	1977—	Clell (Butch) Hobson, Boston	162
1945—	J. Patrick Seerey, Cleveland	97	1978—	Gary Alexander, Oakland-Cleveland	166
1946—	Charles Keller, New York	101	1979—	J. Gorman Thomas, Milwaukee	175
	J. Patrick Seerey, Cleveland	101			

LEADING BASE STEALERS

Year	Player and Club	SB.	Year	Player and Club	SB.
1900—	(Not classed as major)		1910—	Edward Collins, Philadelphia	81
1901—	Frank Isbell Chicago	48	1911—	Tyrus Cobb, Detroit	83
1902—	Fred (Topsy) Hartsel, Philadelphia	54	1912—	J. Clyde Milan, Washington	88
1903—	Harry Bay, Cleveland	46	1913—	J. Clyde Milan, Washington	74
1904—	Elmer Flick, Clev-Harry Bay, Clev	42	1914—	Frederick Maisel, New York	74
1905—	Daniel Hoffman, Philadelphia	46	1915—	Tyrus Cobb, Detroit	96
1906—	Flick, Cleveland-Anderson, Washington	39	1916—	Tyrus Cobb, Detroit	68
1907—	Tyrus Cobb, Detroit	49	1917—	Tyrus Cobb, Detroit	55
1908—	Patrick Dougherty, Chicago	47	1918—	George Sisler, St. Louis	45
1909—	Tyrus Cobb, Detroit	76	1919—	Edward Collins, Chicago	33

LEADING BASE STEALERS—Continued

Year	Player and Club	SB.	Year	Player and Club	SB.
1920	Edgar (Sam) Rice, Washington	63	1950	Dominic DiMaggio, Boston	15
1921	George Sisler, St. Louis	35	1951	Orestes (Minnie) Minoso, Clev-Chi	31
1922	George Sisler, St. Louis	51	1952	Orestes (Minnie) Minoso, Chicago	22
1923	Edward Collins, Chicago	49	1953	Orestes (Minnie) Minoso, Chicago	25
1924	Edward Collins, Chicago	42	1954	Jack Jensen, Boston	22
1925	John Mostil, Chicago	43	1955	Manuel (Jim) Rivera, Chicago	25
1926	John Mostil, Chicago	35	1956	Luis Aparicio, Chicago	21
1927	George Sisler, St. Louis	27	1957	Luis Aparicio, Chicago	28
1928	Charles (Buddy) Myer, Boston	30	1958	Luis Aparicio, Chicago	29
1929	Charles Gehringer, Detroit	27	1959	Luis Aparicio, Chicago	56
1930	Martin McManus, Detroit	23	1960	Luis Aparicio, Chicago	51
1931	W. Benjamin Chapman, New York	61	1961	Luis Aparicio, Chicago	53
1932	W. Benjamin Chapman, New York	38	1962	Luis Aparicio, Chicago	31
1933	W. Benjamin Chapman, New York	27	1963	Luis Aparicio, Baltimore	40
1934	William Werber, Boston	40	1964	Luis Aparicio, Baltimore	57
1935	William Werber, Boston	29	1965	Dagoberto Campaneris, Kansas City	51
1936	Lynford Lary, St. Louis	37	1966	Dagoberto Campaneris, Kansas City	52
1937	Werber, Phila-Chapman, Wash-Bos	35	1967	Dagoberto Campaneris, Kansas City	55
1938	Frank Crosetti, New York	27	1968	Dagoberto Campaneris, Oakland	62
1939	George Case, Washington	51	1969	Tommy Harper, Seattle	73
1940	George Case, Washington	35	1970	Dagoberto Campaneris, Oakland	42
1941	George Case, Washington	33	1971	Amos Otis, Kansas City	52
1942	George Case, Washington	44	1972	Dagoberto Campaneris, Oakland	52
1943	George Case, Washington	61	1973	Tommy Harper, Boston	54
1944	George Stirnweiss, New York	55	1974	William North, Oakland	54
1945	George Stirnweiss, New York	33	1975	John Rivers, California	70
1946	George Case, Cleveland	28	1976	William North, Oakland	75
1947	Robert Dillinger, St. Louis	34	1977	Freddie Patek, Kansas City	53
1948	Robert Dillinger, St. Louis	28	1978	Ronald LeFlore, Detroit	68
1949	Robert Dillinger, St. Louis	20	1979	Willie Wilson, Kansas City	83

SLUGGING LEADERS

Year	Player and Club	Slug. Avg.	Year	Player and Club	Slug. Avg.
1900	(Not classed as major)		1929	George (Babe) Ruth, New York	.697
1901	Napoleon Lajoie, Philadelphia	.630	1930	George (Babe) Ruth, New York	.732
1902	Edward Delahanty, Washington	.589	1931	George (Babe) Ruth, New York	.700
1903	Napoleon Lajoie, Cleveland	.533	1932	James Foxx, Philadelphia	.749
1904	Napoleon Lajoie, Cleveland	.549	1933	James Foxx, Philadelphia	.703
1905	Elmer Flick, Cleveland	.466	1934	H. Louis Gehrig, New York	.706
1906	George Stone, St. Louis	.496	1935	James Foxx, Philadelphia	.636
1907	Tyrus Cobb, Detroit	.473	1936	H. Louis Gehrig, New York	.696
1908	Tyrus Cobb, Detroit	.475	1937	Joseph DiMaggio, New York	.673
1909	Tyrus Cobb, Detroit	.517	1938	James Foxx, Boston	.704
1910	Tyrus Cobb, Detroit	.554	1939	James Foxx, Boston	.694
1911	Tyrus Cobb, Detroit	.621	1940	Henry Greenberg, Detroit	.670
1912	Tyrus Cobb, Detroit	.586	1941	Theodore Williams, Boston	.735
1913	Joseph Jackson, Cleveland	.551	1942	Theodore Williams, Boston	.648
1914	Tyrus Cobb, Detroit	.513	1943	Rudolph York, Detroit	.527
1915	Jacques F. Fournier, Chicago	.491	1944	Robert Doerr, Boston	.5278
1916	Tristram Speaker, Cleveland	.502	1945	George Stirnweiss, New York	.476
1917	Tyrus Cobb, Detroit	.571	1946	Theodore Williams, Boston	.667
1918	George (Babe) Ruth, Boston	.555	1947	Theodore Williams, Boston	.634
1919	George (Babe) Ruth, Boston	.657	1948	Theodore Williams, Boston	.615
1920	George (Babe) Ruth, New York	.847	1949	Theodore Williams, Boston	.650
1921	George (Babe) Ruth, New York	.846	1950	Joseph DiMaggio, New York	.585
1922	George (Babe) Ruth, New York	.672	1951	Theodore Williams, Boston	.556
1923	George (Babe) Ruth, New York	.764	1952	Lawrence Doby, Cleveland	.541
1924	George (Babe) Ruth, New York	.739	1953	Albert Rosen, Cleveland	.613
1925	Kenneth Williams, St. Louis	.613	1954	Theodore Williams, Boston	.635
1926	George (Babe) Ruth, New York	.737	1955	Mickey Mantle, New York	.611
1927	George (Babe) Ruth, New York	.772	1956	Mickey Mantle, New York	.705
1928	George (Babe) Ruth, New York	.709	1957	Theodore Williams, Boston	.731

SLUGGING LEADERS—Continued

Year	Player and Club	Slug. Avg.	Year	Player and Club	Slug. Avg.
1958—	Rocco Colavito, Cleveland	.620	1969—	Reginald Jackson, Oakland	.608
1959—	Albert Kaline, Detroit	.530	1970—	Carl Yastrzemski, Boston	.592
1960—	Roger Maris, New York	.581	1971—	Pedro (Tony) Oliva, Minnesota	.546
1961—	Mickey Mantle, New York	.687	1972—	Richard Allen, Chicago	.603
1962—	Mickey Mantle, New York	.605	1973—	Reginald Jackson, Oakland	.531
1963—	Harmon Killebrew, Minnesota	.555	1974—	Richard Allen, Chicago	.563
1964—	John (Boog) Powell, Baltimore	.606	1975—	Fredric Lynn, Boston	.566
1965—	Carl Yastrzemski, Boston	.536	1976—	Reginald Jackson, Baltimore	.502
1966—	Frank Robinson, Baltimore	.637	1977—	James Rice, Boston	.593
1967—	Carl Yastrzemski, Boston	.622	1978—	James Rice, Boston	.600
1968—	Frank Howard, Washington	.552	1979—	Fredric Lynn, Boston	.637

Wilson Had Five Inside-the-Park Dashes

In what was believed to be the best total of inside-the-park homers by a single player since Kiki Cuyler's eight in 1925, Willie Wilson spanked five of his six homers in 1979 inside the barriers.

The Kansas City Royals speed merchant, who led the American League in stolen bases with 83, had his first inside-the-park homer off Steve Trout at Chicago May 13. His next dash 'round the bases came June 9 at New York vs. Ken Clay in the 13th inning for a 9-8 Royals victory. Six days later, he connected for one in Milwaukee against Bill Castro, a three-run shot in the ninth inning for a 14-11 verdict. Earlier in that game he hit his only homer over the barriers.

Wilson's fourth inside-the-park homer came on August 25 against Boston's Mike Torrez in the first inning at Kansas City. It provided the Royals with a 1-0 decision. The final dash came on September 16 vs. Seattle's Rob Dressler at Royals Stadium.

Jim Essian of the A's hit the only inside-the-park grand slam in 1979. The blow came off Mike Willis of the Blue Jays at Oakland in the fifth inning of a 12-1 A's rout June 10.

LEADING PITCHERS IN WINNING PERCENTAGE

(15 OR MORE VICTORIES)

Year	Pitcher	Club	Won	Lost	Pct.
1901—	Clark Griffith	Chicago	24	7	.774
1902—	William Bernhard	Philadelphia-Cleveland	18	5	.783
1903—	Earl Moore	Cleveland	22	7	.759
1904—	John Chesbro	New York	41	12	.774
1905—	Jess Tannehill	Boston	22	9	.710
1906—	Edward Plank	Philadelphia	19	6	.760
1907—	William Donovan	Detroit	25	4	.862
1908—	Edward Walsh	Chicago	40	15	.727
1909—	George Mullin	Detroit	29	8	.784
1910—	Albert (Chief) Bender	Philadelphia	23	5	.821
1911—	Albert (Chief) Bender	Philadelphia	17	5	.773
1912—	Joseph Wood	Boston	34	5	.872
1913—	Walter Johnson	Washington	36	7	.837
1914—	Albert (Chief) Bender	Philadelphia	17	3	.850
1915—	Ernest Shore	Boston	19	8	.704
	George Foster	Boston	19	8	.704
1916—	Edward V. Cicotte	Chicago	15	7	.682
1917—	Ewell (Reb) Russell	Chicago	15	5	.750
1918—	Samuel Jones	Boston	16	5	.762
1919—	Edward V. Cicotte	Chicago	29	7	.806
1920—	James Bagby	Cleveland	31	12	.721
1921—	Carl Mays	New York	27	9	.750
1922—	Leslie (Joe) Bush	New York	26	7	.788
1923—	Herbert Pennock	New York	19	6	.760
1924—	Walter Johnson	Washington	23	7	.767
1925—	Stanley Coveleski	Washington	20	5	.800
1926—	George Uhle	Cleveland	27	11	.711
1927—	Waite Hoyt	New York	22	7	.759
1928—	Alvin Crowder	St. Louis	21	5	.808
1929—	Robert Grove	Philadelphia	20	6	.769
1930—	Robert Grove	Philadelphia	28	5	.848
1931—	Robert Grove	Philadelphia	31	4	.886
1932—	John Allen	New York	17	4	.810
1933—	Robert Grove	Philadelphia	24	8	.750
1934—	Vernon Gomez	New York	26	5	.839
1935—	Elden Auker	Detroit	18	7	.720
1936—	Monte Pearson	New York	19	7	.731
1937—	John Allen	Cleveland	15	1	.938
1938—	Charles (Red) Ruffing	New York	21	7	.750
1939—	Robert Grove	Boston	15	4	.789
1940—	Lynwood (Schoolboy) Rowe	Detroit	16	3	.842
1941—	Vernon Gomez	New York	15	5	.750
1942—	Ernest Bonham	New York	21	5	.808
1943—	Spurgeon (Spud) Chandler	New York	20	4	.833
1944—	Cecil (Tex) Hughson	Boston	18	5	.783
1945—	Harold Newhouser	Detroit	25	9	.735
1946—	David (Boo) Ferriss	Boston	25	6	.806
1947—	Allie Reynolds	New York	19	8	.704
1948—	John Kramer	Boston	18	5	.783
1949—	Ellis Kinder	Boston	23	6	.793
1950—	Victor Raschi	New York	21	8	.724
1951—	Robert Feller	Cleveland	22	8	.733
1952—	Robert Shantz	Philadelphia	24	7	.774
1953—	Edmund Lopat	New York	16	4	.800
1954—	Sandalio Consuegra	Chicago	16	3	.842
1955—	Thomas Byrne	New York	16	5	.762
1956—	Edward (Whitey) Ford	New York	19	6	.760
1957—	Richard Donovan	Chicago	16	6	.727
	Thomas Sturdivant	New York	16	6	.727
1958—	Robert Turley	New York	21	7	.750
1959—	Robert Shaw	Chicago	18	6	.750
1960—	James Perry	Cleveland	18	10	.643
1961—	Edward (Whitey) Ford	New York	25	4	.862
1962—	Raymond Herbert	Chicago	20	9	.690

LEADING PITCHERS IN WINNING PERCENTAGE—Continued

Year	Pitcher	Club	Won	Lost	Pct.
1963—Edward (Whitey) Ford		New York	24	7	.774
1964—Wallace Bunker		Baltimore	19	5	.792
1965—James (Mudcat) Grant		Minnesota	21	7	.750
1966—Wilfred (Sonny) Siebert		Cleveland	16	8	.667
1967—Joel Horlen		Chicago	19	7	.731
1968—Dennis McLain		Detroit	31	6	.838
1969—James Palmer		Baltimore	16	4	.800
1970—Miguel (Mike) Cuellar		Baltimore	24	8	.750
1971—David McNally		Baltimore	21	5	.808
1972—James A. Hunter		Oakland	21	7	.750
1973—James A. Hunter		Oakland	21	5	.808
1974—Miguel (Mike) Cuellar		Baltimore	22	10	.688
1975—Michael A. Torrez		Baltimore	20	9	.690
1976—William Campbell		Minnesota	17	5	.773
1977—Paul Splittorff		Kansas City	16	6	.727
1978—Ronald Guidry		New York	25	3	.893
1979—R. Michael Caldwell		Milwaukee	16	6	.727

LEADING PITCHERS—EARNED-RUN AVERAGE

(Based on Ten Complete Games Through 1950, Then 154 Innings Until A. L. Expanded in 1961, When It Became 162 Innings)

Year	Pitcher and Club	G.	IP.	ERA.	Year	Pitcher and Club	G.	IP.	ERA.
1913—Johnson, Washington	48	346	1.14	1947—Chandler, New York	17	128	2.46
1914—Leonard, Boston	35	222	1.01	1948—Bearden, Cleveland	37	230	2.43
1915—Wood, Boston	25	157	1.49	1949—Parnell, Boston	39	295	2.78
1916—Ruth, Boston	44	324	1.75	1950—Wynn, Cleveland	32	214	3.20
1917—Cicotte, Chicago	49	346	1.53	1951—Rogovin, Detroit-Chicago	27	217	2.78
1918—Johnson, Washington	39	325	1.27	1952—Reynolds, New York	35	244	2.07
1919—Johnson, Washington	39	290	1.49	1953—Lopat, New York	25	178	2.43
1920—Shawkey, New York	38	267	2.46	1954—Garcia, Cleveland	45	259	2.64
1921—Faber, Chicago	43	331	2.47	1955—Pierce, Chicago	33	206	1.97
1922—Faber, Chicago	43	353	2.80	1956—Ford, New York	31	226	2.47
1923—S. Coveleski, Cleveland	33	228	2.76	1957—Shantz, New York	30	173	2.45
1924—Johnson, Washington	38	278	2.72	1958—Ford, New York	30	219	2.01
1925—S. Coveleski, Washington	32	241	2.84	1959—Wilhelm, Baltimore	32	226	2.19
1926—Grove, Philadelphia	45	258	2.51	1960—Baumann, Chicago	47	185	2.68
1927—Moore, New York	50	213	2.28	1961—Donovan, Washington	23	169	2.40
1928—Braxton, Washington	38	218	2.52	1962—Aguirre, Detroit	42	216	2.21
1929—Grove, Philadelphia	42	275	2.81	1963—Peters, Chicago	41	243	2.33
1930—Grove, Philadelphia	50	291	2.54	1964—Chance, Los Angeles	46	278	1.65
1931—Grove, Philadelphia	41	289	2.06	1965—McDowell, Cleveland	42	273	2.18
1932—Grove, Philadelphia	44	292	2.84	1966—Peters, Chicago	30	205	1.98
1933—Pearson, Cleveland	19	135	2.33	1967—Horlen, Chicago	35	258	2.06
1934—Gomez, New York	38	282	2.33	1968—Tiant, Cleveland	34	258	1.60
1935—Grove, Boston	35	273	2.70	1969—Bosman, Washington	31	193	2.19
1936—Grove, Boston	35	253	2.81	1970—Segui, Oakland	47	162	2.56
1937—Gomez, New York	34	278	2.33	1971—Blue, Oakland	39	312	1.82
1938—Grove, Boston	24	164	3.07	1972—Tiant, Boston	43	179	1.91
1939—Grove, Boston	23	191	2.54	1973—Palmer, Baltimore	38	296	2.40
1940—Feller, Cleveland	43	320	2.62	1974—Hunter, Oakland	41	318	2.49
1941—T. Lee, Chicago	35	300	2.37	1975—Palmer, Baltimore	39	323	2.09
1942—Lyons, Chicago	20	180	2.10	1976—Fidrych, Detroit	31	250	2.34
1943—Chandler, New York	30	253	1.64	1977—Tanana, California	31	241	2.54
1944—Trout, Detroit	49	352	2.12	1978—Guidry, New York	35	274	1.74
1945—Newhouser, Detroit	40	313	1.81	1979—Guidry, New York	33	236	2.78
1946—Newhouser, Detroit	37	293	1.94				

Note—Wilcy Moore pitched only six complete games—he started 12—in 1927, but was recognized as leader because of 213 innings pitched; Ernie Bonham, New York, had 1.91 ERA and ten complete games in 1940, but appeared in only 12 games and 99 innings, and Bob Feller was recognized as leader.

Note—Earned-runs not tabulated in American League prior to 1913.

STRIKEOUT LEADERS—PITCHING

Year - Pitcher and Club	SO.	Year Pitcher and Club	SO.
1900—(Not classed as major)		1941—Robert Feller, Cleveland	260
1901—Denton (Cy) Young, Boston	159	1942—Louis (Bobo) Newsom, Washington	113
1902—George (Rube) Waddell, Philadelphia	210	Cecil (Tex) Hughson, Boston	113
1903—George (Rube) Waddell, Philadelphia	301	1943—Allie Reynolds, Cleveland	151
1904—George (Rube) Waddell, Philadelphia	349	1944—Harold Newhouser, Detroit	187
1905—George (Rube) Waddell, Philadelphia	286	1945—Harold Newhouser, Detroit	212
1906—George (Rube) Waddell, Philadelphia	203	1946—Robert Feller, Cleveland	348
1907—George (Rube) Waddell, Philadelphia	226	1947—Robert Feller, Cleveland	196
1908—Edward Walsh, Chicago	269	1948—Robert Feller, Cleveland	164
1909—Frank Smith, Chicago	177	1949—Virgil Trucks, Detroit	153
1910—Walter Johnson, Washington	313	1950—Robert Lemon, Cleveland	170
1911—Edward Walsh, Chicago	255	1951—Victor Raschi, New York	164
1912—Walter Johnson, Washington	303	1952—Allie Reynolds, New York	160
1913—Walter Johnson, Washington	243	1953—W. William Pierce, Chicago	186
1914—Walter Johnson, Washington	225	1954—Robert Turley, Baltimore	185
1915—Walter Johnson, Washington	203	1955—Herbert Score, Cleveland	245
1916—Walter Johnson, Washington	228	1956—Herbert Score, Cleveland	263
1917—Walter Johnson, Washington	188	1957—Early Wynn, Cleveland	184
1918—Walter Johnson, Washington	162	1958—Early Wynn, Chicago	179
1919—Walter Johnson, Washington	147	1959—James Bunning, Detroit	201
1920—Stanley Coveleski, Cleveland	133	1960—James Bunning, Detroit	201
1921—Walter Johnson, Washington	143	1961—Camilo Pascual, Minnesota	221
1922—Urban Shocker, St. Louis	149	1962—Camilo Pascual, Minnesota	206
1923—Walter Johnson, Washington	130	1963—Camilo Pascual, Minnesota	202
1924—Walter Johnson, Washington	158	1964—Alphonso Downing, New York	217
1925—Robert Grove, Philadelphia	116	1965—Samuel McDowell, Cleveland	325
1926—Robert Grove, Philadelphia	194	1966—Samuel McDowell, Cleveland	225
1927—Robert Grove, Philadelphia	174	1967—James Lonborg, Boston	246
1928—Robert Grove, Philadelphia	183	1968—Samuel McDowell, Cleveland	283
1929—Robert Grove, Philadelphia	170	1969—Samuel McDowell, Cleveland	279
1930—Robert Grove, Philadelphia	209	1970—Samuel McDowell, Cleveland	304
1931—Robert Grove, Philadelphia	175	1971—Michael Lolich, Detroit	308
1932—Charles (Red) Ruffing, New York	190	1972—L. Nolan Ryan, California	329
1933—Vernon Gomez, New York	163	1973—L. Nolan Ryan, California	383
1934—Vernon Gomez, New York	158	1974—L. Nolan Ryan, California	367
1935—Thomas Bridges, Detroit	163	1975—Frank Tanana, California	269
1936—Thomas Bridges, Detroit	175	1976—L. Nolan Ryan, California	327
1937—Vernon Gomez, New York	194	1977—L. Nolan Ryan, California	341
1938—Robert Feller, Cleveland	240	1978—L. Nolan Ryan, California	260
1939—Robert Feller, Cleveland	246	1979—L. Nolan Ryan, California	223
1940—Robert Feller, Cleveland	261		

SHUTOUT LEADERS

Year Pitcher and Club	ShO.	Year Pitcher and Club	ShO.
1900—(Not classed as major)		1916—George H. Ruth, Boston	9
1901—Clark C. Griffith, Chicago	5	1917—Stanley Coveleski, Cleveland	9
Denton T. Young, Boston	5	1918—Walter P. Johnson, Washington	8
1902—Adrian Joss, Cleveland	5	Carl W. Mays, Boston	8
1903—Denton T. Young, Boston	7	1919—Walter P. Johnson, Washington	7
1904—Denton T. Young, Boston	10	1920—Carl W. Mays, New York	6
1905—Edward H. Killian, Detroit	8	1921—Samuel P. Jones, Boston	5
1906—Edward A. Walsh, Chicago	10	1922—George E. Uhle, Cleveland	5
1907—Edward S. Plank, Philadelphia	8	1923—Stanley Coveleski, Cleveland	5
1908—Edward A. Walsh, Chicago	12	1924—Walter P. Johnson, Washington	6
1909—Edward A. Walsh, Chicago	8	1925—Theodore A. Lyons, Chicago	5
1910—John W. Coombs, Philadelphia	13	1926—Edwin L. Wells, Detroit	4
1911—Walter P. Johnson, Washington	6	1927—Horace M. Lisenbee, Washington	4
Edward S. Plank, Philadelphia	6	1928—Herbert J. Pennock, New York	5
1912—Joseph Wood, Boston	10	1929—George F. Blaeholder, St. Louis	4
1913—Walter P. Johnson, Washington	12	Alvin F. Crowder, St. Louis	4
1914—Walter P. Johnson, Washington	10	Samuel D. Gray, St. Louis	4
1915—Walter P. Johnson, Washington	8	Daniel K. MacFayden, Boston	4

SHUTOUT LEADERS—Continued

Year	Pitcher and Club	ShO.
1930—	Clinton H. Brown, Cleveland	3
	George L. Earnshaw, Philadelphia	3
	George W. Pipgras, New York	3
1931—	Robert M. Grove, Philadelphia	4
	Victor G. Sorrell, Detroit	4
1932—	Thomas D. Bridges, Detroit	4
	Robert M. Grove, Philadelphia	4
1933—	Oral C. Hildebrand, Cleveland	6
1934—	Vernon L. Gomez, New York	6
	Melvin L. Harder, Cleveland	6
1935—	Lynwood T. Rowe, Detroit	6
1936—	Robert M. Grove, Boston	6
1937—	Vernon L. Gomez, New York	6
1938—	Vernon L. Gomez, New York	4
1939—	Charles H. Ruffing, New York	5
1940—	Robert W. Feller, Cleveland	4
	Theodore A. Lyons, Chicago	4
	Albert J. Milnar, Cleveland	4
1941—	Robert W. Feller, Cleveland	6
1942—	Ernest E. Bonham, New York	6
1943—	Spurgeon F. Chandler, New York	5
	Paul H. Trout, Detroit	5
1944—	Paul H. Trout, Detroit	7
1945—	Harold Newhouser, Detroit	8
1946—	Robert W. Feller, Cleveland	10
1947—	Robert W. Feller, Cleveland	5
1948—	Robert G. Lemon, Cleveland	10
1949—	Edward M. Garcia, Cleveland	6
	Ellis R. Kinder, Boston	6
	Virgil O. Trucks, Detroit	6
1950—	Arthur J. Houtteman, Detroit	4
1951—	Allie P. Reynolds, New York	7
1952—	Edward M. Garcia, Cleveland	6
	Allie P. Reynolds, New York	6
1953—	Erwin C. Porterfield, Washington	9
1954—	Edward M. Garcia, Cleveland	5
	Virgil O. Trucks, Chicago	5
1955—	William F. Hoeft, Detroit	7
1956—	Herbert J. Score, Cleveland	5
1957—	James A. Wilson, Chicago	5
1958—	Edward C. Ford, New York	7
1959—	Camilo A. Pascual, Washington	6
1960—	Edward C. Ford, New York	4
	James E. Perry, Cleveland	4
	Early Wynn, Chicago	4
1961—	Stephen D. Barber, Baltimore	8
	Camilo A. Pascual, Minnesota	8
1962—	Richard E. Donovan, Cleveland	5
	James L. Kaat, Minnesota	5
	Camilo A. Pascual, Minnesota	5
1963—	Raymond E. Herbert, Chicago	7
1964—	W. Dean Chance, Los Angeles	11
1965—	James T. Grant, Minnesota	6
1966—	Thomas E. John, Chicago	5
	Samuel E. McDowell, Cleveland	5
	Luis C. Tiant, Cleveland	5
1967—	Steven L. Hargan, Cleveland	6
	Joel E. Horlen, Chicago	6
	Thomas E. John, Chicago	6
	Michael S. Lolich, Detroit	6
	James E. McGlothlin, California	6
1968—	Luis C. Tiant, Cleveland	9
1969—	Dennis D. McLain, Detroit	9
1970—	Charles T. Dobson, Oakland	5
	James A. Palmer, Baltimore	5
1971—	Vida Blue, Oakland	8
1972—	L. Nolan Ryan, California	9
1973—	Rikalbert Blyleven, Minnesota	9
1974—	Luis C. Tiant, Boston	7
1975—	James A. Palmer, Baltimore	10
1976—	L. Nolan Ryan, California	7
1977—	Frank Tanana, California	7
1978—	Ronald Guidry, New York	9
1979—	L. Nolan Ryan, California	5
	Michael Flanagan, Baltimore	5
	Dennis Leonard, Kansas City	5

AL Clubs Turned Record 10 Triple Plays

The American League set a major league record with an amazing 10 triple plays in 1979, far better than the previous legue record of seven—last accomplished the AL fielders in 1936.

In the process of reaching the record, the Oakland A's and Boston Red Sox achieved a record-tying three triple plays each. The Toronto Blue Jays turned two triple-killings.

The Texas Rangers and California Angels were each victims of three triple plays.

The World Champion Pittsburgh Pirates had the only National League triple play in 1979.

Eleventh Championship Series

Including

AL Playoff Review

AL Game Box Scores

AL Composite Box Scores

NL Playoff Review

NL Game Box Score

NL Composite Box Score

WILLIE STARGELL displays a star-filled cap while embracing Bert Blyleven after the Pirates NL Championship Series sweep.

Pirates Clinched NL Playoff Sweep
Without Their Stars

By LARRY WIGGE

Can you picture Willie Stargell searching through his locker like a man possessed?

As Willie tells the story, while the Pirates were at Cincinnati for the first two games of their three-game sweep of the National League Championship Series, someone broke into his locker and swiped his final batch of 100 gold cloth stars—those stars he awarded to his teammates for various accomplishments during the season.

"The bag came up missing and still is," lamented Stargell, after he was unanimously selected the Most Valuable Player in the Series for batting .455 with 13 total bases and six RBIs. "It's a dirty trick for someone to pull on us now.

"When I found out they were missing, I ordered 3,000 more. If I have a choice, the entire squad will get a star for this one."

Stargell's contributions were headline material in papers across the country: A three-run, 11th-inning homer that decided a 5-2 win in the opener; a single and double in the Pirates' 10-inning 3-2 triumph in Game 2; a homer and two-run double in the 7-1 clinching victory.

It was sweet revenge for the Pirates' dauntless 38-year-old captain and main inspirational force, even if he couldn't celebrate the conquest of the Reds by awarding stars to his teammates, because the Pirates had been swept by the Reds in the NL playoffs in 1970 and 1975.

And if the Pirates needed extra incentive in their bid to become the first NL East pennant winner since 1973, they found it on the clubhouse wall when they reported for the first game at Riverfront Stadium in Cincinnati on October 2.

Tauntingly displayed was a newspaper clipping in which a major league scout compared the eight starters of each club and gave the Reds the edge at six positions. It was later learned that Pirates' second baseman Phil Garner was behind the newspaper hijinks.

After a 45-minute delay by rain at the start of Game 1, the Pirates, losers in eight of 12 games with the Reds in '79, bolted to a 2-0 lead in the third inning. Garner sliced a homer to right field, Omar Moreno tripled on a drive that eluded the diving Dave Collins in right and Tim Foli contributed a sacrifice fly.

But the Reds rebounded with a pair in the fourth on a single by Dave Concepcion and a homer by George Foster off Pittsburgh starting pitcher John Candelaria.

The deadlock persisted until the top half of the 11th. For two innings in relief of starter Tom Seaver, righthander Tom Hume was in command. But Foli and Dave Parker singled before Stargell's first-pitch homer settled the issue and sent flocks of the 55,006 spectators streaming for the exits.

A single by Concepcion and walks to Foster and Johnny Bench gave Reds' diehards one last hope in their half, before Don Robinson fanned Ray Knight to end the threat.

"Hume has been our best reliever all season," said Cincinnati manager John McNamara when questioned about the possibility of switching to a lefthander against Stargell. "A good pitcher can get anybody out."

After using five pitchers in the first game, Pittsburgh manager Chuck Tanner came right back with six hurlers for a 3-2 verdict in 10 innings in Game 2.

Controversy surrounded the victory, however.

With the score tied 1-1 in the Pirates' half of the fifth, Garner lashed a liner to right field. The Reds' Collins dived for the ball, but second base umpire Frank Pulli ruled a trap. Television replays showed that Collins had made a clean grab.

Garner advanced on a sacrifice by pitcher Jim Bibby and scored on Foli's double, giving the Pirates a 2-1 lead.

"It was my call all the way," said Pulli, refusing a request by McNamara to seek help from John Kibler, umpiring in right field. "I was in no position to see the play," offered Kibler. "If I'd have been asked, I could only have guessed."

The Reds knotted the score with one out in the ninth on a pinch-double by Hector Cruz and another two-bagger by Collins.

The rally continued when Dave Roberts walked Joe Morgan. Don Robinson was summoned by Tanner and proceeded to strike out Concepcion and retire Foster on a groundout.

Then Moreno and Parker singled around a Foli sacrifice in the 10th to make Robinson the winner and saddle Doug Bair with the loss.

GAME OF TUESDAY, OCTOBER 2, AT CINCINNATI (N)

Pittsburgh	AB.	R.	H.	RBI.	PO.	A.	Cincinnati	AB.	R.	H.	RBI.	PO.	A.
Moreno, cf	5	1	1	0	2	0	Collins, rf	5	0	2	0	3	0
Foli, ss	4	0	2	1	1	6	Morgan, 2b	4	0	0	0	3	4
Alexander, pr	0	1	0	0	0	0	Concepcion, ss	5	1	2	0	1	6
B. Robinson, lf	0	0	0	0	0	0	Foster, lf	3	1	1	2	1	0
Parker, rf	4	1	1	0	2	0	Bench, c	3	0	2	0	7	0
Stargell, 1b	4	1	1	3	17	0	Knight, 3b	5	0	0	0	0	1
Milner, lf	5	0	0	0	1	0	Driessen, 1b	4	0	0	0	14	0
Stennett, 2b	0	0	0	0	0	1	Cruz, cf	4	0	0	0	3	0
Madlock, 3b	5	0	2	0	0	4	Seaver, p	2	0	0	0	0	0
Ott, c	5	0	1	0	7	2	Auerbach, ph	1	0	0	0	0	0
Garner, 2b-ss	4	1	2	1	3	5	Hume, p	1	0	0	0	0	2
Candelaria, p	3	0	0	0	0	0	Tomlin, p	0	0	0	0	1	0
Romo, p	0	0	0	0	0	0							
Tekulve, p	0	0	0	0	0	1							
Easler, ph	1	0	0	0	0	0							
Jackson, p	1	0	0	0	0	0							
D. Robinson, p	0	0	0	0	0	0							
Totals	41	5	10	5	33	19	Totals	37	2	7	2	33	13

Pittsburgh	0	0	2	0	0	0	0	0	0	3 — 5
Cincinnati	0	0	0	2	0	0	0	0	0	0 — 2

Pittsburgh	IP.	H.	R.	ER.	BB.	SO.
Candelaria	7	5	2	2	1	4
Romo	⅓	1	0	0	1	1
Tekulve	1⅔	0	0	0	1	0
Jackson (Winner)	1⅔	1	0	0	1	2
D. Robinson (Save)	⅓	0	0	0	1	1

Cincinnati	IP.	H.	R.	ER.	BB.	SO.
Seaver	8	5	2	2	2	5
Hume (Loser)	2⅓	5	3	3	0	1
Tomlin	⅔	0	0	0	1	1

Errors—None. Double plays—Pittsburgh 2, Cincinnati 1. Left on bases—Pittsburgh 7, Cincinnati 7. Three-base hits—Bench, Moreno. Home runs—Garner, Foster, Stargell. Stolen bases—Madlock 2, Collins. Caught stealing—Bench. Sacrifice fly—Foli. Umpires—Kibler, Montague, Dale, Pulli, Stello and Quick. Time—3:14. Attendance—55,006.

A 30-minute rain delay preceded Game 3 as the scene shifted upriver to Pittsburgh on October 5.

Robinson, who saved Game 1, was extremely impressive as he set down five straight batters in the second game.

"This is the best bullpen I've ever had at any managerial level," said Tanner. "Some people think I make pitching moves too quickly. But we've won 100 games this year doing it that way and I'm sure not going to change now."

While Stargell was providing the slugging feats, the Pirates' pitching staff was limiting the once-feared Cincinnati offense to five runs in three games, climaxed by Bert Blyleven's route-going performance, only his fifth complete game of the year and first since August 15.

Blyleven put to rest frequent reports that he couldn't win the big games by becoming the only starter to go the distance. He scattered eight hits and fanned nine, losing his shutout bid in the sixth inning when Bench tagged him for a home run.

And the Bucs' bats went to work early, getting single runs in the first and second and two runs each in the third and fourth. Stargell and Bill Madlock socked homers in the third.

"I've seen a closeness this year," Stargell said. "I saw it the last part of last year. We were 14 games behind and then we started up the mountain.

GAME OF WEDNESDAY, OCTOBER 3, AT CINCINNATI

Pittsburgh	AB.	R.	H.	RBI.	PO.	A.		Cincinnati	AB.	R.	H.	RBI.	PO.	A.
Moreno, cf	5	1	2	0	4	0		Collins, rf	5	0	1	1	0	0
Foli, ss	4	1	2	1	2	1		Morgan, 2b	3	0	0	0	6	6
Parker, rf	5	0	2	1	4	0		Concepcion, ss	5	0	2	0	1	8
Stargell, 1b	3	0	2	0	6	1		Foster, lf	3	0	1	0	3	2
Milner, lf	2	0	0	0	0	0		Bench, c	5	0	0	0	5	1
B. Robinson, lf	2	0	0	0	3	0		Driessen, 1b	4	1	1	0	12	0
Madlock, 3b	5	0	0	1	1	0		Knight, 3b	5	0	2	0	0	2
Ott, c	4	0	2	0	9	1		Geronimo, cf	3	0	0	0	3	0
Garner, 2b	4	1	1	0	1	3		Pastore, p	0	0	0	1	0	0
Bibby, p	0	0	0	0	0	1		Spilman, ph	1	0	0	0	0	0
Jackson, p	0	0	0	0	0	0		Tomlin, p	0	0	0	0	0	0
Romo, p	0	0	0	0	0	0		Hume, p	0	0	0	0	0	0
Tekulve, p	1	0	0	0	0	0		Cruz, ph	1	1	1	0	0	0
Roberts, p	0	0	0	0	0	0		Bair, p	0	0	0	0	0	1
D. Robinson, p	0	0	0	0	0	0								
Totals	35	3	11	3	30	7		Totals	35	2	8	2	30	20

Pittsburgh		0	0	0		1	1	0	0	0	0	1 – 3
Cincinnati		0	1	0		0	0	0	0	0	1	0 – 2

Pittsburgh	IP.	H.	R.	ER.	BB.	SO.
Bibby	7	4	1	1	4	5
Jackson	1/3	0	0	0	0	0
Romo	0*	2	0	0	0	0
Tekulve	1	2	1	1	1	2
Roberts	0†	0	0	0	1	0
D. Robinson (Winner)	1²/₃	0	0	0	0	2
Cincinnati	IP.	H.	R.	ER.	BB.	SO.
Pastore	7	7	2	2	3	1
Tomlin	²/₃	1	0	0	0	1
Hume	1¹/₃	1	0	0	0	1
Bair (Loser)	1	2	1	1	1	0

*Pitched to two batters in eighth.
†Pitched to one batter in ninth.

Errors—None. Double play—Cincinnati 1. Left on bases—Pittsburgh 9, Cincinnati 11. Two-base hits—Concepcion, Foli, Stargell, Cruz, Collins. Stolen bases—Morgan, Knight, Collins. Caught stealing—Concepcion. Sacrifice hits—Bibby 2, Geronimo, Foli. Sacrifice fly—Pastore. Wild pitch—Tekulve. Umpires—Montague, Dale, Pulli, Stello, Quick and Kibler. Time—3:24. Attendance—55,000.

When that season was over, it was 'Whew, I just wish we had another week to play.' "

This season the Bucs didn't need any extra time.

The only things missing from the Pirates' celebration were those Stargell stars. But Willie was sure the 3,000 stars on order would take care of the Championship Series and World Series.

GAME OF FRIDAY, OCTOBER 5, AT PITTSBURGH

Cincinnati	AB.	R.	H.	RBI.	PO.	A.
Collins, rf	4	0	2	0	2	0
Morgan, 2b	4	0	0	0	3	1
Concepcion, ss	4	0	2	0	1	0
Foster, lf	4	0	0	0	1	0
Bench, c	4	1	1	1	5	1
Driessen, 1b	4	0	0	0	6	0
Knight, 3b	4	0	2	0	0	2
Geronimo, cf	4	0	1	0	5	0
LaCoss, p	0	0	0	0	0	1
Norman, p	1	0	0	0	0	0
Leibrandt, p	0	0	0	0	0	0
Auerbach, ph	1	0	0	0	0	0
Soto, p	0	0	0	0	0	0
Spilman, ph	1	0	0	0	0	0
Tomlin, p	0	0	0	0	0	1
Hume, p	0	0	0	0	0	0
Totals	35	1	8	1	24	6

Pittsburgh	AB.	R.	H.	RBI.	PO.	A.
Moreno, cf	2	1	0	0	1	0
Foli, ss	4	0	0	1	0	2
Parker, rf	3	1	1	1	3	0
Stargell, 1b	4	1	2	3	9	1
Milner, lf	2	0	0	0	0	0
B. Robinson, lf	1	0	0	0	0	0
Madlock, 3b	2	1	1	1	0	3
Ott, c	4	0	0	0	9	0
Garner, 2b	4	2	2	0	4	1
Blyleven, p	3	1	1	0	1	1
Totals	29	7	7	6	27	8

```
Cincinnati............................... 0   0  0     0  0  1     0  0  0 – 1
Pittsburgh.............................. 1   1  2     2  0  0     0  1  x – 7
```

Cincinnati	IP.	H.	R.	ER.	BB.	SO.
LaCoss (Loser)	1⅔	1	2	2	4	0
Norman	2	4	4	4	1	1
Leibrandt	⅓	0	0	0	0	0
Soto	2	0	0	0	1	1
Tomlin	1⅔	2	1	0	1	1
Hume	⅓	0	0	0	0	0

Pittsburgh	IP.	H.	R.	ER.	BB.	SO.
Blyleven (Winner)	9	8	1	1	0	9

Error—Geronimo. Left on bases—Cincinnati 7, Pittsburgh 8. Two-base hits—Knight, Stargell. Three-base hit—Garner. Home runs—Stargell, Madlock, Bench. Stolen bases—Moreno, Parker. Sacrifice hits—Moreno, Blyleven. Sacrifice flies—Parker, Foli. Balk—Leibrandt. Umpires—Dale, Pulli, Stello, Quick, Kibler and Montague. Time—2:45. Attendance—42,240.

PITTSBURGH PIRATES' BATTING AND FIELDING AVERAGES

Player—Position	G.	AB.	R.	H.	TB.	2B.	3B.	HR.	RBI.	B.A.	PO.	A.	E.	F.A.
Stargell, 1b	3	11	2	5	13	2	0	2	6	.455	32	2	0	1.000
Garner, 2b-ss	3	12	4	5	10	0	1	1	1	.417	8	9	0	1.000
Foli, ss	3	12	1	4	5	1	0	0	3	.333	3	9	0	1.000
Parker, rf	3	12	2	4	4	0	0	0	2	.333	9	0	0	1.000
Blyleven, p	1	3	1	1	1	0	0	0	0	.333	1	1	0	1.000
Madlock, 3b	3	12	1	3	6	0	0	1	2	.250	1	7	0	1.000
Moreno, cf	3	12	3	3	5	0	1	0	0	.250	7	0	0	1.000
Ott, c	3	13	0	3	3	0	0	0	0	.231	25	3	0	1.000
Alexander, pr	1	0	1	0	0	0	0	0	0	.000	0	0	0	.000
Bibby, p	1	0	0	0	0	0	0	0	0	.000	0	1	0	1.000
Stennett, 2b	1	0	0	0	0	0	0	0	0	.000	0	1	0	1.000
Roberts, p	1	0	0	0	0	0	0	0	0	.000	0	0	0	.000
D. Robinson, p	2	0	0	0	0	0	0	0	0	.000	0	0	0	.000
Romo, p	2	0	0	0	0	0	0	0	0	.000	0	0	0	.000
Easler, ph	1	1	0	0	0	0	0	0	0	.000	0	0	0	.000
Tekulve, p	2	1	0	0	0	0	0	0	0	.000	0	1	0	1.000
Jackson, p	2	1	0	0	0	0	0	0	0	.000	0	0	0	.000
Candelaria, p	1	3	0	0	0	0	0	0	0	.000	0	0	0	.000
B. Robinson, lf	3	3	0	0	0	0	0	0	0	.000	1	0	0	1.000
Milner, lf	3	9	0	0	0	0	0	0	0	.000	1	0	0	1.000
Totals	3	105	15	28	47	3	2	4	14	.267	90	34	0	1.000

CINCINNATI REDS' BATTING AND FIELDING AVERAGES

Player—Position	G.	AB.	R.	H.	TB.	2B.	3B.	HR.	RBI.	B.A.	PO.	A.	E.	F.A.
Concepcion, ss	3	14	1	6	7	1	0	0	0	.429	3	14	0	1.000
Collins, rf	3	14	0	5	6	1	0	0	1	.357	5	0	0	1.000
Knight, 3b	3	14	0	4	5	1	0	0	0	.286	0	5	0	1.000
Bench, c	3	12	1	3	8	0	1	1	1	.250	17	2	0	1.000
Foster, lf	3	10	1	2	5	0	0	1	2	.200	6	2	0	1.000
Cruz, cf-ph	2	5	1	1	2	1	0	0	0	.200	3	0	0	1.000
Geronimo, cf	2	7	0	1	1	0	0	0	0	.143	8	0	1	.889
Driessen, 1b	3	12	1	1	1	0	0	0	0	.083	32	0	0	1.000
Pastore, p	1	0	0	0	0	0	0	0	1	.000	0	0	0	.000
Bair, p	1	0	0	0	0	0	0	0	0	.000	0	1	0	1.000
LaCoss, p	1	0	0	0	0	0	0	0	0	.000	0	1	0	1.000
Leibrandt, p	1	0	0	0	0	0	0	0	0	.000	0	0	0	.000
Soto, p	1	0	0	0	0	0	0	0	0	.000	0	0	0	.000
Tomlin, p	3	0	0	0	0	0	0	0	0	.000	1	1	0	1.000
Norman, p	1	1	0	0	0	0	0	0	0	.000	0	0	0	.000
Hume, p	3	1	0	0	0	0	0	0	0	.000	0	2	0	1.000
Seaver, p	1	2	0	0	0	0	0	0	0	.000	0	0	0	.000
Auerbach, ph	2	2	0	0	0	0	0	0	0	.000	0	0	0	.000
Spilman, ph	2	2	0	0	0	0	0	0	0	.000	0	0	0	.000
Morgan, 2b	3	11	0	0	0	0	0	0	0	.000	12	11	0	1.000
Totals	3	107	5	23	35	4	1	2	5	.215	87	39	1	.992

PITTSBURGH PIRATES' PITCHING RECORDS

Pitcher	G.	GS.	CG.	IP.	H.	R.	ER.	BB.	SO.	HB.	WP.	W.	L.	Pct.	ERA.
D. Robinson	2	0	0	2	0	0	0	3	0	0	1	0	1.000	0.00
Jackson	2	0	0	2	1	0	0	1	2	0	0	1	0	1.000	0.00
Romo	2	0	0	⅓	3	0	0	1	1	0	0	0	0	.000	0.00
Roberts	1	0	0	0	0	0	0	1	0	0	0	0	0	.000	0.00
Blyleven	1	1	1	9	8	1	1	0	9	0	0	1	0	1.000	1.00
Bibby	1	1	0	7	4	1	1	4	5	0	0	0	0	.000	1.29
Candelaria	1	1	0	7	5	2	2	1	4	0	0	0	0	.000	2.57
Tekulve	2	0	0	2⅔	2	1	1	2	2	0	1	0	0	.000	3.38
Totals	3	3	1	30	23	5	5	11	26	0	1	3	0	1.000	1.50

No shutouts. Save—D. Robinson.

CINCINNATI REDS' PITCHING RECORDS

Pitcher	G.	GS.	CG.	IP.	H.	R.	ER.	BB.	SO.	HB.	WP.	W.	L.	Pct.	ERA.
Tomlin	3	0	0	3	1	0	2	3	0	0	0	0	0	.000	0.00
Soto	1	0	0	2	0	0	0	1	0	0	0	0	0	.000	0.00
Leibrandt	1	0	0	⅓	0	0	0	0	0	0	0	0	0	.000	0.00
Seaver	1	1	0	8	5	2	2	2	5	0	0	0	0	.000	2.25
Pastore	1	1	0	7	7	2	2	3	1	0	0	0	0	.000	2.57
Hume	3	0	0	4	6	3	3	0	2	0	0	0	1	.000	6.75
Bair	1	0	0	1	2	1	1	1	0	0	0	0	1	.000	9.00
LaCoss	1	1	0	1⅔	1	2	2	4	0	0	0	0	1	.000	10.80
Norman	1	0	0	2	4	4	4	1	1	0	0	0	0	.000	18.00
Totals	3	3	0	29	28	15	14	13	13	0	0	0	3	.000	4.34

No shutouts or saves.

COMPOSITE SCORE BY INNINGS

Pittsburgh	1	1	4	3	1	0	0	1	0	1	3	– 15
Cincinnati	0	1	0	2	0	1	0	0	1	0	0	– 5

Sacrifice hits—Bibby 2, Geronimo, Foli, Moreno, Blyleven.

Sacrifice flies—Foli 2, Pastore, Parker.

Stolen bases—Madlock 2, Collins 2, Morgan, Knight, Moreno, Parker.

Caught stealing—Bench, Concepcion.

Double plays—Concepcion, Morgan and Driessen 2; Garner, Foli and Stargell; Madlock, Garner and Stargell.

Left on bases—Pittsburgh 7, 9, 8—24; Cincinnati 7, 11, 7—25.

Hit by pitcher—None.

Passed balls—None.

Balk—Leibrandt.

Time of games—First game, 3:14; second game, 3:24; third game, 2:45.

Attendance—First game, 55,006; second game, 55,000; third game, 42,240.

Umpires—Kibler, Montague, Dale, Pulli, Stello and Quick.

Official scorers—Earl Lawson, Cincinnati Post; Dan Donovan, Pittsburgh Press.

Bases-loaded danger is averted as Baltimore's **DOUG DeCINCES** dives for Jim Anderson smash and turns potential extra-base hit into double play to end Angels' fifth-inning threat in fourth game of AL Championship Series.

DeCinces' Stab Stirred Orioles' Memories

By LARRY WIGGE

"I've seen that play a hundred times before," said Baltimore shortstop Mark Belanger. "But by another third baseman."

"I thought of Brooks Robinson," said Brooks Robinson.

Memories. Of diving stops. Of World Series gems. Of Brooks Robinson.

But Brooks was retired and those sparkling plays were now only memories. . . . The California Angels had the bases loaded with one out in the fifth inning, trailing the Baltimore Orioles, 3-0, in the fourth game of the American League Championship Series. The Orioles led the Series two games to one, but the potential tying runs were on the bases.

Shortstop Jim Anderson was at the plate against Scott McGregor with 43,199 Anaheim Stadium fans on their feet, sensing their Angels were going to turn things around.

Anderson swung at the second pitch and hit a vicious one-hopper down the third base line. It looked like at least a double as the ball sped over the bag. Two runs would have scored for sure, maybe three. Doug DeCinces, who had never really escaped the shadow of Brooks Robinson at third base in the eyes of Orioles' rooters, dived to his right and somehow snared the ball. He recovered, straightened up and, while standing on third, threw to first to complete the double play and end the Angels' threat.

"In that situation, you're not going to let Jim Anderson beat you with a double down the line," said DeCinces.

"I feel that play really changed things. It gave us confidence and Scotty really needed that play. When he gets a big play like that to get him out of a jam, he goes like crazy the rest of the game."

McGregor went on to hurl a six-hit shutout and the Orioles won 8-0 for a 3-1 Series triumph and their first visit to the World Series since 1971.

In 16⅔ innings against the Angels in the regular schedule, McGregor permitted only one earned run while winning twice.

Pat Kelly's seventh-inning homer closed out the scoring and was the second three-run blast off California reliever John Montague. However, it was far less dramatic than the first one.

With two out in the 10th inning of the first game, the score deadlocked, 3-3, and DeCinces and Al Bumbry aboard via a single and intentional walk, respectively, pinch-hitter John Lowenstein strolled to the plate against Montague.

Lowenstein, sidelined for much of the latter part of the season because of a severely sprained ankle, sliced a two-strike pitch to the opposite field, just over the left-field wall to break up the game before 52,787 at Baltimore's Memorial Stadium.

"You don't think home run in that situation," Lowenstein remarked. "You just try to hit the ball hard somewhere.

"The ball didn't sink. It didn't die. It just sailed. Yes, I knew it was fair and I knew the game was over. I think that was my first opposite-field home run since 1958 when I was in Little League."

Jim Palmer hurled the first nine innings, yielding seven hits, including a homer and double by Dan Ford, before Don Stanhouse pitched a perfect 10th inning to gain credit for the victory.

The Orioles sent 23-game winner Mike Flanagan to the mound in Game 2 and, after Ford connected off Flanagan in the first inning for his second homer in as many games, the AL Cy Young Award winner was given a 9-1 cushion in the first three innings, only to see it dwindle to one run before Stanhouse slowed the game down to his pace and saved a 9-8 victory.

The Orioles had scored four runs in their half of the first and added four more in the second, highlighted by first baseman Eddie Murray's 400-foot homer, before Kiko Garcia's RBI single in the third made the score 9-1.

After the Angels cuffed Flanagan for single runs in the sixth and seventh, they knocked the lefthander from the mound in the eighth, scoring three more runs, aided by a Murray error.

Stanhouse put gasoline on the fire for Flanagan in the eighth when he yielded a run-scoring single by Don Baylor and a sacrifice fly, reducing Baltimore's lead to 9-6.

In the ninth, Stanhouse permitted a walk, a pinch-double by Willie Davis, an infield out for one run and an RBI single by Carney Lansford, sending Baltimore skipper Earl Weaver to the mound.

"I was going to leave him (Stanhouse) in there until they tied the score," Weaver said later, after watching the Angels load the bases on a single by Ford and an intentional walk to Baylor, before Brian Downing grounded into a forceout to put a halt to the nail-biting.

"I knew we'd get three outs sooner or later," right fielder Ken Singleton said logically. "We got them later, but it was soon enough. With Don, that happens a lot."

"He scares me to death," said catcher Rick Dempsey. "He gives you gray hair 10 years prematurely. But the bottom line is he gets them out."

With no days off for travel, the scene shifted to Anaheim Stadium for Game 3, where high drama once again dominated.

GAME OF WEDNESDAY, OCTOBER 3 AT BALTIMORE (N)

California	AB.	R.	H.	RBI.	PO.	A.	Baltimore	AB.	R.	H.	RBI.	PO.	A.
Miller, cf	5	1	1	0	2	1	Bumbry, cf	4	1	0	0	3	0
Lansford, 3b	4	0	0	0	3	0	Belanger, ss	4	0	1	1	0	5
Ford, rf	4	1	2	2	3	0	Lowenstein, ph	1	1	1	3	0	0
Baylor, dh	4	0	0	0	0	0	Singleton, rf	3	0	0	0	1	0
Carew 1b	4	1	3	0	8	1	Murray, 1b	2	0	0	0	13	0
Downing, c	4	0	0	0	9	0	Kelly, lf	3	1	1	0	3	0
Grich, 2b,	3	0	1	1	1	3	May, dh	4	0	0	0	0	0
Harlow, lf	4	0	0	0	4	0	DeCinces, 3b	3	2	1	1	2	3
Anderson, ss	3	0	0	0	1	2	Dauer, 2b	3	0	1	0	3	3
Davis, ph	1	0	0	0	0	0	Dempsey, c	3	1	1	1	4	1
Campaneris, ss	0	0	0	0	0	0	Crowley, ph	1	0	0	0	0	0
Ryan, p	0	0	0	0	0	0	Palmer, p	0	0	0	0	1	0
Montague, p	0	0	0	0	1	1	Stanhouse, p	0	0	0	0	0	0
Totals	36	3	7	3	29	11	Totals	31	6	6	6	30	14

```
California ............................... 1   0   1      0   0   0      0   0     0 - 3
Baltimore ............................... 0   0   2      1   0   0      0   0   0   3 - 6
```
Two out when winning run scored.

California	IP.	H.	R.	ER.	BB.	SO.
Ryan	7	4	3	1	3	8
Montague (Loser)	2⅔	2	3	3	2	1

Baltimore	IP.	H.	R.	ER.	BB.	SO.
Palmer	9	7	3	3	2	3
Stanhouse (Winner)	1	0	0	0	0	0

Error—Grich. Double plays—California 2. Left on bases—California 5, Baltimore 3. Two-base hits—Ford, Dempsey, Carew, Grich. Home runs—Ford, Lowenstein. Stolen base—Kelly. Caught stealing—Carew, Murray. Sacrifice hit—Dauer. Sacrifice fly—DeCinces. Wild pitch—Ryan. Passed ball—Dempsey. Umpires—Barnett, Ford, Evans, Denkinger, Clark and Kosc. Time—3:10. Attendance—52,787.

Al Bumbry steals second and ignites four-run, first-inning rally for Orioles in second game victory.

GAME OF THURSDAY, OCTOBER 4, AT BALTIMORE

California	AB.	R.	H.	RBI.	PO.	A.
Carew, 1b	5	2	1	1	10	0
Lansford, 3b	5	1	3	3	0	1
Ford, rf	5	1	2	1	0	0
Baylor, dh	4	1	2	1	0	0
Downing, c	4	0	1	1	6	0
Grich, 2b	3	0	0	1	1	3
Clark, lf	3	0	0	0	3	0
Harlow, ph	0	0	0	0	0	0
Miller, cf	4	1	0	0	2	0
Anderson, ss	2	0	0	0	2	3
Rettenmund, ph	0	0	0	0	0	0
Thon, pr-ss	0	1	0	0	0	0
Davis, ph	1	1	1	0	0	0
Frost, p	0	0	0	0	0	0
Clear, p	0	0	0	0	0	0
Aase, p	0	0	0	0	0	0
Totals	36	8	10	8	24	7

Baltimore	AB.	R.	H.	RBI.	PO.	A.
Bumbry, cf	4	2	3	0	3	0
Garcia, ss	3	1	2	2	2	9
Singleton, rf	5	1	1	0	0	0
Murray, 1b	4	2	2	4	13	0
Lowenstein, lf	3	1	0	0	3	0
Kelly, dh	4	1	1	1	0	0
DeCinces, 3b	3	1	1	1	1	2
Dauer, 2b	4	0	0	0	3	5
Dempsey, c	4	0	1	0	2	0
Flanagan, p	0	0	0	0	0	0
Stanhouse, p	0	0	0	0	0	0
Totals	34	9	11	8	27	16

California	1	0	0		0	0	1		1	3	2 – 8
Baltimore	4	4	1		0	0	0		0	0	x – 9

California	IP.	H.	R.	ER.	BB.	SO.
Frost (Loser)	1⅓	5	6	5	3	0
Clear	5⅔	4	3	3	2	3
Aase	1	2	0	0	0	2

Baltimore	IP.	H.	R.	ER.	BB.	SO.
Flanagan (Winner)	7*	6	6	4	1	2
Stanhouse	2	4	2	2	2	0

*Pitched to three batters in eighth.

Errors—Ford, Murray. Double play—California 1. Left on bases—California 6, Baltimore 6. Two-base hits—Carew, Davis. Home runs—Ford, Murray. Stolen bases—Bumbry 2. Sacrifice flies—Grich, Downing. Wild pitch—Clear. Umpires—Ford, Evans, Denkinger, Clark, Kosc and Barnett. Time—2:51. Attendance—52,108.

The Orioles were only two outs away from sweeping the series when the Angels struck back for a 4-3 victory.

Dennis Martinez spaced seven hits in the first eight innings prior to permitting a one-out double to Rod Carew in the ninth, bringing Stanhouse to the mound for the third straight game.

A walk to Downing preceded Bobby Grich's liner to center field where Al Bumbry, unable to hear the crack of the bat because of the roar of the crowd, got a late jump on the ball and dropped it for an error as Carew scored to tie the game, 3-3, with Downing stopping at second.

When Larry Harlow followed with a looping double down the left field line, Downing raced home with the winning run.

One day later it was an altogether different script, written by McGregor, DeCinces, Ken Singleton, Kelly, et al.

"This squad is the best I've ever had," bellowed Weaver. "You can look at the statistics, but I've never had a better team than this. It's the deepest pitching staff I've seen anywhere and we also set a team home run record."

The ecstasy was short-lived for the Angels, who after 19 years of trying, savored fond memories of their finest hour. Gene Autry's dream of having a winner would soon be realized.

But the memories that counted most were those of DeCinces picking himself from the Anaheim Stadium turf to complete the rally-stopping double play and McGregor throttling Angels' hitters on six hits. And . . . we've all seen that play a hundred times before.

GAME OF FRIDAY, OCTOBER 5, AT CALIFORNIA

Baltimore	AB.	R.	H.	RBI.	PO.	A.	California	AB.	R.	H.	RBI.	PO.	A.
Bumbry, cf	5	1	1	0	1	0	Miller, cf	4	0	1	0	7	1
Garcia, ss	3	0	0	0	2	2	Lansford, 3b	4	1	1	0	0	3
Crowley, ph	1	0	1	1	0	0	Ford, rf	4	0	1	1	2	0
Belanger, pr-ss	1	0	0	0	0	0	Baylor, dh	4	1	1	1	0	0
Singleton, rf	4	2	2	0	2	1	Carew, 1b	4	1	2	0	7	0
Murray, 1b	2	0	2	0	8	2	Downing, c	3	1	1	0	8	0
May, dh	3	0	1	1	0	0	Grich, 2b	4	0	0	0	1	1
DeCinces, 3b	3	0	0	1	0	1	Harlow, lf	4	0	1	1	2	0
Roenicke, lf	1	0	0	0	2	1	Anderson, ss	3	0	1	0	0	3
Lowenstein, ph-lf	1	0	0	0	2	0	Tanana, p	0	0	0	0	0	0
Dauer, 2b	4	0	1	0	3	4	Aase, p	0	0	0	0	0	1
Skaggs, c	4	0	0	0	3	1							
D. Martinez, p	0	0	0	0	2	0							
Stanhouse, p	0	0	0	0	0	0							
Totals	32	3	8	3	25	12	Totals	34	4	9	3	27	9

Baltimore	0	0	0	1	0	1	1	0	0–3
California	1	0	0	1	0	0	0	0	2–4

One out when winning run scored.

Baltimore	IP.	H.	R.	ER.	BB.	SO.
D. Martinez	8⅓	8	3	3	0	4
Stanhouse (Loser)	0†	1	1	0	1	0

California	IP.*	H.	R.	ER.	BB.	SO.
Tanana	5*	6	2	2	2	3
Aase (Winner)	4	2	1	1	2	4

*Pitched to three batters in sixth.
†Pitched to three batters in ninth.

Errors—Garcia, Murray, Bumbry. Double plays—Baltimore 2, California 2. Left on bases—Baltimore 8, California 6. Two-base hits—Singleton, Carew, Harlow. Three-base hit—Bumbry. Home run—Baylor. Stolen bases—Lansford, Carew. Sacrifice fly—DeCinces. Hit by pitcher—By Tanana (Roenicke). Umpires—Evans, Denkinger, Clark, Kosc, Barnett and Ford. Time—2:59. Attendance—43, 199.

GAME OF SATURDAY, OCTOBER 6, AT CALIFORNIA

Baltimore	AB.	R.	H.	RBI.	PO.	A.
Bumbry, cf	3	1	0	0	3	0
Garcia, ss	5	0	1	0	2	5
Belanger, ss	0	0	0	0	0	1
Singleton, rf	4	1	3	2	2	0
Murray, 1b	4	1	1	1	10	0
Lowenstein, lf	1	0	0	0	1	0
Roenicke, ph-lf	4	1	1	1	1	0
Kelly, dh	4	1	2	3	0	0
DeCinces, 3b	4	1	2	0	2	2
Smith, 2b	4	0	0	0	1	2
Dauer, 2b	0	0	0	0	1	0
Dempsey, c	3	2	2	1	4	0
McGregor, p	0	0	0	0	0	0
Totals	36	8	12	8	27	10

California	AB.	R.	H.	RBI.	PO.	A.
Carew, 1b	4	0	1	0	9	0
Lansford, 3b	4	0	1	0	4	1
Ford, rf	4	0	0	0	1	0
Baylor, lf	4	0	0	0	4	0
Downing, c	4	0	1	0	4	0
Grich, 2b	3	0	1	0	1	5
Rettenmund, dh	2	0	0	0	0	0
Miller, cf	3	0	2	0	3	0
Anderson, ss	3	0	0	0	1	3
Knapp, p	0	0	0	0	0	0
LaRoche, p	0	0	0	0	0	0
Frost, p	0	0	0	0	0	0
Montague, p	0	0	0	0	0	1
Barlow, p	0	0	0	0	0	0
Totals	31	0	6	0	27	10

Baltimore	0	0	2	1	0	0	5	0	0 – 8
California	0	0	0	0	0	0	0	0	0 – 0

Baltimore	IP.	H.	R.	ER.	BB.	SO.
McGregor (Winner)	9	6	0	0	1	4

California	IP.	H.	R.	ER.	BB.	SO.
Knapp (Loser)	2⅓	5	2	2	1	0
LaRoche	1⅓	2	1	1	1	1
Frost	3	3	4	4	2	1
Montague	1⅓	2	1	1	0	1
Barlow	1	0	0	0	0	0

Error—Garcia. Double plays—Baltimore 3, California 2. Left on bases—Baltimore 6, California 5. Two-base hits—DeCinces, Dempsey, Singleton. Home run—Kelly. Stolen bases—Kelly, Dempsey. Sacrifice fly—Singleton. Wild pitch—Frost. Umpires—Denkinger, Clark, Kosc, Barnett, Ford and Evans. Time—2:56. Attendance—43,199.

BALTIMORE ORIOLES' BATTING AND FIELDING AVERAGES

Player–Position	G.	AB.	R.	H.	TB.	2B.	3B.	HR.	RBI.	B.A.	PO.	A.	E.	F.A.
Crowley, ph	2	2	0	1	1	0	0	0	1	.500	0	0	0	.000
Murray, 1b	4	12	3	5	8	0	0	1	5	.417	44	3	2	.959
Dempsey, c	3	10	3	4	6	2	0	0	2	.400	10	1	0	1.000
Singleton, rf	4	16	4	6	8	2	0	0	2	.375	5	1	0	1.000
Kelly, lf-dh	3	11	3	4	7	0	0	1	4	.364	3	0	0	1.000
DeCinces, 3b	4	13	4	4	5	1	0	0	3	.308	5	8	0	1.000
Garcia, ss	3	11	1	3	3	0	0	0	0	.273	6	16	2	.917
Bumbry, cf	4	16	5	4	6	0	1	0	0	.250	10	0	1	.909
Roenicke, lf-ph	2	5	1	1	1	0	0	0	1	.200	3	1	0	1.000
Belanger, ss-pr	3	5	0	1	1	0	0	0	1	.200	0	6	0	1.000
Dauer, 2b	4	11	0	2	2	0	0	0	0	.182	10	12	0	1.000
Lowenstein, ph-lf	4	6	2	1	4	0	0	1	3	.167	6	0	0	1.000
May, dh	2	7	0	1	1	0	0	0	1	.143	0	0	0	.000
D. Martinez, p	1	0	0	0	0	0	0	0	0	.000	2	0	0	1.000
Palmer, p	1	0	0	0	0	0	0	0	0	.000	1	1	0	1.000
Flanagan, p	1	0	0	0	0	0	0	0	0	.000	0	0	0	.000
McGregor, p	1	0	0	0	0	0	0	0	0	.000	0	0	0	.000
Stanhouse, p	3	0	0	0	0	0	0	0	0	.000	0	0	0	.000
Skaggs, c	1	4	0	0	0	0	0	0	0	.000	3	1	0	1.000
Smith, 2b	1	4	0	0	0	0	0	0	0	.000	1	2	0	1.000
Totals	4	133	26	37	53	5	1	3	25	.278	109	52	5	.970

CALIFORNIA ANGELS' BATTING AND FIELDING AVERAGES

Player–Position	G.	AB.	R.	H.	TB.	2B.	3B.	HR.	RBI.	B.A.	PO.	A.	E.	F.A.
Davis, ph	2	2	1	1	2	1	0	0	0	.500	0	0	0	.000
Carew, 1b	4	17	4	7	10	3	0	0	0	.412	34	1	0	1.000
Ford, rf	4	17	2	5	12	1	0	2	4	.294	6	0	1	.857
Lansford, 3b	4	17	2	5	5	0	0	0	3	.294	4	8	0	1.000
Miller, cf	4	16	2	4	4	0	0	0	0	.250	14	2	0	1.000
Downing, c	4	15	1	3	3	0	0	0	1	.200	27	0	0	1.000
Baylor, dh-lf	4	16	2	3	6	0	0	1	2	.188	4	0	0	1.000
Grich, 2b	4	13	0	2	3	1	0	0	2	.154	4	12	1	.941
Harlow, lf-ph	3	8	0	1	2	1	0	0	1	.125	6	0	0	1.000
Anderson, ss	4	11	0	1	1	0	0	0	0	.091	4	11	0	1.000
Thon, pr-ss	1	0	1	0	0	0	0	0	0	.000	0	0	0	.000
Barlow, p	1	0	0	0	0	0	0	0	0	.000	0	0	0	.000

CALIFORNIA ANGELS' BATTING AND FIELDING AVERAGES (Continued)

Player—Position	G.	AB.	R.	H.	TB.	2B.	3B.	HR.	RBI	B.A.	PO.	A.	E.	F.A.
Campaneris, ss	1	0	0	0	0	0	0	0	0	.000	0	0	0	.000
Clear, p	1	0	0	0	0	0	0	0	0	.000	0	0	0	.000
Knapp, p	1	0	0	0	0	0	0	0	0	.000	0	0	0	.000
LaRoche, p	1	0	0	0	0	0	0	0	0	.000	0	0	0	.000
Ryan, p	1	0	0	0	0	0	0	0	0	.000	0	0	0	.000
Tanana, p	1	0	0	0	0	0	0	0	0	.000	1	2	0	1.000
Montague, p	2	0	0	0	0	0	0	0	0	.000	0	1	0	1.000
Aase, p	2	0	0	0	0	0	0	0	0	.000	0	0	0	.000
Frost, p	2	0	0	0	0	0	0	0	0	.000	0	0	0	.000
Rettenmund, ph-dh	2	2	0	0	0	0	0	0	0	.000	0	0	0	.000
Clark, lf	1	3	0	0	0	0	0	0	0	.000	3	0	0	1.000
Totals	4	137	15	32	48	7	0	3	14	.234	107	37	2	.986

BALTIMORE ORIOLES' PITCHING RECORDS

Pitcher	G.	GS.	CG.	IP.	H.	R.	ER.	BB.	SO.	HB.	WP.	W.	L.	Pct.	ERA.
McGregor	1	1	1	9	6	0	0	1	4	0	0	1	0	1.000	0.00
Palmer	1	1	0	9	7	3	3	2	3	0	0	0	0	.000	3.00
D. Martinez	1	1	0	8⅓	8	3	3	0	4	0	0	0	0	.000	3.24
Flanagan	1	1	0	7	6	6	4	1	2	0	0	1	0	1.000	5.14
Stanhouse	3	0	0	3	5	3	2	3	0	0	0	1	1	.500	6.00
Totals	4	4	1	36⅓	32	15	12	7	13	0	0	3	1	.750	2.97

Shutout—McGregor. No saves.

CALIFORNIA ANGELS' PITCHING RECORDS

Pitcher	G.	GS.	CG.	IP.	H.	R.	ER.	BB.	SO.	HB.	WP.	W.	L.	Pct.	ERA.
Barlow	1	0	0	1	0	0	0	0	0	0	0	0	0	.000	0.00
Ryan	1	1	0	7	4	3	1	3	8	0	1	0	0	.000	1.29
Aase	2	0	0	5	4	1	1	2	6	0	1	1	0	1.000	1.80
Tanana	1	1	0	5	6	2	2	2	3	1	0	0	0	.000	3.60
Clear	1	0	0	5⅔	4	3	3	2	3	0	1	0	0	.000	4.76
LaRoche	1	0	0	1⅓	2	1	1	1	1	0	0	0	0	.000	6.75
Knapp	1	1	0	2⅓	5	2	2	1	0	0	0	0	1	.000	7.71
Montague	2	0	0	4	4	4	4	2	2	0	0	0	0	.000	9.00
Frost	2	1	0	4⅓	8	10	9	5	1	0	1	0	1	.000	18.69
Totals	4	4	0	35⅔	37	26	23	18	24	1	3	1	3	.250	5.80

No shutouts or saves.

COMPOSITE SCORE BY INNINGS

Baltimore	4	4	5	3	0	1	6	0	0	3 –	26
California	3	0	1	1	0	2	1	3	4	0 –	15

Sacrifice hit—Dauer.

Sacrifice flies—DeCinces 2, Grich, Downing, Singleton.

Stolen bases—Bumbry 2, Kelley 2, Lansford, Carew, Dempsey.

Caught stealing—Carew, Murray.

Double plays—Lansford, Grich and Carew 2; Miller and Carew; Anderson, Grich and Carew 2; Roenicke, Garcia and Dauer; Dauer and Murray; Miller and Downing; Smith, Garcia and Murray; Lansford and Carew; DeCinces and Murray; Garcia, Smith and Murray.

Left on bases—Baltimore 3, 6, 8, 6–23; California 5, 6, 6, 5–22.

Hit by pitcher—By Tanana (Roenicke).

Passed ball—Dempsey.

Balks—None.

Time of games—First game, 3:10; second game, 2:51; third game, 2:59; fourth game, 2:56.

Attendance—First game, 52,787; second game, 52,108; third game, 43,199; fourth game, 43,199.

Umpires—Barnett, Ford, Evans, Denkinger, Clark and Kosc.

Official scorers—Jim Henneman, Baltimore News-American; Tracy Ringolsby, Long Beach Independent Press-Telegram.

1979 WORLD SERIES

Including

Review of '79 Series

Official Play-by-Play, Each Game

Official Composite Box Score

World Series Tables—Attendance, Money,

Results

Pirates celebration scene after World Series victory over Orioles.

World Series

WORLD SERIES CHAMPIONS, 1903-1978

New York, A. L.	22	1923-27-28-32-36-37-38-39-41-43-47-49-50-51-52-53-56-58-61-62-77-78
St. Louis, N. L.	8	1926-31-34-42-44-46-64-67
New York, N. L.	6	1905-21-22-33-54 (Giants). 1969 (Mets)
Philadelphia, A.L.	5	1910-11-13-29-30
Boston, A.L.	5	1903-12-15-16-18
Pittsburgh, N.L.	5	1909-25-60-71-79
Cincinnati, N.L.	4	1919-40-75-76
Los Angeles, N.L.	3	1959-63-65
Detroit, A.L.	3	1935-45-68
Oakland, A.L.	3	1972-73-74
Chicago, A.L.	2	1906-17
Chicago, N. L.	2	1907-08
Cleveland, A. L.	2	1920-48
Baltimore, A.L.	2	1966-70
Boston, N. L.	1	1914
Washington, A.L.	1	1924
Brooklyn, N. L.	1	1955
Milwaukee, N.L.	1	1957

American League has won 45, National League 31.

RESULTS OF WORLD SERIES GAMES OF 1979

Game	Where Played	Date	Winner		Winner	Loser	Att.
First	Baltimore	Oct. 10	Baltimore	5-4	Flanagan	Kison	53,735
Second	Baltimore	Oct. 11	Pittsburgh	3-2	D. Rob'son	Stanhouse	53,739
Third	Pittsburgh	Oct. 12	Baltimore	8-4	McGregor	Candelaria	50,848
Fourth	Pittsburgh	Oct. 13	Baltimore	9-6	Stoddard	Tekulve	50,883
Fifth	Pittsburgh	Oct. 14	Pittsburgh	7-1	Blyleven	Flanagan	50,920
Sixth	Baltimore	Oct. 16	Pittsburgh	4-0	Candelaria	Palmer	53,739
Seventh	Baltimore	Oct. 17	Pittsburgh	4-1	Jackson	McGregor	53,733

ROSTERS OF ELIGIBLE PLAYERS FOR WORLD SERIES

Pittsburgh Pirates—Matthew Alexander, James B. Bibby, Rikalbert Blyleven, John R. Candelaria, Michael A. Easler, Timothy J. Foli, Philip M. Garner, Grant D. Jackson, Bruce E. Kison, Leondaus Lacy, Bill Madlock, John D. Milner, Omar R. Moreno, Steven R. Nicosia, N. Edward Ott, David G. Parker, David A. Roberts, Don A. Robinson, William H. Robinson, Enrique Romo, James P. Rooker, Manuel D. Sanguillen, Wilver D. Stargell, Renaldo A. Stennett, Kenton C. Tekulve; Charles W. Tanner, manager; Joseph P. Lonnett, Alex Monchak, Robert R. Skinner, coaches; Tony Bartirome, trainer.

Baltimore Orioles—Benigno F. Ayala, Mark H. Belanger, Alonza B. Bumbry, Terrence M. Crowley, Richard F. Dauer, Douglas V. DeCinces, J. Rikard Dempsey, Michael K. Flanagan, Alfonso R. (Kiko) Garcia, H. Patrick Kelly, John L. Lowenstein, Felix A. (Tippy) Martinez, J. Dennis Martinez, Lee A. May, Scott H. McGregor, Eddie C. Murray, James A. Palmer, Gary S. Roenicke, Kenneth W. Singleton, David L. Skaggs, Billy E. Smith, Donald J. Stanhouse, Samuel L. Stewart, Timothy P. Stoddard, Steven M. Stone; Earl S. Weaver, manager; James G. Frey, Elrod J. Hendricks, Raymond R. Miller, Calvin E. Ripken, Frank Robinson, coaches; Ralph Salvon, trainer.

Bill Robinson was the first Pirates player to greet Willie Stargell after his Series-winning home run in the sixth inning of Game 7.

Stargell Swat Capped Series Turnaround

By LARRY WIGGE

If Reggie Jackson is Mr. October, then Willie Stargell is Mr. October 17.

The last two times the Pittsburgh Pirates have won the World Series, it was Willie Stargell . . . in Baltimore . . . in the seventh game of the Series . . . on October 17.

A glance back in time:

October 17, 1971, Willie, then a 30-year-old left fielder for the Pirates, hit an eighth-inning single and scored the deciding run as the Pirates defeated the Orioles, 2-1, in the seventh game of the World Series at Memorial Stadium.

October 17, 1979, now a 38-year-old first baseman and accepted leader of the club, Willie clouted a two-run, sixth-inning homer that provided the wherewithal for a 4-1 triumph and another Pittsburgh world championship, the fifth in club history.

For his four hits and two RBIs in the clinching encounter, and for his 12 hits, three homers, seven RBIs, and .400 batting average in the seven games, Wilver Dornel Stargell was the unanimous choice for Most Valuable Player of the 76th World Series.

Stargell's homer climaxed an amazing comeback for the Pirates, who trailed three games to one and had just succumbed to a six-run Orioles' eighth-inning explosion to lose 9-6 in Game Four. The Bucs became only the fourth team in history to win a seven-game Series after trailing three to one.

"What can you say about a man who's going to the Hall of Fame?" Pirates' Manager Chuck Tanner said of Stargell. "He came through for us all year and down the stretch he acted like he was 25."

Even with Stargell's heroics, the Bucs, like all champions, needed a lift from the unexpected heroes. Like Jim Rooker.

Until Rooker, the 37-year-old lefthander with only four season victories, took the mound at Three Rivers Stadium October 14, Pirate prospects for success were gloomier than the weather that chilled and showered on the spectators before moderating into the 60s.

"I would have bet against me," Rooker admitted after baffling the Orioles on three hits for five innings. "I told Steve (Nicosia, the Pirates' catcher), 'It's up to you and me to get the rest of the guys over the hump. I'm going to win this one.'"

Bert Blyleven, making his first relief appearance since 1972 when he was with the Minnesota Twins, made truth of Rooker's prediction to Nicosia by hurling four innings of three-hit ball, and the Pirates, just four innings away from elimination, started the long road back with a 7-1 victory.

In addition to the contributions of Rooker and Blyleven, the Pirates pulled together for their skipper. Manager Tanner had learned that his mother, 70-year-old Anne Tanner, had died that morning in Greenville, Pa., 57 miles away.

"He stood 10 feet tall," Stargell said of Tanner. "I learned a lot about the man—not the manager, the man."

What later might be referred to as a snowballing momentum effected by the Bucs' fifth game victory carried over into Baltimore's Memorial Stadium two days later when Pittsburgh evened the series with a 4-0 triumph authored by John Candelaria (six innings) and Kent Tekulve (three innings).

This was the same Candelaria who was battered for five runs in three innings of Game Three and the same Tekulve who was shellacked for three runs in 1⅔ innings in Game Four.

Candelaria scattered six hits and Tekulve surrendered only one safety as the Pirates' tandem combined for the first World Series shutout since Luis Tiant of the Red Sox blanked the Reds, 6-0, in the first game of the 1975 Series.

In Game Seven, until Stargell delivered the blow that dimmed the Orioles' hopes for a third world title, Scott McGregor had scattered four hits and appeared well in command, holding a 1-0 lead.

When Willie strolled to the plate in the sixth inning, he crashed McGregor's first pitch over the right-center field wall to furnish all the runs the Pirates needed for victory.

The homer made a winner out of Grant Jackson, who ironically toiled in the Baltimore bullpen in 1971 when the two teams previously met for the world title.

The Pirates scored two more runs in the ninth inning as Orioles' Manager Earl Weaver paraded a record five pitchers to the mound.

Then a pair of walks opened the Baltimore ninth, once again bringing Tekulve to the mound. The by-play supplied by Stargell was typical of the close-knit Pittsburgh roster.

"I told him," said Willie, " 'Show them why you're the best in the National League and if you don't think you can do that, then you play first base and I'll pitch.' "

But the Orioles' rally fizzled. The Series which had opened so positively for Baltimore flickered by like a bad dream.

It was the Pirates' hopes for a title that were dampened from the outset. The Series began in Baltimore, where rain and cold forced postponement of the opener. Once the Series started, however, the Orioles wasted little time by scoring five runs in the first inning, thanks to a costly throwing error by Pirates' second baseman Phil Garner. ("It was like throwing a bar of soap," said Garner.)

The miscue with the bases loaded accounted for two runs. A wild pitch by Bruce Kison and a home run by Doug DeCinces culminated the rally. The Orioles held on for a 5-4 victory as Mike Flanagan hurled a complete game, despite permitting 11 hits, including four by right fielder Dave Parker.

The Pirates evened the Series the next night. The hero of Game Two was Manny Sanguillen, one of three Pirates (Stargell and Kison were the others) left from the 1971 World Series. With two out in the top of the ninth and Ed Ott on second, Sanguillen was summoned to pinch-hit against Orioles' reliever Don Stanhouse. Sanguillen sliced a two-strike single to right field. First baseman Eddie Murray cut off Ken Singleton's throw to the plate and relayed the ball to catcher Rick Dempsey too late to tag the sliding Ott for a 3-2 Pittsburgh decision.

Baltimore shortstop Kiko Garcia flexed his muscles in the third game—delayed by rain for 67 minutes after 2½ innings with Pittsburgh in front 3-0—by collecting four hits, including a bases-loaded triple to highlight a five-run fourth inning as the Orioles coasted to an 8-4 verdict.

After the Pirates had assumed a 6-3 lead in previously mentioned Game Four, the Orioles seemingly wrapped up the Series with a devastating six-run eighth-inning rally for a 9-6 triumph. Pinch-hitter John Lowenstein doubled for two runs. Another pinch-swinger, Terry Crowley, plated two more runs with a two-base blow. Even pitcher Tim Stoddard, who had never batted in the major leagues, singled for one run, before Al Bumbry drove in the sixth run with a forceout.

But Bill Madlock had four singles to pace the Pirates offensively in their 7-1 fifth-game triumph prior to the 4-0 decision which knotted the Series at three games apiece.

Rich Dauer's homer gave the Orioles a 1-0 lead in the finale. But Willie Stargell ("Pops" to his teammates) put on his power display to become the oldest MVP in the 25-year history of the award.

AT BALTIMORE   Game 1   OCTOBER 10

Pittsburgh	AB.	R.	H.	PO.	A.	E.
Moreno, cf	5	0	0	4	0	0
Foli, ss	5	1	1	1	3	1
Parker, rf	5	1	4	3	0	0
B. Robinson, lf	5	1	1	2	0	0
Stargell, 1b	5	1	1	7	0	1
Madlock, 3b	3	0	0	0	1	0
Nicosia, c	4	0	0	4	1	0
Garner, 2b	4	0	3	3	2	1
Kison, p	0	0	0	0	1	0
Rooker, p	1	0	0	0	2	0
aSanguillen	1	0	0	0	0	0
Romo, p	0	0	0	0	0	0
bLacy	1	0	0	0	0	0
D. Robinson, p	0	0	0	0	0	0
cStennett	1	0	1	0	0	0
Jackson, p	0	0	0	0	0	0
Totals	40	4	11	24	10	3

Baltimore	AB.	R.	H.	PO.	A.	E.
Bumbry, cf	4	1	1	3	0	0
Belanger, ss	3	1	0	1	4	1
Singleton, rf	3	0	1	2	0	0
Murray, 1b	2	1	1	12	1	0
Lowenstein, lf	4	1	0	1	0	0
Roenicke, lf	0	0	0	0	0	0
DeCinces, 3b	3	1	1	0	4	2
Smith, 2b	2	0	1	1	3	0
dDauer, 2b	1	0	1	0	1	0
Dempsey, c	4	0	0	7	0	0
Flanagan, p	4	0	0	2	0	0
Totals	30	5	6	27	15	3

Pittsburgh	0	0	0	1	0	2	0	1	0 – 4
Baltimore	5	0	0	0	0	0	0	0	x – 5

Pittsburgh	IP.	H.	R.	ER.	BB.	SO.
Kison (Loser)	⅓	3	5	4	2	0
Rooker	3⅔	2	0	0	1	2
Romo	1	0	0	0	2	0
D. Robinson	2	0	0	0	1	1
Jackson	1	1	0	0	0	1

Baltimore	IP.	H.	R.	ER.	BB.	SO.
Flanagan (Winner)	9	11	4	2	1	7

Bases on balls—Off Kison 2 (Belanger, Murray), off Rooker 1 (DeCinces), off Romo 2 (Murray, Smith), off D. Robinson 1 (Singleton), off Flanagan 1 (Madlock).

Strikeouts—By Rooker 2 (Belanger, Lowenstein), by D. Robinson 1 (Flanagan), by Jackson 1 (Flanagan), by Flanagan 7 (B. Robinson, Stargell 2, Garner, Moreno 2, Nicosia).

aGrounded out for Rooker in fifth. bReached first base on error for Romo in sixth. cSingled for D. Robinson in eighth. dSingled for Smith in eighth. Runs batted in—Lowenstein, DeCinces 2, Stargell 2, Garner 2. Two-base hits—Parker, Garner. Home runs—DeCinces, Stargell. Stolen base—Murray. Caught stealing—Parker. Sacrifice hit—Bumbry. Wild pitch—Kison. Double play—Madlock, Garner and Stargell. Left on bases—Pittsburgh 10, Baltimore 8. Umpires—Neudecker (A.L.) plate, Engel (N.L.) first base, Goetz (A.L.) second base, Tata (N.L.) third base, McKean (A.L.) left field, Runge (N.L.) right field. Time—3:18. Attendance—53,735.

FIRST INNING

Pittsburgh—Moreno bounced to Smith. Foli flied to Lowenstein. Parker grounded a double down the right field line. Robinson struck out. No runs, one hit, no errors, one left.

Baltimore—Bumbry lined a single to left-center. Belanger walked on four pitches, Bumbry advancing to second. Singleton bounced to Kison, who fumbled the ball but recovered in time to throw Singleton out at first, Bumbry advancing to third and Belanger to second. Murray walked, loading the bases. Lowenstein hit a possible double-play grounder to Garner, who threw the ball past Foli covering at second and into left field for an error, Bumbry and Belanger scoring and Murray advancing to third. With DeCinces batting, Kison made a wild pitch, Murray scoring and Lowenstein advancing to second. DeCinces homered into the left-field bleachers, Lowenstein scoring ahead of him. Smith singled to right. Rooker replaced Kison on the mound for Pittsburgh. Dempsey lined to Foli, who then threw wildly past first base trying to double Smith, who advanced to second on the error. Flanagan tapped in front of the plate to Nicosia, who threw on to first for the out. Five runs, three hits, two errors, one left.

SECOND INNING

Pittsburgh—Stargell struck out. Madlock grounded to DeCinces. Nicosia grounded to Smith. No runs, no hits, no errors, none left.

Baltimore—Bumbry grounded to Rooker. Belanger was called out on strikes. Singleton beat out an infield single to the right of Madlock. Murray singled to center, Singleton stopping at second. Lowenstein struck out. No runs, two hits, no errors, two left.

THIRD INNING

Pittsburgh—Garner was called out on strikes. Rooker bunted to Flanagan, who threw on to first for the out. Moreno lined to Bumbry. No runs, no hits, no errors, none left.

Baltimore—DeCinces walked. Smith grounded into a double play, Madlock to Garner to Stargell. Dempsey grounded to Garner. No runs, no hits, no errors, none left.

Cy Young Award winner Mike Flanagan receives congrats after hurling the Orioles to a 5-4 first game Series victory.

FOURTH INNING

Pittsburgh—Foli singled to center. Parker singled to right, Foli advancing to third. Robinson grounded to DeCinces, Foli holding third and Parker advancing to second. Stargell grounded to Smith, Foli scoring and Parker advancing to third. Madlock walked. Nicosia forced Madlock, Belanger to Smith. One run, two hits, no errors, two left.

Baltimore—Flanagan reached first base safely when his grounder went under the glove of Stargell for an error. Bumbry sacrificed, Rooker to Garner covering first, Flanagan advancing to second. Belanger lined to Moreno. Singleton flied to Parker. No runs, no hits, one error, one left.

FIFTH INNING

Pittsburgh—Garner doubled to left. Sanguillen batted for Rooker and grounded to Belanger, Garner holding second. Moreno struck out. Foli bounced to DeCinces. No runs, one hit, no errors, one left.

Baltimore—Romo came in to pitch for Pittsburgh. Murray walked. Lowenstein flied to Moreno. DeCinces flied to Parker. With Smith batting, Murray stole second. Smith was then walked intentionally. Dempsey flied to Robinson. No runs, no hits, no errors, two left.

SIXTH INNING

Pittsburgh—Parker singled to center. Robinson singled to right, Parker stopping at second. Stargell struck out. Madlock flied to Singleton. Nicosia bounced to the left of DeCinces, who bobbled the ball for an error, loading the bases. Garner grounded a single to left, Parker and Robinson scoring and Nicosia stopping at second. Lacy batted for Romo and bounced to DeCinces, who fumbled the ball and then failed in his effort to tag Nicosia, running from second, the error loading the bases. Moreno flied to Bumbry. Two runs, three hits, two errors, three left.

Baltimore—Don Robinson came in to pitch for Pittsburgh. Flanagan struck out. Bumbry bounced to Foli. Belanger grounded to Foli. No runs, no hits, no errors, none left.

SEVENTH INNING

Pittsburgh—Foli grounded to Belanger. Parker bounced to DeCinces. Bill Robinson flied to Singleton. No runs, no hits, no errors, none left.

Baltimore—Singleton walked. Murray lined to Moreno. Lowenstein flied to Bill Robinson. DeCinces lined to Parker, who made a fine catch in right-center. No runs, no hits, no errors, one left.

EIGHTH INNING

Pittsburgh—Roenicke replaced Lowenstein in left field for Baltimore. Stargell homered into the right-field bleachers. Madlock lined to Bumbry. Nicosia struck out. Garner singled when his high bouncer to third was lost in the lights by DeCinces. Stennett batted for Don Robinson and singled to right, Garner advancing to third. Moreno was called out on strikes. One run, three hits, no errors, two left.

Baltimore—Jackson came in to pitch for Pittsburgh. Dauer batted for Smith and singled to center. Dempsey flied to Moreno. Flanagan, attempting to bunt, struck out. Bumbry forced Dauer, Foli to Garner. No runs, one hit, no errors, one left.

NINTH INNING

Pittsburgh—Dauer stayed in the game at second base for Baltimore. Foli bounced to Belanger. Parker grounded a sharp single to center. With Bill Robinson batting, Flanagan threw to Murray, trapping Parker off first, but Parker was safe at second when he kicked Murray's throw out of the glove of Belanger for an error on the shortstop. Robinson grounded to Dauer, Parker advancing to third. Stargell popped to Belanger in short left-center. No runs, one hit, one error, one left.

AT BALTIMORE   Game 2   OCTOBER 11

Pittsburgh	AB	R	H	PO	A	E		Baltimore	AB	R	H	PO	A	E
Moreno, cf	5	0	1	1	0	0		Bumbry, cf	5	0	0	5	0	0
Foli, ss	4	0	1	0	5	1		Belanger, ss	3	0	0	1	2	0
Parker, rf	4	0	1	1	1	1		cCrowley	0	0	0	0	0	0
Stargell, 1b	4	1	1	12	0	0		T. Martinez, p	0	0	0	0	0	0
Milner, lf	3	1	1	3	0	0		Stanhouse, p	0	0	0	0	0	0
dB. Robinson	1	0	1	0	0	0		Singleton, rf	4	1	1	1	0	0
eAlexander, lf	0	0	0	0	0	0		Murray, 1b	3	1	3	10	2	0
Madlock, 3b	4	0	2	0	4	0		DeCinces, 3b	4	0	0	0	6	1
Ott, c	3	1	1	6	0	0		Lowenstein, lf	3	0	1	1	0	0
Garner, 2b	2	0	1	4	6	0		Smith, 2b	4	0	0	3	0	0
Blyleven, p	2	0	0	0	0	0		Dempsey, c	3	0	1	4	2	0
aEasler	0	0	0	0	0	0		Palmer, p	2	0	0	1	1	0
D. Robinson, p	0	0	0	0	1	0		bKelly	0	0	0	0	0	0
fSanguillen	1	0	1	0	0	0		Garcia, ss	1	0	0	1	0	0
Tekulve, p	0	0	0	0	0	0								
Totals	33	3	11	27	17	2		Totals	32	2	6	27	13	1

Pittsburgh	0	2	0	0 0	0	0	1 – 3
Baltimore	0	1	0	0 1	0	0	0 – 2

Pittsburgh	IP	H	R	ER	BB	SO
Blyleven	6	5	2	2	2	1
D. Robinson (Winner)	2	1	0	0	3	2
Tekulve (Save)	1	0	0	0	0	2

Baltimore	IP	H	R	ER	BB	SO
Palmer	7	8	2	2	2	3
T. Martinez	1*	1	0	0	0	1
Stanhouse (Loser)	1	2	1	1	1	0

*Pitched to one batter in ninth.

Bases on balls—Off Blyleven 2 (Lowenstein, Murray), off D. Robinson 3 (Dempsey, Kelly, Crowley), off Palmer 2 (Garner, Easler), off Stanhouse 1 (Garner).

Strikeouts—By Blyleven 1 (Palmer), by D. Robinson 2 (Bumbry, Singleton), by Tekulve 2 (Dempsey, Garcia), by Palmer 3 (Moreno 2, Ott), by T. Martinez 1 (Stargell).

aWalked for Blyleven in seventh. bWalked for Palmer in seventh. cWalked for Belanger in seventh. dSingled for Milner in ninth. eRan for B. Robinson in ninth. fSingled for D. Robinson in ninth. Runs batted in—Madlock, Ott, Murray 2, Sanguillen. Two-base hit—Murray. Home run—Murray. Caught stealing—Madlock, Alexander. Sacrifice fly—Ott. Wild pitch—Palmer. Double plays—Murray and Palmer; Madlock, Garner and Stargell; Murray, Belanger and Smith; Parker and Ott; Foli, Garner, Madlock and Garner. Left on bases—Pittsburgh 7, Baltimore 8. Umpires—Engel (N.L.) plate, Goetz (A.L.) first base, Tata (N.L.) second base, McKean (A.L.) third base, Runge (N.L.) left field, Neudecker (A.L.) right field. Time—3:13. Attendance—53,739.

FIRST INNING

Pittsburgh—Moreno singled to center. With Moreno running, Foli fouled out to Murray, who threw to Palmer covering first to double up Moreno. Parker grounded to DeCinces. No runs, one hit, no errors, none left.

Baltimore—Bumbry grounded to Garner. Belanger flied to Milner on the warning track. Singleton bounced to Garner. No runs, no hits, no errors, none left.

SECOND INNING

Pittsburgh—Stargell singled to right. Milner singled to center, Stargell stopping at second. Madlock lined a single to right-center, Stargell scoring and Milner advancing to third. Ott flied to Bumbry in deep left-center, Milner scoring after the catch and Madlock holding first. With Garner batting, Madlock was caught stealing, Dempsey to Smith. Garner grounded to Belanger. Two runs, three hits, no errors, none left.

Baltimore—Murray homered into the second deck of stands down the right-field line. DeCinces grounded to Madlock. Lowenstein walked. Smith lined to Garner. Dempsey grounded a single off the glove of Foli, Lowenstein advancing to third when the ball rolled into short center. Palmer struck out. One run, two hits, no errors, two left.

THIRD INNING

Pittsburgh—Blyleven lined to Bumbry. Moreno struck out. Foli singled to right. With Parker batting, Palmer made a wild pitch, Foli advancing to second. Parker grounded to DeCinces. No runs, one hit, no errors, one left.

Baltimore—Bumbry flied to Milner. Belanger lifted a fly to short right where Parker, after calling Garner off the play, dropped the ball for a two-base error. Singleton grounded to Garner, Belanger advancing to third. Murray walked on four pitches. DeCinces grounded to Foli. No runs, no hits, one error, two left.

FOURTH INNING

Pittsburgh—Stargell flied to Lowenstein, who made a sliding catch after misjudging the ball. Milner popped to Murray. Madlock grounded to DeCinces. No runs, no hits, no errors, none left.

ED OTT crosses plate with winning run in top of ninth after Manny Sanguillen's pinch-single gave Pirates 3-2 triumph in Game 2.

Baltimore—Lowenstein singled when Garner could not handle his sharp grounder. Smith grounded into a double play, Madlock to Garner to Stargell. Dempsey bounced to Foli. No runs, one hit, no errors, none left.

FIFTH INNING

Pittsburgh—Ott bunted to Palmer, who threw on to first for the out. Garner singled to center. Blyleven, attempting to sacrifice, bunted into a double play, Murray to Belanger to Smith covering first. No runs, one hit, no errors, none left.

Baltimore—Palmer flied to Milner. Bumbry grounded to Madlock. Belanger flied to Moreno on the warning track in left-center. No runs, no hits, no errors, none left.

SIXTH INNING

Pittsburgh—Moreno bounced to DeCinces. Foli flied to Bumbry. Parker singled to center. Stargell grounded to DeCinces. No runs, one hit, no errors, one left.

Baltimore—Singleton lined a single to left. Murray lined a double into the alley in left-center, Singleton scoring. DeCinces bounced to Foli, Murray advancing to third. With the infield in, Lowenstein lined to Parker, whose throw to Ott easily caught Murray attempting to score after the catch for a double play. One run, two hits, no errors, none left.

SEVENTH INNING

Pittsburgh—Milner flied to Bumbry. Madlock hit a smash to the left of De-Cinces, who made a nice stop but then threw wildly past Murray at first. Madlock was credited with a hit and advanced to second on the error. Ott struck out. Garner was walked intentionally. Easler batted for Blyleven and walked, loading the bases. Moreno struck out. No runs, one hit, one error, three left.

Baltimore—Don Robinson came in to pitch for Pittsburgh. Smith popped to Stargell. Dempsey walked. Kelly batted for Palmer and walked on a 3-2 pitch, Dempsey advancing to second. Bumbry struck out. Crowley batted for Belanger and walked, loading the bases. Singleton struck out. No runs, no hits, no errors, three left.

EIGHTH INNING

Pittsburgh—Garcia came in to play shortstop and Tippy Martinez came in to pitch for Baltimore. Garcia assumed the ninth spot in the batting order and Martinez the second. Foli flied to Singleton. Parker grounded to DeCinces. Stargell was called out on strikes. No runs, no hits, no errors, none left.

Baltimore—Murray looped a single to center. DeCinces bunted to Robinson, whose throw to Foli was dropped for an error on the shortstop. Lowenstein grounded into a double play, Foli to Garner for the force on DeCinces at second, with Garner then throwing to Madlock, who returned the throw to Garner before Murray was tagged out by the second baseman. Lowenstein remained at first during the rundown. Smith bounced to Garner. No runs, one hit, one error, one left.

NINTH INNING

Pittsburgh—Bill Robinson batted for Milner and lined a single to left. Stanhouse replaced Martinez on the mound for Baltimore. Alexander ran for Robinson. With Madlock batting, Alexander was caught stealing, Dempsey to Garcia. Madlock flied to Bumbry in deep center. Ott singled off the chest of Smith on a grounder that took a final explosive hop. Garner walked, Ott advancing to second. Sanguillen batted for Don Robinson and lined a single to right, Ott scoring and Garner advancing to third. Moreno lined to Smith. One run, three hits, no errors, two left.

Baltimore—Alexander remained in the game as a left fielder and Tekulve came in to pitch for Pittsburgh. Dempsey struck out. Garcia was called out on strikes. Bumbry bounced to Foli. No runs, no hits, no errors, none left.

AT PITTSBURGH Game 3 OCTOBER 12

Baltimore	AB.	R.	H.	PO.	A.	E.
Garcia, ss	4	2	4	0	4	0
Ayala, lf	2	1	2	0	0	0
aBumbry, cf	2	1	1	2	0	0
Singleton, rf	5	0	2	4	0	0
Murray, 1b	4	0	0	7	1	0
DeCinces, 3b	5	0	0	0	1	0
Roenicke, cf-lf	5	0	1	5	1	0
Dauer, 2b	5	1	1	2	3	0
Dempsey, c	5	2	2	7	0	0
McGregor, p	3	1	0	0	0	0
Totals	40	8	13	27	10	0

Pittsburgh	AB.	R.	H.	PO.	A.	E.
Moreno, cf	4	1	2	2	1	0
Foli, ss	4	0	0	6	1	1
Parker, rf	3	0	0	2	0	0
B. Robinson, lf	4	0	1	4	1	0
Stargell, 1b	4	2	2	8	1	1
Madlock, 3b	4	0	1	0	0	0
Nicosia, c	4	1	1	8	0	0
Garner, 2b	4	0	1	2	1	0
Candelaria, p	1	0	1	0	0	0
Romo, p	1	0	0	0	1	0
Jackson, p	0	0	0	0	0	0
bLacy	1	0	0	0	0	0
Tekulve, p	0	0	0	1	0	0
Totals	34	4	9	27	11	2

Baltimore	0	0	2	5	0	0	1	0	0 – 8
Pittsburgh	1	2	0	0	0	1	0	0	0 – 4

Baltimore	IP.	H.	R.	ER.	BB.	SO.
McGregor (Winner)	9	9	4	4	0	6

Pittsburgh	IP.	H.	R.	ER.	BB.	SO.
Candelaria (Loser)	3*	8	6	5	2	2
Romo	3⅔	5	2	2	1	4
Jackson	⅓	0	0	0	0	0
Tekulve	2	0	0	0	0	1

*Pitched to four batters in fourth.

Bases on balls—Off Candelaria 2 (Garcia, Murray), off Romo 1 (McGregor).

Strikeouts—By McGregor 6 (B. Robinson 2, Madlock, Parker, Stargell, Moreno), by Candelaria 2 (Singleton, DeCinces), by Romo 4 (Roenicke, Dauer, Dempsey, McGregor), by Tekulve 1 (Roenicke).

aHit by pitcher for Ayala in fourth. bLined out for Jackson in seventh. Runs batted in—Garcia 4, Ayala 2, Singleton, DeCinces, Parker, Madlock, Garner 2. Two-base hits—Garcia, Moreno 2, Garner, Dauer, Stargell, Dempsey. Three-base hit—Garcia. Home run—Ayala. Sacrifice fly—Parker. Wild pitch—Romo. Hit by pitcher—By Romo (Bumbry). Balk—McGregor. Left on bases—Baltimore 9, Pittsburgh 4. Umpires—Goetz (A.L.) plate, Tata (N.L.) first base, McKean (A.L.) second base, Runge (N.L.) third base, Neudecker (A.L.) left field, Engel (N.L.) right field. Time—2:51. Attendance 50,848.

FIRST INNING

Baltimore—Garcia doubled down the right-field line. Ayala looped a single to center, Garcia stopping at third. Singleton struck out. Murray lined to Garner. DeCinces struck out. No runs, two hits, no errors, two left.

Pittsburgh—Moreno doubled to right-center. With Foli batting, McGregor balked, Moreno moving to third. Foli fouled to Dempsey. Parker lined to Roenicke, Moreno scoring after the catch. Robinson struck out. One run, one hit, no errors, none left.

SECOND INNING

Baltimore—Roenicke grounded to Foli. Dauer also grounded to Foli. Dempsey bounced to Foli. No runs, no hits, no errors, none left.

Pittsburgh—Stargell lined a single to center. Madlock was called out on strikes. Nicosia grounded a single to left, Stargell stopping at second. Garner drilled a double to left-center to score Stargell and Nicosia, but when Garner tried to stretch it into a triple he was thrown out, Roenicke to Garcia to DeCinces to Murray to Dauer. Candelaria singled to left. Moreno grounded to Dauer. Two runs, four hits, no errors, one left.

THIRD INNING

Baltimore—McGregor fouled to Stargell. Garcia walked. Ayala hit a 3-2 pitch over the wall in left-center for a home run, Garcia scoring ahead of him. Singleton grounded a single to center. Murray walked, Singleton advancing to second. DeCinces flied to Robinson. Roenicke singled to left, but Singleton was thrown out trying to score, Robinson to Nicosia. Two runs, three hits, no errors, two left.

Pittsburgh—Foli flied to Roenicke. Parker struck out. Robinson singled to left when Ayala misjudged his line drive. Stargell struck out. No runs, one hit, no errors, one left.

Lefthander **SCOTT McGREGOR** scattered nine hits in hurling the Orioles to an 8-4 decision in Game 3.

FOURTH INNING

Baltimore—Dauer doubled to left-center. Dempsey singled to right, Dauer stopping at third. McGregor grounded to Foli, who booted the ball for an error, loading the bases. Garcia tripled to right-center, Dauer, Dempsey and McGregor scoring. Romo replaced Candelaria on the mound for Pittsburgh. Bumbry batted for Ayala and was hit by a pitch. Singleton singled to center, Garcia scoring and Bumbry advancing to third. Murray flied to Parker, both runners holding their bases. DeCinces forced Singleton, Foli to Garner, Bumbry scoring. With Roenicke batting, DeCinces advanced to second on a wild pitch by Romo. Roenicke struck out. Five runs, four hits, one error, one left.

Pittsburgh—Bumbry remained in the game to play center field for Baltimore with Roenicke shifting to left. Madlock flied to Singleton. Nicosia flied to Singleton on the warning track. Garner grounded to Garcia. No runs, no hits, no errors, none left.

FIFTH INNING

Baltimore—Dauer struck out. Dempsey was called out on strikes. McGregor walked. Garcia singled to left, McGregor stopping at second. Bumbry singled to load the bases when Garner made a diving stop to keep his sharp grounder in the infield. Singleton flied to Moreno. No runs, two hits, no errors, three left.

Pittsburgh—Romo flied to Singleton. Moreno doubled into the left-field corner. Foli flied to Roenicke. Parker lined to Singleton at the wall in right. No runs, one hit, no errors, one left.

SIXTH INNING

Baltimore—Murray lined to Robinson. DeCinces grounded to Romo. Roenicke flied to Robinson. No runs, no hits, no errors, none left.

Pittsburgh—Robinson struck out and was tagged out by Dempsey after the ball bounced into the dirt. Stargell doubled to right-center. Madlock singled to center, Stargell scoring. Nicosia flied to Bumbry against the wall in center. Garner flied to Roenicke in deep left. One run, two hits, no errors, one left.

SEVENTH INNING

Baltimore—Dauer flied to Moreno. Dempsey doubled to right-center. McGregor struck out. Garcia blooped a single to center to score Dempsey and advanced to second when Stargell, attempting to throw him out at second after cutting off the throw from the outfield, hit him with the toss for an error. Jackson replaced Romo on the mound for Pittsburgh. Bumbry flied to Robinson. One run, two hits, one error, one left.

Pittsburgh—Lacy batted for Jackson and lined to Dauer, who made a diving catch. Moreno was called out on strikes. Foli flied to Roenicke. No runs, no hits, no errors, none left.

EIGHTH INNING

Baltimore—Tekulve came in to pitch for Pittsburgh. Singleton grounded to Garner. Murray grounded out, Stargell to Tekulve covering first. DeCinces hit a sharp grounder to the right of Foli, who made a diving stop and threw him out at first. No runs, no hits, no errors, none left.

Pittsburgh—Parker grounded to Dauer. Robinson grounded to Garcia. Stargell popped to Murray. No runs, no hits, no errors, none left.

NINTH INNING

Baltimore—Roenicke struck out. Dauer bounced to Foli. Dempsey fouled to Parker. No runs, no hits, no errors, none left.

Pittsburgh—Madlock bounced to Garcia. Nicosia grounded to Dauer. Garner lined to Bumbry. No runs, no hits, no errors, none left.

AT PITTSBURGH Game 4 OCTOBER 13

Baltimore	AB.	R.	H.	PO.	A.	E.
Bumbry, cf	5	1	1	1	1	0
Garcia, ss	5	2	2	6	5	0
Belanger, ss	0	0	0	0	0	0
Singleton, rf	5	0	3	0	0	0
Murray, 1b	5	1	0	8	1	0
DeCinces, 3b	1	1	0	2	0	0
Roenicke, lf	3	0	0	2	0	0
cLowenstein, lf	2	1	1	1	0	0
Dauer, 2b	3	0	1	1	2	0
dSmith, 2b	0	1	0	0	0	0
Skaggs, c	3	1	1	2	2	0
eCrowley	1	0	1	0	0	0
fDempsey, c	0	1	0	3	0	0
D. Martinez, p	0	0	0	0	1	0
Stewart, p	1	0	0	1	2	0
aMay	1	0	0	0	0	0
Stone, p	0	0	0	0	0	0
bKelly	1	0	1	0	0	0
Stoddart, p	1	0	1	0	2	0
Totals	37	9	12	27	16	0

Pittsburgh	AB.	R.	H.	PO.	A.	E.
Moreno, cf	5	0	2	2	0	0
Foli, ss	4	2	3	1	5	0
Parker, rf	5	0	2	1	0	0
Stargell, 1b	5	1	3	8	0	0
Milner, lf	3	1	2	2	0	0
D. Robinson, p	0	0	0	0	0	0
Tekulve, p	0	0	0	0	0	0
gEasler	1	0	0	0	0	0
Madlock, 3b	3	1	2	0	1	1
Ott, c	5	0	1	8	0	0
Garner, 2b	4	1	2	5	7	0
Bibby, p	3	0	0	0	0	0
Jackson, p	0	0	0	0	0	0
B. Robinson, lf	1	0	0	0	0	0
Totals	39	6	17	27	13	1

Baltimore	0	0	3	0	0	0	0	6	0	— 9
Pittsburgh	0	4	0	0	1	1	0	0	0	— 6

Baltimore	IP.	H.	R.	ER.	BB.	SO.
D. Martinez	1⅓	6	4	4	0	0
Stewart	2⅔	4	0	0	1	0
Stone	2	4	2	2	2	2
Stoddart (Winner)	3	3	0	0	1	3

Pittsburgh	IP.	H.	R.	ER.	BB.	SO.
Bibby	6⅓	7	3	2	2	7
Jackson	⅔	0	0	0	0	0
D. Robinson	⅓	2	3	3	1	0
Tekulve (Loser)	1⅔	3	3	3	2	1

Bases on balls—Off Stewart 1 (Milner), off Stone 2 (Foli, Madlock), off Stoddard 1 (Madlock), off Bibby 2 (DeCinces 2), off D. Robinson 1 (DeCinces), off Tekulve 2 (Smith, DeCinces).

Strikeouts—By Stone 2 (Bibby, Stargell), by Stoddard 3 (B. Robinson, Parker, Ott), by Bibby 7 (Garcia, Singleton, Murray 2, Roenicke, Stewart, May), by Tekulve 1 (Garcia).

aStruck out for Stewart in fifth. bSingled for Stone in seventh. cDoubled for Roenicke in eighth. dIntentionally walked for Dauer in eighth. eDoubled for Skaggs in eighth. fRan for Crowley in eighth. gFlied out for Tekulve in ninth. Runs batted in—Bumbry, Garcia 2, Singleton, Lowenstein, Crowley 2, Stoddard, Moreno, Parker, Stargell, Milner, Ott 2. Two-base hits—Madlock, Ott, Garcia, Singleton, Stargell, Milner, Parker, Lowenstein, Crowley. Home run—Stargell. Stolen base—DeCinces. Caught stealing—Madlock. Double plays—D. Martinez, Garcia and Murray; Dauer, Garcia and Murray; Foli, Garner and Murray 2; Garner, Foli and Stargell. Left on bases—Baltimore 6, Pittsburgh 10. Umpires—Tata (N.L.) plate, McKean (A.L.) first base, Runge (N.L.) second base, Neudecker (A.L.) third base, Engel (N.L.) left field, Goetz (A.L.) right field. Time—3:48. Attendance—50,883.

FIRST INNING

Baltimore—Bumbry grounded to Garner. Garcia struck out. Singleton also struck out. No runs, no hits, no errors, none left.

Pittsburgh—Moreno grounded to Garcia. Foli singled to center. Parker grounded into a double play, Martinez to Garcia to Murray. No runs, one hit, no errors, none left.

SECOND INNING

Baltimore—Murray struck out. DeCinces walked. As Roenicke struck out, De-Cinces stole second. Dauer popped to Garner. No runs, no hits, no errors, one left.

Pittsburgh—Stargell hit a 2-2 pitch over the center-field fence for a home run. Milner singled to right. Madlock lined a ground-rule double down the left-field line, Milner stopping at third. Ott cracked a ground-rule double to center, Milner and Madlock scoring. Garner singled to center, but Ott was thrown out trying to score, Bumbry to Murray to Skaggs to DeCinces, Garner taking second on the throw. Stewart replaced Martinez on the mound for Baltimore. Bibby lined to Stewart. Moreno singled to center, Garner scoring. With Foli batting, Moreno was picked off first, Stewart to Murray. Four runs, six hits, no errors, none left.

Baltimore manager **EARL WEAVER** contemplating another move in Game 4. Weaver's pinch-hitters keyed a six-run eighth inning in the 9-6 victory.

THIRD INNING

Baltimore—Skaggs grounded to Madlock, who threw wildly past first base for an error. Stewart struck out. Bumbry singled to center, Skaggs stopping at second. Garcia doubled to left-center, Skaggs and Bumbry scoring. Singleton doubled to the wall in left-center, Garcia scoring. Murray struck out. DeCinces flied to Milner. Three runs, three hits, one error, one left.

Pittsburgh—Foli beat out an infield single to third. Parker flied to Bumbry. Stargell doubled into the right-field corner, Foli stopping at third. Milner was walked intentionally, loading the bases. Madlock grounded into a double play, Dauer to Garcia to Murray. No runs, two hits, no errors, two left.

FOURTH INNING

Baltimore—Roenicke grounded to Madlock, who made a nice backhand stop of the ball and threw on to first for the out. Dauer singled to left. Skaggs grounded into a double play, Foli to Garner to Stargell. No runs, one hit, no errors, none left.

Pittsburgh—Ott lined to Roenicke. Garner singled to left. Bibby, attempting to sacrifice, forced Garner, Stewart to Garcia. Moreno grounded to Garcia, who stepped on second for the force on Bibby. No runs, one hit, no errors, one left.

FIFTH INNING

Baltimore—May batted for Stewart and struck out. Bumbry flied to Milner. Garcia lined to Moreno. No runs, no hits, no errors, none left.

Pittsburgh—Stone came in to pitch for Baltimore. Foli walked. Parker singled to left, Foli stopping at second. Stargell hit a soft pop to DeCinces. Milner doubled inside the line at first, Foli scoring and Parker stopping at third. Madlock was walked intentionally, loading the bases. Ott flied to Roenicke, the runners holding. Garner forced Madlock, Garcia to Dauer. One run, two hits, no errors, three left.

SIXTH INNING

Baltimore—Singleton lined a single to center. Murray grounded into a double play, Garner to Foli to Stargell. DeCinces walked. Roenicke flied to Parker. No runs, one hit, no errors, one left.

Pittsburgh—Bibby was called out on strikes. Moreno grounded to Dauer. Foli singled to right. Parker doubled to left, Foli scoring. Stargell struck out, Skaggs applying the tag after the pitch went into the dirt. One run, two hits, no errors, one left.

SEVENTH INNING

Baltimore—Dauer flied to Moreno. Skaggs singled to left. Kelly batted for Stone and singled when he topped the ball to the right of Stargell, whose throw to Garner covering first was not in time, Skaggs advancing to second. Bumbry grounded into a double play, Foli to Garner to Stargell. No runs, two hits, no errors, one left.

Pittsburgh—Stoddard came in to pitch for Baltimore. Milner popped to Garcia. Madlock walked. With Ott batting, Madlock was caught stealing, Skaggs to Garcia. Ott grounded off the leg of Stoddard to Murray, who stepped on first for the out. No runs, no hits, no errors, none left.

EIGHTH INNING

Baltimore—Don Robinson came in to pitch for Pittsburgh and Bill Robinson replaced Milner in left. Don Robinson assumed the fifth spot in the batting order and Bill Robinson the ninth. Garcia singled to right. Singleton drove a single to left off the glove of Foli, Garcia stopping at second. Murray forced Singleton, Foli to Garner, Garcia advancing to third. DeCinces walked, loading the bases. Tekulve replaced Robinson on the mound for Pittsburgh. Lowenstein batted for Roenicke and doubled into the right-field corner, Garcia and Murray scoring and DeCinces stopping at third. Smith batted for Dauer and was walked intentionally, loading the bases. Crowley batted for Skaggs and, on a 3-2 pitch, doubled into the right-field corner, DeCinces and Lowenstein scoring and Smith stopping at third. Stoddard, with the infield in, bounced a single to left, Smith scoring and Crowley advancing to third. Dempsey ran for Crowley. Bumbry forced Stoddard, Foli to Garner, Dempsey scoring. Garcia struck out. Six runs, five hits, no errors, one left.

Pittsburgh—Lowenstein, Smith and Dempsey remained in the game for Baltimore as left fielder, second baseman and catcher respectively. Garner bounced to Stoddard. Bill Robinson struck out. Moreno singled off the glove of Garcia to short left. Foli grounded to Garcia. No runs, one hit, no errors, one left.

NINTH INNING

Baltimore—Singleton grounded to Garner. Murray grounded to Garner. DeCinces walked. Lowenstein grounded to Garner. No runs, no hits, no errors, one left.

Pittsburgh—Belanger replaced Garcia at shortstop for Baltimore. Parker was called out on strikes. Stargell grounded a single to center. Easler batted for Tekulve and flied to Lowenstein. Madlock singled to center, Stargell advancing to third. Ott struck out. No runs, two hits, no errors, two left.

AT PITTSBURGH   Game 5   OCTOBER 14

Baltimore	AB.	R.	H.	PO.	A.	E.
Garcia, ss	4	0	0	2	1	0
Ayala, lf	1	0	0	2	0	0
bBumbry, cf	1	0	0	1	0	0
Singleton, rf	4	0	0	0	0	0
Murray, 1b	4	0	0	0	0	0
Roenicke, cf-lf	4	1	1	7	1	0
DeCinces, 3b	4	0	2	1	4	0
Dauer, 2b	3	0	0	2	1	0
dLowenstein	1	0	1	0	0	0
Dempsey, c	3	0	2	7	0	0
eCrowley	1	0	0	0	0	0
Flanagan, p	1	0	0	0	2	0
cKelly	1	0	0	0	0	0
Stoddard, p	0	0	0	0	1	1
T. Martinez, p	0	0	0	0	0	0
Stanhouse, p	0	0	0	0	0	1
Totals	32	1	6	24	10	2

Pittsburgh	AB.	R.	H.	PO.	A.	E.
Moreno, cf	4	1	0	3	0	0
Foli, ss	4	2	2	3	7	0
Parker, rf	4	1	2	1	0	0
B. Robinson, lf	4	0	1	2	0	0
Stargell, 1b	3	1	1	10	0	0
Madlock, 3b	4	1	4	0	1	0
Nicosia, c	4	0	0	5	0	0
Garner, 2b	4	1	2	2	3	1
Rooker, p	1	0	0	1	0	0
aLacy	1	0	1	0	0	0
Blyleven, p	1	0	0	0	1	0
Totals	34	7	13	27	12	1

```
Baltimore..............................  0  0  0   0  1  0   0  0  0 – 1
Pittsburgh.............................  0  0  0   0  0  2   2  3  x – 7
```

Baltimore	IP.	H.	R.	ER.	BB.	SO.
Flanagan (Loser)	6	6	2	2	1	6
Stoddard	⅔	2	2	2	0	0
T. Martinez	⅓*	2	1	1	0	0
Stanhouse	1	3	2	2	2	0

Pittsburgh	IP.	H.	R.	ER.	BB.	SO.
Rooker	5	3	1	1	2	2
Blyleven (Winner)	4	3	0	0	1	3

*Pitched to one batter in eighth.

Bases on balls—Off Flanagan 1 (Foli), off Stanhouse 2 (Moreno, Parker), off Rooker 2 (Ayala, Flanagan), off Blyleven 1 (Bumbry).

Strikeouts—By Flanagan 6 (Moreno 2, Parker 2, Rooker, Nicosia), by Rooker 2 (DeCinces, Singleton), by Blyleven 3 (Roenicke, DeCinces, Kelly).

aHad infield single for Rooker in fifth. bFlied out for Ayala in sixth. cStruck out for Flanagan in seventh. dSingled for Dauer in ninth. eFlied out for Dempsey in ninth. Runs batted in—Foli 3, Parker, Stargell, Madlock, Garner. Two-base hits—B. Robinson, Roenicke, Dempsey, Parker. Three-base hit—Foli. Sacrifice hits—B. Robinson, Blyleven. Sacrifice fly—Stargell. Double plays—Garner, Foli and Stargell; Blyleven, Garner, Foli and Stargell. Left on bases—Baltimore 7, Pittsburgh 9. Umpires—McKean (A.L.) plate, Runge (N.L.) first base, Neudecker (A.L.) second base, Engel (N.L.) third base, Goetz (A.L.) left field, Tata (N.L.) right field. Time—2:54. Attendance—50,920.

FIRST INNING

Baltimore—Garcia hit a broken-bat looping liner which Rooker caught behind the mound with a running, over-the-shoulder grab. Ayala grounded to Foli. Singleton flied to Moreno. No runs, no hits, no errors, none left.

Pittsburgh—Moreno struck out. Foli lined to Roenicke. Parker struck out. No runs, no hits, no errors, none left.

SECOND INNING

Baltimore—Murray flied to Parker. Roenicke popped to Stargell. DeCinces struck out. No runs, no hits, no errors, none left.

Pittsburgh—Robinson grounded to DeCinces. Stargell flied to Roenicke. Madlock singled when his grounder to DeCinces took a bad hop. Nicosia flied to Ayala. No runs, one hit, no errors, one left.

THIRD INNING

Baltimore—Dauer popped to Stargell. Dempsey bounced to Madlock. Flanagan flied to Moreno. No runs, no hits, no errors, none left.

Pittsburgh—Garner bunted to Flanagan, who threw on to first for the out. Rooker was called out on strikes. Moreno fouled to Garcia. No runs, no hits, no errors, none left.

FOURTH INNING

Baltimore—Garcia grounded to Foli. Ayala walked. Singleton was called out on strikes. Murray popped to Garner. No runs, no hits, no errors, one left.

Pittsburgh—Foli bounced to DeCinces. Parker struck out. Robinson doubled to right-center. Stargell bounced to Dauer. No runs, one hit, no errors, one left.

Surprise Game 5 starter **JIM ROOKER,** who had won only four times in the regular season, gave Pirates five strong innings to keep their Series hopes alive.

FIFTH INNING

Baltimore—Roenicke doubled to left-center. DeCinces singled to right, Roenicke stopping at third. Dauer grounded into a double play, Garner to Foli to Stargell, Roenicke scoring. Dempsey singled to left. Flanagan walked, Dempsey advancing to second. Garcia forced Flanagan, Foli to Garner. One run, three hits, no errors, two left.

Pittsburgh—Madlock singled to center. Nicosia struck out. Garner flied to Ayala on the warning track. Lacy batted for Rooker and beat out an infield single to third, Madlock stopping at second. Moreno struck out. No runs, two hits, no errors, two left.

SIXTH INNING

Baltimore—Blyleven came in to pitch for Pittsburgh. Bumbry batted for Ayala and flied to Robinson. Singleton grounded to Garner. Murray grounded to Garner, who missed the ball for an error. Roenicke struck out. No runs, no hits, one error, one left.

Pittsburgh—Bumbry remained in the game to play center field for Baltimore with Roenicke shifting to left. Foli walked. Parker singled to center, Foli stopping at second. Robinson sacrificed, Flanagan to Murray, Foli advancing to third and Parker to second. Stargell flied to Bumbry, Foli scoring and Parker advancing to third after the catch. Madlock lined a single to center, Parker scoring. Nicosia grounded to DeCinces, whose low throw was scooped up by Murray for the out. Two runs, two hits, no errors, one left.

SEVENTH INNING

Baltimore—DeCinces struck out. Dauer bounced to Foli. Dempsey doubled to right-center. Kelly batted for Flanagan and struck out. No runs, one hit, no errors, one left.

Pittsburgh—Stoddard came in to pitch for Baltimore. Garner bounced an infield single over the mound. Blyleven, attempting to sacrifice, forced Garner, Stoddard to Garcia. Moreno forced Blyleven, Garcia making a diving stop before flipping to Dauer. With Foli batting, Moreno advanced to second when Stoddard threw wildly in an attempt to pick him off. Foli tripled to right-center, Moreno scoring. Tippy Martinez replaced Stoddard on the mound for Baltimore. Parker doubled to left-center, Foli scoring. Robinson grounded to DeCinces. Two runs, three hits, one error, one left.

EIGHTH INNING

Baltimore—Garcia bounced to Foli. Bumbry walked. Singleton grounded into a double play, Blyleven to Garner to Foli to Stargell. No runs, no hits, no errors, none left.

Pittsburgh—Stargell singled to right. Stanhouse replaced Martinez on the mound for Baltimore. Madlock, with Stargell running, singled to center, Stargell advancing to third. Nicosia fouled to Dempsey, the runners holding. Garner singled to left, Stargell scoring and Madlock stopping at second. Blyleven sacrificed, Murray to Dauer covering first, Madlock advancing to third and Garner to second. Moreno was walked intentionally, loading the bases. Foli singled up the middle, Madlock and Garner scoring and Moreno stopping at second. With Parker batting, Stanhouse threw wildly to first in an attempt to pick off Foli, Moreno advancing to third and Foli to second. Parker was walked intentionally, loading the bases. Robinson popped to DeCinces. Three runs, four hits, one error, three left.

NINTH INNING

Baltimore—Murray flied to Moreno. Roenicke popped to Foli. DeCinces singled to left. Lowenstein batted for Dauer and singled to right, DeCinces stopping at second. Crowley batted for Dempsey and flied out to Robinson. No runs, two hits, no errors, two left.

AT BALTIMORE   Game 6   OCTOBER 16

.Pittsburgh	.AB.	R.	H.	PO.	A.	E.
Moreno, cf	5	1	3	4	0	0
Foli, ss	5	1	2	0	5	0
Parker, rf	4	0	1	3	0	0
Stargell, 1b	4	0	0	8	0	0
Milner, lf	3	0	0	0	0	0
Tekulve, p	1	0	0	0	0	0
Madlock, 3b	3	0	0	1	2	0
Ott, c	4	1	2	6	0	0
Garner, 2b	3	1	2	4	2	0
Candelaria, p	2	0	0	0	1	0
aLacy	1	0	0	0	0	0
B. Robinson, lf	0	0	0	1	0	0
Totals	35	4	10	27	10	0

Baltimore	AB.	R.	H.	PO.	A.	E.
Garcia, ss	3	0	1	1	2	0
eKelly	1	0	0	0	0	0
Belanger, ss	0	0	0	0	0	0
Ayala, lf	3	0	0	2	0	0
fCrowley	1	0	0	0	0	0
Stoddard, p	0	0	0	1	0	0
Singleton, rf	4	0	3	1	0	0
Murray, 1b	4	0	0	5	1	0
DeCinces, 3b	4	0	0	1	3	0
Roenicke, cf	2	0	0	4	0	0
bBumbry, cf	1	0	0	2	0	1
Dauer, 2b	2	0	1	1	1	0
cSmith, 2b	1	0	1	0	0	0
Dempsey, c	3	0	1	7	0	0
Palmer, p	2	0	0	1	0	0
dLowenstein, lf	1	0	0	1	0	0
Totals	32	0	7	27	7	1

Pittsburgh	0	0	0	0	0	0	2	2	0	– 4
Baltimore	0	0	0	0	0	0	0	0	0	– 0

Pittsburgh	IP.	H.	R.	ER.	BB.	SO.
Candelaria (Winner)	6	6	0	0	0	2
Tekulve (Save)	3	1	0	0	0	4

Baltimore	IP.	H.	R.	ER.	BB.	SO.
Palmer (Loser)	8	10	4	4	3	5
Stoddard	1	0	0	0	0	0

Bases on balls—Off Palmer 3 (Milner, Madlock, Parker).

Strikeouts—by Palmer 5 (Candelaria 2, Parker, Stargell, Lacy), by Candelaria 2 (Palmer 2), by Tekulve 4 (Dempsey, Lowenstein, Singleton, DeCinces).

aStruck out for Candelaria in seventh. bFlied out for Roenicke in seventh. cSingled for Dauer in seventh. dStruck out for Palmer in eighth. eFlied out for Garcia in eighth. fGrounded out for Ayala in eighth. Runs batted in—Moreno, Parker, Stargell, B. Robinson. Two-base hits—Foli, Garner. Sacrifice flies—Stargell, B. Robinson. Hit by pitcher—By Palmer (Garner). Double plays—Madlock and Stargell; Foli, Garner and Stargell. Left on bases—Pittsburgh 10, Baltimore 5. Umpires—Runge (N.L.) plate, Neudecker (A.L.) first base, Engel (N.L.) second base, Goetz (A.L.) third base, Tata (N.L.) left field, McKean (A.L.) right field. Time—2:30. Attendance—53,739.

FIRST INNING

Pittsburgh—Moreno bounced a single to center. Foli, with Moreno running, doubled off the glove of DeCinces, Moreno stopping at third. Parker grounded to DeCinces, the runners holding. Stargell fouled to Palmer, who touched first for the out. Milner grounded to Palmer. No runs, two hits, no errors, two left.

Baltimore—Garcia singled to right-center. Ayala flied to Moreno. Singleton singled to left, Garcia stopping at second. Murray grounded into a double play, Madlock stepping on third to force Garcia and then throwing to Stargell to retire Murray. No runs, two hits, no errors, one left.

SECOND INNING

Pittsburgh—Madlock grounded to DeCinces. Ott grounded to Garcia. Garner singled to center. Candelaria struck out. No runs, one hit, no errors, one left.

Baltimore—DeCinces bunted to Candelaria, who fielded the ball along the first base line and threw to Stargell for the out. Roenicke flied to Moreno. Dauer lined to Moreno. No runs, no hits, no errors, none left.

THIRD INNING

Pittsburgh—Moreno flied to Roenicke. Foli grounded to DeCinces. Parker was called out on strikes. No runs, no hits, no errors, none left.

Baltimore—Dempsey singled to center. Palmer struck out, bunting foul on the third strike. Garcia flied to Parker. Ayala lined to Garner. No runs, one hit, no errors, one left.

FOURTH INNING

Pittsburgh—Stargell flied to Roenicke. Milner walked. Madlock walked, Milner advancing to second. Ott forced Madlock, Dauer to Garcia, Milner advancing to third. Garner was hit by a pitch, loading the bases. Candelaria struck out. No runs, no hits, no errors, three left.

Baltimore—Singleton lined a single to right-center. Murray grounded to Madlock, Singleton advancing to second. DeCinces grounded to Foli, Singleton holding second. Roenicke popped to Garner. No runs, one hit, no errors, one left.

FIFTH INNING

Pittsburgh—Moreno lined to Dauer, who made a leaping, backhand catch. Foli fouled to Dempsey. Parker walked. Stargell struck out. No runs, no hits, no errors, one left.

Baltimore—Dauer singled up the middle. Dempsey grounded into a double play, Foli to Garner to Stargell. Palmer struck out. No runs, one hit, no errors, none left.

SIXTH INNING

Pittsburgh—Milner bounced to Garcia. Madlock flied to Singleton on the warning track. Ott singled to left-center. Garner flied to Roenicke. No runs, one hit, no errors, one left.

Baltimore—Garcia flied to Moreno. Ayala hit a soft liner that Foli short-hopped and threw to Stargell for the out. Singleton singled to left. Murray forced Singleton, Foli to Garner. No runs, one hit, no errors, one left.

SEVENTH INNING

Pittsburgh—Lacy batted for Candelaria and struck out. Moreno singled to right. Foli, with Moreno running, beat out an infield hit when Palmer deflected his bouncer, Moreno stopping at second. Parker grounded a single past Dauer into right, Moreno scoring and Foli advancing to third. Stargell flied to Ayala, Foli scoring after the catch and Parker advancing to second. Milner flied to Roenicke. Two runs, three hits, no errors, one left.

Baltimore—Tekulve came in to pitch for Pittsburgh and Bill Robinson went in to play left field. Tekulve assumed the fifth spot in the batting order and Robinson the ninth. DeCinces grounded to Foli. Bumbry batted for Roenicke and flied to Parker. Smith batted for Dauer and singled to right. Dempsey struck out. No runs, one hit, no errors, one left.

EIGHTH INNING

Pittsburgh—Bumbry remained in the game to play center field and Smith to play second base for Baltimore. Madlock flied to Bumbry. Ott singled to right. Garner laced a ground-rule double to left, Ott stopping at third. Robinson lined to Ayala, Ott scoring after the catch and Garner holding second. Moreno singled to center to score Garner and took second when Bumbry juggled the ball for an error. Foli fouled to Dempsey. Two runs, three hits, one error, one left.

Baltimore—Lowenstein batted for Palmer and struck out. Kelly batted for Garcia and flied to Robinson. Crowley batted for Ayala and grounded to Garner. No runs, no hits, no errors, none left.

NINTH INNING

Pittsburgh—Stoddard came in to pitch for Baltimore and assumed the second spot in the batting order. Belanger came in at shortstop and batted first and Lowenstein remained in the game to play left field. Parker flied to Bumbry. Stargell flied to Lowenstein. Tekulve grounded to Murray, who threw to Stoddard covering first for the out. No runs, no hits, no errors, none left.

Baltimore—Singleton struck out. Murray flied to Parker. DeCinces struck out. No runs, no hits, no errors, none left.

AT BALTIMORE   Game 7   OCTOBER 17

Pittsburgh	AB.	R.	H.	PO.	A.	E.
Moreno, cf.	5	1	3	4	0	0
Foli, ss	4	0	1	3	1	0
Parker, rf	4	0	0	2	0	0
B. Robinson, lf	4	1	1	2	0	0
Stargell, 1b	5	1	4	6	1	0
Madlock, 3b	3	0	0	2	1	0
Nicosia, c	4	0	0	6	1	0
Garner, 2b	3	1	1	1	2	0
Bibby, p	1	0	0	1	0	0
aSanguillen	1	0	0	0	0	0
D. Robinson, p	0	0	0	0	0	0
Jackson, p	1	0	0	0	0	0
Tekulve, p	1	0	0	0	0	0
Totals	36	4	10	27	6	0

Baltimore	AB.	R.	H.	PO.	A.	E.
Bumbry, cf	3	0	0	0	0	0
Garcia, ss	3	0	1	0	5	1
eAyala	0	0	0	0	0	0
fCrowley	1	0	0	0	0	0
Stoddard, p	0	0	0	0	1	0
Flanagan, p	0	0	0	0	0	0
Stanhouse, p	0	0	0	0	0	0
T. Martinez, p	0	0	0	0	0	0
D. Martinez, p	0	0	0	0	0	0
Singleton, rf	3	0	1	1	0	0
Murray, 1b	4	0	0	11	0	0
Lowenstein, lf	2	0	2	0	1	0
bRoenicke, lf	2	0	1	0	0	0
DeCinces, 3b	4	0	2	3	3	0
Dempsey, c	3	0	3	0	0	0
gKelly	1	0	0	0	0	0
Dauer, 2b	3	1	1	4	2	0
McGregor, p	1	0	0	1	2	0
cMay	0	0	0	0	0	0
dBelanger, ss	0	0	0	1	1	0
Totals	30	1	4	27	14	2

Pittsburgh	0	0	0	0	0	2	0	0	2 – 4
Baltimore	0	1	0	0	0	0	0	0	0 – 1

Pittsburgh	IP.	H.	R.	ER.	BB.	SO.
Bibby	4	3	1	1	0	3
D. Robinson	⅔	1	0	0	1	0
Jackson (Winner)	2⅔	0	0	0	2	1
Tekulve (Save)	1⅔	0	0	0	1	2

Baltimore	IP.	H.	R.	ER.	BB.	SO.
McGregor (Loser)	8	7	2	2	2	2
Stoddard	⅓	1	1	1	0	0
Flanagan	0*	1	1	1	0	0
Stanhouse	0*	1	0	0	0	0
T. Martinez	0*	0	0	0	0	0
D. Martinez	⅔	0	0	0	0	0

    *Pitched to one batter in ninth.

Bases on balls—Off D. Robinson 1 (McGregor), off Jackson 2 (May, Bumbry), off Tekulve 1 (Singleton), off McGregor 2 (Garner, Madlock).

Strikeouts—By Bibby 3 (Murray 2, Lowenstein), by Jackson 1 (Roenicke), by Tekulve 2 (Roenicke, DeCinces), by McGregor 2 (Parker 2).

aGrounded out for Bibby in fifth. bStruck out for Lowenstein in seventh. cWalked for McGregor in eighth. dRan for May in eighth. eAnnounced as pinch-hitter for Garcia in eighth. fGrounded out for Ayala in eighth. gFlied out for Dempsey in ninth. Runs batted in—Moreno, B. Robinson, Stargell 2, Dauer. Two-base hits—Stargell 2, Garner. Home runs—Dauer, Stargell. Caught stealing—Garcia. Sacrifice hit—Foli. Hit by pitcher—By T. Martinez (Parker), by D. Martinez (B. Robinson). Double play—Belanger and Murray. Left on bases—Pittsburgh 10, Baltimore 6. Umpires—Neudecker (A.L.) plate, Engel (N.L.) first base, Goetz (A.L.) second base, Tata (N.L.) third base, McKean (A.L.) left field, Runge (N.L.) right field. Time—2:54. Attendance—53,733.

FIRST INNING

Pittsburgh—Moreno grounded a single to center. Foli sacrificed, McGregor to Murray, Moreno advancing to second. Parker popped to DeCinces. Robinson popped to DeCinces. No runs, one hit, no errors, one left.

Baltimore—Bumbry grounded to Stargell, who tagged him out sliding into first. Garcia grounded to Garner. Singleton grounded to Stargell, who threw to Bibby covering first for the out. No runs, no hits, no errors, none left.

SECOND INNING

Pittsburgh—Stargell looped a single to left and advanced to second when Lowenstein bobbled the ball for an error. Madlock grounded to Garcia, Stargell holding second. Nicosia fouled to DeCinces. Garner was walked intentionally. Bibby grounded to Dauer, who threw to McGregor covering first for the out. No runs, one hit, one error, two left.

Baltimore—Murray struck out. Lowenstein struck out. DeCinces singled to center. Dempsey grounded to Madlock. No runs, one hit, no errors, one left.

THIRD INNING

Pittsburgh—Moreno lined to Singleton. Foli grounded to Garcia, who made a nice play on a ball hit up the middle before throwing on to Murray for the out. Parker struck out. No runs, no hits, no errors, none left.

Baltimore—Dauer lined the first pitch of the inning into the left-field stands for a home run. McGregor bounced to Foli. Bumbry popped to Foli. Garcia singled to right. With Singleton batting, Garcia was caught stealing, Nicosia to Foli. One run, two hits, no errors, none left.

FOURTH INNING

Pittsburgh—Robinson popped to Dempsey. Stargell hit a soft fly that fell out of the reach of DeCinces in short left for a double. Madlock grounded to Garcia, whose throw to DeCinces in an attempt to retire Stargell was wide for an error, allowing Stargell to reach third and Madlock to reach first. Nicosia lined to Dauer. Garner hit a pop to Murray and was called out for interference when he collided with the first baseman while inside the foul line. No runs, one hit, one error, two left.

Baltimore right fielder **KEN SINGLETON** leaps high near fence but is unable to catch Willie Stargell's Series-clinching homer in seventh game.

Baltimore—Singleton flied to Robinson. Murray struck out. Lowenstein fouled to Madlock. No runs, no hits, no errors, none left.

FIFTH INNING

Pittsburgh—Sanguillen batted for Bibby and grounded to McGregor, who threw on to Murray for the out. Moreno lined to Lowenstein. Foli also lined to Lowenstein. No runs, no hits, no errors, none left.

Baltimore—Don Robinson came in to pitch for Pittsburgh. DeCinces singled to center. Dempsey, after failing in two attempts to sacrifice, flied to Parker, De-'Cinces holding first. Dauer flied to Moreno, DeCinces holding first. McGregor walked on a 3-2 pitch, DeCinces advancing to second. Jackson replaced Robinson on the mound for Pittsburgh. Bumbry fouled to Madlock. No runs, one hit, no errors, two left.

SIXTH INNING

Pittsburgh—Parker grounded to Dauer. Robinson singled off the glove of Garcia into left field. Stargell lifted a high drive to right-center for a home run, Robinson scoring ahead of him. Madlock grounded to DeCinces. Nicosia grounded to Garcia. Two runs, two hits, no errors, none left

Baltimore—Garcia popped to Garner. Singleton flied to Moreno on the warning track. Murray fouled to Stargell. No runs, no hits, no errors, none left.

SEVENTH INNING

Pittsburgh—Garner grounded to DeCinces. Jackson grounded to Garcia. Moreno grounded a single past the left of a diving Dauer into right field. Foli forced Moreno, DeCinces to Dauer. No runs, one hit, no errors, one left.

Baltimore—Roenicke batted for Lowenstein and struck out. DeCinces flied to Moreno. Dempsey flied to Robinson. No runs, no hits, no errors, none left.

EIGHTH INNING

Pittsburgh—Roenicke remained in the game as the left fielder for Baltimore. Parker struck out. Robinson lined to Roenicke. Stargell doubled to left. Madlock was walked intentionally. Nicosia forced Madlock, Garcia to Dauer. No runs, one hit, no errors, two left.

Baltimore—Dauer popped to Foli. May batted for McGregor and walked. Belanger ran for May. Bumbry walked on a 3-2 pitch, Belanger advancing to second. Ayala was announced as a pinch-hitter for Garcia. Tekulve replaced Jackson on the mound for Pittsburgh. Crowley then batted for Ayala and grounded to Garner, Belanger advancing to third and Bumbry to second. Singleton was walked intentionally, loading the bases. Murray lifted a fly to the warning track in right where Parker, after stumbling, made the catch. No runs, no hits, no errors, three left.

NINTH INNING

Pittsburgh—Stoddard came in to pitch for Baltimore and batted second with Belanger remaining in the game as the shortstop. Garner doubled to left. Tekulve, attempting to sacrifice, bunted to Stoddard, who held Garner at second and then threw on to Dauer covering first for the out. Flanagan replaced Stoddard on the mound for Baltimore. Moreno singled to center, Garner scoring. Stanhouse replaced Flanagan on the mound for Baltimore. Foli singled to center, Moreno advancing to third. Tippy Martinez replaced Stanhouse on the mound for Baltimore. Parker, with the count 0-2, was hit by a pitch, loading the bases. Dennis Martinez replaced Tippy Martinez on the mound for Baltimore. Robinson was hit by a pitch, Moreno scoring and the bases remaining loaded. Stargell grounded into a double play, Belanger stepping on second to force Robinson before throwing to Murray to retire Stargell. Two runs, three hits, no errors, two left.

Baltimore—Roenicke struck out. DeCinces struck out. Kelly batted for Dempsey and flied to Moreno. No runs, no hits, no errors, none left.

PITTSBURGH PIRATES' BATTING AND FIELDING AVERAGES

Player—Position	G.	AB.	R.	H.	TB.	2B.	3B.	HR.	RBI.	BB.	IBB.	SO.	B.A.	PO.	A.	E.	F.A.
Stennett, ph	1	1	0	1	1	0	0	0	0	0	0	0	1.000	0	0	0	.000
Garner, 2b	7	24	4	12	16	4	0	0	5	3	2	1	.500	21	23	2	.957
Stargell, 1b	7	30	7	12	25	4	0	3	7	0	0	6	.400	59	2	2	.968
Madlock, 3b	7	24	2	9	10	1	0	0	3	5	2	1	.375	3	10	1	.929
Parker, rf	7	29	2	10	13	3	0	0	4	2	1	7	.345	13	1	1	.933
Moreno, cf	7	33	4	11	13	2	0	0	3	1	1	7	.333	20	1	0	1.000
Foli, ss	7	30	6	10	13	1	1	0	3	2	0	0	.333	8	32	3	.930
Ott, c	3	12	2	4	5	1	0	0	3	0	0	2	.333	20	0	0	1.000
Milner, lf	3	9	2	3	4	1	0	0	1	2	1	0	.333	5	0	0	1.000
Candelaria, p	2	3	0	1	1	0	0	0	0	0	0	2	.333	0	1	0	1.000
Sanguillen, ph	3	3	0	1	1	0	0	0	1	0	0	0	.333	0	0	0	.000
B. Robinson, lf-ph	7	19	2	5	6	1	0	0	2	0	0	4	.263	11	1	0	1.000
Lacy, ph	4	4	0	1	1	0	0	0	0	0	0	1	.250	0	0	0	.000
Nicosia, c	4	16	1	1	1	0	0	0	0	0	0	0	.063	23	2	0	1.000
Alexander, pr-lf	1	0	0	0	0	0	0	0	0	0	0	0	.000	0	0	0	.000
Kison, p	1	0	0	0	0	0	0	0	0	0	0	0	.000	0	1	0	1.000
D. Robinson, p	4	0	0	0	0	0	0	0	0	0	0	0	.000	0	1	0	1.000
Easler, ph	2	1	0	0	0	0	0	0	1	0	0	0	.000	0	0	0	.000
Jackson, p	4	1	0	0	0	0	0	0	0	0	0	0	.000	0	0	0	.000
Romo, p	2	1	0	0	0	0	0	0	0	0	0	0	.000	0	1	0	1.000
Rooker, p	2	2	0	0	0	0	0	0	0	0	0	1	.000	1	2	0	1.000
Tekulve, p	5	2	0	0	0	0	0	0	0	0	0	0	.000	1	0	0	1.000
Blyleven, p	2	3	0	0	0	0	0	0	0	0	0	0	.000	0	1	0	1.000
Bibby, p	2	4	0	0	0	0	0	0	0	0	0	1	.000	1	0	0	1.000
Totals	7	251	32	81	110	18	1	3	32	16	7	35	.323	186	79	9	.967

Sanguillen grounded out for Rooker in fifth inning of first game; singled for D. Robinson in ninth inning of second game; grounded out for Bibby in fifth inning of seventh game.

Lacy reached first base on error for Romo in sixth inning of first game; lined out for Jackson in seventh inning of third game; had infield single for Rooker in fifth inning of fifth game; struck out for Candelaria in seventh inning of sixth game.

Stennett singled for D. Robinson in eighth inning of first game.

Easler walked for Blyleven in seventh inning of second game; flied out for Tekulve in ninth inning of fourth game.

B. Robinson singled for Milner in ninth inning of second game.

Alexander ran for B. Robinson in ninth inning of second game.

BALTIMORE ORIOLES' BATTING AND FIELDING AVERAGES

Player—Position	G.	AB.	R.	H.	TB.	2B.	3B.	HR.	RBI.	BB.	IBB.	SO.	B.A.	PO.	A.	E.	F.A.
Stoddard, p	4	1	0	1	1	0	0	0	1	0	0	0	1.000	1	4	1	.833
Garcia, ss	6	20	4	8	12	2	1	0	6	1	0	3	.400	10	17	1	.964
Singleton, rf	7	28	1	10	11	1	0	0	2	2	1	5	.357	9	0	0	1.000
Ayala, lf-ph	4	6	1	2	5	0	0	1	2	1	0	0	.333	4	0	0	1.000
Skaggs, c	1	3	1	1	1	0	0	0	0	0	0	0	.333	2	2	0	1.000
Dauer, ph-2b	6	17	2	5	9	1	0	1	1	0	0	1	.294	10	10	0	1.000
Dempsey, c-pr	7	21	3	6	8	2	0	0	0	1	0	3	.286	38	2	0	1.000
Smith, 2b-ph	4	7	1	2	2	0	0	0	2	2	0	0	.286	4	3	0	1.000
Crowley, ph	5	4	0	1	2	1	0	0	2	1	0	0	.250	0	0	0	.000
Kelly, ph	5	4	0	1	1	0	0	0	0	1	0	1	.250	0	0	0	.000
Lowenstein, lf-ph	6	13	2	3	4	1	0	0	3	1	0	3	.231	6	0	1	.857
DeCinces, 3b	7	25	2	5	8	0	0	1	3	5	0	5	.200	7	21	3	.903
Murray, 1b	7	26	3	4	8	1	0	1	2	4	0	4	.154	60	7	0	1.000
Bumbry, cf-ph	7	21	3	3	3	0	0	0	1	2	0	1	.143	14	1	1	.938
Roenicke, lf-cf-ph	6	16	1	2	3	1	0	0	0	0	0	6	.125	14	1	0	1.000
D. Martinez, p	2	0	0	0	0	0	0	0	0	0	0	0	.000	0	1	0	1.000
T. Martinez, p	3	0	0	0	0	0	0	0	0	0	0	0	.000	0	0	0	.000
Stanhouse, p	3	0	0	0	0	0	0	0	0	0	0	0	.000	0	0	1	.000
Stone, p	1	0	0	0	0	0	0	0	0	1	0	1	.000	0	0	0	.000
May, ph	2	1	0	0	0	0	0	0	0	0	0	1	.000	0	0	0	.000
Stewart, p	1	1	0	0	0	0	0	0	0	0	0	0	.000	1	2	0	1.000
McGregor, p	2	4	1	0	0	0	0	0	0	2	0	1	.000	1	2	0	1.000
Palmer, p	2	4	0	0	0	0	0	0	0	0	0	3	.000	2	1	0	1.000
Flanagan, p	3	5	0	0	0	0	0	0	0	1	0	2	.000	0	4	0	1.000
Belanger, ss-pr	5	6	1	0	0	0	0	0	0	1	0	1	.000	3	7	1	.909
Totals	7	233	26	54	78	10	1	4	23	26	3	41	.232	186	85	9	.968

Dauer singled for Smith in eighth inning of first game.

Kelly walked for Palmer in seventh inning of second game; singled for Stone in seventh inning of fourth game; struck out for Flanagan in seventh inning of fifth game; flied out for Garcia in eighth inning of sixth game; flied out for Dempsey in ninth inning of seventh game.

Crowley walked for Belanger in seventh inning of second game; doubled for Skaggs in eighth inning of fourth game; flied out for Dempsey in ninth inning of fifth game; grounded out for Ayala in eighth inning of sixth game; grounded out for Ayala in eighth inning of seventh game.

Bumbry hit by pitcher for Ayala in fourth inning of third game; flied out for Ayala in sixth inning of fifth game; flied out for Roenicke in seventh inning of sixth game.

May struck out for Stewart in fifth inning of fourth game; walked for McGregor in eighth inning of seventh game.

Lowenstein doubled for Roenicke in eighth inning of fourth game; singled for Dauer in ninth inning of fifth game; struck out for Palmer in eighth inning of sixth game.

Smith intentionally walked for Dauer in eighth inning of fourth game; singled for Dauer in seventh inning of sixth game.

Roenicke struck out for Lowenstein in seventh inning of seventh game.

Dempsey ran for Crowley in eighth inning of fourth game.

Belanger ran for May in eighth inning of seventh game.

Ayala announced as pinch-hitter for Garcia in eighth inning of seventh game.

PITTSBURGH PIRATES' PITCHING RECORDS

Pitcher	G.	GS.	CG.	IP.	H.	R.	ER.	HR.	BB.	IBB.	SO.	HB.	WP.	W.	L.	Pct.	ERA.
Jackson	4	0	0	4⅔	1	0	0	0	2	0	2	0	0	1	0	1.000	0.00
Rooker	2	1	0	8⅓	5	1	1	0	3	0	4	0	0	0	0	.000	1.04
Blyleven	2	1	0	10	8	2	2	1	3	0	4	0	0	1	0	1.000	1.80
Bibby	2	2	0	10⅓	10	4	3	1	2	0	10	0	0	0	0	.000	2.61
Tekulve	5	0	0	9⅓	4	3	3	0	3	2	10	0	0	0	1	.000	2.89
Romo	2	0	0	4⅔	5	2	2	0	3	1	4	1	1	0	0	.000	3.86
Candelaria	2	2	0	9	14	6	5	1	2	0	4	0	0	1	1	.500	5.00
D. Robinson	4	0	0	5	4	3	3	0	6	0	3	0	0	1	0	1.000	5.40
Kison	1	1	0	⅓	3	5	4	1	2	0	0	0	1	0	1	.000	108.00
Totals	7	7	0	62	54	26	22	4	26	3	41	1	2	4	3	.571	3.19

Saves—Tekulve 3. Shutout—Candelaria and Tekulve (combined).

(NOTE: Pittsburgh individual earned runs do not add up to team total because of rule 10.18(i) applied in Game 3.)

BALTIMORE ORIOLES' PITCHING RECORDS

Pitcher	G.	GS.	CG.	IP.	H.	R.	ER.	HR.	BB.	IBB.	SO.	HB.	WP.	W.	L.	Pct.	ERA.
Stewart	1	0	0	2⅔	4	0	0	1	1	0	0	0	0	0	0	.000	0.00
Flanagan	3	2	1	15	18	7	5	1	2	0	13	0	0	1	1	.500	3.00
McGregor	2	2	1	17	16	6	6	1	2	2	8	0	0	1	1	.500	3.18
Palmer	2	2	0	15	18	6	6	0	5	1	8	1	1	0	1	.000	3.60
Stoddard	4	0	0	5	6	3	3	0	1	0	3	0	0	1	0	1.000	5.40
T. Martinez	3	0	0	1⅓	3	1	1	0	0	0	1	1	0	0	0	.000	6.75
Stone	1	0	0	2	4	2	2	0	2	1	2	0	0	0	0	.000	9.00
Stanhouse	3	0	0	2	6	3	3	0	3	2	0	0	0	0	1	.000	13.50
D. Martinez	2	1	0	2	6	4	4	1	0	0	1	0	0	0	0	.000	18.00
Totals	7	7	2	62	81	32	30	3	16	7	35	3	1	3	4	.429	4.35

Saves—None. Shutouts—None.

COMPOSITE SCORE BY INNINGS

Pittsburgh	1	8	0		1	1	8		4	6	3 – 32
Baltimore	5	1	6		5	1	1		1	6	0 – 26

Sacrifice hits—B. Robinson, Blyleven, Foli, Bumbry.

Sacrifice flies—Ott, Parker, Stargell 2, B. Robinson.

Stolen bases—Murray, DeCinces.

Caught stealing—Parker, Madlock 2, Alexander, Garcia.

Double Plays—Madlock, Garner and Stargell 2; Parker and Ott; Foli, Garner, Madlock and Garner; Foli, Garner and Stargell 3; Garner, Foli and Stargell 2; Blyleven, Garner, Foli and Stargell; Madlock and Stargell; Murray and Palmer; Murray, Belanger and Smith; D. Martinez, Garcia and Murray; Dauer, Garcia and Murray; Belanger and Murray.

Passed balls—None.

Hit by pitcher—By Romo (Bumbry), by Palmer (Garner), by T. Martinez (Parker), by D. Martinez (B. Robinson).

Balk—McGregor.

Bases on balls—Off Kison 2 (Belanger, Murray), off Rooker 3 (DeCinces, Ayala, Flanagan), off Romo 3 (Murray, Smith, McGregor), off D. Robinson 6 (Singleton, Dempsey, Kelly, Crowley, DeCinces, McGregor), off Blyleven 3 (Lowenstein, Murray, Bumbry), off Candelaria 2 (Garcia, Murray), off Bibby 2 (DeCinces 2), off Tekulve 3 (Smith, DeCinces, Singleton), off Jackson 2 (May, Bumbry), off Flanagan 2 (Madlock, Foli), off Palmer 5 (Garner, Easler, Milner, Madlock, Parker), off Stanhouse 3 (Garner, Moreno, Parker), off Stewart 1 (Milner), off Stone 2 (Foli, Madlock), off Stoddard 1 (Madlock), off McGregor 2 (Garner, Madlock).

Strikeouts—By Rooker 4 (Belanger, Lowenstein, DeCinces, Singleton), by D. Robinson 3 (Flanagan, Bumbry, Singleton), by Jackson 2 (Flanagan, Roenicke), by Blyleven 4 (Palmer, Roenicke, DeCinces, Kelly), by Tekulve 10 (Dempsey 2, Garcia 2, Roenicke 2, Lowenstein, Singleton, DeCinces 2), by Candelaria 4 (Singleton, DeCinces, Palmer 2), by Romo 4 (Roenicke, Dauer, Dempsey, McGregor), by Bibby 10 (Garcia, Singleton, Murray 4, Roenicke, Stewart, May, Lowenstein), by Flanagan 13 (B. Robinson, Stargell 2, Garner, Moreno 4, Nicosia 2, Parker 2, Rooker), by Palmer 8 (Moreno 2, Ott, Candelaria 2, Parker, Stargell, Lacy), by T. Martinez 1 (Stargell), by McGregor 8 (B. Robinson 2, Madlock, Parker 3, Stargell, Moreno) by Stone 2 (Bibby, Stargell), by Stoddard 3 (B. Robinson, Parker, Ott).

Left on bases—Pittsburgh 60—10, 7, 4, 10, 9, 10, 10; Baltimore 49—8, 8, 9, 6, 7, 5, 6.

Time of games—First game, 3:18; second game, 3:13; third game, 2:51; fourth game, 3:48; fifth game, 2:54; sixth game, 2:30; seventh game, 2:54.

Attendance—First game, 53,735; second game, 53,739; third game, 50,848; fourth game, 50,883; fifth game, 50,920; sixth game, 53,739; seventh game, 53,733.

Umpires—Neudecker (AL), Engel (NL), Goetz (AL), Tata (NL), McKean (AL), Runge (NL).

Official scorers—J.P. Sarault (Montreal) President of BBWAA; Phil Collier, San Diego Union; Ken Nigro, Baltimore Morning Sun.

Minnesota Invested $75,000 in Major League Draft

Ten players were selected when baseball held its annual major league draft at its winter meetings in Toronto the first week of December. Players who had played three years in the minors and who were left off the parent club's 40-man winter roster were eligible to be purchased by another major league club for $25,000. Each player then had to remain on the major league roster for a minimum of 90 days into the season or be offered back to his former club for $12,500.

The Minnesota Twins led the way with three selections. Their first choice was Guy Sularz, an infielder in the Giants' chain who hit .294 at Phoenix in 1979. In later rounds, the Twins tabbed two pitchers from the Reds' organization, David Moore and Doug Corbett. Moore was 8-12 with a 4.32 ERA at Indianapolis in '79 and Corbett, a reliever for the same club, was 3-6 with eight saves and a 2.95 ERA.

With clubs drafting in inverse order of their '79 finish, the Blue Jays had first call and tabbed third baseman-outfielder Mike Macha, who hit .291 for Richmond and .154 in his six games with the Braves.

The White Sox then selected catcher Bruce Kimm, a .283 hitter at Evansville before the Cubs purchased him from the Tigers in late August. In nine games with the Cubs, Kimm hit .091.

The Indians chose Andres Mora, an outfielder in the Orioles' system who hit .344 with 23 homers at Saltillo in the Mexican League.

The Royals opted for infielder Manny Castillo, a .323 hitter for the Cardinals' Springfield club.

The Angels purchased pitcher Alfredo Martinez from the Mets. Martinez had an 11-8 record and a 3.32 ERA at Jackson. California, however, lost a player when the Brewers selected Mark Brouhard, a 24-year-old outfielder who hit .350 at El Paso and led the Texas League in homers with 28 and RBIs with 107.

The Phillies wrapped things up with their enlistment of Red Sox pitcher Burke Sutter, who was 10-13 with a 4.03 ERA at Pawtucket.

WORLD SERIES RESULTS

Year—Winner   Loser
1903—Boston A. L., 5 games; Pittsburgh N. L., 3 games.
1904—No Series.
1905—New York N. L., 4 games; Philadelphia A. L., 1 game.
1906—Chicago A. L., 4 games; Chicago N. L., 2 games.
1907—Chicago A. L., 4 games; Detroit A. L., 0 games; 1 tie.
1908—Chicago N. L., 4 games; Detroit A. L., 1 game.
1909—Pittsburgh N. L., 4 games; Detroit A. L., 3 games.
1910—Philadelphia A. L., 4 games; Chicago N. L., 1 game.
1911—Philadelphia A. L., 4 games; New York N. L., 2 games.
1912—Boston A. L., 4 games; New York N. L., 3 games; 1 tie.
1913—Philadelphia A. L., 4 games; New York N. L., 1 game.
1914—Boston N. L., 4 games; Philadelphia A. L., 0 games.
1915—Boston A. L., 4 games; Philadelphia N. L., 1 game.
1916—Boston A. L., 4 games; Brooklyn N. L., 1 game.
1917—Chicago A. L., 4 games; New York N. L., 2 games.
1918—Boston A. L., 4 games; Chicago N. L., 2 games.
1919—Cincinnati N. L., 5 games; Chicago A. L., 3 games.
1920—Cleveland A. L., 5 games; Brooklyn N. L., 2 games.
1921—New York N. L., 5 games; New York A. L., 3 games.
1922—New York N. L., 4 games; New York A. L., 0 games; 1 tie.
1923—New York A. L., 4 games; New York N. L., 2 games.
1924—Washington A. L., 4 games; New York N. L., 3 games.
1925—Pittsburgh N. L., 4 games; Washington A. L., 3 games.
1926—St. Louis N. L., 4 games; New York A. L., 3 games.
1927—New York A. L., 4 games; Pittsburgh N. L., 0 games.
1928—New York A. L., 4 games; St. Louis N. L., 0 games.
1929—Philadelphia A. L., 4 games; Chicago N. L., 1 game.
1930—Philadelphia A. L., 4 games; St. Louis N. L., 2 games.
1931—St. Louis N. L., 4 games; Philadelphia A. L., 3 games.
1932—New York A. L., 4 games; Chicago N. L., 0 games.
1933—New York N. L., 4 games; Washington A. L., 1 game.
1934—St. Louis N. L., 4 games; Detroit A. L., 3 games.
1935—Detroit A. L., 4 games; Chicago N. L., 2 games.
1936—New York A. L., 4 games; New York N. L., 2 games.
1937—New York A. L., 4 games; New York N. L., 1 game.
1938—New York A. L., 4 games; Chicago N. L., 0 games.
1939—New York A. L., 4 games; Cincinnati N. L., 0 games.
1940—Cincinnati N. L., 4 games; Detroit A. L., 3 games.
1941—New York A. L., 4 games; Brooklyn N. L., 1 game.
1942—St. Louis N. L., 4 games; New York A. L., 1 game.
1943—New York A. L., 4 games; St. Louis N. L., 1 game.
1944—St. Louis N. L., 4 games; St. Louis A. L., 2 games.
1945—Detroit A. L., 4 games; Chicago N. L., 3 games.
1946—St. Louis N. L., 4 games; Boston A. L., 3 games.
1947—New York A. L., 4 games; Brooklyn N. L., 3 games.
1948—Cleveland A. L., 4 games; Boston N. L., 2 games.
1949—New York A. L., 4 games; Brooklyn N. L., 1 game.
1950—New York A. L., 4 games; Philadelphia N. L., 0 games.
1951—New York A. L., 4 games; New York N. L., 2 games.
1952—New York A. L., 4 games; Brooklyn N. L., 3 games.
1953—New York A. L., 4 games; Brooklyn N. L., 2 games.
1954—New York N. L., 4 games; Cleveland A. L., 0 games.
1955—Brooklyn N. L., 4 games; New York A. L., 3 games.
1956—New York A. L., 4 games; Brooklyn N. L., 3 games.
1957—Milwaukee N. L., 4 games; New York A. L., 3 games.
1958—New York A. L., 4 games; Milwaukee N. L., 3 games.
1959—Los Angeles N. L., 4 games; Chicago A. L., 2 games.
1960—Pittsburgh N. L., 4 games; New York A. L., 3 games.
1961—New York A. L., 4 games; Cincinnati N. L., 1 game.
1962—New York A. L., 4 games; San Francisco N. L., 3 games.
1963—Los Angeles N. L., 4 games; New York A. L., 0 games.
1964—St. Louis N. L., 4 games; New York A. L., 3 games.
1965—Los Angeles N. L., 4 games; Minnesota A. L., 3 games.
1966—Baltimore A. L., 4 games; Los Angeles N. L., 0 games.
1967—St. Louis N. L., 4 games; Boston A. L., 3 games.
1968—Detroit A. L., 4 games; St. Louis N. L., 3 games.
1969—New York N. L., 4 games; Baltimore A. L., 1 game.
1970—Baltimore A. L., 4 games; Cincinnati N. L., 1 game.
1971—Pittsburgh N. L., 4 games; Baltimore A. L., 3 games.
1972—Oakland A. L., 4 games; Cincinnati N. L., 3 games.
1973—Oakland A. L., 4 games; New York N. L., 3 games.
1974—Oakland A. L., 4 games; Los Angeles N. L., 1 game.
1975—Cincinnati N. L., 4 games; Boston A. L., 3 games.
1976—Cincinnati N. L., 4 games; New York A. L., 0 games.
1977—New York A. L., 4 games, Los Angeles N. L., 2 games.
1978—New York A. L., 4 games, Los Angeles N. L., 2 games.
1979—Pittsburgh N. L., 4 games, Baltimore A. L., 3 games.

WORLD SERIES ATTENDANCE, MONEY

Year	Games	Attendance	Gate Receipts	Players' Tot.	W. Share	L. Share
1903	8	100,429	$ 50,000.00	$ 32,612.00	$ 1,182.00	$ 1,316.25
1905	5	91,723	68,436.81	27,394.20	1,142.00	832.22
1906	6	99,845	106,550.00	33,401.70	1,874.63	439.50
1907	5	78,068	101,728.50	54,933.39	2,142.85	1,945.96
1908	5	62,232	94,975.50	46,114.92	1,317.58	870.00
1909	7	145,295	188,302.50	66,924.90	1,825.22	1,274.76
1910	5	124,222	173,980.00	79,071.93	2,062.79	1,375.16
1911	6	179,851	342,364.50	127,910.61	3,654.58	2,436.39
1912	8	252,037	490,833.00	147,572.28	4,024.68	2,566.47
1913	5	151,000	325,980.00	135,164.16	3,246.36	2,164.22
1914	4	111,009	225,739.00	121,898.94	2,812.28	2,031.65
1915	5	143,351	320,361.50	144,899.55	3,780.25	2,520.17
1916	5	162,859	385,590.50	162,927.45	3,910.26	2,834.82
1917	6	186,654	425,878.00	152,888.58	3,669.32	2,442.21
1918	6	128,483	179,619.00	69,527.70	1,102.51	671.09
1919	8	236,928	722,414.00	260,349.66	5,207.07	3,254.36
1920	7	178,737	564,800.00	214,882.74	4,168.00	2,419.60
1921	8	269,976	900,233.00	292,522.23	5,265.00	3,510.00
1922	5	185,947	605,475.00	247,309.71	4,545.71	2,842.86
1923	6	301,430	1,063,815.00	368,783.04	6,143.49	4,112.88
1924	7	283,665	1,093,104.00	331,092.51	5,959.64	3,820.29
1925	7	282,848	1,182,854.00	339,664.19	5,332.72	3,734.60
1926	7	328,051	1,207,864.00	372,300.51	5,584.51	3,417.75
1927	4	201,705	783,217.00	399,440.67	5,782.24	3,985.47
1928	4	199,072	777,290.00	419,736.60	5,813.20	4,181.30
1929	5	190,490	859,494.00	388,086.66	5,620.57	3,782.01
1930	6	212,619	953,772.00	323,865.00	5,038.07	3,536.68
1931	7	231,567	1,030,723.00	320,303.46	4,467.59	3,023.00
1932	4	191,998	713,377.00	363,822.27	5,231.77	4,244.60
1933	5	163,076	679,365.00	284,665.68	4,256.72	3,019.86
1934	7	281,510	1,031,341.00	327,950.46	5,389.57	3,354.68
1935	6	286,672	1,073,794.00	397,360.24	6,544.76	4,198.53
1936	6	302,924	1,204,399.00	460,002.66	6,430.55	4,655.58
1937	5	238,142	985,994.00	459,629.35	6,471.11	4,489.96
1938	4	200,833	851,166.00	434,094.66	5,728.76	4,674.87
1939	4	183,849	745,329.09	431,117.84	5,541.89	4,193.39
1940	7	281,927	1,222,328.21	404,414.04	5,803.62	3,531.81
1941	5	235,773	1,007,762.00	474,184.54	5,943.31	4,829.40
1942	5	277,101	1,105,249.00	427,579.41	6,192.53	3,351.77
1943	5	277,312	1,105,784.00	488,005.74	6,139.46	4,321.96
1944	6	206,708	906,122.00	309,590.91	4,626.01	2,743.79
1945	7	333,457	1,492,454.00	475,579.04	6,443.34	3,930.22
1946	7	250,071	1,052,900.00	304,141.05	3,742.34	2,140.89
1947	7	389,763	1,781,348.92	493,674.82	5,830.03	4,081.19
1948	6	358,362	1,633,685.56	548,214.99	6,772.07	4,570.73
1949	5	236,716	1,129,627.88	490,855.84	5,626.74	4,272.74
1950	4	196,009	953,669.03	486,371.21	5,737.95	4,081.34
1951	6	341,977	1,633,457.47	560,562.37	6,446.09	4,951.03
1952	7	340,706	1,622,753.01	500,003.28	5,982.65	4,200.64
1953	6	307,350	1,779,269.44	691,341.61	8,280.68	6,178.42
1954	4	251,507	1,566,203.38	881,763.72	11,147.90	6,712.50
1955	7	362,310	2,337,515.34	737,853.59	9,768.21	5,598.58
1956	7	345,903	2,183,254.59	758,561.63	8,714.76	6,934.34
1957	7	394,712	2,475,978.94	709,027.55	8,924.36	5,606.06
1958	7	393,909	2,397,223.03	726,044.55	8,759.10	5,896.08
1959	6	420,784	2,628,809.44	893,301.40	11,231.18	7,257.17
1960	7	349,813	2,230,627.88	682,144.82	8,417.94	5,214.64
1961	5	223,247	1,480,059.95	645,928.28	7,389.13	5,356.37
1962	7	376,864	2,878,891.11	893,281.71	9,882.74	7,291.49
1963	4	247,279	1,995,189.09	1,017,546.43	12,794.00	7,874.32
1964	7	321,807	2,243,187.96	696,520.15	8,622.19	5,309.29
1965	7	364,326	2,975,041.60	885,612.21	10,297.43	6,634.36
1966	4	220,791	2,047,142.46	1,044,042.65	11,683.04	8,189.36
1967	7	304,085	2,350,607.10	705,878.44	8,314.81	5,115.23
1968	7	379,670	3,018,113.40	879,761.08	10,936.66	7,078.71
1969	5	272,378	2,857,782.78	1,142,200.93	*18,338.18	*14,904.21
1970	5	253,183	2,599,170.26	1,098,631.14	*18,215.78	*13,687.59
1971	7	351,091	3,049,803.46	1,032,256.90	*18,164.58	*13,906.46
1972	7	363,149	3,954,542.99	1,142,418.35	*20,705.01	*15,080.25
1973	7	358,289	3,923,968.37	1,144,473.44	*24,617.57	*14,950.18
1974	5	260,004	3,007,194.00	2,045,442.79	*22,219.09	*15,703.97
1975	7	308,272	3,380,579.61	*1,826,264.97	*19,060.46	*13,325.87
1976	4	223,009	2,498,416.53	*2,467,835.98	*26,366.68	*19,935.48
1977	6	337,709	3,978,825.33	*2,778,300.31	*27,758.04	*20,899.05
1978	6	337,304	4,650,164.57	*3,301,933.77	*31,236.99	*25,483.21
1979	7	367,597	4,390,766.14	*2,854,824.33	*28,236.87	*22,113.94

*Total combined figures for World Series and League Championship Series.
NOTE—Losers' shares in 1903-05-07 and winners' in 1906-07 include club owners' slices which were added to their teams' player pools.

A view of Seattle's Kingdome at workouts for the players before the 1979 All-Star Game.

1979 ALL-STAR GAME

Review of '79 Game

Official Box Score

Official Play-by-Play

Results of Previous Games

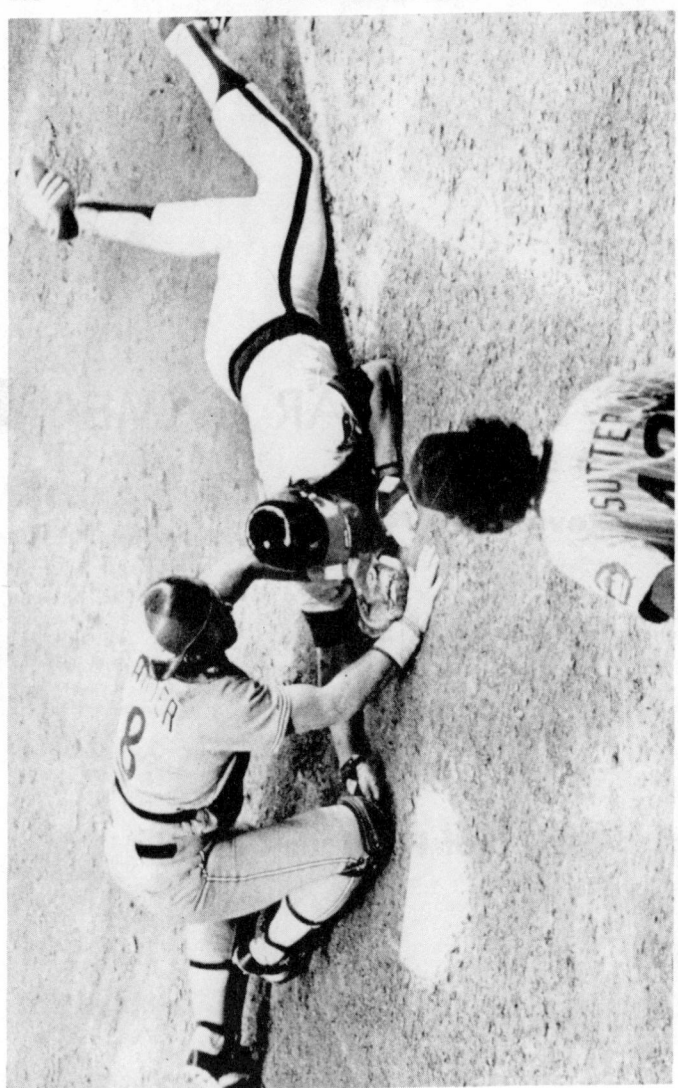

Dave Parker's throw from right field resulted in this bang-bang play at the plate in the eighth inning of the All-Star Game. Catcher Gary Carter blocks the plate and tags Brian Downing out.

Nationals Won 50th All-Star Game
on Bases-Loaded Walk

By JOE MARCIN

Each year the American Leaguers seem to find a different way to lose to the National League in the All-Star Game—and 1979 was no different.

Before the fifth-largest All-Star Game crowd in history—58,905 at Seattle's Kingdome—Lee Mazzilli of the New York Mets walked with the bases loaded in the ninth inning to give the Nationals a 7-6 victory in the 50th All-Star Game.

This was a game the Americans should have won, but didn't because of the arms of Dave Parker and Bruce Sutter, Gary Carter's glove and the bat and eyes of Mazzilli.

It was the eighth straight setback for the Americans and the 16th time in the last 17 summer classics that the game has ended in the Nationals' favor, with the series now, standing at 31-18-1 for the NL after the Americans had won 12 of the first 16 games.

"When you come in there with the bases loaded, you don't have any room to play with," Yankees' ace lefthander Ron Guidry said in something of an understatement after he was called upon to face Mazzilli with two outs in the ninth. "When I'm pitching a game, I can adjust to things like the mound and the game situation. But coming on in relief with the bases loaded when you gotta get one man out is something different for me—you don't have time to adjust."

Cubs' relief ace Sutter hurled two shutout innings to gain the victory, his second straight All-Star triumph. The losing pitcher was Jim Kern of Texas.

It was Kern, who had issued only one homer in 85 innings during the regular season for the Rangers, who served up an eighth-inning, game-tying homer to Mazzilli, then a pinch-hitter for Atlanta's Gary Matthews. Kern also put Guidry on the spot in the ninth when he walked the bases full.

"The homer Mazzilli hit went 317 feet down a 316-foot line in left," bemoaned Kern of the opposite-field homer which tied the game at 6-6. "I didn't want to hang something else, so I went strictly to my fastball and burned myself with it. When I go strictly to my fastball, I start losing control of it."

Three times the AL held one-run leads, 3-2, 5-4 and 6-5, but in each instance the NL battled back to tie before scoring the winning run in the ninth on four bases on balls.

Although nine extra-base hits, including two home runs, caromed off assorted bats, it was the defensive excellence of Parker that commanded the bulk of attention and won MVP honors for the Pittsburgh outfielder.

In the seventh inning, after losing sight of a fly ball off the bat of Jim Rice, Parker pounced on the baseball and fired a strike to third base where Ron Cey tagged out the sliding Boston slugger.

An inning later, after Brian Downing singled and was sacrificed to second, Graig Nettles pulled a single to right. Again Parker responded by rifling a throw to the plate to retire Downing as Carter cut the runner off and forced him to the inside, enhancing the right fielder's throw and making the play.

Carter, naturally, was delighted. He said it might have been the biggest play of his career.

"I might have made a bigger play, but not under conditions like this," Carter beamed. "I thought at first that Downing would try to slide around me so I took a step and made him come inside. The ball got to me just as he slid and I tagged him on the shoulder. I don't think he ever touched the plate."

"I wanted to throw the ball in on one hop, but it took off," said Parker. "It surprised me when it carried all the way. I guess my adrenalin was flowing."

"They (Parker's throws) were right out of a howitzer," said Pittsburgh Manager Chuck Tanner. "Cannon shots," added winning Manager Tom Lasorda.

Parker's two assists set an All-Star Game record for assists by an outfielder. In addition, the MVP collected a single, drove in a run with a sacrifice fly and drew an intentional walk just prior to Mazzilli's game-winning free pass.

The three hour, 11-minute game surpassed the 1954 game at Cleveland for the longest nine-inning contest. Another record was set by Pete Rose when he added a fifth position to his All-Star record by playing first base. And the use of seven NL pitchers tied another record.

Fred Lynn's two-run homer capped a three-run first inning for the Americans to offset a two-run burst by the senior circuit in their half against California's Nolan Ryan. Lynn, unfortunately, had to leave the game fearing that continued play would seriously aggravate a pulled groin muscle he suffered a few days earlier.

So, Bob Lemon's one-day return to managing (he had been fired by the Yankees earlier in 1979 after leading them to the World Series in 1978) was unsuccessful . . . another failure in a series of unsuccessful attempts by the American Leaguers in the All-Star Game.

FIRST INNING

Nationals—Lopes was called out on strikes. Parker struck out. Garvey walked. Schmidt tripled to center, Garvey scoring. Foster doubled down the right-field line, Schmidt scoring. Winfield lined to Rice. Two runs, two hits, no errors, one left.

Americans—Smalley popped to Bowa. Brett walked. Baylor doubled down the left-field line, scoring Brett, who was running with the pitch. Rice popped to Lopes. Lynn homered to right-center, Baylor scoring ahead of him. Yastrzemski flied to Winfield at the fence in right-center. Three runs, two hits, no errors, none left.

SECOND INNING

Nationals—Lemon went in to play center field for the Americans. Boone singled to center. Bowa fouled out to Brett. Brock batted for Carlton and bounced a single over Yastrzemski's head into right field, Boone stopping at second. Lopes hit a bouncer over Ryan's head for an infield single that loaded the bases. Parker flied to Lemon, Boone scoring from third after the catch. Garvey fouled out to Yastrzemski. One run, three hits, no errors, two left.

Americans—Andujar came in to pitch for the Nationals and Matthews went to left field. Porter flied to Matthews. White fouled out to Garvey. Cooper batted for Ryan and walked. Smalley flied to Matthews. No runs, no hits, no errors, one left.

THIRD INNING

Nationals—Stanley came in to pitch for the Americans. Schmidt doubled to right-center. Matthews grounded to Yastrzemski, who threw to third in an attempt to get Schmidt. The throw was too late and Matthews reached first on the fielder's choice. Winfield forced Matthews at second, Brett to White, Schmidt scoring on the play. Boone grounded into a double play, Brett to White to Yastrzemski. One run, one hit, no errors, none left.

Americans—Brett grounded to Garvey. Baylor singled to left and advanced to second on a wild pitch by Andujar. Rice grounded out, Bowa to Garvey, Baylor advancing to third. Lemon was hit by a pitch. Yastrzemski bounced a single up the middle, Baylor scoring and Lemon stopping at second. Porter bounced to Schmidt, whose low throw to first skipped away from Garvey for an error on Schmidt, Lemon scoring and Yastrzemski advancing to third. White forced Porter at second, Schmidt to Lopes. Two runs, two hits, one error, two left.

FOURTH INNING

Nationals—Bowa lined to Smalley. Clark batted for Andujar and grounded out, Yastrzemski to Stanley. Lopes grounded to Smalley. No runs, no hits, no errors, none left.

Americans—Rogers came in to pitch for the Nationals. Kemp batted for Stanley and lined to Lopes. Smalley fouled out to Schmidt. Brett grounded to Bowa. No runs, no hits, no errors, none left.

FIFTH INNING

Nationals—Clear came in to pitch for the Americans. Parker flied to Lemon. Garvey lined to Rice. Schmidt flied to Baylor. No runs, no hits, no errors, none left.

Americans—Carter came in to catch and Cey went to third base for the Nationals. Baylor grounded to Bowa. Rice struck out. Lemon struck out. No runs, no hits, no errors, none left.

SIXTH INNING

Nationals—Matthews popped to Yastrzemski. Winfield doubled to right-center. Carter singled to left, Winfield scoring, and advanced to second on Baylor's throw to the plate. Bowa walked. Rose batted for Rogers and grounded into a double play, White to Smalley to Yastrzemski. One run, two hits, no errors, one left.

Americans—Perry came in to pitch for the Nationals and batted in the third spot with Rose staying in the game at first base to become the first player to play five positions in All-Star competition. Yastrzemski grounded a single to right. Burleson ran for Yastrzemski. Porter doubled to right-center, Burleson stopping at third. Bochte batted for White and, with the infield playing in, bounced a single over Bowa's head into left-center, Burleson scoring and Porter stopping at third. Jackson batted for Clear and Sambito came in to pitch for the Nationals. On a 3-2 pitch, Jackson grounded to Lopes and Porter was caught in a rundown and tagged out, Lopes to Carter to Cey. Bochte advanced to third and Jackson went to second. Smalley was walked intentionally, loading the bases. Brett flied to Winfield in left-center, the runners holding. LaCoss came in to pitch for the Nationals and Reynolds went to short. Reynolds assumed the third spot in the batting order and LaCoss the eighth. Baylor forced Smalley at second, Reynolds to Lopes. One run, three hits, no errors, three left.

SEVENTH INNING

Nationals—Burleson, Bochte and Jackson stayed in the game for the Americans at shortstop, first base and right field, respectively. Rice moved from left field to right field. Grich, Nettles and Downing came in to play second base, third base and catcher, respectively, and Kern came in to pitch. Grich assumed the first spot in the batting order and Kern the third. Morgan batted for Lopes and struck out. Parker beat out an infield single on a smash off Kern's glove. Reynolds grounded out, Nettles to Bochte, Parker advancing to second. Cey grounded to Nettles. No runs, one hit, no errors, one left.

Americans—Morgan remained in the game at second base for the Nationals. Rice hit a pop fly down the right-field line that fell for a double when Parker lost the ball in the lights, but Rice was thrown out trying for third, Parker to Cey. Lemon grounded to Cey. Burleson flied to Winfield. No runs, one hit, no errors, none left.

EIGHTH INNING

Nationals—Mazzilli batted for Matthews and homered down the left-field line. Winfield struck out. Carter popped to Grich. Hernandez batted for LaCoss and struck out swinging. One run, one hit, no errors, none left.

Americans—Mazzilli remained in the game in center field for the Nationals with Winfield shifting to left. Sutter came in to pitch. Downing singled to left-center. Bochte sacrificed Downing to second, Sutter to Morgan covering first. Jackson was walked intentionally. Grich struck out. Nettles singled to right, but Downing was thrown out at the plate on an incredible clothesline peg, Parker to Carter. No runs, two hits, no errors, two left.

NINTH INNING

Nationals—Rose lined to Rice. Morgan walked and advanced to second on a balk by Kern. Parker, after the count reached 2-0, was walked intentionally. Reynolds fouled out to Nettles. Cey walked, loading the bases. Guidry came in to pitch for the Americans. Mazzilli walked, forcing Morgan home from third. Winfield forced Mazzilli at second, Burleson to Grich. One run, no hits, no errors, three left.

Americans—Parrish came in to play third base for the Nationals. Singleton batted for Guidry and grounded to Morgan. Rice struck out. Lemon walked. Burleson struck out. No runs, no hits, no errors, one left.

NATIONALS	AB.	R.	H.	RBI.	PO.	A.
Lopes (Dodgers), 2b	3	0	1	0	4	1
iMorgan (Reds), 2b	1	1	0	0	1	1
Parker (Pirates), rf	3	0	1	1	0	2
Garvey (Dodgers), 1b	2	1	0	0	5	0
Perry (Padres), p	0	0	0	0	0	0
Sambito (Astros), p	0	0	0	0	0	0
Reynolds (Astros), ss	2	0	0	0	0	1
Schmidt (Phillies), 3b	3	2	2	1	1	1
Cey (Dodgers), 3b	1	0	0	0	2	1
Parrish (Expos), 3b	0	0	0	0	0	0
Foster (Reds), lf	1	0	1	1	0	0
Matthews (Braves), lf	2	0	0	0	2	0
jMazzilli (Mets), cf	1	1	1	2	0	0
Winfield (Padres), cf-lf	5	1	1	1	3	0
Boone (Phillies), c	2	1	1	0	0	0
Carter (Expos), c	2	0	1	1	6	1
Bowa (Phillies), ss	2	0	0	0	1	3
LaCoss (Reds), p	0	0	0	0	0	0
kHernandez (Cardinals)	1	0	0	0	0	0
Sutter (Cubs), p	0	0	0	0	0	0
Carlton (Phillies), p	0	0	0	0	0	0
aBrock (Cardinals)	1	0	1	0	0	0
Andujar (Astros), p	0	0	0	0	0	0
cClark (Giants)	1	0	0	0	0	0
Rogers (Expos), p	0	0	0	0	0	0
eRose (Phillies), 1b	2	0	0	0	2	0
Totals	35	7	10	7	27	12

AMERICANS	AB.	R.	H.	RBI.	PO.	A.
Smalley (Twins), ss	3	0	0	0	2	2
Grich (Angels), 2b	1	0	0	2	0
Brett (Royals), 3b	3	1	0	1	2
Nettles (Angels), 3b	1	0	1	0	1	2
Baylor (Angels), lf	4	2	2	1	1	0
Kern (Rangers), p	0	0	0	0	0	0
Guidry (Yankees), p	0	0	0	0	0	0
lSingleton (Orioles)	1	0	0	0	0	0
Rice (Red Sox), rf-lf	5	0	1	0	3	0
Lynn (Red Sox), cf	1	1	1	2	0	0
Lemon (White Sox), cf	2	1	0	0	2	0
Yastrzemski (Red Sox), 1b	3	0	2	1	5	1
fBurleson (Red Sox), ss	2	1	0	0	0	1
Porter (Royals), c	3	0	1	0	2	0
Downing (Angels), c	1	0	1	0	3	0
White (Royals), 2b	2	0	0	0	2	2
gBochte (Mariners), 1b	1	0	1	1	2	0
Ryan (Angels), p	0	0	0	0	0	0
bCooper (Brewers)	1	0	0	0	0	0
Stanley (Red Sox), p	0	0	0	0	1	0
dKemp (Tigers)	1	0	0	0	0	0
Clear (Angels), p	0	0	0	0	0	0
hJackson (Yankees), rf	1	0	0	0	0	0
Totals	35	6	10	5	27	10

Nationals		2	1	1	0	0	1	0	1	1—7
Americans		3	0	2	0	0	1	0	0	0—6

Nationals	IP.	H.	R.	ER.	BB.	SO.
Carlton (Phillies)	1	2	3	3	1	0
Andujar (Astros)	2	2	2	1	1	0
Rogers (Expos)	2	0	0	0	0	2
Perry (Padres)	0*	3	1	1	0	0
Sambito (Astros)	⅔	0	0	0	1	0
LaCoss (Reds)	1⅓	1	0	0	0	0
Sutter (Cubs)	2	2	0	0	2	3

Americans	IP.	H.	R.	ER.	BB.	SO.
Ryan (Angels)	2	5	3	3	1	2
Stanley (Red Sox)	2	1	1	1	0	0
Clear (Angels)	2	2	1	1	1	0
Kern (Rangers)	2⅔	2	2	2	3	3
Guidry (Yankees)	⅓	0	0	0	1	0

*Pitched to three batters in sixth.

Winning pitcher—Sutter. Losing pitcher—Kern.

aSingled for Carlton in second. bWalked for Ryan in second. cGrounded out for Andujar in fourth. dLined out for Stanley in fourth. eGrounded into double play for Rogers in sixth. fRan for Yastrzemski in sixth. gSingled for

White in sixth. hGrounded into force play for Clear in sixth. iStruck out for Lopes in seventh. jHomered for Matthews in eighth. kStruck out for LaCoss in eighth. lGrounded out for Guidry in ninth. Error—Schmidt. Double Plays—Brett, White and Yastrzemski; White, Smalley and Yastrzemski. Left on bases—Nationals 8, Americans 9. Two-base hits—Foster, Baylor, Schmidt, Winfield, Porter, Rice. Three-base hit—Schmidt. Home runs—Lynn, Mazzilli. Sacrifice hit—Bochte. Sacrifice fly—Parker. Wild pitch—Andujar. Hit by pitcher—By Andujar (Lemon). Balk —Kern. Bases on balls—Off Carlton 1 (Brett), off Andujar 1 (Cooper), off Sambito 1 (Smalley), off Sutter 2 (Jackson, Lemon), off Ryan 1 (Garvey), off Clear 1 (Bowa), off Kern 3 (Morgan, Parker, Cey), off Guidry 1 (Mazzilli). Strikeouts—By Rogers 2 (Rice, Lemon), by Sutter 3 (Grich, Rice, Burleson), by Ryan 2 (Lopes, Parker), by Kern 3 (Morgan, Winfield, Hernandez). Umpires—Maloney (A.L.) plate, Weyer (N.L.) first base, Bremigan (A.L.) second base, W. Williams (N.L.) third base, Cooney (A.L.) left field, Rennert (N.L.) right field. Time—3:11. Attendance—58,905. Official scorers—Jean-Paul Sarault, Montreal Metro-Matin; Dick Dozer, Chicago Tribune; Mike Kenyon, Seattle Post-Intelligencer.

RESULTS OF PREVIOUS GAMES

1933—At Comiskey Park, Chicago, July 6. Americans 4, Nationals 2. Managers—Connie Mack, John McGraw. Winning pitcher—Lefty Gomez. Losing pitcher—Bill Hallahan. Attendance—47,595.

1934—At Polo Grounds, New York, July 10. Americans 9, Nationals 7. Managers—Joe Cronin, Bill Terry. Winning pitcher—Mel Harder. Losing pitcher—Van Mungo. Attendance—48,363.

1935—At Municipal Stadium, Cleveland, July 8. Americans 4, Nationals 1. Managers—Mickey Cochrane, Frankie Frisch. Winning pitcher—Lefty Gomez. Losing pitcher—Bill Walker. Attendance—69,831.

1936—At Braves Field, Boston, July 7. Nationals 4, Americans 3. Managers—Charlie Grimm, Joe McCarthy. Winning pitcher—Dizzy Dean. Losing pitcher—Lefty Grove. Attendance—25,556.

1937—At Griffith Stadium, Washington, July 7. Americans 8, Nationals 3. Managers—Joe McCarthy, Bill Terry. Winning pitcher—Lefty Gomez. Losing pitcher— Dizzy Dean. Attendance—31,391.

1938—At Crosley Field, Cincinnati, July 6. Nationals 4, Americans 1. Managers—Bill Terry, Joe McCarthy. Winning pitcher—Johnny Vander Meer. Losing pitcher—Lefty Gomez. Attendance—27,067.

1939—At Yankee Stadium, New York, July 11. Americans 3, Nationals 1. Managers—Joe McCarthy, Gabby Hartnett. Winning pitcher—Tommy Bridges. Losing pitcher—Bill Lee. Attendance—62,892.

1940—At Sportsman's Park, St. Louis, July 9. Nationals 4, Americans 0. Managers—Bill McKechnie, Joe Cronin. Winning pitcher—Paul Derringer. Losing pitcher—Red Ruffing. Attendance—32,373.

1941—At Briggs Stadium, Detroit, July 8. Americans 7, Nationals 5. Managers— Del Baker, Bill McKechnie. Winning pitcher—Ed Smith. Losing pitcher—Claude Passeau. Attendance—54,674.

1942—At Polo Grounds, New York, July 6. Americans 3, Nationals 1. Managers—Joe Cronin, Leo Durocher. Winning pitcher—Spud Chandler. Losing pitcher—Mort Cooper. Attendance—34,178.

1943—At Shibe Park, Philadelphia, July 13 (night game). Americans 5, Nationals 3. Managers—Joe McCarthy, Billy Southworth. Winning pitcher—Dutch Leonard. Losing pitcher—Mort Cooper. Attendance—31,938.

1944—At Forbes Field, Pittsburgh, July 11 (night game). Nationals 7, Americans 1. Managers—Billy Southworth, Joe McCarthy. Winning pitcher—Ken Raffensberger. Losing pitcher—Tex Hughson. Attendance—29,589.

1945—No game played.

1946—At Fenway Park, Boston, July 9. Americans 12, Nationals 0. Managers—Steve O'Neill, Charlie Grimm. Winning pitcher—Bob Feller. Losing pitcher—Claude Passeau. Attendance—34,906.

1947—At Wrigley Field, Chicago, July 8. Americans 2, Nationals 1. Managers—Joe Cronin, Eddie Dyer. Winning pitcher—Frank Shea. Losing pitcher—Johnny Sain. Attendance—41,123.

1948—At Sportsman's Park, St. Louis, July 13. Americans 5, Nationals 2. Managers—Bucky Harris, Leo Durocher. Winning pitcher—Vic Raschi. Losing pitcher—Johnny Schmitz. Attendance—34,009.

1949—At Ebbets Field, Brooklyn, July 12. Americans 11, Nationals 7. Managers—Lou Boudreau, Billy Southworth. Winning pitcher—Virgil Trucks. Losing pitcher—Don Newcombe. Attendance—32,577.

1950—At Comiskey Park, Chicago, July 11. Nationals 4, Americans 3 (14 innings). Managers—Burt Shotton, Casey Stengel. Winning pitcher—Ewell Blackwell. Losing pitcher—Ted Gray. Attendance—46,127.

1951—At Briggs Stadium, Detroit, July 10. Nationals 8, Americans 3. Managers—Eddie Sawyer, Casey Stengel. Winning pitcher—Sal Maglie. Losing pitcher—Ed Lopat. Attendance—52,075.

1952—At Shibe Park, Philadelphia, July 8. Nationals 3, Americans 2 (five innings—rain). Managers—Leo Durocher, Casey Stengel. Winning pitcher—Bob Rush. Losing pitcher—Bob Lemon. Attendance—32,785.

1953—At Crosley Field, Cincinnati, July 14. Nationals 5, Americans 1. Managers—Chuck Dressen, Casey Stengel. Winning pitcher—Warren Spahn. Losing pitcher— Allie Reynolds. Attendance—30,846.

1954—At Municipal Stadium, Cleveland, July 13. Americans 11, Nationals 9. Managers—Casey Stengel, Walter Alston. Winning pitcher—Dean Stone. Losing pitcher—Gene Conley. Attendance—68,751.

1955—At Milwaukee County Stadium, Milwaukee, July 12. Nationals 6, Americans 5 (12 innings). Managers—Leo Durocher, Al Lopez. Winning pitcher—Gene Conley. Losing pitcher—Frank Sullivan. Attendance—45,643.

1956—At Griffith Stadium, Washington, July 10. Nationals 7, Americans 3. Managers—Walter Alston, Casey Stengel. Winning pitcher—Bob Friend. Losing pitcher—Billy Pierce. Attendance—28,843.

1957—At Busch Stadium, St. Louis, July 9. Americans 6, Nationals 5. Managers—Casey Stengel, Walter Alston. Winning pitcher—Jim Bunning. Losing pitcher—Curt Simmons. Attendance—30,693.

1958—At Memorial Stadium, Baltimore, July 8. Americans 4, Nationals 3. Managers—Casey Stengel, Fred Haney. Winning pitcher—Early Wynn. Losing pitcher—Bob Friend. Attendance—48,829.

1959 (first game)—At Forbes Field, Pittsburgh, July 7. Nationals 5, Americans 4. Managers—Fred Haney, Casey Stengel. Winning pitcher—Johnny Antonelli. Losing pitcher—Whitey Ford. Attendance—35,277.

1959 (second game)—At Memorial Coliseum, Los Angeles, August 3. Americans 5, Nationals 3. Managers—Casey Stengel, Fred Haney. Winning pitcher—Jerry Walker. Losing pitcher—Don Drysdale. Attendance—55,105.

1960 (first game)—At Municipal Stadium, Kansas City, July 11. Nationals 5, Americans 3. Managers—Walter Alston, Al Lopez. Winning pitcher—Bob Friend. Losing pitcher—Bill Monbouquette. Attendance—30,619.

1960 (second game)—At Yankee Stadium, New York, July 13. Nationals 6, Americans 0. Managers—Walter Alston, Al Lopez. Winning pitcher—Vern Law. Losing pitcher—Whitey Ford. Attendance—38,362.

1961 (first game)—At Candlestick Park, San Francisco, July 11. Nationals 5, Americans 4 (10 innings). Managers—Danny Murtaugh, Paul Richards. Winning pitcher—Stu Miller. Losing pitcher—Hoyt Wilhelm. Attendance—44,115.

1961 (second game)—At Fenway Park, Boston, July 31. Americans 1, Nationals 1 (nine-inning tie, stopped by rain). Managers—Paul Richards, Danny Murtaugh. Attendance—31,851.

1962 (first game)—At District of Columbia Stadium, Washington, July 10. Nationals 3, Americans 1. Managers—Fred Hutchinson, Ralph Houk. Winning pitcher—Juan Marichal. Losing pitcher—Camilo Pascual. Attendance—45,480.

1962 (second game)—At Wrigley Field, Chicago, July 30. Americans 9, Nationals 4. Managers—Ralph Houk, Fred Hutchinson. Winning pitcher—Ray Herbert. Losing pitcher—Art Mahaffey. Attendance—38,359.

1963—At Municipal Stadium, Cleveland, July 9. Nationals 5, Americans 3. Managers—Alvin Dark, Ralph Houk. Winning pitcher—Larry Jackson. Losing pitcher —Jim Bunning. Attendance—44,160.

1964—At Shea Stadium, New York, July 7. Nationals 7, Americans 4. Managers—Walter Alston, Al Lopez. Winning pitcher—Juan Marichal. Losing pitcher—Dick Radatz. Attendance—50,850.

1965—At Metropolitan Stadium, Bloomington (Minnesota), July 13. Nationals 6, Americans 5. Managers—Gene Mauch, Al Lopez. Winning pitcher—Sandy Koufax. Losing pitcher—Sam McDowell. Attendance—46,706.

1966—At Busch Memorial Stadium, St. Louis, July 12. Nationals 2, Americans 1 (10 innings). Managers—Walter Alston, Sam Mele. Winning pitcher—Gaylord Perry. Losing pitcher—Pete Richert. Attendance—49,936.

1967—At Anaheim Stadium, Anaheim (California), July 11. Nationals 2, Americans 1 (15 innings). Managers—Walter Alston, Hank Bauer. Winning pitcher—Don Drysdale. Losing pitcher—Jim Hunter. Attendance—46,309.

1968—At Astrodome, Houston, July 9 (night). Nationals 1, Americans 0. Managers—Red Schoendienst, Dick Williams. Winning pitcher—Don Drysdale. Losing pitcher—Luis Tiant. Attendance—48,321.

1969—At Robert F. Kennedy Memorial Stadium, Washington, July 23. Nationals 9, Americans 3. Managers—Red Schoendienst, Mayo Smith. Winning pitcher—Steve Carlton. Losing pitcher—Mel Stottlemyre. Attendance—45,259.

1970—At Riverfront Stadium, Cincinnati, July 14 (night). Nationals 5, Americans 4 (12 innings). Managers—Gil Hodges, Earl Weaver. Winning pitcher—Claude Osteen. Losing pitcher—Clyde Wright. Attendance—51,838.

1971—At Tiger Stadium, Detroit, July 13 (night). Americans 6, Nationals 4. Managers—Earl Weaver, George (Sparky) Anderson. Winning pitcher—Vida Blue. Losing pitcher—Dock Ellis. Attendance—53,559.

1972—At Atlanta Stadium, Atlanta, July 25 (night). Nationals 4, Americans 3 (10 innings). Managers—Danny Murtaugh, Earl Weaver. Winning pitcher—Tug McGraw. Losing pitcher—Dave McNally. Attendance—53,107.

1973—At Royals Stadium, Kansas City, July 24 (night). Nationals 7, Americans 1. Managers—George (Sparky) Anderson, Dick Williams. Winning pitcher—Rick Wise. Losing pitcher—Bert Blyleven. Attendance—40,849.

1974—At Three Rivers Stadium, Pittsburgh, July 23 (night): Nationals 7, Americans 2. Managers—Yogi Berra, Dick Williams. Winning pitcher—Ken Brett. Losing pitcher—Luis Tiant. Attendance—50,706.

1975—At Milwaukee County Stadium, Milwaukee, July 15 (night). Nationals 6, Americans 3. Managers—Walter Alston, Alvin Dark. Winning pitcher—Jon Matlack. Losing pitcher—Jim Hunter. Attendance—51,480.

1976—At Veterans Stadium, Philadelphia, July 13 (night). Nationals 7, Americans 1. Managers—George (Sparky) Anderson, Darrell Johnson. Winning pitcher—Randy Jones. Losing pitcher—Mark Fidrych. Attendance—63,974.

1977—At Yankee Stadium, New York, July 19 (night). Nationals 7, Americans 5. Managers—Alfred (Billy) Martin, George (Sparky) Anderson. Winning pitcher—Don Sutton. Losing pitcher—Jim Palmer. Attendance—56,683.

1978—At San Diego Stadium, San Diego, July 11. Nationals 7, Americans 3. Managers—Alfred (Billy) Martin, Thomas Lasorda. Winning pitcher—Bruce Sutter. Losing pitcher—Rich Gossage. Attendance—51,549.

AMERICANS FLEXED MUSCLES IN ORIENT

Twenty-five Americans played in Japan in 1979. Fifteen of the Americans hit at least 20 homers, topped by Charlie Manuel's 37. The entire contingent cracked 512 homers and drove in 2,504 runs.

Second baseman Felix Millan, playing in his second season in Japan, hit .346 to become the first foreigner to lead the Central League in hitting in more than 20 years.

Leron Lee and his younger brother Leon had strong seasons for the Lotte Orions. They combined for 63 home runs and 188 RBIs.

A list of Americans in Japan and their 1979 records follows:

Player—Club	G.	AB.	H.	HR.	RBI.	B.A.
Felix Millan, Yokohama Taiyo Whales	98	364	126	6	41	.346
Leron Lee, Lotte Orions	126	471	157	28	95	.333
Charlie Manuel, Kintetsu Buffaloes	97	333	108	37	94	.324
John Sipin, Yomiuri Giants	117	432	135	27	74	.313
Mike Reinbach, Hanshin Tigers	130	472	146	27	84	.309
Carlos May, Nankai Hawks	117	398	122	26	75	.307
Leon Lee, Lotte Orions	128	484	147	35	93	.304
Bobby Marcano, Hankyu Braves	127	502	150	32	97	.299
Jim Tyrone, Seibu Lions	58	220	64	8	24	.291
Jack Maloof, Seibu Lions	129	503	146	12	48	.290
Chris Arnold, Kintetsu Buffaloes	116	395	114	17	65	.289
Bobby Jones, Chunichi Dragons	110	367	105	16	56	.286
Sam Ewing, Nippon Ham Fighters	119	416	119	15	65	.286
John Scott, Yakult Swallows	112	434	118	28	81	.272
Jim Lyttle, Hiroshima Toyo Carp	130	504	133	23	61	.264
Dave Hilton, Yakult Swallows	105	399	103	19	48	.258
Gene Martin, Yokohama Taiyo Whales	125	417	106	28	83	.254
Wayne Garrett, Chunichi Dragons	115	417	105	20	71	.252
Frank Ortenzio, Nankai Hawks	113	387	96	23	56	.248
Bobby Mitchell, Nippon Ham Fighters	111	365	85	22	60	.233
Bernie Williams, Hankyu Braves	105	291	67	11	30	.230
Lee Stanton, Hanshin Tigers	121	457	103	23	58	.225
Henry Garrett, Hiroshima Toyo Carp	126	395	89	27	59	.225
Tony Muser, Seibu Lions	65	168	33	2	10	.196

Pitcher—Club	G.	W.	L.	IP.	BB.	SO.	ERA.
Rick Kreuger, Yomiuri Giants	18	2	1	29	12	16	4.66

WILLIE STARGELL
• PITTSBURGH PIRATES •
MAJOR LEAGUE
PLAYER OF THE YEAR

HANK PETERS
• BALTIMORE ORIOLES •
MAJOR LEAGUE EXECUTIVE

EARL WEAVER
• BALTIMORE ORIOLES •
MAJOR LEAGUE MANAGER

VERN BENSON
• SYRACUSE •
MINOR LEAGUE MANAGER

GEORGE SISLER JR.
• COLUMBUS, O. •
MINOR LEAGUE EXECUTIVE
IN CLASS AAA

MARK BOMBACK
• VANCOUVER •
MINOR LEAGUE PLAYER

BILL RIGNEY JR.
• MIDLAND •
MINOR LEAGUE EXECUTIVE
IN CLASS AA

The Sporting News

NO. **1**
MEN
of
1979

TOM ROMENESKO
• GREENSBORO •
MINOR LEAGUE EXECUTIVE
IN CLASS A

National League umpire Doug Harvey and his wife are shown walking in one of the many picket lines outside of major league parks in 1979.

REVIEW OF 1979

Including

Summation of Year's Activities

MVP Tables, All-Star Teams

Homers by Parks

With flags at half mast and Thurman Munson's picture shining down on them, Yankees players pay respect to their lost captain. The Yankees honored Munson during pregame ceremonies August 3.

Ump Walkout, Yanks' Troubles Dominated

By CLIFFORD KACHLINE

Prosperity and controversy, record attendance and turmoil, spectacular achievement and tragedy—all intermingled to make 1979 as eventful and historic a year as the long history of professional baseball has witnessed.

A three-month holdout by major league umpires and a spate of discontent and misfortune involving the defending world champion New York Yankees cast a shadow over much of the season. At the same time an unprecedented turnover in division champions combined with a new turnstile high and a sensational World Series to provide a glowing climax to the campaign. Unfortunately, the failure of management and the Players' Association to reach accord on new terms before expiration of their Basic Agreement at year's end posed the possibility of new problems ahead.

The labor dispute with the umpires and the occasionally comic, sometimes tragic aspects of the Yankees' futile bid for a fourth successive pennant were the overriding themes of the year. The arbiters' work stoppage was the longest job action by any group in baseball annals, while the death of Thurman Munson in the crash of his private plane and Billy Martin's on-again, off-again career as manager were only two of many unusual developments on the Yankees.

Origins of the Umpires' Action

The umpires' walkout was a followup to the abortive strike they staged on August 15, 1978, in a bid for more money and summer vacations. That work stoppage lasted just one day when a federal judge in Philadelphia ruled they must live up to their Basic Agreement with the two major leagues—a five-year document extending to December 31, 1980—and issued an injunction ordering them back to work.

After losing that battle in court, members of the Major League Umpires Association were urged by their attorney, Richie Phillips, to try a new approach in 1979. Individually they designated Phillips, a Philadelphia lawyer who also represented National Basketball Association referees, to act as their personal agent in negotiating terms of their '79 contracts.

The new strategy, aimed at individual contracts rather than the collective bargaining agreement, was designed to improve the arbiters' negotiating position. Besides a vacation during the season, the men in blue sought salary increases beyond the "minimum plateaus" stipulated in the Basic Agreement as well as higher per diem payments, job security or tenure and various other improvements.

Rising player salaries, a desire to attain pay parity with officials in other sports and rampant inflation that eroded their per diem allowances triggered the umpires' demands.

"Player salaries indicate a willingness and desire on the part of the owners to present a first-class product," Phillips said. "The umpires are part of that first-class product. I don't say they should be compensated the same as the players, but they are an integral part of the game, always on the road and always performing in pressure situations. Their salaries should reflect these factors."

The Umpires' Basic Agreement

Under their agreement with the two leagues, the umpires' minimum salaries for 1979 and 1980 were set at $17,500 for a first-year man, $22,500 in the fourth year, $27,000 in the seventh, $32,500 in the 10th, $36,000 in the 13th and $39,000 in the 16th. In addition, the pact called for annual minimum raises ranging from $1,000 for those in their second through fifth years, $1,250 for those in their sixth through 10th years and $1,500 for those in their 11th to 20th years. The per diem allowance for 1979 was established at $49 for spring training and $53 for the regular season.

Fifty-one of the 52 umpires scheduled to work in the majors in '79 turned their preferred contracts over to Phillips. The exception was Ted Hendry. He had been added to the American League staff to replace veteran Nestor Chylak, who retired and was appointed an assistant AL umpire supervisor.

According to Phillips, none of the 51 was offered more than $3,000 over the minimum and most were within $1,000 of scale. He said six earned less than $20,000 the previous year, 12 others were under $25,000 and 20 under $30,000, while the highest paid in 1978—other than Chylak—were Ed Vargo and Doug Harvey of the National League and Bill Haller of the American at $38,000 each.

By way of contrast, it was pointed out that a National Basketball Association official with 10 years' experience received a minimum of $45,000 for an 82-game season whereas a major league umpire with the same amount of experience was paid $32,500 for 162 games.

League Presidents React

When no signed contracts were returned, the two league presidents—Lee MacPhail of the American and Chub Feeney of the National—sent identical letters to each of the umpires on February 2. The letters advised that if they failed to sign they would not be permitted to report for duty in spring training and would risk loss of their jobs. The implied threat led Ron Luciano, veteran AL umpire and president of the Umpires Association, to comment: "Typical. I guess they figure we're all expendable and that they can walk into any bar, round up 52 guys and say, 'Hey, here's a blue suit. How about working our games?' "

The three principals—Phillips, Feeney and MacPhail—held several meetings during February, but the impasse continued when the league presidents stood firm. "Other than the players, they (the umpires) are compensated better than any group in baseball," MacPhail said. Feeney pointed out the arbiters also receive $1,500 if they work in the All-Star Game, $6,000 for the League Championship Series and $11,000 for the World Series. "And every other year they participate in one of these events on a rotating basis. One man last year went home with more than $50,000," he added.

With the issue remaining stalemated and the first spring exhibition games only a few days off, Feeney and MacPhail notified their clubs on March 2 to hire local umpires if the regular men in blue failed to sign. The upshot was that semi-pro and sandlot arbiters were pressed into action when the exhibitions began on March 7.

"Some people have the impression we're trying to break the collective bargaining agreement, which is a five-year contract," Phillips commented. "This simply is not true. Our umpires have individual contracts, subject to annual negotiation. The Basic Agreement only sets minimum salaries. Each individual has a right to negotiate beyond the offer the league has extended. This has been the practice through the years."

On March 16, attorneys for the two leagues instituted legal proceedings in the U.S. District Court in Philadelphia. They requested Federal Judge Joseph L. McGlynn, who had issued an injunction against the umpires the previous summer, to reinstate that order. In addition, they asked for fines of $10,000 against the men in blue for every day they remained off the job.

Judge McGlynn's Ruling

Following four days of testimony by league attorneys and several umpires, Judge McGlynn issued a ruling on March 26 denying baseball's motion. "There is no question in my mind that they (the umpires) are entitled to bargain as individuals," the judge said. "I have no authority to order them back to work. They are no longer employees of baseball because they have not signed their contracts."

Meanwhile, the dispute escalated when the umpires received notice from the league presidents that unless they signed by midnight of March 30 they would be released and rehired only if and when there were staff openings.

Five days before the start of the regular season, Phillips and 50 of the umpires—all except Hendry and Paul Pryor—met in Chicago for six and one-half hours. Pryor, an 18-year veteran of the National League, had signed a two-year contract a few weeks earlier. "In this dispute each individual has to make his own decision," he explained. "After much thought, discussion and consideration of the ramifications, my decision was to sign my contract for two years. I had a number of personal reasons that made it necessary for me to sign."

At their March 30 session, the 50 men in blue decided to stick together and rejected new offers from the league. "In no way can this be termed a strike," declared Phillips after the meeting. "It's more of an action. I believe the umpires feel more pride in their decision to see this through as a unit than they have ever felt."

Substitute Umpires Hired

The two leagues subsequently announced they would open the season with officiating crews consisting of one umpire from Triple A and three local arbiters. Each club was instructed to line up the three best local men available to work in home games. "In addition, a supervisor will be in the stands at each game to oversee each operation," MacPhail announced. "The umpires we are bringing in probably will be as good as the bottom half of the ones we have regularly."

That feeling presumably was not shared generally by managers and players. Recognizing the problem, they had refrained from arguing with the substitute arbiters during spring exhibitions. However, several managers and players expressed concern over the prospect of using fill-ins in regular-season contests.

"Everybody's going to realize the regular umpires are better than we thought they were," Jim Palmer, ace Baltimore Orioles pitcher, was quoted in the New York Times. "If they (the owners) want a good product, they're going to have to pay for it. Umpires have the toughest job in baseball. You want games decided by players, not umpires. But now it looks like the umpires could make the difference with a wrong call one way or another."

Although National Association umpires have no union affiliation, eight of the first 12 Triple-A arbiters invited to become major league crew chiefs in the emergency reportedly rejected the opportunity. They were offered two-year and three-year guaranteed contracts, but turned down the chance because of sympathies with their big league brethren. The eight were identified as Drew Coble, Bob Davidson, Gerry Davis, Dan Morrison and John (Rocky) Roe of the American Association and Randy Marsh, Charlie Williams and Mark Johnson of the Pacific Coast League.

Acceptances and Rejections

Those accepting crew chief assignments with the American League, in addition to Hendry, were John Shulock and Fred Spenn from the American Association, Dallas Parks from the International League, Derryl Cousins from the Pacific Coast League and Mike Fitzpatrick and Dick Nelson, former A.A. umpires who were part of the National Association Umpire Development staff. Nelson received his chance when Mark Johnson, after first accepting, backed out. Joining Pryor as crew chiefs in the National League were Lanny Harris, Steve Fields and Dave Pallone from the International League, Fred Brocklander from the Pacific Coast and Dick Tremblay, who last worked in the International in 1971.

Observer-consultants assigned to American League games included Dick Butler, the circuit's umpire supervisor, and assistant supervisors Nestor Chylak, Hank Soar and John Stevens. The National League had its two umpire consultants, Tom Gorman and Al Barlick, and former umpires Ken Burkhart, Emmett Ashford and Ed Sudol served in a supervisory capacity.

When the season opened April 4 in Cincinnati, approximately two dozen arbiters were joined by some union tradesmen in informational picketing outside Riverfront Stadium. The following day 25 umpires plus two NBA referees set up a picket line at Yankee Stadium and 13 arbiters paraded at Dodger Stadium for the inaugural games there. The picketers' signs had two messages: "Baseball Unfair to Umpires" or "Baseball Is Killing the Umpires." Contending they were being locked out, the men in blue said the picket lines were set up "just to inform the public of our stand, not to disrupt the game."

The non-working umpires continued their selective picketing. Stadiums from which nationally-televised games emanated on Saturday over NBC and on Monday night over ABC became special targets. Both networks aired pre-game coverage of the dispute. The arbiters also marched outside the American and National League offices.

Pryor Changes His Mind

After working the inaugural in Cincinnati and then St. Louis' opener two nights later, Pryor experienced a change of heart on April 7. He notified Feeney of his decision and joined his colleagues on the picket line that evening. "I've spent four sleepless nights and finally decided that I couldn't go on like this for 162 games having people call me a scab and other names," he explained.

However, 24 hours later, Pryor, who had drawn heated criticism from his fellow umpires before joining them, was back in uniform on the advice of

PAUL PRYOR had a change of heart April 7 and joined his fellow umpires on the picket lines, after he had worked the openers in Cincinnati and St. Louis.

Phillips. Because of the 10-day termination notice in his contract, Pryor was told by the Umpires Association attorney to remain on the job through April 16. The league then hired Bill Lawson of the Pacific Coast League as a replacement.

On April 16 Hendry gave MacPhail 10 days' notice. "I've been so humiliated working with that caliber of umpires," he told a press conference in New York. Hendry, who had filled in in the American League each of the two previous seasons, signed his first big league contract in February after 11 years in the minors. While few colleagues had sympathy for Pryor, the veteran umpires had shown no hostility toward Hendry. To replace Hendry, the AL called up Rick Reed from the International League.

Umpires Receive Outside Support

The holdouts began receiving backing from other fronts. One umpires' association in Cleveland and another in San Diego voted to prohibit their members from working major league games, and several unions threw their support to the arbiters. In Pittsburgh union officers kicked off the labor war by going on TV on April 13 and urging union members and their families not to attend Pirates games. As a result, the Pirates drew just 10,950 for a Saturday game, April 14, despite a helmet giveaway, and only 3,012 fans turned out on Easter Sunday. The umpires contended the picket line of 200 prompted thousands of fans to turn back.

A game in Detroit on April 21 almost had to be canceled because of the dispute. The grounds crew, electricians and concessions and service employees at Tiger Stadium declined to cross the picket line. However, the umpires later removed the picket line "in the best interest of the fans" and the game was played.

The Turning Point

The turning point in the dispute occurred on April 21 when Phillips, MacPhail and Feeney met in Princeton, N.J. It was their first head-to-head session since breaking off negotiations on March 24. The two leagues, which had notified the umpires that their benefit program, including medical and dental coverage, would expire on April 30, promptly rescinded the directive. Two more meetings were held the following week.

Developments on the field added urgency to the issue. On April 24 at Shea Stadium the fill-in umpires reversed themselves twice during an argument that raged for 28 minutes and wound up issuing a split decision that pleased neither team. Both managers—Joe Torre of the Mets and Joe Altobelli of the Giants—protested the game. And on May 9 the substitute arbiters ejected four managers, one coach and five players amid a flurry of controversy and chaos.

The disputed calls reportedly led the club owners to pressure Feeney and MacPhail to hasten the settlement. An agreement ending the three-month dispute and assuring the umpires of pay increases and summer vacations finally was hammered out during a 14-hour session in New York on May 17. The following day all 52 umpires attended a four-hour meeting in Philadelphia and ratified the pact. After being idle 45 days of the 180-day season, they returned to work on May 19.

Their return spelled the end to a dream experienced by more than 170 local arbiters. One of the group—Al Forman—had umpired in the National League several seasons in the 1960s, but for the others it was the walkout that gave them a shot at the big leagues. For their efforts they earned $108.03 per game, the equivalent of the first-year scale of $17,500.

Local Umpires Listed

The list of local arbiters employed during the dispute follows:

AMERICAN LEAGUE

Baltimore—Robert Roesner, James O'Connor, G. Howard Phipps, Ralph Keister.

Boston—Lester Pratt, Richard Clegg, Clarence Merritt, James McNally, Richard LaPierre, William N. Robinson, Robert F. Clement.

California–Boyd Mauer, Dale Williams, Charles Lupo, Robert Campbell.

Chicago–Marvin Hecht, David Slickenmeyer, Gene Fowler, Woody Urchak, William Sprincz, Alfred Scheel, William Laude, Gary McAvoy.

Cleveland–Harry Farnsworth, Robert Rice, Donald Schirmer, Edward George, Theodore Theilander, Dale Davidson, Russell Terlop.

Detroit–Doug Cossey, Tom Ravashiere, Bob Moyer, Richard Runchey, Amerigo Zuccaro, Joseph Kavulich, John Camp.

Kansas City–Donald Schulte, Harold Easley, Robert G. Jones, Larry Zirbel, Al Purduski, A. Duane Shaw.

Milwaukee–James D. O'Brien, Ken Kirby, Richard Heitzer, Douglas Brown, Mike Farmer, James Mulcahy.

Minnesota–Michael Briscese, George Sweeney, William Ivory, Eugene Kelly, Lawrence Elmer Gallagher, William Fred Hafner, Les Novack, William Follmer.

New York–Merrill Hadry, Thomas O'Connor, Jerry Loeber, Philip Lospitalier, John Mackin, Harold Siroka, Al Forman, James Dunne, Richard Lazar, Lester Fuchs, William E. Henry, Donald Slattery, L. Leonard Riccio, Harry Trimmer.

Oakland–Henry Tillman, Steven Borga, Charles Swenson, Roy Roth, James Cuneo, Tony Patch.

Seattle–Roy Dreke, George Eshelman, Jay Levet, Gale Miller, David Perez, Jack Miller, Homer Bishop, Richard Feaser, Charles Jackson, Buddy Brown, James Marino, Frederick Mabbott.

Texas–Jeff Brown, Johnny F. James, Michael G. Thompson, Joe Bob Taylor.

Toronto–Richard Panas, Joseph Sawchuk, Alan Contant, Peter Schaefer, Adrian Ferreira, Richard Willie, Jr.

NATIONAL LEAGUE

Atlanta–Hank Roundtree, Ed Norris, Lewis Anderson, Jack Baswell, Jack Stansell, Jim Waller.

Chicago–Richard Cavanaugh, Joseph Pomponi, Robert Maher, Dennis Riccio, David Slickenmeyer.

Cincinnati–Leslie Treitel, Roger Grooms, Mick Sharkey, Cliff Schaller, Ed Oliger, Jerry Fick, Richard Urlage, Bill Andress, Ron Jeffers.

Houston–Robert Schroeder, Howard Hanson, Murray Strey, James Rains, Ray Hamil, Robert Davis, Eugene Smith, Howard Jumper.

Los Angeles–Jim Scott, Charles Lupo, Boyd Mauer, Dale Williams, Jack Conn.

Montreal–Michael Spinelli, John Baird, Emilien Cote, Jacques Lauzon.

New York–Harold Siroka, Don Slattery, L. Leonard Riccio, Jerry Loeber, Philip Lospitalier, Merrill Hadry, Mike Barston, William Henry.

Philadelphia–Bob Nelson, Joseph Myers, Tom Telford, Greg Mills, John Schleyer.

Pittsburgh–Joe Schratz, Ron Hutson, Joe Mrvos, Harry Smail, Bob Beck.

St. Louis–Robert Sharp, Ray Perez, Marvin "Bud" Miller, Robert Hantak, Pete Negri, Tom Fleming, James Jones, Joseph Bendekovits, Robert Freels.

San Diego–Terry Bovey, Frank Campagna, Frank Fisher, John Stewart.

San Francisco–James Cuneo, Tony Patch, Roy Roth, Henry Tillman.

Agreement Reached

Under terms of their new agreement, which was extended through 1981, the umpires received salary increases ranging from $4,500 for first-year men to $10,500 for veterans, raising the scale for a 20-year man from $40,000 to $50,000. Most arbiters also were assured two weeks off during each season. The vacation clause, a concession that required both leagues to hire four extra umpires, was considered a major breakthrough for the men in blue. It was estimated the settlement would cost the two leagues $2,500,000 extra over the three-year life of the agreement.

"I'm extremely pleased because we got more than we asked for originally," Phillips said. "We demanded an average salary increase of $10,000 a man, which would have cost the leagues $520,000 a year. We got an average of $7,000 a man plus an average increase of $3,000 in the per diem plus vacations and a no-cut contract, which the umpires had never had."

Terms of the Settlement

Specific terms of the settlement included the following:

—Individual contracts were replaced by fixed salaries based on service.

—Salaries start at $22,000 for a first-year umpire and go to $28,000 for a fifth-year man, $38,000 in the 10th and $45,000 in the 15th year.

—Per diem rate for hotels, meals and transportation was increased from $51 to $67 during the 1979 season, to $72 in 1980 and $77 in 1981.

—Umpires will receive one week off during their first year in the majors and two weeks thereafter, including travel expenses to and from their homes.

—The umpires' pension plan, which was due to expire in 1979, was extended through 1982.

—Spring training compensation was increased from $40 to $50 per game and the spring training per diem to $55.

—Umpires with four years of service will have to work no more than 15 days of spring training.

—National League umpires will receive an additional $1,000 for serving as crew chiefs, the same as AL crew chiefs traditionally received.

—All umpires to be paid retroactively to May 11, the date on which both parties had substantial agreement on the bargaining issues.

—Both leagues agreed there would be no retribution against any of the umpires who walked the picket line.

—In the event of a player strike, umpires will receive 45 days pay.

—Any returnee released in 1980 will receive one full year of suverence pay.

—The umpires acceded to the league's demand that the rotation system to select umpires for the All-Star Game, League Championship Series and World Series be abandoned after 1981 and that the league presidents be permitted thereafter to select the umpires for those special events on a merit basis. The arrangement, however, included certain restrictions: No umpire will work more than one special assignment in a year; no umpire will work on special assignment two years in succession or receive more than two assignments in a three-year period.

Another benfit gained by the umpires involved the "thrift plan" in their pension agreement. Under the plan each arbiter is permitted to put five percent of his salary in savings and the league contributes a matching amount. The new agreement provides the leagues will continue their five percent contribution but waives the umpires' contributions for three years.

To fill out their expanded staffs, the American League decided to retain Shulock, Spenn, Parks and Cousins while the National League kept Harris, Fields, Pallone and Brocklander. They were integrated into crews with the regular arbiters. Of the other substitutes, Reed returned to the International League and Lawson to the Pacific Coast, Tremblay went home to pursue a business venture and Fitzpatrick and Nelson resumed their roles with the minors' umpire development staff.

Bitterness Remained

The lingering undercurrent of bitterness that developed between those who worked and those who went payless during the walkout did not end with the settlement. The eight newcomers generally were shunned by the regulars both on and off the field and treated like social outcasts. On at least one occasion a new man, upon arriving in the umpires' dressing room, found the names of the three regulars taped over their lockers while "SCAB" appeared above his locker. Another rookie arbiter found his equipment vandalized upon reporting to a game. The treatment accorded the new men prompted some writers to refer to them as the "Ostracized Eight."

Richie Phillips Gets Big Fee

While the umpires made significant gains in their new agreement, another big winner in the dispute was Phillips. It was disclosed that the Philadelphia attorney, who had been on a $12,500 a year retainer, was rewarded with a five percent slice from each umpire's annual pay through the league checkoff system. Estimates were that his fee over the three-year life of the contract will amount to more than $250,000.

Problems of the Yankees

For the Yankees the year was even more hectic and traumatic than for the umpires. It was, in fact, a nightmarish year for the New Yorkers, one their fans will never forget. The tragic accident that claimed the life of Munson obviously marked the darkest moment. But disappointment, discontent and turbulence swirled about the team continually. The center of much of the controversy was Billy Martin even though he managed the team only part of the season.

Actually the Yankees' difficulties began prior to spring training. In mid-February coach Ellie Howard came down with a viral infection affecting the muscles around the heart. The ailment hospitalized him for seven weeks and kept him out of uniform all year.

Spring training itself was almost a portent of things to come. The club had high hopes of gaining a third straight world championship following the spectacular finish of 1978 after Bob Lemon replaced Martin as skipper, but the Yankees fared dismally in spring exhibitions. To add to their woes relief ace Rich "Goose" Gossage missed considerable time with a toe infection.

Rich Gossage Injured

Just when Gossage appeared to be rounding into form, the first major blow struck. It came during a post-game clubhouse scuffle between Gossage and Cliff Johnson, husky reserve catcher, on April 19. What presumably began as a friendly needling session erupted into a shoving match, with Gossage suffering a torn ligament in the thumb of his pitching hand. The injury required surgery and sidelined the Yankee reliever until July 12.

Six days after the incident the Yankees announced they were fining the two combatants the equivalent of 10 days' pay each—$18,603 in the case of Gossage, $5,586 for Johnson. The fines later were rescinded when the players filed grievances.

Gossage's absence had a devastating effect as the Yankees quickly fell behind in the race. The altercation also had other repercussions. With the club badly in need of a reliable reliever, ace Ron Guidry volunteered to work out of the bullpen for several weeks. The move wound up costing him a chance at another 20-victory season. And Johnson was traded to Cleveland on June 15.

Billy Martin Returns to Yankees

The next big chapter in the Yankee saga unfolded shortly after the trading deadline. With the team buried in fourth place, owner George Steinbrenner pulled another startling switch. He dismissed Lemon as manager and brought back Martin. The change was officially announced June 18, but the story broke two nights earlier during the Yankees' game at Texas when Rangers owner Brad Corbett, who had learned of Steinbrenner's plans, spilled word to the writers.

BILLY MARTIN fashions the Yankees pin-stripes once again, taking over for manager Bob Lemon in mid-season.

"I think if it (the Yankee season) can be turned around, the (Martin) is the guy to do it," explained Steinbrenner, who was said to feel that Lemon was too easy-going. "Last year I needed someone 180 degrees from what Billy was. This year I need someone 180 degrees from what Lemon was." Martin, who had been scouting for the club, received a contract extending through 1981. Lemon was reassigned to front-office and scouting duties. He also had a contract through 1981.

Martin found a hero's welcome awaiting him upon his arrival in New York. An estimated 80 reporters, broadcasters and photographers plus a horde of fans were on hand at LaGuardia Airport when he arrived early the evening of June 18.

The following night a crowd of 36,211 showed up at Yankee Stadium to celebrate his return. Club officials estimated his appearance attracted an extra 15,000 customers. As a result of the unexpected crush at the turnstiles, the start of the game was delayed 15 minutes. Upon being introduced, Billy received a two-minute standing ovation. Unfortunately, the visiting Toronto Blue Jays spoiled the evening by winning, 5-4.

Originally, Martin wasn't scheduled to resume managerial duties with the Yankees until 1980. That was the timetable announced by Steinbrenner when he rehired Billy the previous summer. However, until a month before his return, there was some doubt that he'd be back because of a suit pending against him.

The legal action resulted from a fight the feisty Martin had with sports-writer Ray Hagar during halftime of a basketball game at Reno, Nev., in November 1978. When Hagar filed suit for assault, Steinbrenner announced his former skipper would have to be exonerated in the incident if he were to come back as Yankees manager. The situation finally was resolved on May 24 when Martin met with Hagar and apologized publicly to the sportswriter, who had agreed to an out-of-court settlement estimated at $7,500. The money supposedly was put up by backers of Reno's professional basketball team.

Martin and Reggie Jackson

Martin's return to the Yankees' helm revived an old problem—the apparently irreconcilable differences between him and slugger Reggie Jackson. Reggie, in the third season of a five-year contract, was on the disabled list with a leg injury when Billy took over from Lemon. On June 25 the Yankees issued a statement disclosing that Jackson had asked the club to put him on waivers so a possible trade could be worked out. Ironically, Reggie and six other Yankees had been placed on the waiver list several days earlier, but Jackson's name was withdrawn when he failed to clear AL waivers.

"No man is indispensable," Steinbrenner was quoted as saying with reference to the Jackson-Martin situation. "You can't ask a manager to crawl on his knees. Certainly Billy has said all the right things (about Jackson) and done all the right things." A statement released by the Yankees added the club "felt strongly that Martin had done everything expected of him in his effort to reconcile differences with Jackson and that it was clearly up to Jackson now."

Yankees officials then provided Martin with an alternative to Reggie by claiming Bobby Murcer from the Chicago Cubs on June 26. When Jackson returned to action a few days later, Martin made a conscious effort to repair old wounds by telling the press: "We need Reggie to win the pennant. We

Rookie umpire Dallas Parks finds Billy Martin back in his old form.

can't do it without him.'' The two antagonists maintained an uneasy truce the remainder of the campaign.

Al Rosen Departs Yankees

It wasn't long, however, before the Yankees found things popping on another front. On July 19 Al Rosen resigned as president of the club following differences with Steinbrenner and Martin. The former Cleveland third base-man had succeeded Gabe Paul as the Yankees prexy early in 1978.

Rosen had indicated unhappiness over his reduced role in baseball opera-tions and an increased involvement with the business end, but the big factor in his decision to quit apparently was the constant criticism and pressure from Steinbrenner. The Yankees boss was said to have come down hard on Rosen over the rescheduling of a July 13 Yankees game at Anaheim. Origi-nally set to start at 7:30, the Friday contest was moved up to 5:30 at the request of the American League to accommodate ABC-TV's national tele-cast. Facing Nolan Ryan in twilight, the New Yorkers managed just one hit in losing, 6-1, and Steinbrenner allegedly hit the roof.

Rosen's departure brought to 12 the number of front-office employees, excluding secretaries, who had left the Yankees since Steinbrenner acquired the club. Rosen subsequently accepted a position with Bally Maufacturing Corp. as executive vice-president in charge of that organization's new casino hotel in Atlantic City, N. J.

George Sisler, Jr., longtime minor league executive and head of the Yankees' Columbus (International) farm team, became the leading choice to fill the vacancy left by Rosen's action. However, the 62-year-old son of the late Hall of Famer rejected the opportunity in favor of staying with his lu-crative position at Columbus, O.

The Death of Thurman Munson

The most shocking blow to befall the Yankees, of course, was the tragic death of Munson. After closing a nine-day trip with a night game in Chicago, August 1, the team enjoyed an open date. Munson took advantage of the occasion to fly home to Canton, O., as he frequently had done throughout the season. He wanted to visit his family and practice landings and takeoffs in his new twin-engine Cessna Citation jet. He had purchased the plane a month earlier. It reportedly cost him $1,400,000.

At 3:02 p.m. on August 2, with Munson at the controls, the craft came down 1,000 feet short of the runway while attempting a landing at Akron-Canton airport and crashed. The 32-year-old Yankees catcher-captain was killed as the plane burst into flames. The two others aboard, David Hall, a flight instructor, and Jerry Anderson, a friend of Munson's, survived although both were injured.

Munson had held a pilot's license for several years, but had limited experience with the jets. Both Steinbrenner and Martin had implored him to give up piloting his own plane.

The night following the mishap a crowd of 51,151 joined in an emotional memorial tribute to the fallen catcher at Yankee Stadium prior to the game against Baltimore. The eight Yankees starters—excluding the catcher—stood motionless at their positions, heads bowed, and the other members of both teams stood on the top steps of their respective dugouts while Terence Cardinal Cooke, archbishop of New York, offered a prayer. Robert Merrill, Metropolitan Opera star, then sang "America The Beautiful," after which cheers and applause thundered through the stadium for nine minutes as Munson's portrait and a message of inspiration were alternately flashed on the scoreboard. The Yankees also announced that Munson's uniform No. 15 would be retired, that his locker would remain vacant in the clubhouse and that a plaque would be placed on the center-field wall in his memory.

On Monday morning, August 6, the entire Yankees team, including wives, flew by charter to Canton for the funeral services. Three members of the Baltimore Orioles—Rick Dempsey, Scott McGregor and Tippy Martinez, all ex-Yankees—as well as Rosen and Joe Torre, Manager of the New York Mets, also joined the Yankees' charter. Commissioner Bowie Kuhn, American League President Lee MacPhail, his assistant, Bob Fishel, and Bob Lemon left Hall of Fame ceremonies in Cooperstown, N. Y., to attend the services, while various other players and club officials also were present. Munson's teammates Lou Piniella and Bobby Murcer participated by reading from the Scriptures and delivering eulogies. Following the services, the Yankees players flew back to New York for that night's series finale against the Orioles, but several of the wives remained to comfort Munson's widow, Diane, and their three children—Tracy, 9; Kelly, 7; and Mike, 4.

Munson was in the first year of a three-year contract calling for an annual salary of $400,000. The pact reportedly did not include the usual clause freeing a team from payments in the event of death while flying a private plane.

Details of the Plane Crash

A coroner's report released September 7 concluded Munson was fully conscious after the crash but died of asphyxiation. The report also stated he did not have his shoulder harness connected at the time of the mishap and as a result his head struck the instrument panel on impact, snapping his spine and paralyzing him.

Following an investigation, the National Transportation Safety Board ruled out mechanical defects as the cause of the crash and blamed it on pilot error. Late in November, Cornhill Insurance Co. Ltd., an associate of Lloyds of London, filed suit seeking to have its policy on Munson's jet declared invalid. The company alleged Munson violated a provision of the policy that required him to fly with a pilot-instructor until he had accumulated 100 hours of flying time in a jet. The firm claimed the Yankees catcher had only 42 hours of flight time.

In New York City steps were taken to honor him. A City Council committee approved a bill calling for renaming a section of East 156th Street outside Yankee Stadium as "Thurman Munson Way."

More Trouble for Martin

Munson's tragic death was hardly the end of the Yankees' woes. Martin found himself entangled in controversy again following an incident in a game at Cleveland, September 18. A story in the New York Times charged the Yankees manager ordered rookie pitcher Bob Kammeyer to hit the Indians' Cliff Johnson, an early-season Yankees player, with a pitch and that Martin gave the young hurler $100 in $20 bills as a reward when he returned to the dugout one batter later. Martin admitted handing the money to his pitcher, but contended it was to pay for dinner and a night on the town for Kammeyer and two fellow rookie hurlers, Paul Mirabella and Rick Anderson.

The episode led to an investigation by MacPhail. On October 4, the American League president announced he found no reason to take disciplinary action against Martin for the incident. While declaring it was apparent a brushback pitch was thrown, MacPhail said he was convinced there was no intent to hit Johnson and that he believed Martin's version that the $100 gift to Kammeyer was for nothing more than a dinner for the three players.

Martin Fights Marshmallow Salesman

Martin's most serious scrape was yet to come. After seeing his team finish a desultory fourth in the AL East, he went pheasant hunting in South Dakota for four days in mid-October with his close friend, Howard Wong, a Minneapolis restaurateur. On returning to Minneapolis the pair made a stop at L'Hotel de France in suburban Bloomington late the evening of October 23 and were engaged in conversation at the bar by Joseph W. Cooper, a 52-year-old marshmallow salesman from Lincolnshire, Ill. Later an altercation developed. Police and hotel security reports charged that Martin hit Cooper after they left the bar. The salesman required 15 stitches to close a cut on his lip.

Publicly, Martin denied striking Cooper and claimed he had fallen. However, Billy reportedly admitted to Steinbrenner through an intermediary that he had hit Cooper. Both the Yankees owner and Commissioner Bowie Kuhn immediately launched investigations.

Yankees Fire Martin

On October 28 the Yankees announced Martin's dismissal as manager. "We just can't have him getting into these things every two months," commented Steinbrenner, who had been supportive of Martin in many of his earlier controversies. "It's not good for the Yankee organization." Martin still had two years remaining on his $120,000 annual contract and continued on the payroll.

Two days after Billy's firing, Cooper broke his silence and gave his version of the incident to the media. "The reason I stayed silent so long was I didn't want Martin to lose his job," the salesman said. "But I couldn't stand all the lies that went around." He then told how the Yankees manager had sucker-punched him after becoming belligerent during a baseball discussion.

Not satisfied to leave well enough alone, Martin released a statement through his agent on October 30. Part of it was aimed at comments by several of Steinbrenner's friends to the effect the Yankees boss was worried about the possibility of Billy getting involved in more serious incidents. "I do not want or need any more of George Steinbrenner's so-called help," the statement read. "He should not be allowed to run my life any more or to interfere with my future in baseball. I will always love baseball and I want the fans to know I will be back."

Kuhn Warns Martin

During his investigation, Commissioner Kuhn had members of his security staff meet with Martin, November 9, and then he met personally with Billy approximately two weeks later. He rendered his verdict on November 29, notifying the ex-manager via letter that he was letting him off with a warning. While saying he had decided not to impose any fine or suspension, the commissioner warned Martin to stay out of future trouble or he would face stern disciplinary action."

"I think you will agree the cumulative effect of these incidents tends to indicate you have not taken every reasonable step to avoid a fight," Kuhn wrote the former Yankees skipper. "You assured me at our meeting, however, that in the future, and notwithstanding possible provocation, you will take every measure to insure that this type of brawling, which places baseball and you personally in such an unfavorable light, will not happen again."

Within two weeks Martin, who some observers feel has a self-destruct button, was in hot water again. After giving a talk at the University of Rhode Island, December 11, he made reference during a question/answer session to Steinbrenner being "sick." MacPhail promptly warned Martin that continued inflammatory remarks about the Yankees and their owner could endanger his return to baseball.

Even with all of the problems and the disappointing fourth-place finish, the Yankees enjoyed at least one bright spot. They had a sensational season at the turnstiles, attracting 2,537,765 at home. It was the second-highest figure in American League history and the fourth straight year they topped two million.

Attendance Reaches All-Time High

Overall, major league attendance totaled 43,550,398 for the regular season. This marked the fourth successive year and the eighth time in the last 11 years that the majors achieved a new gate high. Despite a decrease of more than 485,000, the Los Angeles Dodgers again set the pace with 2,860,954. In addition to the Dodgers and Yankees, six other teams went over the two-million mark. Only Oakland and Seattle in the American League and New York and Atlanta in the National failed to draw one million.

Even the minor leagues enjoyed a turnstile boom. While the majors' turnstile count was up 7.2 percent, the National Association reported an attendance of 15,238,335, representing a gain of 2,226,608 or 17.9 percent over the previous season.

Heated races in three of the four divisions and a complete turnover in first-place finishers contributed to the majors' attendance increase. For the first time since the leagues split into divisions in 1969, not a single defending champion repeated. Only one—the Kansas City Royals—was even in contention, finishing second to the California Angels. Of the other '78 champions, the Dodgers wound up third and the Yankees and Philadelphia Phillies both were fourth.

Storm Clouds on the Horizon

While management was cheering the attendance rise, a new economic battle appeared to be taking shape. Both the major league owners and the Players' Association girded for the collective bargaining sessions mandated by expiration of their Basic Agreement on December 31, 1979, and of the players' pension contract three months later. Heading the opposing camps were Ray Grebey, the owners' chief negotiator as director of the Player Relations Committee, and Marvin Miller, executive director of the Players' Association. Members of the Players Relations Committee included the two league presidents, Feeney and MacPhail, together with Joe Burke of Kansas City, Ed Fitzgerald of Milwaukee, Clark Griffith of Minnesota, Bob Howsam of Cincinnati, John McHale of Montreal and Dan Galbreath of Pittsburgh.

The two sides launched formal negotiations in mid-November, but as the year ended there were no indications that a settlement was imminent. As a matter of fact, concern was being expressed in some quarters that the labor skirmishing might affect the start of the '80 season.

While the disclosure by management that a 60-day notice to terminate the Basic Agreement had been served on October 30 was routine, it did little to improve the atmosphere. Grebey explained the notice was filed under the National Labor Relations Act to "protect the employer from anything that might come from negotiations." Although admitting there was nothing improper about the club's termination notice, Miller pointed out the owners took a similar step in 1975 prior to expiration of the previous agreement and then locked out the players the following spring.

The Owners' War Chest

It also was revealed that the owners set up a "mutual assistance fund," to which teams contributed two percent of their 1979 home gate receipts. According to one official, the fund was intended to make certain that "weaker clubs won't go under in case of a strike." Contributions to the fund from the 1979 season were estimated at around $3,500,000.

While confirming existence of the fund, Grebey said it was no different from a similar fund established by the Players' Association late in 1978. "It provides for needs that might grow out of the negotiations," Grebey said of the owners' fund. A prime source of revenue for the players' war chest, which was estimated at more than $1,000,000, was their licensing program.

The $500,000 Gag

Because of a new cohesiveness among management, details of the proposals being considered by the two sides were sketchy. To maintain a united stand, the owners voted to establish fines of up to $500,000 for any club official who discussed the negotiations publicly. "The problem last time (in 1975) was that everybody was shooting off his mouth," one executive commented. "We have to give them (the negotiators) a chance to conduct this in an orderly fashion without people going off in 26 different directions."

Proposals and Counterproposals

Despite the top-secret nature of the bargaining sessions, the media learned details of some proposals that were put forth. One plan offered by management called for doing away with salary negotiations and arbitration during a player's first six years in the majors. Instead, those falling in this category—about 75 percent of all players—would receive one-year contracts with salaries conforming to an established scale. The owners also were seeking a change in the compensation rule when a club loses a player to free agency, asking that the compensation be another major league player rather than a choice in the amateur draft.

On the other hand, the Players' Association reportedly wanted to reduce free-agent eligibility from six years of major league service to four and was trying to eliminate the five-year period a player must wait before becoming a free agent again.

"Some people felt the game might be in danger because of free agency, but we have found out baseball is in its most prosperous period," a member of the players' Executive Board commented.

The Players' Association also was said to be seeking improvements in pension benefits and the World Series pool, an increase in the major league salary minimum of $21,000 and changes involving scheduling.

Players' Free Agency

The fourth year of the free agency rule found 44 players going that route following the 1979 season. Another—outfielder Ken Griffey of the Cincinnati Reds—missed a chance to join the group because he fell one day short of the required six years. And the Houston Astros narrowly avoided losing outfielder Jose Cruz to free agency by settling a contract dispute with him just before the November 1 deadline. Cruz and his agent had inked a letter of agreement in July covering a five-year pact calling for an estimated $1,800,000. However, disagreement over certain deferred payment procedures held up the actual contract signing.

The New York Yankees reported the most players eligible for free agency—five—while the Chicago White Sox had four. Twenty-seven of the 44 were from American League teams. The complete list of players included in the fourth reentry draft follows:

AMERICAN LEAGUE

Baltimore—Pitcher Don Stanhouse. **Boston**—Catcher Bob Montgomery, first baseman Bob Watson. **California**—Pitcher Nolan Ryan, outfielder Merv Rettenmund. **Chicago**—Catcher Milt May, infielders Don Kessinger and Jorge Orta, outfielder Rusty Torres. **Cleveland**—Pitcher Rick Wise. **Detroit**—None. **Kansas City**—Pitcher Al Hrabosky, shortstop Fred Patek. **Milwaukee**—Outfielder Jim Wohlford. **Minnesota**—Pitcher Dave Goltz, catcher Glenn Borgmann. **New York**—Pitchers Don Hood and Jim Kaat, first baseman George Scott, infielder-outfielder Lenny Randle, outfielder Roy White. **Oakland**—Pitcher Dave Hamilton, infielder Dave Chalk. **Seattle**—Pitcher Wayne

Twitchell, infielder-outfielder Bobby Valentine, outfielder Willie Horton. **Texas**—None. **Toronto**—First baseman Tony Solaita, infielder Tim Johnson.

NATIONAL LEAGUE

Atlanta—Outfielder Rowland Office. **Chicago**—None. **Cincinnati**—Pitcher Fred Norman, second baseman Joe Morgan, outfielder Paul Blair. **Houston**—Outfielder Jesus Alou. **Los Angeles**—Pitcher Lerrin LaGrow. **Montreal**—Pitcher Rudy May, first baseman Tony Perez. **New York**—Pitchers Andy Hassler and Skip Lockwood, first baseman Ed Kranepool. **Philadelphia**—Outfielder Greg Gross. **Pittsburgh**—Pitchers Dock Ellis and Bruce Kison, second baseman Rennie Stennett. **St. Louis**—None. **San Diego**—Outfielder Jay Johnstone. **San Francisco**—Pitcher John Curtis.

The Reentry Draft

The reentry draft was held November 2 at the Plaza Hotel in New York City. Pitcher Dave Goltz turned out to be the top choice. Thirteen clubs named him in the first round, giving him the distinction of being the first player to be chosen that often in the opening round. He was one of four players selected by the maximum of 14 clubs, including their own. The others were Bruce Kison, John Curtis and Rennie Stennett.

Many observers had anticipated that Nolan Ryan would be the prime pick, but his prospective asking price doubtless deterred some teams. Even so, the California Angels' fireballer was named by 13 clubs, including the Angels.

Ten players were not picked by any team. They were Jesus Alou, Glenn Borgmann, Tim Johnson, Don Kessinger, Ed Kranepool, Bob Montgomery, Lenny Randle, Merv Rettenmund, Rusty Torres and Wayne Twitchell. Six others—Paul Blair, Dock Ellis, Jim Kaat, Lerrin LaGrow, George Scott and Tony Solaita—were selected by only one team and thus also became free to dicker with any club.

Nolan Ryan's Big Contract

As expected, Ryan wound up the richest member of the fourth class of free agents. He signed a four-year contract with the Houston Astros calling for $4,500,000, including $1 million per season plus a $250,000 signing bonus and an additional $250,000 for "public relations activities" in 1984. His salary is guaranteed for the first three years.

Although club owners have lamented the upward-spiraling salaries, the first 22 free agents who signed were given contracts worth a guaranteed total of $32 million, according to a year-end survey by Murray Chass of the New York Times. By contrast, the contracts of the 32 free agents signed the previous winter totaled less than $20 million.

The biggest spenders were the Dodgers. They committed themselves to a reported $5.1 million in signing pitchers Dave Goltz and Don Stanhouse and an additional $300,000 for a two-year contract with outfielder Jay Johnstone. The San Francisco Giants guaranteed three free agents—Rennie Stennett, Milt May and Jim Wohlford—a total of $4,825,000.

In all, 15 players signed pacts that offer them the potential of earning $1 million or more. Only 10 players inked contracts worth at least a million dollars in each of the two previous years, while the first free-agent market in 1976 produced 14 millionaires.

NOLAN RYAN   DAVE GOLTZ

A list of free agents besides Ryan who received contracts worth a million dollars or more in 1979 follows:

Rennie Stennett, signed by San Francisco for five years for a guaranteed $3 million, including a salary of $450,000 per season plus a $1 million signing bonus, half of which is deferred at 10 percent interest until retirement.

Dave Goltz, signed by Los Angeles for six years for a total of $3 million. Salary of $425,000 per season and a $450,000 signing bonus.

Bruce Kison, signed by California for $2,465,000 guaranteed. Salary of $160,000 per season for five years, $750,000 signing bonus, $800,000 deferred, $15,000 relocational allowance plus, at the Angels' option, a salary of $376,000 for a sixth year (1985) or $100,000 guaranteed payment if released before 1985.

Al Hrabosky, signed by Atlanta for $2.2 million for five years. Signing bonus of $250,000 and salary of $390,000 per season, with part deferred each year at 10 percent interest and to be paid over a 30-year period at $170,000 a year.

Don Stanhouse, signed by Los Angeles for $2.1 million for five years. Signing bonus of $400,000 and guaranteed salary of $340,000 per season.

Rick Wise, signed by San Diego for $1,950,000 for five years. Signing bonus of $250,000, salary of $300,000 in 1980 and $350,000 guaranteed for next four years.

Bob Watson, signed by New York Yankees for four years for $1,810,000 guaranteed. Signing bonus of $600,000, salary of $250,000 per season for each of first three years, $110,000 in fringe benefits including $10,000 a year for private school for children and premium on life insurance policy, and—at the Yankees' option—a salary of $550,000 for 1983 or a $100,000 guaranteed payment if released before 1983.

John Curtis, signed by San Diego for $1.8 million for five years. Signing bonus of $75,000, salary of $400,000 first year, $325,000 each of next three years and $350,000 in fifth year, with bonus of $25,000 in any year he wins the Cy Young Award.

Milt May, signed by San Francisco for $1.4 million for five years. Signing bonus of $250,000 and salary of $230,000 a year guaranteed.

Jorge Orta, signed by Cleveland for $1,250,000 for five years. Salary of $250,000 a year guaranteed, with $75,000 deferred each year to be paid after retirement.

Tony Perez, signed by Boston for five years for $1,175,000 guaranteed. Signing bonus of $250,000 and salary of $275,000 per season for three years; salary of $300,000 in 1983 and 1984 or $100,000 guaranteed payment if released before 1983, but no payment the following year if released.

Rudy May, signed by New York Yankees for $1 million for three years. Signing bonus of $250,000 and salary of $250,000 per year guaranteed.

Greg Gross, re-signed by Philadelphia for $1 million for five years. Salary of $200,000 a year guaranteed, with bonus of $25,000 for each season he plays at least 100 games and an additional $25,000 a year if he plays in 125 games.

Skip Lockwood, signed by Boston for four years for $775,000 guaranteed and potential of $1,150,000. Signing bonus of $150,000 and salary of $250,000 a year with only first two years guaranteed. Red Sox to decide by November 1, 1981, either to guarantee his 1982 salary or pay him $125,000 if released and to decide by November 1, 1982, either to guarantee his 1983 salary or pay him guaranteed $100,000.

Al Hrabosky's Special Deal

The complexity of some of the contracts was emphasized by Hrabosky's agreement with Atlanta. Having had some experience as a sports broadcaster, the 30-year-old Mad Hungarian harbors ambitions of being a telecaster after his playing days end. Owner Ted Turner of the Braves, who also has a cable system with subscribers in various parts of the nation, was able to outbid other clubs for Hrabosky by promising him a chance at a television career. As a result, Hrabosky received a contract that, while covering only five seasons, will be paying him approximately $170,000 annually through the year 2009.

AL HRABOSKY

TED TURNER

Other free agents who signed for more modest sums were Andy Hassler, inked by the Pittsburgh Pirates for $750,000 for six years; Rowland Office, by the Montreal Expos for $750,000 for four years; Jim Wohlford, by the San Francisco Giants for $713,750 for five years (only three years and $425,000 guaranteed); Fred Norman, by the Montreal Expos for $700,000 for three years (only two years and $450,000 guaranteed); Fred Patek, by the California Angels for $555,000 for three years; Willie Horton, re-signed by the Seattle Mariners for $500,000 for three years, and Jay Johnstone, by Los Angeles for $300,000 for two years.

Salaries Continue to Rise

It wasn't just the free agents, of course, who were reaping bigger rewards. With attendance, ticket prices and television revenue rising, the wage scales in general were escalating. In contrast to the average salary of $24,909 in 1969, player remuneration in the majors averaged $121,000 in 1979.

A survey compiled by the Major League Players' Association and released early in '79 showed the Yankees' payroll the previous year averaged $188,880 per player. The Philadelphia Phillies ranked second at $159,039, followed by the Boston Red Sox at $147,803. The Oakland A's were last at $49,258. In most instances, the average salary was even higher in '79.

Players traveling the free-agency route were being nudged aside in the run for the money by players who negotiated rich new contracts before they could become free agents. At least a dozen players boasted contracts in 1979 that were worth $500,000 or more per season, counting bonuses, salary and deferred payments, leading by year's end, to a $1 million contract per year by Nolan Ryan with Houston.

Big Contracts

High on the 1979 list was Rod Carew, newly acquired by the California Angels, who signed a five-year contract calling for a straight salary reported at $800,000 but containing cost-of-living adjustments in the fourth and fifth years that would bring his average to $900,000. Following Carew was Pete Rose, whose four-year free-agent deal with the Phillies was worth $810,000 annually. Others in the half-million-dollar salary bracket were Dave Parker of Pittsburgh, whose bonus clauses provided a potential $750,000, Jim Rice of the Boston Red Sox and Vida Blue of the San Francisco Giants at an estimated $700,000 each, Catfish Hunter of the New York Yankees at $670,000, Ted Simmons of the St. Louis Cardinals, $665,000; Mike Schmidt of the Phillies, $560,000; Mike Torrez of the Red Sox, $540,000; Reggie Jackson of the Yankees, $532,000; Larry Hisle of the Milwaukee Brewers, $526,000, and Bert Blyleven of the Pirates, $500,000.

Several additional players signed contracts during the year that will place them in the half-million-dollar category in the future. In March the Cincinnati Reds inked slugger George Foster to a three-year pact starting in 1980 that will bring him between $700,000 and $800,000 annually. In November two pitchers—J. R. Richard of the Houston Astros and Phil Niekro of the Atlanta Braves—received equally lucrative contracts. Richard signed a four-year pact worth $3.2 million, while the Braves rewarded Niekro for his 21-victory season at age 40 with a three-year extension said to call for $3,198,000, of which $2,565,000 is to be deferred and spread over nearly 30 years. In addition, Niekro was promised a new Cadillac each of the next three years.

Some Players Go to Arbitration

Obviously not all salary negotiations resulted in amicable settlements. Twelve players went to salary arbitration in the spring of 1979. Eight of them won in that procedure while the four others lost.

The eight who were awarded the salary they were seeking, with the club's offer in parentheses, were: Rodney Scott of the Montreal Expos, $75,000 ($55,000); Dan Spillner of the Cleveland Indians, $80,000 ($67,000); Ed Farmer of the Texas Rangers, $35,000 ($23,000); and five players from the Oakland A's—Dave Heaverlo, $95,000 ($70,000); Rick Langford, $67,000 ($45,000); Jim Essian, $90,000 ($68,000); Jeff Newman, $58,000 ($45,000), and Miguel Dilone, $42,000 ($34,000).

The four who had to settle for the club's offer, with the figure they requested in parentheses, were: Dyar Miller of the California Angels, $72,000 ($110,000); Ike Hampton of the Angels, $20,000 ($33,000); Dale Murray of the New York Mets, $72,000 ($100,000), and Joel Youngblood of the Mets, $78,000 ($91,000). Hampton's salary actually was $1,000 below the major league minimum but was to be raised if he remained with the Angels.

Two other players who were headed for arbitration wound up being released before the proceedings. Pitcher Jim Todd was placed on waivers by the Seattle Mariners the day after notifying the club that he was submitting his salary dispute to arbitration, while outfielder Rich Chiles was similarly released by the Minnesota Twins. Todd, who had been seeking $100,000 from Seattle, later hooked on with Oakland for a reported $41,000. Subsequently, he filed a grievance through the Players' Association and in August was awarded a $43,000 settlement against the Mariners.

The Bob Horner Case

The year's most important arbitration case involved Bob Horner, the Atlanta third baseman who was voted 1978 National League Rookie of the Year. It turned out to be a landmark case that may have sounded the death knell for bonuses to future players signing their first professional contract.

Horner joined the Braves off the Arizona State campus in June, 1978, after being the No. 1 pick in the amateur draft. At the time, he signed a contract that called for the minimum big league salary but included a $150,000 signing bonus and other bonus clauses. As a result, the 21-year-old slugger collected $183,000 for his rookie year.

During the winter a salary squabble developed. Horner's agent, Bucky Woy, contended the bonuses counted as salary and that, since under the rules a player could not be cut more than 20 percent, his client had to be paid at least $146,400 in 1979. The Braves eventually offered him a conditional contract for that amount, but Horner filed for free agency, and both parties filed grievances.

An arbitration hearing to resolve the dispute was held in New York City on May 10-11. Raymond Goetz, 56-year-old law professor at the University of Kansas, was chosen to mediate. In his decision announced June 4, Goetz upheld Horner's contention that his signing bonus was part of his 1978 compensation, but ruled he was not entitled to free agency.

Horner, who missed most of spring training because of the dispute, proceeded to enjoy another banner season for Atlanta. In November he reached agreement with the Braves on a new three-year contract calling for nearly $400,000 per season.

RAY KROC

BOWIE KUHN

WILLIE MAYS

Commissioner Kuhn Is Active

Commissioner Bowie Kuhn also was called upon to rule in several disputes during the year. In one instance he penalized a club owner with the heaviest fine in baseball history. In another controversial situation he forced one of the game's most popular figures to choose between a job in baseball and an opportunity outside the sport.

The victim of the record fine was Ray Kroc, owner of the San Diego Padres. Upset by his team's performance, he announced in mid-August that he was ready to spend $5 million to $10 million to improve the Padres. Unfortunately, in response to a writer's question, the 76-year-old hamburger king mentioned Graig Nettles and Joe Morgan as two players he would go after "if they become free agents."

When the story appeared, the New York Yankees and Cincinnati Reds immediately brought charges of tampering. Acknowledging his mistake, Kroc promptly apologized. "I'm sorry. There was no such intent," he announced. "I made a slip of the tongue. I'm going to consider myself ineligible to bid for Morgan and Nettles and the San Diego club won't draft them if they do become free agents."

Nevertheless, on August 23 the Padres revealed that Kuhn had slapped Kroc with a $100,000 fine on charges of tampering. Outraged by the decision, Kroc announced that, although he would remain as owner, he was stepping down as president of the club and was turning operations of the Padres over to Ballard Smith, his 33-year-old son-in-law. Smith had been serving as executive vice-president.

"I couldn't believe it," Kroc said of the fine. "I had promised we would have nothing to do with either player. But he (Kuhn) stuck it to me anyway."

The Willie Mays Case

Less than three months after his induction into the Baseball Hall of Fame, Willie Mays was ordered by Kuhn to choose between working for baseball or a company owning an Atlantic City hotel gambling casino. The 48-year-old former star still had two seasons remaining on a 10-year contract with the New York Mets to serve as goodwill ambassador and part-time coach at $50,000 a year. Meanwhile, he was offered a 10-year deal with Bally Manufacturing Corp., owner of the hotel casino.

In a telegram to Mays on October 26, the commissioner said he had been informed "that you are about to sign a long-term contract with Bally, in which you are rendering services to promote that company's casino gambling interest. While I appreciate the motivations leading you to this association, it has long been my view that such associations by people in our game are inconsistent with its best interests. Accordingly, while I am not happy at the prospect of losing your active participation in baseball, I must request that you promptly disassociate yourself from your contract with the New York Mets."

Al Rosen, former Yankees president who joined Bally in July, attempted to intercede with Kuhn but to no avail. He pointed out that Willie's role would be to represent Park Place Hotel at golf and tennis tournaments and celebrity events, to visit hospitals, etc. He said Mays would be "obligated to work only 10 days a month, 100 days a year" for Bally.

In explaining his position, Kuhn commented: "My four predecessors (as commissioner) condoned horse racing ties, more or less. I felt that I had to draw the line. I told Charles Finley and directors of the Atlanta Braves back in 1969 to divest themselves of casino stocks and they acquiesced."

Although upset by the commissioner's ultimatum, Mays announced his acceptance of the job with Bally at an October 29 press conference in New York City. "The commissioner told me the only restriction was that I couldn't wear a uniform and represent a team," Willie said. "I can still play in oldtimers' games and do other special events. I can always return to baseball if I give up this job."

Mays' contract with Bally was said to call for a salary of $100,000 annually for three years with a provision for an additional seven years at an escalating salary that would peak at $150,000 in 1989.

Kuhn Fines Jerold Hoffberger

Shortly after the Mays episode came the disclosure that, like Kroc, another owner had been fined by Kuhn. He was Jerold Hoffberger, who was about to step down as head man of the Baltimore Orioles. The commissioner, a stickler for rules, imposed a fine of $2,500 against Hoffberger for having invited Maryland Governor Harry Hughes to throw out the first ball at the second game of the World Series. This, Kuhn declared, violated a rule prohibiting politicians, movie stars and others from throwing out the first ball at a World Series without the commissioner's approval. Contending he had not known of the rule, Hoffberger balked at paying the fine.

Bill Lee Fined by Kuhn

Bill Lee, Montreal Expos southpaw, also was the subject of a Kuhn fine. During spring training he was quoted by a Lynn, Mass., paper as saying he had smoked marijuana. Called onto the carpet by the commissioner's security staff, Lee claimed he had been misquoted, but admitted: "I used to spread some (marijuana) on my buckwheat pancakes other protein health foods when I was in Boston (with the Red Sox)." He subsequently was fined $250 by Kuhn for "conduct detrimental to baseball." Lee, one of the game's free thinkers, later withdrew a grievance and contributed a check for $251— one dollar more than the fine—to St. Mary's Mission in northern Alaska.

The Bill Bordley Case

The commissioner also found it necessary to take action in several other player situations. One involved Bill Bordley, a promising 21-year-old pitcher. The Cincinnati Reds obtained negotiation rights to him in the January draft. However, after conducting a hearing in Los Angeles on February 13, Kuhn ruled that "tampering" by the California Angels made it impossible for the Reds to sign the University of Southern California product.

Finding the Angels "guilty of misconduct in the assurances given Bordley prior to the draft as to their willingness to meet his terms," the commissioner docked the Angels an undisclosed sum and ruled they must surrender one or more future choices in the amateur draft to the Reds. In addition, he instructed Bordley to designate five clubs for a special draft. The young southpaw named the San Francisco Giants, Los Angeles Dodgers, Seattle Mariners, Milwaukee Brewers and Kansas City Royals. In a special drawing held on February 21, the Giants won rights to Bordley and then signed him three days later.

The Minnesota Twins' efforts to deal Rod Carew led to two edicts by the commissoner early in the year. One directive stipulated that no club could negotiate with Carew or his attorney until a trade had been worked out. Later, in his continuing attempt to hold down the exchange of large sums of money in deals, Kuhn ruled no cash could be involved in the Carew swap. As a result, the Twins had to settle for four players—outfielder Ken Landreaux, pitchers Paul Hartzell and Brad Havens and third baseman Dave Engle— when they sent Carew to the California Angels on February 3.

That same day the New York Yankees announced the purchase of two minor leaguers—catcher Bruce Robinson for $400,000 and pitcher Greg Cochran for $100,000—from the Oakland A's. Kuhn promptly ordered the deals held up pending a hearing. Some observers felt the sums involved were excessive for two untried players and suspected the transactions might be a tactic by which the two clubs hoped in some future deal to skirt the $400,000 limit set by the commissioner early in 1977. After meeting with owners George Steinbrenner and Charlie Finley, Kuhn announced approval of the sales on February 16.

The commissioner did, however, nullify a later Yankees' deal, at least temporarily. It involved the swap of outfielder Mickey Rivers to the Texas Rangers on July 30. The Yankees were to receive three players the Rangers had out on option—infielders Domingo Ramos and Gary Gray and outfielder Mike Hart—plus minor leaguer Amos Lewis. On discovering Texas did not have the required waivers on Gray and Hart, Kuhn disallowed the trade. Meanwhile, Rivers had already appeared in a Rangers' game. Forty-eight hours after the original deal, the trade was restructured and the Yankees received Oscar Gamble, Texas' top hitter. In addition, each team agreed to exchange three minor leaguers.

Kuhn Handles Problem of Women Reporters

Another significant directive issued by the commissioner dealt with the subject of women reporters in players' locker rooms. It resulted from litigation brought by Melissa Ludtke Lincoln, a reporter for Sports Illustrated and Time, Inc., against the Yankees and Baseball following an incident in the 1978 World Series. Having reached an understanding with Time, Inc., that led to termination of the litigation, Kuhn issued a notice to all clubs on March 9 urging that all reporters, regardless of sex, be treated equally in the matter of access to locker rooms. It was left to each club to decide whether to open the clubhouses to everyone, to have open and closed periods, or to require that all interviews be conducted in a separate media room.

Ownership of two clubs changed hands in 1979 and another team was sold early in 1980. Meanwhile, efforts to peddle and move the Oakland A's to Denver continued to encounter roadblocks.

Houston Astros Sold

The first club to be sold was the Houston Astros. John J. McMullen, shipbuilding tycoon and naval architect, paid the Ford Motor Credit Co. a reported $19 million in acquiring the Astros and controlling interest in the Astrodomain entertainment/convention complex early in May. Besides the Astros, the deal included the club's lease on the Astrodome, adjacent Astrohall and AstroArena. National League owners approved the sale on May 16.

McMullen, a 61-year-old resident of Montclair, N.J., was a limited partner in ownership of the New York Yankees at the time. Joining him in the Houston venture as a limited partner was David LeFevre, 34, a New York attorney. They later brought in 19 Houston-area investors, including auto race driver A.J. Foyt, as limited partners.

Hoffberger Sells Baltimore Orioles

After trying since 1974 to sell the Baltimore Orioles, Jerold Hoffberger finally succeeded. Edward Bennett Williams, prominent Washington attorney and president of the pro football Washington Redskins, reached agreement on August 2 to buy the Orioles for $12.3 million. Early in the year a group headed by William E. Simon, former Secretary of the Treasury, appeared on the verge of purchasing the club, but that deal fell through. Williams and Jack Kent Cooke, majority owner of the Washington Redskins, were to be Simon's partners. Some months later a Baltimore group made an unsuccessful effort to buy the club.

The sale to Williams, effective at the close of the Orioles stockholders' annual meeting on November 1, prompted speculation the franchise might be moved to Washington. However, Williams immediately announced: "I did not buy the Orioles to move them. . . . So long as the people of Baltimore support the Orioles, they will stay here." Under terms of the club's stadium lease, which still had one year to go, the team could play a maximum of 13 home games away from Baltimore.

The delay in completion of the sale enabled Hoffberger to bask in the glory of the Orioles' pennant success. By drawing 1,681,009 at home, or 495,000 above their previous record, the Birds showed a profit of $1.5 million after taxes for the year. This resulted in declaration of a dividend for the first time since January 1972. Hoffberger estimated dividend distributions would be approximately $7.37 a share to stockholders of Baltimore Baseball Club, Inc., the operating company, and $5.62 per share of Baltimore Orioles, Inc., a holding company. Under terms of the sale, stockholders of Baltimore Baseball Club, Inc., were expected to receive about $47 per share and those of Baltimore Orioles, Inc., about $39 a share. Both figures were more than double the over-the-counter asking price earlier in the year.

In the reorganization that followed completion of the Baltimore transaction, Williams induced Hoffberger to remain as president of the club and added the erstwhile Yankee Clipper, Joe DiMaggio, to the Orioles' board of directors.

New York Mets Change Ownership

The other club to change ownership was the New York Mets. Under Mrs. Joan Payson, who bankrolled the club from its debut season in 1962 until her death late in 1975, the franchise had been extremely profitable. In recent years attendance had dropped sharply, producing heavy financial losses and rumors of a possible sale. From a peak of 2,697,479 in 1970, the gate plummeted to an all-time low of 788,905 in 1979 as the Mets finished in last place for the third successive year.

Mrs. Lorinda de Roulet, daughter of Mrs. Payson and her successor as club president, reportedly had to call upon her 81-year-old father, Charles Shipman Payson, twice during the '79 season to underwrite loans totaling $2 million to keep the club solvent. Payson held 52 percent of the Met stock, while his four children owned 33 percent and M. Donald Grant, former board chairman, had about 11 percent.

Speculation about the Payson family's plans ended November 8 when Mrs. de Roulet notified Met employees that the club definitely was on the market. A three-man committee was appointed to handle arrangements for the sale. It consisted of Louis A. Hoynes, Jr., legal counsel for the National League; William A. Cameron, an attorney for the law firm representing the club, and Gerald F. Schanley of the Arthur Andersen accounting firm.

Bidding War

A two-month bidding war involving as many as 21 groups ensued. It culminated on January 24, 1980, with the announcement that a group headed by the huge New York publishing firm of Doubleday & Co. had bought the club for $21.1 million, a record for a baseball franchise. The other finalist in the bidding was a group led by Earl E. T. Smith, former ambassador to Cuba. Principals among the successful group were Nelson Doubleday, 47-year-old president of the publishing firm and great grand nephew of Abner Doubleday, and two minority stockholders, Fred Wilpon, 43, chairman of the board of Sterling Equities, a Manhassett, L.I., real estate concern, and the City Investing Co.

Oakland Situation On Dead Center

The long, tortuous struggle to solve the Oakland A's situation remained stymied, but as was the case the two previous years major league officials continued to be hopeful that it might be settled before another season rolled around.

Marvin Davis, multi-millionaire Denver oil tycoon, made another attempt to buy the A's and move them to Denver shortly after the '79 season. He and Charlie Finley, Oakland owner, supposedly agreed on a price estimated at $12 million. During a November 7 meeting in Kansas City, other American League owners authorized League President Lee MacPhail to negotiate a settlement with the Oakland-Alameda County Coliseum that would pave the way for the transfer.

Finley's contract with the Coliseum still had eight years to go. While no supporting documents had been signed, the Coliseum board was said to have agreed in principle to a $4 million lease-breaking buyout. The American League reportedly voted a $1 million appropriation for that purpose, while Finley, Davis and Owner Bob Lurie of the San Francisco Giants were to put up $1 million each. With the departure of the A's, the Giants would have the entire Bay Area to themselves.

Proposal Dropped

In February, 1980, however, the transfer proposal was dropped and Finley and the A's remained in Oakland.

Early in 1979 Finley continued his sale of talent to raise cash. As was mentioned previously, he sold two minor league players—catcher Bruce Robinson and pitcher Greg Cochran—to the Yankees in February for $500,000, and on June 15 he sent ace southpaw John Johnson to the Texas Rangers for two players and $400,000 in cash.

With a last-place team, Oakland attendance dipped to depression-era levels. An April 17 night game with the Seattle Mariners attracted only 653 fans—smallest turnout in Coliseum history—while only 750 showed up for a September 18 night game with the Texas Rangers. For the year the A's drew just 306,763, the majors' lowest gate since the A's final season in Philadelphia in 1954.

While the A's were proving less than prosperous, observers concluded that Finley himself was not being squeezed financially by the poor attendance. It was noted that 11 of the club's 25 players were paid the major league minimum, the total payroll was estimated at only $1 million and the A's stadium rental amounted to just $125,000 for the season.

Finley did not attend a single A's game all year, but meanwhile found himself occupied in the courts. He was involved in at least four suits. One brought by Vida Blue, charging fraud in connection with the pitcher's 1976 contract with Oakland, was dismissed early in April. The other cases involved a tax proceeding brought by the IRS, a divorce trial and a suit brought by the Oakland Coliseum board seeking damages totaling $11.5 million for Finley's failure to promote the A's in accordance with a clause in his lease. The divorce trial added to complications in connection with efforts to sell the club because wife Shirley owned 29 percent of Charles O. Finley, Inc., and each of their four children held 10 percent, while Charlie owned 31 percent.

Several other clubs experienced financial difficulties and at various times were the subject of sale rumors. Early in the year two members of the Texas Rangers' board of directors, Ray Nasher and Bill Seay, sought to buy out other stockholders of the financially-troubled club. However, Board Chairman Brad Corbett arranged to push through a vote authorizing issuance of 750,000 new shares of stock at $1 per share to provide needed funds.

The Seattle Mariners likewise encountered ownership problems. In January, Walter Schoenfeld made an abortive effort to buy out his five partners. Later, several Japanese investors expressed an interest in acquiring the Mariners. And in August a nephew of Schoenfeld's, Victor Alhadeff, head of an oil-exploration firm, revealed he was attempting to purchase the team.

New Managers

Four clubs began the '79 season with new managers. Two of them—John McNamara of the Cincinnati Reds and Jim Marshall of the Oakland A's—made it through the season. Two others—Les Moss of the Detroit Tigers and Don Kessinger of the Chicago White Sox—were among 11 managers who were fired during the year. Marshall, however, wasn't quite as lucky as the division-winning McNamara. Finley kept him hanging until February, 1980. Then the unpredictable A's owner announced that Marshall's contract would not be renewed. Only weeks later, Finley surprised the baseball world by selecting Billy Martin to manage his club.

Moss became the first casualty. His initial opportunity as a big league skipper lasted only until June 12 when the Tigers dismissed him in favor of George (Sparky) Anderson. Anderson, whose firing by Cincinnati the previous winter had stunned the baseball world, was given a contract through 1984 at a reported $125,000 annual salary. Coach Dick Tracewski directed the Tigers to a pair of victories while awaiting Anderson's arrival. Moss later joined the Chicago Cubs as a minor league pitching coach.

The second managerial change occurred on June 18 when the Yankees, as related earlier in this account, brought back Billy Martin to replace Bob Lemon.

The next club to make a switch was Cleveland. A 10-game losing streak late in June put Manager Jeff Torborg's job in jeopardy. With Lemon being available, the Indians sought permission to negotiate with the former Yankees skipper. Although Lemon turned down the offer, Torborg tendered his resignation on July 2 with the understanding that he would remain until the close of the season. However, on July 23 the Indians ousted the 37-year-old lame-duck pilot and turned the reins over to coach Dave Garcia. Torborg subsequently joined the Yankees as bullpen coach, while late in the season the Indians rehired Garcia for 1980.

Kessinger, who tried the role of player-manager, saw his first chance as a pilot come to an end on August 2 when he resigned the White Sox helm. Owner Bill Veeck promptly named Tony LaRussa, 34-year-old former infielder, to the post. He had been leading the club's Iowa (American Association) farm team. LaRussa, who passed the Florida bar exam during the off-season, subsequently was given a contract to return in '80.

Phillies Derrick Ozark

After winning division titles the last three years, Danny Ozark paid the price for the Philadelphia Phillies' dismal showing and was ousted on August 31. Dallas Green, the club's farm director and a former pitcher, was appointed interim manager. Like Garcia and LaRussa, he later was rewarded with a contract for 1980.

Less than a year after being voted National League Manager of the Year, Joe Altobelli of the San Francisco Giants was given the ax on September 6. His dismissal followed weeks of turmoil and brittle relations with the press. Coach Dave Bristol succeeded Altobelli and a few days later was given a two-year contract.

Herman Franks, who came out of retirement in 1977 to take the Chicago Cubs' job, resigned September 24. He said the behavior and attitude of some Cubs players prompted him to call it quits. "I've had it right up to here," commented Franks, 65, putting his right hand to his throat. "Some of these players are actually crazy. They don't want to talk to newspaper people and they want separate buses for themselves and the reporters. It's silly things like this that get you fed up. They don't seem to realize that when the newspaper guys don't want to talk to them, then they're really in trouble."

Coach Joe Amalfitano directed the Cubs during the final days of the season, but on October 2 Preston Gomez was appointed as the club's new manager.

Two teams fired their manager on the final day of the season, September 30, and subsequently chose a television announcer and scout as their new leaders. The clubs involved were the San Diego Padres and Toronto Blue Jays.

Coleman Surprise Choice at San Diego

The Padres dismissed Roger Craig and then the next day pulled a real switch by reaching into their television booth and choosing their No. 1 announcer, Jerry Coleman, as their new manager. Coleman, a 55-year-old former Yankees infielder, had been airing San Diego games since 1972.

Toronto dropped Roy Hartsfield, who had piloted the Blue Jays since their founding, and on October 18 elevated Bobby Mattick to the post. Mattick, a 63-year-old former infielder, had been serving as the club's director of player development and top scout. His only previous managerial experience came in rookie and instructional leagues.

Whitey Herzog, winningest manager in the Kansas City Royals' 11-year history, joined the ranks of the unemployed on October 2. Three weeks later, following completion of the World Series, the Royals announced the appointment of Jim Frey, coach of the Baltimore Orioles, as their new manager. Frey thus became the third Orioles coach in three years to move up to the piloting ranks, following Billy Hunter and George Bamberger.

The final managerial switch of 1979 occurred on October 28 when the Yankees fired Martin again and named Dick Howser to replace him. Howser, a former major league infielder, had served as a Yankees coach for 10 years before leaving at the end of the 1978 season to become head baseball coach at his alma mater, Florida State University.

Front-Office Changes

The ranks of top-level executives also underwent numerous changes. One involving the staff of Commissioner Bowie Kuhn resulted in the appointment February 21 of Frank Cashen to the post of administrator. Cashen, executive vice-president of the Baltimore Orioles from 1965 to 1975, succeeded Johnny Johnson, who was elected president of the National Association the previous December. Cashen later joined the New York Mets as their Director of Operations in February of 1980.

The Texas Rangers and the Seattle Mariners figured in two surprising front-office shifts. On January 8 Danny O'Brien resigned as general manager of the Rangers and nine days later signed a four-year contract as president and chief executive officer of the Mariners. Subsequently, Hal Keller quit as Texas' farm director and joined O'Brien in a similar capacity at Seattle.

Lou Brock and Carl Yastrzemski Shine in '79

On the playing field the performances of several veterans overshadowed efforts by younger counterparts. For the fourth time in history two players joined the 3,000-Hit Club in the same season when Lou Brock and Carl Yastrzemski both achieved the mark in '79. Honus Wagner and Nap Lajoie did it in 1914, Tris Speaker and Eddie Collins in 1925 and Hank Aaron and Willie Mays in 1970.

Closing out a brilliant 19-year career, Brock bounced back from a subpar 1978 season to hit .304 at age 40. He attained the 3,000-hit plateau with a single on August 13 at St. Louis' Busch Stadium. By stealing 21 bases, the Cardinals speedster also wound up with a career total of 938 thefts, surpassing by one the former record credited to Billy Hamilton.

Yastrzemski, also 40, joined Brock in the 3,000-hit class when he ripped an eighth-inning single against the Yankees at Fenway Park on September

LOU BROCK   CARL YASTRZEMSKI

12. With 400-plus homers to his credit, the Red Sox star became the first American League player ever to collect 3,000 hits and 400 homers.

Among other veterans, Pete Rose, 38, broke the record he had shared with Ty Cobb by collecting 200 or more hits for the tenth time, while Manny Mota, 41, raised his career pinch-hit total to a record 147. Phil Niekro, 40, won 21 games for the last-place Atlanta Braves and thus tied brother Joe of Houston as the National League's biggest winner. It was the first time two brothers reached the 20-victory class in the same league in the same season.

New Television Contracts

Baseball signed lucrative new television contracts with NBC and ABC in April and also became involved in several television innovations, including entry by the clubs as a unit into cable TV for the first time.

With the majors' four-year agreements with NBC and ABC due to expire at the end of 1979, Tom Villante of the Commissioner's staff negotiated long-term contracts that continue the basic format with the two networks but at greatly increased fees. In contrast to the approximately $92.8 million in revenue produced over the four-year life of the old contracts, the new pacts will bring in more than $175 million over the next four seasons. This represents approximately $1,700,000 annually for each of the 26 clubs—or nearly double the previous network rights fee.

Twenty-two of the 26 clubs joined in a one-year experimental contract for national cable TV. The agreement with UA-Columbia Cablevision provided for live cablecasts on 23 Thursday nights to approximately two million subscribers. To protect local TV contracts, cable systems with subscribers located within 50 miles of a major league park were not permitted to carry the telecasts, which were seen in all states except New Hampshire, Vermont and Maine. The four clubs which did not participate in the arrangement were the Atlanta Braves, Houston Astros, New York Mets and St. Louis Cardinals.

Although baseball grossed less than $500,000 from the cable TV experi-

ment, the project proved successful enough that the majors renewed the
arrangement by signing a two-year contract with UA-Columbia in December.
It calls for cable television coverage of between 40 and 45 games per year,
including numerous doubleheaders with one game from the East or Midwest
followed by a second game from the West Coast.

Most Valuable Player Awards

For the first time in the history of the Most Valuable Player Awards,
there was a tie when Willie Stargell of the Pittsburgh Pirates and Keith
Hernandez of the St. Louis Cardinals deadlocked in the National League vot-
ing. Each wound up with 216 out of a possible 336 points. By contrast, Don
Baylor of the California Angels was an easy winner in the American League
MVP poll, gaining 347 of a possible 364 points. His two nearest rivals, Ken
Singleton of Baltimore (241 points) and George Brett of Kansas City (226),
both finished with more points than the NL co-winners.

In keeping with past practice the voting was done by a committee of two
members of the Baseball Writers' Association from each city. They were
required to cast their ballots between the final day of the regular season and
the opening of the League Championship Series. A 14-point value was assigned to each first-place vote, nine to second, eight to third, etc., on down to
one for tenth place.

Name	1	2	3	4	5	6	7	8	9	10	Tot.
Stargell, Willie	10	3	4	1	—	2	—	—	—	—	216
Hernandez, Keith	4	8	7	2	3	—	—	—	—	—	216
Winfield, Dave	4	3	—	2	6	1	2	2	1	1	155
Parrish, Larry	—	3	5	4	2	1	2	1	2	1	128
Knight, Ray	2	1	2	—	—	1	4	2	1	—	82
Niekro, Joe	1	1	2	½	1	3	2	1	—	1	75½
Sutter, Bruce	—	1	1	—	2	4	2	3	1	1	69
Tekulve, Kent	1	1	1	2	1	—	1	3	—	—	64
Concepcion, Dave	—	3	—	3	—	2	1	—	—	1	63
Parker, Dave	—	—	—	1	3	3	4	—	—	—	56
Kingman, Dave	—	—	—	3	1	—	1	1	6	7	53
Foster, George	—	—	1	1	1	2	—	—	1	1	34
Schmidt, Mike	—	—	1	—	1	1	—	3	—	4	32
Garvey, Steve	—	—	—	—	1	—	2	3	3	1	30
Moreno, Omar	—	—	—	2	—	1	—	—	1	2	23
Rose, Pete	—	—	—	1	—	—	2	—	3	2	23
Carter, Gary	1	—	—	—	—	—	—	—	—	1	15
Madlock, Bill	1	—	—	—	—	—	—	—	—	—	14
Richard, J. R.	—	—	—	—	1	—	—	2	—	—	12
Niekro, Phil	—	—	—	½	—	1	—	1	—	—	11½
Sambito, Joe	—	—	—	—	—	1	1	—	—	—	9
Seaver, Tom	—	—	—	—	—	—	—	1	3	—	9
Bench, Johnny	—	—	—	1	—	—	—	—	—	—	7
Dawson, Andre	—	—	—	—	1	—	—	—	—	—	6
Templeton, Garry	—	—	—	—	—	1	—	—	—	—	5
Matthews, Gary	—	—	—	—	—	—	—	—	2	—	4
Collins, Dave	—	—	—	—	—	—	—	1	—	—	3
Horner, Bob	—	—	—	—	—	—	—	—	—	1	1

The deadlock in the National League created considerable controversy. Although Stargell received ten first-place votes to only four for Hernandez, four writers failed to list the Pirates slugger anywhere on their ten-name ballot while the Cardinals first baseman appeared on all 24 ballots. Hernandez, in fact, was the only player named by all 24 NL writers. The four who failed to include Stargell were identified as Mike Littwin of the Los Angeles Times, Harry Shattuck of the Houston Chronicle, Kenny Hand of the Houston Post and Tim Tucker of the Atlanta Journal. All staunchly defended their choices.

In the American League balloting Baylor drew 20 of the 28 first-place votes in winning by an overwhelming margin. He, Singleton and Brett were listed on all 28 ballots.

Name	1	2	3	4	5	6	7	8	9	10	Tot.
Baylor, Don	20	5	1	2	–	–	–	–	–	–	347
Singleton, Ken	3	10	9	4	1	–	–	1	–	–	241
Brett, George	2	9	11	2	–	1	2	–	1	–	226
Lynn, Fred	–	3	7	4	4	3	2	–	1	½	160½
Rice, Jim	–	–	–	6	7	3	3	3	2	–	124
Flanagan, Mike	3	1	–	2	1	1	1	3	5	1	100
Thomas, Gorman	–	–	–	2	5	5	3	1	1	1	87
Grich, Bobby	–	–	–	1	2	3	2	1	5	3	58
Porter, Darrell	–	–	–	2	1	–	4	3	1	5	52
Bell, Buddy	–	–	–	1	2	3	1	2	1	2	48
Murray, Eddie	–	–	–	–	1	1	3	–	1	½	25½
Kern, Jim	–	–	–	–	1	–	3	2	–	1	25
Marshall, Mike	–	–	–	–	–	3	–	2	1	2	25
Downing, Brian	–	–	–	–	2	–	1	2	1	–	24
Lezcano, Sixto	–	–	–	1	–	1	–	1	1	1	18
Smalley, Roy	–	–	–	–	–	1	–	1	3	2	16
Wilson, Willie	–	–	–	–	–	1	1	1	1	1	15
Kemp, Steve	–	–	–	–	–	–	1	3	–	2	15
Clear, Mark	–	–	–	1	–	1	–	–	–	–	12
Molitor, Paul	–	–	–	–	–	–	1	1	–	1	8
Burleson, Rick	–	–	–	–	1	–	–	–	–	1	7
John, Tommy	–	–	–	–	–	1	–	–	–	–	5
Cooper, Cecil	–	–	–	–	–	–	–	–	2	–	4
Jackson, Reggie	–	–	–	–	–	–	–	1	–	–	3
Horton, Willie	–	–	–	–	–	–	–	–	1	1	3
Ford, Dan	–	–	–	–	–	–	–	–	–	1	1
Guidry, Ron	–	–	–	–	–	–	–	–	–	1	1
Hargrove, Mike	–	–	–	–	–	–	–	–	–	1	1

Mike Flanagan, the Baltimore Orioles' 23-game winner, and Bruce Sutter, relief ace of the Chicago Cubs, captured the Cy Young Awards in their respective leagues. Flanagan was a landslide winner in the American League, being the No. 1 choice on 26 of the 28 ballots. Sutter was the top pick of ten of the 24 members of the Baseball Writers' Association making up the National League selection panel while Houston's Joe Niekro received nine first-place votes. On a basis of five points for first place, three for second and one for third, Sutter edged Niekro, 72 points to 66.

The Cy Young Voting

A breakdown of the 1979 Cy Young Award voting in each league follows:

<table>
<tr><th colspan="5">American League</th><th colspan="5">National League</th></tr>
<tr><th>Pitcher</th><th>1</th><th>2</th><th>3</th><th>Pts.</th><th>Pitcher</th><th>1</th><th>2</th><th>3</th><th>Pts.</th></tr>
<tr><td>Mike Flanagan</td><td>26</td><td>2</td><td>..</td><td>136</td><td>Bruce Sutter</td><td>10</td><td>6</td><td>4</td><td>72</td></tr>
<tr><td>Tommy John</td><td>1</td><td>14</td><td>4</td><td>51</td><td>Joe Niekro</td><td>9</td><td>6</td><td>3</td><td>66</td></tr>
<tr><td>Ron Guidry</td><td>1</td><td>3</td><td>12</td><td>26</td><td>J.R. Richard</td><td>4</td><td>4</td><td>9</td><td>41</td></tr>
<tr><td>Jim Kern</td><td>..</td><td>6</td><td>7</td><td>25</td><td>Tom Seaver</td><td>..</td><td>5</td><td>5</td><td>20</td></tr>
<tr><td>Mike Marshall</td><td>..</td><td>2</td><td>1</td><td>7</td><td>Kent Tekulve</td><td>1</td><td>2</td><td>3</td><td>14</td></tr>
<tr><td>Jerry Koosman</td><td>..</td><td>1</td><td>2</td><td>5</td><td>Phil Niekro</td><td>..</td><td>1</td><td>..</td><td>3</td></tr>
<tr><td>Dennis Eckersley</td><td>..</td><td>..</td><td>1</td><td>1</td><td></td><td></td><td></td><td></td><td></td></tr>
<tr><td>Aurelio Lopez</td><td>..</td><td>..</td><td>1</td><td>1</td><td></td><td></td><td></td><td></td><td></td></tr>
</table>

The Rookie of the Year balloting conducted by the Baseball Writers' Association saw Rick Sutcliffe, Los Angeles Dodgers pitcher, win overwhelmingly in the National League, while two young infielders—John Castino of the Minnesota Twins and Alfredo Griffin of the Toronto Blue Jays—shared honors in the American League. Sutcliffe received 20 of a possible 24 votes in the National League. Houston's Jeff Leonard was runnerup with three votes and Scot Thompson of the Chicago Cubs received the other. In the American League, Castino and Griffin collected seven votes each from the 28-member panel. California's Mark Clear was next with five, while Ron Davis of the New York Yankees, Ross Baumgarten of the Chicago White Sox and Pat Putnam of the Texas Rangers drew three each.

To mark the close of the 1970s, THE SPORTING NEWS chose Pete Rose as its Player of the Decade. He thus joined Stan Musial, Ted Williams and Willie Mays as winners of the Player of the Decade honor.

The Sporting News Awards

The Sporting News' No. 1 Men of the Year designations in the majors went to Willie Stargell, first baseman of the Pittsburgh Pirates; Earl Weaver, manager of the Baltimore Orioles, and Hank Peters, general manager of the Orioles. Winners of TSN awards in the minors were: Player of the Year—Mark Bomback, 22-game winner for the Vancouver (Pacific Coast) Canadians; Manager of the Year—Vern Benson of the Syracuse (International) Chiefs; Executives of the Year—George H. Sisler Jr., of Columbus (International) in Class AAA, William Rigney, Jr., of Midland (Texas) in Class AA and Tom Romenesko of Greensboro (Western Carolinas) in Class A.

In balloting of the National and American League players, THE SPORTING NEWS honored the 1979 performances of Keith Hernandez of the Cardinals as NL Player of the Year; Don Baylor of the Angels as AL Player of the Year; Joe Niekro of the Astros as NL Pitcher of the Year; Mike Flanagan of the Orioles as AL Pitcher of the Year; Jeff Leonard of the Astros as NL Rookie Player of the Year and Rick Sutcliffe of the Dodgers as NL Rookie Pitcher of the Year; Pat Putnam of the Rangers as AL Rookie Player of the Year and Mark Clear of the Angels as AL Rookie Pitcher of the Year; Lou Brock of the Cardinals as NL Comeback Player of the Year; and Willie Horton of the Mariners as AL Comeback Player of the Year. Bruce Sutter of the Cubs won recognition as TSN's NL Fireman of the year, while Jim Kern of the Rangers and Mike Marshall of the Twins tied for AL Fireman of the Year.

THE SPORTING NEWS' 1979 All-Star Teams, as selected by the players themselves, were as follows:

American League: 1B—Cecil Cooper, Milwaukee; 2B—Bobby Grich, California; 3B—George Brett, Kansas City; SS—Roy Smalley, Minnesota; LF—Jim Rice, Boston; CF—Fred Lynn, Boston; RF—Ken Singleton, Baltimore; C—Darrell Porter, Kansas City; RHP—Jim Kern, Texas; LHP—Mike Flanagan, Baltimore; DH—Don Baylor, California.

National League: 1B—Keith Hernandez, St. Louis; 2B—Davey Lopes, Los Angeles; 3B—Mike Schmidt, Philadelphia; SS—Garry Templeton, St. Louis; LF—Dave Kingman, Chicago; CF—Omar Moreno, Pittsburgh; RF—Dave Winfield, San Diego; C—Ted Simmons, St. Louis; RHP—Joe Niekro, Houston; LHP—Steve Carlton, Philadelphia.

Gold Glove winners for fielding excellence, as chosen by each league's managers and coaches, included four members of the Philadelphia Phillies and three from the Boston Red Sox. The all-star defensive choices were: 1B—Cecil Cooper, Milwaukee, in the American League and Keith Hernandez, St. Louis, in the National; 2B—Frank White, Kansas City, and Manny Trillo, Philadelphia; 3B—Buddy Bell, Texas, and Mike Schmidt, Philadelphia; SS—Rick Burleson, Boston, and Dave Concepcion, Cincinnati; OF—Fred Lynn and Dwight Evans, Boston, and Sixto Lezcano, Milwaukee, in the American and Dave Parker, Pittsburgh, Dave Winfield, San Diego, and Garry Maddox, Philadelphia, in the National; C—Jim Sundberg, Texas, and Bob Boone, Philadelphia; and P—Jim Palmer, Baltimore, and Phil Niekro, Atlanta.

Silver Glove winners for fielding supremacy in the minors, were named as follows: 1B—Kelly Snider, Albuquerque (Pacific Coast); 2B—Tom Eaton, Charlotte (Southern); 3B—Blas Santana, Union Laguna (Mexican); SS—Mario Ramirez, Tidewater (International); OF—Dave Augustine, Charleston (International); Dan Wieser, Fort Myers (Florida State), and Ron Roenicke, San Antonio (Texas); C—Ernie Whitt, Syracuse (International); and P—Bob Tufts, Shreveport (Texas).

U.S. Stars Tour Japan

Through arrangements made by the Major League Baseball Promotion Corp., two teams of American and National League All-Stars staged a two-week, post-season tour of Japan. The trip was co-sponsored by Sports Nippon, a group of newspapers in Japan. Approximately 145 persons, including wives, executives and several members of the media, made the jaunt.

The group departed the U.S. on November 3 and the first game was played in Yokohama on November 7. Altogether the two All-Star squads met seven times and, in addition, combined for two other games with a Japanese All-Star squad.

Because of travel difficulties in Japan, the tour proved long and grueling, leading to tensions among the players. Rod Carew, who was bothered by a heel injury, quit the squad and left for home on November 12, and several other playes had to be talked out of returning home early. Generally, however, the trip was acclaimed a success.

The American League All-Star squad consisted of: Pitchers—Dennis Martinez, Baltimore; Mark Clear, California; Sid Monge, Cleveland; Aurelio Lopez, Detroit; Dennis Leonard, Kansas City; Lary Sorensen, Milwaukee; Rick Langford, Oakland, and Floyd Bannister, Seattle; catchers—Rick Dempsey, Baltimore; Lance Parrish, Detroit, and Jim Sundberg, Texas; infielders—Rick Burleson, Boston; Rod Carew and Carney Lansford, California; Cecil Cooper and Paul Molitor, Milwaukee; and Roy Smalley, Minnesota; outfielders—Ken Singleton, Baltimore; Don Baylor, California; Chet Lemon, Chicago; Steve Kemp, Detroit; Willie Wilson, Kansas City; and Bobby Murcer, New York; manager—Earl Weaver, Baltimore; coaches—Jim Frey, Baltimore, and Bobby Winkles, Chicago; trainer—Ralph Salvon, Baltimore; team physician—Dr. Leonard Wallenstein, Baltimore; equipment manager—Bob Sullivan, Milwaukee; and umpire—Bill Haller.

Members of the National League team were: Pitchers—Gene Garber and Phil Niekro, Atlanta; Elias Sosa, Montreal; Tug McGraw, Philadelphia; Jim Bibby, Bert Blyleven and John Candelaria, Pittsburgh; and Bob Forsch, St. Louis; catchers—Joe Ferguson, Los Angeles; John Stearns, New York; and Ted Simmons, St. Louis; infielders—Craig Reynolds, Houston; Steve Garvey, Los Angeles; Larry Bowa and Pete Rose, Philadelphia; Bill Madlock, Pittsburgh; and Ozzie Smith, San Diego; outfielders—Gary Matthews, Atlanta; Dave Kingman, Chicago; George Foster, Cincinnati; Joel Youngblood, New York; Greg Luzinski, Philadelphia; Dave Parker, Pittsburgh; and Lou Brock, St. Louis; manager—Tom Lasorda, Los Angeles; coaches—Chuck Tanner, Pittsburgh, and Roger Craig, San Diego; trainer Bill Buhler, Los Angeles; equipment manager—Mike Murphy, San Francisco; and umpire—Billy Williams.

Heading the list of executives accompanying the group were Commissioner Bowie Kuhn, Frank Cashen, Lee MacPhail, Bob Fishel, Blake Cullen, John McHale, Bill Giles, Calvin Griffith, Clark Griffith, Rudie Schaffer and Joe Podesta, president of the Major League Baseball Promotion Corp.

Scores of the games were as follows: November 8 at Yokohama—Nationals 11, Americans 2; November 8 at Shizuoka—Americans 5, Nationals 5 (ten-inning tie); November 11 at Korakuen Stadium, Tokyo—Americans 6, Nationals 3; November 12 at Seibu—Americans 6, Nationals 5; November 13 at Nagoya—Nationals 12, Americans 9; November 17 at Tokorozawa—Nationals 3, Americans 2; November 18 at Yokohama—Nationals 7, Americans 1.

For winning the series, four games to two with one tie, National League players received $11,000 apiece, while the losing American League stars collected $8,500 each.

The major leaguers closed out their trip with a game against the Japanese All-Stars at Korakuen Stadium in Tokyo on November 20 before a crowd of 42,000. Winners of an earlier game against the Japanese Stars, the Americans lost the finale, 3-2, when Kinji Shimatani belted a three-run homer in the eighth inning. The big turnout brought attendance for the nine games to an estimated 269,000.

Homers by Parks for 1979
NATIONAL LEAGUE

	At Atl.	At Chi.	At Cin.	At Hou.	At L.A.	At Mont.	At N.Y.	At Phil.	At Pitt.	At St.L.	At S.D.	At S.F.	Totals 1979	1978
Atlanta	73	4	7	3	8	1	3	5	3	6	6	8	126	123
Chicago	6	79	2	1	4	4	11	5	8	8	3	4	135	72
Cincinnati	6	5	71	5	7	3	3	8	9	6	4	5	132	136
Houston	4	2	3	15	3	2	1	2	5	4	3	5	49	70
Los Angeles	8	8	8	4	106	3	5	4	4	8	9	11	183	149
Montreal	3	5	6	1	4	68	9	19	10	6	5	7	143	121
New York	5	8	7	0	2	3	30	4	6	4	3	2	74	86
Philadelphia	8	11	5	2	7	4	6	52	10	9	2	3	119	133
Pittsburgh	7	13	6	6	3	8	5	9	74	6	4	7	148	115
St. Louis	11	2	1	3	7	6	10	5	2	48	2	3	100	79
San Diego	11	7	2	4	5	6	3	5	6	2	36	6	93	75
San Francisco	11	7	6	2	5	9	3	6	8	8	7	53	125	117
1979 Totals	153	151	124	46	161	119	88	124	151	113	83	114	1427	
1978 Totals	176	117	135	59	137	95	97	150	118	61	54	77		1276

AT ATLANTA (153): Atlanta (73)—Horner 21, Matthews 18, Murphy 12, Bonnell 9, Lum 4, Burroughs 3, Nolan 2, Royster 2, Spikes 2. **Chicago (6)**—Foote 2, DeJesus, Kingman, Murcer, Ontiveros. **Cincinnati (6)**—Bench, Concepcion, Foster, Knight, Morgan, Seaver. **Houston (4)**—Bergman, Cabell, Cruz, Puhl. **Los Angeles (8)**—Baker 2, Smith 2, Joshua, Lopes, Thomasson, Yeager. **Montreal (3)**—Carter 2, Parrish. **New York (5)**—Cardenal, Hebner, Mazzilli, Montanez, Youngblood. **Philadelphia (8)**—Schmidt 4, Luzinski 2, Rose, Trillo. **Pittsburgh (7)**—B. Robinson 4, Milner, Moreno, Stargell. **St. Louis (11)**—Templeton 3, Tyson 2, Brock, Carbo, Mumphrey, Phillips, Reitz, Simmons. **San Diego (11)**—Tenace 3, Winfield 3, Bevacqua, Briggs, Turner. **San Francisco (11)**—Evans 2, Herndon, Ivie 2, Madlock 2, Clark, McCovey, Tamargo.

AT CHICAGO (151): Atlanta (4)—Burroughs, Hubbard, Lum, Office. **Chicago (79)**—Kingman 25, Martin 13, Foote 10, Buckner 8, Vail 7, DeJesus 4, Dillard 4, Murcer 3, Sizemore 2, Biittner, Krukow, Ontiveros. **Cincinnati (5)**—Concepcion 3, Driessen, Kennedy. **Houston (2)**—Cruz, Richard. **Los Angeles (8)**—Baker 2, Cey 2, Lopes 2, Ferguson, Garvey. **Montreal (5)**—Valentine 2, Carter, Cromartie, Speier. **New York (8)**—Mazzilli 4, Hebner 2, Maddox, Youngblood. **Philadelphia (11)**—Schmidt 5, Boone 2, Maddox 2, Lerch, McBride. **Pittsburgh (13)**—Madlock 3, Milner 3, Parker 2, Berra, Garner, Moreno, Nicosia, Stargell. **St. Louis (2)**—Scott, Simmons. **San Diego (7)**—Tenace 2, Winfield 2, Briggs, Gonzalez, Turner. **San Francisco (7)**—Ivie 3, Clark, Hill, Johnston, McCovey.

AT CINCINNATI (124): Atlanta (7)—Horner 3, Murphy 2, Matthews, Royster. **Chicago (2)**—Buckner 2. **Cincinnati (71)**—Foster 20, Driessen 12, Concepcion 10, Bench 7, Geronimo 4, Knight 4, Morgan 4, Cruz 3, Griffey 3, Auerbach, Correll, Seaver, Summers. **Houston (3)**—Cabell, Cedeno, Watson. **Los Angeles (8)**—Garvey 3, Lopes 2, Cey, Joshua, Russell. **Montreal (6)**—Parrish 3, Perez 2, Staub. **New York (7)**—Flores, Henderson, Mazzilli, Norman, Stearns, Taveras, Youngblood. **Philadelphia (5)**—Maddox, McBride, Rose, Schmidt, Unser. **Pittsburgh (6)**—Parker 2, Milner, Moreno, Nicosia, Stargell. **St. Louis (1)**—Tyson. **San Diego (2)**—Richards, Winfield. **San Francisco (6)**—Ivie 3, Andrews 2, Clark.

AT HOUSTON (46): Atlanta (3)—Horner 2, Hubbard. **Chicago (2)**—Henderson. **Cincinnati (5)**—Foster 4, Knight. **Houston (15)**—Walling 3, Cedeno 2, Cruz 2, Puhl 2, Andujar, Ashby, Bochy, Cabell, Richard, Watson. **Los Angeles (4)**—Baker 2, Russell, Thomas. **Montreal (1)**—Parrish. **New York—None. Philadelphia (2)**—Boone, Schmidt. **Pittsburgh (6)**—Stargell 3, Madlock, Milner, Parker. **St. Louis (3)**—Hendrick, Iorg, Reitz. **San Diego (4)**—Tenace 2, Evans, Richards. **San Francisco (6)**—LeMaster, McCovey.

AT LOS ANGELES (161): Atlanta (8)—Bonnell 2, Burroughs 2, Horner 2, Murphy, Office. **Chicago (4)**—Kingman 2, Foote, Thompson. **Cincinnati (7)**—Griffey 3, Driessen 2, Collins, Morgan. **Houston (3)**—Cedeno 2, Puhl. **Los Angeles (106)**—Garvey 20, Cey 17, Ferguson 16, Lopes 15, Baker 14, Thomasson 6, Yeager 6, Russell 4, Smith 4, Thomas 3, Sutcliffe. **Montreal (4)**—Bernazard, Carter, Dawson, Parrish. **New York (2)**—Kranepool, Mazzilli. **Philadelphia (7)**—Schmidt 4, Luzinski. **Pittsburgh (3)**—Bibby, Moreno, Stargell. **St. Louis (7)**—Scott 2, Simmons 2, Brock, Freed, Templeton. **San Diego (5)**—Gonzalez 2, Winfield 2, Dade. **San Francisco (5)**—Ivie 2, Clark, Evans, Madlock.

AT MONTREAL (119): Atlanta (3)—Matthews. **Chicago (4)**—Kingman 3, Biittner. **Cincinnati (9)**—Bench, Blair, Concepcion. **Houston (2)**—Andujar, Howe. **Los Angeles (5)**—Cey 2, Ferguson, Lopes, Russell. **Montreal (68)**—Parrish 14, Dawson 13, Carter 12, Valentine 12, Perez 7, Cromartie 3, Staub 2, Bahnsen, Cash, Scott, Speier, White. **New York (3)**—Cardenal, Montanez, Stearns. **Philadelphia (4)**—Christenson, Maddox, McBride, Schmidt. **Pittsburgh (8)**—Stargell 3, Garner, Milner, Moreno, Oti, Parker. **St. Louis (6)**—Simmons 2, Hendrick, Hernandez, Reitz, Templeton. **San Diego (6)**—Richards 2, Winfield 2, Gonzalez, Tenace. **San Francisco (9)**—Ivie 3, Clark 2, Evans, Herndon, McCovey, Strain.

AT NEW YORK (88): Atlanta (3)—Burroughs, Matthews, Murphy. **Chicago (11)**—Kingman 6, Ontiveros 2, Foote, Martin, Thompson. **Cincinnati (3)**—Foster 2, Bench. **Houston (1)**—Cruz. **Los Angeles (8)**—Baker, Garvey, Smith, Yeager. **Montreal (9)**—Speier 2, Valentine 2, Cash, Dawson, Parrish, Perez, White. **New York (30)**—Youngblood 8, Hebner 6, Mazzilli 6, Flynn 3, Stearns 3, Henderson 2, Schmidt 2, Maddox. **Pittsburgh (5)**—B. Robinson 3, Easler, Milner. **St. Louis (10)**—Hendrick 3, Hernandez 2, Brock, Reitz, Scott, Simmons, Templeton. **San Diego (6)**—Gonzalez, Tenace, Winfield. **San Francisco (3)**—Clark, Hill, Ivie.

AT PHILADELPHIA (124): Atlanta (5)—Horner 2, Burroughs, Lum, Matthews. **Chicago (5)**—Martin 2, Murcer 2, Foote. **Cincinnati (8)**—Bench 3, Knight 2, Driessen, Foster, Morgan. **Houston (2)**—Cruz, Howe. **Los Angeles (4)**—Cey, Garvey, Lopes, Yeager. **Montreal (19)**—Dawson 5, Parrish 4, Valentine 3, Cromartie 2, Perez 2, Dyer, Schatzeder, Speier. **New York (6)**—Youngblood 3, Flynn, Hebner. **Philadelphia (52)**—Schmidt 16, Luzinski 7, Maddox 6, McBride 6, Trillo 5, Boone 4, Unser 3, Anderson, Mackanin, McCarver, Rader, Rose. **Pittsburgh (9)**—Garner 2, Moreno 2, Parker 2, Foli, Milner, Ott. **St. Louis (5)**—Hendrick, Hernandez, Simmons, Templeton, Tyson. **San Diego (6)**—Tenace 3, Turner, Winfield. **San Francisco (6)**—Ivie 2, Blue, Clark, Evans, Whitfield.

AT PITTSBURGH (151): Atlanta (5)—Matthews 3, Frias, Murphy. **Chicago (8)**—Kingman 3, Buckner 2, Biittner, Martin, Murcer. **Cincinnati (9)**—Bench 3, Blair, Concepcion, Driessen, Foster, Griffey, Morgan. **Houston (5)**—Howe 3, Cabell, Puhl. **Los Angeles (10)**—Thomasson 3, Baker, Ferguson, Garvey, Lopes, Smith. **Montreal (10)**—Carter 2, Dawson 2, Parrish 2, Hutton, Scott, Speier, White. **New York (6)**—Stearns 2, Henderson, Montanez,

Norman, Youngblood. **Philadelphia (10)**—McBride 3, Luzinski 2, Schmidt 2, Maddox, Rose, Unser. **Pittsburgh (74)**—B. Robinson 16, Stargell 16, Parker 14, Milner 7, Garner 6, Ott 4, Lacy 3, Madlock 2, Nicosia 2, Berra, Bibby, Easler, Moreno. **St. Louis (2)**—Hendrick, Hernandez. **San Diego (8)**—Tenace 2, Winfield 2, Almon, Kendall. **San Francisco (8)**—Clark 4, Evans, Littlejohn, Madlock, McCovey.

AT ST. LOUIS (113): Atlanta (5)—Burroughs, Horner, Murphy. **Chicago (8)**—Kingman 4, Buckner 2, Dillard, Martin. **Cincinnati (6)**—Bench 2, Collins, Driessen, Griffey, Knight. **Houston (4)**—Puhl 2, Cabell, Watson. **Los Angeles (9)**—Lopes 3, Smith 2, Baker, Cey, Ferguson, Thomasson. **Montreal (6)**—Carter 2, Cromartie 2, Parrish, Solaita. **New York (4)**—Mazzilli, Norman, Stearns, Youngblood. **Philadelphia (9)**—Luzinski 3, Schmidt 3, Boone, Maddox, Unser. **Pittsburgh (6)**—Stargell 3, Garner, Ott, Parker. **St. Louis (48)**—Simmons 17, Hendrick 7, Hernandez 5, Reitz 4, Brock 2, Carbo 2, Kennedy 2, Mumphrey 2, Templeton 2, Freed, Oberkfell, Scott, Swisher, Tyson. **San Diego (2)**—Briggs, Turner. **San Francisco (8)**—Clark 2, Evans, Herndon, Ivie, Madlock, McCovey, Whitfield.

AT SAN DIEGO (85): Atlanta (6)—Murphy 3, Bonnell, Horner, Nolan. **Chicago (5)**—Kingman 3. **Cincinnati (4)**—Bench, Cruz, Foster, Morgan. **Houston (5)**—Cedeno, Cruz, Puhl. **Los Angeles (8)**—Yeager 3, Cey, Garvey, Guerrero, Lopes, Thomasson. **Montreal (5)**—Carter 2, Dawson 2, Speier. **New York (3)**—Henderson, Montanez, Stearns. **Philadelphia (2)**—Schmidt 2. **Pittsburgh (4)**—Parker 2, Kison, Madlock. **St. Louis (2)**—Hernandez, Simmons. **San Diego (36)**—Winfield 16, Briggs 5, Turner 5, Gonzalez 4, Fahey 3, Tenace 2, Perry. **San Francisco (7)**—Clark 2, Evans 2, Herndon, Hill, Madlock.

AT SAN FRANCISCO (114): Atlanta (8)—Burroughs 2, Matthews 2, Horner, Hubbard, Murphy, Spikes. **Chicago (4)**—Foote, Henderson, Kingman, Martin. **Cincinnati (5)**—Bench 2, Collins, Knight. **Houston (5)**—Cruz 2, Ashby, Cabell, Howe. **Los Angeles (11)**—Cey 3, Thomasson 2, Guerrero, Hatcher, Joshua, Lopes, Thomas, Yeager. **Montreal (7)**—Parrish 2, Valentine 2, Dawson, Perez, Scott. **New York (2)**—Mazzilli, Youngblood. **Philadelphia (3)**—Schmidt 2, Boone. **Pittsburgh (2)**—Stargell 3, Lacy 2, Berra, B. Robinson. **St. Louis (3)**—Hendrick 2, Scott. **San Diego (6)**—Winfield 4, Tenace 2. **San Francisco (53)**—Clark 10, Ivie 10, McCovey 9, Evans 8, North 5, Whitfield 3, Herndon 2, LeMaster 2, Knepper, Madlock, Sadek, Tamargo.

AMERICAN LEAGUE

	At Balt.	At Bos.	At Calif.	At Chi.	At Clev.	At Det.	At K.C.	At Milw.	At Minn.	At N.Y.	At Oak.	At Sea.	At Tex.	At Tor.	Totals 1979	1978
Baltimore	74	6	7	8	11	9	10	8	10	6	13	7	5	7	181	154
Boston	2	121	1	7	7	2	6	14	2	9	3	12	2	6	194	172
California	3	9	71	5	8	4	13	0	7	5	12	11	7	9	164	108
Chicago	3	7	5	56	6	8	5	8	5	4	0	4	10	6	127	106
Cleveland	8	1	3	5	87	4	4	5	5	3	3	3	3	9	138	106
Detroit	5	3	7	4	3	101	3	7	4	6	6	3	6	5	164	129
Kansas City	4	0	4	6	5	4	53	10	4	7	8	9	7	5	116	98
Milwaukee	7	7	4	10	6	11	9	91	6	7	8	5	8	8	185	173
Minnesota	2	0	3	2	2	5	5	4	67	11	9	6	6	5	112	82
New York	7	3	4	2	8	7	3	7	5	77	3	6	6	5	150	125
Oakland	3	3	5	3	1	5	4	4	3	3	88	3	2	2	132	97
Seattle	2	3	5	3	5	8	6	3	4	6	6	69	6	4	132	97
Texas	8	8	2	4	3	8	4	3	4	6	6	6	2	50	140	132
Toronto	3	4	1	2	2	8	1	3	4	6	4	6	2		95	98
1979 Totals	131	180	126	116	159	175	134	172	128	136	111	182	132	124	2006	
1978 Totals	116	166	114	114	87	152	87	144	83	127	103	151	111	125		1680

AT BALTIMORE (131): Baltimore (74)—Singleton 13, DeCinces 10, Murray 10, Roenicke 9, May 8, Kelly 6, Ayala 5, Lowenstein 4, Garcia 3, Bumbry 2, Smith 2, Dauer, Dempsey. **Boston (2)**—Lynn, Watson. **California (3)**—Aikens 2, Lansford. **Chicago (3)**—Morrison 2, Pryor. **Cleveland (8)**—Johnson 3, Harrah 2, Thornton 2, Manning. **Detroit (5)**—Gibson, Parrish, Rodriguez, Staub, Stegman. **Kansas City (4)**—Brett, Cowens, Cruz, Porter. **Milwaukee (7)**—Lezcano 3, Cooper, Davis, Oglivie, Thomas. **Minnesota (2)**—Edwards, Landreaux. **New York (2)**—Chambliss 3, Nettles 2, Gamble, Jackson. **Oakland (3)**—Gross, Newman, Revering. **Seattle (2)**—Bochte, Horton. **Texas (8)**—Bell 2, Putnam 2, Zisk 2, Gamble, Rivers. **Toronto (3)**—Cerone, Woods, Velez.

AT BOSTON (180): Baltimore (6)—Dempsey 2, Roenicke 2, Bumbry, Murray. **Boston (121)**—Lynn 28, Rice 27, Hobson 15, Yastrzemski 15, Evans 12, Watson 7, Fisk 6, Burleson 4, Dwyer 2, Poquette 2, Scott 2, Allenson, Wolfe. **California (9)**—Downing 3, Rudi 3, Lansford 2, Baylor. **Chicago (7)**—Johnson 2, Garr, May, Orta, Soderholm, Squires. **Cleveland (1)**—Harrah. **Detroit (3)**—Parrish 2, Kemp. **Kansas City**—None. **Milwaukee (7)**—Lezcano 2, Bando, Cooper, Davis, Molitor, Thomas. **Minnesota**—None. **New York (3)**—Jackson 2, Nettles. **Oakland (8)**—Newman 2, Page 2, Armas, Gross, Murphy, Revering. **Seattle (5)**—Horton, Jones, Meyer. **Texas (8)**—Ellis 2, Montanez 2, Grubb, Oliver, Soderholm, Zisk. **Toronto (4)**—Mayberry 2, Bosetti, Howell.

AT CALIFORNIA (126): Baltimore (7)—Singleton 3, Dauer, DeCinces, Lowenstein, Smith. **Boston (1)**—Hobson. **California (71)**—Baylor 17, Grich 15, Ford 11, Aikens 9, Lansford 5, Rudi 5, Donohue 3, Downing 3, Carew, DeMiller, Rettenmund. **Chicago (5)**—Bell, Johnson, Lemon, May, Soderholm. **Cleveland (3)**—Johnson 2, Harrah. **Detroit (7)**—Thompson 2, Kemp, Morales, Parrish, Summers, Trammell, Wockenfuss. **Kansas City (4)**—White 2, Brett, Otis. **Milwaukee (7)**—Thomas 3, Cooper, Gantner, Molitor, Oglivie. **Minnesota (3)**—Goodwin, Jackson, Wilfong. **New York (6)**—Chambliss 3, Beniquez, Piniella, Spencer. **Oakland (7)**—Armas 2, Newman, Page. **Seattle (5)**—Horton 2, Bochte, Meyer, Stein. **Texas (2)**—Montanez, Putnam. **Toronto (1)**—Mayberry.

AT CHICAGO (116): Baltimore (8)—Murray 2, Dauer, DeCinces, Dempsey, Lowenstein, Roenicke, Singleton. **Boston (7)**—Rice 2, Allenson, Burleson, Evans, Fisk, O'Berry. **California (6)**—Baylor 4, Downing. **Chicago (56)**—Washington 10, Morrison 9, Lemon 7, Orta 5, Nordhagen 4, Garr 3, May 3, Nahorodny 3, Torres 3, Johnson 2, Bannister, Bosley, Foley, Moore, Pryor, Soderholm, Squires. **Cleveland (5)**—Alexander, Cox, Johnson, Manning, Pruitt. **Detroit (4)**—Morales 2, Parrish, Wockenfuss. **Kansas City (6)**—Brett, Otis, Patek, Porter, Wathan, Wilson. **Milwaukee (4)**—Lezcano 2, Oglivie, Thomas. **Minnesota (3)**—Jackson, Landreaux. **New York (8)**—Piniella 2, Beniquez, Jackson, Johnstone, Narron, Nettles, Spencer. **Oakland (4)**—Gross, Murphy. **Seattle (3)**—Horton 2, Meyer. **Texas (4)**—Jorgensen, Sample, Wills, Zisk. **Toronto (2)**—Carty, Cerone.

AT CLEVELAND (159): Baltimore (11)—Smith 3, Murray 2, Roenicke 2, Dauer, Dempsey, Kelly, Skaggs. **Boston (7)**—Lynn 3, Rice 3, Watson. **California (8)**—Lansford 2, Aikens, Anderson, Baylor, Ford, Grich. **Chicago (6)**—Johnson 2, Lemon, Nordhagen, Torres, Washington. **Cleveland (87)**—Bonds 19, Thornton 17, Harrah 15, Alexander 11, Johnson 10, Hargrove 5, Cox 2, Hassey 2, Norris 2, Rosello 2, Dade, Manning. **Detroit (3)**—LeFlore, Summers, Thompson. **Kansas City (5)**—Otis 2, McRae, Porter, White. **Milwaukee (10)**—Cooper 3, Lezcano 2, Oglivie 2, Davis, Thomas, Yount. **Minnesota (2)**—Adams, Edwards. **New York (7)**—Jackson 2, Dent, Gamble, Johnson, Narron, Piniella. **Oakland (1)**—Heath. **Seattle (5)**—Bochte, Jones, Meyer, Stein, Stinson. **Texas (5)**—Bell, Ellis, Putnam, Roberts, Zisk. **Toronto (2)**—Carty, Woods.

AT DETROIT (175): Baltimore (9)—Bumbry 2, Crowley, Dauer, DeCinces, Kelly, May, Murray, Singleton. **Boston (2)**—Fisk, Yastrzemski. **California (4)**—Grich 2, Ford, Lansford. **Chicago (8)**—Garr 2, Orta 2, Soderholm 2, Foley, Torres. **Cleveland (4)**—Bonds, Hassey, Rosello, Thornton. **Detroit (101)**—Kemp 17, Summers 17, Thompson 13, Parrish 8, LeFlore 7, Morales 7, Wockenfuss 7, Staub 5, Trammell 4, Brookens 3, Jones 3, Rodriguez 3, Whitaker 3, Greene 2, Stegman, Wagner. **Kansas City (4)**—Porter 2, McRae, Terrell. **Milwaukee (6)**—Thomas 2, Cooper, Lezcano, Martinez, Oglivie. **Minnesota (5)**—Adams, Mack, Smalley, Wynegar. **New York (3)**—Jackson, Nettles, White. **Oakland (5)**—Gross 2, Murphy, Piccolo, Revering. **Seattle (8)**—Horton 3, Meyer 2, Jones, Milbourne, Stein. **Texas (8)**—Soderholm 2, Bell, Grubb, Oliver, Rivers, Zisk. **Toronto (8)**—Howell 3, Mayberry 2, Bosetti, Cannon, Velez.

AT KANSAS CITY (134): Baltimore (10)—Roenicke 4, Singleton 3, May 2, Dauer. **Boston (6)**—Wolfe 2, Allenson, Evans, Papi, Yastrzemski. **California (13)**—Baylor 4, Aikens 4, Downing 2, Ford 2, Grich 2, Anderson. **Chicago (5)**—Nahorodny 2, Nordhagen 2, Pryor. **Cleveland (4)**—Alexander, Bonds, Johnson, Thornton. **Detroit (3)**—Wockenfuss 2, Kemp. **Kansas City (55)**—Brett 11, Otis 10, Porter 8, McRae 5, White 5, Cowens 3, LaCock 3, Wilson 3, Braun 2, Hurdle, Quirk, Scott. **Milwaukee (11)**—Thomas 4, Lezcano 2, Yount 2, Cooper, Martinez, Money. **Minnesota (5)**—Jackson 2, Goodwin, Smalley, Wilfong. **New York (7)**—Nettles 2, Spencer 2, Chambliss, Murcer, Stanley. **Oakland (4)**—Chalk, Murphy, Newman, Page. **Seattle (4)**—Horton 2, Bochte, Roberts. **Texas (8)**—Bell 2, Ellis 2, Oliver, Putnam, Sundberg, Wills. **Toronto (1)**—Cerone.

AT MILWAUKEE (172): Baltimore (8)—Murray 2, Bumbry, Dauer, Dempsey, Lowenstein, May, Singleton. **Boston (4)**—Evans 3, Hobson 3, Lynn 2, Watson 2, Yastrzemski 2, Fisk, Scott. **California**—None. **Chicago (8)**—Bell 2, Lemon 2, Chappas, Johnson, May, Nahorodny. **Cleveland (5)**—Alexander, Alston, Bonds, Harrah, Thornton. **Detroit (8)**—Jones, Kemp, Morales, Parrish, Rodriguez, Staub, Thompson, Wockenfuss. **Kansas City (10)**—Otis 3, Brett 2, Wilson 2, Braun, Porter, White. **Milwaukee (91)**—Thomas 22, Oglivie 16, Lezcano 14, Cooper 13, Bando 6, Money 5, Davis 4, Yount 4, Molitor 3, Hisle 2, Moore 2. **Minnesota (4)**—Landreaux, Powell, Smalley, Wynegar. **New York (7)**—Jackson 2, Nettles, Piniella, Randolph, Rivers, Spencer. **Oakland (4)**—Newman 2, Revering 2. **Seattle (4)**—Bochte, Horton, Jones, Meyer. **Texas (6)**—Ellis 2, Putnam 2, Bell, Grubb. **Toronto (3)**—Velez 2, Carty.

AT MINNESOTA (128): Baltimore (10)—Murray 3, May 2, Roenicke 2, Ayala, DeCinces, Lowenstein. **Boston (2)**—Hobson 2. **California (7)**—Aikens 2, Lansford 2, Ford, Grich, Rudi. **Chicago (5)**—Johnson 2, Morrison, Orta, Torres. **Cleveland (5)**—Thornton 2, Cage, Johnson, Norris. **Detroit (5)**—Kemp 2, LeFlore, Thompson, Wockenfuss. **Kansas City (4)**—Porter 2, Cruz, Wathan. **Milwaukee (6)**—Oglivie 3, Thomas 2, Cooper. **Minnesota (77)**—Smalley 19, Jackson 8, Landreaux 8, Adams 6, Edwards 5, Castino 4, Wilfong 4, Wynegar 3, Goodwin 2, Kusick 2, Norwood 2, Rivera 2, Morales, Powell. **New York (5)**—Beniquez, Chambliss, Nettles, Randolph, Spencer. **Oakland (3)**—Newman 2, Revering. **Seattle (2)**—Roberts, Stinson. **Texas (4)**—Grubb 2, Oliver, Putnam. **Toronto (2)**—Velez 2, Howell.

AT NEW YORK (136): Baltimore (6)—Singleton 2, DeCinces, Lowenstein, May, Murray. **Boston (9)**—Hobson 3, Rice 2, Brohamer, Lynn, Sizemore, Yastrzemski. **California (5)**—Aikens 2, Baylor, Carew, Ford. **Chicago (4)**—Lemon 2, Bannister, Torres. **Cleveland (2)**—Bonds, Pruitt. **Detroit (3)**—Kemp, Morales, Stegman. **Kansas City (6)**—Brett 2, Cowens 2, Porter 2. **Milwaukee (7)**—Bando, Davis, Hisle, Martinez, Molitor, Moore, Oglivie. **Minnesota (1)**—Wilfong. **New York (77)**—Spencer 16, Jackson 15, Nettles 11, Chambliss 10, Murcer 7, Gamble 6, Piniella 3, Randolph 2, Rivers 2, White 2, Johnson, Narron, Stanley. **Oakland (8)**—Gross 3, Newman 2, Essian, Murphy, Revering. **Seattle (3)**—Horton, Meyer, Roberts. **Texas (1)**—Bell. **Toronto (2)**—Mayberry, Solaita, Velez, Woods.

AT OAKLAND (111): Baltimore (13)—Roenicke 3, Singleton 3, Dauer 2, May 2, Garcia, Lowenstein, Murray. **Boston (3)**—Evans 2, Hobson. **California (12)**—Grich 4, Downing 2, Rudi 2, Aikens, Baylor, Carew, Mullinks. **Chicago**—None. **Cleveland (5)**—Hargrove 2, Cox, Dade, Thornton. **Detroit (3)**—Parrish, Thompson, Trammell. **Kansas City (6)**—Brett 2, Washington 2, McRae, Porter. **Milwaukee (8)**—Davis 3, Molitor 2, Moore, Thomas, Wohlford. **Minnesota**—None. **New York (3)**—Jackson 2, Munson. **Oakland (46)**—Newman 9, Revering 8, Essian 6, Armas 4, Murphy 4, Page 4, Gross 3, Heath 2, Murray 2, Dilone, Edwards, Henderson, Picciolo. **Seattle**—None. **Texas (6)**—Gamble 2, Putnam 2, Ellis, Roberts. **Toronto (6)**—Mayberry 2, Bosetti, Carty, Davis, Kusick.

AT SEATTLE (182): Baltimore (7)—Singleton 4, Lowenstein, Murray, Roenicke. **Boston (12)**—Lynn 3, Fisk 2, Rice 2, Evans, Hobson, Scott, Watson, Yastrzemski. **California (11)**—Baylor 3, Ford 3, Grich 3, Lansford, Miller. **Chicago (4)**—Kessinger, Morrison, Orta, Torres. **Cleveland (4)**—Bonds 2, Dade, Hargrove. **Detroit (7)**—Greene, Morales, Parrish, Putman, Staub, Thompson, Wockenfuss. **Kansas City (3)**—Hurdle 2, Porter. **Milwaukee (9)**—Thomas 2, Gantner, Lezcano, Martinez, Molitor, Moore, Oglivie, Yount. **Minnesota (8)**—Norwood 2, Smalley 2, Castino, Cubbage, Landreaux, Morales. **New York (6)**—Jackson 2, Piniella 2, Munson, Randolph. **Oakland (12)**—Revering 4, Armas 3, Gross 2, Klutts, Murphy, Page. **Seattle (88)**—Jones 17, Horton 14, Bochte 11, Meyer 11, Roberts 10, Paciorek 6, Cox 4, Stein 4, Stinson 4, Hale 2, Simpson 2, Cruz, Mendoza, Milbourne. **Texas (5)**—Grubb, Mahlberg, Montanez, Wills, Zisk. **Toronto (6)**—Ainge 2, Howell 2, Bailor, Velez.

AT TEXAS (132): Baltimore (5)—Singleton 2, Bumbry, Garcia, Roenicke. **Boston (2)**—Rice, Watson. **California (7)**—Lansford 3, Baylor 2, Anderson, Grich. **Chicago (10)**—Garr 3, Lemon 3, Johnson, May, Soderholm, Washington. **Cleveland (3)**—Hargrove 2, Hassey. **Detroit (3)**—Kemp, Putman, Wockenfuss. **Kansas City (6)**—Brett 3, Braun, Cowens, White. **Milwaukee (7)**—Cooper 2, Oglivie 2, Thomas 2, Bando. **Minnesota (5)**—Landreaux 2, Goodwin, Jackson, Wilfong. **New York (6)**—Beniquez, Dent, Gamble, Munson, Piniella, Scott. **Oakland (4)**—Chalk, Gross, Newman, Wallis. **Seattle (3)**—Roberts 2, Horton. **Texas (69)**—Zisk 10, Bell 9, Oliver 8, Putnam 7, Gamble 5, Ellis 4, Grubb 4, Jorgensen 4, Montanez 4, Rivers 4, Sample 4, Sundberg 3, Wills 2, Blanks. **Toronto (2)**—Bosetti, Cerone.

AT TORONTO (124): Baltimore (7)—May 2, Singleton 2, DeCinces, Kelly, Murray. **Boston (6)**—Hobson 2, Rice 2, Evans, Lynn. **California (9)**—Aikens 2, Baylor 2, Clark, Downing, Ford, Grich, Lansford. **Chicago (6)**—Bell, Johnson, Lemon, Morrison, Orta, Washington. **Cleveland (2)**—Alexander, Thornton. **Detroit (9)**—Parrish 3, Brookens, Kemp, Morales, Staub, Summers, Wockenfuss. **Kansas City (5)**—Cowens 2, McRae 2, Otis. **Milwaukee (6)**—Thomas 3, Davis, Lezcano. **Minnesota (8)**—Wynegar 2, Cubbage, Edwards, Jackson, Landreaux, Norwood, Wilfong. **New York (5)**—Gamble 2, Jackson, Narron, Spencer. **Oakland (4)**—Armas, Essian, Murphy, Newman. **Seattle (2)**—Horton, Meyer. **Texas (6)**—Bell, Jorgensen, Putman, Roberts, Sundberg, Zisk. **Toronto (50)**—Mayberry 13, Carty 8, Howell 8, Velez 8, Bosetti 4, Cerone 3, Griffin 2, Woods 2, Kusick, Solaita, Robertson.

Watson Became First Player in History to Hit for Cycle in Both Leagues

On September 15 Bob Watson rapped out four hits, drove in two runs and became the first Boston player to hit for the cycle in 14 years as the Red Sox pummeled the Orioles, 10-2, at Baltimore.

Watson singled and scored a run in the second inning, doubled in the fourth and tripled in the eighth before hitting a two-run homer off reliever Don Stanhouse in a five-run ninth.

Watson not only became the first Boston player to hit for the cycle since Carl Yastrzemski turned the trick in 1965, but he also became the first player to have accomplished the feat in both leagues. While a member of the Houston Astros, Watson hit for the cycle on June 24, 1977, at the Astrodome against the San Francisco Giants.

There were three other players, all American Leaguers, to hit for the cycle in 1979: George Brett and Frank White of the Royals and Dan Ford of the Angels.

Brett had a single, double, triple and two homers in leading the Royals to a 5-4, 16-inning victory over the Orioles May 28 at Kansas City. Ford had a single, two doubles, a triple and homer August 10, but his Angels lost a 14-inning decision to the Mariners at Anaheim Stadium, 8-6. Finally, White's four hits were part of a 4-0 Royals' victory at California September 26.

Schmidt Homered in Every Park in '79

It wasn't until September 28 that Philadelphia's powerful Mike Schmidt hit a homer at Montreal's Olympic Stadium to give him at least one home run in every National League park in 1979.

Schmidt was the only major leaguer to accomplish the feat. He walloped 16 homers at Philadelphia's Veterans Stadium and connected for a club record 29 round-trippers on the road.

Though Schmidt has led the NL in homers on three occasions, it was the first time in his career that he had homered in every park. Cincinnati's George Foster was the last player to homer in each park, doing so in 1977 when he clubbed 52 homers.

Dave Kingman, the major league leader with 48 homers found the range in every city except Cincinnati, Houston and Philadelphia. AL leader Gorman Thomas, with 45 circuit clouts, only missed at Yankee Stadium.

NO-HITTERS

Including

Review of '79 No-Hitter
Official Box Score

BATTING, PITCHING FEATURES

THE SPORTING NEWS AWARDS

Including

BBWAA Awards

MAJOR LEAGUE FARM SYSTEMS

HALL OF FAME ELECTION

Including

Feature of Electees

All Hall-of-Famers Listed According to Years Selected

The motion of Houston's **KEN FORSCH** in his no-hit performance against the Braves April 7. Forsch walked only two in besting Atlanta, 6-0.

Ken Forsch Made History for No-Hit Brothers

By LARRY WIGGE

The telegram delivered to Ken Forsch during his no-hit celebration April 7 created a special moment in a night of special moments.

"Congratulations on your no-hitter. I know how it feels. Enjoy every minute of it. . . . Your Little Brother."

Bob and Ken Forsch shared a distinction held by 188 other major league pitchers—no-hitters. However, they were the only brother combination in history to achieve the feat.

To further enhance Ken Forsch's gem, it was the earliest no-hitter ever pitched in the majors. Bob Feller threw a no-hitter for the Cleveland Indians on opening day in 1940, but that opener was on April 16.

Forsch's 6-0 no-hitter over the Atlanta Braves was the only no-hitter in the majors in 1979.

"Bob's no-hitter (a 5-0 victory over Philadelphia April 16, 1978) was one of the greatest moments of my life," said Ken. "After tonight, I may never come down from the clouds."

The 32-year-old Astros' righthander, who had a 10-6 mark in 1978 and a 55-62 lifetime won-lost record prior to his '79 debut, walked only two batters and retired 27 of the 29 batters he faced while striking out three and hurling the sixth no-hitter in Houston's 18-year history.

Forsch said he was aware of the no-hitter from the third inning on. "As I sat on the bench, I thought of all the great brother acts in baseball. The Niekros, the Perrys and Dizzy and Paul Dean.

"It's a special feeling to accomplish something no two brothers have ever done," Ken said. "We are a close family. I always root for Bob and he roots for me. He is the greatest guy I know."

Third baseman Enos Cabell speared the game's toughest chance, a one-

Atlanta	AB.	R.	H.	RBI.	E.	Houston	AB.	R.	H.	RBI.	E.
Royster, 3b	4	0	0	0	1	Puhl, rf	4	1	3	1	0
Hubbard, 2b	4	0	0	0	0	Reynolds, ss	3	0	0	0	0
Matthews, rf	3	0	0	0	0	Cedeno, cf	4	1	2	1	0
Burroughs, lf	2	0	0	0	0	Watson, 1b	4	0	0	0	0
Lum, 1b	3	0	0	0	0	Landestoy, 2b	0	0	0	0	0
Murphy, c	3	0	0	0	0	Cabell, 3b-1b	4	1	1	1	0
Bonnell, cf	2	0	0	0	0	Howe, 2b-3b	4	1	1	0	0
Frias, ss	2	0	0	0	1	Cruz, lf	4	1	2	0	0
Beall, ph	1	0	0	0	0	Ashby, c	4	1	2	3	0
Chaney, ss	0	0	0	0	0	FORSCH, p	4	0	0	0	0
McWilliams, p	2	0	0	0	0						
Office, ph	1	0	0	0	0						
Skok, p	0	0	0	0	0						
Devine, p	0	0	0	0	0						
Totals	27	0	0	0	2	Totals	35	6	11	6	0

Atlanta	0	0 0	0 0 0	0 0	0 – 0
Houston	2	0 0	0 0 0	3 1	x – 6

Atlanta	IP.	H.	R.	ER.	BB.	SO.
McWilliams (L. 0-1)	6*	8	5	5	0	3
Skok	1	2	0	0	0	1
Devine	1	1	1	0	0	0

Houston	IP.	H.	R.	ER.	BB.	SO.
FORSCH (W. 1-0)	9	0	0	0	2	3

*Pitched to three batters in seventh.

DP—None. LOB—Atlanta 2, Houston 6. 2B—Cedeno. 3B—Cruz, Ashby. SB—Cabell. SH—Reynolds. T—2:03. A—24,325.

hopper off Glenn Hubbard's bat in the fourth inning. Otherwise, Forsch breezed to the victory.

After Jeff Burroughs walked to open the second, Forsch retired 20 consecutive batters until Barry Bonnell walked with two out in the eighth. One of those eighth-inning outs was Dale Murphy's smash right at shortstop Craig Reynolds, the hardest-hit ball of the game.

Forsch, who had a two-hit game to his credit in 1978 against the Dodgers as his stingiest previous performance, was an uncertain starter until just 24 hours before the game.

"He was bitten by an insect before we left Florida and he had bursitis in his left arm," Houston Manager Bill Virdon explained.

"I was sick as a dog Thursday (April 5)," said Forsch. "I've never had a bite like that."

Next-day Houston starter Joe Niekro, realizing he would have a tough act to follow, asked: "What kind of spider did you say that was that bit you?"

The first brother tandem to hurl no-hitters, Ken and Bob Forsch.

Carlton Took Part in Four Low-Hit Efforts

By CARL CLARK

While American League pitchers could not come up with a no-hitter to match Ken Forsch's, they did twirl a record number of one-hitters in 1979. The 13 fashioned by nine different clubs broke the league record of 12 set in 1910 and 1915 and tied the major league mark set during the 1965 National League season.

In all, 74 low-hit games were pitched compared to 69 in 1978. There were 39 in the AL, divided between 13 one-hitters and 26 two-hitters, and 35 in the NL—10 one-hitters and 24 two-hitters.

Philadelphia, Texas and the Chicago White Sox shared team honors with five low-hitters apiece. The Phillies' total included four one-hit performances, three of which featured Steve Carlton.

Carlton had route-going one-hitters against Houston and New York to push his career total to five, equaling the NL record shared by Tom Seaver, Jim Maloney, Mordecai Brown, Grover Cleveland Alexander and Don Sutton. The Phils' two-time Cy Young lefthander also combined with Tug McGraw to shackle Pittsburgh with one safety in addition to his two-hitter against the Astros.

Nolan Ryan almost matched Carlton headline for headline. He fired an exciting, controversial one-hitter (the seventh of his career) against the Yankees, went all the way in a pair of two-hitters and combined with Jim Barr for a third.

Thrice he came close to becoming the first author of five no-hitters. Opposite-field singles by Mitchell Page and Oscar Gamble with one out in the eighth inning broke up April 21 and June 18 efforts against Oakland and Texas, respectively, and he came even closer against the Yankees July 13 before a national TV audience and a home crowd of 41,805.

Other notables were Cleveland's Rick Waits with one one-hitter and two two-hitters, Ross Baumgarten of the White Sox and Ferguson Jenkins of the Rangers with a one- and two-hitter apiece. Meanwhile, San Francisco's Ed Halicki, Atlanta's Phil Niekro, St. Louis' John Denny and Craig Swan of the Mets had a pair of two-hitters each.

A complete list of one-hit and two-hit games follows:

AMERICAN LEAGUE

One-Hit Games

April 7—Waits, Cleveland vs. Boston, 3-0—Remy, single in sixth.
April 11—Comer (seven innings) and Lyle (two innings), Texas vs. Cleveland, 4-0—Cox, single in third.
April 24—Lemanczyk, Toronto vs. Texas, 2-0—Putnam, single in third.
May   9—Norris, Oakland vs. Baltimore, 4-2—Roenicke, double in seventh.
May 25—Baumgarten, Chicago vs. California, 6-1—Grich, double in seventh.
July   3—Jenkins, Texas vs. Baltimore, 4-0—Lowenstein, single in fifth.
July   5—Langford, Oakland vs. California, 4-0—Downing, single in fifth.
July   7—Medich (six and two-thirds innings) and Kern (two and one-third innings), Texas vs. Toronto, 2-0—Mayberry, single in second.
July   8—Tiant, New York vs. Oakland, 2-0—Henderson, single in third.
July 13—Ryan, California vs. New York, 6-1—Jackson, single in ninth.
July 13—Renko, Boston vs. Oakland, 2-0—Henderson, single in ninth.
July 30—Stone (eight and two-thirds innings) and T. Martinez (one-third inning), Baltimore vs. Milwaukee, 2-1—Moore, homer in third.
Aug. 27—Huffman, Toronto vs. Oakland, 7-0—Essian, single in sixth.

Two-Hit Games

April 13—Clancy (six innings), Toronto vs. Kansas City, 4-1 (stopped by rain)—Otis, single in first; Patek, single in fifth.

April 21–Ryan (seven and two-thirds innings) and Barr (one and one-third innings), California vs. Oakland, 13-1
—Page, single in eighth; Gross, single in eighth.
April 30–Slaton, Milwaukee vs. Cleveland, 8-0–Bonds, single in fourth; Diaz, single in ninth.
May   6–D. Martinez, Baltimore vs. California, 6-0–Baylor, single in seventh; Carew, single in ninth.
May   14–Waits, Cleveland vs. Toronto, 1-0–McKay, single in fourth and double in seventh.
May   17–Kravec (seven innings) and Proly (two innings), Chicago vs. Oakland, 5-1–Essian, single in third; New-
man, homer in seventh.
May   20–Ryan, California vs. Chicago, 4-0–Lemon, single in first; Pryor, single in third.
May   20–John, New York vs. Boston, 2-0–Remy, single in fourth; Lynn, double in fourth.
June   1–Guidry, New York vs. Chicago, 4-0–Lemon, single in second; Bannister, single in ninth.
June   7–Stewart, Baltimore vs. Kansas City, 2-0–Cowens, homer in fifth and single in seventh.
June   7–Jenkins, Texas vs. Milwaukee, 7-1–Cooper, single in first; Gantner, triple in seventh.
June   7–Jenkins, Texas vs. Texas, 5-0–Gamble, single in eighth; Sample, single in ninth.
June 18–Ryan, California vs. New York, 3-0–Chambliss, single in eighth; Dent, single in ninth.
July   5–Sorensen, Milwaukee vs. New York, 5-1–Jackson, single in second; Nettles, triple in second.
July 10–Honeycutt, Seattle vs. New York, 5-1–Jackson, single in second; Nettles, triple in second.
July 22–Scarbery (seven innings) and Farmer (one inning), Chicago vs. Detroit, lost, 1-0–Morales, single in sec-
ond; Thompson, double in fourth.
July 25–Waits, Cleveland vs. Minnesota, 2-0–Rivera, single in seventh; Borgmann, single in ninth.
July 31–Barker (seven and one-third innings) and Monge (one and two-thirds innings), Cleveland vs. Boston,
3-0–Yastrzemski, double in first; Lynn, single in eighth.
Aug.   3–Tiant (eight innings) and Gossage (one inning), New York vs. Baltimore, lost, 1-0–Lowenstein, homer in
second; Bumbry, single in sixth.
Aug.   7–Underwood, Toronto vs. Kansas City, 3-2–Brett, single in second; McRae, homer in third.
Aug.   9–Wortham, Chicago vs. New York, 5-1–Randle, single in third; Piniella, homer in fourth.
Aug. 12–Baumgarten, Chicago vs. Toronto, 7-0 (first game)–Bailor, single in first; Woods, triple in seventh.
Aug. 15–Petry (eight innings) and Underwood (one inning), Detroit vs. California, 6-1–Ford, single in third; Rudi,
single in seventh.
Aug. 30–Medich, Texas vs. Boston, 6-0–Poquette, single in fourth; Watson, single in eighth.
Sept. 4–Koosman, Minnesota vs. Kansas City, 7-0–Wathan, homer in sixth; Wilson, single in ninth.
Sept. 12–Caldwell, Milwaukee vs. Oakland, 7-0–Page, single in second; Picciolo, single in eighth.
Sept. 23–Flanagan (eight innings) and Stanhouse (one inning), Baltimore vs. Cleveland, 3-1 (second game)–
Veryzer, single in fifth; Pruitt, double in seventh.

NATIONAL LEAGUE
One-Hit Games

May   8–Sanderson, Montreal vs. San Francisco, 4-0–Whitfield, single in first.
May   9–Ruthven, Philadelphia vs. San Diego, 2-0–Briggs, double in seventh.
May 11–Rau, Los Angeles vs. Montreal, 7-0–Speier, single in eighth.
June 5–Kison, Pittsburgh vs. San Diego, 7-0–Evans, double in eighth.
June 5–Carlton, Philadelphia vs. Houston, 8-0–Leonard, single in seventh.
June 23–Rogers, Montreal vs. Philadelphia, 3-0–Rader, single in eighth.
June 27–Martinez, St. Louis vs. Montreal, 5-0–Dyer, single in eighth.
July   4–Carlton, Philadelphia vs. New York, 1-0–Maddox, double in seventh.
Sept. 3–Carlton, Philadelphia (seven innings) and McGraw (two innings), Philadelphia vs. Pittsburgh, 2-0 (first
game)–Nicosia, double in sixth.
Sept. 28–Rasmussen, San Diego vs. San Francisco, 2-0–Evans, single in second.

Two-Hit Games

April 16–Lee, Montreal vs. Chicago, 2-0–Foote, single in sixth; Buckner, single in ninth.
April 19–Seaver, Cincinnati vs. Atlanta, 2-0–Frias, double in third; Royster, single in eighth.
April 25–Swan, New York vs. San Francisco, 2-0–Metzger, double in third; Hill, single in eighth.
May 12–Halicki, San Francisco vs. Philadelphia, 4-1–Unser, singles in fourth and ninth.
May 15–Denny, St. Louis vs. Montreal, 1-0–Cromartie, single in first; Parrish, single in second.
May 17–Halicki, San Francisco vs. Houston, 3-0–Cedeno, single in fourth; Cabell, single in ninth.
May 30–Rooker, Pittsburgh vs. Chicago, 9-2–Kingman, homer in fourth; Foote, single in fifth.
June 13–LaCoss (five innings) and Hume (four innings), Cincinnati vs. New York, 4-1–Hebner, single in fourth;
Henderson, single in eighth.
June 15–Swan, New York vs. Atlanta, 2-1–Office, single in fifth; Burroughs, homer in seventh.
June 17–Whitson (seven and one-third innings) and Tekulve (one and two-thirds innings), Pittsburgh vs. Los
Angeles, 5-1–Russell, homer in fourth and single in sixth.
June 19–Andujar, Houston vs. New York, 3-1–Stearns, single in second; Montanez, single in eighth.
July   4–Shirley, San Diego vs. Los Angeles, 6-0–Smith, single in fourth; Thomas, triple in sixth.
July 23–Niekro, Atlanta vs. Pittsburgh, 8-0 (second game)–Parker, single in first; Nicosia, double in eighth.
July 29–Kobel (six innings) and Glynn (one inning), New York vs. Chicago, 4-0 (stopped by rain)–Buckner, single
in second; Sizemore, single in sixth.
Aug.   8–Bonham, Cincinnati vs. Atlanta, 3-1–Bonnell, double in fifth; Matthews, single in eighth.
Aug.   9–Denny, St. Louis vs. New York, 4-0–Mazzilli, single in first; Youngblood, double in fifth.
Aug. 14–Hooton, Los Angeles vs. St. Louis, 9-0–Denny, single in sixth; Reitz, single in seventh.
Aug. 17–Fulgham, St. Louis vs. San Francisco, 3-0–Sadek, double in sixth; McCovey, single in seventh.
Aug. 19–Carlton, Philadelphia vs. Houston, 3-2–Puhl, triple in first; Bochy, single in second.
Aug. 20–Niekro, Houston vs. New York, 8-1–Youngblood, single in second; Stearns, single in fourth.
Aug. 27–Richard, Houston vs. Montreal, 3-0–Valentine, single in fifth; Carter, single in ninth.
Aug. 27–LaCoss (seven innings) and Hume (two innings), Cincinnati vs. Philadelphia, 4-2–Rose, double in first;
Luzinski, single in fourth.
Sept. 3–Reuss, Los Angeles vs. Houston, 1-0–Leonard, single in fifth; Cruz, single in fifth.
Sept. 22–Niekro, Atlanta vs. San Francisco, 10-2–Johnston, single in sixth; LeMaster, single in eighth.

Richard, Ryan Continued Strikeout Magic

By LARRY WIGGE

Houston's J. R. Richard led the majors with 14 10-strikeout games in 1979 and broke his own single-season strikeout record for a National League right-hander by fanning 313.

Richard's strikeout total was 100 better than runnerup Steve Carlton of the Phillies. James Rodney, who surpassed his 303 strikeout total of 1978, finished '79 in a flourish with four consecutive 10-strikeout performances.

At the same time, California's fireballing righthander Nolan Ryan continued to pile up strikeout records in the AL, recording 10 10-strikeout games in '79 to extend his overall 10-or-more strikeout games record to 128. He also led the league in strikeouts for the seventh time in eight years with 223.

Richard and Ryan also were the only pitchers in the majors to log 15-or-more strikeouts in a single game in 1979. Ryan's 16 K's in a 9-1 triumph over Detroit June 9 were tops for the year. It was the 21st time in Ryan's career he had fanned 15 or more batters in one game. Richard twice had 15 strikeouts. He stymied the Braves 4-1 August 3 and on September 21 fanned 15 Reds. In the latter game, Richard retired from the game after 11 innings of a 13-inning 3-2 decision for the Astros.

Following is a complete recap of the 15-strikeout games in 1979:

Date	Pitcher—Club—Opp.	Place	IP.	H.	R.	ER.	BB.	SO.	Result
June 9 —Ryan, Angels vs. Tigers	H	9	4	1	1	2	16	W 9-1
Aug. 3 —Richard, Astros vs. Braves	H	9	6	1	1	3	15	W 4-1
Sept. 21*—Richard, Astros vs. Reds	H	11	7	2	2	1	15	W 3-2

*Not involved in 13-inning decision.

Gaylord Perry of the Padres raised his career strikeout total to 3,141 and moved into second place on the all-time list, passing Bob Gibson. Ryan stepped into fourth place at 2,909, while other active hurlers Tom Seaver of the Reds moved up to fifth at 2,887 and Carlton into 10th at 2,683. Perry, who went into semi-retirement in the final month of the season, trailed only Walter Johnson, who fanned 3,508 in his career.

The following includes a complete list of 10-strikeout games in 1979 and the number of times achieved:

AMERICAN LEAGUE: Baltimore (5)—Flanagan 3, Stone 2. Boston (1)—Eckersley. California (10)—Ryan 10. Chicago—None. Cleveland—None. Detroit (2)—Morris, Underwood. Kansas City—None. Milwaukee—None. Minnesota (2)—Goltz, Redfern. New York (7)—Guidry 7. Oakland (2)—Langford, Norris. Seattle (2)—O. Jones 2. Texas (3)—Jenkins 2, Johnson. Toronto—None.

NATIONAL LEAGUE: Atlanta (3)—Niekro 3. Chicago (3)—Caudill, Krukow, McGlothen. Cincinnati (1)—Seaver. Houston (14)—Richard 14. Los Angeles (1)—Sutton. Montreal—None. New York (1)—Swan. Philadelphia (4)—Carlton 3, Christenson. Pittsburgh (3)—Bibby, Candelaria, Kison. St. Louis (1)—Vuckovich. San Diego (3)—Perry 3. San Francisco—None.

Sutter Won NL Fireman Award; Kern, Marshall Shared AL Honor

By LARRY WIGGE

Cy Young winner Bruce Sutter of the Cubs captured THE SPORTING NEWS Fireman of the Year Award in the National League for 1979.

For the first time since TSN originated the award in 1960, there was a tie when Jim Kern of the Rangers and Mike Marshall of the Twins finished in a deadlock for the American League honor.

After battling for the Fireman Award each of the past two seasons only to have injuries cut short his bid, Sutter tied an NL record for saves in 1979. In addition, he had six relief wins for a total of 43 points. One point is awarded for each relief victory and one point is credited for each save.

Sutter's 37 saves equalled the league mark set by Cincinnati's Clay Carroll in 1972 and matched by San Diego's Rollie Fingers in 1978. Bruce fell one save short of the major league standard established by Detroit's John Hiller in 1973.

Pittsburgh's Kent Tekulve was runnerup with 31 saves and 10 wins for 41 points, two behind Sutter.

Like Sutter, Kern was a first-time winner of the relief award. The Texas righthander retired the final batter in the Rangers' 6-3 victory over California September 29 in the next-to-last game of the season to tie Marshall. Kern finished with 29 saves and 13 wins for 42 points. Marshall had 32 saves and 10 victories. Detroit's Aurelio Lopez and Sid Monge of Cleveland were next with 31 points apiece.

Marshall became the first pitcher ever to collect three Fireman of the Year trophies. He won the honor with the Expos in 1973 and with the Dodgers in 1974.

A complete list of saves and victories in relief by major league pitchers in 1979 follows:

NATIONAL LEAGUE

Pitcher—Club	Saves	Relief Wins	Tot. Pts.	Pitcher—Club	Saves	Relief Wins	Tot. Pts.
Sutter, Chicago	37	6	43	Castillo, Los Angeles	7	2	9
Tekulve, Pittsburgh	31	10	41	Eastwick, Philadelphia	6	3	9
Garber, Atlanta	25	6	31	LaGrow, Los Angeles	4	5	9
Sambito, Houston	22	8	30	Bahnsen, Montreal	5	3	8
Bair, Cincinnati	16	11	27	Glynn, New York	7	1	8
Lavelle, San Francisco	20	7	27	Knowles, St. Louis	6	2	8
Sosa, Montreal	18	8	26	Minton, San Francisco	4	4	8
Fingers, San Diego	13	9	22	Roberts, S.F.-Pittsburgh	4	4	8
Hume, Cincinnati	17	5	22	Andujar, Houston	4	3	7
Jackson, Pittsburgh	14	8	22	D'Acquisto, San Diego	2	5	7
Littell, St. Louis	13	9	22	Griffin, San Francisco	2	5	7
McGraw, Philadelphia	16	4	20	Lee, San Diego	5	2	7
Reed, Philadelphia	5	13	18	Roberge, Houston	4	3	7
Romo, Pittsburgh	5	10	15	Schultz, St. Louis	3	4	7
Tidrow, Chicago	4	11	15	Welch, Los Angeles	5	2	7
Allen, New York	8	6	14	Brett, Los Angeles	2	4	6
Fryman, Montreal	10	3	13	May, Montreal	0	6	6
Borbon, Cin.-San Francisco	5	6	11	Pastore, Cincinnati	4	2	6
Lockwood, New York	9	2	11	Hassler, New York	4	1	5
J. McLaughlin, Atlanta	5	5	10	McGlothen, Chicago	2	3	5
Murray, N.Y.-Montreal	5	5	10	Mura, San Diego	2	3	5
Patterson, Los Angeles	6	4	10				

Pitcher—Club	Saves	Relief Wins	Tot. Pts.	Pitcher—Club	Saves	Relief Wins	Tot. Pts.
Palmer, Montreal	2	3	5	Bruno, St. Louis	0	2	2
Reuss, Los Angeles	3	2	5	Brusstar, Philadelphia	1	1	2
Twitchell, New York	0	5	5	Frazier, St. Louis	0	2	2
Hernandez, Chicago	0	4	4	Hausman, New York	2	0	2
Moffitt, San Francisco	2	2	4	Kison, Pittsburgh	0	2	2
Atkinson, Montreal	1	2	3	M. Mahler, Atlanta	0	2	2
Beckwith, Los Angeles	2	1	3	McEnaney, St. Louis	2	0	2
Bibby, Pittsburgh	0	3	3	B. McLaughlin, Hou.-Atlanta	0	2	2
Bradford, Atlanta	2	1	3	Moore, Chicago	1	1	2
Forster, Los Angeles	2	1	3	Owchinko, San Diego	0	2	2
Rasmussen, San Diego	3	0	3	Reardon, New York	1	1	2
Skok, Atlanta	2	1	3	Sanderson, Montreal	1	1	2
Soto, Cincinnati	0	3	3	Saucier, Philadelphia	1	1	2
Thomas, St. Louis	1	2	3	Schatzeder, Montreal	1	1	2
Tomlin, Cincinnati	1	2	3	Shirley, San Diego	0	2	2

One Save—Hannahs, Los Angeles; Niemann, Houston; Rautzhan, Los Angeles; Sutton, Los Angeles; Whitson, Pittsburgh-San Francisco.

One Relief Win—Bird, Philadelphia; Capilla, Cincinnati-Chicago; Caudill, Chicago; Curtis, San Francisco; Devine, Atlanta; Dixon, Houston; Ellis, New York-Pittsburgh; Forsch, Houston; Grimsley, Montreal; Hough, Los Angeles; Jackson, New York; Kaat, Philadelphia; Kucek, Philadelphia; Ladd, Houston; Moskau, Cincinnati; O'Brien, St. Louis; Orosco, New York; Riccelli, Houston; Sutcliffe, Los Angeles; Throop, Houston.

AMERICAN LEAGUE

Pitcher—Club	Saves	Relief Wins	Tot. Pts.	Pitcher—Club	Saves	Relief Wins	Tot. Pts.
Kern, Texas	29	13	42	Stewart, Baltimore	1	5	6
Marshall, Minnesota	32	10	42	Stoddard, Baltimore	3	3	6
Lopez, Detroit	21	10	31	Tobik, Detroit	3	3	6
Monge, Cleveland	19	12	31	Cleveland, Milwaukee	4	1	5
Stanhouse, Baltimore	21	7	28	Freisleben, Toronto	3	2	5
Clear, California	14	11	25	Lacey, Oakland	4	1	5
Davis, New York	9	14	23	Martin, Kansas City	5	0	5
Drago, Boston	13	10	23	Pattin, Kansas City	3	2	5
Gossage, New York	18	5	23	Rodriguez, Kansas City	2	3	5
Hrabosky, Kansas City	11	9	20	Spillner, Cleveland	1	4	5
McLaughlin, Seattle	14	5	19	Trout, Chicago	4	1	5
Farmer, Tex.-Chicago	14	4	18	Bacsik, Minnesota	0	4	4
Lyle, Texas	13	5	18	Hood, Clev.-New York	2	2	4
LaRoche, California	10	7	17	Kaat, Minnesota	2	2	4
Rawley, Seattle	11	5	16	Mingori, Kansas City	1	3	4
Montague, Sea.-California	7	8	15	Stanley, Boston	1	3	4
Augustine, Milwaukee	5	9	14	Tidrow, New York	2	2	4
Buskey, Toronto	7	6	13	Todd, Oakland	2	2	4
Cruz, Cleveland	10	3	13	Aase, California	2	1	3
Heaverlo, Oakland	9	4	13	Clay, New York	2	1	3
Hiller, Detroit	9	4	13	Ford, Baltimore	2	1	3
T. Martinez, Baltimore	3	10	13	Guidry, New York	2	1	3
Campbell, Boston	9	3	12	Hinton, Chi.-Seattle	2	1	3
Proly, Chicago	9	3	12	Reuschel, Cleveland	1	2	3
McClure, Milwaukee	5	5	10	Ripley, Boston	1	2	3
Castro, Milwaukee	6	3	9	Barr, California	0	2	2
Quisenberry, Kansas City	5	3	8	Busby, Kansas City	0	2	2
Burgmeier, Boston	4	3	7	Hoffman, Chicago	2	0	2
Hamilton, Oakland	5	2	7	D. Jackson, Minnesota	0	2	2
Billingham, Detroit	3	3	6	Jefferson, Toronto	1	1	2
Galasso, Milwaukee	3	3	6	McCatty, Oakland	0	2	2
Redfern, Minnesota	1	5	6	Stein, Seattle	0	2	2
Scarbery, Chicago	4	2	6	Travers, Milwaukee	0	2	2

One Save—Baker, Detroit; Frost, California; Griffin, New York; Kravec, Chicago; LaGrow, Chicago; Rainey, Boston.

One Relief Win—Arroyo, Detroit; Barlow, California; Botting, California; Burnside, Detroit; Burris, New York; Darwin, Texas; Garland, Cleveland; Gura, Kansas City; Hassler, Boston; Honeycutt, Seattle; John, New York; Johnson, Oakland-Texas; Kingman, Oakland; Langford, Oakland; Miller, California-Toronto; Murphy, Toronto; Parrott, Seattle; Rajsich, Texas; Remmerswaal, Boston; Serum, Minnesota; Taylor, Detroit; Vasquez, Seattle; Wilcox, Detroit; Wilkins, Cleveland.

Underwoods Were Featured in 1-0 Game

By CARL CLARK

Students of inside baseball found little from which to learn in 1979. With run-production up by 1,462, or 11.8 percent, there was a corresponding decrease in 1-0 games. Only 31 minimum-score battles were waged (17 in the American League and 14 in the National), the fewest since the 28 of 1961, when there were eight fewer teams. There were 51 such contests in 1978.

Kansas City, Seattle and Montreal paced the majors with three 1-0 victories apiece. The New York Yankees, Oakland, Toronto and Houston each lost three 1-0 struggles.

The individual leaders in 1-0 victories were Dennis Leonard, David Palmer and John Curtis with two. Three pitchers took a pair of 1-0 losses—Tommy Underwood, Ferguson Jenkins and Rick Langford, who also was saddled with two defeats in 1978.

Underwood's second defeat was meliorated by the fact that it came with another Underwood pitching for the opposition. Tommy's 22-year-old brother Pat made his major league debut for Detroit on that May 31 night at Toronto. It was the first time that a pitcher had ever made his debut with his brother on the mound for the enemy. And, with their mother looking on, the lefthanders handed out goose eggs until Jerry Morales blasted a home run to left-center field in the top of the eighth inning. Pat gave up only three hits before Dave Tobik and John Hiller finished up for him after Alfredo Griffin lashed a one-out double in the ninth.

The homer by Morales was one of seven that decided 1-0 contests.

The complete list of 1-0 games, including the winning and losing pitchers and the inning in which the run was scored, follows:

AMERICAN LEAGUE (17)

Date	Winner	Loser	Inning
APRIL—			
25	*Minetto, Oakland	Figueroa, New York	6
MAY—			
2	Ryan, California	Guidry, New York	3
14	Gale, Kansas City	*Bannister, Seattle	8
14	Waits, Cleveland	Underwood, Toronto	1
23	Travers, Milwaukee	Aase, California	7
27	Rainey, Boston	Jefferson, Toronto	3
31	*Underwood, Detroit	Underwood, Toronto	8
JULY—			
22	*Wilcox, Detroit	*Scarbery, Chicago	2
27	*Honeycutt, Seattle	Langford, Oakland	3
28	Eckersley, Boston	Jenkins, Texas	3
AUGUST—			
3	*McGregor, Balt.	*Tiant, New York	2
3	Bannister, Seattle	Keough, Oakland	7
12	Koosman, Minn.	Langford, Oakland	7
25	Leonard, Kan. City	Torrez, Boston	1
SEPTEMBER—			
3	Leonard, Kan. City	Zahn, Minnesota	8
5	*Dressler, Seattle	*Jenkins, Texas	1
18	Kravec, Chicago	Goltz, Minnesota	10

NATIONAL LEAGUE (14)

Date	Winner	Loser	Inning
MAY—			
15	Denny, St. Louis	Rogers, Montreal	9
20†	Williams, Houston	*Perry, San Diego	1
31	Sanderson, Mont.	*Christenson, Phila.	1
JULY—			
4	Carlton, Phila.	Hassler, New York	3
11	Curtis, San Fran.	*Schatzeder, Montreal	7
13	Martinez, St. Louis	*Forsch, Houston	4
14	*Krukow, Chicago	*Bonham, Cincinnati	8
19	Curtis, San Fran.	*Noles, Phila.	4
AUGUST—			
17	Palmer, Montreal	Solomon, Atlanta	9
18	*Christenson, Phila.	Richard, Houston	8
24	*Bonham, Cin.	*Allen, N. York	8
SEPTEMBER—			
3	Reuss, Los Angeles	Niekro, Houston	7
6	*Palmer, Montreal	McGlothen, Chicago	9
17	Niekro, Houston	Owchinko, San Diego	9

*Did not pitch complete game.   †First game of doubleheader.

Rudi, Thornton Were Grand Slam Kings

By CARL CLARK

American League batters, after slugging 47 grand slams in 1978, connected for 50 in 1979 to break the league record of 48 set in 1961. Thirty-one were hit in the National League.

Joe Rudi of the Angels, who led the majors with three grand slams in 1978, again clubbed three slams to share the lead with Cleveland's Andy Thornton.

Willie Mays Aikens, a teammate of Rudi, became the ninth player in major league history to homer with the bases loaded in two consecutive games. The 24-year-old South Carolinian blasted one off Dyar Miller in the second game of a June 13 twinbill at Toronto and came up with another in the first inning the next night against Phil Huffman.

But then watching four runs saunter across the plate was not an unusual experience for Blue Jay hurlers. The staff allowed a major league high of eight grand slams.

The complete list of grand slams, with the inning in which each was hit in parenthesis, follows:

AMERICAN LEAGUE (50)

APRIL—
12 —Yastrzemski, Boston vs. Galasso, Milwaukee ...... (7)
14 —Johnstone, New York vs. LaGrow, Chicago .. (8)
21 —Baylor, California vs. Lacey, Oakland.......... (5)

MAY—
5 —May, Baltimore vs. Aase, California .... (3)
7 —Meyer, Seattle vs. Mirabella, New York .... (5)
8 —Rudi, California vs. Rainey, Boston............... (1)
20 —Thompson, Detroit vs. Wilkins, Cleveland..... (1)
22 —Thornton, Cleveland vs. Lemongello, Tor. ...... (3)

JUNE—
3 —Meyer, Seattle vs. Lemongello, Toronto........ (3)
4 —Oglivie, Milwaukee vs. Baumgarten, Chi...... (1)
4 —Burleson, Boston vs. Rajsich, Texas............. (5)
8 —Ford, California vs. Hiller, Detroit................ (7)
10 —Essian, Oakland vs. Willis, Toronto............. (5)
13 —Allenson, Boston vs. Mingori, Kansas City ... (9)
13† —Aikens, California vs. Miller, Toronto.......... (3)
14 —Aikens, California vs. Huffman, Toronto .... (1)
15 —Davis, Milwaukee vs. Rodriguez, K. City ...... (4)
17 —Bonds, Cleveland vs. Abbott, Seattle .... (8)
18 —Kemp, Detroit vs. Renko, Boston .... (4)
23 —Horton, Seattle vs. Sorensen, Milwaukee ..... (5)

JULY—
3 —Johnson, Cleveland vs. Kravec, Chicago .... (1)
3 —Howell, Toronto vs. Billingham, Detroit .... (1)
4 —Nordhagen, Chicago vs. Waits, Cleveland...... (5)
7 —Rudi, California vs. Stanhouse, Baltimore..... (7)
14 —Bell, Texas vs. Gale, Kansas City................. (2)
15 —Edwards, Minnesota vs. Clancy, Toronto ...... (3)
21 —Randolph, New York vs. Minetto, Oakland.... (5)
23 —Rudi, California vs. Drago, Boston .... (1)
23 —Kelly, Baltimore vs. Heaverlo, Oakland........ (8)
24† —Lowenstein, Baltimore vs. O. Jones, Seattle.. (3)
26 —May, Baltimore vs. Montague, Seattle.......... (4)
29 —Manning, Cleveland vs. Kravec, Chicago....... (2)
31 —Murray, Baltimore vs. Cleveland, Mil........... (9)

AUGUST—
4 —Harrah, Cleveland vs. Johnson, Texas........... (1)
8† —Wockenfuss, Detroit vs. Johnson, Texas........ (3)
23 —Thornton, Cleveland vs. Langford, Oakland . (1)
25 —Baylor, California vs. Moore, Toronto........... (1)
25 —Horton, Seattle vs. Petry, Detroit................ (1)
26* —DeCinces, Baltimore vs. Trout, Chicago........ (1)
27 —Gamble, New York vs. Jenkins, Texas........... (4)
27 —Howell, Toronto vs. Minetto, Oakland.......... (6)

*First game of doubleheader.

†Second game of doubleheader.

SEPTEMBER—
1 —Thornton, Cleveland vs. Barr, California ...... (6)
7 —Carty, Toronto vs. Waits, Cleveland............. (5)
9 —Bonds, Cleveland vs. Buskey, Toronto........... (9)
9 —Dempsey, Baltimore vs. Finch, Seattle.......... (6)
12 —Montanez, Texas vs. Honeycutt, Seattle........ (4)
14 —Gross, Oakland vs. Farmer, Chicago............ (8)
14 —Roberts, Seattle vs. Gura, Kansas City.......... (3)
26 —Bochte, Seattle vs. Haas, Milwaukee .... (7)
28 —Smith, Baltimore vs. Barker, Cleveland........ (2)

NATIONAL LEAGUE (31)

APRIL—
6 —Ferguson, Los Angeles vs. Jones, San Diego.. (1)
8 —Foster, Cincinnati vs. Halicki, San Fran...... (5)
11 —Concepcion, Cincinnati vs. Devine, Atlanta .. (5)
17 —Maddox, Philadelphia vs. Romo, Pittsburgh . (5)
20 —Kingman, Chicago vs. Rogers, Montreal....... (3)

MAY—
1 —Freed, St. Louis vs. Sambito, Houston........... (11)
6 —Carter, Montreal vs. Perry, San Diego........... (5)
9 —Matthews, Atlanta vs. Whitson, Pittsburgh.. (5)
9 —Milner, Pittsburgh vs. Garber, Atlanta .... (9)
15 —Foote, Chicago vs. Espinosa, Philadelphia..... (5)
17 —Buckner, Chicago vs. McGraw, Philadelphia . (5)

JUNE—
11 —Simmons, St. Louis vs. Reuss, Los Angeles... (3)
13 —Scott, St. Louis vs. Sutcliffe, Los Angeles..... (9)
30 —Vail, Chicago vs. Murray, New York .... (11)

JULY—
1* —Kennedy, St. Louis vs. McGraw, Phila........... (8)
13 —Burroughs, Atlanta vs. Rooker, Pittsburgh .. (2)
19 —Knight, Cincinnati vs. McEnaney, St. Louis.. (5)
22* —Concepcion, Cincinnati vs. Hernandez, Chi... (8)
24 —Baker, Los Angeles vs. Brusstar, Phila........... (6)
30* —Hernandez, St. Louis vs. Fryman, Montreal . (4)

AUGUST—
5* —Luzinski, Philadelphia vs. Blyleven, Pitts..... (5)
5* —Milner, Pittsburgh vs. McGraw, Phila........... (9)
10 —Thomas, Los Angeles vs. Knepper, S. Fran.... (2)
11 —Ott, Pittsburgh vs. McGraw, Philadelphia..... (8)
26 —Kison, Pittsburgh vs. Shirley, San Diego ...... (2)

SEPTEMBER—
2 —Lopes, Los Angeles vs. Sutter, Chicago .... (9)
9 —Foote, Chicago vs. Kucek, Philadelphia .... (4)
16† —Cash, Montreal vs. Frazier, St. Louis............. (10)
19* —Schmidt, Philadelphia vs. Romo, Pittsburgh . (7)
25 —Cey, Los Angeles vs. Halicki, San Francisco . (2)
28 —Garvey, Los Angeles vs. Ruhle, Houston....... (8)

Kingman Twice Had 3-Homer Games

By LARRY WIGGE

Dave Kingman of the Cubs became only the sixth player in history to slug three homers in a game twice during the same season in 1979.

Kingman, who led the majors with 48 homers in '79, was the first to account for two three-homer games since Pittsburgh's Willie Stargell accomplished the trick in 1971. Others who have achieved the feat include: Johnny Mize twice (1938, 1940), Ralph Kiner (1947), Ted Williams (1957) and Willie Mays (1961).

Three-homer efforts were in abundance as American Leaguers bashed out seven such games and NL sluggers accounted for four. That total of 11 tied the combined major league record set in 1950. The AL's previous tops in this department was five in 1930 and 1950. The NL high is six, also done in 1950.

Kingman belted three homers in a game in 1976 and again in 1978 to raise his career total to four big-homer games—one shy of the record held by Mize. King Kong's first three-homer game came in a wild 23-22 loss to the Phillies May 17. On July 28, his three-homer production again was wasted in a 6-4 loss to the Mets.

Mike Schmidt of the Phillies had previously blasted four homers in a game April 17, 1976 against the Cubs. Otherwise, only George Brett, who had three homers against Catfish Hunter and the Yankees in the 1978 championship series, had ever achieved the feat before.

A detailed look at the 11-three-homer games in 1979:

Date	Player—Opposition	Place	AB.	R.	H.	2B.	3B.	HR.	RBI.	Result
May 17*	Kingman, Cubs vs. Phillies	H	6	4	3	0	0	3	6	L 22-23
May 18	Murphy, Braves vs. Giants	H	3	3	3	0	0	3	5	W 6-4
May 23	Oliver, Rangers vs. Twins	H	4	3	3	0	0	3	4	W 7-2
July 7	Schmidt, Phillies vs. Giants	H	4	3	3	0	0	3	5	L 6-8
July 8†	Oglivie, Brewers vs. Tigers	H	3	3	3	0	0	3	4	W 5-4
July 14	Washington, White Sox vs. Tigers	H	5	3	3	0	0	3	5	W 12-4
July 22	Brett, Royals vs. Rangers	A	4	3	3	0	0	3	5	W 7-6
July 27	Cooper, Brewers vs. Yankees	H	5	3	3	0	0	3	4	W 6-5
July 28	Kingman, Cubs vs. Mets	A	4	3	4	0	0	3	3	L 4-6
Aug. 29†	Murray, Orioles vs. Twins	A	5	3	3	0	0	3	7	W 7-4
Sept. 1	Lansford, Angels vs. Indians	A	5	3	3	0	0	3	3	W 7-4

*10-inning game.   †First game of doubleheader.   ‡Second game of doubleheader.

Kingman also finished with a total of five multi-homer games, tying Boston's Jim Rice and California's Don Baylor for the major league lead in that department. Following is a list of each player who hit two or more homers in '79 and the number of times achieved:

AMERICAN LEAGUE: Baltimore (6)—Ayala, DeCinces, May, Murray, Roenicke, Singleton. Boston (14)—Rice 5, Lynn 4, Watson 2, Evans, Fisk, Wolfe. California (14)—Baylor 5, Grich 4, Ford 2, Lansford 2, Aikens. Chicago (5)—Lemon, Morrison, Nahorodny, Nordhagen, Washington. Cleveland (6)—Harrah 2, Johnson 2, Hargrove, Norris. Detroit (10)—Kemp 3, Morales 2, Parrish 2, Summers, Thompson, Wockenfuss. Kansas City (4)—Brett 2, Washington, Wilson. Milwaukee (12)—Cooper 4, Thomas 4, Oglivie 3, Lezcano. Minnesota (3)—Edwards, Kusick, Smalley. New York (9)—Spencer 3, Chambliss 2, Murcer 2, Gamble, Nettles. Oakland (7)—Revering 4, Armas, Gross, Heath, Newman. Seattle (3)—Horton 2, R. Jones. Texas (8)—Ellis 2, Oliver 2, Bell, Putnam, Rivers, Soderholm. Toronto (2)—Mayberry, Velez.

NATIONAL LEAGUE: Atlanta (10)—Horner 3, Matthews 3, Murphy 3, Burroughs. Chicago (11)—Kingman 5, Buckner, Dillard, Foote, Martin, Murcer, Vail. Cincinnati (4)—Foster 2, Bench, Knight. Houston—None. Los Angeles (8)—Ferguson 2, Yeager 2, Baker, Cey, Garvey, Lopes. Montreal (10)—Dawson 3, Carter 2, Parrish 2, Valentine 2, Hebner, Mazzilli. Philadelphia (4)—Schmidt 3, McBride. Pittsburgh (9)—B. Robinson 4, Stargell, Milner. St. Louis (4)—Simmons 2, Hendrick, Templeton. San Diego (2)—Winfield 2. San Francisco (7)—Ivie 4, Andrews, Clark, McCovey.

Bowa, Parker Repeated Five-Hit Efforts

By CARL CLARK

A dozen players from each major league collected five hits in a game in 1979. Thirteen had perfect 5-for-5 days. Included on the National League roll call were two players whose names also appeared on the '78 list—Larry Bowa of the Phillies and Dave Parker of the Pirates.

Both repeaters broke through in extra-inning games, as did seven other five-hit men. Parker waited until the next-to-last day of the season to rap five singles in a 7-6, 13-inning loss to Chicago; Bowa had three singles and a pair of doubles and scored four runs in a 23-22, 10-inning conquest of those same Cubs, May 17.

George Brett was nearly a one-man scourge against the Orioles, May 28. He figured in all the Royals' runs in a 16-inning, 5-4 victory, driving in four, scoring three and pounding out a single, double, triple and two home runs. Brett, hitting for the cycle for the first time, led off the 16th with a game-winning homer off Sammy Stewart.

And again this lesson: a five-hit game is much more likely to come from a man playing on the road. That was the story in 16 of the season's 24 cases, bringing the total over the past four years to 78 road-28 home, nearly a 3-1 advantage.

Records of all players with five hits in a game follow:

Date	Player—Opposition	Place	AB.	R.	H.	2B.	3B.	HR.	RBI.	Result
April 15	Downing, Angels vs. A's	A	5	2	5	3	0	0	0	W 8-1
April 27	Bosetti, Blue Jays vs. Brewers	H	5	2	5	1	0	0	1	L 5-8
May 9	Scott, Cards vs. Astros (16 inn.)	A	7	1	5	1	1	0	2	L 4-5
May 12	Remy, Red Sox vs. A's	A	5	1	5	0	0	0	2	W 8-2
May 17	Bowa, Phils vs. Cubs (10 inn.)	A	8	4	5	2	0	0	1	W 23-22
May 26	Bumbry, Orioles vs. Tigers (16 inn.)	A	8	2	5	1	0	1	1	W 7-5
May 28	Brett, Royals vs. Orioles (16 inn.)	H	7	3	5	1	1	2	4	W 5-4
June 19	Garner, Pirates vs. Giants	A	5	1	5	0	1	0	1	W 9-4
July 1	Essian, A's vs. Rangers (15 inn.)	A	8	2	5	1	0	0	1	W 13-12
July 4	Bannister, White Sox vs. Indians	A	6	3	5	1	0	0	3	W 16-4
July 7*	Thompson, Cubs vs. Astros	H	5	0	5	0	0	0	2	W 6-0
July 15	Kemp, Tigers vs. White Sox	A	6	2	5	0	0	0	3	W 14-5
July 20	Scott, Expos vs. Dodgers (11 inn.)	A	5	1	5	0	0	0	2	L 5-6
July 31	Winfield, Padres vs. Braves	A	5	4	5	1	0	1	4	W 10-3
Aug. 10	Ford, Angels vs. Mariners (14 inn.)	H	7	3	5	2	1	1	2	L 6-8
Aug. 26	Cedeno, Astros vs. Phils	A	5	1	5	1	1	0	0	W 4-1
Aug. 27	Simpson, Mariners vs. Indians	A	6	3	5	1	0	0	1	W 6-5
Aug. 27	Otis, Royals vs. Brewers	H	6	1	5	1	0	0	2	W 10-9
Sept. 5	Fahey, Padres vs. Astros (10 inn.)	A	5	0	5	0	0	0	1	L 3-4
Sept. 11	Landestoy, Astros vs. Reds	A	5	2	5	1	0	0	2	L 8-9
Sept. 14	Murphy, Braves vs. Padres	A	5	3	5	0	1	2	3	W 10-7
Sept. 14	Rivers, Rangers vs. Twins	H	5	3	5	0	0	2	2	W 5-3
Sept. 27	Hendrick, Cards vs. Pirates	A	5	3	5	1	0	1	2	W 9-5
Sept. 29	Parker, Pirates vs. Cubs (13 inn.)	H	6	2	5	0	0	0	0	L 6-7

*First game of doubleheader.

For the second year in a row, the season's longest hitting streak belonged to Pete Rose. Although he could not approach his National League record of 44 games, Rose celebrated his first year in a Phillies' uniform by extending his NL record of streaks of 20 or more games to six with a 23-game string in September. The 39-year-old first baseman hit .462 in that stretch (42-for-91) and his 51 hits for the entire month gave him more than 200 hits for an unprecedented tenth time.

Danny Meyer of Seattle and Johnny Grubb of Texas shared American League honors with 21-game skeins in which they had almost identical statistics. Grubb, whose streak began in mid-May, hit .410 with seven homers and 16 RBIs. Meyer, from June 9 through June 30, hit .412 with an identical number of homers and RBIs.

Periods of particular devastation were wrought by several players. Mike Schmidt of the Phillies flexed his muscles over a 17-game span in July, hitting .468 with 12 homers and 28 RBIs. Dave Lopes exploded for nine homers and knocked in 21 Dodgers in 18 games beginning May 27.

California's Bobby Grich, Boston's AL batting king Fred Lynn and Atlanta's Bob Horner each had 20-game streaks. Grich was torrid in June, hitting .400 with nine homers and 20 RBIs. Lynn batted at a .451 clip in the first weeks of August, scorching 11 homers and driving home 23 runs. Horner batted .386 and connected for four homers and 20 RBIs in a score of contests stretching from July 22 to August 7.

Brewer Ben Oglivie hit .508 in his 16-game streak in September.

Only Paul Molitor had two streaks of 15 or more games. The Milwaukee second baseman's first streak extended from June 19 through July 6 and encompassed 16 games, in which he hit .414 and drove in 16 runs. He began September with a 15-game run.

Streaks of 15 or more games were also recorded by these players: 19 games—Warren Cromartie, Expos; Lamar Johnson and Chet Lemon, White Sox; Lee Mazzilli, Mets; Eddie Murray, Orioles; Roy Smalley, Twins; 18 games—Johnny Bench, Reds; 17 games—Joe Morgan, Reds; 16 games—Cecil Cooper, Brewers; Willie Montanez, Rangers; Garry Templeton, Cardinals; 15 games—Al Bumbry, Orioles; Enos Cabell, Jose Cruz and Craig Reynolds, Astros; George Hendrick, Cardinals; Willie Horton, Mariners; Ron LeFlore, Tigers; Rick Manning, Indians; Omar Moreno, Pirates; Mitchell Page, A's; Richie Zisk, Rangers.

Templeton and Brett paced the majors in four-hit games with six apiece. Al Oliver and Bump Wills of the Rangers were next with five each.

The complete list of players with four or more hits in one game follows:

AMERICAN LEAGUE: Baltimore (11)—Dauer 4, Bumbry 2, Murray 2, Singleton 2, Roenicke. Boston (11)—Fisk 2, Watson 2, Brohamer, Evans, Lynn, Papi, Remy, Rice, Yastrzemski. California (20)—Carew 3, Downing 3, Ford 3, Grich 3, Lansford 2, Anderson, Baylor, Campaneris, Davis, Harlow, Rudi. Chicago (12)—Washington 3, Lemon 2, Bannister, Johnson, May, Morrison, Orta, Pryor, Squires. Cleveland (6)—Manning 2, Bonds, Dade, Norris, Thornton. Detroit (6)—Kemp 3, Parrish 2, LeFlore. Kansas City (21)—Brett 6, Wilson 4, Patek 3, LaCock 2, Otis 2, Cowens, Scott, Washington, White. Milwaukee (7)—Molitor 2, Oglivie 2, Cooper, Gantner, Thomas. Minnesota (11)—Smalley 3, Landreaux 2, Powell 2, Castino, Randall, Sofield, Wynegar. New York (9)—Gamble 3, Randolph 3, Jackson 2, Nettles. Oakland (9)—Page 2, Revering 2, Edwards, Essian, Heath, Henderson, Picciolo. Seattle (7)—Bochte 2, Horton 2, Paciorek 2, Simpson. Texas (20)—Oliver 5, Wills 5, Bell 4, Gamble, Grubb, Rivers, Roberts, Sample, Sundberg. Toronto (10)—Bosetti 3, Griffin 3, Howell 2, Mayberry, Woods.

NATIONAL LEAGUE: Atlanta (8)—Frias 2, Horner 2, Hubbard, Miller, Murphy, Royster. Chicago (18)—Buckner 3, Kingman 3, Thompson 3, Sizemore 2, Vail 2, Biittner, DeJesus, Foote, Martin, Ontiveros. Cincinnati (10)—Collins 3, Concepcion 2, Kennedy 2, Griffey, Morgan, Summers. Houston (9)—Howe 2, Reynolds 2, Cabell, Cedeno, Cruz, Landestoy, Puhl. Los Angeles (10)—Baker 3, Russell 2, Thomas 2, Yeager 2, Ferguson. Montreal (10)—Dawson 3, Cromartie 2, Carter, Parrish, Scott, Solaita, Speier. New York (7)—Hebner 2, Taveras 2, Kranepool, Stearns, Youngblood. Philadelphia (11)—Maddox 3, Rose 3, Bowa 2, Boone, Luzinski, McBride. Pittsburgh (11)—Foli 2, Garner 2, Moreno 2, Ott 2, Madlock, Nicosia, Parker. St. Louis (20)—Templeton 6, Hernandez 4, Scott 4, Hendrick 3, Reitz 2, Oberkfell. San Diego (14)—Dade 2, Richards 2, Tenace 2, Winfield 2, Almon, Fahey, Gonzalez, Smith, Turner, Wilhelm. San Francisco (8)—Clark 2, Herndon 2, Ivie 2, Whitfield 2.

Brock, Yaz Stroked 3,000th Hit

By LARRY WIGGE

When most of us look back on the summer of '79, we will remember sitting in long lines of traffic waiting to get gasoline. But in 1979, Lou Brock and Carl Yastrzemski waited for no one—becoming the 14th and 15th players in baseball history to achieve the 3,000-hit plateau.

On August 13, Brock smashed a single off the pitching hand of Chicago righthander Dennis Lamp in the fourth inning at Busch Memorial Stadium for his 3,000th career hit.

Yastrzemski grounded a single into right field against Yankee righthander Jim Beattie in the eighth inning of a game at Fenway Park September 12 for his milestone hit.

It was only the third time in history that two players had accomplished the milestone in the same season. Eddie Collins and Tris Speaker reached the mark in 1925 and Hank Aaron and Willie Mays did it together in 1970.

Brock, who needed 100 hits to reach 3,000 when the season began, ripped through August hitting in the .320 range, after suffering through a miserable .221 average in 1978. Before a gathering of 46,161 on that historical August evening in St. Louis, Brock singled to left field in the first inning. Then, on a 2-and-2 pitch from Lamp in the fourth, Lou lashed a drive off the hurler's hand and flashed past first base.

"The most important thing was to crown my career with a fine performance," Brock would say. "I've always wanted to leave baseball in a blaze of

Stan Musial welcomes Lou Brock to 3,000-hit club.

glory. I've always wanted to orchestrate my own exodus and I'm doing a pretty good job of it."

Brock, who retired after the 1979 season with a career total of 3,023 hits, finished the season with a .304 average.

Yastrzemski needed 131 hits in '79 to reach the 3,000-hit standard. After going through August in the .280s, he slumped while closing in on the coveted plateau. In fact, he had been 0-for-12 and had only one hit in his previous 18 at-bats.

"I came out of my normal realm of hitting. I was anxious. There wasn't a chance to relax," said Yaz. "This was tough, I was almost embarrassed."

Yaz had gone hitless in his first three trips to the plate against starter Catfish Hunter and Beattie, who relieved Hunter in the fifth, before 34,337 Boston fans.

In the memorable eighth, however, Yaz ripped Beattie's first offering, a tailing fastball, past a lunging Yankee second baseman Willie Randolph.

"It just wouldn't have been the same if I had hit in on the road," said Yaz. "After 19 years, I wanted it here, for these people. I never thought about 3,000 hits until after last year. I never accumulated a lot of hits in a season. I know one thing, this was the hardest of the 3,000. I took so long to do it, I guess, because I've enjoyed all those standing ovations you've given me the last three days."

With the 3,000 hits, Yastrzemski became only the fourth player to have that many hits in addition to 400 home runs. Stan Musial, Hank Aaron and Willie Mays were the others.

Yaz finished 1979 with a .270 average. His 140 hits raised his career total to 3,009.

Along with Al Kaline (.297), Brock (.293) and Yastrzemski (.288) are the only members of the 3,000-hit fraternity below the .300-mark in career average.

Brock and Yaz each celebrated his 40th birthday before achieving the 3,000-hit plateau. Only Cap Anson and Honus Wagner before them reached the 3,000 mark at 40-or-over.

With pardons to George Allen's "Over the Hill Gang," Brock coined the performance of himself, Yaz and a chosen few other veterans like Gaylord Perry, Willie McCovey and Willie Stargell as the "On Top of the Hill Club."

Following is a table which includes all the 3,000-hit players:

Player—Years	G.	AB.	R.	H.	2B.	3B.	HR.	Pct.	Age*
Ty Cobb (1905-1928)	3033	11429	2244	4191	724	297	118	.367	34
Hank Aaron (1954-1976)	3298	12364	2174	3771	624	98	755	.305	36
Stan Musial (1941-1963)	3026	10972	1949	3630	725	177	475	.331	37
Tris Speaker (1907-1928)	2789	10208	1881	3515	793	224	115	.344	37
Honus Wagner (1897-1917)	2785	10427	1740	3430	651	252	101	.329	40
Pete Rose (1963-1979)	2668	10824	1747	3372	612	116	154	.312	37
Eddie Collins (1906-1930)	2826	9949	1818	3311	437	186	47	.333	38
Willie Mays (1951-1973)	2992	10881	2062	3283	523	140	660	.302	39
Nap Lajoie (1896-1916)	2475	9589	1503	3251	650	162	82	.339	39
Paul Waner (1926-1945)	2549	9459	1626	3152	603	190	112	.333	39
Cap Anson (1876-1897)	2253	9084	1712	3081	530	129	92	.339	45
Lou Brock (1961-1979)	2616	10332	1610	3023	486	141	149	.293	40
Carl Yastrzemski (1961-1979)	2862	10447	1640	3009	565	56	404	.288	40
Al Kaline (1953-1974)	2834	10116	1622	3007	498	75	399	.297	39
R. Clemente (1955-1972)	2433	9454	1416	3000	440	166	240	.317	38

*Age when 3,000th hit was made.

Mota, Unser Performed Pinch-Hit Feats

Manny Mota of the Dodgers became the all-time major league pinch-hit leader when he laced 15 pinch-blows in 42 at-bats in 1979 to bring his career total to 147 pinch-hits. Smokey Burgess had been the leader with 144.

Another pinch-record established in '79 occurred when Del Unser of the Phillies belted three consecutive pinch-homers. The first homer came June 30 at St. Louis. Unser later homered July 5 against the Mets and July 10 vs. San Diego, both at Veterans Stadium in Philadelphia. His four pinch-homers for the season surpassed by one the number struck by Atlanta's Mike Lum and Pat Kelly of the Orioles.

Of the players who batted at least 10 times as a pinch-hitter, Dave Bergman of the Astros led the National League with a .500 average, getting five-for-10. The American League leader was Bill Nahorodny of the White Sox with a .545 average, going six-for-11.

NATIONAL LEAGUE PINCH-HITTING
(Compiled by Elias Sports Bureau)

Club Pinch-Hitting

Club	AB.	H.	HR.	R.BI.	Pct.	Club	AB.	H.	HR.	R.BI.	Pct.
Chicago	243	65	5	38	.267	Pittsburgh	192	45	5	33	.234
San Francisco	228	60	5	36	.263	Philadelphia	218	50	5	30	.229
Atlanta	205	53	6	33	.259	Cincinnati	180	37	0	15	.206
Montreal	169	43	2	29	.254	New York	228	46	1	20	.202
St. Louis	181	43	4	27	.238	San Diego	237	46	1	28	.194
Los Angeles	190	45	0	13	.237	Totals	2462	578	36	332	.235
Houston	191	45	2	30	.236						

Individual Pinch-Hitting
(10 or More At-Bats)

Player-Club	AB.	H.	HR.	R.BI.	Pct.	Player-Club	AB.	H.	HR.	R.BI.	Pct.
Bergman, Houston	10	5	1	2	.500	Whitfield, San Fran.	31	7	0	5	.226
Stargell, Pittsburgh	15	7	1	6	.467	Freed, St. Louis	27	6	2	6	.222
McCovey, San Francisco	28	11	2	10	.393	Johnston, San Francisco	27	6	0	1	.222
Ivie, San Francisco	23	9	1	8	.391	Auerbach, Cincinnati	23	5	0	3	.217
Maddox, New York	21	8	0	1	.381	Mumphrey, St. Louis	14	3	0	0	.214
Walling, Houston	37	14	1	11	.378	Sanguillen, Pittsburgh	42	9	0	3	.214
Pocoroba, Atlanta	16	6	0	4	.375	Bevacqua, San Diego	29	6	0	8	.207
Herndon, San Francisco	19	7	0	4	.368	Chapman, New York	10	2	0	0	.200
Thompson, Chicago	33	12	0	4	.364	Clines, Chicago	10	2	0	0	.200
Mota, Los Angeles	42	15	0	3	.357	Wilhelm, San Diego	10	2	0	0	.200
Iorg, St. Louis	31	11	1	8	.355	Johnstone, San Diego	16	3	0	2	.188
Dillard, Chicago	17	6	0	0	.353	Joshua, Los Angeles	48	9	0	2	.188
Spikes, Atlanta	47	16	2	13	.340	Tolan, San Diego	16	3	0	2	.188
Lum, Atlanta	52	17	3	11	.327	Lacy, Pittsburgh	33	6	0	2	.182
Cash, Montreal	31	10	0	3	.323	Leonard, Houston	11	2	0	4	.182
Collins, Cincinnati	28	9	0	1	.321	Flores, New York	39	7	0	5	.179
White, Montreal	38	12	0	2	.316	Turner, San Diego	28	5	0	2	.179
Trevino, New York	16	5	0	1	.313	DeFreites, Cincinnati	17	3	0	1	.176
Biittner, Chicago	42	13	1	11	.310	Sexton, Houston	17	3	0	0	.176
Unser, Philadelphia	46	14	4	14	.304	Henderson, Cin-Chi.	52	9	1	5	.173
Tamargo, SF-Mtl	20	6	1	6	.300	Carbo, St. Louis	30	5	1	4	.167
Venable, San Francisco.	17	5	0	0	.294	Chaney, Atlanta	12	2	0	2	.167
Vail, Chicago	42	12	2	12	.286	Staub, Montreal	12	2	0	4	.167
Gross, Philadelphia	51	14	0	3	.275	Kranepool, New York	37	6	0	2	.162
Milner, Pittsburgh	26	7	1	7	.269	Briggs, San Diego	19	3	0	0	.158
Gonzalez, San Diego	15	4	0	3	.267	Solaita, Montreal	13	2	0	1	.154
McCarver, Philadelphia .	39	10	0	3	.256	Richards, San Diego	20	3	0	2	.150
Baldwin, Houston	12	3	0	0	.250	Perkins, San Diego	27	4	0	2	.148
Davalillo, Los Angeles	24	6	0	2	.250	Boisclair, New York	33	5	0	0	.143
Hutton, Montreal	44	11	1	7	.250	Landestoy, Houston	14	2	0	0	.143
B. Robinson, Pittsburgh	12	3	1	5	.250	Cruz, SF-Cin	16	2	0	2	.125
Office, Atlanta	21	5	1	2	.238	Thomasson, Los Angeles	18	2	0	1	.111
Alou, Houston	34	8	0	8	.235	Hodges, New York	29	3	0	2	.103
Cardenal, Philadelphia ..	17	4	0	3	.235	Heep, Houston	10	1	0	1	.100
Kennedy, Cincinnati	17	4	0	0	.235	Summers, Cincinnati	10	1	0	1	.100
Hargrove, San Diego	13	3	0	0	.231	Howe, Houston	11	1	0	1	.091
Norman, New York	13	3	1	3	.231	North, San Francisco	11	1	0	0	.091
Oberkfell, St. Louis	13	3	0	1	.231	Thomas, Los Angeles	11	1	0	0	.091
Andrews, San Francisco	22	5	0	1	.227	Stearns, New York	12	1	0	0	.083
Brock, St. Louis	22	5	0	2	.227	Nolan, Atlanta	14	1	0	0	.071
Easler, Pittsburgh	44	10	2	8	.227	Anderson, Philadelphia .	11	0	0	0	.000
Spilman, Cincinnati	22	5	0	2	.227	Reynolds, San Diego	11	0	0	1	.000

AMERICAN LEAGUE PINCH-HITTING
(Compiled by Sports Information Center)

Club Pinch-Hitting

Club	AB.	H.	HR.	RBI.	Pct.	Club	AB.	H.	HR.	RBI.	Pct.
Milwaukee	46	17	2	9	.370	Chicago	162	40	1	23	.247
Oakland	48	16	1	13	.333	Toronto	52	12	4	14	.231
Baltimore	132	37	4	25	.280	Cleveland	102	21	2	16	.206
New York	106	29	6	24	.274	Minnesota	218	44	0	23	.202
Texas	189	51	5	32	.270	Kansas City	156	31	1	22	.199
California	65	17	0	13	.262	Detroit	106	21	5	24	.198
Seattle	147	38	4	15	.259	Totals	1622	397	35	265	.245
Boston	93	23	0	12	.247						

Individual Pinch-Hitting
(10 or More At-Bats)

Player–Club	AB.	H.	HR.	RBI.	Pct.	Player–Club	AB.	H.	HR.	RBI.	Pct.
Nahorodny, Chicago	11	6	1	5	.545	Moore, Chicago	25	6	0	1	.240
Piniella, New York	12	6	1	3	.500	Johnson, NY-Cleve	17	4	1	3	.235
Kelly, Baltimore	24	11	3	12	.458	Paciorek, Seattle	17	4	1	4	.235
Roberts, Seattle	12	5	0	1	.417	Ayala, Baltimore	13	3	0	0	.231
Milbourne, Seattle	30	12	0	1	.400	Fisk, Boston	13	3	0	1	.231
Rettenmund, California	10	4	0	4	.400	Rivera, Minnesota	26	6	0	6	.231
Oliver, Texas	13	5	0	1	.385	Norris, Cleveland	18	4	0	3	.222
Putnam, Texas	21	8	2	7	.381	Lowenstein, Baltimore	23	5	0	3	.217
Chalk, Tex-Oak	8	3	0	2	.375	Beamon, Seattle	14	3	0	0	.214
Goodwin, Minnesota	11	4	0	2	.364	Morales, Minnesota	42	9	0	1	.214
Norwood, Minnesota	14	5	0	1	.357	Soderholm, Chi-Tex	14	3	0	2	.214
Nordhagen, Chicago	21	7	0	3	.333	Davis, California	24	5	0	1	.208
Pruitt, Cleveland	18	6	0	4	.333	Scott, Bos-KC-NY	10	2	0	0	.200
Dwyer, Boston	22	7	0	5	.318	Jones, Detroit	11	2	0	1	.182
Moore, Milwaukee	19	6	0	3	.316	Orta, Chicago	22	4	0	1	.182
Wilfong, Minnesota	16	5	0	3	.313	Cubbage, Minnesota	17	3	0	2	.176
Summers, Detroit	13	4	2	4	.308	Spencer, New York	17	3	0	1	.176
Washington, Chicago	13	4	0	5	.308	Blanks, Texas	12	2	0	0	.167
Valentine, Seattle	20	6	0	1	.300	LaCock, Kansas City	18	3	0	5	.167
Braun, Kansas City	28	8	0	2	.286	Wathan, Kansas City	31	5	0	6	.161
Gamble, Tex-NY	18	5	2	7	.278	Randall, Minnesota	13	2	0	2	.154
Sample, Texas	18	5	0	4	.278	Poquette, KC-Bos	28	4	0	3	.143
Crowley, Baltimore	40	11	1	6	.275	Powell, Minnesota	15	2	0	2	.133
Aikens, California	11	3	0	2	.273	Jorgensen, Texas	19	2	0	2	.105
Ellis, Texas	26	7	0	7	.269	Kusick, Minn-Tor	10	1	0	0	.100
Quirk, Kansas City	30	8	0	5	.267	Adams, Minnesota	21	2	0	1	.095
Velez, Toronto	19	5	2	6	.263	Alston, Cleveland	11	1	0	0	.091
White, New York	19	5	1	4	.263	Cage, Cleveland	12	1	0	1	.083
Garr, Chi-Calif	23	6	0	3	.261	Torres, Chicago	12	1	0	2	.083
Grubb, Texas	24	6	0	2	.250	Brown, Tor-NY	2	0	0	0	.000
Wockenfuss, Detroit	20	5	2	5	.250						

PINCH-HOMERS FOR 1979

AMERICAN LEAGUE: Baltimore (4)—Kelly 3, Crowley. Boston (0). California (0). Chicago (1)—Nahorodny. Cleveland (2)—Alexander, Johnson. Detroit (5)—Summers 2, Wockenfuss 2, Greene. Kansas City (1)—Otis. Milwaukee (2)—Davis, Oglivie. Minnesota (0). New York (6)—Gamble, Jackson, Johnstone, Piniella, Rivers, White. Oakland (1)—Gross. Seattle (4)—Meyer, Paciorek, Simpson, Stinson. Texas (5)—Putnam 2, Gamble, Roberts, Zisk. Toronto (4)—Carty 2, Velez 2.

NATIONAL LEAGUE: Atlanta (6)—Lum 3, Spikes 2, Office. Chicago (5)—Vail 2, Biittner, Henderson, Martin. Cincinnati (0). Houston (2)—Bergman, Walling. Los Angeles (0). Montreal (2)—Hutton, Valentine. New York (1)—Norman. Philadelphia (5)—Unser 4, McBride. Pittsburgh (5)—Easler 2, Milner, B. Robinson, Stargell. St. Louis (4)—Freed 2, Carbo, Iorg. San Diego (1)—Tenace. San Francisco (5)—McCovey 2, Evans, Ivie, Tamargo.

Goltz Became Elite Reentry Selection

By LARRY WIGGE

Reggie Jackson didn't do it. Neither did Pete Rose. Nor Don Baylor, Rollie Fingers, Sal Bando, Larry Hisle, Rich Gossage, Gene Tenace, Tommy John or Lyman Bostock. None of the big-money free agents of the past seasons.

Enter Dave Goltz.

A 20-game winner in 1977 but only 14-13 in '79 with the Minnesota Twins, Goltz became the first player ever chosen by the maximum 13 clubs in the first round of the reentry draft.

The 30-year-old Goltz, along with pitchers John Curtis and Bruce Kison, and second baseman Rennie Stennett were the only players from the 44 who filed for free agency taken by 13 clubs plus their own team in the fourth annual reentry draft at New York's Plaza Hotel November 2.

The Dodgers signed Goltz along with Baltimore relief ace Don Stanhouse —the first player chosen in the reentry draft by the Toronto Blue Jays—and Jay Johnstone, an outfielder who played for the San Diego Padres in 1979.

Just six days following the draft, the Yankees signed the first two reentry players when first baseman Bob Watson and lefthander Rudy May were inked to long-term contracts.

The biggest names of the draft—fireballing Angels' righthander Nolan Ryan and Cincinnati second baseman Joe Morgan—signed with the Houston Astros. Ryan agreed to a four-year pact worth $4.5 million. Morgan was selected by only four clubs in the reentry proceedings, and Houston wasn't one of them. However, two additional clubs—Houston and the New York Mets—were given negotiating rights December 14 after the Dodgers and Giants, two of the teams that had selected Morgan, had signed their limit of free agents. Morgan signed a one-year Houston contract worth about $250,000 with incentives that could nearly double that figure.

Following is a list of 44 free-agent players and the teams which selected them in the reentry draft. The number in parentheses after each player's name indicates the number of clubs which picked him. The number after each club indicates the round in which the player was chosen. Capital letters indicate the player's former club chose to retain negotiating rights:

JESUS ALOU (0): Not selected.

PAUL BLAIR (1): A's (16).

GLENN BORGMANN (0): Not selected.

DAVE CHALK (4): Giants (6), Indians (7), Rangers (15), A's.

JOHN CURTIS (14): Mariners (1), Twins (1), Indians (2), Cubs (2), Pirates (2), Padres (3), Rangers (3), Royals (3), Angels (3), Expos (3), Brewers (3), Cardinals (4), Dodgers (5), GIANTS.

DOCK ELLIS (1): Rangers (19).

DAVE GOLTZ (14): Braves (1), Padres (1), White Sox (1), Dodgers (1), Phillies (1), Royals (1), Cardinals (1), Angels (1), Reds (1), Expos (1), Red Sox (1), Pirates (1), Brewers (1), TWINS.

GREG GROSS (9): Mets (4), Indians (4), Giants (5), Expos (8), Dodgers (9), A's (10), Padres (11), Pirates (26), PHILLIES.

DAVE HAMILTON (3): Indians (8), Angels (10), A's.

ANDY HASSLER (7): Rangers (20), Angels (20), Blue Jays (21), Padres (21), Cardinals (21), Pirates (24), METS.

DON HOOD (10): Mariners (2), Cubs (4), Red Sox (8), Indians (9), Cardinals (9), Dodgers (10), A's (12), Rangers (12), Pirates (13), YANKEES.

WILLIE HORTON (5): Orioles (4), Yankees (8), A's (9), Royals (9), MARINERS.

AL HRABOSKY (13): Braves (2), Cubs (3), Red Sox (3), Indians (5), Rangers (5), Cardinals (5), Brewers (5), A's (6), Dodgers (6), Pirates (6), Angels (8), Yankees (10), ROYALS.

TIM JOHNSON (0): Not selected.

JAY JOHNSTONE (5): Phillies (7), Dodgers (21), Reds (22), Pirates (25), PADRES.

JIM KAAT (1): Rangers (10).

DON KESSINGER (0): Not selected.

BRUCE KISON (14): Indians (1), Padres (2), Giants (2), Royals (2), Angels (2), Yankees (2), Expos (2), Red Sox (2), Mets (3), Mariners (3), Dodgers (3), Phillies (3), Cardinals (3), PIRATES.

ED KRANEPOOL (0): Not selected.

LERRIN LaGROW (1): Red Sox (9).

SKIP LOCKWOOD (11): Astros (3), Mariners (4), Giants (4), Phillies (5), Red Sox (5), Dodgers (8), Cardinals (8), Pirates (11), Expos (15), Rangers (21), METS.

MILT MAY (11): Orioles (1), Giants (3), A's (4), Rangers (4), Red Sox (4), Pirates (4), Blue Jays (5), Mariners (6), Padres (13), Brewers (13), WHITE SOX.

RUDY MAY (12): Mets (2), Yankees (4), Cubs (5), Pirates (5), Rangers (6), Cardinals (6), Red Sox (6), Padres (8), A's (14), Indians (14), Dodgers (15), EXPOS.

BOB MONTGOMERY (0): Not selected.

JOE MORGAN (4): Giants (8), Padres (16), Dodgers (16), Rangers (17).

FRED NORMAN (8): Twins (2), Expos (11), Padres (12), Cardinals (12), Pirates (12), Indians (13), Dodgers (13), Rangers (13).

ROWLAND OFFICE (9): Indians (6), Brewers (6), Mets (7), Padres (7), Rangers (7), Expos (7), Mariners (8), Phillies (8), Pirates (27).

JORGE ORTA (12): Blue Jays (3), A's (3), Indians (3), Orioles (3), Mariners (9), Brewers (9), Padres (10), Expos (10), Pirates (10), Rangers (11), Dodgers (17), WHITE SOX.

FRED PATEK (5): Angels (4), A's (7), Indians (16), Rangers (16), ROYALS.

TONY PEREZ (9): Twins (3), Yankees (5), Phillies (6), Red Sox (7), Pirates (9), A's (11), Padres (15), Rangers (22), EXPOS.

LENNY RANDLE (0): Not selected.

MERV RETTENMUND (0): Not selected.

NOLAN RYAN (13): Rangers (1), Astros (1), Cardinals (2), Brewers (2), Braves (3), Yankees (3), Pirates (3), Dodgers (4), Padres (5), Expos (5), Indians (12), Giants (13), ANGELS.

GEORGE SCOTT (1): Rangers (14).

TONY SOLAITA (1): Indians (10).

DON STANHOUSE (13): Blue Jays (1), Phillies (2), Brewers (4), Mets (5), A's (5), Dodgers (7), Cardinals (7), Angels (7), Pirates (7), Rangers (8), Padres (14), Indians (15), ORIOLES.

RENNIE STENNETT (14): Mets (1), Giants (1), Cubs (1), Blue Jays (2), A's (2), White Sox (2), Dodgers (2), Rangers (2), Astros (2), Padres (4), Expos (4), Angels (6), Yankees (9), PIRATES.

RUSTY TORRES (0): Not selected.

WAYNE TWITCHELL (0): Not selected.

BOBBY VALENTINE (3): Indians (18), Rangers (18), MARINERS.

BOB WATSON (10): A's (1), Yankees (1), Orioles (2), Phillies (4), Royals (4), Mariners (7), Brewers (7), Angels (9), Expos (9), RED SOX.

ROY WHITE (8): Indians (11), A's (15), Royals (15), Angels (15), Pirates (15), Brewers (15), Mets (16), YANKEES.

RICK WISE (11): White Sox (3), Mariners (5), Angels (5), Padres (6), Yankees (6), Expos (6), Pirates (8), Rangers (9), Phillies (9), A's (13), INDIANS.

JIM WOHLFORD (8): Giants (7), Yankees (7), Blue Jays (8), Mets (8), A's (8), Padres (9), Indians (17), BREWERS.

The following were selected by fewer than two clubs and became free to dicker with any club: Alou, Blair, Borgmann, Ellis, Johnson, Kaat, Kessinger, Kranepool, LaGrow, Montgomery, Randle, Rettenmund, Scott, Solaita, Torres, Twitchell.

The Sporting News AWARDS

THE SPORTING NEWS MVP AWARDS

AMERICAN LEAGUE			NATIONAL LEAGUE		
Year	Player Club	Points		Player Club	Points
1929	Al Simmons, Philadelphia, of	40		No selection	
1930	Joseph Cronin, Washington, ss	52		William Terry, New York, 1b	47
1931	H. Louis Gehrig, New York, 1b	40		Charles Klein, Philadelphia, of	40
1932	James Foxx, Philadelphia, 1b	56		Charles Klein, Philadelphia, of	46
1933	James Foxx, Philadelphia, 1b	49		Carl Hubbell, New York, p	64
1934	H. Louis Gehrig, New York, 1b	51		Jerome Dean, St. Louis, p	57
1935	Henry Greenberg, Detroit, 1b	64		J. Floyd Vaughan, Pitts., ss	42
1936	H. Louis Gehrig, New York, 1b	55		Carl Hubbell, New York, p	61
1937	Charles Gehringer, Detroit, 2b	78		Joseph Medwick, St. Louis, of	70
1938	James Foxx, Boston, 1b	305		Ernest Lombardi, Cincinnati, c	229
1939	Joseph DiMaggio, N. York, of	280		William Walters, Cincinnati, p	303
1940	Henry Greenberg, Detroit, of	292		Frank McCormick, Cinn., 1b	274
1941	Joseph DiMaggio, N. York, of	291		Adolph Camilli, Brooklyn, 1b	300
1942	Joseph Gordon, New York, 2b	270		Morton Cooper, St. Louis, p	263
1943	Spurgeon Chandler, N. Y., p	246		Stanley Musial, St. Louis, of	267
1944	Robert Doerr, Boston, 2b			Martin Marion, St. Louis, ss	
1945	Edward J. Mayo, Detroit, 2b			Thomas Holmes, Boston, of	

THE SPORTING NEWS PLAYER, PITCHER OF YEAR

1948	Louis Boudreau, Cleveland, ss Robert Lemon, Cleveland, p	1948	Stanley Musial, St. Louis, of-1b John Sain, Boston, p
1949	Theodore Williams, Boston, of Ellis Kinder, Boston, p	1949	Enos Slaughter, St. Louis, of Howard Pollet, St. Louis, p
1950	Philip Rizzuto, New York, ss Robert Lemon, Cleveland, p	1950	Ralph Kiner, Pittsburgh, of C. James Konstanty, Phila., p
1951	Ferris Fain, Philadelphia, 1b Robert Feller, Cleveland, p	1951	Stanley Musial, St. Louis, of Elwin Roe, Brooklyn, p
1952	Luscious Easter, Cleveland, 1b Robert Shantz, Philadelphia, p	1952	Henry Sauer, Chicago, of Robin Roberts, Philadelphia, p
1953	Albert Rosen, Cleveland, 3b Erv (Bob) Porterfield, Wash., p	1953	Roy Campanella, Brooklyn, c Warren Spahn, Milwaukee, p
1954	Roberto Avila, Cleveland, 2b Robert Lemon, Cleveland, p	1954	Willie Mays, New York, of John Antonelli, New York, p
1955	Albert Kaline, Detroit, of Edward Ford, New York, p	1955	Edwin Snider, Brooklyn, of Robin Roberts, Philadelphia, p
1956	Mickey Mantle, New York, of W. William Pierce, Chicago, p	1956	Henry Aaron, Milwaukee, of Donald Newcombe, Brooklyn, p
1957	Theodore Williams, Boston, of W. William Pierce, Chicago, p	1957	Stanley Musial, St. Louis, 1b Warren Spahn, Milwaukee, p
1958	Jack Jensen, Boston, of Robert Turley, New York, p	1958	Ernest Banks, Chicago, ss Warren Spahn, Milwaukee, p
1959	J. Nelson Fox, Chicago, 2b Early Wynn, Chicago, p	1959	Ernest Banks, Chicago, ss Samuel Jones, San Francisco, p
1960	Roger Maris, New York, of Charles Estrada, Baltimore, p	1960	Richard Groat, Pittsburgh, ss Vernon Law, Pittsburgh, p
1961	Roger Maris, New York, of Edward Ford, New York, p	1961	Frank Robinson, Cincinnati, of Warren Spahn, Milwaukee, p
1962	Mickey Mantle, New York, of Richard Donovan, Cleveland, p	1962	Maurice Wills, Los Angeles, ss Donald Drysdale, Los Angeles, p
1963	Albert Kaline, Detroit, of Edward Ford, New York, p	1963	Henry Aaron, Milwaukee, of Sanford Koufax, Los Angeles, p

PLAYER, PITCHER OF YEAR—Continued

AMERICAN LEAGUE

1964—Brooks Robinson, Baltimore, 3b
    Dean Chance, Los Angeles, p
1965—Pedro (Tony) Oliva, Minn., of
    James Grant, Minnesota, p
1966—Frank Robinson, Baltimore, of
    James Kaat, Minnesota, p
1967—Carl Yastrzemski, Boston, of
    Jim Lonborg, Boston, p
1968—Ken Harrelson, Boston, of
    Denny McLain, Detroit, p
1969—Harmon Killebrew, Minn., 1b-3b
    Denny McLain, Detroit, p
1970—Harmon Killebrew, Minn., 3b
    Sam McDowell, Cleveland, p
1971—Pedro (Tony) Oliva, Minn., of
    Vida Blue, Oakland, p
1972—Richie Allen, Chicago, 1b
    Wilbur Wood, Chicago, p
1973—Reggie Jackson, Oakland, of
    Jim Palmer, Baltimore, p
1974—Jeff Burroughs, Texas, of
    Jim Hunter, Oakland, p
1975—Fred Lynn, Boston, of
    Jim Palmer, Baltimore, p
1976—Thurman Munson, New York, c
    Jim Palmer, Baltimore, p
1977—Rod Carew, Minnesota, 1b
    Nolan Ryan, California, p
1978—Jim Rice, Boston, of
    Ron Guidry, New York, p
1979—Don Baylor, California, of
    Mike Flanagan, Baltimore, p

NATIONAL LEAUGE

1964—Kenton Boyer, St. Louis, 3b
    Sanford Koufax, Los Angeles, p
1965—Willie Mays, San Francisco, of
    Sanford Koufax, Los Angeles, p
1966—Roberto Clemente, Pittsburgh, of
    Sanford Koufax, Los Angeles, p
1967—Orlando Cepeda, St. Louis, 1b
    Mike McCormick, San Fran., p
1968—Pete Rose, Cincinnati, of
    Bob Gibson, St. Louis, p
1969—Willie McCovey, San Fran., 1b
    Tom Seaver, New York, p
1970—Johnny Bench, Cin., c
    Bob Gibson, St. Louis, p
1971—Joe Torre, St. Louis, 3b
    Ferguson Jenkins, Chicago, p
1972—Billy Williams, Chicago, of
    Steve Carlton, Philadelphia, p
1973—Bobby Bonds, San Francisco, of
    Ron Bryant, San Francisco, p
1974—Lou Brock, St. Louis, of
    Mike Marshall, Los Angeles, p
1975—Joe Morgan, Cincinnati, 2b
    Tom Seaver, New York, p
1976—George Foster, Cincinnati, of
    Randy Jones, San Diego, p
1977—George Foster, Cincinnati, of
    Steve Carlton, Philadelphia, p
1978—Dave Parker, Pittsburgh, of
    Vida Blue, San Francisco, p
1979—Keith Hernandez, St. Louis, 1b
    Joe Niekro, Houston, p

FIREMAN (Relief Pitcher) OF THE YEAR

Year	Player	Club	Player	Club
1960	Mike Fornieles	Boston	Lindy McDaniel	St. Louis
1961	Luis Arroyo	New York	Stu Miller	San Francisco
1962	Dick Radatz	Boston	Roy Face	Pittsburgh
1963	Stu Miller	Baltimore	Lindy McDaniel	Chicago
1964	Dick Radatz	Boston	Al McBean	Pittsburgh
1965	Eddie Fisher	Chicago	Ted Abernathy	Chicago
1966	Jack Aker	Kansas City	Phil Regan	Los Angeles
1967	Minnie Rojas	California	Ted Abernathy	Cincinnati
1968	Wilbur Wood	Chicago	Phil Regan	L.A.-Chicago
1969	Ron Perranoski	Minnesota	Wayne Granger	Cincinnati
1970	Ron Perranoski	Minnesota	Wayne Granger	Cincinnati
1971	Ken Sanders	Milwaukee	Dave Giusti	Pittsburgh
1972	Sparky Lyle	New York	Clay Carroll	Cincinnati
1973	John Hiller	Detroit	Mike Marshall	Montreal
1974	Terry Forster	Chicago	Mike Marshall	Los Angeles
1975	Rich Gossage	Chicago	Al Hrabosky	St. Louis
1976	Bill Campbell	Minnesota	Rawly Eastwick	Cincinnati
1977	Bill Campbell	Boston	Rollie Fingers	San Diego
1978	Rich Gossage	New York	Rollie Fingers	San Diego
1979	Mike Marshall	Minnesota	Bruce Sutter	Chicago
	Jim Kern, Texas			

THE SPORTING NEWS ROOKIE AWARDS

1946—Combined selection—Delmer Ennis, Philadelphia, N. L., of
1947—Combined selection—Jack Robinson, Brooklyn, 1b
1948—Combined selection—Richie Ashburn, Philadelphia, N. L., of

AMERICAN LEAGUE	NATIONAL LEAGUE
Year Player Club	Player Club
1949—Roy Sievers, St. Louis, of	Donald Newcombe, Brooklyn, p
1950—Combined selection—Edward Ford, New York, A. L., p	
1951—Orestes Minoso, Chicago, of	Willie Mays, New York, of
1952—Clinton Courtney, St. Louis, c	Joseph Black, Brooklyn, p
1953—Harvey Kuenn, Detroit, ss	James Gilliam, Brooklyn, 2b
1954—Robert Grim, New York, p	Wallace Moon, St. Louis, of
1955—Herbert Score, Cleveland, p	William Virdon, St. Louis, of
1956—Luis Aparicio, Chicago, ss	Frank Robinson, Cincinnati, of
1957—Anthony Kubek, New York, inf-of	Edward Bouchee, Philadelphia, 1b
(No pitcher named)	Jack Sanford, Philadelphia, p
1958—Albert Pearson, Washington, of	Orlando Cepeda, San Francisco, 1b
Ryne Duren, New York, p	Carlton Willey, Milwaukee, p
1959—W. Robert Allison, Washington, of	Willie McCovey, San Francisco, 1b
1960—Ronald Hansen, Baltimore, ss	Frank Howard, Los Angeles, of
1961—Richard Howser, Kansas City, ss	Billy Williams, Chicago, of
Donald Schwall, Boston, p	Kenneth Hunt, Cincinnati, p
1962—Thomas Tresh, New York, of-ss	Kenneth Hubbs, Chicago, 2b
1963—Peter Ward, Chicago, 3b	Peter Rose, Cincinnati, 2b
Gary Peters, Chicago, p	Raymond Culp, Philadelphia, p
1964—Pedro (Tony) Oliva, Minn., of	Richard Allen, Philadelphia, 3b
Wallace Bunker, Baltimore, p	William McCool, Cincinnati, p
1965—Curtis Blefary, Baltimore, of	Joseph Morgan, Houston, 2b
Marcelino Lopez, California, p	Frank Linzy, San Francisco, p
1966—Tommie Agee, Chicago, of	Tommy Helms, Cincinnati, 3b
James Nash, Kansas City, p	Donald Sutton, Los Angeles, p
1967—Rod Carew, Minnesota, 2b	Lee May, Cincinnati, 1b
Tom Phoebus, Baltimore, p	Dick Hughes, St. Louis, p
1968—Del Unser, Washington, of	Johnny Bench, Cincinnati, c
Stan Bahnsen, New York, p	Jerry Koosman, New York, p
1969—Carlos May, Chicago, of	Coco Laboy, Montreal, 3b
Mike Nagy, Boston, p	Tom Griffin, Houston, p
1970—Roy Foster, Cleveland, of	Bernie Carbo, Cincinnati, of
Bert Blyleven, Minnesota, p	Carl Morton, Montreal, p
1971—Chris Chambliss, Cleveland, 1b	Earl Williams, Atlanta, c
Bill Parsons, Milwaukee, p	Reggie Cleveland, St. Louis, p
1972—Carlton Fisk, Boston, c	Dave Rader, San Francisco, c
Dick Tidrow, Cleveland, p	Jon Matlack, New York, p
1973—Al Bumbry, Baltimore, of	Gary Matthews, San Fran., of
Steve Busby, Kansas City, p	Steve Rogers, Montreal, p
1974—Mike Hargrove, Texas, 1b	Greg Gross, Houston, of
Frank Tanana, California, p	John D'Acquisto, San Francisco, p
1975—Fred Lynn, Boston, of	Gary Carter, Montreal, of-c
Dennis Eckersley, Cleveland, p	John Montefusco, San Francisco, p
1976—Butch Wynegar, Minnesota, c	Larry Herndon, San Francisco, of
Mark Fidrych, Detroit, p	Butch Metzger, San Diego, p
1977—Mitchell Page, Oakland, of	Andre Dawson, Montreal, of
Dave Rozema, Detroit, p	Bob Owchinko, San Diego, p
1978—Paul Molitor, Milwaukee, 2b	Bob Horner, Atlanta, 3b
Rich Gale, Kansas City, p	Don Robinson, Pittsburgh, p
1979—Pat Putnam, Texas, 1b	Jeff Leonard, Houston, of
Mark Clear, California, p	Rick Sutcliffe, Los Angeles, p

MAJOR LEAGUE EXECUTIVE

Year	Executive	Club
1936	Branch Rickey, St. Louis NL
1937	Edward Barrow, New York AL
1938	Warren Giles, Cincinnati NL
1939	Larry MacPhail, Brooklyn NL
1940	W. O. Briggs, Sr., Detroit AL
1941	Edward Barrow, New York AL
1942	Branch Rickey, St. Louis NL
1943	Clark Griffith, Washington AL
1944	Wm. O. DeWitt, St. Louis AL
1945	Philip K. Wrigley, Chicago NL
1946	Thomas A. Yawkey, Boston AL
1947	Branch Rickey, Brooklyn NL
1948	Bill Veeck, Cleveland AL
1949	Robt. Carpenter, Phila'phia NL
1950	George Weiss, New York AL
1951	George Weiss, New York AL
1952	George Weiss, New York AL
1953	Louis Perini, Milwaukee NL
1954	Horace Stoneham, N. York NL
1955	Walter O'Malley, Brooklyn NL
1956	Gabe Paul, Cincinnati NL
1957	Frank Lane, St. Louis NL
1958	Joe L. Brown, Pittsburgh NL
1959	E. J. (Buzzie) Bavasi, L.A. NL
1960	George Weiss, New York AL
1961	Dan Topping, New York AL
1962	Fred Haney, Los Angeles AL
1963	Vaughan (Bing) Devine, St.L.NL
1964	Vaughan (Bing) Devine, St.L.NL
1965	Calvin Griffith, Minnesota AL
1966	Lee MacPhail, Commissioner's Office
1967	Dick O'Connell, Boston AL
1968	James Campbell, Detroit AL
1969	John Murphy, New York NL
1970	Harry Dalton, Baltimore AL
1971	Cedric Tallis, Kansas City AL
1972	Roland Hemond, Chicago AL
1973	Bob Howsam, Cincinnati NL
1974	Gabe Paul, New York AL
1975	Dick O'Connell, Boston AL
1976	Joe Burke, Kansas City AL
1977	Bill Veeck, Chicago AL
1978	Spec Richardson, San Fran. NL
1979	Hank Peters, Baltimore AL

MAJOR LEAGUE MANAGER

Year	Manager	Club
1936	Joe McCarthy, New York AL
1937	Bill McKechnie, Boston NL
1938	Joe McCarthy, New York AL
1939	Leo Durocher, Brooklyn NL
1940	Bill McKechnie, Cincinnati NL
1941	Billy Southworth, St. Louis NL
1942	Billy Southworth, St. Louis NL
1943	Joe McCarthy, New York AL
1944	Luke Sewell, St. Louis AL
1945	Ossie Bluege, Washington AL
1946	Eddie Dyer, St. Louis NL
1947	Bucky Harris, New York AL
1948	Bill Meyer, Pittsburgh NL
1949	Casey Stengel, New York AL
1950	Red Rolfe, Detroit AL
1951	Leo Durocher, New York NL
1952	Eddie Stanky, St. Louis NL
1953	Casey Stengel, New York AL
1954	Leo Durocher, New York NL
1955	Walter Alston, Brooklyn NL
1956	Birdie Tebbetts, Cincinnati NL
1957	Fred Hutchinson, St. Louis NL
1958	Casey Stengel, New York AL
1959	Walter Alston, Los Angeles NL
1960	Danny Murtaugh, Pitts. NL
1961	Ralph Houk, New York AL
1962	Bill Rigney, Los Angeles AL
1963	Walter Alston, Los Angeles NL
1964	Johnny Keane, St. Louis NL
1965	Sam Mele, Minnesota AL
1966	Hank Bauer, Baltimore AL
1967	Dick Williams, Boston AL
1968	Mayo Smith, Detroit AL
1969	Gil Hodges, New York NL
1970	Danny Murtaugh, Pittsb'gh NL
1971	Charlie Fox, San Francisco NL
1972	Chuck Tanner, Chicago AL
1973	Gene Mauch, Montreal NL
1974	Bill Virdon, New York AL
1975	Darrell Johnson, Boston AL
1976	Danny Ozark, Philadelphia NL
1977	Earl Weaver, Baltimore AL
1978	George Bamberger, Milw'kee AL
1979	Earl Weaver, Baltimore AL

MAJOR LEAGUE PLAYER

Year	Player	Club
1936	Carl Hubbell, New York NL
1937	Johnny Allen, Cleveland AL
1938	Johnny Vander Meer, Cinn. NL
1939	Joe DiMaggio, New York AL
1940	Bob Feller, Cleveland AL
1941	Ted Williams, Boston AL
1942	Ted Williams, Boston AL
1943	Spud Chandler, New York AL

MAJOR LEAGUE PLAYER—Continued

Year	Player	Club
1944	Marty Marion, St. Louis NL	
1945	Hal Newhouser, Detroit AL	
1946	Stan Musial, St. Louis NL	
1947	Ted Williams, Boston AL	
1948	Lou Boudreau, Cleveland AL	
1949	Ted Williams, Boston AL	
1950	Phil Rizzuto, New York AL	
1951	Stan Musial, St. Louis NL	
1952	Robin Roberts, Philadelphia NL	
1953	Al Rosen, Cleveland AL	
1954	Willie Mays, New York NL	
1955	Duke Snider, Brooklyn NL	
1956	Mickey Mantle, New York AL	
1957	Ted Williams, Boston AL	
1958	Bob Turley, New York AL	
1959	Early Wynn, Chicago AL	
1960	Bill Mazeroski, Pittsburgh NL	
1961	Roger Maris, New York AL	
1962	Maury Wills, Los Angeles NL	
	Don Drysdale, Los Angeles NL	
1963	Sandy Koufax, Los Angeles NL	
1964	Ken Boyer, St. Louis NL	
1965	Sandy Koufax, Los Angeles NL	
1966	Frank Robinson, Baltimore AL	
1967	Carl Yastrzemski, Boston AL	
1968	Denny McLain, Detroit AL	
1969	Willie McCovey, San Fran. NL	
1970	Johnny Bench, Cin. NL	
1971	Joe Torre, St. Louis NL	
1972	Billy Williams, Chicago NL	
1973	Reggie Jackson, Oakland AL	
1974	Lou Brock, St. Louis NL	
1975	Joe Morgan, Cincinnati NL	
1976	Joe Morgan, Cincinnati NL	
1977	Rod Carew, Minnesota AL	
1978	Ron Guidry, New York AL	
1979	Willie Stargell, Pittsburgh NL	

MINOR LEAGUE EXECUTIVE (HIGHER CLASSIFICATIONS)
(Restricted to Class AAA Starting in 1963)

Year	Executive	Club
1936	Earl Mann, Atlanta, Southern	
1937	Robt. LaMotte, Savannah, Sally	
1938	Louis McKenna, St. Paul, A.A.	
1939	Bruce Dudley, Louisville, A.A.	
1940	Roy Hamey, Kansas City, A.A.	
1941	Emil Sick, Seattle, PCL	
1942	Bill Veeck, Milwaukee, A.A.	
1943	Clar. Rowland, Los Angeles, PCL	
1944	William Mulligan, Seattle, PCL	
1945	Bruce Dudley, Louisville, A.A.	
1946	Earl Mann, Atlanta, Southern	
1947	Wm. Purnhage, Waterloo, I.I.I.	
1948	Ed. Glennon, Bir'ham, Southern	
1949	Ted Sullivan, Indianapolis, A.A.	
1950	Cl. (Brick) Laws, Oakland, PCL	
1951	Robert Howsam, Denver, West.	
1952	Jack Cooke, Toronto, Int.	
1953	Richard Burnett, Dallas, Texas	
1954	Edward Stumpf, Indpls., A.A.	
1955	Dewey Soriano, Seattle, PCL	
1956	Robert Howsam, Denver, A.A.	
1957	John Stiglmeier, Buffalo, Int.	
1958	Ed. Glennon, Bir'ham, Southern	
1959	Ed. Leishman, Salt Lake, PCL	
1960	Ray Winder, Little Rock, Sou.	
1961	Elten Schiller, Omaha, A.A.	
1962	Geo. Sisler, Jr., Rochester, Int.	
1963	Lewis Matlin, Hawaii, PCL	
1964	Ed. Leishman, San Diego, PCL	
1965	Harold Cooper, Columbus, Int.	
1966	John Quinn, Jr., Hawaii, PCL	
1967	Hillman Lyons, Richmond, Int.	
1968	Gabe Paul, Jr., Tulsa, PCL	
1969	Bill Gardner, Louisville, Int.	
1970	Dick King, Wichita, A.A.	
1971	Carl Steinfeldt, Jr., Roch'ter, Int.	
1972	Don Labbruzzo, Evansville, A.A.	
1973	Merle Miller, Tucson, PCL	
1974	John Carbray, Sacramento, PCL	
1975	Stan Naccarato, Tacoma, PCL	
1976	Art Teece, Salt Lake City, PCL	
1977	George Sisler, Jr., Col'bus, Int.	
1978	Willie Sanchez, Albu'que, PCL	
1979	George Sisler, Jr., Col'bus, Int.	

MINOR LEAGUE EXECUTIVE (LOWER CLASSIFICATIONS)
(Separate Awards for Class AA and Class A Started in 1963)

Year	Executive	Club
1950	H. Cooper, Hutch'son, West. A.	
1951	O. W. (Bill) Hayes, T'ple, B.S.	
1952	Hillman Lyons, Danville, MOV	
1953	Carl Roth, Peoria, III	
1954	James Meaghan, Cedar R., III	
1955	John Petrakis, Dubuque, MOV	
1956	Marvin Milkes, Fresno, Calif.	
1957	Richard Wagner, L'coln, West.	
1958	Gerald Waring, Macon, Sally	
1959	Clay Dennis, Des Moines, III	
1960	Hubert Kittle, Yakima, Northw.	
1961	David Steele, Fresno, California	

MINOR LEAGUE EXECUTIVE (LOWER CLASSIFICATIONS) (Continued)
(Separate Awards for Class AA and Class A Started in 1963)

Year	Executive	Club
1962	John Quinn, Jr., S. Jose, Calif.	
1963	Hugh Finnerty, Tulsa, Texas	
	Ben Jewell, M. Valley, Pioneer	
1964	Glynn West, B'ham, Southern	
	Jas. Bayens, Rock Hill, W. Car.	
1965	Dick Butler, Dallas-Ft.W., Tex.	
	Ken. Blackman, Quad C., Midw.	
1966	Tom Fleming, Evansville, South.	
	Cappy Harada, Lodi, California	
1967	Robt. Quinn, Reading, East.	
	Pat Williams, Spar'burg, W. C.	
1968	Phil Howser, Charlotte, South.	
	Merle Miller, Burlington, Midw.	
1969	Charlie Blaney, Albuq., Tex.	
	Bill Gorman, Visalia, Calif.	
1970	Carl Sawatski, Arkansas, Tex.	
	Bob Williams, Bakersfield, Calif.	
1971	Miles Wolff, Savannah, Dixie A.	

Year	Executive	Club
	Ed Holtz, Appleton, Midwest	
1972	John Begzos, S. Antonio, Texas	
	Bob Piccinini, Modesto, Calif.	
1973	Dick Kravitz, Jacksonville, Sou.	
	Fritz Colschen, Clinton, Midw.	
1974	Jim Paul, El Paso, Texas	
	Bing Russell, Portland, N'west	
1975	Jim Paul, El Paso, Texas	
	Cordy Jensen, Eugene, N'west	
1976	Woodrow Reid, Chat'ooga, Sou.	
	Don Buchheister, Ced. Rap., Mid.	
1977	Jim Paul, El Paso, Texas	
	Harry Pells, Quad Cities, Midw.	
1978	Larry Schmittou, Nashville, Sou.	
	Dave Hersh, Appleton, Midw.	
1979	Bill Rigney Jr., Midland, Tex.	
	Tom Romenesko, Greensboro, W.C.	

MINOR LEAGUE MANAGER

Year	Manager	Club
1936	Al Sothoron, Milwaukee, A.A.	
1937	Jake Flowers, Salis'y, East. Sh.	
1938	Paul Richards, Atlanta, South.	
1939	Bill Meyer, Kansas City, A.A.	
1940	Larry Gilbert, Nashville, South.	
1941	Burt Shotton, Columbus, A.A.	
1942	Eddie Dyer, Columbus, A.A.	
1943	Nick Cullop, Columbus, A.A.	
1944	Al Thomas, Baltimore, Int.	
1945	Lefty O'Doul, San Fran., PCL	
1946	Clay Hopper, Montreal, Int.	
1947	Nick Cullop, Milwaukee, A.A.	
1948	Casey Stengel, Oakland, PCL	
1949	Fred Haney, Hollywood, PCL	
1950	Rollie Hemsley, Columbus, A.A.	
1951	Charlie Grimm, Milw., A.A.	
1952	Luke Appling, Memphis, South.	
1953	Bobby Bragan, Hollywood, PCL	
1954	Kerby Farrell, Indpls., A.A.	
1955	Bill Rigney, Minneapolis, A.A.	
1956	Kerby Farrell, Indpls., A.A.	
1957	Ben Geraghty, Wichita, A.A.	

Year	Manager	Club
1958	Cal Ermer, Birmingham, South.	
1959	Pete Reiser, Victoria, Texas	
1960	Mel McGaha, Toronto, Int.	
1961	Kerby Farrell, Buffalo, Int.	
1962	Ben Geraghty, Jackson'le, Int.	
1963	Rollie Hemsley, Indpls., Int.	
1964	Harry Walker, Jacks'vle., Int.	
1965	Grady Hatton, Okla. City, PCL	
1966	Bob Lemon, Seattle, PCL	
1967	Bob Skinner, San Diego, PCL	
1968	Jack Tighe, Toledo, Int.	
1969	Clyde McCullough, Tide., Int.	
1970	Tom Lasorda, Spokane, PCL	
1971	Del Rice, Salt Lake City, PCL	
1972	Hank Bauer, Tidewater, Int.	
1973	Joe Morgan, Charleston, Int.	
1974	Joe Altobelli, Rochester, Int.	
1975	Joe Frazier, Tidewater, Int.	
1976	Vern Rapp, Denver, A.A.	
1977	Tommy Thompson, Arkan., Tex.	
1978	Les Moss, Evansville, A.A.	
1979	Vern Benson, Syracuse, Int.	

MINOR LEAGUE PLAYER

Year	Player	Club
1936	Jn. Vander Meer, Durham, Pied.	
1937	Charlie Keller, Newark, Int.	
1938	Fred Hutchinson, Seattle, PCL	
1939	Lou Novikoff, Tulsa-Los A'les.	
1940	Phil Rizzuto, Kansas City, A.A.	
1941	John Lindell, Newark, Int.	
1942	Dick Barrett, Seattle, PCL	

Year	Player	Club
1943	Chet Covington, Scranton, East.	
1944	Rip Collins, Albany, Eastern	
1945	Gil Coan, Chattanooga, South.	
1946	Sibby Sisti, Indianapolis, A.A.	
1947	Hank Sauer, Syracuse, Int.	
1948	Gene Woodling, S. F., PCL	
1949	Orie Arntzen, Albany, Eastern	

MINOR LEAGUE PLAYER—Continued

Year	Player	Club
1950	Frank Saucier, San Ant'o, Tex.
1951	Gene Conley, Hartford, Eastern
1952	Bill Skowron, Kans. City, A.A.
1953	Gene Conley, Toledo, A.A.
1954	Herb Score, Indianapolis, A.A.
1955	John Murff, Dallas, Texas
1956	Steve Bilko, Los Angeles, PCL
1957	Norm Siebern, Denver, A.A.
1958	Jim O'Toole, Nashville, South.
1959	Frank Howard, Victoria-Spok.
1960	Willie Davis, Spokane, PCL
1961	Howie Koplitz, Bir'ham, South.
1962	Bob Bailey, Columbus, Int.
1963	Don Buford, Indianapolis, Int.
1964	Mel Stottlemyre, Richm'd., Int.
1965	Joe Foy, Toronto, International

Year	Player	Club
1966	Mike Epstein, Rochester, Int.
1967	Johnny Bench, Buffalo, Int.
1968	Merv Rettenmund, Roch'ter, Int.
1969	Danny Walton, Okla. City, A.A.
1970	Don Baylor, Rochester, Int.
1971	Bobby Grich, Rochester, Int.
1972	Tom Paciorek, Albuq'que, PCL
1973	Steve Ontiveros, Phoenix, PCL
1974	Jim Rice, Pawtucket, Int.
1975	Hector Cruz, Tulsa, A.A.
1976	Pat Putnam, Asheville, W. Car.
1977	Ken Landreaux, S.L.C., PCL-El Paso, Tex.
1978	Champ Summers, Indi'polis, A.A.
1979	Mark Bomback, Vancouver, PCL

Baseball Writers' Association Awards
Most Valuable Player Citations

CHALMERS AWARD

	AMERICAN LEAGUE			NATIONAL LEAGUE	
Year	Player Club	Points	Player	Club	Points
1911	Tyrus Cobb, Detroit, of	64	Frank Schulte, Chicago, of		29
1912	Tristram Speaker, Boston, of	59	Lawrence Doyle, N. Y., 2b		48
1913	Walter Johnson, Washington, p	54	Jacob Daubert, Brooklyn, 1b		50
1914	Edward Collins, Phila., 2b	63	John Evers, Boston, 2b		50

LEAGUE AWARDS

	AMERICAN LEAGUE			NATIONAL LEAGUE	
Year	Player Club	Points	Player	Club	Points
1922	George Sisler, St. Louis, 1b	59	No selection		
1923	George Ruth, New York, of	64	No selection		
1924	Walter Johnson, Washington, p	55	Arthur Vance, Brooklyn, p		74
1925	Roger Peckinpaugh, Wash., ss	45	Rogers Hornsby, St. Louis, 2b		73
1926	George Burns, Cleveland, 1b	63	Robert O'Farrell, St. Louis, c		79
1927	H. Louis Gehrig, New York, 1b	56	Paul Waner, Pittsburgh, of		72
1928	Gordon Cochrane, Phila., c	53	James Bottomley, St. Louis, 1b		76
1929	No selection		Rogers Hornsby, Chicago, 2b		60

BASEBALL WRITERS' ASSOCIATION MVP AWARDS

	AMERICAN LEAGUE			NATIONAL LEAGUE	
Year	Player Club	Points	Player	Club	Points
1931	Robert Grove, Philadelphia, p	78	Frank Frisch, St. Louis, 2b		65
1932	James Foxx, Philadelphia, 1b	75	Charles Klein, Phila., of		78
1933	James Foxx, Philadelphia, 1b	74	Carl Hubbell, New York, p		77
1934	Gordon Cochrane, Detroit, c	67	Jerome Dean, St. Louis, p		78
1935	Henry Greenberg, Detroit, 1b	*80	Charles Hartnett, Chicago, c		75
1936	H. Louis Gehrig, New York, 1b	73	Carl Hubbell, New York, p		60
1937	Charles Gehringer, Detroit, 2b	78	Joseph Medwick, St. Louis, of		70

BASEBALL WRITERS' ASSOCIATION MVP AWARDS—Cont.

AMERICAN LEAGUE				NATIONAL LEAGUE		
Year	Player	Club	Points	Player	Club	Points
1938	James Foxx, Boston, 1b		305	Ernest Lombardi, Cincinnati, c		229
1939	Joseph DiMaggio, N. York, of		280	William Walters, Cincinnati, p		303
1940	Henry Greenberg, Detroit, of		292	Frank McCormick, Cinn., 1b		274
1941	Joseph DiMaggio, N. York, of		291	Adolph Camilli, Brooklyn, 1b		300
1942	Joseph Gordon, New York, 2b		270	Morton Cooper, St. Louis, p		263
1943	Spurgeon Chandler, N. Y., p		246	Stanley Musial, St. Louis, of		267
1944	Harold Newhouser, Detroit, p		236	Martin Marion, St. Louis, ss		190
1945	Harold Newhouser, Detroit, p		236	Philip Cavarretta, Chicago, 1b		279
1946	Theodore Williams, Boston, of		224	Stanley Musial, St. Louis, 1b		319
1947	Joseph DiMaggio, N. York, of		202	Robert Elliott, Boston, 3b		205
1948	Louis Boudreau, Cleveland, ss		324	Stanley Musial, St. Louis, of		303
1949	Theodore Williams, Boston, of		272	Jack Robinson, Brooklyn, 2b		264
1950	Philip Rizzuto, New York, ss		284	C. James Konstanty, Phila., p		286
1951	Lawrence Berra, New York, c		184	Roy Campanella, Brooklyn, c		243
1952	Robert Shantz, Phila., p		280	Henry Sauer, Chicago, of		226
1953	Albert Rosen, Cleveland, 3b		*336	Roy Campanella, Brooklyn, c		297
1954	Lawrence Berra, New York, c		230	Willie Mays, New York, of		283
1955	Lawrence Berra, New York, c		218	Roy Campanella, Brooklyn, c		226
1956	Mickey Mantle, N. Y., of		*336	Donald Newcombe, Brkn., p		223
1957	Mickey Mantle, New York, of		233	Henry Aaron, Milwaukee, of		239
1958	Jack Jensen, Boston, of		233	Ernest Banks, Chicago, ss		283
1959	J. Nelson Fox, Chicago, 2b		295	Ernest Banks, Chicago, ss		232½
1960	Roger Maris, New York, of		225	Richard Groat, Pittsburgh, ss		276
1961	Roger Maris, New York, of		202	Frank Robinson, Cincinnati, of		219
1962	Mickey Mantle, New York, of		234	Maurice Wills, Los Angeles, ss		209
1963	Elston Howard, New York, c		248	Sanford Koufax, Los Angeles, p		237
1964	Brooks Robinson, Balti., 3b		269	Kenton Boyer, St. Louis, 3b		243
1965	Zoilo Versalles, Minn., ss		275	Willie Mays, San Francisco, of		224
1966	Frank Robinson, Balti., of		*280	Roberto Clemente, Pitts., of		218
1967	Carl Yastrzemski, Boston, of		275	Orlando Cepeda, St. Louis, 1b		*280
1968	Dennis McLain, Detroit, p		*280	Robert Gibson, St. Louis, p		242
1969	Harmon Killebrew, Minn., 1-3b		294	Willie McCovey, San Fran., of		265
1970	John (Boog) Powell, Balti., 1b		234	Johnny Bench, Cincinnati, c		326
1971	Vida Blue, Oakland, p		268	Joseph Torre, St. Louis, 3b		318
1972	Richie Allen, Chicago, 1b		321	Johnny Bench, Cincinnati, c		263
1973	Reggie Jackson, Oak., of		*336	Pete Rose, Cincinnati, of		274
1974	Jeff Burroughs, Texas, of		248	Steve Garvey, Los Angeles, 1b		270
1975	Fred Lynn, Boston, of		326	Joe Morgan, Cincinnati, 2b		321½
1976	Thurman Munson, N. Y., c		304	Joe Morgan, Cincinnati, 2b		311
1977	Rod Carew, Minn., 1b		273	George Foster, Cincinnati, of		291
1978	Jim Rice, Boston, of		352	Dave Parker, Pittsburgh, of		320
1979	Don Baylor, California, of		347	Willie Stargell, Pittsburgh, 1b		216
				Keith Hernandez, St. Louis, 1b		216

*Unanimous selection.

BASEBALL WRITERS' ASSOCIATION ROOKIE AWARDS

1947—Combined selection—Jack Robinson, Brooklyn, 1b.
1948—Combined selection—Alvin Dark, Boston, N. L., ss.

Year	Player	Club	Votes	Player	Club	Votes
1949	Roy Sievers, St. Louis, of		10	Donald Newcombe, Brkn, p		21
1950	Walter Dropo, Boston, 1b		15	Samuel Jethroe, Boston, of		11
1951	Gilbert McDougald, N. Y., 3b		13	Willie Mays, New York, of		18

BASEBALL WRITERS' ASSOCIATION ROOKIE AWARDS—Cont.

Year	Player	Club	Votes	Player	Club	Votes
1952	Harry Byrd, Philadelphia, p		9	Joseph Black, Brooklyn, p		19
1953	Harvey Kuenn, Detroit, ss		23	James Gilliam, Brooklyn, 2b		11
1954	Robert Grim, New York, p		15	Wallace Moon, St. Louis, of		17
1955	Herbert Score, Cleveland, p		18	William Virdon, St. Louis, of		15
1956	Luis Aparicio, Chicago, ss		22	Frank Robinson, Cincinnati, of		*24
1957	Anthony Kubek, N. Y., inf-of		23	John Sanford, Philadelphia, p		16
1958	Albert Pearson, Washington, of.		14	Orlando Cepeda, S. Fran., 1b		*†21
1959	W. Robert Allison, Wash., of		18	Willie McCovey, San Fran., 1b		*24
1960	Ronald Hansen, Baltimore, ss		22	Frank Howard, Los Angeles, of.		12
1961	Donald Schwall, Boston, p		7	Billy Williams, Chicago, of		10
1962	Thomas Tresh, New York, of-ss .		13	Kenneth Hubbs, Chicago, 2b		19
1963	Gary Peters, Chicago, p		10	Peter Rose, Cincinnati, 2b		17
1964	Pedro (Tony) Oliva, Minn., of		19	Richard Allen, Philadelphia, 3b .		18
1965	Curtis Blefary, Baltimore, of		12	James Lefebvre, Los Ang., 2b		13
1966	Tommie Agee, Chicago, of		16	Tommy Helms, Cincinnati, 3b		12
1967	Rod Carew, Minnesota, 2b		19	Tom Seaver, New York, p		11
1968	Stan Bahnsen, New York, p		17	Johnny Bench, Cincinnati, c		10½
1969	Lou Piniella, Kansas City, of		9	Ted Sizemore, Los Angeles, 2b		14
1970	Thurman Munson, N. Y., c		23	Carl Morton, Montreal, p		11
1971	Chris Chambliss, Cleveland, 1b.		11	Earl Williams, Atlanta, c		18
1972	Carlton Fisk, Boston, c		*24	Jon Matlack, New York, p		19
1973	Al Bumbry, Baltimore, of		13½	Gary Matthews, San Fran., of		11
1974	Mike Hargrove, Texas, 1b		16½	Bake McBride, St. Louis, of		16
1975	Fred Lynn, Boston, of		23	John Montefusco, San Fran., p		12
1976	Mark Fidrych, Detroit, p		22	Butch Metzger, San Diego, p		11
				Pat Zachry, Cincinnati, p		11
1977	Eddie Murray, Balt., dh-1b		12½	Andre Dawson, Montreal, of		10
1978	Lou Whitaker, Detroit, 2b		21	Bob Horner, Atlanta, 3b		12½
1979	John Castino, Minn., 3b		7	Rick Sutcliffe, L.A., p		20
	Alfredo Griffin, Tor., ss		7			

*Unanimous selection. †Three writers did not vote.

CY YOUNG MEMORIAL AWARD

Year	Pitcher	Club	Votes	Year	Pitcher	Club	Votes
1956	Donald Newcombe, Brkn		10	1971	A. L.—Vida Blue, Oakland		†98
1957	Warren Spahn, Milwaukee		15		N. L.—Fergy Jenkins, Chi		†97
1958	Robert Turley, N. Y., A. L.		5	1972	A. L.—Gaylord Perry, Cleve.		†64
1959	Early Wynn, Chicago, A.L.		13		N. L.—Steve Carlton, Phil.		*†120
1960	Vernon Law, Pittsburgh		8	1973	A. L.—Jim Palmer, Balt.		†88
1961	Edward Ford, N. Y., A. L.		9		N. L.—Tom Seaver, N. Y.		†71
1962	Don Drysdale, L.A., N.L.		14	1974	A. L.—Jim Hunter, Oakland.		†90
1963	Sanford Koufax, L.A., N.L.		*20		N. L.—Mike Marshall, L. A.		†96
1964	Dean Chance, L. A., A. L.		17	1975	A. L.—Jim Palmer, Balt.		†98
1965	Sanford Koufax, L.A., N.L.		*20		N. L.—Tom Seaver, N. Y.		†98
1966	Sanford Koufax, L.A., N.L.		*20	1976	A. L.—Jim Palmer, Balt.		†108
1967	A. L.—Jim Lonborg, Boston		18		N. L.—Randy Jones, S. D.		†96
	N. L.—M. McCormick, S. F.		18	1977	A. L.—Sparky Lyle, N.Y.		†56½
1968	A. L.—Dennis McLain, Det.		*20		N. L.—Steve Carlton, Phil.		†104
	N. L.—Bob Gibson, St. L.		*20	1978	A. L.—Ron Guidry, N.Y.		*†140
1969	A. L.—Dennis McLain, Det.		10		N. L.—Gaylord Perry, S.D.		†116
	Mike Cuellar, Balt.		10	1979	A. L.—Mike Flanagan, Balt.		†136
	N. L.—Tom Seaver, N. Y.		23		N. L.—Bruce Sutter, Chi.		†72
1970	A. L.—Jim Perry, Minn.		†55				
	N. L.—Bob Gibson, St. L.		†118				

*Unanimous selection. †Point system used.

Major League Farm Systems for 1980

AMERICAN LEAGUE

BALTIMORE (4): AAA—Rochester. AA—Charlotte. A—Miami. Rookie—Bluefield.

BOSTON (5): AAA—Pawtucket. AA—Bristol, Conn. A—Elmira, Winston-Salem, Winter Haven.

CALIFORNIA (4): AAA—Salt Lake City. AA—El Paso. A—Salinas. Rookie—Idaho Falls.

CHICAGO (3): AAA—Iowa. AA—Glens Falls. A—Appleton.

CLEVELAND (4): AAA—Tacoma. AA—Chattanooga. A—Batavia, Waterloo.

DETROIT (4): AAA—Evansville. AA—Montgomery. A—Lakeland. Rookie—Bristol, Va.

KANSAS CITY (6): AAA—Omaha. AA—Jacksonville. A—Fort Myers, Charleston, S. C. Rookie—Sarasota (2).

MILWAUKEE (5): AAA—Vancouver. AA—Holyoke. A—Burlington, Ia., Stockton. Rookie—Butte.

MINNESOTA (5): AAA—Toledo. AA—Orlando. A—Visalia, Wisconsin Rapids. Rookie—Elizabethton.

NEW YORK (6): AAA—Columbus, O. AA—Nashville. A—Ft. Lauderdale, Greensboro, Oneonta. Rookie—Paintsville.

OAKLAND (4): AAA—Ogden. AA—West Haven. A—Medford, Modesto.

SEATTLE (5): AAA—Spokane. AA—Lynn. A—Alexandria, Bellingham, San Jose, Wausau.

TEXAS (4): AAA—Charleston, W.Va. AA—Tulsa. A—Asheville. Rookie—Sarasota.

TORONTO (5): AAA—Syracuse. AA—Knoxville. A—Kinston, Utica. Rookie—Medicine Hat.

NATIONAL LEAGUE

ATLANTA (5): AAA—Richmond. AA—Savannah. A—Durham, Greenwood. Rookie—Bradenton.

CHICAGO (5): AAA—Wichita. AA—Midland. A—Geneva, Quad Cities. Rookie—Sarasota.

CINCINNATI (6): AAA—Indianapolis. AA—Waterbury. A—Cedar Rapids, Eugene, Tampa. Rookie—Billings.

HOUSTON (4): AAA—Tucson. AA—Columbus, Ga. A—Daytona Beach. Rookie—Sarasota.

LOS ANGELES (5): AAA—Albuquerque. AA—San Antonio. A—Lodi, Vero Beach. Rookie—Lethbridge.

MONTREAL (5): AAA—Denver. AA—Memphis. A—Jamestown, West Palm Beach. Rookie—Calgary.

NEW YORK (5): AAA—Tidewater. AA—Jackson. A—Little Falls, Lynchburg. Rookie—Kingsport.

PHILADELPHIA (6): AAA—Oklahoma City. AA—Reading. A—Bend, Peninsula, Spartanburg. Rookie—Helena.

PITTSBURGH (5): AAA—Portland. AA—Buffalo. A—Salem, Shelby. Rookie—Bradenton.

ST. LOUIS (5): AAA—Springfield, Ill. AA—Arkansas. A—Gastonia, St. Petersburg. Rookie—Johnson City.

SAN DIEGO (5): AAA—Hawaii. AA—Amarillo. A—Grays Harbor, Reno, Walla Walla.

SAN FRANCISCO (5): AAA—Phoenix. AA—Shreveport. A—Clinton, Fresno. Rookie—Great Falls.

Kaline, Snider Elected to Hall of Fame

By LARRY WIGGE

Al Kaline didn't have to wait 15 years like he did for his first World Series. He didn't have to wait through 22 years like he did for his 3,000th hit. No, Al Kaline entered the Hall of Fame on his first ballot—becoming only the 10th player in baseball history to do so.

Kaline received 340 votes out of 385 cast by members of the Baseball Writers' Association of America. Duke Snider joined Kaline in election to the Cooperstown, N.Y., shrine. Snider, who had been passed over for election nine times, polled 333 votes.

With 75 percent of the vote—289 votes—required for election, Don Drysdale was third with 238, Gil Hodges had 230 and Hoyt Wilhelm had 209.

Kaline, who never played a day of minor league ball after signing off the sandlots of Baltimore in 1953, tied a major league record by playing all of his 22 seasons with one club, the Detroit Tigers. In 1955 Al became the youngest American League player ever to win a batting title. The 20-year-old outfielder hit .340 that year.

Though that was Kaline's only batting championship, he hit over .300 nine times in his career, finished with 3,007 hits, 399 homers and an average of .297. Al was chosen AL Player of the Year by THE SPORTING NEWS in 1955 and 1963. He starred in his only World Series appearance, batting .379 with two homers and eight RBIs as the Tigers beat the St. Louis Cardinals in 1968.

Kaline joined Stan Musial, Ted Williams, Mickey Mantle, Willie Mays, Sandy Koufax, Bob Feller, Jackie Robinson, Ernie Banks and Warren Spahn as the only players to be voted into the Hall of Fame on the first ballot.

Chuck Klein, who led or tied for the NL lead in homers three times, won MVP honors in 1932 and the Triple Crown with the Phillies in 1933, and former Boston Owner Tom Yawkey were named by the Veterans Committee. Yawkey bought the Red Sox in 1933.

AL KALINE

DUKE SNIDER

A .295 lifetime hitter, Snider broke in with the Brooklyn Dodgers in 1947. He spent 16 seasons with the Brooklyn-Los Angeles club before putting in one season each with the New York Mets and San Francisco Giants in 1963 and '64.

While Snider was shining in center field in Brooklyn he was constantly compared in New York with Mantle of the Yankees and Mays of the Giants, both of whom were voted into the Hall of Fame on their first ballot.

Duke tied a National League record for most consecutive years with 40 or more homers (five) from 1953 through 1957. He led the NL with 43 homers in 1956 and in RBIs with 136 in 1955. He totaled 407 homers in his career and still holds the World Series record for twice hitting four homers in a single Series. His 11 homers, 26 RBIs and 33 strikeouts for Series play are top marks for NL players. He was named Major League Player of the Year by THE SPORTING NEWS in 1955.

Every Hall of Fame nominee with five percent or more of the vote is included in the following: Al Kaline, 340; Duke Snider, 333; Don Drysdale, 238; Gil Hodges, 230; Hoyt Wilhelm, 209; Jim Bunning, 177; Red Schoendienst, 164; Nelson Fox, 161; Maury Wills, 146; Richie Ashburn, 134; Luis Aparicio, 124; Roger Maris, 111; Mickey Vernon, 96; Harvey Kuenn, 83; Lew Burdette, 66; Don Newcombe, 59; Ted Kluszewski, 50; Orlando Cepeda, 48; Alvin Dark, 43; Bill Mazeroski, 33; Don Larsen, 31; Elston Howard, 29; and Elroy Face, 21.

Following is a complete list of those enshrined in the Hall of Fame prior to 1978 with the vote by which each enrollee was elected:

1936—Tyrus Cobb (222), John (Honus) Wagner (215), George (Babe) Ruth (215), Christy Mathewson (205), Walter Johnson (189), named by Baseball Writers Association of America. Total ballots cast, 226.

1937—Napoleon Lajoie (168), Tristram Speaker (165), Denton (Cy) Young (153), named by the BBWAA. Total ballots cast, 201. George Wright, Morgan G. Bulkeley, Byron Bancroft Johnson, John J. McGraw, Cornelius McGillicuddy (Connie Mack), named by Centennial Commission.

1938—Grover C. Alexander (212), named by BBWAA. Total ballots, 262. Henry Chadwick, Alexander J. Cartwright, named by Centennial Commission.

1939—George Sisler (235), Edward Collins (213), William Keeler (207), Louis Gehrig, named by BBWAA. (Gehrig by special election after retirement from game was announced). Total ballots cast, 274. Albert G. Spalding, Adrian C. Anson, Charles A. Comiskey, William (Buck) Ewing, Charles Radbourn, William A. (Candy) Cummings, named by committee of old-time players and writers.

1942—Rogers Hornsby (182), named by BBWAA. Total ballots cast, 233.

1944—Judge Kenesaw M. Landis, named by committee on old timers.

1945—Hugh Duffy, Jimmy Collins, Hugh Jennings, Ed Delahanty, Fred Clarke, Mike Kelly, Wilbert Robinson, Jim O'Rourke, Dennis (Dan) Brouthers and Roger Bresnahan, named by committee on old-timers.

1946—Jesse Burkett, Frank Chance, Jack Chesbro, Johnny Evers, Clark Griffith, Tom McCarthy, Joe McGinnity, Eddie Plank, Joe Tinker, Rube Waddell and Ed Walsh, named by committee on old timers.

1947—Carl Hubbell (140), Frank Frisch (136), Gordon (Mickey) Cochrane (128) and Robert (Lefty) Grove (123), named by BBWAA. Total ballots, 161.

1948—Herbert J. Pennock (94) and Harold (Pie) Traynor (93), named by BBWAA. Total ballots cast, 121.

1949—Charles Gehringer (159), named by BBWAA in runoff election. Total ballots cast, 187. Charles (Kid) Nichols and Mordecai (Three-Finger) Brown, named by committee on old-timers.

1951—Mel Ott (197) and Jimmie Foxx (179), named by BBWAA. Total ballots cast, 226.

1952—Harry Heilmann (203) and Paul Waner (195), named by BBWAA. Total ballots cast, 234.

1953—Jerome (Dizzy) Dean (209) and Al Simmons (199), named by BBWAA. Total ballots cast, 264. Charles Albert (Chief) Bender, Roderick (Bobby) Wallace, William Klem, Tom Connolly, Edward G. Barrow and William Henry (Harry) Wright, named by the new Committee on Veterans.

1954—Walter (Rabbit) Maranville (209), William Dickey (202) and William Terry (195), named by BBWAA. Total ballots cast, 252.

1955—Joe DiMaggio (223), Ted Lyons (217), Arthur (Dazzy) Vance (205) and Charles (Gabby) Hartnett (195), named by BBWAA. Total ballots cast, 251. J. Franklin (Home Run) Baker and Ray Schalk, named by Committee on Veterans.

1956—Hank Greenberg (164) and Joe Cronin (152), named by BBWAA. Total ballots cast, 193.

1957—Joseph V. McCarthy and Sam Crawford, named by Committee on Veterans.

1959—Zachariah (Zack) Wheat, named by Committee on Veterans.

1961—Max Carey and William Hamilton, named by Committee on Veterans.

1962—Bob Feller (150) and Jackie Robinson (124), named by BBWAA. Total ballots cast, 160. Bill McKechnie and Edd Roush, named by Committee on Veterans.

1963—Eppa Rixey, Edgar (Sam) Rice, Elmer Flick and John Clarkson, named by Committee on Veterans.

1964—Luke Appling (189), named by BBWAA in runoff election. Total ballots cast, 225. Urban (Red) Faber, Burleigh Grimes, Tim Keefe, Heinie Manush, Miller Huggins and John Montgomery Ward, named by Committee on Veterans.

1965—James (Pud) Galvin, named by Committee on Veterans.

1966—Ted Williams (282), named by BBWAA. Total ballots cast, 302. Casey Stengel, named by Committee on Veterans.

1967—Charles (Red) Ruffing (266), named by BBWAA in runoff election. Total ballots cast, 306. Branch Rickey and Lloyd Waner, named by Committee on Veterans.

1968—Joseph (Ducky) Medwick (240), named by BBWAA. Total ballots cast, 283. Leon (Goose) Goslin and Hazen (Kiki) Cuyler, named by Committee on Veterans.

1969—Stan (The Man) Musial (317) and Roy Campanella (270), named by BBWAA. Total ballots cast, 340. Stan Coveleski and Waite Hoyt, named by Committee on Veterans.

1970—Lou Boudreau (232), named by BBWAA. Total ballots cast, 300. Earle Combs, Jesse Haines and Ford Frick, named by Committee on Veterans.

1971—Chick Hafey, Rube Marquard, Joe Kelley, Dave Bancroft, Harry Hooper, Jake Beckley and George Weiss, named by Committee on Veterans. Satchel Paige, named by Special Committee on Negro Leagues.

1972—Sandy Koufax (344), Yogi Berra (339) and Early Wynn (301), named by BBWAA. Total ballots cast, 396. Lefty Gomez, Will Harridge and Ross Youngs, named by Committee on Veterans. Josh Gibson and Walter (Buck) Leonard, named by Special Committee on Negro Leagues.

1973—Warren Spahn (316), named by BBWAA. Total ballots cast, 380. Roberto Clemente (393), in special election by BBWAA in which 424 ballots were cast. Billy Evans, George Kelly and Mickey Welch, named by Committee on Veterans. Monte Irvin, named by Special Committee on Negro Leagues.

1974—Mickey Mantle (322) and Whitey Ford (284), named by BBWAA. Total ballots cast, 365. Jim Bottomley, Sam Thompson and Jocko Conlan, named by Committee on Veterans. James (Cool Papa) Bell, named by Special Committee on Negro Leagues.

1975—Ralph Kiner (273), named by BBWAA. Total ballots cast, 362. Earl Averill, Bucky Harris and Billy Herman, named by Committee on Veterans. William (Judy) Johnson, named by Special Committee on Negro Leagues.

1976—Robin Roberts (337) and Bob Lemon (305), named by BBWAA. Total ballots cast, 388. Roger Connor, Cal Hubbard and Fred Lindstrom, named by Committee on Veterans. Oscar Charleston, named by Special Committee on Negro Leagues.

1977—Ernie Banks (321), named by BBWAA. Total ballots cast, 383. Joe Sewell, Al Lopez and Amos Rusie, named by Committee on Veterans. Martin Dihigo and John Henry Lloyd, named by Special Committee on Negro Leagues.

1978—Eddie Mathews (301), named by BBWAA. Total ballots cast, 379. Larry MacPhail and Addie Joss, named by Committee on Veterans.

1979—Willie Mays (409), named by BBWAA. Total ballots cast, 432. Hack Wilson and Warren Giles, named by Committee on Veterans.

NECROLOGY

MAJOR LEAGUE DEALS

MAJOR LEAGUE HOTELS

MINOR LEAGUE PRESIDENTS

Yankees captain—**THURMAN MUNSON.**

Baseball Mourned Deaths of
Munson . . . O'Malley . . . Giles . . .

By CARL CLARK

A painful numbness. Only that oxymoron explains what Thurman Munson's friends felt when they learned that the New York Yankees' All-Star catcher was dead at 32. Munson, who was practicing takeoffs and landings in his Cessna Citation jet, plunged to his death near Canton-Akron (Ohio) Airport in the late afternoon of August 2, 1979. Aboard the recently purchased aircraft with Munson were a flight instructor and a friend. Both survived, but Munson was burned beyond recognition.

Munson, his numerous requests to be traded to the Cleveland Indians unaccommodated, often took advantage of off-days in the schedule to fly home and be with his wife and three children in Canton. His youngest child, four-year-old Michael, was hyperactive but improved noticeably when Thurman was home.

The American League Rookie of the Year in 1970, Munson was named to THE SPORTING NEWS AL All-Star Team four consecutive years, 1973-76, and was the league's Most Valuable Player in '76. He won three Gold Gloves and hit over .300 five times. He played on world championship clubs in 1977-78 and when the Yankees were swept by Cincinnati in the '76 Series, Munson hit .529 and had a record-tying six consecutive hits.

Munson had a reputation for gruffness and he acknowledged it. "I'm a little too belligerent," he said. "I cuss and swear at people, I yell at umpires and I'm a little too tough at home sometimes. I don't sign as many autographs as I should and I haven't always been very good with the writers."

Apparently, however, this proud and competitive man had a mellow side that he allowed only a few people to see. "For the people who never knew him and didn't like him," said Yankees' Manager Billy Martin, echoing the keenings of many of Munson's teammates, "I feel sorry. He was a great man. I loved him."

There were also two Hall of Famers who died in 1979, Warren Giles and Walter O'Malley.

Giles, the president of the National League from 1952 until his retirement in 1969, was elected to the Hall by the Veterans' Committee one month after his February death in the city where he began his major league career, Cincinnati. He was 82. Giles became the Reds' general manager in 1936, ten years after Branch Rickey had made him president of the St. Louis Cardinals' International League team at Syracuse. In 1939, Cincinnati won its first pennant in 20 years and in 1940 the Reds defeated Detroit in the World Series.

Giles acceded to the NL presidency in 1952 when Ford Frick left that office to become commissioner. Giles and Frick had been locked in a stalemate for the commissionership before Giles withdrew his name.

Warren regarded interleague play and interleague trades as abominations but was a progressive on other issues, one being umpires' salaries. Giles had been a football and basketball official in the Missouri Valley Conference.

Giles took the All-Star Game very seriously and during his term the Nationals won 17 of 22 encounters with the Americans. "Mr. Giles' pre-game speeches to the National League All-Star players were legendary," recalled

WALTER O'MALLEY   WARREN GILES

former Philadelphia Phillies' outfielder Richie Ashburn. "He would walk into the clubhouse and personally talk to each player and by the time he finished talking to the assembled group, you felt it would be a disgrace to lose to the American League."

Giles was presiding when O'Malley opened up the West to baseball with his move of the Dodgers from Brooklyn to Los Angeles in 1958. O'Malley, who joined the organization in 1943 as an attorney, built Dodger Stadium in Chavez Ravine with a $10 million advance from Union Oil of California. At his death, the value of the club was estimated to be at least $50 million, leading some to speculate that O'Malley was baseball's most powerful man.

Not so, said O'Malley. "It's just a lot of bunk to say I run baseball and am more powerful than the commissioner," he said. "If I ran baseball, you can be assured a lot of things would have been done differently, that much of our current structure and rules wouldn't be as they are."

The 75-year-old O'Malley died August 9 at the Mayo Clinic in Rochester, Minn., a year after his team became the first to draw more than three million fans in a season, shattering that barrier by more than 300,000.

Munson's death was not the only sudden or unexpected one in '79. Bill Lucas, 43, the Atlanta Braves' vice-president and the highest-ranking black executive in baseball, was felled by a brain hemorrhage and cardiac arrest. Art Williams, the first black to umpire in the NL, died at 44 six weeks after suffering a brain seizure. And 63-year-old Luke Easter was slain by robbers after cashing paychecks for his fellow employees at TRW, Inc., an aircraft construction firm near Cleveland.

Easter spent his prime in the Negro leagues but still belted 86 homers and drove in 307 runs for Cleveland from 1950-52. "It's too bad he didn't come up to the majors 15 years earlier," said Al Rosen, then Cleveland third baseman and later president of the Yankees. "I would rate his power a nine on a scale of 10. It was enormous."

Other baseball personalities who died in 1979 included Dale Alexander, the AL batting champion in 1932; John Allyn, former owner of the Chicago White Sox; Freddie Fitzsimmons, winner of 217 NL pitching decisions; Stan Hack, third baseman for the Chicago Cubs from 1932-47; Clyde Kluttz, catcher for several major league teams and later a highly regarded talent evaluator for the Yankees, Orioles and A's; Duffy Lewis, outfielder on the Boston Red Sox' world championship teams in 1912-15-16, and Hal Trosky, a first baseman who spent most of his career with Cleveland and who led the AL in RBIs in 1936 with 162.

An alphabetical list of baseball deaths in 1979 follows:

Edward Arthur (Ed) Albrecht, 50, pitcher for the St. Louis Browns in three games in 1949-50, of a heart attack, at Centerville, Ia., December 29.

David (Dale) Alexander, 75, American League batting champion in 1932, at Greenville, Tenn., March 2; began major league career with Detroit in 1929; when he started slowly for the Tigers in 1932, hitting only .250 in 23 games, he was dealt to the Boston Red Sox, where he hit .372 in 101 games to win the batting title with an overall mark of .367; the following season he twisted a knee in a game at Philadelphia and nearly lost his leg when the then new diathermy treatment was applied egregiously, resulting in a third-degree burn and gangrene; a .331 lifetime hitter, he never again played in the majors after that '33 season, laboring in the minors as player and manager until 1951 when he became a scout for the Giants, whom he served until 1963 when he ended his baseball career with a season of scouting for the Milwaukee Braves.

John Allyn, 61, owner and president of the Chicago White Sox from 1969, when he took the reins from his brother Arthur in a stock transaction, until 1975, when he sold the team to a group headed by Bill Veeck, of a heart attack at his home in Winnetka, Ill., April 29; a graduate of Lafayette University, he retained a 20 percent interest in the franchise in the sale to the Veeck group.

Fred N. Ankenman, Sr., 91, president of the St. Louis Cardinals' Texas League club at Houston from 1925-43, at Houston, Tex., February 27.

Kenneth Lowther Ash, 78, pitcher for the Chicago White Sox in 1925 and Cincinnati from 1928-30, at Clarksburg, W. Va., November 15; 6-8 in 55 big league games, he won one of those games by throwing a single pitch—with the Reds in 1930, his first offering to Charley Grimm of Chicago resulted in a triple play.

John Landis Bassler, 84, catcher for Cleveland in 1913-14 and for Detroit from 1921-27, at Santa Monica, Calif., June 29; slow afoot, he notched only 99 doubles, 16 triples and one homer in 2,319 at-bats but was a good contact man, hitting .304 lifetime and .346 in 1924; coached for Cleveland from 1938-40 and for the St. Louis Browns in 1941.

Morton M. (Mort) Berry, 65, publicist for the Philadelphia Phillies from 1956-61, of a heart attack at Philadelphia, Pa., October 17.

Francis Raymond (Ray) Blades, 82, outfielder for the St. Louis Cardinals from 1922-32 and their manager in 1939 and part of 1940, at Lincoln, Ill., May 18; a .301 lifetime hitter, his best year was 1925 when he hit .342; at close of playing days, he began his managing career at Columbus and Rochester, both Redbird farms; he replaced Frankie Frisch in the pilot's seat at St. Louis and, with club in seventh place in June 1940, was ousted in favor of Billy Southworth; he stayed in baseball, however, until the mid-1950s, managing at New Orleans and St. Paul, coaching for Cincinnati, Brooklyn and St. Louis, and coaching and scouting for the Chicago Cubs.

William Clifton (Cliff) Bolton, 72, catcher for Washington in 1931, 1933-36 and 1941 and Detroit in 1937, at Lexington, N.C., April 21; in 1935, the only season in which he played in 100 games, he hit .304.

Herbert Frederick Bremer, 66, catcher for the St. Louis Cardinals from 1937-39, November 28.

William W. (Bill) Brenner, 58, minor league catcher and pitcher and general manager at Sacramento (Pacific Coast League) in 1959, at Portland, Ore., May 17.

William Richard (Bill) Brenzel, 69, catcher for Pittsburgh in 1932 and Cleveland in 1934-35, at Oakland, Calif., June 12; managed at Pocatello, Fresno and Spokane and scouted for the St. Louis Cardinals for three years before joining Brooklyn in 1951; scouting for the Dodgers until his death, he signed Ron Cey, Joe Ferguson, Von Joshua and Lee Lacy.

Jack Butterfield, 50, vice-president in charge of scouting and player development for New York Yankees, of an auto accident, at Paramus, N.J., November 16; he had been with Yankees since 1976 when he was hired as a scout after a distinguished college coaching career; he was field boss at the University of Maine and the University of South Florida; he was named college coach of the year in 1964 when Maine finished third in the NCAA World Series.

Milton John (Milt) Byrnes, 62, outfielder for the St. Louis Browns from 1943-45, at St. Louis, Feburary 1; led American League outfielders in fielding in 1943 when he made only one error in 303 chances.

Charles A. (Charlie) Deal, 87, last surviving member of Boston's 1914 Miracle Braves, at Covina, Calif., September 16; third baseman for Boston club that came from last place in July to take NL crown and sweep A's in Series; played for Detroit in 1912 and part of 1913 before joining Braves; after a season in the Federal League, he played a few games for the St. Louis Browns in 1916 and then finished out with the Chicago Cubs, playing his last major league game in 1921.

Lindsay Fred Deal, 67, an outfielder in four games with Brooklyn in 1939 and a scout for Baltimore from 1955-59, at Little Rock, Ark., April 18.

William Callahan (Bill) DeKoning, Jr., 59, catcher for the New York Giants in three games in 1945, at Palm Harbor, Fla., July 26.

John Drebinger, 88, sportswriter for the New York Times for 40 years and a contributor to The Sporting News, at Greensboro, N.C., October 22.

Luscious (Luke) Easter, 63, a first baseman and occasional outfielder for Cleveland from 1949-54, shot by robbers after cashing paychecks for fellow employees of TRW, Inc., an aircraft construction firm, at Euclid, O., March 29; purchased from the Homestead Greys of the Negro American League by Bill Veeck, he batted .363 and hit 25 homers in 1949 for San Diego of the Pacific Coast League; from 1950-1952 with Cleveland he hit 86 homers and drove in 307 runs; after his final year in the majors, he played in the minors for ten more years; coached for Cleveland in 1969; credited with longest homer at Municipal Stadium in Cleveland, a 477-foot blast off Washington's Joe Haynes on June 23, 1950.

Samuel Sherwood (Sam) Edmonston, 95, pitcher in three games for Washington in 1906-07, at Corpus Christi, Tex., April 12.

Herb Elk, 48, director of media relations for Houston, of a heart attack in a hotel at Philadelphia, August 23; worked for New York Mirror from 1953-61 before getting into public relations; worked for numerous clubs in hockey, baseball and football and edited the Hockey Guide and Hockey Register for The Sporting News.

Allen Clifford (Ace) Elliott, 81, first baseman for the Chicago Cubs in 1923-24, at St. Louis, Mo., May 6.

Claude Enberg, 72, secretary and general manager of Salt Lake City (Pioneer) from 1939-51 and president of the Pioneer League from 1952-74, at Salt Lake City, Utah, October 12; served as vice-president and member of executive committee of the National Association and member of the board of directors of the Pacific Coast League.

Alfred Hubert (Al) Evans, 62, catcher for Washington from 1939-42 and 1944-50 and for the Boston Red Sox in 12 games in 1951, at Kenly, N.C., April 6; after decade of catching knuckleballers Dutch Leonard, Roger Wolff, Johnny Niggeling and Mickey Haefner, he manager at several minor league outposts and later scouted for Washington, Minnesota and San Francisco.

John J. Farrell Sr., 83, traveling secretary for the New York Yankees in the 1940s and a longtime member of the club's public relations team, at Passaic, N.J., November 4.

Frederick Landis (Fat Freddie) Fitzsimmons, 78, National League pitcher for 19 years and manager of the Philadelphia Phillies from August 1943 through July 1945, at Yucca Valley, Calif., November 18; winner of 217 games and loser of 146, he pitched for

New York from 1925-37 and for Brooklyn from 1937-43; 10 times he won 10 or more games for the Giants, including a 20-9 season in 1928; traded at age 35 to Brooklyn for 22-year-old Thomas Baker, he went on to win 47 games before his retirement while Baker won only one; pitched in three World Series (0-3 in four games); coached for the Boston Braves, Chicago Cubs, Kansas City Athletics and Giants; for three years he was general manager of the Brooklyn Dodgers of the NFL.

Fred G. Fleig, 71, National League official from 1951-78, at Walnut Creek, Calif., January 28; began his career with Cincinnati, for whom he served as business manager of several minor league teams, and ultimately became the club's farm director; in 1951 he moved to the league front office where he served as secretary and treasurer until his retirement; his duties included the making of the schedule, handling of money and hiring of umpires.

Willard Roland (Nemo) Gaines, 81, pitcher in four games for the 1921 Washington Senators, January 28.

Alexander Nathaniel (Alex) Gaston, 82, catcher for the New York Giants from 1920-23 and the Boston Red Sox in 1926 and 1929, at Santa Monica, Calif., February 8; brother of Milt Gaston, pitcher in 355 games in 11 American League seasons; the siblings teamed up in only one year, 1929; Alex hit .224 that season and Milt lost 19 games; in a 1926 game between the Red Sox and St. Louis Browns, Alex broke up a no-hit effort by Milt in the seventh inning.

Warren C. Giles, 82, president of the National League from 1952 until his retirement in 1969 and elected to the Hall of Fame by the Veterans' Committee one month after his death at Cincinnati, O., February 7; began career by running Moline's Three-I team and after winning several pennants there he moved on to St. Joseph, Mo., buying that club a few years after his arrival; in 1926 Branch Rickey made him president of the St. Louis Cardinals' International League team at Syracuse; became Cincinnati's general manager in 1936 and three years later the club won its first pennant in 20 years—in 1940 they became world champions; locked in a stalemate for the commissioner's post in 1952 with then NL president Ford Frick, he withdrew his name: Frick became commissioner and Giles succeeded him as head of the senior circuit; opposed to interleague play and interleague trades, he was nonetheless progressive in other areas, such as umpires' salaries; he himself had been a football and basketball official in the Missouri Valley Conference; his presidential term saw the exodus of the Giants and Dodgers from New York and the rise of the NL vis a vis the AL—his league won 17 of the 22 All-Star games during his presidency; named Executive of the Year by THE SPORTING NEWS in 1938; son Bill is executive vice-president of the Philadelphia Phillies.

Ray J. Gillespie, 75, associate editor of the THE SPORTING NEWS and longtime St. Louis sportswriter, of a heart attack, at St. Louis, Mo., February 8; entered profession with St. Louis Star after his high school graduation and only a few years later (1925) picked up his first scoop when he learned from Babe Ruth that Ruth had been suspended and fined $5,000 by manager Miller Huggins for a number of rule violations; after World War II he gained exclusive stories about the raids of major league clubs by the Mexican League through his friendship with the loop's operators, Jorge and Bernardo Pasquel; he was named as a conspirator in a federal court suit filed by the Dodgers, who lost catcher Mickey Owen to the renegade league, but was exculpated.

Frederick Gottlieb Graff, 90, third baseman in four games for 1913 St. Louis Browns, at Chattanooga, Tenn., October 4.

William Turner (Bill) Grieve, 79, an American League umpire from 1938-55, at Yonkers, N.Y., August 17; worked in three World Series (1941-48-53) and two All-Star games (1941 and 1949).

David J. (Dave) Grote, 59, director of public relations for Cincinnati from 1948-50 and for the National League from 1951-75, at San Francisco, Calif., January 2.

Stanley Camfield (Stan) Hack, 70, third baseman for Chicago Cubs from 1932-47 and their manager from 1954-56, at Dixon, Ill., December 15; a .301 lifetime hitter, the lefthanded batter helped the Cubs into four World Series—1932-35-38-45—in which he hit .348; led the league in stolen bases in 1938-39 and in hits in 1940-41; after finishing seventh, sixth and eighth as a manager, he coached for the Cardinals in 1957-58 and when Fred Hutchinson was fired as the St. Louis skipper late in the '58 campaign, Hack managed them for the remainder of the season.

Henry Luther (Hinkey) Haines, 79, outfielder for New York Yankees in 1923 and National Football League quarterback for New York Giants from 1925-28 and Staten Island Stapletons from 1929-31, at Sharon Hill, Pa., January 9.

Charles Russell Hargreaves, 82, catcher for Brooklyn from 1923-28 and for Pittsburgh from 1928-30, at Neptune, N.J., May 9; scouted for Pittsburgh in 1948 and managed at Keokuk (Central Association) in 1949.

Andrew Matthew Harrington, 75, a pinch-hitter in one game for Detroit in 1925, at Boise, Ida., January 29.

John D. Holland, 69, executive with Chicago Cubs from 1957 until his death, at Chicago, July 15; a former minor league catcher, he began his front office career as business manager of the Cubs' Visalia farm club and after stints at Des Moines and Los Angeles joined the parent club, serving as vice-president and general manager until 1976 when he joined the club's board of directors.

Joseph A. (Joe) Iglehart, 88, once the largest individual stockholder in the Baltimore Orioles and the club's chairman of the board, at Lutherville, Md., after being struck by a car in the driveway of his home, November 16.

Melvin David Ingram, 74, player in three games for Pittsburgh in 1929, at Medford, Ore., October 28.

Sigmund (Sig) Jakucki, 69, pitcher who defeated New York Yankees in final game of 1944 season to give St. Louis Browns their only pennant, at Galveston, Tex., May 28; major league career consisted of an 0-3 season for Browns in 1936 and 13-9 and 12-10 marks in 1944-45.

Ricardo Emelino (Rick) Joseph, 39, utilityman for Kansas City Athletics in 1964 and Philadelphia Phillies from 1967-70, of complications arising from diabetes, at Santo Domingo, P.R., September 8; led Phillies in pinch-hits with seven in 1968 and 11 in 1970.

Rudolph (Rudy) Kallio, 86, pitcher for Detroit in 1918-19 and Boston Red Sox in 1925, at Newport, Ore., April 6; won more than 200 games in the Pacific Coast League; served as coach and traveling secretary for Portland (PCL) in 1943 and scouted for Chicago Cubs in 1946.

Francis Eugene (Frankie) Kelleher, 62, outfielder for Cincinnati in 1942-43, at Stockton, Calif., April 13.

Gene Kelly, 60, broadcaster for Philadelphia Phillies from 1950-59 and play-by-play man for several All-Star and World Series games, of a stroke, at Bryn Mawr, Pa., September 18.

Edward Frederick (Babe) Klieman, 61, pitcher for Cleveland from 1943-48, Chicago White Sox and Washington in 1949 and Philadelphia Athletics in 1950, at Homosassa, Fla., November 15; in 222 appearances, most of them in relief, he was 26-28 with a 3.49 ERA.

Clyde Franklin Klutz, 61, major league catcher for nine years and at the time of his death the director of player development for Baltimore, at Salisbury, N.C., May 12; caught for the Boston Braves from 1942-45, the New York Giants in 1945-46, the St. Louis Cardinals in 1946, Pittsburgh in 1947-48, the St. Louis Browns in 1951 and Washington in 1951-52; managed the Philadelphia Athletics' team at Savannah (South Atlantic) in 1954-55 before taking a scouting position with the same organization after the parent club's move to Kansas City; in November 1967 he switched allegiances to the New York Yankees, scouting for them for several years, then becoming a farm system administrator before returning to scouting; in 1976, he joined Baltimore in the same capacity that he held at the time of his death; there he was reunited with Hank Peters, the team's general manager with whom Kluttz had worked in Kansas City, signing and developing many of the players who were to help the Oakland A's to three consecutive world championships; while with New York, he convinced primordial free agent Catfish Hunter to sign with the Yankees, outlining the terms of that historic contract on a dinner napkin.

Walter Henry Kopf, 79, a third baseman in two games for the 1921 New York Giants, at Cincinnati, O., April 30.

Samuel Andrew (Sambo) Leslie, 72, first baseman for the New York Giants from 1929-33, Brooklyn from 1933-35 and again for the Giants from 1936-38, at Pascagoula, Miss., January 21; a .304 lifetime hitter, his best season was 1934 when he hit .332 with nine homers and 102 RBIs.

George Edward (Duffy) Lewis, 91, outfielder for the Boston Red Sox from 1910-1917, the New York Yankees in 1919-1920 and Washington in 1921 and traveling secretary for the Boston and Milwaukee Braves from 1936-61, at Salem, N.H., June 17; was left fielder in Boston outfield considered one of the greatest ever assembled—Tris Speaker was in center and Harry Hooper in right; a .284 lifetime hitter, he helped Boston to world championships in 1912-15-16, batting .444 and .353 in the latter two; after managing in the minors at Mobile, Salt Lake City and several other cities, he served as coach for Boston from 1931-35.

William F. (Bill) Liston, 58, longtime Boston sportswriter and president of the Baseball Writers Association of America in 1978, at Weymouth, Mass., after a cerebral hemorrhage, June 1.

William D. (Bill) Lucas, 43, vice-president and director of operations for Atlanta, at Atlanta, Ga., May 5, three days after being stricken by a brain hemorrhage and cardiac arrest; after spending six years in the minors as an infielder, he became the Braves' assistant farm director in 1965 and later director of player development; at his death, he was functioning as the club's general manager, making him the highest-ranking black executive in baseball; his sister was once married to Hank Aaron.

Fred Turner Martin, 63, pitching coach of Chicago White Sox and one of the players who jumped to the Mexican League after World War II, of cancer, at Chicago, Ill., June 11; was 2-1 as a moundsman for the St. Louis Cardinals in 1946 before leaving for Mexico with teammates Lou Klein and Max Lanier; after a two-year banishment he rejoined the team for the 1949-50 seasons and was 6-0 and 4-2, respectively, giving him a career record of 12-3; managed for four years at Temple, Dallas and St. Cloud and was pitching coach for the Chicago Cubs from 1961-64; became Sox pitching coach after 1978 season; he spent the interim time as a minor league instructor, for the Cubs from 1965-75 and in 1977-78 and for Detroit in 1976; given credit in development of Bruce Sutter's splitfinger fastball.

Martin Joseph (Marty) McHale, 90, pitcher for the Boston Red Sox in 1910-11 and 1916, the New York Yankees from 1913-15 and Cleveland in 1916, at Hempstead, N.Y., May 7; 12-30 in 64 games, he enjoyed more success in vaudeville, where he had an act with Mike Donlin, an outfielder with the New York Giants; Donlin provided the comedy and McHale, the Caruso of Baseball, supplied the songs.

James Irving (Jim) Mooney, 72, lefthanded pitcher for the New York Giants in 1931-32 and the St. Louis Cardinals in 1933-34, of a heart attack at Johnson City, Tenn., April 27; a 17-20 lifetime hurler, he coached for many years at East Tennessee State University, his alma mater.

George Joseph Mucey, 66, scout for the St. Louis Browns and Baltimore from 1948-58 and manager at Greensburg (Pennsylvania State) in 1939, at Washington, Pa., May 30.

Thurman Lee Munson, 32, catcher for the New York Yankees from 1969-79 and the American League MVP in 1976, in a plane crash at Akron-Canton Airport, Canton, O., August 2; played in six All-Star games and three World Series; hit .373 in 16 Series games and .529 in 1976 loss to Cincinnati in which he set several records dealing with hits and consecutive hits; was the Baseball Writers' choice for AL Rookie of the Year in 1970 and was named to THE SPORTING NEWS AL All-Star Team in 1973-4-5-6; won Gold Gloves in 1973-4-5; he hit over .300 five times and three times he drove in 100 or more runs.

Robert Hayes (Bobby) Murray, 80, third baseman in 10 games for Washington in 1923 and manager at several minor league outposts in the 1930's, at Nashua, N.H., January 4.

John B. Old, 78, former sportswriter for Los Angeles Herald-Examiner and for many years a Pacific Coast League correspondent for THE SPORTING NEWS, at Los Angeles, Calif., April 23.

Walter Francis O'Malley, 75, owner of the Los Angeles Dodgers, at the Mayo Clinic in Rochester, Minn., August 9; became associated with the Dodgers in 1943 when he became the club's attorney through his association with a bank that held mortgages on the franchise; with engineering and law degrees he was a millionaire before he entered baseball; by 1950, he owned most of the stock in the team, having purchased the holdings of Branch Rickey; in 1958 he moved the Dodgers from Brooklyn to Los Angeles after selling the Ebbets Field property and Wrigley Field, his minor league park in Los Angeles; he purchased 315 acres of choice real estate in Chavez Ravine and, with a $10 million advance from Union Oil of California, constructed Dodger Stadium; in 1978, the Dodgers drew 3,300,000 fans, the first time a team had drawn more than three million in a season.

Donald E. (Don) Osborn, 70, pitching coach for Pittsburgh in 1963-64, and from 1970-72 and 1974-76, at Torrance, Calif., March 23; pitched in minors for 21 years and managed eight minor league teams; scouted for Pirates in 1958-59.

John Gooding Priest, 88, infielder in nine games with New York Yankees in 1911-12, at Washington, D.C., November 4.

Earl Henry (Gibby) Pruess, outfielder in one game for 1920 St. Louis Browns, August 28.

John L. Reeves, 78, president of the Texas League in 1954 and head of the Fort Worth club in that league from 1945-53, at Fort Worth, Tex., September 18.

Charles Dawson (Charlie) Ripple, 57, pitcher in 11 games for the Philadelphia Phillies from 1944-46, at Wilmington, N.C., May 6.

John Joseph (Bunny) Roser, 77, outfielder who batted .239 in 32 games for the Boston Braves in 1922, at Rocky Hill, Conn., May 6.

Robert Duffy (Bob) Schultz, 55, pitcher for the Chicago Cubs from 1951-53, Pittsburgh in 1953 and Detroit in 1955, at Nashville, Tenn., March 31; in 65 games, he was 9-13 with a 5.16 ERA.

John L. (Jack) Seifert, 71, retired assistant controller of the St. Louis Cardinals, at St. Louis, Mo., March 24.

Harry Leon (Suitcase) Simpson, 53, outfielder for eight seasons, at Akron, O., April 3; nickname derives from peripatetic nature of his career—played for Cleveland from 1951-53 and 1955, Kansas City from 1955-57 and 1958-59, the New York Yankees in 1957-58, and the Chicago White Sox and Pittsburgh in 1959; a .266 lifetime hitter, his best season was in 1955 when he hit .300 in 115 games, 112 of those with Kansas City; at San Diego in 1950, he led the Pacific Coast League in RBIs with 156 and hit .323 with 33 homers.

Cyril Charles (Cy) Slapnicka, 93, player, scout and executive for more than 60 years, at Cedar Rapids, Ia., October 20; pitched for Chicago Cubs in 1911 and Pittsburgh in 1918 and was vice-president and general manager of Cleveland from 1935-40 but achieved greatest fame as a scout; in his 27 years with the Indians, he signed Bob Feller, Herb Score, Hal Trosky, Jim Hegan, Lou Boudreau, Mel Harder and Ken Keltner; also scouted one year for the St. Louis Browns and three for the Chicago Cubs.

Louis J. (Lou) Smith, 71, retired sports editor of the Cincinnati Enquirer and chronicler of the Reds, at Cincinnati, March 21; served as president of the Baseball Writers Association of America in 1952.

Roy Lee Smith, 58, scout for the Philadelphia Phillies from 1960-63, California from 1967-69 and 1973-77 and for Montreal from 1969-73, at Orlando, Fla., December 26.

Vincent Ambrose (Vinnie) Smith, 64, catcher for Pittsburgh in 1941 and 1946 and a National League umpire for nine years, at Virginia Beach, Va., December 14; called balls and strikes in Harvey Haddix' 12 innings of perfect ball for Pittsburgh against Milwaukee Braves in 1959.

Charles Edward (Ed) Stauffer, 81, pitcher for the Chicago Cubs in one game in 1923 and in 20 games for the St. Louis Browns in 1925, at St. Petersburg, Fla., July 2.

Norman (Turkey) Stearns, 78, one of the top players in the Negro leagues, at Detroit, Mich., September 4; played from 1921-42 with the Kansas City Monarchs and Chicago American Giants, but the outfielder who frequently hit 35 or more homers in a season spent his most productive years with the Detroit Stars.

Charles C. (Charley) Stis, 94, a minor league umpire and manager and for 23 years a scout for the St. Louis Browns and Cardinals, Philadelphia Phillies, Chicago White Sox, Boston Braves and Detroit, at Festus, Mo., January 9.

James V. Stouffer, 47, vice-president of Cleveland when his father, Vernon Stouffer, owned the club from 1966-72, at Port Clinton, O., August 28.

Amos Aaron Strunk, 90, American League outfielder for 17 years, at Llanerch, Pa., July 22; played for Philadelphia from 1908-1917 and in 1919-20-24, Boston in 1918-1919 and Chicago from 1920-24; best season for the .283 lifetime hitter was a .332 mark in 1921; in 1923, he led the league in pinch-hits with 12.

Howard Alvin (Dizzy) Sutherland, 56, pitcher and loser in one game for the Washington Senators in 1949, at Washington, D.C., August 26; in his one inning against St. Louis, he walked six and allowed five runs; years later the lefty said he didn't remember much about the game—"I was too busy walking people," he recalled.

Lancelot (Yank) Terry, 68, pitcher for the Boston Red Sox in 1940 and from 1942-45, at Bloomington, Ind., November 4; was 20-28 in the majors, but in 1941 he was named MVP in the Pacific Coast League with a record of 26-8 and a 2.31 ERA for San Diego.

Harold Arthur (Hal) Trosky, 66, first baseman who clubbed 228 homers during his 11-year major league career, at Cedar Rapids, Ia., June 18; the .302 lifetime hitter played for Cleveland from 1933-41 and the Chicago White Sox in 1944 and 1946; migraine headaches which caused him to miss the 1942-43-45 seasons brought an end to his career; best year was 1936 when he hit .343 with 42 homers and a league-leading 162 RBIs.

William Fay (Bill) Vargus, 78, pitcher in 15 games for the Boston Braves in 1925-26, at Cape Cod, Mass., February 12.

Harold Edward (Hal) Wagner, 64, catcher for the Philadelphia Athletics from 1937-44, Boston Red Sox in 1944 and 1946-47, Detroit in 1947-48 and the Philadelphia Phillies in 1948-49, at Riverside, N.J., August 7; hit .330 in 71 games in 1944.

George Edward Washburn, 64, pitcher and loser of one game for the 1941 New York Yankees, at Baton Rogue, La., January 5.

Bert N. Wells, 77, scout for the St. Louis Browns from 1937-39 and for the Brooklyn-Los Angeles Dodgers from 1939 until his death, at Hot Springs, Ark., December 24; served as the Dodgers' Midwest director for nearly 20 years and signed Frank Howard and Don Sutton.

John J. (Poke) Whalen, 87, scout for Pittsburgh from 1945-52, the Philadelphia Athletics in 1953-54, Baltimore from 1954-56 and Cleveland from 1958-63 and a minor league catcher and manager, at Baltimore, Md., December 30.

McKinley Davis (Mack) Wheat, 86, catcher for Brooklyn from 1915-19 and Philadelphia Phillies in 1920-21 and brother of Hall of Famer Zack Wheat, at Los Banos, Calif., August 14; never approached the brilliance of his brother, the longtime Brooklyn outfielder who batted .317 lifetime and once led the league in hitting; Mack never hit higher than .226 and his career average was .204.

Arthur (Art) Williams, 44, the first black to umpire in the National League, at Bakersfield, Calif., February 8, six weeks after suffering a brain seizure; a minor league pitcher for Bakersfield, Visalia, Idaho Falls and Stockton, he umpired in the majors from 1972-77 after serving a three-year apprenticeship in the Pioneer, Midwest, Texas and International leagues.

Rees Gephardt (Steamboat) Williams, 87, pitcher for the St. Louis Cardinals in 1914 and 1916, at Deer River, Minn., June 29; primarily a reliever, he was 6-8 in 41 appearances.

Edward Francis (Eddie) Wilson, 68, outfielder for Brooklyn in 1936-37, at Hamden, Conn., April 11; was batting .347 in 1936 when he suffered a fractured skull after being hit by a pitch thrown by Pittsburgh's Mace Brown.

Raymond Bernard Wolf, 75, first baseman in one game for Cincinnati in 1927, at Fort Worth, Tex., October 6.

Carew Trade, Pirates' Swaps Were Top '79 Deals

By CARL CLARK

Baseball's top two active hitters, Rod Carew and Bill Madlock, were traded in 1979. Together, they possessed nine batting titles and a .332 average. And although neither was past his prime, both were obtained for players of little accomplishment. Carew, after 12 seasons in Minnesota, was dealt to the California Angels. Madlock, traded for the third time in his career, went from San Francisco to the Pittsburgh Pirates.

The Pirates, a fitting name for a world championship team that picked up the left side of its infield in a pair of deals made after the commencement of the '79 season, first sailed into the trading channels two weeks after the season began. They swapped 28-year-old shortstops with the New York Mets, April 19. Frank Taveras, a Pirates' regular since 1974 and the National League's leading base stealer in 1977, was traded for Tim Foli, a more sure-handed fielder but a fractious man who had never batted more than .264 or stolen more than 13 bases.

More than two months later, two weeks after the June 15 intraleague trading deadline, the Bucs acquired Madlock, a two-time NL batting champ with Chicago, along with pitcher Dave Roberts and utilityman Lenny Randle for what most felt was a very reasonable price—pitchers Ed Whitson, Fred Breining and Al Holland, the latter two minor leaguers. Whitson, a hard-throwing 24-year-old righthander, was 2-3 with a 4.34 ERA for the Pirates and performed at the same level for the Giants, finishing the season with a record of 7-11 and a 4.10 ERA.

Madlock had been playing second base for San Francisco but switched to third base for Pittsburgh, allowing Phil Garner to move to second base, his natural position. A moody player, Madlock was unhappy in San Francisco and struggling at the plate. In 85 games with Pittsburgh, he hit .328, stole 21 bases and drove in 44 runs.

When Madlock arrived, Pittsburgh was 37-34, 6½ games behind division-leading Montreal. Thereafter, the Pirates went 61-30 to edge out Montreal for the NL East title by two games. Madlock also hit .375 in the World Series.

Foli, batting behind leadoff man Omar Moreno, hit .291 and drove in 65 runs in 133 games. He hit .333 in both the Championship Series and World Series.

Both players thought that they benefited from the loose, easy-going atmosphere of the Bucs. "A team like this is good not only for me," Madlock said, "but for Foli, too. He was known as a hot-headed crazy guy. But over here, it doesn't make any difference."

In order for the deal with San Francisco to be consummated, Madlock had to clear waivers. How can a player of Madlock's caliber go unclaimed? John Claiborne, St. Louis' general manager, explained. "You could claim everybody, trying to tie a guy up," he said. "But if you keep doing that, two things can happen. Every time I put a waiver list in, they're going to claim seven of mine or every once in a while, they've got a joker they're trying to get rid of . . . you have to be somewhat discreet in whom you claim." Or as Madlock himself said more succinctly, "You get through waivers because it's a you-scratch-my-back-and-I'll-scratch-yours situation."

Carew, owner of seven American League batting crowns and a .334 life-time average, was traded February 3. Carew forced the trade by informing the Twins that he would play out his option in '79 unless he was dealt before February 10.

In return for the 33-year-old first baseman, the Twins received from the Angels outfielder Ken Landreaux, pitcher Paul Hartzell and two minor lea-guers, pitcher Brad Havens and third baseman-outfielder Dave Engle. Landreaux had a productive year, hitting .305 with 15 homers and 83 RBIs; Hartzell worked in the Twins' rotation but was 6-10 with a miserable 5.36 ERA.

Carew, despite sitting out more than six weeks with a thumb injury, was instrumental in the Angels' winning the AL West, their first title ever. Carew hit .318 and scored 78 runs in 110 games. Moreover, the Angels were able to absorb his five-year, $4 million contract with a home attendance of 2,523,575, nearly 800,000 more than their previous high.

The first days of November were busy ones for the New York Yankees, who slipped to fourth place in '79 after two straight world titles. They were involved in two six-player deals. Outfielder Juan Beniquez, catcher Jerry Narron and pitchers Jim Beattie and Rick Anderson were sent to Seattle for pitcher Jim Lewis and outfielder Ruppert Jones. The Yanks also acquired pitcher Tommy Underwood, catcher Rick Cerone and outfielder Thad Wilborn from Toronto in exchange for first baseman Chris Chambliss, shortstop Damaso Garcia and pitcher Paul Mirabella.

The key players from the Yankees' standpoint were Jones, Underwood and Cerone. Jones hit .267 with 21 homers in '79. He drew 85 walks, scored 109 runs and stole 33 bases. Cerone, although he hit only .239 for Toronto, was expected to become New York's catcher. Underwood had a strong second half, going 8-6 with a 2.96 ERA in his last 18 starts.

A week later, the Yankees corraled free agents Bob Watson, a first base-man who hit .337 for Boston and pitcher Rudy May, who was 10-3 with a 2.30 ERA for Montreal.

The winter meetings at Toronto produced only a modicum of trades. In the most noteworthy deals, Detroit traded center fielder Ron LeFlore (.300 with 78 stolen bases in '79) to Montreal for lefthanded pitcher Dan Schatzeder, winner of 10 games, and the Cardinals secured outfielder Bobby Bonds from Cleveland for pitcher John Denny and outfielder Jerry Mumphrey. It was the sixth time that the 33-year-old Bonds, author of 321 home runs and 441 stolen bases, had been traded.

A chronological listing of major league deals and free-agent signings of 1979 follows:

January 4—Blue Jays signed infielder Chuck Scrivener, a free agent, and assigned him to Syracuse.

January 5—Twins re-signed pitcher Mike Marshall, a reentry free agent.

January 9—Dodgers purchased outfielder Von Joshua from Tabasco.

January 9—Blue Jays re-signed designated hitter Rico Carty, a reentry free agent.

January 9—Expos signed pitcher Elias Sosa, a reentry free agent formerly with the A's.

January 15—Mariners re-signed outfielder Tom Paciorek, a reentry free agent.

January 16—Cardinals signed pitcher Darold Knowles, a reentry free agent former-ly with the Expos.

January 17—Orioles released pitcher Nelson Briles.

January 19–Red Sox signed pitcher Steve Renko, a reentry free agent formerly with the A's.

January 19–Pirates signed outfielder-infielder Lee Lacy, a reentry free agent formerly with the Dodgers.

January 20–Cubs signed pitcher Steve Waterbury, a free agent, and assigned him to Wichita.

January 27–Mariners re-signed pitcher Jim Colborn and signed outfielder Willie Horton, reentry free agents; Horton was with the Blue Jays before entering the reentry draft.

January 29–Mariners released first baseman Bob Robertson.

January 30–Orioles re-signed outfielder Al Bumbry, a reentry free agent.

February 1–Mariners re-signed catcher Bill Plummer, a reentry free agent and assigned him to Spokane.

February 3–Twins traded first baseman Rod Carew to Angels for outfielder Ken Landreaux, third baseman Dave Engle and pitchers Paul Hartzell and Brad Havens.

February 3–Yankees purchased pitcher Greg Cochran from A's for an estimated $100,000 and catcher Bruce Robinson for an estimated $400,000; both players were assigned to Columbus, O.

February 7–Twins released pitcher Tom Johnson.

February 7–Padres signed outfielder Steve Brye, a reentry free agent, and assigned him to Hawaii; Brye was with the Pirates before entering the reentry draft.

February 7–Dodgers signed pitcher Andy Messersmith, a free agent.

February 8–Mariners released pitcher Jim Todd.

February 13–Twins traded third baseman Larry Wolfe to Red Sox for third baseman David Coleman, who was assigned to Toledo.

February 13–Twins released outfielder Rich Chiles and pitcher Stan Perzanowski.

February 13–Expos released pitcher Wayne Twitchell.

February 14–Tigers' Evansville affiliate purchased shortstop Dale Soderholm from Twins:

February 15–Cardinals released infielder Jose Baez.

February 15–Braves signed outfielder Mike Lum, a reentry free agent formerly with the Reds.

February 15–Yankees traded outfielder Gary Thomasson to Dodgers for catcher Brad Gulden.

February 19–Cardinals signed pitcher Will McEnaney, a free agent, and assigned him to Arkansas.

February 22–Padres signed catcher Fred Kendall, a reentry free agent formerly with the Red Sox.

February 22–Giants signed pitcher Dave Roberts, a reentry free agent formerly with the Cubs.

February 23–Mariners purchased pitcher Mike Davey from Braves and assigned him to Spokane.

February 23–Dodgers signed pitcher Pete Broberg, a reentry free agent formerly with the A's.

February 23–Phillies traded catcher Barry Foote, second baseman Ted Sizemore, outfielder Jerry Martin and pitchers Derek Botelho and Henry Mack to Cubs for second baseman Manny Trillo, catcher Dave Rader and outfielder Greg Gross.

February 25–Padres signed pitcher Al Fitzmorris, a free agent, and assigned him to Hawaii.

February 26–Brewers traded pitcher Eduardo Rodriguez to Royals for cash and a minor league player to be named later; the teams could not agree upon a player and the deal was settled with cash.

February 28—A's signed pitchers Jim Todd and Dave Hamilton, both free agents.

March 2—Cardinals signed outfielder Bernie Carbo, a reentry free agent formerly with the Indians.

March 5—Astros signed pitcher Brent Strom, a free agent, and assigned him to Columbus, Ga.

March 9—Giants signed outfielder Billy North, a reentry free agent formerly with the Dodgers.

March 13—Mets traded pitcher Mardie Cornejo to Tigers for pitcher Ed Glynn.

March 15—Giants traded outfielder Jim Dwyer to Red Sox for a player to be named later; the teams could not agree upon a player and the deal was settled with cash.

March 15—Indians signed outfielder Billy Baldwin, a free agent, and assigned him to Tacoma.

March 15—Red Sox traded outfielder Mike Easler to Pirates for outfielder George Hill (assigned from Salem to Winston-Salem), pitcher Martin Rivas and cash.

March 19—Phillies released outfielder Dave May and pitcher Butch Metzger.

March 20—Cubs traded catcher Larry Cox to Mariners for outfielder Luis Delgado, assigned from San Jose to Wichita.

March 20—Cubs acquired infielder Steve Dillard from Tigers; Cubs assigned catcher-infielder Ed Putman to Tigers' Evansville affiliate to complete deal, March 24.

March 23—A's released outfielder Dell Alston.

March 23—Mariners released pitcher Frank MacCormack.

March 24—Mariners released pitchers Tommy Brown and Dick Pole.

March 25—Blue Jays purchased outfielder Rogers (Bobby) Brown from Mets.

March 26—Mets released infielder Bobby Valentine.

March 26—Rangers released pitcher Roger Moret.

March 26—Orioles released catcher Elrod Hendricks and named him a fulltime coach.

March 27—Mariners released pitcher Paul Lindblad.

March 27—Phillies traded first baseman-third baseman Richie Hebner and second baseman Jose Moreno to Mets for pitcher Nino Espinosa.

March 27—Blue Jays assigned outfielder Sheldon Mallory to Indians' Tacoma affiliate to complete deal of November 2, 1978, in which Blue Jays obtained pitcher Dave Freisleben.

March 27—Angels signed outfielder Willie Davis, a free agent.

March 27—Astros released pitcher Dan Warthen.

March 27—Brewers purchased first baseman Skip James from Giants and assigned him to Vancouver.

March 28—Mariners released pitchers Jim Colborn and Tom House, catcher Kevin Pasley and outfielder Bobby Thompson.

March 28—Brewers traded pitcher Gary Beare to Phillies for pitcher Dan Boitano; Beare was assigned to Oklahoma City and Boitano to Vancouver.

March 28—Mariners purchased outfielder Joe Simpson from Dodgers.

March 28—Cubs released infielder Mike Sember.

March 29—Blue Jays released pitchers Don Kirkwood and Jeff Byrd.

March 29—Mets released third baseman Lenny Randle.

March 29—Phillies signed outfielder Del Unser, a reentry free agent formerly with the Expos.

March 29—Mariners purchased catcher Terry Bulling from Twins and assigned him to Spokane.

March 30—Cardinals released pitcher Jim Willoughby.

March 30—White Sox released designated hitter Ron Blomberg and pitcher Rich Hinton.

March 30—Expos released pitcher Mike Garman.

March 30—Braves released second baseman-third baseman Rod Gilbreath.

March 30—Twins released infielder Sam Perlozzo.

March 30—Indians traded outfielder Dan Briggs to Padres for a player to be named later; Indians received second baseman Mike Champion to complete deal, April 3, and assigned him to Tacoma.

March 30—Cubs signed pitcher Jim Willoughby, a free agent, and assigned him to Wichita.

March 31—Expos traded second baseman-shortstop Pepe Frias to Braves for pitcher Dave "Chopper" Campbell, who was assigned to Denver.

April 1—Expos' Denver affiliate purchased outfielder Art Gardner from Giants.

April 2—Angels released pitcher Ken Brett.

April 2—White Sox released pitcher Ron Schueler.

April 3—Phillies traded shortstop Todd Cruz to Royals for pitcher Doug Bird; Cruz was assigned to Omaha.

April 3—Braves released pitcher Buzz Capra.

April 4—Giants signed pitcher Tom Griffin, a free agent.

April 4—Mets signed pitcher Wayne Twitchell, a free agent.

April 4—Dodgers released pitcher Pete Broberg.

April 5—Braves signed outfielder Charlie Spikes, a free agent.

April 5—Cardinals released pitcher Paul Siebert.

April 6—Blue Jays signed infielder Mike Sember, a free agent, and assigned him to Syracuse.

April 7—Pirates traded pitcher Jerry Reuss to Dodgers for pitcher Rick Rhoden.

April 9—Pirates signed infielder Rod Gilbreath, a free agent, and assigned him to Portland.

April 10—Mariners signed infielder Bobby Valentine, a free agent.

April 12—Yankees released outfielder Paul Blair.

April 13—White Sox traded pitcher Jack Kucek to Phillies for a player to be named later; Kucek was assigned to Oklahoma City, and second baseman Jim Morrison was assigned to White Sox to complete deal, July 10.

April 15—Brewers signed pitcher Clay Carroll, a free agent, and assigned him to Vancouver.

April 19—Pirates traded shortstop Frank Taveras to Mets for shortstop Tim Foli and pitcher Greg Field, the latter assigned from Tidewater to Portland.

April 19—Blue Jays returned outfielder Bobby Brown to Yankees' Columbus affiliate.

April 21—Giants released pitcher Joe Coleman.

April 23—Blue Jays signed first baseman Bob Robertson, a free agent.

April 27—Astros acquired pitcher George Throop from Royals and assigned him to Charleston, W. Va.; second baseman Keith Drumright was assigned to Royals to complete deal, October 26.

April 30—Twins signed pitcher Ken Brett, a free agent.

May 1—Tigers released infielder Dave Machemer.

May 3—Reds traded pitcher Doug Capilla to Cubs for a player to be named later; Capilla was assigned to Wichita, and Cubs assigned pitcher Mark Gilbert to Reds' Nashville affiliate to complete deal, October 12.

May 4—Rangers traded shortstop Bert Campaneris to Angels for third baseman Dave Chalk.

May 7—Reds signed outfielder Paul Blair, a free agent.

May 9—Cardinals released outfielder Tom Grieve.

May 11—Cubs released outfielder Gene Clines.

May 11—Brewers purchased pitcher Lance Rautzhan from Dodgers.

May 11—Dodgers purchased pitcher Lerrin LaGrow from White Sox.

May 11—Yankees purchased pitcher Jim Kaat from Phils.

May 12—Blue Jays released pitcher Tom Murphy.

May 13—Giants signed third baseman Lenny Randle, a free agent, and assigned him to Phoenix.

May 22—Red Sox released shortstop Frank Duffy.

May 23—Yankees traded pitcher Dick Tidrow to Cubs for pitcher Ray Burris.

May 25—Phillies signed shortstop Bud Harrelson, a free agent.

May 25—Braves traded pitcher Frank LaCorte to Astros for pitcher Michael (Bo) McLaughlin; LaCorte was assigned to Charleston, W. Va.

May 25—Reds traded outfielder Champ Summers to Tigers for a player to be named later; Tigers assigned pitcher Sheldon Burnside to Reds to complete deal, October 25.

May 27—White Sox purchased catcher Milt May from Tigers.

June 4—Twins released pitcher Ken Brett.

June 5—Orioles traded outfielder Larry Harlow to Angels for infielder Floyd Rayford and cash.

June 6—Blue Jays purchased pitcher Dyar Miller from Angels.

June 7—Brewers traded pitcher Randy Stein to Mariners for pitcher Paul Mitchell.

June 7—Mariners purchased pitcher Rob Dressler from Cardinals.

June 11—Dodgers signed pitcher Ken Brett, a free agent.

June 13—Expos purchased catcher John Tamargo from Giants and assigned him to Denver.

June 13—Red Sox traded first baseman George Scott to Royals for outfielder Tom Poquette.

June 13—Astros traded first baseman Bob Watson to Red Sox for pitcher Pete Ladd, a player to be named later and cash; Ladd was assigned from Bristol to Columbus (Ga.) and pitcher Bobby Sprowl was assigned to Astros' Charleston (W. Va.) affiliate to complete deal, June 19.

June 14—Indians traded outfielder-third baseman Paul Dade to Padres for first baseman Mike Hargrove.

June 15—Mets purchased pitcher Andy Hassler from Red Sox.

June 15—Rangers traded third baseman Dave Chalk, catcher Mike Heath and cash to A's for pitcher John Henry Johnson.

June 15—Mets traded pitchers Bob Myrick and Mike Bruhert to Rangers for pitcher Dock Ellis.

June 15—Indians traded pitcher Don Hood to Yankees for catcher Cliff Johnson.

June 15—Padres traded pitcher Dave Wehrmeister to Yankees for outfielder Jay Johnstone.

June 15—White Sox traded third baseman Eric Soderholm to Rangers for pitcher Ed Farmer and first baseman Gary Holle.

June 16—Phillies released pitcher Jim Lonborg.

June 26—Cubs traded outfielder Bobby Murcer to Yankees for pitcher Paul Semall, assigned from Columbus (O.) to Wichita, and cash.

June 27—Blue Jays released first baseman Bob Robertson.

June 28—Cubs purchased outfielder Ken Henderson from Reds.

June 28—Giants traded outfielder Hector Cruz to Reds for pitcher Pedro Borbon.

June 28—Pirates traded pitchers Ed Whitson, Fred Breining and Al Holland to Giants for second baseman-third baseman Bill Madlock, third baseman Lenny Randle and pitcher Dave Roberts; Randle was assigned from Phoenix to Portland, Holland from Portland to Phoenix and Breining from Buffalo to Shreveport.

July 4—Cubs purchased outfielder Miguel Dilone from A's.

July 4—Reds purchased outfielder Sam Mejias from Cubs and assigned him to Indianapolis.

July 5—Padres signed first baseman-outfielder Bobby Tolan, a free agent.

July 6—White Sox traded pitcher Rich Hinton to Mariners for third baseman-outfielder Juan Bernhardt, who remained on the roster of Seattle's Spokane affiliate.

July 20—Expos acquired outfielder Rusty Staub from Tigers; Tigers received catcher Randy Schafer (assigned from Memphis to Evansville) and cash to complete deal, December 3.

July 25—Blue Jays purchased first baseman Craig Kusick from Twins.

July 30—Blue Jays acquired first baseman Tony Solaita from Expos; the contract of pitcher Dyar Miller was formally assigned to the Montreal organization to complete the deal, October 24.

July 31—Angels released catcher Terry Humphrey.

August 1—Rangers traded outfielder Oscar Gamble, third baseman Amos Lewis (assigned from Asheville to Fort Lauderdale) and two players to be named later to Yankees for outfielder Mickey Rivers and three players to be named later; Yankees sent pitchers Bob Polinsky, Neal Mersch and Mark Softy to Rangers, who sent pitchers Gene Nelson and Ray Fontenot to Yankees to complete deal, October 8.

August 2—Mets purchased outfielder Jose Cardenal from Phillies.

August 2—Yankees purchased third baseman-outfielder Lenny Randle from Pirates.

August 6—Mariners released outfielder John Hale.

August 12—Mets traded first baseman Willie Montanez to Rangers for two players to be named later; pitcher Ed Lynch was assigned to Mets, September 18, and first baseman Mike Jorgensen, October 23, to complete deal.

August 17—Cubs traded second baseman Ted Sizemore to Red Sox for cash and a player to be named later; Red Sox assigned catcher Mike O'Berry to Cubs to complete deal, October 23.

August 17—Royals released first baseman George Scott.

August 19—Mariners purchased pitcher Wayne Twitchell from Mets.

August 20—Mets purchased pitcher Ray Burris from Yankees.

August 27—Yankees signed first baseman George Scott, a free agent.

August 28—Dodgers released pitcher Andy Messersmith.

August 29—Angels acquired pitcher John Montague from Mariners for a player to be named later; shortstop Jim Anderson was assigned to Mariners to complete deal, December 5.

August 30—Cubs purchased catcher Bruce Kimm from Tigers.

August 30—Expos purchased pitcher Dale Murray from Mets.

August 31—Orioles purchased outfielder Bob Molinaro from White Sox.

September 20—Angels purchased outfielder Ralph Garr from White Sox.

September 21—Pirates purchased pitcher Dock Ellis from Mets.

October 1—Dodgers released outfielder Manny Mota.

October 3—White Sox purchased outfielder Bob Molinaro from Orioles.

October 3—Cubs released pitcher Ken Holtzman.

October 3—Padres released pitcher Mickey Lolich.

October 4—Mariners released catcher Bill Plummer.

October 15—White Sox signed pitcher Tom Johnson, a free agent, and assigned him to Iowa.

October 17—Cardinals traded second baseman Mike Tyson to Cubs for pitcher Donnie Moore.

October 19—Braves traded pitcher Jamie Easterly to Expos for cash and a player to be named later.

October 23—Blue Jays released pitcher Dave Freisleben and first baseman Craig Kusick.

October 24—Indians released pitcher Paul Reuschel.

October 24—Brewers traded pitcher Lance Rautzhan to Royals for outfielder Kevin Gillen.

October 26—Royals released pitcher Steve Mingori.

October 26—Mets traded pitcher Dwight Bernard to Brewers for pitcher Mark Bomback.

October 31—Mets traded first baseman-third baseman Richie Hebner to Tigers for outfielder Jerry Morales and third baseman Phil Mankowski.

November 1—Mariners traded outfielder Ruppert Jones and pitcher Jim Lewis to Yankees for pitchers Jim Beattie and Rick Anderson, outfielder Juan Beniquez and catcher Jerry Narron.

November 1— Blue Jays traded pitcher Tommy Underwood, catcher Rick Cerone and outfielder Ted Wilborn to Yankees for first baseman Chris Chambliss, infielder Damaso Garcia and pitcher Paul Mirabella.

November 5—Blue Jays purchased shortstop Domingo Ramos from Rangers.

November 8—Yankees signed first baseman Bob Watson, a reentry free agent formerly with the Red Sox, and pitcher Rudy May, a reentry free agent formerly with the Expos.

November 9—Mariners purchased pitcher Dan O'Brien from Cardinals.

November 14—Rangers traded third baseman Eric Soderholm to the Yankees for cash and players to be named later; Rangers received third baseman Amos Lewis (Ft. Lauderdale) and pitcher Ricky Burdette (West Haven) to complete deal, December 13.

November 14—Dodgers signed pitcher Dave Goltz, a reentry free agent formerly with the Twins.

November 16—Red Sox signed first baseman Tony Perez, a reentry free agent formerly with the Expos.

November 16—Angels signed pitcher Bruce Kison, a reentry free agent formerly with the Pirates.

November 17—Dodgers signed pitcher Don Stanhouse, a reentry free agent formerly with the Orioles.

November 19—Astros signed pitcher Nolan Ryan, a reentry free agent formerly with the Angels.

November 20—Braves signed pitcher Al Hrabosky, a reentry free agent formerly with the Royals.

November 20—Padres signed pitcher Rick Wise, a reentry free agent formerly with the Indians.

November 21—Seattle's Spokane affiliate purchased pitcher Kip Young from Tigers.

November 21—Pirates signed pitcher Andy Hassler, a reentry free agent formerly with the Mets.

November 26—Padres signed pitcher John Curtis, a reentry free agent formerly with the Giants.

November 27—Red Sox signed pitcher Skip Lockwood, a reentry free agent formerly with the Mets.

November 27—Expos traded second baseman Dave Cash to Padres for infielder Bill Almon and first baseman-outfielder Dan Briggs.

December 3—Expos signed pitcher Fred Norman, a reentry free agent formerly with the Reds.

December 3—Padres purchased outfielder Von Joshua from Dodgers.

December 3—White Sox traded catcher Bill Nahorodny to Braves for pitcher Rick Wieters, on Savannah roster.

December 4—Dodgers signed outfielder Jay Johnstone, a reentry free agent formerly with the Padres.

December 5—Angels signed shortstop Fred Patek, a reentry free agent formerly with the Royals.

December 5—Blue Jays traded first baseman Chris Chambliss and shortstop Luis Gomez to Braves for outfielder Barry Bonnell, shortstop Pat Rockett and pitcher Joey McLaughlin; Rockett was assigned to Syracuse.

December 5—Tigers traded pitcher Fernando Arroyo to Twins for pitcher Jeff Holly, assigned to Evansville.

December 6—Expos signed outfielder Rowland Office, a reentry free agent formerly with the Braves.

December 6—Brewers traded second baseman Lenn Sakata to Orioles for pitcher John Flinn.

December 6—Royals traded outfielder Al Cowens, shortstop Todd Cruz and a player to be named later to Angels for shortstop Rance Mulliniks and first baseman Willie Mays Aikens.

December 6—Braves traded pitcher Adrian Devine, shortstop Pepe Frias and a player to be named later for pitcher Doyle Alexander and shortstop Larvell Blanks. Originally, Braves outfielder Jeff Burroughs was included in this trade. Burroughs, however, exercised his right to refuse a trade. It was agreed then that if the Braves could eventually obtain Burroughs' consent they would send him to the Rangers as a player to be named later. Failing that, the Rangers would pay the Braves $50,000.

December 6—Indians traded third baseman-outfielder Ted Cox to Mariners for pitchers Rafael Vasquez and Rob Pietroburgo and a player to be named later.

December 7—Orioles traded first baseman Tom Chism to Twins for third baseman Dan Graham.

December 7—Phillies traded infielder Pete Mackanin to Twins for pitcher Paul Thormodsgard, assigned to Oklahoma City.

December 7—Tigers traded third baseman Aurelio Rodriguez to Padres for a player to be named later.

December 7—Tigers traded outfielder Ron LeFlore to Expos for pitcher Dan Schatzeder.

December 7—Cardinals traded outfielder Jerry Mumphrey and pitcher John Denny to Indians for outfielder Bobby Bonds.

December 11—Mets released pitcher Bob Apodaca.

December 12—White Sox purchased pitcher Bill Atkinson from Expos.

December 12—Giants signed catcher Milt May, a reentry free agent formerly with the White Sox; second baseman Rennie Stennett, a reentry free agent formerly with the Pirates; and outfielder Jim Wohlford, a reentry free agent formerly with the Brewers.

December 13—Phillies re-signed outfielder Greg Gross, a reentry free agent.

December 19—Indians signed second baseman-outfielder Jorge Orta, a reentry free agent formerly with the White Sox.

December 19—Giants released second baseman Rob Andrews.

December 20—Mariners re-signed designated hitter Willie Horton, a reentry free agent.

December 21—Indians traded pitcher Larry Andersen to Pirates for pitcher John Burden (on Salem roster) and outfielder Larry Littleton (on Portland roster).

Hotels of Major League Teams

AMERICAN LEAGUE

AT BALTIMORE: Baltimore Hilton—Minnesota. **Cross Keys Inn**—All other clubs.

AT BOSTON: Sheraton-Boston—All clubs.

AT CALIFORNIA: Hyatt House Anaheim—All clubs.

AT CHICAGO: Continental Plaza—Baltimore, Detroit, Milwaukee, New York. **Executive House**—Cleveland, Minnesota, New York, Oakland, Texas. **Hyatt Regency**—California, Kansas City (at Sheraton Plaza August 1, 2, 3), Seattle. **Marriott**—Boston.

AT CLEVELAND: Hollenden House—Boston, Milwaukee, New York. **Bond Court**—All other clubs.

AT DETROIT: Detroit Plaza—Baltimore, Boston, California, Milwaukee, Minnesota, Seattle, Texas, Toronto. **Sheraton Southfield**—Oakland (at Detroit Plaza July 25, 26, 27). **Ponchartrain**—All other clubs.

AT KANSAS CITY: Sheraton Royal—Chicago, Cleveland, Milwaukee, Oakland. **Crown Center**—All other clubs.

AT MILWAUKEE: Chicago (at Marc Plaza May 13, 14, 15), Seattle, Texas (at Pfister September 5, 6, 7). **Pfister**—All other clubs.

AT MINNESOTA: Leamington—Cleveland, Detroit, Milwaukee, New York. **Northstar Inn**—Boston. **Marriott**—All other clubs.

AT NEW YORK: New York Sheraton—All clubs.

AT OAKLAND: Hilton—California, Seattle. **Edgewater Hyatt House**—All other clubs.

AT SEATTLE: Doubletree Inn—Baltimore, California, Kansas City, Texas. **Sea Tac Motor Inn**—Cleveland (at Hilton May 5, 6, 7), Minnesota, Oakland. **Hilton**—All other clubs.

AT TEXAS: Doubletree Inn—Baltimore, Boston, California, Milwaukee, Minnesota. **Inn of the Six Flags**—Oakland (at Rodeway Inn May 30, 31 and June 1). **Sheraton-Dallas**—Toronto. **Rodeway Inn (Arlington)**—All other clubs.

AT TORONTO: Hotel Toronto—All clubs.

NATIONAL LEAGUE

AT ATLANTA: Hilton—Houston, Los Angeles, New York. **Marriott**—All other clubs.

AT CHICAGO: Continental Plaza—San Francisco. **Executive House**—Atlanta. **Hyatt Regency**—Houston, Los Angeles, St. Louis, San Diego. **Marriott**—Cincinnati, Montreal. **Sheraton Plaza**—New York, Philadelphia (at Sheraton O'Hare August 11, 12, 13), Pittsburgh.

AT CINCINNATI: Terrace Hilton—Chicago, Houston, Los Angeles, Montreal. **Stouffer's Inn**—All other clubs.

AT HOUSTON: Shamrock Hilton—Chicago, Los Angeles, Philadelphia (at Stouffer's Greenway Plaza May 16, 17, 18), Pittsburgh, St. Louis. **Marriott**—All other clubs.

AT LOS ANGELES: Los Angeles Hilton—Cincinnati, St. Louis. **Wilshire Hyatt House**—Philadelphia, San Francisco. **Biltmore**—All other clubs.

AT MONTREAL: Loew's La Cite—Atlanta, Cincinnati, New York, St. Louis, San Diego. **Regency Hyatt**—All other clubs.

AT NEW YORK: New York Sheraton—All clubs.

AT PHILADELPHIA: Marriott—Los Angeles. **Stadium Hilton**—Atlanta, Pittsburgh, San Diego. **University City Holiday Inn**—All other clubs.

AT PITTSBURGH: Carlton House—Cincinnati, San Francisco. **Hyatt House**—Houston, Philadelphia. **Marriott**—Atlanta. **Pittsburgh Hilton**—All other clubs.

AT ST. LOUIS: Stouffer's Inn—Cincinnati, Philadelphia. **Marriott Pavilion**—All other clubs.

AT SAN DIEGO: Sheraton Harbor Island–Chicago, Montreal, New York, Pittsburgh, St. Louis. **Town & Country**–All other clubs.

AT SAN FRANCISCO: Sheraton Fisherman's Wharf–Atlanta. **Sheraton Palace**–Houston. **San Francisco Hilton**–All other clubs.

Major League Attendance for 1979

NATIONAL LEAGUE	Home	Away
Atlanta	769,465	1,636,166
Chicago	1,648,587	1,697,549
Cincinnati	2,356,933	1,959,617
Houston	1,900,312	1,588,414
Los Angeles	2,860,954	2,071,730
Montreal	2,102,173	1,713,662
New York	788,905	1,556,732
Philadelphia	2,775,011	1,912,647
Pittsburgh	1,435,454	1,931,851
St. Louis	1,627,256	1,639,983
San Diego	1,456,967	1,606,566
San Francisco	1,456,402	1,863,502

NL 1979 Total—21,178,419

AMERICAN LEAGUE	Home	Away
Baltimore	1,681,009	1,598,750
Boston	2,353,114	2,132,807
California	2,523,575	1,728,537
Chicago	1,280,702	1,524,339
Cleveland	1,011,644	1,478,381
Detroit	1,630,929	1,548,897
Kansas City	2,261,845	1,628,236
Milwaukee	1,918,343	1,417,681
Minnesota	1,070,521	1,471,004
New York	2,537,765	2,224,382
Oakland	306,763	1,389,157
Seattle	844,447	1,381,572
Texas	1,519,671	1,587,236
Toronto	1,431,651	1,261,000

AL 1979 Total—22,371,979

BEST MAJOR LEAGUE ATTENDANCE MARKS

1.	Los Angeles	3,347,845	1978
2.	Los Angeles	2,955,087	1977
3.	Los Angeles	2,860,954	1979
4.	Philadelphia	2,775,011	1979
5.	Los Angeles	2,755,184	1962
6.	Philadelphia	2,700,070	1977
7.	New York Mets	2,697,479	1970
8.	Los Angeles	2,634,474	1974
9.	Cincinnati	2,629,708	1976
10.	Cleveland	2,620,627	1948
11.	Los Angeles	2,617,029	1966
12.	Philadelphia	2,583,389	1978
13.	Los Angeles	2,553,577	1965
14.	Los Angeles	2,539,349	1975
15.	Los Angeles	2,538,602	1963
16.	New York Yankees	2,537,765	1979
17.	Cincinnati	2,532,497	1978
18.	California	2,523,575	1979
19.	Cincinnati	2,519,670	1977
20.	Philadelphia	2,480,150	1976
21.	Los Angeles	2,386,301	1976
22.	New York Yankees	2,373,901	1948
23.	Cincinnati	2,356,933	1979
24.	Boston	2,353,114	1979
25.	New York Yankees	2,335,871	1978

Presidents of Minor Leagues for '80

CLASS AAA

American Association—Joe Ryan, P. O. Box 382, Wichita, Kan. 67201

International League—Harold Cooper, Box 608, Grove City, Ohio 43123

Mexican League—Lic. Antonio Ramirez (Muro), Campos Eliseos 169-202, Mexico 5, D. F., Mexico

Pacific Coast League—Bill Cutler, 2101 E. Broadway Rd., Tempe, Ariz. 85282

CLASS AA

Eastern League—P. Patrick McKernan, Box 26267, Albuquerque, N.M. 87125

Southern League—Billy Hitchcock, Box 528, Opelika, Ala. 36801

Texas League—Carl Sawatski, P. O. Box 5240, Little Rock, Ark. 72205

CLASS A

California League—E. W. (Bill) Wickert, 677 Santa Barbara Road, Berkeley, Calif. 94707

Carolina League—Jim Mills, 516-C Salem Court, Cary, N. C. 27511

Florida State League—George MacDonald, Jr., P. O. Box 414, Lakeland, Fla. 33802

Mexican Center League—Lic. Antonio Ramirez (Muro), Campos Eliseos 169-202, Mexico 5, D. F., Mexico

Midwest League—William K. Walters, P. O. Box 444, Burlington, Ia. 52601

New York-Pennsylvania League—Vincent M. McNamara, 220 Brookside Drive, Buffalo, N. Y. 14220.

Northwest League—Bob Richmond, 1509 Williamette St., Eugene, Ore. 97440

South Atlantic League—John H. Moss, P. O. Box 49, Kings Mountain, N. C. 28086

ROOKIE CLASSIFICATION

Appalachian League—John Leonard, 258 Suncrest Dr., Bristol, Va. 24201 (acting president).

Gulf Coast League—Thomas J. Saffell, 420 Golde Gate Point, Apt. 18, Sarasota, Fla. 33577

Pioneer League—Ralph C. Nelles, P. O. Box 570, Billings, Mont. 59103

JOHN JOHNSON—National Association President.

Official Minor League Averages

Official Averages Of All Triple A, Double A and A Leagues, Plus Rookie Leagues

American Association

CLASS AAA

**Leading Batter
KEITH SMITH
Springfield**

**League President
JOE RYAN**

**Leading Pitcher
BRUCE BERENYI
Indianapolis**

CHAMPIONSHIP WINNERS IN PREVIOUS YEARS

1902 – Indianapolis .683	1935 – Minneapolis .591	1955 – Minneapolis† .597
1903 – St. Paul .657	1936 – Milwaukee† .584	1956 – Indianapolis† .597
1904 – St. Paul .646	1937 – Columbus† .584	1957 – Wichita .604
1905 – Columbus .658	1938 – St. Paul .596	Denver (2nd)‡ .584
1906 – Columbus .615	Kansas City (2nd)‡ .556	1958 – Charleston .589
1907 – Columbus .584	1939 – Kansas City .695	Minneapolis (3rd)‡ .536
1908 – Indianapolis .601	Louisville (4th)‡ .490	1959 – Louisville§ .599
1909 – Louisville .554	1940 – Kansas City .625	Omaha§ .516
1910 – Minneapolis .637	Louisville (4th)‡ .500	Minneapolis (2nd)‡ .586
1911 – Minneapolis .600	1941 – Columbus† .621	1960 – Denver .571
1912 – Minneapolis .636	1942 – Kansas City .549	Louisville (2nd)‡ .556
1913 – Milwaukee .599	Columbus (3rd)‡ .532	1961 – Indianapolis .573
1914 – Milwaukee .590	1943 – Milwaukee .596	Louisville (2nd)‡ .533
1915 – Minneapolis .597	Columbus (3rd)‡ .532	1962 – Indianapolis .605
1916 – Louisville .605	1944 – Milwaukee .667	Louisville (4th)‡ .486
1917 – Indianapolis .588	Louisville (3rd)‡ .574	1963-1968 – Did not operate.
1918 – Kansas City .589	1945 – Milwaukee .604	1969 – Omaha .607
1919 – St. Paul .610	Louisville (3rd)‡ .545	1970 – Omaha* .529
1920 – St. Paul .701	1946 – Louisville† .601	Denver .504
1921 – Louisville .583	1947 – Kansas City .608	1971 – Indianapolis .604
1922 – St. Paul .641	Milwaukee (3rd)‡ .513	Denver* .521
1923 – Kansas City .675	1948 – Indianapolis .649	1972 – Wichita .621
1924 – St. Paul .578	St. Paul (3rd)‡ .558	Evansville* .593
1925 – Louisville .635	1949 – St. Paul .608	1973 – Iowa .610
1926 – Louisville .629	Indianapolis (2nd)‡ .604	Tulsa* .504
1927 – Toledo .601	1950 – Minneapolis .584	1974 – Indianapolis .578
1928 – Indianapolis .593	Columbus (3rd)‡ 549	Tulsa* .567
1929 – Kansas City .665	1951 – Milwaukee† .623	1975 – Evansville* .566
1930 – Louisville .608	1952 – Milwaukee .656	Denver .596
1931 – St. Paul .623	Kansas City (2nd)‡ .578	1976 – Denver* .632
1932 – Minneapolis .595	1953 – Toledo .584	Omaha .574
1933 – Columbus* .604	Kansas City (2nd)‡ .571	1977 – Omaha .563
Minneapolis .562	1954 – Indianapolis .625	Denver* .522
1934 – Minneapolis .570	Louisville (2nd)‡ .556	1978 – Indianapolis .578
Columbus* .556		Omaha* .489

*Won playoff (East vs. West). †Won championship and four-team playoff. ‡Won four-team playoff. §Respective Eastern and Western division winners.

STANDING OF CLUBS AT CLOSE OF SEASON, AUGUST 30

EAST DIVISION

Club	Evan.	Spfd.	Iowa	Ind.	O.C.	Oma.	Den.	Wich.	W.	L.	T.	Pct.	G.B.
Evansville (Tigers)	....	10	15	15	7	12	12	7	78	58	0	.574	.....
Springfield (Cardinals)	14	....	11	14	8	10	7	9	73	63	0	.537	5
Iowa (White Sox)	9	13	....	13	9	7	7	11	69	67	0	.507	9
Indianapolis (Reds)	9	10	11	....	10	7	9	11	67	69	0	.493	11

WEST DIVISION

Oklahoma City (Phillies)	9	8	7	6	....	13	12	17	72	63	0	.533	.....
Omaha (Royals)	4	6	9	9	11	....	15	11	65	71	0	.478	7½
Denver (Expos)	4	9	9	7	11	9	....	13	62	73	0	.459	10
Wichita (Cubs)	9	7	5	5	7	13	11	....	57	79	0	.419	15½

Iowa club represented Des Moines, Iowa.

Major league affiliations in parentheses.

Playoff—Evansville defeated Oklahoma City, four games to two.

Regular-Season Attendance—Denver, 335,684; Evansville, 120,265; Indianapolis, 166,063; Iowa, 136, 138; Oklahoma City, 193,792; Omaha, 157,277; Springfield, 94,910; Wichita, 92,611. Total, 1,296,740. Playoffs, 17,263. No all-star game.

Managers: Denver—Jack McKeon; Evansville—Jim Leyland; Indianapolis—Roy Majtyka; Iowa— Tony LaRussa, Joe Sparks; Oklahoma City, Lee Elia; Omaha—Gordon MacKenzie; Springfield, Hal Lanier; Wichita, Jack Hiatt.

All-Star Team: 1B—Bass, Denver; 2B—Frazier, Iowa; 3B—Castillo, Springfield; SS—Oester, Indianapolis; OF—Pagel, Wichita; Molinaro, Iowa; Smith, Springfield; Utility-Durham, Springfield; Cox, Denver; C—Moreland, Oklahoma City; Kimm, Evansville; P—Robinson, Iowa; Beare, Oklahoma City; Manager—Leyland, Evansville.

(Compiled by Ed Williams, League Statistician, Shawnee, Okla.)

CLUB BATTING

Club	G.	AB.	R.	OR.	H.	TB.	2B.	3B.	HR.	RBI.	SH.	Int. SF.	BB.	HP.	SO.	SB.	CS.	LOB.	Pct.
Denver	135	4413	712	720	1268	1896	218	40	110	649	56	51	589	47	33	625	110	63	1020	.2873
Okla. City	135	4537	733	681	1303	1973	256	45	108	682	42	53	516	43	31	671	91	45	991	.2872
Springfield	136	4524	688	680	1287	1861	220	36	94	641	45	46	476	38	40	582	137	50	986	.284
Iowa	136	4482	681	696	1248	1870	201	41	113	625	41	49	503	33	29	670	130	68	931	.278
Evansville	136	4477	724	617	1233	1859	218	30	116	672	53	41	651	51	47	731	122	58	1055	.275
Wichita	136	4398	620	688	1149	1735	195	34	96	488	65	30	465	40	28	784	92	41	953	.245
Indianapolis	136	4366	527	559	1070	1608	182	34	96	488	65	30	465	40	28	784	92	41	953	.245
Omaha	136	4341	565	621	1058	1587	197	34	88	522	73	27	597	33	35	614	163	64	1002	.244

INDIVIDUAL BATTING

(Leading Qualifiers for Batting Championship—367 or More Plate Appearances)

*Bats lefthanded. †Switch-hitter.

Player and Club	G.	AB.	R.	H.	TB.	2B.	3B.	HR.	RBI.	SH.	SF.	BB.	HP.	SO.	SB.	CS.	Pct.
Smith, Keith, Springfield	119	448	77	157	209	17	4	9	61	1	3	21	0	28	30	11	.350
Pate, Robert, Denver	118	428	85	147	220	26	1	15	63	2	4	60	3	47	13	6	.343
Bass, Randall, Denver*	122	421	91	140	278	28	1	36	105	1	8	97	3	67	2	0	.333
Smith, Lonnie, Oklahoma City	110	451	106	149	214	26	9	7	44	2	1	56	4	52	34	11	.330
Molinaro, Robert, Iowa*	133	475	90	156	228	23	5	13	93	0	9	81	3	26	50	12	.328
Castillo, E. Manuel, Springfield†	127	524	75	169	212	29	4	2	57	7	7	16	0	23	7	5	.323
Peters, Richard, Evansville*	107	387	88	124	170	17	10	3	42	4	3	76	6	34	30	13	.320
Pagel, Karl, Wichita*	136	472	96	149	291	25	0	39	123	1	1	100	1	109	10	3	.316
Gonzalez, Orlando, Okla City*	125	480	87	150	211	29	7	6	76	7	3	65	1	44	16	2	.313
Durham, Leon, Springfield*	127	449	84	139	249	33	4	23	88	0	2	65	4	61	16	4	.310

Departmental Leaders: G—Oester, Pagel, 136; AB—E.M. Castillo, 524; R—L. Smith, 106; H—E.M. Castillo, 169; TB—Pagel, 291; 2B—Moreland, Poff, 34; 3B—Gardner, 11; HR—Pagel, 39; RBI—Pagel, 123; SH—Kinard, 19; SF—Moreland, 13; BB—Pagel, 100; HP—Lentine, 9; SO—Kuntz, 111; SB—Barranca, 75; CS—Barranca, 17.

(All Players—Listed Alphabetically)

Player and Club	G.	AB.	R.	H.	TB.	2B.	3B.	HR.	RBI.	SH.	SF.	BB.	HP.	SO.	SB.	CS.	Pct.
Aguayo, Luis, Okla City	113	370	54	101	148	21	1	8	46	6	7	23	6	82	3	4	.273
Alberts, Francis, Indianapolis	69	241	32	70	105	9	4	6	40	1	4	20	5	37	6	3	.290
Altamirano, Porfirio, Okla City	21	2	0	1	1	0	0	0	0	0	0	0	0	1	0	0	.500
Anderson, Michael, Okla City	9	36	8	10	15	2	0	1	8	0	0	2	1	8	0	1	.278
Angelini, Norman, Denver*	48	5	0	1	1	0	0	0	0	0	0	0	0	2	0	0	.200
Arline, James, Indianapolis*	15	47	6	8	10	2	0	0	0	0	0	4	0	7	0	1	.170
Atkinson, William, Denver*	44	24	4	3	5	0	1	0	2	0	0	0	0	6	0	0	.125
Aviles, Ramon, Oklahoma City	72	252	37	63	72	7	1	0	18	3	0	28	0	19	1	0	.250
Baines, Harold, Iowa*	125	466	87	139	246	25	8	22	87	0	4	33	0	80	5	7	.298
Ballinger, Mark, Omaha	29	2	0	0	0	0	0	0	0	0	0	0	0	1	0	0	.000
Barranca, German, Omaha*	122	472	79	120	176	18	7	8	49	6	4	66	1	42	75	17	.254
Bass, Randall, Denver*	122	421	91	140	278	28	1	36	105	1	8	97	3	67	2	0	.333
Beare, Gary, Oklahoma City	27	5	2	1	1	0	0	0	0	0	0	3	0	3	0	0	.200

Player and Club	G.	AB.	R.	H.	TB.	2B.	3B.	HR.	RBI.	SH.	SF.	BB.	HP.	SO.	SB.	CS.	Pct.
Beene, Fred, Oklahoma City†	27	9	1	1	2	1	0	0	0	1	0	0	0	2	0	0	.111
Bell, Kevin, Iowa	55	191	28	45	84	4	1	11	37	0	1	34	0	42	0	0	.236
Berenyi, Bruce, Indianapolis	26	48	4	6	6	0	0	0	1	8	0	3	1	15	0	0	.125
Bernazard, Antonio, Denver†	82	273	58	82	110	15	2	3	29	2	2	74	2	61	19	15	.300
Bernhardt, Juan, Iowa	25	59	5	18	22	2	1	0	6	0	2	4	0	6	0	0	.305
Bialas, David, Springfield	120	410	66	116	159	27	5	2	60	0	3	55	3	56	6	3	.283
Bosley, Thaddis, Iowa*	95	382	62	101	128	14	5	1	24	1	3	39	1	62	18	9	.264
Botehlo, Derek, Wichita	4	4	0	0	0	0	0	0	0	0	0	1	0	0	0	0	.000
Bowling, Stephen, Indianapolis	3	9	1	2	5	0	0	1	2	0	0	1	0	2	0	0	.222
Brookens, Thomas, Evansville	77	265	51	81	150	23	2	14	46	4	2	33	1	50	10	6	.306
Brown, Darrell, Evansville	23	43	8	11	14	0	0	1	4	1	0	4	0	6	3	1	.256
Brummer, Glenn, Springfield	44	104	19	22	27	2	0	1	11	1	0	13	1	15	3	1	.212
Bruno, Thomas, Springfield	11	8	0	1	1	0	0	0	0	0	0	0	0	5	0	0	.125
Burnside, Sheldon, Indianapolis	39	6	0	0	0	0	0	0	0	2	0	3	0	3	0	0	.000
Bystrom, Martin, Okla City	26	4	0	1	1	0	0	0	0	0	0	1	0	1	0	0	.250
Campbell, David, Denver	42	9	1	2	2	0	0	0	0	0	0	1	0	3	0	0	.222
Capilla, Douglas, Wichita*	29	8	1	0	0	0	0	0	0	3	0	0	0	4	0	0	.000
Cappuzzello, George, Indianapolis ..	19	3	0	1	1	0	0	0	0	0	0	0	0	1	0	0	.333
Carrion, Leonal S., Denver	121	417	57	122	181	17	3	12	71	5	9	46	6	44	10	9	.293
Castillo, E. Manuel, Springfield†	127	524	75	169	212	29	4	2	57	7	7	16	0	23	7	5	.323
Castillo, Martin, Evansville	31	103	11	24	33	4	1	1	6	1	0	11	0	25	0	1	.233
Chamberlain, Thomas, Springfield	12	9	1	1	1	0	0	0	0	1	0	0	0	4	0	0	.111
Chappas, Harry, Iowa†	77	259	36	79	106	6	3	5	32	4	5	35	0	41	18	12	.305
Christenson, Gary, Omaha*	51	2	0	1	1	0	0	0	0	0	0	0	0	0	0	0	.500
Churchill, Norman, Wichita*	11	3	0	0	0	0	0	0	0	0	0	0	0	2	0	0	.000
Colbern, Michael, Iowa	57	214	29	56	97	15	1	8	43	1	0	15	0	47	0	1	.262
Combe, Geoffrey, Indianapolis	14	4	0	0	0	0	0	0	0	0	0	0	0	0	0	0	.000
Corbett, Douglas, Indianapolis	69	9	1	3	3	0	0	0	0	3	0	3	0	0	0	0	.333
Corcoran, Timothy, Evansville*	87	287	40	97	124	15	0	4	50	3	7	42	3	34	8	2	.338
Cox, James, Denver	117	429	56	131	191	20	2	12	77	2	6	28	1	48	0	2	.305
Cram, Gerald, Omaha	35	2	0	0	0	0	0	0	0	0	0	0	0	1	0	0	.000
Cripe, David, Omaha	131	479	66	119	167	26	2	6	46	10	4	57	5	58	8	2	.248
Crowley, Raymond, Denver*	33	88	13	21	33	4	1	2	14	2	1	22	0	10	2	0	.239
Cruz, Henry, Iowa*	120	416	64	117	198	18	6	17	79	2	5	49	5	60	10	4	.281
Cruz, Todd, Omaha	23	91	14	24	53	4	2	7	21	1	0	3	0	15	2	1	.264
Davidson, Randall, Indianapolis	88	212	22	43	55	7	1	1	14	4	2	15	2	18	7	1	.203
Davis, Steven, Wichita	134	500	73	133	201	20	3	14	68	3	4	58	2	73	10	6	.266
DeFreites, Arturo, Indianapolis	65	240	32	62	103	11	3	8	33	0	4	16	2	57	1	0	.258
DeJohn, Mark, Evansville†	112	337	36	77	92	7	1	2	30	18	1	35	5	41	2	2	.228
Delgado, Luis, 19 Wich-17 Om†	36	131	17	24	31	5	1	0	17	3	0	15	2	20	6	3	.183
DeMeo, Robert, Oklahoma City	1	3	0	0	0	0	0	0	0	0	0	0	0	0	0	0	.000
Detherage, Robert, Omaha	97	267	30	63	96	8	5	5	34	3	2	40	1	70	13	5	.236
Dimmel, Michael, Springfield	63	140	26	34	49	6	3	1	15	3	0	16	5	22	4	2	.243
Dineen, Kerry, Oklahoma City*	30	111	20	30	38	6	1	0	12	1	1	28	0	13	1	3	.270
Drury, Kevin, Wichita	61	167	14	37	48	7	2	0	15	0	2	16	1	18	0	2	.222
Dumoulin, Daniel, Indianapolis	18	9	0	0	0	0	0	0	1	4	0	3	0	9	0	0	.000
Duncan, Taylor, Evansville	8	15	0	2	2	0	0	0	2	0	1	0	0	2	0	0	.133
Durham, Leon, Springfield*	127	449	84	139	249	33	4	23	88	0	2	65	4	61	16	4	.310
Duval, Dennis, Indianapolis*	117	294	31	60	71	9	1	0	21	1	0	25	0	55	8	4	.204
Easterly, James, Denver*	20	5	2	1	1	0	0	0	0	0	0	0	0	2	0	0	.200
Edelen, B. Joe, Springfield	15	6	2	2	2	3	1	0	0	0	0	1	0	3	0	0	.333
Enright, George, Omaha	35	107	10	28	36	6	1	0	9	5	0	8	3	17	2	1	.262
Etchandy, Curtis, Iowa	4	17	3	6	10	1	0	1	7	1	1	1	0	4	0	0	.353
Evers, William, Wichita	27	50	8	15	23	2	0	2	14	0	1	17	0	10	2	3	.300
Farkas, Ronald, Springfield	88	242	37	60	80	10	2	2	28	2	8	36	2	35	0	0	.248
Fiala, Neil, Springfield*	21	58	5	18	27	4	1	1	8	0	0	7	2	10	0	0	.310
Figueroa, Jesus, Wichita*	116	426	58	124	142	15	0	1	27	4	0	43	0	38	28	12	.291
Foley, Marvis, Iowa*	77	250	32	70	93	15	1	2	25	3	3	23	5	29	0	2	.280
Frazier, Frederic, Iowa	119	449	66	132	179	26	0	7	44	10	5	44	5	29	3	2	.294
Frazier, George, Springfield	24	2	0	0	0	0	0	0	0	0	0	0	0	1	0	0	.000
Freed, Roger, Springfield	45	126	16	28	53	1	0	8	23	0	1	32	0	25	0	0	.222
Fry, Jerry, Denver	20	44	4	10	16	1	1	1	3	0	0	2	0	13	0	0	.227
Fulgham, John, Springfield	11	7	0	3	3	0	0	0	0	3	0	1	0	4	0	0	.429
Gardner, Arthur, Denver*	124	481	80	134	212	23	11	11	74	3	8	29	5	54	26	16	.279
Gates, Eddie, Denver	19	59	8	13	19	3	0	1	8	1	0	10	3	13	0	0	.220
Gates, Joseph, Iowa*	64	215	25	55	72	9	1	2	24	3	1	19	2	36	9	7	.256
Gaudet, James, Omaha	109	371	33	97	130	13	1	6	33	7	0	24	4	40	3	6	.261
Geisel, J. David, Wichita*	45	7	0	1	1	0	0	0	0	0	0	0	0	5	0	0	.143
Gibson, Kirk, Evansville*	89	327	50	80	130	13	5	9	42	1	1	34	6	110	20	2	.245
Gillen, Kevin, Omaha*	101	322	41	79	115	18	3	4	38	3	3	36	1	32	1	3	.245
Goldetsky, Lawrence, Denver	6	14	1	3	3	0	0	0	0	1	0	0	0	6	0	0	.214
Gonzales, Daniel, Evansville*	40	151	23	51	69	10	1	2	20	0	0	13	1	14	2	5	.338
Gonzalez, Orlando, Okla City*	125	480	87	150	211	29	7	6	76	7	3	65	1	44	16	2	.313
Gordon, Michael, Wichita†	100	303	45	70	134	12	2	16	51	4	4	60	0	76	1	1	.231
Gorinski, Robert, Wichita	41	124	11	27	46	2	1	5	15	0	0	21	0	27	1	0	.218

Player and Club	G.	AB.	R.	H.	TB.	2B.	3B.	HR.	RBI.	SH.	SF.	BB.	HP.	SO.	SB.	CS.	Pct.
Grace, Michael, Indianapolis	125	409	54	112	167	19	6	8	42	3	2	54	0	78	8	5	.274
Granger, Wayne, Denver	24	1	0	0	0	0	0	0	0	0	0	0	0	0	0	0	.000
Greene, Altar, Evansville*	83	292	52	80	148	19	2	15	65	0	3	54	4	51	4	1	.274
Gullickson, William, Denver	14	8	2	5	6	1	0	0	5	0	0	0	0	1	0	0	.625
Gulliver, Glenn, Evansville*	43	123	15	19	38	7	0	4	12	2	1	28	1	21	4	3	.154
Hall, Larry, Iowa*	6	16	1	4	5	1	0	0	3	0	0	1	0	1	0	0	.250
Hemm, K. Warren, Denver*	11	1	0	0	0	0	0	0	0	0	0	0	0	1	0	0	.000
Hernandez, Joseph, Wichita	110	328	43	76	114	17	3	5	30	6	2	23	0	45	5	4	.232
Herr, Thomas, Springfield†	109	423	74	124	174	20	6	6	48	4	6	54	4	51	29	10	.293
Holle, Gary, Iowa	39	121	17	33	51	3	3	3	14	2	1	10	2	18	4	1	.273
Howell, Jay, Indianapolis	24	42	2	9	9	0	0	0	3	3	0	1	0	8	0	0	.214
Hoyt, Dewey, Iowa	9	1	0	0	0	0	0	0	0	0	0	0	1	0	0	0	.000
Hunsaker, Frank, Springfield	38	115	11	38	44	6	0	0	20	1	3	12	0	10	1	0	.330
Hurdle, Clinton, Omaha*	68	220	30	52	83	13	0	6	29	0	1	49	2	42	2	4	.236
Ireland, Timothy, Omaha	109	370	53	97	130	16	1	5	33	13	1	58	7	42	23	9	.262
Isales, Orlando, Oklahoma City	95	303	45	83	125	17	8	3	35	1	3	15	0	54	9	3	.274
James, Arthur, Iowa*	16	46	11	10	14	1	0	1	2	0	0	7	0	4	2	3	.217
James, Robert, Denver	28	19	1	3	4	1	0	0	3	1	0	2	0	8	0	0	.158
Javier, I. Alfredo, Wichita	71	267	36	80	108	13	0	5	41	0	5	8	8	32	7	1	.300
Keatley, Gregory, Wichita	46	162	18	41	69	9	2	5	24	0	0	12	0	37	0	0	.253
Kennedy, Terrence, Springfield*	84	294	35	86	145	18	1	13	64	0	2	32	1	52	0	1	.293
Kimm, Bruce, Evansville	113	382	63	108	158	18	1	10	75	3	6	57	4	46	8	8	.283
Kinard, Rudolph, Omaha	114	355	26	58	72	8	3	0	26	19	2	26	0	44	7	0	.163
Krug, Gary, Wichita†	87	314	37	82	120	15	1	7	39	2	3	12	2	31	1	1	.261
Kuntz, Russell, Iowa	122	394	67	116	198	27	5	15	57	8	3	56	2	111	4	4	.294
Kurosaki, Ryan, Springfield	37	1	0	0	0	0	0	0	0	0	0	2	0	1	0	0	.000
Kusnyer, Arthur, Iowa	48	123	15	25	35	4	0	2	10	0	1	11	1	24	0	0	.203
Landreth, Larry, Denver	13	9	0	0	0	0	0	0	0	1	0	1	0	6	0	0	.000
Landrum, Terry, Springfield	61	193	28	50	80	8	2	6	34	2	4	14	6	35	8	3	.259
Lanier, Harold, Springfield	1	2	0	1	1	0	0	0	0	0	0	0	0	0	0	0	.500
Larson, Daniel, Oklahoma City	24	7	1	1	2	1	0	0	0	0	0	1	0	3	0	0	.143
Leibrandt, Charles, Indianapolis	27	49	3	6	9	0	0	1	3	2	0	5	0	26	0	0	.122
Lentine, James, Springfield	106	383	73	109	173	19	0	15	62	3	3	56	9	39	18	3	.285
Lis, Joseph, Evansville	118	418	71	122	186	16	0	16	80	1	7	60	7	69	1	3	.292
Littlefield, John, Springfield	29	1	0	0	0	0	0	0	0	0	0	0	0	0	0	0	.000
Lyle, Donald, Indianapolis	114	390	41	100	169	16	1	17	62	0	4	46	3	81	7	5	.256
Macha, Kenneth, Denver	31	102	12	27	31	1	0	1	10	1	5	14	1	9	5	0	.265
Machemer, David, Evansville	8	30	2	6	8	0	1	0	1	2	0	6	0	3	1	0	.200
Macko, Steven, Wichita	119	426	56	104	151	27	1	6	44	5	3	46	4	55	13	5	.244
Manos, Peter, Oklahoma City	29	1	0	1	1	0	0	0	2	0	0	0	0	0	0	0	1.000
Manuel, Jerry, Evansville†	130	460	71	116	175	26	3	9	75	6	7	67	5	67	8	5	.252
Martinez, Jose, Oklahoma City	22	1	1	0	0	0	0	0	0	1	0	2	0	1	0	0	.000
Martz, Randy, Wichita*	30	13	2	4	5	1	0	0	1	1	0	6	0	7	0	0	.308
Matuszek, Leonard, Okla. City*	72	228	31	60	87	9	3	4	31	2	3	29	1	35	2	6	.263
May, Davis, Indianapolis	11	14	2	4	4	0	0	0	0	1	0	1	0	3	0	0	.286
McCormack, Donald, Okla. City	115	384	45	100	133	18	3	3	55	2	3	36	3	73	4	0	.260
McEnaney, William, Springfield*	7	1	0	0	0	0	0	0	0	0	0	0	0	0	0	0	.000
Mejias, Samuel, Indianapolis	47	178	21	50	79	15	1	4	25	5	0	18	0	26	5	2	.281
Meoli, Rudolph, Oklahoma City*	20	62	14	15	24	6	0	1	10	1	0	15	0	8	2	1	.242
Miller, Randall, Denver	26	10	0	0	0	0	0	0	0	0	0	1	0	5	0	0	.000
Milner, Eddie, Indianapolis*	30	98	9	18	22	0	2	0	5	1	1	8	1	15	2	1	.184
Molinaro, Robert, Iowa*	133	475	90	156	228	23	5	13	93	0	9	81	3	26	50	12	.328
Moore, David, Indianapolis	30	49	4	10	11	1	0	0	8	2	0	4	0	23	0	1	.204
Moreland, B. Keith, Okla. City	130	494	86	149	249	34	3	20	109	3	13	64	4	56	2	1	.302
Mork, Dennis, Wichita*	7	22	1	9	11	2	0	0	4	0	0	5	0	5	0	1	.409
Morrison, James, Oklahoma City	79	281	59	90	171	15	0	22	61	0	8	40	4	46	10	4	.320
Moskau, Paul, Indianapolis	4	1	2	0	0	0	0	0	0	0	0	2	0	1	0	0	.000
Mutz, Thomas, Indianapolis*	97	253	28	57	86	9	1	6	29	1	3	36	2	45	1	3	.225
Naehring, Mark, Iowa	2	4	0	1	1	0	0	0	0	0	0	2	0	2	0	0	.250
Nettles, James, Omaha*	133	477	65	122	212	31	4	17	86	0	4	83	2	78	14	8	.256
Nyman, Christopher, Iowa	39	98	15	18	32	5	0	3	13	1	1	19	1	17	3	1	.184
Nyman, Nyls, Indianapolis*	44	143	14	27	42	6	0	3	11	1	0	11	0	18	2	1	.189
O'Brien, Daniel, Springfield	22	12	1	5	5	0	0	0	1	1	0	3	0	2	0	0	.417
Oester, Ronald, Indianapolis†	136	509	62	143	180	19	6	2	33	7	2	48	4	60	23	8	.281
O'Neill, Paul, Indianapolis	32	109	11	27	49	4	0	6	18	0	0	6	2	16	0	0	.248
Otten, James, Springfield	33	2	1	1	2	1	0	0	0	0	0	0	0	0	0	0	.500
Pagel, Karl, Wichita*	136	472	96	149	291	25	0	39	123	1	1	100	1	109	10	3	.316
Parker, Darrell, Omaha	24	84	14	19	26	2	1	1	6	1	2	4	0	16	2	1	.226
Pastore, Frank, Indianapolis	10	21	0	2	2	0	0	0	2	0	0	2	0	10	0	0	.095
Patchin, Steven, Evansville	81	247	28	54	87	7	1	8	44	2	0	29	0	50	0	3	.219
Pate, Robert, Denver	118	428	85	147	220	26	1	15	63	2	4	60	3	47	13	6	.343
Penniall, David, Springfield	52	156	16	34	47	5	1	2	19	4	1	14	1	28	1	1	.218
Perkins, Craig, Denver*	17	30	2	3	4	1	0	0	2	0	0	5	1	5	0	0	.100
Peters, Richard, Evansville†	107	387	88	124	170	17	10	3	42	4	3	76	6	34	30	13	.320
Pettini, Joseph, Denver	132	446	70	131	176	21	6	4	46	14	2	58	4	65	11	7	.294

Player and Club	G.	AB.	R.	H.	TB.	2B.	3B.	HR.	RBI.	SH.	SF.	BB.	HP.	SO.	SB.	CS.	Pct.
Phelps, Kenneth, Omaha*	130	430	71	114	206	26	3	20	77	1	3	98	6	72	4	4	.265
Poff, John, Oklahoma City*	132	481	77	141	245	34	5	20	90	4	3	76	4	79	4	4	.293
Putman, Eddy, Evansville	32	104	20	28	52	3	0	7	18	0	0	21	2	25	4	0	.269
Ramos, Roberto, Denver	8	11	0	2	2	0	0	0	2	1	0	0	1	2	0	0	.182
Ramsey, Michael, Springfield†	97	281	28	62	80	9	3	1	27	11	3	19	0	41	11	5	.221
Ratzer, Steven, Denver	42	15	1	2	2	0	0	0	1	0	0	0	6	0	0	.133
Reece, Robert, Denver	91	256	34	58	77	7	0	4	34	7	0	24	1	30	2	0	.227
Riggleman, James, Springfield	35	93	9	22	32	4	0	2	9	0	0	5	2	26	3	1	.237
Riley, George, Wichita*	38	3	0	1	1	0	0	0	0	2	0	2	0	1	0	0	.333
Robinson, Dewey, Iowa	49	1	0	0	0	0	0	0	0	0	0	0	0	0	0	0	.000
Rodriguez, Luis, Oklahoma City	13	53	2	12	18	4	1	0	4	0	0	1	0	7	0	1	.226
Rogers, Charles, Wichita*	27	13	4	4	10	0	0	2	2	3	0	3	0	7	0	0	.308
Rothschild, Lawrence, Ind*	38	28	3	10	14	4	0	0	2	4	1	2	0	5	0	0	.357
Ruling, Stephen, Oklahoma City†	11	2	0	0	0	0	0	0	0	1	0	0	0	1	0	0	.000
Sanchez, Orlando, Oklahoma City*	31	92	14	27	39	5	2	1	9	2	2	4	2	20	1	0	.293
Sarmiento, Manuel, Indianapolis	19	5	0	0	0	0	0	0	0	1	0	0	0	2	0	0	.000
Saucier, Kevin, Oklahoma City*	24	2	1	0	0	0	0	0	0	0	0	0	0	1	0	0	.000
Scanlon, J. Patrick, Denver*	103	307	35	84	115	19	3	2	45	2	3	52	1	47	1	5	.274
Seaman, Kim, Springfield*	33	11	0	0	0	0	0	0	0	0	0	0	4	0	0	.000
Seibert, Kurt, Wichita†	129	420	65	102	134	14	3	4	36	7	4	85	3	54	10	11	.243
Semall, Paul, Wichita	13	13	2	2	4	0	1	0	2	0	0	1	0	2	0	0	.154
Seoane, Manuel, Wichita	22	8	0	2	4	0	1	0	0	0	0	0	0	5	0	0	.250
Sherow, Dennis, Denver	55	159	32	48	63	9	3	0	13	0	1	12	0	34	11	1	.302
Smith, Keith, Springfield	119	448	77	157	209	17	4	9	61	1	3	21	0	28	30	11	.350
Smith, Lonnie, Oklahoma City	110	451	106	149	214	26	9	7	44	2	1	56	4	52	34	11	.330
Soto, Mario, Indianapolis	15	1	0	0	0	0	0	0	0	1	0	0	0	0	0	0	.000
Spilman, Harry, Indianapolis*	71	267	42	77	105	13	3	3	27	1	1	37	0	29	12	2	.288
Staggs, Stephen, Denver	56	155	28	35	57	10	3	2	12	8	2	27	0	21	8	0	.226
Stegman, David, Evansville	133	506	95	153	223	33	2	11	60	5	2	81	2	83	17	3	.302
Stricklen, Don, Wichita	5	15	1	4	4	0	0	0	0	0	1	0	3	0	0	.267
Tamargo, John, Denver†	53	187	35	60	87	11	2	4	29	1	0	23	1	9	0	2	.321
Terlecky, Gregory, Springfield	20	14	3	3	3	0	0	0	3	1	0	1	0	2	0	0	.214
Thomas, Roy, Springfield	17	3	0	1	1	0	0	0	0	0	0	0	1	0	0	.333
Thompson, Michael, Wichita	11	38	10	11	11	0	0	0	3	0	1	5	0	4	1	0	.289
Torrealba, Pablo, Iowa*	22	1	0	1	1	0	0	0	1	0	0	0	0	0	0	1.000
Torres, Angel, Indianapolis*	20	10	0	1	1	0	0	0	1	2	0	0	0	3	0	0	.100
Torres, Raymundo, Iowa	4	14	2	5	7	2	0	0	0	0	0	0	2	0	0	.357
Tracy, James, Wichita*	44	150	26	41	64	9	1	4	18	0	4	21	2	36	0	2	.273
Urrea, John, Springfield	20	6	1	1	1	0	0	0	1	0	2	0	0	0	0	.167
Valentini, Vincent, Wichita	22	15	0	4	6	0	1	0	1	2	0	1	0	7	0	0	.267
Valle, John, Indianapolis	127	408	65	96	189	20	2	23	71	0	3	50	1	85	9	0	.235
Vukovich, John, Oklahoma City	101	382	38	111	169	20	1	12	66	4	6	22	1	56	2	3	.291
Werner, Donald, Indianapolis	99	260	35	66	111	18	3	7	36	3	3	41	5	52	1	4	.254
Wilkerson, Byron, Wichita†	53	4	0	0	0	0	0	0	0	0	0	0	0	2	0	0	.000
Willoughby, James, Wichita†	22	1	0	0	0	0	0	0	0	0	0	0	0	0	0	0	.000
Wolf, Michael 92 Iowa-12 Ok Cy	104	311	30	67	71	2	1	0	30	6	3	27	2	30	4	4	.215
Woodard, Darrell, Wichita†	12	44	5	13	14	1	0	0	2	0	0	7	1	11	4	0	.295
Zdeb, Joseph, Omaha	73	241	25	54	72	7	1	3	26	1	1	37	1	36	5	2	.224

The following pitchers had no plate appearances primarily through use of designated-hitters, listed alphabetically by club, games in parentheses.

DENVER—Dues, Hal (5); Finlayson, Michael (7); Horn, Larry (4); Keener, Joseph (1); Miller, Dyar (15); Siebert, Paul (17).

EVANSVILLE—Arroyo, Fernando (19); Baker, Steven (5); Blair, Theodore (4); Chris, Michael (19); Cornejo, N. Mardie (31); Corr, Larry (12); Graft, Garry (7); Holdsworth, Frederick (23); Martin, John (37); Morris, John (5); Petry, Daniel (15); Rucker, David (2); Shea, Kenneth (2); Steffen, David (19); Taylor, Bruce (18); Tobik, David (19); Treual, Ralph (23); Underwood, Patrick (7); Weaver, Roger (29); Young, Kip (12).

IOWA—Allen, Lloyd (28); Barnes, Richard (3); Burns, R. Britt (7); Contreras, Arnaldo (20); Douglass, Bobby (4); Esser, Mark (43); Evans, Randy (8); Guzman, Luis (3); Hinton, Richard (6); Hoffman, Guy (14); Howard, Fred (7); Johnson, C. Barth (8); Lukevics, Mitchell (18); Moran, C. William (5); Murillo, Ramon (22); Pazik, Michael (2); Rondon, Gilbert (1); Sutton, Johnny (40); Trout, Steven (4).

OKLAHOMA CITY—Arroyo, Carlos (38); Camper, Cardell (2); Fowler, Don (19); Kucek, John (34); Noles, Dickie (13).

OMAHA—Cvejdlik, Kent (17); Daly, Mark (25); Eaton, Craig (26); Hamrick, Stephen (5); Martin, D. Renie (33); McGilberry, Randall (23); Morley, Michael (10); Paschall, William (18); Quisenberry, Daniel (26).

SPRINGFIELD—Edurado, Hector (6); Hamende, Joseph (3); Sykes, Robert (4).

WICHITA—Caudill, William (6); Gault, Raymond (4); Harris, William (3); Moore, Donnie (5); Parker, Mark (2).

GRAND SLAM HOME RUNS—Lentine, Moreland, Patchin, 2 each; Carrion, Colbern, H. Cruz, Detherage, Durham, J. Gates, Greene, Kimm, Landrum, Lis, McCormack, Molinaro, Pagel, Phelps, Poff, Reece, Vukovich.

AWARDED FIRST BASE ON INTERFERENCE—Siebert 2 (Brummer, Macha), Aviles (Ramos), Herr (Mutz), Gorinski (Mutz), Krug (Brummer), Valle (Foley), Vukovich (Gordon), Wolf (Mutz).

CLUB FIELDING

Club	G.	PO.	A.	E.	DP.	PB.	Pct.	Club	G.	PO.	A.	E.	DP.	PB.	Pct.
Wichita	136	3440	1550	116	150	7	.977	Evansville	136	3514	1593	156	107	11	.970
Omaha	136	3494	1447	134	126	9	.974	Iowa	136	3493	1480	156	141	4	.970
Indianapolis	136	3472	1444	140	118	9	.972	Denver	135	3398	1507	171	128	9	.966
Springfield	136	3473	1347	146	125	16	.971	Oklahoma City	135	3475	1453	184	103	17	.964

Triple Play—Indianapolis.

INDIVIDUAL FIELDING

*Throws lefthanded.

FIRST BASEMEN

Player and Club	G.	PO.	A.	E.	DP.	Pct.	Player and Club	G.	PO.	A.	E.	DP.	Pct.
Crowley, Denver*	17	121	13	0	6	1.000	Lis, Evansville	112	1026	62	12	76	.989
Corcoran, Evansville*	29	200	15	1	17	.995	H. Cruz, Iowa*	72	564	42	7	48	.989
Holle, Iowa	39	298	20	2	30	.994	C. Nyman, Iowa	39	255	18	3	28	.989
Durham, Springfield*	30	161	15	1	13	.994	Freed, Springfield	10	84	6	1	6	.989
BASS, Denver	100	885	92	7	91	.993	Poff, Oklahoma City*	90	734	68	10	57	.988
Pagel, Wichita*	19	138	5	1	13	.993	DeFreites, Indianapolis	65	538	45	7	49	.988
Krug, Wichita*	84	744	74	7	85	.992	Alberts, Indianapolis	47	378	35	5	24	.988
Spilman, Indianapolis	15	109	8	1	13	.992	Scanlon, Denver	22	158	20	3	15	.983
Bialas, Springfield	109	880	81	9	92	.991	Matuszek, Okla. City	54	412	39	9	31	.980
Foley, Iowa	12	103	3	1	15	.991	Tracy, Wichita	42	363	20	11	46	.972
Phelps, Omaha*	128	1129	80	13	111	.989							

Triple Play—DeFreites.

(Fewer Than Ten Games)

Player and Club	G.	PO.	A.	E.	DP.	Pct.	Player and Club	G.	PO.	A.	E.	DP.	Pct.
Werner, Indianapolis	9	53	8	0	6	1.000	Farkas, Springfield	1	1	0	0	0	1.000
O. Gonzalez, Okla City*	3	26	1	0	1	1.000	Macha, Denver	1	1	0	0	0	1.000
Riggleman, Springfield	3	17	2	0	3	1.000	Perkins, Denver	1	1	0	0	0	1.000
Davidson, Indianapolis	2	15	1	0	2	1.000	Nettles, Omaha*	9	62	10	1	3	.986
N. Nyman, Indapolis*	4	10	2	0	0	1.000	Patchin, Evansville	9	63	4	2	5	.971
Cox, Denver	1	7	3	0	0	1.000	Valle, Indianapolis	8	69	2	3	5	.959
Kusnyer, Iowa	1	6	0	0	0	1.000	Duncan, Evansville	2	11	0	1	1	.917
Evers, Wichita	2	4	0	0	0	1.000	Fry, Denver	3	8	1	1	2	.900
Staggs, Denver	1	3	0	0	0	1.000	Vukovich, Okla City	1	3	2	1	1	.833

SECOND BASEMEN

Player and Club	G.	PO.	A.	E.	DP.	Pct.	Player and Club	G.	PO.	A.	E.	DP.	Pct.
Fiala, Springfield	21	41	44	1	7	.988	Aviles, Okla City	57	116	170	9	29	.969
Woodard, Wichita	12	29	40	1	21	.986	Davidson, Indianapolis	66	110	171	9	29	.969
Macko, Wichita	50	129	142	4	35	.985	F. Frazier, Iowa	113	240	306	18	85	.968
HERR, Springfield	107	225	324	10	70	.982	Ireland, Omaha	98	225	273	19	68	.963
K. Seibert, Wichita	50	136	144	5	37	.982	Brookens, Evansville	20	33	67	4	13	.962
Barranca, Omaha	33	66	86	3	16	.981	Cox, Denver	21	30	44	3	13	.961
Manuel, Evansville	105	234	363	14	62	.977	Bernazard, Denver	79	178	275	19	59	.960
Drury, Wichita	32	78	89	4	21	.977	Peters, Evansville	17	27	45	3	5	.960
J. Gates, Iowa	19	38	48	2	12	.977	Staggs, Denver	44	84	91	8	19	.956
Morrison, Okla City	61	118	194	9	36	.972	Kinard, Omaha	13	29	35	3	10	.955
Manny Castillo, Sprgfd	17	26	40	2	7	.971	Aguayo, Okla City	18	45	46	5	8	.948
Grace, Indianapolis	90	154	239	12	39	.970							

Triple Play—Grace.

(Fewer Than Ten Games)

Player and Club	G.	PO.	A.	E.	DP.	Pct.	Player and Club	G.	PO.	A.	E.	DP.	Pct.
Davis, Iowa	3	4	8	0	1	1.000	Goldetsky, Denver	5	13	12	1	4	.962
Scanlon, Denver	3	8	4	0	0	1.000	Machemer, Evansville	3	4	6	1	1	.909
DeJohn, Evansville	1	3	1	0	0	1.000	Hall, Iowa	6	6	10	2	2	.889
Farkas, Springfield	1	0	1	0	1	1.000	Ramsey, Springfield	1	3	0	1	0	.750
Wolf, Iowa	7	10	19	1	2	.967							

THIRD BASEMEN

Player and Club	G.	PO.	A.	E.	DP.	Pct.	Player and Club	G.	PO.	A.	E.	DP.	Pct.
J. Gates, Iowa	44	29	85	2	7	.983	Bernhardt, Iowa	18	14	33	3	1	.940
K. Seibert, Wichita	65	51	125	5	16	.972	Cox, Denver	93	62	149	15	11	.934
Marty Castillo, Evan	31	27	66	3	7	.969	Rodriguez, Okla City	12	10	16	2	2	.929
Matuszek, Okla City	12	9	16	1	1	.962	Riggleman, Springfield	13	9	16	2	5	.926
Thompson, Wichita	10	2	23	1	2	.962	Brookens, Evansville	51	38	99	12	4	.919
VUKOVICH, Okla City	99	81	181	11	10	.960	Farkas, Springfield	25	12	21	3	2	.917
Davis, Wichita	64	43	148	8	15	.960	Bell, Iowa	55	39	137	18	11	.907
Cripe, Omaha	131	113	256	19	19	.951	Alberts, Indianapolis	17	12	15	3	1	.900
Gulliver, Evansville	29	24	52	4	4	.950	Wolf, Iowa	23	20	23	5	5	.896
Spilman, Indianapolis	60	45	84	7	8	.949	O'Neill, Indianapolis	32	17	59	10	3	.884
Grace, Indianapolis	43	23	50	4	7	.948	Morrison, Okla City	15	11	32	8	2	.843
Manny Castillo, Spngf.	118	94	191	18	11	.941	Putman, Evansville	25	17	52	13	5	.841
Scanlon, Denver	48	24	72	6	8	.941							

THIRD BASEMEN—Continued

(Fewer Than Ten Games)

Player and Club	G.	PO.	A.	E.	DP.	Pct.	Player and Club	G.	PO.	A.	E.	DP.	Pct.
Foley, Iowa	7	5	14	0	5	1.000	Ireland, Omaha	6	6	16	1	3	.957
Machemer, Evansville	5	4	7	0	3	1.000	Peters, Evansville	5	4	11	1	2	.938
DeJohn, Evansville	2	2	7	0	0	1.000	Macha, Denver	7	8	6	2	1	.875
Staggs, Denver	1	1	3	0	1	1.000	Stricklen, Wichita	4	1	3	1	0	.800
Lis, Evansville	1	1	1	0	0	1.000	Pettini, Denver	1	1	2	1	0	.750
Etchandy, Iowa	2	0	2	0	0	1.000	Drury, Wichita	3	1	5	3	1	.667
Moreland, Okla City	1	0	2	0	0	1.000							

SHORTSTOPS

Player and Club	G.	PO.	A.	E.	DP.	Pct.	Player and Club	G.	PO.	A.	E.	DP.	Pct.
Davis, Wichita	70	109	224	11	48	.968	Wolf, Iowa-Okla City	61	127	200	17	41	.951
T. Cruz, Omaha	23	47	86	5	19	.964	Aguayo, Okla City	91	146	274	22	49	.950
Macko, Wichita	74	118	210	13	52	.962	Pettini, Denver	131	198	413	33	87	.949
DeJOHN, Evansville	109	161	298	19	50	.960	Farkas, Springfield	61	95	147	15	37	.942
Kinard, Omaha	101	157	266	19	57	.957	Ramsey, Springfield	88	134	198	24	50	.933
Barranca, Omaha	14	13	29	2	2	.955	Manuel, Evansville	32	31	71	8	9	.927
Oester, Indianapolis	136	244	397	31	81	.954	Meoli, Okla City	20	32	55	7	6	.926
Chappas, Iowa	75	134	222	17	47	.954	Aviles, Okla City	15	26	32	7	5	.892

Triple Play—Oester.

(Fewer Than Ten Games)

Player and Club	G.	PO.	A.	E.	DP.	Pct.	Player and Club	G.	PO.	A.	E.	DP.	Pct.
Ireland, Omaha	3	2	10	0	1	1.000	Grace, Indianapolis	1	2	1	0	0	1.000
K. Seibert, Wichita	2	5	7	0	2	1.000	Bernhardt, Iowa	1	0	2	0	0	1.000
Cox, Denver	3	5	2	0	0	1.000	Staggs, Denver	6	7	10	1	1	.944
F. Frazier, Iowa	5	2	3	0	0	1.000	Etchandy, Iowa	3	6	11	1	3	.944
Lanier, Springfield	1	3	1	0	0	1.000	Gulliver, Evansville	8	9	17	2	1	.929
Rodriguez, Okla City	1	2	2	0	1	1.000	Machemer, Evansville	1	0	4	1	1	.800

CATCHERS

Player and Club	G.	PO.	A.	E.	DP.	PB.	Pct.	Player and Club	G.	PO.	A.	E.	DP.	PB.	Pct.
Hunsaker, Springfield	36	161	15	1	5	5	.994	Enright, Omaha	35	131	15	3	4	3	.980
Keatley, Wichita	36	174	23	2	0	1	.990	Kimm, Evansville	103	545	73	13	7	9	.979
GORDON, Wichita	88	389	50	5	3	6	.989	Foley, Iowa	59	284	37	7	3	1	.979
Patchin, Evansville	29	155	19	2	1	2	.989	Werner, Indianapolis	71	422	49	12	3	9	.975
Tamargo, Denver	42	208	28	3	3	2	.987	Gaudet, Omaha	105	474	51	14	6	6	.974
Evers, Wichita	19	63	11	1	0	0	.987	Kennedy, Springfield	74	434	38	13	3	10	.973
Kusnyer, Iowa	43	188	28	3	8	1	.986	Mutz, Indianapolis	74	443	48	14	8	5	.972
Colbern, Iowa	53	260	32	5	5	2	.983	Moreland, Okla City	66	397	42	13	5	11	.971
Brummer, Springfield	41	196	12	4	2	1	.981	McCormack, Ok City	72	347	32	13	2	6	.967
Reece, Denver	83	443	50	10	4	5	.980	Macha, Denver	13	74	10	6	3	1	.933

(Fewer Than Ten Games)

Player and Club	G.	PO.	A.	E.	DP.	PB.	Pct.	Player and Club	G.	PO.	A.	E.	DP.	PB.	Pct.
Putman, Evansville	5	30	1	0	1	0	1.000	Fry, Denver	2	3	0	0	0	0	1.000
DeMeo, Okla City	1	6	4	0	0	1	1.000	Bialas, Springfield	1	1	1	0	0	0	1.000
Perkins, Denver	8	6	2	0	1	0	1.000	Ramos, Denver	8	14	3	1	0	1	.944
Freed, Springfield	1	6	0	0	0	0	1.000								

OUTFIELDERS

Player and Club	G.	PO.	A.	E.	DP.	Pct.	Player and Club	G.	PO.	A.	E.	DP.	Pct.
Gillen, Omaha	81	132	7	0	0	1.000	Pagel, Wichita*	99	132	9	3	2	.979
Mejias, Indianapolis	46	112	4	0	0	1.000	K. Smith, Springfield	75	135	3	3	0	.979
D. Gonzales, Evansville	33	44	3	0	1	1.000	Nettles, Omaha*	109	253	6	6	1	.977
Arline, Indianapolis*	13	29	0	0	0	1.000	Poff, Oklahoma City*	53	80	1	2	1	.976
Gorinski, Wichita	11	12	0	0	0	1.000	O. Gonzalez, Okla City*	129	232	5	6	1	.975
K. Seibert, Wichita	13	9	1	0	1	1.000	Molinaro, Iowa	42	65	10	2	0	.974
HERNANDEZ, Wichita	106	237	5	2	1	.992	Valle, Indianapolis	111	164	9	5	2	.972
Corcoran, Evansville*	59	92	8	1	1	.990	Hurdle, Omaha	66	124	14	4	4	.972
Delgado, Wich-Oma*	34	92	1	1	1	.989	Zdeb, Omaha	69	134	1	4	0	.971
Duval, Indianapolis	96	145	12	2	4	.987	Javier, Wichita	71	131	3	4	1	.971
Stegman, Evansville	133	322	12	5	0	.985	Sherow, Denver	46	65	3	2	0	.971
Detherage, Omaha	93	248	11	4	1	.985	Brown, Evansville	20	33	0	1	0	.970
Landrum, Springfield	60	126	5	2	2	.985	Peters, Evansville	79	120	6	4	2	.969
Figueroa, Wichita*	113	211	14	4	1	.983	Durham, Springfield*	98	143	4	5	2	.967
Kuntz, Iowa	118	287	12	5	3	.984	Bosley, Iowa*	78	140	6	5	0	.967
Lentine, Springfield	105	210	11	4	3	.982	Carrion, Denver	115	210	9	8	2	.965
Dimmel, Springfield	54	105	3	2	0	.982	Lyle, Indianapolis	108	183	11	7	3	.965
N. Nyman, Ind*	35	50	2	1	0	.981	Pate, Denver	114	177	10	7	1	.964

OUTFIELDERS—Continued

Player and Club	G.	PO.	A.	E.	DP.	Pct.
Sanchez, Oklahoma City	16	27	0	1	0	.964
Milner, Indianapolis*	25	49	2	2	0	.964
Gardner, Denver*	121	256	16	11	4	.961
L. Smith, Okla City	110	268	13	12	3	.959
Penniall, Springfield	42	67	3	3	0	.959
Baines, Iowa*	121	222	16	11	4	.956
Dineen, Oklahoma City*	30	55	3	3	0	.951
E. Gates, Denver	14	19	0	1	0	.950
H. Cruz, Iowa*	51	88	2	6	1	.938
Greene, Evansville	47	69	3	5	0	.935
Isales, Oklahoma City	85	169	6	13	0	.931
Gibson, Evansville*	65	100	5	9	1	.921

(Fewer Than Ten Games)

Player and Club	G.	PO.	A.	E.	DP.	Pct.
Anderson, Okla City	9	29	1	0	0	1.000
Bialas, Springfield	5	13	1	0	0	1.000
Grace, Indianapolis	4	11	1	0	0	1.000
Crowley, Denver*	5	9	2	0	0	1.000
Macha, Denver	7	9	1	0	0	1.000
Mork, Wichita*	7	9	1	0	0	1.000
A. James, Iowa*	8	8	0	0	0	1.000
D. Parker, Omaha	5	7	0	0	0	1.000
Bowling, Indianapolis	2	5	0	0	0	1.000
Colbern, Iowa	3	2	1	0	0	1.000
Kimm, Evansville	1	3	0	0	0	1.000
Scanlon, Denver	3	2	0	0	0	1.000
Alberts, Indianapolis	4	1	0	0	0	1.000
Machemer, Evansville	2	1	0	0	0	1.000
Tracy, Wichita	1	1	0	0	0	1.000
Werner, Indianapolis	1	1	0	0	0	1.000
Riggleman, Springfield	6	14	0	1	0	.933
Ramsey, Omaha	4	3	0	1	0	.750
R. Torres, Iowa	4	1	0	1	0	.500

PITCHERS

Player and Club	G.	PO.	A.	E.	DP.	Pct.
LEIBRANDT, Indpls*	27	16	41	0	1	1.000
Howell, Indianapolis	24	11	26	0	2	1.000
Petry, Evansville	15	7	24	0	1	1.000
Angelini, Denver*	48	8	17	0	1	1.000
Paschall, Omaha	18	10	13	0	1	1.000
Edelen, Springfield	13	8	15	0	1	1.000
Cornejo, Evansville	31	7	14	0	1	1.000
Cvejdlik, Omaha	17	8	12	0	1	1.000
Martinez, Okla City	21	7	12	0	1	1.000
Lukevics, Iowa	18	5	14	0	1	1.000
Saucier, Okla City*	24	2	15	0	1	1.000
Dumoulin, Indpls	18	3	13	0	1	1.000
Wilkerson, Wichita	53	1	14	0	0	1.000
Geisel, Wichita*	45	6	9	0	0	1.000
Noles, Okla City	12	5	10	0	1	1.000
Rothschild, Indpls	33	4	10	0	0	1.000
Thomas, Springfield	17	4	9	0	0	1.000
Burnside, Indianapolis*	39	3	9	0	0	1.000
Littlefield, Springfield	29	3	9	0	1	1.000
Capilla, Springfield	28	2	10	0	0	1.000
Willoughby, Wichita	22	2	9	0	0	1.000
Altamirano, Okla City	21	3	8	0	1	1.000
Landreth, Denver	12	3	8	0	1	1.000
Morley, Omaha	10	3	7	0	0	1.000
Steffen, Evansville	19	2	7	0	0	1.000
Corr, Evansville	12	5	4	0	0	1.000
Churchill, Wichita*	11	1	8	0	0	1.000
Pastore, Indianapolis	10	2	7	0	1	1.000
Taylor, Evansville	18	3	4	0	0	1.000
Combe, Indianapolis	14	3	4	0	0	1.000
D. Miller, Denver	15	4	2	0	0	1.000
A. Torres, Indianapolis*	19	2	4	0	1	1.000
Fowler, Okla City	19	0	6	0	0	1.000
P. Siebert, Denver*	17	0	5	0	0	1.000
Cappuzzello, Indpls*	19	1	3	0	1	1.000
Soto, Indianapolis	15	0	3	0	0	1.000
Atkinson, Denver	36	26	28	1	1	.982
Eaton, Omaha	26	11	29	1	1	.976
Holdsworth, Evansville	23	12	22	1	1	.976
Berenyi, Indianapolis	25	13	24	1	0	.974
Daly, Omaha*	25	6	30	1	2	.973
Allen, Iowa	28	9	21	1	0	.968
Corbett, Indianapolis	69	4	24	1	1	.966
Easterly, Denver*	20	8	17	1	3	.962
Dave Moore, Indpls	28	10	14	1	1	.960
Chris, Evansville*	19	6	18	1	3	.960
Larson, Okla City	24	11	11	1	3	.957
Martz, Wichita	30	14	28	2	3	.955
F. Arroyo, Evansville	19	7	34	2	2	.953
Gullickson, Denver	11	11	9	1	2	.952
Cram, Omaha	34	6	13	1	1	.950
Ballinger, Omaha	28	13	24	2	2	.949
Murillo, Iowa	22	2	15	1	0	.944
Fulgham, Springfield	11	5	12	1	0	.944
O'Brien, Springfield	22	9	24	2	2	.943
Semall, Wichita	12	5	11	1	2	.941
G. Frazier, Springfield	24	4	11	1	0	.938
Hoffman, Iowa*	13	6	9	1	1	.938
Sutton, Iowa	40	10	34	3	5	.936
Christenson, Omaha*	51	5	24	2	1	.935
Weaver, Evansville	29	10	19	2	1	.935
Beare, Okla City	27	8	19	2	1	.931
Manos, Okla City	29	3	10	1	1	.929
Quisenberry, Omaha	26	4	9	1	2	.929
Chamberlain, Sprngfld	12	4	9	1	0	.929
Ratzer, Denver	40	18	32	4	6	.926
J. Martin, Evansville*	37	4	8	1	0	.923
Riley, Wichita*	38	2	10	1	0	.923
Kucek, Okla City	34	3	9	1	0	.923
Bystrom, Okla City	26	17	28	4	3	.918
Seaman, Springfield*	31	2	9	1	0	.917
Robinson, Iowa	49	7	14	2	1	.913
Treuel, Evansville	23	7	24	3	1	.912
Beene, Okla City	26	11	20	3	2	.912
Urrea, Springfield	20	12	18	3	1	.909
Valentini, Wichita	22	16	22	4	1	.905
McGilberry, Omaha	23	15	13	3	1	.903
Esser, Iowa*	43	5	4	1	0	.900
Young, Evansville	12	3	14	2	2	.895
Contreras, Iowa	20	6	10	2	0	.889
R. Martin, Omaha	33	5	11	2	2	.889
C. Arroyo, Okla City*	38	3	5	1	1	.889
Otten, Springfield	33	1	6	1	0	.875
May, Indianapolis	11	3	4	1	2	.875
Ruling, Okla City	11	3	10	2	0	.867
Kurosaki, Springfield	35	7	12	3	1	.864
Tobik, Evansville	19	2	4	1	0	.857
Terlecky, Springfield	20	5	11	3	0	.842
Rogers, Wichita	26	4	17	4	1	.840
B. James, Denver	26	9	16	5	0	.833
Campbell, Denver	42	1	4	1	0	.833
Sarmiento, Indianapolis	19	2	3	1	0	.833
Torrealba, Iowa*	22	1	8	2	0	.818
Seoane, Wichita	20	9	16	6	1	.806
R. Miller, Denver	26	11	13	6	0	.800
Bruno, Springfield	11	4	6	3	2	.769
Granger, Denver	24	0	3	1	0	.750
Hemm, Denver*	11	0	1	1	0	.500

PITCHERS—Continued

(Fewer Than Ten Games)

Player and Club	G.	PO.	A.	E.	DP.	Pct.
B. Johnson, Iowa	8	4	7	0	0	1.000
Underwood, Evansville*	7	2	9	0	0	1.000
Hamrick, Omaha	5	3	8	0	0	1.000
Donnie Moore, Wichita	5	4	4	0	1	1.000
McEnaney, Springfield*	7	1	6	0	1	1.000
Blair, Evansville*	4	1	6	0	0	1.000
Burns, Iowa*	7	2	4	0	0	1.000
Eduardo, Springfield	6	0	6	0	1	1.000
Moran, Iowa	5	3	3	0	1	1.000
Caudill, Wichita	6	2	2	0	0	1.000
Rondon, Iowa	4	1	3	0	0	1.000
Pazik, Iowa*	2	1	3	0	0	1.000
Finlayson, Omaha	6	0	3	0	0	1.000
Dues, Denver	5	1	2	0	0	1.000
Hinton, Iowa*	5	1	2	0	0	1.000
Harris, Wichita	3	0	3	0	0	1.000
Baker, Evansville	5	1	1	0	0	1.000
Sykes, Springfield*	4	1	1	0	0	1.000

Player and Club	G.	PO.	A.	E.	DP.	Pct.
M. Parker, Wichita	2	1	1	0	0	1.000
Shea, Evansville	2	1	1	0	0	1.000
Guzman, Iowa	3	1	1	0	0	1.000
Rucker, Evansville*	2	0	2	0	0	1.000
Douglass, Iowa*	4	1	0	0	0	1.000
Horn, Denver	4	0	1	0	0	1.000
Moskau, Indianapolis*	2	1	0	0	1	1.000
Camper, Okla City	2	0	1	0	0	1.000
Trout, Iowa*	4	0	10	1	3	.909
Evans, Iowa	8	2	7	1	2	.900
Hoyt, Iowa	9	1	7	1	0	.889
Howard, Iowa	7	2	9	2	0	.846
Barnes, Iowa*	3	0	5	1	0	.833
Morris, Evasville	5	1	3	1	0	.800
Botehlo, Wichita	4	2	1	1	0	.750
Grafton, Evansville	7	0	1	1	0	.500
Keener, Denver	1	0	0	1	0	.000

The following players do not have any recorded accepted chances at the positions indicated; therefore, are not listed in the fielding averages for those particular positions: Barranca, 1b; Bass, of; Bialas, 3b; Carrion, 3b; E. M. Castillo, of-ss; Davidson, of; Duncan, of; Fry, of; Gault, p; Hamende*, p; Keatley, of; Kimm, 3b; Kusyner, p; Moreland, of; Morrison, of; C. Nyman, 2b; Patchin, 3b-p; Spilman, of; Torrealba*, 1b; Werner, 3b. Naehring appeared as pinch-hitter/designated-hitter only.

CLUB PITCHING

Club	G.	CG.	ShO.	Sv.	IP.	H.	R.	ER.	HR.	BB.	Int. BB.	HB.	SO.	WP.	Bk.	ERA.
Indianapolis	136	25	11	30	1157	1054	559	491	66	627	29	26	816	44	7	3.82
Evansville	136	26	11	26	1171	1219	617	516	92	513	45	37	683	73	12	3.97
Omaha	136	28	7	25	1165	1219	621	530	111	457	27	33	536	38	6	4.09
Oklahoma City	135	28	5	20	1158	1200	681	569	104	547	64	32	671	36	14	4.42
Iowa	136	25	5	32	1164	1220	686	595	102	562	24	39	680	63	8	4.60
Springfield	136	28	9	34	1158	1203	680	601	134	501	41	48	741	41	11	4.67
Wichita	136	23	5	25	1147	1218	686	619	131	613	39	20	583	44	8	4.86
Denver	135	32	5	19	1133	1283	720	628	100	541	53	32	687	31	9	4.99

PITCHERS' RECORDS

(Leading Qualifiers for Earned-Run Average Leadership—109 or More Innings)

*Throws lefthanded.

Pitcher—Club	G.	GS.	CG.	ShO.	W.	L.	Sv.	Pct.	IP.	H.	R.	ER.	HR.	BB.	Int. BB.	HB.	SO.	WP.	ERA.
Berenyi, Indianapolis	25	25	6	3	9	9	0	.500	166	134	64	52	0	98	7	4	136	13	2.82
Leibrandt, Indianapolis*	27	26	5	2	8	14	0	.364	162	146	67	53	7	65	2	2	100	2	2.94
Corbett, Indianapolis	69	0	0	0	3	6	8	.333	110	94	38	36	9	39	2	3	77	0	2.95
F. Arroyo, Evansville	19	13	2	0	7	4	0	.636	114	113	50	38	10	34	6	4	39	4	3.00
Eaton, Omaha	26	26	8	1	12	8	0	.600	189	185	85	70	12	48	1	2	61	2	3.33
Urrea, Springfield	20	17	3	0	8	5	2	.615	128	115	60	50	8	58	5	6	64	9	3.52
Beare, Oklahoma City	27	14	3	1	12	1	1	.923	126	132	75	56	13	60	9	5	65	2	4.00
Beene, Oklahoma City	26	12	2	1	10	5	1	.667	114	114	58	51	7	42	7	0	52	1	4.03
Bystrom, Oklahoma City	26	26	7	0	9	5	0	.643	172	174	102	78	15	69	5	7	108	5	4.08
Martz, Wichita	30	26	5	1	8	13	0	.381	178	196	96	81	21	47	2	2	66	4	4.10

Departmental Leaders: G—Corbett, 69; GS—Bystrom, Eaton, B. James, Leibrandt, Martz, 26; CG—Atkinson, 11; ShO—Berenyi, 3; W—Robinson, 13; L—Leibrandt, 14; Sv—Littlefield, 10; Pct.—Beare, .923; IP—Eaton, 189; H—Atkinson, 198; R—B. James, 112; ER—B. James, 98; HR—O'Brien, 22; BB—B. James, 123; IBB—Beare, Robinson, 9; SO—Berenyi, 136; HB—Contreras, 9; WP—Berenyi, 13.

(All Pitchers—Listed Alphabetically)

Pitcher—Club	G.	GS.	CG.	ShO.	W.	L.	Sv.	Pct.	IP.	H.	R.	ER.	HR.	BB.	Int. BB.	HB.	SO.	WP.	ERA.
Allen, Iowa	28	12	3	1	5	6	4	.455	106	113	75	66	6	65	2	4	46	12	5.60
Altamirano, Okla City	21	2	0	0	2	5	0	.286	51	56	25	22	3	27	7	1	41	0	3.88
Angelini, Denver*	48	4	2	1	8	5	5	.615	103	88	49	42	7	43	8	4	77	3	3.67
C. Arroyo, Okla City*	38	4	0	0	3	5	3	.375	74	81	39	34	5	30	3	3	41	1	4.14
F. Arroyo, Evansville	19	13	2	0	7	4	0	.636	114	113	50	38	10	34	6	4	39	4	3.00
Atkinson, Denver	36	23	11	0	9	6	2	.600	187	198	92	86	20	54	4	3	83	2	4.14
Baker, Evansville	5	3	0	0	0	2	0	.000	14	18	13	12	1	10	1	2	15	1	7.71
Ballinger, Omaha	28	16	3	1	5	9	1	.357	127	138	77	65	12	62	2	6	70	9	4.61
Barnes, Iowa*	3	3	0	0	0	1	0	.000	10	12	6	5	3	7	0	1	5	0	4.50
Beare, Oklahoma City	27	14	3	1	12	1	1	.923	126	132	75	56	13	60	9	5	65	2	4.00
Beene, Oklahoma City	26	12	2	1	10	5	1	.667	114	114	58	51	7	42	7	0	52	1	4.03

Pitcher–Club	G.	GS.	CG.	ShO.	W.	L.	Sv.	Pct.	IP.	H.	R.	ER.	HR.	BB.	Int. BB.	HB.	SO.	WP.	ERA.
Berenyi, Indianapolis	25	25	6	3	9	9	0	.500	166	134	64	52	0	98	7	4	136	13	2.82
Blair, Evansville*	4	1	1	0	2	1	0	.667	19	16	3	3	3	3	0	0	7	1	1.42
Botehlo, Wichita	4	4	0	0	1	2	0	.333	19	30	20	18	4	8	0	0	18	2	8.53
Bruno, Springfield	11	10	3	0	3	6	0	.333	57	58	36	28	10	19	3	1	35	1	4.42
Burns, Iowa*	7	6	1	0	2	3	1	.400	41	41	17	15	2	15	0	1	34	1	3.29
Burnside, Indianapolis	39	2	0	0	6	4	5	.600	57	50	22	19	3	33	3	4	48	2	3.00
Bystrom, Oklahoma City.	26	26	7	0	9	5	0	.643	152	174	102	78	15	69	5	7	108	5	4.08
Campbell, Denver	42	2	0	0	2	3	2	.400	81	95	49	36	7	50	5	6	72	1	4.00
Camper, Oklahoma City ..	2	1	0	0	0	0	0	.000	8	10	7	7	2	5	0	1	6	0	7.88
Capilla, Wichita*	28	9	1	0	6	8	4	.429	83	85	44	42	7	51	2	1	45	5	4.55
Cappuzzello, Ind*	19	0	0	0	1	1	3	.500	17	13	6	6	2	3	0	0	13	1	12.71
Caudill, Wichita	6	5	1	1	3	1	0	.750	36	27	11	11	3	17	0	1	36	0	2.75
Chamberlain, Springfield	12	12	3	1	4	4	0	.500	81	74	45	43	9	35	0	7	40	1	4.78
Chris, Evansville*	19	19	3	1	7	8	0	.467	105	113	78	65	10	67	3	4	71	7	5.57
Christenson, Omaha*	51	1	0	0	4	3	7	.571	91	69	33	26	5	43	7	3	63	3	2.57
Churchill, Wichita*	11	7	1	1	4	1	2	.800	53	54	20	20	5	26	0	0	21	6	3.40
Combe, Indianapolis	14	0	0	0	1	0	1	1.000	22	28	12	11	2	16	1	0	7	1	4.50
Contreras, Iowa	20	14	1	0	7	6	0	.538	95	117	69	63	7	41	0	9	66	3	5.97
Corbett, Indianapolis	69	0	0	0	3	6	8	.333	110	94	38	36	9	39	2	3	77	0	2.95
Cornejo, Evansville	31	4	0	0	5	5	2	.500	93	112	64	56	6	35	5	1	37	11	5.42
Corr, Evansville	12	5	0	0	2	2	2	.500	50	60	26	21	4	21	1	1	23	0	3.78
Cram, Omaha	34	3	1	0	2	8	5	.200	83	85	47	40	10	24	3	3	33	2	4.34
Cvejdlik, Omaha	17	17	3	1	7	6	0	.538	108	125	57	55	14	34	1	4	38	4	4.58
Daly, Omaha*	25	25	5	2	7	13	0	.350	156	176	88	74	10	85	0	6	68	3	4.27
Douglass, Iowa*	4	0	0	0	0	0	0	.000	7	6	8	7	0	13	0	0	0	0	9.00
Dues, Denver	5	5	0	0	1	3	0	.250	20	31	21	21	1	19	1	1	3	2	9.45
Dumoulin, Indianapolis ..	18	7	0	0	2	2	0	.500	49	51	33	31	1	59	0	2	19	4	5.69
Easterly, Denver*	20	13	6	2	5	6	2	.455	88	100	40	32	2	39	2	2	55	5	3.27
Eaton, Omaha	26	26	8	1	12	8	0	.600	189	185	85	70	12	48	1	2	61	2	3.33
Edelen, Springfield	13	13	1	0	4	7	0	.364	67	88	53	50	8	34	2	5	39	3	6.72
Eduardo, Springfield	6	6	1	0	2	1	0	.667	37	33	18	17	3	20	0	2	29	2	4.14
Esser, Iowa*	43	6	1	0	1	5	3	.167	68	70	55	50	10	61	1	2	60	10	6.62
Evans, Iowa	8	8	0	0	2	4	0	.333	47	38	23	21	3	24	0	2	30	1	4.02
Finlayson, Denver	6	5	0	0	2	3	0	.400	24	39	26	25	3	13	3	1	3	0	9.38
Fowler, Oklahoma City...	19	1	0	0	2	2	1	.500	47	47	30	26	5	26	5	1	22	1	4.98
G. Frazier, Springfield	24	0	0	0	1	2	6	.333	56	40	17	15	7	23	5	1	56	0	2.41
Fulgham, Springfield	11	11	5	1	6	3	0	.667	77	61	31	27	7	25	1	2	50	0	3.16
Gault, Wichita	4	0	0	0	0	0	0	.000	8	9	4	4	1	9	0	1	5	1	4.50
Geisel, Wichita*	45	1	1	0	5	5	7	.500	79	76	29	22	4	47	4	1	49	3	2.51
Grafton, Evansville	7	0	0	0	0	2	0	.000	11	19	10	8	2	9	2	0	5	1	6.55
Granger, Denver	24	0	0	0	2	4	1	.333	28	38	28	21	3	17	4	2	16	0	6.75
Gullickson, Denver	11	11	1	0	3	3	0	.500	54	65	44	40	10	26	0	1	31	1	6.67
Guzman, Iowa	3	0	0	0	1	0	0	1.000	6	5	4	4	1	3	0	0	3	0	6.00
Hamende, Springfield*	2	0	0	0	0	0	0	.000	9	13	6	6	0	6	0	1	4	0	6.00
Hamrick, Omaha*	5	5	0	0	1	4	0	.200	25	34	18	16	3	15	0	0	8	4	5.76
Harris, Wichita*	3	1	0	0	0	0	0	.000	8	14	9	9	1	6	2	0	2	1	10.13
Hemm, Denver*	11	0	0	0	0	1	0	.000	12	16	9	9	1	6	0	0	6	0	6.75
Hinton, Iowa*	5	4	2	0	2	1	1	.667	30	28	15	11	6	7	0	0	16	0	3.30
Hoffman, Iowa*	13	9	1	0	6	0	2	1.000	70	62	30	26	5	40	3	2	34	5	3.34
Holdsworth, Evansville ...	23	17	3	0	10	6	0	.625	104	113	59	48	7	58	2	1	62	10	4.15
Horn, Denver	4	0	0	0	0	0	0	.000	4	7	10	9	1	8	2	0	1	0	20.25
Howard, Iowa	7	7	1	0	4	1	0	.800	49	34	13	9	3	20	1	0	45	3	1.65
Howell, Indianapolis	24	23	2	2	10	10	0	.500	128	121	82	73	6	84	4	1	79	8	5.13
Hoyt, Iowa	9	7	1	0	1	4	1	.200	43	59	22	22	5	24	0	0	27	3	4.60
B. James, Denver	26	26	2	1	8	13	0	.381	132	139	112	98	11	123	1	6	122	11	6.68
B. Johnson, Iowa	8	8	1	0	1	5	0	.167	50	60	34	27	4	16	0	0	14	1	4.58
Keener, Denver	1	0	0	0	0	0	0	.000	0	4	4	0	0	0	0	0	0	0	.....
Kucek, Oklahoma City ...	34	7	0	0	7	8	7	.467	83	74	40	34	4	63	6	1	62	7	3.69
Kurosaki, Springfield	35	3	0	0	3	5	2	.375	89	102	66	60	10	37	4	3	46	1	6.07
Kusnyer, Iowa	2	0	0	0	0	0	0	.000	3	2	3	3	1	0	1	1	1	1	9.00
Landreth, Denver	12	9	1	0	1	5	0	.167	55	72	42	39	6	29	2	1	35	1	6.38
Larson, Oklahoma City ...	24	24	7	2	9	8	0	.529	146	162	93	78	13	70	3	2	87	7	4.81
Leibrandt, Indianapolis*	27	26	5	2	8	14	0	.364	162	146	67	53	7	65	2	2	100	2	2.94
Littlefield, Springfield	29	0	0	0	6	5	10	.545	46	41	15	15	1	8	4	1	25	0	2.93
Lukevics, Iowa	18	17	4	2	8	6	0	.571	111	135	70	62	5	28	1	4	66	4	5.03
Manos, Oklahoma City	29	0	0	0	3	3	3	.500	52	55	37	35	11	19	4	0	30	2	6.06
J. Martin, Evansville*	37	0	0	0	7	1	2	.875	59	49	12	9	1	25	4	2	53	3	1.37
R. Martin, Omaha	33	0	0	0	6	2	7	.750	63	56	27	22	5	38	8	0	47	3	3.14
Martinez, Oklahoma City	21	21	4	0	4	10	0	.286	106	128	77	62	8	55	6	3	54	4	5.26
Martz, Wichita	30	26	5	1	8	13	0	.381	178	196	96	81	21	47	2	2	66	4	4.10
May, Indianapolis	11	6	0	0	3	0	0	1.000	43	36	21	20	3	26	0	0	16	0	4.19
McEnaney, Springfield* ..	7	0	0	0	0	0	1	.000	13	9	5	3	3	2	0	0	5	0	2.08
McGilberry, Omaha	23	15	3	0	9	7	0	.563	111	115	62	59	14	46	2	1	45	1	4.78
D. Miller, Denver	15	0	0	0	2	0	2	1.000	25	20	6	5	0	12	3	0	18	1	1.80

Pitcher–Club	G	GS	CG	ShO	W	L	Sv	Pct.	IP	H	R	ER	HR	BB	Int. BB	HB	SO	WP	ERA
R. Miller, Denver	26	22	5	1	10	8	0	.556	152	80	72	13	67	6	4	102	3	4.44
Dave Moore, Indianapolis	28	22	6	2	8	12	1	.400	146	142	82	70	14	71	3	5	84	3	4.32
Donnie Moore, Wichita	5	5	1	0	1	3	0	.250	29	29	26	26	4	20	0	1	16	1	8.07
Moran, Iowa	5	0	0	0	0	1	0	.000	9	8	3	3	2	3	0	1	1	0	3.00
Morley, Omaha*	10	10	1	1	3	2	0	.600	58	63	32	31	8	24	1	4	34	1	4.81
Morris, Evansville	5	5	3	0	2	2	0	.500	34	22	13	9	4	18	0	0	28	0	2.38
Moskau, Indianapolis	2	2	0	0	0	0	0	.000	5	2	0	0	0	1	0	0	5	0	0.00
Murillo, Iowa	22	5	1	0	5	1	4	.833	65	55	30	27	4	30	1	2	36	5	3.74
Noles, Oklahoma City	12	12	5	0	6	4	0	.600	76	69	38	33	7	28	1	3	48	5	3.91
O'Brien, Springfield	22	21	6	2	10	5	0	.667	142	156	78	70	22	42	2	6	83	3	4.44
Otten, Springfield	33	3	3	0	5	5	8	.500	77	70	39	36	6	46	5	5	62	4	4.21
M. Parker, Wichita	2	1	0	0	0	1	0	.000	6	6	10	8	0	6	1	0	4	2	12.00
Paschall, Omaha	18	18	4	0	7	8	0	.467	118	144	80	61	17	28	1	3	53	6	4.65
Pastore, Indianapolis	10	10	5	0	7	2	0	.778	68	51	21	21	6	17	0	1	69	3	2.78
Patchin, Evansville	2	0	0	0	0	0	0	.000	3	4	4	4	1	4	0	0	1	1	12.00
Pazik, Iowa*	2	2	0	0	0	2	0	.000	9	12	10	10	2	3	0	1	3	0	10.00
Petry, Evansville	15	15	3	0	4	3	0	.571	91	92	60	49	11	37	0	3	55	6	4.85
Quisenberry, Omaha	26	0	0	0	2	1	5	.667	35	29	15	14	1	10	1	1	16	0	3.60
Ratzer, Denver	40	14	4	0	8	9	4	.471	151	197	88	76	15	22	5	1	50	0	4.53
Riley, Wichita*	38	6	0	0	3	8	5	.273	74	75	53	50	6	53	4	3	53	4	6.08
Robinson, Iowa	49	0	0	0	13	7	9	.650	86	69	32	28	10	43	9	3	76	2	2.93
Rogers, Wichita	26	19	4	1	5	9	0	.357	142	149	80	73	18	64	4	3	69	0	4.63
Rondon, Iowa	4	2	1	0	0	0	0	.000	17	16	7	6	2	6	0	0	13	1	3.18
Rothschild, Indianapolis	33	10	0	0	1	6	6	.143	82	85	52	48	3	56	3	1	68	3	5.27
Rucker, Evansville*	2	2	0	0	1	1	0	.500	13	11	4	4	1	1	0	0	8	0	2.77
Ruling, Oklahoma City	11	10	2	0	3	6	0	.333	58	58	44	42	8	29	1	3	35	1	6.52
Sarmiento, Indianapolis	19	0	0	0	1	0	2	1.000	38	41	14	10	2	11	1	0	34	1	2.37
Saucier, Oklahoma City*	24	1	0	0	2	1	4	.667	47	40	16	11	3	24	7	2	20	0	2.11
Seaman, Springfield*	31	11	0	0	7	4	2	.636	85	101	61	54	14	64	3	1	61	7	5.72
Semall, Wichita	12	12	6	0	5	6	0	.455	87	82	57	49	12	40	0	0	32	3	5.07
Seoane, Wichita	20	18	1	0	6	5	0	.545	106	125	61	57	9	51	3	3	43	6	4.84
Shea, Evansville	2	2	0	0	0	0	0	.000	8	15	6	6	1	3	0	0	3	0	6.75
P. Siebert, Denver*	17	0	0	0	1	3	1	.250	24	22	20	14	0	13	7	0	13	1	5.25
Soto, Indianapolis	15	0	0	0	1	1	2	.500	25	20	11	11	3	18	2	2	38	3	3.96
Steffen, Evansville	19	1	0	0	4	5	0	.333	44	51	27	19	3	18	6	1	28	1	3.89
Sutton, Iowa	40	19	7	0	8	11	4	.421	168	195	103	89	15	72	3	2	69	8	4.77
Sykes, Springfield*	4	1	0	0	0	0	0	.000	5	13	12	9	1	7	1	1	4	1	16.20
Taylor, Evansville	18	0	0	0	3	1	3	.750	29	25	8	8	2	13	0	2	24	2	2.48
Terlecky, Springfield	20	19	2	0	9	5	0	.643	115	150	83	71	14	44	4	4	53	6	5.56
Thomas, Springfield	17	9	1	0	5	6	3	.455	74	79	55	48	11	31	2	2	85	3	5.84
Tobik, Evansville	19	0	0	0	4	0	9	1.000	38	24	6	2	0	13	3	1	45	1	0.47
Torrealba, Iowa*	22	3	0	0	2	3	2	.400	44	68	40	34	5	21	1	3	23	2	6.95
A. Torres, Indianapolis*	19	3	1	0	6	2	3	.750	39	36	14	12	4	14	1	0	23	0	2.77
Treuel, Evansville	23	22	3	1	8	7	0	.533	120	144	79	72	16	51	4	7	44	5	5.40
Trout, Iowa*	4	4	0	0	3	1	0	.750	27	24	10	9	1	19	1	1	12	1	3.00
Underwood, Evansville*	7	7	2	1	2	3	0	.400	48	41	20	15	2	17	1	0	35	3	2.81
Urrea, Springfield	20	17	3	0	8	5	2	.615	128	115	60	50	8	58	5	6	64	9	3.52
Valentine, Wichita	22	21	2	0	5	10	0	.333	131	136	86	76	16	76	3	0	67	4	5.22
Weaver, Evansville	29	8	3	2	8	2	0	.800	99	102	43	41	2	47	4	1	63	8	3.73
Wilkerson, Wichita	53	1	0	0	3	6	2	.333	73	81	56	51	13	71	7	3	42	2	6.29
Willoughby, Wichita	12	0	0	0	2	1	5	.667	34	44	24	22	7	21	7	1	15	0	5.82
Young, Evansville	12	12	3	2	4	4	0	.500	76	75	32	27	5	29	3	7	37	8	3.20

BALKS—Bystrom, 5; Leibrandt, 4; Chris, James, R. Miller, Seoane, Steffen, 3 each; Bruno, Christenson, Contreras, Larson, Morris, Ratzer, Riley, Ruling, Saucier, Taylor, Wilkerson, 2 each; Allen, C. Arroyo, Beene, Burns, Chamberlain, Cornejo, Cvejdlik, Daly, Douglass, Edelen, Evans, Finlayson, Fulgham, Geisel, Howell, Kurosaki, R. Martin, Noles, O'Brien, Otten, Paschall, Pastore, Patchin, Robinson, Soto, Terlecky, Thomas, Urrea, 1 each.

COMBINATION SHUTOUTS—Treuel-J. Martin-Weaver, Treuel-J. Martin, F. Arroyo-Steffen, Rucker-Holdsworth-Steffen, Evansville; Berenyi-Corbett, Moskau-May-Burnside-A. Torres, Indianapolis; Lukevics-Murillo, Howard-Sutton, Iowa; Cvejdlik-Ballinger, Omaha; Edelen-Frazier-McEnaney, Edelen-Kurosaki, Seaman-Thomas, Eduardo-Otten, Urrea-Littlefield, Springfield; Capilla-Riley-Wilkerson, Wichita.

NO-HIT GAMES—Easterly, Denver, defeated Iowa, 10-0, July 14 (seven innings) (PERFECT); Moskau (3 inn.)—May (3 inn.)—Burnside (2 inn.)—A. Torres (1 inn.), Indianapolis, defeated Evansville, 5-0, August 29.

Easterly Hurled Perfecto

Denver lefthander Jamie Easterly became only the third pitcher in the 72-year history of the American Association to hurl a perfect game when he blanked Iowa, 10-0, July 14. Carl DeRose of Kansas City in 1947 and Martin Stuart of Toledo in 1950 had the previous AA perfectos.

Inter-American League

CLASS AAA

NOTE: Inter-American League folded June 30. Following are the most complete statistics available.

STANDING OF CLUBS AT CLOSE OF FIRST HALF, JUNE 17

Club	Mia.	S.D.	Car.	Mar.	Pan.	P.R.	W.	L.	T.	Pct.	G.B.
Miami Amigos	..	2	6	12	14	9	43	17	0	.717	......
Santo Domingo Azucareros	4	..	9	5	4	11	33	21	0	.611	7
Caracas Metropolitanos	2	6	..	6	13	4	31	22	0	.585	8½
Maracaibo Petroleros de Zulia	6	3	3	..	2	13	27	30	0	.474	14½
Panama Banqueros*	4	4	2	3	..	2	15	36	0	.294	23½
Puerto Rico Boricuas*	1	6	2	4	3	..	16	39	0	.291	24½

STANDING OF CLUBS AT CLOSE OF SECOND HALF, JUNE 30

Club	Mia.	Car.	Mar.	S.D.	W.	L.	T.	Pct.	G.B.
Miami Amigos	..	2	2	4	8	4	0	.667	......
Caracas Metropolitanos	2	..	2	2	6	5	0	.545	1½
Maracaibo Petroleros de Zulia	2	0	..	2	4	6	0	.400	3
Santo Domingo Azucareros	0	3	2	..	5	8	0	.385	3½

COMPOSITE STANDING OF CLUBS AT CLOSE OF SEASON, JUNE 30

Club	Mia.	Car.	S.D.	Mar.	Pan.	P.R.	W.	L.	T.	Pct.	G.B.
Miami Amigos	..	8	6	14	14	9	51	21	0	.708	......
Caracas Metropolitanos	4	..	8	8	13	4	37	27	0	.578	10
Santo Domingo Azucareros	4	12	..	7	4	11	38	29	0	.567	10½
Maracaibo Petroleros de Zulia	8	3	5	..	2	13	31	36	0	.463	17½
Panama Banqueros*	4	2	4	3	..	2	15	36	0	.294	25½
Puerto Rico Boricuas*	1	2	6	4	3	..	16	39	0	.291	26½

*Panama and Puerto Rico clubs disbanded upon completion of first half of season.

Playoffs—None; Miami won both halves and was declared league champion.

Regular-Season Attendance—No figures were available.

Managers: Caracas—Jim Busby; Maracaibo—Pat Dobson, Gus Gil, Luis Aparicio; Miami—Dave Johnson; Panama—Chico Salmon, Willie Miranda; Puerto Rico—Jose Santiago; Santo Domingo—Mike Kekich.

(Compiled by Norb Ecksl, Ildefonso Ortega; Miami, Fla.)

CLUB BATTING

Club	G.	AB.	R.	H.	TB.	2B.	3B.	HR.	RBI.	SB.	Pct.
Miami	72	2509	373	724	998	104	25	40	333	100	.289
Santo Domingo	65	1987	214	526	674	74	13	16	179	32	.265
Caracas	64	1892	230	488	635	72	12	17	195	39	.258
Maracaibo	66	1926	185	482	606	66	11	12	160	56	.250
Panama	51	1618	174	396	528	65	14	13	153	23	.245
Puerto Rico	55	1323	114	323	434	48	15	11	129	21	.244

INDIVIDUAL BATTING
(Leading Qualifiers for Batting Championship—160 or More Plate Appearances)

*Bats lefthanded. †Switch-hitter.

Player and Club	G.	AB.	R.	H.	TB.	2B.	3B.	HR.	RBI.	SB.	Pct.
Tyrone, Jim, Miami	68	258	50	94	133	18	3	5	39	12	.364
Brown, Leon, Miami	40	162	40	57	82	8	1	5	29	17	.352
Busby, James C., Caracas	57	234	35	76	90	6	1	2	17	11	.325
Johnson, Larry Doby, Miami	62	224	47	71	107	10	4	6	40	8	.317
Perez, Pastor, Maracaibo	52	167	16	51	69	10	1	2	10	2	.305
Woodard, Darrell, Miami	72	236	48	71	82	6	1	1	17	45	.301
Baez, Jose, Santo Domingo	48	197	14	59	69	8	1	0	17	3	.299
Tyrone, Wayne, Miami	64	241	27	70	111	9	4	8	43	4	.290
Pemberton, Brock, Miami	62	248	33	72	98	10	2	4	51	1	.290
Liranzo, Rafael, Santo Domingo	36	180	23	52	62	7	0	1	14	4	.289

Departmental Leaders: G—Woodard, 72; AB—J. Tyrone, 258; R—J. Tyrone, 50; H—J. Tyrone, 94; TB—J. Tyrone, 133; 2B—J. Tyrone, 18; 3B—Cruz, 6; HR—W. Tyrone, 8; RBI—Pemberton, 51; SB—Woodard, 45.

(All Players—Listed Alphabetically)

Player and Club	G.	AB.	R.	H.	TB.	2B.	3B.	HR.	RBI.	SB.	Pct.
Allen, Kim, Maracaibo	32	119	20	37	45	4	2	0	12	15	.311
Almengor, Victor, Panama	41	138	14	37	48	5	0	2	11	2	.268
Alvarez, J. Orlando, P Rico	42	153	7	38	54	6	2	2	21	0	.248
Anderson, Michael, Pan-Car	12	3	0	0	0	0	0	0	0	0	.000
Andrews, Fred, S Domingo*	17	70	7	14	18	2	1	0	4	0	.200
Attardi, Gerald, S Domingo*	7	1	0	0	0	0	0	0	0	0	.000
Baez, Jose, S Domingo	48	197	14	59	69	8	1	0	17	3	.299
Batton, Chris, S Domingo	15	1	0	0	0	0	0	0	0	0	.000
Begnaud, Gary, Panama	52	180	18	44	64	8	3	2	20	2	.244
Blanco, C. Oswaldo, Caracas	58	194	26	46	72	9	1	5	23	0	.237
Blessit, Isaiah, Maracaibo	12	36	3	8	13	2	0	1	2	0	.222
Bolivar, Flores, Caracas	2	6	0	1	1	0	0	0	1	0	.167
Bravo, Angel, Maracaibo*	15	73	8	21	23	2	0	0	8	1	.288
Breeden, Harold, Miami	60	205	23	46	63	11	0	2	27	1	.224
Brown, Rogers, Puerto Rico†	10	0	1	0	0	0	0	0	0	0	.000
Brown, Curtis, Caracas	56	216	26	61	89	15	2	3	32	6	.282
Brown, Leon, Miami	40	162	40	57	82	8	1	5	29	17	.352
Busby, James C., Caracas*	57	234	35	76	90	6	1	2	17	11	.325
Cantres, Angel, Puerto Rico	28	89	10	20	27	4	0	1	4	1	.225
Cariel, Rafael, Maracaibo	39	131	5	27	30	3	0	0	8	0	.206
Centeno, Jose, Puerto Rico	41	144	21	44	64	7	5	1	18	4	.306
Colina, Victor, Maracaibo	47	161	11	40	42	2	0	0	12	0	.248
Cruz, Ponciano, S Domingo	52	217	30	58	81	11	6	0	18	0	.267
Curbelo, Jorge, Miami	30	80	9	17	18	1	0	0	3	1	.213
Deliza, Juan, S Domingo	42	161	17	44	53	6	0	1	16	5	.273
Drake, George, Panama	12	19	2	1	1	0	0	0	0	0	.053
Evans, Freeman, Maracaibo	33	124	19	33	41	2	0	2	8	15	.266
Fisher, Curt, 20 Pan-6 PR	26	75	7	15	18	3	0	0	2	0	.200
Foster, Leo, Puerto Rico	32	112	11	23	36	6	2	1	5	1	.205
Fuentes, Rigoberto, S Domingo†	24	84	5	21	22	1	0	0	8	0	.250
Gaga, Rafael, S Domingo	3	11	1	1	1	0	0	0	0	0	.091
Garboza, Toribio, Caracas	30	80	9	15	28	2	1	3	12	1	.188
Garcia, Antonio, Maracaibo	36	110	14	30	37	5	1	0	4	0	.273
Garcia, Jose, Panama	23	63	9	14	14	0	0	0	1	0	.222
Gaston, Clarence, S Domingo	40	148	22	48	56	5	0	1	14	1	.324
Gates, Edward, Caracas	10	28	4	8	10	2	0	0	2	0	.286
Gatlin, Mike, Puerto Rico	30	89	8	17	33	3	2	3	9	1	.191
Geigel, German, Puerto Rico*	37	138	16	37	40	1	1	0	7	5	.268
Glass, Robert, Maracaibo†	38	127	7	26	29	3	0	0	9	0	.205
Guarnaccia, John, Panama*	49	164	22	44	54	3	2	1	24	2	.268
Guzman, Eddie, Puerto Rico	1	0	0	0	0	0	0	0	0	0	.000
Hermoso, Remigio, Caracas	17	55	6	16	19	3	0	0	4	1	.291
Hernandez, C. Julio, Puerto Rico	4	14	1	4	4	0	0	0	1	1	.286
Hopkins, Randy, Miami	16	2	0	0	0	0	0	0	0	0	.000
Horvath, Jim, Miami	45	126	15	34	39	2	0	1	13	3	.270
Irwin, Dennis, 2 PR-19 Pan	21	69	10	15	18	3	0	0	1	0	.217
Javier, Ignacio, Santo Domingo	28	101	9	29	45	4	0	4	15	3	.287
Jeter, John, Santo Domingo	56	190	22	49	69	9	1	3	13	10	.258
Johnson, Dave, Miami	10	25	7	6	11	2	0	1	2	0	.240
Johnson, Larry, Miami	62	224	47	71	107	10	4	6	40	8	.317
Kekich, Mike, Santo Domingo	9	4	0	1	1	0	0	0	1	0	.250
Kim Wendell, Miami	45	136	13	37	42	3	1	0	14	3	.272
Leonard, Bernard, 52 Pan-8 Mar	60	232	24	51	85	13	6	3	28	8	.220
Liranzo, R. Rafael, Santo Domingo	36	180	23	52	62	7	0	1	14	4	.289
Llodrat, Fernando, 28 PR-6 SD	34	91	12	21	25	2	1	0	5	1	.231
Lopez, Domingo, Caracas	6	14	0	2	2	0	0	0	0	0	.143
Mangual, Angel, Puerto Rico	5	21	0	4	4	0	0	0	1	0	.190
Marquez, Gonzalo, 24 Car-2 Mar*	26	88	7	16	18	2	0	0	10	0	.182
Martin, Mike, Caracas	12	3	0	0	0	0	0	0	0	0	.000
Martinez, Ron, Miami	14	1	0	0	0	0	0	0	0	0	.000
Martinez, Sebastian, Maracaibo	7	22	3	4	5	1	0	0	0	3	.182
May, David, Santo Domingo*	44	151	16	40	51	5	0	2	9	2	.265
Monasterio, Juan, Caracas	18	67	7	15	27	4	1	2	4	0	.224
Oestreich, Mark, Panama	26	59	6	14	23	4	1	1	9	0	.237
Oliveros, Eddie, Miami	70	249	24	59	80	8	5	1	24	3	.237
Ortiz, Alfredo, Maracaibo	5	11	0	0	0	0	0	0	0	0	.000
Ortiz, Leonardo, Santo Domingo	35	108	9	21	25	2	1	0	8	2	.194
Pasley, Kevin, Santo Domingo	54	193	16	43	54	6	1	1	19	1	.223
Pemberton, Brock, Miami	62	248	33	72	98	10	2	4	51	1	.290
Perez, Pastor, Maracaibo	52	167	16	51	69	10	1	2	10	2	.305
Pettaway, Nathaniel, Maracaibo	34	124	9	25	36	5	0	2	12	1	.202
Phillips, Adolfo, Panama	12	24	2	7	9	0	1	0	2	0	.292
Quintana, Willibaldo, 14 Car-10 Mar	24	73	5	14	21	5	1	0	10	0	.192
Quirk, Eugene, Maracaibo	43	149	21	37	38	1	0	0	8	7	.248
Ramirez, Alexis, Caracas	56	209	26	57	61	4	0	0	19	3	.273
Randall, Aaron, Santo Domingo†	36	134	19	37	58	8	2	3	22	1	.276
Reynolds, Bob, Miami	19	1	0	0	0	0	0	0	0	0	.000

Player and Club	G.	AB.	R.	H.	TB.	2B.	3B.	HR.	RBI.	SB.	Pct.
Richard, Lee, Panama	35	137	16	33	40	5	1	0	11	3	.241
Rivera, Jorge, Puerto Rico	16	43	4	9	11	2	0	0	5	0	.209
Robinson, Henry, 8 Pan-4 Mia†	12	27	3	5	5	0	0	0	1	0	.185
Robles, Pedro, Santo Domingo	3	10	1	3	3	0	0	0	0	0	.300
Rocca, Pedro, Caracas	7	13	3	3	5	0	1	0	0	0	.231
Rodriguez, Felix, Caracas*	42	150	19	40	52	3	3	1	22	6	.267
Rouse, Randy, Panama	23	59	9	15	20	3	1	0	4	0	.254
Sarabia, Antonio, Panama	16	52	1	13	15	2	0	0	4	3	.250
Scott, Mickey, Miami	15	4	0	0	0	0	0	0	0	0	.000
Seidholz, Don, Panama	24	75	7	19	26	4	0	1	11	0	.253
Seoane, Isaac, PR-Mia	30	86	5	26	29	3	0	0	29	0	.302
Smith, Tommy, Miami†	16	53	9	16	23	3	2	0	9	2	.302
Soderholm, Dale, Maracaibo	39	141	9	38	58	9	1	3	20	1	.270
Sposito, Gustavo, Maracaibo	56	174	16	37	42	3	1	0	16	7	.213
Stenholm, Richard, Maracaibo*	29	97	7	27	40	7	0	2	12	1	.278
Sylvester, Jim, Puerto Rico	6	8	0	0	0	0	0	0	0	0	.000
Thomas, Danny, Miami	39	136	21	38	68	8	2	6	20	0	.279
Thompson, Bobby, Maracaibo*	10	36	6	10	17	3	2	0	4	1	.278
Tipa, Steve, Panama	37	117	14	27	42	6	0	3	15	0	.231
Tolan, Robert, Puerto Rico*	30	109	7	31	43	6	0	2	11	2	.284
Torres, Angel, Santo Domingo	18	1	0	0	0	0	0	0	0	0	.000
Tovar, Cesar, Caracas	35	121	17	34	38	4	0	0	15	4	.281
Tyrone, Jim, Miami	68	258	50	94	133	18	3	5	39	12	.364
Tyrone, O. Wayne, Miami	64	241	27	70	111	9	4	8	43	4	.290
Vaz, Luis, Panama	7	9	2	1	1	0	0	0	0	0	.111
Verhelst, Edwing, Caracas	14	32	4	6	9	1	1	0	1	0	.188
Villaran, Miguel, Puerto Rico	28	79	3	18	21	3	0	0	7	0	.228
Wallace, Curtis, 41 PR-3 Mar	44	151	9	32	43	4	2	1	5	6	.212
Wallace, Mike, Miami*.	14	5	1	2	2	0	0	0	0	0	.400
Webb, Hank, Miami	12	1	0	0	0	0	0	0	0	0	.000
Webb, Marvin, 6 Mia-19 Pan	25	89	10	23	28	3	1	0	8	1	.258
Webster, Ramon, Panama*	7	24	1	7	7	0	0	0	5	0	.292
Weicker, George, Caracas	51	184	26	50	63	8	1	1	17	7	.272
Williams, Jimmy, 23 Pan-3 SD	26	95	9	33	39	6	0	0	14	3	.347
Woodard, Darrell, Miami	72	236	48	71	82	6	1	1	17	45	.301
Wrenn, Luther, Maracaibo	10	33	4	12	12	0	0	0	3	0	.364
Zabala, Faustino, Caracas	49	170	13	37	43	6	0	0	11	0	.218

The following pitchers had no plate appearances primarily through use of designated hitters, listed alphabetically by club, games in parentheses:

CARACAS—Barretto, Miguel (9); Caldera, Jose (15); Clark, Dave (2); Hernandez, Angel (9); House, Thomas (13); Lugo, Elias (10); Luna, Luis (2); Metzger, Clarence (2); Moulton, Brian (12); Penalver, Luis (11); Polinsky, Robert (4); Standart, Richard (21).

MARACAIBO—Aponte, Luis (11); Dobson, Patrick (1); Garcia, Dave (10); Hernandez, Carlos (22); Marcano, Gilberto (9); Pazik, Michael (1); Perzanowski, Stanley (23); Ploucher, George (15); Sarmiento, Walfredo (15); Stanton, Michael (5); Thomas, Stanley (19).

MIAMI—Altamirano, Porfirio (16); Curnal, James (1); Granger, Wayne (2); Pena, Orlando (1); Van Bommel, Bill (10); Zamora, Oscar (14).

PANAMA—Alfaro, Jose (10); Bass, Eric (2); Baumgardner, Frank (14); Campbell, Mike (12); Joyce, Kevin (3); Meistickle, Kevin (4); Raboin, Andre (13); Scirripa, Dan (8); Scott, Dan (7); Solis, Angel (12); Velasquez, Anastasio (1); Williams, Alberto (17—1 with Caracas).

PUERTO RICO—Agosto, Juan (10); Albury, Victor (8); Aponte, Bonifacio (12); Baney, Richard (10); Cuellar, Miguel (10—also played with Miami); Souza, Mark (8); Texidor, Esteban (9); Velazquez, Carlos (17); Wrona, Ronald (9).

SANTO DOMINGO—Alcantara, Jose (16); De los Santos, Ramon (17); Griffn, Alan (16); Hughes, James (15); Lewis, D. Curtis (14); Pole, Richard (10); Sealey, Bobby (1); Wallace, David (3).

FIELDING AVERAGES NOT AVAILABLE

CLUB PITCHING

Club	G.	CG.	ShO.	Sv.	IP.	H.	R.	ER.	BB.	SO.	ERA.
Miami	72	22	7	22	626	567	221	162	190	287	2.33
Puerto Rico	55	8	1	6	363	340	144	104	106	131	2.58
Caracas	64	4	2	6	474	488	201	138	143	217	2.62
Santo Domingo	65	4	0	6	535	517	232	186	186	242	3.13
Maracaibo	66	17	5	12	557	550	263	206	175	218	3.59
Panama	51	13	3	4	413	446	239	189	182	212	4.12

PITCHERS' RECORDS
(Leading Qualifiers for Earned-Run Average Leadership—56 or More Innings)

*Throws lefthanded.

Pitcher and Club	G.	CG.	ShO.	W.	L.	Sv.	Pct.	IP.	H.	R.	ER.	BB.	SO.	ERA.
Martinez, Miami	14	4	1	7	1	2	.875	81	54	14	8	26	47	0.89
Altamirano, Miami	16	1	0	5	4	3	.556	57	51	27	13	18	31	2.04
Wallace, Miami	14	2	1	11	1	0	.917	91	88	28	23	18	42	2.27
House, Caracas	13	2	1	5	2	0	.714	84	89	34	22	14	30	2.36

Pitcher and Club	G.	CG.	ShO.	W.	L.	Sv.	Pct.	IP.	H.	R.	ER.	BB.	SO.	ERA.
Cuellar, Puerto Rico-Miami	10	1	0	5	2	0	.714	65	68	21	17	17	26	2.39
Souza, Puerto Rico	8	3	1	1	6	0	.167	60	52	20	16	13	24	2.40
Batton, Santo Domingo	15	3	0	7	4	0	.636	90	85	36	24	26	48	2.40
Scott, Miami	15	7	2	8	4	0	.667	101	90	37	27	25	32	2.41
Penalver, Caracas	11	0	0	3	3	0	.500	68	85	23	22	5	23	2.91
Sarmiento, Maracaibo	15	3	0	6	3	0	.667	83	86	35	27	16	32	2.93

Departmental Leaders: G—Perzanowski, 23; CG—Scott, Zamora, 7; ShO—Scott, Thomas, 2; W—Wallace, 11; L—Thomas, 8; Sv—Reynolds, 11; IP—Thomas, 115; H—Thomas, 126; R—Thomas, 51; ER—Thomas, 43; BB—Hughes, Webb, 35; SO—A. Williams, 52

(All Pitchers-Listed Alphabetically)

Pitcher and Club	G.	CG.	ShO.	W.	L.	Sv.	Pct.	IP.	H.	R.	ER.	BB.	SO.	ERA.
Agosta, Puerto Rico*	10	0	0	3	2	1	.600	31	31	13	9	17	9	2.61
Albury, Puerto Rico*	8	0	0	1	1	2	.500	18	15	4	3	4	15	1.50
Alcantara, Santo Domingo	16	0	0	3	3	1	.500	40	35	15	11	10	18	2.48
Alfaro, Panama	10	1	0	1	4	0	.200	40	45	25	16	20	22	3.60
Altamirano, Miami	16	1	0	5	4	0	.556	57	51	27	13	18	31	2.05
Anderson, Pan-Car*	11	3	1	3	6	3	.333	65	67	38	31	33	36	4.29
Aponte, Puerto Rico	12	0	0	3	2	0	.600	41	34	14	10	19	14	2.20
Aponte, Maracaibo	11	1	0	3	5	0	.375	44	70	30	26	16	19	5.32
Attardi, Santo Domingo*	7	0	0	0	0	0	.000	11	11	3	3	6	2	2.45
Baney, Puerto Rico	10	3	0	3	4	0	.429	62	60	34	24	17	7	3.48
Barretto, Caracas	9	0	0	2	4	0	.333	35	46	14	13	11	9	3.34
Bass, Panama	2	0	0	0	0	0	.000	2	4	1	0	0	0	0.00
Batton, Santo Domingo	15	3	0	7	4	0	.636	90	85	36	24	26	48	2.40
Baumgardner, Panama	14	2	1	3	7	0	.300	74	78	44	33	29	24	4.01
Caldera, Caracas	15	0	0	0	2	1	.000	39	39	18	11	15	21	2.54
Campbell, Panama	12	0	0	1	5	0	.167	22	34	16	14	14	11	5.73
Clark, Caracas	2	0	0	0	0	0	.000	4	10	8	4	2	2	9.00
Cuellar, PR-Mia.	10	1	0	5	2	0	.714	65	68	21	17	17	26	2.35
Curnal, Miami	1	0	0	0	0	0	.000	3	0	0	0	2	1	0.00
De los Santos, Santo Domingo	17	0	0	1	3	3	.250	38	43	13	8	15	25	1.89
Dobson, Maracaibo	1	0	0	0	1	0	.000	1	5	7	7	3	1	63.00
Garcia, Maracaibo	10	0	0	1	2	2	.333	21	19	7	6	15	9	2.57
Granger, Miami	2	0	0	0	0	1	.000	6	10	4	3	1	6	4.50
Griffin, Santo Domingo	16	0	0	6	1	1	.857	54	38	12	10	9	20	1.67
Hernandez, Caracas	9	0	0	2	1	0	.667	33	39	13	9	8	12	2.45
Hernandez, Maracaibo	22	1	0	2	1	2	.667	61	60	24	21	17	17	3.10
Hopkins, Miami	16	0	0	2	1	5	.667	40	29	9	7	19	20	1.58
House, Caracas*	13	2	1	5	2	0	.714	84	89	34	22	14	30	2.36
Hughes, Santo Domingo	15	1	0	5	3	0	.625	84	70	38	36	35	49	3.86
Joyce, 3 Pan-12Mar*	15	0	0	0	2	1	.000	20	13	6	3	13	6	1.35
Kekich, Santo Domingo*	9	0	0	1	4	0	.200	52	56	33	26	28	21	4.50
Lewis, Santo Domingo	14	0	0	3	2	0	.600	27	31	4	4	7	12	1.33
Lugo, Caracas	10	0	0	4	2	0	.667	21	19	6	5	5	8	2.14
Luna, Caracas	2	0	0	1	1	0	.500	12	6	4	3	12	4	2.25
Marcano, Maracaibo	9	1	0	1	6	0	.143	50	56	31	24	16	42	4.32
Martin, Caracas	9	1	1	3	0	0	1.000	48	46	23	15	16	22	2.81
Martinez, Caracas	14	4	1	7	1	2	.875	81	54	14	8	26	47	0.89
Meistickle, Panama	4	0	0	0	1	0	.000	3	5	1	1	1	3	3.00
Metzger, Caracas	2	1	0	2	0	0	1.000	18	8	2	1	5	7	0.50
Moulton, Caracas	12	0	0	1	0	0	1.000	23	22	12	4	16	11	1.57
Pazik, Maracaibo*	1	0	0	0	0	0	.000	⅓	0	0	0	0	0	0.00
Pena, Miami	1	0	0	0	0	0	.000	6	6	2	1	0	2	1.50
Penalver, Caracas	11	0	0	3	3	0	.500	68	85	23	22	5	23	2.91
Perzanowski, Maracaibo	23	0	0	2	3	7	.400	33	33	17	9	17	24	2.45
Ploucher, Maracaibo*	15	2	1	3	5	0	.375	60	59	40	31	27	18	4.65
Pole, Santo Domingo	10	0	0	4	3	0	.571	60	68	37	29	18	19	4.35
Polinsky, Caracas	4	0	0	1	0	0	1.000	15	10	5	4	7	15	2.40
Rabouin, Panama	13	1	0	2	2	0	.500	47	38	25	22	21	31	4.21
Reynolds, Miami	19	0	0	1	2	11	.333	31	27	8	4	9	21	1.16
Sanchez, Caracas	13	0	0	2	4	0	.333	35	39	25	19	19	25	4.89
Sarmiento, Maracaibo	15	3	0	6	3	0	.667	83	86	35	27	16	32	2.93
Schirripa, Panama	8	1	0	2	3	0	.400	33	32	20	17	16	14	4.64
Scott, Panama	7	0	0	2	1	0	.667	11	12	5	3	6	4	2.45
Scott, Miami	15	7	2	8	4	0	.667	101	90	37	27	25	32	2.41
Sealey, Santo Domingo	1	0	0	0	0	0	.000	2	1	1	0	0	4	4.50
Solis, Panama	12	0	0	0	1	0	1.000	41	53	26	23	16	19	5.05
Souza, Puerto Rico	8	3	1	1	6	0	.143	60	52	20	16	13	24	2.40
Standart, Caracas	21	0	0	6	3	2	.667	38	30	14	6	8	28	1.42
Stanton, Maracaibo	5	1	1	3	2	0	.600	30	24	15	9	7	7	2.70
Texidor, Puerto Rico	9	0	0	0	1	0	.000	19	15	7	5	4	11	2.37
Thomas, Maracaibo	19	6	2	6	8	0	.429	115	126	51	43	28	43	3.37
Torres, Santo Domingo*	18	0	0	2	4	0	.333	73	72	35	31	29	27	3.82
Tyrone, Miami	1	1	0	0	1	0	.000	8	8	3	1	4	5	1.13
Velasquez, Panama	1	0	0	0	0	0	.000	1	3	2	0	2	0	0.00
Velasquez, Puerto Rico	17	0	0	0	3	0	.000	24	23	10	7	6	8	2.63
Van Bommel, Miami	10	0	0	2	0	1	1.000	24	17	7	7	23	14	2.63

Pitcher and Club	G.	CG.	ShO.	W.	L.	Sv.	Pct.	IP.	H.	R.	ER.	BB.	SO.	ERA.
Wallace, Santo Domingo	3	0	0	0	0	1	.000	4	6	5	3	3	1	6.75
Wallace, Miami	14	2	1	11	1	0	.917	91	88	28	23	18	42	2.27
Webb, Miami	12	0	0	7	3	0	.700	74	73	39	30	35	38	3.65
Williams, 16 Pan-1 Car	17	5	1	1	7	0	.125	76	79	40	32	27	52	3.79
Wrona, Puerto Rico	9	1	0	2	3	0	.400	43	42	21	13	9	17	2.72
Zamora, Miami	14	7	0	8	4	0	.667	102	114	43	38	11	28	3.35

————————

Inter-American League Failed

The Inter-American League, which collected more bills than fans, closed down June 30, nine weeks short of the conclusion of its planned 130-game season as a new Triple-A circuit.

Miami was declared the champion because the Amigos won the first half of the season, when the loop included six teams, and were atop the standings in the second half.

Time was only one of the commodities the circuit found in short supply during its maiden voyage. The league also had a shortage of fans, community acceptance, radio and television contracts, good weather, on-schedule flights and, ultimately, teams. After 10 weeks, Panama and San Juan could not meet their financial obligations and were disbanded.

The league continued for another two weeks before Caracas Owner Roberto Weill, who was about to lose advertising revenues generated by his two-nation radio networks, telephoned IAL President Bobby Maduro and suggested closing shop for this season.

Maduro took the problem to the other owners. Santo Domingo concurred with Caracas. Miami and Maracaibo wanted to continue, but two teams don't make a league.

The principal cause of the termination was money. Attendance generated some, though not nearly enough to satisfy anyone.

Radio and television contracts had been counted on as an important source. Of the six original franchises, only Caracas, Maracaibo and Santo Domingo had season-long radio contracts. Only Caracas had a television deal for a few early-season games. Panama had no radio package. Miami broadcast one game.

Caracas was easily the backbone of the league, drawing an average of 3,500 fans per game. Miami averaged 1,350, Maracaibo 1,100, Santo Domingo 1,000, Panama 800 and San Juan 650.

Maduro, who resigned his job as major league baseball's coordinator of Latin-American affairs to develop the IAL, said all six teams lost money. The financial drain was so severe that each club was required to post only half of the $50,000 franchise fee.

The IAL was plagued by poor weather and unreliable transportation. Seventy contests were postponed by rain and countless others were played in poor conditions because of downpours. Travel was complicated by the grounding of DC-10 jets.

International League

CLASS AAA

Leading Batter
GARRY HANCOCK
Pawtucket

League President
HAROLD COOPER

Leading Pitcher
SCOTT HOLMAN
Tidewater

CHAMPIONSHIP WINNERS IN PREVIOUS YEARS

1884 – Trenton .520	1924 – Baltimore .709	1953 – Rochester .630
1885 – Syracuse .584	1925 – Baltimore .633	Montreal (2nd)† .586
1886 – Utica .646	1926 – Toronto .657	1954 – Toronto .630
1887 – Toronto .644	1927 – Buffalo .667	Syracuse (4th)§ .510
1888 – Syracuse .723	1928 – Rochester .549	1955 – Montreal .617
1889 – Detroit .649	1929 – Rochester .613	Rochester (4th)† .497
1890 – Detroit .617	1930 – Rochester .629	1956 – Toronto .566
1891 – Buffalo (reg. season) .727	1931 – Rochester .601	Rochester (2nd)†.... .553
Buffalo (supplem'l) .680	1932 – Newark .649	1957 – Toronto .575
1892 – Providence .615	1933 – Newark .622	Buffalo (2nd)† .571
Binghamton* .667	Buffalo (4th)† .494	1958 – Montreal‡ .588
1893 – Erie .606	1934 – Newark .608	1959 – Buffalo .582
1894 – Providence .696	Toronto (3rd)† .559	Havana (3rd)† .523
1895 – Springfield .687	1935 – Montreal .597	1960 – Toronto‡ .649
1896 – Providence .602	Syracuse (2nd)† .565	1961 – Columbus .597
1897 – Syracuse .632	1936 – Buffalo‡ .610	Buffalo (3rd)† .559
1898 – Montreal .586	1937 – Newark‡ .717	1962 – Jacksonville .610
1899 – Rochester .624	1938 – Newark‡ .684	Atlanta (3rd)† .539
1900 – Providence .616	1939 – Jersey City .582	1963 – Syracuse x .533
1901 – Rochester .642	Rochester (2nd)† .556	Indianapolis† .562
1902 – Toronto .669	1940 – Rochester .611	1964 – Jacksonville .589
1903 – Jersey City .642	Newark (2nd)† .594	Rochester (4th)† .532
1904 – Buffalo .657	1941 – Newark .649	1965 – Columbus .582
1905 – Providence .638	Montreal (2nd)† .584	Toronto (3rd)† .556
1906 – Buffalo .607	1942 – Newark .601	1966 – Rochester .565
1907 – Toronto .619	Syracuse (3rd)† .513	Toronto (2nd-tied)† .558
1908 – Baltimore .593	1943 – Toronto .625	1967 – Richmond .574
1909 – Rochester .596	Syracuse (3rd)† .536	Toledo (3rd)† .525
1910 – Rochester .601	1944 – Baltimore‡ .553	1968 – Toledo .565
1911 – Rochester .645	1945 – Montreal .621	Jacksonville (4th)† .514
1912 – Toronto .595	Newark (2nd)† .582	1969 – Tidewater .563
1913 – Newark .625	1946 – Montreal‡ .649	Syracuse (3rd)† .536
1914 – Providence .617	1947 – Jersey City .610	1970 – Syracuse‡ .600
1915 – Buffalo .632	Syracuse (3rd)† .575	1971 – Rochester‡ .614
1916 – Buffalo .586	1948 – Montreal‡ .614	1972 – Louisville .563
1917 – Toronto .604	1949 – Buffalo .584	Tidewater (3rd)† .545
1918 – Toronto .693	Montreal (3rd)† .545	1973 – Charleston .586
1919 – Baltimore .671	1950 – Rochester .609	Pawtucket y† .534
1920 – Baltimore .719	Baltimore (3rd)† .556	1974 – Memphis .613
1921 – Baltimore .717	1951 – Montreal‡ .617	Rochester x‡ .611
1922 – Baltimore .689	1952 – Montreal .629	1975 – Tidewater‡ .610
1923 – Baltimore .677	Rochester (3rd)† .619	

CHAMPIONSHIP WINNERS IN PREVIOUS YEARS—Continued

1976—Rochester	.638	1977—Pawtucket	.571	1978—Richmond (4th)	.511
Syracuse (2nd)†	.590	Charleston (2nd)†	.557	Pawtucket (2nd)	.579

*Won split-season playoff. †Won four-team playoff. ‡Won championsip and four-team playoff. §Defeated Havana in game to decide fourth place, then won four-team playoff. xLeague was divided into Northern, Southern divisions. yLeague divided into American, National divisions. (NOTE—Known as Eastern League in 1884, New York State League in 1885, International League in 1886-87, International Association in 1888, International League in 1889-90, Eastern Association in 1891, and Eastern League from 1892 until 1912.)

STANDING OF CLUBS AT CLOSE OF SEASON, SEPTEMBER 1

Club	Col.	Syr.	Rich.	Tide.	Paw.	Char.	Tol.	Roch.	W.	L.	T.	Pct.	G.B.
Columbus (Yankees)	....	11	11	10	14	12	13	14	85	54	0	.612	......
Syracuse (Blue Jays)	9	....	11	10	5	11	15	16	77	63	0	.550	8½
Richmond (Braves)	9	9	....	11	13	12	9	13	76	64	1	.543	9½
Tidewater (Mets)	10	10	9	....	11	11	11	11	73	67	1	.521	12½
Pawtucket (Red Sox)	6	15	7	9	....	10	8	11	66	74	0	.471	19½
Charleston (Astros)	8	9	8	9	10	....	12	9	65	74	1	.468	20
Toledo (Twins)	6	5	11	9	12	8	....	12	63	76	0	.453	22
Rochester (Orioles)	6	4	7	9	9	10	8	....	53	86	1	.381	32

Tidewater club represented Norfolk and Portsmouth, Va.

Major league affiliations in parentheses.

Playoffs—Columbus defeated Tidewater, three games to one; Syracuse defeated Richmond, three games to two; Columbus defeated Syracuse, four games to three (for Governor's Cup).

Regular-Season Attendance—Charleston, 72,609; Columbus, 599,544; Pawtucket, 147,420; Richmond, 159,864; Rochester, 200,013; Syracuse, 176,539; Tidewater, 111,570; Toledo, 148,592. Total, 1,616,151. Playoffs, 49,678. No all-star game.

Managers: Charleston—Jim Beauchamp; Columbus—Gene Michael; Pawtucket—Joe Morgan; Richmond—Tom Burgess; Rochester—Howard (Doc) Edwards; Syracuse—Vern Benson; Tidewater—Frank Verdi; Toledo—Cal Ermer.

All-Star Team: 1B—Chism, Rochester; 2B—Holt, Columbus; 3B—Stapleton, Pawtucket; SS—Hoffman, Pawtucket; OF—Brown, Columbus; Wilson, Tidewater; Bowen, Pawtucket; C—Gulden, Columbus; DH—Koza, Pawtucket; P—Anderson, Columbus; Boggs, Richmond; Manager—Benson, Syracuse.

(Compiled by Leonard Alley, League Statistician, Richmond, Va.)

CLUB BATTING

Club	G.	AB.	R.	OR.	H.	TB.	2B.	3B.	HR.	RBI.	SH.	SF.	Int. BB.	BB.	HP.	SO.	SB.	CS.	LOB.	Pct.
Columbus	139	4473	609	557	1212	1737	211	31	84	559	51	48	513	38	30	634	107	48	1007	.271
Rochester	140	4487	558	656	1159	1657	188	38	78	504	51	36	425	45	22	589	80	53	884	.258
Charleston	140	4536	549	548	1164	1587	201	27	56	492	31	35	420	26	26	589	49	31	973	.257
Pawtucket	140	4636	582	551	1163	1815	177	23	143	540	34	35	395	24	50	732	22	29	934	.251
Syracuse	140	4605	581	539	1153	1729	195	60	87	535	66	45	420	43	33	803	43	30	929	.250
Richmond	141	4450	548	552	1113	1610	162	52	77	509	63	39	480	39	56	769	164	64	958	.250
Toledo	139	4542	573	591	1132	1653	186	31	91	519	72	39	477	32	20	718	68	38	925	.249
Tidewater	141	4486	527	533	1073	1559	181	43	73	477	44	31	445	26	37	836	126	38	955	.239

INDIVIDUAL BATTING

(Leading Qualifiers for Batting Championship—378 or More Plate Appearances)

*Bats lefthanded. †Switch-hitter.

Player and Club	G.	AB.	R.	H.	TB.	2B.	3B.	HR.	RBI.	SH.	SF.	BB.	HP.	SO.	SB.	CS.	Pct.
Hancock, R. Garry, Pawtucket	111	406	51	132	205	22	3	15	58	0	2	22	2	36	1	5	.325
Chism, Thomas, Rochester*	107	372	60	116	182	25	4	11	60	2	4	50	2	41	1	3	.312
Stapleton, David, Pawtucket	140	553	88	169	249	33	1	15	64	1	6	41	4	40	2	5	.306
Werth, Dennis, Columbus	133	421	69	126	210	27	3	17	74	5	10	88	4	90	3	5	.299
Cruz, Cirilo, Columbus*	109	411	56	122	185	30	3	9	66	3	4	29	1	47	4	1	.297
Vega, Jesus, Toledo	129	450	52	132	201	24	3	13	72	4	9	43	2	63	5	2	.293
Augustine, David, Charleston†	121	430	46	125	168	26	4	3	49	1	7	14	2	45	2	2	.291
Engle, R. David, Toledo	106	363	46	104	144	17	1	7	51	1	1	25	0	54	2	0	.287
Hoffman, Glenn, Pawtucket	139	520	70	148	200	13	3	11	54	6	4	29	10	66	1	1	.285
Iorg, Garth, Syracuse	121	430	65	121	167	23	4	5	39	11	7	46	4	44	2	4	.281

Departmental Leaders: G—Wilson, 141; AB—Stapleton, 553; R—Stapleton, 88; H—Stapleton, 169; TB—Stapleton, 249; 2B—Stapleton, 33; 3B—Miller, 11; HR—Bowen, 28; RBI—Bowen, Keller, 75; SH—Mantick, 15; SF—Werth, 10; BB—Bergman, 95; HP—Miller, 17; SO—Brant, 119; SB—Miller, 76; CS—Miller, 23.

(All Players—Listed Alphabetically)

Player and Club	G.	AB.	R.	H.	TB.	2B.	3B.	HR.	RBI.	SH.	SF.	BB.	HP.	SO.	SB.	CS.	Pct.
Ainge, Daniel, Syracuse	27	101	10	25	33	4	2	0	8	2	0	7	2	20	0	0	.248
Alberts, Francis, Syracuse	19	60	6	14	20	1	1	1	13	1	2	4	0	14	1	0	.233
Alexander, Roger, Richmond	28	2	0	0	0	0	0	0	0	0	0	1	0	1	0	0	.000
Amerson, Archie, Toledo	103	333	39	77	131	13	1	13	45	2	3	34	0	51	6	2	.231

Player and Club	G.	AB.	R.	H.	TB.	2B.	3B.	HR.	RBI.	SH.	SF.	BB.	HP.	SO.	SB.	CS.	Pct.
Anderson, Lawrence, 9 Ch-14 Ri.....	23	7	1	1	1	0	0	0	2	0	0	0	0	4	0	0	.143
Arline, James, Richmond*..............	56	159	20	33	36	1	1	0	13	0	0	23	1	40	7	4	.208
Asselstine, Brian, Richmond*........	21	63	3	17	22	5	0	0	4	1	0	10	0	8	0	2	.270
Augustine, David, Charleston†........	121	430	46	125	168	26	4	3	49	1	7	14	2	45	2	2	.291
Ault, Douglas, Syracuse................	121	444	53	112	185	25	6	12	71	2	5	41	2	58	6	1	.252
Ayala, Benigno, Rochester	17	62	10	22	32	1	3	1	7	1	0	6	1	6	0	1	.355
Baker, David G., Syracuse*............	116	396	42	88	136	17	5	7	43	3	4	31	3	67	1	0	.222
Baldwin, Reginald C., Charleston....	49	180	23	49	76	10	1	5	33	0	1	3	2	10	0	0	.272
Beall, Robert, Richmond†..............	32	104	27	38	57	5	1	4	17	1	1	28	3	21	2	1	.365
Benton, Alfred, Tidewater............	94	313	39	62	82	9	1	3	25	3	1	18	5	54	13	1	.198
Bergman, David, Charleston*........	138	461	78	129	176	23	3	6	58	2	4	95	1	43	9	6	.280
Bernard, Dwight, Tidewater..........	33	3	0	0	0	0	0	0	0	0	1	0	0	0	0	0	.000
Bianco, Thomas, Rochester†..........	91	292	24	64	82	10	1	2	26	1	2	33	1	31	2	1	.219
Boggs, Thomas, Richmond	33	12	0	0	0	0	0	0	2	0	0	1	0	0	0	0	.000
Bonner, Robert, Rochester	4	11	1	3	3	0	0	0	0	0	0	0	0	2	0	0	.273
Bowen, Samuel, Pawtucket............	125	456	68	107	215	16	4	28	75	3	5	60	2	113	4	6	.235
Boyer, Raymond, Pawtucket..........	14	52	7	15	23	3	1	1	9	0	1	8	2	6	1	0	.288
Bradford, Larry, Richmond............	18	1	0	0	0	0	0	0	0	0	0	0	0	1	0	0	.000
Brant, Marshall, Tidewater............	138	488	58	123	214	21	2	22	65	2	6	41	4	119	0	6	.252
Brizzolara, Anthony, Richmond......	9	1	0	0	0	0	0	0	0	0	0	0	0	0	0	0	.000
Brooks, Hubert, Tidewater	5	15	1	6	10	1	0	1	3	0	0	1	0	2	0	0	.400
Brown, Rogers, Columbus*............	70	258	53	90	134	14	3	8	41	1	4	21	1	36	25	7	.349
Bruhert, Michael, Tidewater..........	20	3	0	0	0	0	0	0	0	0	0	0	0	2	0	0	.000
Bryant, Robert, Tidewater*............	18	52	1	8	12	1	0	1	7	3	0	4	0	11	1	1	.154
Buckner, James, 29 Tol.-79 Tide.*..	108	316	37	71	92	14	2	1	27	1	3	21	1	40	15	6	.225
Butera, Barry, Pawtucket*............	108	310	50	96	155	15	1	14	55	1	2	31	2	26	5	3	.310
Butera, Salvatore, Toledo	78	236	20	70	89	13	0	2	29	5	1	23	1	16	0	1	.297
Camp, Rick, Richmond................	22	4	0	0	0	0	0	0	0	0	0	0	0	2	0	0	.000
Cannon, Joseph, Syracuse*............	59	231	41	67	113	14	7	6	24	1	0	11	4	55	11	5	.290
Caughey, Wayne, Toledo*..............	31	105	16	20	26	6	0	0	4	2	0	16	1	11	1	3	.190
Chapman, Kelvin, Tidewater	106	352	45	85	112	14	2	3	37	1	2	45	9	57	17	7	.241
Chapman, Nathan, Columbus*........	60	193	29	52	63	4	2	1	16	2	3	13	3	31	11	4	.269
Chevez, Antonio, Rochester	23	2	0	0	0	0	0	0	0	0	0	0	0	1	0	0	.000
Chism, Thomas, Rochester*	107	372	60	116	182	25	4	11	60	2	4	50	2	41	1	3	.312
Cipot, Edwin, Tidewater*............	124	370	40	92	142	15	4	9	45	2	2	82	3	56	2	2	.249
Coleman, David, Toledo	134	485	65	115	206	23	4	20	63	3	5	59	3	98	1	2	.237
Collins, Donald, Richmond............	34	12	2	1	1	0	0	0	0	0	2	0	0	9	0	0	.083
Corey, Mark, Rochester	92	317	38	79	132	21	1	10	30	2	1	35	3	68	6	5	.249
Cruz, Cirilo, Columbus*................	109	411	56	122	185	30	3	9	66	3	4	29	1	48	4	1	.297
Denton, David, Pawtucket............	114	344	34	69	109	11	1	9	28	3	2	36	5	82	3	1	.201
Diggle, Ronnie, Rochester*	109	353	50	90	149	18	1	13	58	1	1	43	0	63	4	5	.255
Dimmel, Michael, Columbus	21	62	3	15	24	1	1	2	11	0	3	3	0	8	3	1	.242
Doyle, Blake, Rochester*	39	131	23	34	44	2	4	0	21	1	1	16	0	7	1	0	.260
Doyle, Brian, Columbus*..............	39	126	15	32	48	6	2	2	9	2	1	14	0	9	1	0	.254
Drumright, Keith, Charleston*........	76	305	40	107	99	4	0	16	1	3	24	1	17	3	5		.295
Duncan, Taylor, Rochester............	36	132	12	31	43	6	0	2	16	2	1	10	0	15	0	1	.235
Easterly, James, Richmond†..........	10	1	0	0	0	0	0	0	0	0	0	0	0	1	0	0	.000
Eden, E. Michael, Rochester†........	95	333	46	90	121	10	3	5	36	3	3	39	2	23	6	4	.270
Engle, R. David, Toledo..............	106	363	46	104	144	17	1	7	51	1	1	25	0	54	2	0	.287
Estes, Frank, Toledo*..................	62	163	12	40	57	10	2	1	14	3	1	13	0	18	0	2	.245
Ferrer, Sergio, Tidewater†............	29	104	14	20	31	4	2	1	15	4	1	20	1	16	1	0	.192
Fischlin, Michael, Charleston	44	138	13	31	37	4	1	0	8	6	0	11	2	17	4	1	.225
Foster, Otis, Pawtucket	68	210	32	46	63	5	0	4	18	0	3	42	0	23	0	0	.219
Garcia, Damaso, Columbus	39	118	18	32	36	1	0	1	3	5	2	7	0	22	16	5	.271
Gates, Eddie, Charleston..............	30	80	14	23	35	3	0	3	12	2	2	18	1	17	0	0	.288
Glynn, Edward, Tidewater	17	1	0	0	0	0	0	0	0	0	0	0	0	0	0	0	.000
Gorinski, Robert, Tidewater..........	61	179	19	36	65	4	2	7	25	0	0	11	1	53	0	1	.201
Graham, Daniel, Toledo*..............	119	403	48	86	136	19	2	9	55	1	9	54	1	78	1	0	.213
Gulden, Bradley, Columbus*..........	80	230	28	57	85	10	0	6	34	2	4	42	0	31	6	4	.248
Hancock, R. Garry, Pawtucket*	111	406	51	132	205	22	3	15	58	0	2	22	2	36	1	5	.325
Harper, Terry, Richmond..............	108	327	49	99	153	18	3	10	58	1	1	35	6	57	15	2	.303
Hoffman, Glenn, Pawtucket	139	520	70	148	200	13	3	11	54	6	4	29	10	66	1	1	.285
Holman, R. Scott, Tidewater	25	6	1	2	3	1	0	0	1	0	0	0	0	2	0	0	.333
Holt, Roger, Columbus†..............	130	454	72	127	152	16	3	1	33	12	0	69	6	42	8	8	.280
Hough, Stanley, Tidewater............	28	70	9	11	16	2	0	1	5	0	1	7	0	20	0	0	.157
Howard, Wilbur, Charleston	86	291	19	70	80	8	1	0	23	1	3	18	1	32	3	5	.241
Hubbard, Glenn, Richmond............	34	125	21	42	55	5	1	2	17	5	1	14	0	17	2	1	.336
Huizenga, Kenneth, Pawtucket	114	294	23	57	86	14	0	5	23	3	1	15	1	39	0	1	.194
Hunter, Harold, Pawtucket	76	227	18	50	61	9	1	0	23	4	2	26	1	25	0	1	.220
Iorg, Garth, Syracuse	121	430	65	121	167	23	4	5	39	11	7	46	4	44	2	4	.281
Irwin, Dennis, Columbus..............	14	34	0	5	7	2	0	0	0	0	0	2	0	1	0	0	.147
Jackson, Roy Lee, Tidewater..........	33	9	1	1	1	0	0	0	0	0	0	0	0	2	0	0	.111
James, Arthur, Rochester*............	54	199	26	52	78	13	2	3	21	3	1	21	2	18	3	2	.261
Johnson, Larry, Rochester............	40	131	14	41	56	4	1	3	14	1	2	10	0	18	1	1	.313
Jones, Darrell, Columbus................	67	243	32	65	80	13	1	0	23	2	2	16	1	21	2	0	.267

Player and Club	G.	AB.	R.	H.	TB.	2B.	3B.	HR.	RBI.	SH.	SF.	BB.	HP.	SO.	SB.	CS.	Pct.
Keller, Charles, Richmond	126	435	54	111	198	18	3	21	75	2	6	61	3	93	0	1	.255
Kelly, D. Patrick, Syracuse	6	17	0	3	4	1	0	0	0	0	0	0	0	6	0	0	.176
Kennedy, Kevin, Rochester	109	360	28	71	96	8	4	3	32	5	2	26	4	40	0	3	.197
Kerrigan, Joseph, Rochester	64	1	0	0	0	0	0	0	0	0	0	0	0	0	0	0	.000
Koza, David, Pawtucket	101	360	53	86	177	10	0	27	63	0	2	20	8	90	3	1	.239
Krenchicki, Wayne, Rochester*	66	249	21	65	76	7	2	0	22	4	4	16	0	22	6	6	.261
LaCorte, Frank, Charleston	14	0	1	0	0	0	0	0	0	0	0	0	0	0	0	0	.000
LaFrancois, Roger, Pawtucket*	106	305	19	70	99	10	2	5	24	7	1	21	6	43	0	2	.230
Leach, Terry, Richmond	7	1	0	0	0	0	0	0	0	0	0	0	0	1	0	0	.000
Linares, Rufino, Richmond	36	104	9	31	40	4	1	1	13	3	0	4	1	16	3	3	.298
Livingstone, Stuart, Richmond	24	1	0	0	0	0	0	0	0	0	0	0	0	0	0	0	.000
Lopez, Carlos, Rochester	62	234	38	66	98	10	2	6	30	0	4	14	0	43	24	7	.282
Macha, Michael, Richmond	73	254	36	74	116	17	5	5	25	2	2	24	3	45	6	2	.291
Machemer, David, Rochester	69	260	39	76	99	14	3	1	31	8	1	21	1	27	15	3	.292
Maddox, Jerry, Richmond	127	417	49	106	152	15	5	7	53	5	6	59	3	59	2	3	.254
Mahler, Richard, Richmond	24	5	0	0	0	0	0	0	0	0	0	0	0	2	0	0	.000
Mantick, Dennis, Toledo*	107	323	39	77	89	10	1	0	19	15	3	29	2	76	4	6	.238
McKay, David, Syracuse	96	353	54	95	136	14	3	7	53	7	4	39	5	72	8	6	.269
McLaughlin, Joey, Richmond	18	0	0	0	0	0	0	0	0	0	0	1	0	0	0	0	.000
Meoli, Rudolph, Toledo*	51	189	36	50	69	10	3	1	20	0	3	30	0	37	14	3	.265
Merchant, J. Anderson, Pawtucket*	57	151	20	23	35	3	0	3	10	0	1	15	1	14	0	0	.152
Miller, Edward, Richmond†	135	517	73	121	176	18	11	5	37	12	1	41	17	11	76	23	.234
Monasterio, Juan, Tidewater	24	84	9	17	28	6	1	1	7	1	0	4	0	7	0	0	.202
Moreno, Jose, Tidewater†	119	407	49	104	138	17	4	3	49	3	3	50	0	59	20	4	.256
Morogiello, Daniel, Richmond*	31	7	0	2	2	0	0	0	1	1	0	0	0	2	0	0	.286
Myrick, Robert, Tidewater	9	2	0	0	0	0	0	0	0	0	0	0	0	2	0	0	.000
Norman, Daniel, Tidewater	81	297	35	82	128	15	5	7	50	1	2	30	0	40	4	2	.276
O'Berry, P. Michael, Pawtucket	34	78	6	13	17	1	0	1	5	3	1	11	0	24	0	0	.167
Obradovich, James, Charleston*□	119	390	50	90	152	23	0	13	51	2	4	55	3	72	1	0	.231
Orosco, Jesse, Tidewater	16	6	0	1	2	1	0	0	1	1	0	0	0	4	0	0	.167
Owen, Lawrence, Richmond	110	358	32	70	104	7	3	7	29	2	1	29	1	64	0	3	.196
Pacella, John, Tidewater	29	6	2	2	2	0	0	0	0	0	0	0	0	3	0	0	.333
Pankovits, James, Charleston	22	59	7	10	15	3	1	0	3	1	1	6	2	12	1	0	.169
Perez, Ramon, Charleston	99	342	39	80	88	6	1	0	20	5	0	26	0	37	10	2	.234
Petralli, Eugene, Syracuse†	18	56	6	13	15	0	1	0	7	1	2	2	0	11	0	0	.232
Pisker, Donald, Syracuse*	111	385	57	95	157	12	10	10	46	2	3	51	2	111	2	0	.247
Pittman, Joseph, Charleston	5	1	1	0	0	0	0	0	0	0	0	0	0	0	0	0	.000
Powell, Hosken, Toledo*	10	44	14	11	14	3	0	0	6	0	0	6	2	2	1	1	.250
Prewitt, Larry, Tidewater†	9	1	0	0	0	0	0	0	0	0	0	0	0	1	0	0	.000
Pujols, Luis, Charleston	105	345	29	86	126	18	2	6	41	5	0	14	4	60	1	0	.249
Rajsich, Gary, Charleston*	65	218	27	45	75	8	2	6	28	0	3	24	1	27	2	1	.206
Ramirez, Alex, Toledo	27	85	3	20	22	0	1	0	7	3	0	7	0	9	0	0	.235
Ramirez, Mario, Tidewater	132	376	42	82	114	10	2	6	31	9	3	31	0	92	5	2	.218
Ramirez, Orlando, Charleston	4	12	1	1	1	0	0	0	0	0	0	0	0	3	0	0	.083
Ramos, Domingo, 95 Syr-20 Col	115	376	38	92	114	11	4	1	28	11	3	40	3	41	1	0	.245
Reynolds, Michael, Richmond†	52	146	13	29	37	8	0	0	16	3	0	28	2	20	3	5	.199
Rineer, Jeffrey, Rochester*	31	1	0	0	0	0	0	0	0	0	0	0	0	1	0	0	.000
Robertson, Andre, Syracuse	1	4	0	0	0	0	0	0	0	0	0	0	0	0	0	0	.000
Robinson, Bruce, Columbus*	102	316	37	79	120	10	2	9	45	4	3	23	3	41	1	0	.250
Rockett, Patrick, Richmond	85	247	21	55	66	7	2	0	17	9	4	18	5	25	10	3	.223
Rogers, Randell, Tidewater	20	68	10	14	18	2	1	0	4	1	0	6	0	11	0	0	.206
Rosado, Luis, 47 Syr-52 Tide	99	333	35	83	117	20	1	4	29	2	2	22	1	48	0	1	.249
Royster, Willie, Rochester	47	128	17	36	49	4	0	3	13	1	0	7	1	28	2	4	.281
Ruiz, Manuel, Richmond	122	443	52	105	146	15	7	4	53	13	7	38	5	68	22	8	.237
Sain, Thomas, 40 Tol-43 Char	83	249	32	49	73	7	5	1	19	1	3	21	1	30	3	1	.197
Schmitz, Daniel, Columbus*	95	288	31	75	93	6	3	2	32	2	2	58	1	18	2	4	.260
Scott, Michael, Tidewater	17	8	0	0	0	0	0	0	0	0	0	0	0	4	0	0	.000
Sember, Michael, Syracuse	49	140	17	21	32	3	1	2	10	3	1	18	1	56	0	1	.150
Sherrill, Dennis, Columbus	57	158	17	39	56	8	0	3	10	1	1	13	4	36	5	2	.247
Small, G. Henry, Richmond	102	355	39	78	107	9	1	6	35	0	6	19	6	44	2	0	.220
Smith, Garry, Columbus	61	193	20	40	66	11	0	5	25	1	1	16	2	54	7	2	.207
Smith, James, Rochester	130	404	48	96	127	15	2	4	34	11	3	44	3	76	5	2	.238
Smith, Raymond, Toledo	78	233	24	58	75	7	3	3	24	11	0	14	2	19	1	1	.249
Smith, Thomas, Rochester	26	67	7	11	16	2	0	1	9	1	2	4	0	9	1	0	.164
Snell, Nathaniel, Rochester	12	1	0	0	0	0	0	0	0	0	0	0	0	1	0	0	.000
Sofield, Richard, Toledo*	54	177	28	42	60	9	0	3	14	5	0	35	0	40	1	2	.237
Spencer, H. Tom, Charleston	30	106	14	38	51	5	1	2	27	0	0	6	1	9	4	0	.358
Sperring, Robert, Charleston	137	544	71	142	184	23	5	3	49	1	4	40	2	78	0	1	.261
Staiger, Roy, Columbus	104	365	56	95	143	21	0	9	62	3	5	52	1	56	1	1	.260
Stapleton, David, Pawtucket	140	553	88	169	249	33	1	15	64	1	6	41	4	40	2	5	.306
Stenholm, Richard, Columbus*	52	181	21	50	84	12	2	6	23	2	2	12	2	40	1	1	.276
Stephenson, C. Earl, 19 Ro-26 Ti	45	1	0	0	0	0	0	0	0	0	0	0	0	0	0	0	.000
Theiss, Duane, Richmond	11	1	0	0	0	0	0	0	0	0	0	0	0	0	0	0	.000
Thompson, Marvin, Columbus	111	361	45	97	132	16	5	3	49	2	1	47	1	47	10	3	.269
Thurberg, Thomas, P., Tidewater	1	2	0	0	0	0	0	0	0	0	0	0	0	2	0	0	.000

Player and Club	G.	AB.	R.	H.	TB.	2B.	3B.	HR.	RBI.	SH.	SF.	BB.	HP.	SO.	SB.	CS.	Pct.
Till, Steven, Tidewater†	13	32	4	6	7	1	0	0	1	0	0	5	0	11	0	0	.188
Tyler, Michael, Charlotte*	50	143	10	32	34	2	0	0	10	2	0	11	1	29	0	1	.224
Tyrone, Wayne, Rochester	43	139	24	33	53	5	0	5	21	0	1	12	1	23	1	0	.237
Upshaw, Willie, Syracuse*	140	526	71	131	208	25	8	12	68	3	6	52	4	90	3	3	.249
Valdez, Julio, Pawtucket	103	370	43	82	121	12	6	5	31	3	2	18	6	105	2	3	.222
Van de Casteele, Michael, Tide.	32	7	0	0	0	0	0	0	0	2	0	0	0	3	0	0	.000
Vega, Jesus, Toledo	129	450	62	132	201	24	3	13	72	4	9	43	2	63	5	2	.293
Vilorio, Francisco, Toledo	83	282	26	68	86	6	0	4	21	7	1	17	4	29	9	2	.241
Wallace, Michael, Rochester	15	1	0	0	0	0	0	0	0	0	0	0	0	0	0	0	.000
Ward, Gary, Toledo	134	506	75	133	206	16	9	13	67	9	2	58	2	92	17	9	.263
Washington, Ronald, Tidewater	83	273	18	72	96	13	4	1	26	3	4	19	4	56	4	1	.264
Wells, Gregory, Syracuse	99	380	50	104	167	16	4	13	65	2	4	18	2	45	1	0	.274
Werth, Dennis, Columbus	133	421	69	126	210	27	3	17	74	5	10	88	4	90	3	5	.299
Wessinger, James, Richmond	15	49	4	14	17	0	0	1	7	0	1	0	0	.0	0	1	.286
Whisenton, Larry, Richmond*	89	292	43	86	124	10	8	4	35	3	2	44	0	57	14	2	.295
Whitt, Ernest, Syracuse*	114	382	32	95	142	18	4	7	43	7	3	42	0	43	2	1	.249
Wilborn, Thaddeus, Syracuse	61	227	28	56	66	5	1	1	10	10	0	15	1	53	6	9	.247
Wilson, William, Tidewater	141	529	84	141	198	22	10	5	36	6	2	45	8	91	49	12	.267
Woods, Gary, Charleston	97	338	46	90	135	25	1	6	49	2	1	42	1	66	6	6	.266
Youngbauer, Jeffrey, Rochester*	92	307	32	83	121	13	5	5	43	4	3	18	1	26	2	5	.270

The following pitchers had no plate appearances primarily through the use of designated hitters, listed alphabetically by club, games in parentheses):

CHARLESTON—Foucault, Steven (5); Hardy, H. Lawrence (34); Mendoza, Michael (42); Miggins, Mark (37); Miscik, Dennis (10); Niemann, Randy (8); Pladson, Gordon (27); Rothermel, Russell (29); Smith, David, (34); Sprowl, Robert (17–1 with Pawtucket); Strom, Brent (6); Throop, George (10); Williams, Richard (2); Wilson, Gary (19).

COLUMBUS—Anderson, Richard (52); Beattie, James (8); Cochran, Gregory (24); Cooper, Donald (8); Davis, Ronald (11); Griffin, Michael (6); Kammeyer, Robert (27); Lysgaard, James (9); Mersch, Neal (2); Mirabella, Paul (22); Polinsky, Robert (1); Righetti, David (8); Semall, Paul (13); Slagle, Roger (22); Taylor, Steven (12); Wehrmeister, David (17); Welsh, Christopher (36).

PAWTUCKET—Burns, Michael (30); Faust, Alvin (21); Finch, Joel (17); LaRose, H. John (47); Parks, Danny (5); Rainey, Charles (3); Remmerswaal, Wilhelmus (39); Ripley, Allen (23); Schneck, Steven (33); Suter, W. Burke (29); Tudor, John (25); Wallace, David (9); Waller, Richard (30).

RICHMOND—Skok, Craig (8).

ROCHESTER—Bastian, Jose (19); Bernal, Victor (20); Blair, Dennis (7); Boddicker, Michael (15); Fierbaugh, N. Randy (10); Flinn, John (26); Ford, David (15); Franklin, Tony (1); Jones, Larry (10); Pirtle, Gerald (49); Torrez, Pete (8).

SYRACUSE—Benson, Randy (12); Buskey, Thomas (12); Edge, Claude (26); Fore, Charles (16); Garvin, T. Jared (8); Grilli, Stephen (50); Leal, Luis (1); Lemongello, Mark (4); Luebber, Stephen (29); May, Davis (16); Reynolds, Kenneth (19); Robertson, Jay (14); Stieb, David (7); Todd, Jackson (21); Wiley, Mark (27); Willis, Michael (20).

TIDEWATER—Apodaca, Robert (2); Clark, Russell (19); Hausman, Thomas (12); Pearson, Donald (2); Reardon, Jeffrey (30).

TOLEDO—Bacsik, Michael (7); Erickson, Roger (5); Felton, Terry (28); Holly, Jeffrey (38); Jackson, Darrell (14); MacPherson, Bruce (16); Perzanowski, Stanley (4); Serum, Gary (33); Sheehan, Terrence (28); Stanfield, Kevin (29); Thayer, Gregory (46); Thormodsgard, Paul (28); Verhoeven, John (50).

GRAND SLAM HOME RUNS—Keller, 2; S. Butera, Corey, Cruz, Graham, Hancock, Hoffman, Koza, Macha, G. Smith, Werth, Whisenton, Whitt, 1 each.

AWARDED FIRST BASE ON INTERFERENCE—Lopez, 3 (Gulden, LaFrancois, Pujols); Gorinski, 2 (Owen, LaFrancois); Asselstine (Rosado), Diggle (Robinson), Graham (Hausman), Kennedy (S. Butera), Maddox (LaFrancois), McKay (S. Butera), Merchant (Keller), Norman (R. Smith), Staiger (Petralli), Vega (O'Berry).

CLUB FIELDING

Club	G.	PO.	A.	E.	DP.	PB.	Pct.
Columbus	139	3546	1449	108	120	13	.979
Charleston	140	3515	1508	115	112	13	.978
Tidewater	141	3566	1544	136	148	26	.974
Syracuse	140	3678	1537	140	123	6	.973
Richmond	141	3605	1519	144	115	18	.973
Pawtucket	140	3621	1535	147	136	16	.972
Rochester	140	3532	1500	151	112	9	.971
Toledo	139	3644	1546	176	141	11	.967

Triple Plays—None.

INDIVIDUAL FIELDING

FIRST BASEMEN

*Throws lefthanded.

Player and Club	G.	PO.	A.	E.	DP.	Pct.
Hunter, Pawtucket	11	36	6	0	6	1.000
Stapleton, Pawtucket	71	515	58	1	49	.998
WELLS, Syracuse	98	920	63	5	77	.995
Beall, Richmond*	22	187	10	1	17	.995
Werth, Columbus	132	1188	73	9	102	.993
Brant, Tidewater	138	1231	74	11	124	.992
Vega, Toledo	93	890	53	8	92	.992
Small, Richmond	76	634	29	6	56	.991
Tyrone, Rochester	24	199	15	2	23	.991

Player and Club	G.	PO.	A.	E.	DP.	Pct.
Keller, Richmond	49	420	20	4	29	.991
Bergman, Charleston*	93	826	56	8	53	.991
Koza, Pawtucket*	50	442	39	5	38	.990
Chism, Rochester*	95	789	76	13	66	.985
Upshaw, Syracuse*	39	379	16	6	30	.985
Foster, Pawtucket	32	253	18	4	26	.985
Obradovich, Charleston*	48	434	31	8	46	.983
Graham, Toledo	30	245	25	5	13	.982
Bianco, Rochester	22	177	22	4	10	.980

FIRST BASEMEN–Continued

(Fewer than Ten Games)

Player and Club	G.	PO.	A.	E.	DP.	Pct.
Thompson, Columbus	8	52	1	0	5	1.000
Cipot, Tidewater*	6	30	1	0	5	1.000
Baldwin, Charleston	4	28	2	0	1	1.000
Sherrill, Columbus	4	23	1	0	1	1.000
Ault, Syracuse................	2	14	1	0	3	1.000
Alberts, Syracuse	1	10	2	0	2	1.000
Duncan, Rochester	1	9	1	0	1	1.000
Rosado, Tidewater..........	1	9	1	0	2	1.000
Garcia, Columbus...........	2	3	0	0	0	1.000
Br. Doyle, Columbus	1	3	0	0	1	1.000
Robinson, Columbus	1	1	0	0	0	1.000
Coleman, Toledo	10	88	8	1	4	.990
Estes, Toledo*	8	65	6	3	8	.959
Royster, Rochester	2	9	1	1	0	.909
Brown, Columbus............	1	5	1	1	3	.857
Corey, Rochester............	2	10	1	2	0	.846
O'Berry, Pawtucket.........	2	4	0	2	0	.667

SECOND BASEMEN

Player and Club	G.	PO.	A.	E.	DP.	Pct.
Ruiz, Richmond	71	161	209	2	39	.995
M. Ramirez, Tidewater....	27	61	108	1	29	.994
Meoli, Toledo..................	23	43	57	1	12	.990
Eden, Rochester	27	51	89	2	17	.986
MANTICK, Toledo	106	254	319	9	72	.985
Holt, Columbus..............	124	241	309	9	74	.984
Perez, Charleston	43	92	137	4	24	.983
Bl. Doyle, Columbus	37	73	94	3	9	.982
Vilorio, Toledo................	28	42	68	2	14	.982
McKay, Syracuse	76	183	258	9	43	.980
M. Reynolds, Richmond.	42	89	117	5	22	.976
K. Chapman, Tide...........	106	248	303	14	74	.975
Hunter, Pawtucket..........	66	132	177	8	39	.975
Stapleton, Pawtucket......	32	60	88	4	19	.974
Ainge, Syracuse	26	56	77	4	19	.971
Krenchicki, Rochester....	57	123	154	9	31	.969
Hubbard, Richmond	33	82	109	7	28	.965
Drumright, Charleston ..	74	150	220	14	41	.964
Machemer, Rochester....	21	39	62	4	11	.962
Pankovits, Charleston....	22	43	53	4	11	.960
Iorg, Syracuse	37	67	107	8	23	.956
Denton, Pawtucket..........	60	91	119	10	18	.955
Moreno, Tidewater..........	11	21	22	3	0	.935

(Fewer than Ten Games)

Player and Club	G.	PO.	A.	E.	DP.	Pct.
Br. Doyle, Columbus	8	10	23	0	4	1.000
Sherrill, Columbus	7	11	16	0	5	1.000
Bonner, Richmond	4	8	7	0	2	1.000
Bianco, Rochester	3	5	8	0	1	1.000
Sain, Tol-Char	4	3	7	0	2	1.000
Schmitz, Columbus	6	2	5	0	0	1.000
Staiger, Columbus..........	4	2	5	0	1	1.000
Pittman, Charleston	2	1	1	0	1	1.000
Macha, Richmond	1	1	0	0	0	1.000
Sember, Syracuse	2	2	9	1	1	.917
Howard, Charleston	2	2	4	1	0	.857
Rogers, Tidewater	2	4	8	3	2	.800
Tyrone, Rochester	1	1	1	1	1	.667

THIRD BASEMEN

Player and Club	G.	PO.	A.	E.	DP.	Pct.
Sherrill, Columbus	22	12	63	2	5	.974
Stapleton, Pawtucket	45	58	80	4	12	.972
STAIGER, Columbus......	97	60	235	12	22	.961
Sperring, Charleston	81	48	161	9	12	.959
Perez, Charleston	17	12	30	2	3	.955
Eden, Rochester............	43	23	79	5	7	.953
Washington, Tidewater..	70	56	118	9	10	.951
Sain, Charleston	33	23	74	5	6	.951
Bianco, Rochester	34	19	72	5	7	.948
Hoffman, Pawtucket	102	89	175	15	13	.946
Machemer, Rochester ..	21	11	42	3	0	.946
Schmitz, Columbus	15	7	27	2	0	.944
Augustine, Charleston ...	12	8	24	2	0	.941
Maddox, Richmond	126	118	258	24	24	.940
Rogers, Tidewater	12	8	22	2	5	.938
Moreno, Tidewater	75	55	129	13	8	.934
Baker, Syracuse..............	101	76	181	19	15	.931
Duncan, Rochester	33	30	77	8	5	.930
Iorg, Syracuse	35	28	68	8	4	.923
Engle, Toledo	87	72	197	23	22	.921
Graham, Toledo..............	51	42	107	14	13	.914
Tyrone, Rochester	15	11	16	5	1	.844

(Fewer Than Ten Games)

Player and Club	G.	PO.	A.	E.	DP.	Pct.
McKay, Syracuse............	5	6	14	0	1	1.000
Ruiz, Richmond..............	9	0	16	0	1	1.000
Br. Doyle, Columbus	4	2	14	0	0	1.000
Coleman, Toledo	3	1	8	0	0	1.000
Krenchicki, Rochester....	2	1	2	0	0	1.000
Denton, Pawtucket.........	3	2	4	0	0	1.000
Brooks, Tidewater..........	3	1	1	0	0	1.000
Rosado, Tidewater..........	2	2	0	0	0	1.000
Hubbard, Richmond	1	1	0	0	0	1.000
Johnson, Rochester........	1	0	1	0	0	1.000
Thompson, Columbus	8	5	11	2	1	.889
Macha, Richmond	8	2	19	3	1	.875
M. Reynolds, Richmond.	3	0	4	1	0	.800

SHORTSTOPS

Player and Club	G.	PO.	A.	E.	DP.	Pct.
Sherrill, Columbus	15	17	44	0	6	1.000
Wessinger, Richmond	15	20	54	1	9	.987
M. RAMIREZ, Tide.......	105	129	324	8	65	.983
Hoffman, Pawtucket	40	83	111	4	23	.980
Schmitz, Columbus	62	72	165	6	31	.975
Iorg, Syracuse	24	44	75	3	15	.975
Sperring, Charleston	56	76	173	8	31	.969
Meoli, Toledo..................	34	37	96	5	14	.964
Fischlin, Charleston	43	73	134	8	22	.963
J. Smith, Rochester	130	240	358	26	66	.958
Garcia, Columbus...........	33	50	85	6	24	.957
Sember, Syracuse	24	30	76	5	8	.955
Ramos, Syr-Col...............	109	211	323	26	65	.954
Br. Doyle, Columbus	24	36	67	5	6	.954
Rockett, Richmond	82	119	237	18	33	.952
Vilorio, Toledo................	56	94	163	15	40	.945
O. Ramirez, Toledo	27	36	66	6	14	.944
Washington, Tidewater..	23	21	39	4	6	.938
Perez, Charleston	36	47	113	11	18	.936
Valdez, Pawtucket..........	103	178	305	34	60	.934
Ruiz, Richmond	45	58	147	16	27	.928
Caughey, Toledo............	31	56	93	12	21	.925
Ferrer, Tidewater	29	51	89	13	29	.915

SHORTSTOPS—Continued
(Fewer Than Ten Games)

Player and Club	G.	PO.	A.	E.	DP.	Pct.	Player and Club	G.	PO.	A.	E.	DP.	Pct.
Krenchicki, Rochester....	6	5	17	0	1	1.000	Machemer, Rochester.....	3	9	12	2	3	.963
Augustine, Charleston ...	4	7	7	0	1	1.000	A. Ramirez, Charleston..	4	5	7	1	1	.923
Baker, Syracuse............	2	2	7	0	2	1.000	Brooks, Tidewater.........	3	3	7	1	0	.909
Stapleton, Pawtucket ...	3	3	4	0	1	1.000	Holt, Columbus..............	3	4	9	2	2	.867
Bonner, Rochester	1	2	5	0	1	1.000	Eden, Rochester............	4	2	3	1	0	.833
A. Robertson, Syracuse ..	1	1	4	0	1	1.000							

OUTFIELDERS

Player and Club	G.	PO.	A.	E.	DP.	Pct.	Player and Club	G.	PO.	A.	E.	DP.	Pct.
AUGUSTINE, Charl.	103	181	7	0	2	1.000	Cannon, Syracuse..........	59	153	4	5	2	.969
Wilborn, Syracuse	68	168	8	0	1	1.000	N. Chapman, Col.*........	58	121	4	4	0	.969
Spencer, Richmond.......	29	84	1	0	1	1.000	Ward, Toledo................	130	323	12	11	2	.968
Gorinski, Tidewater......	27	37	2	0	0	1.000	Woods, Charleston........	97	253	7	9	0	.967
Whitt, Syracuse	12	15	5	0	1	1.000	Coleman, Toledo...........	110	222	16	8	6	.967
Asselstine, Richmond ...	21	17	0	0	0	1.000	Bergman, Charleston*....	46	84	5	3	0	.967
Stapleton, Pawtucket	11	15	1	0	0	1.000	B. Butera, Pawtucket*....	84	109	5	4	2	.966
Johnson, Rochester	13	15	0	0	0	1.000	Rajsich, Charleston........	65	114	1	4	0	.966
Koza, Pawtucket*..........	12	14	0	0	0	1.000	Boyer, Pawtucket	14	27	1	1	0	.966
Howard, Charleston.......	69	154	6	1	1	.994	Diggle, Rochester	70	136	3	5	1	.965
Corey, Rochester	86	140	6	1	0	.993	Dimmel, Columbus........	20	23	2	1	0	.962
Buckner, Tol-Tide*........	83	127	6	1	1	.993	James, Rochester	47	89	2	4	0	.958
Huizenga, Pawtucket	114	157	4	2	1	.988	Upshaw, Syracuse*........	98	165	8	8	1	.956
Thompson, Columbus ...	82	147	2	2	0	.987	D. Jones, Columbus.......	50	75	6	4	0	.953
Sain, Tol-Charleston	42	75	2	1	1	.987	Amerson, Toledo...........	77	115	4	6	0	.952
Miller, Richmond..........	135	335	13	5	3	.986	Harper, Richmond.........	104	164	9	9	3	.951
Hancock, Pawtucket*	107	166	15	3	3	.984	Ayala, Rochester...........	17	37	0	2	0	.949
Bowen, Pawtucket	125	273	11	5	1	.983	Pisker, Syracuse*..........	95	184	6	11	2	.945
Brown, Columbus	68	166	7	3	1	.983	Moreno, Tidewater........	41	63	2	4	0	.942
Whisenton, Richmond*..	81	163	6	3	1	.983	T. Smith, Rochester	26	46	3	3	0	.942
Youngbauer, Rochester*	92	200	12	4	0	.981	Macha, Richmond	59	105	3	7	0	.939
G. Smith, Columbus*	54	102	2	2	0	.981	Sofield, Toledo.............	51	89	4	6	1	.939
Lopez, Rochester..........	42	97	4	2	0	.981	Bianco, Rochester	14	14	1	1	0	.938
Wilson, Tidewater	141	317	11	7	2	.979	Arline, Richmond..........	34	53	3	4	0	.933
Norman, Tidewater	80	141	13	4	4	.975	Royster, Rochester	27	46	4	5	1	.909
Ault, Syracuse*............	88	146	6	4	2	.974	Monasterio, Tidewater...	22	37	3	4	0	.909
Cruz, Columbus*...........	92	138	5	4	0	.973	Linares, Richmond........	15	22	1	5	0	.821
Cipot, Tidewater*	74	105	4	3	1	.973							

(Fewer Than Ten Games)

Player and Club	G.	PO.	A.	E.	DP.	Pct.	Player and Club	G.	PO.	A.	E.	DP.	Pct.
Stenholm, Columbus*....	6	22	2	0	0	1.000	Merchant, Pawtucket.....	3	1	0	0	0	1.000
Tyler, Charleston..........	6	12	1	0	0	1.000	Reynolds, Richmond......	2	1	0	0	0	1.000
Estes, Toledo*..............	7	8	1	0	1	1.000	Keller, Richmond..........	1	1	0	0	0	1.000
Bryant, Tidewater	4	7	1	0	0	1.000	Till, Tidewater	1	1	0	0	0	1.000
Holt, Columbus	5	7	0	0	0	1.000	Powell, Toledo*............	10	15	1	1	0	.941
Gates, Charleston.........	2	5	0	0	0	1.000	Sember, Syracuse	8	15	0	1	0	.938
Vega, Toledo................	2	5	0	0	0	1.000	Machemer, Rochester....	10	12	0	1	0	.923
Alberts, Syracuse*........	2	2	0	0	0	1.000	Iorg, Syracuse	7	11	0	1	0	.917
Hough, Tidewater.........	3	1	0	0	0	1.000	Beall, Richmond*	3	4	0	1	0	.800

CATCHERS

Player and Club	G.	PO.	A.	E.	DP.	PB.	Pct.	Player and Club	G.	PO.	A.	E.	DP.	PB.	Pct.
Tyler, Charleston..........	35	116	14	0	0	7	1.000	LaFrancois, Paw............	96	489	73	8	4	10	.986
WHITT, Syracuse	88	479	64	3	3	4	.995	Robinson, Columbus ..	82	453	28	7	2	9	.986
Rosado, Syr-Tid............	80	425	51	3	6	10	.994	Irwin, Columbus...........	13	58	3	1	1	2	.984
Merchant, Pawtucket	31	128	16	1	4	3	.993	Johnson, Rochester.......	22	102	6	2	2	2	.982
Gulden, Richmond........	59	326	22	3	1	2	.991	Owen, Richmond..........	110	615	73	13	9	15	.981
Kennedy, Rochester	108	586	56	7	10	5	.989	Benton, Tidewater	82	406	38	9	8	15	.980
Pujols, Charleston........	103	487	41	6	6	6	.989	S. Butera, Toledo..........	75	392	33	11	1	6	.975
Keller, Richmond	36	177	7	2	1	3	.989	R. Smith, Toledo...........	73	358	28	11	3	5	.972
Petralli, Syracuse	18	67	12	1	0	1	.988	Baldwin, Charleston......	13	56	6	2	0	0	.969
Hough, Tidewater.........	17	68	10	1	1	1	.987	O'Berry, Pawtucket	32	164	16	6	2	3	.968

(Fewer Than Ten Games)

Player and Club	G.	PO.	A.	E.	DP.	PB.	Pct.	Player and Club	G.	PO.	A.	E.	DP.	PB.	Pct.
Royster, Rochester	10	65	6	0	0	2	1.000	Till, Tidewater	7	21	2	1	0	1	.958
Werth, Columbus	1	1	0	0	0	0	1.000	Kelly, Syracuse	5	21	1	2	0	0	.917
Reynolds, Richmond ..	1	1	0	0	0	0	1.000								

PITCHERS

Player and Club	G.	PO.	A.	E.	DP.	Pct.	Player and Club	G.	PO.	A.	E.	DP.	Pct.
PLADSON, Charleston ..	27	20	31	0	2	1.000	D. Smith, Charleston......	34	10	18	0	0	1.000
Mendoza, Charleston ...	42	13	22	0	1	1.000	Cochran, Columbus	24	8	20	0	1	1.000
Kerrigan, Rochester	64	9	22	0	1	1.000	Snell, Rochester	12	12	16	0	0	1.000
Morogiello, Richmond*..	31	9	22	0	0	1.000	Chevez, Rochester	23	8	18	0	2	1.000

PITCHERS—Continued

Player and Club	G.	PO.	A.	E.	DP.	Pct.	Player and Club	G.	PO.	A.	E.	DP.	Pct
Collins, Richmond*	34	3	17	0	1	1.000	Faust, Pawtucket	21	7	14	1	2	.955
Holly, Toledo*	38	4	15	0	3	1.000	Pirtle, Rochester	16	7	12	1	2	.950
May, Syracuse	16	2	17	0	1	1.000	Boddicker, Rochester	15	8	11	1	0	.950
Ripley, Pawtucket	23	7	10	0	0	1.000	Edge, Syracuse	26	7	10	1	0	.944
McLaughlin, Richmond	18	2	14	0	1	1.000	Camp, Richmond	22	4	13	1	1	.944
Sprowl, Paw-Char*	17	1	15	0	0	1.000	Holman, Tidewater	25	20	30	3	3	.943
L. Anderson, Char-Rich.	23	3	12	0	1	1.000	R. Jackson, Tidewater	33	8	25	2	1	.943
Remmerswaal, Paw	39	8	7	0	0	1.000	Kammeyer, Columbus	26	8	25	2	0	.943
Waller, Pawtucket	30	7	8	0	2	1.000	Alexander, Richmond	28	10	22	2	2	.941
Benson, Syracuse*	12	2	12	0	1	1.000	Finch, Pawtucket	17	15	28	3	4	.935
Mahler, Richmond	24	2	11	0	0	1.000	Grilli, Syracuse	16	0	14	1	0	.933
Reardon, Tidewater	30	3	8	0	1	1.000	Flinn, Rochester	26	10	16	2	3	.929
Hardy, Charleston	34	4	6	0	1	1.000	R. Anderson, Columbus	52	7	6	1	1	.929
Clark, Tidewater	19	2	8	0	1	1.000	Fore, Syracuse	16	2	11	1	2	.929
Bruhert, Tidewater	20	1	8	0	0	1.000	Orosco, Tidewater*	16	5	8	1	0	.929
Glynn, Tidewater*	17	3	6	0	1	1.000	D. Jackson, Toledo*	14	3	10	1	2	.929
Taylor, Columbus	12	3	6	0	0	1.000	Thormodsgard, Toledo	28	14	28	4	1	.913
LaCorte, Charleston	14	1	7	0	0	1.000	Schneck, Pawtucket	33	12	27	4	0	.907
Theiss, Richmond	11	0	8	0	0	1.000	Rineer, Rochester*	31	7	22	3	2	.906
Rothermel, Charleston*	29	5	2	0	1	1.000	Felton, Toledo	28	16	13	3	0	.906
Willis, Syracuse*	20	1	6	0	0	1.000	G. Wilson, Charleston	19	6	20	3	2	.897
Davis, Columbus	11	2	5	0	0	1.000	Burns, Charleston	30	27	40	8	3	.893
Bernard, Tidewater	33	1	4	0	0	1.000	Thayer, Toledo	46	2	13	2	0	.882
Miggins, Charleston*	37	4	33	1	0	.974	LaRose, Pawtucket*	47	1	13	2	0	.875
Luebber, Syracuse	29	11	26	1	2	.974	Livingstone, Richmond..	24	2	5	1	0	.875
Pacella, Tidewater	29	10	23	1	2	.971	J. Robertson, Syracuse..	14	3	4	1	0	.875
Slagle, Columbus	22	15	17	1	1	.970	Stephenson, Roch-Tide*	45	7	18	4	1	.862
Todd, Syracuse	21	11	21	1	1	.970	Bradford, Richmond*	18	1	5	1	0	.857
MacPherson, Toledo	16	10	21	1	0	.969	Verhoeven, Toledo	50	4	19	4	1	.852
Stanfield, Toledo*	29	6	25	1	3	.969	Bastian, Rochester	19	11	17	5	0	.848
Wiley, Syracuse	27	17	14	1	2	.969	Van de Casteele, Roch...	32	1	10	2	0	.846
Sheehan, Tidewater	28	7	23	1	0	.968	Wehrmeister, Columbus	17	3	13	3	0	.842
Welsh, Columbus*	36	9	20	1	2	.967	Suter, Pawtucket	29	12	18	6	1	.833
Boggs, Richmond	33	12	37	2	2	.961	Wallace, Rochester*	15	3	2	1	0	.833
Semall, Charleston	13	9	15	1	0	.960	Mirabella, Columbus*	22	5	16	5	1	.808
Scott, Tidewater	17	7	16	1	0	.958	Bernal, Rochester	20	3	1	1	0	.800
Ford, Rochester	15	7	16	1	1	.958	K. Reynolds, Syracuse	19	0	14	4	1	.778
Tudor, Pawtucket	25	8	36	2	0	.957	Hausman, Tidewater	12	2	11	4	0	.765

(Fewer Than Ten Games)

Player and Club	G.	PO.	A.	E.	DP.	Pct.	Player and Club	G.	PO.	A.	E.	DP.	Pct.
Niemann, Charleston*	8	6	13	0	0	1.000	Cooper, Columbus	8	0	2	0	0	1.000
Brizzolara, Richmond	9	6	12	0	1	1.000	Skok, Richmond	8	1	1	0	0	1.000
Stieb, Syracuse	7	3	11	0	1	1.000	Leach, Richmond	7	2	0	0	0	1.000
Parks, Pawtucket	5	5	8	0	0	1.000	Perzanowski, Toledo	4	0	2	0	0	1.000
Torrez, Rochester*	8	4	8	0	2	1.000	Easterly, Richmond	10	0	1	0	0	1.000
Erickson, Toledo	5	4	6	0	0	1.000	Foucault, Charleston	5	0	1	0	0	1.000
Blair, Rochester	7	4	5	0	0	1.000	Apodaca, Tidewater	2	1	0	0	0	1.000
Lemongello, Syracuse	4	5	4	0	0	1.000	Cipot, Tidewater*	2	1	0	0	0	1.000
Strom, Charleston*	6	2	5	0	1	1.000	Williams, Charleston	2	0	1	0	0	1.000
Fierbaugh, Rochester	10	3	3	0	0	1.000	Polinsky, Columbus	1	0	1	0	0	1.000
Prewitt, Tidewater	9	3	3	0	1	1.000	Thurberg, Tidewater	1	0	1	0	0	1.000
Wallace, Pawtucket	9	3	1	0	0	1.000	Franklin, Rochester	1	1	0	0	0	1.000
Griffin, Columbus	6	3	1	0	0	1.000	Lysgaard, Columbus	9	6	9	1	3	.938
Serum, Toledo	2	2	2	0	0	1.000	L. Jones, Rochester	10	1	10	1	0	.917
Righetti, Columbus*	6	3	1	0	0	1.000	Beattie, Columbus	8	2	9	1	2	.917
Rainey, Pawtucket	3	0	3	0	0	1.000	Bacsik, Toledo	7	1	2	1	1	.750
Throop, Charleston	10	1	1	0	0	1.000	Myrick, Tidewater*	9	2	0	1	0	.667

The following players do not have any recorded accepted chances at the positions listed in the fielding averages for those particular positions: Beall*, p; Brooks, of; K. Chapman, ss; Brian Doyle*, of; Duncan, 2b; Garvin, p; Grilli, of; Hancock*, 1b; Hoffman, p; Hunter, p; LaFrancois, 1b; Leal, p; Mersch, p; Pearson, p; Sain, p; Small, of; R. Smith, 3b; Staiger, ss; Whitt, 3b.

CLUB PITCHING

Club	G.	CG.	ShO.	Sv.	IP.	H.	R.	ER.	HR.	BB.	Int. BB.	HB.	SO.	WP.	Bk.	ERA.
Syracuse	140	50	13	26	1226	1116	539	458	78	432	12	25	705	63	3	3.36
Pawtucket	140	45	9	18	1207	1087	551	463	95	547	67	34	752	63	5	3.45
Richmond	141	44	10	22	1202	1157	552	470	75	463	31	24	741	98	3	3.52
Charleston	140	45	7	17	1172	1133	548	459	79	363	22	23	611	58	15	3.52
Tidewater	141	23	8	38	1189	1144	533	467	59	430	40	33	686	61	6	3.53
Toledo	139	46	8	16	1215	1182	591	487	88	464	40	53	707	68	5	3.61
Columbus	139	44	9	34	1182	1087	557	497	100	454	27	44	790	65	5	3.78
Rochester	140	28	6	18	1177	1263	656	567	115	422	41	38	678	36	7	4.34

PITCHERS' RECORDS

(Leading Qualifiers for Earned-Run Average Leadership—112 or More Innings)

*Throws lefthanded.

Pitcher—Club	G.	GS.	CG.	ShO.	W.	L.	Sv.	Pct.	IP.	H.	R.	ER.	HR.	BB.	Int. BB.	HB.	SO.	WP.	ERA.
Holman, Tidewater	24	23	7	4	13	7	0	.650	149	125	45	33	4	51	5	3	62	4	1.99
Tudor, Pawtucket*	25	24	9	1	10	11	0	.476	163	145	73	53	14	52	8	0	103	9	2.93
Thormodsgard, Toledo	28	28	11	2	7	13	0	.350	196	186	86	64	17	61	3	12	108	5	2.94
Pladson, Charleston	27	26	14	1	13	14	0	.481	196	181	76	65	10	52	7	2	101	8	2.98
Sprowl, 1 Paw-16 Cha*	17	16	9	2	5	9	0	.357	112	95	48	40	5	38	1	2	70	2	3.21
Todd, Syracuse	21	15	7	0	9	4	1	.692	124	116	48	46	9	35	0	4	59	5	3.34
Luebber, Syracuse	29	28	9	3	11	8	0	.579	183	157	78	69	7	78	0	7	128	12	3.39
Felton, Toledo	28	28	8	3	7	10	0	.412	184	156	89	70	17	74	4	9	127	10	3.42
Collins, Richmond*	34	25	5	3	12	7	0	.632	187	203	84	72	9	64	3	1	119	16	3.47
Mendoza, Charleston	42	17	5	0	11	10	6	.524	150	141	69	59	14	33	0	3	64	9	3.54

Departmental Leaders: G—Kerrigan, 64; GS—Boggs, 33; CG—Boggs, 16; ShO—Holman, 4; W—Kammeyer, 16; L—Rineer, 15; Sv—R. Anderson, 21; Pct.—Finch, .900; IP—Boggs, 227; H—Boggs, 230; R—Boggs, 108; ER—Sheehan, 93; HR—Suter, 23; BB—Schneck, 101; IBB—Burns, Verhoeven, 12; HB—Sheehan, Thormodsgard, 12; SO—Boggs, 138; WP—Boggs, 18.

(All Pitchers—Listed Alphabetically)

Pitcher—Club	G.	GS.	CG.	ShO.	W.	L.	Sv.	Pct.	IP.	H.	R.	ER.	HR.	BB.	Int. BB.	HB.	SO.	WP.	ERA.
Alexander, Richmond	28	24	3	0	6	14	0	.300	133	140	91	78	40	41	1	6	64	11	5.28
Anderson, 9 Char-14 Rich	23	17	5	1	7	5	0	.583	109	104	55	50	12	65	1	0	63	14	4.13
Anderson, Columbus	52	0	0	0	13	3	21	.813	83	53	21	15	6	39	5	3	72	10	1.63
Apodaca, Tidewater	2	2	0	0	0	2	0	.000	4	6	7	7	2	5	0	1	0	0	15.75
Bacsik, Toledo	7	0	0	0	1	1	1	.500	21	19	3	3	0	3	1	1	16	1	1.29
Bastian, Rochester	19	14	3	0	3	3	2	.500	82	77	42	34	9	40	4	1	48	1	3.73
Beall, Richmond*	1	0	0	0	0	0	0	.000	2	2	0	0	0	0	0	1	0	0	0.00
Beattie, Columbus	8	7	4	2	5	1	0	.833	53	31	9	8	1	25	1	2	47	1	1.36
Benson, Syracuse*	12	12	3	3	6	4	0	.600	74	68	35	32	4	14	0	0	41	2	3.89
Bernal, Rochester	20	0	0	0	4	1	0	.800	42	39	18	17	4	18	3	3	24	3	3.64
Bernard, Tidewater	33	0	0	0	1	3	16	.250	61	39	12	12	3	29	5	2	49	6	1.77
Blair, Rochester	7	7	1	0	2	2	0	.500	35	47	25	25	3	11	0	0	21	2	6.43
Boddicker, Rochester	15	12	2	1	4	6	0	.400	72	88	48	48	10	27	1	1	48	4	6.00
Boggs, Richmond	33	33	16	3	15	10	0	.600	227	230	108	91	11	99	5	8	138	18	3.61
Bradford, Richmond*	18	0	0	0	3	1	4	.750	34	22	9	8	2	15	1	4	36	2	2.12
Brizzolara, Richmond	9	9	2	1	4	2	0	.667	66	47	15	14	3	28	4	0	42	9	1.91
Bruhert, Tidewater	20	1	0	0	1	4	5	.200	50	51	22	19	0	11	4	0	21	2	3.42
Burns, Pawtucket	30	28	10	0	8	13	1	.381	187	173	100	86	14	95	12	7	93	8	4.14
Buskey, Syracuse	12	0	0	0	0	0	6	.000	17	15	5	4	1	8	0	1	11	2	2.12
Camp, Richmond	22	0	0	0	3	2	3	.600	55	59	31	26	3	12	1	1	33	5	4.25
Chevez, Rochester	23	14	2	0	2	1	0	.667	96	117	62	55	9	37	2	3	37	0	5.16
Cipot, Tidewater*	2	0	0	0	0	0	0	.000	2	5	4	3	0	2	0	0	2	0	13.50
Clark, Tidewater	19	1	0	0	3	2	0	.600	40	44	26	25	2	19	1	1	22	4	5.63
Cochran, Columbus	24	8	1	0	3	2	1	.600	89	78	41	35	8	43	2	5	60	3	3.54
Collins, Richmond*	34	25	5	3	12	7	0	.632	187	203	84	72	9	64	3	1	119	16	3.47
Cooper, Columbus	8	0	0	0	0	0	2	.000	18	19	11	11	1	11	0	1	14	3	5.50
Davis, Columbus	11	0	0	0	1	0	5	.000	19	13	9	9	-1	15	2	1	10	2	4.26
Easterly, Richmond*	10	0	0	0	0	0	5	.000	14	5	0	0	0	7	1	0	12	1	0.00
Edge, Syracuse	26	4	1	0	5	3	1	.625	104	89	41	28	4	39	0	2	56	13	2.42
Erickson, Toledo	5	5	2	1	3	1	0	.750	34	30	8	6	1	10	0	0	19	1	1.59
Faust, Pawtucket	21	2	2	2	4	3	3	.571	68	62	21	20	1	19	4	1	32	4	2.65
Felton, Toledo	28	28	8	3	7	10	0	.412	184	156	89	70	17	74	4	9	127	10	3.42
Fierbaugh, Rochester	10	4	0	0	1	1	0	.500	40	37	16	16	5	20	1	2	22	0	3.60
Finch, Pawtucket	16	16	4	1	9	1	0	.900	106	93	41	31	2	38	4	5	49	5	2.63
Flinn, Rochester	26	10	3	0	6	6	1	.500	100	92	36	30	4	22	4	8	71	2	2.70
Ford, Rochester	15	15	4	0	6	5	0	.545	109	110	55	43	11	25	1	3	63	4	3.55
Fore, Syracuse	16	16	3	0	6	7	0	.462	102	92	45	37	7	46	0	1	64	3	3.26
Foucault, Charleston	5	0	0	0	0	2	0	.000	7	7	6	6	1	2	0	1	5	2	7.71
Franklin, Rochester	1	0	0	0	0	0	0	.000	1	2	0	0	0	0	0	0	0	0	0.00
Garvin, Syracuse*	8	0	0	0	1	0	0	1.000	9	6	3	2	0	4	0	0	5	0	2.00
Glynn, Tidewater*	17	0	0	0	1	0	5	.000	29	22	10	7	1	9	2	0	16	2	2.17
Griffin, Columbus	6	6	1	0	3	1	0	.750	41	35	9	8	2	13	3	0	34	3	1.76
Grilli, Syracuse	49	0	0	0	9	7	12	.563	103	93	37	23	5	41	5	2	65	6	2.01
Hardy, Charleston	34	0	0	0	2	5	6	.286	45	40	18	15	2	19	1	1	22	5	3.00
Hausman, Tidewater	12	12	0	0	6	4	0	.600	72	75	41	36	5	23	0	4	27	2	4.50
Hoffman, Pawtucket	1	0	0	0	0	0	0	.000	1	1	1	1	1	1	0	0	0	0	9.00
Holly, Toledo*	38	1	0	0	4	3	3	.571	72	71	34	23	2	25	6	1	44	4	2.88
Holman, Tidewater	24	23	7	4	13	7	0	.650	149	125	45	33	4	51	5	3	62	4	1.99
Hunter, Pawtucket	1	0	0	0	0	0	0	.000	1	0	0	0	0	0	0	0	0	0	0.00
Jackson, Toledo*	14	13	4	1	6	5	0	.545	89	80	41	36	8	40	0	2	78	7	3.64

Pitcher—Club	G	GS	CG	ShO	W	L	Sv	Pct.	IP	H	R	ER	HR	BB	Int. BB	HB	SO	WP	ERA
Jackson, Tidewater	33	17	3	1	12	7	5	.632	137	143	63	57	7	33	5	0	89	3	3.74
Jones, Rochester	10	9	1	0	1	7	0	.125	57	63	21	19	5	20	1	0	39	4	3.00
Kammeyer, Columbus	27	27	10	0	16	8	0	.667	172	178	84	75	10	52	0	6	83	6	3.92
Kerrigan, Rochester	64	0	0	0	0	6	11	.625	95	88	41	37	9	49	9	3	55	7	3.51
LaCorte, Charleston	12	11	4	0	4	7	0	.364	79	68	32	24	5	31	0	2	57	0	2.73
LaRose, Pawtucket*	47	1	0	0	2	6	4	.250	53	68	40	29	6	29	5	2	30	3	4.92
Leach, Richmond	7	2	1	0	3	1	1	.750	14	14	3	3	0	4	0	1	12	1	1.93
Leal, Syracuse	1	1	0	0	1	0	0	1.000	6	4	3	3	1	2	0	0	2	0	4.50
Lemongello, Syracuse	4	4	0	0	3	0	0	1.000	25	20	5	5	1	7	0	0	13	1	1.80
Livingstone, Richmond	24	0	0	0	2	1	0	.667	51	59	26	22	7	11	3	0	20	3	3.88
Luebber, Syracuse	29	28	9	3	11	8	0	.579	183	157	78	69	7	78	0	7	128	12	3.39
Lysgaard, Columbus	9	8	1	1	4	2	0	.667	48	46	33	30	7	23	0	0	20	1	5.63
MacPherson, Toledo	16	12	5	0	5	4	0	.556	91	96	44	36	4	28	2	1	33	6	3.56
Mahler, Richmond	24	2	2	0	4	6	4	.400	54	46	26	20	3	18	3	0	40	6	3.33
May, Syracuse	16	16	7	1	6	9	0	.400	103	92	56	46	8	47	3	1	56	4	4.02
McLaughlin, Richmond	18	1	1	0	2	2	4	.500	42	31	16	10	1	18	L	1	33	1	2.14
Mendoza, Charleston	42	17	5	0	11	10	6	.524	150	141	69	59	14	33	0	3	64	9	3.54
Mersch, Columbus	2	0	0	0	0	0	0	.000	3	4	3	3	0	3	0	0	1	0	9.00
Miggins, Charleston*	37	8	0	0	3	5	1	.375	89	100	55	42	4	35	2	6	50	4	4.25
Mirabella, Columbus*	22	20	9	0	11	7	0	.611	144	129	75	62	11	50	2	5	98	8	3.88
Miscik, Charleston*	10	8	1	1	5	3	0	.625	57	51	24	25	4	17	1	2	32	1	3.95
Morogiello, Richmond*	31	31	9	1	12	13	0	.480	200	186	90	79	14	76	3	0	116	10	3.56
Myrick, Tidewater*	9	3	0	0	3	1	1	.750	27	21	10	10	5	9	0	1	21	1	3.33
Niemann, Charleston*	8	6	2	0	3	2	0	.600	47	49	25	21	4	10	0	0	17	1	4.02
Orosco, Tidewater*	16	15	1	0	4	4	0	.500	81	82	45	35	2	43	4	1	55	7	3.89
Pacella, Tidewater	26	24	5	0	7	10	0	.412	142	129	65	58	4	61	2	6	95	4	3.68
Parks, Pawtucket	5	5	0	0	1	2	0	.333	25	25	14	14	5	11	0	2	11	0	5.04
Pearson, Tidewater	2	2	0	0	0	1	0	.000	5	9	4	9	0	4	1	1	5	0	16.20
Perzanowski, Toledo	4	0	0	0	1	0	0	.000	10	12	7	6	2	10	3	2	7	0	5.40
Pirtle, Rochester	49	1	0	0	2	9	1	.182	105	121	69	57	12	36	9	4	68	4	4.89
Pladson, Charleston	27	26	14	1	13	14	0	.481	196	181	76	65	10	52	7	2	101	8	2.98
Polinsky, Columbus	1	1	0	0	0	0	0	.000	5	3	2	2	1	5	0	0	3	0	3.60
Prewitt, Tidewater	8	6	1	1	0	3	0	.250	27	36	24	22	5	18	1	1	18	2	7.33
Rainey, Pawtucket	3	2	1	1	1	0	0	1.000	17	8	0	0	0	3	1	0	9	0	0.00
Reardon, Tidewater	30	1	1	0	5	2	5	.714	69	46	18	16	0	21	1	2	64	3	2.09
Remmerswaal, Pawtucket	39	4	0	0	4	6	7	.400	92	66	22	21	7	35	9	3	93	5	2.05
Reynolds, K., Syracuse*	19	6	0	0	2	4	0	.333	66	71	45	39	8	32	0	1	25	2	5.32
Righetti, Columbus*	8	6	3	2	3	2	0	.600	40	22	13	13	1	19	0	1	44	1	2.93
Rineer, Rochester*	30	26	7	1	5	15	1	.250	162	175	93	79	17	45	2	6	79	1	4.39
Ripley, Pawtucket	23	4	2	1	7	1	1	.875	77	54	13	12	3	28	4	1	51	4	1.40
Robertson, J., Syracuse	14	1	0	0	0	1	3	.000	29	26	14	12	4	10	0	0	21	5	3.72
Rothermel, Charleston*	29	0	0	0	2	0	1	1.000	38	36	14	13	5	13	2	0	20	3	3.08
Sain, Toledo	1	0	0	0	0	0	0	.000	1	1	0	0	0	2	0	0	0	0	0.00
Schneck, Pawtucket	29	28	5	1	8	13	0	.381	143	129	80	74	14	101	6	6	99	4	4.66
Scott, Tidewater	18	15	3	1	8	4	0	.667	99	103	37	35	3	27	1	3	40	8	3.18
Semall, Columbus	13	13	6	1	6	3	0	.667	95	94	45	41	10	28	1	1	48	5	3.88
Serum, Toledo	2	2	1	0	1	1	0	.500	13	15	9	6	4	0	0	0	5	0	4.15
Sheehan, Toledo*	28	23	9	0	10	10	0	.500	148	163	103	93	19	66	2	12	72	9	5.66
Skok, Richmond*	8	0	0	0	3	0	1	1.000	7	18	10	8	2	7	2	0	13	3	4.24
Slagle, Columbus	22	20	3	1	8	11	0	.421	130	138	73	67	16	31	0	2	96	4	4.64
Smith, D., Charleston	34	19	6	3	7	8	1	.467	160	159	80	65	11	44	4	3	90	10	3.66
Snell, Rochester	12	12	4	2	4	7	0	.364	76	72	44	37	10	22	1	2	35	0	4.38
Sprowl, 1 Paw-16 Cha*	17	16	9	2	5	9	0	.357	112	95	44	40	5	38	1	2	70	2	3.21
Stanfield, Toledo*	29	26	10	1	9	13	0	.409	171	180	89	78	12	58	4	8	80	12	4.11
Stephenson, 19Roc-26Tid*	45	2	0	0	2	6	3	.250	75	77	39	31	3	36	8	5	36	4	3.72
Stieb, Syracuse	7	7	4	0	5	2	0	.714	51	39	15	12	0	14	0	2	20	1	2.12
Strom, Charleston*	6	5	1	0	3	0	0	1.000	36	37	13	12	4	9	0	0	7	2	3.00
Suter, Pawtucket	28	28	11	2	10	13	0	.435	174	169	95	78	23	75	4	1	120	9	4.03
Taylor, Columbus	5	1	0	0	3	1	1	.750	51	40	19	18	4	21	0	2	27	4	3.18
Thayer, Toledo	46	1	0	0	4	8	1	.333	84	77	36	33	4	50	3	4	67	7	3.54
Theiss, Richmond	11	1	0	0	1	2	0	.333	24	20	8	8	1	14	2	2	14	3	3.00
Thormodsgard, Toledo	28	28	11	2	7	13	0	.350	196	186	86	64	17	61	3	12	108	5	2.94
Throop, Charleston	10	1	0	0	2	0	2	1.000	17	16	5	5	1	8	1	0	12	3	2.65
Thurberg, Tidewater	1	1	0	0	0	1	0	.000	6	3	2	2	0	3	0	0	4	0	3.00
Todd, Syracuse	21	15	7	0	9	4	1	.692	124	116	48	46	9	35	0	4	59	5	3.34
Torrez, Rochester*	8	7	1	3	2	1	0	.600	41	45	27	24	4	20	0	0	15	0	5.27
Tudor, Pawtucket*	25	24	9	1	10	11	0	.476	163	145	73	53	14	52	8	0	103	9	2.93
Van de Casteele, Tide	32	17	2	1	7	8	0	.467	134	154	70	65	14	38	2	3	71	9	4.37
Verhoeven, Toledo	50	0	0	0	6	6	8	.500	100	96	42	33	2	33	12	1	51	6	2.97
Wallace, D., Pawtucket	9	0	0	0	1	1	0	.000	26	22	10	8	3	18	5	1	16	3	2.77
Wallace, M., Rochester*	15	7	0	0	6	6	0	.000	44	44	42	31	5	33	3	1	32	4	6.34
Waller, Pawtucket	30	0	0	0	2	3	1	.400	66	62	37	34	2	40	5	5	39	5	4.64
Wehrmeister, Columbus	17	9	5	0	2	8	1	.200	75	84	43	41	7	28	5	8	54	4	4.92
Welsh, Columbus*	36	9	0	0	8	4	3	.667	114	120	67	59	14	48	6	7	79	6	4.66

Pitcher—Club	G.	GS.	CG.	ShO.	W.	L.	Sv.	Pct.	IP.	H.	R.	ER.	HR.	BB.	Int. BB.	HB.	SO.	WP.	ERA.
Wiley, Syracuse	27	27	15	2	12	11	0	.522	197	192	88	80	18	45	2	4	111	4	3.65
Williams, Charleston	2	2	0	0	0	1	0	.000	10	15	6	2	0	6	1	0	5	0	1.80
Willis, Syracuse*	20	3	1	0	1	3	3	.250	34	36	21	20	1	10	2	0	28	3	5.29.
Wilson, G., Charleston	19	17	4	0	4	7	0	.364	107	120	58	49	4	32	2	1	52	5	4.12

BALKS—Miggins, 5; L. Anderson, Bastian, Mirabella, Pladson, Slagle, Smith, Stephenson, Waller, 2 each; L. Anderson, Chevez, Clark, Edge, Faust, Garvin, D. Jackson, Kerrigan, Lysgaard, MacPherson, Mahler, Miscik, Morogiello, Orosco, Pacella, Remmerswaal, Rineer, J. Robertson, Sheehan, Sprowl, Strom, Suter, Thormodsgard, Torrez, Van de Casteele, Verhoeven, M. Wallace, G. Wilson, 1 each.

COMBINATION SHUTOUTS—Kammeyer-Beattie, Beattie-R. Anderson, Columbus; Brizzolara-Bradford-Theiss-Easterly, Richmond; Flinn-Kerrigan, Flinn-Bernal, Rochester; May-Grilli, Luebber-Grilli; Luebber-J. Robertson, Lemongello-J. Robertson, Syracuse; Pacella-R. Jackson, Tidewater.

NO-HIT GAMES—None.

Bowen, Butera Had HR Binges

There's little doubt the Syracuse Chiefs saw enough of Pawtucket's Sam Bowen during a three-game series early in the season to last them the whole year.

Bowen clouted a three-run homer in each of the Pawtucket victories May 1 and 2. Then on May 4, he climaxed the power show by belting three homers off pitcher Mark Wiley in a 7-2 decision and three-game sweep over the Chiefs.

Barry Butera, Bowen's teammate, had a three-homer output April 15 against Columbus. Butera's homers came consecutively. On his fourth trip to the plate, Butera doubled off the base of the right-field wall. Both Pawtucket sluggers wound up one home run shy of the league record of four homers in a game last accomplished by Gene Locklear of Columbus, July 14, 1977.

Six Straight Batters Reached Base
—With Only One Run Scoring

The Waterbury A's put six straight men on base and scored only once, but it was enough for Frank Harris, who came out of the A's bullpen for his first start of the season and beat Bristol, 1-0, August 25.

The unique sequence: Shooty Babitt was safe on an error and was thrown out trying to score on a double by Wade Boggs. Kelvin Moore also doubled, driving in Boggs, but Moore tried to stretch his hit into a triple and was thrown out at third base. Eric Attaway, Paul Mize and Rob Klebba followed with successive singles to load the bases before Tad Nowakowski struck out to end the inning.

Mexican League

Leading Batter
JAMES COLLINS
Chihuahua

League President
ANTONIO RAMIREZ, M.

Leading Pitcher
RAFAEL GARCIA
Juarez

CHAMPIONSHIP WINNERS IN PREVIOUS YEARS

1955—Mexico City Tigers* .... .539	1965—Mexico City Tigers .... .590	1973—Saltillo .... .656
1956—Mexico City Reds........... .692	1966—Mexico City Tigers‡ ...... .614	Mexico City Reds x........ .590
1957—Yucatan .... .567	Mexico City Reds........... .571	1974—Jalisco .... .627
Mex. C. Reds (2nd)† .... .550	1967—Jalisco........................... .607	Mexico City Reds x........ .551
1958—Nuevo Laredo .... .625	Mexico City Reds........... .586	1975—Tampico x .... .541
1959—Poza Rica....................... .575	1968—Mexico City Reds........... .586	Cordoba .... .649
Mex. C. Reds (3rd)† .... .507	1969—Reynosa .... .591	1976—Mexico City Reds........... .543
1960—Mexico City Tigers .... .538	1970—Aguila§ .... .580	Union Laguna.............. .547
1961—Veracruz......................... .575	Mexico City Reds........... .607	1977—Mexico City Reds........... .623
1962—Monterrey...................... .592	1971—Jalisco§.......................... .558	Nuevo Laredo x............ .507
1963—Puebla............................ .606	Saltillo .... .593	1978—Aguascalientes x .... .589
1964—Mexico City Reds........... .586	1972—Saltillo........................... .636	Union Laguna .... .523
	Cordoba§ .... .541	

*Defeated Nuevo Laredo, two games to none, in playoff for pennant. †Won four-team playoff. ‡Won split-season playoff. §League divided into Northern, Southern divisions; won two-team playoff. xLeague divided into Northern, Southern zones; sub-divided into Eastern, Western divisions; won eight-team playoff.

STANDING OF CLUBS AT CLOSE OF SEASON, AUGUST 17
NORTHERN ZONE
EASTERN DIVISION

Club	NL.	Mon.	Tam.	PR.	Leo.	Sal.	Jua.	UL.	Coa.	Chi.	Cor.	Tab.	MR.	Ctz.	Yuc.	W.	L.	T.	Pct.	G.B.
N. Laredo.........	..	9	8	4	11	4	6	6	10	1	2	3	4	1	75	60	2	.556	......
Monterrey.........	3	..	6	8	9	2	3	8	5	7	1	3	4	4	3	66	67	3	.496	8
Tampico	4	5	..	4	7	5	3	5	8	6	1	3	2	2	4	59	75	1	.440	15½
Poza Rica........	8	4	8	..	5	3	4	5	6	4	1	2	2	4	1	57	74	0	.435	16
Leon	1	3	5	5	..	5	4	3	4	6	4	4	4	1	3	52	82	0	.388	22½

WESTERN DIVISION

Club	NL.	Mon.	Tam.	PR.	Leo.	Sal.	Jua.	UL.	Coa.	Chi.	Pue.	Ags.	MT.	Dur.	Agu.	W.	L.	T.	Pct.	G.B.
Saltillo.............	7	10	6	9	7	..	7	6	9	11	4	3	6	6	4	95	40	1	.704	......
Juarez..............	6	8	7	8	7	5	..	7	6	8	3	2	5	3	5	80	53	2	.602	14
U. Laguna........	6	4	7	5	9	6	5	..	6	8	1	3	1	2	3	66	70	0	.485	29½
Coahuila	5	7	4	6	8	3	6	6	..	6	1	1	2	4	4	64	70	2	.478	30½
Chihuahua	2	5	6	5	5	1	3	4	4	..	1	3	5	2	5	51	78	4	.395	41

SOUTHERN ZONE
EASTERN DIVISION

Club	Cor.	Tab.	MR.	Ctz.	Yuc.	Pue.	Ags.	MT.	Dur.	Agu.	NL.	Mon.	Tam.	PR.	Leo.	W.	L.	T.	Pct.	G.B.
Cordoba	..	4	6	8	6	8	6	3	7	4	5	5	5	2	76	56	1	.576	......
Tabasco	7	..	6	4	7	5	7	8	5	8	4	3	3	4	2	73	58	5	.557	2½
Mexico Reds	6	6	..	5	7	5	7	7	6	10	3	2	4	4	2	74	64	0	.536	5
Coatzacoalcos ...	4	6	7	..	7	3	4	6	7	2	4	2	4	2	5	66	69	1	.489	11½
Yucatan	5	4	5	5	..	4	5	8	2	9	5	0	2	5	3	62	69	3	.473	13½

WESTERN DIVISION

Club	Cor.	Tab.	MR.	Ctz.	Yuc.	Pue.	Ags.	MT.	Dur.	Agu.	Sal.	Jua.	UL.	Coa.	Chi.	W.	L.	T.	Pct.	G.B.
Puebla	4	7	7	9	8	..	7	5	11	9	2	3	5	4	5	86	51	0	.628	
Aguascalientes	6	4	5	7	6	5	..	5	7	3	3	4	3	4	3	65	67	4	.492	18½
Mexico Tigers	7	4	5	6	3	7	7	..	7	5	0	1	5	4	1	62	73	0	.459	23
Durango	4	6	6	5	10	1	4	5	..	6	0	3	4	2	2	58	74	4	.439	25½
Aguila	5	3	2	5	3	3	7	5	..	1	1	3	2	1		48	85	3	.361	36

Coahuila club represented Monclova and Sabinas.

Tabasco club represented Villahermosa.

Tampico club represented Tampico and Ciudad Madero.

Union Laguna club represented Gomez Palacio and Torreon.

Playoffs—Puebla defeated Tabasco, four games to none; Cordoba defeated Aguascalientes, four games to three; Saltillo defeated Monterrey, four games to three; Ciudad Juarez defeated Nuevo Laredo, four games to three; Puebla defeated Cordoba, four games to one; Ciudad Juarez defeated Saltillo, four games to three; Puebla defeated Ciudad Juarez, four games to three for league championship.

Regular-Season Attendance—Aguascalientes, 233,734; Aguila, 168,524; Chihuahua, 160,609; Ciudad Juarez, 254,439; Coahuila, 142,808; Coatzacoalcos, 223,883; Cordoba, 133,959; Durango, 155,634; Leon, 189,748; Mexico Reds, 405,695; Mexico Tigers, 270,085; Monterrey, 163,634; Nuevo Laredo, 236,605; Poza Rica, 172,225; Puebla, 182,910; Saltillo, 257,646; Tabasco, 441,835; Tampico, 118,268; Union Laguna, 222,839; Yucatan, 453,206. Total, 4,591,286. No all-star game.

Managers—Agascalientes—Jaime Fabela; Aguila—Ronald Camacho, Miguel Sotelo, Rolando Camarero; Chihuahua—Mauro Contreras, Norman McRae; Ciudad Juarez—Jose Guerrero; Coahuila—Victor Fabela; Coatzacoalcos—Miguel Gaspar, Eliseo Rodriguez; Cordoba—Winston Llenas; Durango—Benjamin Cerda; Leon—Benjamin Valenzuela, E. Elizalde, Luis Alcaraz; Mexico Reds—Benjamin Reyes; Mexico Tigers—Domingo Rivera, Luis Garcia Cobos; Monterrey—Marte de Alejandro; Nuevo Laredo—Gerardo Gutierrez; Poza Rica—Emilio Sosa; Puebla—Jorge Fitch; Saltillo—Gregorio Luque; Tabasco—Raul Cano; Tampico—Felipe Leal, Carlos Trevino; Union Laguna—Moises Camacho; Yucatan—Carlos Paz.

All-Star Team: 1B—Williams, Durango; 2B—Navarrete, Saltillo; 3B—Santana, Union Laguna; SS—Jimenez, Puebla; OF—Collins, Chihuahua; Lora, Puebla; Mora, Saltillo; C—Estrada, Puebla; DH—Gonzalez, Chihuahua; P—Garcia, Ciudad Juarez; Munguia, Puebla; Paul, Ciudad Juarez; Manager—Fitch, Puebla.

(Compiled by Ana Luisa Perea de Silva, League Statistician, Mexico, D. F.)

CLUB BATTING

Club	G.	AB.	R.	OR.	H.	TB.	2B.	3B.	HR.	RBI.	SH.	SF.	BB.	Int. BB.	HP.	SO.	SB.	CS.	LOB.	Pct.
Puebla	137	4444	662	462	1323	1685	173	45	33	584	77	53	495	57	31	492	120	92	993	.298
Saltillo	136	4465	684	427	1326	1800	175	40	73	629	71	29	493	77	45	507	93	54	1044	.297
Chihuahua	133	4427	572	657	1302	1748	172	41	64	515	45	38	369	42	50	565	119	99	934	.294
C. Juarez	135	4439	620	468	1279	1667	182	37	44	541	67	38	421	48	53	540	70	56	942	.288
Mexico Reds	138	4749	606	510	1335	1729	169	42	47	524	69	36	437	44	35	503	93	64	1036	.281
Aguascalientes	136	4438	561	532	1242	1618	167	52	35	489	48	43	386	43	35	563	72	73	916	.280
Monterrey	136	4464	538	533	1230	1683	146	56	65	486	77	38	445	47	36	618	102	76	990	.276
Mexico Tigers	135	4344	481	535	1195	1499	142	36	30	430	84	32	383	32	26	533	48	54	911	.275
N. Laredo	137	4528	550	489	1243	1640	161	43	50	494	71	40	409	57	38	612	65	58	1007	.275
Durango	136	4508	531	587	1225	1640	175	33	58	483	53	27	446	49	36	568	62	64	1004	.272
Cordoba	133	4467	554	501	1211	1616	159	45	52	492	48	41	420	47	36	545	27	43	992	.271
U. Laguna	136	4347	480	496	1176	1608	150	45	64	440	49	34	347	39	28	597	75	58	947	.271
Tabasco	136	4491	525	466	1201	1537	147	21	49	470	83	40	419	47	40	640	60	58	982	.267
Coahuila	136	4347	511	527	1144	1539	168	28	57	470	74	34	407	40	29	674	31	50	920	.263
Tampico	135	4509	473	611	1176	1556	155	21	61	411	49	22	376	31	38	729	53	40	985	.261
Coatzacoalcos	136	4373	439	491	1110	1409	149	21	36	387	75	30	425	38	60	521	60	49	1002	.254
Poza Rica	131	4201	392	493	1061	1316	122	35	21	344	81	30	392	39	42	561	73	63	964	.253
Leon	134	4359	519	737	1088	1547	143	23	90	451	44	30	450	32	41	701	59	60	929	.250
Aguila	136	4304	392	556	1050	1358	149	24	37	336	58	23	351	28	40	598	78	43	914	.244
Yucatan	134	4248	430	442	1002	1303	113	19	50	385	96	25	464	42	30	558	55	43	943	.236

INDIVIDUAL BATTING
(Leading Qualifiers for Batting Championship—373 or More Plate Appearances)

*Bats lefthanded. †Switch-hitter.

Player and Club	G.	AB.	R.	H.	TB.	2B.	3B.	HR.	RBI.	SH.	SF.	BB.	HP.	SO.	SB.	CS.	Pct.
Collins, James, Chihuahua*	124	470	95	206	279	35	10	6	60	2	1	53	5	51	33	21	.438
Sanders, Reginald, 89 Tam-21 Ags.	110	410	60	150	232	27	2	17	95	0	7	39	9	41	1	1	.366
Rodriguez, Roberto, Laredo*	110	406	66	147	187	12	14	0	30	9	3	63	0	44	6	13	.362
Lora, Luis, Puebla*	121	472	79	169	209	25	6	1	72	6	8	34	2	31	15	9	.358
Navarrete, Juan, Saltillo*	136	521	110	185	217	15	4	3	61	12	3	53	5	15	40	18	.355
Hairston, Jerry, Durango*	128	427	87	151	219	22	5	12	56	4	4	113	2	34	12	11	.354
Naranjo, Jose, Coahuila†	127	420	60	148	197	28	3	5	56	6	3	52	7	46	2	7	.352
Williams, Walt, 67 Mon-47 Chi	114	409	63	142	207	20	3	13	65	1	3	53	3	27	14	8	.347
Brookins, Joe, 67 Ch-62 Mon	129	481	73	166	234	20	6	12	73	4	7	47	16	27	25	12	.345
Mora, Andres, Saltillo	114	421	79	145	255	31	5	23	102	1	7	37	5	57	3	1	.344

Departmental Leaders: G—Kurpiel, 138; AB—Ramon Hernandez, 563; R—J. Navarrete, 110; H—Collins, 206; TB—Collins, 279; 2B—Collins, 35; 3B—L. Valenzuela, 19; HR—Alcaraz, Murrell, 24; RBI—E. Williams, 112; SH—Villaescusa, Jimenez, 19; SF—Murrell, 11; BB—King, 124; HP—Brookins, 16; SO—C. Juan Martinez, 19; SB—J. Navarrete, 40; CS—Collins, 21.

(All Players—Listed Alphabetically)

Player and Club	G.	AB.	R.	H.	TB.	2B.	3B.	HR.	RBI.	SH.	SF.	BB.	HP.	SO.	SB.	CS.	Pct.
Abarca, David, Aguascalientes......	1	1	0	0	0	0	0	0	0	0	0	0	0	0	0	0	.000
Acuna, Clemente, Puebla.........	20	49	4	15	16	1	0	0	2	0	1	2	0	8	0	0	.306
Aguilar, Enrique, Aguascalientes ...	132	502	72	162	224	23	6	9	66	8	5	31	4	46	19	11	.323
Aguilar, Jose, Puebla†................	83	250	25	70	84	8	3	0	28	4	4	42	1	33	4	2	.280
Aguilera, Hector, Coahuila.........	7	10	0	1	1	0	0	0	1	0	0	1	0	3	0	0	.100
Aguirre, Trinidad, Mex Reds.........	8	17	1	5	8	0	0	1	4	0	0	1	0	1	0	0	.294
Alanis, Hector, Aguila.............	106	249	25	44	51	7	0	0	7	4	1	33	1	47	6	8	.177
Alcaraz, Luis, Leon................	130	446	81	134	229	19	2	24	77	4	7	92	5	93	2	5	.300
Alsup, Robert, Tampico	3	5	0	0	0	0	0	0	0	0	0	0	0	1	0	0	.000
Alvarado, Alejandro, Tampico*......	60	212	34	74	82	5	0	1	22	0	0	25	1	10	3	4	.349
Alvarado, Luis, Yucatan	125	455	46	118	159	12	4	7	42	8	2	45	1	42	26	5	.259
Alvarado, Natanael, Cordoba	106	424	76	109	130	13	4	0	27	6	3	35	4	68	5	5	.257
Alvarez, Juan, Aguascalientes	76	222	16	57	69	10	1	0	21	11	3	12	0	43	1	1	.257
Alvarez, Manuel, Cordoba*.........	128	454	58	128	188	22	4	10	73	5	6	69	2	61	4	1	.282
Alvarez, Orlando, Mex Tigers	10	30	1	5	6	1	0	0	0	0	0	4	0	7	0	0	.167
Andrews, Freddie, Poza Rica........	42	148	16	40	53	4	3	1	22	1	3	14	2	28	0	1	.270
Aranda, Raul, Saltillo.............	55	150	16	34	45	6	1	1	16	3	0	8	2	35	1	1	.227
Aranda, Severo, Poza Rica..........	5	7	2	1	1	0	0	0	0	1	0	1	0	1	0	0	.143
Arano, Samuel, Coatzacoalcos......	1	0	0	0	0	0	0	0	0	0	0	0	0	0	0	0	.000
Arano, Wilfredo, Aguila............	38	66	12	9	9	0	0	0	3	0	0	6	4	9	2	1	.136
Arevalo, Enrique, Durango	34	68	2	16	18	2	0	0	6	0	1	7	0	5	2	1	.235
Armbrister, Edison, 25 Yuc-81 Tam	106	395	56	115	179	13	6	13	62	2	5	34	3	77	14	7	.291
Avizu, Juan, Tabasco	37	88	5	14	15	1	0	0	7	1	1	11	0	28	0	2	.159
Avina, Franco, Coahuila	33	72	8	23	30	2	1	1	6	2	2	3	0	9	2	3	.319
Balaz, John, Juarez................	124	452	87	140	213	20	4	15	85	2	6	67	4	50	3	2	.310
Barajas, Franco, Aguascalientes....	4	6	0	0	0	0	0	0	0	0	0	0	0	1	0	0	.000
Barrera, Nelson, Mex Reds.........	137	540	75	147	215	17	12	9	72	3	4	27	4	78	4	6	.272
Barron, Rafael, Mex Reds..........	48	125	10	34	39	3	1	0	14	1	2	5	0	17	1	2	.272
Batista, Rafael, Cordoba*..........	130	477	66	144	209	31	5	8	68	0	6	71	3	74	0	4	.302
Bellacetin, Juan, Leon*.............	23	58	6	8	11	1	1	0	4	0	1	4	1	8	0	0	.138
Bellacetin, Tomas, Leon*...........	90	268	42	59	62	1	1	0	9	6	0	55	3	22	4	5	.220
Benitez, Jose, Leon	120	427	30	102	138	14	5	4	40	5	1	24	1	64	2	8	.239
Bernal, Arturo, Tabasco*...........	112	358	29	117	132	12	0	1	54	2	10	19	3	32	0	1	.327
Berzunza, William, Yucatan*.......	2	1	0	0	0	0	0	0	0	0	0	0	0	0	0	0	.000
Biagini, Gregory, Coahuila†........	89	304	50	91	174	14	6	19	66	2	3	39	3	50	0	2	.299
Bobadilla, Manuel, Juarez	32	85	9	25	30	5	0	0	11	2	1	5	0	13	0	1	.294
Bojorquez, Jose, Poza Rica	127	441	40	106	137	14	1	5	50	2	7	58	3	81	0	3	.240
Briones, Antonio, Juarez...........	118	465	59	141	156	9	3	0	43	10	1	27	3	33	9	6	.303
Briones, Eleazar, 14 Mo-18 Jua	32	73	7	17	20	0	0	1	6	3	1	7	0	13	0	1	.233
Brookins, Joe, 67 Ch-62 Mon	129	481	73	166	234	20	6	12	73	4	7	47	16	27	25	12	.345
Brown, Leon, Mex Reds............	38	152	25	47	61	9	1	1	17	1	0	10	1	5	1	5	.309
Buckner, Richard, Aguascalientes..	4	11	0	1	1	0	0	0	1	0	0	0	0	3	0	0	.091
Calvo, Bernardo, Puebla	79	279	26	72	81	5	2	0	33	3	0	27	0	21	0	3	.258
Camarero, Rolando, Aguascalientes	73	191	10	43	52	3	0	2	17	4	0	12	1	30	0	0	.225
Camargo, Fernando, Monterrey.....	124	453	54	138	204	22	1	14	57	4	3	41	2	56	3	5	.305
Campos, Carlos, Coatzacoalcos	12	30	3	5	6	1	0	0	3	0	1	1	0	3	0	0	.167
Canada, Romel, Tabasco*..........	131	474	66	139	204	23	3	12	78	1	9	58	10	61	13	7	.293
Cardona, Candelario, Saltillo	90	188	30	54	62	2	3	0	17	4	0	13	2	21	7	5	.287
Carranza, Javier, Coatzacoalcos*...	4	4	0	0	0	0	0	0	0	0	0	0	0	0	0	0	.000
Carreno, Luis, Puebla	88	238	42	58	83	9	2	4	24	4	1	32	2	55	3	6	.244
Castro, Tony, Saltillo*.............	123	422	61	125	173	18	6	6	59	4	1	49	0	58	9	4	.296
Castro, Dave, Leon	3	11	3	1	1	0	0	0	0	0	0	1	0	0	0	0	.091
Castro, Jose Antonio, Aguas	20	18	1	2	2	0	0	0	2	0	1	0	0	4	0	0	.111
Castro, Jose de Jesus, Aguas	39	118	13	28	34	2	2	0	4	1	0	19	1	25	1	3	.237
Centeno, Jose, Tampico*...........	43	163	27	47	61	7	2	1	22	1	1	19	3	16	2	1	.288
Cerda, Benjamin, Durango..........	105	355	24	112	159	20	3	7	71	2	2	28	2	20	1	7	.315
Cervantes, Eduardo, Laredo	17	40	3	13	14	1	0	0	2	0	0	4	0	9	2	0	.325
Cervantes, Refugio, 74 Agu-3 Mon†	77	232	19	48	61	5	1	2	26	0	4	16	1	31	0	0	.207
Charles, Blas, Mex Tigers..........	2	3	0	0	0	0	0	0	0	0	0	0	0	2	0	0	.000
Chavarria, Miguel, Laguna	119	350	49	72	96	9	6	1	12	6	1	16	5	75	12	5	.206
Chavez, Francisco, Mex Tigers......	79	182	15	43	50	7	0	0	10	7	1	17	0	44	0	1	.236
Chavez, Guadalupe, Saltillo*.......	127	504	85	152	185	25	4	0	45	7	1	64	4	30	11	10	.302
Chavez, Jose G., Laguna	16	50	10	12	17	3	1	0	2	0	1	0	1	10	3	0	.240
Chavez, Jose Santos, Laredo*.......	23	27	2	3	3	0	0	0	1	0	0	5	0	5	1	1	.111
Chavez, Juan de Dios, Coatz........	97	297	20	62	71	5	2	0	15	12	0	18	4	41	1	5	.209
Christiansen, Dave, Laguna	132	448	53	122	187	17	6	12	49	5	2	52	3	43	5	4	.272
Collins, James, Chihuahua*.........	124	470	95	206	279	35	10	6	60	2	1	53	5	51	33	21	.438
Colon, Raul, Puebla*..............	54	192	30	74	89	9	2	0	37	1	0	26	2	15	0	3	.385
Contreras, Juan, Laguna	95	260	26	65	87	12	2	2	25	4	3	7	1	54	5	1	.250
Cordova, Ernesto, Tampico	2	3	0	0	0	0	0	0	0	0	0	0	0	1	0	0	.000
Crawford, William, Aguas.*	64	234	33	71	97	15	1	3	29	0	3	26	1	37	4	2	.303
Cruz, Domingo, Cordoba...........	133	488	48	130	177	17	3	8	45	5	3	30	6	51	2	10	.266
Cuellar, Miguel, Coatzacoalcos*....	1	1	0	1	1	0	0	0	0	0	0	0	0	0	0	0	1.000
Cuevas, Ricardo, Poza Rica	47	55	7	14	16	2	0	0	1	1	0	4	0	11	1	3	.255

Player and Club	G.	AB.	R.	H.	TB.	2B.	3B.	HR.	RBI.	SH.	SF.	BB.	HP.	SO.	SB.	CS.	Pct.
Davila, Luis, Juarez	99	302	34	78	101	7	5	2	33	5	2	28	5	50	3	5	.258
De Hoyos, Arnoldo, 40 Coa-56 Yuc*	96	338	24	84	93	9	0	0	22	4	2	24	1	25	2	5	.249
De Los Santos, Jose, Tampico	39	83	7	20	23	1	1	0	2	3	0	2	1	16	1	1	.241
Del Bosque, Alfredo, Monterrey	25	77	7	15	23	2	0	2	11	1	1	5	2	18	0	2	.195
Del Moral, Jose, Aguila	122	447	52	130	181	27	0	8	47	4	1	35	1	50	14	5	.291
Delgado, Manuel, Juarez*	69	166	29	57	80	6	4	3	19	2	0	13	1	26	4	1	.343
Diaz, Albino, 69 Yuc-39 Agu*	108	349	28	73	95	7	3	3	19	11	2	48	2	52	5	5	.209
Diaz, Arsenio, Saltillo	127	462	66	149	228	17	7	16	92	1	6	44	8	65	5	3	.323
Diaz, Arturo, Aguascalientes	1	0	0	0	0	0	0	0	0	0	0	0	0	0	0	0	.000
Diaz, Cesar, Puebla	1	0	1	0	0	0	0	0	0	0	0	0	0	0	0	0	.000
Diaz, Fernando, Leon	9	17	0	2	3	1	0	0	0	0	0	0	0	2	0	0	.118
Diaz, Hector, Leon	61	9	2	1	2	1	0	0	0	0	0	0	0	2	0	0	.111
Duarte, Florentino, Aguascalientes	1	0	1	0	0	0	0	0	0	0	0	0	0	0	0	0	.000
Duran, Gerardo, Chihuahua	38	101	11	22	37	7	1	2	13	4	2	7	1	22	0	0	.218
Duran, Roberto, Poza Rica*	112	343	40	93	135	19	4	5	36	3	2	59	10	42	2	1	.271
Durazo, Hector, Laredo	1	1	0	0	0	0	0	0	0	0	0	0	0	1	0	0	.000
Elguezabal, Jose, Puebla	127	426	72	126	193	20	4	13	69	5	8	61	7	39	20	11	.296
Elizondo, Fernando, Aguila	82	204	13	37	43	2	2	0	11	9	0	16	0	44	3	2	.181
Enriquez, Graciano, Juarez	104	383	36	114	150	21	3	3	49	7	4	13	2	42	2	6	.298
Enriquez, Sergio, Chihuahua	46	68	3	8	8	0	0	0	1	2	0	2	0	21	2	4	.118
Escalante, Victor, Coatzacoalcos	71	183	14	40	50	5	1	1	11	1	2	24	2	46	0	2	.219
Esparza, Julio, Poza Rica	13	22	0	2	3	1	0	0	1	2	0	4	0	3	0	0	.091
Espino, Hector, 27 Le-67 Lag	94	355	48	120	182	17	0	15	70	0	6	30	3	12	1	0	.338
Espinosa, Ernesto, Durango*	84	229	30	56	69	9	2	0	11	5	0	23	3	48	1	2	.245
Espinoza, Ernesto (Torre), Tampico	118	439	41	99	116	10	2	1	23	6	0	32	5	47	1	2	.226
Esqueda, Carlos, Laguna	68	183	11	38	43	5	0	0	6	5	1	9	0	31	0	1	.208
Estrada, Francisco, Puebla	112	399	54	129	156	19	1	2	69	2	5	35	6	17	4	8	.323
Estrada, Pablo, Mex Tigers*	1	1	0	1	1	0	0	0	0	0	0	0	0	0	0	0	1.000
Etchandy, Curtis, Monterrey	45	154	24	39	58	5	4	2	20	3	2	23	0	38	3	0	.253
Faudoa, Victor, Mex Tigers*	84	193	21	54	59	5	0	0	24	2	0	26	0	28	1	3	.280
Felix, Claudio, Tabasco	23	3	3	2	2	0	0	0	0	0	0	1	0	1	0	1	.667
Felix, Fernando, Coahuila	136	498	55	140	190	30	1	6	68	2	9	31	5	61	3	3	.281
Felix, Victor, Tabasco	135	509	73	134	156	16	3	0	40	8	4	71	3	79	12	6	.263
Figueroa, Baldemar, Tampico	72	212	16	49	54	2	0	1	14	4	1	21	0	38	8	4	.231
Figueroa, Leobardo, Juarez	109	386	79	121	145	14	2	2	34	3	1	50	9	28	22	8	.313
Flores, Javier, Leon	36	94	10	13	21	2	0	2	6	1	0	11	2	42	1	1	.138
Flores, Mario, Monterrey	79	212	30	48	62	4	2	2	18	9	1	16	6	40	12	3	.226
Ford, Theodore, Mex Reds	92	328	67	104	164	16	4	12	50	1	5	66	1	39	2	3	.317
Franco, David, Coatzacoalcos	2	1	0	0	0	0	0	0	0	0	0	0	0	1	0	0	.000
Fuentes, Antonio, Poza Rica	39	78	7	20	24	2	1	0	4	1	0	8	0	9	0	1	.256
Gamundi, Timoteo, Poza Rica	130	487	58	127	148	10	4	1	23	14	3	37	8	78	19	10	.261
Garcia, Bulmaro, 72 Yuc-22 Agu	94	303	30	76	88	9	0	1	17	8	0	16	3	32	0	4	.251
Garcia, Humberto, Laredo	133	475	49	109	153	20	0	8	58	5	6	54	3	87	8	3	.229
Garcia, Jesus, Chihuahua	23	50	5	11	14	1	1	0	2	1	1	4	1	13	1	3	.220
Garcia, Jorge, Monterrey	1	2	0	0	0	0	0	0	0	0	0	0	0	1	0	0	.000
Garcia, Pedro, Poza Rica	112	421	46	120	164	20	3	6	41	8	3	39	4	53	21	10	.285
Garcia, Victor, Laredo	2	0	1	0	0	0	0	0	0	0	0	0	0	0	0	0	.000
Garza, Gustavo, Coatzacoalcos*	21	47	5	14	15	1	0	0	7	1	0	2	1	3	1	0	.298
Garzon, Felix, 74 Coa-19 Ags	93	281	24	61	64	10	0	1	29	8	3	35	1	47	3	0	.217
Gaston, Clarence, Leon	24	83	5	28	33	2	0	1	8	1	1	10	1	16	0	1	.337
Gaytan, Ricardo, Tampico	45	112	6	19	21	2	0	0	6	4	0	4	0	33	0	0	.170
George, Frank, Coatzacoalcos	101	356	59	110	152	18	0	8	55	0	4	52	1	64	9	7	.309
Gomez, Alejandro, Laredo	51	96	8	20	24	2	1	0	8	0	0	8	1	18	6	2	.208
Gomez, Graciano, Laredo	131	447	41	111	138	14	5	1	34	6	3	13	5	68	5	8	.248
Gonzalez, Arturo, Monterrey	2	7	0	0	0	0	0	0	0	0	0	0	0	3	0	0	.000
Gonzalez, Efrain, Saltillo	66	153	10	34	42	4	2	0	19	5	0	10	0	38	1	1	.222
Gonzalez, Ernesto, Puebla	38	99	13	21	22	1	0	0	11	4	1	12	1	17	2	1	.212
Gonzalez, Jesus, 10 Leo-88 Ctz	98	339	26	80	92	12	0	0	29	4	4	9	2	48	3	3	.236
Gonzalez, Joseph, Aguascalientes	129	460	67	126	166	9	8	5	61	5	2	44	6	58	15	11	.274
Gonzalez, Mario, Yucatan	5	3	0	1	1	0	0	0	0	0	0	1	0	1	0	0	.333
Gonzalez, Wenceslao, Chihuahua	119	397	48	119	189	10	0	20	87	2	5	64	8	84	1	2	.300
Green, Richard, Aguascalientes†	15	48	0	7	8	1	0	0	3	0	1	9	0	10	1	0	.146
Guarnaccia, John, 20 Ags-27 Tig*	47	141	24	32	43	6	1	1	12	6	0	29	0	23	0	4	.227
Guerra, Claudio, Leon*	25	78	8	20	22	2	0	0	5	0	0	4	0	9	0	0	.256
Guerra, Ricardo, Laredo	109	355	61	103	160	21	3	10	55	3	5	61	8	38	4	0	.290
Guerrero, Leobardo, Aguas.	84	307	43	76	95	2	7	1	22	2	3	30	4	29	12	13	.248
Guillen, Norberto, 14 Yuc-33 Coa	47	109	9	19	24	2	0	1	4	3	1	5	1	15	0	1	.174
Gutierrez, Gerardo, Laredo	53	142	10	24	33	5	2	0	10	2	2	10	2	34	1	2	.169
Gutierrez, Leon, Tabasco	3	0	0	0	0	0	0	0	0	0	0	0	0	0	0	0	.000
Gutierrez, Rogelio, Chihuahua	74	198	26	43	50	7	0	0	9	3	0	26	2	31	6	1	.217
Guzman, Andres, Cordoba	99	287	33	66	88	11	4	1	36	2	6	17	3	70	0	2	.230
Guzman, Horacio, Tampico	109	338	30	68	93	15	2	2	20	8	1	21	4	69	5	3	.201
Guzman, Ramiro, Mex Tigers*	110	355	41	96	114	5	5	1	17	8	1	38	2	44	4	8	.270
Hairston, Jerry, Durango†	128	427	87	151	219	22	5	12	56	4	4	113	2	34	12	11	.354
Hansen, Robert, Yucatan*	69	235	30	63	84	6	0	5	25	1	1	47	1	21	1	2	.268

Player and Club	G.	AB.	R.	H.	TB.	2B.	3B.	HR.	RBI.	SH.	SF.	BB.	HP.	SO.	SB.	CS.	Pct.
Henderson, Joseph, Coatzacoalcos*	21	36	1	5	5	0	0	0	1	1	0	1	0	20	0	0	.139
Heras, Roberto, 26 Tig-7 Yuc	33	73	8	15	18	3	0	0	3	1	0	2	0	22	1	0	.205
Hernandez, Enrique, Coahuila	6	10	2	1	3	0	1	0	0	0	0	0	0	5	0	0	.100
Hernandez, Jorge Luis, Puebla	101	340	43	89	109	11	3	1	46	9	4	20	2	41	1	6	.262
Hernandez, Jose, Durango	132	440	42	92	117	14	1	3	33	8	5	39	5	71	4	6	.209
Hernandez, Juan, Laguna	54	211	30	52	72	6	1	4	22	1	3	12	0	40	6	4	.246
Hernandez, Loreto, Mex Reds	18	40	3	9	9	0	0	0	2	1	0	4	1	11	0	0	.225
Hernandez, Miguel, Coatzacoalcos..	90	223	20	53	60	5	1	0	14	7	2	21	3	30	2	2	.238
Hernandez, Ramon, Mex Reds	135	563	64	156	173	15	1	0	39	11	3	32	2	20	19	8	.277
Hernandez, Raul, Cordoba	5	9	2	1	2	1	0	0	1	1	0	1	0	4	0	0	.111
Hernandez, Rodolfo, Cordoba	129	485	55	131	196	23	3	12	67	5	8	44	5	46	1	4	.270
Hernandez, Salvador, Mex Tigers	31	77	9	20	26	6	0	0	4	4	1	12	0	7	0	0	.260
Huizar, Victor, Laredo	1	1	0	0	0	0	0	0	0	0	0	0	0	0	0	0	.000
Iglesias, Domingo, 15 Ch-101 Agu..	116	328	23	68	83	9	3	0	21	2	1	44	2	78	7	2	.207
Iniguez, Roberto, Coatzacoalcos...	12	22	1	3	5	0	1	0	2	0	0	1	0	8	0	1	.136
Ithier, Pedro, Laredo	52	170	16	40	44	2	1	0	11	5	3	13	2	7	5	5	.235
Jackson, Alfonso, Chihuahua	10	31	0	3	3	0	0	0	2	0	0	0	1	8	0	0	.097
Jimenez, Alfonso, Puebla	132	442	62	135	171	23	5	1	42	19	8	50	1	40	19	16	.305
Juarez, Marcelo, Saltillo	120	461	69	140	163	23	0	0	45	18	2	32	1	31	11	4	.304
King, Harold, Saltillo*	124	375	66	120	195	12	3	19	85	0	5	124	7	70	2	0	.320
Kurpiel, Edward, Mex Reds*	138	499	86	145	225	17	6	17	88	6	7	83	0	60	4	5	.296
Lagunes, Jesus, Aguila*	61	175	17	55	65	4	3	0	8	4	1	12	1	16	6	2	.314
Lara, Armando, Mex Tigers	125	425	42	106	142	14	5	4	47	9	2	38	2	36	4	5	.249
Lara, Cesar, Laredo	25	72	5	9	11	2	0	0	5	5	1	3	1	8	1	0	.125
Lara, Franco Javier, Mex Tigers ..	13	26	0	7	7	0	0	0	3	1	0	1	0	6	0	0	.269
Lara, Francisco, 63 Tig-31 Yuc	94	341	31	90	99	4	1	1	20	9	0	12	3	19	1	5	.264
Lara, Santos, Juarez	4	7	1	2	2	0	0	0	0	0	0	2	0	1	0	0	.286
Lazaro, Alfredo, Coahuila	133	438	45	98	135	10	3	7	51	10	5	42	1	89	4	2	.224
Lazaro, Manuel, Laguna	98	298	26	78	93	8	2	1	21	7	1	22	1	29	5	3	.262
Leal, Marco, Mex Tigers	113	406	39	124	140	12	2	0	32	12	5	27	2	40	6	7	.305
Leon, Maximino, Durango	2	0	1	0	0	0	0	0	0	0	0	0	0	0	0	0	.000
Leon, Richard, Coahuila†	60	230	28	69	88	14	1	1	15.	1	0	20	0	35	2	2	.300
Leyva, Adalberto, Tampico	6	13	0	1	1	0	0	0	0	0	0	0	0	6	0	1	.077
Limon, Jose, Aguila	5	15	0	3	3	0	0	0	0	0	0	0	0	0	0	0	.000
Lindsey, Dave, 37 PR-46 Agu*	83	291	30	62	83	12	0	3	21	2	2	38	2	34	7	5	.213
Lizarraga, Alejandro, Mex Reds	99	344	35	101	131	18	3	2	38	3	3	14	2	38	8	7	.294
Lizarraga, Miguel, Tabasco	69	121	10	29	34	2	0	1	10	4	0	7	1	19	0	0	.240
Lizarraga, Raul, Leon	57	142	15	22	29	4	0	1	7	0	0	17	0	42	0	2	.155
Llenas, Winston, Cordoba	131	487	62	142	193	13	4	10	61	1	4	50	4	42	5	4	.292
Lopez, A. Jaime, Aguascalientes*	5	15	0	3	3	0	0	0	3	0	0	1	0	3	0	0	.200
Lopez, Baudel, Mex Reds*	126	462	62	124	148	14	5	0	38	13	4	73	5	50	9	9	.268
Lopez, E. Jaime, Chihuahua*	110	393	36	118	143	10	6	1	47	4	8	18	2	12	1	6	.300
Lopez, Hector, Mex Tigers	1	1	0	0	0	0	0	0	0	0	0	0	0	0	0	0	.000
Lopez, Lorenzo, Leon	106	365	36	95	124	11	0	6	38	4	4	35	0	56	1	3	.260
Lopez, Raul, Chihuahua*	68	176	18	47	61	11	0	1	19	2	2	6	0	32	2	1	.267
Lopez, Victor, Tabasco	107	331	45	86	122	15	3	5	38	6	1	43	2	49	0	3	.260
Lora, Luis, Puebla*	121	472	79	169	209	25	6	1	72	8	6	34	2	31	15	9	.358
Lugo, Gabriel, Coatzacoalcos	121	451	44	123	172	24	2	7	65	0	6	37	8	41	3	4	.273
Lugo, Manuel, Tampico	2	2	0	0	0	0	0	0	0	0	0	0	1	0	0	0	.000
Lugo, Pedro, Poza Rica	84	246	15	50	59	2	2	1	26	9	1	8	3	28	2	0	.203
Luna, Jose, Monterrey	38	93	6	20	25	2	0	1	4	1	0	10	0	12	1	2	.215
Mares, Hilario, Poza Rica	90	270	31	71	84	11	1	0	19	2	1	18	1	36	0	5	.263
Mariscal, Alfredo, 2 Agu-2 Tab	4	1	2	0	0	0	0	0	0	0	0	0	0	0	0	0	.000
Marquez, Francisco, Yucatan	118	391	39	89	123	10	3	6	39	4	2	41	7	67	1	1	.228
Marquez, Roberto, Coatzacoalcos..	99	292	24	61	64	3	0	0	13	15	2	26	1	40	2	3	.209
Martinez, Antonio, Laredo	1	1	0	0	0	0	0	0	0	0	0	0	0	0	0	0	.000
Martinez, Bernardo, Cordoba	8	21	0	3	4	1	0	0	1	0	0	0	0	7	0	0	.143
Martinez, C. Juan, Monterrey	126	445	54	120	180	21	0	13	74	7	5	49	2	103	1	4	.270
Martinez, G. Juan, Monterrey	6	11	1	1	1	0	0	0	0	0	2	0	0	4	0	0	.091
Matias, John, 82 Tig-40 Agu	122	427	44	143	178	12	4	5	42	1	6	42	3	24	2	5	.335
Matina, Raymond, 83 Agu-39 Yuc..	122	452	46	119	147	14	4	23	11	1	32	2	25	13	9	.263
Melendez, Luis, Yucatan	93	330	31	80	105	9	2	4	40	7	2	25	2	31	0	5	.242
Mendez, Roberto, Durango	127	475	72	132	165	22	4	1	36	7	2	54	1	41	8	5	.278
Mendez, Virgilio, Cordoba	7	7	1	3	3	0	0	0	3	0	0	0	0	2	0	0	.429
Mendoza, Jose, Tabasco	7	10	1	1	1	0	0	0	0	0	0	0	0	3	0	0	.100
Mendoza, Luis, Juarez	125	397	49	112	125	8	1	1	41	11	2	42	4	28	7	5	.282
Mendoza, Margarito, Coahuila	14	12	1	3	5	0	1	0	1	1	0	0	0	2	0	0	.250
Mendoza, Porfirio, Juarez	56	151	17	35	42	5	1	0	9	8	0	14	1	24	3	2	.232
Mendoza, Saul, Yucatan	132	435	60	108	161	18	1	11	51	16	5	95	8	54	10	4	.248
Mere, Luis, Mex Reds	2	1	1	1	1	0	0	0	1	0	0	0	0	0	0	0	1.000
Meza, Rigoberto, 2 Lag-16 Lar	18	0	1	0	0	0	0	0	0	0	0	0	0	0	0	0	.000
Mojica, Bartolo, Leon	41	95	4	12	13	1	0	0	5	0	2	11	1	21	0	2	.126
Molina, Jose, 2 Agu-59 Ags	61	157	10	36	43	7	0	0	18	1	1	7	5	24	0	0	.229
Montiel, Julio, Saltillo	102	274	37	55	63	3	1	1	25	5	3	26	4	25	1	1	.201
Montoya, Raul, Chihuahua	105	427	60	123	146	13	5	0	25	3	2	26	1	19	18	11	.288

Player and Club	G.	AB.	R.	H.	TB.	2B.	3B.	HR.	RBI.	SH.	SF.	BB.	HP.	SO.	SB.	CS.	Pct.
Moore, Curtis, Saltillo*	22	80	16	20	33	5	1	2	13	1	0	14	0	19	0	1	.250
Mora, Andres, Saltillo	114	421	79	145	255	31	5	23	102	1	7	37	5	57	3	1	.344
Mora, Jesus, Leon	45	148	7	37	49	3	0	3	16	0	1	5	0	10	0	2	.250
Morales, Carlos, Tabasco†	17	29	1	5	5	0	0	0	3	1	1	6	1	3	0	0	.172
Morales, Gonzalo, Tabasco	4	1	0	0	0	0	0	0	0	0	0	0	0	0	0	0	.000
Morales, Luis, Cordoba	15	46	5	11	16	0	1	1	4	1	0	3	0	12	0	3	.239
Moreno, Cesar, Tampico	1	1	0	0	0	0	0	0	0	0	0	0	0	0	0	0	.000
Munoz, Edward, Laguna	103	361	44	103	155	11	4	11	41	3	1	39	1	29	4	11	.285
Munoz, Jose Luis, Yucatan	85	203	30	47	65	7	4	1	19	8	0	27	1	40	3	6	.232
Munoz, Romulo, Leon	81	257	20	65	97	11	3	5	28	2	5	20	4	66	1	3	.253
Murrel, Ivan, 41 Pue-90 Leo	131	471	69	134	234	24	2	24	98	0	11	59	6	90	16	4	.285
Naranjo, Jose, Coahuila*	127	420	60	148	197	28	3	5	56	6	3	52	7	46	2	2	.352
Navarrete, Carlos, Coatzacoalcos	132	468	29	108	130	11	4	1	45	10	3	13	10	35	0	7	.231
Navarrete, Juan, Saltillo*	136	521	110	185	217	15	4	3	61	12	3	53	5	15	40	18	.355
Nettles, Morris, Puebla*	132	489	104	155	196	22	5	3	42	5	1	105	0	86	28	15	.317
Noriega, Franco, 14 Agu-72 Chi	86	279	38	71	92	11	2	1	21	3	0	24	3	25	6	3	.254
Oliver, Robert, Aguila	128	465	47	142	226	28	7	14	68	1	4	24	6	50	7	3	.305
Oquendo, Ismael, 87 Lag-24 Tab	111	362	49	93	161	12	1	18	58	3	2	81	2	73	11	4	.257
Ornelas, Jesus, Monterrey	37	95	6	17	21	4	0	0	6	1	1	16	0	21	5	5	.179
Ornelas, Rafael, Yucatan	117	377	39	73	100	4	1	7	36	13	2	43	2	102	4	2	.194
Ornelas, Roberto, Coatzacoalcos	89	194	19	41	54	5	4	0	15	5	0	14	0	31	0	1	.211
Orozco, Arturo, Tampico	125	406	39	98	142	20	3	6	41	0	2	53	6	85	4	4	.241
Ortega, Jose, Aguila	1	0	0	0	0	0	0	0	0	0	0	0	0	0	0	0	.000
Ortiz, Alfredo, Laredo*	31	34	1	6	8	2	0	0	7	1	0	8	0	5	1	0	.176
Ortiz, Armando, 31 Yu-2 Ti-33 Lr	66	183	10	39	43	4	0	0	8	0	1	20	4	41	0	0	.213
Ortiz, Jose, Monterrey	134	491	34	119	155	18	3	4	44	7	5	40	1	53	2	6	.242
Ortiz, Juan, Durango	54	111	10	22	31	4	1	1	9	1	0	12	3	24	0	2	.198
Ortiz, Manuel, Tabasco	3	0	1	0	0	0	0	0	0	0	0	0	0	0	0	0	.000
Osuna, Elpidio, Juarez	105	371	47	108	141	13	1	6	50	1	6	31	3	27	3	2	.291
Palacios, Raul, Tabasco	1	0	1	0	0	0	0	0	0	0	0	0	0	0	0	0	.000
Paredes, Jesus, Laredo	129	481	60	147	181	17	7	1	44	10	6	28	3	73	13	12	.306
Paredes, Raul, Puebla	55	141	19	38	47	5	2	0	10	5	1	4	2	22	5	3	.270
Parra, Manuel, Juarez	123	420	48	120	184	26	4	10	82	0	2	33	8	62	2	3	.286
Payan, Efrain, Yucatan	7	14	1	2	2	0	0	0	1	0	0	5	0	5	0	1	.143
Peralta, Luis, Poza Rica	75	232	17	58	71	6	2	1	23	7	3	14	1	31	1	0	.250
Peralta, Vicente, Cordoba	81	239	20	57	69	8	2	0	23	1	2	22	1	37	3	0	.238
Peraza, Jose, Yucatan	15	15	1	3	5	0	1	0	1	0	0	1	0	3	1	0	.200
Perez, Alfredo, Laguna	110	365	22	105	117	8	2	0	33	4	2	31	5	41	2	7	.288
Perez, Javier, Tampico	6	8	1	0	0	0	0	0	0	0	0	1	0	5	0	0	.000
Perez, Joel, Tabasco	90	340	49	83	121	12	1	8	41	7	5	24	2	51	12	13	.244
Perez, Jose, Aguascalientes*	125	386	49	121	155	14	7	2	38	3	5	37	4	47	2	4	.313
Perez, Miguel, Coatzacoalcos*	17	45	5	8	8	0	0	0	3	0	1	6	1	2	0	0	.178
Pineda, Jose, Aguascalientes	3	0	1	0	0	0	0	0	0	0	0	0	0	0	0	0	.000
Plasencia, Obed, Mex Tigers	120	440	43	136	173	12	2	7	69	1	5	26	6	38	2	3	.309
Plasencia, Rigoberto, Aguila	19	60	4	13	16	3	0	0	7	0	1	4	0	7	0	0	.217
Ponce, Francisco, Tabasco	1	1	0	0	0	0	0	0	0	0	0	0	0	0	0	0	.000
Porras, Ricardo, Coahuila	39	83	9	14	16	0	1	0	4	3	0	2	0	19	0	1	.169
Preciado, Mario, Laguna	2	4	0	0	0	0	0	0	0	0	0	0	0	4	0	0	.000
Quintero, Jose, Durango	3	3	1	1	1	0	0	0	0	0	0	0	0	1	1	0	.333
Quintero, Victor, Saltillo	3	6	1	2	2	0	0	0	0	0	0	1	0	1	1	0	.333
Quinones, Jorge, Leon	51	138	10	26	29	3	0	0	9	2	1	13	0	17	2	2	.188
Quinonez, Ventura, Juarez	5	7	0	3	4	1	0	0	2	0	0	0	0	1	0	0	.429
Quirk, James, Aguascalientes*	19	75	7	18	19	1	0	0	5	0	1	3	0	7	2	1	.240
Ramirez, Gustavo, 16 Agu-88 NL	104	349	38	91	102	8	0	1	22	11	3	25	5	35	6	2	.261
Ramirez, Manuel, Tabasco	131	531	73	151	174	12	4	1	25	10	0	23	3	46	7	5	.284
Rey, Arturo, Aguila	107	330	19	92	120	16	0	4	26	5	1	23	4	48	5	2	.279
Reyes, Juan, Aguascalientes*	6	8	1	0	0	0	0	0	0	0	0	0	0	3	0	0	.000
Rios, Carlos, 62 Dur-54 Lar	116	434	41	111	154	13	3	8	52	7	1	22	0	77	6	11	.256
Rivera, Carlos, Mex Tigers	132	502	64	137	181	21	4	5	47	9	4	26	5	77	14	5	.273
Rivera, Eduardo, Chihuahua	107	352	28	87	98	4	2	1	28	3	1	36	5	34	5	10	.247
Rivero, Gener, Cordoba	131	433	40	103	114	5	3	0	24	12	0	30	1	35	5	8	.238
Robles, Alejandro, Yucatan*	100	368	30	104	118	14	0	0	28	9	1	23	2	18	2	3	.283
Robles, Rigoberto, Tampico	121	463	42	127	155	18	2	2	21	7	2	15	0	66	3	5	.274
Robles, Sergio, Mex Reds	120	422	34	125	142	15	1	0	46	6	3	20	1	33	1	0	.296
Rodriguez, Arturo, Monterrey	81	258	21	70	81	4	2	1	23	1	2	17	0	22	5	3	.271
Rodriguez, Eliseo, Coatzacoalcos	107	309	38	88	122	16	0	6	42	3	1	79	12	32	1	4	.285
Rodriguez, Francisco, Aguas.	125	457	48	125	166	22	5	3	58	3	7	30	3	46	2	3	.274
Rodriguez, Gonzalo, Poza Rica	4	7	2	2	2	0	0	0	1	0	0	1	0	4	0	0	.286
Rodriguez, Guadalupe, Mex Tigers	7	11	1	1	2	1	0	0	0	0	0	1	0	1	0	0	.091
Rodriguez, Jaime, Mex Tigers	9	24	4	5	6	1	0	0	1	0	0	4	0	4	0	0	.208
Rodriguez, Jesus, Juarez	4	5	0	1	1	0	0	0	0	0	0	0	0	1	0	0	.200
Rodriguez, Jose, Yucatan	102	336	34	86	106	9	1	3	29	9	2	27	1	31	1	2	.256
Rodriguez, Juan, Mex Reds†	47	106	12	28	36	5	0	1	17	0	1	12	2	10	0	2	.264
Rodriguez, Juan Franco, Cordoba	50	70	11	15	17	2	0	0	7	2	1	10	1	5	1	0	.214
Rodriguez, Leonardo C., Mont.*	123	456	79	139	199	17	11	7	49	8	5	77	1	65	19	13	.305

Player and Club	G.	AB.	R.	H.	TB.	2B.	3B.	HR.	RBI.	SH.	SF.	BB.	HP.	SO.	SB.	CS.	Pct.
Rodriguez, Leonardo M., Monterrey	111	337	26	83	92	5	2	0	31	13	0	30	2	35	6	3	.246
Rodriguez, Roberto, Laredo*	110	406	66	147	187	12	14	0	30	9	3	63	0	44	6	13	.362
Rodriguez, Rodolfo, Coahuila*	122	442	56	130	150	11	3	1	30	6	1	55	4	46	1	7	.294
Roman, Dagoberto, Mex Reds*	99	329	42	93	116	11	3	2	30	4	0	23	1	47	9	5	.283
Romero, Pedro, Poza Rica	2	5	0	0	0	0	0	0	0	0	0	0	0	1	0	0	.000
Romo, Jesus, Mex Reds	19	38	7	7	9	0	1	0	0	0	0	4	1	9	1	0	.184
Romo, Jose, Tabasco	106	255	31	66	109	12	2	9	39	6	1	32	5	60	1	5	.259
Rondon, Gilberto, Yucatan	1	0	1	0	0	0	0	0	0	0	0	0	0	0	0	0	.000
Roque, Jorge, Coatzacoalcos	115	404	66	122	200	26	5	14	61	0	3	50	6	63	23	11	.302
Rosales, Arturo, Juarez	33	57	6	12	20	6	1	0	2	2	0	1	1	16	1	0	.211
Rosario, Angel, Coatzacoalcos†	132	464	74	144	194	26	3	6	46	2	4	90	2	53	1	5	.310
Rosas, Clemente, Aguascalientes	89	292	24	73	95	20	1	0	34	0	3	15	0	42	0	0	.250
Rubio, Arturo, Tampico	115	391	29	91	102	6	1	1	17	12	4	33	3	47	2	4	.233
Ruiz, Miguel, Laredo	15	38	5	4	4	0	0	0	0	0	0	4	0	10	0	0	.105
Ruiz, Porfirio, Durango	130	456	39	113	146	15	3	4	43	8	3	28	4	50	1	3	.248
Saiz, Francisco, Poza Rica*	122	442	45	120	137	5	6	0	25	7	1	61	4	34	12	8	.271
Salazar, Ronaldo, Aguascalientes	111	372	56	108	139	11	1	6	41	4	1	38	8	50	10	9	.290
Saldana, T. Mario, Leon	122	387	29	70	84	10	2	0	14	9	2	27	0	61	2	6	.181
Samaniego, Gervasio, Coahuila	1	0	1	0	0	0	0	0	0	0	0	0	0	0	0	0	.000
Sanchez, Celerino, Leon	92	326	42	86	124	8	0	10	39	2	1	25	9	32	1	1	.264
Sanchez, Leonides, Poza Rica	112	390	25	98	113	9	3	0	24	10	0	21	2	34	10	7	.251
Sanchez, Juan, Laguna	81	254	12	70	91	10	1	3	26	2	1	10	3	56	0	2	.276
Sanchez, Raul, 59 Lag-70 Leon	129	473	88	148	217	23	11	8	59	8	5	58	7	57	36	15	.313
Sandate, Ricardo, Poza Rica*	1	1	0	0	0	0	0	0	0	0	0	0	0	1	0	0	.000
Sanders, Reg. 89 Tam-21 Aguas	110	410	60	150	232	27	2	17	95	0	7	39	9	41	1	1	.366
Sandoval, Francisco, Aguas.	1	0	0	0	0	0	0	0	0	0	0	0	0	0	0	0	.000
Sandoval, Rodolfo, Poza Rica	26	74	0	11	13	2	0	0	3	2	0	3	0	14	0	1	.149
Santana, Blas, Laguna	131	524	59	172	226	28	4	6	67	1	6	7	1	40	3	1	.328
Sanudo, Asuncion, Mex Tigers	1	1	0	0	0	0	0	0	0	0	0	0	0	0	0	0	.000
Sanudo, Ismael, Saltillo	40	108	11	35	37	2	0	0	7	0	0	5	6	10	1	1	.324
Sauceda, Aristeo, Tampico	1	1	0	0	0	0	0	0	0	0	0	0	0	0	0	0	.000
Sauceda, Oscar, Durango	1	1	0	0	0	0	0	0	0	0	0	0	0	1	0	0	.000
Sauceda, Victor, Chihuahua	131	545	75	153	222	21	6	12	58	5	2	13	14	79	10	14	.281
Serna, Joel, Tabasco	132	457	43	116	152	19	1	5	42	12	3	39	3	83	5	9	.254
Serratos, Ramon, Coatzacoalcos	97	297	34	67	75	4	2	0	7	3	0	25	6	36	24	3	.226
Silverio, Tomas, Mex Tigers*	127	435	70	125	166	18	7	3	55	4	7	82	1	45	9	10	.287
Smith, Calvin, Poza Rica	2	3	0	0	0	0	0	0	0	0	0	0	0	1	0	0	.000
Smith, Cleo, 66 Tam-30 Aguas	96	354	40	88	134	13	3	9	37	0	1	36	1	73	3	4	.249
Smith, Tom, Aguascalientes*	4	9	0	1	1	0	0	0	0	0	0	1	0	0	0	1	.111
Sommers, Jesus, Tampico	122	467	60	131	181	18	1	10	43	0	0	42	2	76	9	3	.281
Sotelo, Emilio, Cordoba	2	3	0	0	0	0	0	0	0	0	0	0	0	2	0	0	.000
Soto, Carlos, Laredo	130	466	57	146	211	21	1	14	77	3	2	37	5	50	0	2	.313
Soto, Gregorio, Aguascalientes	72	192	20	52	64	8	2	0	13	2	0	17	2	31	0	2	.271
Strougher, Steven, Aguas.*	10	36	4	9	16	4	0	1	2	0	0	5	0	1	0	0	.250
Suarez, Miguel, Cordoba*	131	531	77	167	209	12	12	2	52	7	2	36	6	26	1	2	.315
Tellez, Alonso, 7 Chi-29 Mon*	36	101	16	23	37	4	5	0	8	1	2	5	0	13	1	1	.228
Terrazas, Martin, Mex Tigers	122	371	34	87	111	15	3	1	48	11	2	27	3	57	3	2	.235
Thompson, Narciso, 32 PR-71 Leo	103	383	55	102	131	13	2	4	24	6	3	20	1	44	5	5	.266
Torres, Antonio, Chihuahua	34	83	5	15	17	2	0	0	4	3	0	3	0	19	0	2	.181
Torres, Nemesio, Monterrey	78	266	33	71	84	6	2	1	22	12	2	17	4	14	5	5	.267
Torres, Raymundo, Durango	93	360	62	89	131	16	7	4	33	6	1	23	2	56	16	6	.247
Torres, Ricardo, Coahuila	1	3	0	0	0	0	0	0	0	0	0	0	0	0	0	0	.000
Tovar, Jose, Coahuila	110	365	37	76	94	11	2	1	28	17	1	17	2	43	2	5	.208
Trevino, Carlos, Tampico	90	296	24	68	86	6	0	4	29	3	2	26	1	62	1	0	.230
Trevino, Juan, Saltillo	101	340	27	76	100	12	3	2	43	10	1	13	1	32	0	4	.224
Uzcanga, Ali, Laredo	25	52	8	13	16	0	0	1	5	1	0	5	0	15	1	0	.250
Valenzuela, Carlos, Tabasco	111	290	19	68	73	3	1	0	22	7	1	39	2	37	1	0	.234
Valenzuela, Felipe, Tabasco*	50	75	9	19	22	3	0	0	5	3	0	10	0	14	1	2	.253
Valenzuela, Guillermo P., Cordoba*	6	6	0	1	1	0	0	0	0	0	0	2	0	3	0	0	.167
Valenzuela, Guillermo R., Durango	1	0	0	0	0	0	0	0	0	0	0	0	0	0	0	0	.000
Valenzuela, Jose, Coahuila	117	370	34	77	102	10	0	5	33	6	5	24	4	92	2	1	.208
Valenzuela, Leonardo, Monterrey*	130	511	76	162	222	16	19	2	49	5	3	39	2	89	22	14	.317
Valenzuela, Ramon, Durango	1	1	0	0	0	0	0	0	0	0	0	0	0	0	0	0	.000
Valdez, Rodolfo, Leon	1	1	0	0	0	0	0	0	0	0	0	0	0	0	0	0	.000
Valle, Guadalupe, Juarez	110	333	42	81	104	15	4	0	27	5	4	29	2	75	3	5	.243
Vazquez, Efrain, Laredo†	133	507	80	147	206	23	3	10	74	3	6	46	3	49	3	1	.290
Vazquez, Nicolas, Tabasco	94	306	31	84	102	8	2	2	33	6	3	12	3	34	3	1	.275
Vega, Abelardo, Juarez	127	410	73	119	159	26	4	2	52	6	8	62	10	54	8	10	.290
Vega, Manuel, Durango	29	48	2	6	7	1	0	0	0	0	0	4	0	16	0	0	.125
Vega, Valenciano, Coatzacoalcos	105	393	32	103	118	10	1	1	20	14	1	17	1	27	1	0	.262
Velarde, Roman, Durango	118	352	32	90	101	2	3	1	18	7	1	21	8	48	1	2	.256
Villaescusa, Antonio, Mex Reds	117	396	39	105	118	10	0	1	29	19	1	27	5	29	31	8	.265
Villagomez, David, Mex Reds	111	396	43	104	134	19	4	1	39	0	3	26	9	56	3	4	.263
Villalobos, Gonzalo, Aguascalientes	130	465	61	137	168	17	7	0	47	7	5	31	1	54	2	6	.295
Villalobos, Lauro, Tabasco	76	228	19	65	71	6	0	0	18	7	1	11	2	22	2	3	.285

Player and Club	G.	AB.	R.	H.	TB.	2B.	3B.	HR.	RBI.	SH.	SF.	BB.	HP.	SO.	SB.	CS.	Pct.
Villela, Carlos, Laguna	99	280	36	66	92	4	11	0	26	6	1	22	0	64	9	9	.236
Villela, Rigoberto, Durango	120	433	32	114	136	14	1	2	36	1	0	33	3	32	3	7	.263
Washington, Ron, Aguila	42	165	22	43	52	3	3	0	14	4	2	7	4	22	5	1	.261
Williams, Earl, Durango	134	505	69	173	262	25	2	20	112	1	7	48	3	82	8	6	.343
Williams, James, Laredo†	41	152	24	49	62	5	4	0	21	1	2	16	0	9	1	2	.322
Williams, Walter, 67 Mon-47 Chi	114	409	63	142	207	20	3	13	65	1	3	53	3	27	14	8	.347
Wright, Jesse, Leon*	1	1	0	0	0	0	0	0	0	0	0	0	0	1	0	0	.000
Wynn, James, Coahuila	17	54	10	12	15	0	0	1	5	0	0	17	0	10	0	4	.222
Yepez, Francisco, Poza Rica	106	302	22	77	92	5	5	0	29	6	4	20	3	38	4	8	.255
Zamora, Roberto, Mex Tigers	11	4	1	3	4	1	0	0	1	0	0	0	0	6	0	0	.214
Zamudio, Hector, Puebla	119	479	65	138	171	12	9	1	68	8	3	27	3	34	16	9	.288
Zavala, Alfredo, 70 M.Tig-33 Yuc....	103	258	21	55	71	4	3	2	21	5	2	19	1	42	1	3	.213
Zavala, Marcos, Chihuahua	124	427	60	124	178	17	2	11	65	7	9	47	4	85	12	11	.290
Zuniga, Faustino, Aguila	102	323	29	72	86	8	3	0	17	4	0	14	1	54	3	5	.223

The following pitchers had no plate appearances primarily through use of designated hitters, listed alphabetically by club, games in parentheses:

AGUASCALIENTES—Acosta, Cecilio (32); Cervantes, Antonio (5); Cervantes, Lauro (20); Espinosa, Javier (4); Moreno, Angel (32); Pena, Paulino (21); Pina, Horacio (27); Salomon, Porfirio (34); Scott, Mike (6); Valenzuela, Adan (3).

AGUILA—Alfaro, Jose (4); Cuen, Eleno (28); Escalante, Sergio (13); Hansen, Dave (12); Heredia, Ubaldo (25); Morales, Mario (38); Suby, Juan (11); Valdez, Jorge (7).

CHIHUAHUA—Acosta, Eduardo (28); Alvarez, Rigoberto (29); Casas, Arturo (6); Fabela, Wilfredo (29); Guzman, Ramon (53); Martinez, Gabriel (33); Montero, Hernan (1); Morales, Armando (15); Minoz, Adan (23); Nelson, Roger (35); Reyes, Javier (33); Vidana, Manuel (30).

CIUDAD JUAREZ—Aguilar, Rafael (30); Bane, Edward (28); Dimas, Rodolfo (8); Enriquez, Jorge (29); Garcia, Rafael (29); Gutierrez, Porfirio (29); Higuera, Teodoro (2); Longoria, Federico (8); Madrigal, Esteban (4); Paul, Michael (29); Robles, Gregorio (3); Wegener, John (3).

COAHUILA—Buentello, Israel (2); Castro, Benjamin (22); Cavanaugh, Carl (5); Cisneros, Alfonso (39); Garcia, Rogelio (32); Kuk Lee, Ernesto (37); Martinez, A. Franco (24); Monteagudo, Aurelio (38); Romero, Emigdio (16); Silva, Eduardo (33).

COATZACOALCOS—Carranza, Javier (7); Colorado, Salvador (53); Henderson, Joseph (30); Mauleon, Ignacio (7); Miranda, Francisco (27); Quijada, Armando (9); Reynoso, Jesus (17); Rodriguez, Jose (23); Romo, Vicente (32); Uresti, Crisanto (22).

CORDOBA—Antunez, Martin (1); Arano, Ramon (36); Barojas, Salome (41); Beltran, Miguel (17); Cervantes, Luis (3); Lopez, Juan (11); Matus, Nelson (2); Pena, Jose (9); Pulido, Alfonso (20); Quintero, Francisco (27); Ruiz, Cecilio (3); Segui, Diego (30); Sosa, Carlos (42); Vidana, Alejandro (7).

DURANGO—Cazares, Sergio (30); Gutierrez, Guillermo (23); Guzman, Luis (20); Valencia, Ignacio (34); Veintidos, Juan (33).

LEON—Aloi, Dave (6); Bellacetin, Tomas (3); Chavez, Carlos (32); Clark, Jorge (4); Garcia, Nicolas (37); Hernandez, Jaime (3); Lopez, Norberto (21); Moncado, Mario (1); Montoya, Saul (28); Peraza, Vidal (10); Perez, Gregorio (9); Solis, Guillermo (44); Urias, Filiberto (4); Urias, Reyes (1).

MEXICO CITY REDS—Burguette, Alfonso (8); Chavez, Rene (16); Divison, Julio (49); Franco, Pablo (28); Ibarra, Carlos (20); Ochoa, Domingo (29); Orea, Diacono (34); Preciado, Ignacio (6); Trinidad, Jesse (34).

MEXICO CITY TIGERS—Castillejos, J. Marcos (35); Lagunas, Crescencio (28); Pagan, David (6); Raygoza, German (17); Raygoza, Guillermo (26); Sauceda, Ramiro (46); Simpson, Wayne (9); Stover, Michael (2); Villanueva, Luis (38).

MONTERREY—Bernal, Andres (35); Bernal, Othon (10); Butkus, Stanley (40); Cruz, Concepcion (5); De La Torre, Adolfo (30); Esquer, Mercedes (34); McGough, Thomas (16); Reyes, Armando (17); Smith, Myrl (7).

NUEVO LAREDO—Ayon, Andres (3); Bobinger, Mitchell (3); Branch, Roy (27); Guerra, Ricardo (1); Huizar, Victor (23); Icedo, Enrique (20); Salgado, Octavio (25); Seyler, Ronald (3); Solis, Jesus (40); Valdivia, Miguel (2); Vargas, Fidel (2).

POZA RICA—Baruch, Matias (17); Bonfils, Peter (31); Franco, Francisco (22); Garcia, Alfredo (18); Garduza, Jose (18); Hernandez, Angel (41); Hernandez, Rafael (18); Herrera, Juan (4); Purata, Julio (2); Saldana, Eulogio (19); Sombra, Francisco (10); Valenzuela, Hector (28); Vergara, Ciro (3).

PUEBLA—Escarrega, Ernesto (30); Gutierrez, Pablo (30); Lopez, Fernando (25); Munguia, Ramon (42); Pulido, Antonio (20); Rivera, Abraham (25); Soto, Francisco (24).

SALTILLO—Ahumada, Alejo (34); Armas, Tomas (29); Caballero, Juan (17); De La Torre, Ernesto (11); Mennendez, Rolando (31); Pena, Manuel (27); Solis, Miguel (33); Soto, Alvaro (50).

TABASCO—Ayala, Mario (1); Castro, Felipe (2); Conn, Gary (14); Delfin, Justino (45); Feola, Larry (7); Lara, Gilberto (15); Madrigal, Hector (39); Martinez, Javier (19); Nagy, Mike (28); Nieto, Rodolfo (3); Nuno, Ramiro (3); Ochoa, Jose (34); Perez, Cipriano (4).

TAMPICO—Bracamontes, Ignacio (2); Brandt, Randy (22); Centeno, Jose (1); Gamez, Manuel (1); Gamez, Raul (20); Gamez, Rodrigo (2); Granger, Wayne (6); Johnson, Bart (3); Leal, Felipe (1); Lunar, Luis (7); Martinez, Raul (32); Morales, Roberto (28); Perez, Candelario (5); Ramirez, Hermenegildo (2); Reyna, Antonio (1).

UNION LAGUNA—Anderson, Mike (7); Arratia, Javier (10); Beltran, Eleazar (30); Dominguez, Herminio (32); Maytorena, Francisco (27); Ontiveros, Francisco (16); Salinas, Guadalupe (32); Sanchez, Salvador (5); Soto, Ciro (28); Valdez, Humberto (24).

YUCATAN—Castro, Adolfo (28); Jiminez, Juan (29); Kelly, Salvador (1); Meza, Alfredo (13); Moreno, Eleazar (5); Mota, Francisco (26); Rodriguez, Pilar (34); Valenzuela, Fernando (26); Valenzuela, Humberto (8); Vallejano, Rodolfo (27).

TWO CLUBS—Agundez, Victor (5 Aguila, 25 Aguascalientes); Brunet, George (24 Coatzacoalcos, 12 Mexico City Tigers); Campoy, Alejandro (12 Aguila, 2 Mexico City Tigers); Carrasco, Carlos (5 Tampico, 24 Leon); Espinosa, Nestor (1 Coatzacoalcos, 22 Aguila); Gutierrez, Eduardo (15 Monterrey, 13 Aguila); Leon, Cristino (8 Cordoba, 2 Coatzacoalcos); Martinez, Augusto (3 Tabasco, 3 Yucatan); Martinez, Feliz (4 Tampico, 1 Monterrey); Martinez, H. Franco (4 Mexico City Tigers, 39 Cordoba); Matias, John (12 Mexico City Tigers, 1 Aguila); Meistickle, Kevin (10 Aguila, 4 Aguascalientes); Nieblas, Armando (4 Tampico, 13 Ciudad Juarez); Ochoa, Julio (13 Durango, 17 Tampico); Oquendo, Ismael (1 Union Laguna, 2 Tabasco); Pereyra, Miguel (12 Durango, 21 Tabasco); Pollorena, Antonio (11 Union Laguna, 4 Leon); Rodriguez, Manuel (16 Yucatan, 13 Mexico City Tigers); Tovar, Pedro (8 Nuevo Laredo, 8 Union Laguna); Valdez, J. Humberto (6 Coatzacoalcos, 26 Aguila); Valle, Urbano (4 Aguascalientes, 18 Aguila); Valles, Reynaldo (5 Puebla, 6 Yucatan); Verdugo, Roberto (4 Saltillo, 25 Union Laguna); Williams, Gary (4 Leon, 1 Tampico).

GRAND SLAM HOME RUNS—M. Alvarez, 3; R. Guerra, V. Sauceda, 2 each; Armbrister (Yuc) Balaz, Centeno, Cerdo, R. Cervantes (Agu), F. Estrada, Joseph Gonzalez, Rodolfo Hernandez, King, L. Lopez, S. Mendoza, J. Mora, E. Munoz, Rafael Ornelas, Osuna, Parra, Rios (Lar), E. Rivera, E. Rodriguez, Rodolfo Rodriguez, C. Sanchez, Santana, Silverio, C. Soto, Tovar, 1 each.

AWARDED FIRST BASE ON INTERFERENCE—J. Navarrete 5 (Guillen, L. Mendoza, Orozco, L. Peralta, J. Sanchez); P. Ruiz 3 (J. Valenzuela 2, J. Sanchez); Alcaraz (L. Peralta); Camargo (Benitez), Chavarria (Guillen), F. Chavez (Efrain Gonzalez), S. Enriquez (E. Briones), F. Felix (L. Peralta), Garzon (Agu) (M. Hernandez), Kurpiel (M. Lizarraga), R. Lizarraga (J. Valenzuela), L. Lopez (J. Valenzuela), Mares (J. Valenzuela), Oquendo (Orozco), J. Rodriguez (P. Lugo).

CLUB FIELDING

Club	G.	PO.	A.	E.	DP.	PB.	Pct.	Club	G.	PO.	A.	E.	DP.	PB.	Pct.
Cordoba	133	3492	1418	99	117	13	.980	Monterrey	136	3519	1519	159	138	24	.969
Saltillo	136	3447	1645	110	180	14	.979	Nuevo Laredo	137	3561	1422	160	118	20	.969
Mexico	138	3681	1547	123	136	7	.977	Aguila	138	3420	1371	134	114	13	.969
Yucatan	134	3483	1617	129	125	21	.975	Tabasco	136	3573	1570	170	120	21	.968
Durango	136	3537	1504	132	104	26	.974	Poza Rica	133	3378	1357	157	101	11	.968
Ciudad Juarez	135	3510	1560	139	122	10	.973	Coatzacoalcos	136	3522	1538	171	111	8	.967
Puebla	137	3486	1587	142	133	16	.973	Coahuila	136	3462	1490	178	118	12	.965
Aguascalientes	136	3474	1505	140	114	15	.973	Tampico	135	3498	1499	183	115	15	.965
Mexico Tigers	135	3465	1594	149	145	9	.971	Leon	134	3438	1445	189	124	22	.963
Union Laguna	136	3366	1434	144	99	24	.971	Chihuahua	133	3390	1402	196	107	18	.961

Triple Plays—Union Luguna 2, Ciudad Juarez, Coahuila, Leon, Mexico Tigers, Puebla, 1 each.

INDIVIDUAL FIELDING

*Throws lefthanded.

FIRST BASEMEN

Player and Club	G.	PO.	A.	E.	DP.	Pct.	Player and Club	G.	PO.	A.	E.	DP.	Pct.
Quinonez, Leon	19	148	8	0	9	1.000	Martinez, C., Monterrey.	70	579	23	6	60	.990
Lindsey, Aguila-PR*	13	93	5	0	0	1.000	Garcia, H., Laredo	124	1047	55	11	96	.990
Delgado, Juarez*	15	92	2	0	4	1.000	Fuentes, Poza Rica	15	89	4	1	0	.989
Felix, Coahuila	10	91	2	0	5	1.000	Perez, Laguna	13	84	6	1	5	.989
Plasencia, Mex. Tigers ..	81	784	27	2	70	.998	Parra, Juarez	38	334	11	4	26	.989
Trevino, Tampico	35	275	11	1	19	.997	Oliver, Aguila	97	812	34	10	76	.988
Munoz, Leon	44	390	10	2	32	.995	Oquendo, Lag.-Tab.*	77	708	29	9	52	.988
OSUNA, Juarez	100	892	45	5	92	.995	Navarrete, Coatzacoalcos	116	994	56	13	83	.988
Naranjo, Coahuila*	121	1054	38	7	81	.994	Murrel, Puebla-Leon	27	233	9	3	13	.988
Lopez, Chihuahua*	98	875	47	6	65	.994	Bojorquez, Poza Rica	112	988	38	13	88	.987
Castro, Saltillo	47	443	16	3	46	.994	Rodriguez, C. L., Mont.	49	376	18	5	41	.987
Robles, Yucatan*	96	956	62	7	83	.993	Espino, Leon-Laguna	85	744	39	10	51	.987
Batista, Cordoba*	130	1202	46	9	107	.993	King, Saltillo	11	74	2	1	11	.987
Kurpiel, Mex. Reds*	138	1298	84	11	107	.992	Matias, Tig.-Aguila	19	125	9	2	15	.985
Hansen, Yucatan	38	364	10	3	36	.992	Lopez, Tabasco	71	606	47	10	46	.985
Centeno, Tampico*	26	242	6	2	15	.992	Lora, Puebla*	54	498	19	8	38	.985
Sanchez, Leon	12	114	3	1	12	.992	Perez, Aguascalientes	119	909	55	16	76	.984
Williams, Durango	127	1163	69	11	94	.991	Perez, Tabasco	14	134	11	3	14	.980
Arvizu, Tabasco	15	98	10	1	9	.991	Sanders, Tam.-Agua.	89	824	41	18	69	.980
Canada, Tabasco	28	207	6	2	13	.991	Lopez, R., Chihuahua*	43	340	15	8	28	.978
Diaz, Saltillo	85	802	39	8	105	.991	Perez, Coatzacoalcos*	17	119	8	3	11	.977
Colon, Puebla*	54	487	37	5	60	.991	Lopez, Leon	23	209	5	7	22	.968
Cervantes, Agu.-Mont..	31	208	15	2	18	.991	Christiansen, Laguna	10	59	0	2	4	.967
Faudoa, Mex. Tigers*	54	390	21	4	40	.990	Del Bosque, Monterrey	24	189	6	7	20	.965
Calvo, Durango	31	290	12	3	25	.990							

Triple Plays—Christiansen 2; Osuna, C. Sanchez, Colon, Naranjo, Matias (Mex. Tigers).

(Fewer Than Ten Games)

Player and Club	G.	PO.	A.	E.	DP.	Pct.	Player and Club	G.	PO.	A.	E.	DP.	Pct.
Rodriguez, Coat.	6	53	6	0	4	1.000	Morales, C., Tabasco	7	38	1	0	4	1.000
Vazquez, Laredo	7	55	2	0	10	1.000	Soto, Laredo	8	33	0	0	1	1.000
Peralta, Poza Rica	8	43	1	0	6	1.000	Smith, Tampico	5	30	2	0	4	1.000

FIRST BASEMEN—Continued
(Fewer Than Ten Games)

Player and Club	G.	PO.	A.	E.	DP.	Pct.
Escalante, Coatzacoalcos	4	27	1	0	2	1.000
Ortiz, A., Laredo*.	9	25	2	0	4	1.000
Sommers, Tampico	3	21	1	0	4	1.000
Green, Aguila	3	19	2	0	2	1.000
Llenas, Cordoba	3	18	1	0	1	1.000
Orozco, Tampico	2	14	0	0	1	1.000
Hernandez, R., Cordoba.	1	14	0	0	0	1.000
Garza, Coatzacoalcos	5	13	0	0	0	1.000
Camargo, Monterrey	1	12	0	0	1	1.000
Gonzalez, Monterrey	1	10	1	0	1	1.000
Mora, Leon	2	10	0	0	0	1.000
Ortiz, Monterrey	2	8	0	0	1	1.000
Barrera, Mex. Reds	2	8	0	0	1	1.000
Silverio, Mex. Tigers*.	2	8	0	0	0	1.000
Tovar, Coahuila	3	6	0	0	2	1.000
Del Moral, Aguila	2	6	0	0	0	1.000
Guerra, Laredo	1	6	0	0	1	1.000
Marquez, Yucatan	1	6	0	0	0	1.000
Hairston, Durango	1	6	0	0	1	1.000
Arano, Aguila	2	5	0	0	1	1.000
Lopez, Aguascalientes	2	3	0	0	0	1.000
Camarero, Aguila	7	47	1	1	3	.980
Salazar, Aguascalientes	8	42	2	1	3	.978
Alvarez, Aguascalientes	8	56	5	2	3	.968
Cerda, Durango	8	51	2	2	3	.964
Rodriguez, Yucatan	4	23	0	1	2	.958
De Hoyos, Coat.*	5	38	3	2	3	.953
Rosario, Coatzacoalcos	3	17	0	1	1	.944
Garzon, Coa.-Agua.	5	12	1	1	2	.929
Stroughter, Agua.	3	13	0	1	1	.929
Villagomez, Mex. Reds	1	6	1	1	1	.875
Rosales, Juarez	1	0	1	1	0	.500

SECOND BASEMEN

Player and Club	G.	PO.	A.	E.	DP.	Pct.
Ruiz, Laredo	13	25	26	0	6	1.000
Marquez, Coatzacoalcos.	16	16	30	0	6	1.000
Velarde, Durango	17	45	47	1	12	.989
Rodriguez, Cordoba	32	32	48	1	9	.988
NAVARRETE, Saltillo .	127	353	423	10	130	.987
Briones, Juarez	118	318	319	9	87	.986
Ortiz, Monterrey	130	384	331	12	97	.983
Hernandez, Puebla	101	210	295	9	70	.982
Mendez, Durango	123	308	311	12	67	.981
Figueroa, Juarez	18	55	39	2	11	.979
Chavez, Coatzacoalcos.	97	248	218	10	64	.979
Serna, Coatzacoalcos	50	129	143	6	25	.978
Chavez, Mex. Tigers	76	123	148	6	32	.978
Avina, Coahuila	19	41	49	2	9	.978
Villela, Laguna	52	103	120	5	25	.978
Hernandez, R., M. Reds	128	325	322	15	86	.977
Camarero, Aguila	46	104	103	5	22	.976
Alvarado, Yucatan	40	95	111	5	29	.976
Sanchez, Poza Rica	33	75	83	4	19	.975
Llenas, Cordoba	103	264	239	13	61	.975
Garcia, Yuc.-Agu.	94	229	215	12	54	.974
Alcaraz, Leon	121	275	303	16	73	.973
Zavala, Tig.-Yuc.	63	118	137	8	32	.970
Perez, Tabasco	75	196	212	13	47	.969
Escalante, Coatzacoalcos	11	37	23	2	8	.968
Montiel, Saltillo	15	28	33	2	5	.968
Castro, Aguascalientes	37	37	49	3	8	.966
Elizondo, Aguascalientes	50	95	105	7	22	.966
Iglesias, Chi.-Agu.	46	86	85	6	20	.966
Ithier, Laredo	52	150	132	10	45	.966
Lopez, Tabasco	15	53	31	3	7	.966
Elguezabal, Puebla	18	38	45	3	7	.965
Gomez, A., Laredo	19	26	29	2	4	.965
Lugo, Coatzacoalcos	22	51	57	4	9	.964
Hernandez, Mex. Tigers	29	74	79	6	24	.962
Lazaro, Laguna	97	197	184	15	40	.962
Robles, Tampico	117	327	333	26	81	.962
Lizarraga, Leon	12	25	25	2	8	.962
Hernandez, R., Cordoba	18	40	58	4	11	.961
Guerrero, Agua.	82	262	216	21	51	.958
Lazaro, Coahuila	14	41	27	3	9	.958
Garcia, Poza Rica	96	279	229	23	67	.957
Mendoza, P., Juarez	18	35	47	4	11	.953
Tovar, Coahuila	107	272	283	28	55	.952
Carreno, Puebla	12	31	27	3	11	.951
Salazar, Aguascalientes	40	87	90	10	17	.947
Rios, Laredo	40	101	96	12	20	.943
Munoz, Yucatan	28	30	32	4	6	.939
Noriega, Agu.-Chi.	40	88	61	10	11	.937
Ortiza, Yuc.-Tig.-Lar.	28	48	60	8	16	.931
Torres, Chihuahua	32	44	54	10	6	.907

Triple Plays—Alcaraz, A. Briones, J. L., Hernandez, M., Lazaro, A. Zavala.

(Fewer Than Ten Games)

Player and Club	G.	PO.	A.	E.	DP.	Pct.
Aguilar, Aguascalientes	5	13	15	0	4	1.000
Bobadilla, Juarez	6	7	15	0	3	1.000
Cuevas, Poza Rica	4	10	12	0	0	1.000
Serratos, Coatzacoalcos..	7	14	7	0	2	1.000
Salvo, Puebla	2	10	7	0	3	1.000
Andrews, Poza Rica	3	7	4	0	1	1.000
Hernandez, Laguna	1	4	6	0	3	1.000
Gonzalez, Yucatan	5	4	5	0	3	1.000
Romo, Mex. Reds	1	5	3	0	0	1.000
Espinoza, Tampico	1	5	3	0	1	1.000
Rivera, Mex. Tigers	4	4	3	0	1	1.000
Aguirre, Mex. Reds	4	2	4	0	1	1.000
Zamudio, Puebla	1	4	2	0	1	1.000
Alvarado, Cordoba	2	1	4	0	1	1.000
Hairston, Durango	2	1	2	0	0	1.000
Ramirez, Laredo	1	2	1	0	1	1.000
Quintero, Saltillo	1	1	0	0	1	1.000
Leal, Mex. Tigers	1	1	0	0	0	1.000
Acuna, Puebla	9	16	25	1	12	.976
Lara, Laredo	8	38	18	2	6	.966
Montoya, Chihuahua	5	13	10	1	6	.958
Torres, Monterrey	7	18	22	2	7	.952
Contreras, Laguna	9	13	6	1	0	.950
Diaz, F., Leon	4	7	8	1	0	.938
Hernandez, L., M Reds..	8	6	10	2	3	.889
Cervantes, Laredo	5	10	7	3	4	.850
Pineda, Aguascalientes	2	2	1	1	1	.750
Buckner, Aguila	2	4	4	4	0	.667
Rodriguez, Mex. Reds	6	1	1	1	0	.667

SHORTSTOPS

Player and Club	G.	PO.	A.	E.	DP.	Pct.
Iglesias, Aguila	26	31	54	0	12	1.000
Elizondo, Aguila	24	31	42	1	5	.986
RIVERO, Cordoba	131	248	481	14	80	.981
Navarrete, Saltillo	11	15	29	1	2	.978
Cervantes, Laredo	10	16	26	1	3	.977
Acuna, Puebla	11	11	28	1	7	.975
Mendoza, Yucatan	132	241	525	21	77	.973
Villaescusa, Mexico Reds	117	198	380	16	70	.973
Rodriguez, Ags.	125	215	397	18	65	.971
Hernandez, Durango	81	150	240	13	46	.968

SHORTSTOPS—Continued

Player and Club	G.	PO.	A.	E.	DP.	Pct.
Serna, Tabasco	86	138	298	15	49	.967
Gomez, Laredo	10	16	13	1	6	.967
Chavez, Saltillo	127	194	486	24	105	.966
Jimenez, Puebla	132	243	513	27	88	.966
Aguilar, Aguascalientes	12	22	33	2	7	.965
Bobadilla, Juarez	12	17	34	2	6	.962
Leal, Mexico Tigers	113	205	396	25	64	.960
Esqueda, Laguna	68	78	174	11	16	.958
Alanis, Aguila	105	176	275	21	53	.956
Rodriguez, Monterrey	111	193	365	27	73	.954
Santos, Tampico	29	28	89	6	9	.951
Rivera, Mexico Tigers	13	12	27	2	1	.951
Lazaro, Coahuila	114	204	338	28	53	.951
Cuevas, Poza Rica	15	12	26	2	4	.950
Montoya, Chihuahua	98	151	321	25	37	.950
Mendoza, Juarez	30	30	78	6	9	.947
Vega, Coatzacoalcos	23	28	62	5	11	.947
Villela, Laguna	48	60	101	9	16	.947
Saldana, Leon	114	203	404	34	69	.947
Espinosa, Tampico	104	176	305	27	57	.947
Villalobos, Tabasco	65	90	182	16	23	.944

Player and Club	G.	PO.	A.	E.	DP.	Pct.
Yepez, Poza Rica	103	128	287	26	44	.941
Rios, Durango-Laredo	53	101	177	18	19	.939
Uzcanga, Laredo	22	22	68	6	12	.938
Hernandez, L., M. Reds	11	18	27	3	7	.938
Valle, Juarez	108	160	360	35	59	.937
Gonzalez, Leo-Ctz	85	146	258	28	45	.935
Hernandez, Laguna	41	60	125	13	19	.934
Esparza, Poza Rica	10	9	18	2	5	.931
Ramirez, Aguila-Laredo	96	153	261	31	49	.930
Flores, Monterrey	38	46	79	10	10	.926
Escalante, Coatzacoalcos	51	76	146	19	24	.921
Gutierrez, Chihuahua	13	21	23	4	6	.917
Porras, Coahuila	29	36	65	10	13	.909
Romo, Mexico Reds	14	21	27	5	1	.906
Figueroa, Tampico	15	22	35	6	6	.905
Lizarraga, Leon	15	21	26	5	4	.904
Munoz, Yucatan	20	11	31	5	4	.894
Velarde, Durango	16	28	36	8	5	.889
Zavala, Chihuahua	32	60	116	23	23	.884
Lara, Laredo	19	20	38	8	9	.879

Triple Plays—A. Lazaro, Leal, Valle.

(Fewer Than Ten Games)

Player and Club	G.	PO.	A.	E.	DP.	Pct.
Hernandez, Mexico Reds	8	9	18	0	4	1.000
Rodriguez, Cordoba	9	8	11	0	1	1.000
Sanchez, C., Leon	7	11	6	0	0	1.000
Rodriguez, G., M. Tig.	7	2	8	0	0	1.000
Quinonez, Juarez	5	1	7	0	1	1.000
Etchandy, Monterrey	1	2	4	0	0	1.000
Torrez, Monterrey	3	0	4	0	0	1.000
Garcia, H., Laredo	3	2	2	0	1	1.000
Smith, Poza Rica	1	1	3	0	0	1.000
Marquez, Coatzacoalcos	2	1	1	0	1	1.000

Player and Club	G.	PO.	A.	E.	DP.	Pct.
Zavala, Mexico Tigers	3	6	17	1	0	.958
Andrews, Poza Rica	8	18	27	4	4	.918
Washington, Aguila	2	1	8	1	1	.900
Garcia, P., Poza Rica	9	13	21	5	1	.872
Aguirre, Mexico Reds	1	3	3	1	0	.857
Quintero, Saltillo	1	1	5	1	1	.857
Aguilera, Coahuila	7	6	4	2	0	.833
Charles, Mexico Tigers	2	2	0	3	0	.400
Mojica, Leon	1	0	0	1	0	.000

THIRD BASEMEN

Player and Club	G.	PO.	A.	E.	DP.	Pct.
Salazar, Aguascalientes	15	20	28	1	2	.980
Mares, Poza Rica	61	55	127	5	10	.973
Torres, Monterrey	60	82	133	6	13	.973
Rios, Durango	21	22	46	2	6	.971
Alvarado, Yucatan	85	62	213	9	22	.968
SANTANA, Laguna	131	161	327	16	32	.968
Flores, Monterrey	28	26	64	3	8	.968
Montiel, Saltillo	80	51	147	7	21	.966
Vazquez, Laredo	119	115	219	12	28	.965
Garzon, Coat-Ags	62	55	110	6	11	.965
Iglesias, Aguila	47	46	74	5	8	.960
Hernandez, Durango	28	32	61	4	5	.959
Sanudo, Saltillo	32	24	44	3	10	.958
Aquilar, Aguascalientes	118	100	247	16	20	.956
Etchandy, Monterrey	44	35	91	6	7	.955
Vega, Juarez	126	114	302	21	43	.952
Velarde, Durango	85	67	150	11	19	.952
Sanchez, C., Leon	73	58	157	11	18	.951
Arvizu, Tabasco	10	5	14	1	0	.950
Hernandez, Cordoba	73	76	128	11	17	.949
Vega, Durango	20	12	25	2	2	.949
Diaz, Saltillo	38	25	83	6	11	.947
Rivera, Mexico Tigers	120	140	334	27	42	.946
Sanchez, Poza Rica	78	74	167	14	14	.945

Player and Club	G.	PO.	A.	E.	DP.	Pct.
Zavala, Chihuahua	86	85	171	15	18	.945
Marquez, Coatzacoalcos	53	42	111	9	6	.944
Noriega, Agu-Chi	40	36	61	6	4	.942
Barrera, Mexico Reds	137	149	328	31	31	.939
Elguezabal, Puebla	121	81	239	21	19	.938
Sommers, Tampico	106	106	244	24	25	.936
Alvarez, Cordoba	62	54	134	13	10	.935
Munoz, Yucatan	14	11	16	2	1	.931
Zavala, M. Tigers-Yuc.	39	33	74	8	8	.930
Vega, Coatzacoalcos	80	56	168	17	18	.929
Washington, Aguila	41	35	96	10	11	.929
Espinosa, Tampico	16	21	30	4	3	.927
Bobadilla, Juarez	11	6	19	2	0	.926
Biagini, Coahuila	82	88	164	21	19	.923
Del Moral, Aguila	31	42	54	8	4	.923
Ramirez, Tabasco	129	149	287	38	26	.920
Gonzalez, Aguascalientes	38	15	48	6	5	.913
Garcia, Chihuahua	17	10	32	4	1	.913
Flores, Leon	33	24	62	9	9	.905
Gomez, A., Laredo	20	8	27	4	4	.897
Castro, Aguila	17	4	13	2	0	.895
Plasencia, Mexico Tigers	22	19	36	7	5	.887
Figueroa, Tampico	16	19	22	6	3	.872
Lizarraga, Leon	22	29	37	13	4	.835

Triple Plays—Santana 2, Elguezabal, J. Flores.

(Fewer Than Ten Games)

Player and Club	G.	PO.	A.	E.	DP.	Pct.
Orozco, Tampico	3	11	8	0	1	1.000
Iniguez, Coahuila	9	11	5	0	0	1.000
Matina, Agu.-Yuc.	4	6	6	0	1	1.000
Guerra, Laredo	6	5	7	0	0	1.000
Contreras, Laguna	7	5	6	0	2	1.000
Cerda, Durango	6	2	7	0	1	1.000

Player and Club	G.	PO.	A.	E.	DP.	Pct.
Aguirre, Mexico Reds	4	3	6	0	1	1.000
Preciado, Laguna	2	5	3	0	0	1.000
Lopez, Tabasco	2	3	3	0	1	1.000
Cuevas, Poza Rica	7	0	5	0	1	1.000
Barajas, Aguascalientes	4	1	4	0	1	1.000
Guerrero, Aguas	1	1	1	0	0	1.000

THIRD BASEMEN—Continued
(Fewer Than Ten Games)

Player and Club	G.	PO.	A.	E.	DP.	Pct.
Saldana, Leon	4	6	14	1	2	.952
Ramirez, Auguila	9	18	19	2	1	.949
Brookins, Chi-Mont	4	4	8	1	2	.923
Elizondo, Aguila	7	8	14	2	1	.917
Escalante, Coatzacoalcos	4	2	8	1	0	.909
Martinez, C., Monterrey	4	2	8	1	0	.909
Mendoza, Juarez	6	2	7	1	0	.900
Lazaro, Coahuila	2	2	7	1	1	.900
Murrel, Leon	7	5	20	3	1	.893
Zamora, Mexico Tigers	8	0	6	1	0	.857
Mojica, Leon	5	2	8	2	0	.833
Rodriguez, Cordoba	6	0	5	1	0	.833
Lugo, Coatzacoalcos	8	12	19	7	3	.816
Diaz, H., Leon	6	3	1	1	1	.800
Ruiz, Laredo	1	1	3	1	0	.800
Barron, Mexico Reds	6	2	5	2	0	.778
Santos, Tampico	6	2	1	1	0	.750
Payan, Yucatan	3	2	2	2	0	.667
Garcia, Poza Rica	1	1	1	1	0	.667
Perez, Tabasco	2	1	1	1	1	.667

OUTFIELDERS

Player and Club	G.	PO.	A.	E.	DP.	Pct.
Contreras, Laguna	47	71	4	0	1	1.000
Delgado, Juarez*	33	38	4	0	0	1.000
Valenzuela, Tabasco*	27	27	1	0	0	1.000
Gaston, Leon	11	24	0	0	0	1.000
Rodriguez, Mex Reds	17	22	0	0	0	1.000
Martinez, C., Monterrey	10	16	4	0	0	1.000
Chavez, Laredo	22	17	0	0	0	1.000
Chavez, Laguna	11	14	2	0	1	1.000
Campos, Coatzacoalcos	11	8	0	0	0	1.000
Barron, Mex Reds	10	7	0	0	0	1.000
Felix, C., Tabasco	10	5	0	0	0	1.000
Villagomez, Mex Reds	98	187	10	1	2	.995
Guerra, Laredo	65	133	7	1	0	.993
Lopez, Mex Reds	120	254	7	2	0	.992
Rodriguez, Laredo	67	116	5	1	3	.992
Mora, Saltillo	99	181	10	2	2	.990
Del Moral, Aguila	87	185	6	2	1	.990
Davila, Juarez	95	171	4	2	0	.989
Aranda, Saltillo	50	81	2	1	1	.988
Rodriguez, Juarez	78	160	2	2	0	.988
Salazar, Aguascalientes	47	73	8	1	0	.988
Gonzalez, Aguascalientes	126	296	14	4	3	.987
Zamudio, Puebla	112	216	8	3	2	.987
Rosario, Coatzacoalcos	129	210	8	3	2	.986
Diaz, Yucatan-Aguila	106	200	13	3	3	.986
Villela, Durango	111	202	8	3	0	.986
Cardona, Saltillo	81	129	8	2	2	.986
Lizarraga, Mex Reds	92	178	6	3	3	.984
Silverio, Mex Tigers*	127	326	22	6	9	.983
Juarez, Saltillo	120	260	14	5	4	.982
Villalobos, Aguas.	117	253	12	5	2	.981
Ornelas, Yucatan	117	198	11	4	2	.981
Thompson, Poza R.-Leon	91	202	5	4	0	.981
Cruz, Cordoba	133	250	7	5	0	.981
Smith, Tampico-Aguas.	78	152	2	3	1	.981
Gamundi, Poza Rica	130	331	28	7	4	.981
Nettles, Puebla*	132	244	11	5	2	.981
Hairston, Cordoba	116	295	8	6	1	.981
Alvarado, Cordoba	106	290	8	6	0	.980
Suarez, Cordoba*	131	230	10	5	3	.980
Castro, Saltillo*	68	139	4	3	0	.979
Lara, A., Mex Tigers	124	221	14	5	1	.979
Soto, Aguascalientes	61	89	2	2	1	.978
Carreno, Puebla	35	44	1	1	0	.978
Vazquez, Tabasco	77	126	5	3	1	.978
Brown, Mex Reds	36	84	3	2	2	.978
Enriquez, Juarez	75	123	7	3	0	.977
Williams, Laredo	27	38	5	1	0	.977
Figueroa, Juarez	98	158	7	4	2	.976
Lora, Puebla*	72	156	5	4	0	.976
Bellacetin, J., Leon	18	40	1	1	0	.976
Lagunes, Aguila	50	73	6	2	4	.975
Arevalo, Durango	28	38	1	1	0	.975
Wynn, Coahuila	17	38	1	1	0	.975
Rodriguez, C., Mont.	74	144	10	4	4	.975
Roman, Mex Reds*	65	107	8	3	0	.975
Paredes, Laredo	125	248	14	7	3	.974
Duran, Poza Rica*	86	139	9	4	2	.974
Perez, Laguna	86	170	10	5	1	.973
Centeno, Tampico*	17	33	3	1	0	.973
Ornelas, Coahuila	76	90	14	3	3	.972
Torres, Durango	89	197	9	6	1	.972
Rubio, Tampico	90	129	8	4	2	.972
Melendez, Yucatan	87	196	5	6	2	.971
Gomez, G., Laredo	130	281	19	9	2	.971
Collins, Chihuahua*	124	188	11	6	2	.971
Chavarria, Laguna	117	258	7	8	3	.971
Guzman, Tampico	106	242	15	8	2	.970
Sauceda, Chihuahua	131	281	7	9	0	.970
Brookins, Chi.-Mont.	124	209	11	7	1	.969
Guerra, Leon	19	30	1	1	0	.969
Quirk, Aguascalientes*	15	29	2	1	1	.969
Sanchez, Laguna-Leon	127	256	20	9	6	.968
Felix, Coahuila	116	253	21	9	6	.968
Munoz, Laguna	85	169	13	6	4	.968
Valenzuela, L., Mont.	130	331	22	12	2	.967
Matina, Aguas.-Yuca.	118	247	14	9	5	.967
Salz, Poza Rica*	118	223	9	8	1	.967
Rodriguez, Coahuila*	69	103	7	4	0	.965
Bellacetin, T., Leon*	84	178	9	7	3	.964
Roque, Coatzacoalcos	113	255	9	10	0	.964
Lindsey, P.R.-Aguila*	77	126	5	5	1	.963
George, Coahuila	90	169	13	7	4	.963
Guarnaccia, Agua.-M.T*	30	49	2	2	1	.962
Murrel, Puebla-Leon	99	217	10	9	3	.962
Tellez, Ch., Monterrey	33	42	8	2	0	.962
Felix, V., Tabasco	135	311	11	13	2	.961
Rodriguez, A., Mont.	50	67	6	3	3	.961
Lopez, Leon	28	48	0	2	0	.960
Crawford, Aguas.*	18	24	0	1	0	.960
Canada, Tabasco	106	226	10	10	3	.959
Lara, M. Tig.-Ctz.	89	135	6	6	1	.959
Espinosa, Durango*	66	90	4	4	1	.959
Hernandez, Durango	31	40	5	2	1	.957
Balaz, Juarez	120	170	7	8	2	.957
Romo, Tabasco	95	149	5	7	0	.957
Morales, Cordoba	14	21	1	1	0	.957
Ornelas, Monterrey	34	43	0	2	0	.956
Munoz, Leon	30	62	1	3	0	.955
Armbrister, Yuc.-Tam.	101	216	10	11	1	.954
Moore, Saltillo	22	41	0	2	0	.953
Leon, Coahuila*	49	76	3	4	0	.952
De Hoyos, Coa.-Yuca.*	44	58	1	3	0	.952
Serratos, Coatzacoalcos	88	130	7	7	2	.951
Hernandez, Coatz.	24	35	3	2	0	.950
Zuniga, Aguila	94	168	9	10	2	.947
Quinonez, Leon	17	29	3	2	2	.941
Williams, Mont.-Chi.	87	173	10	12	2	.938
Arano, Aguila	12	30	0	2	0	.938
Hernandez, Laguna	11	15	0	1	0	.938
Guzman, Mex Tigers	90	157	4	11	0	.936
Plasencia, Aguila	17	38	4	3	1	.933
Alvarado, Tampico*	59	93	4	7	1	.933
Oquendo, Lag.-Tabasco*	23	49	4	4	2	.930
Garza, Coatzacoalcos	10	12	1	1	0	.929
Marquez, Coatzacoalcos	26	36	2	3	0	.927
Paredes, Puebla	49	85	2	7	0	.926
Enriquez, Chihuahua	17	19	2	2	1	.913

OUTFIELDERS—Continued

Player and Club	G.	PO.	A.	E.	DP.	Pct.	Player and Club	G.	PO.	A.	E.	DP.	Pct.
Rosales, Juarez	25	27	3	3	1	.909	Mora, Leon	18	19	3	5	1	.815
Bojorquez, Poza Rica	14	22	2	3	2	.889	Lopez, Chihuahua*	11	6	1	2	0	.778
Mojica, Leon	10	10	1	2	0	.846	Guzman, Cordoba	10	3	0	1	0	.750

(Fewer Than Ten Games)

Player and Club	G.	PO.	A.	E.	DP.	Pct.	Player and Club	G.	PO.	A.	E.	DP.	Pct.
Ford, Mex Reds	9	13	1	0	0	1.000	Saldana, Leon	2	1	1	0	0	1.000
Mendoza, Tabasco	5	12	0	0	0	1.000	Mares, Poza Rica	4	1	1	0	0	1.000
Figueroa, Tampico	5	9	1	0	0	1.000	Lara, Juarez	2	1	0	0	0	1.000
Stroughter, Aguas.*	4	9	0	0	0	1.000	Gonzalez, Saltillo	2	1	0	0	0	1.000
Martinez, Cordoba	8	8	0	0	0	1.000	Perez, Aguascalientes	9	16	0	1	0	.941
Smith, T., Aguas.	4	8	0	0	0	1.000	Navarrete, Coatzacoalcos	5	14	1	1	0	.938
Garcia, H., Laredo	6	7	0	0	0	1.000	Green, Aguila	7	13	0	1	0	.929
Cuevas, Poza Rica	6	3	1	0	0	1.000	Zavala, Chihuahua	6	12	0	1	0	.923
Aranda, Poza Rica*	5	4	0	0	0	1.000	Diaz, Saltillo	8	20	0	2	0	.909
Munoz, Yucatan	2	4	0	0	0	1.000	Ortiz, Arm., Laredo	7	9	1	1	0	.909
Llenas, Cordoba	2	4	0	0	0	1.000	Martinez, G., Monterrey	6	7	1	1	0	.889
Faudoa, Mex Tigers*	7	3	0	0	0	1.000	Perez, Tampico	5	7	0	1	0	.875
Torres, N., Monterrey	3	3	0	0	0	1.000	Biagini, Coahuila	6	5	0	1	0	.833
Lopez, Aguascalientes*	2	3	0	0	0	1.000	Rodriguez, J., Mex Tigers	8	9	0	2	0	.818
Hernandez, Cordoba	5	2	0	0	0	1.000	Noriega, Chihuahua	3	3	0	1	0	.750
Lugo, Coatzacoalcos	1	2	0	0	0	1.000	Henderson, Coatz.	4	1	0	1	0	.500
Sotelo, Cordoba	1	2	0	0	0	1.000	Wright, Leon*	1	0	0	1	0	.000
Hernandez, Coahuila	2	1	1	0	0	1.000							

CATCHERS

Player and Club	G.	PO.	A.	E.	DP.	PB.	Pct.	Player and Club	G.	PO.	A.	E.	DP.	PB.	Pct.
Ortiz, Durango	23	65	9	0	0	7	1.000	Gutierrez, Laredo	32	108	12	2	3	2	.984
Quinonez, Leon	12	50	4	0	1	1	1.000	Trevino, Saltillo	101	378	75	8	14	11	.983
Navarrete, Coatz.	12	44	9	0	0	0	1.000	Barron, Mex Reds	33	102	10	2	2	2	.982
Sandoval, Poza Rica	15	41	9	0	2	1	1.000	Alvarez, Aguas.	57	236	40	5	4	9	.982
Mendoza, Coahuila	11	9	1	0	0	2	1.000	Valenzuela, C., Tabas.	111	427	65	9	7	12	.982
RODRIGUEZ, Coatz.	85	469	59	2	9	3	.996	Estrada, Puebla	97	452	68	10	1	9	.981
Molina, Ags.-Aguila	59	200	40	1	4	7	.996	Marquez, Yucatan	118	542	98	13	5	20	.980
Guzman, Cordoba	79	330	44	2	1	5	.995	Lugo, Poza Rica	73	348	34	8	7	6	.979
Luna, Monterrey	34	126	21	1	2	3	.993	Gaytan, Tampico	43	155	29	4	4	4	.979
Soto, Laredo	95	547	45	5	8	16	.992	Briones, Mont.-Juarez	30	114	14	3	2	4	.977
Mendoza, L., Juarez	123	693	63	7	3	6	.991	Benitez, Leon	119	497	83	14	6	18	.976
Rivera, Chihuahua	104	542	89	6	11	13	.991	Guerra, Laredo	20	111	12	3	1	2	.976
Hernandez, Coatz.	60	267	31	3	0	5	.990	Orozco, Tampico	106	463	65	13	12	10	.976
Robles, Mex Reds	120	604	79	8	15	5	.988	Guillen, Yuca.-Coah.	45	180	23	5	1	2	.976
Peralta, Cordoba	77	356	32	5	2	8	.987	Rosas, Aguascalientes	87	376	58	11	5	6	.975
Aguilar, Puebla	46	191	14	3	0	7	.986	Sanchez, Laguna	78	305	45	10	4	13	.972
Christiansen, Laguna	66	286	41	5	12	11	.985	Duran, Chihuahua	38	173	17	6	3	5	.969
Valenzuela, Coahuila	116	594	106	11	18	9	.985	Gonzalez, Saltillo	54	164	17	6	5	3	.968
Ruiz, Durango	124	548	86	10	4	18	.984	Peralta, Poza Rica	58	310	33	12	0	4	.966
Terrazas, Mex Tigers	120	479	84	9	13	7	.984	Camargo, Monterrey	97	479	76	21	6	18	.964
Rey, Aguila	98	422	66	8	5	6	.984	Heras, M. Tig.-Yuca.	31	91	11	4	1	2	.962
Lizarraga, Tabasco	67	165	17	3	6	9	.984	Mojica, Leon	12	30	5	4	1	3	.897

Triple Plays—Briones.

(Fewer Than Ten Games)

Player and Club	G.	PO.	A.	E.	DP.	PB.	Pct.	Player and Club	G.	PO.	A.	E.	DP.	PB.	Pct.
Lara, Franco, M. Tig.	6	20	1	0	0	0	1.000	Rodriguez, A., Mont.	1	2	1	0	0	0	1.000
Peraza, Canul, Yuca.	8	12	3	0	0	0	1.000	Quintero, Jose, Dur.	3	1	0	0	0	0	1.000
Jackson, Chihuahua	2	14	1	0	0	0	1.000	Hernandez, J.M., Dur.	4	24	4	1	0	1	.966
Leyva, Tampico	6	13	1	0	1	1	1.000	Noriega, Aguila	3	9	1	1	0	0	.909
Rodriguez, J., Juarez	4	10	2	0	0	3	1.000								

PITCHERS

Player and Club	G.	PO.	A.	E.	DP.	Pct.	Player and Club	G.	PO.	A.	E.	DP.	Pct.
OCHOA, Tabasco	34	5	41	0	2	1.000	Pepeyra, Dur-Tab.	33	3	12	0	1	1.000
Guzman, Durango	20	11	28	0	2	1.000	Hansen, Aguila	12	4	11	0	0	1.000
Moreno, Mon-Tam	37	13	19	0	1	1.000	Franco, Poza Rica	22	4	10	0	0	1.000
Segui, Cordoba	30	6	23	0	0	1.000	Stanley, Monterrey	40	1	12	0	3	1.000
Cordova, Tampico	31	3	25	0	0	1.000	Estrada, Mex Tigers*	36	1	12	0	0	1.000
Ochoa, Mex Reds	39	5	21	0	3	1.000	Agundez, Agu-Ags	30	1	12	0	0	1.000
Brandt, Tampico*	22	2	24	0	1	1.000	Castro, Coahuila	22	1	12	0	1	1.000
Rivera, Puebla	25	9	16	0	0	1.000	Gamez, Raul, Tampico*.	20	0	13	0	0	1.000
Bernal, A., Monterrey	35	3	21	0	1	1.000	Meza, Yucatan*	13	2	11	0	1	1.000
Martinez, Tabasco	19	8	16	0	2	1.000	Reyes, Chihuahua*	33	2	10	0	0	1.000
Sauceda, Mex Tigers	46	4	18	0	2	1.000	Reyes, Monterrey	17	3	9	0	1	1.000
Alvarez, Chihuahua	29	9	12	0	3	1.000	Caballero, Saltillo	17	1	10	0	0	1.000
Soto, Saltillo	50	6	13	0	3	1.000	Maytorena, Laguna	27	1	9	0	0	1.000

PITCHERS—Continued

Player and Club	G.	PO.	A.	E.	DP.	Pct.	Player and Club	G.	PO.	A.	E.	DP.	Pct.
Ibarra, Mex Reds	20	3	7	0	0	1.000	Mariscal, Agu-Tab*	40	9	24	2	0	.943
Cervantes, Ags	20	2	8	0	0	1.000	Bonfils, Poza Rica*	31	6	43	3	1	.942
Castro, Yucatan	28	1	8	0	0	1.000	Durazo, Laredo	23	1	15	1	1	.941
Lopez, Mex Tigers	28	1	8	0	0	1.000	Solis, Leon	44	3	13	1	0	.941
Garduza, Poza Rica	18	4	5	0	0	1.000	Monteagudo, Coahuila ...	38	9	53	4	2	.939
Ontiveros, Laguna	16	2	7	0	0	1.000	Vidana, Chihuahua*	30	8	23	2	1	.939
Munguia, Puebla	42	2	6	0	0	1.000	Valenzuela, Durango	36	6	9	1	1	.938
Uresti, Coatzacoalcos	22	2	6	0	0	1.000	Espinosa, Ctz-Agu	23	4	11	1	0	.938
Pena, Aguascalientes	21	0	8	0	0	1.000	Pollorena, Lag-Leo	15	1	14	1	0	.938
Beltran, Cordoba	17	2	6	0	1	1.000	Mere, Mex Reds	36	18	41	4	5	.937
Valdez, Laguna	24	2	5	0	0	1.000	Ortiz, Laredo*	28	6	50	4	2	.933
Pulido, Cordoba	20	2	5	0	0	1.000	Diaz, Puebla	30	13	29	3	2	.933
Romero, Coahuila	16	1	6	0	0	1.000	Martinez, Tig-Cor*	43	4	10	1	0	.933
Matias, Tig-Agu*	13	0	6	0	0	1.000	Valencia, Durango	34	9	32	3	0	.932
Wright, Leon*	12	0	6	0	0	1.000	Silva, Coahuila	33	8	46	4	4	.931
Arratia, Laguna	10	1	5	0	0	1.000	Munoz, Chihuahua	23	5	22	2	2	.931
Vidana, Cordoba	22	0	5	0	0	1.000	Icedo, Laredo*	20	2	11	1	0	.929
Garcia, Poza Rica*	18	0	5	0	0	1.000	Escarrega, Puebla	30	11	28	3	2	.929
Saucedo, Tampico	16	1	4	0	0	1.000	Vallejano, Yucatan	27	11	28	3	4	.929
Tovar, Lar-Lag	16	2	3	0	0	1.000	Guzman, Chihuahua	53	9	17	2	1	.929
Leon, Cor-Coa	10	0	5	0	0	1.000	Mota, Yucatan	26	5	21	2	0	.929
Hernandez, R., PR	18	0	4	0	0	1.000	Martinez, Tampico	32	1	12	1	0	.929
Nieblas, Tam-Jua	17	0	4	0	0	1.000	Enriquez, Juarez	29	2	11	1	0	.929
Baruch, Poza Rica	17	0	4	0	0	1.000	Miranda, Coatzacoalcos .	27	2	11	1	3	.929
De La Torre, Saltillo	11	1	3	0	1	1.000	Pulido, Puebla	20	2	11	1	0	.929
Sombra, Poza Rica	10	1	3	0	1	1.000	Arano, Cordoba	36	10	28	3	4	.927
Meistickle, Agu-Ags	14	0	3	0	0	1.000	Jimenez, Yucatan	29	10	64	6	6	.925
Quinonez, Leon	12	1	2	0	0	1.000	Gutierrez, Puebla	30	16	44	5	1	.923
Valle, Pue-Yuc*	11	1	2	0	0	1.000	Aguilar, Juarez	30	6	42	4	2	.923
Saldana, Poza Rica	19	0	2	0	0	1.000	Menendez, Saltillo	31	4	20	2	2	.923
Morales, Chihuahua	15	1	1	0	0	1.000	Ponce, Tabasco	17	2	10	1	0	.923
Lopez, Cordoba	11	0	2	0	0	1.000	Campoy, Agu-Tig	13	5	7	1	1	.923
Bernal, Monterrey	10	0	2	0	1	1.000	Moreno, Aguascalientes*	32	12	34	4	2	.920
Salomon, Aguascalientes	34	11	54	1	5	.985	Veintidos, Durango	33	12	34	4	2	.920
Salinas, Durango	32	13	48	1	2	.984	Soto, Laguna*	28	1	22	2	0	.920
Garcia, Juarez	29	4	46	1	2	.980	Limon, Aguila	40	4	30	3	1	.919
Garcia, Leon	37	5	43	1	3	.980	Morales, Tampico	28	5	29	3	1	.919
Garcia, Laredo	31	3	45	1	3	.980	Brunet, Ctz-Tig*	36	4	40	4	1	.917
Saucedo, Durango	40	11	33	1	1	.978	Heredia, Aguila	25	9	24	3	2	.917
Carrasco, Tam-Leo	29	11	31	1	3	.977	Armas, Saltillo*	29	6	27	3	3	.917
Franco, Mex Reds	28	13	28	1	3	.976	Henderson, Ctz	30	10	55	6	2	.915
Dominguez, Laguna*	32	7	33	1	2	.976	Kuk Lee, Coahuila	37	8	54	6	5	.912
Valenzuela, Poza Rica	28	3	32	1	1	.972	Martinez, Chihuahua	33	15	36	5	6	.911
Colorado, Coatzacoalcos.	53	7	27	1	1	.971	Sandate, Poza Rica*	30	9	42	5	0	.911
Sosa, Cordoba	42	3	30	1	0	.971	Lagunas, Mex Tigers	28	10	30	4	1	.909
Villanueva, Mex Tigers*	38	3	29	1	2	.970	Divison, Mex Reds	49	3	17	2	1	.909
Raygoza, Mex Tigers	26	11	20	1	1	.969	Solis, Laredo	40	2	18	2	0	.909
Castillejos, Mex Tigers	35	7	23	1	2	.968	Franco, Coatzacoalcos	32	5	15	2	1	.909
Valdez, Ctz-Agu	32	4	26	1	0	.968	Montoya, Leon*	28	1	9	1	1	.909
Leon, Durango	30	14	44	2	3	.967	Pena, Saltillo*	27	1	9	1	0	.909
Hernandez, A., PR	41	4	24	1	0	.966	Rodriguez, Ctz	23	1	9	1	0	.909
Pina, Aguascalientes	27	9	45	2	3	.964	Madrigal, Tabasco	39	8	21	3	0	.906
Rodriguez, Yucatan	34	5	22	1	2	.964	Chavez, Mex Reds	16	9	20	3	1	.906
Acosta, Aguascalientes	32	4	23	1	2	.964	Escalante, Aguila*	13	2	7	1	0	.900
Abarca, Aguascalientes	21	4	23	1	2	.964	Morales, Aguila	38	2	15	2	2	.895
Ahumada, Saltillo	32	14	64	3	3	.963	Lopez, Puebla	25	6	34	5	2	.889
Chavez, Leon	32	9	40	2	3	.961	Huizar, Laredo*	23	4	28	4	2	.889
Solis, Saltillo	33	8	58	3	8	.957	Soto, Puebla	24	1	7	1	1	.889
Esquer, Monterrey*	34	3	19	1	1	.957	Branch, Laredo	27	3	20	3	1	.885
Romo, Coatzacoalcos	32	10	53	3	6	.955	Rodriguez, Yuc-Tig	29	5	10	2	0	.882
Quintero, Cordoba	27	5	16	1	0	.955	Meza, Lag-Lar	18	3	4	1	0	.875
Rondon, Yucatan	25	8	13	1	1	.955	Lara, Tabasco*	15	0	7	1	0	.875
Fabela, Chihuahua	29	11	29	2	4	.952	Beltran, Laguna	30	6	28	5	1	.872
Cuen, Aguila	28	8	32	2	1	.952	Lugo, Tampico	57	9	18	4	2	.871
Gutierrez, Juarez	29	7	13	1	1	.952	Cazares, Durango*	30	3	16	3	0	.864
McGough, Monterrey	16	5	15	1	0	.952	De La Torre, Monterrey .	30	6	25	5	1	.861
Valenzuela, F., Yucatan*	26	4	35	2	2	.951	Acosta, Chihuahua	28	8	22	5	3	.857
Trinidad, Mex Reds*	34	9	30	2	0	.951	Ochoa, Dgo-Tam*	30	2	16	3	1	.857
Nagy, Tabasco	28	14	42	3	4	.949	Gutierrez, Durango	23	4	14	3	0	.857
Paul, Juarez*	29	9	47	3	1	.949	Gutierrez, Mon-Agu	41	1	11	2	0	.857
Orea, Mex Reds	34	10	27	2	3	.949	Bane, Juarez*	28	8	37	8	3	.849
Conn, Tabasco	14	7	11	1	1	.947	Diaz, Leon	61	4	24	5	0	.848
Barojas, Cordoba	41	8	27	2	6	.946	Reynoso, Coatzacoalcos.	17	4	18	4	2	.846
Gonzalez, Monterrey	36	11	57	4	5	.944	Lopez, Leon	21	3	8	2	0	.846

PITCHERS—Continued

Player and Club	G.	PO.	A.	E.	DP.	Pct.		Player and Club	G.	PO.	A.	E.	DP.	Pct.
Raygoza, Mex Tigers	17	1	4	1	0	.833		Salgado, Laredo	25	1	13	4	0	.778
Garcia, Monterrey	41	3	16	4	0	.826		Garcia, Coahuila	32	3	21	7	0	.774
Delfin, Tabasco	45	1	8	2	0	.818		Cisneros, Coahuila	39	0	6	2	0	.750
Verdugo, Sal-Lag	29	1	11	3	1	.800		Suby, Aguila	11	0	3	1	1	.750
Palacios, Tabasco	24	2	6	2	0	.800		Peraza, Leon	10	1	2	1	0	.750
Martinez, Coahuila*	24	0	4	1	0	.800		Valle, Ags-Agu*	22	0	1	3	0	.250
Nelson, Chihuahua	35	3	16	5	1	.792								

(Fewer Than Ten Games)

Player and Club	G.	PO.	A.	E.	DP.	Pct.		Player and Club	G.	PO.	A.	E.	DP.	Pct.
Cuellar, Coatzacoalcos*	7	6	15	0	2	1.000		Cervantes, Cordoba	3	0	2	0	1	1.000
Lunar, Tampico	7	1	11	0	0	1.000		Bracamontes, Tampico*	2	0	2	0	0	1.000
Feola, Tabasco	7	2	10	0	0	1.000		Buentello, Coahuila	2	0	2	0	0	1.000
Alsup, Tampico	9	1	9	0	0	1.000		Higueras, Juarez	2	0	2	0	0	1.000
Chavez, Laguna	8	0	9	0	0	1.000		Mauleon, Coatzacoalcos	7	0	1	0	0	1.000
Preciado, Mex Reds	6	0	8	0	0	1.000		Cervantes, Ags	5	0	1	0	0	1.000
Pagan, Mex Tigers	6	1	6	0	1	1.000		Moreno, Yucatan	5	0	1	0	0	1.000
Pena, Cordoba	9	1	5	0	0	1.000		Cruz, Monterrey	5	0	1	0	0	1.000
Quijada, Coatzacoalcos	9	1	5	0	1	1.000		Madrigal, Juarez	4	1	0	0	0	1.000
Dimas, Juarez	8	1	5	0	0	1.000		Matus, Cordoba	2	0	1	0	1	1.000
Scott, Aguascalientes	6	1	5	0	2	1.000		Vargas, Laredo	2	0	1	0	0	1.000
Martinez, Tab-Yuc	6	0	5	0	0	1.000		Smith, Monterrey*	7	3	8	1	1	.917
Anderson, Laguna	7	0	5	0	0	1.000		Cavanaugh, Coahuila	5	1	7	1	0	.889
Johnson, Tampico	5	0	4	0	0	1.000		Granger, Tampico	6	1	11	2	0	.857
Williams, Leo-Tam*	5	0	4	0	0	1.000		Perez, Leon*	9	2	4	1	0	.857
Alfaro, Aguila	4	1	3	0	0	1.000		Longoria, Juarez	8	3	3	1	0	.857
Burguette, Mex Reds	8	1	2	0	0	1.000		Bobinger, Laredo*	3	1	4	1	0	.833
Valenzuela, H., Yucatan	8	0	3	0	0	1.000		Ayon, Laredo	3	0	4	1	0	.800
Valdez, J., Aguila	7	1	2	0	0	1.000		Simpson, Mex Tigers	9	1	6	2	0	.778
Martinez, Tam-Mon*	3	0	3	0	0	1.000		Duarte, Aguila	9	1	2	1	0	.750
Wegener, Juarez	2	0	3	0	1	1.000		Sanchez, Laguna*	5	0	2	1	0	.667
Valdivia, Laredo	5	0	3	0	0	1.000		Valenzuela, Ags*	3	0	2	1	0	.667
Casas, Chihuahua	6	0	2	0	0	1.000		Aloi, Leon	6	4	2	4	0	.600
Urias, Leon	4	1	1	0	0	1.000		Vergara, Poza Rica	3	0	0	1	0	.000
Sandoval, Ags	4	0	2	0	0	1.000		Robles, Juarez	3	0	0	2	0	.000

CLUB PITCHING

Club	G.	CG.	ShO.	Sv.	IP.	H.	R.	ER.	HR.	BB.	Int. BB.	HB.	SO.	WP.	Bk.	ERA.
Tabasco	136	52	18	18	1191	1103	466	366	34	433	51	52	499	35	3	2.77
Ciudad Juarez	135	84	19	7	1170	1123	468	361	41	377	25	44	716	52	6	2.78
Yucatan	134	63	19	9	1161	1131	442	368	51	309	30	35	583	59	3	2.85
Puebla	137	66	19	25	1162	1140	462	372	34	364	19	35	571	24	2	2.88
Saltillo	136	67	16	19	1149	1169	427	371	39	328	36	23	471	24	0	2.91
Coatzacoalcos	136	48	17	14	1174	1205	491	392	21	394	47	36	686	30	3	3.01
Nuevo Laredo	137	70	12	15	1187	1127	489	410	65	426	28	29	696	38	3	3.11
Poza Rica	131	56	14	12	1126	1156	493	399	54	321	44	22	625	25	0	3.19
Coahuila	136	65	10	11	1154	1233	527	418	46	409	69	40	651	41	2	3.26
Mexico Reds	138	54	15	19	1227	1263	510	446	35	429	31	31	627	21	7	3.27
Cordoba	133	47	17	12	1164	1156	501	427	48	465	30	28	618	51	2	3.30
Union Laguna	136	51	17	13	1122	1048	496	413	54	447	32	46	519	36	4	3.31
Mexico Tigers	135	39	12	16	1155	1221	535	436	41	441	46	40	483	24	3	3.40
Monterrey	136	42	16	14	1173	1224	533	448	63	499	80	41	563	60	2	3.44
Aguascalientes	136	65	11	6	1158	1137	532	449	49	440	31	36	527	46	2	3.49
Aguila	136	41	13	9	1140	1202	556	459	54	438	50	40	551	36	3	3.62
Durango	135	34	8	18	1166	1285	611	511	76	489	65	49	527	52	3	3.94
Tampico	135	49	10	18	1179	1285	587	501	71	414	53	38	568	52	6	3.82
Chihuahua	133	31	7	13	1130	1301	657	526	56	485	69	51	654	32	2	4.19
Leon	134	31	5	16	1146	1410	737	571	84	427	43	53	490	47	2	4.48

PITCHERS' RECORDS
(Leading Qualifiers for Earned-Run Average Leadership—110 or More Innings)
*Throws lefthanded.

Pitcher—Club	G.	GS.	CG.	ShO.	W.	L.	Sv.	Pct.	IP.	H.	R.	ER.	HR.	BB.	Int. BB.	HB.	SO.	WP.	ERA.
Garica, Juarez	29	29	27	6	20	6	0	.769	260	199	61	49	6	60	1	10	222	12	1.70
Solis, Saltillo	33	32	23	6	25	5	0	.833	259	227	66	53	6	51	4	5	86	5	1.84
Paul, Juarez*	29	29	20	5	21	5	0	.808	241	220	69	50	7	43	4	162	3	1.87
Jimenez, Yucatan	29	23	17	5	16	6	1	.727	210	211	58	44	8	15	4	4	64	1	1.89
Rondon, Yucatan	25	24	17	4	11	8	0	.579	183	136	50	39	3	47	3	160	11	1.92
Ochoa, Tabasco	34	29	13	4	11	9	2	.550	223	187	66	48	3	68	11	12	107	4	1.94
Romo, Coatzacoalcos	32	28	18	10	14	13	1	.519	206	191	59	45	2	41	9	9	127	7	1.97
Colorado, Coatzacoalcos	53	7	3	1	13	4	6	.765	136	115	39	31	0	36	11	3	65	0	2.05
Brandt, Tampico*	22	20	8	1	13	3	0	.813	149	149	44	34	3	34	2	7	99	2	2.05
Heredia, Aguila	25	18	8	3	8	8	2	.500	143	110	47	35	7	46	6	4	102	6	2.20

Departmental Leaders—G—H. Diaz, 61; GS—Kuk Lee, 35; CG—Rafael Garcia, 27; ShO—Romo, 10; W—Solis, 25; L—N. Garcia, Gonzalez, A. Hernandez, Silva, 18; Sv—Munguia, 21; Pct.—Solis, .833; IP—Kuk Lee, 277; H—Kuk Lee, 285; R—N. Garcia, 132; ER—N. Garcia, 110; HR—Carrasco, 16; BB—C. Moreno, 124; IBB—Lugo, 17; HB—C. Moreno, 18; SO—Rafael Garcia, 222; WP—C. Moreno, 20.

(All Pitchers—Listed Alphabetically)

Pitcher—Club	G.	GS.	CG.	ShO.	W.	L.	Sv.	Pct.	IP.	H.	R.	ER.	HR.	BB.	Int. BB.	HB.	SO.	WP.	ERA.
Abarca, Aguascalientes	21	17	5	2	10	4	0	.714	108	115	61	52	5	46	0	0	58	9	4.33
Acosta, Aguascalientes	32	26	9	1	8	13	1	.381	177	194	87	64	6	49	4	8	66	11	3.25
Acosta, Chihuahua	28	26	4	0	6	9	0	.400	129	194	101	73	5	52	5	3	69	5	5.09
Aguilar, Juarez	30	29	12	2	8	16	0	.333	200	215	108	78	7	86	6	8	92	11	3.51
Agundez, 5 Agu-25 Ags	30	0	0	0	2	1	3	.667	64	56	26	20	4	16	7	2	24	0	2.81
Ahumada, Saltillo	32	32	17	5	19	10	0	.655	223	233	89	79	7	77	4	3	122	4	3.19
Alfaro, Aguila	4	3	0	0	0	1	0	.000	13	18	12	11	0	6	0	0	5	0	7.62
Aloi, Leon	6	4	0	0	0	4	0	.000	17	36	23	18	4	4	0	0	10	0	9.53
Alsup, Tampico	9	7	2	0	2	3	0	.400	39	57	26	26	3	15	3	2	18	2	6.00
Alvarez, Chihuahua	29	1	0	0	0	2	0	.000	69	64	30	24	2	34	4	9	31	1	3.13
Anderson, Laguna*	7	4	0	0	2	2	0	.500	25	24	13	9	1	16	0	1	9	2	3.24
Antunez, Cordoba*	1	1	0	0	0	1	0	.000	0	1	5	1	0	3	0	0	0	0	.....
Arano, Cordoba	36	34	21	5	19	13	1	.594	269	249	89	70	14	53	5	7	131	6	2.34
Armas, Saltillo*	29	29	11	2	14	5	0	.737	183	218	88	73	7	27	7	2	58	2	3.59
Arratia, Laguna	10	2	0	0	3	0	2	1.000	29	27	7	7	2	11	1	2	11	0	2.17
Ayala, Tabasco	1	0	0	0	0	0	0	.000	2	4	3	3	0	0	0	0	0	0	13.50
Ayon, Laredo	3	1	1	0	1	1	0	.500	18	15	5	5	0	10	1	1	9	0	2.50
Bane, Juarez*	28	27	18	3	16	10	0	.615	212	199	78	61	12	55	3	5	115	6	2.59
Barojas, Laguna	41	16	4	1	7	6	3	.538	148	143	49	43	6	76	6	8	64	9	2.61
Baruch, Poza Rica	17	3	0	0	2	2	1	.500	38	31	23	20	1	25	1	1	24	1	4.74
Bellacetin, Leon*	3	0	0	0	0	0	0	.000	2	4	3	3	1	4	1	0	0	0	13.50
Beltran, Laguna	30	30	15	3	15	8	0	.652	223	184	73	60	6	96	5	10	128	5	2.42
Beltran, Cordoba	17	5	2	0	3	2	0	.600	47	48	23	23	5	23	1	2	33	3	4.40
Bernal, A., Monterrey	35	6	1	1	7	2	0	.778	123	108	34	32	8	35	8	5	50	3	2.34
Bernal, O., Monterrey	10	0	0	0	1	0	1	1.000	10	7	1	0	0	5	1	0	0	0	0.00
Bobinger, Laredo*	3	3	1	0	0	3	0	.000	19	21	10	8	2	9	0	0	10	0	3.79
Bonfils, Poza Rica*	31	29	13	4	11	11	0	.500	208	189	86	63	5	52	5	3	143	12	2.73
Bracamontes, Tampico*	2	2	0	0	0	2	0	.000	6	6	3	3	1	3	0	0	5	0	4.50
Branch, Laredo	27	24	18	3	17	7	1	.708	189	137	59	48	5	74	2	11	178	9	2.29
Brandt, Tampico*	22	20	8	1	13	3	0	.813	149	149	44	34	3	34	2	7	99	2	2.05
Brunet, 24 Ctz-12 Tig	36	33	15	4	14	17	0	.452	227	221	93	79	4	82	3	2	165	5	3.13
Buentello, Coahuila	2	1	0	0	1	0	0	1.000	7	10	5	5	1	2	0	0	3	2	6.43
Burguette, Mex Reds	8	0	0	0	1	0	0	.000	17	26	16	15	1	13	2	0	6	0	7.94
Butkus, Monterrey	40	0	0	0	8	3	11	.727	70	65	18	15	0	15	7	1	33	0	1.93
Caballero, Saltillo	17	0	0	3	0	0	1	1.000	50	49	16	14	2	12	4	3	16	2	2.52
Campoy, 12 Agu-2 Tig	14	11	1	0	1	7	0	.125	58	81	47	41	4	25	0	5	20	1	6.36
Carranza, Coatzacoalcos*	7	0	0	0	0	0	0	.000	11	10	4	3	0	9	1	0	7	2	2.45
Carrasco, 5 Tam-24 Leo	29	27	8	0	9	11	0	.450	173	197	101	70	16	35	6	7	60	4	3.64
Casas, Chihuahua	6	0	0	0	0	0	0	.000	13	18	11	10	2	4	0	0	5	0	6.92
Castillejos, Mex Tigers	35	17	7	2	10	6	1	.625	153	164	47	42	3	49	6	3	51	0	2.47
Castro, Yucatan	28	1	0	0	1	7	4	.125	58	60	23	21	4	12	4	1	15	3	3.26
Castro, Coahuila	22	7	0	0	3	4	0	.429	67	79	42	35	3	24	5	2	21	3	4.70
Castro, Tabasco	2	0	0	0	0	0	0	.000	2	5	3	3	0	0	0	0	0	0	13.50
Cavanaugh, Coahuila	5	5	3	1	3	2	0	.600	37	36	15	14	4	7	1	2	16	0	3.41
Cazares, Durango*	30	18	6	1	6	11	4	.353	125	133	64	54	8	48	8	7	73	5	3.89
Centeno, Tampico*	1	1	0	0	1	0	0	.000	4	7	2	1	0	1	0	0	1	0	2.25
Cervantes, A., Ags	5	0	0	0	0	0	0	.000	5	9	9	7	1	5	0	0	0	0	12.60
Cervantes, L., Ags	20	2	1	0	4	4	0	.500	53	46	32	24	1	29	2	0	28	2	4.08
Cervantes, Cordoba	3	0	0	0	0	0	0	.000	3	7	5	5	1	1	0	1	1	0	15.00
Chavez, Leon	32	26	6	1	9	12	0	.429	158	191	99	74	13	73	5	7	60	8	4.22
Chavez, Laguna	8	4	1	0	1	0	0	1.000	35	28	18	13	2	17	0	4	26	1	3.34
Chavez, Mex Reds	16	15	10	1	6	8	0	.429	114	101	50	38	2	58	3	1	68	1	3.00
Cisneros, Coahuila	39	2	0	0	3	5	9	.375	67	61	25	14	3	20	2	3	49	2	1.88
Clark, Leon	4	0	0	0	0	1	0	.000	2	7	4	2	2	1	0	0	1	0	9.00
Colorado, Coatzacoalcos*	53	7	3	1	13	4	6	.765	136	115	39	31	0	36	11	3	65	0	2.05
Conn, Tabasco	14	10	1	0	3	5	1	.375	65	68	38	35	2	27	0	2	33	2	4.85
Cordova, Tampico	31	18	3	0	7	8	1	.467	131	168	73	67	10	34	4	2	36	2	4.60
Cruz, Monterrey	5	0	0	0	0	0	0	.000	8	6	4	4	0	2	0	1	5	0	4.50
Cuellar, Coatzacoalcos*	7	7	1	0	2	4	0	.333	38	45	21	14	0	13	1	0	20	0	3.32
Cuen, Aguila	28	25	13	3	12	12	0	.500	190	173	61	47	3	61	2	8	101	1	2.23
De La Torre, Monterrey	30	18	3	1	6	10	2	.375	128	164	71	58	9	33	11	1	33	2	4.08
De La Torre, Saltillo	11	5	1	0	2	3	0	.400	44	45	15	14	0	16	2	1	15	0	2.86
Delfin, Tabasco	45	1	0	0	8	0	9	1.000	82	56	22	15	0	26	3	3	39	1	1.65
Diaz, Puebla	30	30	8	2	16	10	0	.615	196	212	102	87	9	78	4	12	75	7	3.99
Diaz, Leon	61	3	0	0	9	8	15	.529	132	154	64	50	7	38	7	10	70	5	3.41
Dimas, Juarez	8	3	0	0	1	1	0	.500	35	39	16	12	1	10	1	2	8	3	3.09
Divison, Mex Reds	49	0	0	0	4	8	13	.333	90	90	26	21	2	29	7	2	57	2	2.10
Dominguez, Laguna	32	28	10	2	10	15	2	.400	184	180	80	61	0	86	4	7	94	3	3.28

Pitcher–Club	G.	GS.	CG.	ShO.	W.	L.	Sv.	Pct.	IP.	H.	R.	ER.	HR.	BB.	Int. BB.	HB.	SO.	WP.	ERA.
Duarte, Aguila	9	0	0	0	1	0	0	1.000	10	12	4	3	0	3	1	0	3	1	2.70
Durazo, Laredo	23	4	0	0	2	3	2	.400	50	61	39	34	3	25	0	2	30	8	6.12
Enriquez, Juarez	29	4	2	0	4	5	4	.444	74	72	38	27	1	30	2	5	32	9	3.28
Enriquez, Chihuahua	1	0	0	0	0	0	0	.000	1	1	1	0	0	2	0	0	0	0	0.00
Escalante, Aguila*	13	2	0	0	2	0	0	.000	28	24	17	14	1	28	1	0	18	5	4.50
Escarrega, Puebla	30	30	21	5	20	9	0	.690	239	227	74	65	6	55	2	2	144	1	2.45
Espinosa, Durango*	2	0	0	0	0	0	0	.000	4	4	4	4	1	3	0	0	0	2	9.00
Espinosa, Aguascalientes.	4	1	0	0	0	1	0	.000	8	5	6	6	0	4	0	0	5	1	6.75
Espinosa, 1 Ctz-22 Agu	23	19	2	0	4	10	0	.286	114	115	54	40	9	47	6	4	37	4	3.16
Esquer, Monterrey*	34	15	2	1	6	7	0	.462	121	127	59	55	7	63	9	4	63	12	4.09
Estrada, Mex Tigers*	36	3	0	0	1	5	0	.167	83	102	54	40	4	51	9	1	47	7	4.34
Fabela, Chihuahua	29	28	6	0	6	15	0	.286	184	201	107	95	9	79	13	9	94	3	4.65
Feola, Tabasco	7	6	1	0	2	3	0	.400	29	30	21	20	0	22	0	3	8	3	6.21
Franco, Coatzacoalcos.	32	11	1	0	3	8	2	.273	96	118	46	35	2	26	2	1	47	3	3.28
Franco, Poza Rica	22	11	1	0	5	4	0	.556	105	112	45	38	3	50	2	2	43	5	3.26
Franco, Mex Reds	28	18	7	0	9	7	0	.563	146	185	75	68	8	37	2	4	49	0	4.19
Gamez, M., Tampico	1	0	0	0	0	0	0	.000	0	0	0	0	0	1	0	0	1	0	0.00
Gamez, Raul, Tampico*	20	3	0	0	1	5	0	.167	55	57	30	24	5	16	5	1	18	2	3.93
Gamez, Rodrigo, Tam*	2	0	0	0	0	0	0	.000	3	11	4	4	0	1	0	0	0	0	12.00
Gamundi, Poza Rica	1	0	0	0	0	0	0	.000	0	0	0	0	0	0	0	0	0	0	0.00
Garcia, Poza Rica*	18	1	0	0	2	2	0	.500	29	35	17	14	2	13	1	1	13	1	4.34
Garcia, Monterrey	41	5	2	2	10	5	0	.667	121	108	55	41	8	73	9	9	58	9	3.05
Garcia, Leon	37	30	12	2	13	18	0	.419	224	277	132	110	14	56	12	10	69	6	4.42
Garcia, Juarez	29	29	27	6	20	6	0	.769	260	199	61	49	6	60	1	10	222	12	1.70
Garcia, Coahuila	32	14	1	0	6	9	0	.400	109	129	79	57	10	82	12	7	60	8	4.71
Garcia, Laredo	31	30	14	2	18	9	0	.667	238	221	73	60	14	65	3	3	133	7	2.27
Garduza, Poza Rica	18	11	2	1	5	5	2	.500	74	78	32	23	4	19	5	2	27	0	2.80
Gonzalez, Monterrey	36	34	18	3	12	18	0	.400	243	253	113	99	6	105	14	6	144	7	3.67
Granger, Tampico	6	6	1	0	2	1	0	.667	41	47	18	16	1	11	3	1	17	0	3.51
Guerra, Laredo	1	0	0	0	0	0	0	.000	1	0	0	0	0	0	0	0	0	0	0.00
Gutierrez, 15 Mon-13 Agu	28	6	1	0	1	5	2	.167	70	87	36	26	4	33	8	2	31	7	3.34
Gutierrez, Durango	23	10	4	1	5	5	0	.500	89	87	42	30	7	36	6	1	46	3	3.03
Gutierrez, Puebla	30	29	18	2	18	6	0	.750	231	234	78	61	7	46	3	7	89	0	2.38
Gutierrez, Juarez	29	10	5	2	8	5	1	.615	86	89	41	35	1	52	4	7	56	2	3.66
Guzman, Durango	20	18	7	3	8	9	1	.471	136	119	47	41	8	43	3	2	71	10	2.71
Guzman, Chihuahua	53	2	0	0	6	8	6	.429	103	98	44	31	4	46	11	4	89	3	2.71
Hansen, Aguila	12	8	3	0	3	3	0	.500	54	58	26	24	2	18	2	5	28	1	4.00
Henderson, Coatzacoalcos	30	30	12	2	13	13	0	.500	202	204	81	67	7	66	5	5	130	4	2.99
Heredia, Aguila	25	18	8	3	8	8	2	.500	143	110	47	35	9	46	6	4	102	6	2.20
Hernandez, A., Poza Rica	41	22	8	2	7	18	6	.280	180	200	91	81	13	45	12	5	112	0	4.05
Hernandez, Leon	3	1	0	0	0	0	0	.000	5	7	7	6	0	6	0	0	2	0	10.80
Hernandez, R., Poza Rica	18	0	0	0	3	4	2	.429	31	35	10	10	3	6	3	0	16	1	2.90
Herrera, Poza Rica	4	0	0	0	0	0	0	.000	4	6	4	4	0	3	0	0	2	0	9.00
Higuera, Juarez	2	1	0	0	0	1	0	.000	1	4	5	5	0	4	0	0	1	2	45.00
Huizar, Juarez*	23	20	4	1	6	9	0	.400	105	111	66	55	4	61	3	3	57	3	4.71
Ibarra, Mex Reds*	20	5	2	0	1	4	0	.200	61	65	25	24	1	28	1	3	27	4	3.54
Icedo, Laredo*	20	5	0	0	2	2	1	.500	57	63	35	31	2	32	1	1	34	0	4.89
Jimenez, Yucatan	29	23	17	5	16	6	1	.727	210	211	58	44	8	15	4	4	64	1	1.89
Johnson, Tampico	3	3	2	2	2	0	0	1.000	22	19	1	1	0	3	0	0	11	1	0.41
Kelly, Yucatan	1	0	0	0	0	0	0	.000	1	2	0	0	0	0	0	0	0	0	0.00
Kuk Lee, Coahuila	37	35	24	3	19	14	0	.576	277	285	100	78	8	70	10	6	174	5	2.53
Kurpiel, Mex Reds*	1	0	0	0	0	0	0	.000	1	1	0	0	0	0	0	0	0	1	0.00
Lagunas, Mex Tigers*	28	28	10	2	8	11	0	.421	170	190	77	62	6	38	8	3	56	2	3.28
Lara, Tabasco*	15	0	0	0	0	1	2	.000	33	42	18	15	1	15	0	1	14	3	4.09
Leal, Tampico	1	1	0	0	0	0	0	.000	3	4	4	4	0	2	0	0	0	0	36.00
Leal, Mex Tigers	2	0	0	0	0	0	0	.000	4	3	0	0	1	0	0	3	0	0.00
Leon, 8 Cor-2 Coa*	10	1	0	0	1	2	0	.333	15	24	12	10	0	8	1	0	9	1	6.00
Leon, Durango	30	22	8	1	7	12	2	.368	159	202	87	74	10	38	4	11	56	4	4.19
Limon, Aguila	40	20	4	0	8	15	1	.348	164	204	108	96	5	76	9	0	88	9	5.27
Longoria, Juarez	8	0	0	0	0	0	0	.000	20	27	16	15	2	5	3	1	4	1	6.75
Lopez, Puebla	25	25	12	4	11	8	0	.579	170	145	56	46	2	63	4	4	74	7	2.44
Lopez, Mex Tigers	28	4	0	0	2	3	2	.400	51	60	41	33	3	35	1	4	26	1	5.82
Lopez, Cordoba	11	0	0	0	1	1	0	.500	16	25	10	9	2	6	3	0	7	0	5.06
Lopez, Leon	21	8	1	0	2	6	0	.250	69	89	52	42	4	37	2	3	30	4	5.48
Lora, Puebla*	1	0	0	0	0	0	0	.000	3	2	1	0	0	3	0	0	1	0	0.00
Lugo, Tampico	57	2	1	0	10	13	14	.435	116	125	65	53	8	49	17	2	55	5	4.11
Lunar, Tampico	7	7	3	2	2	3	0	.400	46	40	18	17	1	26	0	5	29	6	3.33
Madrigal, Juarez	4	0	0	0	0	1	0	.000	3	7	6	5	0	4	0	0	4	0	15.00
Madrigal, Tabasco	39	26	8	2	17	12	1	.586	207	197	80	60	8	80	10	13	106	7	2.61
Mariscal, 17 Agu-23 Tab*	40	16	2	3	10	2	0	.231	131	153	67	59	8	45	6	2	37	6	4.05
A. Martinez, 3 Tab-3 Yuc.	6	0	0	0	0	0	0	.000	14	22	13	12	0	9	0	1	4	3	7.71
F.Martinez,4Tam-1Mon*.	5	0	0	0	0	0	0	.000	8	21	14	9	2	3	0	0	1	1	10.13
Martinez, Coahuila*	24	1	0	0	0	1	0	.000	26	35	15	9	1	13	4	1	12	1	3.12
Martinez, 4 Tig-39 Cor*	43	5	0	0	7	6	1	.538	80	96	34	29	2	31	5	2	36	3	3.26
Martinez, Chihuahua	33	30	8	3	10	13	0	.435	194	200	116	96	13	103	8	11	113	3	4.45

Pitcher–Club	G	GS	CG	ShO	W	L	Sv	Pct.	IP	H	R	ER	HR	BB	Int. BB	HB	SO	WP	ERA
J. Martinez, Tabasco	19	16	10	1	9	5	1	.643	111	91	38	32	3	27	3	0	47	1	2.59
R. Martinez, Tampico	32	2	0	0	2	4	1	.333	87	109	53	45	4	53	13	2	27	7	4.66
Matias, 12 Tig-1 Agu*	13	5	0	0	3	5	1	.375	48	45	23	18	5	11	0	2	15	1	3.38
Maytorena, Laguna	27	3	1	1	8	4	4	.667	55	39	14	13	4	23	4	0	24	0	2.13
Matus, Cordoba	2	0	0	0	0	0	0	.000	2	2	0	0	0	1	0	1	0	1	0.00
Mauleon, Coatzacoalcos	7	1	0	0	0	1	0	.000	12	20	12	9	0	5	3	1	5	2	6.75
McGough, Monterrey	16	14	3	2	4	6	0	.400	77	98	38	30	7	35	6	2	48	9	3.51
Meistickle, 10 Agu-4 Ags	14	5	2	1	2	5	0	.286	47	37	21	17	4	13	3	0	14	0	3.26
Mennendez, Saltillo	31	31	15	2	18	8	0	.692	215	208	87	80	15	79	6	2	83	3	3.35
Mere, Mex Reds	36	33	11	4	15	8	1	.652	236	226	91	83	6	80	3	10	120	1	3.17
Meza, Yucatan*	13	1	0	0	0	1	1	.000	28	28	16	13	1	10	1	1	12	2	4.18
Meza, 2 Lag-16 Lar	18	1	1	0	0	2	1	.000	40	37	24	23	5	23	1	3	18	4	5.18
Miranda, Coatzacoalcos	27	7	1	0	5	3	2	.625	93	75	33	29	1	50	3	8	51	3	2.81
Moncada, Leon	1	-0	0	0	0	0	0	.000	0	2	1	1	0	0	0	0	0	0	.....
Monteagudo, Coahuila	38	34	24	5	21	12	2	.636	276	280	95	75	6	73	15	8	159	11	2.45
Montero, Chihuahua	1	0	0	0	0	0	0	.000	1	5	4	4	1	0	0	0	1	0	36.00
Montoya, Laredo*	28	8	1	0	2	5	0	.286	67	76	37	29	4	32	0	3	28	4	3.90
Morales, Chihuahua*	15	0	0	0	1	0	0	1.000	29	38	14	12	0	12	4	0	21	2	3.72
Morales, Aguila	38	5	1	1	2	4	3	.333	84	98	42	33	4	22	5	3	28	2	3.54
Morales, Tampico	28	20	1	0	7	8	1	.467	127	122	64	49	11	71	6	8	68	4	3.47
Moreno, Aguascalientes*	32	29	18	1	12	17	0	.414	226	197	92	84	10	90	2	7	124	8	3.35
Moreno, 11 Mon-26 Tam	37	27	8	1	6	16	1	.273	183	181	112	95	10	124	6	18	103	20	4.67
Moreno, Yucatan	5	0	0	0	0	0	0	.000	9	12	4	4	0	5	0	0	8	1	4.00
Mota, Yucatan	26	26	10	4	7	16	0	.304	168	185	68	62	12	34	8	4	79	8	3.32
Munguia, Puebla	42	0	0	0	5	3	21	.625	80	70	32	27	4	23	2	2	49	2	3.04
Munoz, Chihuahua	23	22	5	2	4	13	0	.235	127	153	71	58	5	55	6	3	47	3	4.11
Murrel, Leon	5	0	0	0	0	0	0	.000	5	6	2	0	0	5	1	1	2	0	0.00
Nagy, Tabasco	28	28	16	4	13	12	0	.520	191	172	67	52	5	63	3	9	72	2	2.45
Nelson, Chihuahua	35	7	2	0	8	7	6	.533	94	113	58	40	6	29	6	4	79	5	3.83
Nieblas, 4 Tam-13 Jua	17	3	0	0	1	4	2	.200	35	43	20	12	2	16	1	1	10	3	3.09
Nieto, Tabasco	3	0	0	0	0	0	0	.000	1	5	5	0	0	0	0	0	1	0	0.00
Nuno, Tabasco	3	0	0	0	0	0	0	.000	4	3	2	2	0	3	0	2	2	0	4.50
Ochoa, Mex Reds	39	2	0	0	9	5	5	.643	121	109	38	31	1	40	5	2	52	0	2.31
Ochoa, Tabasco	34	29	13	4	11	9	2	.550	223	187	66	48	3	68	11	12	107	4	1.94
Ochoa, 13 Dur-17 Tam*	30	15	6	2	7	7	0	.500	137	134	68	54	12	50	5	6	55	2	3.55
Ontiveros, Laguna	16	1	0	0	1	3	0	.250	43	44	28	20	4	21	4	3	15	3	4.19
Oquendo, 1 Lag-2 Tab*	3	0	0	0	0	1	0	.000	7	6	3	3	0	7	1	1	8	0	3.86
Orea, Mex Reds	34	32	14	5	18	8	0	.692	230	220	87	76	6	66	5	5	134	10	2.97
Ortiz, Laredo	28	28	18	4	16	10	0	.615	221	209	75	60	13	39	2	0	105	1	2.44
Pagan, Mex Tigers	6	5	2	0	2	3	0	.400	38	35	18	15	1	13	1	2	20	1	3.55
Palacios, Tabasco	24	4	2	0	4	3	0	.571	73	68	32	25	4	27	4	3	18	6	3.08
Paul, Juarez*	29	29	20	5	21	5	0	.808	241	220	69	50	7	43	3	4	162	3	1.87
Pena, Coatzacoalcos	9	8	0	0	2	1	0	1.000	29	37	22	22	4	21	0	1	4	0	6.83
Pena, Saltillo*	27	7	0	0	4	4	1	.500	82	85	34	30	2	41	6	5	39	6	3.29
Pena, Aguascalientes	21	2	1	0	2	3	0	.400	69	70	38	27	3	35	9	0	30	3	3.52
Peraza, Leon	10	1	0	0	0	0	0	.000	23	33	28	22	3	11	0	1	9	3	8.61
Pereyra, 12 Dur-21 Tab	33	1	0	0	3	7	0	.300	77	80	40	35	7	27	8	0	18	0	4.09
Perez, Tampico	5	2	0	0	1	0	0	1.000	18	17	9	8	1	5	1	0	4	1	4.00
Perez, Tabasco	4	0	0	0	0	0	0	.000	6	10	8	5	1	5	0	0	1	1	7.50
Perez, Leon*	9	5	1	0	0	6	1	.000	33	42	26	20	4	13	0	0	16	0	5.45
Pina, Aguascalientes	27	24	15	5	13	8	1	.619	180	172	63	56	5	59	4	9	79	2	2.80
Ponce, Tabasco*	17	3	0	0	1	0	0	1.000	29	38	11	9	2	14	4	1	10	1	2.79
Pollorena, 11 Lag-4 Leon	15	15	8	0	5	8	0	.385	108	116	56	53	12	19	0	3	48	2	4.42
Preciado, Mex Reds	6	2	1	0	1	0	0	1.000	34	27	15	13	0	8	1	0	9	1	4.88
Pulido, Cordoba*	20	5	1	1	3	2	1	.600	47	50	22	22	0	19	2	0	23	5	4.21
Pulido, Puebla	20	4	1	1	5	3	0	.625	69	78	33	19	1	20	0	1	37	1	2.48
Purata, Poza Rica	2	0	0	0	0	0	0	.000	0	4	6	6	0	3	0	0	0	0	.....
Quijada, Coatzacoalcos	9	3	0	0	0	0	0	.000	25	37	17	16	0	10	2	1	10	0	5.76
Quintero, Cordoba	27	21	4	3	9	8	0	.529	135	131	65	53	2	68	2	3	44	8	3.53
Quinonez, Leon	12	3	0	0	1	1	0	.500	24	27	6	5	1	12	2	0	21	2	1.86
Ramirez, Tampico	2	0	0	0	0	0	0	.000	4	3	3	0	3	3	0	0	1	0	0.00
Grm, Raygoza, M Tigers	17	0	0	0	0	2	1	.000	26	38	27	24	2	15	3	1	13	2	8.31
Gll. Raygoza, Mex Tigers	26	23	5	2	9	10	1	.474	150	158	71	60	5	55	2	7	43	4	3.60
Reyes, Monterrey	17	17	5	2	7	3	0	.700	98	99	44	37	8	33	4	2	45	4	3.40
Reyes, Chihuahua*	33	2	0	0	2	2	1	.500	54	71	29	28	4	24	3	2	42	3	4.67
Reyna, Tampico	1	0	0	0	0	0	0	.000	0	2	3	1	0	1	0	0	1	0	.....
Reynoso, Coatzacoalcos	17	13	2	0	6	4	0	.600	87	101	52	33	2	26	1	2	50	2	3.41
Rios, Durango	2	0	0	0	0	0	0	.000	6	3	0	0	0	0	0	0	2	0	0.00
Rivera, Puebla	25	16	4	3	7	7	0	.500	104	103	54	45	4	43	3	6	67	5	3.89
Robles, Juarez	3	0	0	0	0	0	0	.000	3	13	10	7	3	1	0	0	0	0	21.00
Rodriguez, Ctz*	23	4	0	0	1	2	3	.333	49	49	25	19	2	28	4	1	31	2	3.49
Rodriguez, 16 Yuc-13 Tig	29	15	4	0	5	9	0	.357	110	132	62	56	7	37	5	11	20	4	4.58
Rodriguez, Yucatan	34	0	0	0	4	2	3	.667	73	73	23	23	7	19	3	5	39	2	2.84
Romero, Coahuila	16	4	0	0	0	3	0	.000	51	60	31	26	0	17	5	2	14	0	4.59

Pitcher–Club	G.	GS.	CG.	ShO.	W.	L.	Sv.	Pct.	IP.	H.	R.	ER.	HR.	BB.	Int. BB.	HB.	SO.	WP.	ERA.
Romo, Coatzacoalcos	32	28	18	10	14	13	1	.519	206	191	59	45	2	41	9	9	127	7	1.97
Rondon, Yucatan	25	24	17	4	11	8	0	.579	183	136	50	39	3	47	3	3	160	11	1.92
Ruiz, Cordoba	3	0	0	0	0	0	0	.000	4	5	2	2	0	4	0	0	2	0	4.50
Saldana, Poza Rica	19	0	0	0	0	1	0	.000	31	42	19	10	2	12	1	3	16	1	2.90
Salgado, Laredo	25	6	4	0	4	3	3	.571	80	88	40	32	6	27	6	1	47	3	3.60
Salinas, Laguna	32	30	12	5	14	13	0	.519	211	187	84	66	8	48	5	5	90	5	2.82
Salomon, Aguascalientes	34	29	16	2	14	12	1	.538	221	216	87	80	8	87	2	9	100	8	3.26
Samaniego, Coahuila	5	0	0	0	0	0	0	.000	6	6	3	3	1	1	0	0	3	0	4.50
Sanchez, Laguna*	5	0	0	0	0	0	0	.000	10	12	5	5	0	4	0	0	4	1	4.50
Sandate, Poza Rica*	30	29	22	3	16	12	1	.571	240	206	79	62	13	49	5	4	193	4	2.33
Sandoval, Aguascalientes	4	0	0	0	0	0	0	.000	5	11	4	4	0	0	0	0	0	0	7.20
Sanudo, Mex Tigers	3	0	0	0	0	1	0	.000	5	4	3	1	0	2	0	0	2	1	1.80
Sauceda, Mex Tigers	46	0	0	0	3	2	9	.600	79	70	41	30	3	35	5	1	27	1	3.42
Saucedo, Tampico	16	2	0	0	0	1	0	.000	37	54	35	30	6	24	3	3	12	4	7.30
Saucedo, Durango	40	12	6	1	6	10	4	.375	151	162	76	65	13	29	4	4	70	1	3.87
Scott, Aguascalientes	6	4	0	0	0	2	0	.000	24	24	13	12	3	9	0	1	5	0	4.50
Segui, Cordoba	30	29	15	4	15	8	0	.652	230	204	88	75	7	74	5	1	197	5	2.93
Seyler, Laredo*	3	0	0	0	0	1	0	.000	2	7	2	2	0	2	1	0	0	0	9.00
Silva, Coahuila	33	32	13	1	9	18	0	.333	225	232	116	97	9	99	15	9	137	8	3.88
Silverio, Mex Tigers	1	0	0	0	0	0	0	.000	1	0	0	0	0	0	0	0	1	0	0.00
Simpson, Mex Tigers	9	9	1	0	4	3	0	.571	56	51	19	18	4	34	2	4	47	0	2.89
Smith, Monterrey*	7	6	3	0	2	1	0	.667	46	39	11	6	0	12	2	0	25	2	1.17
Solis, Leon	44	5	0	0	3	5	0	.375	117	157	93	67	4	54	8	8	41	6	5.15
Solis, Laredo	40	13	8	1	9	8	6	.529	135	126	52	44	7	50	8	4	66	5	2.93
Solis, Saltillo	33	32	23	6	25	5	0	.833	259	227	66	53	6	51	4	5	86	5	1.84
Sombra, Poza Rica	10	0	0	0	0	0	0	.000	25	31	9	7	1	8	0	0	3	0	2.52
Sosa, Cordoba	42	12	0	0	9	8	4	.529	119	126	68	59	4	58	1	2	53	11	4.46
Soto, Saltillo	50	0	0	0	10	4	18	.714	86	92	27	23	0	23	3	2	52	2	2.41
Soto, Laguna*	28	22	6	1	6	14	0	.300	125	147	78	69	6	61	2	3	42	7	4.97
Soto, Puebla	24	3	2	0	4	4	4	.500	62	68	30	21	1	27	1	1	29	1	3.05
Stover, Mex Tigers	2	0	0	0	0	0	0	.000	3	4	1	1	0	2	0	0	1	0	3.00
Suby, Aguila	11	1	1	0	1	1	0	.500	30	38	13	11	4	10	1	3	10	2	3.30
Tovar, 8 Lar-8 Lag	16	0	0	0	0	4	0	.000	27	32	9	9	4	3	0	0	6	1	3.00
Trinidad, Mex Reds*	34	31	9	4	11	15	0	.423	188	203	87	77	8	70	2	4	105	1	3.69
Uresti, Coatzacoalcos	22	0	0	0	1	2	0	.333	54	63	23	22	2	17	2	3	22	1	3.67
Urias, Leon	4	0	0	0	0	0	0	.000	7	8	3	2	1	5	0	0	4	0	2.57
Urias, Leon	1	0	0	0	0	0	0	.000	3	4	4	3	0	1	0	2	2	0	9.00
Valdez, Aguila	7	0	0	0	1	1	0	.500	7	11	7	5	0	4	0	1	3	0	6.43
Valdez, 6 Ctz-26 Agu	32	9	5	2	3	7	1	.300	123	113	45	37	2	52	12	4	74	0	2.71
Valdez, Laguna	24	0	0	0	0	1	0	.000	47	43	27	26	4	25	1	4	18	2	4.98
Valdivia, Laredo	2	1	0	0	0	1	0	.000	8	6	4	3	0	8	0	0	4	0	3.38
Valencia, Durango	34	27	8	1	9	13	1	.409	159	177	86	74	8	92	15	6	67	8	4.19
Valenzuela, Ags*	3	0	0	0	0	0	0	.000	5	3	2	2	0	6	0	0	4	1	3.60
Valenzuela, Yucatan*	26	26	12	2	10	12	0	.455	181	157	68	50	2	70	0	2	141	1	2.49
Valenzuela, Durango	36	3	0	0	3	3	4	.500	86	104	56	52	2	28	2	1	43	10	5.44
Valenzuela, Poza Rica	28	25	10	2	6	15	0	.286	153	179	69	59	7	31	8	1	28	0	3.47
Valenzuela, Yucatan	8	0	0	0	0	0	0	.000	22	22	9	8	2	6	0	1	11	1	3.27
Valenzuela, Monterrey*	10	4	1	0	1	1	0	.500	20	23	15	13	3	16	0	0	11	0	5.85
Valle, 4 Ags-18 Agu*	22	4	0	0	1	4	0	.200	30	57	31	27	3	19	1	0	9	1	8.10
Vallejano, Durango	27	27	6	3	10	13	0	.435	152	153	67	55	6	60	6	8	35	11	3.26
Valles, 5 Pue-6 Yuc*	11	0	0	0	0	1	0	.000	18	7	7	6	0	16	0	1	12	2	3.00
Vargas, Laredo	2	1	1	0	0	1	0	.000	9	7	2	2	0	1	0	0	3	0	2.00
Veintidos, Durango	33	25	10	1	12	7	2	.632	200	215	79	70	6	80	9	4	122	8	3.15
Verdugo, 4SAL-25LAG	29	1	0	0	2	6	2	.250	51	54	31	21	2	24	6	5	17	3	3.71
Vergara, Poza Rica	3	0	0	0	0	0	0	.000	8	8	3	2	0	5	1	0	5	0	2.25
Vidana, Cordoba	22	1	0	0	2	1	1	.667	42	42	22	18	2	29	0	1	21	1	3.86
Vidana, Chihuahua*	30	15	6	1	8	9	0	.471	133	145	71	55	5	44	9	6	63	4	3.72
Villanueva, Mex Tigers*	38	20	6	1	12	10	1	.545	141	140	55	40	2	46	3	7	63	0	2.55
Wegener, Juarez	3	3	0	0	1	2	0	.333	16	17	10	10	1	16	1	1	10	0	5.63
Williams, 4 Leo-1 Tam*	5	5	0	0	0	3	0	.000	19	20	19	18	1	11	0	3	11	0	8.53
Wright, Leon	12	9	1	0	4	2	0	.667	63	66	33	29	4	24	0	0	47	4	4.14

BALKS—Bane, R. Chavez, Veintidos, 3 each; Cazares, Cordova, Kuk Lee, Nagy, Orea, Sosa, C. Soto, M. Rodriguez, 2 each; C. Acosta, Aguilar, Agundez, A. Bernal, Branch, Carrasco, Castillejos, C. Chavez, A. De La Torre, C. Diaz, Divison, Durazo, Escarrega, D. Franco, P. Franco, Rafael Garcia, Heredia, H. Lopez, J. Martinez, Miranda, A. Morales, M. Morales, C. Moreno, Munoz, Pollorena, Robles, J. M. Rodriguez, Salinas, J. Solis, J. Humberto Valdez, Valencia, F. Valenzuela, Vallejano, 1 each.

COMBINATION SHUTOUTS—Espinosa-Heredia, Heredia-Morales, Cuen-Mariscal-Morales, Aguila; Acosta-Guzman, Chihuahua; Garcia-Gutierrez, Ciudad Juarez;Franco-Colorado, Miranda-Uresti-Franco, Coatzacoalcos; Quintero-Barojas, Segui-H. Franco Martinez, Quintero-Sosa, Cordoba; Guzman-Saucedo, Durango; Garcia-Durazo, Nuevo Laredo; Montoya-Diaz, Solis-Diaz, Leon; Trinidad-Ochoa, Mexico City Reds; Simpson-Matias, Simpson-Villanueva-Lopez, Guillermo Raygoza-Sauceda, Mexico City Tigers; Gonzalez-De La Torre, Reyes-Butkus, A.

Bernal-De La Torre, Monterrey; Garduza-A. Hernandez 2, Poza Rica; Lopez-Soto, Diaz-Munguia, Puebla; Solis-Pena, Saltillo; Madrigal-Delfin, Lara-Madrigal-Ponce-Delfin, Mariscal-Delfin, Conn-Delfin, Madrigal-Mariscal, Ochoa-Madrigal, Mariscal-Pereyra, Tabasco; Granger-Lugo, Tampico; Dominguez-Maytorena, Maytorena-Dominguez, Dominguez-Tovar, Anderson-Arratia, Arratia-Tovar, Union Laguna; Rondon-P. Rodriguez, Yucatan.

NO-HIT GAMES—Solis and Pena, Saltillo, defeated Ciudad Juarez, 1-0, March 25, (seven innings);Gonzalez, Monterrey, tied Ciudad Juarez, 0-0, March 28 (10½ innings); Armas, Saltillo, defeated Monterrey, 5-0, April 13; Monteagudo, Coahuila, defeated Nuevo Laredo, 10-0, May 19 (seven innings); Ochoa, Tabasco, defeated Aguila, 2-0, July 1 (five innins); Lopez, Puebla, defeated Durango, 2-0, July 8 (seven innings); Bonfils, Poza Rica, defeated Tampico, 2-0, August 17 (five innings).

Triple Play Hat Trick

Late in the '79 season at Juarez in the Mexican League, Union Laguna third baseman Blas Santana had one of those rare, record-setting games.

In the first inning with teammates on first and second, Santana grounded into an apparent short-second-first double play. But the runner on second tried to score and he was out, too, for the league's second triple play of the season.

Santana gained revenge in the fifth when he fielded a ground ball and started a triple play against Juarez. Not satisfied yet, Santana speared another grounder in the sixth and started the third triple play of the game.

Protest Upheld, Game Then Forfeited

Clinton's Dodgers clinched the Midwest League's South Division second-half title August 25, a bit earlier than they might have, because of a bizarre series of events which began five days earlier and culminated with the reversal of an umpire's decision and the forfeit of a game by the club's closest challengers, the Quad-Cities Cubs.

The chain of events began in the sixth inning of a Dodger-Cub game August 20 when Clinton pitcher Orel Hershhiser delivered a pitch to Quad-Cities' Wayne Rohlfing just as a Clinton fan threw a ball onto the field.

Plate umpire Randy Bruns called the pitch a strike, bringing an immediate response from Cubs' Manager Jim Napier, whose club trailed at the time, 3-2.

Napier argued that, with the ball on the field, the umpire should have ruled no pitch. Bruns agreed, and that brought an official protest from Dodgers Manager Dick McLaughlin.

The Cubs rallied to win, 4-3, but the victory was overturned August 22 by league President Bill Walters, who reversed Bruns' decision and upheld McLaughlin's protest.

Walters ruled that the game be replayed from the point of the dispute prior to the club's scheduled August 22 doubleheader.

But when Bruns called "play ball" Napier refused to send his players onto the field and Clinton was awarded a 7-0 forfeit victory.

Then the Cubs sent out and swept the Dodgers, 1-0 and 3-2, Tom Spino shutting out the Dodgers on just two hits in the first game, but closing the gap on Clinton by just one game because of the forfeit.

Napier was perhaps operating from a position of strength when he refused to play the game. The Cubs already were assured of a playoff berth, since they won the first-half championship in the South Division.

Pacific Coast League

CLASS AAA

**Leading Batter
MICKEY HATCHER
Albuquerque**

**League President
ROY JACKSON**

**Leading Pitcher
MARK BOMBACK
Vancouver**

CHAMPIONSHIP WINNERS IN PREVIOUS YEARS

Year	Team	Pct.
1903	Los Angeles	.630
1904	Tacoma	.589
	Tacoma§	.571
	Los Angeles§	.571
1905	Tacoma	.583
	Los Angeles*	.604
1906	Portland	.657
1907	Los Angeles	.608
1908	Los Angeles	.585
1909	San Francisco	.623
1910	Portland	.567
1911	Portland	.589
1912	Oakland	.591
1913	Portland	.559
1914	Portland	.574
1915	San Francisco	.570
1916	Los Angeles	.601
1917	San Francisco	.561
1918	Vernon	.569
	Los Angeles (2nd) x	.548
1919	Vernon	.613
1920	Vernon	.556
1921	Los Angeles	.574
1922	San Francisco	.638
1923	San Francisco	.617
1924	Seattle	.545
1925	San Francisco	.643
1926	Los Angeles	.599
1927	Oakland	.615
1928	San Francisco*	.630
	Sacramento§§	.626
	San Francisco§§	.626
1929	Mission	.643
	Hollywood*	.592
1930	Los Angeles	.576
	Hollywood*	.650
1931	Hollywood	.626
	San Francisco*	.608
1932	Portland	.587
1933	Los Angeles	.610
1934	Los Angeles z	.786
	Los Angeles z	.689
1935	Los Angeles	.648
	San Francisco*	.608
1936	Portland‡	.549
1937	Sacramento	.573
	San Diego (3rd)†	.545
1938	Los Angeles	.590
	Sacramento (3rd)†	.537
1939	Seattle	.580
	Sacramento (4th)†	.500
1940	Seattle‡	.629
1941	Seattle‡	.598
1942	Sacramento	.590
	Seattle (3rd)†	.539
1943	Los Angeles	.710
	S. Francisco (2nd)†	.574
1944	Los Angeles	.586
	S. Francisco (3rd)†	.509
1945	Portland	.622
	S. Francisco (4th)†	.525
1946	San Francisco‡	.628
1947	Los Angeles††	.567
1948	Oakland‡	.606
1949	Hollywood‡	.583
1950	Oakland	.590
1951	Seattle‡	.593
1952	Hollywood	.606
1953	Hollywood	.589
1954	San Diego y	.604
1955	Seattle	.552
1956	Los Angeles	.637
1957	San Francisco	.601
1958	Phoenix	.578
1959	Salt Lake City	.552
1960	Spokane	.601
1961	Tacoma	.630
1962	San Diego	.604
1963	Spokane	.620
	Oklahoma City a	.632
1964	Arkansas	.609
	San Diego a	.576
1965	Oklahoma City a	.628
	Portland	.547
1966	Seattle a	.561
	Tulsa	.578
1967	San Diego a	.574
	Spokane	.541
1968	Tulsa a	.642
	Spokane	.586
1969	Tacoma a	.589
	Eugene	.603
1970	Spokane a	.644
	Hawaii	.671
1971	Salt Lake City a	.534
	Tacoma	.545
1972	Albuquerque	.622
	Eugene	.534
1973	Tucson	.583
	Spokane a	.563
1974	Spokane a	.549
	Albuquerque	.535
1975	Salt Lake City	.556
	Hawaii a	.611
1976	Salt Lake City	.625
	Hawaii a	.531
1977	Phoenix a	.579
	Hawaii	.541
1978	Tacoma b	.584
	Albuquerque b	.557

*Won split-season playoff. †Won four-team playoff. ‡Won pennant and four-team playoff. §Tied for second-half title with Tacoma winning playoff. §§Tied for second-half title, with Sacramento winning playoff. ††Ended regular season in tie with San Francisco and won one-game playoff for pennant, then won four-club playoff. xWon playoff from first-place Vernon and awarded championship. yDefeated Hollywood in one-game playoff for pennant. zWon both halves, no playoff. aLeague was divided into Northern, Southern divisions in 1963, 1969-70-71, and Eastern, Western divisions in 1964 through 1968 and 1972 through 1977, won two-team playoff. bLeague divided into Eastern and Western divisions, Tacoma and Albuquerque declared co-champions following cancellation of four-team playoff due to continuing rain and wet grounds. NOTE—Championship awarded to playoff winner, 1936-37.

STANDING OF CLUBS AT CLOSE OF FIRST HALF, JUNE 21

NORTHERN DIVISION						SOUTHERN DIVISION					
Club	W.	L.	T.	Pct.	G.B.	Club	W.	L.	T.	Pct.	G.B.
Hawaii (Padres)	42	32	0	.568	......	Albuquerque (Dodgers)	41	32	0	.562	......
Spokane (Mariners)	39	32	0	.549	1½	Tucson (Rangers)	39	34	0	.534	2
Vancouver (Brewers)	39	36	0	.520	3½	Ogden (A's)	35	39	0	.473	6½
Tacoma (Indians)	34	37	0	.479	6½	Salt Lake City (Angels)	34	40	0	.459	7½
Portland (Pirates)	35	40	0	.467	7½	Phoenix (Giants)	28	44	0	.389	12½

STANDING OF CLUBS AT CLOSE OF SECOND HALF, SEPTEMBER 1

NORTHERN DIVISION						SOUTHERN DIVISION					
Club	W.	L.	T.	Pct.	G.B.	Club	W.	L.	T.	Pct.	G.B.
Vancouver (Brewers)	40	32	0	.556	......	Salt Lake City (Angels)	46	28	0	.622	......
Portland (Pirates)	38	34	0	.528	2	Albuquerque (Dodgers)	45	30	0	.600	1½
Tacoma (Indians)	40	36	0	.526	2	Ogden (A's)	37	36	0	.507	8½
Hawaii (Padres)	30	44	0	.405	11	Tucson (Rangers)	35	40	0	.467	11½
Spokane (Mariners)	29	47	0	.382	13	Phoenix (Giants)	31	44	0	.413	15½

COMPOSITE STANDING OF CLUBS AT CLOSE OF SEASON, SEPTEMBER 1

NORTHERN DIVISION

Club	Van.	Tac.	Port.	Haw.	Spo.	Alb.	SLC	Tuc.	Ogd.	Phx.	W.	L.	T.	Pct.	G.B.
Vancouver (Brewers)	......	9	12	10	15	7	8	5	5	8	79	68	0	.537	......
Tacoma (Indians)	12	....	11	11	10	5	7	7	7	4	74	73	0	.503	5
Portland (Pirates)	10	11	....	9	11	4	6	8	6	8	73	74	0	.497	6
Hawaii (Padres)	12	11	13	....	11	6	3	4	4	8	72	76	0	.486	7½
Spokane (Mariners)	7	12	11	11	....	4	7	6	5	5	68	79	0	.463	11

SOUTHERN DIVISION

Club	Van.	Tac.	Port.	Haw.	Spo.	Alb.	SLC	Tuc.	Ogd.	Phx.	W.	L.	T.	Pct.	G.B.
Albuquerque (Dodgers)	5	7	8	6	8	......	15	15	10	12	86	62	0	.581	......
Salt Lake City (Angels)	4	5	6	9	5	7	....	13	17	14	80	68	0	.541	6
Tucson (Rangers)	7	5	4	8	6	7	9	....	15	13	74	74	0	.500	12
Ogden (A's)	7	5	5	8	7	12	5	7	....	16	72	75	0	.490	13½
Phoenix (Giants)	4	8	4	4	6	10	8	9	6	....	59	88	0	.401	26½

Hawaii club represented Honolulu, Hawaii.

Major league affiliations in parentheses.

Playoffs—Hawaii defeated Vancouver, two games to one; Salt Lake City defeated Albuquerque, two games to none; Salt Lake City defeated Hawaii, three games to none for championship.

Regular-Season Attendance—Albuquerque, 266,586; Hawaii, 176,049; Ogden, 77,027; Phoenix, 162,496; Portland, 159,181; Salt Lake City, 214,825; Spokane, 217,300; Tacoma, 181,443; Tucson, 175,213; Vancouver, 131,367. Total, 1,761,487. Playoffs, 20,072. No all-star game.

Managers: Albuquerque-Del Crandall; Hawaii-Dick Phillips; Ogden-Jose Pagan; Phoenix-Rocky Bridges; Portland-John Lipon; Salt Lake City-Jimy Williams; Spokane-Rene Lachemann; Tacoma-Gene Dusan; Tucson-Rich Donnelly; Vancouver-John Felske.

All-Star Team: 1B-Cacek, Portland; 2B-Sakata, Vancouver; 3B—Hatcher, Albuquerque; SS-Mulliniks, Salt Lake City; OF—Guerrero, Albuquerque; Clark, Salt Lake City; Bourjos, Phoenix; DH-Hampton, Salt Lake City; C-Scioscia, Albuquerque; P-Bomback, Vancouver; Kuhaulua, Hawaii; Manager, Williams, Salt Lake City.

(Compiled by William J. Weiss, League Statistician, San Mateo, Calif.)

CLUB BATTING

Club	G.	AB.	R.	OR.	H.	TB.	2B.	3B.	HR.	RBI.	SH.	SF.	BB.	Int. BB.	HP.	SO.	SB.	CS.	LOB.	Pct.
Albuquerque	148	4939	876	785	1527	2138	252	61	79	799	59	62	581	41	39	633	203	84	1074	.309
Ogden	147	4927	793	866	1420	2028	208	59	94	725	52	54	670	33	12	782	146	67	1123	.288
Portland	147	4947	748	720	1416	1983	233	59	72	670	61	44	524	25	35	651	107	55	1124	.286
Salt Lake City	148	4957	845	776	1404	2198	260	51	144	770	32	47	673	38	26	971	202	83	1097	.283
Tucson	148	4818	760	746	1339	1946	220	69	83	690	60	57	698	48	26	750	138	54	1128	.278
Spokane	147	4900	705	779	1360	1937	265	42	76	634	32	39	486	29	23	678	71	42	1023	.278
Phoenix	147	4947	694	803	1343	1857	225	71	49	619	18	57	547	28	35	695	130	64	1081	.271
Tacoma	147	4816	662	689	1306	1763	202	36	61	596	72	55	585	38	32	688	154	73	1084	.271
Vancouver	147	4869	637	592	1306	1785	209	39	64	576	43	44	547	40	30	590	103	53	1104	.268
Hawaii	148	4755	608	569	1211	1709	196	55	64	556	59	34	551	50	25	678	134	72	991	.255

INDIVIDUAL BATTING

(Leading Qualifiers for Batting Championship—400 or More Plate Appearances)

*Bats lefthanded. †Switch-hitter.

Player and Club	G.	AB.	R.	H.	TB.	2B.	3B.	HR.	RBI.	SH.	SF.	BB.	HP.	SO.	SB.	CS.	Pct.
Hatcher, Michael, Albuquerque	103	420	88	156	239	29	12	10	93	0	5	24	1	32	16	9	.371
Goodwin, Danny, Ogden*	100	370	66	129	225	22	7	20	94	2	4	59	0	62	0	4	.349
Mulliniks, S. Rance, SLC*	116	402	94	138	182	21	7	3	59	0	5	98	4	45	21	11	.343
Scioscia, Michael, Albuquerque*	143	461	80	155	198	34	0	3	68	12	3	73	7	33	5	7	.336
Guerrero, Pedro, Albuquerque	112	453	94	151	268	23	9	22	103	0	5	31	2	84	26	8	.333
Mitchell, Robert, Albuquerque*	123	453	104	148	194	24	8	2	59	4	4	71	3	35	18	11	.327
Harris, John, Salt Lake City*	111	418	63	136	217	38	2	13	88	0	4	52	1	58	5	7	.325
Perconte, John, Albuquerque	143	521	104	168	213	25	7	2	68	10	7	95	1	38	32	4	.322
Walton, Reginald, Spokane	122	463	79	149	227	31	7	11	76	1	3	29	2	71	9	5	.322
Cacek, Craig, Portland	147	565	92	180	278	33	7	17	102	2	6	58	5	40	5	7	.319

Departmental Leaders: G-Cacek, 147; AB-Cosey, Parsons, 566; R-Mangual, 115; H-Cacek, 180; TB-Cacek, 278; 2B-D. Walton, 39; 3B-Parsons, 16; HR-Hampton, 30; RBI-Guerrero, 103; SH-V. Law, 14; SF-Kuecker, 11; BB-Hart, 122; HP-Five tied with 7 each; SO-Mangual, 128; SB-Mangual, 46; CS-Cox, 18.

(All Players—Listed Alphabetically)

Player and Club	G.	AB.	R.	H.	TB.	2B.	3B.	HR.	RBI.	SH.	SF.	BB.	HP.	SO.	SB.	CS.	Pct.
Allietta, Robert, Tacoma	107	319	40	96	121	14	1	3	46	10	3	36	7	21	5	5	.301
Alston, Wendell, Tacoma*	75	310	58	83	109	13	5	1	33	3	5	35	0	28	43	11	.268
Ashford, Thomas, Hawaii	146	509	70	130	206	25	6	13	62	4	7	62	2	91	17	9	.255
Baker, Charles, Hawaii	131	414	35	91	110	15	2	0	30	10	2	18	3	51	0	3	.220
Barrow, Melvin, Tucson	10	39	6	11	12	1	0	0	2	0	0	3	0	4	1	0	.282
Beamon, Charles, Spokane*	52	204	31	72	100	14	4	2	35	0	0	14	1	9	11	3	.353
Beckwith, T. Joseph, Albuquerque	27	3	1	0	0	0	0	0	0	0	0	0	0	0	0	0	.000
Berenguer, Juan, Tacoma	28	2	0	0	0	0	0	0	0	0	0	0	0	2	0	0	.000
Bernal, Victor, Hawaii	17	1	0	0	0	0	0	0	0	0	0	0	0	0	0	0	.000
Bernhardt, Juan, Spokane	98	391	43	106	137	18	2	3	49	0	3	17	2	22	1	2	.271
Berra, Dale, Portland	56	210	37	68	103	13	2	6	32	3	2	19	4	29	2	1	.324
Beswick, James, Hawaii†	144	459	41	98	144	15	5	7	57	0	3	72	3	104	10	7	.214
Biagini, Gregory, Spokane†	19	66	12	16	26	3	2	1	10	0	1	7	0	17	0	0	.242
Biggerstaff, Barry, Hawaii†	13	2	0	1	3	0	1	0	0	0	0	0	0	0	0	0	.500
Botting, Ralph, Salt Lake City*	18	1	0	0	0	0	0	0	0	0	0	2	0	1	0	0	.000
Bourjos, Christopher, Phoenix	142	553	68	167	241	32	9	8	87	1	6	31	5	54	14	10	.302
Boyland, Dorian, Portland*	30	102	10	25	37	6	0	2	12	0	0	10	1	21	2	1	.245
Bradley, J. Richard, Phoenix	63	198	26	38	54	10	0	2	19	0	3	31	1	36	0	1	.192
Bryant, Derek, Ogden	6	19	2	2	2	0	0	0	2	0	1	3	0	0	0	0	.105
Brye, Stephen, Hawaii	75	235	39	58	88	11	2	5	36	4	3	36	1	37	12	3	.247
Bucci, Michael, Tucson	101	332	47	85	112	12	6	1	38	19	1	48	3	43	19	10	.256
Budaska, Mark, Ogden†	97	348	66	101	154	19	2	10	42	1	2	71	0	71	2	3	.290
Bulling, Terry, Spokane	52	160	23	54	78	14	2	2	18	1	0	22	1	18	2	2	.338
Burke, Steven, Spokane	42	0	1	0	0	0	0	0	0	0	0	0	0	0	0	0	.000
Cacek, Craig, Portland	147	565	92	180	278	33	7	17	102	2	6	58	5	40	5	7	.319
Cage, Wayne, Tacoma*	86	315	47	87	146	14	3	13	55	3	2	42	0	77	1	2	.276
Carrithers, Donald, Phoenix	39	3	0	1	1	0	0	0	0	0	0	0	0	0	0	0	.333
Castillo, Anthony, Hawaii	82	230	24	43	56	7	0	2	17	5	0	23	1	38	1	0	.187
Champion, R. Michael, Tacoma	136	501	62	156	192	19	4	3	71	7	6	43	4	78	12	7	.311
Chauncey, Keathel, Tucson*	116	352	67	94	119	11	4	2	33	2	5	53	0	38	19	8	.267
Chiles, Richard, Tacoma*	130	455	58	119	169	29	3	5	61	5	3	47	2	47	11	6	.262
Clark, Robert, Salt Lake City	129	474	85	144	237	30	9	15	91	0	5	47	2	98	16	7	.304
Cliburn, Stanley, Salt Lake City	62	206	15	49	75	12	1	4	26	1	1	15	2	27	1	2	.238
Cosey, D. Ray, Ogden*	144	566	80	178	257	21	11	12	91	4	9	44	0	64	15	12	.314
Cotes, Eugenio, Portland	79	285	39	74	124	14	3	10	45	0	2	20	4	60	14	7	.260
Cox, Jeffrey, Ogden	139	520	102	148	163	10	1	1	37	3	3	87	3	65	45	18	.285
Craig, Rodney, Spokane†	46	181	36	57	75	8	2	2	13	3	1	18	1	18	16	6	.315
Crosby, Edward, Spokane*	103	338	50	81	100	11	4	0	36	3	2	35	2	23	3	1	.240
Cuellar, Robert, Tacoma	37	1	0	0	0	0	0	0	0	0	0	0	0	1	0	0	.000
Darrow, Darrell, Salt Lake City	86	262	24	63	72	9	0	0	22	4	2	24	1	46	2	3	.240
Davalillo, Victor, Albuquerque*	51	139	27	44	59	6	0	3	19	1	1	17	0	13	3	1	.317
Davis, Odie, Tucson	119	376	54	95	122	11	2	4	45	9	2	60	6	98	12	3	.253
Dempsey, Patrick, Ogden	44	149	14	42	51	3	0	2	20	1	0	11	0	16	2	1	.282
Diaz, Baudilio, Tacoma	34	115	5	28	41	7	0	2	11	4	0	5	0	21	0	0	.243
Dilone, Miguel, Ogden†	6	29	5	8	11	1	1	0	6	0	0	1	0	3	4	0	.276
Donohue, Thomas, Salt Lake City ..	15	51	9	13	28	4	1	3	13	0	1	2	0	14	1	2	.255
Duncan, Taylor, 5 Port-22 Tac	27	97	6	16	21	5	0	0	7	0	1	6	0	13	0	0	.165
Dupree, Michael, Hawaii	58	182	21	44	57	5	1	2	19	3	4	16	0	22	0	3	.242
Duran, Daniel, Tucson*	113	388	65	106	159	26	3	7	59	0	8	66	2	56	5	3	.273
Dybzinski, Jerome, Tacoma	132	469	58	119	144	16	3	1	25	13	4	52	7	58	25	10	.254
Dyes, Andrew, Hawaii	106	367	46	98	148	20	3	8	49	2	2	35	4	86	6	3	.267
Edwards, Marshall, Vancouver*	111	385	39	105	123	10	1	2	44	2	3	30	5	25	19	7	.273
Eichelberger, Juan, Hawaii	28	1	0	0	0	0	0	0	0	0	0	0	0	0	0	0	.000
Ellis, Robert, 30 Tac-62 Port	92	331	54	98	148	13	5	9	54	2	8	36	2	59	5	5	.296
Enyart, Terry, Ogden	45	1	0	0	0	0	0	0	0	0	0	0	0	0	0	0	.000

Player and Club	G.	AB.	R.	H.	TB.	2B.	3B.	HR.	RBI.	SH.	SF.	BB.	HP.	SO.	SB.	CS.	Pct.
Estrada, Manuel, Spokane	116	398	66	107	138	26	1	1	34	4	3	46	1	32	13	4	.269
Ewing, William, Salt Lake City	16	66	3	13	17	2	1	0	6	0	0	3	0	20	0	1	.197
Foley, Rick, Salt Lake City	30	1	1	0	0	0	0	0	0	0	0	0	0	1	0	0	.000
Foley, William, Vancouver	28	102	15	26	45	2	1	5	21	0	0	9	1	31	0	0	.255
Garman, Michael, 23 Port-21 Tac	44	1	0	0	0	0	0	0	0	0	0	0	0	1	0	0	.000
George, Frankie, Spokane	16	51	9	16	23	4	0	1	5	0	0	6	1	6	1	1	.314
Gilbreath, Rodney, Portland	112	408	69	119	156	13	9	2	54	8	6	71	1	39	17	5	.292
Gonzales, Daniel, Tucson*	51	198	37	64	113	11	4	10	52	0	3	14	0	18	3	1	.323
Gooch, Ronald, Tucson	72	257	42	82	101	13	3	0	27	7	4	25	1	28	9	5	.319
Goodwin, Danny, Ogden*	100	370	66	129	225	22	7	20	94	2	4	59	0	62	0	4	.349
Grandas, Robert, Ogden	56	204	29	60	78	9	3	1	28	3	4	19	0	33	8	3	.294
Gray, Gary, Tucson	87	315	58	96	175	22	3	17	67	0	5	38	1	43	4	0	.305
Grieve, Thomas, Tucson	93	304	46	81	149	20	3	14	54	2	3	52	3	72	2	2	.266
Guerrero, Pedro, Albuquerque	113	453	94	151	268	33	9	22	103	0	5	31	2	84	26	8	.333
Gutierrez, Israel, Tucson	19	58	9	12	17	3	1	0	7	3	0	8	0	15	2	0	.207
Haines, Dennis, Ogden*	67	226	27	52	72	6	1	4	23	2	2	33	1	32	0	1	.230
Hampton, Isaac, Salt Lake City	106	391	85	113	233	14	8	30	97	0	4	63	3	100	23	5	.289
Hargis, Gary, Portland	103	386	52	107	153	23	4	5	42	9	2	8	1	33	6	2	.277
Harris, John, Salt Lake City*	111	418	63	136	217	38	2	13	88	0	4	52	1	58	5	7	.325
Harris, Victor, Vancouver†	142	509	82	140	206	25	7	9	66	3	6	69	3	48	14	7	.275
Harrison, Mack, Ogden†	94	313	34	72	85	4	3	1	28	8	1	32	0	41	7	6	.230
Hart, J. Michael, Tucson†	139	466	98	141	210	23	11	8	72	4	10	122	2	85	19	4	.303
Hassey, Ronald, Tacoma*	44	157	25	53	72	10	0	3	27	2	3	23	0	15	2	1	.338
Hatcher, Michael, Albuquerque	103	420	88	156	239	29	12	10	93	0	5	24	1	32	16	9	.371
Heath, Michael, Tucson	54	196	21	53	68	8	2	1	28	1	1	16	2	25	2	1	.270
Heidemann, Jack, Spokane	100	339	45	80	101	17	2	0	36	4	7	37	0	53	2	4	.236
Heintzelman, Thomas, Phoenix	69	246	30	60	90	13	1	5	29	1	3	41	2	51	4	1	.244
Henderson, Michael, Vancouver†	6	16	3	5	6	1	0	0	1	0	0	1	0	3	0	0	.313
Henderson, Rickey, Ogden	71	259	66	80	116	11	8	3	26	12	1	53	3	41	44	9	.309
Holland, Alfred, 16 Port-13 Phx	29	4	0	0	0	0	0	0	0	0	0	0	0	2	0	0	.000
Holle, Gary, Tucson	52	208	32	71	98	10	3	3	47	0	1	20	2	29	3	2	.341
Hosley, Timothy, Ogden	82	305	56	92	140	18	3	8	70	2	6	53	4	52	5	2	.302
Jacobs, Ronald, Vancouver	47	100	9	20	24	4	0	0	2	3	0	11	0	17	0	1	.200
James, Philip, Vancouver*	106	342	51	94	146	17	4	9	53	3	8	69	1	56	0	3	.275
Johnston, Gregory, Phoenix*	104	415	64	123	190	17	10	10	72	1	5	44	2	60	16	3	.296
Kearney, Robert, Phoenix	38	124	11	17	27	2	1	2	10	0	0	13	0	20	0	0	.137
Keefe, Kevin, Albuquerque	46	3	1	0	0	0	0	0	0	0	0	0	0	3	0	0	.000
Kolarek, Frank, Ogden	22	68	6	17	22	3	1	0	12	0	3	9	0	16	0	0	.250
Kubski, Gilbert, Salt Lake City*	128	498	83	147	224	33	4	12	54	8	1	39	1	87	31	5	.295
Kuecker, Mark, Phoenix	129	422	48	102	132	19	4	1	55	4	11	51	0	94	3	6	.242
Kuhaulua, Fred, Hawaii*	31	2	0	0	0	0	0	0	0	0	0	0	0	1	0	0	.000
Lantigua, Manuel, Portland	59	185	11	39	45	6	0	0	24	3	5	5	0	30	0	1	.211
Law, Rudy, Albuquerque*	72	270	46	80	88	4	2	0	28	2	4	46	1	27	33	9	.296
Law, Vance, Portland	131	448	62	139	177	16	8	2	52	14	2	47	2	69	8	4	.310
Lewallyn, Dennis, Albuquerque	43	1	0	0	0	0	0	0	0	0	0	0	0	1	0	0	.000
Lieppman, Keith, Ogden	80	275	35	75	114	15	3	6	33	2	2	17	0	31	0	0	.273
Lintz, Larry, Tacoma†	3	12	2	0	0	0	0	0	1	0	0	1	0	1	0	0	.000
Lisi, Riccardo, Tucson	6	13	1	2	3	1	0	0	0	0	0	1	0	5	0	0	.154
Little, D. Jeffery, Phoenix	29	1	0	0	0	0	0	0	0	0	0	0	0	0	0	0	.000
Littlejohn, Dennis, Phoenix	66	239	33	68	104	11	5	5	34	0	6	34	2	52	5	2	.285
Littleton, Larry, Portland	133	459	66	128	188	24	6	8	71	6	2	46	1	82	4	4	.279
Lois, Alberto, Portland	5	9	2	4	6	0	1	0	1	0	0	2	0	1	0	0	.444
Lopez, Juan, Vancouver	113	375	46	99	136	21	5	2	33	5	4	26	1	48	3	3	.264
Lubratich, Steven, Salt Lake City	4	12	3	4	6	2	0	0	2	0	0	1	0	0	0	1	.333
Lucas, Gary, Hawaii*	24	2	0	0	0	0	0	0	0	0	0	0	0	1	0	0	.000
Mahlberg, Gregory, Tucson	87	271	31	60	81	8	2	3	36	6	7	44	3	45	2	4	.221
Mallory, Sheldon, Tacoma*	86	289	48	79	112	11	2	6	33	2	2	52	5	45	26	11	.273
Mangual, Jose, Salt Lake City	136	485	115	131	226	21	4	22	71	3	6	110	2	128	46	13	.270
McCall, Larry, Tucson*	30	3	0	1	3	0	1	0	1	0	0	0	0	1	0	0	.333
McKinney, Lynn, Hawaii†	20	2	1	0	0	0	0	0	0	0	0	1	0	0	0	0	.000
Mitchell, Craig, Ogden	24	1	0	0	0	0	0	0	0	0	0	0	1	0	0	0	.000
Mitchell, Robert, Hawaii*	90	314	41	76	98	7	6	1	34	7	2	41	0	21	16	9	.242
Mitchell, Robert, Albuquerque*	123	453	104	148	194	24	8	2	59	4	4	71	3	35	18	11	.327
Mitchell, Ronald, Portland	56	169	28	39	59	14	3	0	13	0	2	21	2	22	8	4	.231
Mueller, Willard, Vancouver	42	1	0	0	0	0	0	0	0	0	0	0	0	1	0	0	.000
Mulliniks, S. Rance, Salt Lake C*	116	402	94	138	182	21	7	3	59	0	5	98	4	45	21	11	.343
Murray, Richard, Phoenix	125	441	63	116	160	13	8	5	67	0	7	54	1	90	6	6	.263
Narleski, Steven, Tacoma	5	1	0	0	0	0	0	0	0	0	0	0	0	0	0	0	.000
Nordbrook, Timothy, Vancouver	75	213	30	41	54	5	1	2	24	2	3	35	1	28	4	1	.192
Norrid, Timothy, Tacoma*	135	421	61	113	159	16	3	8	55	5	5	64	3	73	4	11	.268
Olivares, Oswaldo, Portland*	127	456	83	137	162	15	5	0	41	4	2	68	6	46	28	9	.300
Oliver, David, Tacoma*	134	493	65	140	174	17	7	1	69	9	7	49	1	42	6	3	.284
Oliver, Richard, Salt Lake City	25	64	13	15	20	2	0	1	4	3	0	24	0	12	2	2	.234
O'Rear, John, Albuquerque	129	437	71	131	184	25	8	4	71	9	8	31	7	64	11	5	.300
Overy, H. Michael, Salt Lake City	57	3	0	1	1	0	0	0	0	0	0	0	0	2	0	0	.333

Player and Club	G.	AB.	R.	H.	TB.	2B.	3B.	HR.	RBI.	SH.	SF.	BB.	HP.	SO.	SB.	CS.	Pct.
Pape, Kenneth, Spokane	45	111	14	35	43	6	1	0	9	1	0	10	0	9	1	2	.315
Parsons, Casey, Phoenix*	142	566	99	175	257	35	16	5	63	4	4	58	5	59	21	10	.309
Pasley, Kevin, Portland	20	54	7	15	17	2	0	0	5	0	1	2	0	2	0	0	.278
Patterson, David, Albuquerque	23	2	0	1	1	0	0	0	0	0	0	0	0	1	0	0	.500
Patterson, Michael, Ogden*	47	179	28	58	95	6	5	7	34	2	1	14	0	37	2	0	.324
Pebley, Edward, Spokane*	21	79	11	24	28	4	0	0	2	0	0	12	0	8	1	1	.304
Peguero, Pablo, Albuquerque	45	106	6	24	32	2	0	2	12	1	1	4	1	22	0	1	.226
Pentz, Eugene, Portland	57	1	0	0	0	0	0	0	0	0	0	0	0	0	0	0	.000
Perconte, John, Albuquerque*	143	521	104	168	213	25	7	2	68	10	7	95	1	38	32	4	.322
Perez, Pascual, Portland	23	0	1	0	0	0	0	0	0	0	0	0	0	0	0	0	.000
Perkins, Broderick, Hawaii*	43	159	19	52	71	9	2	2	17	1	0	10	1	19	5	4	.327
Perlozzo, Samuel, Hawaii	143	532	81	160	207	23	6	4	51	8	3	74	3	39	39	17	.301
Peters, James, Salt Lake City*	83	267	40	67	136	10	4	17	51	1	3	42	0	63	7	5	.251
Pierce, L. Jack, Spokane*	133	472	64	132	215	27	4	16	90	2	6	48	1	92	1	2	.280
Pietroburgo, Robert, Spokane†	33	1	0	0	0	0	0	0	0	0	0	0	0	1	0	0	.000
Pinkerton, C. Wayne, Tucson†	51	154	14	30	43	3	5	0	7	0	1	20	0	32	8	2	.195
Plank, Edward, Phoenix	53	3	1	1	1	0	0	0	0	0	0	0	0	0	0	0	.333
Plummer, William, Spokane	116	369	37	94	122	12	2	4	46	5	5	42	3	66	1	1	.255
Porter, Charles, Salt Lake City	31	0	0	0	0	0	0	0	0	0	0	1	0	0	0	0	.000
Potter, Michael, Spokane	117	407	47	101	136	12	4	5	47	4	1	40	0	87	1	2	.248
Power, Ted, Albuquerque	18	1	0	0	0	0	0	0	0	0	0	0	0	0	0	0	.000
Puryear, Nathaniel, Tacoma	20	0	1	0	0	0	0	0	0	0	0	0	0	0	0	0	.000
Ramirez, Milton, Ogden	63	225	30	64	79	9	0	2	28	3	2	23	0	21	2	0	.284
Ramirez, Orlando, Salt Lake City	27	99	10	21	29	3	1	1	11	0	0	6	2	16	6	2	.212
Ramos, Roberto, Salt Lake City	58	179	27	51	71	9	1	3	21	3	2	24	0	37	4	3	.285
Randle, Leonard, 42 Phx-24 Port†	66	243	42	67	89	13	3	1	25	3	2	35	5	31	15	4	.276
Rayford, Floyd, Salt Lake City	135	551	98	162	241	28	6	13	80	1	4	57	2	105	18	5	.294
Rende, Salvatore, Tacoma*	69	237	34	62	89	6	3	5	31	0	1	40	1	32	2	1	.262
Rex, Michael, Phoenix	126	443	51	103	132	17	3	2	49	1	3	46	3	41	10	3	.233
Reynolds, Donald, Hawaii	51	163	24	45	58	6	2	1	18	1	0	27	1	23	7	2	.276
Roberts, David, Tucson	9	34	4	13	23	4	0	2	10	0	1	3	0	9	1	0	.382
Rodriguez, Michael, Ogden	115	395	61	100	167	22	6	11	65	4	6	55	1	119	4	1	.253
Romero, Edgardo, Vancouver	139	515	65	134	172	26	6	0	39	9	4	52	3	47	9	4	.260
Rowland, Michael, Phoenix	31	3	0	0	0	0	0	0	0	0	0	0	0	0	0	0	.000
Russell, Joseph, Tucson	24	74	2	21	26	5	0	0	3	1	0	7	1	11	0	0	.284
Ryan, Craig, Vancouver*	135	488	58	118	192	22	2	16	81	0	4	40	2	96	3	3	.242
Saferight, Harry, Portland*	129	479	67	127	193	23	5	11	81	2	5	52	3	71	1	1	.265
Sakata, Lenn, Vancouver	118	454	59	136	181	21	3	6	64	1	4	30	3	43	16	7	.300
Sanderlin, Richard, Phoenix	50	156	24	41	56	8	2	1	14	0	1	12	3	14	5	0	.263
Sandt, Thomas, Portland	88	292	47	94	118	14	2	2	42	6	2	36	0	30	1	1	.322
Schaefer, Douglas, Phoenix	15	0	1	0	0	0	0	0	0	0	0	0	0	0	0	0	.000
Schmidt, E. Eugene, Phoenix	24	2	0	1	1	0	0	0	1	0	0	0	0	0	0	0	.500
Scioscia, Michael, Albuquerque*	143	461	80	155	198	34	0	3	68	12	3	73	7	33	5	7	.336
Scott, Martin, Tucson	124	420	58	118	168	14	9	6	61	7	3	57	0	44	4	3	.281
Severns, Billy, Vancouver*	104	371	52	118	136	14	2	0	33	2	0	68	1	9	15	8	.318
Shoemaker, John, Albuquerque*	14	28	1	6	6	0	0	0	3	0	0	3	0	2	1	1	.214
Slater, Robert, Salt Lake City	58	155	25	41	56	10	1	1	22	2	5	23	4	40	6	4	.265
Smith, Steven, Hawaii	18	35	2	8	10	1	0	1	5	0	1	3	2	3	0	2	.229
Snider, Kelly, Albuquerque*	138	494	67	150	205	22	3	9	99	3	10	54	4	61	9	4	.304
Souza, K. Mark, Ogden*	15	1	0	0	0	0	0	0	0	0	0	0	0	1	0	0	.000
Speed, Horace, Tacoma	66	219	35	45	66	5	2	4	18	4	1	45	1	79	9	3	.205
Stevens, Paul, Ogden†	8	21	2	3	3	0	0	0	1	0	0	2	0	8	0	1	.143
Stewart, David, Albuquerque	36	1	1	0	0	0	0	0	1	0	0	0	0	0	0	0	.000
Stillman, Royle, 13 Spo-118 Ogd*	131	492	90	148	207	30	4	7	90	3	7	89	0	68	6	5	.301
Stimac, Craig, Hawaii	102	381	54	104	160	20	6	8	58	1	2	27	4	50	7	2	.273
Strain, Joseph, Phoenix	75	310	47	92	110	13	1	1	26	2	2	24	2	18	7	6	.297
Strawn, C. DeFla, Tucson	11	39	2	5	6	1	0	0	3	0	0	2	0	13	0	0	.128
Stroughter, Stephen, Spokane*	81	300	58	90	154	18	5	12	43	3	2	36	1	35	6	4	.300
Sularz, Guy, Phoenix	144	521	79	153	190	23	4	2	68	2	5	65	5	63	14	9	.294
Sweet, Ricky, Hawaii†	135	452	59	116	156	17	4	5	52	5	4	76	0	31	4	4	.257
Swiacki, William, Albuquerque	30	0	1	0	0	0	0	0	0	0	0	0	0	0	0	0	.000
Taveras, Alejandro, Albuquerque	119	402	55	104	126	12	5	0	55	12	6	51	1	36	13	11	.259
Tennant, Michael, Albuquerque	15	0	1	0	0	0	0	0	0	0	0	0	0	0	0	0	.000
Tevlin, Creighton, Vancouver*	109	400	57	115	158	23	4	4	40	5	0	58	2	28	8	5	.288
Thon, Richard, Salt Lake City	38	162	25	47	58	3	1	2	21	1	1	15	1	16	14	3	.290
Tipa, Stephen, Salt Lake City	3	0	1	0	0	0	0	0	0	0	0	0	0	0	0	0	.000
Torres, Alfredo, Portland	1	3	1	1	1	0	0	0	1	0	0	0	0	0	0	1	.333
Vasquez, Rafael, Spokane	23	4	1	1	1	0	0	0	0	0	0	0	0	0	0	0	.250
Venable, W. McKinley, Phoenix*	38	150	27	46	59	5	4	0	11	0	0	24	1	20	17	6	.307
Walterhouse, Richard, Portland*	25	94	9	16	20	4	0	0	5	0	0	11	0	19	1	1	.170
Walton, Daniel, Spokane†	146	522	71	135	219	39	0	15	81	1	5	60	7	103	2	2	.259
Walton, Reginald, Spokane	122	463	79	149	227	31	7	11	76	1	3	29	2	71	9	5	.322
Washington, LaRue, Tucson	76	320	65	99	136	13	6	4	38	0	2	39	0	31	24	6	.309
Wehrmeister, David, Hawaii	15	0	1	0	0	0	0	0	0	0	0	0	0	0	0	0	.000
Westmoreland, Claude, Alb	118	369	65	102	167	23	3	12	55	1	4	44	6	84	28	6	.276

Player and Club	G.	AB.	R.	H.	TB.	2B.	3B.	HR.	RBI.	SH.	SF.	BB.	HP.	SO.	SB.	CS.	Pct.
White, Myron, Albuquerque*	107	374	63	106	157	13	4	10	65	3	4	37	5	93	8	7	.283
Whitmer, Daniel, Salt Lake City	66	210	25	48	68	8	0	4	31	5	3	25	1	55	0	1	.229
Wilhelm, James, Hawaii	87	313	50	87	137	16	8	6	51	8	1	31	0	59	10	4	.278
Williams, Michael, Albuquerque*.	62	1	0	1	1	0	0	0	0	0	0	0	0	0	0	0	1.000
Wiltbank, Benjamin, Portland	13	0	1	0	0	0	0	0	0	0	0	0	0	0	0	0	.000
Wirth, Alan, Ogden	24	1	0	0	0	0	0	0	0	0	0	0	0	0	0	0	.000
Yancy, Hugh, Tacoma	96	313	46	87	109	13	0	3	34	4	9	40	4	31	10	1	.278
Yost, Edgar, Vancouver	130	419	43	110	135	12	2	3	53	8	6	18	3	75	8	4	.263
Yurak, Jeffrey, Vancouver†	56	179	27	45	71	6	1	6	22	0	1	31	4	35	4	0	.251

The following pitchers had no plate appearances primarily through the use of designated hitters, listed alphabetically by club, games in parentheses:

ALBUQUERQUE—Castillo, Robert (16); Goulding, Richard (1); Hannahs, Gerald* (28); Heredia, Ubaldo (2); Hughes, James (17); Shirley, Steven* (11).

HAWAII—Armstrong, Michael (3); Blair, Dennis (16); Carroll, Joe (6); Fierbaugh, N. Randall* (7); Fitzmorris, Alan† (8); Kinney, Dennis* (20); Lee, Mark (21); Tellmann, Thomas (44); Wilkes, Gregory (18).

OGDEN—Abraham, Brian* (32); Bell, Ronald* (20); Bradley, S. Bert† (6); Braun, Barton (4); Camacho, Ernie (21); Green, C. Randall (13); Greenfield, Monroe (49); Jones, Jeffrey (28); Kingman, Brian (13); Lysander, Richard (50); McCatty, Steven (8); Morgan, Michael (13).

PHOENIX—Bordley, William* (27); Cline, Steven (26); Cornutt, Terry (38); Hammon, Randal (21); Hypes, Kyle† (10); Nastu, Philip* (7).

PORTLAND—Arias, Juan (2); Cliburn, Stewart (7); Coleman, Joseph† (32); Field, Gregory (23); Jones, T. Frederick* (33); Kaiser, Robert† (4); Nelson, Roger (1); Pagan, David (9); Pazik, Michael* (6); Pole, Richard (13); Scurry, Rodney* (35); Smith, James (1); Standart, Richard* (10); Warthen, Daniel† (49); Willoughby, James (24).

SALT LAKE CITY—Boone, Daniel* (50); Crisler, T. Joel (16); Dorsey, James (28); Eddy, Steven (11); Ferris, Robert (30); Millsop, Robert (4); Perez, Carlos (49); Schrom, Kenneth (3); Schuler, David (26).

SPOKANE—Anderson, Karl (19); Biercevicz, Gregory (24); Davey, Michael (66); Decker, George (29); Dressler, Robert (10); Lance, Gary† (54); Lewis, James (28); Simond, Robert* (13); Stein, W. Randolph (16—12 with Vancouver); Wheelock, Gary (21).

TACOMA—Albury, Victor* (13); Andersen, Larry (27); Borchers, Rickey (24); Brennan, Thomas (27); Heimer, Todd* (7); Melson, Gary (26); Nicholson, Carl (6); Stanton, Michael† (8); Wihtol, Alexander (49); Wright, Jesse* (5).

TUCSON—Allard, Brian (25); Babcock, Robert (41); Bianchi, Steven (39); Brown, Thomas (39—19 with Tacoma); Bruhert, Michael (21); Darwin, Danny (13); Jakubowski, Stanley (21); Kainer, Donald (28); Lynch, Edward (27); Moharter, David* (4); Myrick, Robert (22); Rajsich, David* (5); Smith, Myrl (18); Umbarger, James* (26).

VANCOUVER—Boitano, Danny (53); Bomback, Mark (33); Carroll, Clay (12); Carroll, Edgar* (16); Galasso, Robert* (6); Keeton, Rickey (32); Ogawa, Kunikazu (28); Olsen, Richard (14); Quiros, Gustavo (35); Replogle, Andrew (29).

GRAND SLAM HOME RUNS—Cage, Cotes, Ellis (Tacoma 1-Portland 1), 2 each; Beswick, Bourjos, Gonzales, Guerrero, Hampton, Kubski, Patterson, Perconte, Perlozzo, Peters, Pierce, Rayford, Rodriguez, Ryan, Sweet, Washington, 1 each.

AWARDED FIRST BASE ON INTERFERENCE—Saferight 8 (Scioscia 3, Allietta, Diaz, Hosley, Mahlberg, Whitmer); Berra 3 (Kearney 2, Scioscia); White 3 (Hosley 2, Heath); R. Law (Heath); Mangual (Scioscia); M. Patterson (Scioscia); O. Ramirez (Scioscia); Westmoreland (Hosley); Wilhelm (Lantigua); Yost (Whitmer).

CLUB FIELDING

Club	G.	PO.	A.	E.	DP.	PB.	Pct.
Vancouver	147	3802	1714	124	162	9	.978
Hawaii	148	3831	1692	140	164	14	.975
Portland	147	3756	1558	156	136	10	.971
Salt Lake City	148	3811	1626	167	122	17	.970
Tucson	148	3775	1593	168	151	16	.970

Club	G.	PO.	A.	E.	DP.	PB.	Pct.
Tacoma	147	3822	1608	180	135	13	.968
Albuquerque	148	3770	1519	180	141	31	.967
Phoenix	147	3782	1679	189	152	18	.967
Spokane	147	3742	1597	190	150	17	.966
Ogden	147	3783	1713	226	141	19	.961

Triple Plays—Tucson, Tacoma, Phoenix.

INDIVIDUAL FIELDING

*Throws lefthanded.

FIRST BASEMEN

Player and Club	G.	PO.	A.	E.	DP.	Pct.
Holle, Tucson*	17	171	11	0	16	1.000
SNIDER, Albuquerque*	132	1087	70	2	93	.998
James, Vancouver*	93	888	52	3	94	.997
J. Harris, SLC*	108	1022	80	5	86	.995
Duran, Tucson*	96	793	44	5	78	.994
Rende, Tacoma*	56	500	30	3	42	.994
Sweet, Hawaii	42	351	31	3	33	.992
O'Rear, Albuquerque	17	126	6	1	15	.992
Cacek, Portland	146	1201	138	14	117	.990
Ryan, Vancouver	59	533	41	6	51	.990
Sularz, Phoenix	28	243	17	3	16	.989

Player and Club	G.	PO.	A.	E.	DP.	Pct.
Cage, Tacoma*	76	660	73	9	64	.988
Perkins, Hawaii*	43	385	33	5	46	.988
Pierce, Spokane	130	1172	80	17	115	.987
Stimac, Hawaii	53	487	33	7	49	.987
Budaska, Ogden*	54	542	31	9	59	.985
Goodwin, Ogden	88	832	46	14	66	.984
Beamon, Spokane*	12	108	11	2	8	.983
Scott, Tucson	39	320	16	6	31	.982
Murray, Phoenix	119	1043	86	26	114	.977
Dupree, Hawaii	19	152	18	5	18	.971
Hampton, Salt Lake C	34	262	18	10	18	.966

Triple Plays—Rende, Murray.

FIRST BASEMEN—Continued
(Fewer Than Ten Games)

Player and Club	G.	PO.	A.	E.	DP.	Pct.
Grieve, Tucson	7	55	2	0	9	1.000
Lieppman, Ogden	6	44	2	0	4	1.000
Alston, Tacoma	6	38	3	0	5	1.000
Darrow, Salt Lake C	3	19	2	0	2	1.000
Kubski, Salt Lake	3	15	4	0	2	1.000
R. L. Mitchell, Port	3	13	3	0	0	1.000
Hosley, Ogden	1	12	0	0	0	1.000
Johnston, Phoenix*	1	10	2	0	0	1.000
Boyland, Portland*	1	9	1	0	1	1.000
Bradley, Phoenix	1	7	0	0	0	1.000
Stillman, Ogden*	1	4	0	0	1	1.000
Ashford, Hawaii	1	3	0	0	0	1.000
Biggerstaff, Hawaii*	1	3	0	0	0	1.000
D. Walton, Spokane	1	3	0	0	1	1.000
Shoemaker, Alb	3	2	0	0	0	1.000
Guerrero, Albuquerque	1	2	0	0	0	1.000
Norrid, Tacoma	9	71	5	1	4	.987
Gray, Tucson	6	58	1	1	4	.983
Bernhardt, Spokane	7	45	3	1	2	.980
Heintzelman, Phoenix	3	36	5	1	2	.976
Rayford, Salt Lake C	4	28	2	1	1	.968
Allietta, Tacoma	6	24	1	1	4	.962
Plummer, Spokane	3	22	0	1	3	.957
Westmoreland, Alb	6	39	3	2	7	.955
Pape, Spokane	2	15	1	1	1	.941
Ramos, Salt Lake City	2	14	2	2	1	.889
W. Foley, Vancouver	1	7	0	1	1	.875

SECOND BASEMEN

Player and Club	G.	PO.	A.	E.	DP.	Pct.
PERLOZZO, Hawaii	142	309	447	9	105	.988
Lopez, Vancouver	17	28	42	1	7	.986
Hargis, Portland	79	163	219	7	47	.982
Sandt, Portland	23	56	48	2	14	.981
Thon, Salt Lake City	10	19	34	1	5	.981
Mulliniks, Salt Lake C	11	23	29	1	3	.981
Sakata, Vancouver	117	266	407	14	92	.980
Gooch, Tucson	72	164	226	8	53	.980
Rex, Phoenix	75	165	214	8	58	.979
Pinkerton, Tucson	30	66	107	4	22	.977
Gilbreath, Portland	39	83	101	5	21	.974
Heidemann, Spokane	88	169	300	13	64	.973
Slater, Salt Lake C	55	95	148	7	18	.972
R. Oliver, SL City	22	60	77	4	23	.972
V. Harris, Vancouver	16	26	42	2	9	.971
Cox, Ogden	138	302	501	25	104	.970
D. Oliver, Tacoma	129	250	363	22	74	.965
Strain, Phoenix	75	169	238	15	47	.964
Estrada, Spokane	54	113	156	10	55	.964
Darrow, Salt Lake C	69	114	150	11	31	.960
Washington, Tucson	36	79	87	7	23	.960
Perconte, Albuquerque	143	278	403	35	88	.951
V. Law, Portland	12	42	33	4	9	.949
Yancy, Tacoma	23	35	48	6	7	.933

Triple Play—D. Oliver.

(Fewer Than Ten Games)

Player and Club	G.	PO.	A.	E.	DP.	Pct.
Roberts, Tucson	9	11	16	0	4	1.000
S. Smith, Hawaii	6	6	13	0	2	1.000
R. D. Mitchell, Hawaii	3	5	10	0	2	1.000
Shoemaker, Alb	3	5	9	0	4	1.000
Bernhardt, Spokane	2	6	7	0	3	1.000
Stevens, Ogden	1	5	4	0	2	1.000
Pape, Spokane	2	2	7	0	1	1.000
Davis, Tucson	1	3	4	0	2	1.000
M. Henderson, Van	1	2	4	0	1	1.000
Nordbrook, Vancouver	1	2	4	0	0	1.000
Dupree, Hawaii	1	0	1	0	0	1.000
Pebley, Spokane	5	13	13	1	4	.963
Harrison, Ogden	9	11	21	2	6	.941
Gutierrez, Tucson	8	12	16	2	0	.933
O'Rear, Albuquerque	5	11	12	2	1	.920
Rayford, SL City	2	4	7	1	2	.917
Champion, Tacoma	3	5	5	1	0	.909
Randle, Portland	1	5	2	1	3	.875
Lintz, Tacoma	3	5	6	2	1	.846
Crosby, Spokane	2	1	4	1	1	.833

Triple Play—Gutierrez.

THIRD BASEMEN

Player and Club	G.	PO.	A.	E.	DP.	Pct.
Darrow, Salt Lake C	13	13	14	0	2	1.000
V. Law, Portland	42	42	90	2	10	.985
Scott, Tucson	86	68	150	7	13	.969
O. Ramirez, SL City	14	8	21	1	2	.967
RAYFORD, SL City	120	91	285	17	20	.957
Randle, Phx-Port	43	36	98	6	6	.957
Gilbreath, Portland	55	48	119	8	13	.954
Hatcher, Albuquerque	77	55	150	10	7	.953
O'Rear, Albuquerque	74	59	118	10	13	.947
Champion, Tacoma	117	68	214	16	12	.946
Ashford, Hawaii	141	131	314	26	31	.945
Bucci, Tucson	68	59	130	11	7	.945
Bernhardt, Spokane	75	72	127	12	10	.943
Nordbrook, Vancouver	54	31	117	9	13	.943
Sandt, Portland	20	16	29	3	4	.938
Lopez, Vancouver	88	40	147	13	13	.935
Heintzelman, Phoenix	42	30	94	9	15	.932
Pape, Spokane	13	9	18	2	3	.931
Duncan, Port-Tac	16	14	25	3	2	.929
Estrada, Spokane	33	22	49	6	5	.922
Sularz, Phoenix	32	23	56	7	11	.919
Lieppman, Ogden	48	25	92	12	8	.907
Walterhouse, Portland	19	19	27	5	2	.902
Biagini, Spokane	17	15	30	5	2	.900
Rodriguez, Ogden	98	65	201	30	23	.899
Rex, Phoenix	37	33	69	12	10	.895
Yancy, Tacoma	16	15	26	6	4	.872
V. Harris, Vancouver	10	3	10	2	2	.867
R. L. Mitchell, Portland	12	5	14	7	1	.731

Triple Play—Scott.

(Fewer Than Ten Games)

Player and Club	G.	PO.	A.	E.	DP.	Pct.
Romero, Vancouver	3	4	6	0	0	1.000
Lubratich, SL City	3	0	10	0	0	1.000
Guerrero, Albuquerque	3	3	5	0	0	1.000
Norrid, Tacoma	6	2	6	0	0	1.000
R. D. Mitchell, Hawaii	2	2	3	0	0	1.000
Pierce, Spokane	2	1	3	0	0	1.000
Hassey, Tacoma	2	1	2	0	1	1.000
Pebley, Spokane	2	1	2	0	1	1.000
Berra, Portland	1	1	2	0	0	1.000
Taveras, Albuquerque	1	0	3	0	0	1.000
Pinkerton, Tucson	2	2	0	0	0	1.000
Mahlberg, Tucson	2	0	2	0	1	1.000

THIRD BASEMEN—Continued
(Fewer Than Ten Games)

Player and Club	G.	PO.	A.	E.	DP.	Pct.	Player and Club	G.	PO.	A.	E.	DP.	Pct.
Sakata, Vancouver	2	0	2	0	0	1.000	Crosby, Spokane	4	1	6	1	0	.875
Ellis, Portland	1	0	2	0	0	1.000	Yurak, Vancouver	4	3	3	1	0	.857
Plummer, Spokane	9	5	11	1	4	.941	R. Oliver, SL City	3	2	3	1	0	.833
M. Henderson, Van.	3	3	10	1	1	.929	Shoemaker, Alb	5	8	14	5	1	.815
Stimac, Hawaii	7	1	9	1	2	.909	Gutierrez, Tucson	3	1	5	3	0	.667
Harrison, Ogden	4	7	1	1	0	.889	Scioscia, Albuquerque	3	0	1	1	0	.500

SHORTSTOPS

Player and Club	G.	PO.	A.	E.	DP.	Pct.	Player and Club	G.	PO.	A.	E.	DP.	Pct.
R.D. Mitchell, Hawaii	21	34	41	1	12	.987	Crosby, Spokane	92	153	254	26	61	.940
Pinkerton, Tucson	19	29	58	2	8	.978	Davis, Tucson	117	217	356	38	79	.938
MULLINIKS, SLC	106	181	302	16	63	.968	Gilbreath, Portland	10	14	31	3	3	.938
Berra, Portland	47	67	156	8	32	.965	Kuecker, Phoenix	129	195	342	36	71	.937
Rex, Phoenix	14	20	54	3	5	.961	Thon, Salt Lake City	28	51	86	10	10	.932
Romero, Vancouver	134	215	414	26	97	.960	Pebley, Spokane	14	24	53	6	10	.928
Dybzinski, Tacoma	132	269	409	30	91	.958	O'Rear, Albuquerque	35	56	90	12	22	.924
Taveras, Albuquerque	118	199	305	23	64	.956	M. Ramirez, Ogden	62	106	198	27	45	.918
Baker, Hawaii	130	216	396	29	92	.955	Washington, Tucson	15	20	35	5	9	.917
Nordbrook, Vancouver	15	25	56	4	9	.953	Sularz, Phoenix	10	17	19	4	2	.900
V. Law, Portland	78	117	185	16	33	.950	Estrada, Spokane	26	35	79	13	15	.898
Lieppman, Ogden	11	9	28	2	7	.949	Champion, Tacoma	16	16	33	6	7	.891
Hargis, Portland	16	25	46	4	10	.947	Pate, Spokane	14	17	41	8	5	.879
Harrison, Ogden	74	120	242	21	41	.945							

Triple Play—Kuecker.

(Fewer Than Ten Games)

Player and Club	G.	PO.	A.	E.	DP.	Pct.	Player and Club	G.	PO.	A.	E.	DP.	Pct.
Heidemann, Spokane	8	10	21	0	6	1.000	Lopez, Vancouver	7	5	17	1	5	.957
Ashford, Hawaii	3	7	7	0	3	1.000	S. Smith, Hawaii	6	7	11	2	2	.900
Bucci, Tucson	2	2	4	0	0	1.000	Darrow, Salt Lake C	4	4	5	1	1	.900
Rayford, Salt Lake C	7	11	22	1	2	.971	Stevens, Ogden	3	6	7	2	1	.867
D. Oliver, Tacoma	6	9	16	1	3	.962	O. Ramirez, SL City	9	20	23	9	4	.827

OUTFIELDERS

Player and Club	G.	PO.	A.	E.	DP.	Pct.	Player and Club	G.	PO.	A.	E.	DP.	Pct.
Reynolds, Hawaii	46	76	6	0	1	1.000	Bernhardt, Spokane	17	33	1	1	0	.971
Stimac, Hawaii	46	76	5	0	1	1.000	Speed, Spokane	65	124	4	4	0	.970
Washington, Tucson	29	63	2	0	0	1.000	Potter, Spokane	117	206	13	7	4	.969
George, Spokane	16	36	1	0	0	1.000	White, Albuquerque*	103	180	6	6	2	.969
Craig, Spokane	45	113	2	1	1	.991	Grandas, Ogden	56	123	3	4	0	.969
Brye, Hawaii	63	104	4	1	1	.991	Bourjos, Phoenix	139	276	24	10	4	.968
TEVLIN, Vancouver*	104	180	11	2	1	.9896	Mangual, Salt Lake C	104	206	8	7	0	.968
V. Harris, Vancouver	110	274	9	3	1	.9895	Randle, Portland	21	59	1	2	0	.968
Parsons, Phoenix	141	232	12	3	3	.988	Hart, Tucson	136	265	11	10	3	.965
Littleton, Portland	133	317	10	5	0	.985	Olivares, Portland*	117	177	17	7	5	.965
Ellis, Tac-Port.	79	118	11	2	4	.985	Grieve, Tucson	80	128	10	5	0	.965
Westmoreland, Alb	36	64	2	1	1	.985	Norrid, Tacoma	94	178	8	7	0	.964
Beswick, Hawaii	141	278	17	5	6	.983	R. Henderson, Ogden	71	149	6	6	1	.963
Strougther, Spokane	79	143	9	3	0	.981	M. Patterson, Ogden	44	74	4	3	0	.963
Clark, Salt Lake City	126	328	12	7	4	.980	Davalillo, Albuquerque	15	24	1	1	1	.962
Chiles, Tacoma*	118	188	11	4	2	.980	Alston, Tacoma	63	132	10	6	2	.959
R. Law, Albuquerque*	64	142	2	3	1	.980	Dyes, Hawaii	35	42	4	2	0	.958
Johnston, Phoenix*	103	273	8	6	1	.979	R.S. Mitchell, Hawaii	20	41	5	2	1	.958
Chauncey, Tucson*	108	228	7	5	2	.979	Mallory, Tacoma*	75	168	1	8	0	.955
Beamon, Spokane*	40	85	3	2	0	.978	Cotes, Portland	70	118	9	6	0	.955
R.V. Mitchell, Alb*	119	279	21	7	3	.977	Dupree, Hawaii	25	40	2	2	2	.955
Gonzales, Tucson	50	76	4	2	2	.976	R.L. Mitchell, Portland	41	77	5	4	0	.953
Hatcher, Albuquerque	33	72	6	2	2	.975	Duran, Tucson*	22	37	1	2	0	.950
Wilhelm, Hawaii	87	187	4	5	2	.974	Bucci, Tucson	31	54	2	3	0	.949
Guerrero, Albuquerque	97	183	4	5	2	.974	Yurak, Vancouver	28	34	2	2	0	.947
Edwards, Vancouver*	99	200	11	6	4	.972	Peters, Salt Lake City	78	149	9	9	1	.946
Cosey, Ogden*	126	203	7	6	1	.972	Barrow, Tucson	10	28	2	2	1	.938
Severns, Vancouver*	101	168	8	5	3	.972	Sanderlin, Phoenix	26	35	5	3	1	.930
Stillman, Spo-Ogd*	100	158	17	5	2	.972	Ryan, Vancouver	11	12	0	1	0	.923
R. Walton, Spokane	120	298	7	9	0	.971	Boyland, Portland*	11	21	1	2	0	.917
Kubski, Salt Lake City	122	254	14	8	1	.971	Hampton, Salt Lake C	27	53	1	6	0	.900
Venable, Phoenix	38	96	4	3	4	.971	Yancy, Tacoma	25	21	1	4	1	.846
Budaska, Ogden*	38	61	6	2	1	.971							

Triple Play—Alston.

OUTFIELDERS—Continued
(Fewer Than Ten Games)

Player and Club	G.	PO.	A.	E.	DP.	Pct.
Gilbreath, Portland	7	16	0	0	0	1.000
Dilone, Ogden	6	14	0	0	0	1.000
Estrada, Spokane	5	12	0	0	0	1.000
Gutierrez, Tucson	4	10	1	0	0	1.000
Nordbrook, Vancouver	6	8	0	0	0	1.000
Harrison, Ogden	5	6	1	0	0	1.000
Walterhouse, Portland	4	6	0	0	0	1.000
Sandt, Portland	3	6	0	0	0	1.000
Lois, Portland	3	5	1	0	0	1.000
Lieppman, Ogden	3	3	0	0	0	1.000
Biagini, Spokane	2	3	0	0	0	1.000
James, Vancouver	1	3	0	0	0	1.000
Bryant, Ogden	3	2	1	0	0	1.000
Lisi, Tucson	4	2	0	0	0	1.000
Tipa, Salt Lake City	3	2	0	0	0	1.000
Donohue, Salt Lake C	2	2	0	0	0	1.000
Sularz, Phoenix	2	2	0	0	0	1.000
Yost, Vancouver	1	2	0	0	0	1.000
Allietta, Tacoma	1	2	0	0	0	1.000
Holle, Tucson*	1	1	0	0	0	1.000
Rodriguez, Ogden	9	12	1	2	0	.867
Stevens, Ogden	2	4	0	1	0	.800
Bradley, Phoenix	2	1	1	1	1	.667
Champion, Tacoma	1	1	0	1	0	.500

CATCHERS

Player and Club	G.	PO.	A.	E.	DP.	PB.	Pct.
Pasley, Portland	18	73	12	0	1	1	1.000
Donohue, SL City	12	52	4	0	0	2	1.000
Littlejohn, Phoenix	62	299	48	2	5	11	.994
Hassey, Tacoma	38	281	42	2	3	3	.994
Jacobs, Vancouver	40	134	21	1	4	1	.994
ALLIETTA, Tacoma	83	387	45	5	6	8	.989
Mahlberg, Tucson	78	339	49	5	2	5	.987
Whitmer, SL City	63	251	41	4	4	7	.986
Yost, Vancouver	124	604	64	10	8	8	.985
Bulling, Spokane	50	218	31	4	3	8	.984
Peguero, Albuquerque	22	54	7	1	3	1	.984
Sweet, Hawaii	85	412	41	8	8	7	.983
Scioscia, Albuquerque	127	690	86	15	19	22	.981
Castillo, Hawaii	76	401	41	9	4	7	.980
Diaz, Tacoma	31	223	24	5	4	2	.980
Lantigua, Portland	56	288	33	7	3	4	.979
Bradley, Phoenix	54	265	40	7	9	6	.978
Stan Cliburn, SLC	60	257	33	7	4	1	.976
Plummer, Spokane	102	467	49	13	9	9	.975
Saferight, Portland	88	425	37	12	9	5	.975
Kolarek, Ogden	22	116	14	4	0	3	.970
Kearney, Phoenix	35	183	27	7	2	1	.968
Heath, Tucson	38	183	24	7	4	6	.967
Hosley, Ogden	51	296	30	12	2	7	.964
Haines, Ogden	38	206	23	10	5	5	.958
Ramos, Salt Lake C	25	98	12	5	1	6	.957
Dempsey, Ogden	41	213	24	11	2	4	.956
Russell, Tucson	24	98	23	6	1	2	.953
Ramos, Salt Lake C	25	98	12	5	1	6	.957
Westmoreland, Alb	17	86	13	7	0	8	.934

(Fewer Than Ten Games)

Player and Club	G.	PO.	A.	E.	DP.	PB.	Pct.
Bucci, Tucson	5	5	0	0	0	0	1.000
Strawn, Tucson	9	50	5	3	1	3	.948
Hampton, SL City	4	14	0	1	0	1	.933
Norrid, Tacoma	4	8	1	1	0	0	.900

PITCHERS

Player and Club	G.	PO.	A.	E.	DP.	Pct.
BORDLEY, Phoenix*	27	11	27	0	1	1.000
Dorsey, Salt Lake C	28	12	21	0	2	1.000
R. Foley, Salt Lake C	30	11	21	0	2	1.000
Scurry, Portland*	35	7	25	0	1	1.000
Plank, Phoenix	53	12	19	0	1	1.000
Camacho, Ogden	21	10	21	0	2	1.000
Kuhaulua, Hawaii*	29	4	27	0	4	1.000
Blair, Hawaii	16	13	15	0	1	1.000
Keefe, Albuquerque	44	7	21	0	4	1.000
Mueller, Vancouver	41	7	15	0	1	1.000
Darwin, Tucson	13	7	15	0	1	1.000
Boitano, Vancouver	53	5	16	0	1	1.000
Olsen, Vancouver	14	7	12	0	1	1.000
Schuler, Salt Lake C*	26	5	14	0	1	1.000
Ogawa, Vancouver	28	6	12	0	0	1.000
C. Perez, Salt Lake C	49	5	13	0	0	1.000
Kinney, Hawaii*	20	5	13	0	2	1.000
Simond, Spokane*	12	5	13	0	1	1.000
Pole, Portland	13	8	8	0	0	1.000
Power, Albuquerque	18	3	13	0	3	1.000
Decker, Spokane	29	4	11	0	0	1.000
Cline, Phoenix	25	4	10	0	1	1.000
Schaefer, Phoenix	14	4	9	0	1	1.000
Albury, Tacoma*	13	3	10	0	0	1.000
Davey, Spokane*	66	2	11	0	0	1.000
Bianchi, Tucson	39	3	9	0	0	1.000
Hughes, Albuquerque	17	2	8	0	0	1.000
Souza, Ogden*	15	1	8	0	0	1.000
C. Mitchell, Ogden	24	2	6	0	0	1.000
Standart, Portland	10	4	3	0	0	1.000
Brown, Tac-Tuc	39	6	7	0	0	1.000
D. Patterson, Alb	23	4	2	0	0	1.000
Lee, Hawaii	21	3	3	0	0	1.000
Bernal, Hawaii	16	1	5	0	1	1.000
Jakubowski, Tucson	21	5	0	0	0	1.000
E. Carroll, Vancouver*	16	0	5	0	1	1.000
Biggerstaff, Hawaii*	12	1	1	0	0	1.000
Bomback, Vancouver	33	17	43	1	7	.984
Keeton, Vancouver	32	18	34	1	4	.981
Replogle, Vancouver	29	10	27	1	4	.974
Ferris, Salt Lake C	30	18	16	1	0	.971
P. Perez, Portland	20	15	18	1	2	.971
Morgan, Ogden	13	4	28	1	0	.970
Wehrmeister, Hawaii	13	8	20	1	1	.966
Lance, Spokane	54	7	20	1	0	.964
Wheelock, Spokane	18	8	17	1	1	.962
Dressler, Spokane	10	4	20	1	0	.960
Brennan, Tacoma	26	12	35	2	1	.959
Vasquez, Spokane	22	11	12	1	2	.958
Lucas, Hawaii*	24	11	33	2	2	.957
Quiros, Vancouver	35	12	31	2	3	.956
Wihtol, Tacoma	49	5	16	1	4	.955
Andersen, Tacoma	27	14	24	2	3	.950
Warthen, Portland*	49	12	24	2	1	.947
Allard, Tucson*	22	8	26	2	2	.944
Coleman, Portland	32	10	7	1	0	.944
Garman, Port-Tac	44	9	8	1	0	.944
Overy, Salt Lake City	57	7	10	1	0	.944
Wiltbank, Portland	12	5	12	1	0	.944
Swiacki, Albuquerque	29	16	33	3	2	.942

PITCHERS—Continued

Player and Club	G.	PO.	A.	E.	DP.	Pct.
Schmidt, Phoenix	24	21	11	2	0	.941
Eddy, Salt Lake City	11	8	8	1	3	.941
J. Jones, Ogden	28	9	21	2	0	.938
Wirth, Ogden	23	6	24	2	3	.938
Lysander, Ogden	50	2	13	1	0	.938
Carrithers, Phoenix	36	11	32	3	5	.935
Umbarger, Tucson*	26	4	25	2	2	.935
McCall, Tucson	29	10	17	2	0	.931
Lynch, Tucson	27	18	21	3	0	.929
Holland, Port-Phx*	29	13	26	3	1	.929
Kainer, Tucson	28	9	30	3	3	.929
Porter, Salt Lake C	31	11	15	2	1	.929
Berenguer, Tacoma	26	11	15	2	1	.929
Lewis, Spokane	28	15	35	4	2	.926
Abraham, Ogden*	31	7	29	3	2	.923
Little, Phoenix*	28	5	19	2	1	.923
Tellmann, Hawaii	44	4	20	2	1	.923
Kingman, Ogden	13	4	8	1	0	.923
Bell, Ogden	20	8	15	2	0	.920
Borchers, Tacoma*	24	9	25	3	5	.919
T.F. Jones, Portland*	33	13	20	3	4	.917
R. Castillo, Alb	16	2	9	1	1	.917
Myrick, Tucson*	22	1	10	1	1	.917
Rowland, Phoenix	30	13	30	4	0	.915
Cuellar, Tacoma	37	7	14	2	0	.913
Puryear, Tacoma	19	11	19	3	1	.909
McKinney, Hawaii	19	8	22	3	0	.909
Willoughby, Portland	24	7	3	1	0	.909
Green, Ogden	13	6	13	2	1	.905

Player and Club	G.	PO.	A.	E.	DP.	Pct.
Pentz, Portland	57	9	9	2	2	.900
Cornutt, Phoenix	38	3	15	2	1	.900
Wilkes, Hawaii	18	3	6	1	0	.900
Lewallyn, Albuquerque..	43	4	22	3	1	.897
Beckwith, Albuquerque .	27	8	17	3	0	.893
Burke, Spokane	40	7	18	3	3	.893
Boone, Salt Lake City*	50	3	20	3	1	.885
Babcock, Tucson	41	0	14	2	1	.875
M. Smith, Tucson*	18	1	6	1	1	.875
Hannahs, Albuquerque*	26	5	15	3	0	.870
Hammon, Phoenix	21	6	20	4	0	.867
Enyart, Ogden*	44	3	10	2	0	.867
Anderson, Spokane	19	4	15	3	0	.864
Stein, Van-Spo	16	10	15	4	1	.862
Tennant, Albuquerque ..	14	3	3	1	0	.857
C. Carroll, Van	12	1	5	1	1	.857
Crisler, SL City	16	7	11	3	0	.857
Pietroburgo, Spo*	32	0	6	1	0	.857
Williams, Alb*	62	4	13	3	0	.850
Bierceviez, Spokane	24	11	22	6	0	.846
Eichelberger, Hawaii	28	7	24	6	1	.838
Field, Portland	23	7	8	3	0	.833
Shirley, Albuquerque*	11	2	8	2	0	.833
Hypes, Phoenix	10	0	5	1	1	.833
Botting, SL City*	18	2	12	3	0	.824
Melson, Tacoma	26	14	8	5	2	.815
Bruhert, Tucson	21	6	4	4	3	.714
Stewart, Albuquerque	28	6	16	9	1	.710

(Fewer Than Ten Games)

Player and Club	G.	PO.	A.	E.	DP.	Pct.
Stewart Cliburn, Port	7	4	4	0	1	1.000
J. Carroll, Hawaii	6	3	3	0	0	1.000
Bradley, Ogden	6	2	4	0	0	1.000
Wright, Tacoma*	5	0	6	0	0	1.000
McCatty, Ogden	8	1	3	0	0	1.000
Millsop, SL City	4	1	3	0	0	1.000
Galasso, Vancouver	6	1	2	0	0	1.000
Rajsich, Tucson*	5	1	2	0	0	1.000
Braun, Ogden	4	0	3	0	0	1.000
Heredia, Albuquerque..	2	0	3	0	0	1.000
Pagan, Portland	9	1	1	0	0	1.000
Dupree, Hawaii	4	1	1	0	0	1.000
Sandt, Portland	2	1	1	0	0	1.000
Nelson, Portland	1	1	1	0	0	1.000
Fierbaugh, Hawaii	7	0	2	0	0	1.000

Player and Club	G.	PO.	A.	E.	DP.	Pct.
Kaiser, Portland	4	0	2	0	1	1.000
Moharter, Tucson*	4	0	2	0	0	1.000
S. Smith, Hawaii	1	0	2	0	0	1.000
Greenfield, Ogden	4	0	1	0	0	1.000
Armstrong, Hawaii	3	0	1	0	0	1.000
Davalillo, Alb*	3	0	1	0	0	1.000
Schrom, Salt Lake C	3	0	1	0	0	1.000
Stanton, Tacoma	8	2	11	1	2	.929
Nastu, Phoenix*	7	2	5	1	0	.875
Nicholson, Tacoma	6	0	5	1	1	.833
Pazik, Portland*	6	3	0	1	0	.750
Heimer, Tacoma*	7	0	3	1	0	.750
Fitzsimmons, Hawaii	8	3	6	3	0	.750
J. Smith, Portland	1	1	1	1	0	.667

The following players do not have any recorded accepted chances at the positions indicated; therefore, are not listed in the fielding averages for those particular positions: Abraham*, of; Arias, p; Ashford, 2b; Beamon*, p; Budaska*, p; Crosby, p; R. Foley, of; Goulding, p; Hargis, of; Harrison, p; Kubski, p; Lieppman, p; Littlejohn, p; R. D. Mitchell, p; R. L. Mitchell, p; Murray, of; Narleski, p; Pape, of; Peguero, of; Peters*, p; Plummer, p; Saferight, of; Sanderlin, p, 3b; Stevens, p; Stimac, p; Vasquez, of; Yancy, 1b.

CLUB PITCHING

Club	G.	CG.	ShO.	Sv.	IP.	H.	R.	ER.	HR.	BB.	Int. BB.	HB.	SO.	WP.	Bk.	ERA.
Hawaii	148	50	17	23	1277	1191	569	495	79	580	24	30	763	67	6	3.49
Vancouver	147	44	12	28	1267	1257	592	526	69	464	21	25	692	51	4	3.74
Tacoma	147	34	12	37	1274	1266	689	573	73	634	41	33	847	61	10	4.05
Portland	147	18	10	29	1252	1383	720	626	89	567	20	30	712	71	3	4.50
Spokane	147	34	5	25	1247	1457	779	627	72	502	21	19	635	51	6	4.53
Phoenix	147	26	5	19	1261	1433	803	641	65	643	64	29	684	97	6	4.57
Tucson	148	34	4	23	1258	1476	747	643	60	491	21	37	614	55	4	4.60
Salt Lake City	148	27	7	32	1270	1396	777	671	85	564	45	36	622	68	12	4.76
Albuquerque	148	22	6	38	1257	1360	786	667	81	722	49	18	765	93	10	4.78
Ogden	147	40	9	19	1261	1413	866	728	114	695	72	24	783	76	15	5.20

PITCHERS' RECORDS
(Leading Qualifiers for Earned-Run Average Leadership—118 or More Innings)

*Throws lefthanded.

Pitcher–Club	G.	GS.	CG.	ShO.	W.	L.	Sv.	Pct.	IP.	H.	R.	ER.	HR.	Int. BB.	BB.	HB.	SO.	WP.	ERA.
Bomback, Vancouver	33	33	16	5	22	7	0	.759	246	225	87	70	3	67	0	7	151	8	2.56
Lucas, Hawaii*	24	24	9	4	10	7	0	.588	178	151	64	55	15	58	1	3	98	1	2.78
Kuhaulua, Hawaii*	29	18	8	4	10	7	1	.588	157	141	57	49	6	64	1	2	99	4	2.81
Lance, Spokane	54	10	2	0	10	8	5	.556	147	161	73	48	3	56	5	4	73	3	2.94
Brennan, Tacoma	26	26	8	3	12	7	0	.632	176	176	70	62	8	38	4	6	102	3	3.17
Cuellar, Tacoma	37	4	1	0	3	7	4	.300	127	127	61	47	6	53	9	2	69	4	3.33
Eichelberger, Hawaii	28	27	14	4	13	9	0	.591	195	151	79	73	8	137	3	5	159	17	3.37
Keefe, Albuquerque	44	3	1	0	7	0	4	1.000	121	118	52	46	10	63	6	4	71	2	3.42
J. Jones, Ogden	28	25	6	1	13	7	0	.650	175	152	79	68	8	89	7	5	126	6	3.50
Melson, Tacoma	26	21	5	1	6	9	0	.400	137	134	69	54	6	68	2	7	105	3	3.55

Departmental Leaders: G—Davey, 66; GS—Bomback, 33; CG—Bomback, 16; ShO—Bomback, 5; W—Bomback, 22; L—Wirth, 15; Sv—Boitano, 18; Pct.—Bomback, .759; IP—Bomback, 246; H—McCall, 239; R—Swiacki, 120; ER—Dorsey, 103; HR—Bell, 18; BB—Eichelberger, 137; IBB—Plank, 16; HB—Bomback, Melson, Pentz, Porter, 7; SO—Berenguer, 220; WP—Bordley, 20.

(All Pitchers—Listed Alphabetically)

Pitcher–Club	G.	GS.	CG.	ShO.	W.	L.	Sv.	Pct.	IP.	H.	R.	ER.	HR.	Int. BB.	BB.	HB.	SO.	WP.	ERA.
Abraham, Ogden*	31	17	5	1	8	9	1	.471	148	187	101	85	13	82	9	4	92	7	5.17
Albury, Tacoma*	13	9	0	0	5	3	0	.625	53	64	29	27	5	25	1	0	20	2	4.58
Allard, Tucson	22	22	3	0	10	6	0	.625	138	159	81	69	6	54	0	4	70	2	4.50
Andersen, Tacoma	27	12	4	0	10	6	4	.625	112	124	59	50	5	32	2	3	52	2	4.02
Anderson, Spokane	19	19	1	0	2	13	0	.133	105	124	84	75	7	60	0	2	56	2	6.43
Arias, Portland	2	0	0	0	0	1	0	.000	4	8	4	4	0	4	0	0	3	1	9.00
Armstrong, Hawaii	3	0	0	0	0	0	1	.000	7	6	2	2	1	5	0	0	4	0	2.57
Babcock, Tucson	41	0	0	0	5	3	15	.625	64	53	27	23	0	33	1	3	54	5	3.23
Beamon, Spokane*	1	0	0	0	0	0	0	.000	1	1	0	0	1	0	0	0	0	0	0.00
Beckwith, Albuquerque	27	15	1	0	8	8	6	.500	113	119	74	58	11	46	3	1	64	11	4.62
Bell, Ogden	20	19	2	1	4	8	0	.333	96	117	85	63	18	45	7	0	49	6	5.91
Berenguer, Tacoma	26	26	4	0	8	8	0	.500	166	128	101	90	11	129	1	3	220	17	4.88
Bernal, Hawaii	16	0	0	0	2	2	0	.000	20	15	15	13	3	20	1	3	11	2	6.75
Bianchi, Tucson	39	2	0	0	3	2	0	.600	67	83	42	34	3	39	1	6	18	5	4.57
Biercevicz, Spokane	24	22	5	1	10	10	0	.500	141	166	91	74	15	41	1	2	66	7	4.72
Biggerstaff, Hawaii*	12	1	0	0	1	1	0	.000	23	27	12	9	1	8	0	1	6	1	3.52
Blair, Hawaii	16	15	2	0	6	6	0	.500	102	99	58	55	11	52	2	2	64	7	4.85
Boitano, Vancouver	53	0	0	0	6	8	18	.429	81	78	34	33	3	42	7	2	48	12	3.67
Bomback, Vancouver	33	33	16	5	22	7	0	.759	246	225	87	70	3	67	0	7	151	8	0.56
Boone, Salt Lake City*	50	0	0	0	9	2	8	.818	83	90	35	28	6	23	5	1	48	5	3.04
Borchers, Tacoma*	24	16	3	1	7	5	1	.583	109	108	75	53	11	60	3	1	38	4	4.38
Bordley, Phoenix*	27	27	6	0	8	11	0	.421	156	181	106	79	11	94	5	3	84	20	4.56
Botting, Salt Lake City*	18	14	4	1	5	8	0	.385	92	110	51	49	10	50	4	1	42	3	4.79
Bradley, Ogden	6	3	1	0	0	2	0	.000	27	27	16	14	1	14	1	0	12	1	4.67
Braun, Ogden	4	1	0	0	0	0	0	.000	12	21	11	11	1	4	1	1	6	1	8.25
Brennan, Tacoma	26	26	8	3	12	7	0	.632	176	176	70	62	8	38	4	6	102	3	3.17
Brown, 19 Tac–20 Tuc	39	0	0	0	2	3	5	.400	74	87	45	37	7	27	3	0	37	3	4.50
Bruhert, Tucson	21	5	1	0	4	3	0	.571	60	79	39	29	2	25	2	0	21	2	4.35
Budaska, Ogden*	1	0	0	0	0	0	0	.000	0	0	2	2	0	3	0	1	0	0	.....
Burke, Spokane	40	1	0	0	3	1	2	.750	82	116	80	62	3	40	0	3	42	12	6.80
Camacho, Ogden	21	17	2	0	7	9	0	.438	97	102	86	71	14	70	5	2	60	10	6.59
Carrithers, Phoenix*	36	8	2	0	7	4	0	.636	133	154	72	61	5	65	7	3	75	17	4.13
C. Carroll, Vancouver	12	0	0	0	2	1	0	.000	22	38	23	22	3	6	1	2	18	1	9.00
E. Carroll, Vancouver*	16	0	0	0	1	1	0	.500	23	18	13	11	1	22	0	0	20	4	4.30
J. Carroll, Hawaii	6	5	0	0	1	2	0	.333	31	39	20	19	3	16	0	0	20	1	5.52
R. Castillo, Albuquerque	16	5	1	0	4	3	0	.571	45	49	34	28	1	31	1	0	42	4	5.60
Stewart Cliburn, Portland	7	6	0	0	3	2	0	.600	33	43	19	18	2	17	0	1	17	3	4.91
Cline, Phoenix	25	0	0	0	2	2	4	.500	43	50	24	16	2	35	8	0	26	3	3.35
Coleman, Portland	32	0	0	0	5	1	3	.833	55	53	18	17	3	20	2	0	34	3	2.78
Cornutt, Phoenix	38	0	0	0	5	4	5	.556	74	79	32	26	1	37	3	2	34	1	3.16
Crisler, Salt Lake City	16	15	0	0	3	3	0	.500	72	75	53	41	2	41	1	4	29	5	5.13
Crosby, Spokane	1	0	0	0	0	0	0	.000	1	0	2	2	0	4	0	0	0	0	18.00
Cuellar, Tacoma	37	4	1	0	3	7	4	.300	127	127	61	47	6	53	9	2	69	4	3.33
Darwin, Tucson	13	13	4	1	6	6	0	.500	95	89	43	38	1	42	2	6	65	5	3.60
Davalillo, Albuquerque*	3	0	0	0	0	0	0	.000	6	3	1	0	1	0	0	3	0	0.00
Davey, Spokane*	66	1	0	0	4	4	12	.500	92	103	46	40	4	39	4	0	64	1	3.91
Decker, Spokane	29	4	0	0	3	2	5	.600	53	51	21	18	0	34	4	0	29	4	3.06
Dorsey, Salt Lake City	28	28	6	2	10	12	0	.455	168	176	113	103	14	100	2	2	92	9	5.52
Dressler, Spokane	10	10	4	0	3	4	0	.429	74	76	36	31	2	24	1	0	39	3	3.77
Dupree, Hawaii	4	1	1	1	0	0	0	1.000	11	10	4	3	1	5	0	0	6	0	2.45
Eddy, Salt Lake City	11	11	3	1	4	3	0	.571	72	75	38	26	1	34	1	2	24	2	3.25
Eichelberger, Hawaii	28	27	14	4	13	9	0	.591	195	151	79	73	8	137	3	5	159	17	3.37

Pitcher–Club	G	GS	CG	ShO	W	L	Sv	Pct.	IP	H	R	ER	HR	BB	Int. BB	HB	SO	WP	ERA
Enyart, Ogden*	44	0	0	0	1	3		.250	84	109	64	56	7	55	4	1	56	7	6.00
Ferris, Salt Lake City	30	22	4	0	14	7	0	.667	166	161	92	83	10	71	3	6	98	6	4.50
Field, Portland	23	22	4	0	4	13	0	.235	117	153	75	63	6	33	3	2	58	2	4.85
Fierbaugh, Hawaii	7	0	0	0	0	0		.000	16	17	12	11	2	10	0	1	5	1	6.19
Fitzmorris, Hawaii	8	8	0	0	2	2	0	.500	39	36	18	16	0	12	1	1	12	7	3.69
R. Foley, Salt Lake City	30	23	3	0	5	11	0	.313	144	201	116	96	8	60	3	4	89	8	6.00
Galasso, Vancouver	6	0	0	0	1	0	1	1.000	11	5	0	0	0	2	0	0	9	1	0.00
Garman, 23 Pt–21 Tac	44	0	0	0	6	3	10	.667	87	104	53	45	7	31	2	2	38	2	4.66
Goulding, Albuquerque	1	1	0	0	0	1	0	.000	1	7	6	6	0	2	0	0	1	0	54.00
Green, Ogden	13	13	4	1	5	7	0	.417	80	104	59	51	7	29	5	1	33	2	5.74
Greenfield, Ogden	4	0	0	0	0	0	0	.000	6	12	11	11	1	8	3	0	6	1	16.50
Hammon, Phoenix	21	18	3	0	2	13	0	.133	112	159	94	77	3	46	4	1	43	6	6.19
Hannahs, Albuquerque*	26	20	3	1	11	8	0	.579	136	137	88	78	8	98	4	0	99	13	5.16
Harrison, Ogden	1	0	0	0	0	0	0	.000	5	5	3	3	1	2	0	0	1	0	5.40
Heimer, Tacoma*	7	0	0	0	1	1	0	.500	20	14	16	11	1	32	0	0	14	3	4.95
Heredia, Albuquerque	2	2	0	0	0	0	0	.000	9	11	6	5	0	9	0	0	6	2	5.00
Holland, 16 Pt–13 Phx*	29	28	3	1	10	10	0	.500	174	173	99	87	13	87	0	2	140	14	4.50
Hughes, Albuquerque	17	0	0	0	3	1	1	.750	36	34	14	12	2	24	3	0	27	2	3.00
Hypes, Phoenix*	10	0	0	0	0	0	0	.000	20	27	33	26	3	31	0	2	7	12	11.70
Jakubowski, Tucson	21	0	0	0	1	4	2	.200	31	51	40	36	7	14	0	1	16	0	10.45
J. Jones, Ogden	28	25	6	1	13	7	0	.650	175	152	79	68	8	89	7	5	126	8	3.50
T. F. Jones, Portland*	33	22	8	2	12	8	3	.600	173	185	84	69	9	53	1	0	112	9	3.59
Kainer, Tucson	28	28	5	0	6	13	0	.316	167	222	114	99	9	56	5	4	69	7	5.34
Kaiser, Portland*	4	2	0	0	0	1	0	.000	10	15	10	10	1	9	0	0	2	1	9.00
Keefe, Albuquerque	44	3	1	0	7	0	4	1.000	121	118	52	46	10	63	4	4	71	2	3.42
Keeton, Vancouver	32	32	12	3	15	14	0	.517	203	187	102	85	11	82	2	3	96	4	3.77
Kingman, Ogden	13	13	4	1	7	2	0	.778	83	90	47	43	3	38	2	3	62	7	4.66
Kinney, Hawaii*	20	12	3	0	4	11	2	.267	87	106	54	46	6	31	2	1	50	2	4.76
Kubski, Salt Lake City	1	0	0	0	0	0	0	.000	1	0	0	0	0	0	0	0	0	0	0.00
Kuhaulua, Hawaii*	29	18	8	4	10	7	1	.588	157	141	57	49	6	64	1	2	99	4	2.81
Lance, Spokane	54	10	2	0	10	8	5	.556	147	161	73	48	3	56	5	4	73	3	2.94
Lee, Hawaii	21	2	0	0	4	1	8	.800	41	39	9	8	0	16	4	1	20	5	1.76
Lewallyn, Albuquerque	43	10	3	1	10	8	14	.556	125	139	66	52	7	36	7	2	71	6	3.74
Lewis, Spokane	28	28	8	1	13	11	0	.542	183	206	95	75	10	56	2	3	98	5	3.69
Lieppman, Ogden	1	0	0	0	0	0	0	.000	3	4	4	4	1	3	0	0	1	2	12.00
Little, Phoenix*	28	25	3	0	7	13	0	.350	140	179	110	92	9	76	2	4	72	17	5.91
Littleton, Portland	1	0	0	0	0	0	0	.000	2	3	3	1	1	0	0	0	0	0	13.50
Lucas, Hawaii*	24	24	9	4	10	7	0	.588	174	150	57	55	15	58	1	3	98	1	2.78
Lynch, Tucson	27	25	6	2	10	11	0	.476	156	184	96	84	8	37	1	2	65	7	4.85
Lysander, Ogden	50	0	0	0	10	3	7	.769	84	94	54	44	1	46	10	0	60	3	4.39
McCall, Tucson	29	28	14	1	14	10	0	.583	212	239	108	89	12	38	0	1	88	7	3.78
McCatty, Ogden	8	0	0	0	1	1	5	.500	20	12	7	7	3	18	2	0	16	1	3.15
McKinney, Hawaii	19	18	7	2	7	10	0	.412	126	122	60	51	6	52	0	3	64	7	3.64
Melson, Tacoma	26	21	5	1	6	9	0	.400	137	134	69	54	6	68	2	7	105	3	3.55
Millsop, Salt Lake City	4	0	0	0	0	0	0	.000	10	20	14	14	1	8	1	1	3	0	12.60
C. Mitchell, Ogden	24	3	0	0	2	2	1	.500	44	69	74	49	5	35	4	1	23	3	10.02
R. D. Mitchell, Hawaii	1	0	0	0	0	0	0	.000	2	2	4	4	0	4	0	0	2	2	18.00
R. L. Mitchell, Portland	1	0	0	0	0	0	0	.000	⅓	0	0	0	0	0	0	0	0	0	0.00
Moharter, Tucson*	4	0	0	0	0	1	0	.000	6	5	2	2	0	2	1	0	1	1	3.00
Morgan, Ogden	13	13	6	0	5	5	0	.500	101	93	48	39	5	49	2	3	42	7	3.48
Mueller, Vancouver	41	12	1	0	7	3	3	.700	131	145	73	65	11	41	2	1	51	4	4.47
Myrick, Tucson*	22	3	1	0	3	4	1	.429	42	48	24	23	1	31	4	3	31	2	4.93
Narleski, Tacoma	4	1	0	0	1	1	0	.500	11	7	7	5	1	5	1	0	4	1	4.09
Nastu, Phoenix*	7	7	0	0	1	1	0	.500	38	38	17	14	4	15	0	2	27	0	3.32
Nelson, Portland	1	0	0	0	0	0	0	.000	2	3	4	3	0	1	0	0	2	0	13.50
Nicholson, Tacoma	6	6	0	0	1	2	0	.333	30	43	27	23	3	22	0	1	20	6	6.90
Ogawa, Vancouver	28	1	0	0	1	7	4	.125	67	72	43	40	6	27	1	2	43	1	5.37
Olsen, Vancouver	14	14	1	0	4	3	0	.571	80	84	53	33	7	38	0	3	53	6	3.71
Overy, Salt Lake City	57	0	0	0	11	6	13	.647	105	102	47	43	6	45	11	2	69	7	3.69
Pagan, Portland	9	0	0	0	2	0	1	1.000	21	24	13	13	1	8	0	2	12	1	5.57
D. Patterson, Alb	23	0	0	0	2	1	6	.667	25	16	4	0	0	6	1	0	20	1	0.00
Pazik, Portland*	6	2	0	0	1	1	1	.500	16	17	9	7	0	5	0	1	7	2	3.94
Pentz, Portland	57	0	0	0	5	6	12	.455	81	78	44	39	6	57	5	7	66	5	4.33
C. Perez, Salt Lake City	49	0	0	0	4	3	8	.571	96	97	53	43	4	50	8	3	53	9	4.03
P. Perez, Portland	20	20	0	1	9	7	0	.563	103	121	70	63	9	47	0	1	51	5	5.50
Peters, Salt Lake City*	1	0	0	0	0	0	0	.000	2	2	1	1	0	1	0	0	0	1	4.50
Pietroburgo, Spokane*	32	0	0	0	1	4	1	.200	54	62	40	37	6	17	0	0	33	1	6.17
Plank, Phoenix	53	0	0	0	4	8	10	.333	91	92	45	32	3	53	16	1	47	6	3.16
Plummer, Spokane	2	0	0	0	0	0	0	.000	1	3	2	2	0	0	0	0	0	0	18.00
Pole, Portland	13	12	2	1	5	1	0	.833	71	77	35	34	3	11	0	1	23	5	4.31
Porter, Salt Lake City	31	19	2	0	5	9	0	.357	137	164	100	87	12	44	4	7	41	8	5.72
Power, Albuquerque	18	17	2	0	5	5	0	.500	101	95	59	54	2	82	3	1	69	8	4.63
Puryear, Tacoma	19	19	6	1	7	10	0	.412	115	127	74	63	4	67	2	4	50	4	4.93
Quiros, Vancouver	35	15	7	0	6	9	1	.400	148	150	65	60	9	41	1	5	72	5	3.65

Pitcher–Club	G.	GS.	CG.	ShO.	W.	L.	Sv.	Pct.	IP.	H.	R.	ER.	HR.	BB.	Int. BB.	HB.	SO.	WP.	ERA.
Rajsich, Tucson*	5	0	0	0	1	0	2	1.000	6	1	0	0	0	4	0	0	1	0	0.00
Replogle, Vancouver	29	29	5	0	11	12	0	.478	185	202	96	92	12	71	6	1	87	3	4.48
Rowland, Phoenix	30	25	8	1	10	12	0	.455	191	209	98	77	10	59	7	3	102	2	3.63
Sanderlin, Phoenix	1	0	0	0	0	0	0	.000	2	4	0	0	0	0	0	0	1	0	0.00
Sandt, Portland	2	0	0	0	0	0	0	.000	4	5	6	2	2	6	0	0	1	0	4.50
Schaefer, Phoenix	14	8	1	0	1	5	0	.167	56	52	34	30	4	29	2	0	26	4	4.82
Schmidt, Phoenix	24	17	1	0	6	12	0	.333	122	140	96	75	5	60	10	6	57	3	5.53
Schrom, Salt Lake City	3	0	0	0	1	0	1	1.000	4	3	0	0	0	3	0	0	3	0	0.00
Schuler, Salt Lake City*	26	16	5	1	10	4	2	.714	118	120	64	57	11	34	2	3	36	1	4.35
Scurry, Portland*	35	15	1	0	5	5	0	.500	122	121	64	56	11	72	1	2	94	7	4.13
Shirley, Albuquerque*	11	11	1	1	5	5	0	.500	58	66	35	33	2	30	1	0	27	1	5.12
Simond, Spokane*	12	12	1	0	2	6	0	.250	67	90	53	39	4	42	0	1	38	4	5.24
J. Smith, Portland	1	1	0	0	0	1	0	.000	6	8	5	5	1	3	0	0	4	0	7.50
M. Smith, Tucson*	18	2	0	0	4	1	0	.800	48	60	30	26	3	35	2	2	22	6	4.88
S. Smith, Hawaii	1	0	0	0	0	0	0	.000	2	2	0	0	0	0	0	0	1	1	0.00
Souza, Ogden*	15	1	0	0	3	2	0	.600	41	42	23	20	3	20	0	2	25	2	4.39
Standart, Portland	10	3	0	0	1	3	0	.250	26	32	22	21	4	8	1	1	16	0	7.27
Stanton, Tacoma	8	7	3	1	3	3	0	.500	45	43	17	12	1	23	3	2	34	4	2.40
Stein, 12 Van-4 Spo	16	15	2	1	7	2	0	.778	95	79	35	23	3	33	1	1	59	2	2.18
Stevens, Ogden	1	0	0	0	0	0	0	.000	3	3	2	2	1	0	0	0	0	0	18.00
Stewart, Albuquerque	28	26	5	1	11	12	1	.478	170	198	112	99	14	81	4	1	105	9	5.24
Stimac, Hawaii	1	1	0	0	0	1	0	.000	4	4	3	3	0	2	0	0	1	2	6.75
Swiacki, Albuquerque	29	28	5	1	13	6	0	.684	187	212	120	98	14	100	8	6	100	14	4.72
Tellmann, Hawaii	44	0	0	0	4	8	7	.333	83	98	37	27	5	40	5	1	51	4	2.93
Tennant, Albuquerque	14	8	0	0	2	4	0	.333	41	53	39	36	2	38	0	0	12	5	7.90
Umbarger, Tucson*	26	20	0	0	6	10	1	.375	133	166	85	80	6	69	2	5	73	4	5.41
Vasquez, Spokane	22	21	9	0	8	11	0	.421	126	153	90	75	11	50	1	2	63	4	5.36
Warthen, Portland*	49	11	1	0	10	9	3	.526	154	139	69	61	11	80	5	4	92	7	3.56
Wehrmeister, Hawaii	13	13	9	2	8	5	0	.615	96	70	24	20	4	24	2	5	56	1	1.88
Wheelock, Spokane	18	15	2	0	7	5	0	.583	97	118	53	47	7	30	2	2	19	3	4.36
Wihtol, Tacoma	49	0	0	0	5	5	16	.500	85	73	24	23	4	38	8	2	73	5	2.44
Wilkes, Hawaii	18	3	0	0	2	4	1	.333	56	60	36	29	7	24	2	1	34	2	4.66
Williams, Albuquerque*	62	2	0	0	5	0	4	1.000	82	103	76	64	6	75	8	3	48	15	7.02
Willoughby, Portland	24	2	0	0	3	2	5	.600	60	61	29	19	4	9	0	5	28	3	2.85
Wiltbank, Portland	12	12	0	0	2	6	0	.250	54	64	46	36	2	44	1	3	20	8	6.00
Wirth, Ogden	23	22	10	2	6	15	0	.286	155	170	101	88	15	85	10	0	112	8	5.11
Wright, Tacoma*	5	0	0	0	0	1	0	.000	8	12	13	13	0	9	0	1	4	2	14.63

BALKS—J. Jones 5; Souza 4; Bordley, Melson, 3 each; Camacho, Dorsey, Ferris, Foley, Hammon, Ogawa, C. Perez, Porter, Shirley, Simond, Swiacki, Tellmann, Tennant, 2 each; Abraham, Andersen, Bell, Berenguer, Blair, Boone, Brennan, Cuellar, Darwin, Davey, Field, Fierbaugh, Garman (Port), Green, Heredia, Holland (Port.), Keefe, Keeton, Kinney, Lance, McKinney, Millsop, Myrick, Narleski, Nicholson, Power, Quiros, Schmidt, Schuler, M. Smith, Stewart, Umbarger, Vasquez, Wheelock, Wihtol, 1 each.

COMBINATION SHUTOUTS—Powers-Williams-Lewallyn, Albuquerque; Bell-Lysander-Enyant, Jones-Mitchell, Ogden; Nastu-Cornutt, Nastu-Schmidt, Schaefer-Cornutt-Plank, Phoenix; Perez-Pentz, Perez-Warthen, Scurry-Garman, Scurry-Pentz, Warthen-Jones, Wiltbank-Arias, Wiltbank-Warthen-Garman, Portland; Eddy-Boone, Foley-Perez, Salt Lake City; Lewis-Davey, Simond-Vasquez-Pietroburgo, Stein-Davey, Spokane; Berenguer-Garman, Berenguer-Garman, Borchers-Garman, Brennan-Wihtol, Melson-Wihtol, Tacoma; Keeton-Boitano, Olsen-Boitano, Olsen-Mueller, Vancouver.

NO-HIT GAMES—None.

Bomback Had 22-7 Record

Mark Bomback became the first Triple-A pitcher to win 20 games in one season since 1966 when he scattered 10 hits and was the beneficiary of four double plays, pitching the Vancouver Canadians to a 7-2 triumph over Ogden, August 18. The 26-year-old righthander was the first 20-game winner in the Triple-A classification since Denver's Jimmy Ollom 13 years earlier.

Berenguer Tied PCL Strikeout Standard

Striking out six Vancouver batters August 28, Juan Berenguer raised his strikeout total to a record-tying 220. The Tacoma righthander had an 18-strikeout performance earlier in the season en route to his mammoth total. He tied the mark of former Tacoma hurler Al Stanek (1964). Berenguer was prevented from establishing a new record when he was recalled by the New York Mets immediately following his feat.

Eastern League

CLASS AA

**Leading Batter
DAVID SCHMIDT
Bristol**

**League President
PAT McKERNAN**

**Leading Pitcher
BOB WALK
Reading**

CHAMPIONSHIP WINNERS IN PREVIOUS YEARS

Year	Team	Pct.
1923	Williamsport	.661
1924	Williamsport	.654
1925	York§	.583
	Williamsport§	.583
1926	Scranton	.627
1927	Harrisburg	.630
1928	Harrisburg	.603
1929	Binghamton	.597
1930	Wilkes-Barre	.572
1931	Harrisburg	.597
1932	Wilkes-Barre	.561
1933	Binghamton	.690
1934	Scranton	.694
	Williamsport*	.603
1935	Scranton	.657
	Binghamton*	.580
1936	Scranton*	.609
	Elmira	.629
1937	Elmira†	.622
1938	Binghamton	.622
	Elmira (3rd)‡	.522
1939	Scranton†	.571
1940	Scranton	.568
	Binghamton (2nd)‡	.554
1941	Wilkes-Barre	.630
	Elmira (3rd)‡	.514
1942	Albany	.600
	Scranton (2nd)‡	.593
1943	Scranton	.630
	Elmira (2nd)‡	.568
1944	Hartford	.723
	Binghamton (4th)‡	.474
1945	Utica	.615
	Albany (3rd)‡	.564
1946	Scranton†	.691
1947	Utica†	.652
1948	Scranton†	.636
1949	Albany	.664
	Binghamton (4th)‡	.500
1950	Wilkes-Barre‡	.652
1951	Wilkes-Barre	.612
	Scranton (2nd)†	.562
1952	Albany	.603
	Binghamton (2nd)‡	.562
1953	Reading	.682
	Binghamton (2nd)‡	.636
1954	Wilkes-Barre	.576
	Albany (3rd)‡	.540
1955	Reading	.613
	Allentown (2nd)‡	.565
1956	Schenectady†	.609
1957	Binghamton	.607
	Reading (3rd)‡	.529
1958	Lancaster x	.568
	Binghamton (6th)‡	.493
1959	Springfield†	.607
1960	Williamsport y	.551
	Springfield (3rd)y	.496
1961	Springfield	.612
1962	Williamsport	.593
	Elmira (2nd)‡	.514
1963	Charleston	.593
1964	Elmira	.586
1965	Pittsfield	.607
1966	Elmira	.633
1967	Binghamton z	.586
	Elmira	.532
1968	Pittsfield	.604
	Reading (2nd)‡	.579
1969	York	.640
1970	Waterbury a	.560
	Reading a	.553
1971	Three Rivers	.569
	Elmira a	.561
1972	West Haven b	.600
	Three Rivers	.559
1973	Reading b	.551
	Pittsfield	.551
1974	Thetford Mines (2nd)c	.536
	Pittsfield (2nd)	.496
1975	Reading	.613
	Bristol*	.587
1976	Three Rivers	.601
	West Haven d	.576
1977	West Haven e	.623
	Three Rivers	.551
1978	Reading	.642
	Bristol*	.580

*Won split-season playoff. †Won championship and four-team playoff. ‡Won four-team playoff. §Tied for pennant, York winning playoff. xLeague was divided into Northern, Southern divisions and played a split season; Lancaster over-all season leader. yPlayoff finals canceled after one game because of rain with Williamsport and Springfield declared playoff co-champions. zLeague was divided into Eastern, Western divisions; Binghamton won playoff. aTied for pennant, Waterbury winning playoff. bLeague was divided into American, National divisions; won playoff. cLeague was divided into American and National divisions; won four-team playoff. dLeague was divided into Northern, Southern divisions, won playoff. eLeague was divided into New England and Canadian-American divisions, won playoff. (NOTE—Known as New York-Pennsylvania League prior to 1938.)

STANDING OF CLUBS AT CLOSE OF FIRST HALF, JUNE 22

Club	W.	L.	T.	Pct.	G.B.	Club	W.	L.	T.	Pct.	G.B.
West Haven (Yankees)	42	28	0	.600	......	Buffalo (Pirates)	36	33	0	.522	5½
Reading (Phillies)	37	32	0	.536	4½	Holyoke (Brewers)	33	37	0	.471	9
Bristol (Red Sox)	37	33	0	.529	5	Waterbury (A's)	24	46	0	.343	18

STANDING OF CLUBS AT CLOSE OF SECOND HALF, SEPTEMBER 1

Club	W.	L.	T.	Pct.	G.B.	Club	W.	L.	T.	Pct.	G.B.
West Haven (Yankees)	41	28	0	.594	......	Buffalo (Pirates)	36	34	0	.514	5½
Reading (Phillies)	40	29	0	.580	1	Holyoke (Brewers)	30	39	0	.435	11
Bristol (Red Sox)	36	33	0	.522	5	Waterbury (A's)	25	45	0	.357	16½

COMPOSITE STANDING OF CLUBS AT CLOSE OF SEASON, SEPTEMBER 1

Club	W.H.	Read.	Bris.	Buf.	Hol.	Wat.	W.	L.	T.	Pct.	G.B.
West Haven (Yankees)	....	17	13	15	16	22	83	56	0	.597	....
Reading (Phillies)	11	....	17	13	18	18	77	61	0	.558	5½
Bristol (Red Sox)	15	10	....	12	19	17	73	66	0	.525	10
Buffalo (Pirates)	13	14	16	....	13	16	72	67	0	.518	11
Holyoke (Brewers)	11	.10	9	15	....	18	63	76	0	.453	20
Waterbury (A's)	6	10	11	12	10	....	49	91	0	.350	34½

Major league affiliations in parentheses.

Playoffs—None.

Regular-Season Attendance—Bristol, 66,844; Buffalo, 133,148; Holyoke, 50,207; Reading, 84,200; Waterbury, 30,339; West Haven, 71,302. Total, 436,040. No playoffs or all-star game.

Managers: Bristol—Tony Torchia; Buffalo—Steve Demeter; Holyoke—George Farson; Reading—Jim Snyder; Waterbury—Ed Nottle; West Haven—Carl Merrill.

All-Star Team: 1B—Valley, Buffalo; 2B—McDonald, Buffalo; 3B—Boggs, Bristol; SS—Soto, Holyoke; OF—Lancellotti, Buffalo; Lefebvre, West Haven; Salazar, Buffalo; Vukovich, Reading; C—Pena, Buffalo; DH—Schmidt, Bristol; Utility—Loviglio, Reading; P—Righetti, West Haven; Walk, Reading; Manager—Merrill, West Haven.

(Compiled by Howe News Bureau, Chicago, Ill.)

CLUB BATTING

Club	G.	AB.	R.	OR.	H.	TB.	2B.	3B.	HR.	RBI.	SH.	SF.	BB.	Int. BB.	HP.	SO.	SB.	CS.	LOB.	Pct.
Buffalo	139	4613	790	777	1291	2138	183	35	198	723	27	49	569	33	33	839	109	58	960	.280
Reading	138	4418	637	545	1216	1707	182	51	69	567	48	55	409	26	49	673	169	83	897	.275
Bristol	139	4473	674	612	1200	1723	200	28	89	588	50	37	575	24	30	730	114	58	1007	.268
West Haven	139	4443	679	578	1188	1730	175	41	95	597	72	43	603	23	43	634	99	68	1016	.267
Holyoke	139	4381	601	692	1138	1695	175	38	102	549	51	43	485	23	31	714	78	64	933	.260
Waterbury	140	4388	543	720	1063	1505	159	41	67	478	58	33	517	17	37	662	156	79	958	.242

INDIVIDUAL BATTING

(Leading Qualifiers for Batting Championship—378 or More Plate Appearances)

*Bats lefthanded.　†Switch-hitter.

Player and Club	G.	AB.	R.	H.	TB.	2B.	3B.	HR.	RBI.	SH.	SF.	BB.	HP.	SO.	SB.	CS.	Pct.
Schmidt, David, Bristol	117	371	78	123	212	32	0	19	73	1	3	83	2	89	10	3	.332
Boggs, Wade, Bristol†	113	406	56	132	153	17	2	0	41	2	1	66	1	21	11	3	.325
Salazar, Luis, Buffalo	139	561	108	181	289	17	5	27	86	5	4	44	5	119	21	11	.323
McDonald, Jerry W., Buffalo*	107	372	82	119	171	12	2	12	60	3	1	89	2	28	12	12	.320
Pena, Antonio, Buffalo	134	515	89	161	287	16	4	34	97	1	1	30	2	83	5	4	.313
Baker, Kenneth, West Haven*	111	379	67	115	152	12	2	7	40	5	1	57	1	35	10	7	.303
Loviglio, John, Reading	131	504	92	148	189	21	4	4	52	11	7	52	3	53	55	12	.294
Vukovich, George, Reading	138	501	80	147	220	14	10	13	88	2	14	65	2	52	16	11	.293
Lefebvre, Joseph, West Haven*	138	487	85	142	253	28	10	21	107	5	9	79	4	61	5	6	.292
Soto, Thomas, Holyoke	126	424	47	123	147	17	2	1	39	16	4	21	2	26	1	5	.290

Departmental Leaders: G—Salazar, 139; AB—Salazar, 561; R—Salazar, 108; H—Salazar, 181; TB—Lancellotti, 296; 2B—Schmidt, 32; 3B—Walker, 12; HR—Lancellotti, 41; RBI—Lancellotti, Lefebvre, 107; SH—Harris, 22; SF—Vukovich, 14; BB—Jerry McDonald, 89; HP—Dempsey, 16; SO—Torres, 120; SB—Loviglio, 55; CS—Walker, 16.

(All Players—Listed Alphabetically)

Player and Club	G.	AB.	R.	H.	TB.	2B.	3B.	HR.	RBI.	SH.	SF.	BB.	HP.	SO.	SB.	CS.	Pct.
Alburtis, Roland, Bristol	125	405	63	99	157	16	0	14	59	0	5	56	0	82	0	1	.244
Alexander, Matthew, Buffalo†	32	134	26	42	67	10	0	5	16	0	1	12	0	18	13	0	.313
Armstead, V. Albert, Waterbury	44	125	20	34	48	1	2	3	14	2	2	22	5	45	17	3	.272
Attaway, Eric, Waterbury*	40	122	11	27	29	2	0	0	5	5	2	14	1	27	0	0	.221
Babitt, M. Shooty, Waterbury	133	484	68	129	184	25	6	6	55	1	10	44	3	47	19	13	.267
Bailey, Daryl, Holyoke	1	2	0	0	0	0	0	0	0	0	0	0	0	1	0	0	.000
Baker, Kenneth, West Haven*	111	379	67	115	152	12	2	7	40	5	1	57	1	35	10	7	.303
Barnes, Michael, Buffalo*	25	73	22	22	34	3	0	3	11	1	0	27	0	16	2	2	.301
Bass, Kevin, Holyoke†	135	490	69	129	176	15	4	8	54	7	3	37	4	77	17	10	.263
Berger, Kenneth, Reading*	45	141	21	35	45	3	2	1	13	2	1	17	0	24	7	2	.248

Player and Club	G.	AB.	R.	H.	TB.	2B.	3B.	HR.	RBI.	SH.	SF.	BB.	HP.	SO.	SB.	CS.	Pct.
Bevington, Terry, Holyoke	85	214	26	54	78	12	0	4	21	3	2	31	3	31	8	7	.252
Boggs, Wade, Bristol†	113	406	56	132	153	17	2	0	41	2	1	66	1	21	11	3	.325
Bonaparte, Elijah, Reading*	119	428	65	121	154	19	4	2	47	5	10	38	2	74	31	12	.283
Boyer, Raymond, Bristol	109	344	55	92	111	9	2	2	50	10	3	41	11	42	20	8	.267
Callahan, Patrick, West Haven	80	218	30	62	83	13	4	0	16	3	2	30	0	43	2	0	.284
Castro, Jose I., Reading	20	76	11	23	27	2	1	0	7	2	0	4	0	11	0	1	.303
Chapman, Nathan, West Haven*	55	214	36	59	90	8	4	5	23	2	0	26	0	21	11	11	.276
Cicatiello, Gary, Buffalo*	18	58	9	14	20	3	0	1	6	1	0	8	0	7	2	0	.241
Conroy, Timothy, Waterbury*	2	2	1	0	0	0	0	0	0	0	0	0	0	1	0	0	.000
Cook, G. Timothy, Holyoke	1	0	1	0	0	0	0	0	0	0	0	0	0	0	0	0	.000
Cotes, Eugenio, Buffalo	39	124	19	27	43	4	0	4	14	1	2	12	3	28	12	5	.218
Curry, Steven, Reading	11	36	6	7	10	0	0	1	2	1	0	6	0	5	3	1	.194
Davis, Michael, Waterbury*	97	351	51	77	114	9	5	6	39	7	5	47	4	58	15	11	.219
Dayett, Brian, West Haven	135	465	58	119	181	21	4	11	74	3	7	55	2	90	11	8	.256
De La Rosa, Jesus, Buffalo	27	94	9	24	31	4	0	1	9	0	1	4	0	23	2	3	.255
Dempsey, Peter, Reading	130	430	64	120	179	24	4	9	62	9	7	22	16	84	9	15	.279
Djakonow, Powel, Buffalo	86	262	41	54	103	7	3	12	34	2	0	35	3	49	2	2	.206
Driver, Ronald, Holyoke	1	1	0	0	0	0	0	0	0	0	0	0	0	1	0	0	.000
Duncan, Columbus, Holyoke	9	27	3	5	7	2	0	0	2	0	0	3	0	11	0	0	.185
Duran, Richard, Holyoke	39	118	15	30	40	5	1	1	13	0	1	13	2	17	0	1	.254
Ellison, J. Jeffrey, Buffalo*	4	10	2	2	5	0	0	1	2	0	0	6	0	1	0	0	.200
Espino, Juan, West Haven	95	296	40	70	107	11	1	8	44	1	3	30	9	69	1	1	.236
Evans, Ronald, Bristol	62	164	37	44	65	8	2	3	25	3	4	45	1	34	6	1	.268
Foley, William, Holyoke	96	333	46	90	164	16	2	18	74	0	4	42	6	82	0	1	.270
Foster, Otis, Bristol	46	146	22	39	50	2	0	3	21	0	1	26	0	16	1	1	.267
Fournier, Bruce, Waterbury*	127	422	46	105	151	18	5	6	41	3	3	55	2	30	3	6	.249
Galante, Joseph, Buffalo	1	0	1	0	0	0	0	0	0	0	0	0	0	0	0	0	.000
Gedman, Richard, Bristol*	130	470	48	129	192	25	1	12	63	3	2	49	4	95	0	3	.274
Grandas, Robert, Waterbury	59	221	44	55	79	4	4	4	24	4	1	27	1	28	28	4	.249
Griffin, Michael, West Haven	1	1	1	0	0	0	0	0	0	0	0	0	0	0	0	0	.000
Hall, Rocky, Holyoke†	10	6	2	2	2	0	0	0	1	0	0	0	0	1	0	0	.333
Harer, Wayne, West Haven†	104	386	62	110	140	13	4	3	45	2	1	54	1	40	5	6	.285
Harris, D. Mark, West Haven*	116	323	43	63	68	5	0	0	26	22	0	39	0	40	4	3	.195
Henderson, Michael, Holyoke†	112	402	68	114	146	13	8	1	21	9	5	71	0	26	6	6	.284
Hernaiz, Jesus, Reading	1	2	0	0	0	0	0	0	0	0	0	0	0	1	0	0	.000
Irwin, Dennis, West Haven	33	102	14	27	51	10	1	4	16	0	1	9	2	19	0	0	.265
Jarquin, Gersan, Holyoke	45	118	10	19	23	2	1	0	8	2	0	8	0	15	2	3	.161
Jemison, Gregory, West Haven*	13	45	8	14	17	1	1	0	1	2	0	8	0	6	7	2	.311
Johnston, J. Mark, West Haven*	123	366	65	97	169	15	3	17	60	2	6	82	10	52	9	6	.265
Jones, Joe L., Reading	79	231	25	55	80	10	0	5	25	5	0	18	0	41	3	1	.238
Jurak, Edward, Bristol	135	435	50	96	117	17	2	0	41	17	4	44	4	63	7	4	.221
Klebba, Robert, Waterbury	87	284	14	54	64	4	0	2	25	3	2	22	2	45	2	3	.190
Kolarek, Frank, Waterbury	21	58	5	4	4	0	0	0	3	1	0	6	1	14	0	0	.069
Kraus, Jeffrey, Reading	103	270	35	63	85	5	4	3	30	2	1	24	7	53	8	9	.233
Lancellotti, Richard, Buffalo*	138	506	95	145	296	14	7	41	107	0	13	59	5	88	6	4	.287
Laribee, Russell, Bristol*	115	364	65	100	176	18	2	18	72	2	5	47	4	73	18	3	.275
Lefebvre, Joseph, West Haven*	138	487	85	142	253	28	10	21	107	5	9	79	4	61	5	6	.292
Lois, Alberto, Buffalo	11	40	8	11	19	1	2	1	0	0	0	4	1	11	1	0	.275
Lollar, W. Timothy, West Haven*	65	122	16	28	46	3	0	5	15	1	2	16	2	38	3	2	.230
Lora, Ramon, Reading	84	282	29	83	114	17	4	2	37	1	2	10	1	36	2	3	.294
Loviglio, John, Reading	131	504	92	148	189	21	4	4	52	11	7	52	3	53	55	12	.294
MacAuley, J. Andrew, Buffalo†	62	221	40	63	84	8	2	3	17	4	2	25	4	29	9	3	.285
MacWhorter, Keith, Bristol	1	1	0	0	0	0	0	0	0	0	0	0	0	0	0	0	.000
Manos, Peter, Reading	1	1	0	0	0	0	0	0	0	0	0	0	0	0	0	0	.000
Matuszek, Leonard, Reading*	32	108	19	31	57	9	4	3	16	0	0	16	1	13	2	1	.287
McDonald, James E., West Haven*	19	65	7	12	14	2	0	0	10	0	3	7	1	4	1	2	.185
McDonald, Jerry W., Buffalo*	107	372	82	119	171	12	2	12	60	3	1	89	2	28	12	12	.320
McGee, Willie, West Haven	49	115	21	28	36	3	1	1	8	3	0	13	1	17	7	1	.243
McMillan, Thomas, Buffalo	97	334	49	85	112	14	2	3	35	3	5	37	0	65	12	4	.254
McNeely, Ronald, Waterbury*	127	440	59	106	129	9	4	2	37	11	2	65	2	29	25	9	.241
Meyer, Scott, Waterbury	129	465	37	99	149	26	3	6	57	3	2	27	2	67	2	4	.213
Minker, Allan, Waterbury	28	78	13	15	15	0	0	0	10	4	0	21	2	8	4	0	.192
Mize, Paul, Waterbury	65	193	22	52	62	5	1	1	22	3	2	28	4	33	2	5	.269
Moore, Kelvin, Waterbury	83	317	46	106	173	19	3	14	56	1	1	19	1	76	12	2	.334
Nowakowski, Tadeusz, Waterbury†	10	32	4	4	4	0	0	0	2	0	0	2	0	12	0	0	.125
Ongarato, Michael, Bristol	124	437	69	113	175	24	4	10	51	3	3	31	1	61	11	7	.259
Patterson, Michael, Waterbury*	84	286	42	78	130	12	5	10	40	0	0	35	0	41	18	8	.273
Pena, Antonio, Buffalo	134	515	89	161	287	16	4	34	97	1	1	30	2	83	5	4	.313
Poole, Bruce, Bristol*	1	1	0	0	0	0	0	0	0	0	0	0	0	0	0	0	.000
Popovich, Nicholas, Reading	123	446	55	118	174	25	2	9	56	1	2	43	1	86	2	1	.265
Purcell, Gary, Bristol	70	220	27	48	59	9	1	0	19	3	1	19	1	47	0	6	.218
Quinones, Rene, Holyoke	1	1	0	0	0	0	0	0	0	0	0	0	0	1	0	0	.000
Reed, Steven, Holyoke	1	1	0	0	0	0	0	0	0	0	0	0	0	0	0	0	.000
Robbins, LeRoy, Waterbury	122	395	48	96	143	22	2	7	40	4	1	58	7	81	7	8	.243
Rodriguez, Luis Ernesto, Reading	92	313	55	95	129	5	10	3	36	2	1	20	1	29	21	3	.304

Player and Club	G.	AB.	R.	H.	TB.	2B.	3B.	HR.	RBI.	SH.	SF.	BB.	HP.	SO.	SB.	CS.	Pct.
Rush, Lawrence, Holyoke	137	484	56	131	204	19	3	16	76	3	8	26	2	103	22	6	.271
Salazar, Luis, Buffalo	39	561	108	181	289	17	5	27	86	5	4	44	5	119	21	11	.323
Sanchez, Orlando, Reading*	70	219	23	71	102	11	1	6	30	2	4	13	5	30	3	5	.324
Schmidt, David, Bristol	117	371	78	123	212	32	0	19	73	1	3	83	2	89	10	3	.332
Schmitz, Daniel, West Haven*	20	69	5	21	24	3	0	0	13	3	2	10	1	4	3	1	.304
Schuster, R. Mark, Holyoke*	130	418	65	107	185	15	6	17	66	2	2	65	0	77	6	2	.256
Sherrill, Dennis, West Haven	21	66	5	14	14	0	0	0	2	0	0	9	5	7	2	2	.212
Shoebridge, Terence, Holyoke	15	36	5	7	10	0	0	1	4	1	1	4	1	8	0	0	.194
Showalter, W. Nathaniel, WH*	129	469	71	131	162	7	3	6	51	17	2	36	2	30	8	6	.279
Smith, Bobby G., Holyoke*	126	382	53	89	128	18	6	3	28	3	2	46	1	48	9	15	.233
Smithson, B. Mike, Bristol	1	0	0	0	0	0	0	0	0	0	0	0	0	0	0	0	.000
Soto, Thomas, Holyoke	126	424	47	123	147	17	2	1	39	16	4	21	2	26	1	5	.290
Splitt, Steven, Holyoke*	71	241	21	59	83	15	0	3	24	0	1	7	1	52	5	3	.245
Steele, Carlton, Bristol	54	115	15	25	26	1	0	0	8	0	0	13	1	18	0	2	.217
Stenholm, Richard, West Haven*	16	62	11	19	27	5	0	1	10	0	1	10	0	7	1	0	.306
Stevens, Paul, Waterbury†	38	112	14	22	27	3	1	0	8	6	0	24	0	20	2	3	.196
Swift, Weldon, Holyoke	2	1	1	0	0	0	0	0	0	0	1	0	1	0	0	0	.000
Tabler, Patrick, West Haven	56	190	33	57	96	15	3	6	36	1	3	36	2	44	9	4	.300
Torres, Alfredo, Buffalo	129	485	58	137	211	31	5	11	86	2	7	40	3	120	3	2	.282
Tronerud, Ricky, Waterbury	1	0	0	0	0	0	0	0	0	0	1	0	0	0	0	0	.000
Valley, Charles, Buffalo*	132	479	81	129	237	31	1	25	98	1	9	87	4	71	2	1	.269
Virgil, Osvaldo, Reading	128	429	57	99	142	17	1	8	66	3	6	61	10	81	7	6	.231
Vukovich, George, Reading	138	501	80	147	220	14	10	13	88	2	14	65	2	52	16	11	.293
Walker, Cleotha, Bristol†	123	498	75	132	199	19	12	8	57	6	4	44	0	77	29	16	.265
Walterhouse, Richard, Buffalo*	59	215	39	51	87	6	0	10	33	3	1	39	0	58	4	5	.237
Whiting, Don, Holyoke*	129	441	75	125	203	22	1	18	78	4	5	72	2	83	1	3	.283
Wilson, James D., Bristol	35	96	14	28	31	3	0	0	8	1	0	11	0	12	1	1	.292
Wyatt, Porter, Holyoke†	22	43	7	7	10	0	0	1	5	0	1	4	1	11	1	1	.163
Young, Ernest, Buffalo†	42	130	12	24	42	2	2	4	11	0	2	11	1	25	1	0	.185
Yurak, Jeffrey, Holyoke†	58	197	31	47	89	4	4	10	35	1	4	34	6	41	0	1	.239

The following pitchers had no plate appearances primarily through use of designated hitters, listed alphabetically by club, games in parentheses:

BRISTOL—Baum, Mark (14); Birrell, Robert (18); Denman, Brian (28); Faust, Alvin (26); Hurst, Bruce (16); King, Jerome (25); Ladd, Peter (18); Parks, Danny (11); Stephenson, Kevin (23).

BUFFALO—Alcala, Santo (7); Arias, Juan (24); Breining, Fred (12); Cliburn, Stewart (15); Cyburt, Philip (5); Dravecky, David (35); Evans, Ricky (28); Gelinas, Marc (13); Griffin, Alan (1); Johnston, James (2); Long, Robert E. (44); Martinez, Ignacio (20); Rock, Robert (9); Smith, James C. (13); Weismiller, Robert (38); Wiltbank, Benjamin (11).

HOLYOKE—Boyce, Randall (26); Carroll, Edgar (25); Cort, Barry (10); Hinds, Samuel (20); Landreth, Larry (5); Olsen Richard (13); Rautzhan, Clarence (11); Riggar, Calvin (3).

READING—Abreu, Armand (9); Anderson, Lawrence (1); Brusstar, Warren (1); Camper, Cardell (22); Fowler, Don (19); Hart, Thomas (2); Munninghoff, Scott (26); Noles, Dickie (1); Reed, Jerry (45); Ruling, Stephen (15); Shiera, Norman (10); Speck, R. Clifford (9); Thomason, M. Erskine (18); Walk, Robert (24); Welborn, Sammye (22).

WATERBURY—Atherton, Keith (4); Beard, C. David (25); Bradley, S. Bert (5); Braun, Barton (20); Clapham, Mark (3); DeBarr, Dennis (22); Green, C. Randall (13); Groover, Lawrence (35); Harris, Frank (25—2 with Bristol); Moore, Robert (17); Retzer, Edwin (16); Wyszynski, Dennis (31).

WEST HAVEN—Burdette, Ricky (4); Cochran, Gregory (3); Cooper, Donald (28); Filer, Thomas (24); Led Duke, Daniel (46); Lewis, Timothy (30); Lysgaard, James (11); McGaffigan, Andrew (23); Mersch, Neal (16); Polinsky, Robert (11); Righetti, David (11); Softy, Mark (14); Taylor, Steven (10).

GRAND-SLAM HOME RUNS—Jerry McDonald, Salazar, 2 each; Bonaparte, Dayett, Jones, Lancellotti, Lefebvre, Meyer, Pena, Robbins, Valley, Walterhouse, Whiting, 1 each.

AWARDED FIRST BASE ON INTERFERENCE—Bevington 2 (Gedman, Virgil); Schuster 2 (Espino 2); Shoebridge (Gedman); Whiting (Torres).

CLUB FIELDING

Club	G.	PO.	A.	E.	DP.	PB.	Pct.	Club	G.	PO.	A.	E.	DP.	PB.	Pct.
Reading	138	3462	1582	159	124	21	.969	Holyoke	139	3440	1514	173	113	18	.966
West Haven	139	3523	1448	168	112	24	.967	Waterbury	140	3479	1434	209	146	36	.959
Bristol	139	3498	1502	169	123	31	.967	Buffalo	139	3555	1458	238	130	13	.955

Triple Play—Waterbury.

INDIVIDUAL FIELDING

*Throws lefthanded.

FIRST BASEMEN

Player and Club	G.	PO.	A.	E.	DP.	Pct.	Player and Club	G.	PO.	A.	E.	DP.	Pct.
Torres, Buffalo	6	29	2	0	2	1.000	Cicatiello, Buffalo*	1	1	0	0	1	1.000
Johnston, West Haven	4	17	4	0	4	1.000	Popovich, Reading	70	664	67	3	56	.996
Rush, Holyoke	3	6	1	0	0	1.000	Harer, West Haven*	47	359	44	2	27	.995
Bevington, Holyoke	1	6	0	0	0	1.000	Foster, Bristol	35	253	16	2	30	.993
Sanchez, Reading	1	3	0	0	0	1.000	Lollar, West Haven*	17	137	9	1	12	.993
Splitt, Holyoke*	1	2	0	0	0	1.000	SCHUSTER, Holyoke*	126	1070	87	10	93	.991

FIRST BASEMEN—Continued

Player and Club	G.	PO.	A.	E.	DP.	Pct.
Valley, Buffalo#	130	1063	108	12	109	.990
Alburtis, Bristol	100	871	65	9	71	.990
Showalter, W Haven*	62	524	49	6	48	.990
Ongarato, Bristol	8	74	9	1	5	.988
Matuszek, Reading	17	140	15	2	13	.987
Duran, Holyoke	18	128	10	2	8	.986
Jones, Reading	58	495	47	8	40	.985
Robbins, Waterbury	31	230	11	4	25	.984
K. Moore, Waterbury*	80	700	35	13	73	.983
Minker, Waterbury	28	237	18	5	25	.981
Walterhouse, Buffalo	7	49	2	1	3	.981
McDonald, W Haven*	18	137	14	4	10	.974
De La Rosa, Buffalo	5	36	2	1	2	.974
Attaway, Waterbury*	3	24	2	1	3	.963
Patterson, Waterbury	1	9	1	1	1	.909
Schmidt, Bristol	1	1	0	1	0	.500

Triple Play—Minker.

SECOND BASEMEN

Player and Club	G.	PO.	A.	E.	DP.	Pct.
Soto, Holyoke	10	21	20	0	4	1.000
McMillan, Buffalo	7	12	22	0	2	1.000
Boggs, Bristol	3	7	7	0	2	1.000
Walterhouse, Buffalo	3	8	6	0	2	1.000
McNeely, Waterbury	3	5	5	0	1	1.000
Dempsey, Reading	1	1	1	0	1	1.000
Bevington, Holyoke	4	1	1	0	1	1.000
Kraus, Reading	1	0	1	0	0	1.000
Henderson, Holyoke	91	196	241	8	61	.982
Ongarato, Bristol	16	47	45	2	11	.979
Rodriguez, Reading	9	17	29	1	1	.979
LOVIGLIO, Reading	131	211	451	15	76	.978
Mize, Waterbury	18	33	48	2	12	.976
Jarquin, Holyoke	35	54	84	4	9	.972
Djakonow, Buffalo	9	17	15	1	5	.970
Johnston, West Haven	81	171	206	13	32	.967
Harris, West Haven	11	15	13	1	5	.966
Walker, Bristol	122	252	357	23	66	.964
Babitt, Waterbury	124	275	383	29	87	.958
McDonald, Buffalo	97	175	298	21	55	.957
Tabler, West Haven	56	122	169	13	42	.957
MacAuley, Buffalo	12	18	40	4	4	.935
Barnes, Buffalo	17	34	36	7	10	.909
Wyatt, Holyoke	16	22	29	6	7	.895
Hall, Holyoke	3	2	4	1	1	.857

Triple Play—Babitt.

THIRD BASEMEN

Player and Club	G.	PO.	A.	E.	DP.	Pct.
Henderson, Holyoke	2	1	1	0	1	1.000
Jarquin, Holyoke	1	1	1	0	1	1.000
Sherrill, West Haven	3	1	1	0	0	1.000
Foley, Holyoke	1	1	0	0	0	1.000
Soto, Holyoke	1	0	1	0	0	1.000
Rodriguez, Reading	42	33	79	3	4	.974
Salazar, Buffalo	10	9	27	1	3	.973
Dempsey, Reading	45	36	67	3	9	.972
Popovich, Reading	33	29	50	3	5	.963
BOGGS, Bristol	98	76	188	13	17	.953
Young, Buffalo	11	7	11	1	0	.947
Rush, Holyoke	137	130	276	27	24	.938
Dayett, West Haven	135	86	226	24	17	.929
Djakonow, Buffalo	73	62	117	15	6	.923
Wilson, Bristol	5	2	9	1	0	.917
Fournier, Waterbury	120	108	203	29	32	.915
Matuszek, Reading	13	5	27	3	1	.914
Evans, Bristol	42	33	69	13	4	.887
Klebba, Waterbury	13	13	29	6	1	.875
Walterhouse, Buffalo	24	17	36	9	4	.855
Kraus, Reading	5	2	9	2	1	.846
Alexander, Buffalo	27	12	36	9	3	.842
Lefebvre, West Haven	6	4	11	3	0	.833
Lora, Reading	3	3	1	1	0	.800
Robbins, Waterbury	8	5	6	3	1	.786
Barnes, Buffalo	3	3	6	3	2	.750
Ongarato, Bristol	2	0	2	2	0	.500

Triple Play—Fournier.

SHORTSTOPS

Player and Club	G.	PO.	A.	E.	DP.	Pct.
Jarquin, Holyoke	6	7	16	0	3	1.000
Djakonow, Buffalo	4	1	1	0	1	1.000
SOTO, Holyoke	119	192	356	15	63	.973
Sherrill, West Haven	19	36	55	3	8	.968
Stevens, Waterbury	26	45	54	4	18	.961
Mize, Waterbury	49	78	146	11	36	.953
Harris, West Haven	104	157	278	24	55	.948
Rodriguez, Reading	41	77	129	12	24	.945
MacAuley, Buffalo	50	105	130	15	34	.940
Schmitz, West Haven	20	30	49	5	9	.940
Jurak, Bristol	135	208	374	40	76	.936
Boggs, Bristol	11	11	18	2	2	.935
Dempsey, Reading	81	123	245	27	54	.932
Klebba, Waterbury	71	123	174	24	31	.925
Castro, Reading	20	39	59	8	10	.925
Henderson, Holyoke	25	46	64	10	8	.917
McMillan, Buffalo	90	177	220	38	53	.913
Lefebvre, West Haven	4	0	3	1	0	.750

OUTFIELDERS

Player and Club	G.	PO.	A.	E.	DP.	Pct.
Wilson, Bristol	27	39	2	0	0	1.000
Stevens, Waterbury	7	20	2	0	1	1.000
Alburtis, Bristol	7	13	1	0	0	1.000
Schmidt, Bristol	8	10	2	0	0	1.000
Lora, Reading	12	11	1	0	1	1.000
Cicatiello, Buffalo*	8	10	0	0	0	1.000
Evans, Bristol	10	10	0	0	1	1.000
McDonald, Buffalo	5	9	0	0	0	1.000
Babitt, Waterbury	3	3	1	0	1	1.000
De La Rosa, Buffalo	4	4	0	0	0	1.000
Duran, Holyoke	5	4	0	0	0	1.000
Rodriguez, Reading	3	3	0	0	0	1.000
Tabler, West Haven	2	2	0	0	0	1.000
Klebba, Waterbury	1	1	0	0	0	1.000
Meyer, Waterbury	1	1	0	0	0	1.000
Grandas, Waterbury	55	125	4	1	1	.992
Harer, West Haven*	53	125	2	2	0	.984
Steele, Bristol	46	58	2	1	0	.984
BOYER, Bristol	107	231	7	4	2	.983
Ongarato, Bristol	95	156	7	3	1	.982
Showalter, West Haven*	32	51	3	1	1	.982
Kraus, Reading	94	179	9	4	1	.979
Lefebvre, West Haven	131	238	16	6	2	.977
McNeely, Waterbury	69	118	3	3	0	.976

OUTFIELDERS—Continued

Player and Club	G.	PO.	A.	E.	DP.	Pct.	Player and Club	G.	PO.	A.	E.	DP.	Pct.
Vukovich, Reading	137	238	13	8	3	.969	Bonaparte, Reading*	118	177	14	12	1	.941
McGee, West Haven	47	88	3	3	0	.968	Sanchez, Reading	33	62	2	4	0	.941
Attaway, Waterbury*	32	58	3	2	2	.968	Laribee, Bristol	97	163	6	11	3	.939
Johnston, West Haven	13	26	3	1	0	.967	Davis, Waterbury*	90	208	7	15	2	.935
Salazar, Buffalo	132	312	15	12	3	.965	Armstead, Waterbury	38	66	5	5	0	.934
Baker, West Haven*	94	147	4	6	2	.962	Alexander, Buffalo	6	14	0	1	0	.933
Yurak, Holyoke	46	73	2	3	0	.962	Splitt, Holyoke	69	94	2	7	1	.932
Lois, Buffalo	11	24	1	1	0	.962	Lancellotti, Buffalo*	138	190	13	16	2	.927
Chapman, W Haven*	55	143	1	6	0	.960	Torres, Buffalo	90	177	9	15	1	.925
Berger, Reading*	43	80	3	4	0	.954	Whiting, Holyoke	62	95	4	8	0	.925
Patterson, Waterbury	72	135	5	7	2	.952	Stenholm, West Haven*	6	8	0	1	0	.889
Smith, Holyoke*	119	204	9	11	0	.951	Cotes, Buffalo	25	44	0	7	0	.863
Robbins, Waterbury	61	109	4	6	1	.950	Jemison, West Haven	13	18	0	3	0	.857
Purcell, Bristol	68	89	4	5	1	.949	Walterhouse, Buffalo	7	12	0	2	0	.857
Bass, Holyoke*	135	280	16	17	1	.946							

CATCHERS

Player and Club	G.	PO.	A.	E.	DP.	PB.	Pct.	Player and Club	G.	PO.	A.	E.	DP.	PB.	Pct.
Shoebridge, Holyoke	13	48	4	0	0	1	1.000	Lora, Reading	37	185	18	5	1	6	.976
Young, Buffalo	2	11	1	0	0	0	1.000	Irwin, West Haven	29	142	18	4	2	5	.976
Lefebvre, West Haven	1	5	0	0	0	0	1.000	Schmidt, Bristol	56	301	40	9	5	10	.974
Steele, Bristol	1	1	0	0	0	0	1.000	Pena, Buffalo	128	768	120	26	14	10	.972
Callahan, West Haven	30	133	21	2	1	7	.987	Bevington, Holyoke	69	333	42	11	3	6	.972
GEDMAN, Bristol	90	497	58	11	6	21	.981	Kolarek, Waterbury	17	88	10	3	1	2	.970
Virgil, Reading	104	532	64	12	10	15	.980	Nowakowski, Water	10	49	8	2	1	1	.966
Meyer, Waterbury	117	540	86	14	9	33	.978	Torres, Buffalo	12	58	3	3	0	3	.953
Espino, West Haven	91	509	57	13	4	12	.978	Duran, Holyoke	7	11	3	2	0	2	.875
Foley, Holyoke	69	338	58	9	3	9	.978								

PITCHERS

Player and Club	G.	PO.	A.	E.	DP.	Pct.	Player and Club	G.	PO.	A.	E.	DP.	Pct.
QUINONES, Holyoke	40	8	24	0	2	1.000	R. Moore, Waterbury	17	3	24	1	1	.964
Hinds, Holyoke	20	10	20	0	2	1.000	Hernaiz, Reading	20	17	10	1	2	.964
Cliburn, Buffalo	15	9	20	0	2	1.000	Driver, Holyoke*	38	7	17	1	1	.960
Stephenson, Bristol	23	9	16	0	2	1.000	Led Duke, West Haven	46	8	13	1	0	.955
Lysgaard, West Haven	11	9	12	0	1	1.000	Denman, Bristol	28	24	37	3	5	.953
Faust, Bristol	26	10	11	0	1	1.000	Gelinas, Buffalo	13	8	11	1	0	.950
Lewis, West Haven*	30	4	17	0	1	1.000	Hurst, Bristol*	16	2	17	1	0	.950
Olsen, Holyoke	13	4	16	0	0	1.000	Fowler, Reading	19	4	15	1	0	.950
Wyszynski, Waterbury	31	5	12	0	3	1.000	Boyce, Holyoke*	26	7	29	2	1	.947
Weismiller, Buffalo	38	6	10	0	0	1.000	Filer, West Haven	24	21	30	3	1	.944
Speck, Reading	9	7	8	0	2	1.000	Smithson, Bristol	48	10	24	2	4	.944
Mersch, West Haven	16	8	7	0	0	1.000	Righetti, West Haven*	11	3	14	1	0	.944
Bradley, Waterbury	5	1	12	0	1	1.000	Lollar, West Haven*	22	7	26	2	1	.943
Wiltbank, Buffalo	11	3	10	0	1	1.000	King, Bristol	25	12	21	2	1	.943
Ladd, Bristol	18	2	9	0	0	1.000	Long, Buffalo	44	4	12	1	1	.941
Cochran, West Haven	3	2	8	0	0	1.000	Walk, Reading	24	15	31	3	0	.939
Cyburt, Buffalo*	5	2	7	0	0	1.000	Galante, Buffalo	16	7	8	1	2	.938
Retzer, Waterbury	16	3	6	0	1	1.000	Reed, Reading	45	5	10	1	1	.938
Harris, Bri-Wat	25	4	5	0	0	1.000	Breining, Buffalo	12	7	6	1	0	.929
Cort, Holyoke	10	5	3	0	0	1.000	Arias, Buffalo	24	11	27	3	5	.927
Polinsky, West Haven	11	2	6	0	0	1.000	Reed, Holyoke	46	7	17	2	0	.923
Clapham, Waterbury	3	1	4	0	0	1.000	Poole, Bristol*	21	2	10	1	2	.923
Hart, Reading	2	0	4	0	0	1.000	Beard, Waterbury	25	9	24	3	2	.917
Bailey, Holyoke	5	1	3	0	1	1.000	Cooper, West Haven	28	4	7	1	1	.917
Valley, Buffalo*	10	0	4	0	0	1.000	Evans, Buffalo	28	3	17	2	1	.909
Landreth, Holyoke	5	0	3	0	0	1.000	Swift, Holyoke	29	8	12	2	1	.909
Brusstar, Reading	1	0	2	0	0	1.000	Rautzhan, Holyoke*	11	5	13	2	1	.900
Johnston, Buffalo	2	0	2	0	0	1.000	Welborn, Reading	18	8	10	2	2	.900
Lefebvre, West Haven	2	1	1	0	1	1.000	DeBarr, Waterbury*	22	6	12	2	1	.900
Alcala, Buffalo	7	2	0	0	0	1.000	McGaffigan, West Haven	23	11	15	3	0	.897
Alburtis, Bristol	1	0	1	0	0	1.000	Tronerud, Waterbury	21	13	12	3	2	.893
Anderson, Reading	1	0	1	0	0	1.000	Thomason, Reading	18	10	6	2	1	.889
Griffin, Buffalo	1	0	1	0	0	1.000	Abreu, Reading*	9	2	6	1	1	.889
Noles, Reading	1	0	1	0	0	1.000	Cook, Holyoke	26	13	22	5	0	.875
Burdette, West Haven*	4	1	0	0	0	1.000	Rock, Buffalo	9	3	4	1	0	.875
Munninghoff, Reading	26	26	44	1	5	.986	Manos, Reading	12	3	4	1	0	.875
MacWhorter, Bristol	37	17	23	1	2	.976	Softy, West Haven	14	3	4	1	0	.875
Parks, Bristol	11	7	30	1	0	.974	Taylor, West Haven	10	4	9	2	1	.867
Groover, Waterbury*	35	12	23	1	0	.972	Smith, Buffalo	13	7	17	4	2	.857
Camper, Reading	22	17	14	1	1	.969	Atherton, Waterbury	4	2	4	1	0	.857
Green, Waterbury	13	9	21	1	0	.968	Griffin, West Haven	17	8	20	6	1	.824
Dravecky, Buffalo*	35	6	24	1	2	.968	Martinez, Buffalo	20	3	11	3	0	.824

PITCHERS—Continued

Player and Club	G.	PO.	A.	E.	DP.	Pct.
Birrell, Bristol*	17	2	7	2	0	.818
Braun, Waterbury	20	3	6	2	0	.818
Ruling, Reading	15	3	12	4	0	.789
Conroy, Waterbury*	25	2	16	5	1	.783

Player and Club	G.	PO.	A.	E.	DP.	Pct.
Baum, Bristol	14	2	8	3	0	.769
Shiera, Reading*	10	0	3	1	1	.750
Carroll, Holyoke*	25	0	3	4	1	.429
Riggar, Holyoke*	3	1	0	4	1	.200

Curry, Rea, Duncan, Hol and Ellison appeared as designated hitters and/or pinch-hitters only.

CLUB PITCHING

Club	G.	CG.	ShO.	Sv.	IP.	H.	R.	ER.	HR.	BB.	Int. BB.	HB.	SO.	WP.	Bk.	ERA.
Reading	138	54	10	21	1154	1088	545	446	80	487	36	38	671	47	3	3.48
West Haven	139	41	10	24	1174	1116	578	484	109	427	22	25	755	60	5	3.71
Bristol	139	41	5	27	1166	1141	612	505	96	552	41	56	750	64	6	3.90
Waterbury	140	58	4	9	1160	1252	720	570	92	543	23	32	624	82	7	4.42
Holyoke	139	33	7	22	1147	1176	692	576	104	550	9	36	678	93	7	4.52
Buffalo	139	30	5	28	1185	1323	777	621	139	599	15	36	774	81	3	4.72

PITCHERS' RECORDS

(Leading Qualifiers for Earned-Run Average Leadership—112 or More Innings)

*Throws lefthanded.

Pitcher—Club	G.	GS.	CG.	ShO.	W.	L.	Sv.	Pct.	IP.	H.	R.	ER.	HR.	BB.	Int. BB.	HB.	SO.	WP.	ERA.
Walk, Reading	24	24	11	1	12	7	0	.632	185	156	62	46	11	77	4	10	135	9	2.24
Griffin, West Haven	17	17	5	1	7	6	0	.533	125	120	53	41	9	26	0	3	66	1	2.95
Ruling, Reading	15	15	7	2	8	4	0	.667	112	91	41	37	2	51	3	9	78	8	2.97
Beard, Waterbury	25	24	20	0	10	14	0	.417	191	192	87	64	14	63	9	2	111	7	3.02
MacWhorter, Bristol	37	17	7	1	11	10	4	.524	166	165	76	57	2	72	8	17	101	6	3.09
Lollar, West Haven*	22	16	3	0	8	5	0	.615	119	122	55	42	12	36	3	1	60	2	3.18
Lewis, West Haven*	30	14	3	1	11	6	3	.647	118	110	54	44	10	42	2	2	67	9	3.36
Quinones, Holyoke	40	12	4	1	10	8	5	.556	136	111	60	53	9	70	2	4	94	6	3.51
Hurst, Bristol*	16	15	8	1	9	4	0	.692	113	108	56	45	13	49	4	3	91	2	3.58
Filer, West Haven	24	23	9	1	12	8	0	.600	154	132	73	62	15	53	2	7	80	5	3.62

Departmental Leaders: G—Smithson, 48; GS—Munninghoff, 26; CG—Beard, 20; ShO—Denman, 3; W—Denman, Munninghoff, 14; L—Beard, Conroy, 14; Sv—Led Duke, 14; Pct.—J. Reed, .733; IP—Beard, 191; H—Denman, 194; R—Cook, 108; ER—Cook, 94; HR—Cook, 24; BB—Conroy, 119; IBB—Beard, Cooper, J. Reed, 9; HB—MacWhorter, 17; SO—Walk, 135; WP—Conroy, 22.

(All Pitchers—Listed Alphabetically)

Pitcher—Club	G.	GS.	CG.	ShO.	W.	L.	Sv.	Pct.	IP.	H.	R.	ER.	HR.	BB.	Int. BB.	HB.	SO.	WP.	ERA.
Abreu, Reading*	9	0	0	0	1	1	0	.500	18	15	8	8	1	11	1	2	9	3	4.00
Alburtis, Bristol	1	0	0	0	0	0	0	.000	2	2	1	1	0	2	0	0	0	0	4.50
Alcala, Buffalo	7	0	0	0	0	0	1	.000	22	24	20	15	3	11	1	4	16	2	6.14
Anderson, Reading	1	1	0	0	0	1	0	.000	2	6	8	7	2	4	0	0	0	0	31.50
Arias, Buffalo	24	23	4	0	7	7	0	.500	138	170	104	81	23	53	2	4	65	9	5.28
Atherton, Waterbury	4	4	0	0	0	3	0	.000	21	28	23	13	2	13	2	1	11	0	5.57
Bailey, Holyoke	5	0	0	0	0	0	1	.000	12	14	8	4	1	3	0	0	9	0	3.00
Baum, Bristol	14	12	2	0	2	4	0	.333	65	61	50	43	12	53	1	7	53	8	5.95
Beard, Waterbury	25	24	20	0	10	14	0	.417	191	192	87	64	14	63	9	2	111	7	3.02
Birrell, Bristol*	17	3	0	0	1	1	1	.500	35	40	24	14	2	24	1	3	33	4	3.60
Boyce, Holyoke*	26	16	4	1	7	7	2	.500	118	130	77	64	9	57	1	5	62	12	4.88
Bradley, Waterbury	5	5	3	1	2	2	0	.500	45	36	11	10	2	13	0	0	8	0	2.00
Braun, Waterbury	20	0	0	0	2	3	0	.400	33	45	20	15	1	11	2	0	24	5	4.09
Breining, Buffalo	12	12	3	2	5	4	0	.556	82	77	39	24	4	41	0	1	73	5	2.63
Brusstar, Reading	1	0	0	0	0	1	0	.000	2	1	0	0	0	0	0	1	0	0	0.00
Burdette, West Haven*	4	3	0	0	1	1	0	.500	18	24	10	10	1	7	0	0	9	2	5.00
Camper, Reading	22	21	6	0	8	7	1	.533	129	139	64	53	11	32	1	6	68	3	3.70
Carroll, Holyoke*	26	0	0	0	2	3	5	.400	48	40	25	23	4	31	1	1	45	8	4.31
Clapham, Waterbury	3	2	2	0	0	2	0	.000	16	16	9	8	0	13	0	1	5	2	4.50
Cliburn, Buffalo	15	15	7	0	6	6	0	.500	103	110	50	37	5	43	1	3	62	6	3.23
Cochran, West Haven	3	3	0	0	2	1	0	.667	25	17	7	6	1	5	0	1	16	1	2.16
Conroy, Waterbury*	25	25	4	1	7	14	0	.333	138	115	95	80	6	119	0	12	106	22	5.22
Cook, Holyoke	26	24	5	0	4	11	0	.267	150	161	108	94	24	81	0	2	98	13	5.64
Cooper, West Haven	28	0	0	0	6	4	6	.600	54	49	31	26	6	30	9	0	44	8	4.33
Cort, Holyoke	10	7	3	0	3	4	0	.429	47	56	31	27	7	9	0	0	31	3	5.17
Cyburt, Buffalo*	5	4	1	1	1	2	0	.333	18	32	19	18	7	10	0	0	12	0	9.00
DeBarr, Waterbury*	22	7	2	0	2	8	0	.200	68	91	52	44	4	29	0	3	34	5	5.29
Denman, Bristol	28	25	12	3	14	10	0	.583	188	194	88	77	14	54	6	4	97	5	3.69
Dravecky, Buffalo*	35	13	1	1	6	7	2	.462	114	125	71	54	11	59	0	4	81	8	4.26
Driver, Holyoke*	38	10	4	1	4	8	3	.333	102	129	80	67	13	46	2	6	49	7	5.91
Evans, Buffalo	28	8	2	1	7	9	2	.438	109	115	64	55	10	58	2	2	76	8	4.54
Faust, Bristol	26	1	0	0	3	1	2	.750	64	70	23	21	5	17	3	2	29	2	2.95
Filer, West Haven	24	23	9	1	12	8	0	.600	154	132	73	62	15	53	2	7	80	5	3.62
Fournier, Waterbury	1	0	0	0	0	0	0	.000	1	4	3	3	0	0	0	1	0	0	27.00

Pitcher–Club	G.	GS.	CG.	ShO.	W.	L.	Sv.	Pct.	IP.	H.	R.	ER.	HR.	BB.	Int. BB.	HB.	SO.	WP.	ERA.
Fowler, Reading	19	0	0	0	3	5	5	.375	48	31	13	8	3	17	5	0	24	1	1.50
Galante, Buffalo	16	13	1	0	5	3	0	.625	71	92	50	38	7	32	2	3	53	4	4.82
Gelinas, Buffalo	13	13	4	0	4	7	0	.364	64	67	52	41	3	54	0	2	29	4	5.77
Green, Waterbury	13	13	5	0	3	7	0	.300	92	112	52	39	7	19	0	2	40	1	3.82
Griffin, Buffalo	1	0	0	0	0	0	0	.000	4	2	2	2	2	0	0	0	3	0	4.50
Griffin, West Haven	17	17	7	2	8	7	0	.533	125	120	53	41	9	26	0	3	66	1	2.95
Groover, Waterbury*	35	20	11	0	9	13	2	.409	165	181	106	81	15	70	4	5	85	6	4.42
Harris, 2 Bri-23 Wat	25	2	1	1	2	4	4'	.333	44	41	23	15	4	15	3	3	29	1	3.07
Hart, Reading	2	2	1	0	0	1	0	.000	14	11	7	6	3	3	0	0	6	0	3.86
Hernaiz, Reading	20	10	4	1	6	3	0	.667	93	87	41	38	9	27	1	1	50	2	3.68
Hinds, Holyoke	20	19	5	2	8	8	0	.500	123	134	70	59	12	62	0	5	52	10	4.32
Hurst, Bristol*	16	15	8	1	9	4	0	.692	113	108	56	45	13	49	4	3	91	2	3.58
Johnston, Buffalo	2	0	0	0	0	1	0	.000	7	8	6	3	1	6	0	1	4	0	3.86
King, Bristol	25	24	2	0	7	11	0	.389	143	122	81	71	10	111	4	1	110	4	4.47
Ladd, Bristol	18	0	0	0	3	1	9	.750	29	11	2	2	1	8	1	2	26	3	0.62
Landreth, Holyoke	5	5	1	0	0	3	0	.000	25	29	16	16	3	7	0	2	12	1	5.76
Led Duke, West Haven	46	0	0	0	8	4	14	.667	93	89	37	33	8	26	2	3	63	3	3.19
Lefebvre, West Haven	2	0	0	0	0	0	0	.000	5	5	2	2	0	1	0	0	4	2	3.60
Lewis, West Haven*	34	14	3	1	11	6	3	.647	118	110	54	44	10	42	2	2	67	9	3.36
Lollar, West Haven*	22	16	3	0	8	5	0	.615	119	122	55	42	12	36	3	1	60	2	3.18
Long, Buffalo	44	0	0	0	4	10	10	.286	92	98	52	35	10	54	4	3	73	5	3.42
Lysgaard, West Haven	11	9	2	1	3	6	0	.333	62	63	40	40	7	21	1	2	39	4	5.81
MacWhorter, Bristol	37	17	7	1	11	10	4	.524	166	165	76	57	2	72	8	17	101	6	3.09
Manos, Reading	12	0	0	0	1	4	5	.200	31	33	9	9	2	3	1	0	20	1	2.61
Martinez, Buffalo	20	6	0	0	5	3	1	.625	75	76	41	39	11	32	0	3	58	7	4.68
McGaffigan, West Haven.	23	23	8	2	10	6	0	.625	144	136	75	61	13	54	2	1	113	11	3.81
Mersch, West Haven	16	2	1	0	2	2	0	.500	38	48	32	29	9	15	0	0	25	1	6.87
R. Moore, Waterbury	17	17	3	0	5	7	0	.417	85	86	64	56	8	69	0	1	42	13	5.93
Munninghoff, Reading	26	26	15	2	14	9	0	.609	188	172	94	78	9	94	6	2	87	11	3.73
Noles, Reading	1	1	1	0	0	1	0	.000	9	7	5	4	1	4	0	2	2	0	4.00
Olsen, Holyoke	13	12	3	0	9	2	0	.818	83	72	32	23	6	35	0	2	61	6	2.49
Ongarato, Bristol	1	0	0	0	0	0	0	.000	1	1	0	0	0	0	0	0	1	0	0.00
Parks, Bristol	11	11	4	0	6	4	0	.600	84	72	37	29	8	34	2	4	37	5	3.11
Polinsky, West Haven	11	0	0	0	0	1	1	.000	22	29	14	12	3	13	1	2	17	2	4.91
Poole, Bristol*	21	6	0	0	4	1	0	.800	52	60	39	34	6	26	2	0	32	3	5.88
Quinones, Holyoke	40	12	4	1	10	8	5	.556	136	111	60	53	9	70	2	4	94	6	3.51
Rautzhan, Holyoke*	11	11	2	0	6	4	0	.600	73	56	25	25	1	31	1	1	41	3	3.08
Reed, Reading	45	0	0	0	11	4	9	.733	80	67	25	17	3	28	9	0	37	0	1.91
Reed, Holyoke	46	1	1	0	7	5	5	.583	94	77	48	37	5	43	2	1	56	10	3.54
Retzer, Waterbury	16	4	2	1	1	3	0	.250	49	53	34	27	8	29	1	1	31	6	4.96
Riggar, Holyoke*	3	3	0	0	0	3	0	.000	18	13	15	9	0	14	0	0	9	1	4.50
Righetti, West Haven*	11	11	3	0	4	3	0	.571	69	45	23	15	3	45	0	1	78	5	1.96
Rock, Buffalo	9	8	1	0	5	1	0	.833	48	61	36	32	8	24	0	0	22	5	6.00
Ruling, Reading	15	15	7	2	8	4	0	.667	112	91	41	37	2	51	3	9	78	8	2.97
Shiera, Reading*	10	0	0	0	1	0	1	0.000	22	19	16	12	1	15	3	2	11	0	4.91
Smith, Buffalo	13	13	6	0	9	0	0	1.000	94	94	54	46	11	44	0	3	57	1	4.40
Smithson, Bristol	48	13	2	0	8	12	11	.400	132	128	82	69	14	53	5	9	89	16	4.70
Softy, West Haven	14	8	1	0	4	1	0	.800	68	70	42	33	5	29	0	1	35	1	4.37
Speck, Reading	9	5	0	0	3	5	0	.375	56	60	33	27	8	21	0	1	39	2	4.34
Stephenson, Bristol	23	12	4	0	5	7	0	.417	93	107	53	42	9	47	2	0	48	6	4.06
Swift, Holyoke	29	19	1	0	3	10	1	.231	118	144	90	76	10	61	0	7	59	13	5.80
Taylor, West Haven	10	10	1	0	4	1	0	.800	60	57	30	28	7	24	0	1	39	3	4.20
Thomason, Reading	18	11	1	0	6	2	0	.750	85	100	50	34	5	25	2	0	39	6	3.60
Tronerud, Waterbury	21	17	5	0	3	8	1	.273	117	164	93	79	9	47	2	0	42	7	6.08
Valley, Buffalo*	10	0	0	0	2	0	1	1.000	25	17	6	6	1	9	1	0	19	0	2.16
Walk, Reading	24	24	11	1	12	7	0	.632	185	156	62	46	11	77	4	10	135	7	2.24
Weismiller, Buffalo	38	0	0	0	5	1	11	.833	75	85	58	47	12	28	2	0	46	5	5.64
Welborn, Reading	18	18	3	1	3	7	0	.300	80	93	70	63	9	75	0	3	65	1	7.09
Wiltbank, Buffalo	11	11	0	0	1	3	0	.143	43	70	53	48	10	41	0	3	22	12	10.05
Wyszynski, Waterbury	31	0	0	0	3	3	2	.500	95	88	48	41	12	35	3	2	63	6	3.88

BALKS—MacWhorter, Quinones, 3 each; Beard, Boyce, Conroy, McGaffigan, Rock, 2 each; Birrell, Bradley, Braun, Gelinas, Griffin, Groover, Hinds, Lollar, Lysgaard, Olsen, Ongarato, Poole, Ruling, Shiera, Walk.

COMBINATION SHUTOUTS—Swift-Quinones, Hinds-Driver, Holyoke; Welborn-Fowler, Hernaiz-Reed, Camper-Brusstar, Reading; Righetti-Cooper, McGaffigan-Cooper, Lollar-Mersch-Cooper, West Haven.

NO-HIT GAMES—None.

Southern League

CLASS AA

Leading Batter
JOE CHARBONEAU
Chattanooga

League President
BILLY HITCHCOCK

Leading Pitcher
SCOTT BROWN
Nashville

CHAMPIONSHIP WINNERS IN PREVIOUS YEARS

1904–Macon 598	1930–Greenville* 620	1957–Augusta 636
1905–Macon 625	Macon 643	Charlotte (2nd)† 562
1906–Savannah 637	1931-35–Did not operate.	1958–Augusta 550
1907–Charleston 620	1936–Jacksonville..............652	Macon (3rd)† 500
1908–Jacksonville.............694	Columbus* 650	1959–Knoxville..................557
1909–Chattanooga*............738	1937–Columbus 572	Gastonia (4th)† 504
Augusta 702	Savannah (3rd)† 565	1960–Columbia 597
1910–Columbus 588	1938–Savannah 574	Savannah (3rd)† 561
1911–Columbus* 681	Macon (2nd)† 570	1961–Asheville..................635
Columbia 710	1939–Columbus 601	1962–Savannah 662
1912–Jacksonville*............679	Augusta (2nd)† 597	Macon (3rd)† 576
Columbus 632	1940–Savannah 627	1963–Augusta* 661
1913–Savannah 754	Columbus (2nd)† 583	Lynchburg 662
Savannah 593	1941–Macon 643	1964–Lynchburg 579
1914–Savannah* 667	Columbia (2nd)† 636	1965–Columbus 572
Albany 650	1942–Charleston 620	1966–Mobile 629
1915–Macon 588	Macon (2nd)† 585	1967–Birmingham 604
Columbus* 686	1943-45–Did not operate.	1968–Asheville..................614
1916–Augusta* 617	1946–Columbus 568	1969–Charlotte 579
Columbia 631	Augusta (4th)† 547	1970–Columbus 569
1917–Charleston 741	1947–Columbus 575	1971–Did not operate as league–
Columbia* 667	Savannah (2nd)† 563	clubs were members of Dixie Asso-
1918–Did not operate.	1948–Charleston 572	ciation.
1919–Columbia 585	Greenville (3rd)† 549	1972–Asheville..................583
1920–Columbia 633	1949–Macon‡ 623	Montgomery§ 561
1921–Columbia 642	1950–Macon‡ 588	1973–Montgomery§ 580
1922–Charleston 625	1951–Montgomery 607	Jacksonville.................559
1923–Charlotte* 653	1952–Columbia 649	1974–Jacksonville..............565
Macon 580	Montgomery (3rd)† 558	Knoxville§....................533
1924–Augusta 612	1953–Jacksonville..............679	1975–Orlando 587
1925–Spartanburg.............620	Savannah (2nd)† 571	Montgomery§ 545
1926–Greenville 662	1954–Jacksonville..............593	1976–Montgomery x 591
1927–Greenville 622	Savannah (2nd)† 571	Orlando 540
1928–Asheville..................664	1955–Columbia 636	1977–Montgomery x 628
1929–Asheville..................605	Augusta (3rd)† 543	Jacksonville.................522
Knoxville* 634	1956–Jacksonville‡...........621	1978–Knoxville x 611
		Savannah 500

*Won split-season playoff. †Won four-club playoff. ‡Won championship and four-club playoff. §League was divided into Eastern and Western divisions; won playoff. xLeague was divided into Eastern and Western divisions and played split-season. Playoff winner.

STANDING OF CLUBS AT CLOSE OF FIRST HALF, JUNE 24

EASTERN DIVISION

Club	W.	L.	T.	Pct.	G.B.
Charlotte (Orioles)	41	25	1	.621	......
Columbus (Astros)	39	27	0	.591	2
Savannah (Braves)	28	33	1	.459	10½
Orlando (Twins)	31	39	0	.443	12
Jacksonville (Royals)	27	37	0	.422	13

WESTERN DIVISION

Club	W.	L.	T.	Pct.	G.B.
Memphis** (Expos)	36	34	0	.514	......
Montgomery** (Tigers)	36	34	0	.514	......
Nashville (Reds)	35	34	0	.507	½
Chattanooga (Indians)	32	35	0	.478	2½
Knoxville (White Sox)	30	37	0	.448	4½

STANDING OF CLUBS AT CLOSE OF SECOND HALF, SEPTEMBER 2

EASTERN DIVISION

Club	W.	L.	T.	Pct.	G.B.
Columbus (Astros)	45	32	0	.584	......
Jacksonville (Royals)	42	35	2	.545	3
Charlotte (Orioles)	32	44	0	.421	12½
Orlando (Twins)	29	42	0	.408	13
Savannah (Braves)	32	50	1	.390	15½

WESTERN DIVISION

Club	W.	L.	T.	Pct.	G.B.
Nashville (Reds)	48	27	1	.640	......
Memphis (Expos)	46	28	0	.622	1½
Chattanooga (Indians)	43	34	0	.558	6
Knoxville (White Sox)	35	39	0	.473	12½
Montgomery (Tigers)	26	47	0	.356	21

**Memphis and Montgomery finished first half of split season with identical won and lost records. Memphis defeated Montgomery in one game playoff July 18 for first half Western Division Championship. League President ruled that neither a win or loss shall be credited to either team. However, all individual and club batting, fielding and pitching statistics are included in final statistics.

COMPOSITE STANDING OF CLUBS AT CLOSE OF SEASON, SEPTEMBER 2

WESTERN DIVISION

Club	Nash.	Mem.	Chat.	Knx.	Mon.	Col.	Char.	Jax.	Orl.	Sav.	W.	L.	T.	Pct.	G.B.
Nashville (Reds)	...	8	10	7	10	8	11	8	10	11	83	61	1	.576	......
Memphis (Expos)	8	...	8	9	9	9	6	10	13	10	82	62	0	.569	1
Chattanooga (Indians)	6	8	...	9	9	9	8	9	10	7	75	69	0	.521	8
Knoxville (White Sox)	9	7	7	...	8	5	8	6	7	8	65	76	0	.461	16½
Montgomery (Tigers)	6	7	7	8	...	6	7	6	8	7	62	81	0	.434	20½

EASTERN DIVISION

Club	Nash.	Mem.	Chat.	Knx.	Mon.	Col.	Char.	Jax.	Orl.	Sav.	W.	L.	T.	Pct.	G.B.
Columbus (Astros)	8	7	7	11	10	...	8	11	11	11	84	59	0	.587	......
Charlotte (Orioles)	5	10	8	8	9	7	...	9	7	10	73	69	1	.514	10½
Jacksonville (Royals)	8	6	7	9	10	5	6	...	9	9	69	72	2	.489	14
Orlando (Twins)	6	3	6	7	7	5	9	7	...	10	60	81	0	.426	23
Savannah (Braves)	5	6	9	8	9	5	6	6	6	...	60	83	2	.420	24

Major league affiliations in parentheses.

Playoffs—Columbus, second half leader, defeated Charlotte, first half leader, two games to none for Eastern Division championship. Nashville, second half leader, defeated Memphis, first half leader, two games to one for Western Division championship. Nashville (Western Division Champion) defeated Columbus (Eastern Division Champion), three games to one for League Championship.

Regular-Season Attendance—Charlotte, 122,336; Chattanooga, 107,780; Columbus, 108,076; Jacksonville, 114,546; Knoxville, 62,876; Memphis, 226,832; Montgomery, 98,487; Nashville, 515,482; Orlando, 41,021; Savannah, 85,001. Total, 1,482,437. Playoff, 28,624. All-star game, 6,727.

Managers—Charlotte, Jimmy Williams; Chattanooga, Woody Smith; Columbus, Jim Johnson; Jacksonville, Joe Jones; Knoxville, Gordon Lund; Memphis, Billy Gardner; Montgomery, Denny Sommers; Nashville, George Scherger; Orlando, Roy McMillan; Savannah, Eddie Haas.

All-Star Team—1B—Logan, Charlotte; 2B—Raines, Memphis; 3B—Naehring, Knoxville; SS—Bonner, Charlotte; OF—Charboneau, Charlotte; Heep, Columbus; Walker, Nashville; C—Knicely, Columbus; DH—Hostetler, Memphis; Utility—Householder, Nashville; Castillo, Montgomery; P—Chamberlain, Jacksonville; Combe, Nashville; Robbins, Montgomery; Manager—Johnson, Columbus.

(Compiled by Howe News Bureau, Chicago, Ill.)

CLUB BATTING

Club	G.	AB.	R.	OR.	H.	TB.	2B.	3B.	HR.	RBI.	SH.	SF.	BB.	Int. BB.	HP.	SO.	SB.	CS.	LOB.	Pct.
Columbus	143	4625	702	547	1280	1987	223	35	138	648	56	45	433	38	36	554	73	40	982	.277
Knoxville	141	4391	620	671	1205	1693	191	33	77	544	43	45	503	21	39	749	133	64	989	.274
Chattanooga	144	4564	698	704	1234	1839	203	21	120	625	55	38	574	32	23	725	130	49	989	.270
Jacksonville	143	4499	626	609	1210	1668	191	21	75	569	67	42	633	31	24	642	192	55	1059	.269
Nashville	145	4588	624	563	1207	1731	188	60	72	556	83	44	561	48	35	655	141	43	1054	.263
Memphis	145	4726	716	617	1235	1906	204	58	117	646	38	37	645	34	29	833	114	47	1089	.261
Montgomery	144	4554	581	663	1165	1630	191	20	78	504	64	37	593	31	46	586	126	55	1092	.256
Charlotte	143	4587	637	622	1167	1735	207	26	103	576	34	36	509	24	26	808	158	62	952	.254
Orlando	141	4421	580	684	1108	1635	193	35	88	525	64	39	541	18	32	695	69	29	1000	.251
Savannah	145	4615	597	701	1154	1663	176	30	91	532	37	36	592	29	33	823	113	46	1078	.250

INDIVIDUAL BATTING
(Leading Qualifiers for Batting Championship—389 or More Plate Appearances)

*Bats lefthanded.   †Switch-hitter.

Player and Club	G.	AB.	R.	H.	TB.	2B.	3B.	HR.	RBI.	SH.	SF.	BB.	HP.	SO.	SB.	CS.	Pct.
Charboneau, Joseph, Chattanooga .	109	372	70	131	222	24	2	21	78	3	4	47	1	49	6	1	.352
Heep, Daniel, Columbus*	138	523	103	171	274	30	5	21	84	2	4	49	3	32	7	3	.327
Sutherland, Leonardo, Knoxville* ..	124	452	65	144	175	14	7	1	38	6	1	37	2	61	30	8	.319
Walker, Duane, Nashville*	143	545	97	165	250	28	15	9	57	3	2	89	2	67	46	10	.303
Webb, Dennis, Jacksonville*	126	438	65	132	141	7	1	0	19	7	2	76	3	36	30	7	.301
Pasillas, J. Andrew, Knoxville	114	386	43	115	162	21	1	8	61	4	3	29	6	49	2	1	.298
Gross, George, Columbus	129	464	75	138	205	29	4	10	76	7	7	40	5	56	15	6	.297
Menees, H. Eugene, Nashville	145	553	84	164	205	18	4	5	54	18	4	46	6	43	6	3	.297
Naehring, Mark, Knoxville	128	402	67	118	168	13	5	9	71	8	4	99	3	75	7	1	.294
Johnson, Anthony, Memphis	141	504	82	147	235	28	9	14	85	0	3	78	3	115	25	6	.292

Departmental Leaders: G—Barnes, Hostetler, Menees, Raines, 145; AB—Porter, 555; R—Raines, 104; H—Heep, 171; TB—Heep, 274; 2B—Wiedenbauer, 31; 3B—Walker, 15; HR—Knicely, 33; RBI—Hostetler, 114; SH—Menees, 18; SF—Stokke, 11; BB—K. Smith, 102; IBB—Hostetler, 13; HP—Bush, 8; SO—Hazewood, 137; SB—Harris, 68; CS—Greene, 19.

(All Players—Listed Alphabetically)

Player and Club	G.	AB.	R.	H.	TB.	2B.	3B.	HR.	RBI.	SH.	SF.	BB.	HP.	SO.	SB.	CS.	Pct.
Adams, W. Craig, Chattanooga	7	19	2	1	4	0	0	1	1	1	0	0	0	7	0	0	.053
Aldrich, Russell, Nashville*	18	14	2	2	5	0	0	1	1	0	0	2	0	2	0	0	.143
Allen, Roderick, Knoxville	86	281	32	75	109	12	2	6	45	0	7	20	1	58	5	2	.267
Alvarez, Jose L., Savannah	29	1	0	0	0	0	0	0	0	0	0	1	0	0	0	0	.000
Armstrong, Michael, Nashville	34	13	2	1	1	0	0	0	0	0	0	1	0	2	0	0	.077
Baldwin, Reginald, Columbus	22	75	8	22	31	3	0	2	12	1	1	3	2	4	0	1	.293
Bando, Christopher, Chattanooga†	21	62	5	15	21	4	1	0	7	0	0	12	0	6	1	0	.242
Barnes, Richard, Knoxville	25	0	1	0	0	0	0	0	0	0	0	0	0	0	0	0	.000
Barnes, William, Nashville	145	500	54	133	196	19	4	12	77	4	7	27	4	64	5	3	.266
Bedrosian, Stephen, Savannah	13	6	0	1	1	0	0	0	0	0	0	0	0	2	0	0	.167
Benson, Steve, Orlando	121	448	67	108	146	15	4	5	38	7	4	53	2	54	20	5	.241
Bonilla, Juan, Chattanooga	138	550	80	150	191	26	0	5	59	5	6	34	2	39	3	5	.273
Bonner, Robert, Charlotte	119	460	55	134	190	29	3	7	67	1	5	20	3	43	3	1	.291
Bozich, Gary, 42 Orl.-39 Mont.	81	234	32	48	61	11	1	0	18	3	3	36	2	40	6	1	.205
Brazell, Ted, Montgomery	59	180	16	40	57	8	0	3	22	1	0	22	2	17	0	1	.222
Brett, Russell, Charlotte	115	409	51	97	143	21	2	7	48	3	3	34	3	111	11	1	.237
Brill, Timothy, Savannah	29	78	4	8	11	0	0	1	2	3	0	13	1	30	0	0	.103
Brown, Darrell, Montgomery	95	384	40	98	131	17	2	4	32	3	6	15	2	24	30	11	.255
Brown, Scott E., Nashville	27	41	2	2	2	0	0	0	2	5	1	2	0	29	0	0	.049
Buffamoyer, John, Charlotte	50	137	11	34	46	9	0	1	8	0	0	21	1	29	0	0	.248
Bush, R. Randall, Orlando*	76	243	33	62	96	12	2	6	34	1	2	50	8	50	1	1	.255
Buszka, John, Chattanooga*	97	257	41	67	85	12	0	2	30	4	4	58	2	25	2	2	.261
Cappuzzello, George, Nashville	44	20	1	2	2	0	0	0	2	1	0	1	0	8	0	0	.100
Castillo, Martin, Montgomery	74	274	47	84	130	17	1	9	47	5	1	30	3	45	1	1	.307
Chamberlain, Craig, Jacksonville	22	2	0	0	0	0	0	0	0	0	0	0	1	0	0	0	.000
Charboneau, Joseph, Chattanooga .	109	372	70	131	222	24	2	21	78	3	4	47	1	49	6	1	.352
Chiti, H. Dominic, Savannah*	25	2	0	0	0	0	0	0	0	0	0	0	0	0	0	0	.000
Christopher, Scott, Charlotte†	38	135	16	30	47	9	1	2	16	0	1	16	0	11	8	2	.222
Cole, Timothy, Savannah*	24	3	0	0	0	0	0	0	0	0	0	0	0	0	0	0	.000
Colzie, Richard, Chattanooga	48	172	36	58	69	11	0	0	19	1	1	23	1	13	15	6	.337
Combe, Geoffrey, Nashville	54	9	0	0	0	0	0	0	0	3	0	0	0	3	0	0	.000
Cooper, Gary N., Savannah†	107	390	49	90	108	8	2	2	32	6	0	62	2	81	19	9	.231
Cornell, Jeffery, Jacksonville	50	0	1	0	0	0	0	0	0	0	0	0	0	0	0	0	.000
Cowley, Joe, Savannah	25	2	0	1	2	1	0	0	0	0	0	0	0	1	0	0	.500
Crowley, Raymond, Memphis*	66	226	57	64	114	13	2	11	43	1	2	63	0	43	2	2	.283
Cypret, Gregory, Columbus	10	13	2	3	3	0	0	0	1	1	0	0	0	1	0	0	.231
Dahl, Gregory, Columbus	41	120	14	25	41	2	1	4	11	3	0	11	2	27	0	1	.208
Dasen, Ted, Montgomery*	133	457	57	118	193	16	1	19	77	2	7	67	3	76	6	4	.258
Dawley, William, Nashville	25	41	5	4	5	1	0	0	1	5	0	4	0	14	0	0	.098
DeLaCruz, Miguelito, Savannah	2	6	1	3	3	0	0	0	2	0	0	1	0	0	0	0	.500
DeLeon, Luis, Chattanooga†	93	288	40	76	100	9	3	3	30	12	2	26	5	40	14	5	.264
Derryberry, Timothy, Charlotte*	56	182	28	44	73	8	0	7	29	0	1	23	3	38	1	0	.242
Douglas, Stephen, Orlando	112	430	54	119	175	21	7	7	43	10	2	23	2	58	4	4	.277
Duncan, Richard, Nashville*	97	268	30	76	100	14	2	2	36	3	6	46	2	25	1	1	.284
Duncan, Taylor, Montgomery	13	38	6	13	21	2	0	2	7	1	2	9	0	7	1	0	.342
Eaton, Tom, Charlotte	105	341	49	94	112	16	1	0	33	6	2	54	3	23	25	13	.276
Elliott, Clayton, Savannah	120	419	59	107	187	26	3	16	74	0	6	57	2	88	3	4	.255
Engle, Ricky, Memphis*	27	8	1	1	1	0	0	0	1	0	0	0	5	0	0	1	.125
Ervin, Todd, Montgomery*	104	343	41	93	112	10	3	1	37	11	2	66	2	21	2	3	.271
Eschen, James, Jacksonville†	115	372	58	108	150	14	2	8	71	1	5	69	1	27	10	4	.290
Estes, Frank, Orlando*	46	166	23	48	59	9	1	0	24	2	2	27	0	17	4	2	.289
Etchandy, Curtis, Knoxville	11	29	2	4	5	1	0	0	1	0	1	3	0	8	1	0	.138
Evans, Godfrey, Memphis	59	181	19	40	50	3	2	1	12	5	1	33	1	30	2	4	.221
Faedo, Leonardo, Orlando	103	336	35	91	119	13	3	3	34	11	2	29	0	22	2	0	.271

Player and Club	G.	AB.	R.	H.	TB.	2B.	3B.	HR.	RBI.	SH.	SF.	BB.	HP.	SO.	SB.	CS.	Pct.
Ferreyra, Raul, Nashville	61	12	1	1	1	0	0	0	0	2	0	2	0	4	0	0	.083
Filkins, Leslie, Montgomery*	109	357	51	99	145	17	1	9	43	2	4	39	4	51	7	4	.277
Flannery, John, Knoxville	124	386	37	85	107	10	0	4	33	1	4	31	1	53	6	4	.220
Followell, Vern, Montgomery†	43	148	11	39	44	5	0	0	19	3	3	24	2	17	3	1	.264
Forbes, Andres, Savannah	22	67	3	13	15	2	0	0	5	1	1	4	0	6	0	1	.194
Fucci, Dominic, Knoxville*	66	194	25	47	65	8	2	2	20	3	1	38	3	45	10	6	.242
Ganger, Robert, Jacksonville	18	1	0	0	0	0	0	0	0	0	0	0	0	0	0	0	.000
Garcia, Daniel, Jacksonville*	136	440	70	127	152	19	3	0	41	9	2	100	3	52	36	8	.289
Gardner, Vassie, Chattanooga	53	186	31	58	89	8	1	7	25	1	0	25	0	37	16	4	.312
Garrison, Venoy, Montgomery	19	67	4	15	17	2	0	0	8	0	1	12	3	9	2	0	.224
Glass, Robert, Montgomery†	42	134	10	35	42	5	1	0	10	3	1	14	0	3	0	0	.261
Goldetsky, Lawrence, Memphis	51	138	20	35	49	6	4	0	15	1	0	19	2	40	3	0	.254
Gonzalez, Jorge, Montgomery	11	34	3	5	5	0	0	0	5	1	0	0	0	8	0	0	.147
Gray, Lorenzo, Knoxville	116	402	68	101	132	12	2	5	32	4	2	60	7	61	22	9	.251
Greene, Steven F., Charlotte†	98	362	63	88	112	12	6	0	27	3	1	64	0	58	49	19	.243
Gross, George, Columbus	129	464	75	138	205	29	4	10	76	7	7	40	5	56	15	6	.297
Gullickson, William, Memphis	16	6	1	1	2	1	0	0	0	1	0	0	0	2	0	0	.167
Gulliver, Glenn, Montgomery*	75	226	45	59	102	15	2	8	30	2	2	76	3	17	5	5	.261
Gustavson, Duane, Jacksonville	52	128	7	30	37	4	0	1	11	2	1	23	1	23	0	2	.234
Hallberg, Lance, Orlando	90	315	45	93	133	13	3	7	44	2	2	37	2	44	4	2	.295
Hamilton, Robert, Nashville*	84	119	17	34	45	6	1	1	15	4	0	23	1	13	1	1	.286
Hammond, Steven, Savannah*	61	218	30	61	86	15	2	2	40	2	2	24	2	16	1	0	.280
Hampton, Raphael, Montgomery	139	495	74	132	190	28	3	8	44	10	2	79	5	69	31	11	.267
Hanley, John, Knoxville	69	233	28	66	85	8	1	3	34	2	4	24	1	54	0	2	.283
Harper, Arvis, Columbus†	23	55	8	12	16	4	0	0	6	2	0	7	0	5	1	1	.218
Harris, LaMart, Jacksonville†	124	445	71	117	139	13	0	3	28	12	1	52	2	61	68	14	.263
Harvey, M. Craig, Chattanooga	5	13	0	3	3	0	0	0	2	0	0	2	0	0	0	0	.231
Haslerig, J. William, Savannah*	130	457	62	127	182	22	3	9	61	0	2	49	2	60	19	7	.278
Hazewood, Drungo, Charlotte	122	398	60	92	170	11	2	21	64	2	3	55	41	37	9	3	.231
Heath, Kelly, Jacksonville	129	422	67	115	168	26	3	7	61	6	5	58	1	52	8	9	.273
Heep, Daniel, Columbus*	138	523	103	171	274	30	5	21	84	2	4	49	3	32	7	3	.327
Heimer, Todd, Chattanooga*	32	0	1	0	0	0	0	0	0	0	0	0	0	0	0	0	.000
Hemm, K. Warren, Memphis*	15	2	0	2	3	1	0	0	0	0	0	0	0	0	0	0	1.000
Herz, Steven, Orlando	82	261	34	64	85	9	0	4	20	6	0	28	5	24	1	1	.245
Hill, Anthony, Knoxville	95	359	54	99	125	20	3	0	23	6	2	23	1	57	29	13	.276
Hill, Elmore, Jacksonville	45	182	19	33	60	3	0	8	20	0	1	15	1	39	0	0	.181
Hogg, David, Jacksonville	109	334	40	84	125	12	1	9	49	6	4	58	2	59	3	0	.251
Holmstedt, Victor, Chattanooga	20	1	0	0	0	0	0	0	0	0	0	0	0	0	0	0	.000
Hostetler, David, Memphis	145	548	77	148	244	28	4	20	114	0	4	70	6	110	2	1	.270
Householder, Paul, Nashville	142	488	93	138	236	24	7	20	95	3	6	84	5	63	21	12	.283
Hubbard, Donald, Chattanooga	28	106	11	20	28	3	1	1	9	1	2	5	0	20	2	3	.189
Hughes, Gregory T., Nashville	38	39	8	4	4	0	0	0	1	4	0	4	1	19	0	0	.103
Hughes, Stephen, Nashville	15	24	1	1	1	0	0	0	0	2	0	2	0	7	0	0	.042
Huppert, David, Charlotte	102	300	37	67	98	12	2	5	37	4	3	46	2	62	0	4	.223
Ingle, Randy, Savannah	18	60	9	17	29	3	0	3	7	0	0	4	1	13	0	0	.283
Isaac, Luis, Chattanooga	39	92	7	21	22	1	0	0	5	0	0	11	0	13	1	0	.228
Jackson, Melvin, Montgomery	113	375	45	84	104	12	4	0	26	10	4	31	0	42	17	2	.224
James, Arthur, Knoxville*	27	97	16	37	53	10	0	2	10	0	0	6	0	11	3	3	.381
Johnson, Anthony, Memphis	141	504	82	147	235	28	9	14	85	0	3	78	3	115	25	6	.292
Johnson, Ronald, Jacksonville	17	61	8	15	27	6	0	2	10	0	1	6	1	9	2	1	.246
Kelly, William, Nashville	33	49	7	7	9	2	0	0	1	6	0	5	0	22	0	0	.143
Kittle, Ron, Knoxville	53	157	28	43	72	9	1	6	26	0	1	12	4	47	0	1	.274
Klimas, Philip, Columbus	122	386	54	98	160	19	2	13	59	3	2	59	4	60	0	1	.254
Knicely, Alan, Columbus	120	422	77	122	239	12	3	33	76	6	1	61	4	77	2	1	.289
Lahti, Jeffrey, Nashville	6	3	0	1	2	1	0	0	1	0	0	0	0	2	0	0	.333
Laskey, William, Jacksonville	15	1	0	0	0	0	0	0	0	0	0	0	0	0	0	0	.000
Laudner, Timothy, Orlando	45	141	17	34	50	7	0	3	20	5	1	19	0	19	0	1	.241
Lea, Charles, Memphis	24	5	0	1	1	0	0	0	1	0	0	1	0	1	0	0	.200
Leach, Terry, Savannah	40	1	0	0	0	0	0	0	0	0	0	0	0	1	0	0	.000
Linares, Rufino, Savannah	53	198	35	65	102	11	1	8	37	0	4	24	3	13	11	3	.328
Logan, H. Daniel, Charlotte*	136	485	83	137	223	19	2	21	79	1	9	64	0	77	0	1	.282
LoGrande, Angelo, Chattanooga	127	439	60	108	190	20	1	20	76	2	1	39	4	128	4	3	.246
Lombardo, Richard, Nashville*	17	1	0	0	0	0	0	0	0	0	0	1	0	0	0	0	.000
Loucks, Scott, Columbus†	9	8	3	1	1	0	0	0	1	1	1	1	0	1	1	0	.125
Lovins, Steven, Memphis	50	2	0	0	0	0	0	0	0	0	0	1	0	2	0	0	.000
Lucas, Mark, Savannah*	2	5	0	1	1	0	0	0	0	0	0	0	0	0	0	0	.200
Lucy, Frank, Montgomery	60	210	22	52	75	6	1	5	22	1	0	9	4	44	0	2	.248
Maher, Mark, Orlando	19	50	3	9	10	1	0	0	5	3	0	9	0	10	0	0	.180
Martinez, Ronald, Montgomery	126	450	54	121	159	20	0	6	43	5	0	47	7	66	17	9	.269
Maxwell, Martyn, Orlando	33	113	12	27	42	9	0	2	18	0	0	7	0	15	1	1	.239
Mayer, Robert, Nashville†	18	29	3	4	5	1	0	0	1	3	0	0	1	7	0	0	.138
McCann, Francis, Jacksonville	127	460	50	128	189	25	3	10	84	8	6	40	3	80	16	5	.278
McManaman, Steven, Orlando	104	372	38	85	142	19	1	12	56	0	3	44	1	122	1	1	.228
McWhirter, Kevin, Orlando	96	341	51	80	137	11	2	14	52	3	2	35	1	49	8	2	.235
Menees, H. Eugene, Nashville	145	553	84	164	205	18	4	5	54	18	4	46	6	43	6	3	.297

Player and Club	G.	AB.	R.	H.	TB.	2B.	3B.	HR.	RBI.	SH.	SF.	BB.	HP.	SO.	SB.	CS.	Pct.
Mesa, Ivan, Knoxville	5	11	0	3	4	1	0	0	2	0	1	1	1	2	0	0	.273
Meyers, Jay Dee, Montgomery	17	44	4	7	8	1	0	0	1	0	0	5	1	16	1	0	.159
Michael, Steven, Memphis*	56	178	19	32	45	6	2	1	16	1	1	19	0	20	1	3	.180
Miller, Mark, Nashville	59	88	5	22	25	3	0	0	5	0	0	16	1	21	0	0	.250
Miller, Michael, Savannah†	97	289	30	68	82	6	1	2	26	4	4	47	2	71	6	4	.235
Milner, Eddie, Nashville*	104	369	70	97	166	12	12	11	51	3	2	48	3	39	35	2	.263
Morley, Michael, Jacksonville†	16	2	0	0	0	0	0	0	0	0	0	0	0	0	0	0	.000
Mullins, Francis, Knoxville	53	164	21	44	63	5	1	4	22	1	2	14	2	26	1	1	.268
Naehring, Mark, Knoxville	128	402	67	118	168	13	5	9	71	8	4	99	3	75	7	1	.294
Nandin, Robert, Montgomery†	17	61	9	12	14	0	1	0	1	1	0	8	0	4	0	0	.197
Nyman, Christopher, Knoxville	86	302	59	93	171	20	2	18	67	0	5	47	4	38	8	7	.308
O'Keeffe, Richard, Nashville*	11	11	0	1	1	0	0	0	0	0	0	0	0	4	0	0	.091
Ondina, Michael, Jacksonville*	35	101	9	22	31	3	0	2	14	1	1	14	0	27	1	1	.218
Pankovits, James, Columbus	92	346	53	91	137	10	3	10	45	6	6	28	0	40	2	3	.263
Parker, Darrell, Jacksonville†	79	282	42	90	140	22	2	8	56	3	4	23	1	31	5	2	.319
Pasillas, J. Andrew, Knoxville..........	114	386	43	115	162	21	1	8	61	4	3	29	6	49	2	1	.298
Perez, Joel, Knoxville	17	56	14	16	25	3	0	2	7	0	0	7	0	10	0	0	.286
Perez, Julio, Memphis*	38	137	19	32	39	4	0	1	18	1	3	21	0	4	1	1	.234
Phillips, K. Anthony, Memphis†	52	156	31	44	61	4	2	3	11	3	1	19	1	13	3	2	.282
Pittman, John, Orlando	114	389	64	91	163	17	5	15	51	3	3	63	2	80	2	0	.234
Pittman, Joseph, Columbus.............	100	382	56	108	140	13	2	5	27	9	0	29	5	36	15	6	.283
Porter, Robert, Savannah*	143	555	80	143	213	19	6	13	49	0	5	64	7	100	11	6	.258
Pratt, Louis, Savannah*	30	2	0	0	0	0	0	0	0	0	0	0	0	1	0	0	.000
Price, Joseph, Nashville	22	33	2	2	4	0	1	0	1	1	0	2	0	13	0	0	.061
Raines, Timothy, Memphis†	145	552	104	160	220	25	10	5	50	2	3	90	3	51	59	12	.290
Rajsich, Gary, Columbus*	66	232	43	68	143	25	4	14	53	1	5	23	3	33	6	6	.293
Ramirez, Rafael, Savannah	113	386	47	80	133	17	3	10	39	5	3	34	1	78	7	0	.207
Ramos, Richard, Memphis	15	7	0	1	1	0	0	0	1	1	0	0	0	1	0	0	.143
Rausch, Albert, Chattanooga	133	464	72	135	194	19	2	12	73	7	4	43	2	52	14	5	.291
Redus, Gary, Nashville	36	109	7	19	23	2	1	0	7	1	1	18	1	27	8	3	.174
Rende, Salvatore, Chattanooga*	71	233	53	75	148	11	1	20	56	1	1	44	2	40	3	0	.322
Rhomberg, Kevin, Chattanooga........	132	440	84	118	178	21	6	9	53	8	4	81	1	93	36	8	.268
Ripken, Calvin, Charlotte	17	61	6	11	22	0	1	3	8	1	0	3	0	13	1	0	.180
Rivera, David, Chattanooga	112	374	41	84	128	14	3	8	42	2	3	27	0	93	10	4	.225
Rooney, Patrick, Memphis	125	458	52	115	191	18	5	16	69	2	3	44	0	118	4	2	.251
Rosario, Simon, Columbus	8	23	3	6	8	2	0	0	2	0	0	1	0	5	0	0	.261
Royster, Willie, Charlotte	2	6	3	3	6	3	0	0	2	0	0	1	0	1	0	0	.500
Santo Domingo, Rafael, Nashville†	108	322	38	101	148	24	7	3	49	5	4	35	6	45	11	2	.314
Schafer, Randall, Memphis	94	327	43	87	164	11	3	20	66	2	2	20	2	66	1	1	.266
Scoras, John, Memphis	121	393	58	92	136	17	6	5	46	6	7	54	3	73	1	4	.234
Seidholz, Donn, Knoxville...............	4	3	0	1	1	0	0	0	0	0	0	0	0	0	0	0	.333
Sherow, Dennis, Memphis	28	111	18	28	33	3	1	0	6	0	0	17	0	17	5	2	.252
Simunic, Douglas, Memphis	64	203	15	42	57	9	0	2	18	4	2	20	2	34	0	1	.207
Smith, Billy L., Columbus	27	2	0	0	0	0	0	0	0	0	0	0	0	1	0	0	.000
Smith, Bryn, Memphis....................	27	10	0	1	1	0	0	0	0	2	0	0	0	5	0	0	.100
Smith, Jackie, Knoxville..................	32	1	0	0	0	0	0	0	0	0	0	0	0	0	0	0	.000
Smith, Jeffrey, Columbus*	99	314	39	84	117	11	2	6	38	1	5	44	0	39	3	1	.268
Smith, Kenneth, Savannah*.............	141	449	71	112	162	12	4	10	51	1	2	102	4	101	18	7	.249
Snitker, Brian, Savannah	75	259	26	66	102	10	1	8	30	2	0	12	0	50	1	1	.255
Sofield, Richard, Orlando*	30	101	9	27	38	4	2	1	13	0	0	22	0	16	6	2	.267
Sohns, Thomas, Nashville*	135	412	36	94	116	6	5	2	35	1	5	39	0	41	7	5	.228
Spence, Sam, Chattanooga	25	1	0	0	0	0	0	0	0	0	0	0	0	0	0	0	.000
Spencer, H. Thomas, Knoxville	78	272	37	69	100	16	3	3	35	3	4	25	0	27	7	3	.254
Stokke, Douglas, Columbus	142	497	71	128	185	21	3	10	69	9	11	23	2	21	2	2	.258
Strom, Brent, Columbus	7	2	0	1	1	0	0	0	0	0	0	0	0	1	0	0	.500
Sutherland, Leonardo, Knoxville* ..	124	452	65	144	175	14	7	1	38	6	1	37	2	61	30	8	.319
Thayer, Scott, Savannah.................	8	26	2	3	6	0	0	1	3	0	2	3	0	7	2	0	.115
Thomas, Vernon, Charlotte	126	450	65	123	191	22	2	14	69	2	3	52	3	93	29	10	.273
Tobias, Grayling, Savannah	81	317	50	79	98	11	4	0	24	3	2	39	1	30	5	4	.249
Tomski, Jeffrey, Chattanooga	105	275	39	64	98	13	0	7	36	5	2	80	2	50	1	1	.233
Torres, A. Raymundo, Knoxville	10	34	6	14	20	2	2	0	4	0	1	6	1	6	1	0	.412
Town, Randall, Nashville	13	15	0	1	1	0	0	0	1	3	0	0	0	5	0	0	.067
Trucks, Phil, Knoxville	61	170	18	31	50	5	1	4	12	5	2	19	2	60	1	3	.182
Twitty, Jeffrey, Jacksonville*	14	1	0	0	0	0	0	0	0	0	0	0	0	0	0	0	.000
Tyson, Terry, Chattanooga	62	220	24	50	69	7	0	4	24	2	4	17	1	19	2	2	.227
Ullger, Scott, Orlando	126	412	66	111	164	21	4	8	50	6	8	69	6	73	7	4	.269
Upshaw, John, Montgomery	57	180	28	37	56	7	0	4	21	3	1	23	4	31	0	0	.206
Van Gorder, David, Nashville	137	461	58	131	178	27	1	6	64	2	6	62	2	66	0	1	.284
Vilorio, Francisco, Orlando	26	94	8	21	27	3	0	1	11	1	2	3	2	10	5	3	.223
Walker, Duane, Nashville*	143	545	97	165	250	28	15	9	57	3	2	89	2	67	46	10	.303
Wallach, Timothy, Memphis	75	257	50	84	162	16	4	18	51	2	3	37	5	53	0	2	.327
Waller, Reginald, Columbus	65	207	25	55	91	11	2	7	24	0	2	21	0	42	6	0	.266
Webb, Dennis, Jacksonville*	126	438	65	132	141	7	1	0	19	7	2	76	3	36	30	7	.301
Wessinger, James, Savannah	83	335	49	100	130	16	1	4	37	4	2	34	6	31	7	2	.299
Westendorf, Philip, Jacksonville	141	472	72	127	184	24	3	9	63	6	7	68	4	100	3	0	.269

Player and Club	G.	AB.	R.	H.	TB.	2B.	3B.	HR.RBI.SH.			SF.	BB.	HP.	SO.	SB.	CS.	Pct.
Westmoreland, Claude, Jack..........	1	3	0	0	0	0	0	0	0	0	0	0	0	2	0	0	.000
Whisenton, Larry, Savannah*	48	166	20	37	52	5	2	2	18	1	2	19	0	33	6	1	.223
Whitfield, Robert, Charlotte	90	304	39	63	84	10	1	3	32	2	2	16	4	54	7	0	.207
Wiedenbauer, Thomas, Columbus..	141	554	68	147	195	31	4	3	64	3	0	33	6	74	12	8	.265
Wieters, Richard, Savannah...........	36	3	1	3	4	1	0	0	1	0	0	0	0	0	0	0	1.000
Wilkinson, Ron, Orlando	22	72	3	12	13	1	0	0	3	4	1	3	0	7	0	0	.167
Willett, Joel, Nashville	8	1	0	0	0	0	0	0	0	0	0	2	0	0	0	0	.000
Williams, Dallas, Charlotte*...........	133	519	68	144	209	25	2	12	52	8	3	38	0	51	15	8	.277
Yarbrough, William, Jacksonville...	111	352	47	82	125	13	3	8	42	6	2	31	1	43	10	2	.233
Yoder, Kris, Savannah	77	235	19	49	53	2	1	0	18	6	1	38	0	41	2	0	.209
Youngbauer, Jeffrey, Charlotte*....	11	38	3	6	9	1	1	0	5	1	0	2	0	7	0	0	.158

The following pitchers had no plate appearances, primarily through use of designated hitters, listed alphabetically by club, games in parentheses.

CHARLOTTE—Bastian, Jose (4); Boddicker, Michael (14); Carey, Brooks (8); Chevez, Antonio (9); George, William (7); Jones, Larry (19); Mayo, Ricky (40); McArthur, Gregory (24); Pensiero, Russell (18); Presley, Billy (42); Rowe, Thomas (28); Schneider, Jeffery (42); Snell, Nathaniel (10); Torrez, Pete (21); Welchel, Donald (13).

CHATTANOOGA—Arnold, John (13); Arp, Ronnie (5); Borchers, Rickey (5); Fuson, Robin (5); Glaser, G. Gordon (41); Hussey, Robert (4); McGough, Thomas (16); Narleski, Steven (39); Nicholson, Carl (22); Ploucher, George (4); Richard, Raymond (16); Teising, John (40); Wilder, Troy (13).

COLUMBUS—Aponte, C. Ricardo (25); Boxberger, Rodney (21); Cajide, Alberto (5); Ladd, Peter (13); Leatherwood, Delrick (28); Leland, Stanley (5); MacDonald, James (10); Meridith, Ronald (26); Miscik, Dennis (13); Morris, Frederick (32); Quealey, Steven (2); Roberge, Bertrand (12); Troedson, Thad (35).

JACKSONVILLE—Casbolt, William (8); Dubee, Richard (18); Grzybek, Benjamin (17); Hamrick, Stephen (20); Hanslovan, Jeffrey (10); Hendricks, Erik (14); Jones, Michael C. (26); Martin, D. Renie (8); Reichenbach, Michael (10); Shattinger, Jeffery (22); Skinner, John (4).

KNOXVILLE—Barnicle, Theodore (20); Burns, R. Britt (20); Dotson, Richard (25); Gutierrez, Guillermo (5); Guzman, Julio (4); Hoyt, Dewey (37); Lukevics, Mitchell (8); Monroe, Lawrence (29); Moran, C. William (10); Murillo, Ramon (21); Patterson, Reginald (4); Platel, Mark (12); Teutsch, Mark (17); Vasquez, Dennis (1); Woods, Ronald (13).

MEMPHIS—Dues, Hal (7); Finlayson, Michael (11); Gingrich, Jeffrey (35); Tenenini, Robert (42); Williams, Richard Anthony (33).

MONTGOMERY—Blair, Theodore (17); Cassetto, David (16); Codiroli, Christopher (8); Corr, Larry (27); Geiger, Burwell (4); Grafton, Garry (34); Holdsworth, Frederick (8); Jackowiak, Jeffrey (3); MacCormack, Frank (6); Martin, John R. (11); Polvi, Michael (27); Robbins, Bruce (13); Rucker, David (28); Shea, Kenneth (12); Smith, Jack (23); Steffen, David (16); Ujdur, Gerald (19); Viefhaus, Stephen (25).

ORLANDO—Alonso, Julio (16); Blake, Robert (17); Brueggemann, Jeffrey (28); Clapham, Mark (17); Dobbs, Gary (2); Gideon, James (7); Havens, Bradley (19); Isaacs, Joe Keith (11); Kinnunen, Michael (17); Lewis, D. Curtis (11); MacPherson, Bruce (10); Mapel, Steven (11); Mertens, Warren (32); Reyes, Jose (7); Sarmiento, Wilfredo (6); Veselic, Robert (28).

SAVANNAH—Graven, Timothy (27); Livingstone, Stuart (13); Lucia, Daniel (11); Pettaway, Felix (6); Shields, W. Michael (27); Wright, Jesse (8).

GRAND SLAM HOME RUNS—Charboneau, Nyman, 2 each. Brazell, Bush, Eschen, Gross, Hampton, Heep, Hogg, Hostetler, Logan, Maxwell, McWhirter, Milner, Ondina, Ramirez, Schafer, J. Smith, Stokke, Tomski, Van Gorder, Walker, Wessinger, Whitfield, Williams, 1 each.

AWARDED FIRST BASE ON INTERFERENCE—Crowley (Snitker); Douglas (Huppert); Householder (Herz); McManaman (Knicely); Perez (Snitker); Porter (Pasillas); Rajsich (Yoder); Trucks (Knicely).

CLUB FIELDING

Club	G.	PO.	A.	E.	DP.	PB.	Pct.	Club	G.	PO.	A.	E.	DP.	PB.	Pct.
Columbus	143	3549	1611	137	145	26	.974	Nashville	145	3675	1520	181	90	9	.966
Charlotte	143	3616	1643	155	161	15	.971	Montgomery	144	3595	1523	189	124	26	.964
Chattanooga	144	3560	1519	153	150	22	.971	Knoxville	141	3393	1383	177	139	13	.964
Memphis	145	3711	1558	161	129	14	.970	Orlando	141	3487	1664	194	164	12	.964
Jacksonville	143	3551	1386	156	116	24	.969	Savannah	145	3613	1582	217	126	20	.960

Triple Plays—None.

INDIVIDUAL FIELDING

*Throw lefthanded.

FIRST BASEMEN

Player and Club	G.	PO.	A.	E.	DP.	Pct.	Player and Club	G.	PO.	A.	E.	DP.	Pct.
Van Gorder, Nashville....	9	55	4	0	4	1.000	Spencer, Knoxville..........	1	5	0	0	1	1.000
Naehring, Knoxville.......	4	38	5	0	2	1.000	Westmoreland, Jacks	1	5	0	0	0	1.000
Garcia, Jacksonville*.....	4	27	0	0	2	1.000	Seidholz, Knoxville.........	3	5	0	0	0	1.000
Whitfield, Charlotte.......	3	24	0	0	4	1.000	Ondina, Jacksonville.......	1	4	0	0	1	1.000
Martinez, Montgomery...	4	21	2	0	2	1.000	Glass, Montgomery	1	4	0	0	0	1.000
Aldrich, Nashville..........	10	17	1	0	1	1.000	Cypret, Columbus...........	1	3	0	0	0	1.000
Brazell, Montgomery	1	13	1	0	2	1.000	Simunic, Memphis..........	1	3	0	0	1	1.000
Estes, Orlando*..............	1	13	0	0	0	1.000	Scoras, Memphis............	1	2	0	0	0	1.000
Johnson, Jacksonville.....	2	7	0	0	0	1.000	Pittman, Columbus	2	2	0	0	1	1.000
Baldwin, Columbus........	1	6	0	0	2	1.000	Wallach, Memphis..........	32	283	20	1	22	.997

FIRST BASEMEN—Continued

Player and Club	G.	PO.	A.	E.	DP.	Pct.
GROSS, Columbus	129	1242	65	6	110	.9954
Smith, Savannah	135	1182	85	7	106	.9945
Nyman, Knoxville	84	695	52	5	78	.993
Logan, Charlotte*	136	1225	81	10	133	.992
Hostetler, Memphis	113	959	55	9	94	.991
Duncan, Nashville	84	641	49	6	34	.991
LoGrande, Chattanooga.	48	409	22	4	49	.991
Buszka, Chattanooga*	39	303	18	3	33	.991
Duncan, Montgomery	13	106	7	1	10	.991
Hanley, Knoxville	23	185	9	2	21	.990
Snitker, Savannah	11	85	1	1	10	.989
Rende, Chattanooga*	65	547	43	7	57	.988
Garrison, Montgomery	19	156	5	2	15	.988

Player and Club	G.	PO.	A.	E.	DP.	Pct.
Westendorf, Jacksonville	141	1119	96	16	98	.987
Dasen, Montgomery	77	643	46	10	64	.986
Santo Domingo, Nash.	60	520	35	9	41	.984
Pittman, Orlando	69	640	39	12	73	.983
Bush, Orlando*	71	653	38	13	73	.982
Lucy, Montgomery	31	244	18	5	14	.981
J. Smith, Columbus	13	93	10	2	12	.981
Gray, Knoxville	25	163	16	4	19	.978
Brett, Charlotte	3	25	2	1	5	.964
Fucci, Knoxville*	5	31	4	2	4	.946
Gulliver, Montgomery	1	14	1	1	1	.938
Thomas, Charlotte	3	25	1	2	5	.929

SECOND BASEMEN

Player and Club	G.	PO.	A.	E.	DP.	Pct.
Vilorio, Orlando	3	6	10	0	2	1.000
Stokke, Columbus	1	3	5	0	2	1.000
Phillips, Memphis	1	5	1	0	1	1.000
Goldetsky, Memphis	3	1	5	0	0	1.000
Westendorf, Jacksonville	1	2	3	0	1	1.000
Santo Domingo, Nash.	3	2	3	0	0	1.000
Heath, Jacksonville	1	1	2	0	1	1.000
Gray, Knoxville	1	1	1	0	1	1.000
Rajsich, Columbus	1	1	0	0	0	1.000
Naehring, Knoxville	1	0	1	0	0	1.000
EATON, Charlotte	103	250	303	5	89	.991
Forbes, Savannah	22	51	50	2	12	.981
Benson, Orlando	91	193	308	10	75	.980
Menees, Nashville	144	311	374	16	60	.977
Pankovits, Columbus	91	226	240	11	68	.977
Flannery, Memphis	58	146	136	7	45	.976
Eschen, Jacksonville	26	57	63	3	11	.976

Player and Club	G.	PO.	A.	E.	DP.	Pct.
Bonilla, Chattanooga	138	332	360	18	104	.975
Pittman, Columbus	55	131	157	8	36	.973
Ingle, Savannah	10	17	19	1	5	.973
Wessinger, Savannah	83	212	227	13	59	.971
Hill, Knoxville	85	185	213	12	52	.971
Bonner, Charlotte	28	54	81	4	20	.971
Raines, Memphis	145	341	413	23	93	.970
Ervin, Montgomery	103	225	264	15	56	.970
Bozich, Orl-Mon	59	138	178	10	53	.969
Jackson, Montgomery	28	68	56	4	13	.969
Miller, Savannah	31	66	83	5	18	.968
Webb, Jacksonville	121	257	261	18	56	.966
Wilkinson, Orlando	9	24	27	2	7	.962
Tyson, Chattanooga	5	9	10	1	4	.950
Rhomberg, Chattanooga	3	3	11	1	2	.933
Greene, Charlotte	16	44	37	6	10	.931

THIRD BASEMEN

Player and Club	G.	PO.	A.	E.	DP.	Pct.
Eschen, Jacksonville	19	18	32	0	5	1.000
Gulliver, Montgomery	5	6	10	0	2	1.000
Bando, Chattanooga	3	3	8	0	0	1.000
Yarbrough, Jacksonville	3	4	6	0	0	1.000
Greene, Charlotte	2	2	6	0	1	1.000
Wilkinson, Orlando	2	1	5	0	0	1.000
Cypret, Columbus	5	2	2	0	0	1.000
Nyman, Knoxville	1	1	2	0	1	1.000
Lucas, Savannah	2	1	1	0	0	1.000
Perez, Memphis	31	24	84	5	8	.956
Nandin, Montgomery	5	6	15	1	3	.955
SCORAS, Memphis	100	89	193	14	24	.953
Whitfield, Charlotte	23	18	56	4	2	.949
McCann, Jacksonville	126	128	227	21	30	.944
Naehring, Knoxville	111	74	207	17	21	.943
Rausch, Chattanooga	79	66	165	14	18	.943
Pittman, Columbus	31	26	69	6	10	.941
Klimas, Columbus	113	102	274	24	22	.940
Jackson, Montgomery	22	18	50	5	7	.932
Ripkin, Charlotte	15	13	26	3	1	.929
Goldetsky, Memphis	10	7	6	1	0	.929
Ullger, Orlando	100	86	200	23	22	.926
Gray, Knoxville	12	9	28	3	2	.925

Player and Club	G.	PO.	A.	E.	DP.	Pct.
Vilorio, Orlando	23	33	40	6	4	.924
Benson, Orlando	8	5	19	2	3	.923
Barnes, Nashville	142	123	291	35	21	.922
Brett, Charlotte	102	72	211	24	24	.922
Castillo, Montgomery	74	70	174	22	16	.917
Elliott, Savannah	120	103	261	34	26	.915
Followell, Montgomery	6	1	9	1	2	.909
Rhomberg, Chattanooga	26	24	69	10	7	.903
Perez, Knoxville	15	11	35	5	4	.902
Maxwell, Orlando	9	7	16	3	3	.885
Sohns, Nashville	8	4	11	2	1	.882
Wallach, Memphis	10	7	15	3	1	.880
Miller, Memphis	12	8	21	4	1	.879
Tyson, Chattanooga	40	34	81	16	6	.878
Thayer, Savannah	8	4	17	4	2	.840
Dasen, Montgomery	14	15	21	7	2	.837
Etchandy, Knoxville	4	2	7	2	1	.818
Ingle, Savannah	4	2	6	2	0	.800
Santo Domingo, Nash.	2	1	3	1	0	.800
Bozich, Orl-Mon	21	11	29	11	4	.784
Bonner, Charlotte	2	4	3	2	0	.778
Householder, Nashville	1	2	1	1	0	.750

SHORTSTOPS

Player and Club	G.	PO.	A.	E.	DP.	Pct.
Naehring, Knoxville	4	3	18	0	3	1.000
Rhomberg, Chattanooga	4	2	12	0	0	1.000
Pankovits, Columbus	1	0	13	0	1	1.000
Cypret, Columbus	2	3	6	0	3	1.000
Tyson, Chattanooga	2	0	4	0	0	1.000
Gray, Knoxville	30	40	72	3	23	.974
Rausch, Chattanooga	48	65	127	7	24	.965
Bonner, Charlotte	86	132	318	18	68	.962
STOKKE, Columbus	140	194	466	30	85	.957
Goldetsky, Memphis	35	61	106	8	15	.954
Gulliver, Montgomery	69	79	180	13	18	.952

Player and Club	G.	PO.	A.	E.	DP.	Pct.
Perez, Memphis	9	14	25	2	1	.951
Whitfield, Charlotte	60	74	172	13	40	.950
Followell, Montgomery	37	68	132	11	25	.948
DeLeon, Chattanooga	93	141	273	23	66	.947
Faedo, Orlando	103	153	352	30	73	.944
Eschen, Jacksonville	22	27	57	5	4	.944
Heath, Jacksonville	126	166	346	31	57	.943
Sohns, Nashville	116	163	352	32	47	.941
Evans, Memphis	59	112	205	22	40	.935
Mullins, Knoxville	51	57	150	17	26	.924
Ramirez, Savannah	105	134	282	38	51	.916

SHORTSTOPS—Continued

Player and Club	G.	PO.	A.	E.	DP.	Pct.
Phillips, Memphis	47	63	133	18	14	.916
Flannery, Knoxville	59	81	147	22	30	.912
Jackson, Montgomery	29	40	95	13	19	.912
Wilkinson, Orlando	11	21	30	5	5	.911
Miller, Savannah	51	69	168	24	32	.908
S. Hughes, Nashville	9	10	19	3	3	.906
Benson, Orlando	21	35	77	12	19	.903
Etchandy, Knoxville	7	6	12	2	4	.900
Nandin, Montgomery	12	13	29	6	7	.875
Mesa, Knoxville	5	7	12	3	2	.864
Ullger, Orlando	9	8	18	6	6	.813
Santo Domingo, Nash.	24	37	48	21	4	.802

OUTFIELDERS

Player and Club	G.	PO.	A.	E.	DP.	Pct.
Waller, Columbus	64	123	4	0	0	1.000
Fucci, Knoxville*	59	103	5	0	2	1.000
Parker, Jacksonville	48	81	2	0	0	1.000
Torres, Knoxville	10	28	0	0	0	1.000
Harper, Columbus	20	27	1	0	0	1.000
Flannery, Knoxville	8	16	2	0	1	1.000
Adams, Chattanooga	6	17	0	0	0	1.000
Dasen, Montgomery	8	12	0	0	0	1.000
Crowley, Memphis*	5	8	0	0	0	1.000
Hanley, Knoxville	8	8	0	0	0	1.000
Smith, Savannah	4	6	0	0	0	1.000
Jackson, Montgomery	6	6	0	0	0	1.000
Johnson, Jacksonville	1	4	0	0	0	1.000
Eschen, Jacksonville	5	4	0	0	0	1.000
Gustavson, Jacksonville	2	2	1	0	1	1.000
Royster, Charlotte	2	3	0	0	0	1.000
Rende, Chattanooga*	2	3	0	0	0	1.000
Gonzalez, Montgomery	5	3	0	0	0	1.000
Ullger, Orlando	2	1	1	0	0	1.000
Bonner, Charlotte	1	0	1	0	0	1.000
Miller, Savannah	1	1	0	0	0	1.000
Schafer, Memphis	1	1	0	0	0	1.000
Smith, Knoxville*	1	1	0	0	0	1.000
Rhomberg, Chattanooga	86	209	4	2	1	.991
HOUSEHOLDER, Nash.	141	246	16	3	5	.989
Christopher, Charlotte	34	63	2	1	0	.985
Wiedenbauer, Columbus	141	345	22	6	4	.984
Tobias, Memphis*	80	169	5	3	0	.983
Milner, Nashville*	100	259	9	5	1	.982
Hamilton, Nashville*	42	50	5	1	0	.982
Rooney, Memphis	123	253	9	5	2	.981
Colzie, Chattanooga	40	100	3	2	0	.981
Greene, Charlotte	26	48	4	1	0	.981
Hazewood, Charlotte	122	187	11	4	1	.980
Douglas, Orlando	107	182	5	4	2	.979
Hallberg, Orlando	86	125	7	3	1	.978
Yarbrough, Jacksonville	103	203	5	5	3	.977
Haslerig, Savannah	106	233	11	6	2	.976
Hampton, Montgomery	133	235	8	6	2	.976
Brown, Montgomery	95	232	7	6	0	.976
McWhirter, Orlando	89	196	7	5	1	.976
Scoras, Memphis	23	41	0	1	0	.976
Hubbard, Chattanooga	27	37	3	1	0	.976
Cooper, Savannah	99	218	12	6	1	.975
Charboneau, Chat.	102	187	7	5	2	.975
Heep, Columbus*	138	211	12	6	3	.974
Sofield, Orlando	30	73	2	2	0	.974
James, Knoxville*	22	37	1	1	0	.974
Martinez, Montgomery	98	175	8	5	2	.973
Rivera, Chattanooga	94	171	8	5	3	.973
Ondina, Jacksonville	31	68	1	2	0	.972
Williams, Charlotte*	133	319	16	10	2	.971
Harris, Jacksonville	124	272	15	9	3	.970
Gardner, Chattanooga	52	153	4	5	0	.969
Garcia, Jacksonville*	134	229	13	8	2	.968
Rajsich, Columbus*	66	104	7	4	1	.965
Michael, Memphis*	48	101	5	4	2	.964
Porter, Savannah*	99	174	7	7	2	.963
Filkins, Montgomery*	97	146	11	6	3	.963
Redus, Nashville	34	74	3	3	0	.963
Spencer, Knoxville	68	120	8	5	1	.962
Buszka, Chattanooga*	41	45	2	2	0	.959
Youngbauer, Charlotte	11	18	4	1	0	.957
Whisenton, Savannah*	45	59	6	3	0	.956
Gray, Knoxville	50	81	4	4	0	.955
Allen, Knoxville	68	98	6	5	1	.954
Walker, Nashville*	143	237	9	12	1	.953
Linares, Savannah	22	40	1	2	1	.953
Maxwell, Orlando	16	20	0	1	0	.952
Sutherland, Knoxville*	117	256	11	14	0	.950
Thomas, Charlotte	108	185	7	10	2	.950
McManaman, Orlando	94	124	10	7	2	.950
Hammond, Savannah	60	100	5	6	0	.946
Sherow, Memphis	27	51	2	3	0	.946
Johnson, Memphis	139	236	15	17	1	.937
Kittle, Knoxville	30	30	0	5	0	.857
Loucks, Columbus	3	6	0	1	0	.857
Brett, Charlotte	2	3	0	1	0	.750
Trucks, Knoxville	3	1	0	1	0	.500

CATCHERS

Player and Club	G.	PO.	A.	E.	DP.	PB.	Pct.
Brazell, Montgomery	37	189	27	0	4	5	1.000
Bando, Chattanooga	13	58	5	0	1	0	1.000
Harvey, Chattanooga	5	14	1	0	0	1	1.000
De La Cruz, Savan.	2	12	2	0	0	0	1.000
Aldrich, Nashville	1	7	1	0	0	0	1.000
Lucy, Montgomery	25	144	16	1	4	8	.994
VAN GORDER, Nash.	131	726	74	6	7	6	.993
Schafer, Memphis	90	518	34	5	4	7	.991
Upshaw, Montgomery	56	338	23	4	5	9	.989
Dahl, Columbus	40	154	21	2	3	9	.989
Huppert, Charlotte	100	543	73	10	7	8	.984
Tomski, Chattanooga	103	435	52	9	5	17	.982
Isaac, Chattanooga	37	140	21	3	4	4	.982
Yoder, Savannah	76	375	33	8	5	9	.981
Pasillas, Knoxville	92	491	44	11	8	8	.980
Baldwin, Columbus	12	37	9	1	0	1	.979
Hogg, Jacksonville	104	650	69	17	10	18	.977
Simunic, Memphis	60	290	47	8	5	7	.977
Laudner, Orlando	43	224	29	6	3	9	.977
Brill, Savannah	28	147	8	4	3	7	.975
Herz, Orlando	81	440	50	13	6	3	.974
Knicely, Columbus	94	446	51	15	3	16	.971
Miller, Nashville	29	120	16	4	1	3	.971
Trucks, Knoxville	53	282	24	10	3	4	.968
Buffamoyer, Char.	50	213	23	8	5	7	.967
Gustavson, Jacks.	44	217	18	8	0	6	.967
Glass, Montgomery	22	122	16	5	4	1	.965
Maher, Orlando	19	60	8	3	4	0	.958
Meyers, Montgomery	17	57	7	3	0	3	.955
Snitker, Savannah	43	244	10	14	1	4	.948
Kittle, Knoxville	3	14	1	1	0	1	.938

PITCHERS

Player and Club	G.	PO.	A.	E.	DP.	Pct.
LEATHERWOOD, Col*	28	14	26	0	1	1.000
Polvi, Montgomery	26	14	24	0	1	1.000
Engle, Memphis*	27	9	25	0	2	1.000
Leach, Savannah	40	4	24	0	1	1.000

PITCHERS—Continued

Player and Club	G.	PO.	A.	E.	DP.	Pct.
Clapham, Orlando	17	6	21	0	5	1.000
Jones, Jacksonville*	26	12	14	0	0	1.000
Meridith, Columbus*	26	9	16	0	2	1.000
Morley, Jacksonville*	16	5	17	0	1	1.000
Price, Nashville*	22	3	19	0	1	1.000
Monroe, Knoxville	29	10	12	0	1	1.000
MacPherson, Orlando	10	3	18	0	1	1.000
Bedrosian, Savannah	13	4	16	0	0	1.000
Gullickson, Memphis	16	4	15	0	2	1.000
Corr, Montgomery	27	6	13	0	1	1.000
Blake, Orlando*	17	2	16	0	0	1.000
Ramos, Memphis	15	6	11	0	1	1.000
Mayo, Charlotte	40	5	12	0	1	1.000
Tenenini, Memphis	42	5	12	0	1	1.000
Presley, Charlotte	42	5	11	0	2	1.000
Wilder, Chattanooga*	13	4	11	0	1	1.000
Woods, Knoxville	13	5	10	0	1	1.000
Sarmiento, Orlando	6	8	6	0	0	1.000
George, Charlotte*	7	3	11	0	1	1.000
Finlayson, Memphis	11	2	12	0	0	1.000
McArthur, Charlotte	14	6	8	0	1	1.000
Dues, Memphis	7	3	10	0	1	1.000
Roberge, Columbus	12	4	9	0	0	1.000
Nicholson, Chattanooga	22	4	9	0	0	1.000
Lukevics, Knoxville	8	2	10	0	2	1.000
Holdsworth, Mont	8	1	10	0	0	1.000
Martin, Jacksonville	8	4	7	0	0	1.000
Hamrick, Jacksonville*	20	3	8	0	1	1.000
Narleski, Chattanooga	39	0	11	0	0	1.000
Patterson, Knoxville	4	4	6	0	2	1.000
Shields, Savannah	27	1	9	0	0	1.000
Strom, Columbus*	7	1	8	0	0	1.000
O'Keefe, Nashville*	9	2	7	0	0	1.000
Grafton, Montgomery	34	2	7	0	1	1.000
Borchers, Chattanooga*	5	3	5	0	1	1.000
Livingstone, Savannah	13	4	4	0	0	1.000
Teutsch, Knoxville	17	1	6	0	1	1.000
Morris, Columbus*	32	1	6	0	1	1.000
Chevez, Charlotte	9	4	2	0	0	1.000
Hanslovan, Jacks*	10	1	5	0	1	1.000
Reichenbach, Jacks	10	3	3	0	1	1.000
Twitty, Jacksonville*	14	0	6	0	0	1.000
Hemm, Memphis*	15	0	6	0	0	1.000
Burns, Knoxville*	20	0	6	0	1	1.000
Geiger, Montgomery	4	0	5	0	0	1.000
Cajide, Columbus	5	2	3	0	0	1.000
Quealey, Columbus	2	2	2	0	0	1.000
Ploucher, Chattanooga*	4	1	3	0	0	1.000
Willett, Nashville	8	1	3	0	0	1.000
Lombardo, Nashville*	17	1	3	0	0	1.000
Murillo, Knoxville	21	1	3	0	0	1.000
Guzman, Knoxville	3	1	2	0	0	1.000
Bastian, Charlotte	4	1	2	0	0	1.000
Casbolt, Jacksonville*	8	0	3	0	0	1.000
Martin, Montgomery*	11	2	1	0	0	1.000
McGough, Chattanooga	16	2	1	0	0	1.000
Reyes, Orlando	7	0	2	0	0	1.000
Lewis, Orlando	11	0	2	0	0	1.000
S. Hughes, Nashville	1	0	1	0	0	1.000
Spencer, Knoxville	1	0	1	0	0	1.000
Vasquez, Knoxville	1	0	1	0	0	1.000
Dobbs, Orlando*	2	0	1	0	0	1.000
Trucks, Knoxville	2	0	1	0	0	1.000
Moran, Knoxville	10	1	0	0	0	1.000
Veselic, Orlando	28	15	34	1	6	.980
Dubee, Jacksonville	28	8	26	1	2	.971
Kinnunen, Orlando	17	6	27	1	2	.971
Kelly, Nashville	30	12	21	1	3	.971
Holmstedt, Chattanooga	20	2	26	1	2	.966
Dawley, Nashville	25	6	22	1	2	.966
Torrez, Charlotte*	21	10	45	2	2	.965
Laskey, Jacksonville	15	8	19	1	2	.964
Schneider, Charlotte*	42	7	20	1	1	.964
Heimer, Chattanooga*	32	2	21	1	3	.958

Player and Club	G.	PO.	A.	E.	DP.	Pct.
Ferreyra, Nashville	61	6	17	1	0	.958
Blair, Montgomery*	17	6	16	1	1	.957
Combe, Nashville	54	6	15	1	0	.955
Barnes, Knoxville*	22	11	27	2	3	.950
Boddicker, Charlotte	14	5	14	1	2	.950
Grzybek, Jacksonville	17	9	10	1	2	.950
Chiti, Savannah	25	11	26	2	1	.949
Lea, Memphis	24	17	19	2	1	.947
Gingrich, Memphis	35	8	27	2	5	.946
Richard, Chattanooga	16	4	30	2	3	.944
Rucker, Montgomery*	28	7	27	2	2	.944
Cassetto, Montgomery	16	2	15	1	0	.944
Brown, Nashville	27	2	15	1	0	.944
Chamberlain, Jacks.	22	11	21	2	1	.941
Miscik, Columbus*	13	3	13	1	1	.941
Havens, Orlando*	19	2	14	1	1	.941
Teising, Chattanooga*	40	2	14	1	0	.941
Alvarez, Savannah	29	14	47	4	4	.938
Cole, Savannah	24	4	26	2	1	.938
MacDonald, Columbus	10	2	13	1	0	.938
Williams, Memphis*	33	3	12	1	1	.938
Dotson, Knoxville	25	6	22	2	1	.933
G. Hughes, Nashville	25	13	14	2	0	.931
Codiroli, Montgomery	8	2	11	1	1	.929
Jones, Charlotte	19	5	8	1	3	.929
Troedson, Columbus	35	1	12	1	0	.929
Smith, Memphis	27	13	24	3	1	.925
Glaser, Chattanooga	39	14	23	3	3	.925
Mertens, Orlando	32	2	46	4	3	.923
Fuson, Chattanooga	5	2	10	1	1	.923
Lovins, Memphis	50	5	7	1	0	.923
Cappuzzello, Nashville*	44	5	18	2	0	.920
Spence, Chattanooga	25	11	34	4	2	.918
Carey, Charlotte*	8	2	9	1	0	.917
Hendricks, Jacksonville	13	5	6	1	2	.917
Brueggemann, Orlando	28	3	8	1	1	.917
Hoyt, Knoxville	37	3	8	1	0	.917
B. Smith, Columbus	27	7	33	4	4	.909
Pratt, Savannah*	30	4	26	3	2	.909
Pensiero, Charlotte	18	2	8	1	2	.909
Wieters, Savannah	36	12	37	5	3	.907
Boxberger, Columbus	21	8	21	3	1	.906
Welchel, Charlotte	13	4	15	2	2	.905
Steffen, Montgomery	16	3	15	2	0	.900
Snell, Charlotte	10	2	7	1	1	.900
Barnicle, Knoxville*	20	4	12	2	2	.889
Lucia, Savannah	11	2	6	1	0	.889
Arnold, Chattanooga*	13	0	8	1	0	.889
Viefhaus, Montgomery	25	11	20	4	0	.886
Mayer, Nashville*	15	5	18	3	0	.885
Shea, Montgomery	12	4	11	2	1	.882
Cowley, Savannah	25	9	20	4	1	.879
Smith, Montgomery	23	4	10	2	0	.875
Robbins, Montgomery*	13	5	21	4	2	.867
Smith, Knoxville*	31	8	18	4	0	.867
Schattinger, Jacksonville	22	3	10	2	0	.867
Graven, Savannah*	27	1	17	3	1	.857
Leland, Columbus	5	1	5	1	0	.857
Gideon, Orlando	7	4	2	1	1	.857
Wright, Savannah*	8	2	4	1	0	.857
Ujdur, Montgomery	19	2	4	1	0	.857
Rowe, Charlotte	28	8	33	7	2	.854
Mapel, Orlando	11	5	12	3	1	.850
Town, Nashville	13	2	15	3	1	.850
Isaacs, Orlando	11	4	12	3	1	.842
Ladd, Columbus	13	2	3	1	0	.833
Ganger, Jacksonville	18	0	5	1	0	.833
Aponte, Columbus	25	5	7	3	0	.800
Cornell, Jacksonville	49	3	9	3	0	.800
Armstrong, Nashville	32	2	6	2	0	.800
Arp, Chattanooga	5	0	4	1	0	.800
Pettaway, Savannah	6	0	4	1	0	.800
MacCormack, Mont	6	0	7	2	0	.778
Platel, Knoxville	12	1	6	2	0	.778

PITCHERS—Continued

Player and Club	G.	PO.	A.	E.	DP.	Pct.		Player and Club	G.	PO.	A.	E.	DP.	Pct.
Alonso, Orlando*	16	5	4	3	0	.750		Gutierrez, Knoxville*	5	0	2	1	0	.667
Skinner, Jacksonville	4	1	2	1	0	.750		Lahti, Nashville	6	1	2	4	0	.429
Jackowiak, Montgomery	3	0	2	1	0	.667								

Hussey, p, did not have any recorded accepted chances; therefore, is not listed in the fielding averages for that position. Derryberry, Hill and Rosario appeared as designated hitters and/or pinch hitters only.

CLUB PITCHING

Club	G.	CG.	ShO.	Sv.	IP.	H.	R.	ER.	HR.	BB.	Int. BB.	HB.	SO.	WP.	Bk.	ERA.
Nashville	145	16	8	41	1225	1190	563	460	92	429	47	15	795	49	4	3.38
Columbus	143	61	15	15	1183	1104	547	464	79	577	22	31	576	72	13	3.53
Jacksonville	143	37	12	23	1184	1099	609	504	83	600	35	35	711	66	3	3.83
Memphis	145	45	10	29	1237	1252	617	537	88	515	35	34	749	67	3	3.91
Charlotte	143	38	8	33	1205	1221	622	533	102	588	29	28	712	58	14	3.98
Savannah	145	31	8	20	1204	1186	701	551	101	648	33	47	710	51	8	4.12
Montgomery	144	31	6	20	1198	1203	663	574	88	641	56	35	803	71	10	4.31
Knoxville	141	32	6	31	1131	1166	671	567	94	548	17	42	748	50	16	4.51
Orlando	141	61	7	20	1162	1290	684	584	88	465	7	27	655	45	11	4.52
Chattanooga	144	40	9	25	1187	1254	704	605	144	564	25	29	600	55	9	4.59

PITCHERS' RECORDS
(Leading Qualifiers for Earned-Run Average Leadership—115 or More Innings)

*Throws lefthanded.

Pitcher, Club	G.	GS.	CG.	ShO.	W.	L.	Sv.	Pct.	IP.	H.	R.	ER.	HR.	BB.	Int. BB.	HB.	SO.	WP.	ERA.
Brown, Nashville	27	19	3	1	9	2	1	.818	131	103	40	35	12	43	1	2	109	2	2.40
Chamberlain, Jax	22	22	11	3	12	9	0	.571	160	142	57	46	10	45	3	6	117	7	2.59
Smith, Columbus	27	26	19	2	14	9	0	.609	201	187	77	59	6	68	4	3	76	9	2.64
Ferreyra, Nashville	61	0	0	0	5	9	6	.357	116	128	47	35	7	24	9	1	53	1	2.72
Alvarez, Savannah	29	24	9	1	11	11	0	.500	186	165	87	62	16	73	3	5	120	5	3.00
Leatherwood, Columbus*	28	26	15	4	15	11	0	.577	202	180	82	69	7	103	1	10	95	14	3.07
Hughes, Nashville	25	24	2	1	11	4	0	.733	120	115	56	43	5	63	3	2	67	6	3.23
Smith, Memphis	27	27	10	1	11	10	0	.524	184	175	80	69	10	74	7	2	115	9	3.38
Torrez, Charlotte*	21	21	8	2	7	9	0	.438	144	152	86	56	13	62	2	2	67	8	3.50
Smith, Knoxville*	31	11	2	0	6	9	0	.500	122	127	61	48	6	35	0	1	77	3	3.54

Departmental Leaders: G—Ferreyra, 61; GS—Dubee, Rowe, Veselic, 28; CG—Billy Smith, 19; ShO—Leatherwood, 4; W—Leatherwood, 15; L—Mertens, 15; Sv—Combe, 27; Pct.—Hughes, .733; IP—Leatherwood, 202; H—Veselic, 220; R—Chiti, 114; ER—Chiti, 94; HR—Nicholson, 27; BB—M. Jones, 109; IBB—Corr, 10; HB—Barnes, Cowley, Gingrich, 13; SO—Veselic, 151; WP—M. Jones, 16.

(All Pitchers—Listed Alphabetically)

Pitcher, Club	G.	GS.	CG.	ShO.	W.	L.	Sv.	Pct.	IP.	H.	R.	ER.	HR.	BB.	Int. BB.	HB.	SO.	WP.	ERA.
Alonso, Orlando*	16	0	0	0	0	2	0	.000	26	25	20	16	0	12	0	0	26	1	5.54
Alvarez, Savannah	29	24	9	1	11	11	0	.500	186	165	87	62	16	73	3	5	120	5	3.00
Aponte, Columbus	25	0	0	0	3	3	3	.500	47	43	24	20	4	31	5	1	31	1	3.83
Armstrong, Nashville	32	0	0	0	5	1	3	.833	64	58	30	24	9	29	2	3	53	3	3.38
Arnold, Chattanooga*	13	6	0	0	4	3	0	.571	48	47	33	27	4	35	1	1	29	1	5.06
Arp, Chattanooga	5	5	1	0	1	4	0	.200	28	37	16	14	2	10	0	1	7	1	4.50
Barnes, Knoxville*	22	22	3	0	8	8	0	.500	131	136	79	61	4	86	4	13	91	8	4.19
Barnicle, Knoxville*	20	16	4	0	3	11	0	.214	89	95	64	56	12	50	2	3	46	6	5.66
Bastian, Charlotte	4	3	0	0	1	0	0	.000	11	8	7	6	0	16	0	0	5	1	4.91
Bedrosian, Savannah	13	13	4	2	5	5	0	.500	89	71	36	30	2	58	1	1	73	3	3.03
Blair, Montgomery*	17	10	2	0	3	5	0	.375	66	71	42	36	3	34	3	2	34	4	4.91
Blake, Orlando*	17	11	5	0	3	6	0	.333	82	94	48	45	11	37	0	2	41	2	4.94
Boddicker, Charlotte	14	14	8	2	9	3	0	.750	102	82	40	34	9	36	2	3	89	4	3.00
Borchers, Chattanooga*	5	5	3	1	2	2	0	.500	31	22	9	9	3	9	0	0	22	0	2.61
Boxberger, Columbus	21	21	3	1	6	7	0	.462	122	127	89	65	12	92	1	4	50	11	4.80
Brazell, Montgomery	1	0	0	0	0	0	0	.000	1	2	2	2	1	0	0	0	0	0	18.00
Brown, Nashville	27	19	3	1	9	2	1	.818	131	103	40	35	12	43	1	2	109	2	2.40
Brueggemann, Orlando	28	0	0	0	4	3	10	.571	50	50	32	22	3	34	0	1	34	2	3.96
Burns, Montgomery*	20	19	4	1	6	10	1	.375	110	126	68	59	5	37	0	0	92	1	4.83
Cajide, Columbus	5	3	0	0	0	2	0	.000	22	26	18	17	2	15	0	1	11	3	6.95
Cappuzzello, Nashville*	44	3	0	0	8	4	4	.667	82	89	34	22	3	31	2	0	72	7	2.41
Carey, Charlotte*	8	7	2	1	4	2	0	.667	51	49	24	21	4	13	0	1	34	0	3.71
Casbolt, Jacksonville*	8	0	0	0	1	1	0	.500	10	14	6	3	1	13	3	1	6	1	2.70
Cassetto, Montgomery	16	16	5	0	5	9	0	.357	93	88	65	56	10	50	4	1	48	1	5.42
Chamberlain, Jax	22	22	11	3	12	9	0	.571	160	142	57	46	10	45	3	6	117	7	2.59
Chevez, Charlotte	9	2	0	0	2	0	1	1.000	24	24	10	10	2	11	0	0	11	1	3.75
Chiti, Savannah*	25	25	4	0	7	13	0	.350	153	172	114	94	24	74	2	2	48	6	5.53

Pitcher–Club	G	GS	CG	ShO	W	L	Sv	Pct.	IP	H	R	ER	HR	BB	Int. BB	HB	SO	WP	ERA
Clapham, Orlando	17	9	2	0	2	8	0	.200	74	104	58	54	5	39	1	3	29	5	6.57
Codiroli, Montgomery	8	8	1	0	2	3	0	.400	49	41	24	18	4	27	0	0	34	3	3.31
Cole, Savannah*	24	24	2	1	6	11	0	.353	137	141	110	90	11	98	0	2	74	6	5.91
Combe, Nashville	54	0	0	0	5	5	27	.500	87	66	29	20	2	30	9	2	84	8	2.07
Cornell, Jacksonville	49	1	1	0	6	10	9	.375	86	62	41	33	4	52	5	1	76	6	3.45
Corr, Montgomery	27	0	0	0	6	3	6	.667	59	53	14	13	2	25	10	4	34	3	1.98
Cowley, Savannah	25	23	6	3	7	9	1	.438	144	115	74	60	13	81	2	13	103	6	3.75
Dawley, Nashville	25	24	4	2	9	9	0	.500	140	144	72	62	12	41	6	1	84	2	3.99
Dobbs, Orlando*	2	0	0	0	0	0	0	.000	6	7	8	3	0	3	0	0	1	2	4.50
Dotson, Knoxville	25	25	10	1	9	9	0	.500	163	133	81	67	14	88	2	3	133	5	3.70
Dubee, Jacksonville	28	28	3	2	8	13	0	.381	158	187	105	85	10	64	8	1	68	6	4.84
Dues, Memphis	7	7	1	0	2	2	0	.500	44	51	24	20	4	19	1	0	12	2	4.09
Engle, Memphis*	27	27	4	0	6	8	0	.429	161	162	95	84	20	68	0	0	103	6	4.70
Ferreyra, Nashville	61	0	0	0	5	9	6	.357	116	128	47	35	7	24	9	1	53	1	2.72
Finlayson, Memphis	11	8	3	0	4	3	0	.571	56	61	29	27	6	17	1	0	24	3	4.34
Fuson, Chattanooga	5	5	1	0	0	3	0	.000	31	27	15	15	3	18	1	2	17	2	4.35
Ganger, Jacksonville	18	0	0	0	0	3	0	.000	31	27	11	8	7	11	0	0	13	0	2.25
Geiger, Montgomery	4	1	0	0	2	0	4	.000	28	20	8	7	3	11	0	0	13	1	2.12
George, Charlotte*	7	7	2	0	2	4	0	1.000	17	11	4	4	0	11	0	0	13	1	2.12
Gideon, Orlando	7	6	4	0	2	3	0	.333	43	55	29	24	8	25	0	1	26	4	5.02
Gingrich, Memphis	35	10	5	2	8	9	1	.400	43	47	25	20	5	18	0	2	13	4	4.19
Glaser, Chattanooga	39	13	6	0	8	7	3	.533	127	151	69	54	12	49	4	13	66	10	3.83
Grafton, Montgomery	34	0	0	0	7	5	3	.583	73	74	32	29	2	52	5	3	55	5	3.58
Graven, Savannah*	27	3	0	0	3	3	2	.500	52	60	21	9	2	25	4	2	25	2	1.56
Grzybek, Knoxville	17	14	2	0	0	7	0	.000	83	91	62	56	7	62	2	2	31	4	6.07
Gullickson, Memphis	16	16	8	1	10	3	0	.769	116	110	52	47	9	42	1	1	115	5	3.65
Gutierrez, Knoxville	5	0	0	1	0	0	1	1.000	15	15	12	9	1	12	0	3	6	0	5.40
Guzman, Knoxville	3	3	0	0	2	0	0	1.000	21	13	11	9	3	7	0	0	14	0	3.86
Hamrick, Jacksonville*	20	3	0	0	1	2	1	.333	47	59	32	26	5	26	3	2	23	3	4.98
Hanslovan, Jacksonville*	10	9	1	1	3	2	0	.600	50	42	24	24	6	32	0	0	25	3	4.32
Havens, Orlando*	19	14	4	0	4	10	1	.286	94	128	85	76	9	50	0	1	63	7	7.28
Heimer, Chattanooga	32	9	4	0	10	3	3	.769	120	103	59	49	8	74	2	3	92	8	3.68
Hemm, Memphis*	15	3	0	0	2	2	0	.500	37	52	25	23	4	22	1	1	15	1	5.59
Hendricks, Jacksonville	5	0	0	3	1	0	0	.750	47	36	27	21	3	51	0	8	46	6	4.02
Holdsworth, Montgomery	8	8	6	1	3	4	0	.467	118	139	74	59	13	41	1	1	46	6	4.50
Holmstedt, Chattanooga	20	20	6	1	7	8	0	.429	60	55	24	21	1	31	2	0	46	5	3.15
Hoyt, Knoxville	37	0	0	0	9	5	12	.643	82	80	29	27	5	35	2	4	60	0	2.96
Hughes, Nashville	25	24	2	1	11	4	0	.733	120	115	56	43	5	63	3	2	67	6	3.23
Hussey, Chattanooga	4	2	0	0	0	1	0	.000	9	14	12	12	2	9	0	0	8	1	12.00
Isaac, Chattanooga	1	0	0	0	0	0	0	.000	3	10	7	7	0	0	0	3	1	21.00
Isaacs, Orlando	11	9	2	0	2	5	1	.286	57	73	46	42	3	22	0	3	21	5	6.63
Jackowiak, Montgomery..	3	0	0	0	0	3	0	.000	6	11	11	9	0	12	0	0	3	1	13.50
Jones, Charleston	19	19	4	1	10	3	0	.769	135	127	63	59	9	77	1	4	100	10	3.93
Jones, Jacksonville*	26	26	8	2	9	13	0	.409	167	142	92	76	13	100	3	1	116	16	4.10
Kelly, Nashville	30	22	5	1	13	6	0	.684	149	164	65	60	13	16	5	1	76	4	3.62
Kinnunen, Orlando	17	16	8	0	6	6	0	.500	118	129	63	54	7	45	1	0	55	3	4.12
Ladd, Columbus	13	4	2	1	6	1	4	.857	41	24	13	12	3	23	0	4	31	2	2.63
Lahti, Nashville	6	0	0	0	2	0	0	1.000	16	10	4	3	0	5	1	0	12	2	1.69
Laskey, Jacksonville	15	15	3	1	4	3	0	.571	97	78	44	38	6	46	0	5	53	4	3.53
Lea, Memphis	24	24	3	1	8	8	0	.500	162	161	88	79	11	71	2	6	81	9	4.39
Leach, Savannah	40	0	0	0	2	9	2	.182	92	77	33	20	4	26	5	2	68	2	1.96
Leatherwood, Columbus*	28	26	15	4	15	11	0	.577	202	180	82	69	7	103	1	10	95	14	3.07
Leland, Columbus	5	5	1	0	1	2	0	.333	31	30	17	14	3	14	0	0	13	1	4.06
Lewis, Orlando	11	0	0	0	0	4	3	.000	22	17	11	9	2	11	1	0	10	1	3.68
Livingstone, Savannah	13	0	0	0	3	0	3	1.000	22	24	10	6	2	6	1	1	12	0	2.45
Lombardo, Nashville*	17	0	0	0	3	2	0	.600	26	26	18	14	1	17	2	0	14	2	4.85
Lovins, Memphis	50	0	0	0	11	5	18	.688	79	58	26	23	1	43	6	3	67	9	2.62
Lucia, Savannah	11	7	1	0	2	5	0	.286	38	50	31	30	5	29	1	4	28	1	7.11
Lukevics, Knoxville	8	7	3	1	4	3	0	.571	48	48	26	24	4	11	0	1	28	0	4.50
MacCormack, Mont	6	4	0	0	0	3	0	.000	30	20	25	18	1	40	2	1	29	11	5.40
MacDonald, Columbus	10	10	2	0	3	6	0	.500	58	65	33	30	4	18	0	0	30	3	4.66
MacPherson, Orlando	10	10	2	1	5	2	0	.714	67	66	29	27	4	27	0	1	45	4	3.63
Mapel, Orlando	11	11	5	1	7	3	0	.700	80	65	27	24	8	18	0	6	52	2	2.70
Martin, Jacksonville	8	0	0	3	1	3	0	.750	18	10	3	2	0	4	0	1	14	0	1.00
Martin, Montgomery*	11	0	0	0	2	0	4	1.000	27	15	8	6	3	9	1	0	18	1	2.00
Maxwell, Orlando	1	0	0	0	0	0	0	.000	⅓	0	0	0	0	0	0	0	0	0	0.00
Mayer, Nashville*	15	15	0	0	3	3	0	.500	81	78	39	37	1	52	3	0	58	4	4.11
Mayo, Charlotte	40	1	0	0	4	5	8	.444	88	80	42	37	2	60	7	2	41	7	3.78
McArthur, Charlotte	14	12	2	1	4	7	0	.364	71	70	49	45	9	52	4	6	27	4	5.70
McGough, Chattanooga	16	2	0	0	2	2	4	.500	41	48	24	21	3	22	1	1	29	3	4.61
Meridith, Columbus	26	23	8	3	9	11	1	.450	149	150	75	71	14	78	3	6	63	4	4.29
Mertens, Orlando	32	20	12	0	10	15	3	.400	177	202	98	82	15	55	1	3	75	4	4.17
Miller, Savannah	1	0	0	0	0	0	0	.000	2	3	3	3	0	0	0	0	0	0	13.50
Miscik, Columbus*	13	13	3	1	8	2	0	.800	90	90	40	35	7	42	0	0	44	7	3.50

Pitcher—Club	G	GS	CG	ShO	W	L	Sv	Pct.	IP	H	R	ER	HR	BB	Int. BB	HB	SO	WP	ERA
Monroe, Knoxville	29	12	2	0	4	8	2	.333	107	103	73	62	15	72	1	2	65	10	5.21
Moran, Knoxville	10	0	0	0	0	2	4	.000	17	17	9	7	5	7	0	2	8	0	3.71
Morley, Jacksonville*	16	16	7	0	8	4	0	.667	109	96	43	35	11	40	3	3	63	2	2.89
Morris, Columbus*	32	1	0	0	3	1	2	.750	45	48	25	25	4	25	5	0	29	4	5.00
Murillo, Knoxville	21	4	0	0	3	1	9	.750	40	50	23	18	1	13	0	3	26	2	4.05
Narleski, Chattanooga	39	0	0	0	11	6	12	.647	78	69	32	30	11	22	6	2	44	3	3.46
Nicholson, Chattanooga	22	17	5	0	1	8	0	.111	96	116	87	81	27	64	4	3	52	4	7.59
O'Keeffe, Nashville*	9	7	0	0	0	6	0	.000	29	31	24	20	3	13	1	1	15	0	6.21
Patterson, Knoxville	4	4	1	0	2	1	0	.667	25	22	12	9	0	15	0	1	7	0	3.24
Pensiero, Charlotte	18	4	1	0	0	4	2	.000	56	72	37	35	9	17	1	0	24	2	5.63
Pettaway, Savannah	6	2	0	0	2	2	0	.500	15	18	17	16	4	10	0	0	12	1	9.60
Platel, Knoxville	12	12	2	0	4	5	0	.444	62	80	36	32	3	32	2	0	26	8	4.65
Ploucher, Chattanooga*	4	4	1	0	1	2	0	.333	20	23	11	11	0	17	0	0	8	0	4.95
Polvi, Montgomery	26	16	3	1	6	5	0	.545	110	118	60	49	7	35	4	5	49	5	4.01
Pratt, Savannah*	30	13	2	1	5	8	0	.385	105	114	73	65	9	71	2	4	73	11	5.57
Presley, Charlotte	42	1	1	0	7	4	18	.636	56	40	15	9	2	27	2	0	43	3	1.45
Price, Nashville*	22	20	2	2	6	6	0	.500	109	101	58	48	13	41	1	1	69	6	3.96
Quealey, Columbus	2	1	1	0	1	0	0	1.000	8	6	2	2	1	4	0	1	7	1	2.25
Ramos, Memphis	15	15	7	3	8	2	0	.800	105	109	44	42	8	24	3	1	76	0	3.60
Reichenbach, Jacksonville	10	0	0	0	0	0	0	.000	22	36	21	15	1	11	0	0	6	3	6.14
Reyes, Orlando	7	1	0	0	0	1	0	.000	23	27	18	18	4	8	1	1	9	1	7.04
Richard, Chattanooga	16	16	6	0	5	5	0	.500	109	93	47	37	10	38	2	6	41	3	3.06
Robbins, Montgomery*	13	12	2	0	7	1	0	.875	88	80	34	29	5	37	3	0	86	5	2.97
Roberge, Columbus	12	3	3	1	4	2	1	.667	54	32	7	6	3	10	1	0	47	1	1.00
Rowe, Charlotte	28	28	4	0	11	14	0	.440	167	200	113	93	16	76	5	6	90	3	5.01
Rucker, Montgomery*	28	11	1	0	4	7	1	.364	96	97	56	49	6	66	3	7	64	3	4.59
Sarmiento, Orlando	6	6	3	1	4	2	0	.667	41	36	15	12	2	15	0	1	29	1	2.63
Schattinger, Jacks	22	0	0	0	8	2	3	.800	46	42	19	16	0	26	3	2	17	2	3.13
Schneider, Charlotte*	42	1	0	0	3	7	4	.300	105	102	51	40	6	48	3	5	42	4	5.59
Shea, Montgomery	12	10	3	0	3	4	0	.429	74	71	49	46	10	38	5	2	42	4	5.59
Shields, Savannah	27	0	0	0	4	1	7	.800	42	40	12	9	1	21	5	1	21	2	1.93
Skinner, Jacksonville	4	4	1	1	1	2	0	.333	29	19	14	12	1	11	0	1	16	2	3.72
Smith, Columbus	27	26	19	2	14	9	0	.609	201	187	77	59	6	68	4	3	76	9	2.64
Smith, Memphis	27	27	10	1	11	10	0	.524	184	175	80	69	10	74	7	2	115	9	3.38
Smith, Montgomery	23	7	1	0	2	9	1	.182	77	91	60	55	9	38	2	5	42	3	6.43
Smith, Knoxville*	31	11	2	0	6	6	0	.500	122	127	61	48	6	35	0	1	77	3	3.54
Snell, Charlotte	10	10	1	0	5	2	0	.714	65	65	30	27	8	29	1	1	42	1	3.74
Spence, Chattanooga	25	25	5	0	12	8	0	.600	163	162	82	67	19	77	3	5	79	7	3.70
Spencer, Knoxville	1	0	0	0	0	0	0	.000	3	5	4	4	2	0	0	0	0	0	12.00
Steffen, Montgomery	16	5	3	1	5	5	0	.500	90	100	59	51	6	45	2	1	83	5	5.10
Strom, Columbus*	7	7	4	1	3	3	0	.500	47	39	22	19	7	19	0	0	24	3	3.64
Teising, Chattanooga*	40	2	0	0	5	6	3	.455	80	92	66	47	10	54	1	1	41	7	5.29
Tenenini, Memphis	42	3	0	0	8	3	5	.727	98	116	52	44	2	42	5	3	50	5	4.04
Teutsch, Knoxville	17	0	0	0	2	2	0	.500	37	40	31	29	7	13	1	2	27	2	7.05
Torrez, Charlotte*	21	21	8	2	7	9	0	.438	144	152	65	56	13	62	2	2	67	8	3.50
Town, Nashville	13	11	0	0	3	2	0	.600	57	56	32	27	9	15	0	1	20	2	4.26
Troedson, Columbus	35	0	0	0	8	2	4	.800	64	57	23	20	2	35	2	1	25	8	2.81
Trucks, Knoxville	2	0	0	0	0	0	0	.000	6	3	5	5	1	2	0	2	5	0	7.50
Twitty, Jacksonville*	14	0	0	0	0	0	3	1.000	25	23	11	9	2	4	2	1	21	1	3.24
Ujdur, Montgomery	19	3	0	0	2	5	0	.286	37	48	27	23	8	16	2	1	30	5	5.59
Vasquez, Knoxville	1	1	1	0	1	0	0	1.000	7	6	1	0	0	4	0	0	3	2	0.00
Veselic, Orlando	28	28	13	3	11	10	0	.524	201	220	101	80	10	71	2	3	151	1	3.58
Viefhaus, Montgomery	25	20	4	0	3	12	0	.200	144	156	67	60	10	75	8	3	98	7	3.75
Welchel, Charlotte	13	13	5	0	5	4	0	.556	86	95	47	37	5	39	1	1	40	2	3.87
Wieters, Savannah	36	11	3	0	4	6	4	.400	115	114	70	51	6	68	4	8	45	6	3.99
Wilder, Chattanooga*	13	13	2	2	6	1	0	.857	74	89	46	44	5	29	1	0	26	1	5.35
Willett, Nashville	8	0	0	0	1	2	0	.333	16	21	15	10	2	9	0	0	9	0	5.63
Williams, Memphis*	33	5	1	0	5	7	5	.417	68	46	33	25	1	44	4	4	25	8	3.31
Woods, Knoxville	13	5	0	0	1	5	1	.167	47	67	46	41	6	29	3	2	34	3	7.85
Wright, Savannah*	8	0	0	0	0	0	0	.000	12	22	10	6	1	5	1	2	8	0	4.50
Yarbrough, Jacksonville	1	0	0	0	0	0	0	.000	1	0	0	0	0	3	0	0	0	0	0.00

BALKS—Cajide, 8; Burns, 6; Chamberlain, 5; Monroe, Torrez, 4 each; Boddicker, Cassetto, Pratt, Spence, Steffen, 3 each; Corr, Cowley, Dotson, Glaser, Grzybek, L. Jones, Kinnunen, Mapel, Mertens, Narleski, Richard, Rowe, B. L. Smith, 2 each; Barnes, Brown, Brueggemann, Cole, Dawley, Dobbs, Engle, Gideon, Gutierrez, Havens, Hughes, M. Jones, Leatherwood, Lucia, MacPherson, Mayer, Mayo, Pensiero, Ramos, Robbins, Roberge, Schneider, Jack Smith, Tenenini, Troedson, Vasquez, Wieters, Woods, 1 each.

COMBINATION SHUTOUTS—Bastian-Chevez-Mayo, Charlotte; Borchers-Narleski, Spence-Glaser, Glaser-Heimer, Holmstedt-Teising, Richard-Teising, Chattanooga; Leatherwood-Aponte, Columbus; Laskey-Schattinger 2, Jacksonville; Barnes-Murillo, Dotson-Murillo, Monroe-Burns, Knoxville; Hemm-Tenenini, Williams-Lovins 2, Memphis; Polvi-Martin, Viefhaus-Geiger, Montgomery; Kelly-Combe, Nashville; Clapham-Mertens, Orlando.

NO-HIT GAMES—None.

Texas League

CLASS AA

Leading Batter
JAMES TRACY
Midland

League President
CARL SAWATSKI

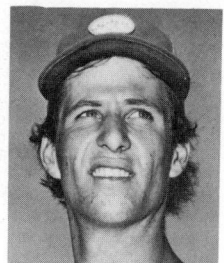

Leading Pitcher
GREG HARRIS
Jackson

CHAMPIONSHIP WINNERS IN PREVIOUS YEARS

1888 – Dallas .... .671	1919 – Shreveport* .... .677	1942 – Beaumont .... .605
1889 – Houston .... .551	Fort Worth .... .651	Shreveport (2nd)§ .... .576
1890 – Galveston .... .705	1920 – Fort Worth .... .703	1943-44-45 – Did not operate.
1892 – Houston .... .741	Fort Worth .... .750	1946 – Fort Worth .... .656
Houston .... .613	1921 – Fort Worth .... .691	Dallas (2nd)§ .... .591
1895 – Dallas .... .754	Fort Worth .... .662	1947 – Houston‡ .... .623
Fort Worth* .... .750	1922 – Fort Worth .... .694	1948 – Fort Worth‡ .... .601
1896 – Fort Worth .... .757	Fort Worth .... .711	1949 – Fort Worth .... .649
Houston* .... .679	1923 – Fort Worth .... .632	Tulsa (2nd)§ .... .584
Galveston .... .548	1924 – Fort Worth .... .689	1950 – Beaumont .... .595
1897 – San Antonio† .... .657	Fort Worth .... .763	San Antonio (4th)§ .... .513
Galveston† .... .717	1925 – Fort Worth .... .711	1951 – Houston‡ .... .619
1898 – League disbanded.	Fort Worth y .... .653	1952 – Dallas .... .571
1899 – Galveston .... .632	1926 – Dallas .... .574	Shreveport (3rd)§ .... .522
Galveston .... .762	1927 – Wichita Falls .... .654	1953 – Dallas‡ .... .571
1900-01 – Did not operate.	1928 – Houston* .... .679	1954 – Shreveport .... .559
1902 – Corsicana .... .866	Wichita Falls .... .731	Houston (2nd)§ .... .553
Corsicana .... .682	1929 – Dallas* .... .588	1955 – Dallas .... .581
1903 – Paris-Waco .... .615	Wichita Falls .... .620	Shreveport (3rd)§ .... .540
Dallas* .... .648	1930 – Wichita Falls .... .697	1956 – Houston‡ .... .623
1904 – Corsicana* .... .615	Fort Worth* .... .632	1957 – Dallas .... .662
Fort Worth .... .800	1931 – Houston** .... .625	Houston (2nd)§ .... .630
1905 – Fort Worth .... .545	Houston .... .734	1958 – Fort Worth .... .582
1906 – Fort Worth .... .677	1932 – Beaumont* .... .640	Cor. Christi (3rd)§ .... .507
Cleburne x .... .609	Dallas .... .727	1959 – Victoria .... .589
1907 – Austin .... .629	1933 – Houston .... .623	Austin (2nd)§ .... .548
1908 – San Antonio .... .664	San Antonio (4th)§ .... .523	1960 – Rio Grande Valley .... .590
1909 – Houston .... .601	1934 – Galveston‡ .... .579	Tulsa (3rd) .... .528
1910 – Dallas† .... .586	1935 – Oklahoma City‡ .... .590	1961 – Amarillo .... .643
Houston† .... .586	1936 – Dallas .... .604	San Antonio (3rd)§ .... .532
1911 – Austin .... .575	Tulsa (3rd)§ .... .519	1962 – El Paso .... .571
1912 – Houston .... .626	1937 – Oklahoma City .... .635	Tulsa (2nd)§ .... .550
1913 – Houston .... .620	Fort Worth (3rd)§ .... .535	1963 – San Antonio .... .564
1914 – Houston† .... .671	1938 – Beaumont .... .635	Tulsa (3rd)§ .... .529
Waco† .... .671	1939 – Houston .... .606	1964 – San Antonio‡ .... .607
1915 – Waco .... .592	Fort Worth (4th)§ .... .540	1965 – Tulsa .... .574
1916 – Waco .... .587	1940 – Houston‡ .... .652	Albuquerque xx .... .550
1917 – Dallas .... .600	1941 – Houston .... .673	1966 – Arkansas .... .579
1918 – Dallas .... .584	Dallas (4th)§ .... .519	1967 – Albuquerque .... .557

CHAMPIONSHIP WINNERS IN PREVIOUS YEARS—Continued

1968—Arkansas	.586	Association.		Midland xxx	.604
El Paso xx	.562	1972—Alexandria	.600	1976—Amarillo xx	.600
1969—Amarillo	.593	El Paso xx	.557	Shreveport	.515
Memphis xx	.504	1973—San Antonio	.590	1977—El Paso	.600
1970—Albuquerque**	.615	Memphis xx	.558	Arkansas a	.485
Memphis	.507	1974—Victoria xx	.581	1978—El Paso a	.593
1971—Did not operate as league—		El Paso	.555	Jackson	.567
clubs were members of Dixie		1975—Lafayette xxx	.558		

*Won split-season playoff. †No playoff for title. ‡Finished first and won four-club playoff. §Won four-club playoff. xTitle to Cleburne by default. yTied with Dallas in second half and won playoff for championship. zFort Worth disbanded. **Tied with Beaumont at end of first half and won title in best-of-five series played as part of second half schedule. xxLeague divided into Eastern, Western divisions; won two-team playoff. xxxLeague divided into Eastern, Western divisions; declared co-champions when playoffs were not completed. aLeague divided into Eastern and Western divisions and played split-season; won playoffs. NOTE—Championship awarded to winner of four-team playoff, 1933-51; first-place team and playoff winner co-champions, 1952-64.

STANDNG OF CLUBS AT CLOSE OF FIRST HALF, JUNE 24

EASTERN DIVISION						WESTERN DIVISION					
Club	W.	L.	T.	Pct.	G.B.	Club	W.	L.	T.	Pct.	G.B.
Arkansas (Cardinals)	42	27	0	.609	......	San Antonio (Dodgers)	36	30	0	.545	......
Jackson (Mets)	33	29	0	.532	5½	Midland (Cubs)	38	32	0	.543	......
Shreveport (Giants)	30	33	0	.476	9	Amarillo (Padres)	35	36	0	.493	3½
Tulsa (Rangers)	25	35	0	.417	12½	El Paso (Angels)	26	43	0	.377	11½

STANDING OF CLUBS AT CLOSE OF SECOND HALF, SEPTEMBER 1

EASTERN DIVISION						WESTERN DIVISION					
Club	W.	L.	T.	Pct.	G.B.	Club	W.	L.	T.	Pct.	G.B.
Shreveport (Giants)	43	29	0	.597	......	Midland (Cubs)	38	27	0	.585	......
Arkansas (Cardinals)	34	30	0	.531	5	El Paso (Angels)	35	32	0	.522	4
Jackson (Mets)	37	36	0	.507	6½	San Antonio (Dodgers)	33	32	0	.508	5
Tulsa (Rangers)	33	40	0	.452	10½	Amarillo (Padres)	19	46	0	.292	19

COMPOSITE STANDING OF CLUBS AT CLOSE OF SEASON, SEPTEMBER 1

EASTERN DIVISION

Club	Ark.	Shrev.	Jack.	Tul.	Mid.	S.A.	ElP.	Amar.	W.	L.	T.	Pct.	G.B.
Arkansas (Cardinals)	....	15	19	20	6	5	5	6	76	57	0	.571	......
Shreveport (Giants)	17	....	12	19	7	3	7	8	73	62	0	.541	4
Jackson (Mets)	13	19	....	19	4	4	5	6	70	65	0	.519	7
Tulsa (Rangers)	12	13	13	....	3	3	6	8	58	75	0	.436	18

WESTERN DIVISION

Club	Ark.	Shrev.	Jack.	Tul.	Mid.	S.A.	ElP.	Amar.	W.	L.	T.	Pct.	G.B.
Midland (Cubs)	3	3	6	7	....	18	19	20	76	59	0	.563	......
San Antonio (Dodgers)	3	7	6	4	14	....	18	17	69	62	0	.527	5
El Paso (Angels)	5	3	5	4	13	14	....	17	61	75	0	.449	15½
Amarillo (Padres)	4	2	4	2	12	15	15	....	54	82	0	.397	22½

Arkansas club represented Little Rock, Ark.

Major league affiliations in parentheses.

Playoffs—Arkansas defeated Shreveport, two games to none for Eastern Division Championship. San Antonio defeated Midland, two games to one for Western Division Championship. Arkansas (Eastern Division Champion) defeated San Antonio (Western Division Champion), three games to none for League Championship.

Regular-Season Attendance—Amarillo, 57,667; Arkansas, 183,643; El Paso, 266,475; Jackson, 68,340; Midland, 89,915; San Antonio, 63,990; Shreveport, 47,333; Tulsa, 48,844. Total, 826,207. Playoff, 9,777. All-Star game, 5,689.

Managers: Amarillo—Glenn Ezell, Rusty Gerhardt; Arkansas—Tommy Thompson; El Paso—Larry (Moose) Stubing; Jackson—Bob Wellman; Midland—Randy Hundley; San Antonio—Don LeJohn; Shreveport—Andy Gilbert; Tulsa—Jim Schaffer.

All-Star Team: 1B—DeSa, Arkansas; 2B—Flannery, Amarillo; 3B—Brooks, Jackson; SS—Weiss, San Antonio; OF—Brouhard, El Paso; Roenicke, San Antonio; Lezcano, Midland; C—Davis, Jackson; DH—Grandy, Midland; Utility—Lisi, Tulsa; P—Davis, Arkansas; Harris, Jackson; Searage, Arkansas; Tufts, Shreveport; Manager—Gilbert, Shreveport.

(Compiled by Ed Williams, League Statistician, Shawnee, Okla.)

CLUB BATTING

Club	G.	AB.	R.	OR.	H.	TB.	2B.	3B.	HR.	RBI.	SH.	SF.	Int. BB.	BB.	HP.	SO.	SB.	CS.	LOB.	Pct.
Midland	135	4518	854	750	1410	2016	215	47	99	747	50	46	592	18	34	660	200	105	971	.312
El Paso	136	4679	798	862	1437	2185	271	39	133	741	64	538	25	26	608	92	48	1060	.307
Amarillo	136	4454	618	811	1232	1752	203	24	87	559	37	30	491	17	26	743	98	59	999	.277
Arkansas	133	4289	589	474	1181	1652	226	37	57	532	38	34	436	21	37	591	81	46	961	.275
Tulsa	133	4209	570	653	1148	1592	183	36	63	504	32	27	436	15	46	634	130	60	926	.273
San Antonio	131	4199	630	594	1140	1688	213	31	91	544	73	24	567	18	28	659	197	77	946	.271
Shreveport	135	4210	579	494	1134	1619	168	25	89	529	59	37	524	22	46	678	60	41	989	.269
Jackson	135	4085	495	495	1081	1522	171	30	70	441	30	35	417	28	35	616	118	52	899	.265

INDIVIDUAL BATTING

(Leading Qualifiers for Batting Championship—367 or More Plate Appearances)

*Bats lefthanded. †Switch-hitter.

Player and Club	G.	AB.	R.	H.	TB.	2B.	3B.	HR.	RBI.	SH.	SF.	BB.	HP.	SO.	SB.	CS.	Pct.
Tracy, James, Midland*	86	301	75	107	170	16	1	15	67	2	3	63	4	41	7	8	.355
Brouhard, Mark, El Paso	132	517	97	181	308	29	7	28	107	0	8	61	5	83	4	1	.350
Flannery, Timothy, Amarillo*	125	524	88	181	234	23	6	6	71	2	1	30	0	36	17	12	.345
Rosinski, Brian, Midland*	118	381	70	126	173	22	2	7	74	7	1	54	6	63	14	8	.331
Smith, Christopher, Tulsa†	98	354	46	117	159	18	3	6	54	0	2	36	3	32	4	1	.331
Lezcano, Carlos, Midland	124	457	94	149	228	28	9	11	82	5	2	50	5	86	23	16	.326
Barrios, Jose, Shreveport	118	410	56	133	210	18	4	17	84	3	6	31	4	83	1	1	.324
Lubratich, Steven, El Paso	101	388	66	125	175	20	3	8	69	7	9	27	2	27	7	3	.322
Weiss, Gary, San Antonio*	125	455	82	146	205	27	4	8	66	13	3	76	.2	81	28	9	.321
Santos, Edgardo, San Antonio	107	396	60	126	198	26	2	14	65	5	1	24	2	57	13	5	.318
DeSa, Joseph, Arkansas*	130	463	71	147	228	32	5	13	86	1	5	44	13	65	3	3	.317

Departmental Leaders: G—Bertoni, Greer, 136; AB—Martin, 542; R—Rohn, 122; H—Brouhard, Flannery, 181; TB—Brouhard, 308; 2B—Harper, 37; 3B—Grandy, 10; HR—Brouhard, 28; RBI—Brouhard, 107; SH—Fiala, 17; SF—Bertoni, 14; BB—Rohn, 105; HP—Bogener, 17; SO—Greer, 153; SB—Wilson, 56; CS—Wilson, 24.

(All Players—Listed Alphabetically)

Player and Club	G.	AB.	R.	H.	TB.	2B.	3B.	HR.	RBI.	SH.	SF.	BB.	HP.	SO.	SB.	CS.	Pct.
Alfaro, Jesus, Midland	77	298	62	105	151	16	0	10	50	3	8	42	1	27	11	3	.352
Anderson, Richard, Jackson	25	23	1	6	8	2	0	0	1	0	0	2	0	4	0	0	.261
Aranzamendi, Jorge, Arkansas	58	137	17	35	48	9	2	0	10	2	1	8	0	25	0	0	.255
Ashby, Gary, Amarillo*	119	451	54	139	.188	29	4	4	63	6	4	22	0	94	10	5	.308
Backman, Walter, Jackson†	110	404	63	114	141	11	5	2	19	3	1	35	5	50	23	5	.282
Baez, Jesse, San Antonio	23	82	9	16	23	4	0	1	8	1	0	8	0	14	0	1	.195
Baldwin, Brian, San Antonio	9	2	0	0	0	0	0	0	0	0	0	0	0	2	0	0	.000
Barbe, James, Tulsa	102	343	43	87	111	15	0	3	36	1	0	42	1	68	1	3	.254
Barrios, Jose, Shreveport	118	410	56	133	210	18	4	17	84	3	6	31	4	83	1	1	.324
Barrow, Melvin, Tulsa	90	336	50	98	127	11	3	4	39	2	2	34	3	36	26	10	.292
Barton, Kenneth, Shreveport†	129	460	62	119	176	18	3	11	63	8	4	62	0	37	3	3	.259
Battey, Earl, Amarillo	103	343	45	101	135	20	1	4	39	2	1	31	5	38	8	3	.294
Beal, Calvin, Midland	4	0	1	0	0	0	0	0	0	0	0	0	0	0	0	0	.000
Beltre, Sergio, Jackson	125	374	38	91	141	19	2	9	50	6	3	31	3	67	11	5	.243
Bertolotti, Fulvio, Arkansas	9	24	3	2	3	1	0	0	1	0	0	0	0	6	1	0	.083
Bertoni, Jeffery, El Paso	136	502	83	147	208	27	5	8	66	8	14	59	2	74	23	7	.293
Bhagwat, Thomas, El Paso	102	355	72	106	186	27	1	17	61	2	2	75	1	50	5	2	.299
Bishop, Michael, El Paso	75	276	51	89	155	15	3	15	51	0	4	54	1	60	1	3	.322
Bodie, Keith, Jackson	133	435	45	113	152	16	4	5	37	3	2	37	4	63	16	8	.260
Bogener, Terry, Tulsa*	108	352	52	111	149	22	5	2	44	3	1	44	17	36	21	6	.315
Bradley, Mark, San Antonio	98	328	46	95	145	18	4	8	55	3	8	63	3	79	23	8	.290
Breining, Fred, Shreveport	10	11	0	2	2	0	0	0	1	0	0	0	0	4	0	0	.182
Brenly, Robert, Shreveport	64	193	33	57	94	8	1	9	30	0	0	19	2	38	0	0	.295
Brewster, Richard, El Paso	117	473	79	141	183	18	9	2	52	9	7	45	0	24	22	12	.298
Brooks, Hubert, Jackson	112	406	68	124	158	21	2	3	28	3	1	51	4	59	14	8	.305
Brouhard, Mark, El Paso	132	517	97	181	308	29	7	28	107	0	8	61	5	83	4	1	.350
Bryant, Robert, Jackson*	79	227	41	69	102	11	2	6	36	2	1	32	6	32	13	8	.304
Budner, Scott, Shreveport†	37	58	6	16	17	1	0	0	2	3	0	2	0	3	0	0	.276
Cacciatore, Paul, Jackson	24	22	0	3	4	1	0	0	0	0	0	0	0	7	0	0	.136
Calvert, Mark, Shreveport	8	8	1	2	2	0	0	0	0	0	0	0	0	2	0	0	.250
Capowski, James, 28 Tul-1 Amar.	29	96	13	25	26	1	0	0	6	1	1	5	1	23	2	0	.260
Capra, Nick, Tulsa	66	212	29	59	75	7	0	3	26	2	1	23	2	32	16	5	.278
Carney, Roland, Tulsa*	108	405	51	100	146	17	4	7	35	4	4	33	0	43	13	9	.247
Chamberlain, Thomas, Arkansas	13	13	1	1	1	0	0	0	0	0	0	3	0	7	0	0	.077
Chevolek, Thomas, El Paso*	23	1	0	1	1	0	0	0	0	0	0	0	0	0	1	0	1.000
Clark, Russell, Jackson	20	1	1	0	0	0	0	0	0	0	0	0	0	1	0	0	.000
Cline, Steven, Shreveport	16	8	0	1	1	0	0	0	0	0	0	1	0	4	0	0	.125
Crow, Donald, San Antonio	55	177	15	34	44	7	0	1	16	4	1	16	0	23	2	1	.192
Cummings, Robert, Shreveport	12	41	4	11	13	2	0	0	3	0	0	2	0	7	0	0	.268
Davis, Christopher, Arkansas	43	4	0	0	0	0	0	0	0	0	0	0	0	0	0	0	.000
Davis, Jody, Jackson	132	433	57	128	222	23	4	21	91	0	9	63	3	93	3	2	.296
Delany, Dennis, Arkansas	95	286	24	72	90	12	0	2	38	4	1	30	2	36	0	2	.252
DeLeon, Luis, Arkansas	2	2	0	0	0	0	0	0	0	0	0	0	1	0	0	0	.000
DelVecchio, James, San Antonio	64	179	21	40	50	5	1	1	13	7.	1	14	1	23	7	1	.233
Derryberry, Timothy, Amarillo*	55	192	29	49	72	9	1	4	32	1	3	43	2	46	4	4	.255
DeSa, Joseph, Arkansas*	130	463	71	147	228	32	5	13	86	1	5	44	13	65	3	3	.317
Dimmel, Michael, Arkansas	5	6	0	1	1	0	0	0	0	0	0	0	0	2	0	0	.167
Dixon, F. Daniel, Tulsa	11	26	0	4	5	1	0	0	3	0	0	1	1	5	0	0	.154
Dotson, J. Eugene, Arkansas	129	451	81	138	220	32	7	12	66	0	4	51	3	81	16	10	.306
Edelen, Benny Joe, Arkansas	12	9	0	1	1	0	0	0	1	0	0	0	0	2	0	0	.111
Eduardo, Hector, Arkansas	20	27	1	5	7	2	0	0	3	0	0	1	0	6	0	0	.185
Ellison, J. Jeffrey, Amarillo†	9	19	5	2	3	1	0	0	1	0	0	10	0	4	0	0	.105
Elrod, James, Shreveport	38	103	5	16	22	3	0	1	5	3	1	11	3	21	0	0	.155
Evers, William, Midland	3	7	0	2	2	0	0	0	0	0	0	3	1	1	0	0	.286

Player and Club	G.	AB.	R.	H.	TB.	2B.	3B.	HR.	RBI.	SH.	SF.	BB.	HP.	SO.	SB.	CS.	Pct.
Fiala, Neil, Arkansas*	105	369	51	107	132	11	4	2	36	17	8	49	2	44	8	5	.290
Fierro, Javier, Midland	80	272	40	70	124	15	3	11	54	3	4	23	0	40	4	4	.257
Flannery, Timothy, Amarillo*	125	524	88	181	234	23	6	6	71	2	1	30	0	36	17	12	.345
Fobbs, Larry, San Antonio	121	392	53	93	145	16	3	10	55	6	3	78	0	43	14	10	.237
Glinatsis, Michael, Shreveport	26	31	0	0	0	0	0	0	0	3	0	0	1	13	0	0	.000
Gooch, Ronald, Tulsa	53	192	16	52	60	6	1	0	22	3	3	25	4	27	3	5	.271
Goulding, Richard, San Antonio	25	9	0	1	1	0	0	0	1	1	0	0	0	1	0	0	.111
Grandy, Eric, Midland	133	492	102	150	221	18	10	11	84	1	8	72	5	70	45	13	.305
Greer, Brian, Amarillo	136	489	66	112	189	21	1	18	79	3	7	70	1	153	18	6	.229
Grote, Robert, Jackson	23	24	2	4	4	0	0	0	1	4	0	2	0	9	0	0	.167
Gutierrez, Julian, Arkansas	19	69	11	19	25	2	2	0	5	1	1	5	0	6	2	0	.275
Hacker, Richard, Amarillo	6	14	1	2	2	0	0	0	1	0	0	2	0	1	0	0	.143
Hamner, J. Peter, Jackson	37	1	1	1	1	0	0	0	0	0	0	0	0	0	0	0	1.000
Hargesheimer, Alan, Shreveport	25	24	2	2	4	0	1	0	0	3	0	4	0	11	0	0	.083
Harper, Brian, El Paso	132	531	85	167	252	37	3	14	90	3	9	50	2	47	10	2	.315
Harris, Greg, Jackson†	26	31	2	3	3	0	0	0	2	0	0	1	0	12	0	0	.097
Harrison, Douglas, San Antonio	24	11	0	1	1	0	0	0	1	1	0	0	0	4	0	0	.091
Hayes, Brian, San Antonio*	11	1	0	0	0	0	0	0	0	0	0	0	0	0	0	0	.000
Hayes, William, Midland	107	377	51	113	168	21	2	10	55	6	2	31	4	85	4	3	.300
Heaton, Michael, El Paso†	32	0	1	0	0	0	0	0	0	0	0	0	0	0	0	0	.000
Heimueller, Gorman, Shreveport*	29	10	0	3	5	2	0	0	1	0	0	3	0	3	0	0	.300
Hernandez, Leonardo, San Antonio	36	128	19	32	45	7	0	2	11	0	0	8	0	15	0	0	.250
Hicks, Joseph, Amarillo	118	405	77	114	184	23	4	13	67	5	1	63	4	53	25	9	.281
Holton, Brian, San Antonio	13	7	1	0	0	0	0	0	0	1	0	0	0	3	0	0	.000
Hough, Stanley, Jackson	13	47	4	6	7	1	0	0	1	0	0	1	0	7	0	0	.128
Howard, Michael, Jackson†	131	447	43	102	127	13	3	2	42	0	5	43	2	50	31	9	.228
Howe, Steve, San Antonio*	13	8	0	1	1	0	0	0	0	0	0	0	0	1	0	0	.125
Humphry, Brandt, El Paso	121	447	71	136	214	30	3	14	72	0	3	19	2	70	1	7	.304
Hunsaker, Frank, Arkansas	32	118	15	40	44	4	0	0	12	0	1	9	0	9	0	0	.339
Hypes, Kyle, Shreveport†	13	6	0	1	2	1	0	0	0	0	0	1	0	1	0	0	.167
Ilertsen, Dane, Amarillo	129	454	52	127	187	22	1	12	74	2	5	55	5	89	1	0	.280
Johnson, David, Arkansas	27	21	1	1	1	0	0	0	1	1	0	1	0	2	0	0	.048
Johnson, Randall, Jackson	86	228	23	67	80	7	0	2	20	0	2	25	3	18	0	2	.294
Jones, Donny, El Paso	26	92	12	21	25	4	0	0	9	1	1	3	0	21	0	1	.228
Kearney, Robert, Shreveport	63	224	27	60	83	9	1	4	24	4	1	13	2	36	0	2	.268
Kirchenwitz, Arno, Arkansas*	24	19	0	1	1	0	0	0	2	0	0	0	0	3	0	0	.053
Krug, Gary, Midland*	44	168	31	65	88	5	3	4	38	2	4	9	2	21	3	1	.387
Landis, Craig, Shreveport	126	436	66	132	185	24	1	9	59	2	5	61	12	58	13	3	.303
Lane, Richard, Jackson	6	15	1	1	1	0	0	0	0	0	0	2	0	2	0	0	.067
Lanning, David, San Antonio*	23	79	6	16	20	4	0	0	3	1	0	6	0	9	0	0	.203
Landrum, Terry, Arkansas	71	265	44	71	110	20	5	3	33	2	1	25	1	37	15	8	.268
Lashley, Mickey, San Antonio	42	5	0	1	1	0	0	0	0	0	0	0	0	4	0	0	.200
Lezcano, Carlos, Midland	124	457	94	149	228	28	9	11	82	5	2	50	5	86	23	16	.326
Lisi, Riccardo, Midland	120	435	86	133	241	32	5	22	84	0	3	51	3	83	7	1	.306
Littlefield, John, Arkansas	26	5	0	0	0	0	0	0	0	0	0	0	0	1	0	0	.000
Lubratich, Steven, El Paso	101	388	66	125	175	20	3	8	69	7	9	27	2	27	7	3	.322
Lunar, Luis, Jackson	8	2	0	0	0	0	0	0	0	0	0	0	0	1	0	0	.000
Mabee, Victor, Tulsa	7	24	2	4	4	0	0	0	1	1	0	0	0	7	0	0	.167
MacDonald, Ronald, Jackson	133	458	62	132	209	21	4	16	74	6	8	47	4	42	5	2	.288
Martin, Jared, Midland*	129	542	85	168	194	18	4	0	73	11	2	42	2	66	33	17	.310
Martinez, Alfredo, Jackson	24	28	0	3	3	0	0	0	1	1	0	1	0	14	0	0	.107
May, Ted, Midland*	21	59	7	19	29	1	0	3	12	1	2	10	0	17	0	0	.322
McDonald, Russell, San Antonio	29	10	2	3	3	0	0	0	1	1	0	1	0	1	0	0	.300
McMath, Shelton, Tulsa	39	125	16	24	39	6	0	3	21	1	2	16	0	38	3	1	.192
Mendoza, David, Shreveport	21	10	0	0	09	0	0	0	0	1	0	0	0	4	0	0	.000
Miller, Richard, Jackson*	31	80	8	16	20	4	0	0	7	0	0	7	1	11	2	1	.200
Mitchell, Howard, Shreveport	121	405	65	113	151	16	2	6	50	6	6	63	3	50	7	5	.279
Moffitt, G. Scott, El Paso	129	506	90	159	228	34	1	11	70	1	3	54	4	27	13	5	.314
Mustad, Eric, Amarillo	32	0	1	0	0	0	0	0	0	0	0	0	0	0	0	0	.000
Nipp, Mark, San Antonio	24	9	1	1	1	0	0	0	2	0	0	0	0	5	0	0	.111
Oliver, Richard, El Paso	85	297	41	81	100	10	3	1	36	3	1	41	1	34	6	4	.273
Olmsted, Alan, Arkansas	12	11	1	1	1	0	0	0	1	0	0	2	0	4	0	0	.091
O'Neill, Paul, Amarillo	49	162	16	36	65	6	1	7	19	0	1	12	0	22	0	1	.222
Parker, Mark, Midland*	24	4	0	0	0	0	0	0	0	0	0	0	0	3	0	0	.000
Pastors, Gregory, Amarillo	40	130	17	35	54	5	1	4	12	4	1	13	2	25	1	3	.269
Pechek, Wayne, Shreveport*	92	267	50	83	96	9	2	0	37	3	1	53	4	28	10	10	.311
Penniall, David, Arkansas	55	197	32	48	65	6	1	3	26	0	4	20	1	32	9	3	.244
Perez, Francisco, Jackson	77	222	21	56	77	10	1	3	20	1	2	21	0	31	0	1	.252
Power, Ted, San Antonio	10	2	0	0	0	0	0	0	0	0	0	0	0	2	0	0	.000
Prewitt, Larry, Jackson	16	24	0	2	2	0	0	0	0	0	0	0	0	11	0	0	.083
Ramirez, Jack, Tulsa	51	158	18	35	43	5	0	1	14	1	2	9	2	20	6	3	.222
Ransom, Jeffrey, Shreveport†	43	145	10	40	48	6	1	0	14	2	0	7	1	20	0	0	.276
Reed, Curtis, Amarillo*	76	269	32	81	111	9	3	5	25	0	1	27	0	51	3	4	.301
Richards, David, San Antonio	21	71	4	17	21	4	0	0	2	1	0	3	1	6	0	0	.239
Richardt, Michael, Tulsa	68	272	50	89	131	17	5	5	24	3	0	14	2	24	10	6	.327

Player and Club	G.	AB.	R.	H.	TB.	2B.	3B.	HR.	RBI.	SH.	SF.	BB.	HP.	SO.	SB.	CS.	Pct.
Riggleman, James, Arkansas	46	110	17	30	42	9	0	1	23	0	3	13	.1	23	5	0	.273
Rincon, Andrew, Arkansas	3	4	0	0	0	0	0	0	0	0	0	0	0	0	0	0	.000
Roenicke, Ronald, San Antonio†	130	464	82	140	215	24	6	13	69	5	3	99	2	77	47	15	.302
Rohn, Daniel, Midland*	128	489	122	150	203	26	6	5	52	1	5	105	1	35	30	19	.307
Roof, Eugene, Arkansas	128	478	86	145	206	22	3	11	53	1	1	72	7	49	10	7	.303
Rosinski, Brian, Midland*	118	381	70	126	173	22	2	7	74	7	1	54	6	63	14	8	.331
Roy, Patrick, Shreveport	40	11	0	0	0	0	0	0	0	0	0	0	0	1	0	0	.000
Ruiz, August, San Antonio*	13	4	0	0	0	0	0	0	0	0	0	0	0	2	0	0	.000
Runnells, Thomas, Shreveport†	128	435	45	102	128	10	2	4	32	9	5	44	1	55	4	3	.234
Russell, Joseph, Tulsa	84	263	37	60	82	8	1	4	35	3	2	29	3	34	0	4	.228
Sander, Richard, San Antonio	17	5	0	1	1	0	0	0	0	0	0	0	0	2	0	0	.200
Santos, Edgardo, San Antonio	107	396	60	126	198	26	2	14	65	5	1	24	2	57	13	5	.318
Scheetz, Michael, Shreveport	11	22	0	1	1	0	0	0	0	0	0	3	0	7	0	0	.045
Searage, Raymond, Arkansas*	43	7	1	1	1	0	0	0	0	1	0	0	0	2	0	0	.143
Segelke, Herman, Midland	29	3	0	0	0	0	0	0	0	0	0	0	0	3	0	0	.000
Shames, Bradley, Amarillo	53	153	26	38	43	3	1	0	16	3	3	30	2	16	0	2	.248
Shirley, Steven, San Antonio*	13	2	0	0	0	0	0	0	0	0	0	0	0	1	0	0	.000
Shoemaker, John, San Antonio*	60	192	31	47	51	4	0	0	13	3	1	22	1	11	1	2	.245
Slettvet, Douglas, Jackson	2	2	1	0	0	0	0	0	0	0	0	1	0	0	0	0	.000
Smith, Christopher, Tulsa†	98	354	46	117	159	18	3	6	54	0	2	36	3	32	4	1	.331
Smith, Daniel, Jackson	44	7	1	2	4	0	1	0	0	1	0	0	0	1	0	0	.286
Smith, Steven, Amarillo	89	380	54	109	131	14	1	2	29	3	1	24	2	10	8	4	.287
Soriano, Hilario, San Antonio	37	115	8	28	34	6	0	0	16	4	1	7	0	20	1	0	.243
Strawn, C. DeFla, Tulsa	58	186	20	52	69	7	2	2	22	1	2	18	1	43	2	1	.280
Strelitz, Leonard, Arkansas	27	27	2	5	5	0	0	0	1	0	1	0	1	5	0	0	.185
Szymarek, Paul, Shreveport*	24	68	9	24	38	4	2	2	18	0	0	3	1	17	1	0	.353
Thomas, Randall, Arkansas†	111	349	42	88	105	11	0	2	34	2	3	27	4	42	3	1	.252
Thompson, Michael, Midland	30	97	13	17	19	2	0	0	8	3	2	11	2	7	4	2	.175
Thurmond, Mark, Amarillo*	19	2	1	0	0	0	0	0	0	0	0	1	0	0	0	0	.000
Till, Steven, Jackson†	54	141	13	36	54	11	2	1	11	0	1	14	0	30	0	1	.255
Tingley, Ronald, Amarillo	30	90	16	23	32	4	1	1	6	1	0	14	0	17	2	0	.256
Tisdale, Freddie, Arkansas*	'97	297	33	78	110	20	3	2	37	0	4	23	1	29	1	2	.263
Tolleson, J. Wayne, Tulsa	130	418	43	98	124	9	7	1	36	4	3	56	3	79	16	5	.234
Tracy, James, Midland*	86	301	75	107	170	16	1	15	67	2	3	63	4	41	7	8	.355
Trevino, A. Ted, Midland	17	45	9	10	17	1	0	2	7	0	0	9	0	8	0	2	.222
Tucker, Michael, Shreveport	20	12	0	1	1	0	0	0	2	0	1	0	0	5	0	0	.083
Tufts, Robert, Shreveport*	26	28	1	3	5	2	0	0	0	3	0	1	0	12	0	0	.107
Turgeon, Michael, Midland†	130	461	79	137	206	25	7	10	83	3	3	61	1	78	13	8	.297
Valentine, Vincent, Midland	5	1	0	0	0	0	0	0	0	0	0	0	0	0	0	0	.000
Venable, W. McKinley, Shreveport*	18	69	11	16	21	1	2	0	3	0	0	7	0	6	5	2	.232
Vessey, Thomas, Amarillo	76	234	22	50	65	6	0	3	14	3	0	27	3	57	0	5	.214
Violette, John, Jackson	3	3	0	2	2	0	0	0	0	0	1	0	1	0	0	0	.667
VonOhlen, David, Jackson*	37	1	0	0	0	0	0	0	0	0	0	0	0	1	0	0	.000
Waller, E. Tyrone, Arkansas	126	432	48	122	177	29	4	6	54	1	1	42	2	60	8	4	.282
Walterhouse, Richard, Amarillo*	40	141	15	31	55	8	2	4	11	2	1	17	0	30	1	1	.220
Weiss, Gary, San Antonio†	125	455	82	146	205	27	4	8	66	13	3	76	2	81	28	9	.321
White, Myron, San Antonio*	31	128	20	38	67	7	2	6	25	1	0	7	0	14	3	0	.297
Whitehead, Steven, El Paso*	42	146	25	33	63	9	0	7	28	1	1	30	3	50	0	0	.226
Whitmer, Daniel, El Paso	43	148	25	50	87	11	1	8	29	0	2	20	3	41	0	1	.338
Wilkins, Steve, Shreveport*	117	337	59	100	183	20	0	21	64	0	4	81	8	86	2	1	.297
Williams, Ray, Arkansas	44	3	0	0	0	0	0	0	0	1	0	0	0	2	0	0	.000
Wilson, Michael, San Antonio	130	492	105	155	214	27	7	6	42	12	1	82	7	42	56	24	.315
Winslow, Daniel, Arkansas	23	63	6	20	25	3	1	0	11	0	0	9	0	3	0	1	.317
Witt, Harold, Arkansas	14	23	1	2	3	1	0	0	0	0	0	1	0	7	0	0	.087
Wojcik, James, Shreveport	1	0	0	0	0	0	0	0	0	0	0	0	0	0	0	0	.000
Woodard, Darrell, Midland†	21	64	13	22	23	1	0	0	6	2	0	7	0	9	9	1	.344
Woodbrey, Mark, Shreveport*	106	378	67	96	131	14	3	5	37	5	3	55	4	66	14	11	.254
Zebley, Elwood, Tulsa	5	16	0	2	3	1	0	0	2	0	0	0	0	5	0	0	.125
Zouras, Michael, San Antonio	127	446	65	108	202	27	2	21	82	1	1	53	9	117	2	1	.242

The following pitchers had no plate appearances primarily through use of designated hitters, listed alphabetically by club, games in parentheses:

AMARILLO—Armstrong, Michael (7); Biggerstaff, Barry †(15); Carroll, Joe (20); Chiffer, Floyd (43); Gerhardt, A. Russell †(12); Hirschy, Francis (23); Hunziker, Kent †(14); Pickert, Gary *(28); Stablein, George (27); Wilkes, Gregory (22); Yandle, John (37).

ARKANSAS—Gott, James (2).

EL PASO—Border, Robert (17); Brown, Steven (10); Comstock, Keith †(16); Crisler, J. Joel (12); Gronlund, David (21); Miller, Mark *(26); Phillips, Charles *(32); Rennicke, Randall *(38); Rommel, Richard (4); Schrom, Kenneth (25); Steck, David (8); Stover, Michael (21); Vallone, James (16).

MIDLAND—Albert, Jeffrey (11-7 with San Antonio); Allen, Michael (43); Butler, W. Thomas (24); Clark, Robert *(2); Earley, William (30); Ledbetter, Charles (23); Mack, Henry (27); McClain, Joe (2); Mercer, Mark *(40); Perlman, Jonathan (18); Smith, Lee (35); Turner, Darrell (39).

SAN ANTONIO—Bain, Paul (5); Nobles, James (3).

SHREVEPORT—Schmidt, E. Eugene (5).

TULSA—Butcher, John †(26); Crutcher, David (26); Finch, Steven (12); Fossas, E. Anthony *(2); Gleaton, Jerry *(5); Jakubowski, Stanley (15); Kelly, Harold (8); Lamson, Charles *(24); Nickerson, James (7); Nielsen, Stephen (24); Rainbolt, Rayburn (36); Vasquez, Jerry (7); Whitehouse, Leonard *(25).

GRAND SLAM HOME RUNS—Barrios, 5; Beltre, Szymarek, 2 each; Barton, Bertoni, Bishop, Brenly, Brouhard, Bryant, Capra, Greer, Humphry, Kearney, Rohn, Roof, Rosinski, Whitehead, Wilkins, Zouras, 1 each.

AWARDED FIRST BASE ON INTERFERENCE—Bertoni 9 (Russell 2, Crow, W. Hayes, Kearney, Soriano, Tingley, Vessey, Winslow); Bhagwat 2 (J. Davis, Tingley); Landrum (J. Davis); Mitchell (J. Davis).

CLUB FIELDING

Club	G.	PO.	A.	E.	DP.	PB.	Pct.	Club	G.	PO.	A.	E.	DP.	PB.	Pct.
Arkansas	133	3326	1413	130	129	8	.973	Tulsa	133	3239	1473	172	144	9	.965
Shreveport	135	3322	1568	149	148	20	.970	Jackson	135	3201	1314	162	96	18	.965
El Paso	136	3481	1527	166	157	27	.968	San Antonio	131	3330	1428	185	118	22	.963
Midland	135	3433	1519	172	170	13	.966	Amarillo	136	3374	1480	224	125	29	.956

Triple Plays—None.

INDIVIDUAL FIELDING

*Throws lefthanded.

FIRST BASEMEN

Player and Club	G.	PO.	A.	E.	DP.	Pct.	Player and Club	G.	PO.	A.	E.	DP.	Pct.
Lubratich, El Paso	15	128	9	0	14	1.000	Bishop, El Paso	75	653	44	11	65	.984
Shoemaker, San Ant	52	443	30	2	44	.996	Howard, Jackson	51	418	19	7	34	.984
BARBE, Tulsa	97	850	61	6	92	.993	Humphry, El Paso	48	410	17	7	51	.984
Tracy, Midland	86	799	31	6	95	.993	Perez, Jackson	44	341	28	6	29	.984
Krug, Midland*	43	367	19	3	53	.992	Ilertsen, Amarillo	63	534	24	10	48	.982
DeSa, Arkansas*	126	1129	71	11	102	.991	Lisi, Tulsa	33	311	25	6	37	.982
R. Johnson, Jackson	12	92	5	1	6	.990	Pechek, Shreveport*	12	102	4	2	11	.981
Roenicke, San Antonio*	38	154	8	2	13	.988	Ashby, Amarillo*	74	585	53	14	58	.979
Barrios, Shreveport	116	1071	62	15	113	.987	J. Davis, Jackson	26	184	13	5	14	.975
Zouras, San Antonio	65	558	41	9	56	.985							

(Fewer Than Ten Games)

Player and Club	G.	PO.	A.	E.	DP.	Pct.	Player and Club	G.	PO.	A.	E.	DP.	Pct.
Walterhouse, Amarillo	4	35	1	0	4	1.000	Brenly, Shreveport	8	62	3	1	7	.985
Rosinski, Midland	2	10	1	0	2	1.000	MacDonald, Jackson	6	50	3	1	1	.981
Barton, Shreveport	1	8	0	0	0	1.000	Capowski, Tulsa	5	33	3	1	1	.973
Hunsaker, Arkansas	1	5	0	0	1	1.000	Fierro, Midland	8	30	4	2	5	.944
Wilkins, Shreveport	3	4	0	0	1	1.000	Riggleman, Arkansas	2	16	0	1	0	.941
Slettvett, Jackson	1	1	0	0	0	1.000	Evers, Midland	2	14	0	1	2	.933
C. Smith, Tulsa	1	1	0	0	0	1.000	Whitmer, El Paso	2	11	1	1	2	.923
Tisdale, Arkansas	9	63	7	1	6	.986							

SECOND BASEMEN

Player and Club	G.	PO.	A.	E.	DP.	Pct.	Player and Club	G.	PO.	A.	E.	DP.	Pct.
Richardt, Tulsa	67	162	218	6	77	.984	Rohn, Midland	128	315	429	19	120	.975
Del Vecchio, San Ant	14	23	36	1	7	.983	Gooch, Tulsa	51	127	143	8	39	.971
MacDONALD, Jackson	126	259	341	11	63	.982	Barton, Shreveport	126	294	344	26	87	.961
Lubratich, El Paso	51	114	137	5	25	.980	Flannery, Amarillo	120	280	353	27	81	.959
Gutierrez, Arkansas	18	46	53	2	10	.980	Fobbs, San Antonio	119	244	296	29	70	.949
Oliver, El Paso	85	190	273	10	74	.979	Capra, Tulsa	14	21	33	5	11	.915
Fiala, Arkansas	105	217	301	12	63	.977	Mitchell, Shreveport	11	24	22	5	5	.902

(Fewer Than Ten Games)

Player and Club	G.	PO.	A.	E.	DP.	Pct.	Player and Club	G.	PO.	A.	E.	DP.	Pct.
Walterhouse, Amarillo	8	18	12	0	3	1.000	Witt, Arkansas	1	1	1	0	0	1.000
Tisdale, Arkansas	5	8	18	0	3	1.000	Wojcik, Shreveport	1	1	1	0	0	1.000
Fierro, Midland	6	11	11	0	5	1.000	Hacker, Amarillo	4	10	16	1	6	.963
Brewster, El Paso	5	7	8	0	4	1.000	Woodard, Midland	5	12	11	1	2	.958
O'Neill, Amarillo	2	4	8	0	1	1.000	Backman, Jackson	5	14	8	1	1	.957
Howard, Jackson	1	2	6	0	0	1.000	Aranzamendi, Arkansas	7	14	17	3	5	.912
Thompson, Midland	4	2	4	0	0	1.000	R. Johnson, Jackson	3	10	6	2	1	.889
Vessey, Amarillo	2	3	2	0	2	1.000	Capowski, Amarillo	1	0	2	5	0	.286
Ramirez, Tulsa	1	3	0	0	1	1.000							

THIRD BASEMEN

Player and Club	G.	PO.	A.	E.	DP.	Pct.	Player and Club	G.	PO.	A.	E.	DP.	Pct.
Perez, Jackson	10	6	16	0	0	1.000	WALLER, Arkansas	121	105	275	26	36	.936
O'Neill, Amarillo	47	30	95	4	9	.969	Mitchell, Shreveport	89	65	215	19	24	.936
Lubratich, El Paso	31	29	62	3	9	.968	Turgeon, Midland	124	100	226	25	37	.929
Lanning, San Antonio	23	19	55	4	5	.949	Ramirez, Tulsa	49	24	99	10	13	.925
R. Johnson, Jackson	29	21	42	4	4	.940	Wilkins, Shreveport	18	7	30	3	5	.925

THIRD BASEMEN—Continued

Player and Club	G.	PO.	A.	E.	DP.	Pct.
Humphry, El Paso	71	57	146	17	17	.923
Walterhouse, Amarillo	24	16	43	5	4	.922
Brooks, Jackson	92	55	158	19	12	.918
Capra, Tulsa	49	35	125	15	16	.914
Capowski, Tulsa	17	14	28	4	4	.913
Battey, Amarillo	69	51	114	16	5	.912
Del Vecchio, San Ant	19	7	34	4	2	.911
Riggleman, Arkansas	11	8	22	3	1	.909

Player and Club	G.	PO.	A.	E.	DP.	Pct.
Brenly, Shreveport	16	7	32	4	3	.907
C. Smith, Tulsa	22	10	28	4	0	.905
Whitehead, El Paso	36	27	70	11	7	.898
Hernandez, San Ant	33	19	51	8	3	.897
Elrod, Shreveport	27	16	58	9	2	.892
Bodie, Jackson	12	8	26	5	1	.872
Zouras, San Antonio	58	52	121	28	11	.861

(Fewer Than Ten Games)

Player and Club	G.	PO.	A.	E.	DP.	Pct.
Fierro, Midland	8	3	19	0	1	1.000
Gooch, Tulsa	2	1	7	0	0	1.000
Hacker, Amarillo	2	1	1	0	0	1.000
Barton, Shreveport	1	0	1	0	0	1.000

Player and Club	G.	PO.	A.	E.	DP.	Pct.
Witt, Arkansas	1	0	1	0	0	1.000
Thompson, Midland	6	4	10	1	1	.933
Shoemaker, San Ant	2	4	2	2	1	.750
Barbe, Midland	1	0	0	1	0	.000

SHORTSTOPS

Player and Club	G.	PO.	A.	E.	DP.	Pct.
Mitchell, Shreveport	11	15	31	0	9	1.000
RUNNELLS, Shreveport	125	190	413	19	79	.969
Bertoni, El Paso	136	250	424	27	103	.961
Aranzamendi, Arkansas	37	39	80	5	14	.960
Thomas, Arkansas	110	176	296	20	58	.959
Fierro, Midland	53	93	177	12	46	.957
Alfaro, Midland	75	115	232	19	58	.948
Weiss, San Antonio	125	220	410	35	83	.947

Player and Club	G.	PO.	A.	E.	DP.	Pct.
Howard, Jackson	10	12	22	2	1	.944
Tolleson, Tulsa	129	179	413	41	84	.935
Backman, Jackson	104	170	251	30	46	.933
Pastors, Amarillo	39	54	121	13	28	.931
S. Smith, Amarillo	89	124	270	35	50	.918
Brooks, Jackson	25	37	60	10	12	.907
Del Vecchio, San Ant	10	8	14	3	2	.880

(Fewer Than Ten Games)

Player and Club	G.	PO.	A.	E.	DP.	Pct.
Tisdale, Arkansas	2	2	6	0	1	1.000
Flannery, Amarillo	5	7	21	1	2	.966
Woodard, Midland	6	8	19	1	3	.964

Player and Club	G.	PO.	A.	E.	DP.	Pct.
Thompson, Midland	5	2	13	1	2	.938
Capra, Tulsa	3	4	15	2	2	.905
Walterhouse, Amarillo	6	6	12	4	2	.818

CATCHERS

Player and Club	G.	PO.	A.	E.	DP.	PB.	Pct.
Hunsaker, Arkansas	29	149	15	0	4	0	1.000
Jones, El Paso	22	114	24	0	2	2	1.000
Till, Jackson	40	215	23	1	1	3	.996
Brenly, Shreveport	26	114	18	1	6	4	.992
Crow, San Antonio	55	269	39	4	2	9	.987
Soriano, San Antonio	36	202	25	3	2	9	.987
Cummings, Shrev	12	68	6	1	0	4	.987
Trevino, Midland	16	58	11	1	2	0	.986
DELANY, Arkansas	88	395	30	7	5	7	.984
Hayes, Midland	105	497	80	10	5	12	.983
J. Davis, Jackson	90	477	68	10	6	13	.982
Baez, San Antonio	23	139	29	3	2	3	.982

Player and Club	G.	PO.	A.	E.	DP.	PB.	Pct.
Kearney, Shreveport	60	312	49	7	4	7	.981
Ransom, Shreveport	32	140	16	3	2	4	.981
Shames, Amarillo	52	293	34	7	4	8	.979
Whitmer, El Paso	21	111	19	3	2	5	.977
Vessey, Amarillo	68	378	37	10	7	14	.976
Winslow, Arkansas	17	76	4	2	0	1	.976
Russell, Tulsa	79	422	60	14	7	6	.972
Strawn, Tulsa	52	241	39	8	6	3	.972
Tingley, Amarillo	20	119	17	4	2	7	.971
May, Midland	16	67	7	4	1	1	.949
Richards, San Ant	21	106	21	7	2	1	.948
Harper, El Paso	96	443	66	29	5	19	.946

(Fewer Than Ten Games)

Player and Club	G.	PO.	A.	E.	DP.	PB.	Pct.
Zebley, Tulsa	5	30	2	0	0	0	1.000
Hough, Jackson	5	21	2	0	0	0	1.000
Evers, Midland	1	6	1	0	0	0	1.000
Bishop, El Paso	1	3	0	0	0	1	1.000

Player and Club	G.	PO.	A.	E.	DP.	PB.	Pct.
Bertolotti, Arkansas	9	43	5	1	0	0	.980
Lane, Jackson	5	23	3	1	0	1	.963
Scheetz, Shreveport	7	35	2	2	0	1	.949

OUTFIELDERS

Player and Club	G.	PO.	A.	E.	DP.	Pct.
Howard, Jackson	72	134	8	0	1	1.000
Tisdale, Arkansas	20	25	4	0	0	1.000
Szymarek, Shreveport	16	20	1	0	0	1.000
Tingley, Amarillo	10	14	0	0	0	1.000
ROENICKE, San Ant*	108	272	10	2	2	.993
Penniall, Arkansas	53	131	1	1	0	.992
Bryant, Jackson	70	112	4	1	0	.992
Lezcano, Midland	123	338	11	5	2	.986
Lisi, Tulsa	72	142	3	2	2	.986
Wilkins, Shreveport	85	129	5	2	0	.985
Bhagwat, El Paso	66	113	6	2	2	.983
White, San Antonio*	31	49	5	1	0	.982

Player and Club	G.	PO.	A.	E.	DP.	Pct.
McMath, Tulsa	32	43	2	1	0	.978
Woodbrey, Shreveport	101	231	5	6	1	.975
Barrow, Tulsa	87	178	10	5	1	.974
Wilson, San Antonio	116	243	9	7	8	.973
Brouhard, El Paso	104	171	10	5	2	.973
Landrum, Arkansas	70	134	7	4	3	.972
Brewster, El Paso	111	256	8	8	2	.971
Roof, Arkansas	126	217	12	7	5	.970
Venable, Shreveport	18	28	2	1	0	.968
Santos, San Antonio	46	84	5	3	0	.967
Moffitt, El Paso	129	335	18	13	5	.964
Dotson, Arkansas	127	244	16	10	7	.963

OUTFIELDERS—Continued

Player and Club	G.	PO.	A.	E.	DP.	Pct.
Bogener, Tulsa*	97	-152	6	6	2	.963
Carney, Tulsa*	95	148	7	6	2	.963
Ashby, Amarillo*	45	72	5	3	0	.963
Bodie, Jackson	119	183	18	8	4	.962
Martin, Midland*	128	293	24	13	5	.961
Bradley, San Antonio	94	163	10	7	0	.961
Landis, Shreveport	123	197	16	9	4	.959
Pechek, Shreveport*	55	86	4	4	2	.957
Beltre, Jackson	119	235	7	12	1	.953
Hicks, Amarillo	118	200	15	11	0	.951
Reed, Amarillo	75	103	13	6	1	.951
Brenly, Shreveport	12	16	2	1	1	.947
Greer, Amarillo	135	335	13	21	3	.943
Rosinski, Midland	87	107	8	7	0	.943
Miller, Jackson	21	32	0	2	0	.941
Battey, Amarillo	24	27	1	2	1	.933
Grandy, Midland	57	102	4	8	3	.930
C. Smith, Tulsa	14	15	0	2	0	.882

(Fewer Than Ten Games)

Player and Club	G.	PO.	A.	E.	DP.	Pct.
R. Johnson, Jackson	9	21	0	0	0	1.000
Derryberry, Amarillo	8	13	1	0	0	1.000
Riggleman, Arkansas	5	10	0	0	0	1.000
Budner, Shreveport*	7	7	1	0	0	1.000
Thompson, Midland	6	6	2	0	0	1.000
Witt, Arkansas	4	4	0	0	0	1.000
Lubratich, El Paso	3	4	0	0	1	1.000
Fierro, Midland	6	3	0	0	0	1.000
Turgeon, Midland	4	3	0	0	0	1.000
Heimueller, Shreveport*	2	3	0	0	0	1.000
Till, Jackson	3	2	0	0	0	1.000
MacDonald, Jackson	1	2	1	0	0	1.000
Krug, Midland*	1	2	0	0	0	1.000
Del Vecchio, San Ant.	3	1	0	0	0	1.000
Roy, Shreveport	2	1	0	0	0	1.000
Dimmel, Arkansas	1	1	0	0	0	1.000
Harper, El Paso	1	1	0	0	0	1.000
Jones, El Paso	1	1	0	0	0	1.000
Woodard, Midland	7	10	0	1	0	.909
Hough, Jackson	7	9	1	1	0	.909
Dixon, Tulsa	9	11	0	2	0	.846
Capowski, Tulsa	3	2	0	1	0	.667

PITCHERS

Player and Club	G.	PO.	A.	E.	DP.	Pct.
TUFTS, Shreveport	26	15	45	0	1	1.000
Eduardo, Arkansas	20	10	33	0	1	1.000
Butcher, Tulsa	26	19	18	0	2	1.000
Budner, Shreveport*	24	8	22	0	0	1.000
Tucker, Shreveport	20	4	23	0	2	1.000
Gronlund, El Paso	21	3	21	0	1	1.000
Vallone, El Paso*	16	4	19	0	0	1.000
Heaton, El Paso	30	11	11	0	2	1.000
Edelen, Arkansas	12	5	17	0	1	1.000
Chamberlain, Arkansas	13	5	13	0	1	1.000
Littlefield, Arkansas	26	4	13	0	1	1.000
Rennicke, El Paso	38	7	8	0	0	1.000
C. Davis, Arkansas	43	1	12	0	3	1.000
Mercer, Tulsa*	40	2	11	0	0	1.000
Shirley, San Antonio	13	0	13	0	0	1.000
Roy, Shreveport	38	2	8	0	0	1.000
Chevolek, El Paso*	23	1	8	0	0	1.000
Cline, Shreveport	16	3	5	0	1	1.000
Von Ohlen, Jackson*	37	0	7	0	0	1.000
Hunziker, Amarillo	14	2	4	0	1	1.000
Gerhardt, Amarillo	12	1	3	0	0	1.000
Butler, Midland*	24	0	3	0	0	1.000
Stablein, Amarillo	27	15	37	1	1	.981
Glinatsis, Shreveport	26	10	29	1	4	.975
Nipp, San Antonio	24	6	25	1	0	.969
Grote, Jackson	21	8	23	1	4	.969
Goulding, San Antonio	25	10	19	1	2	.967
Crutcher, Tulsa	26	8	20	1	1	.966
Anderson, Jackson	25	6	22	1	0	.966
D. Johnson, Arkansas*	26	5	21	1	2	.963
Mendoza, Shreveport	21	4	22	1	2	.963
D. Smith, Jackson	44	3	20	1	0	.958
Crisler, El Paso	12	2	21	1	0	.958
Heimueller, Shreveport*	27	3	18	1	1	.955
Yandle, Amarillo	37	2	18	1	1	.952
Howe, San Antonio	13	1	19	1	1	.952
Lamson, Tulsa*	24	5	14	1	3	.950
Parker, Midland	24	10	24	2	1	.944
Border, El Paso	17	2	15	1	2	.944
L. Smith, Midland	35	4	13	1	1	.944
Whitehouse, Tulsa*	25	2	15	1	2	.944
Mustad, Amarillo	27	15	33	3	2	.941
Hirschy, Amarillo	23	3	13	1	1	.941
Sander, San Antonio	17	5	11	1	1	.941
Hamner, Jackson	37	5	10	1	0	.938
Earley, Midland*	30	9	35	3	3	.936
Hargesheimer, Shreve.	24	10	34	3	2	.936
Williams, Arkansas	44	1	13	1	0	.933
Thurmond, Amarillo*	17	2	12	1	1	.933
Phillips, El Paso*	32	3	10	1	1	.929
Breining, Shreveport	10	4	9	1	0	.929
Allen, Midland	43	8	4	1	0	.923
Brown, El Paso	10	3	9	1	2	.923
Strelitz, Arkansas	27	22	22	4	2	.917
Hayes, San Antonio*	11	3	8	1	1	.917
Lashley, San Antonio	42	0	10	1	0	.909
Stover, El Paso	21	4	6	1	2	.909
Comstock, El Paso*	16	0	10	1	0	.909
Nielsen, Tulsa	24	21	26	5	3	.904
Biggerstaff, Amarillo	15	5	13	2	4	.900
Russ Clark, Jackson	20	0	9	1	1	.900
Harris, Jackson	24	12	32	5	1	.898
Harrison, San Antonio	24	11	24	4	1	.897
Rainbolt, Tulsa	36	5	11	2	0	.889
Albert, Mid-San Ant.	11	3	5	1	0	.889
Pickert, Amarillo*	28	6	24	4	3	.882
Martinez, Jackson	24	8	22	4	2	.882
Ledbetter, Midland	23	3	12	2	2	.882
Jakubowski, Tulsa	15	6	9	2	0	.882
Miller, El Paso*	26	8	21	4	0	.879
Kirchenwitz, Arkansas	24	6	8	2	0	.875
Finch, Tulsa	12	6	8	2	1	.875
Segelke, Midland	29	6	26	5	4	.865
Schrom, El Paso	25	5	20	4	1	.862
Holton, San Antonio	13	4	8	2	1	.857
McDonald, San Antonio	29	3	24	5	2	.844
Carroll, Amarillo	20	9	23	6	1	.842
Olmsted, Arkansas*	12	1	14	3	1	.833
Hypes, Shreveport*	13	2	3	1	1	.833
Searage, Arkansas*	42	4	9	3	0	.813
Prewitt, Jackson	16	5	7	3	1	.800
Perlman, Midland	18	4	14	5	2	.783
Ruiz, San Antonio*	13	2	5	2	0	.778
Power, San Antonio	10	3	4	2	0	.778
Mack, Midland	27	3	13	6	0	.727
Turner, Midland	39	3	5	3	1	.727
Cacciatore, Jackson	24	3	15	7	1	.720
Chiffer, Amarillo	43	2	6	4	1	.667
Wilkes, Amarillo	22	0	3	2	0	.600

PITCHERS—Continued

(Fewer Than Ten Games)

Player and Club	G.	PO.	A.	E.	DP.	Pct.	Player and Club	G.	PO.	A.	E.	DP.	Pct.
Armstrong, Amarillo......	7	0	7	0	3	1.000	Rincon, Arkansas	3	0	2	0	0	1.000
Gleaton, Tulsa*..............	5	1	5	0	1	1.000	Rommel, El Paso	4	0	1	0	0	1.000
Steck, El Paso	8	0	5	0	0	1.000	DeLeon, Arkansas	2	1	0	0	0	1.000
Tisdale, Arkansas	3	3	2	0	0	1.000	Fossas, Tulsa*..............	2	0	1	0	0	1.000
Beal, Midland	3	2	3	0	1	1.000	Calvert, Shreveport	8	4	4	1	1	.889
Bain, San Antonio	5	0	4	0	1	1.000	Kelly, Tulsa	8	3	4	1	1	.875
Baldwin, San Antonio	9	1	2	0	0	1.000	Lunar, Jackson	8	2	5	1	1	.875
Schmidt, Shreveport	5	0	3	0	1	1.000	Valentini, Midland	5	3	9	3	0	.800
Vasquez, Tulsa	7	1	1	0	0	1.000	Nickerson, Tulsa	7	1	1	1	0	.667
Violette, Jackson..........	3	1	1	0	0	1.000							

The following players do not have any recorded accepted chances at the positions indicated; therefore, are not listed in the fielding averages for those particular positions: Aranzamendi, 3b; Barrow, p; Robert Clark*, p; Gott, p; Humphry, p; McClain, p; Mitchell, c; Nobles*, p; Ramirez, ss; Reed, 3b; Shames, 2b; Tisdale, 3b. Ellison and Mabee appeared as designated-hitters/pinch-hitters only.

CLUB PITCHING

Club	G.	CG.	ShO.	Sv.	IP.	H.	R.	ER.	HR.	BB.	Int. BB.	HB.	SO.	WP.	Bk.	ERA.
Arkansas	133	28	10	26	1109	1107	474	402	58	416	20	47	622	54	5	3.26
Shreveport	135	56	13	15	1107	1074	494	403	67	467	23	37	611	46	11	3.28
Jackson	135	46	13	26	1067	1001	495	394	56	480	30	32	687	54	4	3.32
San Antonio	131	43	8	16	1110	1112	594	492	83	560	26	28	657	51	7	3.99
Tulsa	133	41	6	20	1080	1232	653	536	77	466	22	38	661	59	12	4.47
Midland	135	39	6	24	1144	1363	750	629	123	553	18	23	586	71	7	4.95
Amarillo	136	28	7	18	1124	1396	811	674	82	479	17	34	736	52	7	5.39
El Paso	136	29	0	16	1160	1478	862	747	143	580	8	39	629	48	8	5.80

PITCHERS' RECORDS

(Leading Qualifiers for Earned-Run Average Leadership—109 or More Innings)

*Throws lefthanded.

Pitcher–Club	G.	GS.	CG.	ShO.	W.	L.	Sv.	Pct.	IP.	H.	R.	ER.	HR.	BB.	Int. BB.	HB.	SO.	WP.	ERA.
Harris, Jackson	25	25	11	2	9	11	0	.450	163	125	58	41	6	81	5	3	89	5	2.26
Tufts, Shreveport*..........	26	26	12	2	14	10	0	.583	176	175	60	48	10	69	5	5	75	1	2.45
Eduardo, Arkansas	20	20	7	3	10	4	0	.714	134	102	50	39	4	70	2	5	90	10	2.62
Budner, Shreveport*........	24	24	11	3	8	12	0	.400	162	148	67	54	11	61	3	7	110	8	3.00
McDonald, San Antonio	29	9	4	1	9	3	1	.750	121	123	56	41	5	45	4	2	74	7	3.05
Nipp, San Antonio	24	23	10	2	11	8	0	.579	155	150	71	54	8	68	1	7	83	3	3.14
D. Johnson, Arkansas*.....	26	26	4	2	10	5	0	.667	143	136	67	52	12	80	3	5	80	12	3.27
Lamson, Tulsa*..............	24	24	12	0	11	8	0	.579	156	162	76	57	7	62	2	3	84	10	3.29
Martinez, Jackson	24	24	5	3	11	8	0	.579	157	152	71	58	10	74	2	4	108	6	3.32
Grote, Jackson	21	21	8	3	9	10	0	.474	128	145	62	49	4	43	3	2	65	4	3.45

Departmental Leaders: G–Williams, D. Smith, 44; GS–Mustad, Stablein, Strelitz, 27; CG–Lamson, Tufts, 12; ShO–Budner, Eduardo, Grote, Martinez, Nielsen, 3; W–Tufts, 14; L–Stablein, 15; Sv–Lashley, 12; Pct.–Phillips, .833; IP–Segelke, 184; H–Stablein, 235; R–Miller, 135; ER–Stablein, 116; HR–Parker, 34; BB–Mack, 116; IBB–Rainbolt, 6; HB–Cacciatore, 14; SO–Budner, Carroll, 110; WP–Cacciatore, 13.

(All Pitchers—Listed Alphabetically)

Pitcher–Club	G.	GS.	CG.	ShO.	W.	L.	Sv.	Pct.	IP.	H.	R.	ER.	HR.	BB.	Int. BB.	HB.	SO.	WP.	ERA.
Albert, 4 Mid-7 SA..........	11	2	0	0	1	3	1	.250	25	38	25	20	2	10	0	1	12	2	7.20
Allen, Midland	43	0	0	0	4	3	10	.571	66	57	29	23	4	27	5	1	52	3	3.14
Anderson, Jackson..........	25	21	7	1	8	11	0	.421	131	124	72	56	5	43	2	3	71	4	3.85
Armstrong, Amarillo	7	4	1	0	2	3	0	.400	31	32	15	12	2	14	1	1	34	1	3.48
Bain, San Antonio	5	5	0	0	0	2	0	.000	13	21	26	24	2	4	0	0	9	2	16.62
Baldwin, San Antonio	9	5	1	0	1	1	0	.500	31	48	33	27	8	18	1	0	24	5	7.84
Barrow, Tulsa	1	0	0	0	0	0	0	.000	1	0	0	0	0	0	0	0	0	0	0.00
Beal, Midland	3	2	1	0	1	0	0	1.000	14	16	9	9	1	10	0	1	8	1	5.79
Biggerstaff, Amarillo*......	15	9	1	0	1	6	0	.143	64	94	54	47	4	16	1	1	27	3	6.61
Border, El Paso	17	15	2	0	4	7	0	.364	85	121	74	68	12	36	0	2	38	6	7.20
Breining, Shreveport	10	8	5	1	4	2	0	.667	60	50	12	8	2	17	2	0	50	4	1.20
Brown, El Paso	10	10	5	0	4	4	0	.500	73	80	45	43	9	26	0	1	51	0	5.30
Budner, Shreveport*........	24	24	11	3	8	12	0	.400	162	148	67	54	11	61	3	7	110	8	3.00
Butcher, Tulsa	26	25	6	1	9	12	0	.429	155	197	106	88	9	53	2	6	82	7	5.11
Butler, Midland*............	24	0	0	0	2	3	1	.400	20	27	16	14	3	13	0	2	15	0	7.20
Cacciatore, Jackson	24	24	7	0	10	8	0	.556	136	141	85	68	13	64	0	14	103	13	4.50
Calvert, Shreveport	8	8	2	0	2	2	0	.500	40	56	36	28	3	32	3	1	17	4	6.30
Carroll, Amarillo	20	19	7	2	6	9	0	.400	131	142	84	63	8	59	5	4	110	8	4.33

Pitcher–Club	G.	GS.	CG.	ShO.	W.	L.	Sv.	Pct.	IP.	H.	R.	ER.	HR.	BB.	Int. BB.	HB.	SO.	WP.	ERA.
Chamberlain, Arkansas ..	13	13	5	1	9	4	0	.692	93	82	32	29	5	26	0	5	70	1	2.81
Chevolek, El Paso*	23	0	0	0	4	2	5	.667	37	44	19	14	6	17	3	1	28	0	3.41
Chiffer, Amarillo	43	0	0	0	3	2	4	.600	82	121	72	64	8	38	1	4	62	9	7.02
Robert Clark, Midland* ..	2	0	0	0	0	0	0	.000	3	9	11	11	0	5	0	0	2	3	33.00
Russ. Clark, Jackson	20	0	0	0	0	1	5	.000	29	22	12	7	1	13	3	0	22	1	2.17
Cline, Shreveport	16	0	0	0	7	3	1	.700	39	30	14	11	3	17	3	1	21	1	2.54
Comstock, El Paso*	16	8	1	0	2	5	0	.286	63	95	64	50	12	35	0	2	18	5	7.14
Crisler, El Paso	12	12	3	0	6	4	0	.600	89	90	50	36	8	37	2	4	51	2	3.64
Crutcher, Tulsa	26	24	7	0	9	13	0	.409	157	179	102	91	13	77	0	5	88	6	5.22
C. Davis, Arkansas	43	0	0	0	3	6	9	.333	74	75	20	19	1	25	4	5	48	4	2.31
DeLeon, Arkansas	2	0	0	0	0	0	0	.000	3	1	2	2	1	2	0	0	4	0	6.00
Earley, Midland*	30	21	10	0	13	6	0	.684	164	180	87	74	19	62	2	4	94	9	4.06
Edelen, Arkansas	12	12	1	0	4	4	0	.500	71	79	37	37	4	16	0	6	32	1	4.69
Eduardo, Arkansas	20	20	7	3	10	4	0	.714	134	102	50	39	4	70	2	5	90	10	2.62
Finch, Tulsa	12	12	3	1	2	7	0	.222	68	70	35	27	5	20	0	2	50	2	3.57
Fossas, Tulsa*	2	2	0	0	1	1	0	.500	11	14	10	8	1	4	0	3	3	1	6.55
Gerhardt, Amarillo*	12	0	0	0	0	0	0	.000	25	42	25	22	2	15	1	2	14	2	8.28
Gleaton, Tulsa*	5	5	1	0	3	2	0	.600	35	37	19	19	3	15	0	0	21	1	4.89
Glinatsis, Shreveport	26	25	9	2	9	8	0	.529	167	162	81	73	8	68	1	7	76	6	3.93
Gott, Arkansas	2	1	0	0	0	1	0	.000	5	3	6	3	0	13	0	0	7	2	5.40
Goulding, San Antonio	25	19	6	2	7	9	1	.438	147	147	76	65	16	52	4	6	79	2	3.98
Gronlund, El Paso	21	15	1	0	6	8	0	.429	94	131	74	66	6	68	0	3	53	4	6.32
Grote, Jackson	21	21	8	3	9	10	0	.474	128	145	62	49	4	43	3	2	65	4	3.45
Hamner, Jackson	37	0	0	0	2	3	4	.400	58	56	26	22	3	14	3	2	32	3	3.41
Hargesheimer, Shreve......	24	4	5	0	6	10	0	.375	141	165	96	71	5	60	0	6	80	5	4.53
Harris, Jackson	25	25	11	2	9	11	0	.450	163	125	58	41	6	81	5	3	89	5	2.26
Harrison, San Antonio	24	24	7	1	11	8	0	.579	160	155	85	77	7	95	2	3	82	7	4.33
Hayes, San Antonio*	11	0	0	0	1	2	1	.333	30	20	10	8	0	12	2	0	6	0	2.40
Heaton, El Paso	30	14	4	0	4	10	1	.286	129	182	104	97	26	49	0	5	54	2	6.77
Heimueller, Shreveport* ..	27	1	0	0	3	2	0	.600	58	58	29	25	7	31	0	1	29	2	3.88
Hirschy, Amarillo	23	12	4	0	7	10	0	.412	97	105	55	44	8	36	2	3	55	4	4.08
Holton, San Antonio	13	7	3	0	3	5	0	.375	51	50	24	21	2	25	3	2	40	3	3.71
Howe, San Antonio*	13	13	5	1	6	2	0	.750	95	78	36	33	11	22	1	3	57	1	3.13
Humphry, El Paso	1	0	0	0	0	0	0	.000	1	2	5	5	1	3	0	0	2	0	45.00
Hunziker, Amarillo	14	2	0	0	1	0	0	.000	39	59	45	37	3	23	1	0	21	0	8.54
Hypes, Shreveport*	13	0	0	0	2	1	2	.667	37	28	18	12	1	17	2	3	18	0	2.92
Jakubowski, Tulsa	15	2	0	0	3	3	3	.500	56	50	18	13	2	22	5	1	40	1	2.09
D. Johnson, Arkansas*	26	26	4	2	10	5	0	.667	143	136	67	52	12	80	3	5	80	12	3.27
Kelly, Tulsa	8	2	1	0	0	3	0	.000	28	37	26	17	4	16	0	0	21	1	5.46
Kirchenwitz, Arkansas	24	16	2	0	5	5	0	.500	99	120	56	47	10	20	2	1	30	5	4.27
Lamson, Tulsa*	24	24	12	0	11	8	0	.579	156	162	76	57	7	62	2	3	84	10	3.29
Lashley, San Antonio	42	0	0	0	6	8	12	.429	69	66	27	26	9	42	3	0	36	5	3.39
Ledbetter, Midland	23	10	3	0	4	6	1	.400	92	109	55	50	9	35	1	0	37	2	4.89
Littlefield, Arkansas	26	1	1	0	2	4	7	.333	58	52	17	14	3	11	2	4	31	0	2.17
Lunar, Jackson	8	0	0	0	2	1	0	.000	22	25	18	15	1	28	4	1	17	5	6.14
Mack, Midland	27	25	2	1	10	4	0	.714	144	156	99	79	8	116	1	3	102	8	4.94
Martinez, Jackson	24	24	5	3	11	8	0	.579	157	152	71	58	10	74	2	4	108	6	3.32
McClain, Midland	2	0	0	0	0	0	0	.000	1	3	3	3	0	2	0	0	0	0	27.00
McDonald, San Antonio ...	29	9	4	1	9	3	1	.750	121	123	56	41	5	45	4	2	74	7	3.05
Mendoza, Shreveport*	21	12	7	1	9	4	0	.692	97	85	37	34	8	42	1	1	53	2	3.15
Mercer, Tulsa*	40	0	0	0	3	2	8	.600	70	73	36	31	3	37	3	4	62	1	3.99
Miller, El Paso*	26	26	5	0	8	11	0	.421	155	212	135	111	15	84	0	5	75	9	6.45
Mustad, Amarillo	27	27	3	0	11	12	0	.478	152	167	104	89	10	80	0	9	101	6	5.27
Nickerson, Tulsa	7	0	0	0	1	0	0	1.000	17	27	15	14	2	11	0	2	12	1	7.41
Nielsen, Tulsa	24	18	6	3	8	7	2	.533	131	159	70	53	7	42	2	5	63	10	3.64
Nipp, San Antonio	24	23	10	2	11	8	0	.579	155	150	71	54	8	68	1	7	83	3	3.14
Nobles, San Antonio*	3	0	0	0	1	0	0	.000	7	10	3	2	0	4	1	0	13	1	2.57
Olmsted, Arkansas	12	12	4	1	3	4	0	.429	71	83	42	37	3	20	0	4	46	5	4.69
Parker, Midland	24	22	8	2	11	8	0	.579	156	205	111	90	34	29	1	2	71	8	5.19
Perlman, Midland	18	13	4	0	4	8	1	.333	96	133	76	49	9	32	2	0	34	4	4.59
Phillips, El Paso*	32	2	1	0	10	2	6	.833	74	75	30	25	3	27	1	5	49	3	3.04
Pickert, Amarillo*	28	26	4	2	8	12	0	.400	154	191	124	102	16	75	0	6	95	7	5.96
Power, San Antonio	10	10	4	1	5	1	0	.833	64	69	44	37	4	43	0	3	52	3	5.20
Prewitt, Jackson	16	13	5	2	7	2	0	.778	91	63	29	25	1	64	3	0	70	6	2.47
Rainbolt, Tulsa	36	0	0	0	3	5	7	.375	71	61	33	28	5	56	6	5	53	5	3.55
Rennicke, El Paso	38	0	0	0	2	2	2	.500	66	82	46	38	7	21	0	4	32	3	5.18
Rincon, Arkansas	3	3	0	0	1	2	0	.333	16	18	8	8	1	5	0	2	7	0	4.50
Rommel, El Paso	4	0	0	0	0	1	0	.000	6	8	3	3	0	3	0	1	2	1	4.50
Roy, Shreveport	38	0	0	0	4	3	10	.429	43	39	15	14	4	28	3	0	41	9	2.93
Ruiz, San Antonio*	13	0	0	0	1	6	0	.143	37	32	25	19	1	30	0	1	25	2	4.62
Sander, San Antonio	17	8	3	0	4	2	0	.667	67	79	42	31	4	36	1	1	36	5	4.16
Schmidt, Shreveport	5	0	0	0	0	0	0	.000	14	11	4	4	0	4	0	2	12	2	2.57
Schrom, El Paso	25	25	7	0	7	8	0	.467	168	204	111	97	19	75	1	3	107	2	5.20
Searage, Arkansas*	42	0	0	0	10	4	3	.714	89	73	27	22	4	46	2	4	63	4	2.22

Pitcher–Club	G.	GS.	CG.	ShO.	W.	L.	Sv.	Pct.	IP.	H.	R.	ER.	HR.	BB.	Int. BB.	HB.	SO.	WP.	ERA.
Segelke, Midland	29	26	9	1	13	8	0	.619	184	227	116	107	21	83	1	6	81	11	5.23
Shirley, San Antonio*	13	8	2	0	3	3	0	.500	51	45	26	23	5	39	3	0	35	5	4.06
D. Smith, Jackson	44	4	1	1	10	5	9	.667	102	104	45	41	10	42	3	1	76	7	3.62
L. Smith, Midland	35	9	0	0	9	5	0	.643	104	122	65	57	7	85	1	1	46	12	4.93
Stablein, Amarillo	27	27	6	1	8	15	0	.348	168	235	132	116	7	57	4	4	88	8	6.21
Steck, El Paso	8	7	0	0	0	4	0	.000	24	44	48	44	5	39	0	0	11	1	16.50
Stover, El Paso	21	0	0	0	1	5	1	.167	35	41	24	21	4	20	0	2	24	1	5.40
Strelitz, Arkansas	27	27	0	0	9	9	0	.500	159	208	80	68	6	42	2	3	67	5	3.85
Thurmond, Amarillo*	17	8	2	1	3	5	0	.375	62	89	52	39	9	31	0	0	46	1	5.66
Tisdale, Arkansas	3	2	2	1	2	0	1	1.000	20	10	1	0	0	8	0	1	12	0	0.00
Tucker, Shreveport	20	7	5	2	6	4	2	.600	73	67	25	21	5	21	0	3	29	2	2.59
Tufts, Shreveport*	26	26	12	2	14	10	0	.583	176	175	60	48	10	69	5	5	75	1	2.45
Turner, Midland	39	0	0	0	3	4	8	.429	55	63	38	34	5	29	4	2	25	6	5.56
Valentini, Midland	5	5	2	1	2	2	0	.500	33	37	20	18	2	14	0	0	13	2	4.91
Vallone, El Paso*	16	2	0	0	3	2	1	.600	60	67	30	29	10	40	1	1	34	0	4.35
Vasquez, Tulsa	7	5	1	0	0	5	0	.000	22	40	32	26	9	6	0	1	3	2	10.64
Violette, Jackson	3	3	2	0	0	3	0	.000	17	16	6	6	2	4	1	0	8	0	3.18
Von Ohlen, Jackson*	37	0	0	0	4	1	7	.800	34	28	11	7	0	10	1	2	26	0	1.85
Whitehouse, Tulsa*	25	14	4	1	5	7	0	.417	102	126	75	64	7	45	2	1	79	11	5.65
Wilkes, Amarillo	22	1	0	0	4	2	10	.667	41	35	12	7	0	15	1	0	32	0	1.54
Williams, Arkansas	44	0	0	0	8	5	7	.615	72	65	29	25	4	32	3	2	35	5	3.13
Yandle, Amarillo*	37	1	0	0	1	5	4	.167	77	84	37	31	5	20	0	0	51	3	3.62

BALKS—Budner, 5; Finch, Lamson, Segelke, 3 each; Cacciatore, Crutcher, Eduardo, Hargesheimer, Jakubowski, Mendoza, Miller, Mustad, Nielsen, Yandle, 2 each; Allen, Anderson, Baldwin, Beal, Calvert Carroll, Chevolek, Chiffer, Comstock, Crisler, C. Davis, Edelen, Goulding, Hamner, Harrison, Hayes, Heaton, Howe, D. Johnson, Lashley, Ledbetter, Perlman, Phillips, Pickert, Power, Roy, Stablein, 1 each.

COMBINATION SHUTOUTS—Mustad-Hirschy, Amarillo; Chamberlain-Williams, Edelen-C. Davis, Arkansas; Prewitt-Smith, Jackson; Parker-Earley-Turner, Midland; Glinatsis-Roy, Tufts-Tucker-Hypes, Shreveport.

NO-HIT GAMES—Anderson, Jackson defeated Shreveport, 8-0, May 12; Glinatsis, Shreveport defeated Jackson, 1-0, June 15 (first game, seven innings); Whitehouse, Tulsa defeated Shreveport, 2-0, June 22 (second game, seven innings); Goulding, San Antonio defeated Amarillo, 5-0, July 4.

Barrios Clubbed Five Grand Slams

Shreveport first baseman Jose Barrios belted his fifth grand slam homer of the season in the first game of a doubleheader July 9 against Jackson.

At the time, no other player had hit more than one grand slam. But the 6-4 righthanded hitter fell one short of the Texas League record of six grand slams by Roy Ostergard of Galveston in 1923.

Boddicker Set Strikeout Mark

Charlotte righthander Mike Boddicker set a Southern League mark by fanning 18 batters in an 8-2 victory at Knoxville, June 7. Boddicker struck out the side in the second, fourth and ninth innings en route to eclipsing the league's previous record of 16 strikeouts. The previous record-holders included: Jim Nash of Mobile (1966), Steve Tissot of Montgomery (1971) and Jim Reid of Jacksonville (1972).

California League

CLASS A

STANDING OF CLUBS AT CLOSE OF FIRST HALF, JUNE 20

NORTHERN DIVISION						SOUTHERN DIVISION					
Club	W.	L.	T.	Pct.	G.B.	Club	W.	L.	T.	Pct.	G.B.
Lodi (Dodgers)	42	28	0	.600	......	Visalia (Twins)	44	26	0	.629	......
Reno (Padres)	36	34	0	.514	6	San Jose (Mariners)	40	30	0	.571	4
Stockton (Brewers)	34	34	0	.486	8	Salinas (Angels)	35	35	0	.500	9
Modesto (A's)	30	40	0	.429	12	Fresno (Giants)	34	36	0	.486	10
Santa Clara (Co-op)	23	47	0	.329	19	Bakersfield (Independent)	32	38	0	.457	12

STANDING OF CLUBS AT CLOSE OF SECOND HALF, SEPTEMBER 1

NORTHERN DIVISION						SOUTHERN DIVISION					
Club	W.	L.	T.	Pct.	G.B.	Club	W.	L.	T.	Pct.	G.B.
Stockton** (Brewers)	39	32	0	.549	.....	San Jose (Mariners)	49	21	0	.700	......
Reno (Padres)	38	33	0	.535	1	Visalia (Twins)	42	28	0	.600	7
Modesto	36	34	0	.514	2½	Salinas (Angels)	34	36	0	.486	15
Lodi (Dodgers)	25	44	0	.362	13	Fresno (Giants)	32	37	0	.464	16½
Santa Clara (Co-op)	24	46	0	.343	14½	Bakersfield (Independent)	31	39	0	.443	18

**Stockton and Reno finished second half regular season tied for first place in the Northern Division. Stockton defeated Reno in a single-game tie-breaker.

COMPOSITE STANDING OF CLUBS AT CLOSE OF SEASON, SEPTEMBER 1
NORTHERN DIVISION

Club	Reno	Sto.	Lodi	Mod.	S.C.	S.J.	Vis.	Sal.	Fr.	Bak.	W.	L.	T.	Pct.	G.B.
Reno (Padres)	....	7	13	12	16	5	2	6	7	6	74	67	0	.525	......
Stockton (Brewers)	16	....	9	15	10	4	6	4	6	3	73	68	0	.518	1
Lodi (Dodgers)	9	14	....	9	16	2	4	3	4	6	67	72	0	.482	6
Modesto (A's)	10	8	14	....	16	3	3	4	2	6	66	74	0	.471	7½
Santa Clara (Co-op)	8	12	6	6	....	3	1	5	2	4	47	93	0	.336	26½

SOUTHERN DIVISION

Club	Reno	Sto.	Lodi	Mod.	S.C.	S.J.	Vis.	Sal.	Fr.	Bak.	W.	L.	T.	Pct.	G.B.
San Jose (Mariners)	5	6	8	7	7	....	12	12	15	17	89	51	0	.636	......
Visalia (Twins)	8	4	6	7	9	10	....	14	12	16	86	54	0	.614	3
Salinas (Angels)	4	6	7	6	5	12	8	....	10	11	79	71	0	.493	20
Fresno (Giants)	3	4	5	8	7	11	12	....	....	8	66	73	0	.475	22½
Bakersfield (Independent)	4	7	4	4	6	5	7	11	15	....	63	77	0	.450	26

Major league affiliates in parentheses.

Playoffs—Stockton, second half leader, defeated Lodi, first half leader, two games to none for Northern Division championship. San Jose, second half leader, defeated Visalia, first half leader, two games to one for Southern Division championship. San Jose (Southern Division Champion) defeated Stockton (Northern Division Champion), three games to two for League Championship.

Regular-season attendance—Bakersfield, 44,546; Fresno, 74,985; Lodi, 44,102; Modesto, 61,037; Reno, 59,422; Salinas, 53,023; San Jose, 71,320; Santa Clara, 19,952; Stockton, 25,901; Visalia, 50,199. Total—504,487. No all-star game. Playoffs, 10,717.

Managers: Bakersfield—Ron Mihal; Fresno—Jack Mull; Lodi—Stan Wasiak; Modesto—Gaylen Pitts; Reno—Eddie Watt; Salinas—Chris Cannizzaro; San Jose—Bob Didier; Santa Clara—Joe Volpi; Stockton—Lee Sigman; Visalia—Tom Kelly.

All-Star Team: 1B—Funderburk, Visalia; 2B—Lane, Fresno; 3B—Pearsey, Visalia; SS—Concepcion, Bakersfield; OF—Brunson, Stockton; Garrison, Lodi; Henderson, San Jose; Negron, San Jose; C—Cadahia, Visalia; DH—Marshall, Lodi; P—Biko, Visalia; Green, Visalia; McGee, San Jose; Miller, Reno; Show, Reno; Manager—Kelly, Visalia.

(Compiled by William J. Weiss, League Statistician, San Mateo, Calif.)

CLUB BATTING

Club	G.	AB.	R.	OR.	H.	TB.	2B.	3B.	HR.	RBI.	SH.	SF.	BB.	Int. BB.	HP.	SO.	SB.	CS.	LOB.	Pct.
Lodi	139	4641	592	774	1336	1890	228	25	92	686	57	46	658	23	48	805	151	72	1105	.288
San Jose	140	4607	804	616	1323	1908	205	40	100	695	54	52	544	42	39	782	276	122	927	.287
Bakersfield	140	4659	788	903	1295	1934	240	36	109	686	41	32	675	21	36	824	152	68	1078	.278
Visalia	140	4657	876	702	1278	1914	197	47	115	760	34	69	713	35	41	842	156	53	1042	.274
Modesto	140	4705	790	850	1280	1777	183	34	62	685	39	36	710	20	30	846	186	68	1127	.272
Reno	141	4728	814	729	1274	1886	187	52	107	701	57	35	738	22	43	965	162	49	1151	.269
Santa Clara	140	4576	692	984	1197	1623	183	27	63	615	31	37	682	31	29	897	122	72	1063	.262
Stockton	141	4631	654	594	1208	1660	178	56	54	578	34	39	586	23	36	843	142	63	1029	.261
Fresno	139	4678	779	763	1220	1871	219	39	118	680	49	44	628	36	47	857	111	40	1054	.261
Salinas	140	4567	651	715	1114	1640	167	40	93	555	46	27	560	18	22	1043	144	90	943	.244

INDIVIDUAL BATTING

(Leading Qualifiers for Batting Championship—378 or More Plate Appearances)

*Bats lefthanded.   †Switch-hitter.

Player and Club	G.	AB.	R.	H.	TB.	2B.	3B.	HR.	RBI.	SH.	SF.	BB.	HP.	SO.	SB.	CS.	Pct.
Marshall, Michael, Lodi	137	525	101	186	301	37	3	24	116	2	5	71	4	86	22	7	.354
Negron, Miguel, San Jose*	135	466	90	153	189	20	5	2	62	0	6	38	4	57	14	17	.328
Garrison, Marvin, Lodi	130	502	103	164	231	29	4	10	51	6	5	95	3	94	28	19	.327
Pearsey, Leslie, Visalia	133	531	111	173	278	27	9	20	121	3	7	68	4	88	12	4	.326
DeVito, Frederick, Modesto	117	456	65	145	213	32	3	10	83	6	5	27	6	57	7	2	.318
Rametta, Steven, Bakersfield	95	348	61	108	171	22	1	13	59	1	2	29	4	44	4	1	.310
Funderburk, Mark, Visalia	128	484	106	150	265	20	1	31	109	1	8	56	7	101	11	3	.310
Maler, James, San Jose	139	523	89	162	274	30	5	24	100	0	5	40	4	102	11	7	.310
Alvarez, John, Reno	134	510	89	156	256	28	9	18	100	3	5	67	5	69	4	2	.306
Gutierrez, Julian, Santa Clara	91	350	61	106	126	8	3	2	38	1	0	66	0	57	36	21	.303

Departmental Leaders: G—Brunansky, 140; AB—Hardy, 553; R—Pearsey, 111; H—Marshall, 186; TB—Marshall, 301; 2B—Marshall, 37; 3B—Brunson, 10; HR—Funderburk, 31; RBI—Pearsey, 121; SH—Carnes, 13; SF—Elder, 12; BB—Nichols, 107; HP—Walker, 11; SO—Gilbert, 132; SB—Weston, 66; CS—Weston, 25.

(All Players—Listed Alphabetically)

Player and Club	G.	AB.	R.	H.	TB.	2B.	3B.	HR.	RBI.	SH.	SF.	BB.	HP.	SO.	SB.	CS.	Pct.
Adamson, Wade, Visalia	35	1	0	0	0	0	0	0	0	0	0	0	0	1	0	0	.000
Almon, John, Reno	124	395	68	105	163	15	2	13	69	7	0	99	0	108	11	7	.266
Alvarez, John, Reno	134	510	89	156	256	28	9	18	100	3	5	67	5	69	4	2	.306
Anthony, Thomas, Fresno	104	382	60	98	144	16	9	4	44	4	4	54	5	49	11	4	.257
Arias, Rodolfo, 40 SJ-4 SC	44	77	6	11	11	0	0	0	2	3	0	10	1	22	0	2	.143
Armstead, V. Albert, Modesto	70	249	31	51	82	5	4	6	27	2	1	34	2	93	17	7	.205
Attaway, Eric, Santa Clara*	88	295	50	84	90	4	1	0	41	2	1	87	2	36	8	5	.285
Baez, Jesse, Lodi	32	102	18	28	41	10	0	1	15	0	0	16	0	17	0	0	.275
Barr, Timothy, Visalia*	39	1	0	0	0	0	0	0	0	0	0	0	0	0	0	0	.000
Bedrosian, David, Santa Clara	19	56	13	12	16	4	0	0	7	2	0	14	0	21	2	0	.214
Beerbower, Dan, Bakersfield	5	17	1	1	2	1	0	0	2	1	1	2	0	4	0	0	.059
Bennett, James, Santa Clara*	137	479	66	123	204	22	4	17	80	3	8	61	3	89	10	6	.257
Berger, Kenneth, Visalia*	76	264	61	63	90	11	5	2	25	3	2	46	3	51	11	2	.239
Berry, Dana, Modesto*	102	337	53	83	128	17	2	8	55	0	3	52	2	93	2	4	.246

Player and Club	G.	AB.	R.	H.	TB.	2B.	3B.	HR.	RBI.	SH.	SF.	BB.	HP.	SO.	SB.	CS.	Pct.
Bertolotti, Fulvio, Santa Clara	72	248	38	68	107	15	0	8	55	0	4	17	1	38	0	0	.274
Bishop, Michael, Salinas	62	218	47	67	119	11	1	13	45	1	1	42	0	48	0	2	.307
Blakley, Robert, Reno	132	518	82	140	188	15	6	7	55	11	3	47	3	129	32	10	.270
Boggs, Mark, Santa Clara	22	3	0	0	0	0	0	0	0	0	0	0	0	0	0	0	.000
Bolla, Anthony, Fresno	12	24	2	4	5	1	0	0	1	2	0	2	0	7	0	0	.167
Bothwell, Monte, Bakersfield*	17	53	7	11	14	3	0	0	5	0	1	6	0	17	0	0	.208
Bradley, Mark, Lodi	31	101	24	28	38	5	1	1	14	0	3	36	1	25	12	4	.277
Brenly, Robert, Fresno	56	212	49	65	107	11	2	9	37	1	1	28	4	31	6	3	.307
Broders, John, Bakersfield*	25	83	11	25	29	4	0	0	13	1	0	16	1	11	5	3	.301
Brooks, Keith, Fresno†	48	156	27	38	45	5	1	0	7	2	0	13	3	35	3	0	.244
Brown, Bobby, Lodi*	49	158	32	45	80	11	0	8	28	1	1	36	1	39	8	3	.285
Brunansky, Thomas, Salinas	140	485	85	131	225	23	1	23	76	0	6	100	5	116	20	15	.270
Brunson, Eddie, Stockton	138	500	88	149	204	23	10	4	71	5	4	69	6	93	15	7	.298
Brunswick, Thomas, Modesto	77	306	41	82	98	9	2	1	41	5	1	33	0	34	3	4	.268
Buice, DeWayne, Fresno	46	4	0	1	1	0	0	0	0	0	0	1	0	2	0	0	.250
Byrd, Jeffrey, San Jose	26	0	1	0	0	0	0	0	0	1	0	0	0	0	0	0	.000
Cadahia, Auerlio, Visalia	91	281	45	80	113	15	0	6	59	5	8	40	2	23	2	2	.285
Caira, Dennis, Santa Clara†	43	166	25	35	54	7	3	2	23	4	1	11	0	40	0	2	.211
Carnes, Scott, Salinas	134	494	67	112	145	17	5	2	46	13	4	59	4	80	17	7	.227
Cheesman, Barry, Salinas	26	48	4	11	14	0	0	1	5	1	0	11	0	21	1	0	.229
Cias, Darryl, Modesto	56	180	26	51	66	8	2	1	33	1	3	25	1	35	4	2	.283
Concepcion, Onix, Bakersfield	127	504	88	151	224	25	3	14	75	6	6	60	6	60	17	9	.300
Cordova, Rocky, Lodi	42	1	0	0	0	0	0	0	0	0	0	0	0	0	0	0	.000
Cox, Mobil, Reno	35	125	21	28	46	6	3	2	14	2	1	19	3	24	1	1	.224
Craig, Rodney, San Jose†	64	238	51	75	101	7	5	3	27	6	2	39	0	25	35	9	.315
Croft, Paul, Visalia	69	250	68	71	115	11	3	9	39	1	2	48	6	71	24	4	.284
Cuarezma, Julio, Stockton	11	29	5	8	13	3	1	0	5	0	0	4	0	4	0	0	.267
Cummings, Robert, Fresno	17	59	6	12	15	0	0	1	7	1	0	1	1	12	0	0	.203
Cyburt, Richard, Fresno	45	121	17	22	25	3	0	0	6	6	1	20	2	11	5	1	.182
Dailey, R. Anthony, Salinas*	118	401	50	105	124	11	4	0	27	3	3	24	0	45	16	13	.262
Daniel, Daniel, Bakersfield†	114	376	65	100	159	18	4	11	59	7	0	51	3	87	5	3	.266
Davis, Charles, Fresno†	134	490	91	132	229	24	5	21	95	4	7	80	3	91	30	4	.269
Davis, Michael, Modesto*	41	161	48	63	81	10	4	0	19	0	0	34	0	20	13	5	.391
Dempsey, Patrick, Modesto	57	208	25	53	65	3	3	1	25	2	2	22	1	22	6	1	.255
DeVito, Frederick, Modesto	117	456	65	145	213	32	3	10	83	6	5	27	6	57	7	2	.318
Dixon, Roy, Bakersfield	23	57	9	7	10	1	1	0	6	1	1	10	0	16	3	0	.123
Doss, Richard, Fresno	72	253	37	70	112	12	3	8	33	3	2	26	0	53	2	1	.277
Duncan, Columbus, Stockton	71	254	35	51	89	6	4	8	40	0	3	36	0	62	2	1	.201
Dunn, James, Fresno	35	134	23	33	36	3	0	0	10	4	1	13	0	15	2	1	.246
Duran, Richard, Stockton	64	232	40	76	110	17	1	5	47	2	3	33	3	33	5	1	.328
Eagan, D. Thomas, Santa Clara	100	313	53	80	113	14	2	5	37	0	2	62	3	70	4	3	.256
Eakin, Gordon, Modesto	37	96	9	20	27	5	1	0	18	1	2	11	0	21	3	1	.208
Elder, David, San Jose	138	508	101	152	236	28	7	14	104	6	12	72	7	89	42	13	.299
Ennis, Jerry, Visalia	131	491	75	135	179	22	5	4	63	3	8	53	6	73	11	7	.275
Feinberg, Kenneth, Fresno	36	134	14	36	46	5	1	1	16	0	3	13	0	16	0	1	.269
Fiorante, Gary, 12 SC-10 SJ-10 SC	32	3	0	2	2	0	0	0	0	0	0	0	0	0	0	0	.667
Fireovid, Stephen, Reno†	26	2	3	1	1	0	0	0	0	0	0	1	0	0	0	0	.500
Flammang, J. Christopher, SJ*	123	306	50	84	106	15	2	1	44	6	2	30	1	42	22	7	.275
Foster, Robert, Lodi	47	0	0	0	0	0	0	0	0	0	0	0	0	0	0	0	.000
Franjul, Miguel, Lodi	126	480	60	130	161	17	1	4	62	9	5	30	2	83	16	4	.271
Frederickson, Mark, Bakersfield	17	35	5	7	8	1	0	0	0	0	0	8	1	4	1	0	.200
Funderburk, Mark, Visalia	128	484	106	150	265	20	1	31	109	1	8	56	7	101	11	3	.310
Gardner, Vassie, Bakersfield	77	310	67	101	144	14	7	5	41	2	1	48	0	52	30	9	.326
Garrett, Lynn, Bakersfield	17	58	12	16	25	0	3	0	11	0	1	12	2	14	2	0	.276
Garrison, Marvin, Lodi	130	502	103	164	231	29	4	10	51	6	5	95	3	94	28	19	.327
Gelfarb, Stephen, Modesto*	6	6	1	2	2	0	0	0	1	0	0	2	0	0	0	0	.333
Gilbert, Dennis, Salinas	135	488	77	118	175	14	8	9	65	1	0	55	0	132	9	7	.242
Gladden, C. Daniel, Fresno†	60	228	41	70	90	9	1	3	31	4	1	17	3	30	17	9	.307
Gonzalez, Filiberto, 25 Sal-82 SC*	107	370	54	106	160	20	2	10	63	1	2	33	3	68	4	6	.286
Gonzalez, Richard, Bakersfield	130	447	71	110	176	21	0	15	61	4	1	59	5	82	5	4	.246
Gosse, M. John, Modesto	43	2	0	0	0	0	0	0	0	0	0	0	0	1	0	0	.000
Greb, Jay, Modesto	33	100	13	15	18	3	0	0	8	1	0	16	0	25	2	1	.150
Green, David, Stockton	136	500	68	131	189	16	9	8	70	2	6	42	1	95	20	8	.262
Green, Steven, Visalia	27	3	0	0	0	0	0	0	0	0	0	0	0	2	0	0	.000
Greer, Randy, Visalia*	118	385	82	101	129	14	4	2	48	2	7	81	4	54	22	4	.262
Grimes, Steven, Santa Clara	130	478	76	136	181	22	1	7	73	3	3	77	3	82	12	4	.285
Gutierrez, Julian, Santa Clara	91	350	61	106	126	8	3	2	38	0	1	66	0	57	36	21	.303
Guzman, Hector, Lodi†	3	1	1	0	0	0	0	0	0	0	0	0	0	0	0	0	.000
Gwosdz, Douglas, Reno	85	258	37	67	98	7	3	6	40	6	4	39	4	65	7	2	.260
Haley, J. Michael, Bakersfield	54	216	43	79	126	18	4	7	31	0	1	26	1	26	10	3	.366
Hamilton, James, Salinas	95	265	30	54	72	7	1	3	25	3	2	16	0	55	15	8	.204
Hardwick, Willie, Reno	29	1	1	1	2	1	0	0	0	0	0	0	0	0	0	1	1.000
Hardy, Frank, Reno*	135	553	69	153	199	21	5	5	79	3	3	57	2	86	5	2	.277
Harris, Tracy, 5 SJ-66 SC	71	5	1	1	1	0	0	0	0	0	0	1	0	3	0	0	.200
Harryman, Jeffrey, Bakersfield*	18	2	0	0	0	0	0	0	0	0	0	1	0	0	0	0	.000

Player and Club	G.	AB.	R.	H.	TB.	2B.	3B.	HR.	RBI.	SH.	SF.	BB.	HP.	SO.	SB.	CS.	Pct.
Hawkins, M. Andrew, Reno	29	5	1	2	3	1	0	0	2	0	0	0	0	1	0	0	.400
Henderson, David, San Jose	136	507	103	152	262	23	3	27	99	0.	6	56	4	115	19	4	.300
Hernandez, Leonardo, Lodi	61	257	48	82	122	12	2	8	52	0	2	15	1	20	4	1	.319
Hertel, Richard, 44 SC-18 Reno	62	254	35	69	87	10	1	2	29	1	2	20	2	58	16	2	.272
Holman, Q. Dale, Lodi*	73	254	41	73	116	7	3	10	56	2	5	32	5	51	2	1	.287
Hunziker, Kent, Santa Clara†	23	6	0	1	2	1	0	0	0	0	0	0	0	2	0	0	.167
Incaviglia, Tony, Santa Clara	108	322	64	84	118	18	2	4	41	5	3	85	4	99	10	1	.261
Jamerson, Donald, Fresno*	57	169	30	33	48	5	2	2	18	2	2	36	6	40	3	3	.195
Johnson, Abner, 19 Vis-6 Bak	25	1	0	0	0	0	0	0	0	0	0	0	0	1	0	0	.000
Johnson, Gregory, Salinas	28	1	0	0	0	0	0	0	0	0	0	0	0	1	0	0	.000
Johnson, Jerry, Reno	124	438	85	129	196	19	6	12	72	3	1	89	4	87	12	4	.295
Jones, Donny, Salinas	26	72	8	18	25	2	1	1	14	2	0	12	0	16	2	0	.250
Jones, Thomas, Santa Clara	9	7	3	2	2	0	0	0	2	0	0	0	0	1	0	0	.286
Keedy, C. Patrick, Salinas	52	125	22	26	41	3	0	4	15	1	0	22	2	50	12	1	.208
Kelley, Bradley, Bakersfield	32	1	0	0	0	0	0	0	0	0	0	0	0	0	0	0	.000
Kelley, Steven, Bakersfield	27	49	8	14	22	1	2	1	7	0	0	4	0	6	0	1	.286
Kelly, J. Thomas, Visalia*	2	0	0	0	0	0	0	0	0	0	0	1	0	0	0	0	.000
Kemp, Rodney, Lodi*	91	309	47	79	99	10	2	2	42	2	3	39	2	45	9	8	.256
Kingsolver, Kurtis, Stockton	8	19	1	2	2	0	0	0	0	0	0	10	0	7	1	0	.105
Kittrell, Rickey, Fresno*	23	1	0	0	0	0	0	0	0	0	0	0	0	0	0	0	.000
Klebba, Robert, Santa Clara	31	116	14	29	31	2	0	0	7	1	0	8	0	9	4	4	.250
Kneuer, Frank, Modesto	22	64	7	13	20	1	0	2	11	0	0	7	1	14	0	0	.203
Lake, Steven, Stockton	94	329	36	93	129	12	3	6	40	5	5	10	3	41	2	4	.283
Lane, Jerry, Fresno	127	492	100	140	269	36	3	29	88	1	3	55	5	74	8	1	.285
Lanning, David, Lodi*	36	129	11	37	46	6	0	1	20	0	2	19	0	22	1	4	.287
Ledbetter, Gareth, Bakersfield	17	42	8	6	10	2	1	0	4	0	0	12	1	13	0	0	.143
Lee, Terry, Bakersfield*	104	364	67	108	180	27	0	15	71	1	2	56	4	83	8	3	.297
Lemon, Leo, Salinas†	100	266	29	58	71	6	2	1	21	7	1	28	3	74	16	13	.218
Leonard, Bernardo, Visalia	4	19	2	6	9	3	0	0	1	0	0	1	0	5	2	0	.316
Lettrich, Stephen, Santa Clara†	27	6	0	2	2	0	0	0	0	0	0	0	0	3	0	0	.333
Lohse, John, Bakersfield	117	410	60	110	148	27	4	1	59	1	4	50	3	56	12	4	.268
Loman, Douglas, Stockton*	138	521	76	144	211	22	9	9	65	0	4	64	4	81	16	8	.276
Loureiro, Mark, Fresno*	40	126	9	33	42	6	0	1	16	0	0	7	0	21	0	1	.262
Maddon, Joseph, Santa Clara	20	60	8	15	17	2	0	0	7	0	1	3	0	9	0	0	.250
Maler, James, San Jose	139	523	89	162	274	30	5	24	100	0	5	40	4	102	11	7	.310
Malkin, John, Lodi	21	68	10	10	11	1	0	0	3	0	0	14	0	18	1	0	.147
Mann, Leo, Lodi	27	76	16	22	24	2	0	0	6	3	0	8	1	8	2	4	.289
Manning, M. Allen, Stockton	129	367	50	66	94	15	2	3	26	2	2	70	6	115	9	3	.180
Markham, Robert, Modesto*	135	465	97	134	184	21	1	9	63	1	4	103	4	107	23	4	.288
Marrero, William, Visalia	15	47	7	10	14	1	0	1	6	0	0	9	0	25	0	0	.213
Marshall, Michael, Lodi	137	525	101	186	301	37	3	24	116	2	5	71	4	86	22	7	.354
Martin, J. Michael, Reno*	83	255	38	62	90	7	0	7	30	2	0	25	5	48	0	0	.243
Martinson, Evon, Lodi	84	259	37	65	88	11	0	4	33	4	2	33	2	69	2	0	.251
Maxwell, Martin, Visalia	26	93	26	31	61	7	1	7	19	0	1	16	1	21	1	3	.333
McDonald, Blane, Visalia	96	320	49	87	142	21	2	10	62	2	8	29	3	47	4	3	.272
McHenry, Vance, San Jose	107	307	44	65	81	6	2	2	30	12	2	40	6	63	21	13	.212
Mejia, Alfredo, Lodi	30	91	9	20	28	5	0	1	9	1	1	13	1	21	0	0	.220
Mercado, Orlando, San Jose	110	335	53	86	138	18	2	10	54	3	7	47	0	78	7	2	.257
Minker, Allen, Modesto	76	265	47	75	115	13	0	9	48	1	2	47	4	32	2	1	.283
Moore, Alvin, Visalia	108	331	60	89	129	5	4	9	56	0	2	75	0	55	10	4	.269
Moore, Kelvin, Modesto	51	199	45	64	119	5	1	16	55	0	1	33	2	58	2	1	.322
Morley, James, Fresno	28	82	13	14	18	1	0	1	9	1	1	11	1	13	1	0	.171
Morris, Donald, Modesto	136	540	77	153	215	24	4	10	99	5	6	48	3	71	18	8	.283
Negron, Miguel, San Jose*	135	467	66	153	189	20	5	2	62	0	6	38	4	57	14	17	.328
Nelson, James, Bakersfield	116	378	58	106	166	20	2	12	65	3	3	64	1	75	7	5	.280
Nichols, Alfred, Bakersfield†	122	403	81	102	144	16	4	6	51	3	3	107	4	94	37	11	.253
Nocciolo, Mark, Salinas	116	356	60	83	127	12	4	8	38	5	2	56	2	80	9	3	.233
Nowakowski, Tadeusz, S Clara†	54	176	15	39	52	6	2	1	13	2	0	8	3	48	1	2	.222
Nowland, David, San Jose	77	125	21	31	39	6	1	0	15	3	3	12	3	30	4	3	.248
Omo, Robert, Fresno†	28	1	0	0	0	0	0	0	0	0	0	0	0	0	0	0	.000
Packard, Edward, Santa Clara	21	57	6	10	10	0	0	0	4	0	1	12	0	25	0	0	.175
Parker, Michael, 51 SC-79 Reno	130	449	87	103	154	17	5	8	65	1	8	93	7	99	5	1	.229
Pastors, Gregory, Reno	84	316	48	93	130	16	3	5	53	3	4	38	4	55	11	1	.294
Patterson, Larry, San Jose	70	161	14	51	65	8	0	2	34	0	1	23	0	32	3	1	.317
Pearsey, Leslie, Visalia	133	531	111	173	278	27	9	20	121	3	7	68	4	88	12	4	.326
Pebley, Edward, San Jose*	88	250	47	80	106	19	2	1	31	3	3	35	1	30	16	9	.320
Putman, Randy, 78 SC-49 Reno*	127	403	57	92	118	10	2	4	48	4	5	70	1	66	3	0	.228
Rabouin, Andre, Bakersfield	6	0	0	0	0	0	0	0	0	0	0	0	0	0	0	1	.000
Rametta, Steven, Bakersfield	95	348	61	108	171	22	1	13	59	1	2	29	4	44	4	1	.310
Ramirez, Orlando, Bakersfield	32	118	16	26	33	1	0	2	9	2	0	7	0	15	2	0	.220
Ramirez, Russell, Stockton	36	92	9	20	27	1	3	0	14	0	2	21	0	24	5	1	.217
Ransom, Jeffery, Fresno†	62	216	29	55	76	7	1	4	22	0	3	32	2	47	2	1	.255
Reed, Curtis, Reno†	56	217	48	71	101	14	5	2	28	1	1	42	2	31	2	5	.327
Reichenbach, Michael, Bakersfield*	14	26	2	3	3	0	0	0	1	0	0	2	0	8	0	0	.115
Reis, Dale, Bakersfield	10	1	0	0	0	0	0	0	0	0	0	0	0	0	0	0	.000

Player and Club	G.	AB.	R.	H.	TB.	2B.	3B.	HR.	RBI.	SH.	SF.	BB.	HP.	SO.	SB.	CS.	Pct.
Richards, David, Lodi	7	23	2	8	9	1	0	0	5	0	0	3	0	4	0	0	.348
Richmond, Albert, Reno	134	472	90	114	188	19	5	15	74	4	4	87	3	126	55	8	.242
Riffel, J. Branner, Salinas	100	289	28	78	101	10	2	3	41	0	0	21	1	57	3	3	.270
Rivera, German, Lodi	36	139	26	26	37	6	1	1	17	0	1	11	1	24	4	0	.187
Roberts, Steven, Modesto	48	139	23	31	47	1	0	5	19	0	0	37	1	25	7	0	.223
Robinson, Henry, Bakersfield†	28	67	6	11	14	1	1	0	4	5	0	21	0	8	0	0	.164
Robinson, Howard, Santa Clara†	16	59	7	9	11	2	0	0	2	0	0	6	0	14	4	3	.153
Rodriguez, Ivan, Stockton	128	434	47	92	113	9	3	2	38	7	1	43	1	92	8	4	.212
Romero, Andres, Visalia*	117	393	54	105	157	20	7	6	67	4	6	53	3	67	19	8	.267
Rothford, James, Fresno	118	434	61	130	220	26	5	18	85	3	4	34	7	111	1	1	.300
Rowe, Harold, Fresno	102	303	56	64	109	15	0	10	55	2	5	66	3	73	7	2	.211
Ruzek, Don, Lodi	49	152	35	41	49	6	1	0	24	1	1	47	2	38	5	2	.270
Sarno, Gary, Bakersfield	40	3	0	0	0	0	0	0	0	0	0	0	0	2	0	0	.000
Schexnayder, Wade, Salinas	79	196	24	31	46	4	1	3	17	0	1	19	1	78	7	3	.158
Schultz, Greg, Lodi	32	97	12	28	39	5	0	2	14	4	0	17	1	12	1	2	.289
Sconiers, Daryl, Salinas*	108	365	60	105	167	17	6	11	50	2	4	42	1	80	7	4	.288
Semones, Timothy, Bakersfield*	53	106	13	29	37	6	1	0	19	2	1	14	0	26	0	0	.274
Serrano, Martin, Santa Clara	61	172	26	43	46	3	0	0	18	1	1	26	1	20	10	8	.250
Shoebridge, Terence, Stockton	59	174	19	47	50	3	0	0	12	1	1	35	5	28	3	2	.270
Shoemaker, John, Lodi*	6	18	0	2	2	0	0	0	1	0	0	2	0	1	1	1	.111
Show, Eric, Reno	29	2	1	0	0	0	0	0	0	0	0	0	0	1	0	0	.000
Skorochocki, John, Stockton*	123	456	78	137	175	18	7	2	55	6	4	64	5	36	15	7	.300
Skow, Gary, Santa Clara	19	53	12	13	25	3	0	3	7	0	0	12	0	14	0	0	.245
Skube, Robert, Stockton*	1	5	1	1	1	0	0	0	0	0	0	1	0	2	1	0	.200
Slémbecker, George, Visalia†	127	412	69	96	142	14	4	8	46	2	6	68	1	99	6	5	.233
Smith, Ronald, Visalia†	86	258	45	55	63	4	2	0	33	6	3	56	1	42	13	2	.213
Spillane, Paul, Modesto	36	112	6	18	24	1	1	1	17	2	2	21	1	31	1	3	.161
Springman, William, Salinas	108	366	43	88	144	23	3	9	50	5	2	12	1	76	9	5	.240
Stevens, Paul, Modesto†	63	218	56	64	78	12	1	0	23	6	2	67	1	26	16	6	.294
Stevenson, John, Reno	46	180	41	45	63	6	3	2	15	6	0	25	1	32	14	4	.250
Stockley, Paul, Modesto	58	171	30	39	51	5	2	1	10	3	0	21	0	44	2	1	.228
Swoope, C. William, Lodi	122	420	72	116	197	32	2	15	65	6	7	43	10	72	7	7	.276
Thomas, Franklin, Stockton	96	367	58	103	121	12	3	0	35	4	0	51	0	43	42	17	.281
Thompson, Michael, Bakersfield	30	113	20	38	53	6	0	3	22	1	4	6	0	9	4	1	.336
Thomson, Douglas, 13 Sal-28 SC	41	3	0	0	0	0	0	0	0	0	0	0	0	2	0	0	.000
Thon, Francis, Fresno	18	43	3	8	9	1	0	0	3	1	1	2	0	5	3	0	.186
Tingley, Ronald, Santa Clara	52	143	11	29	35	4	1	0	17	3	2	18	0	37	0	3	.203
Tipa, Stephen, Salinas	29	70	6	16	24	5	0	1	13	1	1	3	2	17	1	0	.229
Torassa, George, Fresno	34	93	8	14	18	4	0	0	7	5	1	10	0	38	0	1	.151
Valenzuela, Fernando, Lodi	3	0	0	0	0	0	0	0	0	1	0	0	0	0	0	0	.000
Valgardson, Don, Stockton*	98	352	37	88	130	19	1	7	53	0	4	34	2	85	0	0	.250
Villaescusa, Juan, Lodi*	13	30	6	11	11	0	0	0	6	0	0	2	0	5	0	0	.367
Walker, John, Lodi	121	449	82	135	160	15	5	0	47	11	5	76	11	51	27	5	.301
Wardlow, Michael, Fresno	22	2	0	0	0	0	0	0	0	0	0	1	0	0	0	0	.000
Webb, Marvin, Bakersfield	21	81	9	26	36	5	1	1	11	0	1	6	0	10	1	0	.321
Weston, Alfred, San Jose	137	522	110	150	189	15	6	4	45	12	3	81	2	36	66	25	.287
White, Michael, 77 SJ-14 SC-19 SJ	110	346	58	92	148	14	0	14	64	1	3	21	7	68	16	13	.266
Wiggins, David, Fresno*	106	379	79	112	162	20	6	6	69	1	3	80	1	55	5	3	.296
Wilkinson, Ronald, Visalia†	26	92	16	26	28	2	0	0	7	1	1	12	0	16	8	2	.283
Woodard, Michael, Modesto*	118	431	90	124	144	8	3	2	31	3	2	70	1	37	61	17	.288
Woods, Michael, Fresno*	32	106	14	24	28	4	0	0	12	1	1	14	0	24	5	1	.226
Ziccardi, John, Fresno*	16	37	10	11	16	5	0	0	9	1	0	13	1	3	0	0	.297

The following pitchers had no plate appearances, primarily through use of designated hitters, listed alphabetically by club, games in parentheses.

BAKERSFIELD—Batton, Christopher (5); Baumgardner, Frank (4); Bowers, Gary (18); Conaty, Peter (40); Costello, Timothy* (16); Gray, Chester (25); Harness, John (3); Heard, Glenn (6); Lucarelli, Francis (6); Mathey, Douglas (17); Milke, George (13); Noonan, John (9); Pekarcik, Lawrence (2); Waldrop, C. Kevin (10); Wright, David (17).

FRESNO—Alexander, Patrick (23); Bungarz, Michael* (15); Fisher, Glenn (25); Hartwig, Daniel (3); Marietta, Louis (6); Moyer, Gregory (36); Murphy, Robert (5); Pisel, Ronald (26); Schopp, William (7); Stember, Jeffrey (20); Tucker, Michael (17).

LODI—Aragon, Reinaldo (7); Bain, Paul† (20); Baldwin, Brian (12); Bass, Jerry (18); Hayes, Brian* (23); Holton, Brian (10); Malden, Christopher (26); Nobles, James (27); O'Neill, Timothy (18); Perry, Stephen (15); Powers, Larry (14); Ruiz, August* (8); Scheller, Rodney* (14); Schmidt, Eric* (11); Sutcliffe, Terry (12).

MODESTO—Atherton, Keith (21); Bigos, Walter (31); Bradley, S. Bert (9); Braun, Barton (18); Corzel, Kennedy (13); Dougherty, Charles (9); Harris, D. Craig (9); Holloway, Richard (11); Jensen, Ronald (25); Lund, Frederick (33); Mantsch, Ronnie (20); McCarthy, David F.* (6); Schubert, Donald (28); Van Marter, Donald (12); Wyszynski, Dennis (3); Yesenchak, Michael* (14).

RENO—Church, Sydney* (41); Dixon, Troy (27); Hamm, Timothy (6); Jannusch, David (26); Johnson, Donald* (27); Miller, K. Randall (51); Patton, Gregory (11).

SALINAS—Boyle, Gary (33); Brown, Steven (17); Cannizzaro, Christopher (1); Chevolek, Thomas* (20); Conner, Jeffrey* (30); Duran, David (17); Healey, Robert (19); Morrison, Perry (41); Rommel, Richard (51); Skaggs, Jackie (1); Steirer, Ricky (29); Vallone, James† (22); Walters, Michael (11); Witt, Michael (30); Wysocki, Paul (6—4 with Santa Clara).

SAN JOSE—Anderson, Karl (9); Bainer, Michael (17); Black, Harry* (17); Diaz, Carlos (26); Edge, Alvin (6); Harrison, Brian (10); Knight, Steven (53); Krajewski, Christopher (57—25 with Santa Clara); McGee, Ronald (26); Naumann, Richard* (27); Smith, David (42); Smith, Douglas (26); Stoddard, Robert (20).

SANTA CLARA—Davis, Robert (11); Givens, Paul (9—7 with San Jose); Hills, John* (35); Hobbs, Jack (32—23 with San Jose); Holmes, Jack* (3); Keen, Daniel (26—2 with Reno); Nobles, David (29—8 with Fresno); Phillips, Charles* (7); Volpi, Joseph* (1); Wulfemeyer, Mark (15).

STOCKTON—Ako, Gerald (54); Bailey, Daryl (22); Christison, Steven (18); Cocanower, James (21); Cort, Barry (13); Curran, David (22); DiPino, Frank* (16); Jenkins, Jerry (3); LaPoint, David* (27); Montgomery, Larry (27); Nicholson, Richard (36); Riggar, Calvin* (8); Sigman, S. Lee† (2); Torres, Anthony (25).

VISALIA—Belk, Charles (21); Biko, Thomas* (30); Pettaway, Felix (24); Reichard, Clyde (58); Salagan, Charles* (16); VanderLaan, Steven* (14); Wagner, Steven (27).

GRAND SLAM HOME RUNS—Alvarez 2; Bertolotti, Bishop, Brunswick, Concepcion, Croft, Daniel, C. Davis, R. Duran, Gilbert, Henderson, Holman, Incaviglia, Jamerson, J. Johnson, Kneuer, Lane, Lee, Loman, A. Moore, Richmond, Swoope, 1 each.

AWARDED FIRST BASE ON INTERFERENCE—Henderson 5 (Nelson 2, Cadahia, Gwosdz, Tingley); Funderburk 3 (Patterson 2, Gwosdz); Springman 2 (Cadahia, Mercado); Blakley (Dempsey); Carnes (Gwosdz); C. Davis (Jones); F. Gonzalez (Martin); Grimes (Shoebridge); Hernandez (Shoebridge); Manning (Baez); Nowakowski (Cadahia); Reed (Lake); Romano (Dempsey); Shoebridge (Martin); Thomas (Martin).

NO-HIT GAME—LaPoint, Stockton, defeated Reno, 4-0, July 25.

CLUB FIELDING

Club	G.	PO.	A.	E.	DP.	PB.	Pct.	Club	G.	PO.	A.	E.	DP.	PB.	Pct.
Stockton	141	3648	1482	187	118	22	.965	Visalia	140	3653	1668	221	113	23	.960
Reno	141	3638	1553	191	126	42	.965	Fresno	139	3595	1613	247	118	53	.955
Salinas	140	3624	1490	192	132	26	.964	Modesto	140	3588	1444	243	109	16	.954
San Jose	140	3634	1573	203	128	30	.962	Bakersfield	140	3568	1597	278	169	24	.949
Lodi	139	3556	1537	210	130	17	.960	Santa Clara	140	3538	1528	326	124	44	.940

Triple Play—Lodi.

INDIVIDUAL FIELDING

FIRST BASEMEN

*Throws lefthanded

Player and Club	G.	PO.	A.	E.	DP.	Pct.	Player and Club	G.	PO.	A.	E.	DP.	Pct.
Bishop, Salinas	40	354	15	0	29	1.000	Hardy, Reno*	125	1096	92	18	99	.985
Skorochocki, Stockton	35	254	10	1	21	.996	Berry, Modesto	74	631	31	10	59	.985
R. Duran, Stockton	43	352	16	2	34	.995	Marshall, Lodi	137	1173	71	20	101	.984
Semones, Bakersfield*	20	143	6	1	20	.993	Putman, SC-Reno	88	721	44	.13	62	.983
R. Gonzalez, Bakersfield	16	127	8	1	10	.993	Minker, Modesto	62	498	35	9	32	.983
SCONIERS, Salinas*	97	804	42	7	77	.992	Attaway, Santa Clara*	23	220	12	4	15	.983
Broders, Bakersfield	18	125	6	1	15	.992	Bothwell, Bakersfield*	12	107	6	2	9	.983
Valgardson, Stockton*	42	378	22	5	23	.988	Funderburk, Visalia	108	1031	74	20	69	.982
Romero, Visalia*	21	150	12	2	19	.988	F. Gonzalez, Sal-SC*	48	389	29	8	35	.981
Maler, San Jose	139	1260	75	17	111	.987	Loureiro, Fresno	27	175	18	4	14	.980
Duncan, Stockton	32	289	11	4	26	.987	Rothford, Fresno	106	977	54	22	73	.979
Riffel, Salinas	12	75	2	1	5	.987	Rametta, Bakersfield	52	482	17	11	55	.978
Robinson, Bakersfield	17	126	10	2	19	.986	K. Moore, Modesto	10	68	2	3	5	.959

(Fewer Than Ten Games)

Player and Club	G.	PO.	A.	E.	DP.	Pct.	Player and Club	G.	PO.	A.	E.	DP.	Pct.
Feinberg, Fresno	9	77	4	0	6	1.000	Gelgarb, Modesto*	1	2	0	0	0	1.000
Cadahia, Visalia	4	23	2	0	2	1.000	Pearsey, Visalia	7	71	4	1	7	.987
Patterson, San Jose	5	15	0	0	1	1.000	Ledbetter, Bakersfield	6	54	1	1	7	.982
Klebba, Santa Clara	2	9	1	0	1	1.000	White, Santa Clara	4	47	3	1	3	.980
Lee, Bakersfield	2	9	0	0	1	1.000	Reichenbach, Bakers.	4	29	2	1	6	.969
Mercado, San Jose	1	7	1	0	2	1.000	McDonald, Visalia	9	54	3	2	4	.966
Berger, Visalia*	2	7	1	0	1	1.000	Ziccardi, Fresno*	9	79	2	3	5	.964
Hertel, Reno	1	7	0	0	1	1.000	Frederickson, Bakers.	2	21	2	1	2	.958
R. Smith, Visalia	2	6	1	0	1	1.000	Nelson, Bakersfield	7	38	4	2	2	.955
Wiggins, Fresno*	2	5	2	0	1	1.000	Martinson, Lodi	4	17	2	1	3	.950
Cheesman, Salinas	2	4	0	0	1	1.000	Slembecker, Visalia	2	16	0	1	2	.941
Kelly, Visalia*	1	3	1	0	0	1.000	Webb, Bakersfield	1	10	0	1	0	.909
Holman, Lodi	1	2	1	0	0	1.000	Richards, Lodi	1	8	0	1	3	.889
Hamilton, Salinas	2	2	0	0	0	1.000	Brunson, Stockton	1	0	0	1	0	.000
Brunansky, Salinas	1	2	0	0	1	1.000	Nowakowski, S. Clara	1	0	0	1	0	.000

SECOND BASEMEN

Player and Club	G.	PO.	A.	E.	DP.	Pct.
Walker, Lodi	13	35	33	0	7	1.000
Rowe, Fresno	27	51	66	2	15	.983
Thon, Fresno	17	32	45	2	5	.975
ENNIS, Visalia	104	218	293	15	61	.971
Thomas, Stockton	94	195	233	14	44	.968
J. Johnson, Reno	114	248	300	18	61	.968
Franjul, Lodi	117	263	311	19	63	.968
Lee, Bakersfield	24	58	78	5	19	.965
R. Smith, Visalia	34	63	97	6	19	.964
Weston, San Jose	132	269	347	24	79	.963
Wilkinson, Visalia	12	25	25	2	6	.962
Skorochocki, Stockton	49	104	118	9	27	.961
Brunswick, Modesto	20	36	49	4	4	.955
Serrano, Santa Clara	11	18	24	2	4	.955
Daniel, Bakersfield	98	224	260	25	80	.951
Springman, Salinas	99	217	227	25	67	.947
Stevens, Modesto	12	40	32	4	9	.947
Gutierrez, Santa Clara	87	209	241	27	49	.943
Woodard, Modesto	110	230	253	30	51	.942
Lane, Fresno	102	199	247	29	56	.939
R. Gonzalez, Bakersfield	11	27	19	3	11	.939
Cox, Reno	23	46	45	6	13	.938
Hamilton, Salinas	47	85	98	13	22	.934
Robinson, Santa Clara	15	26	38	7	7	.901
Bedrosian, Santa Clara	19	41	47	11	14	.889

Triple Play—Franjul.

(Fewer Than Ten Games)

Player and Club	G.	PO.	A.	E.	DP.	Pct.
Pebley, San Jose	9	18	20	0	8	1.000
Shoemaker, Lodi	5	18	19	0	6	1.000
Alvarez, Reno	8	11	17	0	1	1.000
Klebba, Santa Clara	4	8	8	0	2	1.000
Webb, Bakersfield	4	6	10	0	4	1.000
McHenry, San Jose	3	7	6	0	3	1.000
Hertel, Reno	3	6	4	0	2	1.000
Slembecker, Visalia	3	4	6	0	2	1.000
Nowland, San Jose	2	3	4	0	1	1.000
Eakin, Modesto	1	2	1	0	1	1.000
Incaviglia, San Clara	1	2	0	0	0	1.000
Reed, Reno	1	0	1	0	0	1.000
Cuarezma, Stockton	5	12	16	1	6	.966
Thompson, Bakers	6	12	9	1	2	.955
Grimes, Santa Clara	4	12	9	1	4	.955
Schultz, Lodi	8	20	18	2	6	.950
O. Ramirez, Bakersfield	4	9	9	1	3	.947
Gladden, Fresno	4	7	9	1	2	.941
Caira, Santa Clara	3	9	6	3	1	.833
Dunn, Fresno	2	1	4	1	1	.833
Schexnayder, Salinas	2	4	0	1	1	.800
Tingley, Santa Clara	1	3	0	2	1	.600
Lettrich, Santa Clara	1	1	0	1	0	.500
Cheesman, Salinas	1	0	1	1	0	.500

THIRD BASEMEN

Player and Club	G.	PO.	A.	E.	DP.	Pct.
PEARSEY, Visalia	119	90	284	22	23	.944
Hamilton, Salinas	39	24	53	5	5	.939
Keedy, Salinas	44	35	87	8	11	.938
Roberts, Modesto	26	15	45	4	4	.938
Edler, San Jose	135	111	309	29	26	.935
Doss, Fresno	72	60	197	18	12	.935
R. Smith, Visalia	17	4	39	3	3	.935
Klebba, Santa Clara	24	14	57	6	5	.922
Skorochocki, Stockton	21	20	37	5	6	.919
Alvarez, Reno	123	93	261	32	12	.917
Rametta, Bakersfield	31	21	56	7	7	.917
DeVito, Modesto	107	84	240	31	14	.913
Brenly, Fresno	55	39	133	17	12	.910
Manning, Stockton	125	94	249	35	24	.907
Lanning, Lodi	35	26	66	10	6	.902
Bishop, Salinas	22	21	34	6	4	.902
Rowe, Fresno	19	20	43	7	2	.900
Putnam, SC-Reno	16	9	18	3	1	.900
O. Ramirez, Bakersfield	27	17	44	7	7	.897
Schexnayder, Salinas	69	42	114	21	14	.881
Slembecker, Visalia	10	5	16	3	2	.875
Incaviglia, Santa Clara	78	71	165	34	13	.874
Hernandez, Lodi	61	52	143	29	8	.871
Parker, Reno	11	7	17	4	0	.857
Grimes, Santa Clara	16	14	33	8	2	.855
Rivera, Lodi	36	24	84	19	9	.850
Lee, Bakersfield	11	8	19	5	3	.844
R. Gonzalez, Bakers	49	45	103	32	13	.822
Serrano, Santa Clara	19	17	29	10	2	.821
Thompson, Bakers	10	7	23	7	3	.811
Nelson, Bakersfield	10	8	17	6	4	.806

Triple Play—Hernandez.

(Fewer Than Ten Games)

Player and Club	G.	PO.	A.	E.	DP.	Pct.
Schultz, Lodi	4	2	11	0	1	1.000
Robinson, Bakersfield	3	1	11	0	2	1.000
Pebley, San Jose	5	1	9	0	1	1.000
J. Johnson, Reno	2	2	4	0	0	1.000
Frederickson, Bakers	3	3	2	0	0	1.000
F. Gonzalez, Salinas*	1	0	5	0	2	1.000
Thomas, Stockton	1	0	4	0	0	1.000
Eakin, Modesto	1	1	2	0	0	1.000
Duncan, Stockton	1	0	3	0	0	1.000
Maxwell, Visalia	2	1	1	0	0	1.000
Nocciolo, Salinas	2	0	2	0	0	1.000
R. Dixon, Bakersfield	1	1	0	0	0	1.000
Patterson, San Jose	1	0	1	0	0	1.000
Wilkinson, Visalia	1	0	1	0	0	1.000
Brunswick, Modesto	8	5	15	2	2	.909
Broders, Bakersfield	3	5	3	1	1	.889
Webb, Bakersfield	6	4	15	3	3	.864
Hertel, SC-Reno	6	5	19	4	5	.857
Cuarezma, Stockton	3	1	3	2	1	.667
Ruzek, Lodi	3	1	1	1	0	.667
Maddon, Santa Clara	2	1	1	1	0	.667
Skow, Santa Clara	2	1	2	2	0	.600
Stevens, Modesto	2	5	2	5	0	.583
Nowland, Salinas	3	2	2	4	0	.500
R. Ramirez, Stockton	1	1	0	1	0	.500
Almon, Reno	1	0	0	1	0	.000

SHORTSTOPS

Player and Club	G.	PO.	A.	E.	DP.	Pct.
Ruzek, Lodi	25	34	78	4	11	.966
Skorochocki, Stockton	15	19	34	2	5	.964
Mann, Lodi	27	40	65	4	14	.963
Wilkinson, Visalia	11	16	33	2	6	.961
Nowland, San Jose	24	31	56	4	18	.956
Daniel, Bakersfield	12	12	31	2	6	.956

SHORTSTOPS—Continued

Player and Club	G.	PO.	A.	E.	DP.	Pct.	Player and Club	G.	PO.	A.	E.	DP.	Pct.
McHENRY, San Jose	100	156	305	25	54	.949	Stockley, Modesto	57	92	139	17	28	.931
Pastors, Reno	81	118	255	21	48	.947	Stevenson, Reno	46	84	139	17	31	.929
Carnes, Salinas	134	174	411	34	62	.945	Concepcion, Bakersfield.	125	227	454	55	85	.925
Dunn, Fresno	33	32	109	9	19	.940	Rowe, Fresno	52	53	146	18	18	.917
Rodriguez, Stockton	127	189	377	37	65	.939	Pebley, San Jose	35	47	77	12	11	.912
Slembecker, Visalia	112	143	362	33	49	.939	Stevens, Modesto	28	55	68	12	13	.911
Walker, Lodi	87	144	255	26	44	.939	R. Smith, Visalia	23	39	69	11	12	.908
Cyburt, Fresno	45	52	119	12	15	.934	Greb, Modesto	32	33	90	14	19	.898
Grimes, Santa Clara	92	157	275	31	49	.933	Woods, Fresno	24	32	57	14	8	.864
Eakin, Modesto	32	49	101	11	14	.932	Hertel, S. C.-Reno	42	54	107	27	11	.856

Triple Play—Walker

(Fewer Than Ten Games)

Player and Club	G.	PO.	A.	E.	DP.	Pct.	Player and Club	G.	PO.	A.	E.	DP.	Pct.
Gutierrez, Santa Clara	2	7	5	0	1	1.000	Alvarez, Reno	6	7	20	2	1	.931
Klebba, Santa Clara	1	3	8	0	2	1.000	Schultz, Lodi	7	9	26	3	5	.921
Cuarezma, Stockton	3	3	7	0	3	1.000	R. Dixon, Bakersfield	6	8	13	3	3	.875
Gladden, Fresno	2	4	4	0	1	1.000	Serrano, Santa Clara	6	4	14	3	2	.857
Manning, Stockton	2	3	3	0	1	1.000	Brunswick, Modesto	2	6	5	2	0	.846
Pearsey, Visalia	1	1	2	0	0	1.000	Thomas, Stockton	1	2	2	1	0	.800
Franjul, Lodi	1	0	2	0	1	1.000	Hamilton, Salinas	7	1	7	3	1	.727
Keedy, Salinas	8	12	22	1	6	.971	Incaviglia, Santa Clara	3	4	9	6	1	.684
Cox, Reno	8	11	35	2	8	.958	Guzman, Lodi	1	0	0	1	0	.000

OUTFIELDERS

Player and Club	G.	PO.	A.	E.	DP.	Pct.	Player and Club	G.	PO.	A.	E.	DP.	Pct.
Reed, Reno	50	62	9	0	2	1.000	A. Moore, Visalia	84	114	9	5	0	.961
Garrett, Bakersfield	17	32	4	0	1	1.000	Gladden, Fresno	44	45	3	2	2	.960
Roberts, Modesto	11	26	0	0	0	1.000	Gardner, Bakersfield	77	156	4	7	0	.958
Riffel, Salinas	26	21	2	0	1	1.000	Blakley, Reno	116	148	11	7	3	.958
R. Dixon, Bakersfield	15	21	2	0	0	1.000	Lohse, Bakersfield	95	166	15	8	2	.958
Webb, Bakersfield	10	20	3	0	1	1.000	Markham, Modesto*	135	294	14	14	2	.957
Incaviglia, Santa Clara	14	14	2	0	0	1.000	Lemon, Salinas	83	151	2	7	0	.956
Frederickson, Baker.	10	7	1	0	0	1.000	Romero, Visalia	73	124	5	6	0	.956
Morley, Fresno	10	7	1	0	0	1.000	Bradley, Lodi	31	39	3	2	1	.955
Maxwell, Visalia	10	2	1	0	0	1.000	Bennett, Santa Clara*	123	239	9	12	4	.954
ALMON, Reno	116	212	12	3	3	.987	Eagan, Santa Clara	82	114	9	6	2	.953
Berger, Visalia*	71	146	8	2	1	.987	Lane, Fresno	13	15	3	1	0	.947
Henderson, San Jose	132	264	18	4	3	.986	Armstead, Modesto	70	170	3	10	1	.945
Wiggins, Fresno*	105	201	6	4	3	.981	Brooks, Fresno*	30	29	4	2	0	.943
D. Green, Stockton	134	282	8	6	1	.980	Nichols, Bakersfield	110	193	19	13	8	.942
Brunansky, Salinas	140	279	11	6	1	.980	Feinberg, Fresno	25	25	5	2	2	.938
Anthony, Fresno	90	174	15	4	7	.979	Bertolotti, Santa Clara	10	15	0	1	0	.938
R. Ramirez, Stockton	28	35	3	1	1	.974	Thompson, Bakersfield	10	14	1	1	0	.938
Gilbert, Stockton	133	234	21	7	7	.973	Jamerson, Fresno	54	64	8	5	0	.935
Swoope, Lodi	117	188	18	6	5	.972	Attaway, Santa Clara*	63	79	6	6	2	.934
Negron, San Jose*	98	130	10	4	3	.972	Lee, Bakersfield	21	21	7	2	0	.933
Nowland, San Jose	43	32	1	1	0	.971	Tipa, Salinas	13	11	3	1	0	.933
Greer, Visalia*	108	191	5	6	0	.970	Haley, Bakersfield	54	100	7	8	4	.930
Richmond, Reno	111	168	20	6	1	.969	White, SJ-SC-SJ	66	92	8	8	4	.926
Flammang, San Jose*	108	111	13	4	3	.969	M. Davis, Modesto*	39	76	3	7	0	.919
Loman, Stockton*	136	258	12	9	1	.968	C. Davis, Fresno	73	111	10	11	1	.917
Kemp, Lodi	91	110	7	4	0	.967	Funderburk, Visalia	15	7	3	1	0	.909
Caira, Santa Clara	40	86	3	3	2	.967	Croft, Visalia	63	102	10	13	0	.896
Garrison, Lodi	119	248	4	9	2	.966	B. Brown, Lodi	35	42	4	6	0	.885
Morris, Modesto	122	184	15	7	0	.966	Packard, Santa Clara,	16	20	3	3	0	.885
Parker, S. C.-Reno	65	80	6	3	0	.966	Ennis, Visalia	15	13	2	2	0	.882
Dailey, Salinas	66	79	7	3	0	.966	Marrero, Visalia	10	7	0	1	0	.875
Craig, San Jose	45	54	1	2	0	.965	F. Gonzalez, Sal-S. C.*	44	48	2	8	1	.862
Brunson, Stockton	120	172	12	7	2	.963	Skorochocki, Stockton	10	15	2	3	0	.850
Holman, Lodi	53	74	3	3	0	.963	K. Moore, Modesto*	34	48	1	11	0	.817
Stevens, Modesto	15	25	1	1	0	.963							

(Fewer Than Ten Games)

Player and Club	G.	PO.	A.	E.	DP.	Pct.	Player and Club	G.	PO.	A.	E.	DP.	Pct.
Lake, Stockton	5	10	1	0	0	1.000	R. Gonzalez, Bakersfield	2	5	0	0	0	1.000
Ransom, Fresno	3	9	1	0	0	1.000	Patterson, San Jose	2	5	0	0	0	1.000
Beerbower, Bakersfield.	5	6	0	0	0	1.000	Hamilton, Salinas	4	3	0	0	0	1.000
Broders, Bakersfield	5	6	0	0	0	1.000	Skow, Santa Clara	4	3	0	0	0	1.000
Maddon, Santa Clara	5	5	1	0	0	1.000	Lettrich, Santa Clara	1	3	0	0	0	1.000
O. Ramirez, Bakersfield.	2	3	3	0	0	1.000	Putman, Santa Clara	2	2	0	0	0	1.000
Semones, Bakersfield*	3	5	0	0	0	1.000	Robinson, Bakersfield	2	2	0	0	0	1.000

OUTFIELDERS—Continued
(Fewer Than Ten Games)

Player and Club	G.	PO.	A.	E.	DP.	Pct.
Boggs, Santa Clara	1	2	0	0	0	1.000
Sarno, Bakersfield	1	2	0	0	0	1.000
Reis, Bakersfield	1	1	0	0	0	1.000
Skube, Stockton*	1	1	0	0	0	1.000
Leonard, Visalia	4	14	0	1	0	.933
Minker, Modesto	5	6	1	1	0	.875
Pebley, San Jose	4	4	1	1	0	.833

Player and Club	G.	PO.	A.	E.	DP.	Pct.
Tingley, Santa Clara	4	7	0	2	0	.778
Rametta, Bakersfield	7	5	1	2	0	.750
T. Jones, Santa Clara	4	1	2	1	0	.750
Nowakowski, S. C.	1	1	1	1	0	.667
Schultz, Lodi	2	1	0	1	0	.500
Ziccardi, Fresno*	2	1	0	1	0	.500

CATCHERS

Player and Club	G.	PO.	A.	E.	DP.	PB.	Pct.
Malkin, Lodi	20	131	9	1	2	4	.993
Cias, Modesto	42	237	29	3	1	6	.989
MARTINSON, Lodi	74	432	68	6	4	4	.9881
Gwosdz, Reno	82	583	51	8	2	20	.9875
Lake, Stockton	83	504	73	8	7	12	.986
Patterson, San Jose	32	193	12	3	1	4	.986
D. Jones, Salinas	25	146	30	3	1	2	.983
R. Gonzalez, Baker.	47	239	31	5	4	5	.982
Mejia, Lodi	26	135	31	3	3	5	.982
Nocciolo, Salinas	108	629	92	14	11	20	.981
Torassa, Fresno	33	192	20	4	3	10	.981
Shoebridge, Stockton	59	344	49	8	0	9	.980
Tingley, Santa Clara	42	251	42	6	4	7	.980
Spillane, Modesto	36	223	25	5	3	3	.980
Mercado, San Jose	99	622	70	17	4	24	.976

Player and Club	G.	PO.	A.	E.	DP.	PB.	Pct.
Maddon, Santa Clara	11	71	6	2	0	5	.975
Martin, Reno	69	439	36	13	3	22	.973
McDonald, Visalia	76	414	59	13	2	11	.973
Nelson, Bakersfield	94	468	77	16	9	19	.971
Bertolotti, S.C.	47	269	36	9	8	12	.971
Dempsey, Modesto	53	307	42	11	2	5	.969
Ransom, Fresno	51	365	40	14	7	20	.967
C. Davis, Fresno	42	228	33	9	4	17	.967
Arias, San Jose-SC	42	175	21	7	1	2	.966
Cadahia, Visalia	80	455	56	19	3	12	.964
Baez, Lodi	26	174	32	8	3	4	.963
Cummings, Fresno	16	97	7	4	1	4	.963
Cheesman, Salinas	23	92	7	4	1	4	.961
Kneuer, Modesto	15	86	14	6	1	2	.943
Nowakowski, S. C.	41	249	42	21	4	18	.933

Triple Play—Baez.

(Fewer Than Ten Games)

Player and Club	G.	PO.	A.	E.	DP.	PB.	Pct.
Lane, Fresno	8	49	7	0	1	0	1.000
Richards, Fresno	8	39	3	0	0	0	1.000
Schexnayder, Salinas	1	1	0	0	0	0	1.000
Bolla, Fresno	8	28	6	1	0	2	.971
Robinson, Bakersfield	6	23	8	1	3	0	.969

Player and Club	G.	PO.	A.	E.	DP.	PB.	Pct.
Skow, Santa Clara	8	50	6	2	0	2	.966
Kingsolver, Stockton	8	40	9	2	1	0	.961
Ledbetter, Bakersfield	7	29	4	2	1	0	.943
R. Duran, Stockton	3	16	1	4	0	1	.810

PITCHERS

Player and Club	G.	PO.	A.	E.	DP.	Pct.
LaPOINT, Stockton*	27	6	29	0	1	1.000
Montgomery, Stockton	26	8	25	0	1	1.000
Moyer, Fresno	35	12	19	0	1	1.000
Atherton, Modesto	21	7	24	0	1	1.000
Boyle, Salinas	33	6	21	0	4	1.000
Miller, Reno	51	12	10	0	1	1.000
Lund, Modesto	33	5	17	0	0	1.000
Gosse, Modesto*	43	3	16	0	1	1.000
Baldwin, Lodi	12	7	11	0	0	1.000
Scheller, Lodi	14	6	12	0	0	1.000
Hayes, Lodi*	23	3	13	0	0	1.000
Tucker, Fresno	17	4	10	0	1	1.000
Bigos, Modesto	31	2	12	0	1	1.000
Wulfemeyer, SC	15	5	9	0	0	1.000
Mantsch, Modesto	20	3	10	0	2	1.000
DiPino, Stockton*	16	3	10	0	0	1.000
Ako, Stockton	54	2	11	0	0	1.000
O'Neill, Lodi	18	2	9	0	0	1.000
Church, Reno*	41	4	6	0	0	1.000
Waldrop, Bakersfield	10	2	8	0	1	1.000
Black, San Jose*	17	2	7	0	0	1.000
Milke, Bakersfield	13	5	3	0	0	1.000
Gray, Bakersfield*	25	2	5	0	2	1.000
Yesenchak, Modesto*	14	2	5	0	0	1.000
Powers, Lodi	14	0	7	0	0	1.000
Holloway, Modesto	11	1	5	0	1	1.000
Diaz, San Jose*	26	1	4	0	0	1.000
Braun, Modesto	18	0	5	0	1	1.000
Christison, Stockton	18	1	3	0	0	1.000
D. Duran, Salinas	17	1	2	0	0	1.000
Schmidt, Lodi*	11	1	2	0	1	1.000
Wright, Bakersfield	17	0	3	0	1	1.000
Schubert, Modesto	28	9	36	1	2	.978
Show, Reno	28	14	28	1	1	.977

Player and Club	G.	PO.	A.	E.	DP.	Pct.
Biko, Visalia*	30	9	31	1	3	.976
Torres, Stockton	25	9	26	1	1	.972
S. Green, Visalia	27	22	34	2	1	.966
Steirer, Salinas	29	12	15	1	0	.964
Cordova, Lodi	42	7	19	1	2	.963
S. Brown, Salinas	17	7	19	1	1	.963
Kittrell, Fresno*	21	5	21	1	0	.963
Fireovid, Reno	26	18	31	2	3	.961
Alexander, Fresno*	23	9	35	2	2	.957
Jannusch, Reno	26	10	11	1	1	.955
Vallone, Salinas*	22	1	17	1	1	.947
Foster, Lodi	47	4	13	1	0	.944
Barr, Visalia	38	13	20	2	2	.943
David Smith, San Jose	42	11	22	2	3	.943
Jensen, Modesto*	25	9	23	2	1	.941
Wagner, Visalia	27	19	26	3	0	.938
Douglas Smith, Reno	26	9	21	2	4	.938
Chevolek, Salinas*	20	5	10	1	0	.938
G. Johnson, Salinas	27	3	26	2	3	.935
T. Dixon, Reno	27	16	26	3	4	.933
Bass, Lodi	18	9	5	1	1	.933
Sutcliffe, Lodi	12	7	7	1	3	.933
Buice, Fresno	46	5	9	1	0	.933
Byrd, San Jose	26	8	32	3	2	.930
Rommel, Salinas	51	6	20	2	2	.929
Reichard, Visalia	58	3	10	1	0	.929
Hunziker, Santa Clara	20	7	28	3	3	.921
Wardlow, Fresno	22	4	19	2	0	.920
Boggs, Santa Clara	20	6	16	2	3	.917
Belk, Visalia	19	4	7	1	0	.917
Bungarz, Fresno*	15	0	11	1	0	.917
Fisher, Fresno	25	7	14	2	0	.913
Malden, Lodi	26	4	17	2	0	.913
Perry, Lodi	15	8	12	2	1	.909

PITCHERS—Continued

Player and Club	G.	PO.	A.	E.	DP.	Pct.
Healey, Salinas	19	7	13	2	1	.909
Mathey, Bakersfield	17	6	14	2	2	.909
Nicholson, Stockton	36	5	15	2	1	.909
Witt, Salinas	30	5	15	2	0	.909
Koen, Reno-SC*	26	2	18	2	0	.909
Morrison, Salinas	41	4	6	1	1	.909
Costello, Bakersfield*	16	2	8	1	0	.909
Sarno, Bakersfield	39	15	24	4	0	.907
Hills, Santa Clara*	35	6	23	3	2	.906
D. Johnson, Reno*	27	14	24	4	2	.905
Corzel, Modesto	13	2	7	1	0	.900
Knight, San Jose	52	5	10	2	0	.882
Conner, Salinas*	30	4	11	2	0	.882
S. Kelley, Bakersfield	12	3	12	2	1	.882
Harris, SJ-SC	69	6	22	4	1	.875
B. Kelley, Bakersfield	31	9	19	4	1	.875
Naumann, San Jose*	27	3	11	2	0	.875
Harryman, Bakersfield*	17	4	3	1	0	.875
Hardwick, Reno	28	3	4	1	0	.875
Semones, Bakersfield*	15	2	5	1	1	.875
Harrison, San Jose	10	1	6	1	0	.875
Pettaway, Visalia	24	10	17	4	1	.871
McGee, San Jose	26	9	43	8	4	.867
R. Davis, Santa Clara	11	4	8	2	0	.857
Curran, Stockton	22	7	10	3	0	.850
Hawkins, Reno	27	10	33	8	3	.843
Krajewski, SC-SJ	57	10	21	6	4	.838
Conaty, Bakersfield	40	4	16	4	3	.833
Stoddard, San Jose	20	1	19	4	1	.833
Van Marter, Modesto	12	4	6	2	0	.833
Lettrich, Santa Clara	23	8	11	4	2	.826
Pisel, Fresno	26	7	12	4	1	.826
Holton, Lodi	10	6	8	3	1	.824
Bailey, Stockton	22	1	8	2	1	.818
Fiorante, SC-SJ-SC	32	4	9	3	2	.813
Adamson, Visalia	34	5	16	5	1	.808
Bain, Lodi	20	5	15	5	3	.800
Thomson, Sal-SC	41	3	17	5	1	.800
Stember, Fresno	20	2	2	1	0	.800
Omo, Fresno*	28	3	20	6	0	.793
Hobbs, SJ-SC*	32	7	18	7	0	.781
J. Nobles, Lodi*	27	2	5	2	0	.778
Vander Laan, Visalia	14	.5	5	3	0	.769
Cocanower, Stockton	20	10	16	8	1	.765
A. Johnson, Vis-Bak	20	5	14	6	0	.760
Cort, Stockton	13	1	7	3	0	.727
Patton, Reno	11	3	3	3	0	.667
D. Nobles, Fr-SC	29	0	8	4	0	.667
Bowers, Bakersfield	18	1	5	3	1	.667
Walters, Salinas	21	2	3	3	1	.625
Bainer, San Jose	17	0	1	2	0	.333
Salagan, Visalia*	16	0	1	3	0	.250

(Fewer Than Ten Games)

Player and Club	G.	PO.	A.	E.	DP.	Pct.
McCarthy, Modesto*	6	1	4	0	0	1.000
Lucarelli, Bakersfield	6	2	2	0	0	1.000
Reichenbach, Bakersf'd	5	1	3	0	0	1.000
Wysocki, SC-Sal	6	0	4	0	0	1.000
Jenkins, Stockton	3	2	1	0	0	1.000
Schopp, Fresno	7	1	2	0	0	1.000
Hamm, Reno	6	0	3	0	1	1.000
Kelly, Visalia*	1	0	3	0	1	1.000
Edge, San Jose	6	2	0	0	0	1.000
Baumgardner, Bakersf'd	4	0	2	0	0	1.000
Pekarcik, Bakersfield	2	0	2	0	0	1.000
Grimes, Santa Clara	5	1	0	0	0	1.000
Givens, SJ-SC*	9	0	1	0	0	1.000
Harness, Bakersfield	3	0	1	0	0	1.000
Riffel, Salinas	1	0	1	0	0	1.000
Phillips, Santa Clara*	7	3	7	1	0	.909
Bradley, Modesto	9	1	9	1	0	.909
Valenzuela, Lodi*	3	1	9	1	0	.909
Batton, Bakersfield	5	4	5	1	0	.900
Rabouin, Bakersfield	5	1	6	1	0	.875
Riggar, Stockton	8	1	5	1	0	.857
Anderson, San Jose	9	3	7	2	0	.833
Reis, Bakersfield*	9	2	3	1	0	.833
Dougherty, Modesto*	8	2	3	1	0	.833
Hartwig, Fresno	3	0	4	1	0	.800
Ruiz, Lodi*	8	0	4	1	0	.800
Harris, Modesto	9	3	4	2	1	.778
Aragon, Lodi	7	2	1	1	0	.750
Marietta, Fresno	6	0	2	1	0	.667
Noonan, Bakersfield*	9	1	2	2	0	.600

The following players do not have any recorded accepted chances at the positions indicated; therefore, are not listed in the fielding averages for those particular positions: Arias, p; Brunson, 3b; Brunswick, p; Cannizzaro, p; Carnes, 2b; R. Duran, of; Eakin, of; Frederickson, p; Galfarb*, of; Gwosdz, of; Hamliton, c-p; Heard*, p; Holmes*, p; Keedy, of; Lemon, 2b; Murphy, p; Rametta, 2b; Riffel, 2b; Roberts, ss; Schexnayder, of; Sigman, p; Skaggs, p; R. Smith, of; Tingley, p; Volpi*, p; Weston, of; Wysztnski, p.

CLUB PITCHING

Club	G.	CG.	ShO.	Sv.	IP.	H.	R.	ER.	HR.	BB.	Int. BB.	HB.	SO.	WP.	Bk.	ERA.
Stockton	141	36	8	20	1216	1117	594	483	51	558	21	25	888	56	8	3.57
San Jose	140	31	10	29	1211	1031	616	499	60	698	26	50	950	118	8	3.71
Visalia	140	29	6	32	1218	1280	703	568	79	542	20	23	834	90	8	4.20
Salinas	140	20	5	25	1208	1265	715	578	100	595	86	36	818	75	4	4.31
Reno	141	34	4	24	1213	1248	729	596	90	616	12	30	1005	106	14	4.42
Fresno	139	26	6	23	1198	1253	763	604	88	663	12	30	948	114	20	4.54
Lodi	139	26	8	23	1185	1216	778	639	102	798	27	32	879	131	19	4.85
Modesto	140	38	2	23	1196	1419	850	691	125	533	32	38	783	56	14	5.20
Bakersfield	140	34	5	18	1189	1405	903	703	125	620	19	30	729	106	11	5.32
Santa Clara	140	20	1	11	1179	1291	984	752	105	851	10	60	870	156	14	5.74

PITCHERS' RECORDS

(Leading Qualifiers for Earned-Run Average Leadership—112 or More Innings)

*Throws lefthanded.

Pitcher–Club	G	GS	CG	ShO	W	L	Sv	Pct.	IP	H	R	ER	HR	BB	Int. BB	HB	SO	WP	ERA
S. Brown, Salinas	17	17	4	0	10	5	0	.667	123	109	52	33	3	57	5	2	89	7	2.41
David Smith, San Jose	42	19	3	0	15	6	4	.714	156	125	65	46	5	62	2	7	113	13	2.65
McGee, San Jose	26	25	10	3	15	6	0	.714	186	146	78	57	8	87	1	6	111	14	2.76
Ako, Stockton	54	1	0	0	11	2	9	.846	113	115	42	36	3	32	8	3	70	2	2.87
Montgomery, Stockton	26	24	9	2	11	8	0	.579	174	147	66	56	8	40	3	0	105	3	2.90
Fisher, Fresno	25	17	4	3	9	4	1	.692	132	123	56	43	10	70	0	6	111	6	2.93
Byrd, San Jose	26	23	4	0	12	6	0	.667	151	97	72	50	6	117	1	15	161	17	2.98
Stoddard, San Jose	20	16	3	1	7	5	0	.583	120	78	45	40	6	58	1	2	104	7	3.00
LaPoint, Stockton*	27	25	11	3	12	10	0	.545	180	144	74	63	5	85	0	1	208	7	3.15
Biko, Visalia*	30	28	10	2	14	9	0	.609	177	184	81	62	6	79	4	5	101	3	3.15

Departmental Leaders: G—Harris, 69; GS—Biko, Steirer, 28; CG—LaPoint, Steirer, 11; ShO—Fisher, Holton, LaPoint, McGee, Douglas Smith, 3; W—Green, 16; L—Hills, 18; Sv—Reichard, 19; Pct.—Ako, .846; IP—Green, 208; H—Hawkins, 232; R—Hills, 147; ER—Hawkins, 117; HR—Sarno, 21; BB—Byrd, 117; IBB—G. Johnson, Morrison, 10; HP—Byrd, 15; SO—LaPoint, 208; WP—Wardlow, 27.

(All Pitchers—Listed Alphabetically)

Pitcher–Club	G	GS	CG	ShO	W	L	Sv	Pct.	IP	H	R	ER	HR	BB	Int. BB	HB	SO	WP	ERA
Adamson, Visalia	34	16	3	2	11	5	. 2	.688	146	136	75	67	8	72	3	1	121	10	4.13
Ako, Stockton	54	1	0	0	11	2	9	.846	113	115	42	36	3	32	8	3	70	2	2.87
Alexander, Fresno*	23	18	4	1	7	7	1	.500	131	140	81	63	9	70	0	4	68	12	4.33
Anderson, San Jose	9	8	1	0	5	3	0	.625	49	49	23	21	2	17	0	3	47	3	3.86
Aragon, Lodi	7	0	0	0	0	0	0	.000	18	15	8	4	2	12	0	0	18	8	2.00
Arias, San Jose	1	0	0	0	0	0	0	.000	1	4	4	4	1	2	0	0	0	0	36.00
Atherton, Modesto	21	21	9	0	9	8	0	.529	146	190	107	97	18	51	4	3	103	1	5.98
Bailey, Stockton	22	0	0	0	3	2	4	.600	38	48	30	16	0	17	0	1	24	0	3.79
Bain, Lodi	20	19	2	0	5	8	0	.385	93	104	71	60	3	97	0	3	70	14	5.81
Bainer, San Jose	17	1	0	0	2	1	1	.667	25	30	19	19	2	20	1	0	19	6	6.84
Baldwin, Lodi	12	12	3	1	6	3	0	.667	80	74	37	32	4	36	0	2	49	4	3.60
Barr, Visalia	38	10	2	0	10	3	4	.769	115	112	57	43	5	48	4	3	99	13	3.37
Bass, Lodi	18	0	0	0	2	2	2	.500	53	48	29	27	7	38	1	3	30	5	4.58
Batton, Bakersfield	5	5	1	0	1	3	0	.250	27	43	27	23	4	16	0	0	14	3	7.67
Baumgardner, Baker.	4	4	1	0	0	2	0	.000	23	22	15	13	1	9	0	0	10	3	5.09
Belk, Visalia	19	1	0	0	4	1	3	.800	29	34	16	13	3	11	1	1	9	0	4.03
Bigos, Modesto	31	0	0	0	4	2	5	.667	61	65	26	19	3	28	3	2	49	2	2.80
Biko, Visalia*	30	28	10	2	14	9	0	.609	177	184	81	62	6	79	4	5	101	3	3.15
Black, San Jose*	17	2	0	0	1	1	1	.000	27	17	11	9	1	16	1	2	24	2	3.00
Boggs, Santa Clara	20	15	0	0	3	11	1	.214	101	111	76	65	3	55	1	8	66	10	5.79
Bowers, Bakersfield	18	8	1	0	4	5	2	.444	62	53	38	32	2	65	3	2	47	11	4.65
Boyle, Salinas	33	1	0	0	3	2	2	.600	73	82	28	23	2	26	6	1	42	3	2.84
Bradley, Modesto	9	4	2	0	2	2	1	.500	35	28	19	15	4	10	0	1	24	0	3.86
Braun, Modesto	18	0	0	0	8	1	4	.889	34	32	10	9	5	13	0	0	17	0	2.38
S. Brown, Salinas	17	17	4	0	10	5	0	.667	123	109	52	33	3	57	5	2	89	7	2.41
Brunswick, Modesto	1	0	0	0	0	0	0	.000	3	1	0	0	0	0	0	0	0	0	0.00
Buice, Fresno	46	0	0	0	7	5	3	.583	97	83	51	40	9	44	4	2	86	12	3.71
Bungarz, Fresno*	15	1	0	0	1	1	1	.500	41	34	19	14	3	25	0	0	33	3	3.07
Byrd, San Jose	26	23	4	0	12	6	0	.667	151	97	72	50	6	117	1	15	161	17	2.98
Cannizzaro, Salinas	1	0	0	0	0	0	0	.000	3	1	0	0	0	2	0	0	4	0	0.00
Chevolek, Salinas*	20	0	0	0	1	1	2	.500	41	29	12	10	4	20	5	3	48	3	2.20
Christison, Stockton	18	3	2	0	1	8	0	.111	48	51	35	26	2	37	1	6	36	3	4.88
Church, Reno*	41	0	0	0	3	4	0	.250	68	65	30	26	5	44	4	2	62	4	3.44
Cocanower, Stockton	20	8	1	0	2	4	1	.333	78	73	42	36	4	45	1	5	36	8	4.15
Conaty, Bakersfield	40	4	1	0	5	4	8	.556	101	124	69	56	4	45	3	2	63	8	4.99
Conner, Salinas*	30	15	1	1	6	5	0	.545	109	110	64	53	9	60	8	6	67	9	4.38
Cordova, Lodi	42	0	0	0	6	5	5	.545	97	84	47	39	7	74	5	2	62	11	3.62
Cort, Stockton	13	13	1	0	3	4	0	.429	70	66	31	26	2	15	0	2	48	5	3.34
Corzel, Modesto	13	12	3	0	2	4	0	.333	83	94	50	43	5	25	2	1	42	3	4.66
Costello, Bakersfield*	16	11	2	0	5	3	0	.625	64	83	61	49	11	27	0	0	39	5	6.89
Curran, Stockton	22	12	4	0	8	6	1	.571	99	97	48	39	5	42	1	2	65	8	3.55
R. Davis, Santa Clara	11	10	1	0	3	5	0	.375	50	71	52	39	4	35	0	2	47	4	5.85
Diaz, San Jose*	26	0	0	0	4	1	3	.800	24	26	18	17	1	13	1	0	36	1	6.38
DiPino, Stockton*	16	15	1	0	5	3	0	.625	99	92	45	38	3	46	0	0	67	1	3.45
T. Dixon, Reno	27	26	7	0	9	13	0	.409	175	169	90	74	13	88	0	10	146	17	3.81
Dougherty, Modesto*	8	8	0	0	3	5	0	.375	41	53	54	46	6	21	0	1	26	2	10.10
D. Duran, Salinas	17	0	0	0	1	2	3	.333	51	57	34	31	11	21	3	1	28	3	5.47
Edge, San Jose	6	2	0	0	0	2	0	.000	10	14	11	10	1	8	0	1	10	3	9.00
Fiorante, 22 SC-10 SJ	32	2	0	0	0	2	0	.000	46	64	74	52	6	66	3	1	28	7	10.17
Fireovid, Reno	26	26	7	0	13	9	0	.591	168	182	92	76	9	65	0	3	135	17	4.07
Fisher, Fresno	25	17	4	3	9	4	1	.692	132	123	56	43	10	70	0	6	111	6	2.93
Foster, Lodi	47	0	0	0	5	10	8	.333	74	70	58	53	10	67	7	1	69	14	6.45

Pitcher–Club	G.	GS.	CG.	ShO.	W.	L.	Sv.	Pct.	IP.	H.	R.	ER.	HR.	BB.	Int. BB.	HB.	SO.	WP.	ERA.
Frederickson, Bakersville	1	0	0	0	0	0	0	.000	2	1	1	0	0	2	0	0	0	0	0.00
Givens, 7 SJ-2 SC*	9	0	0	0	0	0	0	.000	7	5	18	18	2	18	0	2	2	11	23.14
Gosse, Modesto*	43	8	3	0	5	4	7	.556	104	121	68	52	9	30	3	1	80	5	4.50
Gray, Bakersfield*	25	1	1	0	2	1	0	.667	43	49	39	35	10	25	2	2	30	5	7.33
S. Green, Visalia	27	27	8	1	16	6	0	.727	208	222	104	81	10	38	1	6	98	5	3.50
Grimes, Santa Clara	5	0	0	0	0	1	1	1.000	5	4	1	1	0	3	0	0	4	2	1.80
Hamilton, Salinas	1	1	0	0	0	0	0	.000	0	1	1	1	0	0	0	0	0	0	.....
Hamm, Reno	6	1	0	0	0	0	0	.000	13	22	13	9	1	6	0	1	6	2	6.23
Hardwick, Reno	28	0	0	0	5	0	2	1.000	70	70	66	51	6	69	0	1	62	13	6.56
Harness, Bakersfield	3	0	0	0	0	0	0	1.000	4	6	4	4	0	3	0	0	2	2	9.00
C. Harris, Modesto	9	9	1	0	5	4	0	.556	47	49	40	22	3	38	0	6	27	9	4.21
T. Harris, 5 SJ-64 SC	69	1	0	0	7	4	4	.636	106	100	81	66	2	113	2	9	106	-26	5.60
Harrison, San Jose	10	0	0	0	1	1	0	.500	12	14	10	8	3	15	0	1	8	0	6.00
Harryman, Bakersfield*	17	10	3	0	4	6	0	.400	73	91	57	47	11	39	0	0	42	14	5.79
Hartwig, Fresno	3	3	0	0	0	1	0	.000	15	21	15	14	0	12	0	0	7	2	8.40
Hawkins, Reno	27	27	7	1	8	13	0	.381	188	232	143	117	12	97	3	2	130	13	5.60
Hayes, Lodi*	23	5	2	0	5	1	2	.833	53	51	30	21	4	35	3	1	27	4	3.57
Healey, Salinas	19	17	0	0	5	5	0	.500	86	105	58	47	8	34	2	3	41	5	4.92
Heard, Bakersfield*	6	1	0	0	1	0	0	1.000	7	6	8	5	0	8	0	0	13	0	6.43
Hills, Santa Clara*	35	26	6	0	7	18	0	.280	175	194	147	103	14	116	1	4	125	19	5.30
Hobbs, 23 SJ-9 SC*	32	22	2	0	11	6	1	.647	150	172	117	90	13	112	1	3	151	23	5.40
Holloway, Modesto	11	3	0	0	2	1	0	1.000	34	42	31	28	3	32	1	2	25	2	7.41
Holmes, Santa Clara	3	0	0	0	1	0	0	.000	3	9	9	8	1	2	0	1	1	0	24.00
Holton, Lodi	10	10	6	3	7	0	0	1.000	72	47	26	21	2	32	1	5	72	4	2.63
Hunziker, Santa Clara	20	16	4	0	4	11	0	.267	111	120	82	56	11	54	1	5	76	13	4.54
Jannusch, Reno	26	8	2	0	2	4	0	.333	80	76	45	43	10	44	2	1	68	10	4.84
Jenkins, Stockton	3	2	0	0	0	1	0	.000	10	12	11	7	2	7	0	1	6	0	6.30
Jensen, Modesto*	25	25	6	1	9	8	0	.529	173	172	93	74	17	73	3	2	129	12	3.85
A. Johnson, 19 Vis-5 Bk	24	17	2	0	5	10	0	.333	103	124	103	84	13	80	1	2	42	15	7.34
D. Johnson, Reno*	27	26	6	1	11	10	0	.524	169	189	108	91	14	79	1	4	97	15	4.85
G. Johnson, Salinas	27	22	2	1	9	10	0	.474	139	157	101	86	17	85	10	5	88	7	5.57
Keen, 2 Reno-24 SC*	26	17	4	0	3	7	0	.300	127	129	91	75	14	74	1	11	99	11	5.31
B. Kelley, Bakersfield	31	22	8	1	10	6	0	.625	164	191	108	83	16	58	0	7	92	6	4.55
S. Kelley, Bakersfield	12	12	2	0	3	6	0	.333	76	86	58	35	10	29	1	0	45	6	4.14
Kelly, Visalia*	1	1	0	0	1	0	0	1.000	8	5	3	2	0	7	0	0	2	0	2.25
Kittrell, Fresno*	21	17	3	0	4	8	1	.333	116	132	58	46	8	32	0	2	64	7	3.57
Knight, San Jose	52	2	1	0	3	5	9	.375	86	74	28	26	3	42	8	3	62	6	2.72
Krajewski, 25 SC-32 SJ	57	6	1	0	6	4	12	.600	143	149	78	65	10	58	2	2	97	11	4.09
LaPoint, Stockton*	27	25	11	3	12	10	0	.545	180	144	74	63	5	85	0	1	208	7	3.15
Lettrich, Santa Clara	23	13	0	0	3	6	0	.333	90	98	77	59	12	84	0	5	54	19	5.90
Lucarelli, Bakersfield	6	1	0	0	1	2	0	.333	16	16	12	11	0	14	0	1	16	1	6.19
Lund, Modesto	33	14	4	1	7	8	0	.467	112	149	92	74	16	61	2	6	71	7	5.95
Malden, Lodi	26	26	2	1	10	10	0	.500	148	164	104	85	10	104	3	3	130	21	5.17
Mantsch, Modesto	20	0	0	0	2	3	3	.400	44	41	14	11	1	17	4	3	22	2	2.25
Marietta, Fresno	6	0	0	0	0	0	0	.000	9	16	17	15	2	10	0	2	5	0	15.00
Mathey, Bakersfield	17	16	4	1	4	9	0	.308	94	108	60	46	6	34	2	0	53	4	4.40
McCarthy, Modesto*	6	1	0	0	0	0	0	.000	18	29	22	14	4	7	0	0	14	0	7.00
McGee, San Jose	26	25	10	3	15	6	0	.714	186	146	78	57	8	87	1	6	111	14	2.76
Milke, Bakersfield	13	9	1	1	2	4	0	.333	57	69	43	39	7	35	0	2	30	12	6.16
Miller, Reno	51	0	0	0	12	5	18	.706	80	54	25	16	4	32	5	2	85	7	1.80
Montgomery, Stockton	26	24	9	2	11	8	0	.579	174	147	66	56	8	40	3	0	105	3	2.90
Morrison, Salinas	41	1	0	0	3	2	3	.600	61	54	27	19	2	41	10	3	64	3	2.80
Moyer, Fresno	35	15	4	0	7	10	7	.412	139	168	93	76	10	60	1	2	95	9	4.92
Murphy, Fresno	5	0	0	0	0	0	0	.000	9	13	8	6	1	6	1	0	7	2	6.00
Naumann, San Jose*	27	5	0	0	3	3	0	.500	50	58	42	42	7	32	1	0	23	5	7.56
Nicholson, Stockton	36	6	2	0	3	9	5	.250	86	81	54	42	2	64	7	2	60	7	4.40
D. Nobles, 8 Fr-21 SC	29	2	0	0	3	5	1	.375	62	85	74	60	9	57	4	3	37	4	8.71
J. Nobles, Lodi*	27	8	0	0	5	4	3	.556	80	97	64	57	14	60	1	2	65	5	6.41
Noonan, Bakersfield*	9	2	0	0	1	3	1	.250	28	40	30	20	3	24	0	3	33	3	6.43
Omo, Fresno*	28	20	3	0	8	9	0	.471	138	158	96	75	14	80	1	1	116	7	4.89
O'Neill, Lodi	18	0	0	0	1	5	0	.167	47	48	27	22	7	14	0	2	49	2	4.21
Patton, Reno	11	0	0	0	1	0	0	.000	28	36	31	18	3	17	1	0	26	3	5.79
Pekarcik, Bakersfield	2	0	0	0	1	0	0	.000	1	1	2	2	0	3	0	0	0	1	18.00
Perry, Lodi	15	15	4	1	3	5	0	.375	92	88	58	46	6	51	0	2	64	12	4.50
Pettaway, Visalia	24	13	0	0	5	7	2	.417	116	137	82	66	11	56	3	1	76	9	5.12
Phillips, Santa Clara*	7	6	2	0	1	5	0	.167	38	48	39	26	6	13	0	3	25	4	6.16
Pisel, Fresno	26	22	2	1	9	11	0	.450	123	118	82	75	8	79	2	1	83	16	5.49
Powers, Lodi	14	14	0	0	5	3	0	.625	67	80	58	48	7	53	1	1	42	10	6.45
Rabouin, Bakersfield	5	3	0	0	2	1	0	.667	25	24	15	8	1	24	0	1	28	2	2.88
Reichard, Visalia	58	0	0	0	5	5	19	.500	70	48	21	19	3	39	2	1	92	9	2.44
Reichenbach, Bakersfield	5	3	0	0	0	1	0	.000	10	28	28	27	2	13	0	1	4	1	24.30
Reis, Bakersfield*	9	0	0	0	0	0	1	.000	21	26	16	14	4	10	0	0	13	3	6.00
Riffel, Salinas	1	0	0	0	0	0	0	.000	2	1	0	0	0	1	0	0	0	0	0.00
Riggar, Stockton*	8	7	0	0	2	3	0	.400	35	43	39	32	7	34	0	0	23	4	8.23

Pitcher—Club	G.	GS.	CG.	ShO.	W.	L.	Sv.	Pct.	IP.	H.	R.	ER.	HR.	BB.	Int. BB.	HB.	SO.	WP.	ERA.
Rommel, Salinas	51	1	0	0	10	7	10	.588	71	59	46	35	7	39	9	3	65	7	4.44
Ruiz, Lodi*	8	3	0	0	0	3	0	.000	20	34	28	21	4	23	0	1	15	6	9.45
Salagan, Visalia*	16	2	0	0	1	0	0	1.000	38	43	28	23	2	28	0	2	36	8	5.45
Sarno, Bakersfield	39	9	4	0	8	6	3	.571	139	155	91	70	21	51	4	3	73	5	4.53
Scheller, Lodi	14	14	5	0	4	7	0	.364	81	95	61	51	7	39	2	1	37	2	5.67
Schmidt, Lodi*	11	0	0	0	0	0	0	.000	23	29	24	21	3	17	0	0	15	1	8.22
Schopp, Fresno	7	1	0	0	0	1	0	.000	20	28	26	19	0	20	0	2	20	5	8.55
Schubert, Modesto	28	23	7	0	8	13	1	.381	160	182	113	95	17	60	3	3	99	6	5.34
Semones, Bakersfield*	15	9	1	0	3	8	0	.273	62	81	55	42	7	44	1	3	29	8	6.10
Show, Reno	28	27	5	1	13	9	0	.591	169	144	79	67	12	92	2	14	186	5	3.57
Sigman, Stockton	2	0	0	0	0	0	0	.000	2	0	0	0	0	1	0	0	0	0	0.00
Skaggs, Salinas	1	1	0	0	0	0	0	.000	3	3	0	0	0	0	0	0	1	0	0.00
David Smith, San Jose	42	19	3	0	15	6	4	.714	156	125	65	46	5	62	2	7	113	13	2.65
Douglas Smith, San Jose.	26	21	7	3	11	7	0	.611	140	120	67	55	8	78	4	9	77	14	3.54
Steirer, Salinas	29	28	11	2	11	13	0	.458	193	210	106	83	15	66	9	6	119	11	3.87
Stember, Fresno	20	3	0	0	4	2	0	.667	44	43	38	25	7	29	0	1	41	4	5.11
Stoddard, San Jose	20	16	3	1	7	5	0	.583	120	78	45	40	6	58	1	2	104	7	3.00
Sutcliffe, Lodi	12	10	2	0	2	4	0	.333	65	68	37	30	5	33	1	3	47	7	4.15
Thomson, 13 Sal-28 SC	41	6	1	0	3	8	3	.273	105	113	84	59	10	66	3	5	81	7	5.06
Tingley, Santa Clara	1	0	0	0	0	0	0	.000	4	5	1	1	0	2	0	0	2	1	9.00
Torres, Stockton	25	25	5	0	12	8	0	.600	183	149	77	66	8	93	0	2	140	8	3.25
Tucker, Fresno	17	2	1	0	4	0	3	1.000	55	53	18	15	2	21	0	1	38	2	2.45
Valenzuela, Lodi*	3	3	0	0	1	2	0	.333	24	21	10	3	0	13	2	0	18	1	1.13
Vallone, Salinas*	22	0	0	0	2	1	5	.667	41	32	12	11	2	18	4	1	31	2	2.41
Vander Laan, Visalia	14	0	0	0	2	0	2	1.000	32	44	30	21	2	12	0	1	20	1	5.91
Van Marter, Modesto	12	12	1	0	1	9	0	.100	61	87	67	53	11	42	0	3	32	2	7.82
Volpi, Santa Clara*	1	0	0	0	0	0	0	.000	1	0	0	0	0	1	0	0	1	0	0.00
Wagner, Visalia	27	26	5	0	13	9	0	.591	196	214	114	93	16	84	1	1	143	21	4.27
Waldrop, Bakersfield	10	10	3	2	5	1	0	.833	53	54	31	21	1	18	0	2	31	2	3.57
Walters, Salinas	11	8	0	0	0	4	0	.000	35	47	34	33	3	23	6	1	17	1	8.49
Wardlow, Fresno	22	20	5	0	6	11	1	.353	112	96	74	51	4	82	1	4	161	27	4.10
Witt, Salinas	30	26	2	0	8	10	0	.444	141	156	96	80	13	70	7	1	94	11	5.11
Wright, Bakersfield	17	0	0	0	1	3	3	.250	17	25	23	15	4	12	3	0	17	1	7.94
Wulfemeyer, Santa Clara	15	13	1	0	3	7	0	.300	58	57	59	48	2	77	0	3	52	14	7.45
Wysocki, 4 SC-2 Sal	6	3	0	0	1	2	0	.333	20	27	25	22	0	26	0	1	7	3	9.90
Wyszynski, Modesto	3	0	0	0	0	1	0	.000	4	2	0	0	0	2	0	0	3	0	0.00
Yesenchak, Modesto*	14	0	0	0	1	1	0	.500	34	60	44	39	3	23	4	4	19	3	10.32

BALKS—Hardwick 6; Perry, Pisel, 5 each; Atherton 4; Bungarz, Fisher, Hobbs (SJ 1-SC 2), Hunziker, Keen (SC), LaPoint, Schubert, Semones, Show, VanMarter, Wardlow, 3 each; Bain, Baldwin, Biko, Chevolek, Christison, Cordova, T. Harris (SC), Hills, Jensen, Mathey, McGee, Moyer, Douglas Smith, Wagner, Wysocki (SC 1-Sal 1), 2 each; Adamson, Alexander, Bass, Bowers, Church, Diaz, DiPino, Dixon, Duran, Fireovid, Foster, Gray, Green, Hawkins, Jannusch, B. Kelley, S. Kelley, Kelly, Kittrell, Lettrich, Lucarelli, Lund, Malden, Montgomery, Nicholson, J. Nobles, Omo, O'Neill, Rabouin, Ruiz, Salagan, Scheller, David Smith, Stember, Stoddard, Valenzuela, Yesenchak, 1 each.

COMBINATION SHUTOUTS—Pisel-Moyer, Fresno; Hayes-Foster, Sutcliffe-Nobles, Lodi; Show-Church, Reno; Witt-Vallone, Salinas; Bainer-Byrd-Naumann-Knight, McGee-Knight, Naumann-Knight, San Jose; Wulfemeyer-Harris, Santa Clara; Di Pino-Bailey, Montgomery-Ako, Torres-Montgomery, Stockton; Adamson-Reichard, Visalia.

NO-HIT GAME—La Point, Stockton, defeated Reno, 4-0, July 25.

Wasiak Managed 4,000th Game in Minors

Stan Wasiak, who began his managerial career in 1950, reached another milestone in his 30-year managing career June 10 when he managed in his 4,000th minor league game. Unfortunately, his Lodi Dodgers bowed to Stockton, 6-5. Excluding postseason contests, Wasiak's record after the '79 season stood at 2141-1939 (.525).

Carolina League

CLASS A

CHAMPIONSHIP WINNERS IN PREVIOUS YEARS

1945 – Danville .... .681	1958 – Danville .... .576	1968 – Salem (West.)............... .607
1946 – Greensboro† .... .599	Burlington (4th)† .... .511	Ral-Dur (East.)........... .597
Raleigh (2nd)† .... .563	1959 – Raleigh .... .600	H P-Thom. y (W.)........ .493
1947 – Burlington................... .613	Wilson (2nd)† .... .550	1969 – Rocky M (East.)........... .569
Raleigh (3rd)† .... .574	1960 – Greensboro‡ .... .636	Salem (West.) .... .542
1948 – Raleigh .... .592	Burlington................ .586	Ral-Dur z (East.) .... .560
Martinsville (2nd)† ...... .570	1961 – Wilson .... .594	1970 – Winston-Salem‡........... .586
1949 – Danville .... .601	1962 – Durham .... .636	Burlington................ .597
Burlington (4th)† .... .500	Wilson .... .600	1971 – Peninsula‡................... .647
1950 – Winston-Salem* .... .693	Kinston (2nd)† .... .593	Kinston................... .623
1951 – Durham .... .600	1963 – Kinston§..................... .538	1972 – Salem‡....................... .657
Wins-Salem (2nd)† .... .583	Greensboro§.............. .590	Burlington................ .632
1952 – Raleigh .... .581	Wilson (2nd)† .... .535	1973 – Lynchburg.................. .588
Reidsville (4th)† .... .536	1964 – Kinston§..................... .572	Winston-Salem‡........... .557
1953 – Raleigh .... .593	Winston-Salem§† .... .590	1974 – Salem......................... .671
Danville (2nd)† .... .572	1965 – Peninsula§.................. .597	Salem................... .582
1954 – Fayetteville* .... .628	Durham§................ .580	1975 – Rocky Mount .... .667
1955 – HP-Thomasville .... .580	Tidewater† .... .528	Rocky Mount .... .614
Danville (2nd)† .... .533	1966 – Kinston§..................... .547	1976 – Winston-Salem .... .618
1956 – HP-Thomasville .... .591	Winston-Salem§ .... .586	Winston-Salem .... .551
Fayetteville (4th)† ...... .523	Rocky Mount† .... .533	1977 – Lynchburg.................. .591
1957 – Durham .... .632	1967 – Durham x (West.)......... .536	Peninsula‡................ .556
HP-Thomasville .... .622	Raleigh (East.)........... .542	1978 – Peninsula.................... .696
		Lynchburg‡................ .614

*Won championship and four-club playoff. †Won four-club playoff. ‡Won split-season playoff. §League was divided into Eastern, Western divisions. xWon eight-club, two-division playoff.
  yWon eight-club, two-division playoff against Raleigh-Durham.
  zWon eight-club, two-division playoff against Burlington.

STANDING OF CLUBS AT CLOSE OF FIRST HALF, JUNE 21

Club	W.	L.	T.	Pct.	G.B.	Club	W.	L.	T.	Pct.	G.B.
Winston-Salem (Red Sox)	44	26	0	.629	......	Kinston (Blue Jays)	33	36	0	.478	10½
Alexandria (Mariners)	38	29	0	.567	4½	Lynchburg (Mets)	31	36	0	.463	11½
Peninsula (Phillies)	35	32	0	.522	7½	Salem (Pirates)	22	44	0	.333	20

STANDING OF CLUBS AT CLOSE OF SECOND HALF, SEPTEMBER 1

Club	W.	L.	T.	Pct.	G.B.	Club	W.	L.	T.	Pct.	G.B.
Winston-Salem (Red Sox)	41	29	1	.586	......	Peninsula (Phillies)	33	36	0	.478	7½
Alexandria (Mariners)	36	33	0	.522	4½	Salem (Pirates)	32	38	0	.457	9
Kinston (Blue Jays)	34	33	1	.507	5½	Lynchburg (Mets)	30	37	0	.448	9½

COMPOSITE STANDING OF CLUBS AT CLOSE OF SEASON, SEPTEMBER 1

Club	W.-S.	Alex.	Pen.	Kin.	Lyn.	Salem	W.	L.	T.	Pct.	G.B.
Winston-Salem (Red Sox)	....	13	17	20	16	19	85	55	1	.607	......
Alexandria (Mariners)	15	....	16	12	15	16	74	62	0	.544	9
Peninsula (Phillies)	11	11	....	13	17	16	68	68	0	.500	15
Kinston (Blue Jays)	8	15	15	....	12	17	67	69	1	.493	16
Lynchburg (Mets)	12	12	10	13	....	14	61	73	0	.455	21
Salem (Pirates)	9	11	10	11	13	....	54	82	0	.397	29

Major League affiliations in parentheses.

Peninsula represented Hampton, Va.

Playoffs – None.

Regular-Season Attendance – Alexandria, 34,614; Kinston, 38,569; Lynchburg, 53,400; Peninsula, 44,050; Salem, 43,036; Winston-Salem, 68,702. Total, 282,371. All-star game, 1,081. No playoffs.

Managers: Alexandria – Bobby Floyd; Kinston – Duane Larson; Lynchburg – Jack Aker; Peninsula – Ron Clark; Salem – Jim Mahoney; Winston-Salem – Bill Slack.

All-Star Team: 1B—Walker, Peninsula; 2B—Barnes, Salem; Dennis, Kinston; 3B—Wheeler, Kinston; SS—Gardenhire, Lynchburg; McDonald, Peninsula; OF—Dernier, Peninsula; Nichols, Winston-Salem; Sauer, Winston-Salem; C—Kelly, Kinston; Ortiz, Salem; DH—Lombarski, Peninsula; P—Clark, Alexandria; Gause, Peninsula; Hart, Peninsula; Manager—Slack, Winston-Salem.

(Compiled by Howe News Bureau, Chicago, Ill.)

CLUB BATTING

Club	G.	AB.	R.	OR.	H.	TB.	2B.	3B.	HR.	RBI.	SH.	SF.	BB.	Int. BB.	HP.	SO.	SB.	CS.	LOB.	Pct.
Kinston	137	4449	590	596	1173	1580	167	57	42	515	33	37	435	20	42	750	85	33	962	.264
Winston-Salem	141	4664	675	599	1225	1673	174	50	58	562	77	38	573	22	44	829	193	63	1098	.263
Peninsula	136	4409	605	572	1158	1575	174	45	51	521	49	27	477	20	29	745	153	37	960	.263
Lynchburg	134	4225	548	558	1084	1521	192	37	57	473	91	33	508	19	35	841	84	49	991	.257
Alexandria	136	4219	589	595	1030	1423	161	23	62	488	51	43	516	24	39	756	211	60	905	.244
Salem	136	4295	558	645	1045	1436	168	35	51	500	52	39	583	27	36	843	102	30	1024	.243

INDIVIDUAL BATTING

(Leading Qualifiers for Batting Championship—378 or More Plate Appearances)

*Bats lefthanded. †Switch-hitter.

Player and Club	G.	AB.	R.	H.	TB.	2B.	3B.	HR.	RBI.	SH.	SF.	BB.	HP.	SO.	SB.	CS.	Pct.
Kelly, D. Patrick, Kinston	96	350	48	108	146	23	6	1	50	1	6	17	8	66	10	0	.309
Dennis, Eduardo, Kinston	126	472	70	145	184	19	4	4	52	4	3	14	3	38	18	11	.307
Lombarski, Thomas, Peninsula*	118	434	64	133	172	16	4	5	70	2	1	51	1	60	2	2	.306
Barnes, Michael, Salem*	109	340	60	102	157	25	3	8	64	6	4	109	7	89	6	3	.300
Wheeler, Ralph, Kinston	132	493	69	145	194	24	5	5	69	6	3	48	6	43	6	0	.294
Nichols, T. Reid, Winston-Salem	134	532	107	156	227	25	5	12	59	4	3	56	12	47	66	12	.293
Sauer, Jack, Winston-Salem	137	470	68	137	181	21	7	3	74	7	6	63	3	68	16	9	.291
Dernier, Robert, Peninsula	135	491	102	143	178	19	2	4	42	12	4	80	5	58	77	10	.291
Bryant, Erwin, Winston-Salem	120	442	57	127	144	9	4	0	47	7	3	56	1	25	18	6	.287
Korbe, Gregory, Lynchburg	118	409	55	117	166	21	5	6	62	12	4	48	2	73	8	0	.286

Departmental Leaders: G—Sauer, 137; AB—Nichols, 532; R—Nichols, 107; H—Nichols, 156; TB—Nichols, 227; 2B—G. Walker, 27; 3B—Silverman, 12; HR—Pellant, 18; RBI—Fitzgerald, 75; SH—Dernier, Korbe, 12; SF—Fitzgerald, 11; BB—Barnes, 109; HP—Nichols, 12; SO—Nanni, 132; SB—Dernier, 77; CS—Lindsay, 16.

(All Players—Listed Alphabetically)

Player and Club	G.	AB.	R.	H.	TB.	2B.	3B.	HR.	RBI.	SH.	SF.	BB.	HP.	SO.	SB.	CS.	Pct.
Arias, Rodolfo, Alexandria	16	40	2	7	7	0	0	0	2	1	0	2	0	10	0	0	.175
Aubin, D. Gerald, Salem	29	107	14	24	30	3	0	1	13	0	0	4	2	40	8	0	.224
Ballard, Glenn, Peninsula	78	259	27	61	78	11	0	2	25	2	3	21	4	36	0	0	.236
Barfield, Jesse, Kinston	136	477	66	126	184	24	5	8	71	2	3	49	9	126	6	0	.264
Barnes, Michael, Salem*	109	340	60	102	157	25	3	8	64	6	4	109	7	89	6	3	.300
Bonnette, Robert, Kinston	7	26	4	6	9	0	0	1	2	0	0	0	0	5	0	0	.231
Brooks, Craig, Winston-Salem*	114	377	71	102	170	16	8	12	62	4	2	68	3	85	17	5	.271
Bryant, Erwin, Winston-Salem	120	442	57	127	144	9	4	0	47	7	3	56	1	25	18	6	.287
Calderon, Jose R., Salem*	32	2	0	0	0	0	0	0	0	0	0	0	0	2	0	0	.000
Castillo, Albert, Kinston*	47	104	18	22	23	1	0	0	7	2	1	28	1	21	1	0	.212
Castro, Jose, Peninsula	66	245	37	67	104	10	3	7	32	2	0	22	0	27	6	1	.273
Connors, Edward, Winston-Salem.	88	300	42	77	116	14	2	7	35	5	2	31	2	76	0	1	.257
Coyne, Michael, Kinston	110	329	35	71	88	4	5	1	33	5	3	44	1	66	7	3	.216
Crawford, John L., Kinston*	81	228	33	59	96	14	4	5	30	0	0	33	1	76	0	0	.259
Crawford, Steven, Winston-Salem.	29	3	1	2	2	0	0	0	1	0	1	0	1	0	0	0	.667
Cuervo, Edward, Lynchburg†	104	335	48	98	112	10	2	0	30	9	0	26	5	52	19	7	.293
Culmer, Wilfred, Peninsula	33	107	10	16	17	1	0	0	7	0	3	14	0	50	3	0	.150
Curry, Steven, Peninsula	119	389	68	104	167	21	6	10	51	3	4	82	0	73	19	5	.267
Cyburt, Philip, Salem*	18	2	0	0	0	0	0	0	0	0	0	0	0	2	0	0	.000
Darr, Michael, Kinston	25	3	0	0	0	0	0	0	0	0	0	0	0	1	0	0	.000
Davis, Robert C., Salem	14	1	0	0	0	0	0	0	0	0	0	1	0	0	0	0	.000
De La Rosa, Bienvenido, Salem*.	94	280	47	62	68	6	0	0	17	5	3	38	2	52	19	3	.221
Dennis, Eduardo, Kinston	126	472	70	145	184	19	4	4	52	4	3	14	3	38	18	11	.307
Dernier, Robert, Peninsula	135	491	102	143	178	19	2	4	42	12	4	80	5	58	77	10	.291
Elder, John, Lynchburg*	88	258	28	59	78	14	1	1	22	4	2	29	0	66	1	3	.229
Emala, David, Salem	128	384	59	81	118	15	2	6	47	3	1	93	5	93	7	5	.211
Ereu, William, Kinston†	34	109	16	30	38	2	3	0	14	1	2	8	1	15	3	0	.275
Farr, Steven, Salem	27	0	0	0	0	0	0	0	0	0	0	1	0	0	0	0	.000
Faulconer, Charles, Salem	3	9	1	0	0	0	0	0	0	0	0	2	1	5	0	0	.000
Federici, Richard, Salem*	128	474	56	125	152	18	3	1	44	5	6	39	1	46	26	6	.264
Fitzgerald, Michael, Lynchburg	117	368	55	93	156	16	4	13	75	7	11	54	8	84	0	2	.253
Fusari, Donald, Peninsula*	25	3	0	0	0	0	0	0	0	0	0	0	1	0	0	0	.000
Gabella, James, Alexandria	50	123	15	27	38	6	1	1	14	7	2	8	0	24	1	1	.220
Gardenhire, Ronald, Lynchburg	70	277	36	82	113	13	3	4	27	9	1	21	0	45	9	5	.296
Gelinas, Marc, Salem	7	1	0	0	0	0	0	0	0	0	0	0	0	1	0	0	.000
Gentile, Gene, Winston-Salem*	121	404	66	108	152	19	5	5	56	8	4	64	3	71	13	5	.267
Giles, Brian, Lynchburg	86	278	40	83	109	16	2	2	33	3	4	47	3	52	4	4	.299
Gossett, Jeffery, Lynchburg†	112	386	56	98	166	25	2	13	53	5	3	24	4	120	2	1	.254

Player and Club	G.	AB.	R.	H.	TB.	2B.	3B.	HR.	RBI.	SH.	SF.	BB.	HP.	SO.	SB.	CS.	Pct.
Hair, Wesley, Salem*	21	81	7	15	18	1	1	0	7	0	1	5	1	24	0	0	.185
Harrington, Ronald, Win-Salem	34	93	14	20	25	0	1	1	13	1	2	24	1	34	1	1	.215
Hernandez, Pedro J., Kinston	122	430	50	98	126	13	6	1	35	1	1	44	1	72	8	5	.228
Hillenga, Brent, Salem*	103	324	37	72	121	13	3	10	57	5	8	74	1	62	0	3	.222
Hobbs, Rodney, Alexandria	126	417	61	107	150	15	2	8	61	4	4	62	2	94	51	8	.257
Holland, Elwood, Alexandria*	99	292	50	65	78	6	2	1	26	1	3	51	2	26	36	4	.223
Howard, David W., Lynchburg	72	243	29	62	102	9	5	7	23	3	0	28	2	64	6	2	.255
Hudson, Christopher, Alexandria	90	253	36	66	90	9	3	3	30	4	2	38	3	55	4	0	.261
Ibarra, Miguel, Peninsula	92	310	33	80	111	7	3	6	44	5	0	14	3	55	0	0	.258
Kaeterle, Mark, Winston-Salem	61	179	24	29	50	6	0	5	19	4	2	19	2	61	0	0	.162
Kelly, D. Patrick, Kinston	96	350	48	108	146	23	6	1	50	1	6	17	8	66	10	0	.309
Koke, Kyle, Alexandria	119	368	47	97	115	10	1	2	39	5	2	41	4	47	16	5	.271
Korbe, Gregory, Lynchburg	118	409	55	117	166	21	5	6	62	12	4	48	2	73	8	0	.286
Kuvinka, Scott, Salem	69	239	30	44	77	11	2	6	31	3	2	10	4	64	3	0	.184
Lajszky, Werner, Alexandria	1	0	0	0	0	0	0	0	0	0	0	1	0	0	0	0	.000
Lane, Richard, Lynchburg	61	207	18	52	59	7	0	0	17	5	0	23	0	20	1	1	.251
Lauer, James, Lynchburg†	116	373	48	95	132	20	4	3	28	7	3	55	5	27	9	12	.255
Lebo, Michael, Kinston*	83	243	21	52	72	7	5	1	29	1	5	43	3	76	0	0	.214
Lickert, John, Winston-Salem	112	356	42	97	126	14	3	3	43	6	3	58	4	49	8	2	.272
Lindsay, Charles, Alexandria†	116	419	69	98	110	4	4	0	22	9	2	31	8	79	48	16	.234
Lombarski, Thomas, Peninsula*	118	434	64	133	172	16	4	5	70	2	1	51	1	60	2	2	.306
MacAuley, John, Salem†	63	242	40	73	83	8	1	0	20	2	2	16	1	31	10	1	.302
Matamoros, Carlos, Alexandria	102	391	43	97	128	21	2	2	37	8	3	26	5	38	19	9	.248
McDonald, Manuel, Peninsula	134	466	52	128	156	22	3	0	40	3	2	17	1	35	10	5	.275
Mee, Thomas, Alexandria*	80	204	34	53	70	5	3	2	24	1	4	36	1	19	4	1	.260
Messmer, James, Salem	13	41	2	4	4	0	0	0	1	1	0	5	0	8	0	0	.098
Miloszewski, Frank, Salem*	25	1	0	0	0	0	0	0	0	0	0	0	0	0	0	0	.000
Mirabel, Eduardo, Lynchburg*	99	329	35	76	117	18	7	3	35	4	2	33	2	93	1	0	.231
Moore, Michael, Alexandria*	134	452	55	101	157	26	0	10	58	2	5	57	5	111	5	3	.223
Mugele, James, Winston-Salem	37	115	16	26	39	8	1	1	9	1	3	13	2	26	0	3	.226
Nanni, Tito, Alexandria*	113	402	49	91	130	19	1	6	48	0	5	38	0	132	15	4	.226
Nicely, Anthony, Salem	2	7	0	1	1	0	0	0	0	0	0	0	0	2	0	0	.143
Nichols, T. Reid, Winston-Salem	134	532	107	156	227	25	5	12	59	4	3	56	12	47	66	12	.293
Noonan, James, Lynchburg	50	137	19	32	42	8	1	0	13	6	2	18	0	33	1	2	.234
Notarino, Anthony, Salem	15	0	1	0	0	0	0	0	0	0	0	0	0	0	0	0	.000
Olszak, Thomas, Salem	36	118	12	28	50	4	3	4	13	1	0	18	1	22	0	0	.237
Ortiz, Adalberto, Salem	108	396	35	112	152	21	2	5	66	5	6	26	2	55	0	0	.283
Pace, Michael, Peninsula†	87	276	43	70	92	10	6	0	25	5	2	36	3	66	20	4	.254
Palmer, Richard, Kinston	8	11	1	3	3	0	0	0	1	0	0	2	0	4	0	0	.273
Pedrique, Alfredo, Lynchburg	19	49	2	11	13	2	0	0	3	3	0	2	1	7	1	0	.224
Pellant, Gary, Alexandria†	132	441	77	123	205	24	2	18	70	2	6	73	4	66	10	6	.279
Perez, Benjamin, Kinston	121	411	63	103	116	13	0	0	33	3	3	33	3	30	11	4	.251
Quade, Michael, Salem	77	281	35	76	94	9	3	1	26	6	1	35	0	47	3	2	.270
Randolph, John, Alexandria*	70	197	24	46	63	7	2	2	23	4	3	18	0	16	1	1	.234
Reyes, Wascar, Salem	66	242	36	55	62	3	2	0	16	2	2	38	1	29	15	5	.227
Roman, Noel, Winston-Salem	116	426	57	115	142	13	7	0	45	6	5	29	4	64	27	9	.270
Roman, Rosendo, Lynchburg	11	4	2	2	3	0	0	0	2	0	0	0	0	1	0	0	.500
Rossen, Robert, Lynchburg*	39	100	9	22	35	5	1	2	10	6	0	9	2	21	2	1	.220
Santana, Rafael, Kinston	27	0	1	0	0	0	0	0	0	0	0	0	0	0	0	0	.000
Sauer, Jack, Winston-Salem	137	470	68	137	181	21	7	3	74	7	6	63	3	68	16	9	.291
Silverman, Robert, Kinston	136	504	57	123	162	9	12	2	43	2	3	50	3	59	12	10	.244
Skow, Gary, Alexandria	25	62	10	16	23	4	0	1	9	0	0	11	1	14	0	0	.258
Slettvet, Douglas, Lynchburg	66	161	12	31	48	6	1	3	15	4	0	31	2	57	0	0	.193
Smith, Ronald B., Peninsula†	17	53	3	7	8	1	0	0	6	0	0	12	2	4	0	1	.132
Smith, Stanley, Winston-Salem	107	384	38	101	154	18	4	9	61	8	1	31	3	78	2	3	.263
Sullivan, Colin, Peninsula*	65	196	20	37	55	7	1	3	21	4	3	26	0	51	0	0	.189
Swain, Steven, Peninsula*	84	273	36	78	104	17	3	1	37	3	0	24	4	63	3	1	.286
Tavera, Miguel, Winston-Salem†	117	385	52	90	100	6	2	0	27	11	1	32	1	86	22	7	.234
Teston, Phillip, Peninsula	43	1	0	0	0	0	0	0	0	0	0	0	0	0	0	0	.000
Thompson, C. Leonard, W-S	39	101	7	20	20	0	0	0	7	5	1	10	1	16	0	0	.198
Thurberg, Thomas, Lynchburg	34	0	1	0	0	0	0	0	0	0	0	1	0	0	0	0	.000
Troyan, Donald, Lynchburg*	114	330	47	70	93	8	3	3	31	3	2	49	0	81	10	6	.212
Tyler, David, Winston-Salem	28	0	1	0	0	0	0	0	0	0	0	0	0	0	0	0	.000
Valle, David, Alexandria	58	169	17	36	59	5	0	6	25	3	2	23	4	24	1	2	.213
Velazquez, Alfredo J., Kinston	16	37	2	9	9	0	0	0	1	0	0	2	0	13	0	0	.243
Waag, William, Salem	62	215	29	54	75	11	2	2	21	1	0	15	2	31	3	1	.251
Walker, Gregory, Peninsula*	122	446	59	125	190	27	4	10	61	7	2	40	4	92	6	3	.280
Walker, W. Keith, Kinston	38	76	8	22	36	5	0	3	18	1	1	7	1	25	1	0	.289
Warren, Charles, Lynchburg*	103	311	43	77	94	11	3	0	29	5	2	42	1	38	11	3	.248
Wells, Gregory, Kinston	37	146	28	52	95	9	2	10	27	0	3	12	1	13	2	0	.356
Wheeler, Ralph, Kinston	132	493	69	145	194	24	5	5	69	6	3	48	6	43	6	0	.294
Whittemore, Reginald, W-Salem*	34	97	12	18	25	5	1	0	4	0	0	18	1	40	3	1	.186
Wick, R. Michael, Salem	55	154	17	33	49	2	1	4	20	2	1	18	3	38	1	1	.214
Williams, Wayne, Peninsula	123	460	50	108	142	5	10	3	60	1	3	38	2	73	7	5	.235
Wotus, Ronald, Salem	8	26	4	8	8	0	0	0	2	1	0	3	0	3	0	0	.308

The following pitchers had no plate appearances primarily through use of designated hitters, listed alphabetically by club, games in parentheses:

ALEXANDRIA—Adair, M. Richard (13); Batten, Mark (11); Best, Karl (24); Cary, Jeff (58); Clark, Bryan (23); Garrity, Peter (35); Graser, Richard (31); Hallgren, Tim (17); Martinez, Randy (10); Minnick, Donald (21); Musselman, R. Ronald (27); Rudiman, Paul (8); Salva, Elisas (5); Simond, Robert (15); Snyder, Brian (6).

KINSTON—Baltz, W. Nicholas (4); Benson, V. Randall (7); Buckley, David (30); Coughlin, Gregory (1); Cuellar, Miguel A. (11); Dejak, Thomas (33); Flores, Jesse (26); Gambrell, P. Greg (2); Kiser, Orvin (2); Ricks, Edward (21); Robertson, Jay (38); Smith, David Allen (6); Stoeber, Mark (14); Wiens, Randy Roy (8); Wright, Terry Kem (14).

LYNCHBURG—Bozeman, Randall (18); Brazell, Donald (40); Brown, Randall S. (20); Coghen, Alexander (12); Corrado, Gary (13); Franklin, R. Jeffrey (24); Johnson, Glen (22); Lowry, Michael (21); Pearson, Donald (18); Pitts, Randy (3); Shermeyer, Keith (24); Violette, John (22).

PENINSULA—Abreu, Armand (27); Acosta, Oscar (23); Adams, Daryl (25); Gause, Ernest (24); Gonzalez, Marcos Antonio (33); Hart, Thomas (23); Lasek, James (17); Martinez, Ronald Lee (3); Moore, Gregory (20); Shiera, Norman (8); Speck, R. Clifford (26).

SALEM—Barez, Angel (2); Britt, Douglas (35); Burden, John (28); DeLeon, Paulo (26); Demery, Lawrence (3); Jimenez, Luis (19); Nicholson, Larry (15); Parke, James (12); Peterson, Eric (4); Powell, Charles (10); Rick, Dean (1); Rock, Robert (12); Taylor, Johnny (15).

WINSTON-SALEM—Baum, Mark (14); Cooke, Richard (14); Howard, Michael S. (33); Hulbert, Alvin (31); Madden, Andrew (9); Pecka, Keith (31); Rivas, Martin (36); Schoppee, David (37); Shields, Stephen (24); Weppner, Daniel (23).

GRAND-SLAM HOME RUNS—Connors, Federici, Gentile, Hobbs, Korbe, Lombarski, Wheeler, 1 each.

AWARDED FIRST BASE ON INTERFERENCE—Dernier (Fitzgerald); Lauer (Ortiz); Pellant (Ortiz); Quade (Arias).

CLUB FIELDING

Club	G.	PO.	A.	E.	DP.	PB.	Pct.
Peninsula	136	3433	1454	205	115	21	.960
Kinston	137	3434	1443	214	103	34	.958
Lynchburg	134	3344	1571	218	145	18	.958
Alexandria	136	3393	1532	225	114	45	.956
Salem	136	3377	1516	224	122	28	.956
Winston-Salem	141	3667	1543	257	104	28	.953

Triple Plays—None.

INDIVIDUAL FIELDING

*Throws lefthanded.

FIRST BASEMEN

Player and Club	G.	PO.	A.	E.	DP.	Pct.
Mee, Alexandria	3	15	2	0	1	1.000
Bonnette, Kinston	2	13	0	0	3	1.000
Ortiz, Salem	2	7	0	0	1	1.000
Warren, Lynchburg*	1	2	0	0	1	1.000
Federici, Salem*	63	534	35	3	43	.995
Hillenga, Salem*	71	609	43	7	54	.989
Wheeler, Kinston	52	409	35	5	34	.989
Wells, Kinston	37	351	26	5	27	.987
Kaeterle, Winston-Salem	59	461	31	7	31	.986
MOORE, Alexandria	134	1172	77	20	100	.984
Smith, Winston-Salem	69	582	38	11	48	.983
Walker, Peninsula	113	973	53	19	80	.982
Swain, Peninsula	17	165	3	3	15	.982
Kelly, Kinston	14	98	9	2	7	.982
Troyan, Lynchburg*	114	971	82	21	107	.980
Whittemore, W-Salem	27	224	6	5	16	.979
Slettvet, Lynchburg	39	266	21	7	32	.976
Crawford, Kinston*	12	95	6	3	6	.971
Lombarski, Peninsula	7	55	2	2	5	.966
Lebo, Kinston	20	179	8	7	12	.964
Wick, Salem	5	33	2	2	4	.946
Wotus, Salem	1	12	1	1	1	.929
Hudson, Alexandria	2	2	0	1	0	.667

SECOND BASEMEN

Player and Club	G.	PO.	A.	E.	DP.	Pct.
Gabella, Alexandria	5	11	14	0	4	1.000
Castro, Peninsula	18	45	42	2	7	.978
Cuervo, Lynchburg	22	49	64	3	16	.974
Giles, Lynchburg	80	180	271	13	64	.972
Perez, Kinston	40	65	106	5	15	.972
Randolph, Alexandria	35	72	91	5	15	.970
BRYANT, Win-Sal	113	232	341	19	59	.9679
Matamoros, Alexandria	102	246	293	18	67	.9676
Barnes, Salem	78	170	225	14	49	.966
Curry, Peninsula	108	223	327	22	74	.962
Dennis, Kinston	101	225	269	21	49	.959
Noonan, Lynchburg	37	59	122	8	26	.958
Tavera, Winston-Salem	35	63	78	8	12	.946
Smith, Peninsula	12	29	23	3	3	.945
Reyes, Salem	58	107	135	20	19	.924
Roman, Winston-Salem	6	6	15	3	3	.875
Ereu, Kinston	2	1	6	1	0	.875
Roman, Lynchburg	1	1	0	1	0	.500

THIRD BASEMEN

Player and Club	G.	PO.	A.	E.	DP.	Pct.
Lane, Lynchburg	3	2	5	0	0	1.000
Nichols, Winston-Salem	1	1	0	0	1	1.000
Wotus, Salem	7	5	21	1	1	.963
Castro, Peninsula	36	20	72	4	3	.958
Barnes, Salem	22	18	71	5	6	.947
Dernier, Peninsula	14	16	15	2	1	.939
Bonnette, Kinston	4	5	10	1	4	.938
Emala, Salem	37	33	82	8	5	.935
McDonald, Peninsula	9	5	24	2	2	.935
Perez, Kinston	57	52	103	11	10	.934
Wheeler, Kinston	78	56	148	16	9	.927
Kuvinka, Salem	64	57	113	15	14	.919
PELLANT, Alexandria	120	89	235	30	20	.915
Lombarski, Peninsula	79	58	158	20	15	.915
Cuervo, Lynchburg	28	11	42	6	2	.898
Gossett, Lynchburg	109	71	200	32	24	.894

THIRD BASEMEN—Continued

Player and Club	G.	PO.	A.	E.	DP.	Pct.	Player and Club	G.	PO.	A.	E.	DP.	Pct.
Tavera, Winston-Salem	67	39	86	15	4	.893	Messmer, Salem	5	5	4	2	1	.818
Gabella, Alexandria	18	7	34	5	3	.891	Hair, Salem	5	5	5	3	0	.769
Connors, Winston-Salem	81	42	129	29	7	.855	Bryant, Winston-Salem	6	4	9	4	0	.765
Hernandez, Kinston	5	4	6	2	1	.833	Roman, Winston-Salem	6	1	9	5	0	.667
Noonan, Lynchburg	2	1	4	1	1	.833							

SHORTSTOPS

Player and Club	G.	PO.	A.	E.	DP.	Pct.	Player and Club	G.	PO.	A.	E.	DP.	Pct.
Tavera, Winston-Salem	1	1	4	0	2	1.000	Randolph, Alexandria	27	21	59	7	8	.920
Curry, Peninsula	1	3	0	0	1	1.000	MacAuley, Salem	63	104	180	25	29	.919
Barnes, Salem	1	0	1	0	0	1.000	Nichols, Winston-Salem	5	6	13	2	0	.905
Dennis, Kinston	25	48	61	4	10	.965	Hernandez, Kinston	113	145	283	46	46	.903
Waag, Salem	62	85	187	14	39	.951	Cuervo, Lynchburg	47	58	115	22	20	.887
Bryant, Winston-Salem	4	10	9	1	4	.950	Mugele, Winston-Salem	34	44	97	18	18	.887
McDONALD, Peninsula	125	194	399	33	70	.947	Smith, Peninsula	5	6	7	2	0	.867
Gardenhire, Lynch	69	120	252	21	57	.947	Lane, Lynchburg	4	8	11	3	2	.864
Koke, Alexandria	118	180	376	38	71	.936	Gabella, Alexandria	5	3	3	1	0	.857
Pedrique, Lynchburg	18	22	63	6	12	.934	Emala, Salem	12	13	32	11	4	.804
Noonan, Lynchburg	7	9	15	2	4	.923	Ereu, Kinston	2	2	5	2	0	.778
Roman, Winston-Salem	104	158	328	42	53	.920	Wheeler, Kinston	2	1	1	1	1	.667

OUTFIELDERS

Player and Club	G.	PO.	A.	E.	DP.	Pct.	Player and Club	G.	PO.	A.	E.	DP.	Pct.
Swain, Peninsula	33	56	1	0	0	1.000	Tavera, Winston-Salem	22	48	2	3	0	.943
Olszak, Salem	29	40	5	0	1	1.000	Emala, Salem	72	87	7	6	0	.940
Faulconer, Salem	3	4	0	0	0	1.000	Brooks, Winston-Salem	36	44	2	3	0	.939
Wheeler, Kinston	4	3	0	0	0	1.000	Pace, Peninsula	69	101	4	7	1	.938
Nicely, Salem	2	2	0	0	0	1.000	Nanni, Alexandria*	105	150	5	11	1	.934
Roman, Lynchburg	2	2	0	0	0	1.000	Hobbs, Alexandria	122	207	9	16	1	.931
Wick, Salem	1	0	1	0	0	1.000	Sullivan, Peninsula	58	97	11	8	1	.931
Cuervo, Lynchburg	3	1	0	0	0	1.000	Aubin, Salem	24	50	3	4	0	.930
Skow, Alexandria	3	1	0	0	0	1.000	Castillo, Kinston*	31	37	1	3	0	.927
LAUER, Lynchburg*	113	240	6	4	0	.984	De La Rosa, Salem*	84	139	12	12	2	.926
Quade, Salem	77	184	9	4	2	.980	Hillenga, Salem*	28	43	5	4	0	.923
Silverman, Kinston	136	224	14	5	4	.979	Williams, Peninsula	123	202	20	19	6	.921
Dernier, Peninsula	121	315	8	8	1	.976	Korbe, Lynchburg	52	84	2	8	0	.915
Warren, Lynchburg*	95	149	3	4	1	.974	Hair, Salem	7	8	1	1	0	.900
Coyne, Kinston	105	167	9	5	1	.972	Rossen, Lynchburg*	36	51	1	6	0	.897
Elder, Lynchburg	61	90	5	3	1	.969	Hudson, Alexandria	16	14	1	2	1	.882
Lindsay, Alexandria	114	271	7	10	0	.965	Culmer, Peninsula	22	45	4	7	0	.875
Nichols, Winston-Salem	130	239	23	10	1	.963	Ereu, Kinston	14	22	5	4	0	.871
Gentile, Winston-Salem*	117	209	6	9	0	.960	Holland, Alexandria	12	12	0	2	0	.857
Howard, Lynchburg	69	87	10	4	0	.960	Smith, Winston-Salem	10	5	0	1	0	.833
Federici, Salem*	64	107	9	5	2	.959	Mirabel, Salem*	28	35	1	9	0	.800
Mee, Alexandria	49	58	2	3	1	.952	Ortiz, Salem	3	2	0	1	0	.667
Sauer, Winston-Salem	135	189	16	11	1	.949	Kelly, Kinston	1	0	1	1	0	.500
Barfield, Kinston	136	284	19	17	1	.947	Noonan, Lynchburg	1	0	0	1	0	.000

CATCHERS

Player and Club	G.	PO.	A.	E.	DP.	PB.	Pct.	Player and Club	G.	PO.	A.	E.	DP.	PB.	Pct.
Kuvinka, Salem	2	13	0	0	0	1	1.000	Wick, Salem	37	190	23	5	1	10	.977
Arias, Alexandria	16	89	8	1	0	5	.990	Hudson, Alexandria	62	324	30	9	3	17	.975
Thompson, Wins-Sal	39	233	15	3	2	7	.988	Ballard, Peninsula	60	364	39	11	6	7	.973
LICKERT, Wins-Sal	110	707	77	10	3	19	.987	Ibarra, Peninsula	78	408	57	14	3	14	.971
Kelly, Kinston	77	508	53	9	5	13	.984	Slettvet, Lynchburg	24	108	20	4	0	1	.970
Harrington, Wins-Sal	9	48	3	1	0	2	.981	Valle, Alexandria	54	290	44	11	5	15	.968
Fitzgerald, Lyn'burg	81	424	60	10	6	14	.980	Skow, Alexandria	16	87	4	4	0	8	.958
Lebo, Kinston	57	327	36	8	5	16	.978	Velazquez, Kinston	9	29	7	2	1	3	.947
Lane, Lynchburg	38	202	25	5	2	3	.978	Palmer, Kinston	6	30	3	2	1	2	.943
Ortiz, Salem	102	625	84	17	12	17	.977								

PITCHERS

Player and Club	G.	PO.	A.	E.	DP.	Pct.	Player and Club	G.	PO.	A.	E.	DP.	Pct.
FRANKLIN, Lynchburg	24	8	25	0	0	1.000	Rock, Salem	12	4	10	0	0	1.000
Pecka, Winston-Salem*	31	5	26	0	0	1.000	Wright, Kinston	14	2	12	0	0	1.000
Schoppee, Wins-Sal	37	8	18	0	2	1.000	Shermeyer, Winston-Salem	24	3	11	0	2	1.000
Gause, Peninsula*	24	2	22	0	0	1.000	Batten, Alexandria	11	3	8	0	0	1.000
Fusari, Peninsula*	24	4	13	0	0	1.000	Cooke, Winston-Salem*	14	1	9	0	0	1.000
Tyler, Winston-Salem	25	6	10	0	0	1.000	Gelinas, Salem	7	2	7	0	0	1.000
Benson, Kinston*	7	3	12	0	0	1.000	Stoeber, Kinston	14	1	7	0	0	1.000

PITCHERS—Continued

Player and Club	G.	PO.	A.	E.	DP.	Pct.
Abreu, Peninsula*	27	2	6	0	1	1.000
Peterson, Salem*	4	2	4	0	0	1.000
Taylor, Salem	15	0	5	0	0	1.000
Barez, Salem	2	0	4	0	0	1.000
Snyder, Alexandria*	6	2	2	0	0	1.000
Powell, Salem*	10	0	4	0	0	1.000
Demery, Salem	3	1	2	0	0	1.000
Rudiman, Alexandria	8	1	2	0	0	1.000
Pitts, Lynchburg	3	0	2	0	0	1.000
Baltz, Kinston	4	0	2	0	0	1.000
Martinez, Peninsula	3	0	1	0	0	1.000
Best, Alexandria	24	9	27	1	1	.973
Adair, Alexandria	13	3	30	1	1	.971
Lasek, Peninsula	17	10	23	1	2	.971
Clark, Alexandria*	23	13	40	2	2	.964
Dejak, Kinston*	33	4	18	1	1	.957
Violette, Lynchburg	22	14	26	2	1	.952
Cuellar, Kinston	11	6	13	1	0	.950
Buckley, Kinston*	30	9	37	3	3	.939
Farr, Salem	26	5	26	2	0	.939
Hart, Peninsula	23	4	26	2	1	.938
DeLeon, Peninsula	26	7	23	2	1	.938
Teston, Peninsula	43	4	11	1	0	.938
Lowry, Lynchburg	21	13	15	2	1	.933
Notarino, Salem	14	4	9	1	1	.929
Cary, Alexandria	57	5	20	2	0	.926
Musselman, Alexandria	27	4	20	2	0	.923
Robertson, Kinston	38	1	23	2	0	.923
Britt, Salem*	35	5	18	2	2	.920
Brown, Lynchburg	20	8	14	2	0	.917
Acosta, Peninsula	23	3	18	2	0	.913
Madden, Wins-Sal	9	3	7	1	0	.909
Coghen, Lynchburg	12	0	10	1	1	.909
Cyburt, Salem*	18	2	26	3	0	.903
Moore, Peninsula	20	5	13	2	0	.900
Ricks, Kinston	21	6	12	2	1	.900
Miloszewski, Salem*	25	9	35	5	3	.898
Crawford, Wins-Sal	29	18	34	6	3	.897
Davis, Salem	14	4	13	2	0	.895
Gonzalez, Peninsula	33	2	15	2	0	.895
Adams, Peninsula	25	8	17	3	1	.893
Johnson, Lynchburg	22	6	27	4	1	.892
Smith, Kinston	6	1	7	1	1	.889
Weppner, Wins-Sal*	23	4	19	3	0	.885
Simond, Alexandria*	15	7	31	5	3	.884
Burden, Salem	28	4	11	2	1	.882
Calderon, Salem*	32	2	13	2	0	.882
Santana, Kinston	26	9	28	5	2	.881
Rivas, Winston-Salem	36	5	17	3	1	.880
Brazell, Lynchburg	40	6	8	2	1	.875
Martinez, Alexandria*	10	0	7	1	1	.875
Bozeman, Lynchburg	18	5	8	2	0	.867
Thurberg, Lynchburg	34	4	9	2	1	.867
Speck, Peninsula	26	2	17	3	0	.864
Howard, Wins-Sal	33	4	26	5	1	.857
Minnick, Alexandria*	21	6	18	4	4	.857
Hallgren, Alexandria	17	2	10	2	0	.857
Hulbert, Wins-Sal	31	5	12	3	0	.850
Walker, Kinston*	15	2	9	2	0	.846
Flores, Kinston	26	6	5	2	1	.846
Darr, Kinston	25	6	26	6	0	.842
Wiens, Kinston	8	3	2	1	0	.833
Corrado, Lynchburg*	13	2	3	1	0	.833
Graser, Alexandria*	31	0	5	1	0	.833
Pearson, Lynchburg	18	7	14	5	2	.808
Baum, Winston-Salem	14	4	8	3	0	.800
Shiera, Peninsula*	8	1	3	1	1	.800
Nicholson, Salem*	15	3	8	3	0	.786
Garrity, Alexandria	35	10	16	9	1	.743
Shields, Winston-Salem	24	7	20	13	1	.675
Salva, Alexandria	5	0	2	1	0	.667
Jimenez, Salem	19	0	1	1	0	.500

The following players do not have any recorded accepted chances at the positions indicated; therefore, are not listed in the fielding averages for those particular positions: Coughlin*, p; Gambrell*, p; Kiser, p; Parke, p; Rick*, p. Lajszky appeared as pinch-hitter only.

CLUB PITCHING

Club	G.	CG.	ShO.	Sv.	IP.	H.	R.	ER.	HR.	BB.	Int. BB.	HB.	SO.	WP.	Bk.	ERA.
Winston-Salem	141	43	12	34	1222	1148	599	439	50	536	26	34	954	78	7	3.23
Lynchburg	134	45	9	14	1115	1037	558	424	40	493	32	30	691	68	20	3.42
Peninsula	136	43	8	16	1144	1109	572	448	48	488	27	37	727	72	8	3.52
Kinston	137	25	8	22	1145	1127	596	455	52	528	20	38	835	97	12	3.58
Alexandria	136	38	9	27	1131	1103	595	455	39	548	10	52	763	72	12	3.62
Salem	136	30	4	16	1126	1191	645	506	92	499	17	34	794	65	7	4.04

PITCHERS' RECORDS
(Leading Qualifiers for Earned-Run Average Leadership—112 or More Innings)

*Throws lefthanded.

Pitcher—Club	G.	GS.	CG.	ShO.	W.	L.	Sv.	Pct.	IP.	H.	R.	ER.	HR.	BB.	Int. BB.	HB.	SO.	WP.	ERA.
Hart, Peninsula	23	23	12	3	14	6	0	.700	162	115	49	40	6	71	1	3	132	11	2.22
Howard, Winston-Salem	33	16	7	0	12	3	2	.800	149	107	49	38	4	62	1	4	161	11	2.30
Clark, Alexandria*	23	23	13	3	14	5	0	.737	167	124	57	49	3	112	0	9	116	27	2.64
Franklin, Lynchburg	24	24	9	2	9	11	0	.450	154	131	66	50	8	65	1	2	107	8	2.92
Violette, Lynchburg	22	22	12	1	10	10	0	.500	153	135	63	50	10	39	3	3	94	5	2.94
Gause, Peninsula	24	24	7	3	11	8	0	.579	156	148	70	51	11	41	0	2	86	4	2.94
Crawford, Winston-Salem	29	28	15	3	11	11	0	.500	211	208	88	69	4	67	3	2	127	13	2.94
Shields, Winston-Salem	24	22	5	0	11	8	0	.579	152	149	78	51	9	80	3	1	152	13	3.02
Acosta, Peninsula	23	21	7	0	10	7	0	.588	163	147	67	55	7	63	2	2	75	8	3.04
Darr, Kinston	25	24	4	1	10	9	0	.526	154	158	86	55	3	106	3	5	109	16	3.21

Departmental Leaders: G—Cary, 57; GS—Crawford, 28; CG—Crawford, 15; ShO—Clark, Crawford, DeLeon, Gause, Hart, 3; W—Clark, Hart, 14; L—Miloszewski, 12; Sv—Cary, 21; Pct.—Howard, .800; IP—Crawford, 211; H—Crawford, 208; R—Miloszewski, 90; ER—Adams, Crawford, 69; HR—DeLeon, Miloszewski, 14; BB—Clark, 112; IBB—Gonzalez, Teston, 8; HB—Moore, 12; SO—Howard, 161; WP—Clark, 27.

(All Pitchers—Listed Alphabetically)

Pitcher–Club	G	GS	CG	ShO	W	L	Sv	Pct.	IP	H	R	ER	HR	BB	Int. BB	HB	SO	WP	ERA
Abreu, Peninsula*	27	0	0	0	1	1	3	.500	36	35	21	17	0	14	1	2	31	1	4.25
Acosta, Peninsula	23	21	7	0	10	7	0	.588	163	147	67	55	7	63	2	2	75	8	3.04
Adair, Alexandria	13	12	2	1	6	5	0	.545	80	86	29	25	1	26	1	3	53	7	2.81
Adams, Peninsula	25	23	8	2	7	10	0	.412	137	156	81	69	4	56	0	7	99	11	4.53
Baltz, Kinston	4	0	0	0	0	0	1	.000	10	9	9	8	1	7	0	0	8	1	7.20
Barez, Salem	2	2	0	0	0	2	0	.000	6	12	11	8	2	6	0	4	2	1	12.00
Batten, Alexandria	11	8	0	0	3	4	0	.429	59	73	41	34	4	11	0	2	33	2	5.19
Baum, Winston-Salem	14	14	3	0	10	1	0	.909	91	67	39	34	1	69	4	7	94	9	3.36
Benson, Peninsula*	7	4	4	2	3	2	0	.600	40	34	16	12	0	10	0	0	23	2	2.70
Best, Alexandria	24	24	8	0	8	11	0	.421	167	150	74	60	6	85	1	8	108	10	3.23
Bozeman, Lynchburg	18	7	1	0	4	4	0	.500	62	81	51	41	3	44	1	2	20	3	5.95
Brazell, Lynchburg	40	0	0	0	3	5	12	.375	63	49	17	13	0	17	5	0	33	2	1.86
Britt, Salem*	35	1	0	0	3	8	6	.273	78	66	36	33	6	35	1	5	57	4	3.81
Brown, Lynchburg	20	20	6	0	5	10	0	.333	117	101	65	51	4	67	4	3	50	6	3.92
Buckley, Kinston*	30	17	4	0	9	10	0	.474	148	158	79	61	9	55	3	6	95	12	3.71
Burden, Salem	28	0	0	0	5	3	5	.625	45	42	17	13	2	12	1	1	39	2	2.60
Calderon, Salem*	32	2	1	1	3	4	1	.429	87	89	43	35	6	40	3	4	70	4	3.62
Cary, Alexandria	57	0	0	0	7	5	21	.583	83	65	32	24	4	38	4	4	82	2	2.60
Clark, Alexandria*	23	23	13	3	14	5	0	.737	167	124	57	49	3	112	0	9	116	27	2.64
Coghen, Lynchburg	12	8	2	0	1	4	0	.200	51	45	36	28	2	28	0	4	39	5	4.94
Connors, Winston-Salem	1	0	0	0	0	0	0	.000	1	0	0	0	0	1	0	0	0	0	0.00
Cooke, Winston-Salem*	14	0	0	0	0	1	0	.000	32	41	21	15	0	15	2	1	20	4	4.22
Corrado, Lynchburg*	13	0	0	0	0	2	0	.000	28	28	10	7	0	10	2	0	10	1	2.25
Coughlin, Kinston*	1	0	0	0	0	0	0	.000	1	2	0	0	0	1	0	0	0	0	0.00
Crawford, Winston-Salem	29	28	15	3	11	11	0	.500	211	208	88	69	4	67	3	2	127	13	2.94
Cuellar, Kinston	11	9	2	1	3	5	1	.375	63	60	38	18	2	22	0	4	31	5	2.57
Cyburt, Salem*	18	13	3	0	6	3	1	.667	97	107	38	32	4	28	2	3	57	1	2.97
Darr, Kinston	25	24	4	1	10	9	0	.526	154	158	86	55	3	106	3	5	109	16	3.21
Davis, Salem	14	9	1	0	1	4	0	.200	48	64	43	28	5	36	0	1	27	5	5.25
Dejak, Kinston*	33	6	1	0	6	6	0	.500	95	92	42	36	1	32	5	3	78	6	3.41
DeLeon, Salem	26	18	5	3	9	8	0	.529	124	107	58	51	14	45	1	2	88	4	3.70
Demery, Salem	3	3	0	0	0	1	0	.000	8	12	7	6	1	3	0	0	8	1	6.75
Farr, Salem	26	15	5	0	3	10	1	.231	119	138	81	66	7	47	1	3	105	5	4.99
Flores, Kinston	26	16	1	1	7	6	1	.538	123	117	65	46	6	43	1	4	95	8	3.37
Franklin, Lynchburg	24	24	9	2	9	11	0	.450	154	131	66	50	8	65	1	2	107	8	2.92
Fusari, Peninsula*	24	2	0	0	2	2	0	.000	47	62	42	23	4	23	2	3	28	1	4.40
Gabella, Alexandria	1	0	0	0	0	0	0	.000	1	0	0	0	0	0	0	0	0	0	0.00
Gambrell, Kinston*	2	0	0	0	0	0	0	.000	3	1	1	1	0	1	0	1	3	0	3.00
Garrity, Alexandria	35	9	2	0	11	3	2	.786	104	125	62	46	1	29	1	7	48	1	3.98
Gause, Peninsula*	24	24	7	3	11	8	0	.579	156	148	70	51	11	41	0	2	86	4	2.94
Gelinas, Salem	7	7	1	0	1	5	0	.167	38	39	19	16	3	16	1	1	20	4	3.79
Gonzalez, Peninsula	33	2	1	0	4	6	1	.400	84	95	35	28	6	33	8	0	53	6	3.00
Graser, Peninsula*	31	1	0	0	2	3	2	.400	37	43	35	26	3	33	1	1	32	3	6.32
Hallgren, Alexandria	17	7	0	0	2	6	0	.250	52	78	45	39	3	10	0	2	31	0	6.75
Hart, Peninsula	23	23	12	3	14	6	0	.700	162	115	49	40	6	71	1	3	132	11	2.22
Howard, Winston-Salem	33	16	7	0	12	3	2	.800	149	107	49	38	4	62	1	4	161	11	2.30
Hulbert, Winston-Salem	31	4	0	0	3	2	2	.600	67	81	54	38	6	37	2	2	43	6	5.10
Jimenez, Salem	19	0	0	0	2	1	1	.667	25	32	22	13	5	16	0	1	14	1	4.68
Johnson, Lynchburg	22	17	6	2	6	9	0	.400	140	147	79	58	5	41	3	6	81	5	3.73
Kiser, Kinston	2	0	0	0	0	1	0	.000	3	1	3	3	0	5	0	0	1	0	9.00
Lasek, Peninsula	17	14	4	0	4	7	0	.364	91	83	41	31	3	38	2	1	64	9	3.07
Lowry, Lynchburg	21	20	6	2	10	5	0	.667	117	105	57	48	5	63	3	3	71	14	3.69
Madden, Winston-Salem	9	9	0	0	1	2	0	.333	31	23	22	13	0	25	0	1	11	4	3.77
Martinez, Alexandria*	10	4	0	0	0	3	0	.000	29	34	30	26	3	24	1	1	15	3	8.07
Martinez, Peninsula	3	1	0	0	0	1	0	.000	7	12	9	8	1	7	0	0	4	1	10.29
Miloszewski, Salem*	25	25	5	0	8	12	0	.400	134	151	90	65	14	72	2	2	86	7	4.37
Minnick, Alexandria*	21	18	3	1	6	5	1	.545	97	77	55	35	2	61	0	7	63	8	3.25
Moore, Peninsula	20	19	1	0	4	10	0	.286	95	113	76	61	2	59	2	12	43	10	5.78
Musselman, Alexandria	27	9	1	0	3	4	1	.429	90	87	44	31	5	30	1	3	60	1	3.10
Nichols, Winston-Salem	1	0	0	0	0	0	0	.000	1	5	5	5	1	2	0	0	0	0	45.00
Nicholson, Salem*	15	15	6	0	7	6	0	.538	103	94	33	27	6	36	0	0	80	4	2.36
Notarino, Salem	14	4	0	0	1	2	1	.333	49	62	23	22	4	7	1	0	23	3	4.04
Parke, Salem	12	2	0	0	1	0	0	1.000	27	24	12	11	2	8	0	0	18	0	3.67
Pearson, Lynchburg	18	16	3	0	5	10	0	.333	110	118	65	45	3	44	3	0	90	7	3.68
Pecka, Winston-Salem*	31	9	0	0	6	6	2	.500	96	101	54	32	8	47	3	4	63	5	3.00
Peterson, Salem*	4	4	0	0	0	3	0	.000	16	21	17	13	2	8	0	1	7	2	7.31
Pitts, Lynchburg	3	0	0	0	1	0	0	1.000	7	2	1	1	0	8	0	1	3	0	1.29
Powell, Salem*	10	3	0	0	1	2	0	.333	28	38	19	17	4	16	1	0	29	2	5.46
Rick, Salem*	1	0	0	0	0	0	0	.000	3	5	3	3	0	2	0	0	0	0	9.00
Ricks, Kinston	21	13	3	0	2	7	0	.222	91	95	70	53	4	68	0	2	65	11	5.24
Rivas, Winston-Salem	36	9	5	1	11	6	6	.647	118	108	61	49	8	30	3	4	93	1	3.74
Robertson, Kinston	38	0	0	0	7	5	9	.583	84	72	28	22	5	33	5	2	69	8	2.36
Rock, Salem	12	12	3	0	2	8	0	.200	63	66	57	38	5	45	3	3	40	6	5.43

Pitcher–Club	G.	GS.	CG.	ShO.	W.	L.	Sv.	Pct.	IP.	H.	R.	ER.	HR.	BB.	Int. BB.	HB.	SO.	WP.	ERA.
Rudiman, Alexandria........	8	0	0	0	0	0	0	.000	16	9	8	6	0	21	0	1	13	2	3.38
Salva, Alexandria	5	0	0	0	0	1	0	.000	10	22	18	13	0	7	0	0	7	1	11.70
Santana, Kinston	26	23	4	0	10	7	1	.588	142	143	65	55	8	57	0	4	102	9	3.49
Schoppee, Winston-Salem	37	0	0	0	3	4	19	.429	62	50	23	17	0	14	2	2	47	5	2.47
Shermeyer, Lynchburg	24	0	0	0	0	2	0	.000	45	39	22	12	0	27	4	2	27	8	2.40
Shields, Winston-Salem ...	24	22	5	0	11	8	0	.579	152	149	78	51	9	80	3	1	152	13	3.02
Shiera, Peninsula*...........	8	1	0	0	1	0	0	1.000	13	17	14	14	0	13	0	1	8	1	9.69
Simond, Alexandria*........	15	15	8	2	9	4	0	.692	107	107	54	34	4	39	0	1	82	4	2.86
Smith, Kinston.................	6	0	0	0	0	3	0	.000	26	33	20	14	2	18	1	1	22	4	4.85
Snyder, Alexandria*.........	6	0	0	0	0	3	0	.000	26	33	20	14	2	18	1	1	22	4	4.85
Speck, Peninsula	26	6	3	0	6	3	5	.667	77	65	30	24	2	39	3	0	58	1	2.81
Stoeber, Kinston	14	0	0	0	2	1	3	.667	23	20	5	4	0	6	2	2	18	1	1.57
Tavera, Winston-Salem ...	2	0	0	0	0	0	0	.000	3	4	6	6	0	7	0	0	1	0	18.00
Taylor, Salem	15	0	0	0	1	0	0	1.000	28	22	16	9	0	21	0	3	24	9	2.89
Teston, Peninsula	43	0	0	0	6	7	5	.462	74	61	37	27	2	31	8	5	46	8	3.28
Thurberg, Lynchburg	34	0	0	0	7	2	2	.778	67	56	26	20	0	40	3	4	66	4	2.69
Tyler, Winston-Salem	25	10	3	2	9	4	3	.692	82	58	19	13	1	38	2	2	70	0	1.43
Violette, Lynchburg	22	22	12	1	10	10	0	.500	153	135	63	50	10	39	3	3	94	5	2.94
Walker, Kinston*..............	15	10	2	1	4	3	1	.571	71	55	21	20	8	26	0	2	63	6	2.54
Weppner, Win-Salem*	23	20	5	2	8	7	0	.533	126	147	80	59	8	42	1	4	72	7	4.21
Wheeler, Kinston	1	0	0	0	0	0	0	.000	2	6	3	3	0	0	0	0	2	0	13.50
Wiens, Kinston	8	0	0	0	2	1	2	.667	19	22	11	11	1	6	0	1	13	2	5.21
Wright, Kinston................	14	9	0	0	2	3	3	.400	48	49	34	33	2	32	0	1	38	6	6.19

BALKS—Bozeman, Smith, Violette, 4 each; Minnick, Pearson, 3 each; Baum, Johnson, Lowrey, Moore, Musselman, Rudiman, Shermeyer, Shields, Shiera, Taylor, 2 each; Best, Brown, Cary, Corrado, Cuellar, Cyburt, Darr, Davis, Dejak, DeLeon, Flores, Franklin, Fusari, Garrity, Gause, Gonzalez, Miloszewski, Ricks, Rivas, Rock, Santana, Simond, Snyder, Speck, Stoeber, Tyler, Walker, Weppner, 1 each.

COMBINATION SHUTOUTS—Adair-Cary, Alexandria; Darr-Wright, Walker-Wright, Kinston; Franklin-Thurberg-Brazell, Pearson-Brazell, Lynchburg; Shields-Schoppee, Baum-Schoppee, Weppner-Howard-Tyler, Tyler-Pecka, Winston-Salem.

NO-HIT GAME—Hart, Peninsula, defeated Salem, 5-0 June 2, first game, seven innings (PERFECT GAME).

Pellant Pulled HR Switch

Gary Pellant, a 23-year-old third baseman for Alexandria of the Carolina League, accomplished a feat done only once before in Organized Ball when he hit a home run from each side of the plate in the same inning of a 20-7 victory over Salem.

Pellant highlighted a big seventh inning for the Mariners April 30 by homering from the right side of the plate leading off the frame, then connecting lefthanded with one man aboard later in the inning.

A check of the records showed that former major league outfielder Ellis Burton turned the same trick for Toronto's International League club on May 3, 1961. In Toronto's home opener of that season against Jersey City, Burton hit a two-run homer batting lefthanded, then hit a grand slam batting righthanded in a 10-run eighth inning.

Miller Set Record for Shutout Innings

Reno reliever Randy Miller set a California League record for consecutive shutout innings July 18 when he completed his 15th consecutive shutout appearance. Miller's streak began June 12 and covered 24 innings. The previous league record was 22 innings set by Bob Foderaro of San Jose in 1968.

Florida State League

CLASS A

CHAMPIONSHIP WINNERS IN PREVIOUS YEARS

1919–Sanford* .605	1947–St. Augustine .625	1963–Sarasota .645
Orlando* .703	Gainesville (2nd)‡ .584	Sarasota .667
1920–Tampa .654	1948–Orlando .643	1964–Fort Lauderdale† .629
Tampa .722	Daytona B'ch (2nd)‡ .616	St. Petersburg .594
1921–Orlando .635	1949–Gainesville .635	1965–Fort Lauderdale .627
1922–St. Petersburg .503	St. Augustine (3rd)‡ .556	Fort Lauderdale .634
St. Petersburg .618	1950–Orlando .629	1966–Leesburg† .781
1923–Orlando .667	DeLand (3rd)‡ .590	St. Petersburg .700
Orlando .678	1951–DeLand§ .643	1967–St. Petersburg y .691
1924–Lakeland .695	1952–DeLand x .704	Orlando .638
Lakeland .683	Palatka (3rd)‡ .569	1968–Miami .613
1925–St. Petersburg .667	1953–Daytona Beach† .657	Orlando z .579
Tampa† .696	DeLand .703	1969–Miami a .606
1926–Sanford .647	1954–Jacksonville Beach .629	Orlando .606
Sanford .623	Lakeland† .594	1970–Miami b .662
1927–Orlando† .600	1955–Orlando .671	St. Petersburg .600
Miami .661	Orlando .643	1971–Miami b .667
1928-35–Did not operate.	1956–Cocoa .614	Daytona Beach .586
1936–Gainesville .542	Cocoa .671	1972–Miami c .562
St. Augustine (4th)† .492	1957–Palatka .629	Daytona Beach .606
1937–Gainesville§ .616	Tampa† .681	1973–St. Petersburg d .575
1938–Leesburg .626	1958–St. Petersburg .732	West Palm Beach .580
Gainesville (2nd)‡ .615	St. Petersburg .681	1974–West Palm Beach d .598
1939–Sanford§ .787	1959–Tampa .591	Ft. Lauderdale .626
Orlando (4th)‡ .507	St. Petersburg† .612	1975–St. Petersburg d .652
1940–Daytona Beach .619	1960–Lakeland .731	Miami .581
Orlando (4th)‡ .507	Palatka† .614	1976–Tampa .559
1941–St. Augustine .659	1961–Tampa† .710	Lakeland d .536
Leesburg (4th)‡ .488	Sarasota .696	1977–Lakeland d .616
1942-45–Did not operate.	1962–Sarasota .689	West Palm Beach .583
1946–Orlando§ .681	Fort Lauderdale† .623	1978–Lakeland .565
		Miami§ .539

*Split-season playoff abandoned after each team won three games. †Won split-season playoff. ‡Won four-club playoff. §Won championship and four-club playoff. xWon both halves of split season.

yLeague divided into Eastern and Western divisions with split season. St. Petersburg and Orlando won both halves of split season; St. Petersburg won playoff.

zLeague divided into Eastern and Western divisions. Miami won regular-season pennant on basis of highest won-lost percentage. Orlando won four-club playoff involving first two teams in each division.

aLeague divided into Southern and Central divisions. Miami won playoff between division leaders. (NOTE—Pennant awarded to playoff winner in 1936.)

bLeague divided into Eastern and Western divisions. Miami won regular-season pennant on basis of highest won-loss percentage, and also won four-club playoff involving first two teams in each division.

cLeague divided into Eastern and Western divisions. Won four-club playoff involving first two teams in each division.

dLeague divided into Northern and Southern divisions. Won four-club playoff involving first two teams in each division.

STANDING OF CLUBS AT CLOSE OF FIRST HALF, JUNE 23

NORTHERN DIVISION

Club	W.	L.	T.	Pct.	G.B.
Winter Haven (Red Sox)	40	32	1	.556	.....
Tampa (Reds)	38	34	0	.528	2
Dunedin (Blue Jays)	36	34	0	.514	3
St. Petersburg (Cardinals)	35	35	1	.500	4
Lakeland (Tigers)	22	50	0	.306	18

SOUTHERN DIVISION

Club	W.	L.	T.	Pct.	G.B.
Ft. Lauderdale (Yankees)	46	26	0	.639	.....
West Palm Beach (Expos)	42	30	0	.583	4
Ft. Myers (Royals)	38	32	2	.543	7
Daytona Beach (Astros)	32	38	0	.457	13
Miami (Orioles)	27	45	0	.375	19

STANDING OF CLUBS AT CLOSE OF SECOND HALF, SEPTEMBER 1

NORTHERN DIVISION

Club	W.	L.	T.	Pct.	G.B.
Winter Haven (Red Sox)	39	26	0	.600	....
Tampa (Reds)	36	26	2	.581	1½
Dunedin (Blue Jays)	32	35	0	.478	8
St. Petersburg (Cardinals)	29	36	1	.446	10
Lakeland (Tigers)	28	37	0	.431	11

SOUTHERN DIVISION

Club	W.	L.	T.	Pct.	G.B.
Ft. Lauderdale (Yankees)	46	25	0	.648	....
West Palm Beach (Expos)	37	35	0	.514	9½
Miami (Orioles)	33	36	0	.478	12
Ft. Myers (Royals)	31	37	0	.456	13½
Daytona Beach (Astros)	24	42	3	.364	19½

COMPOSITE STANDING OF CLUBS AT CLOSE OF SEASON, SEPTEMBER 1

NORTHERN DIVISION

Club	WH.	Tam.	Dun.	StP.	Lak.	FtL.	WPB	FtM.	Mia.	DB.	W.	L.	T.	Pct.	G.B.
Winter Haven (Red Sox)	....	10	13	12	16	2	2	3	5	16	79	58	1	.577	....
Tampa (Reds)	10	....	10	11	15	2	5	5	3	13	74	60	2	.552	3½
Dunedin (Blue Jays)	9	10	....	15	9	2	2	5	5	11	68	69	0	.496	11
St. Petersburg (Cardinals)	7	10	5	....	17	3	1	0	5	12	64	71	2	.474	14
Lakeland (Tigers)	6	4	13	5	....	3	6	2	3	8	50	87	0	.365	29

SOUTHERN DIVISION

Club	WH.	Tam.	Dun.	StP.	Lak.	FtL.	WPB	FtM.	Mia.	DB.	W.	L.	T.	Pct.	G.B.
Ft. Lauderdale (Yankees)	6	6	6	5	5	....	19	20	20	5	92	51	0	.643	....
W. Palm Beach (Expos)	6	3	6	8	2	13	....	16	19	6	79	65	0	.549	13½
Ft. Myers (Royals)	5	3	3	3	6	11	16	....	17	5	69	69	2	.500	20½
Miami (Orioles)	3	5	3	3	5	12	13	12	....	4	60	81	0	.426	31
Daytona Beach (Astros)	6	9	10	9	12	3	2	1	4	....	56	80	3	.412	32½

Major League affiliations in parentheses.

Playoffs—Winter Haven (Northern Division Champion) defeated Ft. Lauderdale (Southern Division Champion), three games to none, for League Championship.

Regular-Season Attendance—Daytona Beach, 50,109; Dunedin, 36,676; Ft. Lauderdale, 76,762; Ft. Myers, 59,194; Lakeland, 54,017; Miami, 41,313; St. Petersburg, 157,669; Tampa, 93,303; West Palm Beach, 125,213; Winter Haven, 28,002. Total, 722,258. Playoff, 2,344. No all-star game.

Managers: Daytona Beach—Carlos Alfonso; Dunedin—Denis Menke; Fort Lauderdale—Doug Holmquist; Fort Myers—Gene Lamont; Lakeland—Fred Hatfield; Miami—Lance Nichols; St. Petersburg—Sonny Ruberto; Tampa—Mike Compton; West Palm Beach—Larry Bearnarth; Winter Haven—Rac Slider. .

All-Star Team: 1B—Thompson, Dunedin; 2B—Rivas, St. Petersburg; 3B—Esasky, Tampa; SS—Ripken, Miami; OF—Denman, Miami; Graham, Winter Haven; Moseby, Dunedin; C—Bjorkman, St. Petersburg; Christmas, Tampa; DH—Johnson, Ft. Myers; Utility—Herring, Tampa; Santana, Ft. Lauderdale; P—Boris, Ft. Lauderdale; Ojeda, Winter Haven; Ryder, Ft. Lauderdale; Scherrer, Tampa; Manager-Slider, Winter Haven.

(Compiled by Howe News Bureau, Chicago, Ill.)

CLUB BATTING

Club	G.	AB.	R.	OR.	H.	TB.	2B.	3B.	HR.	RBI.	SH.	SF.	BB.	Int. BB.	HP.	SO.	SB.	CS.	LOB.	Pct.
Dunedin	137	4366	567	588	1125	1542	158	29	67	504	35	35	420	34	36	788	65	33	955	.258
Daytona Beach	139	4191	516	631	1073	1326	134	25	23	443	48	33	519	29	54	668	168	94	953	.256
Ft. Lauderdale	143	4586	549	412	1173	1530	151	34	46	472	68	40	518	32	38	806	179	65	1093	.256
W. Palm Beach	144	4620	559	480	1173	1480	146	19	41	492	70	42	581	25	36	687	109	65	1114	.254
Winter Haven	138	4375	555	462	1093	1365	145	23	27	483	62	43	599	29	48	835	155	48	1095	.250
Miami	141	4504	473	557	1120	1458	158	45	30	411	77	31	438	22	47	866	105	48	1010	.249
Tampa	136	4259	455	414	1046	1323	116	28	35	386	65	28	478	49	35	747	164	90	965	.246
Lakeland	137	4265	495	606	1043	1351	136	35	34	430	59	32	512	27	43	704	95	68	984	.245
St. Petersburg	137	4244	499	500	1032	1301	160	20	23	405	54	41	565	41	30	719	111	93	940	.243
Ft. Myers	140	4330	480	488	1027	1328	133	27	38	428	41	23	469	25	27	790	169	54	948	.237

INDIVIDUAL BATTING
(Leading Qualifiers for Batting Championship—389 or More Plate Appearances)

*Bats lefthanded.   †Switch-hitter.

Player and Club	G.	AB.	R.	H.	TB.	2B.	3B.	HR.	RBI.	SH.	SF.	BB.	HP.	SO.	SB.	CS.	Pct.
Rivas, Raymond, St. Petersburg*	126	434	59	145	170	13	3	2	39	3	3	66	2	27	13	13	.334
Moseby, Lloyd, Dunedin*	129	446	89	148	237	23	6	18	84	0	1	63	10	103	16	12	.332
Johnson, Ronald D., Ft. Myers	116	381	47	117	164	19	2	8	58	0	3	55	2	30	5	4	.307
Ripken, Calvin, Miami	105	393	51	119	164	28	1	5	54	4	1	31	1	64	4	3	.303
Young, Kenneth, Winter Haven*	113	400	65	121	157	15	6	3	51	10	4	53	1	72	36	6	.303
Thompson, Timothy, Dunedin*	126	456	64	134	212	19	4	17	77	3	5	43	4	77	1	0	.294
Morrison, Steven, West Palm B*	135	494	54	144	172	17	4	1	50	3	5	50	4	63	10	5	.291
Herring, Paul, Tampa	121	413	53	120	159	15	3	6	43	2	7	47	1	41	16	12	.291
Tolman, Timothy, Daytona Beach	131	422	62	122	144	13	3	1	53	2	6	74	5	50	12	8	.289
Franklin, Glen, West Palm B*	120	447	66	129	162	12	3	5	52	9	4	54	4	46	24	14	.289

Departmental Leaders: G—Balboni, 140; AB—Balboni, 504; R—Moseby, 89; H—Moseby, 148; TB—Moseby, 237; 2B—Ripken, 28; 3B—Denman, 9; HR—Balboni, 26; RBI—Balboni, 91; SH—Lawless, 13; SF—Barrett, 9; BB—Loucks, 77; HP—Moseby, Toman, Tovar, 10; SO—Balboni, 154; SB—Lawless, 60; CS—Mota, 21.

(All Players—Listed Alphabetically)

Player and Club	G.	AB.	R.	H.	TB.	2B.	3B.	HR.	RBI.	SH.	SF.	BB.	HP.	SO.	SB.	CS.	Pct.
Abone, Joseph, West Palm Bch	1	1	0	0	0	0	0	0	0	0	0	0	0	0	0	0	.000
Adams, Ricky Lee, Daytona Bch	107	305	31	89	105	12	2	0	26	4	2	23	5	33	11	11	.292
Aldrich, Russell, Tampa*	105	373	36	99	141	11	5	7	56	3	3	33	6	41	8	5	.265
Anderson, Scott W., West PB	2	2	1	1	1	0	0	0	1	0	1	0	1	0	0	0	.500
Atkinson, James J., West PB	29	74	11	17	18	1	0	0	7	2	0	13	1	20	0	1	.230
Auten, James, West Palm Beach	56	181	16	34	39	5	0	0	8	3	1	21	3	25	1	0	.188
Balboni, Stephen, Ft. Laud	140	504	69	127	228	19	2	26	91	0	5	69	6	154	2	1	.252
Ballard, Byron, Ft. Laud†	1	0	1	0	0	0	0	0	1	0	1	0	0	0	0	0	.000
Barrett, Martin, Winter Haven	57	178	25	53	63	7	0	1	28	3	9	22	2	10	4	1	.298
Batter, Ronald, Ft. Myers	30	73	8	19	22	1	1	0	6	0	0	8	0	12	1	2	.260
Belmonte, Nicholas, West PB	5	15	1	4	6	2	0	0	1	0	1	0	0	1	0	0	.267
Beltran, Julio, Daytona Beach	109	300	40	77	88	6	1	1	27	1	0	18	4	34	30	13	.257
Benda, Robert, Lakeland	135	455	56	114	149	19	5	2	37	7	3	44	4	74	11	11	.251
Bender, Dei Eric, Winter Haven	49	152	16	33	40	7	0	0	12	4	0	11	1	44	2	0	.217
Berti, Thomas, Lakeland*	19	66	4	11	11	0	0	0	5	1	0	7	0	17	1	1	.167
Biancalana, Roland, Ft. Myers	125	357	44	71	92	7	4	2	32	8	4	63	1	78	21	7	.199
Bjorkman, George, St. Pete†	118	384	56	95	147	21	2	9	53	1	6	73	8	82	5	6	.247
Boris, Paul, Ft. Lauderdale	1	0	0	0	0	0	0	0	0	0	1	0	0	0	0	0	.000
Bowman, Donald, Miami	89	317	32	79	111	15	1	5	34	3	1	26	7	71	4	2	.249
Boyce, Robert, Miami	28	88	6	21	26	2	0	1	4	0	0	10	0	15	1	2	.239
Bresnahan, Raymond, Ft. Myers	128	472	66	107	126	12	2	1	34	2	3	55	0	89	25	6	.227
Brito, Jose C., Tampa	29	54	4	5	8	0	0	1	2	4	0	1	1	20	0	1	.093
Brown, Jeffrey, Lakeland*	55	188	29	50	72	8	4	2	14	1	0	25	4	26	2	1	.266
Buckle, Larry T., Tampa	10	17	0	1	1	0	0	0	0	0	0	1	0	9	0	0	.059
Bumstead, Mark, St. Petersburg	72	198	19	32	38	6	0	0	10	0	3	30	2	46	2	4	.162
Burchett, Kerry, St. Petersburg	4	10	1	2	4	0	1	0	0	0	0	0	0	6	0	0	.200
Burdette, Ricky, Ft. Laud	1	1	0	0	0	0	0	0	0	0	0	0	0	0	0	0	.000
Burtt, Gregory, Miami	108	327	31	85	105	10	5	0	29	6	2	24	4	93	2	3	.260
Caldwell, Ronnie, West PB	3	2	0	0	0	0	0	0	0	0	0	1	0	0	0	0	.000
Calise, Michael, St. Petersburg	25	88	10	21	27	3	0	1	9	0	0	12	1	21	0	2	.239
Campbell, Mark, Daytona Beach	28	61	9	15	17	2	0	0	4	2	0	9	3	8	2	2	.246
Campbell, Ron, Ft. Lauderdale	22	42	4	9	9	0	0	0	5	0	1	5	0	12	0	1	.214
Caraballo, Jose, St. Petesburg	2	2	0	0	0	0	0	0	0	0	0	0	0	0	0	0	.000
Cazares, Jose, St. Petersburg	18	38	6	4	4	0	0	0	1	0	0	1	0	7	0	0	.105
Christmas, Stephen, Tampa*	122	377	50	99	139	18	2	6	39	1	5	72	2	30	5	5	.263
Christopher, Scott, Miami	71	265	38	66	89	7	8	0	12	4	0	19	2	15	17	8	.249
Cirbo, Dennis, St. Petersburg	72	206	13	43	57	9	1	1	24	6	5	18	1	23	1	5	.209
Colbert, Richard, Winter Haven	73	163	25	26	31	3	1	0	9	4	0	36	5	43	2	5	.160
Collazo, Julio, Winter Haven	52	167	19	45	59	8	0	2	15	1	0	22	0	33	1	0	.269
Collins, Stephen, Winter Haven	1	1	0	0	0	0	0	0	0	0	0	0	0	1	0	0	.000
Connor, Domingo, Dunedin	13	28	3	5	5	0	0	0	0	0	0	0	0	8	0	0	.179
Corey, Juan, Miami	49	131	10	26	30	4	0	0	8	3	0	13	4	36	0	0	.198
Crafort, Samuel, Dunedin†	112	399	64	88	99	7	2	0	26	2	3	58	0	119	23	4	.221
Crawford, John, Lakeland	35	108	12	28	28	0	0	0	9	4	0	10	1	5	2	0	.259
Cypret, Gregory, Daytona Beach	110	393	57	110	127	15	1	0	40	6	4	46	4	33	11	10	.280
Davidson, James, Ft. Myers	37	107	14	21	30	4	1	1	7	0	0	13	1	28	3	2	.196
DeLeon, Luis A., St. Petersburg	1	0	0	0	0	0	0	0	0	1	0	0	0	0	0	0	.000
DelMonte, John, St. Pete	69	215	19	52	68	10	0	2	16	0	1	33	1	47	8	5	.242
Dempsey, J. Michael, Dunedin	1	1	0	1	1	0	0	0	1	0	0	0	0	0	0	0	1.000
Denman, John, Miami	115	393	61	110	161	12	9	7	44	4	3	65	1	87	33	6	.280
Dewey, Duane, Ft. Myers	8	23	2	2	2	0	0	0	0	1	0	0	0	11	0	1	.087
Dixon, Roy, Lakeland	12	35	2	5	6	1	0	0	1	0	1	1	0	11	0	0	.143
Dye, Scott A., Tampa	51	14	1	2	2	0	0	0	1	3	0	2	1	9	0	0	.143
Eaton, Tom, Miami	3	7	0	1	1	0	0	0	0	0	0	2	0	1	0	0	.143
Echstenkamper, T. Michael, Ft. L.	3	6	1	1	2	1	0	0	1	0	0	0	0	2	0	0	.167
Edwards, Allen, Miami	1	0	1	0	0	0	0	0	0	0	0	0	0	0	0	0	.000
Ereu, William, Dunedin†	48	175	19	42	50	2	3	0	9	2	1	5	1	29	2	0	.240
Esasky, Nicholas, Tampa	124	439	52	118	170	16	3	10	66	1	1	44	8	97	3	6	.269
Espinoza, Steven, Miami	71	214	32	48	52	2	1	0	17	6	2	35	2	43	3	7	.224
Fabiano, James, Winter Haven	90	241	42	52	76	9	3	3	31	6	1	60	3	52	7	2	.216
Fabrizio, Kurt, Miami*	117	380	38	97	135	18	4	4	45	12	7	44	4	46	4	1	.255
Fick, Charles, West Palm Bch	31	67	9	14	16	2	0	0	1	1	0	10	2	9	0	1	.209
Fields, Bruce, Lakeland*	70	220	30	52	60	4	2	0	17	3	1	41	3	45	4	9	.236
Foley, Thomas, Tampa	125	414	38	95	119	12	6	0	37	5	3	37	1	39	5	4	.229
Franklin, Glen, West PB*	120	447	66	129	162	12	3	5	52	9	4	54	4	46	24	14	.289
Gadowski, Dennis, St. Pete*	1	1	0	0	0	0	0	0	0	0	0	0	0	0	0	0	.000
Galarraga, Andres, West PB	7	23	3	3	3	0	0	0	1	0	2	1	1	11	0	0	.130
Garcia, David J., Ft. Laud*	26	76	8	21	25	2	1	0	6	1	1	10	1	16	0	0	.276
Garcia, Nelson, St. Pete†	103	351	43	98	111	11	1	0	28	4	5	46	5	36	12	8	.279
Gates, Michael, West Palm Bch*	78	289	44	82	97	9	3	0	27	9	3	30	2	31	5	3	.284
Gavillan, Pedro, West PB†	18	45	3	7	9	2	0	0	5	1	0	3	2	5	0	0	.156
George, Jerry, West Palm Bch*	43	128	20	38	48	7	0	1	15	4	2	26	2	26	1	1	.297
Gibson, Paul, Tampa	24	42	0	5	6	1	0	0	3	2	0	2	0	10	0	1	.119
Gill, Frank, Winter Haven*	107	329	52	92	108	13	0	1	40	4	7	38	1	23	23	2	.280

Player and Club	G.	AB.	R.	H.	TB.	2B.	3B.	HR.	RBI.	SH.	SF.	BB.	HP.	SO.	SB.	CS.	Pct.
Gilmore, Andrew, Ft. Laud.*	109	320	31	66	89	11	0	4	44	2	6	44	1	42	1	1	.206
Glass, Robert, Ft. Myers†	7	11	1	4	4	0	0	0	0	1	0	2	0	0	0	0	.364
Goffena, Thomas, Dunedin	83	271	31	62	65	3	0	0	23	8	3	36	1	44	3	5	.229
Gonzalez, Jorge, Lakeland	44	164	14	39	45	2	2	0	21	1	2	4	1	16	0	0	.238
Good, James, Lakeland	58	180	13	38	55	5	0	4	17	2	0	11	1	66	0	0	.211
Graham, Lee, Winter Haven*	117	404	65	103	119	9	2	1	31	4	1	60	5	46	40	13	.255
Grossini, LeRoy, St. Petersburg	122	372	41	69	79	8	1	0	31	12	3	55	2	58	10	10	.185
Haley, J. Michael, Ft. Myers	43	134	14	32	39	2	1	1	19	1	1	14	2	26	3	2	.239
Hall, David, West Palm Bch	127	452	48	112	167	12	2	13	66	3	1	61	1	107	7	4	.248
Harper, Arvis, Daytona Beach†	31	113	12	27	30	3	0	0	11	0	2	10	0	16	8	2	.239
Harper, Daryl, Ft. Myers†	53	123	12	27	30	3	0	0	12	5	0	15	0	15	6	1	.220
Headford, Grant, Miami	20	47	1	5	5	0	0	0	1	2	1	5	1	20	0	0	.106
Hendrickson, Stanley, Miami	10	10	1	2	2	0	0	0	1	0	0	1	1	4	0	0	.200
Herring, Paul, Tampa	121	413	53	120	159	15	3	6	43	2	7	47	1	41	16	12	.291
Hodgson, Paul, Dunedin	127	446	45	112	151	13	4	6	57	1	3	28	4	75	2	2	.251
Holland, John, Daytona Beach	42	138	11	26	32	3	0	1	18	0	1	7	7	37	0	0	.188
Hook, Edwin, Miami	1	1	0	0	0	0	0	0	0	0	0	0	0	0	0	0	.000
Houston, Kevin, Daytona Beach*	1	1	0	0	0	0	0	0	0	0	0	0	0	1	0	0	.000
Howell, Randy, St. Petersburg	25	63	10	14	16	2	0	0	2	0	0	5	2	24	3	2	.222
Hudler, Rex, Ft. Lauderdale	116	414	37	104	123	14	1	1	25	7	4	15	5	73	23	7	.251
Ingraham, Patrick, Tampa	103	295	19	72	87	8	2	1	15	5	0	29	0	74	12	8	.244
Irwin, Dennis, Ft. Lauderdale	2	11	1	3	7	1	0	1	1	0	0	0	0	3	1	0	.273
Jackson, Douglas, Daytona Bch	1	1	0	0	0	0	0	0	0	0	0	0	0	1	0	0	.000
Jackson, Patrick, Ft. Myers	28	84	7	20	24	2	1	0	2	0	0	12	0	5	2	0	.238
Jendra, Richard, Tampa	72	128	20	32	34	2	0	0	14	2	2	31	0	28	2	2	.250
Johnson, Craig, Lakeland	89	299	37	73	119	10	3	10	41	2	3	51	1	67	8	5	.244
Johnson, Howard, Lakeland†	132	456	49	107	137	9	3	3	49	3	6	69	6	85	18	8	.235
Johnson, Ronald, Ft. Myers	116	381	47	117	164	19	2	8	58	0	3	55	2	30	5	4	.307
Jones, David, St. Petersburg	2	3	1	1	1	0	0	0	0	0	0	0	0	0	0	0	.333
Jordan, Timothy, Ft. Laud	130	426	53	120	157	17	7	2	40	3	1	49	4	72	32	6	.282
Jorn, David, St. Petersburg	2	6	0	1	1	0	0	0	0	0	0	0	0	2	0	0	.167
Josephson, Paul, West Palm Bch	2	3	0	0	0	0	0	0	0	0	0	0	0	3	0	0	.000
Keen, George, West Palm Bch	7	18	2	3	3	0	0	0	1	0	0	1	2	5	0	0	.167
Kelly, Michael, Dunedin*	123	397	46	107	155	15	0	11	45	3	3	52	2	73	1	4	.270
Kenaga, Jeffrey, Lakeland*	60	187	17	44	57	8	1	1	21	2	1	12	1	26	1	3	.235
Khoury, Peter, Ft. Laud	102	294	29	74	91	10	2	1	19	6	1	30	3	40	5	5	.252
Kuchar, William, Tampa*	53	144	10	24	30	3	0	1	12	2	1	18	0	40	1	0	.167
Lansford, Phillip, Dunedin	106	335	33	66	83	5	0	4	36	6	6	19	3	68	0	1	.197
Lawless, Thomas, Tampa	131	469	66	126	148	9	5	1	39	13	4	70	1	92	60	17	.269
Leach, Richard, Lakeland*	48	168	21	51	69	10	1	2	23	0	2	27	2	15	4	3	.304
Lebo, Michael, Dunedin*	18	52	8	14	16	2	0	0	4	0	0	6	0	16	0	0	.269
Lee, Ronald, Winter Haven	28	85	11	24	32	5	0	1	6	3	0	11	1	13	4	0	.282
Lewis, Amos, Ft. Lauderdale	15	42	4	5	5	0	0	0	1	1	0	8	0	11	0	0	.119
Lewis, J. Tod, Ft. Myers	88	248	18	42	54	6	0	2	25	3	1	26	3	71	3	3	.169
Lindberg, Ronald, Lakeland	3	6	0	1	1	0	0	0	0	0	0	0	0	1	0	0	.167
Lombardo, Richard, Tampa*	17	10	1	5	6	1	0	0	2	0	0	2	0	4	0	0	.500
Loucks, Scott, Daytona Beach	108	338	80	83	101	6	3	2	18	3	1	77	2	77	46	13	.246
Manriques, Fred, Dunedin	5	15	0	2	2	0	0	0	0	0	0	0	0	5	0	0	.133
Marrero, William, Miami	29	76	2	9	11	0	1	0	4	2	1	4	2	31	2	0	.118
Marston, Anderson, Miami	13	40	3	10	12	2	0	0	4	0	0	9	0	9	0	0	.250
McGee, Willie, Ft. Laud.	46	176	25	56	73	8	3	1	18	2	0	17	0	34	16	4	.318
McIntyre, James, St. Pete.	93	277	27	60	74	11	0	1	18	4	1	29	2	78	7	6	.217
Medina, Valentin, Daytona Beach	76	185	22	52	68	12	2	0	26	3	1	12	4	29	3	2	.281
Mendon, D. Kevin, West Palm B.	1	1	0	0	0	0	0	0	0	0	0	0	0	0	0	0	.000
Meyer, Gregory, Tampa	28	24	1	5	6	1	0	0	1	0	0	8	1	8	0	0	.208
Michael, Steven, West Palm B.*	41	160	17	38	50	4	1	2	19	3	0	13	0	17	5	3	.238
Miklosi, Jerry, Winter Haven	43	133	15	37	44	5	1	0	20	3	3	12	2	16	0	0	.278
Miller, William E., Ft. Myers	1	0	1	0	0	0	0	0	0	0	0	0	0	0	0	0	.000
Mills, J. Bradley, West Palm B.*	78	258	43	70	99	12	1	5	30	2	4	58	1	20	8	3	.271
Milner, Brian, Dunedin	38	133	7	25	32	5	1	0	11	0	1	7	0	21	2	0	.188
Mizerock, John, Daytona Beach	53	152	13	39	56	6	1	3	12	3	0	27	0	23	1	0	.257
Morgan, John, Winter Haven	49	154	11	33	42	3	0	2	17	0	0	11	3	19	0	0	.214
Moriarty, Dermot, Ft. Myers*	73	184	14	41	59	5	2	3	28	1	2	21	0	21	3	1	.223
Moroff, Daniel, Ft. Laud.	66	182	9	38	51	5	1	2	19	3	2	25	2	47	0	0	.209
Morrison, Steven, West Palm B.*	135	494	54	144	172	17	4	1	50	3	5	50	4	63	10	5	.291
Moseby, Lloyd, Dunedin*	129	446	89	148	237	23	6	18	84	0	1	63	10	103	16	12	.332
Mota, Jose, Tampa†	122	441	58	121	130	7	1	0	18	6	0	33	7	76	45	21	.274
Motley, Darryl, Ft. Myers	123	447	47	106	154	20	2	8	45	3	2	30	4	83	19	3	.237
Murelli, Donald, Miami	43	139	11	40	40	0	0	0	7	2	0	3	1	24	2	0	.288
Nandin, Robert, Lakeland†	102	369	60	103	121	12	3	0	27	11	2	63	2	41	23	13	.279
Nave, D. Garland, Miami	9	15	0	1	1	0	0	0	0	1	0	3	0	6	1	0	.067
Neely, Alex, Tampa	1	0	0	0	0	0	0	0	0	1	0	0	0	0	0	0	.000
Neuenschwander, Douglas, Tampa	45	11	3	4	4	0	0	0	1	1	0	3	0	6	1	0	.364
O'Connor, Daniel, Lakeland	28	41	3	8	12	1	0	1	9	0	0	8	1	9	0	0	.195
O'Connor, Jack, West Palm B.*	1	1	0	0	0	0	0	0	0	0	0	0	1	0	0	0	.000

Player and Club	G.	AB.	R.	H.	TB.	2B.	3B.	HR.	RBI.	SH.	SF.	BB.	HP.	SO.	SB.	CS.	Pct.
Paris, Kelly, St. Pete.†	118	388	52	110	137	15	3	2	53	10	4	40	2	39	25	10	.284
Parker, C. Robert, Winter Haven	81	254	29	58	66	6	1	0	20	0	3	26	6	44	1	1	.228
Paula, Julio, Dunedin	13	26	7	7	9	2	0	0	2	1	0	1	0	9	0	0	.269
Paulino, Jose, Ft. Lauderdale	110	306	46	83	94	5	3	0	22	8	0	29	5	58	23	10	.271
Pautt, Juan, Winter Haven	50	140	17	33	41	4	2	0	23	1	2	34	3	41	4	3	.236
Pavlik, John, Miami	6	7	0	0	0	0	0	0	0	1	0	0	0	2	0	0	.000
Pena, Adalberto, Daytona Beach†	113	341	26	66	82	11	-1	1	23	9	1	23	2	83	4	4	.194
Perez, David, West Palm Beach	38	95	12	21	28	3	2	0	6	1	0	10	1	21	0	1	.221
Perez, Julio, West Palm Beach*	59	184	13	45	48	3	0	0	21	1	4	20	0	7	2	3	.245
Petralli, Eugene, Dunedin†	52	184	18	53	69	13	0	1	24	0	0	12	1	20	1	1	.288
Phillips, K. Anthony, W. Palm B*	60	203	30	47	54	5	1	0	18	5	3	36	0	26	7	6	.232
Pimentel, Carlos, Tampa	34	84	4	12	14	2	0	0	5	1	1	2	0	17	0	2	.143
Plante, Daniel, Ft. Lauderdale	91	268	19	62	68	6	0	0	23	10	2	30	2	37	2	0	.231
Purdy, William, Miami	1	1	0	0	0	0	0	0	0	0	0	0	0	0	0	0	.000
Quetti, Russell, Winter Haven	100	330	36	70	85	9	0	2	38	5	4	43	3	49	4	1	.212
Ray, John, Daytona Beach†	24	68	6	15	23	1	2	1	10	1	0	11	1	11	3	2	.221
Ray, Larry, Daytona Beach*	62	211	24	54	73	8	1	3	29	1	1	25	0	49	2	1	.256
Richard, Timothy, Miami	19	37	2	9	9	0	0	0	3	4	0	4	2	11	0	1	.243
Rincon, Andrew, St. Petersburg	2	3	0	0	0	0	0	0	0	0	0	1	0	1	0	0	.000
Ripken, Calvin, Miami	105	393	51	119	164	28	1	5	54	4	1	31	1	64	4	3	.303
Rivas, Raymond, St. Petersburg*	126	434	59	145	170	13	3	2	39	3	3	66	2	27	13	13	.334
Robbins, Wesley, Ft. Lauderdale	112	394	55	108	137	17	0	4	53	3	6	47	0	40	32	11	.274
Roberson, Ell, Lakeland	6	15	2	3	3	0	0	0	0	0	0	4	0	5	0	0	.200
Robertson, Andre, Dunedin	70	264	35	57	81	14	2	2	18	3	0	16	2	50	2	1	.216
Rodriguez, Eduardo, Miami	120	388	41	89	112	12	4	1	25	9	1	19	3	85	9	1	.229
Rodriguez, Victor, Miami	67	228	23	70	87	10	2	1	31	3	1	18	2	19	2	0	.307
Roeder, Steven, West Palm Beach	15	23	5	5	5	0	0	0	0	2	0	3	0	7	3	1	.217
Rosario, Simon, Daytona Beach	103	357	35	109	143	15	5	3	60	0	4	23	2	40	5	5	.305
Ross, R. Charles, Miami*	116	388	29	92	120	16	3	2	38	4	6	45	3	29	2	1	.237
Rowe, Peter, Dunedin	94	282	39	72	98	14	0	4	33	2	4	41	5	23	1	1	.255
Royster, Willie A., Miami	39	130	11	42	53	8	0	1	11	0	1	10	2	26	6	3	.323
Ruffler, Kevin, Daytona Beach	97	286	16	56	69	4	0	3	27	3	2	39	3	52	3	6	.196
Ryal, Mark, Ft. Myers*	107	360	27	79	105	12	1	4	34	6	2	20	2	66	4	3	.219
Sagers, Bobby, Lakeland*	8	19	1	3	3	0	0	0	2	0	0	3	0	6	0	0	.158
Sandberg, Charles, Winter Haven†	71	213	22	51	72	8	2	3	26	5	2	39	1	44	0	0	.239
Santana, Rafael F., Ft. Lauderdale	133	472	62	124	145	9	6	0	41	12	7	36	1	53	12	5	.263
Santarone, Richard, Ft. Laud.	4	3	0	0	0	0	0	0	0	1	0	0	0	1	0	0	.000
Sarrett, Daniel, Tampa	32	63	4	14	16	2	0	0	2	1	0	11	1	12	1	0	.222
Schardt, Andreas, Lakeland*	51	155	23	46	69	11	0	4	25	0	3	12	1	26	0	0	.297
Scherrer, William, Tampa*	31	57	5	12	13	1	0	0	8	2	0	1	0	13	0	2	.211
Schoeller, Michael, Lakeland*	76	253	24	69	87	11	2	1	30	0	3	38	1	28	3	1	.273
Shelby, John, Miami†	132	478	50	96	128	11	6	3	38	7	4	44	5	120	13	10	.201
Sheridan, Patrick, Ft. Myers	67	235	25	66	76	4	3	0	16	3	1	27	0	29	14	6	.281
Sherman, Steven, St. Petersburg†	1	1	0	0	0	0	0	0	0	0	0	0	0	0	0	0	.000
Shimp, Tommy Joe, West Palm B.	2	4	0	1	1	0	0	0	0	0	0	0	0	1	0	0	.250
Shines, Anthony R., West Palm B.†	122	406	44	104	129	13	0	4	53	2	6	56	4	58	9	6	.256
Silver, Larry, St. Petersburg	3	11	0	2	2	0	0	0	0	0	0	3	0	3	0	0	.182
Skaggs, Steven, Tampa	20	36	1	3	3	0	0	0	1	2	0	3	1	18	0	0	.083
Spreckles, Keith, St. Petersburg†	37	119	18	28	40	5	2	1	15	1	4	19	0	28	7	2	.235
Staffon, Gregory, West Palm B.	1	1	0	0	0	0	0	0	0	0	0	0	0	0	0	0	.000
Steele, Michael, Lakeland	7	13	1	0	0	0	0	0	0	0	0	3	2	4	0	0	.000
Stryker, Ronald, Tampa	55	8	2	3	4	1	0	0	0	2	0	0	0	3	0	0	.375
Stuper, John, St. Petersburg	2	1	0	0	0	0	0	0	0	0	0	1	0	1	0	0	.000
Sullivan, Marc, Winter Haven	31	92	8	19	23	2	1	0	10	2	1	4	2	15	1	0	.207
Tabler, Patrick, Ft. Lauderdale	75	247	39	78	104	12	4	2	33	1	1	51	5	46	4	3	.316
Taylor, James, Tampa	12	26	2	11	11	0	0	0	2	0	0	2	0	3	0	0	.423
Taylor, Melvin, West Palm B*	19	58	5	11	14	3	0	0	3	0	0	14	0	13	1	1	.190
Thompson, Timothy, Dunedin*	126	456	64	134	212	19	4	17	77	3	5	43	4	77	1	0	.294
Toal, Arthur, Lakeland	90	289	29	69	94	15	2	2	30	11	3	22	4	45	5	5	.239
Tobias, Grayling, West Palm B.†	49	155	21	48	57	5	2	0	20	4	2	20	1	16	12	8	.310
Tolman, Timothy, Daytona Beach.	131	422	62	122	144	13	3	1	53	2	6	74	5	50	12	8	.289
Toman, Thomas, Daytona Beach*	109	308	36	67	79	6	0	2	26	10	3	56	10	40	14	10	.218
Toothman, Jeffrey, St. Petersburg*	101	281	20	63	76	11	1	0	29	4	1	27	0	57	5	5	.224
Tovar, Raul, Ft. Myers	103	335	39	90	106	12	2	0	30	2	0	28	10	75	13	5	.269
Town, Randall, Tampa	21	35	2	3	3	0	0	0	0	2	0	1	0	6	0	0	.086
Tucker, Wilson, Lakeland*	26	82	13	23	28	2	0	1	7	2	1	9	1	8	2	3	.280
Turner, Ira, Ft. Myers	118	405	52	100	143	12	5	7	48	3	2	24	2	119	32	5	.247
Turnes, Jose, Daytona Beach	19	27	1	7	10	3	0	0	4	0	0	4	0	10	3	0	.259
Upshaw, John, Lakeland	50	152	23	31	43	3	0	3	13	7	1	21	2	41	4	2	.204
Villaman, Rafael, Ft. Laud.	95	313	48	80	101	12	3	1	19	7	0	31	2	48	25	11	.256
Viltz, Escamillo, Tampa†	96	264	23	51	65	6	1	2	19	3	1	19	4	52	5	4	.193
Wadsworth, Timothy, W. Haven	46	125	9	25	33	5	0	1	11	1	0	28	0	36	0	1	.200
Walker, Tony, Tampa	9	21	0	4	4	0	0	0	0	1	0	2	0	5	1	0	.190
Waller, Reginald, Daytona Beach.	60	183	33	59	79	8	3	2	29	0	5	34	2	40	10	5	.322
Watkins, James, Winter Haven	68	233	27	65	80	7	1	2	19	0	1	39	0	25	14	5	.279

Player and Club	G.	AB.	R.	H.	TB.	2B.	3B.	HR.	RBI.	SH.	SF.	BB.	HP.	SO.	SB.	CS.	Pct.
Whitehead, Cecil, Miami	8	24	0	3	4	1	0	0	1	0	0	4	0	8	0	0	.125
Whitfield, N. Jerome, West Palm B.	54	195	19	47	68	0	0	7	29	2	1	10	1	52	1	1	.241
Wieghaus, Thomas, West Palm B	121	382	41	83	104	15	0	2	35	6	2	44	1	44	0	2	.217
Wieser, Daniel, Ft. Myers†	113	354	40	83	98	12	0	1	32	3	2	55	0	32	15	3	.234
Wilber, Robert, Lakeland	4	6	0	1	1	0	0	0	0	0	0	0	0	1	0	0	.167
Wilder, Clifton, Lakeland	43	144	21	38	43	1	2	0	9	0	0	14	0	16	5	2	.264
Winborn, Waldo, Lakeland	9	8	4	2	4	0	1	0	1	0	0	0	0	5	0	0	.250
Winters, Matthew, Ft. Laud*	34	89	8	14	21	2	1	1	10	0	2	22	1	17	1	0	.157
Witt, Harold, St. Petersburg	28	88	7	13	17	1	0	1	7	1	1	7	1	25	1	2	.148
Wolters, Michael, St. Petersburg	91	255	45	63	82	17	1	0	19	2	1	54	0	37	6	3	.247
Wood, Andre, Dunedin	127	456	59	130	177	21	7	4	55	4	5	33	3	50	11	2	.285
Wren, Frank, West Palm Beach	74	252	30	65	82	14	0	1	24	5	3	24	2	50	13	1	.258
Wright, Jackie, Winter Haven	128	425	38	107	125	9	3	1	51	6	2	38	8	79	12	8	.252
Wright, Michael, Lakeland	104	342	30	80	103	15	1	2	47	2	3	25	6	41	2	1	.234
Yanus, Raymond, W.P. Bch	1	1	0	0	0	0	0	0	0	0	0	0	0	1	0	0	.000
Young, Kenneth, Winter Haven*	113	400	65	121	157	15	6	3	51	10	4	53	1	72	36	6	.303
Zayas, Felipe, St. Petersburg	120	447	42	116	150	17	4	3	51	4	3	45	1	71	6	10	.260

The following pitchers had no plate appearances primarily through use of designated hitters, listed alphabetically by club, games in parentheses.

DAYTONA BEACH—Aponte, C. Ricardo (16); de los Santos, German (21); Finch, Michael (5); Hessler, John (25); Lazorko, Jack (17); Leland, Stanley (22); Lohuis, Mark (13); MacDonald, James (16); Melendez, Diego (14); Perry, W. Patrick (12); Petersen, Gregory (12); Quealey, Steven (16); Rice, Andrew (19); Robinson, R. Donald (44); Smith, K. Blaine (11); Strom, Brent (10); Troedson, Thad (12); Welenc, Douglas (3).

DUNEDIN—Baltz, W. Nicholas (21); Coughlin, Gregory (6); Cuellar, Miguel A. (6); Cullen, Michael (2); Fore, Charles (5); Frank, Gary (14); Gill, John (13); Leal, Luis (21); Liber, Mark (15); Mohorcic, Dale (23); Morgan, Richard (41); Puleo, Charles (22); Smith, David (18); Stieb, David (8); Stoeber, Mark (31).

FT. LAUDERDALE—Carlucci, Richard (34); Gleckel, Scott (30); Hernandez, Carlos (20); Luongo, Ronald (14); Lysgaard, James (3); McLeod, Michael (20); Ricci, Frank (3); Ryder, Brian (25); Slagle, Roger (3); Softy, Mark (5); Steffen, Karl (2); Taylor, Jeffrey (24).

FT. MYERS—Begue, Roger (10); DiLorenzo, Christopher (20); Fischer, Daniel (10); Ganger, Robert (16); Grzybek, Benjamin (3); Hammaker, C. Atlee (1); Hanslovan, Jeffrey (14); Hardtke, Elwaine (3); Hasbach, David (10); Hendricks, Erik (16); Kurtz, Kenneth (11); Laskey, William (13); Pippin, Craig (34); Prince, Raymond (8); Reichenbach, Michael (4); Ryan, Frank (10); Schattinger, Jeffery (20); Skinner, John (7); Twitty, Jeffrey (3); Weatherford, Robert (19—9 with West Palm Beach).

LAKELAND—Bailey, Howard (25); Beecroft, Michael (6); Bresnen, Robert (12); Cascadden, Brian (3); Cassetto, David (11); Chretian, Gordon (13); Flynn, John (1); Geiger, Burwell (21); Jackowiak, Jeffrey (22); Janton, Joseph (2); Klank, William (25); Lackey, John (15); Nelson, Randy (15); Pashnick, Larry (28); Richards, Kevin (14); Robbins, Bruce (7); Shea, Kenneth (13); Simerly, James (38); Smith, Jack (11); Wheeler, James (1).

MIAMI—Carey, Brooks (19); George, William (14); Gonzalez, Julian (13); McArthur, Gregory (19); Norris, Timothy (9); Peralta, Luis (11); Rachuba, Michael (32); Ramirez, D. Allan (14); Salagan, Charles (13); Vander Laan, Steven (21); Welchel, Donald (14); White, Peder (24).

ST. PETERSBURG—Citarella, Ralph (7); Colon, Rafael (2); David, Mark (42); Gott, James (4); Morton, Dennis (13); Murphy, John (3); Olmsted, Alan (23); Otten, James (1); Sykes, Robert (4).

TAMPA—Moore, Mark (1).

WEST PALM BEACH—Coppol, Walter (1); Dooner, Glenn (39); Fadhel, Antonio (1); Hartsock, Gary (12); Kenner, Joseph (2); Ramos, Richard (13); Torres, Miguel (4).

WINTER HAVEN—Baldwin, Oscar (3); Burtt, Dennis (35); Carlander, Paul (19); Dale, D.`Charles (5); Davis, William A. (26); Givens, Gary (29); Grant, William (of) (1); Hurst, Bruce (12); Johnson, Clinton (31); Kane, Kevin (21); Ojeda, Robert (29); Sprowl, Robert (13).

GRAND SLAM HOME RUNS—Motley, Thompson, 2 each; Aldrich, Holland, Moseby, Shelby, Wieghaus, M. Wright, 1 each.

AWARDED FIRST BASE ON INTERFERENCE—Thompson 4 (Lewis 2, Bjorkman, Holland); Morrison 2 (Bjorkman, Morgan); Christopher (Upshaw); Herring (Colbert); Hudler (Corey); Jordan (Fick); Lee (Christmas); Rosario (Christmas); Watkins (Christmas); Wieser (Fick).

CLUB FIELDING

Club	G.	PO.	A.	E.	DP.	PB.	Pct.	Club	G.	PO.	A.	E.	DP.	PB.	Pct.
Winter Haven	138	3519	1464	151	114	20	.971	Lakeland	137	3384	1490	184	118	27	.964
St. Petersburg	137	3477	1524	158	138	19	.969	Ft. Myers	140	3471	1291	183	107	24	.963
Tampa	136	3452	1526	159	125	28	.969	West Palm Beach	144	3696	1469	204	131	13	.962
Ft.Lauderdale	143	3668	1559	173	123	23	.968	Dunedin	137	3374	1524	203	117	26	.960
Miami	141	3588	1558	186	147	30	.965	Daytona Beach	139	3346	1405	234	109	29	.953

Triple Plays—Winter Haven, St. Petersburg, West Palm Beach.

INDIVIDUAL FIELDING

*Throws lefthanded.

FIRST BASEMEN

Player and Club	G.	PO.	A.	E.	DP.	Pct.	Player and Club	G.	PO.	A.	E.	DP.	Pct.
Colbert, Winter Haven	5	44	3	0	2	1.000	Wright, Lakeland	30	241	13	2	15	.992
Christmas, Tampa	6	38	6	0	4	1.000	Johnson, Ft. Myers	14	104	6	1	8	.991
Morrison, W. Palm Bch	3	21	0	0	2	1.000	Bowman, Miami	60	491	36	6	52	.989
Turnes, Daytona Bch	4	14	0	0	1	1.000	Bender, Winter Haven	45	374	27	5	30	.988
Paulino, Ft. Laud	1	10	1	0	0	1.000	Marrero, Miami	9	77	6	1	9	.988
Waller, Daytona Bch	1	9	0	0	0	1.000	Schardt, Winter Haven	38	271	23	4	28	.987
Bjorkman, St. Pete	1	7	1	0	1	1.000	Thompson, Dunedin*	105	1009	58	15	79	.986
Wolters, St. Pete	1	7	0	0	2	1.000	Fabrizio, Miami*	80	580	43	9	60	.986
Wilber, Lakeland	1	6	0	0	1	1.000	Sandberg, Winter Haven	57	431	33	7	33	.985
J. Perez, West Palm Bch	3	5	1	0	2	1.000	Toman, Daytona Beach*	16	119	7	2	5	.984
Gonzalez, Lakeland	1	4	0	0	1	1.000	Ruffler, Daytona Beach	19	117	6	2	10	.984
Galarraga, W. Palm Bch	1	2	1	0	1	1.000	Shines, West Palm Bch	106	860	53	16	73	.983
Davidson, Ft. Myers	1	3	0	0	0	1.000	Whitfield, W. Palm Bch	34	273	21	5	32	.983
Herring, Tampa	1	0	2	0	0	1.000	Turner, Ft. Myers	94	746	36	16	68	.980
Upshaw, Lakeland	1	1	0	0	1	1.000	Ross, Miami	5	48	1	1	4	.980
Crawford, Lakeland	1	1	0	0	0	1.000	Tolman, Daytona Beach	92	658	57	17	64	.977
Jendra, Tampa	1	1	0	0	0	1.000	Schoeller, Lakeland	57	469	34	13	45	.975
Kuchar, Tampa*	41	346	12	1	27	.997	Moriarty, Ft. Myers*	44	333	19	9	19	.975
Bumstead, St. Pete	33	265	18	1	36	.996	Kelly, Dunedin*	30	261	11	7	26	.975
Paris, St. Pete	33	212	22	1	22	.996	Ingraham, Tampa	17	144	10	4	11	.975
Cypret, Daytona Bch	33	192	15	1	16	.995	Dixon, Lakeland	8	59	3	2	8	.969
Toothman, St. Pete*	85	726	36	5	61	.993	Wadsworth, Win. Haven	15	105	8	4	4	.966
Aldrich, Tampa	84	684	35	5	65	.993	Gavillan, W. Palm Bch	4	24	3	2	4	.931
Toal, Lakeland	48	406	24	3	36	.993	Tabler, Ft. Laud	2	9	0	1	0	.900
BALBONI, Ft. Laud	140	1297	97	11	106	.992	Winborn, Lakeland	1	5	0	1	2	.833

Triple Plays—Toothman, Sandberg.

SECOND BASEMEN

Player and Club	G.	PO.	A.	E.	DP.	Pct.	Player and Club	G.	PO.	A.	E.	DP.	Pct.
Ereu, Dunedin	4	7	10	0	0	1.000	Fabiano, Winter Haven	68	135	155	13	19	.957
J. Perez, West Palm Bch	5	5	12	0	1	1.000	Harper, Ft. Myers	18	20	39	3	7	.952
Tabler, Ft. Laud	2	5	12	0	2	1.000	Espinoza, Miami	5	8	12	1	4	.952
Morrison, W. Palm Bch	25	48	57	2	11	.981	Adams, Daytona Bch	102	189	279	24	49	.951
Robertson, Dunedin	10	21	31	1	6	.981	Lee, Winter Haven	21	34	42	4	10	.950
Barrett, Winter Haven	52	124	144	6	40	.978	Gill, Winter Haven	10	21	16	2	3	.949
LAWLESS, Tampa	129	296	376	17	82	.975	Phillips, West Palm Bch	40	89	111	11	20	.948
Benda, Lakeland	106	230	319	14	67	.975	V. Rodriguez, Miami	20	40	50	5	11	.947
E. Rodriguez, Miami	118	280	353	18	84	.972	Berti, Lakeland	14	39	42	5	6	.942
Hudler, Ft. Laud	15	29	38	2	9	.971	Eaton, Miami	3	6	10	1	2	.941
Wolters, St. Pete	32	57	104	5	21	.970	Medina, Daytona Beach	25	42	52	7	11	.931
Jendra, Tampa	8	17	15	1	5	.970	Paula, Dunedin	3	4	9	1	0	.929
Santana, Ft. Laud	23	32	56	3	16	.967	D. Perez, West Palm Bch	26	67	59	10	21	.926
Toal, Lakeland	17	36	50	3	7	.966	Bumstead, St. Pete	4	6	6	1	1	.923
Villaman, Ft. Laud	93	169	293	17	48	.965	Beltran, Daytona Bch	14	24	32	5	5	.918
Rivas, St. Pete	112	251	306	21	79	.964	Campbell, Daytona Bch	14	25	30	5	7	.917
Wood, Dunedin	123	263	435	28	82	.961	Richard, Miami	4	6	12	2	2	.900
Gates, West Palm Bch	55	107	163	11	30	.961	Campbell, Ft. Laud	9	13	10	3	2	.885
Bresnahan, Ft. Myers	127	261	344	26	54	.959	Ripken, Miami	1	3	4	1	0	.875
Garcia, Ft. Laud	16	29	41	3	6	.959	J. Ray, Daytona Beach	1	3	3	1	0	.857

Triple Plays—Barrett, Gates.

THIRD BASEMEN

Player and Club	G.	PO.	A.	E.	DP.	Pct.	Player and Club	G.	PO.	A.	E.	DP.	Pct.
Calise, St. Pete	11	9	20	0	2	1.000	Bumstead, St. Pete	17	7	22	2	4	.935
Collazo, Winter Haven	11	7	11	0	0	1.000	Santana, Ft. Laud	45	17	80	7	7	.933
Petralli, Dunedin	4	5	8	0	1	1.000	V. Rodriguez, Miami	34	26	55	6	7	.931
Roeder, West Palm Bch	3	1	6	0	2	1.000	Cypret, Daytona Bch	63	61	97	12	10	.929
D. Perez, West Palm Bch	2	2	4	0	0	1.000	Lansford, Dunedin	99	97	160	20	12	.928
E. Rodriguez, Miami	1	2	3	0	0	1.000	Esasky, Tampa	122	91	234	27	18	.923
Bowman, Miami	4	1	4	0	0	1.000	Berti, Lakeland	4	4	7	1	1	.917
Paula, Dunedin	3	1	2	0	0	1.000	Goffena, Dunedin	27	17	45	6	4	.912
Lee, Winter Haven	2	0	2	0	0	1.000	Motley, Ft. Myers	122	109	183	29	11	.910
Espinoza, Miami	11	10	22	1	1	.970	Paris, St. Pete	87	79	207	29	24	.908
Wieser, Ft. Myers	15	9	16	1	2	.962	H. Johnson, Lakeland	98	86	150	24	7	.908
J. Perez, West Palm Bch	7	7	15	1	1	.957	Toal, Lakeland	10	11	13	3	2	.889
Mills, West Palm Bch	70	66	110	9	11	.951	Miklosi, Winter Haven	4	2	6	1	0	.889
Harper, Ft. Myers	9	4	15	1	5	.950	Beltran, Daytona Bch	22	17	26	6	6	.878
Benda, Lakeland	29	19	60	5	2	.940	Moroff, Ft. Lauderdale	58	31	82	16	9	.876
Ripken, Miami	58	63	122	12	17	.939	Morrison, W. Palm Bch	63	30	121	22	9	.873
WRIGHT, Win. Haven	126	74	254	22	19	.937	Tolman, Daytona Beach	30	26	36	9	3	.873
Wolters, St. Pete	36	20	66	6	4	.935	J. Ray, Daytona Bch	16	17	29	7	1	.868

THIRD BASEMEN—Continued

Player and Club	G.	PO.	A.	E.	DP.	Pct.
Tabler, Ft. Lauderdale ...	22	14	25	6	3	.867
Richard, Miami	14	8	18	4	2	.867
Fabiano, Winter Haven .	5	2	11	2	1	.867
Jendra, Tampa	16	11	27	6	2	.864
Boyce, Miami	24	22	38	10	3	.857
Campbell, Daytona Bch.	5	3	3	1	1	.857
Lewis, Ft. Lauderdale	15	6	17	4	2	.852
Ereu, Dunedin	11	6	15	4	0	.840
Hudler, Ft. Lauderdale ..	25	13	26	8	1	.830
Marrero, Miami	8	7	11	4	0	.818
Medina, Daytona Bch.	26	15	29	10	5	.815
Franklin, W. Palm Bch.	3	0	3	1	1	.750
Ruffler, Daytona Bch	2	0	2	1	0	.667

Triple Plays—J. Perez, Wright.

SHORTSTOPS

Player and Club	G.	PO.	A.	E.	DP.	Pct.
Toal, Lakeland	4	6	6	0	2	1.000
J. Ray, Daytona Bch	4	1	6	0	1	1.000
Fabiano, Winter Haven .	2	2	4	0	1	1.000
Benda, Lakeland	1	0	2	0	0	1.000
Boyce, Miami	1	1	1	0	0	1.000
Shelby, Miami	1	2	0	0	0	1.000
J. Perez, West Palm Bch	19	36	57	1	7	.989
Santana, Ft. Laud	72	111	215	6	42	.982
Bumstead, St. Pete	7	18	16	1	3	.971
Miklosi, Winter Haven	36	60	102	5	18	.970
Murelli, Miami	43	80	108	8	21	.959
Cypret, Daytona Bch.	35	37	81	5	13	.959
GROSSINI, St. Pete	121	223	363	26	79	.958
Nandin, Lakeland	102	213	353	28	65	.953
Foley, Tampa	122	223	394	35	71	.946
Cazares, St. Pete	13	22	28	3	4	.943
Biancalana, Ft. Myers	125	236	342	36	65	.941
Quetti, Winter Haven	100	156	289	28	46	.941
Robertson, Dunedin	60	111	214	21	36	.939
Espinoza, Miami	54	66	183	17	30	.936
Goffena, Dunedin	54	84	158	18	37	.931
Ripken, Miami	52	83	135	17	37	.928
Jendra, Tampa	20	20	37	5	6	.919
Harper, Ft. Myers	21	22	43	6	9	.915
Hudler, Ft. Laud.	78	121	250	35	43	.914
H. Johnson, Lake	29	38	90	12	14	.914
Lindberg, Lakeland	2	2	8	1	2	.909
Pena, Daytona Bch.	112	152	290	45	48	.908
Gates, West Palm Bch.	22	24	65	9	12	.908
Franklin, W. Palm Bch.	88	157	209	38	47	.906
Ereu, Dunedin	24	30	69	11	9	.900
Phillips, West Palm Bch	19	31	45	10	11	.884
Lee, Winter Haven	5	7	15	3	1	.880
D. Perez, W. Palm Bch.	5	7	7	3	4	.824
Beltran, Daytona Bch	4	2	7	2	1	.818
Manriques, Dunedin	4	4	7	3	0	.786

Triple Play—Bumstead.

OUTFIELDERS

Player and Club	G.	PO.	A.	E.	DP.	Pct.
WIESER, Ft. Myers	96	139	8	0	3	1.000
Christopher, Miami	71	108	9	0	2	1.000
Michael, W. Palm Bch*.	41	105	2	0	0	1.000
Haley, Ft. Myers	40	83	2	0	0	1.000
Kenaga, Lakeland	43	77	2	0	1	1.000
Kelly, Dunedin*	40	61	2	0	0	1.000
Bowman, Miami	15	27	7	0	3	1.000
Aldrich, Miami	25	33	0	0	0	1.000
Pimentel, Tampa	25	30	1	0	0	1.000
Wright, Lakeland	15	22	1	0	0	1.000
Atkinson, W. Palm Bch .	17	22	0	0	0	1.000
Bumstead, St. Pete	10	17	0	0	0	1.000
Marston, Miami	10	15	1	0	0	1.000
Fabiano, Winter Haven .	7	15	0	0	0	1.000
Taylor, W. Palm Bch*...	8	12	0	0	0	1.000
Shines, West Palm Bch ..	6	11	0	0	0	1.000
Walker, Tampa	6	10	0	0	0	1.000
Whitfield, W. Palm Bch .	8	7	1	0	0	1.000
Keen, West Palm Bch ..	3	7	0	0	0	1.000
H. Johnson, Lakeland ..	2	6	0	0	0	1.000
Calise, St. Pete	3	6	0	0	0	1.000
V. Rodriguez, Miami ...	3	5	0	0	0	1.000
Turner, Ft. Myers	3	3	2	0	0	1.000
Goffena, Dunedin	3	4	0	0	0	1.000
Tolman, Daytona Bch ..	3	4	0	0	0	1.000
Pavlik, Miami	4	4	0	0	0	1.000
Echstenkamper, Ft.L.	2	3	0	0	0	1.000
Dixon, Lakeland	1	2	0	0	0	1.000
Espinoza, Miami	1	2	0	0	0	1.000
Ballard, Ft. Laud	1	1	0	0	0	1.000
Campbell, Daytona Bch.	1	1	0	0	0	1.000
Colbert, Winter Haven ..	1	1	0	0	0	1.000
Petralli, Dunedin	1	1	0	0	0	1.000
Fick, West Palm Bch ...	2	1	0	0	0	1.000
Hudler, Ft. Laud.	2	1	0	0	0	1.000
Hendrickson, Miami ...	3	1	0	0	0	1.000
Sheridan, Ft. Myers	66	142	8	1	0	.993
Jordan, Ft. Laud.	111	207	8	2	2	.991
Tobias, West Palm Bch*	49	103	2	1	0	.991
Watkins, Winter Haven .	67	151	10	2	1	.988
Gill, Winter Haven	92	153	8	2	4	.988
DelMonte, St. Pete	67	146	3	2	1	.987
Robbins, Ft. Laud.	46	77	1	1	0	.987
Ryal, Ft. Myers*	103	199	15	3	2	.986
Brown, Lakeland	35	70	2	1	1	.986
Spreckles, St. Pete	34	67	3	1	1	.986
Mota, Tampa	113	232	10	4	1	.984
Loucks, Daytona Bch	100	164	13	3	4	.983
Denman, Miami	105	207	13	4	3	.982
C. Johnson, Lakeland ..	85	148	6	3	0	.981
McGee, Ft. Laud	45	103	3	2	1	.981
Waller, Daytona Bch ..	49	92	5	2	2	.980
Witt, St. Pete	27	48	2	1	0	.980
Hall, West Palm Bch ...	121	251	16	6	5	.978
Graham, Winter Haven*	113	176	4	4	1	.978
Howell, St. Pete.	20	44	0	1	0	.978
McIntyre, St. Pete*	91	161	7	4	0	.977
Khoury, Ft. Laud.	94	160	6	4	3	.976
Fields, Lakeland	56	120	2	3	2	.976
Morrison, W. Palm Bch.	47	78	2	2	1	.976
Leach, Lakeland*	45	104	8	3	1	.974
Young, Winter Haven* .	65	108	3	3	1	.974
Pautt, Winter Haven	50	68	7	2	1	.974
George, West Palm Bch .	25	35	1	1	1	.973
Shelby, Miami	129	252	22	8	7	.972
Viltz, Tampa	82	161	15	5	3	.972
Beltran, Daytona Bch.	41	68	1	2	0	.972
Toman, Daytona Bch* ..	77	90	9	3	1	.971
Paulino, Ft. Laud.	104	150	10	5	2	.970
Wren, West Palm Bch ..	68	92	5	3	1	.970
Garcia, St. Pete	76	134	12	5	3	.967
Burtt, Miami	76	106	6	4	0	.966
L. Ray, Daytona Bch....	57	78	4	3	0	.965
Hodgson, Dunedin	125	215	14	9	4	.962
Herring, Tampa	116	160	17	7	2	.962
Headford, Miami	19	24	1	1	1	.962
Auten, West Palm Bch ..	56	94	5	4	1	.961
Harper, Daytona Bch ..	27	44	3	2	2	.959

OUTFIELDERS—Continued

Player and Club	G.	PO.	A.	E.	DP.	Pct.
Good, Lakeland	53	83	8	4	0	.958
Moseby, Dunedin	129	190	11	9	1	.957
Parker, Winter Haven	60	83	3	4	0	.956
Crafort, Dunedin	110	247	6	12	1	.955
Tovar, Ft. Myers	102	187	6	9	1	.955
Tabler, Ft. Laud	48	74	4	4	2	.951
Tucker, Lakeland	24	38	1	2	0	.951
Zayas, St. Pete	103	130	22	8	3	.950
Davidson, Ft. Myers	33	33	3	2	1	.947
Schoeller, Lakeland	13	18	0	1	0	.947

Player and Club	G.	PO.	A.	E.	DP.	Pct.
Wilder, Lakeland	40	64	4	4	3	.944
Ingraham, Tampa	75	109	6	7	1	.943
Roberson, Lakeland	5	14	1	1	1	.938
Winters, Ft. Laud	23	28	1	2	0	.935
Rosario, Daytona Bch	86	118	7	9	2	.933
Gonzalez, Lakeland	8	11	1	1	0	.923
Toal, Lakeland	2	10	0	1	0	.909
Marrero, Miami	8	10	0	1	0	.909
Paula, Dunedin	4	4	0	1	0	.800
Connor, Dunedin	12	5	1	3	0	.667
Roeder, West Palm Bch	2	0	0	1	0	.000

CATCHERS

Player and Club	G.	PO.	A.	E.	DP.	PB.	Pct.
Gavillan, W. Palm B	12	61	7	0	1	0	1.000
Taylor, Tampa	7	34	6	0	0	2	1.000
Nave, Miami	9	33	6	0	2	0	1.000
Aldrich, Tampa	2	12	3	0	1	2	1.000
Campbell, Day. Bch	4	7	0	0	0	0	1.000
Paulino, Ft. Laud	1	2	1	0	0	0	1.000
Keen, West Palm Bch	1	2	0	0	0	0	1.000
Caraballo, St. Pete	2	2	0	0	0	0	1.000
Santarone, Ft. Laud	2	1	0	0	0	0	1.000
Ruffler, Daytona Bch	62	400	38	5	6	11	.989
Sullivan, W. Haven	31	146	20	2	2	7	.988
WIEGHAUS, WPB	116	742	95	11	10	8	.987
Lebo, Dunedin	14	64	11	1	0	2	.987
Corey, Miami	35	197	19	3	1	8	.986
Colbert, Win. Haven	65	333	27	6	1	5	.984
Royster, Miami	37	217	32	4	5	5	.984
Plante, Ft. Laud	91	492	46	10	7	13	.982
Mizerock, Day. Bch	45	255	25	5	3	15	.982
Crawford, Lakeland	35	180	26	4	3	4	.981
Jackson, Ft. Myers	28	191	19	4	3	3	.981
Morgan, Win. Haven	49	258	25	6	3	6	.979

Player and Club	G.	PO.	A.	E.	DP.	PB.	Pct.
Petralli, Dun	45	200	34	5	0	11	.979
Turnes, Daytona Bch	14	42	4	1	0	1	.979
Christmas, Tampa	114	646	113	17	9	17	.978
Bjorkman, St. Pete	100	556	67	14	7	12	.978
Gilmore, Ft. Laud	70	359	25	9	2	10	.977
Rowe, Dunedin	81	406	40	11	3	12	.976
Batter, Ft. Myers	30	105	19	3	2	2	.976
Cirbo, St. Pete	38	203	22	6	1	7	.974
O'Connor, Lakeland	26	66	6	2	0	5	.973
Lewis, Ft. Myers	88	454	37	14	2	17	.972
Upshaw, Lakeland	48	193	31	7	1	6	.970
Wright, Lakeland	38	189	34	7	5	11	.970
Wadsworth, WH	22	118	12	4	2	2	.970
Fick, West Palm Bch	29	135	20	5	1	5	.969
Ross, Miami	71	404	61	17	2	17	.965
Sarrett, Tampa	32	112	22	5	2	7	.964
Holland, Daytona Bch	34	190	21	8	3	2	.963
Dewey, Ft. Myers	5	23	0	1	0	0	.958
Milner, Dunedin	4	16	4	1	1	1	.952
Steele, Lakeland	7	20	7	3	0	1	.900
Glass, Ft. Myers	3	6	0	1	0	2	.857

PITCHERS

Player and Club	G.	PO.	A.	E.	DP.	Pct.
GLECKEL, Ft. Laud*	30	12	30	0	2	1.000
Burchett, St. Pete	27	12	25	0	1	1.000
Rincon, St. Pete	25	8	21	0	0	1.000
Burtt, Winter Haven	35	7	21	0	1	1.000
Stryker, Tampa	55	5	16	0	0	1.000
Josephson, W. P. Beach	31	4	16	0	3	1.000
DiLorenzo, Ft. Myers	20	5	14	0	1	1.000
Ramos, W. P. Beach	13	5	13	0	1	1.000
Boris, Ft. Lauderdale	45	5	13	0	1	1.000
Welchel, Miami	14	5	12	0	0	1.000
Carey, Miami*	19	3	14	0	0	1.000
Simerly, Lakeland	34	5	12	0	0	1.000
Robbins, Lakeland*	7	1	15	0	2	1.000
Caldwell, W. P. Beach	12	4	12	0	2	1.000
Vander Laan, Miami	21	7	9	0	1	1.000
Morgan, Dunedin	41	3	13	0	0	1.000
Stieb, Dunedin	8	6	9	0	0	1.000
Burdette, Ft. Laud*	25	4	11	0	0	1.000
Shea, Lakeland	13	3	11	0	0	1.000
Lazorko, Daytona Beach	17	4	10	0	2	1.000
Carlander, Win Haven	19	7	7	0	1	1.000
Robinson, DayBeach	44	5	9	0	0	1.000
Sprowl, Winter Haven*	13	4	8	0	0	1.000
Richards, Lakeland	14	3	9	0	0	1.000
Carlucci, Ft. Laud	34	3	9	0	0	1.000
Laskey, Ft. Myers	13	2	9	0	1	1.000
White, Miami	23	5	6	0	0	1.000
Pippin, Ft. Myers	34	5	6	0	0	1.000
Strom, Daytona Beach*	10	1	9	0	1	1.000
Buckle, Tampa	10	3	6	0	0	1.000
Begue, Ft. Myers	10	0	8	0	0	1.000
Salagan, Miami*	13	3	5	0	0	1.000
Grzybek, Ft. Myers	3	2	5	0	0	1.000
Gonzalez, Miami*	13	2	5	0	0	1.000

Player and Club	G.	PO.	A.	E.	DP.	Pct.
Morton, St. Pete*	13	0	7	0	0	1.000
Fore, Dunedin	5	1	5	0	1	1.000
Cuellar, Dunedin	6	2	4	0	0	1.000
Norris, Miami	9	2	4	0	0	1.000
Bresnen, Lakeland*	12	0	6	0	0	1.000
Aponte, Daytona Beach	16	2	4	0	0	1.000
de los Santos, D. Beach	21	2	4	0	0	1.000
Sherman, St. Pete*	36	1	5	0	0	1.000
Baldwin, Winter Haven	3	2	3	0	0	1.000
Slagle, Ft. Lauderdale	3	0	5	0	0	1.000
Citarella, St. Pete	7	0	5	0	0	1.000
Liber, Dunedin*	15	1	4	0	0	1.000
Quealey, Daytona Beach	16	1	4	0	0	1.000
Lysgaard, Ft. Laud	3	2	2	0	0	1.000
Dale, Winter Haven	5	1	3	0	0	1.000
Troedson, Day Beach	12	1	3	0	0	1.000
Ricci, Ft. Lauderdale	3	1	2	0	0	1.000
Softy, Ft. Lauderdale	5	1	2	0	0	1.000
Kurtz, Ft. Myers	11	0	3	0	0	1.000
Ganger, Ft. Myers	16	2	1	0	0	1.000
Wheeler, Lakeland	1	0	2	0	0	1.000
Janton, Lakeland	2	0	2	0	0	1.000
Cascadden, Lakeland*	3	0	2	0	1	1.000
Murphy, St. Pete*	3	2	0	0	0	1.000
Reichenbach, Ft. Myers	4	0	2	0	0	1.000
Peralta, Miami	11	1	1	0	0	1.000
Hartsock, W. P. Beach	12	0	2	0	1	1.000
Fadhel, W. P. Beach	1	0	1	0	0	1.000
Otten, St. Pete	1	0	1	0	0	1.000
Keener, W. P. Beach	2	0	1	0	0	1.000
Twitty, Ft. Myers*	3	1	0	0	0	1.000
Welenc, Daytona Beach	3	0	1	0	0	1.000
Torres, W. P. Beach	4	1	0	0	0	1.000
Finch, Daytona Beach*	5	0	1	0	0	1.000

PITCHERS—Continued

Player and Club	G.	PO.	A.	E.	DP.	Pct.
Coughlin, Dunedin*	6	0	1	0	0	1.000
Neely, Tampa	8	0	1	0	0	1.000
Taylor, Ft. Laud	24	26	23	1	1	.980
Ryder, Ft. Lauderdale	25	13	25	1	3	.974
Puleo, Dunedin	22	12	25	1	0	.974
Gibson, Tampa*	24	3	26	1	1	.967
Pashnick, Lakeland	28	9	20	1	0	.967
Collins, Winter Haven	33	9	19	1	2	.966
Givens, Winter Haven	29	15	38	2	2	.964
MacDonald, Day Beach.	16	8	18	1	2	.963
Meyer, Tampa*	28	6	19	1	3	.962
David, St. Pete	39	3	19	1	2	.957
Ojeda, Winter Haven*	29	10	52	3	6	.954
Shimp, W. P. Beach	27	12	28	2	0	.952
Hurst, Winter Haven*	12	3	17	1	4	.952
Ramirez, Miami	14	6	13	1	1	.950
Anderson, W. P. Beach ..	17	7	12	1	0	.950
Fischer, Ft. Myers	10	4	14	1	2	.947
Chretian, Lakeland	13	3	15	1	1	.947
Brito, Tampa	28	3	15	1	1	.947
McLeod, Ft. Lauderdale.	20	8	9	1	1	.944
Jones, St. Pete	23	5	12	1	0	.944
Scherrer, Tampa*	25	3	30	2	4	.943
Abone, W. P. Beach	16	9	23	2	2	.941
Luongo, Ft. Lauderdale .	14	5	11	1	0	.941
Davis, Winter Haven	26	7	9	1	1	.941
Stuper, St. Pete	42	4	12	1	1	.941
Neuenschwander, Tam ..	45	2	14	1	1	.941
Ballard, Ft. Lauderdale .	22	15	31	3	1	.939
Lackey, Lakeland	15	10	20	2	1	.938
Skaggs, Tampa	20	11	19	2	2	.938
Kane, Winter Haven	21	4	11	1	1	.938
Johnson, Winter Haven .	31	3	12	1	0	.938
Purdy, Miami	47	1	14	1	1	.938
Gill, Dunedin	13	1	13	1	0	.933
Leal, Dunedin	21	4	10	1	1	.933
Dempsey, Dunedin	22	2	12	1	0	.933
Mendon, W. P. Beach	28	9	32	3	3	.932
Olmsted, St. Pete*	23	6	21	2	3	.931
Baltz, Dunedin	22	9	27	3	2	.923
Town, Tampa	19	4	19	2	1	.920
Houston, Daytona Bch*	22	5	17	2	1	.917
Jackowiak, Lakeland	22	11	11	2	0	.917
Smith, Lakeland	10	7	4	1	0	.917
Petersen, Day Beach	12	5	6	1	0	.917
Klank, Lakeland	25	5	6	1	2	.917
Hernandez, Ft. Laud*	20	7	34	4	2	.911
Ryan, Ft. Myers	10	3	7	1	1	.909
Mohorcic, Dunedin	23	5	22	3	3	.900
Gadowski, St. Pete	14	1	8	1	1	.900
Frank, Dunedin	14	6	3	1	0	.900
Yanus, W. P. Beach	16	5	4	1	0	.900
Lombardo, Tampa*	17	0	9	1	0	.900
Rice, Daytona Beach*	19	2	7	1	2	.900
Schattinger, Ft. Myers	20	11	15	3	1	.897
Bailey, Lakeland*	25	3	23	3	1	.897
Jorn, St. Pete	24	9	23	4	1	.889
Hendricks, Ft. Myers	16	4	12	2	1	.889
Miller, Ft. Myers	20	7	9	2	0	.889
Stoeber, Dunedin	31	4	12	2	1	.889
Hasbach, Ft. Myers	10	3	5	1	0	.889
McArthur, Miami	18	4	4	1	0	.889
O'Connor, W. P. Beach*	24	6	17	3	3	.885
Melendez, Day Beach ...	14	2	13	2	0	.882
Staffon, W. P. Beach	14	4	17	3	2	.875
George, Miami*	14	2	18	3	0	.870
Dye, Tampa	51	2	11	2	0	.867
Hessler, Day Beach	25	16	29	7	3	.865
Smith, Dunedin	18	9	9	3	0	.857
Edwards, Miami	32	9	9	3	1	.857
Cassetto, Lakeland	11	4	13	3	0	.850
Hanslovan, Ft. Myers* ..	14	0	11	2	2	.846
Weatherford, WPB-Ft.M	19	3	8	2	1	.846
Hardtke, Ft. Myers	20	7	4	2	1	.846
DeLeon, St. Pete	59	4	7	2	1	.846
Leland, Daytona Beach..	22	10	22	6	1	.842
Hook, Miami	23	11	19	6	1	.833
Rachuba, Miami*	31	4	21	5	1	.833
Skinner, Ft. Myers	7	0	5	1	1	.833
Dooner, W. P. Beach	39	4	10	3	1	.824
Jackson, Day Beach	28	3	15	4	1	.818
Perry, Daytona Beach*..	12	1	8	2	2	.818
Prince, Ft. Myers	7	1	3	1	1	.800
Lohuis, Daytona Beach..	13	0	4	1	0	.800
Smith, Daytona Beach ..	11	3	4	2	0	.778
Gott, St. Pete	4	0	4	2	0	.667
Nelson, Lakeland	15	2	2	2	0	.667
Beecroft, Lakeland	6	1	1	1	0	.667
Geiger, Lakeland	21	2	2	3	1	.571
Steffen, Ft. Laud*	2	0	1	1	0	.500
Sykes, St. Pete*	2	0	1	1	0	.500

The following players do not have any recorded accepted chances; therefore, are not listed in the fielding averages for those positions: Belmonte, of; Colon, p; Coppol*, p; Cullen, p; Flynn, p; Grant, of; Hammaker*, p; Moore*, p; Sagers, 2b. Irwin, Silver and Whitehead appeared as designated hitters and/or pinch-hitters only.

CLUB PITCHING

Club	G.	CG.	ShO.	Sv.	IP.	H.	R.	ER.	HR.	BB.	Int. BB.	HB.	SO.	WP.	Bk.	ERA.
Ft. Lauderdale	143	48	25	26	1223	1069	412	327	29	428	19	34	825	50	8	2.41
West Palm Beach	144	63	17	10	1232	1089	480	357	48	511	15	48	870	44	18	2.61
Tampa	136	30	19	20	1151	962	414	337	31	479	35	33	745	55	6	2.64
Winter Haven	138	42	19	26	1173	999	462	366	36	510	15	29	801	71	6	2.81
Ft. Myers	140	53	18	16	1157	1036	488	391	27	558	30	32	717	64	4	3.04
St. Petersburg	137	30	9	26	1159	1142	500	416	32	459	47	57	686	54	6	3.23
Miami	141	42	9	18	1196	1201	557	437	37	544	25	47	795	74	14	3.29
Dunedin	137	45	16	21	1125	1166	588	482	52	452	28	33	630	47	14	3.86
Daytona Beach	139	38	8	17	1115	1089	631	484	31	657	41	43	842	102	14	3.91
Lakeland	137	38	5	13	1128	1152	606	493	40	501	57	49	599	70	24	3.93

PITCHERS' RECORDS
(Leading Qualifiers for Earned-Run Average Leadership—115 or More Innings)
*Throws lefthanded.

Pitcher–Club	G.	GS.	CG.	ShO.	W.	L.	Sv.	Pct.	IP.	H.	R.	ER.	HR.	Int. BB.	BB.	HB.	SO.	WP.	ERA.
Taylor, Ft. Lauderdale	24	23	7	4	13	2	0	.867	156	157	46	29	2	29	4	3	68	8	1.67
Scherrer, Tampa*	25	24	10	4	12	3	0	.800	159	126	43	32	0	65	2	2	140	9	1.81
Ryder, Ft. Lauderdale	25	25	10	6	15	5	0	.750	171	135	49	44	5	76	0	1	156	6	2.32
Burtt, Winter Haven	35	20	9	2	11	10	3	.524	152	113	53	40	5	74	2	2	109	6	2.37
Brito, Tampa	28	26	8	3	11	7	0	.611	167	126	57	45	7	82	2	5	154	9	2.43
Ojeda, Winter Haven*	29	29	8	2	15	7	0	.682	200	163	66	54	5	84	1	5	150	6	2.43
Mendon, W Palm Beach	28	28	12	3	13	11	0	.542	196	188	79	53	6	69	2	10	143	6	2.43
Carey, Miami*	19	19	10	2	10	7	0	.588	125	118	44	34	5	23	0	5	116	4	2.45
Shimp, W Palm Beach	27	23	15	3	13	8	0	.619	188	157	68	54	6	83	1	7	138	3	2.59
Leal, Dunedin	21	21	7	4	12	2	0	.857	150	137	51	44	5	45	1	2	90	2	2.64

Departmental Leaders: G—DeLeon, 59; GS—Givens, Ojeda, 29; CG—Shimp, 11; ShO—Ryder, 6; W—Boris, Givens, 16; L—Leland, 13; Sv—DeLeon, Morgan, 14; Pct.—Taylor, .867; IP—Givens, 206; H—Burchett, 205; R—Hessler, 98; ER—Bailey, 72; HR—Bailey, 11; BB—Hessler, 132; IBB—Bailey, DeLeon, 10; HB—Bailey, 12; SO—Ryder, 156; WP—Hessler, 28.

(All Pitchers—Listed Alphabetically)

Pitcher–Club	G.	GS.	CG.	ShO.	W.	L.	Sv.	Pct.	IP.	H.	R.	ER.	HR.	Int. BB.	BB.	HB.	SO.	WP.	ERA.
Abone, West Palm Beach	16	13	7	2	5	8	2	.385	105	88	32	19	3	26	0	3	65	3	1.63
Anderson, W Palm Beach	17	9	2	0	3	4	0	.429	87	48	27	20	2	58	2	6	45	8	2.69
Aponte, Daytona Beach	16	2	0	0	2	0	2	1.000	30	25	7	6	0	9	1	0	20	1	1.80
Bailey, Lakeland*	25	24	5	1	8	12	0	.400	142	147	83	72	11	64	10	12	76	10	4.56
Baldwin, Winter Haven	3	3	0	0	0	2	0	.000	10	19	7	4	0	1	0	1	8	0	3.60
Ballard, Ft. Lauderdale	22	22	6	2	4	9	0	.308	140	134	76	58	2	64	3	10	74	7	3.73
Baltz, Dunedin	22	19	11	3	10	11	0	.476	143	135	61	43	5	37	6	1	70	6	2.71
Barrett, Winter Haven	1	0	0	0	0	0	0	.000	1	0	0	0	0	0	0	0	1	0	0.00
Beecroft, Lakeland	6	6	0	0	0	4	0	.000	21	21	24	23	1	23	1	1	17	3	9.86
Begue, Ft. Myers	10	1	1	0	1	3	0	.000	25	25	9	9	0	6	0	0	12	1	3.24
Boris, Ft. Lauderdale	45	3	2	0	16	8	12	.667	110	91	30	25	5	19	1	0	76	2	2.05
Bresnen, Lakeland*	12	0	0	0	1	1	0	.000	20	20	7	7	0	13	1	1	13	0	3.15
Brito, Tampa	28	26	8	3	11	7	0	.611	167	126	57	45	7	82	2	5	154	9	2.43
Buckle, Tampa	10	9	0	0	2	2	0	.500	47	39	27	23	1	29	1	5	30	2	4.40
Burchett, St. Pete	27	27	7	0	8	10	0	.444	184	205	81	71	5	38	5	9	99	5	3.47
Burdette, Ft. Laud*	25	4	1	1	8	2	2	.800	73	58	17	13	2	16	2	1	43	0	1.60
Burtt, Winter Haven	35	20	9	2	11	10	3	.524	152	113	53	40	5	74	2	2	109	6	2.37
Caldwell, W Palm Bch	12	12	3	1	6	3	0	.667	72	75	30	28	1	35	0	4	39	3	3.50
Carey, Miami*	19	19	10	2	10	7	0	.588	125	118	44	34	5	23	0	5	116	4	2.45
Carlander, Winter Haven	19	6	2	0	1	5	1	.167	68	78	48	41	5	29	1	1	28	6	5.43
Carlucci, Ft. Laud	34	0	0	0	2	1	9	.667	67	64	14	13	2	19	0	2	57	6	1.75
Cascadden, Lakeland*	3	1	1	0	0	1	0	.000	7	7	9	4	0	9	1	0	3	5	5.14
Cassetto, Lakeland	11	8	2	0	3	5	0	.375	64	57	40	18	5	28	4	4	37	1	2.53
Chretian, Lakeland	13	11	5	1	3	6	0	.333	90	84	37	30	2	24	2	1	31	3	3.00
Citarella, St. Pete	7	4	1	1	0	0	0	.000	26	31	8	5	0	11	0	2	10	0	1.73
Collins, Winter Haven	33	16	2	1	9	7	3	.563	135	122	60	48	2	87	2	5	90	20	3.20
Colon, St. Petersburg	2	0	0	0	0	0	0	.000	5	4	1	1	0	1	0	1	2	0	1.80
Coppol, West Palm Bch*	1	0	0	0	0	0	0	.000	1	1	3	2	0	4	0	0	1	1	18.00
Coughlin, Dunedin*	6	1	0	0	1	0	0	.000	14	16	12	12	2	15	0	4	0	7.71
Cuellar, Dunedin	6	4	3	1	3	0	1	1.000	33	25	6	5	0	13	0	2	13	1	1.36
Cullen, Dunedin	2	0	0	0	0	0	0	.000	5	3	5	2	1	2	0	0	0	0	3.60
Dale, Winter Haven	5	0	0	0	2	1	0	.667	7	12	4	4	0	0	0	1	5	3	5.14
David, St. Petersburg	39	0	0	0	4	6	3	.400	63	59	32	27	2	38	4	6	25	6	3.86
Davis, Winter Haven	26	0	0	0	2	2	4	.500	77	53	29	25	2	57	4	5	51	3	2.92
DeLeon, St. Petersburg	59	0	0	0	8	3	14	.727	92	63	20	15	3	28	10	5	100	4	1.47
de los Santos, Daytona B.	21	0	0	0	1	0	0	1.000	26	16	15	11	0	29	2	1	10	1	3.81
Dempsey, Dunedin	22	8	2	0	2	7	2	.222	83	97	59	50	4	33	2	2	45	5	5.42
DiLorenzo, Ft. Myers	20	13	4	0	3	8	0	.273	88	76	36	29	1	42	1	1	62	6	2.97
Dooner, West Palm Bch	39	1	1	0	5	3	6	.625	69	71	27	18	4	21	2	7	50	2	2.35
Dye, Tampa	51	1	0	0	12	3	6	.800	100	81	24	20	0	24	2	5	74	2	1.80
Edwards, Miami	32	14	4	0	6	8	1	.429	126	112	62	43	0	74	2	5	73	10	3.07
Fadhel, West Palm Beach	1	0	0	0	0	0	0	.000	1	0	0	0	0	1	0	0	0	0	0.00
Finch, Daytona Bch*	5	0	0	0	1	0	0	1.000	4	1	0	0	0	0	0	0	6	0	0.00
Fischer, Ft. Myers	10	10	7	3	3	5	0	.375	66	64	23	18	1	10	1	0	44	0	2.45
Flynn, Lakeland	1	0	0	0	0	0	0	.000	1	2	0	0	0	0	0	0	0	0	0.00
Fore, Dunedin	5	5	0	0	2	3	0	.400	31	27	18	13	1	14	0	0	28	2	3.77
Frank, Dunedin	14	4	0	0	2	2	0	.500	43	52	36	31	3	31	1	2	33	3	6.49
Gadowski, St. Pete	14	14	0	0	3	4	0	.429	66	79	43	35	3	39	1	3	25	3	4.77
Ganger, Ft. Myers	16	0	0	0	5	3	5	.625	32	26	8	4	0	11	4	0	27	0	1.13
Geiger, Lakeland	21	3	0	0	2	4	0	.333	51	70	37	29	0	26	4	2	34	4	5.12
George, Miami*	14	14	4	2	5	5	0	.500	84	90	43	30	4	37	0	3	66	4	3.21
Gibson, Tampa*	24	22	2	0	3	8	0	.273	129	121	56	44	5	46	7	4	58	5	3.07

Pitcher–Club	G.	GS.	CG.	ShO.	W.	L.	Sv.	Pct.	IP.	H.	R.	ER.	HR.	BB.	Int. BB.	HB.	SO.	WP.	ERA.
Gill, Winter Haven	3	0	0	0	0	0	0	.000	3	6	3	2	0	3	0	0	2	0	6.00
Gill, Dunedin	13	11	2	0	1	7	0	.125	59	64	35	27	5	34	1	1	23	2	4.12
Givens, Winter Haven	29	29	10	3	16	12	0	.571	206	189	85	61	9	67	3	6	89	7	2.67
Gleckel, Ft. Laud*	30	23	8	0	9	7	0	.563	178	180	69	57	4	42	6	1	115	6	2.88
Gonzalez, Miami*	13	13	3	0	8	3	0	.727	78	75	28	25	3	21	0	0	77	5	2.88
Gott, St. Petersburg	4	4	0	0	0	3	0	.000	18	18	13	13	0	13	0	1	9	0	6.50
Grzybek, Ft. Myers	3	3	2	0	1	2	0	.333	18	18	10	10	1	11	1	0	10	2	5.00
Hammaker, Ft. Myers*	1	1	0	0	0	1	0	.000	5	9	5	1	0	0	0	0	5	0	1.80
Hanslovan, Ft. Myers*	14	14	6	2	8	4	0	.667	95	91	43	38	1	38	2	0	55	2	3.60
Hardtke, Ft. Myers	20	14	4	1	6	6	0	.500	99	91	42	34	3	53	3	0	60	2	3.09
Hartsock, W Palm Beach.	12	0	0	0	2	2	0	.500	20	24	14	8	2	13	2	1	13	0	3.60
Hasbach, Ft. Myers	10	3	2	1	6	1	0	.857	42	37	15	12	1	16	0	1	19	7	2.57
Hendricks, Ft. Myers	16	15	3	0	4	6	1	.400	106	82	59	46	3	98	2	11	102	6	3.91
Hernandez, Ft. Laud*	20	16	4	2	5	7	0	.417	95	73	34	27	1	84	1	7	63	5	2.56
Hessler, Daytona Beach	25	25	7	1	8	11	0	.421	130	104	98	70	1	132	1	7	139	28	4.85
Hook, Miami	23	23	3	0	3	9	0	.250	135	158	74	50	4	56	1	3	77	6	3.33
Houston, Daytona Beach	22	20	3	0	7	6	0	.538	123	105	71	55	2	94	2	6	86	11	4.02
Hurst, Winter Haven*	12	12	4	2	8	2	0	.800	84	57	22	18	2	20	0	2	64	7	1.93
Ingraham, Tampa	1	0	0	0	0	0	0	.000	1	2	4	2	0	2	0	0	2	0	18.00
Jackowiak, Lakeland	22	20	4	0	5	9	0	.357	120	115	73	58	4	71	2	8	58	13	4.35
Jackson, Daytona Bch.	28	15	7	2	4	8	0	.333	110	123	70	51	2	71	3	5	80	12	4.17
Janton, Lakeland	2	2	0	0	0	1	0	.000	5	12	8	8	0	0	0	0	4	0	14.40
Johnson, Winter Haven	31	0	0	0	5	2	12	.714	61	41	17	15	2	22	1	0	54	4	2.21
Jones, St. Petersburg	23	11	0	0	7	6	4	.538	93	86	36	32	2	39	6	6	47	5	3.10
Jorn, St. Petersburg	24	24	8	2	10	9	0	.526	143	164	72	60	7	42	6	4	74	6	3.78
Josephson, W Palm Bch.	31	1	0	7	4	1	.636	94	81	33	31	6	31	4	4	68	5	2.97
Kane, Winter Haven	21	11	4	3	7	2	3	.778	90	63	31	22	3	33	0	0	60	3	2.20
Keener, W Palm Beach	2	2	0	0	0	0	0	.000	6	2	1	0	0	2	0	1	1	0	0.00
Kelly, Dunedin*	1	0	0	0	0	0	0	.000	2	1	0	0	0	1	0	0	1	0	0.00
Klank, Lakeland	25	2	0	0	0	0	3	.000	49	59	36	31	3	28	2	1	27	5	5.69
Kurtz, Ft. Myers	11	5	2	1	2	1	0	.667	29	30	11	11	2	9	0	1	13	1	3.41
Lackey, Lakeland	15	15	8	1	6	8	0	.429	111	103	37	32	0	20	5	1	54	5	2.59
Laskey, Ft. Myers	13	13	6	3	7	4	0	.636	93	71	24	23	7	35	0	2	72	1	2.23
Lazorko, Daytona Beach.	17	0	0	0	2	1	3	.667	29	38	15	15	0	12	0	0	17	3	4.66
Leal, Dunedin	21	21	7	4	12	2	0	.857	150	137	51	44	5	45	1	2	90	2	2.64
Leland, Daytona Beach	22	19	5	0	5	13	0	.278	130	127	67	54	3	62	5	7	111	6	3.74
Liber, Dunedin*	15	0	0	0	2	3	.000	18	25	12	11	1	11	2	1	12	2	5.50
Lohuis, Daytona Beach	13	0	0	0	2	0	.000	32	27	12	9	1	21	3	0	27	6	2.53
Lombardo, Tampa*	17	6	0	0	1	3	1	.250	45	39	24	14	0	20	4	1	24	3	2.80
Luongo, Ft. Lauderdale	14	10	5	2	8	2	0	.800	75	48	17	14	2	19	0	4	64	3	1.68
Lysgaard, Ft. Laud	3	3	1	1	1	1	0	.500	17	6	5	4	1	4	0	1	16	0	2.12
MacDonald, Daytona Bch	16	15	7	2	7	7	0	.500	105	98	42	33	4	25	2	1	65	2	2.83
McArthur, Miami	18	1	0	0	2	4	0	.333	39	39	21	21	3	38	3	9	22	4	4.85
McLeod, Ft. Lauderdale.	20	6	0	0	6	3	2	.667	78	71	33	26	2	27	0	2	45	6	3.00
Melendez, Daytona Bch	14	6	1	0	2	4	0	.333	56	51	43	30	1	52	4	7	39	7	4.82
Mendon, West Palm Bch.	28	28	12	3	13	11	0	.542	196	188	79	53	6	69	2	10	143	6	2.43
Meyer, Tampa*	28	13	2	1	5	4	0	.556	85	70	34	25	4	47	2	0	41	3	2.65
Miklosi, Winter Haven	3	0	0	0	0	0	0	.000	4	2	1	1	0	2	1	0	2	0	2.25
Miller, Ft. Myers	20	16	3	0	5	9	0	.357	104	105	54	44	2	66	3	3	41	12	3.81
Mohorcic, Dunedin	23	15	6	2	4	7	0	.364	106	134	59	52	5	27	1	3	52	3	4.42
Moore, Tampa*	1	0	0	0	0	0	0	.000	2	1	0	0	0	0	0	0	0	0	0.00
Morgan, Dunedin	41	0	0	0	5	5	14	.500	72	79	36	34	5	20	4	4	51	2	4.25
Moriarty, Ft. Myers*	1	0	0	0	0	0	0	.000	0	1	5	5	0	4	0	0	0	0	
Morton, St. Petersburg	13	7	1	1	1	3	0	.250	42	39	24	20	1	26	1	1	30	6	4.29
Murphy, St. Pete*	3	3	0	0	1	2	0	.333	9	12	8	7	0	9	0	0	6	5	7.00
Neely, Tampa	8	0	0	0	0	2	0	.000	9	10	5	5	1	6	0	0	5	1	5.00
Nelson, Lakeland	15	0	0	0	2	1	1	.667	21	15	18	16	1	11	3	2	5	2	6.86
Neuenschwander, Tampa	45	0	0	0	9	5	5	.643	82	82	35	25	0	31	4	2	51	4	2.74
Norris, Miami	9	0	0	0	0	0	0	.000	20	26	18	16	1	18	2	1	7	4	7.20
O'Connor, W Palm Bch*	24	22	6	3	9	7	0	.563	146	125	60	46	8	63	0	0	87	1	2.84
Ojeda, Winter Haven*	29	29	8	2	15	7	0	.682	200	163	66	54	5	84	1	5	150	6	2.43
Olmsted, St. Pete*	23	12	6	2	8	5	2	.615	101	91	31	25	1	27	3	2	70	3	2.23
Otten, St. Petersburg	1	1	0	1	0	0	0	1.000	9	1	1	1	0	5	1	0	5	1	1.00
Pashnick, Lakeland	28	28	6	1	8	9	1	.471	149	146	72	58	5	67	6	4	70	8	3.50
Peralta, Miami	11	0	0	0	4	2	.000	16	13	8	8	0	11	3	1	12	1	4.50
Perry, Daytona Bch*	12	7	1	0	2	3	0	.400	51	64	31	30	1	16	3	0	30	1	5.29
Petersen, Daytona Bch	12	8	2	1	2	5	1	.286	57	47	28	26	6	24	0	1	37	3	4.11
Pippin, Ft. Myers	34	0	0	0	4	4	2	.500	68	56	23	20	2	43	3	1	47	9	2.65
Prince, Ft. Myers	7	1	0	0	1	1	0	.500	23	33	11	8	0	9	0	0	8	1	3.13
Puleo, Dunedin	22	22	6	1	10	10	0	.500	123	126	72	61	6	61	1	3	77	6	4.46
Purdy, Miami	47	1	0	0	4	6	7	.400	102	108	42	32	2	35	3	4	44	8	2.82
Quealey, Daytona Bch	16	0	0	1	1	4	.500	22	12	2	2	0	9	2	2	26	0	0.82
Rachuba, Miami*	31	19	5	2	7	11	2	.389	135	125	69	60	5	85	3	5	102	7	4.00
Ramirez, Miami	14	14	5	1	3	9	0	.250	93	97	40	27	3	35	1	1	54	3	2.61

Pitcher–Club	G	GS	CG	ShO	W	L	Sv	Pct.	IP	H	R	ER	HR	BB	Int. BB	HB	SO	WP	ERA.
Ramos, West Palm Beach	13	13	10	3	10	2	0	.833	106	80	25	22	6	24	0	0	95	0	1.87
Reichenbach, Ft. Myers	4	0	0	0	2	0	2	1.000	12	9	3	3	0	4	1	0	10	0	2.25
Ricci, Ft. Lauderdale	3	1	1	2	0	0	1	1.000	14	9	2	1	0	8	1	0	11	0	0.64
Rice, Daytona Beach*	19	2	0	0	1	2	1	.333	20	13	11	6	0	22	2	2	12	1	2.70
Richards, Lakeland	14	4	1	1	3	2	0	.600	45	50	19	17	1	24	3	5	16	3	3.40
Rincon, St. Petersburg	25	24	5	2	10	9	0	.526	158	153	74	59	4	66	7	10	89	7	3.36
Robbins, Lakeland*	7	3	0	1	4	0	0	.200	49	46	18	18	0	18	2	1	31	1	3.31
Robinson, Daytona Bch	44	0	0	0	3	5	3	.375	53	67	31	25	1	33	7	2	48	6	4.25
Ryan, Ft. Myers	10	10	3	1	2	6	0	.250	75	70	33	25	1	12	5	1	25	1	3.00
Ryder, Ft. Lauderdale	25	25	10	6	15	5	0	.750	171	135	49	44	5	76	0	1	156	6	2.32
Salagan, Miami*	13	5	0	0	2	4	0	.333	35	34	24	18	2	32	2	1	28	2	4.63
Schattinger, Ft. Myers	20	13	4	1	5	5	1	.500	92	88	48	34	1	52	0	1	56	12	3.33
Scherrer, Tampa*	25	24	10	4	12	3	0	.800	159	126	43	32	0	65	2	2	140	9	1.81
Shea, Lakeland	13	8	2	0	2	7	0	.222	59	60	34	29	3	28	3	0	49	1	4.42
Sherman, St. Pete*	36	1	0	0	1	3	1	.250	40	36	13	12	0	12	1	1	27	0	2.70
Shimp, West Palm Beach	27	23	15	3	13	8	0	.619	188	157	68	54	6	83	1	7	138	3	2.59
Simerly, Lakeland	34	3	0	0	4	8	7	.333	66	62	31	24	2	33	5	6	43	5	3.27
Skaggs, Tampa	20	20	3	1	4	7	0	.364	126	104	43	42	7	67	2	5	46	7	3.00
Skinner, Ft. Myers	7	7	6	3	5	1	0	.833	52	28	9	7	1	15	0	0	29	1	1.21
Slagle, Ft. Lauderdale	3	2	1	0	1	1	0	.500	15	13	5	4	0	6	1	1	12	0	2.40
Smith, Daytona Beach	11	10	2	1	4	5	0	.444	55	71	40	26	5	14	0	0	37	3	4.25
Smith, Dunedin	18	14	6	2	7	5	0	.583	106	89	42	34	5	46	1	4	52	9	2.89
Smith, Lakeland	10	5	1	0	3	3	0	.500	57	54	23	19	2	14	3	0	34	3	3.00
Softy, Ft. Lauderdale	5	4	1	0	2	2	1	.500	27	24	8	6	0	12	0	1	20	0	2.00
Sprowl, Winter Haven*	13	11	3	1	3	6	0	.333	76	81	36	31	1	31	0	1	88	6	3.67
Staffon, W Palm Beach	21	17	4	1	5	9	0	.357	103	95	58	41	3	60	0	4	82	9	3.58
Steffen, Ft. Laud*	2	1	0	0	0	1	0	.000	7	11	7	6	1	3	0	0	5	1	7.71
Stieb, Dunedin	8	8	2	1	5	0	0	1.000	51	54	30	24	0	28	1	4	38	3	4.24
Stoeber, Dunedin	31	5	0	0	5	7	1	.417	87	102	54	39	4	34	7	3	41	1	4.03
Strom, Daytona Bch*	10	8	2	0	4	4	0	.500	54	71	32	25	4	18	2	1	32	7	4.17
Stryker, Tampa	55	1	0	0	7	11	8	.389	85	72	30	26	3	40	6	1	53	4	2.75
Stuper, St. Petersburg	42	1	0	0	2	5	2	.286	93	84	38	28	3	54	3	3	62	8	2.71
Sykes, St. Petersburg*	4	4	1	0	0	3	0	.000	15	11	5	5	1	12	0	2	6	0	3.00
Taylor, Ft. Lauderdale	24	23	7	4	13	2	0	.867	156	157	46	29	2	29	4	3	68	6	1.67
Torres, W Palm Beach	4	0	0	0	0	0	0	.000	6	6	6	5	0	8	1	0	6	1	7.50
Town, Tampa	19	14	5	2	8	5	0	.615	112	89	36	34	3	20	3	3	67	6	2.73
Troedson, Daytona Bch	12	0	0	0	0	1	3	.000	15	14	8	4	0	7	1	1	8	2	2.40
Twitty, Ft. Myers*	3	0	0	0	0	0	0	.000	5	2	0	0	0	2	0	0	6	0	0.00
Vander Laan, Miami	21	4	1	0	3	2	2	.600	59	66	26	23	1	31	4	2	26	5	3.51
Weatherford, 9WP-10FM.	19	1	0	0	0	2	1	.000	42	38	21	14	0	31	5	0	25	1	3.00
Welchel, Miami	14	14	7	0	5	6	0	.455	95	86	34	31	2	34	1	4	53	6	2.94
Welenc, Daytona Beach	3	2	1	0	0	2	0	.000	13	15	8	6	0	7	1	0	12	2	4.15
Wheeler, Lakeland	1	0	0	0	0	0	0	.000	2	2	0	0	0	0	0	0	0	0	0.00
White, Miami	23	0	0	0	2	3	4	.400	55	54	22	19	4	14	1	3	38	5	3.11
Yanus, West Palm Beach	16	3	2	0	1	3	1	.250	38	34	8	6	1	4	0	1	26	1	1.42

BALKS—Hook, Pashnick, 5 each; Bresnen, Caldwell, Frank, Leland, J. Smith, 4 each; Abone, Bailey, Hendricks, Ryder, Shimp, Staffon, Stuper, 3 each; Carlucci, J. Gill, Jackowiak, Klank, Leal, Lohuis, O'Connor, Puleo, Purdy, Rachuba, D. Smith, Stryker, Welenc, 2 each; Anderson, Ballard, Beecroft, Brito, Burtt, Collins, Dale, DeLeon, DiLorenzo, Edwards, Fore, Geiger, George, Gibson, Givens, Gleckel, Gonzalez, Hurst, Ingraham, Jackson, Jorn, Josephson, Lackey, Lazorko, Luongo, Melendez, Mendon, Meyer, Norris, Ojeda, Olmsted, Quealey, Ramirez, Rice, Simerly, Stieb, Strom, 1 each.

COMBINATION SHUTOUTS—Leland-Robinson, Daytona Beach; Puleo-Morgan, Cuellar-Morgan, Dunedin; Ryder-McLeod, Ryder-Carlucci, Luongo-McLeod-Boris, Gleckel-Boris, Hernandez-Carlucci, Softy-Boris, Ft. Lauderdale; Hardtke-Begue, Miller-Pippin, Ft. Myers; Gonzalez-Vander Laan, Gonzalez-Peralta, Miami; Rincon-Stuper-DeLeon, St. Petersburg; Scherrer-Neely-Stryker, Brito-Dye, Scherrer-Dye-Brito-Lombardo-Stryker, Gibson-Dye 2, Buckle-Stryker, Scherrer- Dye 2, Tampa; Yanus-Josephson, West Palm Beach; Sprowl-Kane, Hurst-Burtt, Burtt-Kane, Collins-Burtt, Burtt-Collins, Winter Haven.

NO-HIT GAMES—Leal, Dunedin, defeated Tampa, 2-0, May 11; J. O'Connor, West Palm Beach, defeated Ft. Myers, 1-0, June 28; Puleo, Dunedin, defeated St. Petersburg, 3-0, August 13, second game, seven innings.

WPB Pitchers Finished What They Started

West Palm Beach pitchers compiled a string of 12 consecutive complete games and 11 victories during a two-week span in June. And just one day after the streak had ended June 27 Expos' starter Jack O'Connor threw a nine-inning no-hitter at Fort Myers, beating the Royals, 1-0.

Midwest League

CLASS A

CHAMPIONSHIP WINNERS IN PREVIOUS YEARS

1947–Belleville	.667	1959–Waterloo	.613	1969–Appleton	.648
Belleville	.672	Waterloo	.613	Appleton	.690
1948–West Frankfort*	.708	1960–Waterloo	.629	1970–Quincy z	.691
1949–Centralia	.627	Waterloo	.677	Quad Cities	.581
Paducah (4th)†	.454	1961–Waterloo	.613	1971–Appleton	.642
1950–Centralia‡	.675	Quincy z	.594	Quad Cities a	.548
1951–Paris§	.700	1962–Dubuque z	.667	1972–Appleton	.598
Danville (4th)†	.432	Waterloo	.625	Danville a	.584
1952–Danville x	.685	1963–Clinton	.710	1973–Wisconsin Rapids a	.562
Decatur (3rd)†	.584	Clinton	.629	Danville	.537
1953–Decatur*	.576	1964–Clinton	.667	1974–Appleton	.593
1954–Decatur	.587	Fox Cities z	.667	Danville a	.517
Danville (2nd)‡	.528	1965–Burlington	.667	1975–Waterloo a	.727
1955–Dubuque*	.587	Burlington	.677	Quad Cities	.624
1956–Paris y	.656	1966–Fox Cities z	.689	1976–Waterloo a	.600
Dubuque	.603	Cedar Rapids	.762	Cedar Rapids	.595
1957–Decatur y	.683	1967–Wisconsin Rapids	.685	1977–Waterloo	.580
Clinton	.623	Appleton z	.587	Burlington a	.511
1958–Michigan City	.623	1968–Decatur	.656	1978–Appleton a	.708
Waterloo z	.613	Quad Cities z	.648	Burlington	.500

*Won championship and our-club playoff. †Won four-club playoff. ‡Playoff finals canceled because of bad weather. xWon first half of split-season and tied Paris for second-half title. yWon first-half title and four-team playoff. zWon split-season playoff. (NOTE–Known as Illinois State League in 1947-48 and Mississippi-Ohio Valley League from 1949 through 1955.)

aLeague divided into Northern and Southern divisions and played split-season. Playoff winner.

STANDING OF CLUBS AT CLOSE OF FIRST HALF, JUNE 19

NORTHERN DIVISION

Club	W.	L.	T.	Pct.	G.B.
Waterloo (Indians)	42	25	0	.627	....
Appleton (White Sox)	38	29	1	.567	4
Wausau (Co-op)	29	37	0	.439	12½
Wisconsin Rapids (Twins)	26	41	0	.388	16

SOUTHERN DIVISION

Club	W.	L.	T.	Pct.	G.B.
Quad Cities (Cubs)	38	27	1	.585	....
Burlington (Brewers)	33	35	0	.485	6½
Clinton (Dodgers)	31	35	0	.470	7½
Cedar Rapids (Giants)	30	38	0	.441	9½

STANDING OF CLUBS AT CLOSE OF SECOND HALF, AUGUST 30

NORTHERN DIVISION

Club	W.	L.	T.	Pct.	G.B.
Wausau (Co-op)	40	24	1	.625	....
Waterloo (Indians)	39	29	0	.574	3
Wisconsin Rapids (Twins)	34	31	1	.523	6½
Appleton (White Sox)	25	43	0	.368	17

SOUTHERN DIVISION

Club	W.	L.	T.	Pct.	G.B.
Clinton (Dodgers)	43	24	0	.642	......
Quad Cities (Cubs)	39	29	0	.574	4½
Cedar Rapids (Giants)	28	40	0	.412	15½
Burlington (Brewers)	20	48	0	.294	23½

COMPOSITE STANDINGS OF CLUBS AT CLOSE OF SEASON, AUGUST 30

NORTHERN DIVISION

Club	Q.C.	Cln.	C.R.	Bur.	Wat.	Wau.	Apl.	W.R.	W.	L.	T.	Pct.	G.B.
Waterloo (Indians)	10	9	14	8	..	14	14	12	81	54	0	.600	....
Wausau (Co-op)	9	5	11	9	9	..	13	13	69	61	1	.531	9½
Appleton (White Sox)	8	8	6	8	10	11	..	12	63	72	1	.467	18
Wisconsin Rapids (Twins)	5	9	9	6	12	7	12	..	60	72	1	.455	19½

SOUTHERN DIVISION

Club	Q.C.	Cln.	C.R.	Bur.	Wat.	Wau.	Apl.	W.R.	W.	L.	T.	Pct.	G.B.
Quad Cities (Cubs)	..	12	15	19	6	7	7	11	77	56	1	.579	....
Clinton (Dodgers)	10	..	15	17	7	10	8	7	74	59	0	.556	3
Cedar Rapids (Giants)	9	9	..	16	2	5	10	7	58	78	0	.426	20½
Burlington (Brewers)	5	7	8	..	8	7	8	10	53	83	0	.390	25½

Quad Cities represented Davenport and Bettendorf, Ia., and Moline and Rock Island, Ill.

Major league affiliations in parentheses.

Playoffs—Waterloo, first half leader, defeated Wausau, second half leader, two games to one, for Northern Division championship. Quad Cities, first half leader, defeated Clinton, second half leader, two games to one, for Southern Division championship. Quad Cities (Southern Division Champion), defeated Waterloo (Northern Division Champion), two games to one for League Championship.

Regular-Season Attendance—Appleton, 72,011; Burlington, 55,001; Cedar Rapids, 73,206; Clinton, 41,949; Quad Cities, 89,256; Waterloo, 70,196; Wausau, 43,059; Wisconsin Rapids, 41,239. Total, 485,915. Playoffs, 12,804. All-star game, 3,427.

Managers: Appleton—Jim Breazeale; Burlington—Duane Espy; Cedar Rapids—Wayne Cato; Clinton—Dick McLaughlin; Quad Cities—Jim Napier; Waterloo—Cal Emery; Wausau—Tom Robson; Wisconsin Rapids—Rick Stelmaszek.

All-Star Team: 1B—Anderson, Waterloo; 2B—Plinski, Cedar Rapids; 3B—Peltz, Waterloo; SS—Mesa, Appleton; OF—Stockstill, Wausau; Gilbert, Quad Cities; Webster, Clinton; C—Johnson, Wausau; DH—Hudgens, Waterloo; P—Clark, Quad Cities; Jones, Burlington; Joyce, Clinton; Rambus, Waterloo; Sutherland, Cedar Rapids; Manager —Robson, Wausau.

(Compiled by Howe News Bureau, Chicago, Ill.)

CLUB BATTING

Club	G.	AB.	R.	OR.	H.	TB.	2B.	3B.	HR.	RBI.	SH.	SF.	BB.	Int. BB.	HP.	SO.	SB.	CS.	LOB.	Pct.
Waterloo	135	4357	707	571	1157	1779	207	20	125	625	54	37	623	22	32	820	147	69	989	.266
Clinton	133	4160	608	566	1098	1431	174	27	35	494	38	52	496	18	49	557	232	98	919	.265
Wausau	131	4199	706	644	1091	1655	192	24	108	610	33	42	642	22	42	749	96	34	1007	.260
Appleton	136	4429	682	698	1135	1659	199	38	83	585	37	49	659	17	36	934	116	42	1092	.256
Quad Cities	134	4183	665	570	1071	1453	164	39	40	553	61	45	695	15	36	752	230	79	1026	.256
Wis. Rapids	133	4161	596	645	1047	1493	170	15	82	521	47	33	534	6	45	750	86	28	952	.252
Cedar Rapids	136	4294	619	737	1076	1488	169	27	63	528	26	33	586	16	46	812	250	102	971	.251
Burlington	136	4420	613	765	1040	1439	171	30	56	510	21	35	623	18	38	885	194	79	994	.235

INDIVIDUAL BATTING

(Leading Qualifiers for Batting Championship—367 or More Plate Appearances)

*Bats lefthanded.   †Switch-hitter.

Player and Club	G.	AB.	R.	H.	TB.	2B.	3B.	HR.	RBI.	SH.	SF.	BB.	HP.	SO.	SB.	CS.	Pct.
Webster, Mitchell, Clinton†	123	473	95	154	191	17	7	2	40	8	2	58	6	58	54	21	.326
Gilbert, Mark, Quad Cities†	117	407	80	128	154	12	7	0	55	4	3	65	8	51	50	22	.314
Hubbard, Donald, Waterloo	90	338	50	105	161	21	1	11	69	3	5	33	2	43	8	8	.311
Alvarez, Roberto, Waterloo	111	355	55	108	153	19	4	6	50	7	4	48	8	40	9	7	.304
Peltz, Peter, Waterloo	122	403	94	122	168	22	3	6	66	0	2	95	1	48	25	8	.303
Johnson, Bobby, Wausau	124	433	89	131	223	20	0	24	79	1	3	89	3	78	4	0	.303
Hicks, Joseph, A., Quad Cities	132	461	78	138	210	23	5	13	74	5	5	75	4	77	24	6	.299
Benson, Mark, Cedar Rapids	118	388	68	114	161	24	4	5	59	2	7	82	4	53	23	2	.294
Hudgens, David, Waterloo*	127	422	87	123	239	34	2	26	85	2	6	78	4	97	18	7	.291
Sax, Stephen, Clinton	115	386	64	112	137	15	2	2	52	2	7	57	3	30	25	8	.290

Departmental Leaders: G—Lozado, 136; AB—Lozado, 525; R—Plinski, 98; H—Webster, 154; TB—Stockstill, 248; 2B—Hudgens, Winterfeldt, 34; 3B—Daniels, 8; HR—Anderson, 30; RBI—Stockstill, 101; SH—Boelter, Mohr, 13; SF —Elliott, Kizer, 10; BB—Peltz, 95; HP—Jirschele, 11; SO—White, 122; SB—Plinski, 72; CS—Gilbert, 22.

(All Players—Listed Alphabetically)

Player and Club	G.	AB.	R.	H.	TB.	2B.	3B.	HR.	RBI.	SH.	SF.	BB.	HP.	SO.	SB.	CS.	Pct.
Adams, W. Craig, Waterloo	26	76	11	21	34	4	0	3	10	0	0	20	0	16	3	2	.276
Agapay, Felix, Appleton*	23	51	13	18	22	4	0	0	9	0	0	19	0	7	5	0	.353
Ahlert, Jerome, Quad Cities	5	11	1	3	3	0	0	0	1	0	0	2	1	3	1	0	.273
Alvarez, Roberto, Waterloo	111	355	55	108	153	19	4	6	50	7	4	48	8	40	9	7	.304
Anderson, Thomas, Waterloo	127	408	72	112	221	17	1	30	92	3	5	67	0	115	4	2	.275
Bahns, Edward, Appleton*	89	297	40	70	110	11	4	7	44	1	3	36	1	54	1	0	.236
Bailey, Vincent, Burlington	134	500	67	119	143	12	3	2	52	3	2	56	1	84	26	20	.238
Baker, Gregory, Cedar Rapids	42	141	21	31	52	10	1	3	21	1	2	25	4	42	5	2	.220
Bargfeldt, John, Quad Cities*	5	1	2	1	1	0	0	0	0	0	0	2	0	0	0	0	1.000
Bauer, Phillip, Appleton	63	230	36	48	54	4	1	0	13	0	2	50	0	29	4	4	.209
Benson, Mark, Cedar Rapids	118	388	68	114	161	24	4	5	59	2	7	82	4	53	23	2	.294
Beyers, Tom, Clinton	74	271	33	82	112	12	3	4	34	0	6	19	3	19	7	4	.303
Bienek, Vincent, Appleton	113	414	64	117	161	27	4	3	58	1	2	56	3	70	7	1	.283
Bilardello, Dann, Clinton	52	142	18	34	44	4	0	2	15	1	1	18	1	11	2	6	.239
Boelter, Tarry, Wis. Rapids	109	329	33	78	92	6	1	2	33	13	2	29	4	81	3	2	.237
Bohnet, Robert, Wis. Rapids	71	252	45	68	90	7	0	5	20	1	3	48	2	45	2	2	.270
Boothe, Charles, Cedar Rapids	38	101	9	25	31	6	0	0	11	1	0	21	0	23	1	1	.248
Bradley, Mark, Clinton	29	63	12	11	19	2	0	2	2	0	0	16	3	29	4	4	.175
Bravo, Luis, Wis. Rapids	109	395	57	100	125	15	5	0	32	5	2	38	5	32	41	10	.253
Breazeale, James, Appleton*	36	84	18	30	52	5	1	5	24	0	3	13	1	8	0	0	.357
Cannon, Stanley, Wis. Rapids*	50	168	25	39	49	5	1	1	12	5	3	26	0	38	9	2	.232
Carroll, Timothy, Quad Cities	19	44	8	8	9	1	0	0	6	2	0	8	0	12	3	0	.182
Castillo, M. Carmelo, Waterloo	49	138	25	28	44	5	1	3	12	2	1	20	1	29	15	4	.203
Chaney, Bruce, Waterloo	39	102	8	19	29	3	2	1	12	0	1	18	0	31	0	3	.186
Clark, Marcus, Waterloo*	3	10	3	6	10	1	0	1	1	0	0	1	0	1	0	0	.600

Player and Club	G.	AB.	R.	H.	TB.	2B.	3B.	HR.	RBI.	SH.	SF.	BB.	HP.	SO.	SB.	CS.	Pct.
Colletti, Manuel, Wis. Rapids†	69	223	33	46	51	5	0	0	19	5	1	62	0	34	6	1	.206
Colzie, Richard, Waterloo	14	23	6	9	11	2	0	0	4	0	1	0	1	4	1	0	.391
Cook, John, Wausau	37	106	25	25	30	5	0	0	8	1	2	22	4	19	7	1	.236
Craig, R. Dean, Wausau†	93	296	51	71	96	14	1	3	32	5	2	48	4	44	1	1	.240
Cruz, Jesus, Cedar Rapids*	8	9	2	0	0	0	0	0	0	0	0	0	0	4	0	0	.000
Cuarezma, Julio, Burlington	70	266	33	55	70	12	0	1	24	0	3	29	3	17	10	6	.207
Cummings, Robert, Cedar Rapids..	56	184	29	38	45	4	0	1	12	0	2	29	0	34	11	6	.207
Curry, Charles, Cedar Rapids	61	193	26	58	90	12	1	6	24	2	1	28	0	48	2	2	.301
Daniels, David, Appleton	113	395	59	104	134	5	8	3	43	7	4	66	1	83	31	9	.263
Davis, Stanley, Burlington†	126	441	76	113	195	21	2	19	81	0	5	73	4	95	36	11	.256
Davis, V. Samuel, Waterloo	119	386	57	90	129	15	0	8	40	6	3	37	1	63	18	6	.233
Deer, Robert, Cedar Rapids	29	86	7	18	23	0	1	1	16	0	1	7	0	34	3	1	.209
Dierberger, George, Wis. Rapids..	121	384	69	109	180	21	1	16	69	3	0	70	10	88	2	0	.284
Doss, Richard, Cedar Rapids	53	198	27	48	68	8	3	2	27	1	0	15	1	30	16	5	.242
Dovalis, Alexander, Wis. Rapids	28	87	11	24	29	5	0	0	7	0	1	11	0	17	0	0	.276
Duckhorn, Steven, Cedar Rapids	1	0	1	0	0	0	0	0	0	0	0	0	0	0	0	0	.000
Duncan, Columbus, Burlington	26	101	17	23	36	7	0	2	11	0	1	11	0	28	0	1	.228
Elliott, Mark, Clinton*	103	326	38	88	117	15	1	4	55	5	10	23	4	27	4	5	.270
English, James, Appleton	17	55	5	16	17	1	0	0	3	1	0	6	0	12	1	0	.291
Evans, Johnny, Burlington	121	412	69	113	154	21	1	6	62	2	5	71	10	59	3	5	.274
Freeman, M. Todd, Burlington	12	32	5	6	10	1	0	1	2	1	0	9	0	19	2	1	.188
Gaffney, William, Wausau	34	99	17	26	31	3	1	0	15	1	3	16	0	16	3	0	.263
Gandy, Chris, Clinton	49	144	18	30	48	4	1	4	12	2	0	14	5	33	2	0	.208
Garrett, Lynn, Waterloo	67	215	34	46	64	7	1	3	20	3	3	32	0	34	6	5	.214
Gbur, Paul, Appleton†	65	186	29	41	61	8	0	4	22	1	2	39	1	54	4	2	.220
Gilbert, Mark, Quad Cities†	117	407	80	128	154	12	7	0	55	4	3	65	8	51	50	22	.314
Gilmartin, Daniel, Burlington	36	104	9	16	19	3	0	0	9	5	1	18	3	31	1	1	.154
Glass, Timothy, Waterloo	98	314	50	77	128	9	0	14	52	0	1	50	1	101	5	3	.245
Gloyd, Timothy, Clinton	52	155	14	30	36	4	1	0	12	2	1	16	0	21	21	5	.194
Godley, Michael, Quad Cities*	13	30	3	8	10	2	0	0	2	2	0	7	0	4	3	0	.267
Gonzalez, Luis Antonio, Wis Rapids	2	3	0	0	0	0	0	0	0	0	0	0	0	0	0	0	.000
Gray, Lorenzo, Appleton	17	67	24	21	31	4	0	2	8	0	2	12	1	8	18	1	.313
Grout, Ronald, Wis Rapids	127	471	60	117	191	26	6	16	80	3	4	48	3	71	0	0	.248
Gutierrez, Israel, Wausau	33	111	10	28	36	3	1	1	9	0	1	11	1	22	0	2	.252
Hall, Larry, Appleton	60	211	20	47	56	4	1	1	22	1	3	37	4	32	7	4	.223
Hall, Rocky, Burlington†	84	291	47	68	74	2	2	0	31	4	2	52	2	37	26	3	.234
Hallstrom, William, Waterloo	103	315	36	88	104	14	1	0	20	10	2	26	7	39	12	1	.279
Hanley, John, Appleton	38	131	20	39	63	9	0	5	28	0	1	20	3	29	1	1	.298
Hart, Michael, Wausau	52	177	34	46	60	9	1	1	21	2	0	33	1	23	3	0	.260
Hedrick, Craig, Cedar Rapids*	66	193	28	39	61	11	1	3	28	1	0	30	4	53	7	6	.202
Henderson, Matthew, Wis Rapids*.	97	310	44	83	118	15	1	6	44	2	3	53	3	77	5	4	.268
Hernandez, Leonardo, Clinton	29	113	24	38	54	8	1	2	23	3	2	6	0	12	3	0	.336
Hernandez, Nicholas, Burlington	87	275	36	57	91	11	4	5	26	0	1	43	2	66	2	1	.207
Hicks, Joseph A., Quad Cities	132	461	78	138	210	23	5	13	74	5	5	75	4	77	24	6	.299
Hinson, Gary, Waterloo	52	191	21	39	53	8	0	2	23	1	1	15	2	37	3	3	.204
Hodgson, Gordon, Quad Cities	102	296	42	72	100	11	7	1	38	0	4	47	3	62	7	2	.243
Hubbard, Donald, Waterloo	90	338	50	105	161	21	1	11	69	3	5	33	2	43	8	8	.311
Hudgens, David, Waterloo*	127	422	87	123	239	34	2	26	85	2	6	78	4	97	18	7	.291
Hudson, Rodney, Waterloo	18	40	5	5	10	2	0	1	5	2	0	11	0	10	0	0	.125
Irvine, Edward, Burlington	71	306	37	76	99	8	6	1	16	1	2	22	1	32	22	11	.248
Jirschele, Michael, Wausau	127	407	64	98	142	15	4	7	54	3	2	77	11	78	7	3	.241
Johnson, Bobby, Wausau	124	433	89	131	223	20	0	24	79	1	3	89	3	78	4	0	.303
Johnson, Michael, Appleton	65	198	52	57	92	16	2	5	32	5	1	58	7	54	13	8	.288
Johnson, Randall S., Appleton*	105	339	57	89	151	25	5	9	46	2	4	61	5	66	2	1	.263
Keating, Dennis, Appleton	105	360	48	100	140	11	4	7	51	3	6	22	1	74	12	4	.278
Killebrew, Cameron, Wausau	55	163	26	33	60	6	0	7	29	2	2	27	1	64	3	0	.202
Kittle, Ron, Appleton	35	120	18	31	42	3	1	2	12	0	0	15	0	46	0	0	.258
Kizer, Harold, Quad Cities	75	273	38	80	107	14	5	1	48	4	10	33	2	42	11	2	.293
Kornfeld, Craig, Quad Cities	123	459	78	119	150	18	5	1	44	8	3	51	3	40	41	11	.259
Kyzer, Richard, Wis Rapids	106	377	53	88	117	8	0	7	47	4	7	24	3	30	3	1	.233
Lopez, Antonio, Wis Rapids..	130	505	78	144	220	25	3	15	71	0	1	25	5	53	11	3	.285
Lozado, William, Burlington	136	525	66	124	169	21	6	4	48	3	4	47	4	102	23	5	.236
Lucarelli, Vito, Appleton	68	209	29	57	102	14	2	9	36	3	4	27	2	72	1	1	.273
Mabee, Victor, Wausau	81	276	46	79	111	13	2	5	34	1	3	22	2	39	4	3	.286
Maher, Mark, Wis Rapids	44	138	22	35	61	3	1	7	26	1	1	22	4	28	2	0	.254
Maldonado, Candido, Clinton	50	158	25	37	58	13	1	2	26	0	4	17	1	29	5	4	.234
Malkin, John, Clinton	16	38	2	3	3	0	0	0	0	0	2	0	0	12	0	0	.079
Maples, Stephen, Clinton	53	113	10	21	28	5	1	0	13	5	0	10	2	35	5	2	.186
Marietta, Louis, Cedar Rapids	2	4	1	1	1	0	0	0	0	0	0	0	0	2	0	0	.250
Martinez, Tommy, Waterloo	13	32	1	10	13	0	0	1	6	1	0	0	1	15	1	1	.313
May, Ted, Quad Cities*	58	157	28	33	62	11	0	6	35	3	1	50	2	51	4	3	.210
McCrary, Arnold, Wausau *	92	296	47	76	104	9	2	5	31	2	3	36	2	31	19	3	.257
McMurray, Steven, Waterloo	63	148	24	28	45	5	0	4	17	4	1	24	0	37	1	0	.189
Mesa, Ivan, Appleton	108	392	60	111	157	21	2	7	50.	7	5	31	2	51	5	2	.283
Messmer, James, Quad Cities	47	153	17	38	41	3	0	0	17	2	1	18	2	23	3	2	.248

Player and Club	G.	AB.	R.	H.	TB.	2B.	3B.	HR.	RBI.	SH.	SF.	BB.	HP.	SO.	SB.	CS.	Pct.
Mitchell, James W., Quad Cities*	116	347	54	100	119	16	0	1	64	1	6	82	1	39	19	4	.288
Mohler, S. Keith, Clinton	32	91	12	18	21	3	0	0	11	0	0	8	3	17	5	2	.198
Mohr, Edwin, Quad Cities	106	330	36	61	79	15	0	1	34	13	3	39	1	78	2	7	.185
Moore, Edmund, Quad Cities	1	1	0	1	1	0	0	0	0	0	0	0	0	0	0	0	1.000
Morgan, William, Quad Cities	115	357	68	84	111	8	5	3	28	6	0	79	4	82	30	9	.235
Morton, Stanley, Cedar Rapids*	26	63	3	9	9	0	0	0	3	0	0	6	0	21	0	0	.143
Nelson, M. Kim, Wis Rapids	41	126	20	31	41	7	0	1	15	2	3	27	0	39	1	0	.246
Norwood, Steven, Burlington	1	1	0	0	0	0	0	0	0	0	0	0	0	1	0	0	.000
Oliver, Bruce, Cedar Rapids	106	325	41	64	90	11	0	5	36	0	3	45	8	86	10	6	.197
Oppenheimer, Juan, Cedar Rapids	26	49	5	9	13	1	0	1	7	0	1	13	0	7	2	1	.184
Owen, David, Quad Cities	45	129	23	18	21	3	0	0	4	3	0	38	0	25	14	2	.140
Padula, James, Burlington	83	254	31	60	84	13	1	3	30	0	1	51	0	92	6	0	.236
Payne, James, Wausau	107	375	55	97	122	12	2	3	42	5	1	35	6	80	21	6	.259
Peltz, Peter, Waterloo	122	403	94	122	168	22	3	6	66	0	2	95	1	48	25	8	.303
Plinski, Paul, Cedar Rapids	130	479	98	136	180	18	7	4	36	1	5	75	6	62	72	21	.284
Pone, Vincent, Burlington	43	121	17	31	38	7	0	0	9	1	1	24	3	42	1	1	.256
Rabb, John, Cedar Rapids†	125	447	63	118	196	19	1	19	90	2	7	36	6	75	7	7	.264
Raines, Ned, Cedar Rapids	111	329	51	86	97	11	0	0	25	1	1	51	0	53	39	10	.261
Ramirez, Russell, Burlington	36	108	16	22	36	6	1	2	12	0	1	19	0	29	3	2	.204
Rich, Kean, Cedar Rapids	25	49	6	7	10	3	0	0	8	0	0	18	0	21	2	2	.143
Rivera, German, Clinton	100	338	43	82	122	18	5	4	42	0	5	30	6	50	9	4	.243
Robbins, John Lee, Clinton*	97	297	52	86	101	13	1	0	38	0	2	52	0	47	22	7	.290
Robins, George, Burlington*	21	67	9	15	20	3	1	0	8	0	1	9	1	10	0	4	.224
Robinson, James, Burlington	91	319	31	66	79	6	2	1	30	0	3	20	1	82	12	5	.207
Rodriguez, Jose A., Wis Rapids	45	124	11	24	29	5	0	0	8	3	0	8	3	42	0	0	.194
Rohlfing, Wayne, Quad Cities	81	242	35	67	102	13	2	6	42	1	5	19	2	70	3	2	.277
Rojas, Francisco, Cedar Rapids*	99	296	26	79	103	12	0	4	36	1	0	29	5	45	11	5	.267
Rosenberg, Brendan, Wis Rapids	63	200	30	53	88	16	2	5	32	0	1	30	1	51	1	3	.265
Saavedra, Edwin, Waterloo	111	387	60	107	142	15	4	4	30	8	1	46	2	54	15	9	.276
Sax, David, Clinton	97	282	37	76	114	18	1	6	49	2	7	43	2	31	7	5	.270
Sax, Stephen, Clinton	115	386	64	112	137	15	2	2	52	2	7	57	3	30	25	8	.290
Schultz, Greg, Clinton	10	33	5	10	12	2	0	0	5	0	1	8	0	3	1	2	.303
Seegers, Patrick, Burlington	42	103	21	19	22	3	0	0	14	1	1	37	1	30	5	2	.184
Sheehy, Mark, Clinton	73	250	32	72	86	14	0	0	23	3	2	18	5	20	11	5	.288
Shepston, Michael, Quad Cities	72	192	30	42	56	6	1	2	25	1	1	43	2	32	3	3	.219
Shumate, Jack, Wis Rapids	4	10	3	3	3	0	0	0	1	0	0	1	0	4	0	0	.300
Skube, Robert, Burlington*	54	194	26	57	100	14	1	9	45	0	1	28	2	28	16	0	.294
Smith, Clay, Clinton*	51	174	17	38	47	4	1	1	15	2	1	16	3	33	2	0	.218
Spino, Thomas, Quad Cities	2	2	1	1	1	0	0	0	1	0	0	0	0	0	0	0	.500
Stockstill, David, Wausau*	127	459	88	130	248	23	7	27	101	1	4	84	2	54	3	1	.283
Stoltenberg, Scott, Wis Rapids	19	59	4	5	9	1	0	1	5	0	1	6	1	20	0	0	.085
Sutton, Philip, Cedar Rapids	127	477	64	120	142	10	6	0	51	9	2	52	2	64	29	15	.252
Szymarek, Paul, Cedar Rapids	17	49	14	14	40	2	0	8	16	0	0	11	1	15	6	2	.286
Taylor, Michael, Wausau*	44	141	20	34	50	3	2	3	21	4	2	16	0	27	7	1	.241
Teutsch, Mark, Appleton	1	0	1	0	0	0	0	0	0	0	0	0	0	0	0	0	.000
Thompson, Michael S., Wausau	20	73	11	16	26	4	0	2	9	0	1	10	0	8	4	2	.219
Thon, Francis, Cedar Rapids	59	194	22	53	63	6	2	0	14	2	0	10	5	25	4	7	.273
Torassa, George, Cedar Rapids	18	40	3	9	13	1	0	1	8	2	1	3	0	15	0	1	.225
Trevino, A. Ted, Quad Cities	40	137	19	33	51	6	0	4	20	2	0	18	0	29	3	0	.241
Turner, Lloyd, Wausau	38	107	20	19	23	1	0	1	10	0	0	11	1	27	3	2	.178
Tyson, Terry, Waterloo	13	54	7	14	21	4	0	1	11	2	0	2	1	5	4	1	.259
Villaescusa, Juan, Clinton*	4	6	0	0	0	0	0	0	0	0	0	0	0	1	0	0	.000
Vuksan, Jeffrey, Appleton	80	253	20	42	65	12	1	3	31	3	5	18	4	60	1	1	.166
Walker, Andrew, Quad Cities†	63	155	25	36	45	2	2	1	16	2	3	20	1	32	9	4	.232
Webster, Mitchell, Clinton†	123	473	95	154	191	17	7	2	40	8	2	58	6	58	54	21	.326
White, David, Appleton	128	429	68	97	149	15	2	11	52	2	2	69	0	122	3	3	.226
Wiggins, Alan, Clinton†	95	296	57	76	81	3	1	0	27	3	1	65	2	40	43	14	.257
Williams, Dan, Appleton*	3	7	0	0	0	0	0	0	1	0	0	4	0	3	0	0	.000
Winterfeldt, Todd, Wausau	105	393	57	103	164	34	0	9	68	3	8	49	1	59	7	5	.262
Woods, Ronald, Appleton	1	1	0	0	0	0	0	0	0	0	0	0	0	0	0	0	.000
Zisk, John, Wausau	92	288	46	79	129	18	1	10	47	2	5	54	3	80	0	4	.274

The following pitchers had no plate appearances primarily through use of designated hitters, listed alphabetically by club, games in parentheses:

APPLETON—Estrada, Luis (26); Evans, Randy (4); Friedrich, Gary (1); Hickey, Kevin (30); Hoffman, Guy (2); Hoffmann, Jerome (13); Jackman, Mark (20); Johnson, Charles (14); Maitland, Michael (21); Northey, Clifford (1); Platel, Mark (16); Richartz, Scott (22); Shaffer, Duane (3); Sivik, Michael (27); Smith, Jackie (1); Soth, Paul (23); Umdenstock, Robert (26); Vasquez, Dennis (19); Walters, Victor (11).

BURLINGTON—Boyce, Randall (6); DeHart, Gregory (4); Diaz, Roberto (43); Edwards, Larry (13); Gibson, Robert (25); Gibson, Steven (15); Gierhan, Samuel (6); Jones, Douglas R. (28); Kranitz, Richard (13); Lepson, Mark (24); Madden, Michael (5); Manderfield, Steve (32); Maxson, J. Daniel (15).

CEDAR RAPIDS—Anderson, Kelly (44); Bellomo, William (25); Chue, Jose (5); Cosio, Raymundo (7); Fisher, Glenn (5); Henderson, Robert (36); Martinez, Michael (13); Matrisciano, Ronald (17); Stadler, Jeffrey (26); Stember, Jeffrey (9); Sutherland, Matthew (25); Thornton, David (3); Wing, Harry (12).

CLINTON—Albert, Jeffrey (11); Alexander, Roberto (19); Bryant, Franklin (6); Ferst, Larry (23); Hershiser, Orel (15); Johnson, Kent (10); Joyce, Kevin F. (39); LaPointe, David P. (9); Nelson, Rodney (22); Oroz, Felix (14); Pena, Alejandro (21); Reeves, Mathew (25); Schmidt, Eric (13); White, Robert (8); Wickensheimer, Clinton (14); Wilczewski, Francis (8); Wright, Larry (23).

QUAD CITIES—Churchill, Norman (20); Clark, J. Randall (24); Cole, Joey (10); Madden, Robert (23); McClain, Joe (30); McClure, Richard (49); Morris, Thomas (20); Viskas, Steven (25); Wright, Michael R. (25).

WATERLOO—Asbell, John (2); Bullinger, D. Matthews (39); Dwyer, Scott (8); Fuson, Robin (20); Ganci, Louis (6); Hendry, Keith (24); Hoban, John (10); Hussey, Robert (12); Johnson, Gregory S. (32); Jones, Kirk (10); Leach, Ron (11); Rambis, Randall (41); Regan, Francis (8); Richard, Raymond (7); Walters, John (22); Warnecke, David (11); White, Larry (1); Wilder, Troy (12).

WAUSAU—Barnhart, Richard (29-2 with Waterloo); Cassidy, Reid (20-14 with Waterloo); Christianson, Alec (53); Davis, Ted (22); Eason, W. Gregory (5); Gaff, Brent (20); Goff, Wallace (15); Keenan, Kerry (16); Littrell, Jack (29); Lowe, Donald (26); Owens, Thomas (26); Romero, Ramon (17); Stutzriem, Gerald (10).

WISCONSIN RAPIDS—Belk, Charles (21); Blake, Robert (13); Dobbs, Gary (29); Francingues, Kenneth (21); Grove, James (4); Gurholt, Jack (13); Havens, Bradley (10); Jones, Robert A. (2); Kromy, Ted (29); Lamkey, William (19); Malone, Rubio (11); Mapel, Steven (15); Minarcin, John (15); Mulligan, Robert (3); Riley, Michael (6); Ungs, Michael (32); Voigt, Paul (14).

GRAND SLAM HOME RUNS—S. Davis, Lopez, 2 each; Bahns, Dierberger, Grout, Hicks, Hubbard, B. Johnson, M. Johnson, Killebrew, Kizer, Kyzer, Lozado, Mabee, Payne, Peltz, D. Sax, Skube, 1 each.

AWARDED FIRST BASE ON INTERFERENCE—Vuksan 4 (N. Hernandez 2, Glass, McMurray); Rich 3 (Craig, Glass, N. Hernandez); Plinski 2 (Padula, Shepston); S. Davis (Dierberger); Gbur (Dierberger); Jirschele (Bilardello); Mabee (Dierberger); Mohler (N. Hernandez); Peltz (B. Johnson).

CLUB FIELDING

Club	G.	PO.	A.	E.	DP.	PB.	Pct.	Club	G.	PO.	A.	E.	DP.	PB.	Pct.
Quad Cities	134	3370	1478	196	114	25	.961	Cedar Rapids	136	3375	1452	218	126	29	.957
Wausau	131	3246	1411	202	126	20	.958	Waterloo	135	3450	1426	235	119	35	.954
Clinton	133	3270	1362	205	101	30	.958	Wisconsin Rapids	133	3246	1384	240	97	22	.951
Appleton	136	3429	1444	219	118	10	.957	Burlington	138	3491	1529	290	117	33	.945

Triple Play—Burlington.

INDIVIDUAL FIELDING

FIRST BASEMEN

*Throws lefthanded.

Player and Club	G.	PO.	A.	E.	DP.	Pct.	Player and Club	G.	PO.	A.	E.	DP.	Pct.
Wiggins, Clinton	10	81	4	0	8	1.000	Duncan, Burlington	26	224	13	4	17	.983
Hodgson, Quad Cities	6	47	1	0	2	1.000	Evans, Burlington	32	300	19	6	29	.982
English, Appleton	5	29	2	0	3	1.000	Hicks, Quad Cities	130	1180	78	26	97	.980
D. Sax, Clinton	2	17	1	0	1	1.000	Anderson, Waterloo*	109	926	71	20	82	.980
Williams, Appleton*	2	15	0	0	1	1.000	Hanley, Appleton	8	47	3	1	9	.980
Davis, Waterloo	4	14	1	0	2	1.000	Zisk, Wausau	71	596	32	15	57	.977
Hubbard, Waterloo	2	12	1	0	0	1.000	Craig, Wausau	65	584	18	14	52	.977
White, Appleton	1	12	0	0	1	1.000	Lopez, Wisconsin Rapids	33	278	18	7	18	.977
Daniels, Appleton	1	4	1	0	0	1.000	Hudgens, Waterloo*	29	235	15	6	18	.977
Clark, Waterloo*	1	1	0	0	0	1.000	Grout, Wisconsin Rapids	72	595	43	18	46	.973
Curry, Cedar Rapids	35	306	16	3	19	.991	R. Johnson, Apl*	35	276	13	8	24	.973
Gray, Appleton	11	97	7	1	8	.990	Skube, Burlington*	4	31	3	1	3	.971
OLIVER, Cedar Rapids	95	806	38	9	75	.989	Gandy, Clinton	33	246	11	11	17	.959
Bahns, Appleton*	84	649	50	8	54	.989	Oppenheimer, C Rapids	14	81	1	4	5	.953
Bohnet, Wis Rapids	30	266	15	3	22	.989	Alvarez, Waterloo	4	14	2	1	1	.941
Elliott, Clinton*	98	808	61	11	66	.988	Doss, Cedar Rapids	3	22	3	2	2	.926
Davis, Burlington	77	696	33	11	51	.985	Hedrick, Cedar Rapids	2	12	0	1	1	.923

Triple Play—Davis, Burlington.

SECOND BASEMEN

Player and Club	G.	PO.	A.	E.	DP.	Pct.	Player and Club	G.	PO.	A.	E.	DP.	Pct.
Wiggins, Clinton	8	17	16	0	2	1.000	Payne, Wausau	7	11	7	1	1	.947
Kizer, Quad Cities	1	3	2	0	1	1.000	Smith, Clinton	25	28	38	4	8	.943
Gloyd, Clinton	1	2	1	0	0	1.000	Hall, Appleton	46	110	125	15	31	.940
Gray, Appleton	1	2	1	0	1	1.000	Gbur, Appleton	30	65	61	8	18	.940
Lozado, Burlington	1	1	2	0	1	1.000	Raines, Cedar Rapids	23	40	60	7	6	.935
Peltz, Waterloo	1	0	2	0	0	1.000	Padula, Burlington	2	8	6	1	2	.933
White, Appleton	1	0	1	0	0	1.000	Hinson, Waterloo	49	93	100	14	26	.932
Gonzalez, Wis Rapids	2	1	0	0	0	1.000	Messmer, Quad Cities	17	38	43	6	9	.931
Hallstrom, Waterloo	30	64	93	3	21	.981	Gilmartin, Burlington	25	55	63	9	11	.929
BOELTER, Wis Rapids	105	225	251	12	59	.975	Thon, Cedar Rapids	55	94	150	19	35	.928
Plinski, Cedar Rapids	63	121	155	7	38	.975	Hall, Burlington	48	100	140	20	25	.923
Sheehy, Clinton	73	139	179	12	42	.964	Dovalis, Wis Rapids	10	23	25	4	2	.923
Alvarez, Waterloo	64	120	145	11	24	.960	Gutierrez, Wausau	3	5	5	1	0	.909
Jirschele, Wausau	126	285	333	27	99	.958	S. Sax, Clinton	34	65	66	14	18	.903
Cuarezma, Burlington	60	128	165	15	32	.951	English, Appleton	8	18	18	4	4	.900
Bauer, Appleton	59	138	134	14	23	.951	Ahlert, Quad Cities	5	7	2	1	2	.900
Kornfeld, Quad Cities	116	267	286	29	61	.950	Rodriguez, Wis Rapids	23	39	37	9	7	.894
							Robins, Burlington	6	12	7	4	1	.826

Triple Play—Gilmartin.

THIRD BASEMEN

Player and Club	G.	PO.	A.	E.	DP.	Pct.
Hall, Appleton	6	12	16	0	3	1.000
Gutierrez, Wausau	9	2	19	0	4	1.000
Hanley, Appleton	2	1	5	0	1	1.000
Hudson, Waterloo	1	0	3	0	0	1.000
Hallstrom, Waterloo	1	0	2	0	0	1.000
Hinson, Waterloo	1	0	1	0	0	1.000
Padula, Burlington	1	0	1	0	0	1.000
Ramirez, Burlington	1	0	1	0	0	1.000
Smith, Clinton	1	0	1	0	0	1.000
Jirschele, Wausau	2	0	1	0	0	1.000
WINTERFELDT, Wau.	105	70	243	16	17	.951
Rohlfing, Quad Cities	19	8	26	2	1	.944
Rivera, Clinton	98	74	199	17	16	.941
Hernandez, Clinton	29	22	66	6	1	.936
Mitchell, Quad Cities	111	79	230	22	21	.934
Doss, Cedar Rapids	50	52	117	14	15	.923
Cuarezma, Burlington	10	12	12	2	1	.923
Plinski, Cedar Rapids	42	34	94	11	9	.921
Hubbard, Waterloo	10	8	15	2	1	.920
Nelson, Wis Rapids	39	31	86	11	5	.914
D. Sax, Clinton	4	1	9	1	0	.909
Peltz, Waterloo	114	78	239	32	17	.908
Raines, Cedar Rapids	37	27	77	11	11	.904
White, Appleton	126	102	258	39	17	.902
Kyzer, Wisconsin Rapids	74	74	155	25	14	.902
Rabb, Cedar Rapids	7	8	8	2	1	.889
Freeman, Burlington	11	11	19	4	3	.882
Thompson, Wausau	18	15	29	6	2	.880
Gray, Appleton	4	3	4	1	0	.875
Evans, Burlington	40	35	61	14	3	.873
Gilmartin, Burlington	10	6	20	4	1	.867
Messmer, Quad Cities	24	14	37	8	3	.864
Oliver, Cedar Rapids	3	4	7	2	0	.846
Hall, Appleton	33	18	71	17	4	.840
Bohnet, Wis Rapids	21	11	40	11	3	.823
Alvarez, Waterloo	22	8	31	9	1	.813
Wiggins, Clinton	4	3	5	2	1	.800
Gbur, Appleton	4	0	4	1	0	.800
Pone, Burlington	42	23	58	25	3	.764
Davis, Waterloo	2	3	3	2	1	.750
S. Sax, Clinton	4	1	4	2	0	.714
Walker, Quad Cities	2	2	0	1	0	.667

SHORTSTOPS

Player and Club	G.	PO.	A.	E.	DP.	Pct.
Gilmartin, Burlington	1	2	5	0	1	1.000
English, Appleton	2	4	3	0	0	1.000
Keating, Appleton	2	1	4	0	0	1.000
Raines, Cedar Rapids	2	1	1	0	1	1.000
Mitchell, Quad Cities	2	1	0	0	0	1.000
Chaney, Waterloo	39	41	110	6	23	.962
Gaffney, Wausau	34	59	98	7	15	.957
Boelter, Wis. Rapids	4	7	13	1	2	.952
Owen, Quad Cities	45	56	139	11	25	.947
Gbur, Appleton	23	27	58	5	17	.944
Kizer, Quad Cities	72	89	227	19	35	.943
SUTTON, Cedar Rapids	125	167	356	34	67	.939
Hall, Appleton	7	4	11	1	0	.938
Gutierrez, Wausau	9	9	20	2	4	.935
Mesa, Appleton	106	151	295	32	58	.933
Schultz, Clinton	9	14	27	3	4	.932
Colletti, Wis. Rapids	69	79	184	20	32	.929
Tyson, Waterloo	13	13	38	4	6	.927
Lozado, Burlington	135	244	445	64	81	.915
Dovalis, Wis. Rapids	12	17	34	5	4	.911
Payne, Wausau	92	94	265	36	44	.909
Hallstrom, Waterloo	75	91	180	27	33	.909
Plinski, Cedar Rapids	14	15	25	4	4	.909
Wiggins, Clinton	62	79	173	30	28	.894
Gloyd, Clinton	50	62	133	23	24	.894
Alvarez, Waterloo	25	37	54	11	12	.892
Kyzer, Wis. Rapids	32	43	99	18	14	.888
Smith, Clinton	16	12	33	6	4	.882
Rodriguez, Wis. Rapids	20	27	70	16	3	.858
Kornfeld, Quad Cities	4	9	15	4	4	.857
Messmer, Quad Cities	6	6	18	4	4	.857
Peltz, Waterloo	5	1	5	1	0	.857
Walker, Quad Cities	12	6	26	6	2	.842
Turner, Wausau	4	5	15	5	4	.800
Rivera, Clinton	3	5	6	4	1	.733
Cuarezma, Burlington	1	0	0	1	0	.000

Triple Play—Lozado.

OUTFIELDERS

Player and Club	G.	PO.	A.	E.	DP.	Pct.
Hart, Wausau	42	79	3	0	1	1.000
R. Johnson, Appleton*	41	62	4	0	1	1.000
Killebrew, Wausau	27	37	1	0	0	1.000
Szymarek, Cedar Rapids	13	19	1	0	0	1.000
Wiggins, Clinton	11	16	0	0	0	1.000
Carroll, Quad Cities	10	14	1	0	0	1.000
Godley, Quad Cities	13	10	0	0	0	1.000
Davis, Burlington	6	9	0	0	0	1.000
Payne, Wausau	3	5	1	0	0	1.000
Plinski, Cedar Rapids	5	6	0	0	0	1.000
Clark, Waterloo*	2	3	0	0	0	1.000
Robins, Burlington*	2	2	1	0	0	1.000
Gray, Appleton	2	2	0	0	0	1.000
Bohnet, Wis. Rapids	1	1	0	0	0	1.000
D. Sax, Clinton	4	1	0	0	0	1.000
Beyers, Clinton	74	152	6	3	2	.981
Hubbard, Waterloo	80	129	5	3	2	.978
Cannon, Wis. Rapids*	48	86	5	2	1	.978
Hanley, Appleton	24	39	5	1	2	.978
Maldonado, Clinton	48	81	5	2	1	.977
Hedrick, Cedar Rapids	59	79	5	2	0	.977
GILBERT, Quad Cities	114	198	3	5	2	.976
Seegers, Burlington	36	76	7	2	0	.976
Garrett, Waterloo	60	76	4	2	1	.976
Saavedra, Waterloo	104	188	8	6	3	.970
Morton, Cedar Rapids*	23	31	1	1	0	.970
Mohr, Quad Cities	104	149	7	5	1	.969
Bradley, Clinton	25	29	2	1	0	.969
Robinson, Burlington	88	154	20	6	5	.967
Robbins, Clinton	69	110	6	4	1	.967
Cook, Wausau	31	54	4	2	1	.967
Webster, Clinton*	122	272	10	10	2	.966
Davis, Waterloo	114	219	16	9	6	.963
Adams, Waterloo	23	48	4	2	0	.963
Bailey, Burlington	134	243	11	10	2	.962
Stockstill, Wausau	124	157	20	7	2	.962
S. Sax, Clinton	49	45	5	2	0	.962
Henderson, Wis. Rapids	92	155	12	7	1	.960
Rich, Cedar Rapids	15	21	3	1	0	.960
McCrary, Wausau*	85	134	6	6	2	.959
Irvine, Burlington	69	150	9	7	3	.958
Morgan, Quad Cities	114	192	7	9	3	.957
Rosenberg, Wis. Rapids	62	124	5	6	0	.956
Daniels, Appleton	109	208	9	11	0	.952
Benson, Cedar Rapids	106	174	6	9	1	.952
M. Johnson, Appleton	56	122	10	7	4	.950
Mabee, Wausau	57	90	6	5	3	.950
Bravo, Wis. Rapids	106	200	13	12	1	.947
Rabb, Cedar Rapids	27	32	3	2	1	.946
Hodgson, Quad Cities	54	47	5	3	0	.945
Bienek, Appleton*	100	155	5	10	0	.941
Keating, Appleton	79	139	10	10	1	.937

OUTFIELDERS—Continued

Player and Club	G.	PO.	A.	E.	DP.	Pct.
Raines, Cedar Rapids.....	39	81	7	6	1	.936
Skube, Burlington*.....	43	92	7	7	0	.934
Baker, Cedar Rapids.....	40	91	7	7	2	.933
Rojas, Cedar Rapids*.....	86	128	10	10	4	.932
Stoltenberg, Wis. Rapids	18	26	1	2	0	.931
Mohler, Clinton.............	19	26	1	2	0	.931
Ramirez, Burlington.....	33	33	0	3	0	.917
Turner, Wausau.............	27	30	2	3	1	.914
Deer, Cedar Rapids.....	27	35	1	4	0	.900
Taylor, Wausau.............	15	27	0	3	0	.900
Walker, Quad Cities.....	25	17	1	2	0	.900
Hudgens, Waterloo*.....	10	9	0	1	0	.900
Lopez, Wis. Rapids.....	81	118	7	15	0	.893
Rohlfing, Quad Cities..	5	7	1	1	1	.889
Agapay, Appleton.....	10	8	0	1	0	.889
Castillo, Waterloo.....	38	54	1	7	1	.887
Cruz, Cedar Rapids*.....	6	6	1	1	0	.875
Kittle, Appleton.....	6	6	0	1	0	.857
Colzie, Waterloo.....	8	6	0	1	0	.857
Padula, Burlington.....	4	5	0	1	0	.833
Zisk, Wausau.....	4	3	0	1	0	.750
Oppenheimer, C. Rapids	4	4	0	2	0	.667

CATCHERS

Player and Club	G.	PO.	A.	E.	DP.	PB.	Pct.
Shumate, Wis. Rapids	4	14	0	0	1		1.000
Dovalis, Wis. Rapids ..	5	9	2	0	0		1.000
Breazeale, Appleton	1	2	0	0	0		1.000
Hicks, Quad Cities......	1	1	1	0	0	4	1.000
SHEPSTON, Q. Cities	70	443	61	4	9	6	.992
Bilardello, Clinton ..	50	283	31	3	5	7	.991
Hudson, Waterloo.....	16	95	13	1	3	5	.991
Trevino, Quad Cities ..	35	221	25	3	1	6	.988
Malkin, Clinton........	16	75	9	1	1	4	.988
May, Quad Cities	38	210	25	3	3	9	.987
Lucarelli, Clinton	61	378	46	7	4	2	.984
Vuksan, Appleton	77	442	68	10	9	8	.981
Craig, Wausau	26	179	19	4	0	1	.980
Boothe, Cedar Rapids.	24	124	23	3	4	4	.980
Lopez, Wis. Rapids ...	7	45	4	1	0	2	.980
Cummings, C. Rapids	45	263	45	7	5	13	.978
Maples, Clinton	53	237	33	6	1	9	.978
Johnson, Wausau ..	109	666	86	18	9	19	.977
Dierberger, Wis. Rap..	101	597	84	16	6	15	.977
Torassa, C. Rapids......	14	69	8	2	0	1	.975
Glass, Waterloo........	83	491	28	14	7	18	.974
D. Sax, Clinton........	44	207	22	6	0	10	.974
Padula, Burlington ...	68	372	72	14	7	13	.969
Rabb, Cedar Rapids ..	61	352	47	13	7	11	.968
Hernandez, Burl.	71	389	48	15	5	20	.967
Kittle, Appleton	5	27	1	1	0	0	.966
Maher, Wis. Rapids ..	21	97	17	5	0	3	.958
McMurray, Waterloo..	63	288	35	16	4	12	.953

PITCHERS

Player and Club	G.	PO.	A.	E.	DP.	Pct.
Ferst, Clinton	23	4	29	0	0	1.000
Morris, Quad Cities*.....	20	3	22	0	0	1.000
Richard, Waterloo	7	4	19	0	1	1.000
Moore, Quad Cities	28	6	13	0	0	1.000
C. Johnson, Appleton	14	5	13	0	0	1.000
Blake, Wis. Rapids*.....	13	6	11	0	2	1.000
S. Gibson, Burlington.....	15	4	13	0	1	1.000
Maxson, Burlington	15	5	12	0	1	1.000
Teutsch, Appleton	26	4	13	0	3	1.000
Dobbs, Wis. Rapids	29	4	11	0	0	1.000
Anderson, Cedar Rapids	43	3	12	0	0	1.000
Lamkey, Wis. Rapids ...	19	3	11	0	0	1.000
Havens, Wis. Rapids*...	10	1	11	0	1	1.000
Gurholt, Wis. Rapids*...	13	4	8	0	0	1.000
Madden, Burlington	5	1	10	0	1	1.000
Goff, Wausau*.....	15	1	10	0	1	1.000
Wing, Cedar Rapids	12	2	5	0	0	1.000
Schmidt, Clinton*.....	13	0	7	0	0	1.000
Chue, Cedar Rapids.....	3	1	5	0	0	1.000
LaPointe, Clinton	9	1	5	0	0	1.000
Hoban, Waterloo.....	10	1	5	0	0	1.000
Johnson, Clinton.....	10	2	4	0	0	1.000
Matrisciano, Ced. Rapids	17	3	3	0	0	1.000
Gierhan, Burlington	6	1	3	0	1	1.000
Warnecke, Waterloo	11	2	2	0	0	1.000
Francingues, Wis. Rap..	21	0	4	0	1	1.000
Grove, Wis. Rapids*.....	4	1	2	0	0	1.000
Boyce, Burlington*.....	6	2	1	0	0	1.000
Wilczewski, Clinton	8	1	2	0	0	1.000
Cole, Quad Cities	10	0	3	0	0	1.000
Martinez, Cedar Rapids .	13	0	3	0	0	1.000
Barnhart, Wat-Wau	29	0	3	0	0	1.000
Northey, Appleton	1	0	2	0	0	1.000
Smith, Appleton*.....	1	0	2	0	0	1.000
Hoffman, Appleton*.....	2	0	2	0	0	1.000
Riley, Wis. Rapids	6	1	1	0	0	1.000
Cosio, Cedar Rapids	7	1	1	0	0	1.000
Stutzriem, Wausau*.....	10	1	1	0	0	1.000
White, Waterloo	1	0	1	0	0	1.000
Shaffer, Appleton	3	0	1	0	0	1.000
UNGS, Wis. Rapids	32	11	25	1	0	.973
Hickey, Appleton*.....	29	12	22	1	3	.971
Hendry, Waterloo	24	11	22	1	1	.971
Marietta, Cedar Rapids..	28	11	20	1	0	.969
Johnson, Waterloo	32	8	23	1	1	.969
Oroz, Clinton*.....	14	3	24	1	0	.964
Jones, Burlington	28	11	43	2	2	.964
Viskas, Quad Cities	25	8	18	1	1	.963
Reeves, Clinton*.....	25	4	21	1	1	.962
Sivik, Appleton	27	10	15	1	0	.962
Christianson, Wausau ...	53	5	20	1	2	.962
Duckhorn, Cedar Rapids	26	11	27	2	2	.950
Spino, Quad Cities*.....	28	10	43	3	3	.946
Richartz, Appleton	18	8	9	1	2	.944
Wright, Clinton	23	14	36	3	3	.943
Kranitz, Clinton	13	11	22	2	2	.943
Hershiser, Clinton	15	6	9	1	2	.938
Vasquez, Appleton	19	2	13	1	0	.938
Churchill, Quad Cities*..	20	3	11	1	2	.933
Estrada, Appleton	26	5	9	1	0	.933
Minarcin, Wis. Rapids...	15	11	15	2	2	.929
Platel, Appleton	16	5	21	2	2	.929
Clark, Quad Cities	24	11	40	4	3	.927
Fuson, Waterloo	20	13	25	3	1	.927
Walters, Waterloo	21	8	17	2	1	.926
Mapel, Wis. Rapids	25	5	31	3	1	.923
Stadler, Cedar Rapids ...	26	7	17	2	0	.923
Romero, Wausau*.....	17	1	11	1	0	.923
Jackman, Appleton*.....	20	0	12	1	0	.923
Sutherland, C. Rapids*..	25	10	25	3	1	.921
Maitland, Appleton*.....	20	2	21	2	0	.920
Madden, Quad Cities	23	2	21	2	2	.920
Wilder, Waterloo*.....	12	3	19	2	2	.917
Rambis, Waterloo	41	10	12	2	0	.917
Diaz, Burlington	43	5	17	2	1	.917
Bargfeldt, Quad Cities ...	25	3	8	1	1	.917
R. Gibson, Burlington ...	25	7	25	3	2	.914
Bellomo, Cedar Rapids...	25	10	32	4	0	.913
Davis, Wausau	22	11	29	4	4	.909
Wickensheimer, Clinton	14	2	18	2	1	.909
Bullinger, Waterloo*.....	39	4	6	1	0	.909
Owens, Wausau	26	5	22	3	1	.900

PITCHERS—Continued

Player and Club	G.	PO.	A.	E.	DP.	Pct.	Player and Club	G.	PO.	A.	E.	DP.	Pct.
Kromy, Wis. Rapids	29	8	19	3	2	.900	Alexander, Clinton	19	10	9	3	1	.864
Cassidy, Wat-Wau	20	6	12	2	0	.900	Umdenstock, Appleton	26	6	12	3	0	.857
Pena, Clinton	21	5	13	2	0	.900	DeHart, Burlington	6	1	5	1	0	.857
Woods, Appleton	23	6	12	2	1	.900	Soth, Appleton	23	4	18	4	1	.846
Hoffmann, Appleton	13	1	8	1	1	.900	Leach, Waterloo*	11	3	8	2	0	.846
Joyce, Clinton*	39	2	7	1	0	.900	Nelson, Clinton	22	3	8	2	0	.846
Norwood, Burlington	22	5	19	3	1	.889	Littrell, Wausau	29	1	9	2	2	.833
Dwyer, Waterloo	8	1	7	1	0	.889	Bryant, Clinton	6	1	4	1	0	.833
Walters, Appleton	11	1	7	1	1	.889	Jones, Waterloo	10	1	4	1	0	.833
Gaff, Wausau	20	4	27	4	2	.886	McClain, Quad Cities	30	4	15	4	2	.826
Henderson, Ced. Rapids.	36	6	16	3	2	.880	Wright, Quad Cities*	25	3	11	3	1	.824
Lowe, Wausau	26	5	23	4	2	.875	Lepson, Burlington	24	9	22	7	2	.816
Edwards, Burlington*	13	3	11	2	1	.875	Belk, Wis. Rapids	21	0	4	1	1	.800
Eason, Wausau*	5	0	7	1	0	.875	Ganci, Waterloo	6	2	4	2	0	.750
Regan, Waterloo	8	2	5	1	0	.875	Malone, Wis. Rapids*	11	1	5	2	1	.750
Voigt, Wis. Rapids	14	2	5	1	0	.875	Albert, Clinton	11	1	2	1	0	.750
Manderfield, Bur*	32	0	7	1	1	.875	McClure, Quad Cities	49	2	6	3	1	.727
Stember, Cedar Rapids ..	9	3	10	2	1	.867	Jones, Wis. Rapids*	2	0	1	1	0	.500
Hussey, Waterloo	12	8	11	3	0	.864	Evans, Appleton	4	1	0	1	0	.500
Keenan, Wausau	16	4	15	3	1	.864	White, Clinton*	8	0	1	1	0	.500
							Thornton, Cedar Rapids	3	0	0	1	0	.000

The following players did not have any recorded accepted chances; therefore, are not listed in the fielding averages at those positions; Asbell, p; Fisher, p; Friedrich*, p; Martinez, of; Mulligan. p. Villaescusa appeared as designated hitter and pinch-hitter only.

CLUB PITCHING

Club	G.	CG.	ShO.	Sv.	IP.	H.	R.	ER.	HR.	BB.	Int. BB.	HB.	SO.	WP.	Bk.	ERA.
Waterloo	135	43	11	26	1150	999	571	423	78	636	20	28	826	64	9	3.31
Clinton	133	35	12	23	1090	944	566	430	49	533	11	49	775	89	17	3.55
Quad Cities	134	29	12	24	1123	983	570	454	45	617	24	39	841	87	9	3.64
Wisconsin Rapids	133	47	8	9	1082	1091	645	474	116	508	11	33	723	51	7	3.94
Wausau	131	41	6	18	1082	1085	644	513	79	615	20	34	813	62	8	4.27
Appleton	136	16	4	25	1143	1218	698	568	78	707	27	43	804	77	15	4.47
Burlington	136	57	3	8	1164	1258	765	593	82	588	9	37	702	104	10	4.59
Cedar Rapids	136	44	5	16	1125	1137	737	581	85	654	12	61	775	101	9	4.65

PITCHERS' RECORDS

(Leading Qualifiers for Earned-Run Average Leadership—109 or More Innings)

*Throws lefthanded.

Pitcher—Club	G.	GS.	CG.	ShO.	W.	L.	Sv.	Pct.	IP.	H.	R.	ER.	HR.	BB.	Int. BB.	HB.	SO.	WP.	ERA.
Jones, Burlington	28	20	16	3	10	10	0	.500	190	144	63	37	5	73	1	8	115	5	1.75
Fuson, Waterloo	20	20	12	3	12	4	0	.750	149	113	58	41	9	89	3	4	107	9	2.48
Clark, Quad Cities	24	24	9	2	16	5	0	.762	171	144	64	48	4	63	2	0	86	9	2.53
Viskas, Quad Cities	25	24	4	3	14	6	0	.700	161	120	59	49	4	66	1	4	135	9	2.74
Reeves, Clinton*	25	24	7	3	8	8	0	.500	142	129	57	45	4	74	1	7	88	8	2.85
Gaff, Wausau	20	20	10	2	10	5	0	.667	145	147	71	48	10	48	1	3	99	7	2.98
Mapel, Wis. Rapids	15	15	11	1	8	7	0	.533	117	96	48	39	10	37	0	4	89	0	3.00
Ungs, Wis.Rapids	32	19	8	2	9	9	1	.500	171	156	86	59	17	68	4	5	104	4	3.11
Spino, Quad Cities*	24	23	6	1	9	9	1	.500	162	141	74	57	9	81	3	4	102	10	3.17
Sutherland, Ced. Rap*	25	25	9	0	13	8	0	.619	167	145	86	63	6	113	1	2	118	11	3.40
Kromy, Wis Rapids	29	22	11	2	8	11	0	.421	159	177	87	60	17	38	0	5	87	5	3.40

Departmental Leaders: G—Christianson, 53; GS—Duckhorn, Owens, 26; CG-D. Jones, 16; ShO—Fuson, D. Jones, Reeves, Viskas, 3; W—Clark, 16; L—Duckhorn, 17; Sv-Joyce, McClure, 14; Pct.–J. Walters, .846; IP-D. Jones, 190; H—Lepson, 183; R—Duckhorn, 128; ER—Duckhorn, 114; HR—Duckhorn, Kromy, Ungs, 17; BB—Duckhorn, 117; IBB—Christianson, 8; HB—Duckhorn, 16; SO—Owens, 136; WP—Duckhorn, 21.

(All Pitchers—Listed Alphabetically)

Pitcher—Club	G.	GS.	CG.	ShO.	W.	L.	Sv.	Pct.	IP.	H.	R.	ER.	HR.	BB.	Int. BB.	HB.	SO.	WP.	ERA.
Albert, Clinton	11	0	0	0	4	0	1	1.000	20	14	4	3	1	7	1	0	13	1	1.35
Alexander, Clinton	19	19	4	1	8	5	0	.615	106	100	61	46	4	45	2	7	66	6	3.91
Anderson, Cedar Rapids ..	43	8	2	0	6	9	9	.400	92	90	63	49	9	61	4	1	77	8	4.79
Asbell, Waterloo	2	0	0	0	0	0	0	.000	3	5	4	4	0	5	0	0	6	0	12.00
Bargfeldt, Quad Cities	25	1	1	1	4	2	2	.667	49	47	30	24	2	34	4	5	39	3	4.41
Barnhart, 2 Wat-27 Wau ..	29	0	0	0	2	2	5	.500	45	41	32	25	1	44	2	1	55	4	5.00
Belk, Wis Rapids	21	0	0	1	1	2	0	.500	37	33	18	13	5	8	1	1	26	2	3.16
Bellomo, Cedar Rapids..	25	20	5	2	6	9	0	.400	134	142	81	60	12	50	1	8	99	12	4.03
Blake, Wis Rapids*	13	9	4	1	7	2	0	.778	81	68	34	25	4	37	0	1	58	2	2.78

Pitcher–Club	G.	GS.	CG.	ShO.	W.	L.	Sv.	Pct.	IP.	H.	R.	ER.	HR.	BB.	Int. BB.	HB.	SO.	WP.	ERA.
Boyce, Burlington*	6	0	0	0	1	0	2	1.000	14	9	4	4	0	6	0	0	7	0	2.57
Bryant, Clinton	6	2	0	0	0	1	0	.000	17	21	16	13	0	21	3	2	8	4	6.88
Bullinger, Waterloo*	39	0	0	0	5	5	5	.500	47	49	31	21	4	28	2	1	49	2	4.02
Cassidy, 14 Wat-6 Wau	20	19	5	2	6	7	0	.462	120	106	61	46	10	84	1	2	70	7	3.45
Christianson, Wau	53	0	0	0	10	7	12	.588	91	64	29	20	6	44	8	2	85	2	1.98
Chue, Cedar Rapids	3	3	0	0	0	2	0	.000	14	20	12	6	0	11	0	0	5	2	3.86
Churchill, Quad Cities*	20	4	0	0	4	3	1	.571	48	55	35	24	2	21	0	3	39	3	4.50
Clark, Quad Cities	24	24	9	2	16	5	0	.762	171	144	64	48	4	63	2	0	86	9	2.53
Cole, Quad Cities	10	0	0	0	2	0	0	1.000	18	24	20	19	1	15	0	1	13	5	9.50
Colzie, Waterloo	3	0	0	0	0	0	0	.000	3	4	1	1	0	2	0	0	1	0	3.00
Cosio, Cedar Rapids	7	1	0	0	1	1	1	.500	16	21	18	17	1	14	0	0	16	6	9.56
Davis, Wausau	22	22	9	1	12	9	0	.571	148	151	83	68	13	69	2	4	94	4	4.14
DeHart, Burlington	6	6	0	0	0	4	0	.000	28	36	33	23	3	22	0	3	16	6	7.39
Diaz, Appleton	43	3	2	0	8	6	5	.571	133	155	84	69	13	35	2	4	60	11	4.67
Dobbs, Wis Rapids*	29	5	0	0	1	7	3	.125	56	73	55	43	10	35	1	3	51	7	6.91
Duckhorn, Cedar Rapids	26	26	9	1	6	17	0	.261	156	150	128	104	17	117	1	16	78	21	6.00
Dwyer, Waterloo	8	4	0	0	1	2	0	.333	23	28	18	16	0	13	1	0	15	3	6.26
Eason, Wausau*	5	5	1	0	3	1	0	.750	34	27	17	15	3	26	0	1	13	0	3.97
Edwards, Burlington*	13	5	1	0	1	2	0	.333	49	67	39	30	5	28	1	1	19	4	5.51
Estrada, Appleton	26	12	1	1	3	7	0	.300	103	107	63	52	9	70	1	3	85	6	4.54
Evans, Appleton	4	0	0	1	0	0	1	1.000	11	5	1	1	0	7	0	0	19	0	0.82
Ferst, Clinton	23	12	1	0	6	10	1	.375	106	98	54	48	7	49	0	3	61	10	4.08
Fisher, Cedar Rapids	5	0	0	0	0	0	0	.000	6	7	5	3	1	5	0	0	8	2	4.50
Francingues, Wis Rapids	21	0	0	0	1	1	2	.500	30	33	25	18	4	22	2	0	25	3	5.40
Friedrich, Appleton*	1	1	0	0	0	0	0	.000	1	2	3	3	0	1	0	0	0	0	27.00
Fuson, Waterloo	20	20	12	3	12	4	0	.750	149	113	58	41	9	89	3	4	107	9	2.48
Gaff, Wausau	20	20	10	2	10	5	0	.667	145	147	71	48	10	48	1	3	99	7	2.98
Ganci, Waterloo	6	0	0	0	0	0	0	.000	15	17	11	8	1	8	0	1	15	2	4.80
R. Gibson, Burlington	25	17	9	0	5	12	1	.294	137	152	99	84	9	81	2	1	111	11	5.52
S. Gibson, Burlington	15	15	3	0	5	8	0	.385	67	92	63	55	2	42	0	4	36	12	7.39
Gierhan, Burlington	6	1	0	0	0	1	0	.000	11	10	7	6	0	10	0	3	3	3	4.91
Goff, Wausau*	15	11	0	0	2	6	0	.250	62	68	49	42	3	51	1	3	72	2	6.10
Grove, Wis Rapids	4	1	0	0	0	1	0	.000	7	14	11	11	1	11	0	0	3	2	14.14
Gurholt, Wis Rapids	13	9	4	0	2	3	0	.400	66	66	44	29	10	35	0	0	43	4	3.95
Havens, Wis Rapids*	10	10	4	0	6	1	0	.857	73	62	35	34	13	18	0	0	80	5	4.19
Henderson, Cedar Rapids	36	2	0	0	3	3	3	.500	81	85	55	45	5	55	3	6	59	7	5.00
Hendry, Waterloo	24	17	7	0	7	8	1	.467	123	133	79	67	12	67	3	2	73	4	4.90
Hershiser, Clinton	15	4	1	0	4	0	2	1.000	43	43	13	10	2	17	0	2	33	5	2.09
Hickey, Appleton*	29	15	4	0	5	10	3	.333	121	122	64	48	2	71	3	3	100	5	3.57
Hoban, Waterloo	10	8	0	0	5	2	0	.714	43	32	26	22	4	37	0	0	18	3	4.60
Hoffman, Appleton*	2	0	0	0	0	1	0	.000	5	2	0	0	0	1	0	0	4	1	0.00
Hoffman, Appleton	13	0	0	0	2	4	1	.333	24	23	14	13	3	14	4	0	11	2	4.88
Hussey, Waterloo	12	12	4	1	5	5	0	.500	83	65	36	33	7	40	1	1	56	6	3.58
Jackman, Appleton*	20	4	1	0	2	3	4	.400	55	53	30	21	1	29	1	2	40	5	3.44
C. Johnson, Appleton	14	10	0	0	4	4	0	.500	65	67	45	38	3	47	2	4	50	4	5.26
Johnson, Waterloo	32	8	2	1	5	6	5	.455	102	93	48	32	7	36	2	3	67	3	2.82
Johnson, Clinton	10	0	0	0	1	0	0	1.000	18	13	11	2	6	0	0	10	2	5.50	
Jones, Burlington	28	20	16	3	10	10	0	.500	190	144	63	37	5	73	1	8	115	5	1.75
Jones, Waterloo	10	0	0	0	1	1	0	.500	18	17	15	14	1	11	1	1	17	4	7.00
Jones, Wis Rapids*	2	2	0	0	0	2	0	.000	5	9	14	6	1	10	0	1	2	1	10.80
Joyce, Clinton*	39	0	0	0	5	3	14	.625	62	38	20	17	3	26	1	1	90	7	2.47
Keenan, Wausau	16	11	3	0	6	6	0	.500	86	89	56	39	6	42	1	4	74	4	4.08
Kranitz, Burlington	13	13	8	0	4	9	0	.308	100	111	50	36	6	41	1	2	95	9	3.24
Kromy, Wis Rapids	29	22	11	2	8	11	0	.421	159	177	87	60	17	38	0	5	87	5	3.40
Lamkey, Wis Rapids	19	0	0	0	7	2	1	.778	44	31	15	9	3	26	2	5	21	0	1.84
LaPointe, Clinton	9	4	0	0	3	1	0	.750	31	37	32	19	0	19	1	2	14	3	5.52
Leach, Waterloo*	11	11	3	0	5	3	0	.625	79	60	42	37	4	40	3	2	79	1	2.51
Lepson, Burlington	24	24	9	0	5	13	0	.278	144	183	114	86	13	75	0	6	59	10	5.38
Littrell, Wausau	29	3	0	0	3	2	1	.600	73	95	55	41	4	41	0	1	38	7	5.05
Lowe, Wausau	26	15	4	1	6	6	0	.500	105	108	79	65	10	62	3	4	67	11	5.57
Madden, Burlington	5	4	0	0	2	1	0	.667	32	21	11	7	0	15	0	0	23	3	1.97
Madden, Quad Cities	23	19	2	0	8	6	0	.571	107	70	56	47	5	97	0	9	81	5	3.95
Maitland, Appleton*	20	17	0	0	4	9	0	.308	123	84	68	62	0	44	6	6	66	4	6.73
Malone, Wis Rapids*	11	11	0	0	3	6	0	.333	43	45	45	29	4	46	0	0	27	7	6.07
Manderfield, Burlington*	32	1	0	0	3	5	0	.375	64	50	53	38	2	73	0	5	51	10	5.34
Mapel, Wis Rapids	15	15	11	1	8	7	0	.533	117	96	48	39	10	37	0	4	89	0	3.00
Marietta, Cedar Rapids	28	13	5	0	8	7	0	.533	133	151	80	64	5	49	0	6	78	10	4.33
Martinez, Cedar Rapids	13	0	0	0	1	3	0	.250	22	22	12	9	2	13	1	0	22	1	3.68
Matrisciano, C Rapids	17	3	0	0	0	2	1	.000	40	49	43	37	3	33	0	5	29	1	8.33
Maxson, Burlington	15	5	0	0	1	3	0	.250	59	84	49	37	9	12	1	0	30	7	5.64
McClain, Quad Cities	30	14	3	0	3	5	3	.375	104	96	61	44	5	62	5	4	80	9	3.81
McClure, Quad Cities	49	0	0	0	7	2	14	.778	66	52	28	20	2	37	5	1	61	11	2.73
Minarcin, Wis Rapids	15	10	2	0	2	9	0	.182	84	113	69	48	8	47	0	5	35	2	5.14
Moore, Quad Cities	28	1	0	0	2	4	1	.333	61	71	38	32	3	34	2	3	52	5	4.72

Pitcher–Club	G	GS	CG	ShO	W	L	Sv	Pct.	IP	H	R	ER	HR	BB	Int. BB	HB	SO	WP	ERA
Morris, Quad Cities*	20	3	1	0	0	7	1	.000	55	52	26	24	2	19	3	0	34	3	3.93
Mulligan, Wis Rapids	3	1	0	0	0	1	0	.000	5	11	8	7	2	5	0	0	2	0	12.60
Nelson, Clinton	22	0	0	0	5	4	1	.556	41	35	26	12	0	26	1	4	20	5	2.63
Northey, Appleton	1	1	0	0	0	0	0	.000	2	4	4	3	1	2	0	0	1	0	13.50
Norwood, Burlington	22	22	9	0	8	9	0	.471	135	144	94	81	15	75	1	3	77	13	5.40
Oroz, Clinton*	14	13	3	2	7	3	0	.700	85	69	37	26	4	30	0	0	54	6	2.75
Owens, Wausau	26	26	12	1	9	14	0	.391	176	169	91	76	10	97	2	5	136	12	3.89
Pena, Clinton	21	5	0	0	3	3	0	.500	71	53	39	33	5	44	1	4	57	6	4.18
Platel, Clinton*	16	9	3	0	5	2	2	.714	85	92	38	27	5	34	0	1	40	3	2.86
Rambis, Waterloo	41	1	0	0	8	4	13	.667	78	53	31	15	5	35	1	6	48	5	1.73
Reeves, Clinton*	25	24	7	3	8	8	0	.500	142	129	57	45	4	74	1	7	88	8	2.85
Regan, Waterloo	8	1	0	0	0	1	0	.000	24	22	22	15	0	16	0	0	18	5	5.63
Richard, Waterloo	7	7	3	0	5	1	0	.833	51	39	11	8	3	18	1	0	37	2	1.41
Richartz, Appleton	18	11	2	0	2	7	0	.222	74	101	61	50	5	36	1	2	32	8	6.08
Riley, Wis Rapids	6	6	0	0	1	2	0	.333	21	23	14	13	4	18	0	1	10	3	5.57
Romero, Wausau*	17	11	0	0	4	1	0	.800	66	77	53	48	6	53	0	4	53	7	6.55
D. Sax, Clinton	1	0	0	0	1	0	0	1.000	2	2	0	0	0	1	0	0	1	0	0.00
Schmidt, Clinton*	13	10	3	0	0	7	0	.000	56	56	43	26	3	38	0	0	27	4	4.18
Shaffer, Appleton	3	0	0	0	0	0	0	.000	7	9	4	3	0	5	0	0	2	3	3.86
Sivik, Appleton	27	19	1	0	7	8	0	.467	108	118	78	69	5	89	0	2	72	12	5.75
Smith, Appleton*	1	1	0	0	1	0	0	1.000	5	3	0	0	0	1	0	1	8	0	0.00
Soth, Appleton	23	20	2	1	10	5	0	.667	103	106	55	49	10	59	2	7	73	3	4.28
Spino, Quad Cities*	28	23	6	1	9	9	1	.500	162	141	74	57	9	81	3	4	102	10	3.17
Stadler, Cedar Rapids	26	25	12	1	10	13	0	.435	175	166	95	75	14	98	1	11	129	12	3.86
Stember, Cedar Rapids	9	9	2	1	3	3	0	.500	56	51	34	29	9	21	0	5	35	5	4.66
Stutzriem, Wausau*	10	1	0	0	0	1	0	.000	16	18	14	12	1	19	0	1	12	1	6.75
Sutherland, Ced. Rap*	25	25	9	0	13	8	0	.619	167	145	86	63	6	113	1	2	118	11	3.40
Teutsch, Appleton	26	0	0	0	4	4	3	.500	61	63	34	30	1	32	2	4	50	2	4.43
Thornton, Cedar Rapids ..	3	0	0	0	0	0	0	.000	3	4	7	4	0	5	0	0	4	1	12.00
Umdenstock, Appleton	26	11	1	0	6	5	1	.545	91	100	52	43	3	67	2	1	58	10	4.25
Ungs, Wis Rapids	32	19	8	2	9	9	1	.500	171	156	86	59	17	68	4	5	104	4	3.11
Vasquez, Appleton	19	1	0	0	0	2	3	.000	44	35	23	18	3	21	4	3	23	6	3.68
Viskas, Quad Cities	25	24	6	3	14	6	0	.700	161	120	59	49	4	66	1	4	135	9	2.74
Voigt, Wis Rapids	14	13	3	1	4	7	0	.364	84	82	37	31	3	47	1	2	50	4	3.32
Walters, Waterloo	21	20	2	0	11	2	0	.846	113	106	61	47	9	80	1	5	76	4	3.74
Walters, Appleton	11	1	0	0	2	1	3	.667	29	36	22	17	0	20	1	3	30	3	5.28
Warnecke, Waterloo	11	0	0	0	0	0	1	.000	18	15	7	5	0	13	0	0	14	1	2.50
White, Waterloo	1	1	0	0	0	1	0	.000	6	4	4	1	0	2	0	0	8	2	1.50
White, Clinton*	8	2	0	0	1	1	0	.500	22	22	19	19	4	24	0	0	22	4	7.77
Wickensheimer, Clinton ..	14	14	5	0	7	3	0	.700	89	63	34	25	4	29	0	3	77	2	2.53
Wilczewski, Clinton	8	1	0	0	0	2	1	.000	15	12	16	13	0	21	0	5	11	3	7.80
Wilder, Waterloo*	12	12	7	2	7	3	0	.700	87	68	30	19	5	31	0	1	67	2	1.97
Wing, Cedar Rapids	12	1	0	0	1	1	2	.500	27	34	18	16	1	11	0	1	18	2	5.33
Woods, Appleton	23	3	1	0	5	1	4	.833	59	47	23	15	2	35	4	3	40	3	2.29
Wright, Clinton	23	23	11	2	11	8	0	.579	163	139	80	64	6	56	0	9	123	13	3.53
Wright, Quad Cities*	25	21	1	1	8	7	1	.533	122	112	79	66	6	88	0	5	119	15	4.87

BALKS—Hickey, 5; Alexander, Leach, Oroz, 4 each; Estrada, Gaff, Norwood, Owens, Spino, M. Wright, 3 each; Albert, Duckhorn, Fuson, D. Jones, Kromy, Maitland, Pena, Richartz, Stadler, 2 each; Anderson, Blake, Boyce, Christianson, Cosio, Dobbs, Dwyer, Eason, Edwards, Ferst, R. Gibson, Henderson, Hoban, G. Johnson, Joyce, Kranitz, M. Madden, Matrisciano, McClain, Morris, Mulligan, Nelson, Reeves, Soth, Stember, Ungs, Vasquez, Viskas, Voigt, Walters, L. Wright, 1 each.

COMBINATION SHUTOUTS—Smith-Woods, Umdenstock-Hickey, Appleton; Reeves-Joyce, Wickensheimer-Schmidt-Joyce, Alexander-Joyce, Wickensheimer-Oroz-Reeves-Hershiser, Clinton; Madden-Bargfedt, Clark-Churchill, Spino-McClure, Clark-McClain, Quad Cities; Dwyer-Barnhart, Hoban-Rambis, Johnson-Bullinger, Waterloo; Riley-Belk, Wisconsin Rapids.

NO-HIT GAMES—None.

Released Players Had One Last Game

They didn't have any other plans for the evening of July 24, so first baseman Charlie Lord and third baseman Steve Bryan hung around and played for Salem after being cut from the roster that afternoon.

Axed, together with outfielder Dan Supple, for what General Manager Jim Hughes said were financial reasons, Lord and Bryan played against Eugene and had three of the Senators' eight hits in a 4-2 loss to the Emeralds. The three had been given the choice of leaving or playing one last game. Supple took the first option.

NY-Pennsylvania League

CLASS A

CHAMPIONSHIP WINNERS IN PREVIOUS YEARS

1939—Olean* .... .631	Jamestown (2nd)† .... .643
1940—Olean* .... .625	1953—Jamestown* .... .704
1941—Jamestown .... .618	1954—Corning* .... .621
Bradford (2nd)† .... .549	1955—Hamilton* .... .656
1942—Jamestown* .... .672	1956—Wellsville* .... .617
1943—Lockport .... .591	1957—Wellsville .... .632
Wellsville (3rd)† .... .532	Erie (2nd)† .... .598
1944—Lockport .... .608	1958—Wellsville .... .556
Jamestown (2nd)† .... .565	Geneva (2nd)† .... .548
1945—Batavia* .... .677	1959—Wellsville† .... .635
1946—Jamestown‡ .... .672	1960—Erie .... .643
Batavia‡ .... .672	Wellsville (2nd)† .... .535
1947—Jamestown* .... .690	1961—Geneva .... .616
1948—Lockport* .... .603	Olean (4th)† .... .512
1949—Bradford* .... .635	1962—Jamestown .... .580
Olean (2nd)† .... .568	Auburn (3rd)† .... .521
1950—Hornell .... .653	1963—Auburn .... .585
Hornell (3rd)† .... .568	Batavia (3rd)† .... .485
1951—Olean .... .622	1964—Auburn§ .... .622
Hornell (3rd)† .... .568	1965—Binghamton .... .677
1952—Hamilton .... .659	

Binghamton .... .607
1966—Auburn x .... .620
Binghamton .... .646
1967—Auburn .... .667
1968—Auburn .... .645
Oneonta (2nd)* .... .558
1969—Oneonta .... .662
1970—Auburn .... .623
1971—Oneonta .... .662
1972—Niagara Falls .... .686
1973—Auburn .... .667
1974—Oneonta .... .768
1975—Newark .... .688
Newark .... .714
1976—Elmira .... .727
Elmira .... .703
1977—Oneonta y .... .671
Batavia .... .600
1978—Oneonta .... .729
Geneva z .... .718

*Won championship and four-club playoff. †Won four-club playoff. ‡Jamestown and Batavia declared co-champions; Batavia defeated Jamestown in final of four-club playoff. §Won championship and two-club playoff. xWon split-season playoff. yLeague divided into Eastern and Western Divisions; won playoff. zLeague divided into Wrigley and Yawkey Divisions; won playoff. (NOTE—Known as Pennsylvania-Ontario-New York League from 1939 through 1956.)

STANDING OF CLUBS AT CLOSE OF SEASON, AUGUST 30

YAWKEY DIVISION

Club	Ont.	Elm.	L.F.	Utica	Aub.	Gen.	Jtn.	Bat.	New.	N.F.	W.	L.	T.	Pct.	G.B.
Oneonta (Yankees)	..	3	7	7	5	3	3	5	4	5	42	26	0	.618	......
Elmira (Red Sox)	4	..	4	4	5	1	5	4	2	5	34	35	0	.493	8½
Little Falls (Mets)	1	4	..	2	6	1	3	4	5	5	31	39	1	.443	12
Utica (Blue Jays)	1	3	4	..	3	2	1	3	4	4	25	41	0	.379	16
Auburn (Co-op)	2	3	2	2	..	1	3	2	3	4	22	45	0	.328	19½

WRIGLEY DIVISION

Geneva (Cubs)	5	6	7	6	7	..	5	4	5	5	50	19	0	.725	......
Jamestown (Expos)	4	3	5	7	5	2	..	7	7	3	43	27	1	.614	7½
Batavia (Indians)	3	4	4	5	6	3	1	..	5	6	37	34	0	.521	14
Newark (Independent)	3	6	3	4	5	3	1	3	..	4	32	39	0	.451	19
N. Falls (Independent)	3	3	3	4	3	3	5	2	4	..	30	41	0	.423	21

Major league affiliations in parentheses.

Playoff—Oneonta defeated Geneva, two games to one.

Regular-Season Attendance—Auburn, 37,459; Batavia, 41,376; Elmira, 35,071; Geneva, 22,828; Jamestown, 32,325; Little Falls, 27,873; Newark, 14,152; Niagara Falls, 29,908; Oneonta, 38,446; Utica, 19,100. Total, 298,538. Playoffs, 3,046. No all-star game.

Managers: Auburn—Tom Kotchman, Batavia—Tom Trebelhorn, Elmira—Dick Berardino, Geneva—Bob Hartsfield, Jamestown—Pat Daugherty, Little Falls—Matt Galante, Newark—Mal Fichman, Niagara Falls—Duane Shaffer, Oneonta—Art Mazmanian, Utica—John McLaren.

All-Star Team: 1B—Upton, Geneva; 2B—Johnson, Jamestown; 3B—Swires, Oneonta; SS—Fletcher, Geneva; OF—Adams, Jamestown; Caprio, Newark; Castillo, Batavia; Hall, Geneva; C—Buffamoyer, Oneonta; Siciliano, Little Falls; DH—Stemberger, Utica; Utility—J. Brown, Niagara Falls; P—Blyth, Geneva; Hardy, Geneva; Steffan, Oneonta; Tolliver, Oneonta; Managers—Daugherty, Jamestown; Hartsfield, Geneva.

(Compiled by Howe News Bureau, Chicago, Ill.)

CLUB BATTING

Club	G.	AB.	R.	OR.	H.	TB.	2B.	3B.	HR.	RBI.	SH.	SF.	BB.	Int. BB.	HP.	SO.	SB.	CS.	LOB.	Pct.
Geneva	69	2415	470	267	697	1023	106	20	60	402	15	27	358	14	21	344	63	32	569	.289
Jamestown	71	2320	436	350	643	901	87	26	33	378	20	32	394	11	23	316	98	19	582	.277
Elmira	69	2250	431	395	602	850	108	25	30	369	40	20	417	10	28	380	51	14	580	.268
Newark	71	2256	373	405	589	795	98	21	22	312	44	26	427	10	25	410	55	12	639	.261
Utica	66	2232	359	472	579	815	88	11	42	308	14	13	323	5	29	544	66	28	530	.259
Oneonta	68	2128	354	291	537	778	75	23	40	305	23	23	387	2	16	387	89	12	518	.252
Batavia	71	2242	357	342	559	796	89	17	38	299	17	20	374	13	25	469	100	32	566	.249
Niagara Falls	71	2318	372	418	575	807	84	32	28	321	17	31	366	11	23	480	119	26	562	.248
Auburn	67	2189	304	449	527	715	69	25	23	256	16	17	325	5	20	435	69	20	539	.241
Little Falls	71	2295	358	425	538	747	80	15	33	299	27	23	438	14	30	436	94	22	619	.234

INDIVIDUAL BATTING

(Leading Qualifiers for Batting Championship—194 or More Plate Appearances)

*Bats lefthanded. †Switch-hitter.

Player and Club	G.	AB.	R.	H.	TB.	2B.	3B.	HR.	RBI.	SH.	SF.	BB.	HP.	SO.	SB.	CS.	Pct.
Stemberger, Brian, Utica	63	198	43	71	106	9	1	8	41	0	1	36	3	31	6	5	.359
Adams, Kalvin, Jamestown	69	280	53	99	140	9	13	2	69	1	5	17	2	31	3	2	.354
Mattingly, Donald, Oneonta*	53	166	20	58	81	10	2	3	31	0	2	30	0	6	2	2	.349
Johnson, Wallace, Jamestown†	70	284	60	96	137	11	6	6	42	3	2	40	0	14	14	5	.338
Atkinson, James, Jamestown	68	238	57	77	117	11	4	7	60	3	4	54	1	38	12	1	.324
Garrett, Augustine, Little Falls*	53	180	35	58	91	6	0	9	44	0	1	24	1	40	4	2	.322
Caprio, Larry, Newark	62	228	38	73	101	11	1	5	44	0	3	39	0	41	5	1	.320
Williams, Dan, Niagara Falls*	58	191	31	61	103	11	2	9	50	0	6	43	2	27	2	0	.319
Malespin, Gustavo, Elmira	59	207	43	66	94	5	4	5	43	1	0	43	0	12	3	0	.319
Pruitt, R. Lee, Elmira*	69	254	50	80	119	16	1	7	58	0	1	41	3	46	2	2	.315
Hall, Melvin, Geneva*	66	251	49	79	116	18	5	3	53	2	3	35	1	41	4	3	.315

Departmental Leaders: G—McCann, Simmons, 71; AB—W. Johnson, 284; R—Glynn, 71; H—Adams, 99; TB—Adams, 140; 2B—Diaz, 19; 3B—Adams, 13; HR—Grant, LaVigne, Martinez, Petryschuk, Upton, Winters, 10; RBI—Adams, 69; SH—McCann, 16; SF—Upton, 7; BB—Csefelvay, 71; HP—Dembowski, 14; SO—V. Williams, 74; SB—Naclerio, 38; CS—Baker, Kelley, 8.

(All Players—Listed Alphabetically)

Player and Club	G.	AB.	R.	H.	TB.	2B.	3B.	HR.	RBI.	SH.	SF.	BB.	HP.	SO.	SB.	CS.	Pct.
Ackerman, Paul, Newark	8	23	5	5	7	0	0	0	2	0	0	0	0	3	0	0	.217
Ackley, John, Elmira	25	51	8	10	15	2	0	1	11	0	1	18	0	9	2	1	.196
Adams, Kalvin, Jamestown	69	280	53	99	140	9	13	2	69	1	5	17	2	31	3	2	.354
Agapay, Felix, Niagara Falls*	55	156	31	39	71	9	4	5	32	0	2	32	1	29	11	0	.250
Angulo, Hector, Oneonta	7	9	1	0	0	0	0	0	0	0	0	0	0	5	0	0	.000
Anicich, Michael, Little Falls	59	203	24	47	82	13	2	6	39	0	3	35	2	45	2	2	.232
Atkinson, James, Jamestown	68	238	57	77	117	11	4	7	60	3	4	54	1	38	12	1	.324
Baker, Ricky, Batavia†	61	228	38	66	78	5	2	1	16	2	2	28	3	33	20	8	.289
Barker, Christopher, Auburn	36	111	12	29	38	1	4	0	15	1	0	11	1	31	1	1	.261
Barnett, R. David, Jamestown†	34	81	12	16	16	0	0	0	4	1	1	20	0	23	4	0	.198
Beck, James, Little Falls*	47	127	28	31	37	6	0	0	12	0	3	32	0	25	13	2	.244
Berroa, Eduardo, Elmira	24	33	5	6	7	1	0	0	5	0	0	4	0	6	0	0	.182
Bessard, Lloyd, Elmira	50	163	27	46	67	11	2	2	45	2	2	25	5	27	3	0	.282
Bonnette, Robert, Utica	42	158	35	53	70	8	0	3	26	0	1	31	3	25	5	2	.335
Brown, Jeffery M., Niagara Falls†	56	196	36	53	71	12	0	2	27	3	3	36	2	27	15	6	.270
Brown, Keith, Niagara Falls*	57	204	32	54	79	10	3	3	41	0	5	24	4	42	5	2	.265
Brummer, Thomas, Elmira*	57	169	30	48	62	5	3	1	25	5	3	19	2	15	3	1	.284
Bryan, A. Curt, Little Falls	6	8	1	2	4	0	1	0	2	0	0	1	0	0	0	0	.250
Buffamoyer, David, Oneonta	54	164	30	37	52	8	2	1	22	1	3	42	1	24	5	0	.226
Butterfield, Brian, Oneonta	58	179	25	39	42	1	1	0	13	4	1	24	1	27	8	2	.218
Cabrera, Carlos, Utica	36	101	11	24	34	1	0	3	13	1	1	12	1	33	0	2	.238
Cannon, Michael, Auburn	16	55	7	14	24	4	0	2	8	0	0	5	0	15	0	1	.255
Caprio, Larry, Newark	62	228	38	73	101	11	1	5	44	0	3	39	0	41	5	1	.320
Castillo, M. Carmelo, Batavia	36	128	29	43	77	8	1	8	28	0	2	21	1	27	7	2	.336
Cecchetti, George, Batavia*	70	231	33	54	87	11	2	6	44	0	3	41	3	38	5	2	.234
Chaney, Bruce, Batavia	22	74	11	12	23	2	0	3	11	4	3	12	0	15	1	0	.162
Clark, Marcus, Batavia*	44	155	24	47	64	7	2	2	26	1	0	18	4	35	5	2	.303
Clatterbuck, Donald, Newark*	64	190	36	57	67	7	0	1	28	6	4	56	2	22	9	1	.300
Coletta, Matthew, Newark	41	127	28	27	38	6	1	1	19	2	4	28	0	20	2	0	.213
Compton, Bruce, Oneonta	33	82	18	15	20	0	1	1	14	1	1	31	1	27	1	2	.183
Connor, Domingo, Utica	36	108	13	23	27	4	0	0	10	0	1	9	1	29	1	1	.213
Creten, C. Gregg, Geneva	23	62	9	15	19	1	0	1	7	0	0	6	0	9	0	0	.242
Csefelvay, John, Little Falls*	69	228	51	60	85	11	4	4	33	2	3	71	5	19	13	0	.263
Dann, Thomas, Newark*	10	0	0	0	0	0	0	0	0	0	0	0	0	0	0	0	.000
DeLoach, Richard, Geneva*	55	187	29	48	86	10	2	8	32	3	3	35	0	42	1	1	.257
Dembowski, Stephen, Newark	62	198	56	55	75	8	3	2	21	3	1	61	14	34	14	3	.278
Demeter, Todd, Oneonta	66	198	32	50	83	3	3	8	38	0	4	52	5	67	4	0	.273
Dennis, Roberto, Oneonta	41	99	19	27	32	1	2	0	11	2	1	5	0	14	6	1	.273
Diaz, Michael, Geneva	63	237	45	74	116	19	1	7	36	0	1	24	5	24	1	0	.312

Player and Club	G.	AB.	R.	H.	TB.	2B.	3B.	HR.	RBI.	SH.	SF.	BB.	HP.	SO.	SB.	CS.	Pct.
Doby, Larry, Niagara Falls†	59	183	30	39	59	5	3	3	25	0	5	29	5	57	12	1	.213
Echstenkamper, T. Michael, One....	53	186	37	48	91	15	2	8	39	0	1	30	1	33	11	0	.258
Eddins, Glenn, Elmira	45	125	21	26	35	7	1	0	13	5	3	18	3	22	0	0	.208
Encarnacion, Jose, Oneonta	2	1	1	0	0	0	0	0	0	0	0	1	0	1	0	0	.000
Escobar, Jose, Utica	62	204	44	54	71	5	3	2	21	4	0	40	0	52	4	3	.265
Fazzio, Daryl, Batavia*	3	7	4	3	6	1	1	0	3	0	0	5	0	2	0	0	.429
Fiori, Joseph, Geneva	27	76	13	19	20	1	0	0	9	1	0	16	0	7	1	0	.250
Fletcher, Rick, Auburn	20	41	7	6	6	0	0	0	0	0	0	5	2	7	0	1	.146
Fletcher, Scott, Geneva	67	261	59	81	111	12	3	4	43	1	2	56	5	29	10	3	.310
Fortman, David, Niagara Falls	34	109	11	22	26	4	0	0	7	1	0	14	0	35	0	0	.202
Fortune, Steven, Elmira*	57	159	28	44	61	6	1	3	35	3	2	44	1	42	1	0	.277
Franjul, A. Alejandro, Utica	33	68	8	17	19	2	0	0	5	1	1	15	0	19	4	0	.250
Freedman, Kerry, Auburn	7	0	1	0	0	0	0	0	0	0	0	0	0	0	0	0	.000
Frobel, Douglas, Auburn*	35	118	16	34	54	4	2	4	31	1	1	13	1	31	1	0	.288
Garcia, David, Oneonta*	24	65	7	19	23	4	0	0	7	1	1	17	0	8	9	0	.292
Garrett, Augustine, Little Falls....	53	180	35	58	91	6	0	9	44	0	1	24	1	40	4	2	.322
Gavillan, Pedro, Jamestown	28	79	9	16	18	0	1	0	5	4	0	8	3	3	0	0	.203
Gbur, Paul, Niagara Falls†	34	119	21	30	44	5	3	1	16	1	1	17	1	41	6	0	.252
Girata, Daniel, Oneonta	47	147	19	26	40	6	1	2	19	1	1	23	2	27	8	1	.177
Glynn, Eugene, Jamestown	64	208	71	61	89	16	3	2	36	0	5	70	4	34	26	1	.293
Goss, James, Newark*	47	151	21	38	67	5	3	6	38	2	6	43	0	34	1	1	.252
Grant, Thomas, Geneva*	48	148	35	45	82	5	1	10	32	2	3	23	0	18	1	1	.304
Greenfield, Richard, Little Falls	52	140	17	26	29	1	0	0	15	7	0	20	2	33	3	0	.186
Grier, Mark, Newark	6	12	3	4	5	1	0	0	1	0	0	3	0	3	1	0	.333
Gutierrez, Joaquin, Elmira	63	183	29	46	54	4	2	0	14	6	0	19	3	25	1	1	.251
Guzman, Luis, Utica	50	154	16	34	57	7	2	4	26	1	0	12	0	26	7	0	.221
Hagemann, Kenneth, Auburn*	64	229	30	58	74	10	3	0	24	1	1	40	2	34	2	0	.253
Hall, Melvin, Geneva*	66	251	49	79	116	18	5	3	53	2	3	35	1	41	4	3	.315
Hardie, Gary, Little Falls	70	243	29	43	56	8	1	1	22	3	2	40	4	62	5	2	.177
Hartsock, Gary, Jamestown	20	1	1	0	0	0	0	0	0	0	0	0	0	0	0	0	.000
Heller, John, Little Falls*	23	62	6	12	17	1	2	0	8	1	0	10	0	12	1	1	.194
Hennessy, Michael, Little Falls†	44	140	20	21	25	2	1	0	10	3	1	27	3	33	5	2	.150
Henriquez, Ralph, Newark	53	182	21	52	62	5	1	1	19	3	1	20	1	25	4	1	.286
Hill, Bill, Little Falls	39	139	27	36	40	4	0	0	4	1	0	18	3	34	24	4	.259
Hinson, Gary, Batavia	67	225	33	60	82	10	0	4	30	4	2	42	1	36	10	2	.267
Hodge, Ralph, Batavia	8	23	2	2	3	1	0	0	0	0	1	0	8	0	0	0	.087
Holt, David, Elmira*	62	162	38	42	74	11	3	5	22	3	1	56	2	24	8	2	.259
Hudson, Rodney, 14 Aub-34 Bat....	48	136	31	39	50	3	1	2	18	3	0	36	3	10	1	1	.287
Huffstickler, Danny, Elmira	41	110	24	33	39	4	1	0	16	2	1	26	3	29	1	1	.300
Hutson, Ted, Auburn	36	108	4	18	23	2	0	1	8	1	1	15	1	47	2	2	.167
Hyatt, Richard, Auburn	12	39	5	13	19	3	0	1	2	0	0	3	0	11	1	1	.333
Johnson, Gregory, Batavia*	10	30	6	6	7	1	0	0	3	0	0	11	0	5	0	0	.200
Johnson, Wallace, Jamestown†	70	284	60	96	137	11	6	6	42	3	2	40	0	14	14	5	.338
Keck, Daniel, Auburn	37	126	12	26	41	6	0	3	22	0	1	13	2	26	2	1	.206
Kelley, Michael, Geneva*	65	282	62	83	98	8	2	1	29	0	3	30	1	23	24	8	.294
Korbes, Dean, Niagara Falls*	1	0	0	0	0	0	0	0	0	0	0	1	0	0	0	0	.000
Kwist, Randall, Auburn	60	198	24	46	59	6	2	1	21	2	1	27	1	19	2	0	.232
LaCasse, Michael, Newark	60	207	22	46	56	7	0	1	22	1	2	10	1	32	1	0	.222
Lagergren, Frederick, Auburn	59	199	29	41	55	6	1	2	19	1	2	50	2	36	4	5	.206
Land, R. William, Newark	20	46	10	15	21	3	0	1	11	1	0	5	0	8	2	0	.326
Lanz, Scott, Newark	2	5	0	0	0	0	0	0	0	0	0	0	0	0	0	0	.000
LaPorte, Michael, Batavia*	4	6	0	0	0	0	0	0	0	0	0	1	1	2	0	0	.000
LaVigne, Randall, Geneva	63	252	44	79	122	9	2	10	50	2	3	25	3	43	7	2	.313
Leal, Carlos, Utica	40	116	10	21	25	4	0	0	15	1	0	19	1	41	1	2	.181
Lee, Eddie, Elmira	63	237	48	54	80	11	3	3	23	4	0	38	4	48	22	4	.228
Lessard, Michael, Utica†	58	194	39	53	68	10	1	1	26	0	3	38	2	28	10	4	.273
Liggins, Danny, Auburn	15	58	5	19	20	1	0	0	7	0	1	4	1	10	6	0	.328
Likely, Albert, Niagara Falls	37	113	7	20	25	0	1	1	12	0	3	11	0	33	0	0	.177
Locascio, Lawrence, Batavia	26	81	11	23	30	4	0	1	12	2	1	9	0	9	4	1	.284
Loeffler, Christopher, Jame*	42	124	14	21	31	3	2	1	21	1	3	21	0	23	0	0	.169
Lopez, Jack, Batavia	54	174	28	40	46	0	3	0	17	0	0	30	1	34	14	2	.230
MacDonald, Kevin, Newark	13	26	3	4	4	0	0	0	1	0	7	1	12	0	0		.154
Mainieri, Paul, Niagara Falls	60	190	39	48	62	8	3	0	16	4	4	45	3	44	12	3	.253
Malespin, Gustavo, Elmira	59	207	43	66	94	5	4	5	43	1	0	43	0	12	3	0	.319
Martinez, Tommy, Batavia	55	214	29	60	99	9	0	10	38	0	2	10	3	51	5	1	.280
Mata, Victor, Oneonta	60	224	36	60	74	6	1	2	23	3	2	23	3	31	11	2	.268
Mattingly, Donald, Oneonta*	53	166	20	58	81	10	2	3	31	0	2	30	0	6	2	3	.349
McCann, Joseph, Newark	71	267	50	67	92	9	8	0	35	16	0	41	0	39	9	1	.251
McQueen, Steven, Elmira	22	41	10	14	18	2	1	0	8	1	0	15	0	8	0	0	.341
Meier, Bryan, Batavia	36	108	11	19	24	5	0	0	11	1	0	21	0	33	2	2	.176
Mercedes, Adolfo, Oneonta	25	46	4	7	9	0	1	0	6	1	0	3	2	12	1	0	.152
Millhauser, Glenn, Geneva*	21	29	10	7	7	0	0	0	6	0	0	8	1	11	1	0	.241
Millner, Timothy, Geneva	12	1	0	0	0	0	0	0	0	0	0	0	0	0	0	0	.000
Mitchell, Weston, Batavia	42	150	18	40	51	11	0	0	20	0	2	20	0	24	11	3	.267
Mizzi, Douglas, Little Falls	19	1	0	0	0	0	0	0	0	0	0	0	0	0	0	0	.000

Player and Club	G.	AB.	R.	H.	TB.	2B.	3B.	HR.	RBI.	SH.	SF.	BB.	HP.	SO.	SB.	CS.	Pct.
Murray, Jerry, Auburn	12	39	1	3	3	0	0	0	1	0	0	2	0	13	0	0	.077
Naclerio, Ronald, Niagara Falls*	57	202	44	55	65	2	1	2	15	1	0	35	1	20	38	5	.272
Nataupsky, Harold, Auburn	31	87	13	20	29	1	1	2	10	2	0	13	0	25	2	1	.230
Nicolet, Donald, 17 Bat-18 Aub	35	83	11	15	20	5	0	0	9	1	2	28	0	30	2	2	.181
Niggebrugge, Paul, Little Falls	68	235	40	58	93	12	1	7	40	0	0	49	5	40	5	2	.247
O'Connor, J. Paul, 6 Aub-3 New*	9	14	1	5	7	1	0	0	3	0	0	4	0	3	0	0	.357
Olson, Mitchell, Niagara Falls	58	190	28	45	59	4	5	0	22	0	0	36	1	34	9	5	.237
Ortega, Kirk, Geneva	20	42	7	12	14	2	0	0	3	0	2	3	7	2	1	.286
Osmulski, Frank, Batavia	22	34	4	6	7	1	0	0	2	0	0	15	0	13	1	1	.176
Palmer, Richard, Utica	20	55	5	14	20	4	1	0	10	0	2	15	0	15	0	1	.255
Pascarella, Andrew, Newark	67	245	34	69	97	18	2	2	37	1	2	47	2	43	5	2	.282
Paula, Julio, Utica*	11	38	5	11	12	1	0	0	6	1	0	4	0	10	2	0	.289
Payano, Vidal, Oneonta	18	17	5	2	2	0	0	0	2	0	0	6	0	7	1	0	.118
Pedrique, Alfredo, Little Falls	33	92	3	21	25	0	2	0	11	1	1	6	1	12	3	1	.228
Perez, Juan, Utica*	49	145	32	40	53	7	0	2	15	0	1	20	3	21	8	1	.276
Petryschuk, Edward, Utica	58	209	31	61	103	10	1	10	45	0	2	31	4	40	3	1	.292
Piechota, Joseph, Jamestown*	69	228	28	56	70	6	1	2	37	3	4	40	2	25	2	0	.246
Pruitt, R. Lee, Elmira*	69	254	50	80	119	16	1	7	58	0	1	41	3	46	2	2	.315
Pustorino, Frederick, L. Falls	22	38	3	4	5	1	0	0	4	0	0	5	1	10	0	0	.105
Raineri, Eugene, Auburn*	5	17	2	3	5	0	1	0	0	0	0	1	0	2	1	0	.176
Rehbaum, Christopher, Batavia*	28	95	17	16	22	1	1	1	9	0	0	16	3	27	3	1	.168
Rigoli, Joseph, Newark	29	61	8	14	22	4	0	2	8	2	0	8	3	12	0	0	.230
Rittweger, William, Little Falls	69	265	42	60	75	5	2	2	24	8	5	36	2	43	9	4	.226
Rodriguez, Eduardo, Oneonta	29	24	6	5	5	0	0	0	3	0	0	7	0	10	0	0	.208
Roeder, Steven, Jamestown	66	226	43	59	83	7	1	5	31	1	1	37	7	54	19	3	.261
Romero, Ramon, Niagara Falls†	47	133	14	24	28	2	1	0	10	5	0	12	1	33	1	2	.180
Ronshausen, Ted, Niagara Falls*	23	64	8	17	20	3	0	0	6	0	3	8	1	17	1	1	.266
Rose, Kevin, Newark	16	46	6	13	16	3	0	0	4	2	1	11	0	7	0	0	.283
Rossen, Robert, Auburn*	7	21	1	4	7	3	0	0	2	0	0	3	0	5	0	0	.190
Samaniego, Arturo, Elmira	58	149	26	38	57	13	0	2	28	2	5	13	2	16	2	0	.255
Sanchez, Arturo, Niagara Falls*	26	70	14	18	27	2	2	1	14	0	1	5	0	13	5	0	.257
Santarone, Richard, Oneonta	19	44	4	7	8	1	0	0	3	0	0	5	0	12	0	0	.159
Schervish, Michael, Jamestown	64	237	36	62	93	12	2	5	40	0	4	27	4	11	9	2	.262
Seilheimer, Ricky, Niagara Falls*	24	89	10	16	28	3	3	1	13	0	0	4	0	22	1	0	.180
Serrano, E. Andres, Elmira	27	50	11	11	14	3	0	0	4	3	5	0	13	0	0	.220
Shapiro, Howard, Geneva*	49	140	32	35	46	2	0	3	15	1	0	24	1	12	5	4	.250
Siciliano, Marc, Little Falls	56	165	27	51	73	10	0	4	29	0	2	57	1	24	2	0	.309
Simmons, D. Wayne, Jamestown*	71	261	41	66	83	11	0	2	23	3	2	34	0	40	8	5	.253
Smith, Keith, Oneonta	56	119	19	29	29	0	0	0	9	10	1	33	0	30	9	3	.244
Spicer, Leonard, Newark*	18	59	10	10	12	2	0	0	3	1	0	6	0	13	0	0	.169
Stemberger, Brian, Utica	63	198	43	71	106	9	1	8	41	0	1	36	3	31	6	5	.359
Stricklen, Don, Geneva	36	95	13	23	33	4	0	2	10	0	1	5	0	9	1	2	.242
Swires, Glenn, Oneonta	65	247	49	70	114	14	6	6	41	1	1	28	0	28	5	1	.283
Tapia, Santiago, Utica†	44	99	17	12	13	1	0	0	3	0	9	5	39	9	0	.121
Teller, Jeems, Elmira	30	58	18	16	25	4	1	1	11	1	0	17	0	13	2	0	.276
Tillman, Kerry, Little Falls	6	22	4	7	9	0	1	0	4	1	2	3	0	2	5	0	.318
Torres, Samuel, Batavia	17	24	2	3	3	0	0	0	0	0	1	0	10	0	0	.125
Turner, Lloyd, 2 Bat-59 Aub	61	203	39	49	75	7	5	3	29	4	3	28	1	46	8	3	.241
Upton, Jack, Geneva	69	274	45	82	133	15	3	10	63	3	7	35	0	39	4	2	.299
Vaiana, James, Jamestown*	23	61	11	12	22	1	3	1	7	0	1	24	0	14	1	0	.197
Vail, Jeffery, Utica	21	22	3	6	7	1	0	0	2	0	0	6	0	13	0	0	.273
Vasquez, Francisco, Elmira	40	99	15	22	29	3	2	0	8	2	1	13	0	21	1	2	.222
Velasquez, Alfredo, Utica	50	167	27	46	68	8	1	4	20	0	0	18	3	46	2	1	.275
Viggiano, Michael, Little Falls	6	8	1	1	1	0	0	0	0	0	0	1	0	6	0	0	.125
Viola, Lance, Newark	38	100	13	26	36	7	0	1	9	3	1	15	1	26	1	2	.260
Wagner, Kent, Jamestown	5	13	0	2	2	0	0	0	3	0	0	1	0	6	0	0	.154
Wells, John, Auburn	61	201	41	52	65	3	2	2	16	2	2	44	3	33	20	2	.259
White, Harry, Newark*	30	81	13	15	20	2	0	1	7	0	1	20	0	29	1	0	.185
Wilder, Clifton, Auburn	61	243	42	68	86	9	3	1	28	0	3	23	1	24	18	1	.280
Williams, Dan, Niagara Falls*	58	191	31	61	103	11	2	9	50	0	6	43	2	27	2	0	.319
Williams, Vincent, Utica	54	196	20	39	62	6	1	5	27	2	0	7	3	74	4	5	.199
Winters, Matthew, Oneonta*	62	188	40	53	93	6	2	10	38	0	4	56	1	42	9	0	.282
Woods, Victor, Batavia	47	121	27	25	43	7	4	1	15	0	2	25	4	44	9	3	.207
Zelmanski, Gary, Niagara Falls	40	119	16	34	40	4	1	0	15	2	1	13	1	6	1	1	.286

The following pitchers had no plate appearances primarily through use of designated hitters, listed alphabetically by club, games in parentheses:

AUBURN—Camp, Michael (10); Collyer, Rick (15); Dwyer, Scott (9–4 with Batavia); Fitzhugh, Kevin (13); Florey, Timothy (9); Gorey, Rick (10); Hodgins, Robert (2); Hundley, John (25); Krill, Michael (9); LaPointe, David P. (11); Ostrow, Frank (4); Owens, Alan (5); Paradise, M. Scott (2); Reynoso, Rafael (14); Tulacz, Randall (2).

BATAVIA—Anthony, Dane (13); Asbell, John (17); Bajus, Mark (3); Bauman, Alan (5); Bohnet, John (12); Clancy, Thomas (6); Fee, Ronald (7); Hrynko, Lawrence (24); Jackubowicz, Michael (4); Larison, Jerry (10); Maki, Matthew (8); Merry, George (10); Norman, Terry (13); Nuismer, N. Jack (10); Regan, Francis (10); Roche, Stephen (13); Stutzriem, Gerald (9); White, Larry (12).

ELMIRA—Birrell, Robert (6); Davis, Parker (13); DeSanto, Thomas (16); Fredlund, Jay (19); Gering, Scott (18);

Hayford, Donald (21); McCarthy, Thomas (18); Moloney, William (21); Saunders, Mark (16); Schaefer, Steven (16); Tremblay, Wayne (7).

GENEVA—Blyth, Robert (26); Crawford, Russell (2); Gault, Raymond (5); Hardy, Bryan (11); McManus, James (11); Mims, Gerry (11); Renwick, Richard (15); Soff, Raymond (9); Thompson, Michael E. (13); Vaji, Mark (5); Wilkins, Mark (13).

JAMESTOWN—Baker, John (6); Byrket, Blake (1); Cates, Timothy (14); Flowers, David (15); Huber, Randolph (2); Kellogg, Kerry (9); Maher, Buddy (17); Montgomery, Thomas (17); Musum, Craig (14); Reed, Mark (8); St. Claire, Randy (4); Sattler, William (13); Taylor, Jeffrey (13).

LITTLE FALLS—Damiter, Theodore (29); Foust, Algernan (13); Green, James (10); Henley, Douglas (15); Hilton, Gary (9); Paquette, Darryl (11); Rosario, Victor (19); Semprini, John (16); Shockley, P. Lee (12); Tancredi, Michael (16); Welch, Mark (15); Zwolinski, Mark (12).

NEWARK—Adams, Carl Ray (14); Baker, Bruce (4); Clay, Bill (21); Gainer, Keith (1); Ganch, Timothy (4); Goeggelman, Paul (19); Karl, Brian (9); Mayles, B. Allen (9); McArow, Mathew (6); Nicastro, Stephen (23); Oleksak, Michael (3); Overton, Michael (12); Russo, Gavin (6); Wright, B. Mitchell (14).

NIAGARA FALLS—Davis, Keefe (13); Fallon, Robert (15); Fishback, Robert (13); Friedrich, Gary (3); Holbrook, Alan (13); Keating, Thomas (14); Maitland, Michael (4); Mills, William (20); Ortega, Daniel (12); Patterson, Reginald (10); Samuel, Jay (7); Sivik, Michael (1); Walters, Victor (25).

ONEONTA—Andersen, Edward (16); Copeland, Gregory (1); Ervey, Albert (16); Filson, W. Peter (1); Franks, John (13); Gnacinski, Paul (7); Irot, Kevin (7); Kaufman, Kurt (17); Nurthen, John (15); Seneca, John (11); Steffan, Karl (17); Toliver, Freddie (12); Wever, Stefan (10).

UTICA—Burger, Bradley (3); Cuevas, Armengol (13); DeRatt, A. LaMont (13); Ford, Randy (16); Holton, Mark (2); Lunar, Manuel (19); Mudano, Mario (16); O'Dowd, Thomas (14); Oravec, Robert (19); Pimentel, Rafael (16); White, P. Richard (27).

GRAND SLAM HOME RUNS—Guzman, 2; Bessard, Compton, Creten, S. Fletcher, Grant, Lessard, Malespin, Petryschuk, Upton, Velasquez, Wells, V. Williams, 1 each.

AWARDED FIRST BASE ON INTERFERENCE—Hagemann 3 (Siciliano 2, Osmulski); LaCasse 2 (Heller, Hudson); Locascio 2 (Heller, Palmer); Gutierrez (Pusterino); Mattingly (Osmulski).

CLUB FIELDING

Club	G.	PO.	A.	E.	DP.	PB.	Pct.	Club	G.	PO.	A.	E.	DP.	PB.	Pct.
Geneva	69	1833	745	80	55	24	.970	Newark	71	1761	774	135	75	18	.949
Jamestown	71	1791	751	107	60	10	.960	Oneonta	68	1717	657	130	62	15	.948
Elmira	69	1743	643	118	47	21	.953	Niagara Falls	71	1803	765	163	78	24	.940
Little Falls	71	1828	728	129	57	19	.952	Utica	66	1698	708	158	65	23	.938
Batavia	71	1771	798	131	63	19	.951	Auburn	67	1678	646	156	56	39	.937

Triple Play—Little Falls.

*Throws lefthanded.

INDIVIDUAL FIELDING

FIRST BASEMEN

Player and Club	G.	PO.	A.	E.	DP.	Pct.	Player and Club	G.	PO.	A.	E.	DP.	Pct.
Beck, Little Falls*	25	166	14	0	17	1.000	Anicich, Little Falls	52	392	22	5	33	.988
Winters, Oneonta	3	20	0	0	1	1.000	Piechota, Jamestown*	69	565	26	8	52	.987
Hodge, Batavia	4	14	2	0	4	1.000	Fortune, Elmira	51	347	28	5	20	.987
Keck, Auburn	2	12	1	0	2	1.000	Pruitt, Elmira	26	186	15	3	19	.985
Mattingly, Oneonta*	2	12	0	0	3	1.000	Petryschuk, Utica	56	459	22	8	47	.984
Siciliano, Little Falls	1	9	2	0	1	1.000	Pascarella, Newark	66	587	33	11	61	.983
Bonnette, Utica	1	6	1	0	0	1.000	Lessard, Utica	7	42	2	1	2	.978
Santarone, Oneonta	1	7	0	0	0	1.000	Williams, Niagara F*	54	446	28	11	50	.977
Hudson, Batavia	1	5	0	0	0	1.000	Likely, Niagara Falls*	7	60	3	2	5	.969
Agapay, Niagara Falls*	2	5	0	0	0	1.000	Hagemann, Auburn*	63	487	27	17	44	.968
Frobel, Auburn	1	3	0	0	2	1.000	K. Brown, NF*	15	115	4	4	12	.967
Pustorino, Little Falls	1	2	0	0	0	1.000	Viola, Newark	6	49	1	2	3	.962
Torres, Batavia	1	2	0	0	0	1.000	Johnson, Batavia	3	21	4	1	2	.962
O'Connor, Newark	1	1	0	0	1	1.000	Vail, Utica	8	52	4	4	7	.933
Teller, Elmira	1	1	0	0	0	1.000	Schervish, Jamestown	2	11	0	1	0	.917
UPTON, Geneva	69	595	38	7	53	.9890	Kwist, Auburn	2	17	1	2	1	.900
Cecchetti, Batavia*	68	574	30	7	50	.9885	Adams, Jamestown	3	14	1	2	1	.882
Demeter, Oneonta	64	540	20	7	55	.988							

Triple Play—Anicich.

SECOND BASEMEN

Player and Club	G.	PO.	A.	E.	DP.	Pct.	Player and Club	G.	PO.	A.	E.	DP.	Pct.
Mitchell, Batavia	5	7	13	0	1	1.000	Hinson, Batavia	34	84	104	4	22	.979
Murray, Auburn	3	4	6	0	2	1.000	Glynn, Jamestown	16	39	50	2	11	.978
Goss, Newark	1	2	3	0	2	1.000	McCann, Newark	47	110	146	6	31	.977
Rigoli, Newark	1	1	2	0	0	1.000	Gutierrez, Elmira	24	52	58	3	12	.973
Pedrique, Little Falls	3	1	2	0	0	1.000	Creten, Geneva	14	27	31	2	7	.967
Girata, Oneonta	1	1	0	0	0	1.000	Clatterbuck, Newark	19	38	43	3	12	.964
Romero, Niagara Falls*	1	0	1	0	0	1.000	Lopez, Jamestown	33	73	83	6	21	.963
Shapiro, Geneva	45	92	96	1	25	.995	Fiori, Geneva	21	34	50	4	5	.955
Lessard, Utica	32	59	87	1	19	.993	RITTWEGER, LF	69	195	176	19	37	.951

SECOND BASEMEN—Continued

Player and Club	G.	PO.	A.	E.	DP.	Pct.
Garcia, Oneonta	16	28	48	4	13	.950
Fletcher, Auburn	11	17	20	2	2	.949
Johnson, Jamestown	56	157	155	17	34	.948
Lagergren, Auburn	57	142	139	16	27	.946
Butterfield, Oneonta	50	89	117	12	17	.945
Escobar, Utica	26	64	48	7	15	.941
Mainieri, Niagara F.	60	144	171	20	45	.940
Guzman, Utica	8	16	10	2	2	.929
Gbur, Niagara Falls	5	8	5	1	1	.929
Bryan, Little Falls	4	4	8	1	2	.923
Samaniego, Elmira	48	77	76	13	13	.922
J. Brown, Niagara F.	12	18	23	4	2	.911
Dembowski, Newark	10	18	24	5	5	.894
Serrano, Elmira	19	25	21	6	4	.885
Franjul, Utica	11	14	19	5	6	.868
Turner, Batavia	2	3	1	1	0	.800
Payano, Oneonta	14	14	19	10	4	.767

Triple Play—Rittweger.

THIRD BASEMEN

Player and Club	G.	PO.	A.	E.	DP.	Pct.
Guzman, Utica	3	4	6	0	1	1.000
Hodge, Batavia	3	2	5	0	0	1.000
Stemberger, Utica	4	3	4	0	0	1.000
Niggebrugge, LF	1	0	5	0	0	1.000
Zelmanski, Niagara F.	1	2	1	0	0	1.000
Escobar, Utica	1	2	0	0	0	1.000
Creten, Geneva	2	0	2	0	0	1.000
Adams, Jamestown	1	1	0	0	0	1.000
Fiori, Geneva	1	0	1	0	0	1.000
Lagergren, Auburn	1	1	0	0	0	1.000
Viggiano, Little Falls	3	0	1	0	1	1.000
Glynn, Jamestown	10	11	18	1	2	.967
Hinson, Batavia	33	30	58	4	6	.957
SWIRES, Oneonta	56	41	107	7	13	.955
MacDonald, Newark	12	7	13	1	1	.952
Lessard, Utica	15	13	32	3	5	.938
Stricklen, Geneva	28	17	50	5	1	.931
J. Brown, Niagara F.	20	16	29	4	3	.918
Clatterbuck, Newark	48	61	95	15	12	.912
DeLoach, Geneva	54	39	82	12	6	.910
Lopez, Batavia	4	3	7	1	1	.909
Kwist, Auburn	41	35	77	12	10	.903
Bonnette, Utica	38	39	81	14	8	.896
Goss, Newark	17	10	37	6	3	.887
Hyatt, Auburn	10	11	20	4	2	.886
Meier, Batavia	32	18	63	11	5	.880
Paula, Utica	8	5	17	3	0	.880
Hardie, Little Falls	70	55	130	26	13	.877
Eddins, Elmira	43	35	60	14	4	.872
Olson, Niagara Falls	48	54	87	21	10	.870
Roeder, Jamestown	61	51	93	22	9	.867
Huffstickler, Elmira	39	31	57	17	3	.838
Gbur, Niagara Falls	7	7	8	3	1	.833
Girata, Oneonta	13	7	17	5	4	.828
Frobel, Batavia	17	15	30	11	1	.804
Mercedes, Oneonta	11	6	13	5	2	.792
Torres, Batavia	4	3	4	2	1	.778
Velasquez, Utica	2	3	2	2	0	.714
Keck, Auburn	4	3	11	6	0	.700
Turner, Batavia	1	1	1	1	0	.667
Bryan, Little Falls	1	0	0	1	0	.000
McQueen, Elmira	3	0	0	1	0	.000

SHORTSTOPS

Player and Club	G.	PO.	A.	E.	DP.	Pct.
Fiori, Geneva	3	2	7	0	4	1.000
Swires, Oneonta	3	3	3	0	1	1.000
Lessard, Utica	1	2	1	0	1	1.000
Glynn, Jamestown	1	1	1	0	0	1.000
Olson, Niagara Falls	1	2	0	0	0	1.000
Millhauser, Geneva	1	1	0	0	0	1.000
FLETCHER, Geneva	67	99	195	18	33	.942
Gutierrez, Elmira	42	45	99	9	14	.941
Turner, Batavia-Auburn	60	99	152	16	27	.940
Chaney, Batavia	22	36	81	8	10	.936
McCann, Newark	42	82	81	13	17	.926
Mitchell, Batavia	36	57	121	15	16	.922
Butterfield, Oneonta	9	10	12	2	2	.917
Greenfield, Little Falls	51	68	129	18	22	.916
J. Brown, Niagara Falls	24	37	65	10	13	.911
Vasquez, Elmira	38	27	72	10	9	.908
Simmons, Oneonta	71	105	227	34	39	.907
LaCasse, Newark	47	58	139	21	25	.904
Escobar, Utica	35	59	83	15	17	.904
Smith, Oneonta	56	65	115	21	18	.896
Lopez, Batavia	18	28	50	10	14	.886
Gbur, Niagara Falls	17	15	39	7	7	.885
Pedrique, Little Falls	31	55	88	19	13	.883
Stemberger, Utica	16	20	40	8	6	.882
Romero, Niagara Falls	44	60	124	27	28	.872
Franjul, Utica	18	22	47	11	7	.863
Viggiano, Little Falls	3	4	5	2	1	.818
Bonnette, Utica	5	1	16	4	4	.810
Rodriguez, Oneonta	28	14	21	9	4	.795
McQueen, Elmira	11	10	17	7	5	.794
Murray, Auburn	10	20	8	2	2	.789
Fletcher, Auburn	5	1	4	5	0	.500
Stricklen, Geneva	3	0	1	1	0	.500
Garcia, Oneonta	1	0	1	1	0	.000

Triple Play—Pedrique.

OUTFIELDERS

Player and Club	G.	PO.	A.	E.	DP.	Pct.
Clark, Batavia*	16	20	2	0	0	1.000
Grant, Geneva	15	18	1	0	0	1.000
Teller, Elmira	9	11	1	0	0	1.000
Kwist, Auburn	3	6	1	0	1	1.000
Dembowski, Newark	3	4	2	0	1	1.000
J. Brown, Niagara Falls	5	6	0	0	0	1.000
Tillman, Little Falls	2	4	1	0	0	1.000
Olson, Niagara Falls	7	4	1	0	0	1.000
Millhauser, Geneva	8	5	0	0	0	1.000
Mercedes, Oneonta	2	4	0	0	0	1.000
Angulo, Oneonta	3	4	0	0	0	1.000
Girata, Oneonta	4	4	0	0	0	1.000
LaPorte, Batavia	3	2	0	0	0	1.000
Torres, Batavia	9	2	0	0	0	1.000
Pruitt, Elmira	47	78	1	1	0	.988
Barnett, Jamestown	29	59	3	1	0	.984
KELLEY, Geneva*	64	143	9	3	2	.9806
Schervish, Jamestown	60	94	7	2	1	.9805
Hill, Little Falls	23	39	1	1	0	.976
Lee, Elmira	61	122	8	4	1	.970
Coletta, Newark	37	57	6	2	4	.969
Viola, Newark	18	26	5	1	2	.969
Agapay, Niagara Falls*	51	54	7	2	2	.968
Niggebrugge, Lit. Falls.	64	112	7	4	0	.967
Goss, Newark	28	53	5	2	0	.967
Glynn, Jamestown	18	27	2	1	1	.967
K. Brown, Nia. Falls*	32	50	7	2	1	.966
Mata, Oneonta	59	100	9	4	2	.965
Leal, Utica	40	52	3	2	0	.965
Naclerio, Niagara Falls*	53	104	4	4	2	.964

OUTFIELDERS—Continued

Player and Club	G.	PO.	A.	E.	DP.	Pct.
Guzman, Utica	32	49	4	2	0	.964
LaVigne, Geneva	53	92	13	4	2	.963
Malespin, Elmira	56	96	8	4	3	.963
Hennessy, Little Falls*	42	76	3	3	0	.963
Echstenkamper, One	53	68	2	3	0	.959
Cannon, Auburn	13	22	1	1	0	.958
Atkinson, Jamestown	60	103	6	5	3	.956
Csefelvay, Little Falls*	57	103	3	5	1	.955
Adams, Jamestown	57	96	9	5	0	.955
Wilder, Auburn	56	138	7	7	3	.954
Caprio, Newark	61	136	6	7	0	.953
Woods, Batavia	37	54	5	3	0	.952
Bessard, Elmira	43	68	3	4	0	.947
Hall, Geneva*	63	113	5	7	1	.944
Doby, Niagara Falls	42	64	3	4	0	.944
Rose, Newark	14	17	0	1	0	.944
Compton, Geneva	15	16	0	1	0	.941
Winters, Oneonta	55	59	2	4	1	.938
Liggins, Auburn	12	15	0	1	0	.938
Dennis, Oneonta	26	39	3	3	0	.933
Wells, Auburn	53	102	7	8	1	.932
Baker, Batavia	55	66	1	5	0	.931
Land, Newark	17	24	2	2	0	.929
Castillo, Batavia	28	56	4	5	1	.923
Garrett, Little Falls	15	23	1	2	0	.923
Raineri, Auburn*	4	10	1	1	0	.917
Rossen, Auburn*	6	10	1	1	0	.917
Barker, Auburn	24	26	3	3	0	.906
Mattingly, Oneonta*	17	17	2	2	1	.905
White, Newark	26	43	4	5	1	.904
Nicolet, Batavia-Auburn	30	59	4	7	0	.900
Rehbaum, Batavia	28	39	4	5	2	.896
Gbur, Niagara Falls	9	15	2	2	1	.895
Martinez, Batavia	47	62	5	8	0	.893
Sanchez, Niagara Falls*	19	23	2	3	1	.893
Spicer, Newark*	14	32	1	4	0	.892
Perez, Utica*	43	56	3	8	1	.881
Williams, Utica	50	96	3	14	1	.876
Keck, Auburn	25	35	5	6	2	.870
Berroa, Elmira	20	12	1	2	0	.867
Likely, Niagara Falls*	22	24	1	4	0	.862
Beck, Little Falls*	16	23	1	4	0	.857
Cabrera, Utica	10	10	1	2	0	.846
Tapia, Utica	38	51	5	11	1	.836
Connor, Utica	29	29	3	7	1	.821
Henriquez, Newark	7	8	0	3	0	.727
Rigoli, Newark	2	1	0	1	0	.500
Stemberger, Utica	1	0	0	1	0	.000

CATCHERS

Player and Club	G.	PO.	A.	E.	DP.	PB.	Pct.
Vaiana, Jamestown	19	106	7	0	0	4	1.000
Grier, Newark	6	21	0	0	0	2	1.000
Fazzio, Batavia	3	17	1	0	0	2	1.000
Viola, Newark	3	14	1	0	0	2	1.000
Seilheimer, Nia. Falls	1	5	0	0	0	0	1.000
Schervish, Jamestown	1	2	0	0	0	0	1.000
Gavillan, Jamestown	28	157	18	1	1	4	.994
Holt, Elmira	21	127	4	1	1	10	.992
Loeffler, Jamestown	31	175	20	2	1	2	.990
Ortega, Geneva	14	74	7	1	1	5	.988
BRUMMER, Elmira	49	292	22	4	3	8	.987
Diaz, Geneva	61	423	35	7	1	19	.985
Girata, Oneonta	17	105	17	2	2	4	.984
Siciliano, Little Falls	51	291	30	7	2	12	.979
Pustorino, Little Falls	19	82	9	2	1	4	.978
Ackerman, Newark	8	39	4	1	0	3	.977
Fortman, Nia. Falls	30	179	16	5	5	12	.975
Buffamoyer, Oneonta	47	374	36	11	3	9	.974
Heller, Little Falls	18	96	10	3	0	3	.972
Santarone, Oneonta	15	59	7	2	0	2	.971
Hudson, Aub.-Bat.	41	228	29	8	5	9	.970
Palmer, Utica	20	136	15	5	3	9	.968
Locascio, Batavia	25	176	20	7	2	4	.966
Rigoli, Newark	26	100	9	4	2	4	.965
Henriquez, Newark	46	175	32	8	4	7	.963
Velasquez, Utica	45	247	28	11	3	7	.962
Ackley, Elmira	16	70	6	3	1	3	.962
Cabrera, Utica	12	23	2	1	0	7	.962
Natupapky, Auburn	30	139	10	6	1	13	.961
Ronshausen, N.F.	19	100	12	5	0	6	.957
Osmulski, Batavia	21	92	10	5	0	7	.953
Hutson, Auburn	36	187	19	11	2	23	.949
Zelmanski, Nia. Falls	31	155	21	10	1	6	.946

PITCHERS

Player and Club	G.	PO.	A.	E.	DP.	Pct.
FORD, Utica*	16	8	25	0	1	1.000
Millner, Geneva	12	8	16	0	0	1.000
Fishback, Niagara F	13	10	14	0	2	1.000
Fallon, Niagara Falls*	15	4	19	0	1	1.000
Moloney, Elmira*	21	2	17	0	1	1.000
White, Utica	27	7	11	0	3	1.000
Gorey, Auburn	10	7	10	0	0	1.000
O'Dowd, Utica	14	3	14	0	0	1.000
Hartsock, Jamestown	19	3	12	0	0	1.000
Gering, Elmira	18	4	10	0	0	1.000
Blyth, Geneva	25	4	10	0	0	1.000
Dann, Newark*	9	3	10	0	1	1.000
Vaji, Geneva*	5	1	11	0	0	1.000
McArow, Newark	6	1	11	0	0	1.000
Hardy, Geneva*	11	3	9	0	0	1.000
Damiter, Little Falls	29	0	12	0	1	1.000
Krill, Auburn*	9	2	9	0	0	1.000
Holbrook, Niagara F	13	4	7	0	2	1.000
Cates, Jamestown	13	2	9	0	0	1.000
Schaefer, Elmira	16	3	8	0	0	1.000
Karl, Newark	9	5	5	0	0	1.000
Shockley, Little Falls	12	3	7	0	1	1.000
Norman, Batavia*	13	4	5	0	0	1.000
Maitland, Batavia F*	4	0	8	0	0	1.000
Dwyer, Bat-Aub	9	2	6	0	0	1.000
Korbes, Niagara Falls*	10	1	7	0	0	1.000
Davis, Niagara Falls	13	1	7	0	0	1.000
Nurthen, Oneonta	15	1	7	0	1	1.000
Semprini, Little Falls	16	1	7	0	0	1.000
Hrynko, Batavia	24	1	7	0	0	1.000
Foust, Little Falls	13	3	4	0	1	1.000
Lunar, Utica	19	3	4	0	0	1.000
Kellogg, Jamestown	9	0	6	0	0	1.000
Flowers, Jamestown*	15	1	5	0	0	1.000
Mizzi, Little Falls*	19	1	5	0	0	1.000
DeRatt, Utica	13	2	3	0	2	1.000
Kaufman, Oneonta	17	1	4	0	1	1.000
Gault, Geneva	5	0	4	0	0	1.000
Reed, Jamestown*	8	0	4	0	0	1.000
Stutzriem, Batavia*	9	0	4	0	1	1.000
Adams, Newark	14	1	3	0	1	1.000
Tancredi, Little Falls	16	1	3	0	0	1.000
Paradise, Auburn*	2	1	2	0	0	1.000
Burger, Utica	3	2	1	0	0	1.000
Oleksak, Newark*	3	0	3	0	0	1.000
Samuel, Niagara Falls	7	0	3	0	0	1.000
Mims, Geneva*	11	0	3	0	1	1.000
Cuevas, Utica	12	0	3	0	0	1.000
Zwolinski, Little F*	12	0	3	0	0	1.000
Reynoso, Auburn	14	0	3	0	0	1.000
Gainer, Newark	1	1	1	0	0	1.000
Tulacz, Auburn*	2	0	2	0	0	1.000
Kwist, Auburn	4	1	1	0	0	1.000
Ostrow, Auburn	4	1	1	0	0	1.000

PITCHERS—Continued

Player and Club	G.	PO.	A.	E.	DP.	Pct.
Owens, Auburn	5	0	2	0	0	1.000
Clancy, Batavia	6	1	1	0	0	1.000
Tremblay, Elmira*	7	2	0	0	0	1.000
Merry, Batavia*	10	0	2	0	0	1.000
Vail, Utica	10	1	1	0	0	1.000
LaPointe, Auburn	11	0	2	0	1	1.000
Rosario, Little Falls*	19	0	2	0	0	1.000
Likely, Niagara Falls*	1	1	0	0	0	1.000
Sivik, Niagara Falls	1	1	0	0	0	1.000
Crawford, Geneva	2	1	0	0	0	1.000
Hodgins, Auburn	2	1	0	0	0	1.000
Friedrich, Niagara F*	3	0	1	0	0	1.000
Jackubowicz, Batavia	4	0	1	0	0	1.000
Bauman, Batavia*	5	0	1	0	0	1.000
Maki, Batavia*	8	0	1	0	0	1.000
Toliver, Oneonta	13	9	8	1	0	.964
Montgomery, James*	17	2	21	1	1	.958
Fitzhugh, Auburn	16	6	15	1	0	.955
Pimentel, Utica	16	5	15	1	1	.952
Fredlund, Elmira	19	6	14	1	0	.952
Anthony, Batavia	13	8	11	1	0	.950
Mudano, Utica*	16	3	16	1	0	.950
Sattler, Jamestown	13	2	16	1	0	.947
Thompson, Geneva*	13	5	12	1	3	.944
Wilkins, Geneva	13	6	11	1	1	.944
Hayford, Elmira	21	7	10	1	0	.944
Regan, Batavia	10	4	11	1	1	.938
Bohnet, Batavia*	12	3	12	1	1	.938
Musum, Jamestown*	12	1	14	1	1	.938
Soff, Geneva	9	5	23	2	2	.933
Roche, Batavia	13	3	11	1	0	.933
Mayles, Newark	9	3	10	1	0	.929
Henley, Little Falls	15	10	14	2	2	.923
Overton, Newark	12	2	10	1	0	.923
Patterson, Niagara Falls	10	3	8	1	1	.917
Ortega, Niagara Falls*	12	3	8	1	0	.917
Stemberger, Utica	14	3	18	2	3	.913
Renwick, Geneva	15	7	14	2	0	.913
Welch, Little Falls*	15	3	17	2	0	.909
Camp, Auburn	10	2	8	1	1	.909
Taylor, Jamestown*	13	3	15	2	1	.900
Freedman, Auburn	6	1	8	1	1	.900
Nuismer, Batavia	10	2	7	1	0	.900
Seneca, Oneonta	11	1	8	1	1	.900
White, Batavia	12	1	7	1	0	.889
Davis, Elmira*	13	1	7	1	0	.889
McCarthy, Elmira	18	3	5	1	1	.889
Wever, Oneonta	10	4	10	2	0	.875
Paquette, Little Falls	11	4	3	1	0	.875
Andersen, Oneonta	14	1	11	2	2	.857
Saunders, Elmira	16	5	7	2	1	.857
Maher, Jamestown	15	0	6	1	0	.857
Mills, Niagara Falls	20	1	5	1	0	.857
Wright, Newark	14	7	16	4	0	.852
Steffan, Oneonta*	14	6	10	3	0	.842
Florey, Auburn	9	1	9	2	1	.833
McManus, Geneva	11	0	10	2	1	.833
Ervey, Oneonta	16	3	7	2	1	.833
Russo, Newark	6	3	2	1	0	.833
Fee, Batavia*	7	3	2	1	0	.833
Collyer, Auburn*	15	1	4	1	0	.833
Goeggelman, Newark	19	2	3	1	0	.833
Oravec, Utica	19	1	8	2	0	.818
Walters, Niagara Falls	25	1	7	2	0	.800
Baker, Newark	4	1	3	1	0	.800
Irot, Oneonta	7	0	4	1	3	.800
Clay, Newark	21	2	2	1	0	.800
Keating, Niagara Falls	14	4	7	3	0	.786
DeSanto, Elmira	16	7	4	3	1	.786
Asbell, Batavia	17	2	10	4	0	.750
Birrell, Elmira*	6	2	4	2	0	.750
Larison, Batavia	10	1	2	1	0	.750
Nicastro, Newark	23	2	1	1	1	.750
Franks, Oneonta	13	1	9	4	3	.714
Hundley, Auburn*	25	3	2	2	0	.714
Green, Little Falls	10	1	3	2	0	.667

The following players had no recorded accepted chances; therefore are not listed in the fielding averages for those positions: Bajus, p; Baker, p; Byrket, p; Copeland, p; Filson*, p; Ganch*, p; Gnacinski, p; Hilton, p; Holton, p; Huber, p; St. Claire, p; Wagner, of. Encarnacion and Lanz appeared as designated hitters and/or pinch-hitters only.

CLUB PITCHING

Club	G.	CG.	ShO.	Sv.	IP.	H.	R.	ER.	HR.	BB.	Int. BB.	HB.	SO.	WP.	Bk.	ERA.
Oneonta	68	19	7	19	572	480	291	208	17	346	1	30	504	59	5	3.27
Geneva	69	19	8	10	611	525	267	228	33	309	10	25	477	46	0	3.36
Batavia	71	7	4	16	590	567	342	255	36	363	7	18	446	44	2	3.89
Jamestown	71	29	4	9	597	578	350	279	29	385	11	20	409	30	4	4.21
Elmira	69	3	2	11	581	584	395	301	27	403	16	29	449	57	4	4.66
Niagara Falls	71	12	1	8	601	610	418	322	20	439	3	29	417	67	2	4.82
Little Falls	71	6	2	10	609	632	425	328	39	407	8	23	439	42	1	4.84
Newark	71	18	0	9	587	645	405	322	27	316	17	15	320	38	3	4.94
Auburn	67	20	1	5	559	581	449	333	54	436	3	33	355	62	6	5.36
Utica	66	16	2	10	566	644	472	366	67	405	19	18	385	56	7	5.82

PITCHERS' RECORDS
(Leading Qualifiers for Earned-Run Average Leadership—58 or More Innings)

*Throws lefthanded.

Pitcher—Club	G.	GS.	CG.	ShO.	W.	L.	Sv.	Pct.	IP.	H.	R.	ER.	HR.	BB.	Int. BB.	HB.	SO.	WP.	ERA.
Wever, Oneonta	10	9	4	2	6	3	0	.667	66	43	24	13	1	36	0	3	70	5	1.77
Renwick, Geneva	15	10	3	1	8	1	1	.889	93	79	23	19	2	31	1	4	66	3	1.84
Thompson, Geneva*	13	5	2	0	5	1	1	.833	65	44	19	14	5	26	3	0	63	1	1.94
Bohnet, Batavia*	12	10	1	0	6	3	0	.667	59	41	19	13	4	37	0	0	65	3	1.98
Moloney, Elmira*	21	0	0	0	8	1	4	.889	60	35	22	14	2	27	2	0	59	2	2.10
Toliver, Oneonta	13	13	1	0	10	2	0	.833	77	46	28	18	3	66	0	1	71	9	2.10
Andersen, Oneonta	14	7	3	1	4	3	2	.571	65	52	19	16	2	23	0	4	39	1	2.22
Millner, Geneva	12	12	6	1	9	1	0	.900	94	69	27	25	6	36	0	1	52	7	2.39
Regan, Batavia	10	10	2	0	5	4	0	.556	62	49	29	19	3	28	0	1	54	7	2.76
Hardy, Geneva*	11	11	5	3	7	1	0	.875	84	72	29	26	4	17	0	3	82	3	2.79

Departmental Leaders: G—Damiter, 29; GS—Ford, Welch, 15; CG—Sattler, 10; ShO—Hardy, 3; W—Toliver, 10; L—Pimentel, 10; Sv—Hrynko, Kaufman, 9; Pct.—Millner .900; IP—Ford, 104; H—Ford, 120; R—Wright, 67; ER—Ford, 52; HR—Fitzhugh, 11; BB—O'Dowd, 69; IBB—Goeggelman, 9; HB—Hundley, 7; SO—Hardy, Sattler, 82; WP—Camp, 17.

(All Pitchers–Listed Alphabetically)

Pitcher–Club	G	GS	CG	ShO	W	L	Sv	Pct.	IP	H	R	ER	HR	BB	Int. BB	HB	SO	WP	ERA
Adams, Newark	14	0	0	0	0	1	2	.000	29	34	20	20	1	27	0	2	18	10	6.21
Andersen, Oneonta	14	7	3	1	4	3	2	.571	65	62	29	16	2	23	0	4	39	1	2.22
Anthony, Batavia	13	12	2	0	5	6	0	.455	81	86	41	32	4	30	0	0	61	4	3.56
Asbell, Batavia	17	7	1	0	2	6	1	.250	56	59	38	30	4	32	1	2	44	6	4.82
Bajus, Batavia*	3	0	0	0	0	0	0	.000	4	3	3	3	1	5	0	1	1	0	6.75
Baker, Newqrk*	4	2	0	0	1	1	0	.500	15	19	18	11	2	11	0	0	5	0	6.60
Baker, Jamestown	6	3	1	0	0	2	0	.000	11	19	15	15	0	13	0	2	11	0	12.27
Bauman, Batavia*	5	2	0	0	2	1	1	.667	16	16	10	7	1	15	0	0	20	0	3.94
Birrell, Elmira*	6	0	0	0	1	1	3	.500	13	10	4	1	0	5	0	1	19	1	0.69
Blyth, Geneva	26	0	0	0	8	2	7	.800	55	42	19	17	4	41	5	2	63	6	2.78
Bohnet, Batavia*	12	10	1	0	6	3	0	.667	59	41	19	13	4	37	0	0	65	3	1.98
Burger, Utica	3	0	0	0	0	0	0	.000	3	3	3	2	0	T	1	0	2	2	6.00
Byrket, Jamestown	1	0	0	0	0	0	0	.000	0	0	2	2	0	4	0	0	0	0	....
Camp, Auburn	10	9	0	0	1	6	0	.143	38	40	51	40	5	66	0	4	20	17	9.47
Cates, Jamestown	13	7	3	0	5	4	0	.556	64	66	35	24	1	46	0	1	33	4	3.38
Clancy, Batavia	6	0	0	0	0	1	0	.000	12	22	14	12	0	10	1	0	4	0	9.00
Clay, Newark	21	0	0	0	0	1	1	.500	42	47	26	22	2	18	1	4	27	2	4.71
Collyer, Auburn*	15	1	0	0	0	2	1	.000	36	27	22	11	0	35	0	1	35	9	2.75
Copeland, Oneonta	1	0	0	0	0	0	0	.000	⅓	0	1	0	0	2	0	0	1	0	0.00
Crawford, Geneva	2	0	0	0	1	0	0	1.000	5	4	3	3	0	1	0	0	5	0	5.40
Cuevas, Utica	12	0	0	0	0	0	0	.000	18	26	37	32	3	30	2	1	20	1	16.00
Damiter, Little Falls	29	0	0	0	5	5	7	.500	57	50	26	22	1	30	2	1	37	2	3.47
Dann, Newark*	9	9	2	0	1	5	0	.167	48	58	33	26	0	24	0	0	38	3	4.88
Davis, Niagara Falls	13	3	0	0	1	1	0	.500	40	44	29	27	3	32	0	3	15	3	6.08
Davis, Elmira*	13	11	0	0	2	2	0	.500	49	46	35	27	2	44	0	3	42	6	4.96
DeRatt, Elmira	13	3	0	0	1	2	2	.333	33	36	27	19	7	33	0	0	25	5	5.18
DeSanto, Elmira	16	10	0	0	2	5	0	.286	54	60	53	47	6	65	2	4	31	12	7.83
Dwyer, 4 Bat-5 Aub	9	7	0	0	0	5	0	.000	33	42	35	22	4	27	1	3	7	6	6.00
Ervey, Oneonta	16	6	1	0	3	2	3	.600	54	46	21	14	1	24	0	5	50	3	2.33
Fallon, Niagara Falls*	15	12	1	0	3	7	0	.300	83	70	48	32	3	66	0	1	52	6	3.47
Fee, Batavia*	7	1	0	0	1	0	1	1.000	17	17	8	3	0	12	0	1	12	0	1.59
Filson, Oneonta*	1	0	0	0	0	0	0	.000	⅔	0	0	0	0	0	0	0	1	0	0.00
Fishback, Niagara Falls	13	12	4	0	5	6	0	.455	89	91	48	34	2	24	0	1	43	2	3.44
Fitzhugh, Auburn	13	13	6	0	3	9	0	.250	90	92	64	49	11	51	0	4	69	8	4.90
Florey, Auburn	9	7	0	0	1	4	0	.200	36	32	33	28	1	39	0	3	21	1	7.00
Flowers, Jamestown*	14	4	1	0	1	4	4	.200	42	32	34	25	5	45	2	0	34	3	5.36
Ford, Utica*	16	15	5	1	7	6	0	.538	104	120	65	52	7	55	0	4	78	12	4.50
Foust, Little Falls	13	2	0	0	0	2	0	.000	32	28	22	19	2	35	3	2	23	1	5.34
Franks, Oneonta	13	10	3	0	5	2	0	.714	58	67	48	40	2	44	0	4	37	8	6.21
Fredlund, Elmira	19	10	2	0	5	3	0	.625	85	78	41	29	4	42	1	3	62	7	3.07
Freedman, Auburn	6	5	2	0	2	1	0	.667	39	34	19	16	3	20	1	1	31	7	3.69
Friedrich, Niagara Falls*	3	3	0	0	0	1	0	.500	15	17	15	13	0	15	0	1	16	2	7.80
Gainer, Newark	1	1	0	0	0	0	0	.000	2	3	2	2	0	3	0	0	0	0	9.00
Ganch, Newark*	4	1	0	0	0	1	0	.000	3	13	10	8	0	2	0	1	1	0	24.00
Gault, Geneva	5	5	0	0	0	3	0	.000	9	10	28	27	1	32	0	6	11	6	27.00
Gering, Elmira	18	11	0	0	5	6	0	.455	70	83	53	37	1	36	1	5	50	5	4.76
Gnacinski, Oneonta	7	2	0	0	1	1	1	.500	16	5	7	5	0	14	0	2	20	2	2.81
Goeggelman, Newark	19	0	0	0	2	4	3	.333	33	32	14	12	2	27	9	0	27	2	3.27
Gorey, Auburn	10	10	6	0	1	8	0	.111	69	77	52	38	6	40	0	4	34	0	4.96
Green, Little Falls	10	8	0	0	2	3	0	.400	33	38	34	24	1	32	0	1	33	3	6.55
Hardy, Geneva	11	11	5	3	7	1	0	.875	84	72	29	26	4	17	0	3	82	3	2.79
Hartsock, Jamestown	19	6	4	0	7	4	0	.636	71	78	40	33	2	29	3	3	38	1	4.18
Hayford, Elmira	21	3	0	0	2	3	1	.400	56	55	37	33	1	45	5	2	54	2	5.30
Henley, Little Falls	15	10	3	1	4	6	1	.400	77	68	50	37	3	30	0	3	44	2	4.32
Hilton, Little Falls	8	0	0	0	0	0	0	.000	14	12	8	7	1	8	0	0	12	1	4.50
Hodgins, Auburn	2	0	0	0	0	0	0	.000	4	15	16	11	4	1	0	0	1	1	24.75
Holbrook, Niagara Falls	13	0	0	0	0	1	1	.500	36	47	37	32	2	27	2	3	28	8	8.00
Holton, Utica	2	0	0	0	0	0	0	.000	2	0	0	0	3	0	0	0	2	0	0.00
Hrynko, Batavia	24	2	0	0	1	2	9	.667	37	30	10	9	0	11	1	0	23	0	2.19
Huber, Jamestown	2	0	0	0	0	0	0	.000	2	3	7	7	0	3	0	0	3	0	31.50
Hundley, Auburn*	25	0	0	0	7	3	1	.700	48	45	37	25	4	37	0	7	38	1	4.69
Irot, Oneonta	7	1	0	0	0	1	0	.000	29	24	21	14	2	30	0	3	21	7	4.34
Jackubowicz, Batavia	4	0	0	0	0	0	0	.000	7	9	6	6	0	5	0	0	4	0	7.71
Karl, Newark	9	9	2	0	3	5	0	.375	52	57	33	29	3	22	1	0	13	3	5.02
Kaufman, Oneonta	17	0	0	0	4	1	9	.800	30	10	3	3	0	16	1	0	50	2	0.90
Keating, Niagara Falls	14	9	0	0	2	5	0	.286	38	64	66	48	4	54	0	3	19	6	11.37
Kellogg, Jamestown	9	0	0	0	1	1	4	.500	21	15	8	4	0	13	3	0	20	2	1.71
Korbes, Niagara Falls*	10	3	1	0	2	2	0	.500	38	29	19	15	0	30	0	3	34	6	3.55
Krill, Auburn*	9	8	5	1	5	2	0	.714	64	52	24	20	3	45	1	0	37	0	2.81
Kwist, Auburn	4	0	0	0	0	0	0	.000	4	6	1	1	0	2	0	0	4	0	2.25
Larison, Batavia	10	3	0	0	2	1	0	.667	21	24	13	9	1	18	1	1	10	2	3.86
LaPointe, Auburn	11	2	1	0	1	0	1	1.000	35	37	28	22	6	18	0	3	10	4	5.66
Likely, Niagara Falls*	1	0	0	0	0	0	0	.000	4	9	7	4	0	5	0	0	1	2	9.00
Lunar, Utica	19	0	0	0	0	1	0	.000	38	67	52	36	6	24	2	1	29	3	8.53

Pitcher—Club	G.	GS.	CG.	ShO.	W.	L.	Sv.	Pct.	IP.	H.	R.	ER.	HR.	BB.	Int. BB.	HB.	SO.	WP.	ERA.
Maher, Jamestown	15	9	3	1	8	3	1	.727	66	49	28	21	1	41	0	4	46	2	2.86
Maitland, Niagara Falls*	4	4	1	0	2	2	0	.500	29	27	9	8	1	9	0	0	26	3	2.48
Maki, Batavia*	8	0	0	0	1	1	0	.500	10	16	11	10	3	10	0	1	4	2	9.00
Mayles, Newark	9	6	0	0	4	1	0	.800	39	42	29	25	2	41	0	1	17	4	5.77
McArow, Newark	6	6	2	0	3	2	0	.600	41	46	34	23	0	22	0	1	38	1	5.05
McCarthy, Elmira	18	4	0	0	2	6	1	.250	46	67	50	36	2	37	2	2	26	4	7.04
McManus, Geneva	11	1	0	0	2	1	0	.667	27	43	24	18	1	18	0	1	10	1	6.00
Merry, Batavia*	10	1	0	0	0	0	0	.000	15	21	13	8	2	11	0	0	14	3	4.80
Millner, Geneva	12	12	6	1	9	1	0	.900	94	69	27	25	6	36	0	1	52	7	2.39
Mills, Niagara Falls	20	4	0	0	2	3	3	.400	49	43	37	27	0	55	1	0	45	8	4.96
Mims, Geneva*	11	0	0	0	0	1	1	.000	18	18	10	9	0	19	0	0	21	2	4.50
Mizzi, Little Falls	19	7	0	0	4	4	0	.500	52	53	34	26	4	36	2	1	44	8	4.50
Moloney, Elmira*	21	0	0	0	8	1	4	.889	60	35	22	14	2	27	2	0	59	2	2.10
Montgomery, Jamestown*	17	5	2	1	5	1	3	.833	59	64	35	25	5	36	0	1	36	2	3.81
Mudano, Utica	16	5	0	0	2	3	1	.400	46	67	45	34	9	21	2	0	23	5	6.65
Musum, Jamestown*	12	11	3	0	2	2	0	.500	66	67	34	31	4	37	2	0	31	3	4.23
Nicastro, Newark	23	3	2	0	6	5	3	.545	70	68	54	44	5	42	4	3	59	6	5.66
Norman, Batavia*	13	7	0	0	3	3	3	.500	48	42	31	22	3	31	0	4	42	2	4.13
Nuismer, Batavia	10	7	0	0	2	3	0	.400	39	35	18	13	2	21	0	0	35	5	3.00
Nurthen, Oneonta	15	0	0	0	1	2	0	.333	39	34	19	14	0	23	0	2	29	8	3.23
O'Dowd, Utica	14	14	0	0	4	7	0	.364	67	62	58	45	9	69	1	1	43	6	6.04
Oleksak, Newark*	3	3	1	0	0	2	0	.000	16	18	7	7	1	10	0	0	8	0	3.94
Oravec, Utica	19	3	0	0	2	3	3	.400	44	50	30	25	6	24	2	1	29	4	5.11
Ortega, Niagara Falls*	12	11	1	0	3	7	0	.300	55	54	39	33	1	46	0	4	42	6	5.40
Ostrow, Auburn	4	3	0	0	1	2	0	.333	15	21	14	8	1	5	0	0	5	1	4.80
Overton, Auburn	12	11	1	0	1	4	0	.200	60	64	37	29	4	20	2	2	24	2	4.35
Owens, Auburn	5	1	0	0	0	1	0	.000	9	9	11	11	1	12	0	1	11	1	11.00
Paquette, Little Falls	11	11	1	0	3	3	0	.500	57	55	35	25	0	39	0	3	30	1	3.95
Paradise, Auburn*	2	1	0	0	0	1	0	.000	12	12	8	1	13	0	1	7	2		8.00
Patterson, Niagara Falls.	10	6	4	0	5	1	0	.833	55	43	17	14	1	21	0	4	44	6	2.29
Pimentel, Utica	16	13	3	0	3	10	0	.231	69	78	65	48	7	52	3	3	35	6	6.26
Reed, Jamestown*	8	0	0	0	1	0	0	1.000	17	28	16	14	0	12	1	1	13	1	7.41
Regan, Batavia	10	10	2	0	5	4	0	.556	62	49	28	19	3	28	0	1	54	7	2.76
Renwick, Geneva	15	10	3	1	8	1	1	.889	93	79	23	19	2	31	1	4	66	3	1.84
Reynoso, Auburn	14	0	0	0	0	1	0	.000	30	40	28	21	4	21	0	1	18	5	6.30
Roche, Batavia	13	4	0	0	2	2	1	.500	41	43	35	28	6	28	1	1	22	4	6.15
Rosario, Little Falls	19	0	0	0	1	0	1	1.000	24	32	24	16	5	15	1	0	25	2	6.00
Russo, Newark	6	6	3	0	3	1	0	.750	41	31	21	18	1	16	0	0	5	1	3.95
St. Claire, Jamestown	4	0	0	0	0	1	0	.000	5	11	10	10	1	3	0	2	1	1	18.00
Samuel, Niagara Falls	7	2	0	0	0	2	0	.000	22	31	18	14	1	18	0	0	9	4	5.73
Sattler, Jamestown	13	13	9	1	8	2	0	.800	96	83	42	33	5	50	0	3	82	8	3.09
Saunders, Elmira	16	8	0	0	3	4	1	.429	64	63	45	35	5	43	1	1	46	12	4.92
Schaefer, Elmira	16	12	1	0	4	4	0	.500	78	81	49	36	3	50	2	6	56	6	4.15
Semprini, Little Falls	16	3	0	0	2	2	1	.500	42	51	27	24	4	28	0	1	21	7	5.14
Seneca, Oneonta	11	6	3	1	3	3	0	.500	50	43	26	23	1	22	0	2	36	5	4.14
Shockley, Little Falls	12	11	0	0	2	6	0	.250	62	75	50	39	5	47	0	3	51	4	5.66
Sivik, Niagara Falls	1	1	0	0	0	1	0	.000	3	5	4	4	0	5	0	0	1	1	12.00
Soff, Geneva	9	8	0	0	3	2	0	.600	56	48	26	23	2	34	0	5	38	4	3.70
Steffan, Oneonta*	14	14	4	0	5	7	0	.417	89	100	64	48	5	46	0	4	80	8	4.85
Stemberger, Utica	14	11	2	1	4	4	0	.500	65	59	30	21	3	30	2	2	42	5	2.91
Stutzriem, Batavia*	9	1	0	0	1	1	0	.500	16	14	10	4	0	18	1	1	7	0	2.25
Tancredi, Little Falls	16	3	0	0	1	3	0	.250	36	45	35	30	4	38	0	3	20	4	7.50
Taylor, Jamestown	13	13	3	1	5	3	0	.625	77	63	44	35	5	53	0	3	61	3	4.09
Thompson, Geneva*	13	5	2	0	5	1	1	.833	65	44	19	14	5	26	3	0	63	1	1.94
Toliver, Oneonta	13	13	1	0	10	2	0	.833	77	46	28	18	3	66	0	1	71	9	2.10
Tremblay, Elmira*	7	0	0	0	0	1	0	1.000	8	6	6	6	1	9	0	1	4	0	6.75
Tulacz, Auburn*	2	2	0	0	0	1	0	.000	11	10	12	8	0	15	0	1	10	1	6.55
Vail, Utica	10	0	0	0	0	0	0	.000	25	22	14	13	4	16	1	1	13	1	4.68
Vaji, Geneva*	5	4	0	0	1	1	0	.500	20	13	10	10	2	16	0	0	11	8	4.50
Velasquez, Utica	2	0	0	0	0	0	0	.000	4	3	1	1	0	4	0	0	2	0	2.25
Walters, Niagara Falls	25	1	0	0	4	2	5	.667	46	36	25	17	2	32	0	6	42	4	3.33
Welch, Little Falls*	15	15	2	1	5	5	0	.500	96	104	61	46	9	41	0	4	66	4	4.31
Wever, Oneonta	10	9	4	2	6	3	0	.667	66	43	24	13	1	36	0	3	70	5	1.77
White, Batavia	12	2	1	0	3	0	0	1.000	41	30	24	21	2	30	1	5	21	4	4.61
White, Utica	27	2	0	0	2	5	4	.286	48	51	45	38	6	38	3	4	44	4	7.13
Wilkins, Geneva	13	13	3	0	6	5	0	.545	83	83	49	39	6	38	1	3	54	5	4.23
Wright, Newark	14	14	5	0	7	6	0	.538	94	113	67	46	4	31	0	1	40	4	4.40
Zwolinski, Little Falls*	12	12	1	0	2	1	0		28	21	19	13	0	28	0	1	33	3	4.18

BALKS—Reynoso, 3; Adams, Cates, Cuevas, Mooney, Schaefer, Stemberger, Toliver, Wever, 2 each; Anthony, Asbell, Fishback, Freedman, Gorey, Green, Kaufman, Lunar, Mayles, Mills, Mudano, O'Dowd, Sattler, Taylor, Tulacz, 1 each.

COMBINATION SHUTOUTS—Regan-Anthony, Anthony-Stutzreim, Nuismer-Hrynko, Anthony-Stutzreim-Norman, Batavia; Schaefer-Davis, Davis-Moloney, Elmira; Millner-Thompson, Vaji-Renwick, Wilkins-Blyth, Jamestown; Ortega-Walters, Niagara Falls; Toliver-Kaufman, Wever-Gnacinski, Ervey-Kaufman, Oneonta.

NO-HIT GAMES—None.

Northwest League

CLASS A

CHAMPIONSHIP WINNERS IN PREVIOUS YEARS

1901—Portland .... .675	1940—Spokane........................... .587	1962—Wenatchee*.................... .574
1902—Butte............................. .608	Tacoma (4th)†............. .500	Tri-City .... .580
1903—Butte............................. .578	1941—Spokane........................... .669	1963—Lewiston.................... .594
1904—Boise............................. .625	1942—Vancouver .... .594	Yakima*........................ .613
1905—Vancouver...................... .586	1943-45—Did not operate.	1964—Eugene .... .636
Everett*................... .667	1946—Wenatchee...................... .622	Yakima*........................ .611
1906—Tacoma.......................... .600	1947—Vancouver .... .566	1965—Lewiston.................... .667
1907—Aberdeen .... .625	1948—Spokane........................... .614	Tri-City*....................... .681
1908—Vancouver...................... .578	1949—Yakima............................. .660	1966—Tri-City .... .679
1909—Seattle........................... .653	Vancouver (2nd)†........... .615	1967—Medford...................... .607
1910—Spokane......................... .596	1950—Yakima............................. .613	1968—Tri-City .... .600
1911—Vancouver...................... .628	1951—Spokane........................... .655	1969—Rogue Valley................ .633
1912—Seattle........................... .600	1952—Victoria........................... .631	1970—Lewiston a .... .538
1913—Vancouver...................... .600	1953—Salem............................... .635	Coos Bay-No. Bend......... .563
1914—Vancouver...................... .632	Spokane*........................ .590	1971—Tri-City a .... .625
1915—Seattle........................... .564	1954—Vancouver*...................... .636	Bend .... .538
1916—Spokane......................... .622	Lewiston....................... .629	1972—Lewiston a .... .675
1917—Great Falls .... .592	1955—Salem............................... .646	Walla Walla .... .513
1918—Seattle........................... .588	Eugene*......................... .639	1973—Walla Walla b .... .638
1919—Seattle........................... .590	1956—Yakima............................. .691	Portland .... .563
1920—Victoria......................... .600	Yakima........................... .619	1974—Bellingham .... .619
1921—Yakima........................... .710	1957—Eugene .... .576	Eugene c........................ .571
Yakima......................... .660	Wenatchee*.................... .647	1975—Portland .... .545
1922—Calgary§........................ .600	1958—Lewiston......................... .621	Eugene d........................ .684
1923-36—Did not operate.	Yakima*......................... .594	1976—Portland .... .556
1937—Wenatchee..................... .603	1959—Salem............................... .623	Walla Walla d .... .639
Tacoma*..................... .627	Yakima*......................... .563	1977—Bellingham e .... .618
1938—Yakima........................... .583	1960—Yakima‡.......................... .638	Portland .... .667
Bellingham (2nd)†....... .511	Yakima........................... .562	1978—Grays Harbor f .... .671
1939—Wenatchee..................... .601	1961—Lewiston*........................ .621	Eugene............................ .514
Tacoma (2nd)†........ .533	Yakima........................... .600	

*Won split-season playoff. †Won four-club playoff. §League disbanded June 18. aLeague divided into Northern and Southern divisions, declared champion under league rules. (NOTE—Known as Pacific Northwest League 1901-02, Pacific National League 1903-04, Northwestern League 1905-18, Pacific Coast International League 1919-22 and Western International League 1937-54.) bLeague divided into Eastern and Western divisions, declared champion under league rules. cLeague divided into Eastern and Western divisions; won two-team playoff. dLeague divided into Northern and Southern divisions; won two-team playoff. eLeague divided into Affiliate and Independent divisions; won two-team playoff. fDeclared league champion after winning one-game playoff. Balance of playoff canceled due to rain and wet grounds.

STANDING OF CLUBS AT CLOSE OF SEASON, AUGUST 30

NORTHERN DIVISION

Club	W.W.	Bell.	Vic.	G.H.	C.O.	Med.	Sal.	Eug.	W.	L.	T.	Pct.	G.B.
Walla Walla (Padres)	..	10	4	12	2	2	5	5	40	30	0	.571	....
Bellingham (Mariners)	6	..	8	13	1	5	4	4	41	31	0	.569	....
Victoria (Independent)	12	8	..	11	1	3	1	5	41	31	0	.569	....
Grays Harbor (Mets)	3	3	5	..	2	3	0	3	19	52	0	.268	21½

SOUTHERN DIVISION

Central Oregon (Phillies)	3	5	5	4	..	8	9	9	43	28	0	.606	....
Medford (Athletics)	4	1	3	3	8	..	10	9	38	33	0	.535	5
Salem (Independent)	1	2	5	6	7	6	..	6	33	39	0	.458	10½
Eugene (Reds)	1	2	1	3	7	6	10	..	30	41	0	.423	13

Central Oregon represented Bend, Ore.

Grays Harbor represented Aberdeen and Hoquiam, Wash.

Major league affiliations in parentheses.

Playoff—Central Oregon defeated Walla Walla, two games to one.

Regular-Season Attendance—Bellingham, 31,741; Central Oregon, 18,610; Eugene, 66,156; Grays Harbor, 16,665; Medford, 34,656; Salem, 15,904; Victoria, 9,073; Walla Walla, 20,358. Total, 213,163. Playoffs, 1,812. No all-star game.

Managers: Bellingham—Jeffrey Scott; Central Oregon—Tom Harmon; Eugene—Greg Riddoch; Grays Harbor—Danny Monzon; Medford—Richard Morales; Salem—Gene Lanthorn; Victoria—Bill Bryk; Walla Walla—Curt Daniels.

All-Star Team: 1B—Drzayich, Victoria; 2B—Clark, Bellingham; 3B—Seefried, Salem; SS—Franco, Central Oregon; OF—Garrett, Medford; Estepa, Bellingham; Cain, Walla Walla; C—Orensky, Central Oregon; DH—Lulay, Walla Walla; Utility—Durrman, Medford; P—Barba, Walla Walla; Froelich, Walla Walla; Koziol, Victoria; Ramsey, Eugene; Runyan, Salem; Manager—Harmon, Central Oregon.

(Compiled by William J. Weiss, League Statistician, San Mateo, Calif.)

CLUB BATTING

Club	G.	AB.	R.	OR.	H.	TB.	2B.	3B.	HR.	RBI.	SH.	SF.	Int. BB.	BB.	HP.	SO.	SB.	CS.	LOB.	Pct.
Victoria	72	2412	430	358	665	955	120	25	40	381	29	31	400	10	26	420	65	46	603	.276
Salem	72	2450	414	408	668	879	88	39	15	350	56	24	359	13	34	402	89	47	587	.273
Cent. Oregon	71	2449	435	328	649	965	98	34	50	394	21	23	275	10	26	556	112	43	499	.265
Medford	71	2383	376	402	627	841	89	28	23	316	17	28	339	7	19	401	120	36	561	.263
Bellingham	72	2390	396	353	620	872	103	19	37	319	19	23	346	9	30	478	92	51	537	.259
Walla Walla	70	2299	371	355	562	766	71	20	31	318	38	24	437	15	25	532	91	33	601	.244
Eugene	71	2387	316	375	579	779	75	25	25	259	29	14	322	17	34	471	90	24	584	.243
Grays Harbor	71	2290	278	437	535	684	74	12	17	232	19	24	334	9	23	554	68	25	573	.234

INDIVIDUAL BATTING

(Leading Qualifiers for Batting Championship—194 or More Plate Appearances)

*Bats lefthanded.   †Switch-hitter.

Player and Club	G.	AB.	R.	H.	TB.	2B.	3B.	HR.	RBI.	SH.	SF.	BB.	HP.	SO.	SB.	CS.	Pct.
Rabassa, Pedro, Victoria*	62	181	46	69	108	19	4	4	35	2	2	58	2	37	11	3	.381
Durrman, James, Medford*	62	214	43	75	124	9	5	10	50	0	3	48	1	29	5	1	.350
Clark, Roy, Bellingham	49	182	38	61	80	12	2	1	23	3	4	19	1	11	10	3	.335
Garrett, Bobby, Medford	71	286	66	95	115	10	5	0	32	1	5	39	4	23	58	11	.332
Franco, Julio, Central Oregon	71	299	57	98	153	15	5	10	45	2	2	24	3	59	22	9	.328
Lulay, Douglas, Walla Walla	70	275	48	88	134	15	5	7	62	6	0	26	6	56	10	6	.320
McKinney, Gregory, Eugene*	50	163	25	50	69	5	4	2	19	2	2	38	5	44	1	3	.307
Codiroli, Michael, Bellingham	51	171	36	52	63	7	2	0	17	5	2	35	8	35	14	4	.304
Estepa, Ramon, Bellingham	71	265	55	80	126	16	3	8	51	0	3	45	1	41	10	7	.302
Cain, Aaron, Walla Walla	69	240	59	72	104	8	3	6	42	3	2	61	3	39	23	3	.300

Departmental Leaders: G—Drzayich, Estepa, Franco, Garrett, G. Jackson, Rincones, 71; AB—Rincones, 301; R—Garrett, 66; H—Franco, 98; TB—Franco, 153; 2B—Rabassa, 19; 3B—Seefried, 8; HR—Durrman, Franco, 10; RBI—Lulay, 62; SH—Majam, 9; SF—Drzayich, Seefried, 6; BB—Majam, 82; HP—Codiroli, G. Jacksn, 8; SO—Fryer, 82; SB—Garrett, 58; CS—Burton, Garrett, 11.

(All Players-Listed Alphabetically)

Player and Club	G.	AB.	R.	H.	TB.	2B.	3B.	HR.	RBI.	SH.	SF.	BB.	HP.	SO.	SB.	CS.	Pct.
Acosta, Jorge, Bellingham	44	87	11	17	17	0	0	0	9	0	2	9	2	22	2	1	.195
Adams, Norman, Eugene*	12	13	1	3	3	0	0	0	2	1	0	0	0	3	0	0	.231
Allen, James, Bellingham	21	85	11	14	20	3	0	1	13	0	1	9	0	10	1	0	.165
Altobelli, Michael, Medford	56	216	35	55	79	8	5	2	27	6	1	18	4	26	6	3	.255
Angius, Robert, Central Oregon*	37	124	18	26	33	2	1	1	11	1	0	12	1	35	4	1	.210
Aponte, Edwin, Bellingham	38	118	19	37	54	11	0	2	17	0	0	11	2	14	0	2	.314
Bangert, Gregory, Eugene*	16	19	0	1	1	0	0	0	1	2	0	4	0	16	0	0	.053
Baugh, D. Dean, Central Oregon	41	137	20	24	38	2	0	4	21	2	2	19	3	41	1	2	.175
Bauman, Brad, Salem	52	180	23	40	50	5	1	1	25	8	1	21	2	28	2	2	.222
Beal, Calvin, Victoria	45	94	23	28	38	4	3	0	5	0	0	8	2	26	7	6	.298
Belmonte, Nicholas, 31 Sal—11 Vic.	42	146	29	38	58	5	6	1	25	5	2	15	7	25	13	4	.260
Blackman, Steven, Salem*	47	168	22	58	78	11	3	1	26	0	0	19	1	30	10	6	.345
Bodman, Lewis, Salem	61	135	23	35	41	4	1	0	9	6	1	16	7	23	1	0	.259
Bryan, James, Salem	25	67	14	18	23	5	0	0	6	1	0	8	0	20	1	0	.269
Burnett, Oscar, Medford	14	33	5	4	4	0	0	0	5	0	0	4	0	7	0	0	.121
Burton, James, Victoria	66	239	54	57	86	10	2	5	29	5	4	44	3	31	12	11	.238
Cain, Aaron, Walla Walla	69	240	59	72	104	8	3	6	42	3	2	61	3	39	23	3	.300
Chamberlain, William, G Harbor	65	221	24	56	76	8	0	4	34	1	5	35	5	64	1	1	.253
Chambers, Albert, Bellingham*	55	166	26	41	53	4	1	2	22	1	1	33	0	51	13	8	.247
Chelette, J. Mark, Bellingham*	11	38	12	12	24	3	0	3	10	0	0	8	0	2	2	1	.316
Cias, Darryl, Medford	16	56	11	20	32	5	2	1	11	0	0	9	1	13	0	0	.357
Clark, Roy, Bellingham	49	182	38	61	80	12	2	1	23	3	4	19	1	11	10	3	.335
Codiroli, Michael, Bellingham	51	171	36	52	63	7	2	0	17	5	2	35	8	35	14	4	.304
Colby, Charles, Bellingham	39	52	12	12	17	3	1	0	4	0	0	8	1	20	5	5	.231
Cook, John, Bellingham*	3	8	4	2	4	0	1	0	2	0	0	0	0	1	1	0	.250
Cooper, Marques, Grays Harbor	10	33	3	7	8	1	0	0	4	0	0	2	0	13	1	0	.212
Cummins, L. Michael, Salem	66	255	31	76	97	14	2	1	46	1	1	22	4	38	2	2	.298
DeJiulio, Frank, Eugene*	18	32	0	7	7	0	0	0	1	0	1	1	1	10	0	0	.219
Denby, Darryl, Grays Harbor	64	214	27	52	65	5	1	2	16	5	2	10	2	57	9	1	.243
DeSimone, Gerald, Walla Walla†	67	225	39	64	82	10	4	0	32	4	2	65	1	36	13	3	.284
Diaz, Enrique, Bellingham	65	237	28	52	68	9	2	1	23	1	1	23	2	53	3	3	.219
Diaz, Mario, Bellingham	32	96	12	19	24	2	0	1	5	3	0	5	1	17	0	3	.198

Player and Club	G.	AB.	R.	H.	TB.	2B.	3B.	HR.	RBI.	SH.	SF.	BB.	HP.	SO.	SB.	CS.	Pct.
Dorsey, Thomas, Victoria*	39	131	24	42	74	9	4	5	24	1	1	16	1	33	1	2	.321
Drzayich, Emil, Victoria*	71	271	41	77	121	18	1	8	61	0	6	27	6	44	1	0	.284
Duff, David, Grays Harbor	57	202	17	48	74	16	2	2	24	1	3	29	2	31	2	4	.238
Dunbar, Bryan, Grays Harbor	21	63	6	7	9	2	0	0	3	0	0	13	0	23	0	0	.111
Durrman, James, Medford*	62	214	43	75	124	9	5	10	50	0	3	48	1	29	5	1	.350
Dwyer, Michael, Walla Walla	19	42	8	6	6	0	0	0	3	0	0	11	0	19	0	0	.143
Echenique, Orlando, Grays Harbor	45	139	13	25	34	4	1	1	14	0	3	29	0	36	0	3	.180
Edwards, Brian, Victoria	22	65	12	19	20	1	0	0	11	1	0	7	3	14	2	1	.292
Eiler, Dale, Bellingham	30	81	14	26	42	5	1	3	17	0	2	18	1	17	0	1	.321
Elliott, Douglas, Medford	66	231	35	63	73	6	2	0	29	7	3	31	4	43	15	1	.273
Elliott, William, Eugene*	3	1	0	0	0	0	0	0	0	0	0	0	0	0	0	0	.000
Estepa, Ramon, Bellingham	71	265	55	80	126	16	3	8	51	0	3	45	1	41	10	7	.302
Flannery, Kevin, Eugene*	1	2	1	0	0	0	0	0	0	0	0	0	0	1	0	0	.000
Franco, Julio, Central Oregon	71	299	57	98	153	15	5	10	45	2	2	24	3	59	22	9	.328
Freitas, John, Victoria	15	46	9	18	24	3	0	1	13	0	0	12	0	5	0	0	.391
Frierson, Michael, 15 Bel-18 Salt	33	90	15	20	21	1	0	0	5	1	0	4	2	25	13	3	.222
Fryer, Paul, Central Oregon	62	231	39	57	87	12	3	4	30	0	2	23	1	82	4	4	.247
Fuson, Grady, Salem	45	126	16	25	30	3	1	0	12	5	1	16	1	34	2	3	.198
Gaffney, William, Bellingham	4	9	2	1	1	0	0	0	0	0	0	3	0	3	0	1	.111
Gandy, Chris, Victoria	28	81	9	16	21	3	1	0	10	0	3	9	2	28	0	1	.198
Garcia, Agustin, Grays Harbor	57	180	22	32	44	6	3	0	13	0	2	28	2	54	3	2	.178
Garrett, Bobby, Medford	71	286	66	95	115	10	5	0	32	1	5	39	4	23	58	11	.332
Gausepohl, Daniel, Walla Walla	66	268	47	66	95	5	3	6	31	4	2	32	1	43	17	9	.246
Geren, Robert, Walla Walla	54	151	19	26	31	5	0	0	16	1	1	32	0	39	0	0	.172
Getter, Russell, Eugene*	26	65	7	15	19	4	0	0	8	3	3	17	3	21	0	0	.231
Gonzalez, Francisco, Walla Walla	68	229	34	53	69	8	1	2	40	3	5	53	3	47	0	3	.231
Greb, Jay, Medford	33	98	11	17	19	2	0	0	9	3	2	11	1	31	1	1	.173
Harper, Therron, Medford	54	199	32	54	78	12	0	4	37	0	2	23	4	39	4	2	.271
Hart, Michael, Bellingham*	4	8	0	1	1	0	0	0	0	1	0	1	0	3	1	0	.125
Harvey, Steven, Central Oregon	54	197	29	50	71	5	2	4	19	5	1	13	1	42	1	5	.254
Hayne, William, Salem	17	0	1	0	0	0	0	0	0	0	0	0	0	0	0	0	.000
Henry, Chris, Bellingham*	45	121	24	32	40	8	0	0	18	0	3	29	0	20	5	2	.264
Hollenbach, Charlton, Eugene	26	9	3	1	1	0	0	0	0	0	0	8	0	3	0	0	.111
Hood, Michael, Bellingham	26	72	7	16	18	2	0	0	3	1	0	7	1	16	0	1	.222
Hopkins, Nickie, Victoria	34	98	8	24	30	4	1	0	8	0	1	16	0	19	0	0	.245
Hover, Lee, Eugene†	65	251	43	67	83	3	5	1	26	7	0	36	3	39	22	7	.267
Jackson, Byron, Eugene	19	24	5	5	6	1	0	0	3	0	0	6	0	6	0	0	.208
Jackson, Gregory, Eugene	71	275	43	72	117	16	1	9	45	1	3	23	8	30	4	1	.262
Johnson, Kevin, Salem†	6	14	1	2	2	0	0	0	0	0	0	2	0	4	0	2	.143
Johnson, Steven, Walla Walla*	47	102	15	16	16	0	0	0	6	2	0	25	2	39	6	2	.157
Jones, Thomas, Walla Walla	19	39	5	11	13	2	0	0	5	3	1	4	0	7	1	0	.282
Kennedy, Michael, Medford†	8	24	5	8	8	0	0	0	1	1	0	3	0	3	0	0	.333
King, Kevin, Bellingham	49	147	20	39	74	4	2	9	32	0	0	21	0	54	2	0	.265
Kintz, Nicholas, Victoria	60	214	36	64	80	11	1	1	32	6	1	34	0	27	7	3	.299
Kirsch, Paul, Salem*	69	258	45	70	83	7	3	0	29	3	3	22	1	15	6	5	.271
Kneuer, Frank, Medford	35	113	9	27	34	7	0	0	15	0	2	10	0	14	1	1	.239
Lacey, Shaun, Medford	63	224	26	47	59	5	2	1	23	2	4	16	0	41	6	3	.210
Lais, John, Grays Harbor*	37	117	17	26	31	3	1	0	11	0	0	28	0	32	2	0	.222
Lajszky, Werner, Bellingham	52	154	24	41	67	7	2	5	24	0	1	22	3	45	3	0	.266
Lansford, Joseph, Walla Walla	44	146	17	21	41	2	0	6	31	1	4	25	0	71	1	0	.144
LaVielle, Scott, Grays Harbor	31	93	8	21	26	2	0	1	11	0	1	10	3	23	0	0	.226
Ledbetter, Gareth, Victoria	39	145	20	41	69	8	1	6	33	1	5	14	2	25	0	0	.283
Linhart, C. Greg, Central Oregon	70	233	44	53	64	5	3	0	33	3	2	30	2	34	15	0	.227
Littlefield, David, Central Oregon	26	83	15	23	33	7	0	1	13	0	2	18	0	22	0	1	.277
Lord, Charles, Salem	15	36	6	7	10	0	0	1	2	1	0	4	0	5	0	0	.194
Lulay, Douglas, Walla Walla	70	275	48	88	134	15	5	7	62	6	0	26	6	56	10	6	.320
Majam, Rosben, Salem†	66	223	56	63	82	10	1	3	30	9	1	82	1	47	16	7	.283
Masone, Anthony, Eugene	48	182	27	46	80	8	4	6	26	0	1	18	0	37	2	1	.253
Mateo, Wilson, Eugene	7	13	1	2	2	0	0	0	0	0	0	0	0	4	0	0	.154
McBrain, John, Medford*	17	51	6	11	12	1	0	0	1	0	0	7	0	15	0	0	.216
McGill, Anthony, Central Oregon	68	283	55	83	110	9	3	4	55	3	3	22	3	73	26	6	.293
McGrue, Anthony, Walla Walla	10	24	4	4	5	1	0	0	2	0	0	4	0	8	2	0	.167
McKinney, Charles, Eugene	12	5	0	1	1	0	0	0	1	1	1	0	2	0	0	0	.200
McKinney, Gregory, Eugene*	50	163	25	50	69	5	4	2	19	2	2	38	5	44	1	3	.307
Molina, Hilton, Eugene	19	11	1	1	2	0	0	0	2	0	0	2	0	9	0	0	.091
Moore, Thomas, Salem	69	284	42	84	108	9	6	1	41	4	1	22	4	31	9	9	.296
Moretti, Roy, Victoria	36	2	0	0	0	0	0	0	0	0	0	0	0	2	0	0	.000
Morganti, Douglas, Victoria	61	201	47	57	91	10	0	8	30	3	2	50	0	29	6	4	.284
Murphy, Roderick, Victoria	59	178	32	44	59	6	3	1	27	4	1	33	2	19	6	3	.247
Nelson, Chester, Victoria*	13	31	3	2	2	0	0	0	2	1	1	1	0	10	0	0	.065
Nolan, L. Shane, Victoria	17	25	3	5	5	0	0	0	4	1	0	5	0	5	0	0	.200
Oquendo, Jose, Grays Harbor	64	220	24	50	61	8	0	1	14	2	1	33	1	45	9	6	.227
Orensky, Herbert, Central Oregon*	61	199	30	59	104	13	7	6	47	1	2	45	1	34	5	2	.296
Owings, M. Andrew, Cent. Oregon†	47	176	36	43	80	10	6	5	33	1	3	5	2	30	5	1	.244
Parent, Mark, Walla Walla	40	126	15	24	31	4	0	1	11	3	2	8	0	31	0	0	.190

Player and Club	G.	AB.	R.	H.	TB.	2B.	3B.	HR.	RBI.	SH.	SF.	BB.	HP.	SO.	SB.	CS.	Pct.
Perkins, Drew, Eugene†	36	126	15	28	38	5	1	1	17	1	0	20	6	18	7	0	.222
Pignotti, John, Medford	33	93	12	21	28	1	0	2	7	0	1	12	1	13	2	0	.226
Pittman, Larry, Grays Harbor	52	171	19	40	52	1	1	3	17	0	1	21	3	55	0	1	.234
Porte, Carlos, Eugene	29	94	5	24	28	2	1	0	9	1	0	7	0	15	1	0	.255
Potts, Robert, Victoria	19	54	10	17	26	6	0	1	10	1	1	7	1	7	2	1	.315
Presley, James, Bellingham	48	138	20	27	36	4	1	1	12	3	0	19	4	21	7	3	.196
Purpura, Daniel, Victoria	68	237	29	60	71	5	3	0	36	1	3	39	0	39	2	6	.253
Pyle, John, Salem	56	185	26	49	70	5	2	4	34	2	4	26	2	27	12	3	.265
Rabassa, Pedro, Victoria*	62	181	46	69	108	19	4	4	35	2	2	58	2	37	11	3	.381
Ramsey, Michael, Eugene	17	21	4	2	2	0	0	0	0	2	0	3	0	7	1	0	.095
Randle, Daniel, Medford*	38	108	13	29	32	3	0	0	17	0	2	10	0	16	2	2	.269
Reppucci, Peter, Eugene	47	132	15	31	42	9	1	0	15	3	0	22	1	27	8	1	.235
Rincones, Hector, Eugene	71	301	36	82	103	8	5	1	38	1	2	20	1	39	20	2	.272
Rivera, Luis, Bellingham†	39	112	16	29	34	3	1	0	16	0	3	12	1	11	6	3	.259
Robinson, Howard, Medford†	57	210	30	51	63	6	3	0	17	2	1	34	1	54	14	6	.243
Rodriguez, Alfredo, Walla Walla*	43	101	9	16	23	4	0	1	11	2	4	23	2	38	3	1	.158
Rothey, Mark, Eugene*	18	29	3	7	7	0	0	0	2	0	0	2	0	4	0	0	.241
Sanchez, Alejandro, Cent. Oregon	54	204	31	55	78	10	2	3	38	2	2	14	3	44	11	7	.270
Sarrett, Daniel, Eugene	26	97	14	24	31	4	0	1	3	0	0	7	1	13	0	1	.247
Schields, Steven, Medford	59	206	34	51	66	10	1	1	36	1	5	46	0	34	10	5	.248
Seefried, John, Salem	66	215	52	64	101	9	8	4	40	8	6	53	5	36	2	1	.298
Smith, Curtis, Walla Walla	21	1	0	1	1	0	0	0	0	0	0	0	0	0	0	0	1.000
Souza, Ronald, Grays Harbor	55	182	27	42	44	2	0	0	11	2	0	28	1	36	7	3	.231
Stamper, Timothy, Eugene	12	21	1	4	4	0	0	0	2	0	0	2	0	4	0	0	.190
Stevenson, John, Walla Walla	24	79	14	27	34	3	2	0	5	2	0	17	2	13	5	1	.342
Stropolo, Christopher, Eugene*	43	125	24	25	31	1	1	1	7	0	0	34	2	25	14	3	.200
Sullivan, Michael, Eugene	20	55	4	4	4	0	0	0	1	1	0	3	1	30	0	0	.073
Supple, Daniel, Salem	23	63	10	15	20	1	2	0	11	0	1	8	0	22	5	1	.238
Tarnow, Gregory, Walla Walla	18	27	1	2	2	0	0	0	2	0	0	2	0	18	0	0	.074
Taylor, James, Eugene	26	74	8	19	26	2	1	1	9	1	1	12	2	19	3	0	.257
Thomson, Scott, Grays Harbor	3	7	3	2	2	0	0	0	1	0	0	3	0	0	1	0	.286
Thys, Gregory, Walla Walla	63	224	44	65	79	4	2	2	19	4	1	49	5	28	10	5	.290
Tillman, Kerry, Grays Harbor	60	217	33	64	85	10	1	3	30	1	3	34	0	42	18	3	.295
Valdez, Jose, Eugene	29	81	12	19	28	3	0	2	12	1	1	6	0	19	1	0	.235
Waller, Kevin, Eugene	57	166	18	39	44	3	1	0	11	0	0	30	0	26	6	5	.235
Weis, David, Victoria	18	0	2	0	0	0	0	0	0	0	0	0	0	0	0	0	.000
White, Alvin, Central Oregon	65	248	55	73	106	8	2	7	41	1	1	44	5	52	17	5	.294
Wilber, Robert, Medford	19	44	5	6	8	0	1	0	2	0	0	8	1	16	0	1	.136
Williams, Derek, Central Oregon	14	35	6	5	8	0	0	1	8	0	1	6	1	8	1	0	.143
Williams, Joseph, Medford	61	208	33	56	80	10	4	2	26	1	0	41	1	27	11	0	.269
Young, Steven, 24 Vic-28 Salem	52	167	39	38	44	2	2	0	21	5	3	42	0	24	10	6	.228

The following pitchers had no plate appearances primarily through use of designated hitters, listed alphabetically by club, games in parentheses:

BELLINGHAM—Batten, Mark (3); Black, Harry* (2); Cahill, Mark (12); Diaz, Carlos (2); Georger, Joseph (23); Harrison, Brian (1); Hunger, Christopher (11); Martin, William (20); Martinez, Randy* (6); Murray, Jed (18); Naumann, Richard* (11); Nunez, Edwin (6); Randolph, Robert (14); Salva, Elias (13); Steger, Kevin* (12); Stranski, H. Scott (11).

CENTRAL OREGON—Barnett, Robert (13); Faulk, M. Kelly (14); Goff, Wallace* (10); Guardia, Oscar (17); Lenaburg, Brad (18); Lynes, Michael* (23); Marshall, C. Harvey (10); Martinez, M. Dean (12); Palmieri, John* (15); Redmond, Roger (18); Shoemaker, Martin (6); Wright, James† (14).

GRAYS HARBOR—Anderson, Jesse (15); Bettendorf, Jeffrey (9); Burkman, Randall* (5); Buttles, David (8); Cooperider, James* (14); Graves, Ronald (19); Michael, David (12); Miller, Thomas* (21); Plummer, Joseph (21); Smith, David (14); Spicer, Kevin† (14); Sunderlage, Jeffrey* (11).

MEDFORD—Call, Keith (13); Cleland, Bret (1); Dougherty, Charles (13); Ferguson, Mark (12); Harris, D. Craig (8); Mantsch, Ronnie (10); Marlow, Stephen (13); Oliver, Steven* (16); Slattery, Peter (8); Tolli, William (16); Van Marter, Donald (16); Wood, Robert (16); Yesenchak, Michael* (21).

SALEM—Aspenleiter, Richard (21); Baker, Bruce (6); Brennan, Thomas* (12—8 with Bellingham); Howell, Peter (8); Jordan, Anthony (8—4 with Bellingham); Martin, Ricky* (15); Odekirk, Richard* (14); Runyan, Mark (25); Somers, Richard* (17); Vasche, Thomas (19).

VICTORIA—Avallone, Mario (7); Candiotti, Thomas (12); Caraher, John† (14); Hartery, Stephen* (19); Hays, John (1); Holt, Randy (4); Koziol, Edward (20); Mathey, Douglas (8).

WALLA WALLA—Barba, Michael (21); Brokop, Thomas (8); Danielson, Daniel (14); Froelich, David (13); Hamm, Timothy (14); Patton, Gregory (12); Peterson, Rodney (15); Sijer, Daniel* (13); Wilson, Philip (14); Wyrick, Courtney (15).

GRAND SLAM HOME RUNS—G. Jackson 2; Harper, Lansford, Lulay, Orensky, Stopolo, 1 each.

AWARDED FIRST BASE ON INTERFERENCE—DeSimone (Duff), G. Jackson (Parent), Kintz (Littlefield).

CLUB FIELDING

Club	G.	PO.	A.	E.	DP.	PB.	Pct.	Club	G.	PO.	A.	E.	DP.	PB.	Pct.
Victoria	72	1885	753	124	70	21	.955	Eugene	71	1861	731	144	63	35	.947
Walla Walla	70	1858	837	131	60	38	.953	Bellingham	72	1893	722	155	68	27	.944
Central Oregon	71	1884	830	136	67	22	.952	Salem	72	1921	866	166	54	25	.944
Medford	71	1856	762	143	59	23	.948	Grays Harbor	71	1792	748	176	54	39	.935

Triple Play—Victoria.

INDIVIDUAL FIELDING

FIRST BASEMEN

*Throws lefthanded.

Player and Club	G.	PO.	A.	E.	DP.	Pct.	Player and Club	G.	PO.	A.	E.	DP.	Pct.
Kirsch, Salem*	10	71	5	0	2	1.000	E. Diaz, Bellingham	64	524	26	15	51	.973
G. JACKSON, Eugene*	71	632	15	8	54	.988	White, Central Oregon	39	353	26	11	43	.972
Rodriguez, W Walla	15	120	8	2	13	.985	Thys, Walla Walla	14	114	13	4	7	.969
Angius, C Oregon*	35	313	18	6	19	.982	Cummins, Salem	12	90	4	3	5	.969
Drzayich, Victoria	71	566	31	12	64	.980	Chamberlain, G Harbor	32	247	18	11	24	.960
J. Williams, Medford	61	512	19	11	44	.980	Dwyer, Walla Walla	16	104	4	5	4	.956
Pyle, Salem	46	414	22	11	30	.975	Pittman, Grays Harbor	36	261	9	14	14	.951
Lansford, W Walla	24	204	21	6	23	.974	Lord, Salem	13	68	5	4	5	.948

Triple Play—Drzayich.

(Fewer Than Ten Games)

Player and Club	G.	PO.	A.	E.	DP.	Pct.	Player and Club	G.	PO.	A.	E.	DP.	Pct.
Acosta, Bellingham	8	50	2	0	9	1.000	Echenique, G Harbor	3	5	0	0	1	1.000
Cias, Medford	4	36	6	0	2	1.000	Reppucci, Eugene	2	5	0	0	0	1.000
Geren, Walla Walla	4	32	2	0	4	1.000	Getter, Eugene	1	5	0	0	2	1.000
Gandy, Victoria	5	30	3	0	4	1.000	Harper, Medford	1	3	0	0	1	1.000
Lajszky, Bellingham	4	24	3	0	2	1.000	Lais, Grays Harbor*	5	52	6	1	4	.983
Bryan, Salem	3	21	0	0	1	1.000	Durrman, Medford	6	54	1	1	7	.982
Kintz, Victoria	3	10	0	0	1	1.000	Lulay, Walla Walla	7	67	1	2	4	.971
Pignotti, Medford	1	6	0	0	0	1.000							

SECOND BASEMEN

Player and Club	G.	PO.	A.	E.	DP.	Pct.	Player and Club	G.	PO.	A.	E.	DP.	Pct.
D. ELLIOTT, G Harbor	59	165	143	7	36	.978	Rivera, Bellingham	28	60	55	7	11	.943
Gonzalez, Walla Walla	27	63	66	3	8	.977	Majam, Salem	44	130	106	15	19	.940
Thys, Walla Walla	44	103	109	8	26	.964	Clark, Bellingham	49	92	123	14	35	.939
Garcia, Grays Harbor	12	23	30	2	3	.964	Robinson, Medford	53	132	122	19	25	.930
Purpura, Victoria	67	173	133	12	52	.962	Hover, Eugene	61	120	138	23	32	.918
Linhart, Central Oregon	70	169	208	15	50	.962	Fuson, Salem	16	25	31	5	5	.918
Blackman, Salem	11	20	21	2	3	.953	Greb, Medford	10	14	29	5	5	.896

Triple Play—Purpura.

(Fewer Than Ten Games)

Player and Club	G.	PO.	A.	E.	DP.	Pct.	Player and Club	G.	PO.	A.	E.	DP.	Pct.
Baugh, Central Oregon	3	6	3	0	0	1.000	Porte, Eugene	24	16	2	7		.952
M. Diaz, Bellingham	2	5	4	0	0	1.000	Young, Salem	7	22	17	2	6	.951
Jones, Walla Walla	1	4	1	0	0	1.000	Kennedy, Medford	5	6	11	1	3	.944
Oquendo, Grays Harbor	1	2	2	0	0	1.000	Murphy, Victoria	9	15	15	3	4	.909
Reppucci, Eugene	1	2	1	0	1	1.000	Frierson, Bellingham	2	5	3	1	1	.889
Kintz, Victoria	1	1	0	0	0	1.000	Perkins, Eugene	4	14	7	3	2	.875
Schields, Medford	8	19	26	1	6	.978	Souza, Grays Harbor	3	3	3	2	1	.750

THIRD BASEMEN

Player and Club	G.	PO.	A.	E.	DP.	Pct.	Player and Club	G.	PO.	A.	E.	DP.	Pct.
M. Diaz, Bellingham	13	8	12	0	0	1.000	Rodriguez, Walla Walla	16	13	27	6	3	.870
Freitas, Victoria	11	5	25	2	4	.938	Lacey, Medford	63	49	119	26	8	.866
Porte, Eugene	19	15	43	4	2	.935	Aponte, Bellingham	34	28	48	12	5	.864
Gonzalez, Walla Walla	35	29	70	9	8	.917	Lajszky, Bellingham	23	16	35	8	4	.864
SEEFRIED, Salem	66	69	182	26	15	.906	Reppucci, Eugene	20	3	33	6	2	.857
Morganti, Victoria	36	25	77	11	10	.903	Perkins, Eugene	30	9	45	10	6	.844
Baugh, Central Oregon	17	15	34	6	3	.891	DeSimone, Walla Walla	19	13	41	10	1	.844
Kintz, Victoria	30	27	61	12	5	.880	Garcia, Grays Harbor	31	27	59	18	4	.827
Souza, Grays Harbor	36	22	69	13	7	.875	Rivera, Bellingham	10	3	7	4	1	.714
Fryer, Central Oregon	57	33	112	21	8	.873							

(Fewer Than Ten Games)

Player and Club	G.	PO.	A.	E.	DP.	Pct.	Player and Club	G.	PO.	A.	E.	DP.	Pct.
Harper, Medford	5	3	3	0	0	1.000	Young, Salem	1	1	3	0	0	1.000
Stevenson, W Walla	2	2	2	0	0	1.000	Kennedy, Medford	2	2	1	0	0	1.000
Echenique, G Harbor	1	1	3	0	0	1.000	Fuson, Salem	1	0	2	0	0	1.000

THIRD BASEMEN—Continued

(Fewer Than Ten Games)

Player and Club	G.	PO.	A.	E.	DP.	Pct.	Player and Club	G.	PO.	A.	E.	DP.	Pct.
Bryan, Salem	6	5	11	1	1	.941	Chamberlain, G Harbor.	5	3	1	3	1	.571
Chelette, Bellingham	9	8	25	4	2	.892	Durrman, Medford	2	1	1	2	0	.500
Thys, Walla Walla	3	1	7	1	0	.889	D. Elliott, Grays Harbor	1	1	0	1	0	.500
Getter, Eugene	3	6	6	2	1	.857	Lulay, Walla Walla	2	0	1	2	0	.333
Taylor, Eugene	7	4	11	3	1	.833	Schields, Medford	1	0	0	1	0	.000
Burnett, Medford	3	4	3	3	0	.700							

SHORTSTOPS

Player and Club	G.	PO.	A.	E.	DP.	Pct.	Player and Club	G.	PO.	A.	E.	DP.	Pct.
MURPHY, Victoria	49	67	144	12	30	.946	Blackman, Salem	14	20	37	7	6	.891
Rincones, Eugene	71	126	225	24	40	.936	Bryan, Salem	13	21	35	7	5	.889
Stevenson, W Walla	22	39	74	8	7	.934	Fuson, Salem	11	22	41	9	3	.875
Schields, Medford	54	80	158	17	29	.933	Oquendo, G Harbor	63	88	175	40	27	.868
DeSimone, W Walla	47	76	169	19	31	.928	Presley, Bell	47	42	127	27	21	.862
Franco, C Oregon	69	103	256	31	45	.921	Garcia, G Harbor	10	7	18	4	4	.862
Majam, Salem	18	22	66	8	5	.917	Greb, Medford	22	35	56	17	11	.843
Young, Vic-Sal	42	53	126	17	15	.913	Colby, Bellingham	17	16	26	10	6	.808
M. Diaz, Bellingham	18	15	53	8	10	.895							

(Fewer Than Ten Games)

Player and Club	G.	PO.	A.	E.	DP.	Pct.	Player and Club	G.	PO.	A.	E.	DP.	Pct.
Owings, C Oregon	5	3	13	0	5	1.000	Thys, Walla Walla	1	3	3	1	0	.857
Gaffney, Bell	4	3	7	0	0	1.000	Souza, Salem	2	0	4	1	0	.800
Porte, Eugene	1	2	1	0	0	1.000	K. Johnson, Sal	6	7	8	4	1	.789
Rodriguez, W Walla	1	1	1	0	0	1.000	Kintz, Victoria	4	1	9	3	2	.769
Chamberlain, GH	1	0	1	0	0	1.000	Kennedy, Medford	1	0	0	2	0	.000
Jones, W Walla	2	3	4	1	0	.875							

OUTFIELDERS

Player and Club	G.	PO.	A.	E.	DP.	Pct.	Player and Club	G.	PO.	A.	E.	DP.	Pct.
McBrain, Medford	15	24	1	0	0	1.000	White, C Oregon	22	24	0	1	0	.960
Wilber, Medford	11	13	2	0	0	1.000	Randle, Medford*	23	41	4	2	1	.957
Bauman, Salem	11	14	0	0	0	1.000	Estepa, Bellingham	71	117	11	6	5	.955
ALTOBELLI, Med	56	107	11	1	3	.992	Chambers, Bell*	50	63	1	3	0	.955
Beal, Victoria	33	54	3	1	0	.983	Waller, Eugene	50	100	4	5	1	.954
Kirsch, Salem*	56	96	15	2	5	.982	Sanchez, C Oregon	53	97	6	5	0	.954
Cain, Walla Walla	67	96	7	2	1	.981	Dorsey, Victoria	19	33	1	2	0	.944
Moore, Salem	61	95	4	2	0	.980	Harper, Medford	35	44	5	3	0	.942
Gausepohl, W Walla	66	127	6	3	1	.978	Baugh, C Oregon	17	28	4	2	0	.941
Garrett, Medford	71	116	9	3	0	.977	Belmonte, Sal-Vic	34	40	6	3	2	.939
Stropolo, Eugene*	40	80	4	2	1	.977	King, Bellingham*	22	31	0	2	0	.939
Morganti, Victoria	21	32	1	1	1	.971	Harvey, C Oregon	54	79	8	6	0	.935
Kintz, Victoria	21	30	3	1	0	.971	Rabassa, Victoria*	54	66	4	5	0	.933
Burton, Victoria	64	146	8	5	1	.969	Reppucci, Eugene	17	26	1	2	0	.931
Lulay, Walla Walla	61	115	8	4	3	.969	Denby, Grays Harbor	62	111	9	9	0	.930
Codiroli, Bell*	49	89	4	3	1	.969	Bodman, Salem	59	88	3	7	0	.929
Tillman, G Harbor	60	140	7	5	4	.967	Chamberlain, GH	27	43	3	4	0	.920
Frierson, Bell-Sal	28	55	2	2	1	.966	Echenique, G Harbor	23	20	2	2	0	.917
Valdez, Eugene	19	27	0	1	0	.964	Potts, Victoria	18	19	2	2	0	.913
McGill, C Oregon	68	152	5	6	1	.963	Supple, Salem	14	11	2	2	2	.867
Masone, Eugene	47	77	2	3	2	.963	S. Johnson, WW*	19	25	0	4	0	.862
Acosta, Bellingham	37	25	1	1	0	.963	G. McKinney, Eug.	47	59	1	11	0	.845
Lais, Grays Harbor*	29	46	3	2	2	.961							

(Fewer Than Ten Games)

Player and Club	G.	PO.	A.	E.	DP.	Pct.	Player and Club	G.	PO.	A.	E.	DP.	Pct.
Burnett, Medford	8	8	0	0	0	1.000	Parent, W Walla	1	1	0	0	0	1.000
Pignotti, Medford	8	8	0	0	0	1.000	Jones, Walla Walla	5	0	1	0	0	1.000
Lajszky, Bellingham	9	7	0	0	0	1.000	Hart, Bellingham*	2	8	1	1	0	.900
Robinson, Med	3	5	0	0	0	1.000	Souza, Grays Harbor	8	6	2	1	0	.889
Nolan, Victoria	6	3	0	0	0	1.000	Thomson, G Harbor	2	4	0	1	0	.800
Hover, Eugene	2	3	0	0	0	1.000	Cooper, G Harbor	8	9	0	3	0	.750
Mateo, Eugene	2	3	0	0	0	1.000	Fryer, C Oregon	4	5	0	2	0	.714
Fuson, Salem	4	1	0	0	0	1.000	McGrue, Walla Walla	4	2	0	1	0	.667
Freitas, Victoria	1	1	0	0	0	1.000							

CATCHERS

Player and Club	G.	PO.	A.	E.	DP.	PB.	Pct.	Player and Club	G.	PO.	A.	E.	DP.	PB.	Pct.
Gotter, Eugene	18	114	18	0	0	4	1.000	HENRY, Bell	39	260	18	2	2	9	.993
Nelson, Victoria	10	55	5	0	0	0	1.000	Taylor, Eugene	16	121	16	1	2	8	.993

CATCHERS—Continued

Player and Club	G.	PO.	A.	E.	DP.	PB.	Pct.
Dunbar, G Harbor	12	67	18	1	1	10	.988
LaVielle, GH	13	68	11	1	1	5	.988
Orensky, C Oregon	45	311	33	6	3	12	.983
Durrman, Medford	28	198	28	4	0	16	.983
Ledbetter, Victoria	38	280	28	6	1	4	.981
Eiler, Bellingham	20	139	9	3	0	8	.980
Duff, Grays Harbor	51	344	69	9	7	24	.979
Parent, W Walla	38	228	34	6	3	15	.978
Cummins, Salem	39	199	23	5	4	11	.978
Pignotti, Medford	13	70	7	2	1	4	.975
Bauman, Salem	40	247	33	8	2	14	.972

Player and Club	G.	PO.	A.	E.	DP.	PB.	Pct.
Hood, Bellingham	23	202	18	7	2	10	.969
Hopkins, Victoria	13	74	8	3	1	6	.965
Tarnow, W Walla	17	53		2	0	4	.965
Sarrett, Eugene	26	162	23	7	1	10	.964
Geren, W Walla	37	183	23	9	0	19	.958
Clas, Medford	4	22	1	1	0	0	.958
Kneuer, Medford	29	213	31	11	1	3	.957
D. Williams, CO	7	21	1	1	1	4	.957
Edwards, Victoria	22	116	16	8	0	7	.943
Littlefield, CO	24	131	14	9	3	6	.942
Sullivan, Eugene	19	103	13	9	0	13	.928

PITCHERS

Player and Club	G.	PO.	A.	E.	DP.	Pct.
HAMM, Walla Walla	14	8	27	0	2	1.000
Tolli, Medford	16	6	17	0	1	1.000
Cahill, Bellingham	12	2	18	0	1	1.000
Lenaburg, C Oregon	18	7	9	0	1	1.000
Marshall, C Oregon	10	4	11	0	0	1.000
Hayne, Salem	15	1	14	0	2	1.000
Stamper, Eugene	10	3	11	0	1	1.000
Hollenbach, Eugene*	26	4	9	0	2	1.000
Barba, Walla Walla	21	2	10	0	0	1.000
Candiotti, Victoria	12	3	8	0	0	1.000
Molina, Eugene	19	1	10	0	0	1.000
Plummer, Grays Harbor	21	3	7	0	1	1.000
W. Martin, Bellingham	20	3	6	0	1	1.000
Stranski, Bellingham	11	3	6	0	1	1.000
Ramsey, Eugene	16	1	8	0	0	1.000
Wood, Medford	16	1	6	0	1	1.000
Weis, Victoria	16	2	4	0	1	1.000
Peterson, Walla Walla	15	2	4	0	1	1.000
Hunger, Bellingham	10	2	4	0	0	1.000
Lynes, Central Oregon*	23	1	5	0	1	1.000
Redmond, C Oregon	18	1	5	0	0	1.000
Naumann, Bellingham*	11	2	3	0	0	1.000
Sunderlage, G Harbors	11	0	5	0	0	1.000
Marlow, Medford	13	1	3	0	0	1.000
C. Smith, Walla Walla	20	0	4	0	2	1.000
Guardia, Central Oregon	17	0	4	0	0	1.000
Michael, Grays Harbor	12	1	2	0	0	1.000
Barnett, Central Oregon	13	0	3	0	1	1.000
Wilson, Walla Walla	13	0	3	0	0	1.000
Faulk, Central Oregon	14	14	18	1	1	.970
Koziol, Victoria	20	8	20	1	1	.966
Danielson, Walla Walla	14	9	15	1	1	.960
Call, Medford	13	7	15	1	0	.957
Odekirk, Salem*	14	10	26	2	2	.947
Rothey, Eugene*	17	4	11	1	0	.938
Hartery, Victoria*	19	5	21	2	1	.929
Palmieri, C Oregon*	16	6	19	2	1	.926

Player and Club	G.	PO.	A.	E.	DP.	Pct.
Yesenchak, Medford*	21	2	10	1	0	.923
Murray, Bellingham	18	1	11	1	1	.923
Froelich, Walla Walla	13	3	20	2	1	.920
Van Marter, Medford	16	3	8	1	0	.917
R. Martin, Salem*	15	4	6	1	0	.909
Patton, Walla Walla	12	0	10	1	1	.909
Oliver, Medford*	16	2	7	1	1	.900
Aspenleiter, Salem	21	4	31	4	1	.897
Randolph, Bellingham	13	5	12	2	2	.895
Runyan, Salem	25	8	17	3	1	.893
Mantsch, Medford	10	1	7	1	0	.889
Georger, Bellingham	23	3	12	2	2	.882
Cooperider, G Harbor*	14	3	11	2	0	.875
Adams, Eugene	12	0	7	1	1	.875
Sijer, Walla Walla*	13	6	21	4	0	.871
Dougherty, Medford*	13	4	15	3	0	.864
Wright, Central Oregon	14	5	7	2	2	.857
D. Smith, Grays Harbor	14	2	9	2	0	.846
Ferguson, Medford	12	1	10	2	0	.846
Somers, Salem*	17	3	7	2	0	.833
B. Jackson, Eugene	18	2	16	4	3	.818
Miller, Grays Harbor	21	1	8	2	0	.818
C. McKinney, Eugene	11	0	9	2	0	.818
Graves, Grays Harbor	19	7	6	3	1	.813
Spicer, Grays Harbor	14	2	11	3	0	.813
Wyrick, Walla Walla	15	6	15	5	1	.808
DeJulio, Eugene	18	3	12	4	0	.789
Vasche, Salem	19	3	14	5	2	.773
Brennan, Bell-Sal	12	1	5	2	0	.750
M. D. Martinez, C Ore	12	1	2	1	0	.750
Bangert, Eugene*	16	1	13	5	2	.737
Salva, Bellingham	13	4	14	7	0	.720
Caraher, Victoria	14	2	8	4	0	.714
Goff, Central Oregon*	10	1	4	2	1	.714
Moretti, Victoria	36	2	9	5	0	.688
Anderson, Grays Harbor	15	1	9	5	0	.667
Steger, Bellingham	12	1	3	2	0	.667

(Fewer Than Ten Games)

Player and Club	G.	PO.	A.	E.	DP.	Pct.
Mathey, Victoria	8	5	13	0	2	1.000
Beal, Victoria	8	2	11	0	1	1.000
Avallone, Victoria	7	4	8	0	0	1.000
Nunez, Bellingham	6	2	4	0	0	1.000
Harris, Medford	8	2	3	0	0	1.000
Slattery, Medford	8	0	5	0	0	1.000
Brokop, Walla Walla	8	1	3	0	0	1.000
R. Martinez, Bell*	6	1	3	0	0	1.000
Burkman, G Harbor*	4	1	3	0	1	1.000
Shoemaker, C Oregon	6	1	2	0	0	1.000
Wilber, Medford	3	1	2	0	0	1.000
Black, Bellingham*	2	0	2	0	0	1.000

Player and Club	G.	PO.	A.	E.	DP.	Pct.
C. Diaz, Bellingham*	2	0	1	0	0	1.000
Flannery, Eugene	1	0	1	0	0	1.000
Buttles, Grays Harbor	8	2	8	2	0	.833
Holt, Victoria	4	0	5	1	0	.833
Bettendorf, G Harbor	9	3	4	2	0	.778
Nolan, Victoria	5	1	2	1	0	.750
Jordan, Bell-Sal	8	3	1	2	0	.667
Baker, Salem	6	1	3	2	0	.667
Howell, Salem	8	0	4	2	0	.667
Batten, Bellingham	3	1	0	1	0	.500
W. Elliott, Eugene*	3	0	1	1	0	.500

The following players do not have any recorded accepted chances at the positions indicated; therefore, are not listed in the fielding averages for those particular positions: Angius*, of; Beal, 3b; Burnett, p; Burton, ss; Cleland, p; Gandy, of; Garcia, of; Harrison, p; Hays*, p; Jones, 1b; Kneuer, 1b; Masone, p; Orensky, of; Owings, 2b; Pyle, c; Rodriguez, 2b; Taylor, 1b.

CLUB PITCHING

Club	G.	CG.	ShO.	Sv.	IP.	H.	R.	ER.	HR.	BB.	Int. BB.	HB.	SO.	WP.	Bk.	ERA.
Central Oregon	71	13	2	12	628	597	328	263	28	299	11	24	438	51	2	3.77
Bellingham	72	8	5	11	631	610	353	271	27	362	20	25	577	46	6	3.87
Victoria	72	18	2	13	628	624	358	276	33	338	4	28	502	35	4	3.96
Salem	72	21	2	11	640	662	408	296	24	339	23	37	405	56	5	4.16
Walla Walla	70	17	2	15	619	603	355	289	36	353	9	26	446	60	2	4.20
Eugene	71	3	1	10	620	558	375	293	25	385	7	16	497	59	3	4.25
Medford	71	14	5	15	619	616	402	311	32	347	5	29	489	56	4	4.52
Grays Harbor	71	13	2	8	597	635	437	322	33	389	11	32	460	51	5	4.85

PITCHERS' RECORDS
(Leading Qualifiers for Earned-Run Average Leadership–58 or More Innings)

*Throws lefthanded.

Pitcher–Club	G.	GS.	CG.	ShO.	W.	L.	Sv.	Pct.	IP.	H.	R.	ER.	HR.	BB.	Int. BB.	HB.	SO.	WP.	ERA.
Georger, Bellingham	23	0	0	0	6	5	5	.545	62	52	23	15	2	37	7	4	89	5	2.18
Lenaburg, C Oregon	18	5	2	1	4	4	2	.500	70	49	22	17	1	33	1	2	52	3	2.19
Moretti, Victoria	36	1	0	0	6	5	10	.545	82	67	33	20	1	52	2	1	86	2	2.20
DeJiulio, Eugene	18	10	0	0	4	7	3	.364	95	63	30	24	1	26	0	0	100	3	2.27
Aspenleiter, Salem	21	11	7	0	5	7	1	.417	105	112	41	27	1	26	6	9	43	1	2.31
Randolph, Bellingham	13	9	0	0	6	2	1	.750	67	63	31	18	2	30	0	2	56	5	2.42
Candiotti, Victoria	12	9	3	0	5	1	1	.833	70	63	23	19	1	16	1	3	66	2	2.44
Call, Medford	13	10	6	2	7	1	0	.875	76	65	30	23	5	26	0	1	60	3	2.72
Dougherty, Medford*	13	13	3	1	5	3	0	.625	91	94	42	28	3	19	0	1	68	3	2.77
Froelich, Walla Walla	13	13	7	2	6	5	0	.545	100	83	39	32	7	26	1	3	87	7	2.88

Departmental Leaders: G–Moretti, 36; GS–Koziol, 16; CG–Aspenleiter, Froelich, 7; ShO–Call, Froelich, Stranski, 2; W–Koziol, 9; L–Cooperider, 9; Sv–Moretti, 10; Pct.–Call, .875; IP–Koziol, 125; H–Koziol, 114; R–Vasche, 66; ER–Koziol, 53; HR–Koziol, Sunderlage, 8; BB–Cooperider, 69; IBB–Georger, 7; HB–Koziol, 10; SO–Koziol, 104; WP–Bettendorf, 13.

(All Pitchers–Listed Alphabetically)

Pitcher–Club	G.	GS.	CG.	ShO.	W.	L.	Sv.	Pct.	IP.	H.	R.	ER.	HR.	BB.	Int. BB.	HB.	SO.	WP.	ERA.
Adams, Eugene	12	7	0	0	1	0	0	1.000	40	56	29	26	2	24	1	1	21	4	5.85
Anderson, Grays Harbor	15	9	3	3	5	0	3	.375	87	85	48	31	2	45	3	5	82	6	3.21
Aspenleiter, Salem	21	11	7	0	5	7	1	.417	105	112	41	27	1	26	6	9	43	1	2.31
Avallone, Victoria	7	7	2	0	3	2	0	.600	38	50	28	24	6	19	0	3	22	1	5.68
Baker, Salem	6	2	0	0	0	1	0	.000	21	32	20	17	0	4	0	3	7	0	7.29
Bangert, Eugene*	16	5	0	0	3	3	1	.500	61	46	33	25	4	46	1	1	39	12	3.69
Barba, Walla Walla	21	0	0	0	4	3	5	.571	37	17	19	15	0	40	3	0	46	7	3.65
Barnett, Central Oregon	13	1	0	0	1	0	0	.000	24	24	19	16	2	25	0	3	13	4	6.00
Batten, Bellingham	3	0	0	0	1	1	0	.500	10	11	7	4	1	5	0	1	6	0	3.60
Beal, Victoria	8	6	1	0	2	1	0	.667	34	39	34	25	1	36	0	2	21	3	6.62
Bettendorf, G Harbor	9	9	1	0	1	4	0	.200	44	50	33	20	3	33	0	6	36	13	4.09
Black, Bellingham*	2	0	0	0	0	0	0	.000	5	3	0	0	0	5	0	0	8	0	0.00
Brennan, 8 Bell-4 Sal*	12	5	0	0	0	4	0	.000	43	57	44	31	3	33	0	4	36	2	6.49
Brokop, Walla Walla	8	4	0	0	1	2	0	.333	20	19	21	17	0	31	0	0	4	3	7.65
Burkman, Grays Harbor*	4	3	0	0	1	2	0	.333	20	16	10	5	1	11	0	0	23	1	2.25
Burnett, Medford	1	0	0	0	0	0	0	.000	2	6	7	7	0	5	0	0	2	0	31.50
Buttles, Grays Harbor	8	5	1	0	1	3	1	.250	38	44	24	20	2	23	1	1	26	1	4.74
Cahill, Bellingham	12	12	1	0	6	2	0	.750	69	76	37	27	2	31	1	1	45	6	3.52
Call, Medford	13	10	6	2	7	1	0	.875	76	65	30	23	5	26	0	1	60	3	2.72
Candiotti, Victoria	12	9	3	0	5	1	1	.833	70	63	23	19	1	16	1	3	66	2	2.44
Caraher, Victoria	14	9	3	0	5	5	0	.500	65	61	42	27	3	40	0	3	51	7	3.74
Cleland, Medford	1	0	0	0	0	0	0	.000	3	7	6	4	0	1	0	0	3	0	12.00
Cooperider, Grays Har*	14	14	4	1	3	9	0	.250	72	66	63	44	3	69	2	2	52	5	5.50
Danielson, Walla Walla	14	5	0	0	3	2	1	.600	68	68	29	23	3	37	2	3	45	9	3.04
DeJiulio, Eugene	18	10	0	0	4	7	3	.364	95	63	30	24	1	26	0	0	100	3	2.27
C. Diaz, Bellingham*	2	0	0	0	0	2	0	.000	8	5	0	0	0	2	0	0	8	0	0.00
Dougherty, Medford*	13	13	3	1	5	3	0	.625	91	94	42	28	3	19	0	1	68	3	2.77
W. Elliott, Eugene*	3	0	0	0	0	0	0	.000	7	6	8	6	2	8	0	3	3	7.71
Faulk, Central Oregon	14	14	5	0	8	4	0	.667	102	100	52	36	5	35	2	1	70	8	3.18
Ferguson, Central Oregon	12	12	0	0	1	8	0	.111	57	63	54	36	3	36	0	3	46	8	5.68
Flannery, Eugene	1	1	0	0	0	1	0	.000	6	5	5	4	1	0	0	2	1	6.00
Froelich, Walla Walla	13	13	7	2	6	5	0	.545	100	83	39	32	7	26	1	3	87	7	2.88
Georger, Bellingham	23	0	0	0	6	5	5	.545	62	52	23	15	2	37	7	4	89	5	2.18
Goff, Central Oregon*	10	10	1	0	4	4	0	.500	59	52	31	24	1	38	0	1	76	8	3.66
Graves, Grays Harbor	19	6	1	0	3	6	1	.333	65	60	43	30	1	30	1	5	40	5	4.15
Guardia, Central Oregon	17	0	0	0	1	1	2	.500	17	19	7	6	0	15	0	2	15	3	3.18
Hamm, Walla Walla	14	14	4	0	8	6	0	.571	94	107	49	39	5	31	0	2	52	4	3.73
Harris, Medford	8	4	1	0	1	1	0	.500	29	29	26	23	3	31	0	2	27	4	7.14
Harrison, Bellingham	1	0	0	0	0	0	0	.000	2	1	0	0	1	0	0	4	0	0.00

OFFICIAL BASEBALL GUIDE

Pitcher–Club	G	GS	CG	ShO	W	L	Sv	Pct.	IP	H	R	ER	HR	BB	Int. BB	HB	SO	WP	ERA
Hartery, Victoria*	19	11	1	0	7	6	1	.538	88	86	46	30	4	51	1	1	61	7	3.07
Hayne, Salem	15	2	0	0	5	2	1	.714	49	61	44	34	3	38	3	5	28	10	6.24
Hays, Victoria*	1	0	0	0	0	1	0	.000	1	6	6	6	0	1	0	0	1	1	54.00
Hollenbach, Eugene*	26	2	0	0	3	3	5	.500	57	60	35	25	0	36	3	1	50	1	3.95
Holt, Victoria	4	3	0	0	1	1	0	.500	15	15	5	5	0	15	0	1	5	2	3.00
Howell, Salem	8	1	0	0	0	2	0	.000	18	27	21	14	0	9	0	1	9	1	7.00
Hunger, Bellingham	10	1	0	0	0	2	0	.000	22	29	22	18	0	17	1	1	14	3	7.36
B. Jackson, Eugene	18	5	2	0	5	3	0	.625	72	59	29	25	5	31	0	4	38	1	3.13
Jordan, 4 Bell-4 Salem	8	4	1	0	1	1	0	.500	20	7	20	19	0	46	0	0	27	5	8.55
Koziol, Victoria	20	16	5	0	9	3	0	.750	125	114	65	53	8	56	0	10	104	4	3.82
Lenaburg, C Oregon	18	5	2	1	4	4	2	.500	70	49	22	17	1	33	1	2	52	3	2.19
Lynes, Central Oregon*	23	0	0	0	2	2	4	.500	40	39	19	15	5	14	3	1	32	1	3.38
Mantsch, Medford	10	0	0	0	5	1	3	.833	21	9	4	3	0	5	1	0	17	0	1.29
Marlow, Medford	13	2	0	0	0	2	0	.000	14	24	31	23	2	29	0	0	9	6	14.79
Marshall, Central Oregon	10	10	0	0	5	3	0	.625	70	74	34	28	2	12	0	4	36	5	3.60
R. Martin, Salem*	15	9	3	0	4	5	0	.444	72	70	46	37	3	34	4	3	52	1	4.63
W. Martin, Bellingham	20	0	0	0	3	2	3	.600	39	20	11	9	0	29	3	2	41	1	2.08
M. D. Martinez, Cen. Ore.	12	2	0	0	3	1	0	.750	19	29	19	17	0	14	0	1	15	3	8.05
R. Martinez, Bell*	6	2	0	0	0	0	0	.000	15	19	23	19	1	20	0	0	16	1	11.40
Masone, Eugene	2	0	0	0	0	0	0	.000	3	1	2	1	0	1	0	0	3	1	3.00
Mathey, Victoria	8	7	3	1	3	1	0	.750	48	49	20	18	3	15	0	1	33	1	3.38
C. McKinney, Eugene	11	4	0	0	1	1	0	.500	30	30	20	15	2	31	0	1	20	7	4.50
Michael, Grays Harbor	12	1	0	0	0	1	0	.000	25	35	26	22	1	19	0	1	15	2	7.92
Miller, Grays Harbor*	21	1	0	0	4	5	4	.444	50	48	38	29	4	32	2	1	44	0	5.22
Molina, Eugene	19	4	1	0	2	3	1	.400	39	40	30	27	2	27	1	2	24	3	6.23
Moretti, Victoria	36	1	0	0	6	5	10	.545	82	67	33	20	1	52	2	1	86	2	2.20
Murray, Bellingham	18	1	0	0	5	1	0	.833	50	47	16	11	0	16	4	0	51	2	1.98
Naumann, Bellingham*	11	5	0	0	0	4	0	.000	30	47	31	24	1	19	0	2	17	5	7.20
Nolan, Victoria	5	2	0	0	0	4	0	.000	22	34	28	23	4	10	0	0	26	3	9.41
Nunez, Bellingham	6	6	2	0	4	1	0	.800	39	39	14	9	3	5	0	1	30	1	2.08
Odekirk, Salem*	14	12	2	0	3	5	0	.375	87	90	63	43	7	50	0	3	45	6	4.45
Oliver, Medford*	16	4	0	0	1	1	1	.500	50	60	32	23	3	29	0	2	44	5	4.14
Palmieri, Central Ore*	15	14	3	1	6	3	0	.667	90	81	48	42	2	47	0	2	45	3	4.20
Patton, Walla Walla	12	9	0	0	2	2	0	.500	45	54	38	37	7	31	0	7	15	4	7.40
Peterson, Walla Walla	15	4	1	0	4	2	0	.667	44	45	30	24	2	22	0	3	42	10	4.91
Plummer, Grays Harbor	21	0	0	0	0	5	2	.000	44	50	37	22	3	33	2	4	34	3	4.50
Ramsey, Eugene*	16	14	0	0	7	8	0	.467	77	70	62	49	2	65	1	2	83	7	5.73
Randolph, Bellingham	13	9	0	0	6	2	1	.750	67	63	31	18	2	30	0	2	56	5	2.42
Redmond, Central Oregon	18	0	0	0	3	2	4	.600	37	37	19	17	4	15	4	0	28	4	4.14
Rothey, Eugene*	17	10	0	0	2	7	0	.222	76	65	57	38	1	63	0	1	63	9	4.50
Runyan, Salem	25	6	4	0	6	4	7	.600	79	71	43	32	2	49	6	4	61	10	3.65
Salva, Bellingham	13	1	0	0	4	4	0	.500	73	66	37	30	4	40	2	5	41	4	3.70
Shoemaker, Central Ore	6	0	0	0	1	1	0	.500	9	11	9	7	1	6	0	0	10	2	7.00
Sijer, Walla Walla*	13	9	3	0	4	2	0	.667	73	67	39	31	5	39	0	2	52	3	3.82
Slattery, Medford	8	0	0	0	1	0	1	1.000	21	14	16	14	1	14	0	1	16	3	6.00
C. Smith, Walla Walla	20	0	0	0	4	0	1	1.000	50	36	15	14	0	18	2	3	26	3	3.82
D. Smith, Grays Harbor	14	12	3	1	3	5	0	.375	70	81	40	34	3	31	0	2	60	3	4.37
Somers, Salem*	17	12	1	1	4	6	1	.400	79	83	44	30	1	32	2	1	51	9	3.42
Spicer, Grays Harbor*	14	5	0	0	0	4	0	.000	38	41	38	28	2	40	0	5	31	9	6.63
Stamper, Eugene	10	9	0	0	2	7	0	.286	57	57	35	28	4	26	0	3	51	7	4.42
Steger, Bellingham	12	6	1	0	1	1	0	.500	42	42	31	27	1	33	2	3	45	8	5.79
Stranski, Bellingham	11	11	3	2	5	3	0	.625	63	46	26	23	4	30	0	1	77	4	3.43
Sunderlage, Grays Har*	11	6	0	0	0	3	0	.000	44	59	37	37	8	23	0	0	17	3	7.57
Tolli, Medford	16	11	2	0	6	5	0	.545	87	70	36	30	4	59	1	6	66	6	3.10
Van Marter, Medford	16	8	0	0	6	5	4	.545	66	76	52	43	3	40	2	4	56	5	5.86
Vasche, Salem	19	14	3	0	5	5	1	.500	101	96	66	48	7	60	2	6	75	12	4.28
Weis, Victoria	16	1	0	0	0	3	1	.000	40	40	28	26	2	27	0	3	26	2	5.85
Wilber, Medford	3	0	0	0	0	0	0	.000	10	12	7	4	0	5	0	1	6	2	3.60
Wilson, Walla Walla	13	1	0	0	0	1	0	.000	22	29	18	16	0	25	0	0	22	0	6.55
Wood, Medford	16	4	1	0	2	4	3	.333	40	37	27	24	3	26	0	5	36	8	5.40
Wright, Central Oregon	14	14	2	0	6	2	0	.750	89	82	49	38	5	45	1	7	46	7	3.84
Wyrick, Walla Walla	15	11	2	0	4	5	2	.444	84	78	58	41	7	53	1	3	55	10	4.39
Yesenchak, Medford*	21	3	1	0	3	2	3	.600	53	50	32	26	2	22	1	3	33	4	4.42

BALKS—Anderson, Avallone, Runyan, Salva, 2 each; Brennan (Bell), Candiotti, Dougherty, Ferguson, Graves, Koziol, R. Martin, W. Martin, McKinney, Michael, Naumann, Patton, Plummer, Ramsey, Redmond, Somers, Stamper, Steger, Tolli, Vasche, Wilson, Wood, Wright, 1 each.

COMBINATION SHUTOUTS—Murray-Martin, Randolph-Martin, Salva-Murray, Bellingham; Bangert-Hollenbach, Eugene; Dougherty-Mantsch, Tolli-Mantsch, Medford; Somers-Aspenleiter, Salem.

NO-HIT GAMES—None.

Western Carolinas League

CLASS A

CHAMPIONSHIP WINNERS IN PREVIOUS YEARS

1948—Lincolnton*	.627	1963—Greenville†	.576
1949—Newton-Conover	.667	Salisbury	.631
Ruth'ford Co. (2nd)†	.627	1964—Rock Hill	.672
1950—Newton-Conover	.627	Salisbury‡	.631
Lenoir (2nd)†	.626	1965—Salisbury	.641
1951—Morganton	.645	Rock Hill‡	.603
Shelby (2nd)†	.604	1966—Spartanburg	.682
1952—Lincolnton	.649	Spartanburg	.767
Shelby (2nd)†	.645	1967—Spartanburg	.730
1953-59—League inactive.		Spartanburg	.567
1960—Lexington	.707	1968—Spartanburg	.597
Salisbury (2nd)†	.650	Greenwood‡	.597
1961—Salisbury	.627	1969—Greenwood‡	.587
Shelby (4th)†	.481	Shelby	.565
1962—Statesville	.563	1970—Greenville	.576
Statesville	.700	Greenville	.619

1971—Greenwood	.631
Greenwood	.759
1972—Spartanburg‡	.788
Greenville	.652
1973—Spartanburg‡	.646
Gastonia	.619
1974—Gastonia	.606
Gastonia	.672
1975—Spartanburg	.543
Spartanburg	.614
1976—Asheville	.544
Greenwood‡	.600
1977—Greenwood	.557
Gastonia‡	.590
1978—Greenwood	.614
Greenwood	.565

*Won championship and four-club playoff. †Won four-club playoff. ‡Won split-season playoff. (NOTE—Known as Western Carolina League from 1948 through 1962.)

STANDING OF CLUBS AT CLOSE OF FIRST HALF, JUNE 20

Club	W.	L.	T.	Pct.	G.B.	Club	W.	L.	T.	Pct.	G.B.
Greenwood* (Braves)	39	31	0	.557	......	Greensboro (Reds)	35	33	0	.515	3
Gastonia (Cardinals)	39	31	0	.557	......	Spartanburg (Phillies)	33	37	0	.471	6
Asheville (Rangers)	36	32	0	.529	2	Shelby (Pirates)	24	42	0	.364	13

*Greenwood defeated Gastonia 9-8 (10 innings) on July 4 to win first half championship. League president ruled results of this game were to be included in second half standings.

STANDING OF CLUBS AT CLOSE OF SECOND HALF, AUGUST 31

Club	W.	L.	T.	Pct.	G.B.	Club	W.	L.	T.	Pct.	G.B.
Spartanburg (Phillies)	40	29	0	.580	......	Shelby (Pirates)	32	36	1	.471	7½
Greenwood (Braves)	39	29	0	.574	½	Greensboro (Reds)	30	38	0	.441	9½
Asheville (Rangers)	39	31	1	.557	1½	Gastonia (Cardinals)	26	43	0	.377	14

COMPOSITE STANDING OF CLUBS AT CLOSE OF SEASON, AUGUST 31

Club	Gwd.	Ash.	Spar.	Gbr.	Gas.	Shel.	W.	L.	T.	Pct.	G.B.
Greenwood (Braves)	....	14	16	14	19	15	78	60	0	.565	......
Asheville (Rangers)	14	....	15	19	13	14	75	63	1	.543	3
Spartanburg (Phillies)	12	13	....	13	19	16	73	66	0	.525	5½
Greensboro (Reds)	13	9	14	....	13	16	65	71	0	.478	12
Gastonia (Cardinals)	9	15	9	15	....	17	65	74	0	.468	13½
Shelby (Pirates)	12	12	12	10	10	....	56	78	1	.418	20

Major league affiliations in parentheses.

Playoff—Greenwood defeated Spartanburg, three games to one.

Regular-Season Attendance—Asheville, 42,012; Gastonia, 58,089; Greensboro, 165,596; Greenwood, 37,010; Shelby, 15,570; Spartanburg, 28,960. Total, 347,237. Playoff, 1,532.

Managers: Asheville-Wayne Terwilliger; Gastonia-Johnny Lewis; Greensboro-Jim Lett; Greenwood-Al Gallagher; Shelby-Tom Zimmer; Spartanburg-Bill Dancy.

All-Star Team: 1B—Vargus, Shelby; 2B—Doyle, Asheville; 3B—Borucki, Spartanburg; SS—Hall, Greenwood; OF—Bell, Spartanburg; Rudd, Greenwood; Walker, Greensboro, C-Rubino, Shelby; DH—Gonzalez, Asheville; Utility—Hammond, Greenwood; Pierce, Gastonia; P—Davis, Spartanburg; Farr, Asheville; Gore, Greenwood; Lahti, Greensboro; Manager—Gallagher, Greenwood.

(Compiled by Howe News Bureau, Chicago, Ill.)

CLUB BATTING

Club	G.	AB.	R.	OR.	H.	TB.	2B.	3B.	HR.	RBI.	SH.	SF.	BB.	Int. BB.	HP.	SO.	SB.	CS.	LOB.	Pct.
Greenwood	138	4426	708	654	1194	1619	178	32	61	588	35	44	623	51	50	734	282	98	1012	.270
Asheville	139	4388	721	683	1142	1747	204	28	115	615	31	48	523	39	43	765	179	60	872	.260
Gastonia	139	4564	623	608	1169	1632	186	23	77	545	54	38	542	36	37	873	88	41	1041	.256
Spartanburg	139	4564	633	593	1142	1621	183	46	68	544	45	25	499	33	52	929	140	66	980	.250
Greensboro	136	4320	590	626	1041	1437	169	19	63	494	78	30	646	40	51	1021	127	53	1068	.241
Shelby	135	4136	564	675	992	1516	155	30	103	476	44	20	436	34	45	906	139	71	784	.240

INDIVIDUAL BATTING

(Leading Qualifiers for Batting Championship—378 or More Plate Appearances)

*Bats lefthanded.   †Switch-hitter.

Player and Club	G.	AB.	R.	H.	TB.	2B.	3B.	HR.	RBI.	SH.	SF.	BB.	HP.	SO.	SB.	CS.	Pct.
Perry, Gerald, Greenwood*	109	400	69	133	185	17	4	9	71	1	3	56	2	63	35	13	.333
Doyle, Jeffrey, D., Gastonia†	138	531	90	168	227	28	5	7	70	14	9	59	1	25	14	10	.316
Bell, George, Spartanburg	130	491	78	150	270	24	15	22	102	1	4	26	6	98	10	5	.305
Borucki, Raymond, Spartanburg	136	499	83	149	208	32	6	5	83	1	6	74	2	51	13	7	.299
Cowger, Tracy, Asheville	117	408	68	120	158	21	1	5	57	2	10	24	3	48	9	3	.294
Ross, Angelo, Spartanburg	102	382	63	112	137	11	4	2	33	2	1	33	5	47	32	13	.293
Pierce, Walter, Gastonia	136	513	69	150	218	26	3	12	97	4	4	61	4	84	2	2	.292
Gonzalez, Luis, Asheville*	114	389	67	113	222	25	3	26	87	0	8	36	1	70	3	1	.290
Rudd, Ronald, Greenwood*	115	418	60	121	151	17	2	3	41	4	1	39	2	70	41	14	.289
Hall, Albert, Greenwood†	105	368	84	106	122	10	3	0	38	3	6	60	10	43	66	10	.288

Departmental Leaders: G—Doyle, Sandberg, 138; AB—Sandberg, 539; R—Doyle, 90; H—Doyle, 168; TB—Bell, 270; 2B—Borucki, 32; 3B—Bell, 15; HR—H. Vargas, 31; RBI—Bell, 102; SH—Doyle, 14; SF—Cowger, L. Vargas, 10; BB—Kable, 95; HP—Walker, 17; SO—Kiess, 149; SB—Hall, 66; CS—Sinatro, Washington, 15.

(All Players—Listed Alphabetically)

Player and Club	G.	AB.	R.	H.	TB.	2B.	3B.	HR.	RBI.	SH.	SF.	BB.	HP.	SO.	SB.	CS.	Pct.
Alduey, Juan, Greenwood	1	2	0	0	0	0	0	0	0	0	0	0	0	1	0	0	.000
Alicea, Miguel, Spartanburg	4	7	0	1	2	1	0	0	1	0	1	0	5	0	0	.143
Andino, Raul, Shelby	25	80	12	17	28	5	0	2	4	1	1	16	0	11	6	1	.213
Arigoni, Scott, Gastonia	1	2	0	0	0	0	0	0	0	0	0	0	1	0	0	.000
Arroyo, Felipe, Greenwood	2	3	0	0	0	0	0	0	0	0	0	0	2	0	0	.000
Baez, Berquis, Shelby	22	72	9	15	18	1	1	0	7	0	0	11	0	18	6	2	.208
Barez, Angel, Shelby	1	2	0	1	1	0	0	0	0	0	0	0	0	0	0	.500
Baskerville, Phillip, Gastonia*	41	132	17	34	50	8	1	2	9	0	0	21	2	31	3	1	.258
Baugh, Dean, Spartanburg	15	31	6	6	15	3	0	2	3	0	0	1	1	9	0	0	.194
Behenna, Richard, Greenwood	1	1	0	0	0	0	0	0	0	1	0	0	0	0	0	.000
Bell, George, Spartanburg	130	491	78	150	270	24	15	22	102	1	4	26	6	98	10	5	.305
Black, Charles, Greenwood*	30	79	10	18	18	0	0	0	8	0	0	12	2	7	3	1	.228
Borucki, Raymond, Spartanburg	136	499	83	149	208	32	6	5	83	1	6	74	2	51	13	7	.299
Brauer, Robert, Shelby	50	135	30	28	37	2	2	1	13	5	1	25	1	37	12	4	.207
Brown, Michael E., Shelby	1	1	0	0	0	0	0	0	0	0	0	0	0	0	0	.000
Buckhorn, Glenn, Greenwood	70	227	38	60	95	9	1	8	47	0	2	52	0	65	1	2	.264
Burroughs, Darren, Spartanburg	6	9	2	2	2	0	0	0	1	0	2	0	3	0	0	.222
Butler, Brett, Greenwood*	35	117	26	37	50	2	4	1	11	1	1	24	0	27	20	6	.316
Cabassa, Carlos, Spartanburg*	2	1	0	0	0	0	0	0	0	0	0	0	1	0	0	.000
Caira, Dennis, Gastonia†	54	145	11	29	37	6	1	0	13	1	0	9	0	33	2	2	.200
Carman, Donald, Spartanburg*.	3	3	0	1	1	0	0	0	0	0	0	0	1	0	0	.333
Carvajal, Crucito, Shelby	1	1	0	0	0	0	0	0	0	0	0	0	0	0	0	.000
Childs, Michael, Asheville	19	39	3	5	11	2	2	0	4	0	0	8	0	10	0	0	.128
Cicatiello, Gary, Shelby*	22	64	9	15	26	4	2	1	4	0	0	5	1	12	3	0	.234
Cline, Donald, 14 Shel-10 Grnwd	24	2	0	0	0	0	0	0	0	0	0	0	0	1	0	0	.000
Cline, Robin, Gastonia	12	29	2	5	5	0	0	0	2	0	0	4	0	5	0	0	.172
Corbett, Raymond, Greensboro*	100	300	38	79	111	6	1	8	42	3	3	45	2	66	1	3	.263
Cowger, Tracy, Asheville	117	408	68	120	158	21	1	5	57	2	10	24	3	48	9	3	.294
Cuevas, Miguel, Spartanburg	4	5	0	0	0	0	0	0	0	0	0	0	0	2	0	0	.000
Culmer, Wilfred, Spartanburg	68	228	35	70	111	17	3	6	46	0	1	18	10	68	12	2	.307
Daniels, Jessie C., Shelby*	43	151	20	46	65	9	2	2	16	3	0	10	0	31	4	6	.305
Daves, W. Edward, Gastonia	32	91	14	15	28	1	0	4	15	0	0	12	0	21	1	0	.165
Davis, Mark, Spartanburg*	5	13	1	1	1	0	0	0	0	2	0	0	1	0	0	.077
De La Cruz, Miguelito, Grnwd	27	64	3	12	13	1	0	0	4	0	2	0	13	0	0	.188
DeVincenzo, John, Spartanburg	3	3	0	0	0	0	0	0	0	0	0	0	1	0	0	.000
Dixon, F. Daniel, Asheville	21	55	6	12	14	2	0	0	7	3	1	2	0	9	0	0	.218
Doyle, Jeffrey D., Gastonia†	138	531	90	168	227	28	5	7	70	14	9	59	1	25	14	10	.316
Dyer, John, Greenwood*	37	115	16	35	55	8	0	4	21	0	2	12	0	35	0	0	.304
Engel, Charles, Greensboro	118	381	46	90	110	14	3	0	44	8	2	53	1	85	1	1	.236
Faulconer, Charles, Shelby	38	107	12	21	28	4	0	1	10	3	1	15	1	33	6	3	.196
Feliz, Adolfo, Greensboro	115	412	52	100	141	23	6	2	40	7	3	40	5	66	17	8	.243
Fleming, Steven, Shelby	16	48	2	5	7	2	0	0	6	0	1	8	0	17	0	1	.104
Forbes, Andre, Greenwood	69	259	39	84	107	13	2	2	35	2	1	31	2	16	15	3	.324

Player and Club	G.	AB.	R.	H.	TB.	2B.	3B.	HR.	RBI.	SH.	SF.	BB.	HP.	SO.	SB.	CS.	Pct.
Frobel, Douglas, Shelby*	48	130	11	24	36	3	0	3	13	3	2	6	1	37	0	0	.185
Garnett, Bradley, Shelby*	103	311	36	61	114	10	2	13	44	1	0	29	2	103	5	5	.196
Gonzalez, Luis, Asheville*	114	389	67	113	222	25	3	26	87	0	8	36	1	70	3	1	.290
Gore, B. Lance, Greenwood*	1	1	0	0	0	0	0	0	0	1	0	0	0	0	0	0	.000
Guinn, Wayne, Greensboro	34	55	10	14	19	2	0	1	5	7	0	8	0	23	0	0	.255
Gutierrez, Israel, Asheville	54	174	21	45	61	8	1	2	21	1	5	16	1	30	6	2	.259
Hair, Wesley, Shelby*	87	293	33	70	96	13	2	3	22	4	0	29	0	62	8	6	.239
Hall, Albert, Greenwood*	105	368	84	106	122	10	3	0	38	3	6	60	10	43	66	10	.288
Hammond, Steven, Greenwood*	58	201	34	65	92	17	2	2	37	0	1	23	2	12	3	2	.323
Harskamp, John, Gastonia	25	82	9	16	24	2	0	2	10	0	1	7	2	24	0	0	.195
Henson, Michael, Spartanburg	49	137	14	28	33	5	0	0	14	2	3	9	1	42	0	0	.204
Hibner, David, Asheville	97	212	42	39	73	2	1	10	28	3	1	56	2	102	9	5	.184
Hicks, Robert, Gastonia	78	268	21	62	75	8	1	1	16	4	1	12	4	74	1	1	.231
Hoenstine, David, Greensboro	113	374	53	97	119	12	2	2	37	6	2	69	4	64	14	6	.259
Hover, Lee, Greensboro	39	108	17	22	27	3	1	0	4	3	2	14	0	35	7	2	.204
Howell, Randy, Gastonia	33	107	18	26	43	5	0	4	19	1	2	12	2	36	2	0	.243
Hunsaker, Frank, Gastonia	23	78	19	28	43	6	0	3	18	0	0	19	1	7	0	1	.359
Jackson, Larry, Greensboro	21	36	5	7	8	1	0	0	2	0	0	4	0	22	0	0	.194
Jacobson, Kevin, Greensboro	128	438	56	108	151	24	2	5	61	8	4	73	6	48	2	4	.247
Jimenez, Luis, Shelby	2	2	0	0	0	0	0	0	0	0	0	0	0	1	0	0	.000
Kable, David, Gastonia*	131	432	60	95	172	15	1	20	72	2	4	95	9	135	1	2	.220
Kiess, Paul, Spartanburg*	137	485	44	110	144	17	1	5	38	6	2	48	3	149	3	3	.227
Kripner, Michael, Greensboro†	80	214	25	49	65	7	0	3	24	1	1	40	8	73	5	2	.229
Kuchar, William, Greensboro	32	74	8	16	18	2	0	0	8	0	0	27	0	31	0	0	.216
Lahti, Jeffrey, Greensboro	53	16	3	5	8	1	1	0	2	2	0	2	1	3	0	0	.313
Lang, Robert, Shelby	2	2	0	1	2	1	0	0	0	0	0	1	0	0	0	0	.500
LaRosa, William, Gastonia	1	1	0	0	0	0	0	0	0	0	0	0	0	0	0	0	.000
Lesley, Bradley, Greensboro	19	26	2	5	6	1	0	0	2	6	0	3	0	9	0	0	.192
Lett, Roosevelt, Gastonia	10	23	1	6	6	0	0	0	2	0	0	0	0	6	0	0	.261
Lewis, Amos, Asheville	88	264	56	73	151	11	2	21	62	0	2	53	4	98	1	5	.277
Liggins, Danny, Gastonia	22	85	10	18	21	1	1	0	8	0	1	7	1	21	5	1	.212
Littlefield, David, Spartanburg	14	41	5	9	14	2	0	1	6	0	0	5	0	8	0	0	.220
LoCascio, John, Greensboro*	48	27	5	3	4	1	0	0	3	3	1	6	0	13	0	0	.111
Lucas, Mark, Greenwood	61	167	23	45	53	4	2	0	20	2	1	25	1	26	5	3	.269
Lucia, Daniel, Greenwood	1	1	0	0	0	0	0	0	0	0	0	2	0	0	0	0	.000
Martin, Mark, Greenwood	46	137	8	22	25	3	0	0	6	1	1	9	0	16	2	3	.161
Martinez, Ignacio, Shelby	1	0	0	0	0	0	0	0	0	0	0	1	0	0	0	0	.000
Matthews, Jeffrey, Greenwood	86	237	32	64	76	10	1	0	24	3	2	39	0	26	2	1	.270
McArdle, James, Greensboro	108	364	43	100	143	15	2	8	57	2	2	49	0	59	7	2	.275
McCauley, Stanley, Gastonia	52	160	20	32	46	8	0	2	12	2	0	18	0	35	1	0	.200
McGivney, Thomas, Asheville*	35	85	11	16	26	4	0	2	14	2	0	14	0	19	0	0	.188
McKinney, Gregory, Greensboro*	50	142	25	29	40	5	0	2	9	0	1	25	3	45	2	5	.204
McKnight, James, Gastonia†	30	84	2	11	14	3	0	0	7	2	0	5	0	10	0	0	.131
Merulla, Tony, Shelby	85	229	34	57	83	11	0	5	34	2	1	41	6	45	4	2	.249
Miller, David, Asheville†	110	339	66	86	110	14	2	2	25	6	1	40	7	48	44	8	.254
Mills, Rhadames, Gastonia	135	507	67	143	187	20	6	4	53	12	3	44	2	78	31	13	.282
Moore, Mark, Greensboro†	6	10	4	4	4	0	0	0	2	1	0	1	0	4	0	0	.400
Morton, Dennis, Gastonia*	1	1	0	1	1	0	0	0	0	0	0	0	0	0	0	0	1.000
Mueller, Timothy, Gastonia	92	332	37	76	118	12	3	8	45	0	2	25	5	70	0	0	.229
Navaretti, Aaron, Spartanburg	91	239	29	39	48	3	3	0	10	3	2	44	2	47	3	2	.163
Neal, E. Earl, Spartanburg	116	414	62	98	176	19	4	17	68	5	2	42	5	103	11	6	.237
Neely, Alex, Greensboro	13	14	0	0	0	0	0	0	0	2	0	2	0	11	0	0	.000
Nelson, Patrick, Asheville	1	1	0	0	0	0	0	0	0	0	0	0	0	1	0	0	.000
Neufang, Gerald, Asheville	15	43	4	9	10	1	0	0	6	0	0	4	0	4	0	0	.209
Noble, Charles, Greenwood*	8	11	1	1	2	1	0	0	0	2	0	4	0	7	0	0	.091
O'Keeffe, Richard, Greensboro*	18	30	2	7	10	3	0	0	8	2	1	2	0	6	0	0	.233
Olszak, Thomas, Shelby	25	83	14	22	29	4	0	1	14	0	2	8	3	15	1	3	.265
Ortiz, Albert, Asheville*	96	307	61	83	112	17	3	2	33	0	3	62	3	32	22	5	.270
Perry, Gerald, Greenwood*	109	400	69	133	185	17	4	9	71	1	3	56	2	63	35	13	.333
Pierce, Walter, Gastonia	136	513	69	150	218	26	3	12	97	4	4	61	4	84	2	2	.292
Pill, Michael, Shelby	3	8	0	2	2	0	0	0	2	0	0	1	0	3	0	0	.250
Pittman, Michael, Gastonia	1	1	0	0	0	0	0	0	0	0	0	0	0	0	0	0	.000
Poff, James, Shelby	97	304	36	67	97	14	2	4	36	3	1	30	5	64	17	5	.220
Prior, Daniel, Spartanburg	4	4	0	0	0	0	0	0	0	0	0	0	0	1	0	0	.000
Proulx, Patrick, Gastonia	39	93	12	17	19	2	0	0	3	1	0	5	1	19	2	0	.183
Ramos, George, Greenwood	57	137	33	36	47	5	0	2	11	1	0	31	5	27	14	6	.263
Rasmussen, James, Spartanburg	7	12	0	2	2	0	0	0	2	1	0	2	0	3	0	0	.167
Ray, Arthur, Shelby	2	2	1	1	1	0	0	0	0	0	0	1	0	0	0	0	.500
Redus, Gary, Greensboro	83	309	79	86	152	17	1	16	52	1	2	58	1	61	41	8	.278
Reese, Stanley, Asheville*	104	377	55	90	154	17	1	15	50	0	1	36	1	41	5	5	.239
Reimer, Mark, Shelby	20	60	9	9	21	3	0	3	9	0	1	5	2	15	1	0	.150
Reynolds, Larry, Asheville†	39	139	23	43	52	5	2	0	15	2	0	14	0	23	17	3	.309
Richardt, Michael, Asheville	75	283	61	88	121	15	3	4	41	5	4	29	3	22	22	3	.311
Righetti, Steven, Asheville	94	265	37	60	103	14	1	9	42	1	2	15	7	61	1	2	.226
Rios, Carlos, Shelby	128	391	46	97	118	7	4	2	34	9	0	38	1	56	20	14	.248

Player and Club	G.	AB.	R.	H.	TB.	2B.	3B.	HR.	RBI.	SH.	SF.	BB.	HP.	SO.	SB.	CS.	Pct.
Rodriguez, Angel, Shelby	29	76	4	16	28	3	0	3	11	0	0	1	1	15	1	1	.211
Rodriguez, Jose, Shelby	117	357	48	85	120	12	4	5	29	9	2	33	3	99	11	4	.238
Rogers, James, Greenwood	2	1	0	0	0	0	0	0	0	2	0	2	0	1	0	0	.000
Rollins, Rip, Spartanburg	25	32	0	3	6	3	0	0	3	1	0	6	0	14	0	0	.094
Ross, Angelo, Spartanburg	102	382	63	112	137	11	4	2	33	2	1	33	5	47	32	13	.293
Roush, Mark, Greenwood	2	2	0	0	0	0	0	0	0	0	0	0	0	1	0	0	.000
Rubino, Patrick, Shelby	122	367	64	97	156	11	0	16	52	0	4	67	5	65	8	5	.264
Rudd, Ronald, Greenwood*	115	418	60	121	151	17	2	3	41	4	1	39	2	70	41	14	.289
Russell, Robert, Gastonia	1	2	0	0	0	0	0	0	0	1	0	0	0	1	0	0	.000
Ryan, Gil, Greenwood	3	7	1	1	1	0	0	0	0	0	0	1	0	3	0	0	.143
Salazar, Terrell, Shelby	56	184	24	50	79	9	1	6	25	0	1	13	2	29	5	3	.272
Sandberg, Ryne, Spartanburg	138	539	83	133	180	21	7	4	47	8	0	64	1	95	21	7	.247
Scanlon, Kenneth, Greenwood	48	147	19	28	31	3	0	0	10	1	0	18	3	26	5	1	.190
Shields, W. Michael, Greenwood	1	1	0	0	0	0	0	0	0	0	0	0	0	1	0	0	.000
Siebert, Thomas, Shelby	1	1	0	0	0	0	0	0	0	0	0	0	0	0	0	0	.000
Sinatro, Matthew, Greenwood	120	385	54	97	142	16	4	7	57	4	4	42	6	59	25	15	.252
Smith, Everette, Gastonia	34	100	16	18	24	3	0	1	9	0	2	14	0	21	0	0	.180
Smith, Michael T., Greenwood	3	8	3	4	5	1	0	0	2	1	0	1	0	2	0	0	.500
Sorel, Michael, Greensboro	84	252	23	41	46	5	0	0	14	6	1	29	1	53	1	2	.163
Spreckles, Keith, Gastonia	69	239	46	74	103	17	0	4	29	2	2	52	1	52	11	2	.310
Straker, Lester, Greensboro	29	42	2	7	7	0	0	0	1	4	0	4	0	17	0	0	.167
Supel, Bobby, Greenwood	31	93	8	19	22	3	0	0	12	0	0	20	0	29	5	1	.204
Tanzi, Robert, Asheville	83	240	28	63	79	13	0	1	29	1	2	27	1	31	5	4	.263
Taylor, Johnny, Shelby	2	2	0	2	3	1	0	0	1	0	0	0	0	0	0	0	1.000
Teixeira, Peter, Greenwood	1	4	0	1	1	0	0	0	1	0	0	0	0	2	0	0	.250
Thayer, Scott, Greenwood	78	243	42	52	98	14	1	10	39	2	2	36	5	64	0	1	.214
Thompson, Milton, Greenwood*	53	145	31	27	39	4	1	2	16	5	5	32	3	39	16	3	.186
Thomson, Philip, Spartanburg*	81	201	34	44	54	7	0	1	22	1	0	41	5	30	3	1	.219
Turco, Steve, Gastonia*	116	366	60	93	111	7	1	3	23	8	2	38	2	55	9	6	.254
Ulrich, Jeffery, Spartanburg	94	309	34	66	83	11	0	2	29	4	2	44	6	66	4	2	.214
Vargas, Hediberto, Shelby	126	440	76	124	250	23	5	31	78	0	2	26	6	101	8	3	.282
Vargas, Leonel, Greenwood	125	455	74	127	191	21	5	11	73	0	10	54	7	58	24	13	.279
Veale, Jerry, Greenwood	1	1	0	0	0	0	0	0	0	0	0	0	0	0	0	0	.000
Venger, Tad, Greensboro*	91	253	30	56	85	14	0	5	30	1	1	25	2	96	2	1	.221
Waag, William, Shelby	60	210	33	56	68	3	3	1	10	0	0	16	4	28	13	3	.267
Walker, Tony, Greensboro	114	404	58	112	151	12	0	9	41	1	3	56	17	109	26	9	.277
Washington, Keith, Spartanburg*	121	423	49	106	116	6	2	0	30	4	2	26	4	70	27	15	.251
White, Alvin, Spartanburg	32	53	11	12	18	1	1	1	7	0	0	11	1	11	1	3	.226
Willett, Joel, Greensboro	35	28	3	3	9	0	0	2	5	2	1	6	0	14	1	0	.107
Winslow, Daniel, Gastonia	52	160	22	51	59	8	0	0	14	2	2	23	0	13	7	3	.319
Wojton, Walter, Shelby	3	5	0	1	1	0	0	0	0	0	0	0	0	0	0	0	.000
Woodward, Donald, Spartanburg	2	2	0	0	0	0	0	0	0	0	0	0	0	1	0	0	.000
Wright, George, Asheville	115	379	53	97	134	17	4	4	40	3	3	35	9	51	13	11	.256
Zaske, L. Jeffrey, Shelby	1	1	0	0	0	0	0	0	0	0	0	0	0	0	0	0	.000
Zimmer, Thomas, Shelby	1	5	1	2	2	0	0	0	1	0	0	0	0	1	0	0	.400
Zitek, Jeffrey, Asheville*	117	390	61	98	154	16	2	12	55	2	5	52	1	54	22	3	.251

The following pitchers had no plate appearances primarily through use of designated hitters, listed alphabetically by club, games in parentheses):

ASHEVILLE—Chapman, David (19); Farr, James (24); Hartwig, Daniel (11); Kwolek, Charles (10); Lazorko, Jack (23); McWilliams, James M. (2); Mosby, Linvel (24); Nelson, W. Eugene (33); Nickerson, James (25); Scott, Jeffrey (3); Tam, Andrew (16); Vickers, Michael (27); Williams, Wesley (25).

GASTONIA—Gadowski, Dennis (9); Gott, James (19); Harshbarger, John (5); Johnson, Jerry D. (36); Jones, David R. (6); Little, Martin (35); Riggins, Mark (8); Silva, Freddie (25); Thomas, William C. (25); Vasche, Thomas (7); Vega, Axel (22).

GREENSBORO—Hayes, Ben (1); Torres, Nelson (2).

GREENWOOD—Balogh, Kevin (17); Kerdolff, Russell (7); Kitts, Dewayne (18); Lawrence, Stephen (8); North, Roy (3).

SHELBY—Dodd, Lance (20); Guerra, Fernando (13); Huey, John (14); Kirby, Dennis (7); Peralta, Sergio (12).

SPARTANBURG—Shoemaker, Martin (3).

GRAND SLAM HOME RUNS—Bell, Cowger, Felix, Gonzalez, Neal, Pierce, Redus, Sinatro, H. Vargas, L. Vargas, 1 each.

AWARDED FIRST BASE ON INTERFERENCE—Thayer 4 (Cowger, Daves, Merulla, Rubino), Harskamp (Sinatro), Henson (A. Rodriguez), McArdle (Rubino), J. Rodriguez (Ulrich).

CLUB FIELDING

Club	G.	PO.	A.	E.	DP.	PB.	Pct.	Club	G.	PO.	A.	E.	DP.	PB.	Pct.
Spartanburg	139	3578	1533	200	121	27	.9623	Asheville	139	3464	1485	247	110	27	.952
Gastonia	139	3552	1550	203	110	24	.9617	Shelby	135	3301	1211	228	104	26	.952
Greensboro	136	3461	1329	235	106	27	.953	Greenwood	138	3482	1512	264	108	22	.950

Triple Plays—None.

INDIVIDUAL FIELDING

FIRST BASEMEN

*Throws lefthanded.

Player and Club	G.	PO.	A.	E.	DP.	Pct.
Thayer, Greenwood	14	119	7	0	9	1.000
Salazar, Shelby	4	24	1	0	3	1.000
White, Spartanburg	4	18	1	0	3	1.000
Ortiz, Asheville*	2	13	1	0	2	1.000
Winslow, Gastonia	1	9	0	0	1	1.000
Garnett, Shelby*	2	5	0	0	0	1.000
KABLE, Gastonia	127	1128	68	10	89	.992
Kuchar, Greensboro	23	193	13	2	14	.990
Vargas, Shelby	118	863	49	10	72	.989
Righetti, Asheville	23	154	5	2	2	.988

Player and Club	G.	PO.	A.	E.	DP.	Pct.
Engel, Greensboro	108	879	61	12	68	.987
Reese, Asheville	62	482	33	7	41	.987
Frobel, Shelby	18	138	10	2	10	.987
McCauley, Gastonia	13	108	12	2	9	.984
Kiess, Spartanburg*	137	1290	61	24	109	.983
Hoenstine, Greensboro	7	56	1	1	3	.983
Perry, Greenwood	107	881	59	91	69	.980
Dyer, Greenwood*	21	195	6	4	14	.980
Gonzalez, Asheville*	63	549	26	26	36	.957
De La Cruz, Greenwood	3	14	2	2	1	.889

SECOND BASEMEN

Player and Club	G.	PO.	A.	E.	DP.	Pct.
Hoenstine, Greensboro	5	10	13	0	1	1.000
Brauer, Shelby	2	1	5	0	0	1.000
McKnight, Gastonia	2	1	2	0	2	1.000
Ortiz, Asheville*	1	1	0	0	0	1.000
Black, Greenwood	27	61	58	2	11	.983
Buckhorn, Greenwood	10	22	23	1	6	.978
DOYLE, Gastonia	136	295	400	18	69	.975
Gutierrez, Asheville	50	89	131	6	18	.973
Forbes, Greenwood	47	109	146	8	26	.970
Richardt, Asheville	74	173	212	16	37	.960
Lucas, Greenwood	6	12	10	1	3	.957
Poff, Shelby	58	111	136	12	31	.954
Navaretti, Spartanburg	90	200	207	20	49	.953

Player and Club	G.	PO.	A.	E.	DP.	Pct.
Waag, Shelby	51	95	110	10	21	.953
Reynolds, Asheville	11	18	23	2	3	.953
Redus, Greensboro	74	154	192	20	47	.945
Scanlon, Greenwood	47	100	123	13	21	.945
Daniels, Shelby	35	60	62	8	12	.938
Feliz, Greensboro	50	73	105	12	18	.937
Thomson, Spartanburg	66	121	157	19	41	.936
Righetti, Asheville	8	8	20	2	2	.933
Tanzi, Asheville	2	4	7	1	0	.917
Hover, Greensboro	15	15	25	4	2	.909
Matthews, Greenwood	8	20	18	4	6	.905
Proulx, Gastonia	6	7	9	2	0	.889
Mills, Gastonia	1	2	0	1	0	.667

THIRD BASEMEN

Player and Club	G.	PO.	A.	E.	DP.	Pct.
Hammond, Greenwood	1	3	2	0	0	1.000
Proulx, Gastonia	2	0	4	0	0	1.000
A. Rodriguez, Shelby	1	1	0	0	0	1.000
Hoenstine, Greensboro	16	15	25	1	2	.976
Frobel, Shelby	14	12	23	1	1	.972
BORUCKI, Spart.	132	109	311	19	18	.957
Righetti, Asheville	44	34	73	5	5	.955
Poff, Shelby	29	25	34	4	5	.937
Jacobson, Greensboro	121	87	230	28	20	.919
Forbes, Greenwood	11	4	30	3	3	.919
Pierce, Gastonia	135	121	260	34	14	.918
Lucas, Greenwood	33	26	42	7	5	.907
Hair, Shelby	46	46	67	12	4	.904
Tanzi, Asheville	61	50	109	17	5	.903
Supel, Greenwood	16	8	29	4	4	.902

Player and Club	G.	PO.	A.	E.	DP.	Pct.
Thayer, Greenwood	8	9	17	3	1	.897
Buckhorn, Greenwood	60	54	107	23	12	.875
Ramos, Greenwood	3	2	5	1	0	.875
Matthews, Greenwood	20	6	41	7	3	.870
Thomson, Spartanburg	6	5	8	2	1	.867
Lewis, Asheville	53	40	69	17	14	.865
Salazar, Shelby	22	8	22	5	2	.857
McKnight, Gastonia	3	2	4	1	0	.857
J. Rodriguez, Shelby	20	18	34	9	4	.852
Baugh, Spartanburg	5	4	4	2	1	.800
Brauer, Shelby	14	8	13	6	3	.778
McCauley, Gastonia	1	1	2	1	0	.750
Gutierrez, Asheville	4	4	4	3	0	.727
Harskamp, Gastonia	1	1	1	1	0	.667

SHORTSTOPS

Player and Club	G.	PO.	A.	E.	DP.	Pct.
Brauer, Shelby	3	1	5	0	1	1.000
Thomson, Spartanburg	2	1	2	0	0	1.000
Hair, Shelby	1	1	0	0	0	1.000
Neufang, Asheville	1	1	0	0	0	1.000
Proulx, Gastonia	23	26	58	3	10	.966
SANDBERG, Spart.	138	134	467	35	80	.945
Turco, Gastonia	99	141	282	28	49	.938
Harskamp, Gastonia	21	24	65	6	9	.937
Sorel, Greensboro	80	119	174	23	27	.927
Rios, Shelby	127	230	316	48	63	.919

Player and Club	G.	PO.	A.	E.	DP.	Pct.
Zitek, Asheville	114	163	364	49	49	.915
Tanzi, Asheville	12	11	21	3	3	.914
Matthews, Greenwood	55	64	146	25	18	.894
Lewis, Asheville	15	14	31	6	5	.882
McKnight, Gastonia	16	16	32	7	3	.873
Feliz, Greensboro	59	85	144	36	33	.864
Hall, Greenwood	95	120	288	72	45	.850
Waag, Shelby	8	11	14	5	3	.833
Gutierrez, Asheville	1	0	1	1	0	.500
Nickerson, Asheville	1	0	0	2	0	.000

OUTFIELDERS

Player and Club	G.	PO.	A.	E.	DP.	Pct.
Butler, Greenwood*	34	45	2	0	0	1.000
Thayer, Greenwood	30	44	2	0	1	1.000
Liggins, Gastonia	22	35	1	0	0	1.000
Olszak, Shelby	23	34	2	0	0	1.000
Dixon, Asheville	18	28	3	0	0	1.000
Ramos, Greenwood	27	25	0	0	0	1.000
White, Spartanburg	7	17	0	0	0	1.000
Turco, Gastonia	10	15	2	0	0	1.000
Poff, Shelby	10	14	1	0	0	1.000
McCauley, Gastonia	11	11	3	0	0	1.000
Merulla, Shelby	5	7	1	0	0	1.000

Player and Club	G.	PO.	A.	E.	DP.	Pct.
A. Rodriguez, Shelby	12	8	0	0	0	1.000
Righetti, Asheville	8	7	0	0	0	1.000
Forbes, Greenwood	7	4	0	0	0	1.000
McKnight, Gastonia	2	3	0	0	0	1.000
Frobel, Shelby	3	3	0	0	0	1.000
Lett, Gastonia	7	3	0	0	0	1.000
Sinatro, Greenwood	1	2	0	0	0	1.000
De La Cruz, Greenwood	2	2	0	0	0	1.000
Perry, Greenwood	4	2	0	0	0	1.000
Taylor, Shelby	1	1	0	0	0	1.000
MILLER, Ash	103	151	10	2	1	.988

OUTFIELDERS—Continued

Player and Club	G.	PO.	A.	E.	DP.	Pct.
Andino, Shelby	24	40	5	1	0	.978
Spreckles, Gastonia	65	112	9	3	3	.976
Baskerville, Gastonia	28	40	0	1	0	.976
Ortiz, Asheville*	89	108	11	3	3	.975
Wright, Asheville	115	245	22	7	6	.974
Washington, Spartan	116	226	19	7	4	.972
McArdle, Greensboro	97	164	12	5	3	.972
Cicatiello, Shelby	22	29	5	1	0	.971
Thompson, Greenwood	50	85	8	3	1	.969
Hicks, Gastonia	77	114	4	4	0	.967
Faulconer, Shelby	36	52	6	2	1	.967
Hover, Greensboro	17	28	1	1	0	.967
Mills, Gastonia	132	224	21	9	4	.965
Bell, Spartanburg	114	206	14	8	1	.965
Ross, Spartanburg	93	175	14	7	2	.964
Baez, Shelby	21	52	1	2	0	.964
Vargas, Greenwood	124	188	6	8	1	.960
Hoenstine, Greensboro	76	93	4	4	1	.960
Reynolds, Asheville	29	43	5	2	1	.960
Rudd, Greenwood	110	151	11	7	0	.959
Walker, Greensboro	106	215	11	10	3	.958
Hibner, Asheville	81	132	13	7	2	.954
Hammond, Greenwood	44	73	7	4	3	.952
J. Rodriguez, Shelby	97	190	6	10	2	.951
Redus, Greensboro	7	18	1	1	0	.950
Reimer, Shelby	20	33	1	2	0	.944
Venger, Greensboro	69	96	11	7	2	.939
Howell, Gastonia	29	43	3	3	1	.939
Neal, Spartanburg	73	115	6	9	1	.931
Caira, Gastonia	49	46	6	4	0	.929
Fleming, Shelby	15	27	1	3	0	.903
Smith, Gastonia	18	24	3	3	0	.900
Daniels, Shelby	2	9	0	1	0	.900
Hair, Shelby	35	50	1	6	0	.895
Supel, Greenwood	9	7	1	1	1	.889
Garnett, Shelby*	84	122	5	16	3	.888
Brauer, Shelby	27	34	2	5	0	.878
McKinney, Greensboro	43	58	4	9	0	.873
Culmer, Spartanburg	28	40	2	8	1	.840
Vargas, Shelby	3	5	0	1	0	.833
Childs, Asheville	6	7	1	2	0	.800

CATCHERS

Player and Club	G.	PO.	A.	E.	DP.	PB.	Pct.
Neufang, Asheville	13	71	10	0	1	0	1.000
McCauley, Gastonia	4	8	0	0	0	1	1.000
Hair, Shelby	1	1	0	0	0	1	1.000
RUBINO, Shelby	104	636	91	9	8	20	.988
Hunsaker, Gastonia	12	70	12	1	1	0	.988
Ulrich, Spartanburg	92	559	69	8	6	14	.987
Sinatro, Greenwood	102	639	69	11	8	15	.985
Corbett, Greensboro	78	587	55	12	7	15	.982
Martin, Greenwood	39	244	30	6	3	7	.979
Mueller, Gastonia	71	482	54	13	1	13	.976
Merulla, Shelby	37	201	21	6	1	5	.974
Kripner, Greensboro	60	449	49	14	9	12	.973
Cowger, Asheville	108	642	91	23	9	20	.970
Henson, Spartanburg	40	248	11	8	1	11	.970
Winslow, Gastonia	48	280	41	11	6	8	.967
McGivney, Asheville	31	155	18	6	1	7	.966
Cline, Gastonia	8	45	3	2	1	1	.960
De La Cruz, Grnwd	11	62	6	3	1	0	.958
Littlefield, Spar	12	73	10	4	3	2	.954
Daves, Gastonia	7	49	7	3	0	1	.949
A. Rodriguez, Shelby	8	32	1	2	0	1	.943
Cuevas, Spartanburg	2	3	1	1	0	0	.800

PITCHERS

Player and Club	G.	PO.	A.	E.	DP.	Pct.
RASMUSSEN, Spar	26	8	20	0	4	1.000
Alicea, Spartanburg	25	3	24	0	4	1.000
Pill, Shelby	12	5	15	0	0	1.000
Ray, Shelby	10	8	11	0	1	1.000
Little, Gastonia	35	3	15	0	1	1.000
Carman, Spartanburg*	37	1	10	0	1	1.000
Kerdolff, Greenwood	7	2	7	0	0	1.000
Pittman, Gastonia*	14	1	7	0	0	1.000
Carvajal, Shelby	30	2	5	0	0	1.000
Peralta, Shelby	12	2	4	0	1	1.000
Riggins, Gastonia*	8	0	5	0	0	1.000
Taylor, Shelby	11	2	3	0	0	1.000
Huey, Shelby	14	1	4	0	0	1.000
Scott, Asheville	3	1	3	0	1	1.000
Guerra, Shelby	13	1	3	0	0	1.000
Tam, Asheville	16	1	5	0	1	1.000
Lang, Shelby	2	2	1	0	0	1.000
Vasche, Gastonia	7	0	2	0	0	1.000
Lucas, Greenwood	1	0	1	0	0	1.000
McWilliams, Ash*	2	0	1	0	0	1.000
Thayer, Greenwood	2	0	1	0	0	1.000
Torres, Greensboro	2	0	1	0	0	1.000
Lawrence, Greenwood	8	0	1	0	0	1.000
Martinez, Shelby	16	0	1	0	0	1.000
Ryan, Greenwood	21	10	19	1	2	.967
Burroughs, Spar*	2	2	27	1	1	.967
Johnson, Gastonia	36	8	20	1	2	.966
Teixeira, Grnwd	13	7	20	1	3	.964
Silva, Gastonia	25	6	21	1	3	.964
Lahti, Greensboro	53	5	22	1	1	.964
Mosby, Shelby	24	3	20	1	1	.958
Lucia, Greenwood	14	6	15	1	0	.955
Gore, Greenwood*	45	2	16	1	2	.947
LoCascio, Grnsboro*	48	5	13	1	1	.947
Alduey, Greenwood	13	7	10	1	0	.944
Vickers, Asheville*	27	10	22	2	1	.941
Guinn, Greensboro	34	15	31	3	4	.939
Farr, Asheville	24	8	22	2	4	.938
Kitts, Greenwood*	18	1	14	1	2	.938
Rogers, Greenwood	20	13	31	3	1	.936
Williams, Asheville	25	15	28	3	0	.935
Arigoni, Gastonia*	15	2	11	1	0	.929
Balogh, Greensboro	17	1	12	1	0	.929
Roush, Greenwood	17	4	9	1	0	.929
O'Keeffe, Grnsboro*	18	2	22	2	1	.923
Brown, Shelby	24	6	17	2	1	.920
Cline, Shelby-Grnwd	24	5	18	2	2	.920
E. Nelson, Ashe	33	7	26	3	5	.917
Cabassa, Spar*	32	5	15	2	2	.909
Noble, Greensboro*	8	3	7	1	1	.909
Arroyo, Greenwood	17	3	7	1	1	.909
Lesley, Greensboro	19	6	28	4	0	.895
Behenna, Greenwood	8	6	11	2	0	.895
Moore, Greensboro*	35	3	14	2	1	.895
Prior, Spartanburg	51	4	13	2	2	.895
Neely, Greensboro	52	2	15	2	0	.895
LaRosa, Gastonia	56	3	12	2	0	.882
Thomas, Gastonia	25	7	22	4	0	.879
Kirby, Shelby	7	1	6	1	0	.875
Smith, Greenwood	18	9	11	3	0	.870
Jimenez, Shelby	16	3	10	2	2	.867
Morton, Gastonia*	19	4	9	2	0	.867
Siebert, Shelby	16	5	14	3	2	.864
DeVincenzo, Spar	50	3	15	3	0	.857
Hartwig, Asheville	11	7	9	3	0	.842
Davis, Spartanburg*	26	6	20	5	0	.839
Willett, Greensboro	34	9	6	3	0	.833
Wojton, Shelby	34	2	13	3	0	.833
Kwolek, Asheville*	10	1	4	1	0	.833
Barez, Shelby	16	9	20	6	1	.829
Jackson, Greensboro	21	5	14	4	3	.826
Vega, Gastonia	22	8	15	5	1	.821

PITCHERS—Continued

Player and Club	G.	PO.	A.	E.	DP.	Pct.
Rollins, Spartanburg	25	1	17	4	0	.818
Gadowski, Gastonia	9	1	8	2	0	.818
Lazorko, Asheville	23	3	6	2	1	.818
Straker, Greensboro	29	11	24	8	2	.814
Russell, Gastonia	27	6	15	5	1	.808
Woodward, Spar	31	1	7	2	0	.800
Shields, Greenwood	12	0	4	1	0	.800
Chapman, Asheville	19	3	8	3	0	.786
Nickerson, Asheville	25	3	9	4	1	.750
Jones, Gastonia	6	2	7	3	1	.750
Harshbarger, Gas	5	1	2	1	0	.750
Zaske, Shelby	25	2	11	5	0	.722
P. Nelson, Ashe	26	2	13	6	1	.714
Veale, Greenwood	22	3	9	5	0	.706
Dodd, Shelby	20	1	6	3	0	.700
Gott, Gastonia	19	1	8	4	0	.692
Hayes, Greensboro	11	0	1	2	0	.333

The following pitchers had no recorded accepted chances; therefore are not listed in the fielding averages: North, Shoemaker. Zimmer appeared as a designated hitter only.

CLUB PITCHING

Club	G.	CG.	ShO.	Sv.	IP.	H.	R.	ER.	HR.	BB.	Int. BB.	HB.	SO.	WP.	Bk.	ERA.
Spartanburg	139	34	12	22	1193	1133	593	456	76	483	51	47	830	76	16	3.44
Gastonia	139	19	11	28	1184	1078	608	477	77	623	79	63	905	103	20	3.63
Greenwood	138	35	12	14	1161	1147	644	477	78	478	28	56	852	101	21	3.70
Greensboro	136	19	9	29	1154	1087	626	480	100	514	36	39	980	85	13	3.74
Asheville	139	42	7	23	1155	1201	683	528	80	545	29	32	828	79	11	4.11
Shelby	135	30	5	19	1100	1034	675	516	76	626	10	41	833	87	21	4.22

PITCHERS' RECORDS
(Leading Qualifiers for Earned-Run Average Leadership—112 or More Innings)

*Throws lefthanded.

Pitcher—Club	G.	GS.	CG.	ShO.	W.	L.	Sv.	Pct.	IP.	H.	R.	ER.	HR.	BB.	Int. BB.	HB.	SO.	WP.	ERA.
Johnson, Gastonia	36	12	5	2	10	6	3	.625	156	153	62	46	10	60	10	4	111	7	2.65
Silva, Gastonia	25	17	3	2	7	3	0	.700	119	102	50	36	3	54	4	5	64	4	2.72
Burroughs, Spar*	26	26	8	1	13	8	0	.619	183	158	79	62	12	71	1	11	180	11	3.05
Russell, Gastonia	27	25	5	1	10	9	0	.526	154	137	74	53	9	51	8	6	130	6	3.10
Davis, Spartanburg*	26	26	9	5	11	9	0	.550	166	147	76	59	18	49	7	3	135	10	3.20
Thomas, Gastonia	25	25	2	1	9	7	0	.563	131	124	68	47	4	65	1	3	91	8	3.23
LoCascio, Greensboro*	48	12	2	1	7	7	5	.500	127	124	57	46	2	64	6	3	117	9	3.26
Farr, Asheville	24	21	10	0	14	7	0	.667	167	171	82	61	10	30	2	5	122	6	3.29
Vickers, Asheville*	27	24	5	3	11	7	0	.611	164	168	87	63	12	61	2	5	122	6	3.46
Rasmussen, Spar	26	26	7	2	9	9	0	.500	173	166	90	68	13	66	5	7	114	3	3.54

Departmental Leaders: G—LaRosa, 56; GS—Guinn, 28; CG—Farr, Williams, 14; ShO—Davis, 5; W—Farr, 14; L—Mosby, 14; Sv—Lahti, LaRosa, 13; Pct.—W. E. Nelson .722; IP—Burroughs, 183; H—Guinn, 181; R—Mosby, 105; ER—Mosby, 82; HR—Davis, 18; BB—Mosby, 113; IBB—LaRosa, 16; HB—Burroughs, 11; SO—Burroughs, 180; WP—Gott, 21.

(All Pitchers—Listed Alphabetically)

Pitcher—Club	G.	GS.	CG.	ShO.	W.	L.	Sv.	Pct.	IP.	H.	R.	ER.	HR.	BB.	Int. BB.	HB.	SO.	WP.	ERA.
Alduey, Greenwood	13	12	5	1	8	1	0	.889	81	82	36	27	5	20	0	3	51	4	3.00
Alicea, Spartanburg	25	25	5	2	9	6	0	.600	146	163	80	70	8	61	3	6	75	8	4.23
Arigoni, Gastonia*	15	14	0	0	4	7	0	.364	68	60	42	36	6	54	2	1	47	8	4.76
Arroyo, Greenwood	17	6	3	1	5	2	0	.714	58	53	37	23	6	23	2	3	69	8	3.57
Balogh, Greenwood	17	5	2	1	4	2	0	.667	59	57	28	19	3	25	3	3	44	2	2.90
Barez, Shelby	16	16	3	0	5	9	0	.357	104	93	52	43	9	49	0	6	88	17	3.72
Behenna, Greenwood	8	5	1	0	0	6	0	.000	43	38	30	25	3	32	0	3	22	7	5.23
Brauer, Shelby	1	0	0	0	0	0	0	.000	1	1	1	1	0	1	0	0	0	0	9.00
Brown, Shelby	24	22	3	1	6	9	0	.400	114	111	86	67	11	76	0	11	85	11	5.29
Burroughs, Spartanburg*	26	26	8	1	13	8	0	.619	183	158	79	62	12	71	1	11	180	11	3.05
Cabassa, Spartanburg*	32	1	0	0	4	2	0	.667	61	39	24	17	1	38	8	4	40	4	2.51
Carman, Spartanburg*	37	8	3	1	6	3	0	.667	78	72	36	34	3	28	2	2	70	3	3.92
Carvajal, Shelby	30	0	0	0	5	4	0	.556	56	58	25	16	0	21	1	3	40	3	2.57
Chapman, Asheville	19	1	0	0	1	1	0	.500	38	39	17	13	1	22	3	3	40	3	3.08
Cicatiello, Shelby	1	0	0	0	0	0	0	.000	2	2	1	1	1	1	1	0	1	0	4.46
Cline, 14 Shel-10 Gwd	24	20	6	2	7	9	0	.438	121	114	70	43	3	52	1	7	135	10	3.20
Davis, Spartanburg*	26	26	9	5	11	9	0	.550	166	147	76	59	18	49	7	3	135	10	3.20
De La Cruz, Greenwood	1	0	0	0	0	0	0	.000	4	1	1	1	1	3	0	0	1	0	2.25
DeVincenzo, Spar	50	0	0	0	10	5	12	.667	72	61	24	14	2	23	3	1	39	5	1.75
Dodd, Shelby	20	8	1	0	1	6	0	.143	55	65	64	51	5	66	0	0	30	9	8.35
Farr, Asheville	24	21	10	0	14	7	0	.667	167	171	82	61	10	30	2	5	122	6	3.29
Gadowski, Gastonia	9	9	1	0	1	6	0	.143	51	56	43	33	10	26	6	3	44	2	5.82
Gore, Greenwood*	45	2	0	0	13	11	7	.542	100	95	65	41	8	26	6	5	102	5	3.69
Gott, Gastonia	19	11	1	0	5	5	0	.500	77	63	57	48	8	88	5	9	44	21	5.61
Guerra, Shelby	13	1	0	0	0	1	0	.000	23	30	22	18	3	21	0	4	15	3	7.04
Guinn, Greensboro	34	28	4	0	12	10	1	.545	172	181	94	76	9	93	3	9	134	16	3.98

Pitcher–Club	G	GS	CG	ShO	W	L	Sv	Pct.	IP	H	R	ER	HR	BB	Int. BB	HB	SO	WP	ERA
Harshbarger, Gastonia	5	2	0	0	0	2	0	.000	19	23	9	8	3	7	0	1	6	0	3.79
Hartwig, Asheville	11	8	1	0	5	4	0	.556	51	72	31	27	2	24	0	0	27	0	4.76
Hayes, Greensboro	11	0	0	0	1	0	0	1.000	13	11	11	8	1	7	0	0	8	1	5.54
Huey, Shelby	14	3	0	0	0	2	1	.000	36	40	24	18	1	18	0	0	35	4	4.50
Jackson, Greensboro	21	16	1	0	5	4	0	.556	105	77	59	45	14	52	0	3	96	8	3.86
Jimenez, Shelby	16	11	5	0	6	1	2	.857	84	67	31	24	4	23	2	0	70	4	2.57
Johnson, Gastonia	36	12	5	2	10	6	3	.625	156	133	62	46	10	60	10	4	111	7	2.65
Jones, Gastonia	6	4	0	0	2	1	0	.667	29	22	10	6	0	9	1	1	25	3	1.86
Kerdolff, Greenwood	7	5	1	0	3	0	0	1.000	36	28	13	4	0	8	2	2	21	2	1.00
Kirby, Shelby	7	6	0	0	1	1	0	.500	31	32	25	19	2	28	1	1	13	4	5.52
Kitts, Greenwood*	18	1	0	0	2	2	0	.500	39	35	18	14	3	12	1	1	27	3	3.23
Kwolek, Asheville	10	9	0	0	1	1	0	.500	37	39	27	23	3	31	0	1	28	6	5.59
Lahti, Greensboro	53	2	1	1	7	2	13	.778	92	83	43	29	8	33	6	4	89	9	2.84
Lang, Shelby	2	0	0	0	1	1	0	.500	15	14	7	6	2	4	0	1	7	0	3.60
LaRosa, Gastonia	56	0	0	0	4	8	13	.333	91	72	38	30	6	45	16	8	82	11	2.97
Lawrence, Greenwood ..	8	0	0	0	0	1	0	.000	12	6	2	2	1	5	0	1	8	1	1.50
Lazorko, Asheville	23	0	0	0	4	3	0	.571	37	33	19	13	2	12	5	1	22	4	3.16
Lesley, Greensboro	19	18	3	0	3	7	0	.300	101	112	67	52	12	34	0	2	62	7	4.63
Little, Gastonia	35	3	1	1	7	3	0	.700	68	70	46	41	5	44	5	6	42	12	5.43
LoCascio, Greensboro*	48	12	2	1	7	7	5	.500	127	124	57	46	2	64	6	3	117	9	3.26
Lucas, Greenwood	1	0	0	0	0	0	0	.000	⅓	0	0	0	0	0	0	0	0	0	0.00
Lucia, Greenwood	14	14	5	2	9	3	0	.750	97	81	41	33	8	25	1	5	73	11	3.06
Martin, Greenwood	1	0	0	0	0	0	0	.000	1	4	8	8	0	5	0	1	2	1	72.00
Martinez, Shelby	16	0	0	0	2	2	3	.500	35	20	14	12	1	13	0	1	58	3	3.09
Matthews, Greenwood ..	1	0	0	0	0	0	0	.000	1	0	0	0	0	0	0	0	0	0	0.00
McWilliams, Asheville* ..	1	0	0	0	0	0	0	.000	1	0	0	0	0	0	0	0	0	0	0.00
Merulla, Shelby	2	0	0	0	0	0	0	.000	2	5	4	4	0	1	1	0	3	0	18.00
Moore, Greensboro*	1	0	0	0	0	0	0	.000	3	1	0	0	0	0	0	0	4	0	0.00
Morton, Gastonia*	35	1	0	0	5	3	4	.625	55	47	18	16	4	17	5	6	61	0	2.62
Mosby, Asheville	19	1	0	0	0	1	2	.333	59	62	30	25	4	20	6	5	58	4	3.81
Neely, Greensboro	52	2	0	0	8	14	0	.364	112	125	105	82	8	113	1	4	83	18	6.59
P. Nelson, Asheville	26	14	5	1	7	7	0	.500	122	130	80	70	10	66	4	2	100	9	5.16
W. E. Nelson, Asheville ...	33	17	7	1	13	5	4	.722	155	149	77	62	13	44	2	6	96	4	3.60
Nickerson, Asheville	25	1	0	0	1	3	6	.250	61	58	35	16	5	26	4	1	54	1	2.36
Noble, Greensboro*	8	6	1	1	3	3	0	.500	41	30	16	11	5	15	0	1	35	1	2.41
North, Greenwood	3	3	1	0	1	1	0	.500	18	19	10	7	2	10	2	0	13	2	3.50
O'Keeffe, Greensboro*	18	16	4	1	6	7	1	.462	96	99	53	41	11	34	0	2	78	6	3.84
Peralta, Shelby	12	0	0	0	0	0	0	.000	21	24	9	6	2	9	1	0	13	0	2.57
Pill, Shelby	12	11	5	0	4	5	0	.444	83	74	42	32	6	27	2	3	45	1	3.47
Pittman, Gastonia*	14	0	0	0	1	1	2	.500	22	19	8	8	1	18	3	2	25	5	3.27
Prior, Spartanburg	51	0	0	0	2	8	9	.200	85	86	43	30	3	40	10	4	60	4	3.18
Rasmussen, Spartanburg ..	26	26	7	2	9	9	0	.500	173	166	90	68	13	66	5	7	114	8	3.54
Ray, Shelby	10	10	3	0	3	7	0	.300	51	45	33	28	3	35	0	2	47	4	4.94
Riggins, Gastonia*	8	1	1	0	0	3	1	.000	25	22	6	6	2	11	2	0	22	2	2.16
Rogers, Greenwood	20	16	4	2	7	8	1	.467	109	108	60	26	4	29	5	4	54	9	2.15
Rollins, Spartanburg	25	25	2	0	5	10	0	.333	154	165	97	73	13	61	5	3	81	17	4.27
Roush, Greensboro	17	4	0	0	2	3	0	.400	52	64	43	36	7	33	3	7	46	4	6.23
Russell, Gastonia	27	25	5	1	10	9	0	.526	154	137	74	53	9	51	8	6	130	6	3.10
Ryan, Greenwood	21	16	3	1	7	4	1	.636	106	98	66	47	6	61	1	2	66	10	3.99
Scott, Asheville	3	0	0	0	1	0	0	1.000	16	11	4	3	0	2	1	0	12	0	1.69
Shields, Greenwood	12	0	0	0	1	0	0	1.000	19	15	3	2	0	6	1	1	13	1	0.95
Shoemaker, Spartanburg ..	3	0	0	0	2	0	0	1.000	5	1	0	0	1	0	0	0	5	0	0.00
Siebert, Shelby	16	14	4	0	7	6	0	.538	87	91	55	38	12	32	1	3	39	6	3.93
Silva, Gastonia	25	17	3	2	7	3	0	.700	119	102	50	36	3	54	4	5	64	4	2.72
Smith, Greenwood	18	17	3	0	7	6	0	.538	104	116	64	57	13	40	0	9	73	9	4.93
Straker, Greensboro	29	27	1	0	7	10	0	.412	141	123	83	62	7	75	1	1	121	14	3.96
Tam, Asheville	16	0	0	0	1	1	0	.500	29	45	30	24	2	24	3	1	17	6	7.45
Taylor, Shelby	11	1	0	0	3	1	1	.750	31	26	17	11	1	18	0	4	36	7	3.19
Teixeira, Greenwood	13	12	3	0	4	3	1	.571	86	92	48	38	5	17	1	3	76	6	3.98
Thayer, Greenwood	2	0	0	0	0	0	0	.000	5	11	15	11	1	6	0	2	3	1	19.80
Thomas, Gastonia	25	25	0	0	9	7	0	.563	131	124	68	47	4	65	6	3	91	8	3.23
Torres, Greensboro	2	0	0	0	0	0	0	.000	1	3	2	2	0	0	0	0	0	0	18.00
Vasche, Gastonia	7	1	0	0	0	1	0	.000	5	11	15	11	1	6	2	2	0	0	18.00
Veale, Greenwood	22	14	3	0	2	3	1	.000	11	12	10	9	2	7	2	0	5	1	7.36
Vega, Gastonia	22	14	0	0	4	0	0	.375	97	111	67	48	2	71	1	3	73	13	4.45
Vickers, Asheville*	27	24	5	3	11	7	0	.611	164	168	87	63	12	61	2	5	122	6	3.46
Willett, Greensboro	34	8	2	0	4	7	2	.364	111	98	62	45	16	35	3	2	80	5	3.65
Williams, Asheville	25	23	10	2	8	10	0	.444	162	156	85	67	12	89	1	2	129	18	3.72
Wojton, Shelby	34	0	0	0	0	0	0	.000	2	1	0	0	0	0	0	0	1	0	0.00
Woodward, Spartanburg .	31	2	0	0	2	6	6	.250	50	55	44	28	4	56	2	2	71	4	3.04
Zaske, Shelby	25	16	1	0	5	10	0	.333	100	91	80	58	7	96	0	5	88	10	5.22
Zitek, Asheville	1	0	0	0	0	0	0	.000	1	1	0	0	0	0	0	0	1	0	0.00

BALKS–Alicea, Davis, Mosby, 5 each; Barez, Burroughs, Ryan, 4 each; Kirby, LoCascio, Pittman, Siebert, Thomas, Vega, 3 each; Alduey, Arigoni, Arroyo, Balogh, Brown, Gadowski, Guerra, Jackson, Johnson, Lahti,

Lucia, Neely, O'Keeffe, Rogers, Russell, Veale, Zaske, 2 each; Behenna, DeVincenzo, Gore, Gott, Hartwig, Kitts, Lesley, Little, Martin, Martinez, P. Nelson, W. E. Nelson, Peralta, Pill, Prior, Riggins, Roush, Straker, Tam, Taylor, Vickers, Williams, Wojton, 1 each.

COMBINATION SHUTOUTS—Silva-LaRosa, Silva-Johnson, Russell-LaRosa, Johnson-Riggins, Gastonia; Straker-LoCascio, Guinn-LoCascio, Straker-Moore, Straker-Neely-Lahti, Guinn-O'Keeffe, Greensboro; Alduey-Shields, Smith-Shields, Rogers-Gore, Ryan-Kitts, Greenwood; Siebert-Carvajal, Kirby-Wojton, Shelby; Rollins-Prior, Spartanburg.

NO-HIT GAMES—None.

Greenwood Stole Record

The Greenwood Braves stole five bases on August 21 against Spartanburg to enable them to set a league record for steals with 270. The previous record of 267 stolen bases was set by Asheville in 1977.

Greensboro Walked Over Shelby

You've heard the one about the pitcher who couldn't locate the plate with both hands and a flashlight?

Shelby had four of them August 13.

They combined to issue 19 bases on balls to Greensboro batters, tying a league record for a nine-inning game and providing the Hornets with a "walk-over" 9-3 victory.

It could have been a lot worse for the Pirates. Greensboro left the bases loaded in four innings.

Things started innocently enough as Shelby starter Art Ray set the Hornets down 1-2-3 in the first inning. In the second, however, he issued five free passes, forcing in two runs. Before Ray got the hook in the fourth, he'd walked nine, and Greensboro had built up a 4-1 lead—without getting a hit.

Three successors combined for 10 more free tickets.

Greensboro first baseman Bill Kuchar went 0-for-1 officially, but picked up three RBIs by drawing bases-loaded walks. And third baseman Kevin Jacobson didn't have a time at bat, but he went into the WCL books with a record-tying five walks.

Geneva Had Pinch-Hit Bonanza

Tom Grant of Geneva hit a three-run pinch-homer in the ninth inning July 13 for a 7-7 tie. Grant stayed in the game, but when his turn to bat came around in the 11th, Don Strickland was sent in as a pinch-hitter. Strickland belted a solo homer to give Geneva a 10-8 victory over Utica.

Utica Faced Great Hardship

As if losing 20 of your first 25 games of the season wasn't bad enough, Utica Manager John McLaren saw his club suffer the worst defeat in the team's three-year history July 15 when they lost to Geneva, 29-4. Cubs' shortstop Scott Fletcher had seven hits, including a home run, four doubles and eight RBIs. Adding insult to injury, Geneva scored 15 of those runs in the ninth inning.

Appalachian League

SUMMER CLASS A CLASSIFICATION

CHAMPIONSHIP WINNERS IN PREVIOUS YEARS

1921—Greenville .608	1945—Kingsport‡ .670	1963—Bluefield .652
Johnson City* .627	1946—New River‡ .675	1964—Johnson City .662
1922—Bristol .557	1947—Pulaski .648	1965—Salem .614
1923—Knoxville .635	New River (3rd)† .516	1966—Marion .623
1924—Knoxville* .642	1948—Pulaski‡ .680	1967—Bluefield .627
Bristol .607	1949—Bluefield‡ .721	1968—Marion .583
1925—Greenville .667	1950—Bluefield .600	1969—Pulaski a .576
1926-36—Did not operate.	Bluefield z .745	Johnson City .544
1937—Elizabethton .559	1951—Kingsport‡ .659	1970—Bluefield .638
Pennington Gap* .580	1952—Johnson City .595	1971—Bluefield a .609
1938—Elizabethton .664	Welch (3rd)† .509	Kingsport .559
Greenville (3rd)† .571	1953—Welch* .705	1972—Bristol a .588
1939—Elizabethton‡ .597	Johnson City .672	Covington .586
1940—Johnson City§ .726	1954—Bluefield‡ .619	1973—Bluefield .757
Elizabethton .750	1955—Salem** .689	1974—Bristol a .754
1941—Johnson City .614	1956—Did not operate.	Bluefield .536
Elizabethton* .661	1957—Bluefield .701	1975—Marion .515
1942—Bristol .667	1958—Johnson City .662	Johnson City a .603
Bristol x .660	1959—Morristown .603	1976—Johnson City a .714
1943—Bristol .755	1960—Wytheville .614	Bluefield .600
Bristol y .617	1961—Middlesboro .591	1977—Kingsport .623
1944—Kingsport‡ .575	1962—Bluefield .671	1978—Elizabethton .594

*Won split-season playoff. †Won four-team playoff. ‡Won championship and four-team playoff. §Johnson City, first-half winner, won playoff involving six clubs. xWon both halves and defeated second-place Elizabethton in playoff. yWon both halves, but Erwin won four-team playoff. zWon both halves, but Bristol won two-club playoff. **Salem and Johnson City declared playoff co-champions when weather forced cancellation of final series. aLeague was divided into Northern, Southern divisions; declared league champion, based on highest won-lost percentage.

STANDING OF CLUBS AT CLOSE OF SEASON, AUGUST 31

Club	Pvl.	Kpt.	Eliz.	Blu.	J.C.	Bri.	W.	L.	T.	Pct.	G.B.
Paintsville (Yankees)	..	10	11	10	9	12	52	13	1	.800	......
Kingsport (Braves)	4	..	10	4	9	12	39	31	0	.557	15½
Elizabethton (Twins)	3	4	..	8	11	11	37	33	1	.529	17½
Bluefield (Orioles)	2	10	6	..	9	6	33	35	0	.485	20½
Johnson City (Cardinals)	3	5	3	5	..	9	25	43	0	.368	28½
Bristol (Tigers)	1	2	3	8	5	..	19	50	0	.275	35

Major league affiliations in parentheses.

Playoffs—None.

Regular-Season Attendance—Bluefield, 23,630; Bristol, 11,555; Elizabethton, 16,660; Johnson City, 29,591; Kingsport, 26,085; Paintsville, 21,214. Total—128,735. No playoffs or all-star game.

Managers: Bluefield—Wilbert (Junior) Miner; Bristol—Joe Lewis; Elizabethton—Fred Waters; Johnson City—Nick Leyva; Kingsport—Gene Hassell; Paintsville—Bill Livesey.

All-Star Team: 1B—Guerra, Paintsville; 2B—Garcia, Kingsport; 3B—Nixon, Paintsville; SS—Runge, Kingsport; OF—Schuman, Bluefield; Teegarden, Paintsville; M. Thompson, Kingsport; C—Austin, Elizabethton; DH—Miller, Elizabethton; P—Filson, Paintsville; Ricci, Paintsville; Manager—Livesay, Paintsville.

(Compiled by Howe News Bureau, Chicago, Ill.)

CLUB BATTING

Club	G.	AB.	R.	OR.	H.	TB.	2B.	3B.	HR.	RBI.	SH.	SF.	BB.	Int. BB.	HP.	SO.	SB.	CS.	LOB.	Pct.
Paintsville	66	1860	403	218	520	747	83	21	34	354	34	19	349	13	7	311	50	25	440	.280
Elizabethton	71	2210	402	353	585	899	116	12	58	348	16	17	331	7	25	382	40	10	505	.280
Kingsport	70	2037	415	363	536	865	102	13	67	345	30	30	348	12	26	372	74	15	457	.265
Johnson City	68	2071	299	436	516	733	74	19	35	245	22	7	200	7	22	356	57	21	486	.263
Bluefield	68	1934	338	320	481	700	81	18	34	270	20	15	323	10	23	369	49	15	488	.249
Bristol	69	2110	274	441	474	668	66	16	32	232	16	16	299	5	14	396	45	20	504	.225

INDIVIDUAL BATTING
(Leading Qualifiers for Batting Championship—189 or More Plate Appearances)

*Bats lefthanded.   †Switch-hitter.

Player and Club	G.	AB.	R.	H.	TB.	2B.	3B.	HR.	RBI.	SH.	SF.	BB.	HP.	SO.	SB.	CS.	Pct.
Miller, Kevin, Elizabethton	70	241	47	81	142	14	1	15	74	0	2	34	3	44	0	1	.336
Teegarden, Robert, Paintsville	65	212	66	70	134	14	4	14	74	0	3	49	2	32	3	0	.330
Bohnet, Robert, Elizabethton	55	174	38	56	98	14	2	8	38	2	2	38	1	23	1	0	.322
Guerra, Randall, Paintsville*	63	212	43	65	107	15	0	9	65	2	2	37	0	28	2	0	.307
Christensen, James, Elizabethton	56	206	41	63	98	17	3	4	23	2	4	23	0	8	7	0	.306
Rogers, M. Glen, Paintsville*	60	181	50	55	64	7	1	0	22	12	3	46	1	23	3	6	.304
Gayden, Huey, Paintsville*	62	214	50	65	77	6	3	0	34	4	0	29	2	19	12	4	.304
Blake, Angelo, Bluefield	59	185	32	56	89	11	2	6	31	3	2	47	2	23	6	4	.303
Schuman, David, Bluefield	58	190	28	57	76	4	5	2	31	0	1	27	6	48	2	1	.300
Runge, Paul, Kingsport	66	229	57	67	96	11	0	6	45	3	3	56	2	31	19	4	.293

Departmental Leaders: G—K. Miller, 70; AB—K. Miller, Roman, 241; R—Teegarden, 66; H—K. Miller, 81; TB—K. Miller, 142; 2B—Christensen, 17; 3B—Schuman, 5; HR—H. Williams, 16; RBI—K. Miller, Teegarden, 74; SH—Rogers, 12; SF—Dieters, 6; BB—Nixon, 57; HP—Schuman, H. Williams, 6; SO—Komminsk, 74; SB—Komminsk, 20; CS—Roman, 7.

(All Players—Listed Alphabetically)

Player and Club	G.	AB.	R.	H.	TB.	2B.	3B.	HR.	RBI.	SH.	SF.	BB.	HP.	SO.	SB.	CS.	Pct.
Agras, Alfredo, Elizabethton	11	17	4	4	5	0	0	0	0	0	0	4	0	6	0	0	.235
Austin, Richard, Elizabethton	48	156	22	48	68	11	0	3	24	0	1	18	3	23	2	0	.308
Ayer, Jonathan, Johnson City	65	218	35	63	96	15	3	4	25	2	0	40	2	27	17	1	.289
Bailey, Welby, Kingsport	34	93	17	23	30	4	0	1	14	0	3	16	0	26	0	0	.247
Baker, Christopher, Bristol	57	195	13	48	63	3	3	2	32	0	1	9	3	34	3	2	.246
Baldwin, Kenneth, Bristol*	46	150	21	33	65	7	2	7	20	0	1	14	2	30	0	1	.220
Barraco, Anthony, Bristol†	39	113	10	23	29	3	0	1	11	0	1	12	0	25	0	0	.204
Baskerville, Phillip, Johnson City*.	20	68	11	18	29	0	1	3	9	0	0	12	0	15	2	1	.265
Behenna, Richard, Kingsport	1	1	0	1	1	0	0	0	0	0	0	0	0	0	0	0	1.000
Benedict, Scott, Paintsville	36	84	6	16	20	4	0	0	9	2	0	11	0	24	0	0	.190
Beswick, Rick, Elizabethton†	42	154	29	36	52	10	0	2	18	0	1	25	2	26	4	1	.234
Black, Charles, Kingsport*	11	33	5	10	10	0	0	0	2	1	0	4	0	1	0	0	.303
Blake, Angelo, Bluefield	59	185	32	56	89	11	2	6	31	3	2	47	2	23	6	4	.303
Bohnet, Robert, Elizabethton	55	174	38	56	98	14	2	8	38	2	2	38	1	23	1	0	.322
Bowen, Billy, Kingsport*	61	222	38	59	100	12	1	9	39	7	2	30	0	33	2	2	.266
Bowman, Bruss, Bluefield†	45	102	14	17	25	5	0	1	12	0	0	20	1	29	1	1	.167
Boyce, Robert, Bluefield	4	12	2	3	3	0	0	0	1	0	0	5	1	0	0	0	.250
Brandt, Kevin, Elizabethton	45	137	18	22	28	3	0	1	9	2	0	19	2	41	0	0	.161
Brito, Enrique, Elizabethton†	5	12	3	2	2	0	0	0	0	0	0	1	0	2	0	0	.167
Bulcock, Derek, Elizabethton	42	131	19	33	35	2	0	0	8	0	0	22	0	17	4	1	.252
Camara, Tony, Bristol	48	130	17	33	44	5	0	2	16	1	3	26	0	23	1	0	.254
Caraballo, Jose, Johnson City	18	32	2	5	6	1	0	0	5	1	0	2	0	10	0	0	.156
Carlson, Brad, Elizabethton	29	85	12	18	29	2	0	3	14	0	1	5	2	23	0	1	.212
Chevalier, Reginald, Johnson City..	1	2	0	0	0	0	0	0	0	0	0	0	0	2	0	0	.000
Christensen, James, Elizabethton ..	56	206	41	63	98	17	3	4	23	2	4	23	0	8	7	0	.306
Clark, Terry, Johnson City	1	0	0	0	0	0	0	0	0	0	0	0	0	0	0	0	.000
DeLeon, John, Bluefield	32	85	13	17	25	1	2	1	8	0	0	8	3	40	0	0	.200
Dieters, James, Johnson City*	66	192	32	51	81	8	2	6	31	0	6	47	3	28	8	3	.266
Dovalis, Alexander, Elizabethton	44	128	19	33	45	8	2	0	19	0	3	14	1	13	0	0	.258
Driver, Jon, Bristol	30	82	7	12	18	3	0	1	6	0	0	2	1	11	0	0	.146
Espinosa, Steven, Bluefield	49	144	24	40	48	6	1	0	12	4	0	30	1	19	3	0	.278
Fields, Bruce, Bristol*	41	138	23	32	41	4	1	1	7	0	0	21	0	28	5	2	.232
Fink, Bill, Johnson City*	38	97	16	21	35	4	2	2	6	2	1	22	1	19	2	2	.216
Fisher, Keith, Bristol	58	177	24	39	68	7	2	6	23	1	4	33	0	49	4	1	.220
Followell, Vernon, Bristol†	26	103	16	33	50	5	0	4	17	1	1	16	0	6	5	1	.320
Gaetti, Gary, Elizabethton	56	230	50	59	120	15	2	14	42	3	0	43	2	40	6	2	.257
Gagne, Gregory, Paintsville	41	106	10	19	27	2	3	0	7	1	0	13	0	25	2	1	.179
Garcia, Michael, Kingsport	53	158	39	45	74	9	1	6	31	3	3	46	0	13	7	1	.285
Gayden, Huey, Paintsville*	62	214	50	65	77	6	3	0	34	4	0	29	2	19	12	4	.304
Guerra, Randall, Paintsville*	63	212	43	65	107	15	0	9	65	2	2	37	0	28	2	0	.307
Hage, Joseph, Paintsville*	37	70	14	23	35	2	2	2	19	0	2	13	0	7	1	2	.329
Hall, Kurt, Paintsville	24	50	10	11	14	3	0	0	4	0	0	5	1	12	1	1	.220
Hardy, William, Bristol	35	104	16	27	31	2	1	0	9	0	3	4	3	17	4	1	.260
Harskamp, James, Johnson City	53	179	25	44	65	6	3	3	24	2	2	16	3	35	2	2	.246
Harvey, Nelson, Bluefield	14	28	4	3	6	0	0	1	3	0	0	4	0	8	0	0	.107
Harvey, Randall, Bristol*	46	123	14	22	35	6	2	1	12	2	1	13	1	44	2	2	.179
Harvey, Ronald, Bristol	13	25	6	2	2	0	0	0	1	0	1	9	1	10	1	0	.080
Hawthorne, Kyle, Bluefield	25	84	13	18	35	2	0	5	22	0	1	12	2	15	2	0	.214
Hendrickson, Stanley, Bluefield	62	205	44	58	81	11	0	4	24	1	0	48	1	26	12	5	.283
Hicks, Robert, Johnson City	6	24	3	8	12	4	0	0	6	0	0	0	0	5	0	0	.333
Howser, Thomas, Paintsville	39	76	15	19	20	1	0	0	7	1	1	24	0	9	8	1	.250
Hrbek, Kent, Elizabethton*	17	59	5	12	17	2	0	1	11	0	0	7	0	15	2	0	.203
Ingle, Randy, Kingsport	38	148	25	47	77	9	3	5	29	2	3	14	2	22	0	2	.318

Player and Club	G.	AB.	R.	H.	TB.	2B.	3B.	HR.	RBI.	SH.	SF.	BB.	HP.	SO.	SB.	CS.	Pct.
Ivie, Lonnie, Bluefield	30	79	7	17	20	3	0	0	9	1	2	4	0	15	0	0	.215
Jacoby, Brook, Kingsport	8	28	3	7	9	2	0	0	1	0	0	2	0	5	0	0	.250
Jensen, T. Alan, Elizabethton	22	59	6	15	23	2	0	2	10	3	1	5	0	15	0	1	.254
Jerman, Steven, Johnson City*	42	114	13	27	36	2	2	1	11	1	0	8	1	6	0	0	.237
Jurena, Mark, Bluefield*	62	221	49	61	95	15	2	5	26	0	2	36	1	25	12	3	.276
Keck, Daniel, Bluefield	6	18	3	3	4	1	0	0	3	0	0	4	1	2	0	0	.167
Komminsk, Brad, Kingsport	59	185	37	41	73	9	1	7	34	1	1	48	1	74	20	2	.222
Kopala, Michael, Johnson City	4	5	0	0	0-	0	0	0	1	0	0	1	0	2	0	0	.000
Lett, Roosevelt, Johnson City	45	129	20	33	46	4	0	3	15	0	1	19	4	31	5	2	.256
Liggins, Danny, Johnson City	1	1	0	0	0	0	0	0	0	0	0	0	0	0	0	0	.000
Lindberg, Ronald, Bristol	20	56	14	18	28	1	3	1	6	2	0	18	1	10	0	2	.321
Martinez, Luis, Bluefield*	16	30	3	5	8	1	1	0	1	1	0	7	0	10	3	1	.167
Martinez, Manuel, Bluefield	11	28	3	7	8	1	0	0	7	0	0	5	0	4	0	0	.250
Matos, Carlos, Johnson City	40	121	12	26	34	5	0	1	10	0	0	10	1	35	2	0	.215
McCauley, Stanley, Johnson City	5	18	1	2	2	0	0	0	0	0	0	3	0	1	1	0	.111
McKnight, Mark, Bristol	8	31	5	4	5	1	0	0	2	0	0	2	0	4	1	0	.129
McNealy, Derwin, Paintsville*	32	76	12	20	31	5	0	2	13	2	0	7	0	22	1	1	.263
Melton, Michael, Johnson City	16	41	5	8	14	1	1	1	4	0	0	5	1	19	0	0	.195
Mesa, Jose, Elizabethton	21	68	9	18	25	4	0	1	8	1	0	5	2	8	0	0	.265
Miller, Kevin, Elizabethton	70	241	47	81	142	14	1	15	74	0	2	34	3	44	0	1	.336
Miller, Randolph, Bluefield	22	63	6	13	15	2	0	0	7	1	0	4	1	6	1	0	.206
Murelli, Donald, Bluefield	8	26	2	4	5	1	0	0	2	0	0	2	0	2	0	0	.154
Nixon, Ottis, Paintsville	63	203	58	58	77	10	3	1	25	3	1	57	0	40	5	3	.286
Ortiz, Luis, Paintsville	39	106	18	27	46	3	2	4	26	1	2	9	0	27	4	1	.255
Palmer, Robert, Bluefield	36	106	11	20	31	4	2	1	19	2	0	18	1	17	1	0	.189
Patten, Kevin, Kingsport	58	187	29	45	69	7	1	5	30	1	2	18	5	27	9	1	.241
Perlongo, John, Johnson City*	45	112	16	26	30	2	1	0	11	2	0	20	1	17	4	0	.232
Presko, Timothy, Johnson City	23	72	16	21	27	0	0	2	11	2	0	6	1	10	1	2	.292
Proulx, Patrick, Johnson City	1	1	0	0	0	0	0	0	0	0	0	0	0	0	0	0	.000
Reeder, Michael, Bristol	24	62	8	13	25	0	0	4	5	0	0	7	1	17	1	1	.210
Reiter, Gary, Kingsport*	1	1	0	0	0	0	0	0	0	0	0	0	0	0	0	0	.000
Richard, Timothy, Bluefield	10	39	6	7	9	0	1	0	2	0	0	7	0	14	1	0	.179
Roberson, Ell, Bristol	55	174	19	47	61	10	2	0	24	0	2	36	0	35	4	4	.270
Rodriguez, Ruben, Johnson City	23	35	6	6	9	3	0	0	3	0	0	6	2	19	1	0	.171
Rogers, M. Glen, Paintsville*	60	181	50	55	64	7	1	0	22	12	3	46	1	23	3	6	.304
Roman, Luis, Johnson City*	64	241	37	66	85	10	0	3	25	3	2	23	2	28	9	7	.274
Rudolph, Jeffrey, Paintsville	36	85	12	23	35	4	1	2	15	1	1	14	1	11	0	2	.271
Runge, Paul, Kingsport	66	229	57	67	96	11	0	6	45	3	3	56	2	31	19	4	.293
Salas, Mark, Johnson City*	53	144	23	35	58	4	2	5	23	3	0	11	0	14	2	0	.243
Sanchez, Jose, Johnson City†	17	30	3	6	7	1	0	0	2	3	1	3	0	3	1	1	.200
Scanlon, Kenneth, Kingsport	37	107	24	26	29	1	1	0	7	2	2	27	3	10	2	1	.243
Schriner, Terry, Bluefield	23	55	6	13	13	0	0	0	3	3	1	9	1	15	2	0	.236
Schuman, David, Bluefield	58	190	28	57	76	4	5	2	31	0	1	27	6	48	2	1	.300
Sheets, Larry, Bluefield*	3	12	2	4	6	2	0	0	2	0	1	0	0	0	0	0	.333
Shefte, Richard, Elizabethton	61	185	41	44	51	5	1	0	26	2	1	38	4	23	3	1	.238
Smith, Freddie, Bluefield	1	2	0	1	1	0	0	0	0	0	0	0	0	0	0	0	.500
Sporrer, Gregory, Paintsville	58	164	28	42	53	7	2	0	27	5	4	28	0	26	7	3	.256
Steele, Michael, Bristol	24	55	5	7	8	1	0	0	1	0	1	15	0	16	1	0	.127
Stefero, John, Bluefield*	59	200	37	55	94	11	2	8	42	4	5	22	1	35	2	0	.275
Stieb, Steven, Kingsport	50	175	26	39	60	13	1	2	16	2	4	14	2	40	0	2	.223
Stocker, Bruce, Elizabethton	39	143	37	38	54	5	1	3	20	0	1	27	3	41	11	2	.266
Stoltenberg, Scott, Elizabethton	4	12	0	1	2	1	0	0	0	1	0	2	0	4	0	0	.083
Stovall, Don, Elizabethton	6	11	2	2	5	0	0	1	2	0	0	1	0	5	0	0	.182
Teegarden, Robert, Paintsville	65	212	66	70	134	14	4	14	74	0	3	49	2	32	3	0	.330
Tejeda, Felix, Johnson City	37	118	11	31	34	3	0	0	17	0	1	3	0	7	0	0	.263
Thompson, Milton, Kingsport*	26	94	22	31	50	8	4	1	11	4	1	16	1	17	13	0	.330
Thompson, Tommy, Kingsport*	51	150	32	46	79	6	0	9	33	3	2	22	2	8	2	0	.307
Tucker, Wilson, Bristol*	31	114	19	31	42	5	0	2	20	1	0	18	0	11	. 5	1	.272
Washington, Henry, Bristol	63	215	21	45	47	2	0	0	14	3	0	26	1	14	8	2	.209
Williams, Charles, Bluefield*	15	23	0	1	1	0	0	0	1	0	0	3	0	12	0	0	.043
Williams, Harold, Kingsport	65	225	44	52	111	11	0	16	52	1	4	34	6	59	0	0	.231
Winborn, Waldo, Bristol	13	32	6	5	6	1	0	0	4	1	0	15	0	12	2	0	.156
Zimmerer, George, Paintsville	28	30	6	8	8	0	0	0	4	0	0	7	0	4	1	0	.267
Zunino, Gary, Johnson City	22	77	5	19	27	1	2	1	9	0	0	4	0	17	0	0	.247

The following pitchers had no plate appearances primarily through use of designated hitters, listed alphabetically by club, games in parentheses:

BLUEFIELD: Conradi, Fred (17); Davis, George (10); Maples, Timothy (10); Norris, Timothy (12); Pfeiffer, David (18); Swaggerty, William (17); Wick, David (20); Woodall, Lawrence (12); Zedonek, Gary (14).

BRISTOL: Beecroft, Michael (11); Bollens, Scott (19); Cascadden, Brian (8); Collyer, Richard (4); Desjarlais, Keith (11); Dunn, Steven (13); Fox, Paul (7); Justus, Timothy (13); Krill, Michael (2); Nail, Charles (11); Perry, Jerry (15); Power, John (11); Sanchez, Luis (8); Vaughn, R. Scott (12); Vorisek, Robert (5); Warren, Michael (13); Wheeler, James (18).

ELIZABETHTON: Arrington, Samuel (13); Everett, Conrad (19); Fagely, Timothy (10); Hodge, Ed (14); Jones, Robert A. (9); Jackson, Ralph (5); Konopa, Robert (13); May, Larry (11); Mulligan, Robert (8); Orosco, Boyce (6); Palica, Wayne (10); Persandi, George (9); Riley, Michael (3); Sterk, William (4); Thomas, Christopher (11).

JOHNSON CITY: Bright, David (10); Brooks, Robert (12); Citarella, Ralph (4); Colon, Rafael (14); Dozier, Thomas (11); Fish, Timothy (11); Gonzalez, Jesus (14); Gotay, Ruben (2); Ostrow, Frank (12); Perez, Jose (2); Pinkston, Lynn (16); Pittman, Michael (5); Rincon, John (18); Santin, L. Rodolfo (6); Taylor, Jeffery H. (10); Tejeda, Hector (10); Warburton, Jeffrey (13); Weaver, Earl (13).

KINGSPORT: Ames, Kenneth (8); Castaigne, Arcilio (23); Coatney, Ricky (10); Coghill, David (10); Fuller, Timothy (6); Haley, Bill (3); Hibbett, G. Wendell (6); Kennedy, Robert (9); Kitts, Dewayne (1); Norris, Gregory (18); North, Roy (6); Payne, Michael (7); Rabun, Kenneth (8).

PAINTSVILLE: Akchurin, Erol (4); Beyler, Jeffrey (4); Booker, David (7); Budweg, Richard (8); Campbell, James (8); De Maria, George (7); Diaz, Gumercindo (13); Filson, W. Peter (13); Free, D. Michael (11); Lein, Christopher (12); Melgar, Luis (2); Murphy, Brian (13); Ricci, Frank (9); Vanderplas, B. Jeffrey (1).

GRAND SLAM HOME RUNS—K. Miller 2; Bohnet, Gaetti, Guerra, Runge, H. Williams, 1 each.

AWARDED FIRST BASE ON INTERFERENCE—Harskamp (Austin), Ivie (Jensen), Patten (Salas).

CLUB FIELDING

Club	G.	PO.	A.	E.	DP.	PB.	Pct.	Club	G.	PO.	A.	E.	DP.	PB.	Pct.
Paintsville	66	1495	635	79	43	8	.964	Bristol	69	1600	586	98	49	9	.957
Johnson City	68	1629	702	95	57	11	.961	Bluefield	68	1544	629	114	49	15	.950
Kingsport	70	1593	686	102	57	13	.957	Elizabethton	71	1696	604	139	49	10	.943

Triple Plays—None.

INDIVIDUAL FIELDING
FIRST BASEMEN

*Throws lefthanded.

Player and Club	G.	PO.	A.	E.	DP.	Pct.	Player and Club	G.	PO.	A.	E.	DP.	Pct.
Driver, Bristol	17	97	7	0	11	1.000	Miller, Elizabethton	35	272	11	4	18	.986
McCauley, Johnson City	3	17	1	0	2	1.000	Hrbek, Bluefield	16	126	11	2	7	.986
Rudolph, Paintsville	3	10	1	0	2	1.000	Dieters, Johnson City	22	168	11	3	19	.984
Hage, Paintsville*	2	7	0	0	4	1.000	Hawthorne, Bluefield	15	143	8	3	9	.981
Dovalis, Elizabethton	1	6	0	0	1	1.000	Hicks, Johnson City	6	42	1	1	1	.977
T. Thompson, Kingsport	1	6	0	0	0	1.000	DeLeon, Bluefield	29	218	9	6	13	.974
Sanchez, Johnson City	1	3	0	0	0	1.000	Bohnet, Elizabethton	22	187	9	6	18	.970
Bowen, Kingsport*	2	3	0	0	0	1.000	Randy, Harvey, Bristol*	30	230	16	8	13	.969
GUERRA, Paintsville*...	60	450	32	3	32	.994	Bowman, Bluefield*	27	169	16	7	18	.964
Perlongo, Johnson City*	44	347	16	3	29	.992	Winborn, Bristol	11	104	5	5	8	.956
Camara, Bristol	14	107	6	1	15	.991	Austin, Elizabethton	1	12	1	1	0	.929
Williams, Kingsport	65	557	34	8	56	.987							

SECOND BASEMEN

Player and Club	G.	PO.	A.	E.	DP.	Pct.	Player and Club	G.	PO.	A.	E.	DP.	Pct.
McKnight, Bristol	6	10	20	0	3	1.000	Sanchez, Johnson City ...	11	18	20	2	6	.950
Richard, Bluefield	2	3	5	0	1	1.000	Dovalis, Elizabethton	35	72	92	9	18	.948
Fields, Bristol	1	2	3	0	2	1.000	Baldwin, Bristol	38	86	73	9	10	.946
Stoltenberg, Eliz	1	3	1	0	1	1.000	Black, Kingsport	11	22	28	3	4	.943
Lindberg, Bristol	3	1	2	0	1	1.000	Miller, Bluefield	18	34	45	5	11	.940
Stocker, Elizabethton	1	1	0	0	1	1.000	Washington, Bristol	19	27	47	5	11	.937
Ortiz, Paintsville	25	31	46	1	10	.987	Howser, Paintsville	20	34	40	5	7	.937
Sporrer, Paintsville	23	43	17	1	12	.984	Zimmerer, Paintsville ...	20	18	25	3	4	.935
Espinoza, Bluefield	8	19	17	1	5	.973	Ron Harvey, Bristol	6	5	8	1	2	.929
Garcia, Kingsport	21	40	59	4	15	.961	Blake, Bluefield	40	100	90	16	13	.922
Jerman, Johnson City	40	74	101	8	25	.956	Scanlon, Kingsport	36	78	111	16	24	.922
F. Tejeda, Johnson City .	23	50	48	5	12	.951	Beswick, Elizabethton	7	13	21	4	4	.895
Bulcock, Elizabethton ...	26	49	67	6	14	.951	Brito, Elizabethton	5	5	3	1	0	.889

THIRD BASEMEN

Player and Club	G.	PO.	A.	E.	DP.	Pct.	Player and Club	G.	PO.	A.	E.	DP.	Pct.
McCauley, Johnson City	2	1	6	0	0	1.000	Gaetti, Elizabethton	56	44	105	18	10	.892
Ron Harvey, Bristol	5	2	5	0	1	1.000	Keck, Bluefield	5	5	11	2	1	.889
Baldwin, Bristol	5	3	3	0	0	1.000	Stoltenberg, Eliz	3	5	3	1	0	.889
Zimmerer, Paintsville	2	2	2	0	1	1.000	Camara, Bristol	30	23	31	7	6	.885
Espinoza, Bluefield	1	3	0	0	0	1.000	Harskamp, Johnson City	34	42	59	14	8	.878
Scanlon, Kingsport	1	1	2	0	0	1.000	Ingle, Kingsport	38	32	69	14	7	.878
Bohnet, Elizabethton	1	1	1	0	0	1.000	Miller, Elizabethton	4	3	4	1	1	.875
F. Tejeda, Johnson City .	1	0	2	0	0	1.000	Stefero, Bluefield	49	34	90	18	8	.873
Lindberg, Bristol	12	8	31	1	8	.975	T. Thompson, Kingsport	8	7	17	4	3	.857
Washington, Bristol	21	14	40	2	3	.964	Ayer, Johnson City	8	6	20	5	4	.839
NIXON, Paintsville	62	52	120	10	12	.945	Boyce, Bluefield	3	3	7	3	0	.769
Shefte, Elizabethton	9	6	8	1	0	.933	Howser, Paintsville	1	0	2	1	0	.667
Garcia, Kingsport	18	11	26	3	5	.925	Ortiz, Paintsville	3	0	2	1	0	.667
Dieters, Johnson City	28	23	51	7	3	.914	Harvey, Bluefield	4	4	11	8	1	.652

SHORTSTOPS

Player and Club	G.	PO.	A.	E.	DP.	Pct.	Player and Club	G.	PO.	A.	E.	DP.	Pct.
Harskamp, Johnson City	3	3	8	0	0	1.000	Washington, Bristol	24	33	59	6	8	.939
Howser, Paintsville	1	1	1	0	0	1.000	AYER, Johnson City	48	54	122	12	22	.936
Jerman, Johnson City	1	0	2	0	0	1.000	Runge, Kingsport	66	104	194	24	38	.925
T. Thompson, Kingsport	1	1	1	0	0	1.000	Shefte, Elizabethton	49	70	129	17	17	.921
Ortiz, Paintsville	1	1	0	0	0	1.000	Lindberg, Bristol	5	10	12	2	2	.917
Zimmerer, Paintsville	1	0	1	0	0	1.000	Presko, Johnson City	20	22	54	7	9	.916
Richard, Bluefield	8	11	40	1	2	.981	Reeder, Bristol	19	21	40	6	4	.910
Followell, Bristol	26	56	88	4	15	.973	Bulcock, Elizabethton	14	20	48	9	6	.883
Murelli, Bluefield	7	19	12	1	5	.969	Gagne, Paintsville	31	28	62	14	6	.865
Gaetti, Elizabethton	10	26	29	3	8	.948	Williams, Bluefield	10	2	17	3	4	.864
Sporrer, Paintsville	43	34	67	6	13	.944	Nixon, Paintsville	3	2	2	1	1	.800
Espinoza, Bluefield	42	61	124	12	20	.939	Smith, Bluefield	1	1	1	3	1	.400

OUTFIELDERS

Player and Club	G.	PO.	A.	E.	DP.	Pct.	Player and Club	G.	PO.	A.	E.	DP.	Pct.
Matos, Johnson City	40	87	3	0	0	1.000	Jurena, Bluefield	61	100	10	5	1	.957
Tucker, Bristol	28	45	3	0	0	1.000	Teegarden, Paintsville	63	80	8	4	2	.957
Baskerville, John. City	20	31	0	0	0	1.000	Stocker, Elizabethton	38	59	6	3	0	.956
Ayer, Johnson City	8	20	2	0	2	1.000	Gayden, Paintsville*	60	98	5	5	1	.954
Rodriguez, Johnson City	18	17	2	0	0	1.000	Carlson, Elizabethton	17	17	2	1	1	.950
Jacoby, Kingsport	8	9	0	0	0	1.000	McNealy, Paintsville*	17	18	0	1	0	.947
Garcia, Kingsport	2	6	0	0	0	1.000	Bowen, Kingsport*	57	74	9	5	0	.943
Ortiz, Paintsville	3	5	0	0	0	1.000	Lett, Johnson City	44	61	3	4	0	.941
Bailey, Kingsport	1	1	0	0	0	1.000	Hardy, Bristol	30	47	4	4	0	.927
DeLeon, Bluefield	1	1	0	0	0	1.000	Roman, Johnson City*	62	115	16	11	2	.923
T. Thompson, Kingsport	1	1	0	0	0	1.000	Baker, Bristol	56	65	7	6	1	.923
Sheets, Bluefield	2	1	0	0	0	1.000	Brandt, Elizabethton	45	48	2	6	0	.893
CHRISTENSEN, Eliz.	55	81	1	1	0	.9880	Randy Harvey, Bristol	5	7	1	1	0	.889
Rogers, Paintsville	53	72	9	1	1	.9878	L. Martinez, Bluefield*	12	15	0	2	0	.882
Roberson, Bristol	54	73	5	1	0	.987	Hage, Paintsville*	6	6	1	1	0	.875
M. Thompson, Kingsport	26	58	4	1	1	.984	Schriner, Bluefield	12	7	0	1	0	.875
Komminsk, Kingsport	59	112	1	2	0	.983	Beswick, Elizabethton	33	76	2	12	1	.867
Patten, Kingsport	48	86	9	2	0	.979	Agras, Elizabethton	7	11	2	2	0	.867
Fields, Bristol	41	79	2	2	0	.976	Mesa, Elizabethton	19	26	5	5	2	.861
Fink, Johnson City	35	68	3	2	2	.973	Miller, Elizabethton	8	6	0	1	0	.857
Schuman, Bluefield	51	86	4	3	0	.968	Washington, Bristol	1	2	0	1	0	.667
Hendrickson, Bluefield	61	71	4	3	0	.962	Stieb, Kingsport	1	0	0	1	0	.000

CATCHERS

Player and Club	G.	PO.	A.	E.	DP.	PB.	Pct.	Player and Club	G.	PO.	A.	E.	DP.	PB.	Pct.
Bailey, Kingsport	16	81	5	0	0	3	1.000	Stieb, Kingsport	49	257	38	4	0	10	.987
Melton, Johnson City	15	59	6	0	0	0	1.000	Ivie, Bluefield	23	128	14	3	0	6	.979
Caraballo, John. City	17	48	2	0	0	2	1.000	Salas, Johnson City	48	194	19	6	2	10	.973
M. Martinez, Kingsport	5	20	0	0	0	4	1.000	Fisher, Bristol	29	151	20	5	1	5	.972
Stovall, Elizabethton	5	19	0	0	1	0	1.000	Rudolph, Paintsville	28	157	13	5	0	5	.971
T. Thompson, Kings.	4	13	0	0	0	0	1.000	Steele, Bristol	24	118	11	4	1	1	.970
Hardy, Bristol	1	11	1	0	0	1	1.000	Stefero, Bluefield	5	24	5	1	0	2	.967
Baldwin, Bristol	1	3	0	0	0	0	1.000	Austin, Elizabethton	44	247	20	10	1	6	.964
Chevalier, John. City	1	2	1	0	0	0	1.000	Jensen, Elizabethton	22	122	4	5	1	4	.962
Randy Harvey, Bris*	1	2	0	0	0	0	1.000	Driver, Bristol	10	45	1	3	0	0	.939
Wheeler, Bristol	1	2	0	0	0	0	1.000	Barraco, Bristol	16	73	3	5	0	2	.938
PALMER, Bluefield	36	193	21	1	3	3	.995	Dovalis, Elizabethton	6	15	0	1	0	0	.938
Benedict, Paintsville	33	220	15	2	0	2	.992	Agras, Elizabethton	3	10	0	1	0	0	.909
Hall, Paintsville	21	90	2	1	0	1	.989	Kopala, Johnson City	4	6	3	1	0	0	.900

PITCHERS

Player and Club	G.	PO.	A.	E.	DP.	Pct.	Player and Club	G.	PO.	A.	E.	DP.	Pct.
HODGE, Elizabethton*	14	6	15	0	0	1.000	Perry, Bristol	15	2	6	0	0	1.000
Bollens, Bristol	19	4	13	0	2	1.000	Norris, Kingsport	18	4	4	0	0	1.000
De Maria, Paintsville	7	6	8	0	0	1.000	Free, Paintsville	11	1	6	0	0	1.000
Davis, Bluefield	10	4	9	0	2	1.000	Warburton, John. City*	13	1	6	0	0	1.000
Brooks, Johnson City	12	4	9	0	0	1.000	Pinkston, Johnson City	16	3	4	0	0	1.000
Cascadden, Bristol*	8	3	9	0	0	1.000	Citarella, Johnson City	4	1	5	0	0	1.000
Behenna, Kingsport	12	3	9	0	0	1.000	Fuller, Kingsport	6	3	3	0	0	1.000
Gonzalez, Johnson City	14	3	9	0	0	1.000	Ames, Kingsport	8	2	4	0	0	1.000
Zedonek, Bluefield	14	3	9	0	1	1.000	Taylor, Johnson City*	10	0	6	0	0	1.000
Clark, Johnson City	23	2	9	0	1	1.000	Nail, Bristol	11	0	6	0	0	1.000
Coghill, Kingsport*	10	4	6	0	0	1.000	Pfeiffer, Bluefield	18	1	5	0	0	1.000
Woodall, Bluefield*	12	1	9	0	1	1.000	Castaigne, Kingsport	23	3	3	0	0	1.000
Orosco, Elizabethton	6	0	9	0	0	1.000	Jones, Elizabethton*	9	0	5	0	0	1.000
Desjarlais, Bristol	11	3	6	0	0	1.000	Maples, Bluefield	10	1	4	0	1	1.000
Thomas, Elizabethton	11	2	6	0	0	1.000	Ostrow, Johnson City	12	0	5	0	1	1.000

PITCHERS—Continued

Player and Club	G	PO	A	E	DP	Pct.
Colon, Johnson City	14	1	4	0	0	1.000
Wick, Bluefield*	20	1	4	0	0	1.000
Jackson, Elizabethton	5	2	2	0	0	1.000
Fagely, Elizabethton*	10	1	3	0	0	1.000
Murphy, Paintsville*	13	0	4	0	0	1.000
Rincon, Johnson City	18	2	2	0	0	1.000
Collyer, Bristol*	4	0	3	0	0	1.000
Fox, Bristol	7	0	3	0	0	1.000
Rabun, Kingsport	8	2	1	0	1	1.000
Persandi, Elizabethton*	9	0	3	0	0	1.000
Bright, Johnson City	10	1	2	0	0	1.000
Haley, Kingsport	3	0	2	0	0	1.000
Riley, Elizabethton	3	0	2	0	0	1.000
Sterk, Elizabethton	4	1	1	0	1	1.000
Power, Bristol	11	1	1	0	0	1.000
Vanderplas, Paintsville	1	0	1	0	0	1.000
Gotay, Johnson City	2	1	0	0	0	1.000
Guerra, Paintsville*	2	0	1	0	1	1.000
Krill, Bristol*	2	0	1	0	0	1.000
Melgar, Paintsville	2	1	0	0	0	1.000
T. Thompson, Kingsport	2	0	1	0	0	1.000
Randy Harvey, Bristol*	3	0	1	0	0	1.000
H. Tejeda, Johnson City	10	0	1	0	0	1.000
Wheeler, Bristol	17	7	15	1	1	.957
Norris, Bluefield	12	8	9	1	0	.944
Campbell, Paintsville	8	2	14	1	0	.941
Swaggerty, Bluefield	17	8	8	1	0	.941
May, Elizabethton	11	3	10	1	2	.929
Konopa, Elizabethton*	13	3	9	1	0	.923
Ricci, Paintsville	9	5	6	1	0	.917
Sanchez, Bristol	8	4	6	1	1	.909
Beecroft, Bristol	11	3	6	1	0	.900
Lein, Paintsville	12	3	6	1	1	.900
Budweg, Paintsville*	8	3	5	1	0	.889
Mulligan, Elizabethton	8	1	7	1	0	.889
Filson, Paintsville*	13	3	12	2	0	.882
Coatney, Kingsport	9	2	5	1	2	.875
Dozier, Johnson City	11	3	4	1	0	.875
Fish, Johnson City*	11	1	6	1	0	.875
Pittman, Johnson City*	5	2	4	1	0	.857
Payne, Kingsport	7	0	6	1	1	.857
Weaver, Johnson City	13	0	10	2	0	.833
Warren, Bristol	13	2	3	1	0	.833
Palica, Bristol	10	7	2	2	0	.818
Smith, Bluefield	14	6	6	3	0	.800
Conradi, Bluefield*	17	0	4	1	0	.800
Reiter, Kingsport*	16	1	6	2	3	.778
Everett, Elizabethton	19	1	2	1	0	.750
North, Paintsville	6	1	4	2	0	.714
Vaughn, Bristol	12	0	5	2	0	.714
Dunn, Bristol*	13	2	3	2	0	.714
Arrington, Elizabethton	13	3	4	3	0	.700
Beyler, Paintsville*	4	0	2	1	1	.667
Justus, Bristol	13	1	1	1	0	.667
Hibbett, Kingsport*	6	2	1	2	0	.600
Kennedy, Kingsport	9	2	1	2	0	.600
Akchurin, Paintsville	4	0	2	2	0	.500
Garcia, Kingsport	1	0	0	1	0	.000

The following pitchers had no recorded accepted chances; therefore, are not listed in the fielding averages for that position: Booker, Diaz, Kitts*, Perez*, Santin, Vorisek*. Liggins, Proulx and Zunino appeared as designated hitters and/or pinch-hitters only.

CLUB PITCHING

Club	G	CG	ShO.	Sv.	IP	H	R	ER	HR	BB	Int. BB	HB	SO	WP.	Bk.	ERA
Paintsville	66	36	8	11	498	401	218	184	31	270	1	22	446	22	8	3.32
Bluefield	68	22	3	9	515	460	320	239	34	284	3	9	351	34	7	4.18
Elizabethton	71	23	4	7	565	559	353	285	36	274	10	14	393	31	9	4.54
Kingsport	70	15	4	12	531	516	363	273	55	306	1	20	327	17	3	4.63
Johnson City	68	6	2	13	543	635	436	356	54	341	12	25	287	31	4	5.90
Bristol	69	16	1	5	533	541	441	354	50	439	27	27	382	44	9	5.98

PITCHERS' RECORDS
(Leading Qualifiers for Earned-Run Average Leadership—56 or More Innings)

*Throws lefthanded.

Pitcher–Club	G	GS	CG	ShO	W	L	Sv	Pct.	IP	H	R	ER	HR	BB	Int. BB	HB	SO	WP	ERA
Filson, Paintsville*	13	13	9	3	9	0	0	1.000	91	51	19	17	1	39	1	1	118	1	1.68
Ricci, Paintsville	9	8	6	2	7	0	0	1.000	56	40	14	11	3	20	0	3	66	1	1.77
Reiter, Kingsport*	16	5	4	2	5	4	2	.556	58	46	26	17	3	34	0	3	43	3	2.64
Norris, Bluefield	13	9	4	0	3	3	1	.500	75	63	35	29	5	39	0	1	46	1	3.48
Woodall, Bluefield*	12	11	5	0	6	5	0	.545	73	60	45	29	5	29	0	0	55	2	3.77
Konopa, Elizabethton*	13	11	4	1	5	6	0	.455	74	60	41	31	4	34	1	0	54	3	3.88
Davis, Bluefield	10	10	3	1	4	4	0	.500	58	44	34	25	3	32	3	3	63	1	4.18
Bollens, Bristol	19	4	2	0	6	4	1	.600	56	42	34	26	3	32	1	1	56	1	4.33
Hodge, Elizabethton*	14	13	6	1	8	4	0	.667	81	82	46	39	6	21	1	1	46	0	4.55
Behenna, Kingsport	12	12	6	0	5	3	0	.625	83	76	52	42	12	42	0	4	36	1	4.55

Departmental Leaders: G—Castaigne, Clark, 23; GS—Colon, 14; CG—Filson, 9; ShO—Filson, 3; W—Filson, 9; L—Fish, 8; Sv—Clark, 8; Pct.—Filson, Ricci, 1.000; IP—Filson, 91; H—Colon, 94; R—Colon, 65; ER—Colon, 56; HR—Behenna, Colon, 12; BB—Beecroft, 52; IBB—Pinkston, Vaughn, 5; HB—Lein, 5; SO—Filson, 118; WP—Justus, 11.

(All Pitchers—Listed Alphabetically)

Pitcher–Club	G	GS	CG	ShO	W	L	Sv	Pct.	IP	H	R	ER	HR	BB	Int. BB	HB	SO	WP	ERA
Akchurin, Paintsville	4	4	2	0	4	0		1.000	29	25	16	14	5	11	0	0	24	3	4.34
Ames, Kingsport	8	8	2	0	0	1	4	.200	43	52	31	26	6	18	0	2	17	3	5.44
Arrington, Elizabethton	13	12	4	1	5	3	0	.625	75	86	49	38	3	29	0	2	39	4	4.56
Beecroft, Bristol	11	11	2	0	1	6	0	.143	51	43	30	24	2	52	3	1	25	4	4.24
Behenna, Kingsport	12	12	6	0	5	3	0	.625	83	76	52	42	12	42	0	4	36	1	4.55

Pitcher—Club	G.	GS.	CG.	ShO.	W.	L.	Sv.	Pct.	IP.	H.	R.	ER.	HR.	BB.	Int. BB.	HB.	SO.	WP.	ERA.
Beyler, Paintsville*	4	1	1	0	2	0	0	1.000	13	14	9	9	1	14	0	0	7	0	6.23
Bollens, Bristol	19	4	2	0	6	4	1	.600	56	42	34	26	3	32	3	3	43	1	4.18
Booker, Paintsville	7	1	0	0	0	0	0	.000	16	12	7	5	0	16	0	2	13	2	2.81
Bright, Johnson City	10	2	0	0	2	0	0	1.000	20	27	15	14	3	15	0	0	11	2	6.30
Brooks, Johnson City	12	9	2	0	4	3	0	.571	57	70	37	35	2	20	0	0	11	2	6.30
Budweg, Paintsville*	8	7	4	0	5	1	0	.833	51	44	30	28	4	43	0	3	37	0	4.94
Campbell, Paintsville	8	8	4	0	5	2	0	.714	53	46	32	26	4	40	0	0	38	6	4.42
Cascadden, Bristol*	8	7	3	0	1	5	0	.167	34	45	38	35	8	21	1	0	19	3	9.26
Castaigne, Kingsport	23	1	0	0	4	3	5	.571	43	48	26	23	5	24	0	1	42	0	4.81
Citarella, Johnson City	4	1	0	0	2	0	0	.000	21	23	15	13	1	12	1	0	16	1	5.57
Clark, Johnson City	23	0	0	0	4	2	8	.667	32	31	10	7	1	11	2	0	16	1	1.97
Coatney, Kingsport	9	7	1	0	3	1	0	.750	36	29	13	13	2	20	0	2	28	0	3.25
Coghill, Kingsport*	10	10	0	0	3	4	0	.429	50	55	45	34	7	33	0	3	26	3	6.12
Collyer, Bristol*	4	0	0	0	1	1	0	.500	8	5	5	5	0	8	1	2	2	1	5.63
Colon, Johnson City	14	14	0	0	4	6	0	.400	64	94	65	56	12	34	0	5	42	4	7.88
Conradi, Bluefield*	17	1	0	0	2	2	1	.500	39	29	16	13	2	32	0	1	30	6	3.00
Davis, Bluefield	10	10	3	1	4	4	0	.500	58	44	34	25	3	30	0	2	54	4	3.88
De Maria, Paintsville	7	7	4	1	3	2	0	.600	43	35	16	13	3	14	0	1	32	1	2.72
Desjarlais, Bristol	11	8	2	0	2	5	0	.286	45	55	40	31	3	14	0	1	32	1	2.72
Diaz, Paintsville	3	1	0	0	0	0	0	1.000	6	5	3	3	1	4	0	0	3	1	4.50
Dozier, Johnson City	11	7	0	0	1	3	0	.250	35	48	28	20	2	15	0	1	12	2	5.14
Dunn, Bristol*	13	0	0	0	1	1	0	.500	23	17	9	9	1	22	2	0	20	3	3.52
Everett, Elizabethton	19	0	0	0	3	2	4	.600	28	22	9	9	1	13	2	1	31	0	2.89
Fagely, Elizabethton*	10	0	0	0	3	1	0	.750	33	31	19	14	1	21	1	1	31	4	3.82
Filson, Paintsville*	13	13	9	3	9	0	0	1.000	91	51	19	17	1	39	1	1	118	1	1.68
Fish, Johnson City*	11	5	0	0	2	8	0	.200	25	41	40	31	2	26	1	0	21	1	11.16
Fox, Bristol	7	0	0	0	0	0	0	.000	14	14	11	10	1	12	0	0	8	1	6.43
Free, Paintsville	11	0	0	0	6	0	4	1.000	28	19	6	5	1	13	0	1	32	2	1.61
Fuller, Kingsport	6	1	0	0	2	0	0	1.000	22	11	6	5	0	8	0	1	15	0	2.05
Garcia, Kingsport	1	0	0	0	0	0	0	.000	2	3	3	2	0	1	0	0	0	0	9.00
Gonzalez, Johnson City	14	3	0	0	3	0	0	1.000	37	32	25	22	5	35	0	2	27	6	5.35
Gotay, Johnson City	2	0	0	0	1	0	0	.000	2	1	1	0	0	4	0	0	1	0	0.00
Guerra, Paintsville	2	1	1	0	1	0	1	1.000	8	6	4	4	2	2	0	0	8	0	4.50
Haley, Kingsport	3	2	0	0	0	1	1	.000	8	6	4	4	2	2	0	0	8	0	4.50
Harvey, Bristol*	3	3	0	0	0	1	0	.000	17	11	8	6	1	5	0	0	6	0	7.20
Hibbett, Kingsport*	6	0	0	0	0	0	0	1.000	11	7	4	4	0	5	0	0	7	0	3.27
Hodge, Elizabethton*	14	13	6	1	8	4	0	.667	81	82	46	39	6	21	1	1	56	1	2.45
Jackson, Elizabethton	5	0	0	0	1	1	0	.500	16	13	6	6	1	3	1	1	11	4	4.33
Jones, Elizabethton*	9	2	0	0	1	1	0	.500	19	23	20	18	1	8	1	0	11	5	3.38
Justus, Bristol	13	2	0	0	0	1	0	.000	19	29	32	22	3	19	1	1	18	0	8.53
Kennedy, Kingsport	9	4	1	0	0	2	0	.000	23	41	36	31	2	28	0	3	13	4	12.13
Kitts, Kingsport*	1	0	0	0	0	0	0	.000	2	3	1	1	0	1	0	0	0	0	
Konopa, Elizabethton*	13	11	4	1	5	6	0	.455	74	60	41	31	4	34	1	0	55	2	3.77
Krill, Bristol*	2	0	0	0	0	0	0	.000	8	8	5	2	1	5	1	0	9	0	2.25
Lein, Paintsville	12	8	3	0	4	5	0	.444	64	71	41	36	3	24	0	8	44	3	5.06
Maples, Bluefield	10	6	3	0	3	4	0	.429	41	31	27	25	2	28	0	1	34	2	5.49
May, Elizabethton	11	9	4	1	3	5	0	.375	65	61	43	37	4	32	1	2	46	7	5.12
Melgar, Paintsville	2	1	0	0	1	0	0	1.000	6	5	4	3	0	2	0	5	7	1	4.50
Mulligan, Elizabethton	8	3	2	0	2	1	2	.667	38	31	11	6	0	10	1	1	25	0	1.42
Murphy, Paintsville*	13	2	2	0	5	0	5	1.000	33	27	12	11	3	23	0	2	23	1	3.00
Nail, Bristol	11	6	1	0	0	3	0	.000	30	46	50	39	0	44	0	4	15	2	11.70
Norris, Kingsport	18	3	0	0	6	2	3	.750	52	52	32	29	7	33	0	0	48	0	5.02
Norris, Bluefield	13	9	4	0	3	3	1	.500	57	52	32	29	7	33	0	0	48	0	5.02
North, Kingsport	6	6	0	0	4	1	0	.800	37	24	15	11	4	12	0	1	17	1	2.68
Orosco, Elizabethton	6	1	0	0	1	2	1	.333	16	23	15	11	1	3	0	1	5	0	6.19
Ostrow, Johnson City	12	0	0	0	0	2	0	.000	29	26	25	18	3	16	0	0	15	1	5.59
Palica, Elizabethton	10	7	2	0	3	2	0	.600	46	49	38	23	7	29	2	2	26	4	4.50
Payne, Kingsport	7	7	1	0	2	3	0	.400	30	30	23	13	0	17	1	0	14	0	3.90
Perez, Johnson City*	2	0	0	0	0	0	0	.000	1	1	2	0	0	3	0	0	0	0	18.00
Perry, Bristol	5	2	0	0	0	4	0	.200	45	42	25	22	2	22	4	2	45	2	4.40
Persnadi, Elizabethton*	9	0	0	0	0	0	0	.000	17	22	19	18	1	13	0	0	14	0	9.53
Pfeiffer, Bluefield	18	0	0	0	0	2	1	.500	31	32	24	22	4	18	1	0	14	1	6.39
Pinkston, Johnson City	16	0	0	0	0	3	0	.000	17	15	15	10	0	25	5	0	6	4	5.29
Pittman, Johnson City*	5	0	0	0	0	0	0	.000	17	15	15	10	0	25	5	0	6	4	5.29
Power, Bristol	11	0	0	0	0	3	0	.000	21	20	11	10	0	10	0	0	8	1	0.60
Rabun, Kingsport	8	0	0	0	1	2	0	.333	18	13	13	10	3	11	0	1	17	2	4.71
Reiter, Kingsport*	16	5	4	2	5	4	2	.556	58	46	26	17	7	34	0	3	43	3	2.64
Ricci, Paintsville	9	8	6	2	7	0	0	1.000	56	40	14	11	3	20	0	2	66	1	1.77
Riley, Elizabethton	3	3	0	0	0	0	0	.000	10	10	8	7	1	7	0	2	6	1	6.30
Rincon, Johnson City	18	0	0	0	1	1	2	.500	32	31	20	19	5	17	2	4	12	1	5.34
Sanchez, Bristol	8	8	2	0	2	3	0	.400	29	34	37	35	3	37	1	1	26	1	10.86
Santin, Johnson City	6	0	0	0	0	0	0	.000	4	6	3	3	0	3	0	0	1	1	6.75
Smith, Bluefield	14	8	1	0	3	3	0	.500	45	54	29	26	2	21	0	0	37	3	5.20
Sterk, Elizabethton	4	4	0	0	0	3	0	.000	17	15	13	12	1	19	0	0	9	2	6.35

Pitcher–Club	G.	GS.	CG.	ShO.	W.	L.	Sv.	Pct.	IP.	H.	R.	ER.	HR.	Int. BB.	BB.	HB.	SO.	WP.	ERA.
Swaggerty, Bluefield	17	9	3	0	5	3	0	.625	68	76	45	36	5	28	0	0	36	8	4.76
Taylor, Johnson City*	10	6	0	0	0	3	1	.000	33	45	29	24	4	14	0	3	12	1	6.55
H. Tejeda, Johnson City	10	0	0	0	0	0	0	.000	11	22	15	13	3	10	0	0	4	1	10.64
Thomas, Elizabethton	11	4	1	0	2	2	0	.500	30	31	16	16	2	16	0	0	3	0	4.80
Thompson, Kingsport	2	0	0	0	0	0	0	.000	5	10	5	5	2	1	0	0	3	0	9.00
Vanderplas, Paintsville*	1	1	0	0	0	0	0	.000	4	3	0	0	0	2	0	0	0	0	0.00
Vaughn, Bristol	12	7	0	0	0	5	0	.000	39	37	31	27	9	34	5	4	26	3	6.23
Vorisek, Bristol*	5	0	0	0	0	0	0	.000	4	1	1	1	0	8	0	1	1	0	2.25
Warburton, Johnson C*	13	5	1	0	1	4	0	.200	43	45	36	31	5	41	1	4	20	1	6.49
Warren, Bristol	13	4	1	0	0	3	0	.000	36	32	27	16	6	40	0	1	43	3	4.00
Weaver, Johnson City	13	13	1	0	3	5	0	.375	65	70	53	37	6	29	0	1	35	5	5.12
Wheeler, Bristol	17	6	3	0	3	5	2	.375	55	63	42	32	3	22	2	2	29	3	5.24
Wick, Bluefield*	20	2	1	0	2	3	5	.400	39	26	12	9	2	25	1	1	31	1	2.08
Woodall, Bluefield*	12	11	5	0	6	5	0	.545	73	60	45	29	5	29	0	0	43	4	3.58
Zedonek, Bluefield	14	8	2	0	1	4	1	.200	46	45	33	25	4	34	1	3	26	3	4.89

BALKS—Filson, 4; Konopa, Swaggerty, Vaughn, 3 each; Cascadden, Colon, Conradi, Jackson, May, Murphy, Power, 2 each; Akchurin, Ames, Bollens, Clark, Coatney, Free, Hodge, Palica, Pfeiffer, Pinkston, Reiter, Smith, Vorisek, 1 each.

COMBINATION SHUTOUTS—Davis-Zedonek-Pfeiffer, Woodall-Wick, Bluefield; Beecroft-Perry, Bristol; Warburton-Fish-Clark, Brooks-Ostrow, Johnson City; Coatney-Castaigne 2, Kingsport; De Maria-Ricci, Filson-Lein, Paintsville.

NO-HIT GAMES—Filson, Paintsville, defeated Kingsport, 10-0, August 7, second game (seven innings).

Paintsville Had Best Percentage in Baseball

The Paintsville Yankees won 25 of their first 31 games under Bill Livesay, 38, who had never managed before professionally. They went on to a 52-13 record and .800 won-lost percentage, which was the best in baseball in 1979.

Mercifully, there were no post-season playoffs in the Appalachian League; the Yankees finished 15½ games ahead of their closest challengers, the Kingsport Braves.

Left Was All Right With Pettis

Gary Pettis had batted righthanded all his life. That is, until Angels scout Loyd Christopher noticed Pettis signed his contract with his left hand.

Had the Idaho Falls infielder been born a generation earlier, he might have been the subject of one of those forced elementary schoolroom conversion attempts to make him write righthanded as well.

The results by Pettis after the Angels made him switch-hit were amazing. The Oakland native tied the Pioneer League record for triples with 10, collecting most of them while batting lefthanded. His first hit at home in '79 was an inside-the-park home run, and he got it batting lefthanded. His seasonal batting average was .318.

Gulf Coast League

SUMMER CLASS A CLASSIFICATION

CHAMPIONSHIP WINNERS IN PREVIOUS YEARS

1964—Sarasota Braves............ .610	1969—Montreal.................... .585	1973—Texas .... .732
1965—Bradenton Astros .... .632	1970—Chicago A.L. .... .600	1974—Chicago N.L. .... .702
1966—New York A.L. .... .667	1971—Kansas City................ .755	1975—Texas .... .774
1967—Kansas City................. .614	1972—Chicago N.L. a .... .651	1976—Texas .... .704
1968—Oakland..................... .650	Kansas City a.......... .651	1977—Chicago-AL .... .731
		1978—Texas.................... .600

(Note—Known as Sarasota Rookie League in 1964 and Florida Rookie League in 1965.) aDeclared co-champions; no playoff.

STANDING OF CLUBS AT CLOSE OF SEASON, AUGUST 27

Club	Hous.	Texas	K.C. Gold	Atl.	K.C. Blues	Pitt.	Chi. NL	W.	L.	T.	Pct.	G.B.
Houston	..	5	4	4	6	8	6	33	19	0	.635	......
Texas	4	..	7	5	5	7	5	33	21	0	.611	1
Kansas City-Golds..........	4	2	..	4	5	7	7	29	23	0	.558	4
Atlanta.......................	5	4	5	..	3	3	6	26	28	0	.481	8
Kansas City-Blues..........	3	4	4	6	..	4	3	24	29	0	.453	9½
Pittsburgh	1	2	2	6	4	..	5	20	32	0	.385	13
Chicago-NL..................	2	4	1	3	6	3	..	19	32	0	.373	13½

Houston declared league champion on basis of highest won-lost percentage.

Club names indicate major league connections.

Games played at Bradenton and Sarasota, Fla.

Regular-Season Attendance—At Payne Park, Sarasota, 7,226; no admission charged at other parks. No playoffs. All-star game, 1,000.

Managers: Atlanta—Pedro Gonzalez; Chicago-NL—Ken Rudolph; Houston—Julio Linares; Kansas City-Blues —Brian Murphy; Kansas City-Golds—Jose Martinez; Pittsburgh—Elwood (Woody) Huyke; Texas—Andy Hancock.

(Compiled by Howe News Bureau, Chicago, Ill.)

CLUB BATTING

Club	G.	AB.	R.	OR.	H.	TB.	2B.	3B.	HR.	RBI.	SH.	SF.	BB.	Int. BB.	HP.	SO.	SB.	CS.	LOB.	Pct.
K.C.-Golds........	52	1729	325	255	495	687	67	28	23	279	11	27	234	10	14	213	77	31	403	.286
K.C.-Blues........	53	1692	253	303	459	624	60	24	19	219	7	25	255	8	20	234	51	21	424	.271
Texas	54	1817	302	271	491	603	63	14	7	251	16	22	321	11	15	231	93	35	473	.270
Chicago-NL........	51	1754	306	367	453	562	55	18	6	248	19	20	313	6	16	293	67	27	454	.258
Atlanta.............	54	1788	302	280	460	627	70	17	21	251	17	21	264	6	16	244	45	28	425	.257
Houston	52	1733	256	205	440	545	67	10	6	202	11	21	262	12	15	263	63	31	440	.254
Pittsburgh	52	1703	225	288	412	536	45	20	13	175	7	15	181	7	11	255	82	32	353	.242

INDIVIDUAL BATTING
(Leading Qualifiers for Batting Championship—146 or More Plate Appearances)

*Bats lefthanded.   †Switch-hitter.

Player and Club	G.	AB.	R.	H.	TB.	2B.	3B.	HR.	RBI.	SH.	SF.	BB.	HP.	SO.	SB.	CS.	Pct.
Brewer, Michael, KC-Golds............	51	205	38	76	105	7	5	4	47	0	5	12	1	23	18	7	.371
Wilson, J. Michael, Chicago-NL........	39	144	38	52	58	6	0	0	10	2	1	26	0	16	21	7	.361
Patterson, S. Craig, KC-Blues........	50	171	30	59	70	7	2	0	24	1	5	32	1	13	10	2	.345
Atkinson, James, KC-Blues*..........	47	165	26	56	75	9	2	2	27	0	3	25	1	9	4	2	.339
Stockstill, John, Chicago-NL..........	41	133	10	45	53	1	2	1	28	0	2	18	0	12	2	1	.338
Arroyo, Hector, KC-Golds*...........	46	181	32	60	65	3	1	0	17	1	1	24	0	19	16	6	.331
Jabalera, Francisco, Houston*........	49	192	32	63	68	5	0	0	19	4	2	22	3	26	6	7	.328
Ray, John, Houston†.................	37	132	25	41	60	8	1	3	25	1	3	32	3	4	7	3	.311
Townley, Robin, KC-Golds............	48	181	43	56	68	10	1	0	17	0	3	30	5	21	12	4	.309
Scott, Donald, Texas‡................	45	146	18	45	57	7	1	1	29	1	5	31	0	17	4	1	.308

Departmental Leaders: G—Dikos, 54; AB—Brewer, 205; R—Townley, 43; H—Brewer, 76; TB—Brewer, 105; 2B— De Sena, 13; 3B—Rosa, 7; HR—Dikos, Doak, Sosa, 5; RBI—Brewer, 47; SH—Luzon, 7; SF—Palmer, 7; BB—Primante, 45; HP—Ball, Townley, Wynne, 5; SO—Triplett, 43; SB—J.M. Wilson, 21; CS—Brewer, Jabalera, J.M. Wilson, 7.

(All Players—Listed Alphabetically)

Player and Club	G.	AB.	R.	H.	TB.	2B.	3B.	HR.	RBI.	SH.	SF.	BB.	HP.	SO.	SB.	CS.	Pct.
Allen, S. Shane, Chicago-NL	39	146	23	42	55	6	2	1	17	0	1	9	1	22	3	1	.288
Araujo, Juan, Chicago-NL*	1	2	0	2	2	0	0	0	2	0	0	1	0	0	1	0	1.000
Arias, Ruben, Pittsburgh	21	66	5	14	15	1	0	0	4	0	0	4	0	9	2	1	.212
Arroyo, Hector, KC-Golds*	46	181	32	60	65	3	1	0	17	1	1	24	0	19	16	6	.331
Ashley, Larry, Houston	17	39	4	6	7	1	0	0	4	1	0	6	1	21	1	3	.154
Atkinson, James, KC-Blues*	47	165	26	56	75	9	2	2	27	0	3	25	1	9	4	2	.339
Austin, Terry, Houston	29	78	10	16	19	1	1	0	12	0	1	20	2	15	4	2	.205
Ayala, Eric, Atlanta	38	167	25	43	47	4	0	0	15	2	1	8	2	7	4	3	.257
Baker, Stanley, Texas	43	119	19	34	37	3	0	0	14	5	1	41	1	12	3	5	.286
Ball, Robert, Texas	43	168	30	47	59	9	0	1	21	1	3	23	5	29	18	5	.280
Barnette, Johnny, KC-Golds	36	102	23	30	36	3	0	1	13	0	0	14	0	15	4	1	.294
Bastien, Rodger, Texas	39	139	21	31	41	3	2	1	17	0	1	25	0	17	7	1	.223
Batter, Ronald, KC-Golds	2	7	0	4	6	0	1	0	0	0	0	2	1	0	0	0	.571
Bazan, Pedro, Chicago-NL*	42	129	27	34	44	8	1	0	24	0	1	24	4	15	0	0	.264
Beaudoin, Michael, Texas	32	117	12	35	38	3	0	0	9	0	0	18	0	10	4	5	.299
Belmonte, Phillip, Chicago-NL	36	109	26	35	42	5	1	0	15	1	1	24	0	14	4	2	.321
Benjamin, Julio, Houston	20	66	8	14	14	0	0	0	6	1	0	8	0	7	0	0	.212
Biafore, Anthony, Chicago-NL	40	114	19	22	30	4	2	0	13	3	2	26	1	31	1	2	.193
Black, Charles, Atlanta*	13	45	11	15	18	3	0	0	3	0	0	16	0	4	1	4	.333
Boozer, Eugene, Atlanta*	9	0	0	0	0	0	0	0	0	0	0	0	0	0	0	0	.000
Brewer, Michael, KC-Golds	51	205	38	76	105	7	5	4	47	0	5	12	1	23	18	7	.371
Brito, Ruben, Pittsburgh	11	37	6	9	13	1	0	1	6	0	0	1	0	5	0	0	.243
Burgin, Russell, KC-Golds	9	11	4	3	3	0	0	0	1	0	0	5	0	2	0	0	.273
Bush, John, Texas	13	40	8	10	15	2	0	1	5	0	0	6	1	8	1	3	.250
Butler, Brett, Atlanta*	30	111	36	41	67	7	5	3	20	1	1	19	1	15	5	4	.369
Caballero, Jose, Pittsburgh	27	91	11	25	30	3	1	0	14	0	1	2	1	16	0	2	.275
Childs, Michael, Texas	25	85	19	27	34	3	2	0	19	0	1	13	0	11	10	1	.318
Cooper, Junior, KC-Golds	41	146	28	34	61	6	6	3	22	1	1	16	1	29	4	1	.233
De Aza, Manuel, Houston	42	153	21	40	45	5	0	0	17	1	2	13	2	16	10	2	.261
De Sena, Sergio, Houston	48	192	26	43	58	13	1	0	22	3	2	16	1	32	5	2	.224
Dewey, Duane, KC-Blues	23	59	10	14	23	5	2	0	4	0	1	14	0	6	1	1	.237
Dikos, Gregory, Atlanta	54	196	36	48	74	9	1	5	32	0	4	36	2	27	0	0	.245
Dixon, F. Daniel, Pittsburgh	7	29	5	7	7	0	0	0	2	0	0	1	1	4	3	1	.241
Doak, Leon, KC-Golds	31	111	21	30	49	2	1	5	20	1	0	5	1	19	3	2	.270
Donofrio, Larry, Texas*	27	86	11	20	25	5	0	0	11	2	2	14	1	13	1	1	.233
Doran, William, Houston	44	164	21	42	51	6	0	1	16	2	1	19	1	16	3	3	.256
Espinoza, Alvaro, Houston	11	32	3	7	7	0	0	0	5	1	0	4	0	6	0	0	.219
Espinoza, Ernesto, Houston	8	25	3	2	2	0	0	0	1	0	1	1	1	8	1	0	.080
Felt, James, Pittsburgh	52	179	27	39	62	5	3	4	24	0	1	29	0	29	15	6	.218
Ferguson, Bret, Atlanta	6	1	0	0	0	0	0	0	0	0	0	0	0	0	0	0	.000
Ford, Kenneth, Pittsburgh	40	147	28	36	51	5	2	2	19	0	3	13	0	20	9	0	.245
Gainey, Telmanch, Houston*	21	61	5	14	17	1	1	0	7	1	1	10	0	26	2	1	.230
Garray, Allan, KC-Golds	42	128	22	33	53	4	2	4	19	0	1	24	1	17	2	0	.258
Gil, Carlos, Chicago-NL	12	0	1	0	0	0	0	0	0	0	0	0	0	0	0	0	.000
Goodman, William, Texas	18	65	10	16	18	2	0	0	2	3	0	13	0	10	4	2	.246
Grahek, Lawrence, KC-Golds*	26	59	18	23	38	8	2	1	13	0	3	16	0	8	6	1	.390
Guerrero, Inocencio, Atlanta	23	80	16	18	24	3	0	1	15	1	1	10	0	17	0	1	.225
Gulaskey, Robert, Pittsburgh	2	7	0	3	3	0	0	0	1	0	0	0	1	0	0	0	.429
Henriquez, Pablo, Pittsburgh†	37	131	22	36	39	3	0	0	8	0	0	8	0	19	8	4	.275
Infante, Ulises, KC-Blues	33	102	20	34	38	2	1	0	17	0	2	25	1	16	7	1	.333
Irvin, Otis, KC-Golds	15	33	2	2	2	0	0	0	5	0	2	6	0	6	1	0	.061
Jabalera, Francisco, Houston*	48	192	32	63	68	5	0	0	19	4	2	22	3	26	6	7	.328
Jackson, Patrick, KC-Blues	27	60	6	12	12	0	0	0	9	0	3	7	0	5	0	0	.200
Jacoby, Brook, Atlanta	42	160	24	43	65	11	1	3	35	1	2	21	1	23	4	5	.269
Jansen, Charles, KC-Blues	32	109	16	30	41	5	0	2	12	0	2	19	1	10	6	1	.275
Johnson, Thomas, Chicago-NL	25	69	9	15	18	3	0	0	6	0	1	8	0	18	4	0	.217
Jones, Christopher, Houston	31	93	15	24	29	3	1	0	6	2	1	18	1	10	6	2	.258
Knoll, David, Chicago-NL	26	50	12	9	10	1	0	0	2	3	0	15	0	17	0	0	.180
Lockett, James, Chicago-NL*	45	144	25	39	47	6	1	0	23	3	4	33	2	17	.5	3	.271
Lois, Alberto, Pittsburgh	2	4	3	1	1	0	0	0	0	0	0	0	0	1	1	0	.250
Lucious, Jesse, KC-Blues	19	56	6	12	13	1	0	0	4	1	0	9	0	19	1	2	.214
Luethy, David, KC-Golds	49	170	28	38	50	7	1	1	28	5	2	27	1	14	4	2	.224
Luzon, Robert, Atlanta	53	189	23	34	39	5	0	0	12	7	1	20	2	27	9	1	.180
Made, Rafael, Pittsburgh	36	103	7	22	26	4	0	0	5	1	0	8	0	15	2	3	.214
Martinez, Anardy, Pittsburgh	27	85	8	23	23	0	0	0	6	2	3	2	0	9	6	1	.271
Martinez, Angel, Chicago-NL*	45	147	20	33	42	5	2	0	20	1	2	24	3	30	1	1	.244
Martinez, Carmelo, Chicago-NL	40	143	18	29	36	4	0	1	23	1	3	17	1	20	0	0	.203
Matos, Alexander, Atlanta	17	1	0	0	0	0	0	0	0	0	0	0	0	0	0	0	.000
McGehee, C. Connor, Pittsburgh*	44	152	30	45	60	4	4	1	15	0	1	33	1	26	13	2	.296
McMath, Shelton, Texas	3	11	3	2	6	1	0	1	2	0	0	2	0	2	1	0	.182
Mennemeier, Mark, KC-Blues	38	128	26	31	43	3	0	3	16	0	0	22	2	13	0	1	.242
Mork, Dennis, Chicago-NL*	38	123	26	40	58	4	4	2	24	0	1	16	0	14	3	2	.325
Neal, Arthur, Atlanta	13	41	4	8	10	0	1	0	6	0	1	4	0	4	0	1	.195
Neufang, Gerald, Texas	10	24	4	6	6	0	0	0	3	0	1	6	0	2	0	0	.250

Player and Club	G.	AB.	R.	H.	TB.	2B.	3B.	HR.	RBI.	SH.	SF.	BB.	HP.	SO.	SB.	CS.	Pct.
Nunez, Hector, Atlanta	25	65	8	16	18	2	0	0	10	1	2	11	2	14	0	0	.246
O'Brien, Peter, Texas*	50	189	39	46	60	10	2	0	31	1	2	36	0	8	1	1	.243
Orzel, David, Texas†	10	1	0	0	0	0	0	0	0	0	0	0	0	0	0	0	.000
Owen, Dave, Chicago-NL	10	23	8	7	7	0	0	0	4	0	0	7	0	2	9	2	.304
Owens, Texas	1	2	0	0	0	0	0	0	0	0	0	0	0	0	0	0	.000
Palmer, Michael, KC-Golds	50	190	35	54	79	10	3	3	38	0	7	20	3	23	8	5	.284
Patterson, S. Craig, KC-Blues	50	171	30	59	70	7	2	0	24	1	5	32	1	13	10	2	.345
Pederson, Russell, KC-Blues	22	61	8	15	19	1	0	1	7	1	0	5	0	12	1	1	.246
Pocoroba, Joseph, Atlanta	42	141	18	37	43	4	1	0	12	1	1	22	1	17	4	1	.262
Porter, Denny, KC-Golds*	17	39	5	10	13	3	0	0	10	1	0	8	0	2	0	0	.256
Primante, Valintino, Houston†	42	121	24	35	46	6	1	1	27	0	5	45	0	23	7	1	.289
Purdy, Christopher, KC-Blues†	24	54	5	8	13	1	2	0	6	0	0	12	0	9	2	1	.148
Quezada, Rafael, Atlanta	43	121	19	31	36	5	0	0	11	0	2	18	2	14	2	3	.256
Ray, John, Houston†	37	132	25	41	60	8	1	3	25	1	3	32	3	4	7	3	.311
Reasonover, Larry, Texas	23	52	4	13	17	1	0	1	4	0	1	5	2	14	2	1	.250
Reedy, W. Robert, Pittsburgh†	26	82	13	17	25	4	2	0	13	1	3	25	2	15	4	3	.207
Reynolds, Larry, Texas	17	74	23	26	29	1	1	0	6	1	0	10	0	4	18	2	.351
Robinson, Gregory, Texas	6	22	0	5	7	2	0	0	3	0	0	2	0	3	0	0	.227
Robles, Ruben, Houston	2	4	0	0	0	0	0	0	0	0	0	0	0	0	0	0	.000
Rodriguez, Angel, Pittsburgh	42	158	14	34	49	4	4	1	21	1	1	10	4	21	5	1	.215
Rodriguez, Julio, KC-Blues	36	117	23	29	35	4	1	0	9	0	1	17	4	24	5	1	.248
Rodriguez, Manuel, Pittsburgh	22	78	7	14	17	0	0	1	9	0	0	2	0	26	0	0	.179
Romey, Stephen, Texas	20	54	7	15	15	0	0	6	0	1	4	3	9	0	2	.278
Rosa, Angel, KC-Blues*	38	117	15	31	56	5	7	2	11	2	0	10	2	25	1	1	.265
Salazar, Terrell, Pittsburgh	3	12	3	5	5	0	0	0	1	0	0	0	0	1	0	0	.417
Schaefer, James, Texas*	42	148	26	43	49	6	0	0	27	1	0	17	2	6	9	2	.291
Scott, Donald, Texas†	45	146	18	45	57	7	1	1	29	1	5	31	0	17	4	1	.308
Showell, Keith, Texas*	28	90	14	22	22	0	0	0	14	0	3	15	0	15	5	1	.244
Silverio, Luis, KC-Blues	5	14	2	4	7	3	0	0	0	0	0	2	0	4	0	0	.286
Smith, Sidney, Chicago-NL†	30	65	13	11	11	0	0	0	7	2	0	17	0	16	3	3	.169
Snaith, Andrew, Pittsburgh	38	120	10	30	39	3	0	2	11	1	1	17	1	20	2	2	.250
Snider, Ronald, KC-Golds*	51	164	26	42	59	4	5	1	27	2	2	22	0	14	4	2	.256
Sosa, Miguel, Atlanta	44	171	25	48	75	8	2	5	26	1	1	11	0	42	7	3	.281
Stafford, Charles, Texas	28	84	17	25	29	2	1	0	12	1	1	20	0	27	7	0	.298
Stockstill, John, Chicago-NL	41	133	10	45	53	1	2	1	28	0	2	18	0	12	2	1	.338
Strucher, Mark, Houston	29	96	18	21	29	5	0	1	13	1	2	18	1	13	1	0	.219
Swaggerty, F. Glenn, Chi-NL	14	0	1	0	0	0	0	0	0	0	0	0	0	0	0	0	.000
Tanzi, Robert, Texas	12	47	7	13	15	2	0	0	6	0	0	9	0	5	0	1	.277
Thomas, Marc, Houston	42	134	16	34	40	6	0	0	11	0	1	15	0	20	3	2	.254
Tjader, James, Texas.	6	27	4	5	16	0	4	1	5	0	0	3	0	5	0	1	.185
Townley, Robin, KC-Golds	48	181	43	56	68	10	1	0	17	0	3	30	5	21	12	4	.309
Triplett, Robert, Chicago-NL*	41	129	18	18	25	0	2	1	14	3	0	22	2	43	6	1	.140
Veith, Anthony, Chicago-NL*.	4	6	2	4	5	1	0	0	3	0	0	4	1	1	0	0	.667
Velasquez, Richard, Texas.	3	7	2	0	0	0	0	0	0	0	0	3	0	3	0	0	.000
Vranesh, Keith, KC-Blues	41	118	15	26	43	2	3	3	18	1	2	14	1	36	0	0	.220
Wellman, Brad, KC-Blues	48	170	24	44	56	6	0	2	24	0	3	26	2	17	5	3	.259
Wheeler, Timothy, Pittsburgh	20	57	8	9	13	2	1	0	3	0	1	10	1	9	3	0	.158
Wherry, Clifton, Houston	47	184	33	47	64	7	5	0	21	2	1	31	1	22	11	5	.255
Whistler, Randall, Atlanta	27	65	13	15	22	2	1	1	15	0	2	20	0	14	1	0	.231
Williams, Jaime, Houston	13	40	2	7	8	1	0	0	1	0	0	3	0	8	0	0	.175
Williams, Larry, KC-Golds	10	2	0	0	0	0	0	0	0	0	0	0	0	1	0	0	.000
Williams, Preston, Atlanta	42	137	25	36	53	5	3	2	22	1	1	39	1	21	3	0	.263
Wilson, J. Michael, Chicago-NL	39	144	38	52	58	6	0	0	12	2	1	26	0	16	21	7	.361
Wilson, Luis, Atlanta	29	96	20	27	36	2	2	1	17	1	1	8	2	19	4	2	.281
Wolff, David, Pittsburgh	5	18	2	3	5	0	1	0	1	0	0	1	0	2	1	0	.167
Wotus, Ronald, Pittsburgh	40	147	16	40	53	6	2	1	14	1	0	13	0	10	5	6	.272
Wynne, Marvell, KC-Blues*	50	190	21	54	80	6	4	4	28	1	3	12	5	16	9	4	.284
Zebley, Elwood, Texas.	10	20	4	5	8	1	1	0	5	0	0	3	0	1	0	0	.250

The following pitchers had no plate appearances primarily through use of designated hitters, listed alphabetically by club, games in parentheses:

ATLANTA—Driestadt, Joe (11); Haley, Bill (9); Hibbett, Wendell (6); Kerdolff, Russell (7); Mouse, Francis (17—1 with Houston); Nice, William (11—2 with Pittsburgh); Rabun, Kenneth (10); Rymer, Carlos (8); Sellers, Willie (14); Valdez, Juan (10).

CHICAGO-NL—Cole, Joey (10); Crout, James (14); Gorman, Eric (16); Kyles, Stanley (8); Miglio, John (13); Scheiwe, Mark (13); Trapani, William (14); Watson, David (10); Weissmann, Craig (12).

HOUSTON—Bonine, Eddie (20); Brown, Lawrence (21); Bryan, Sam (1); De Paula, Elvido (1); Finch, Michael (5); Graham, Barry (6); Hernandez, Manuel (9); Lohuis, Mark (4); McIntosh, Joseph (4); Paris, Sacarias (10); Penate, Adalio (10); Perry, W. Patrick (9); Petersen, Gregory (3); Quealey, Steven (1); Ray, William (8); Regalado, Uvaldo (4); Rice, Andrew (1); Ross, Mark (2); Ruiz, Quico (10); Smith, Kenneth Blaine (1); Welenc, Douglas (9); Yan, Roberto (9).

KANSAS CITY-BLUES—Begue, Rodger (3); Canfield, James (14); Hasbach, David (1); Lackey, James (14); Laughton, James (11); Olsen, Lewis (16); Porter, Cleveland (12); Sanford, Edmund (12); Smith, Ronald (19); Timlin, Timothy (12); Woodworth, Brian (10); Vila, Antonio (15).

KANSAS CITY-GOLDS—Albright, David (12); Biedenkapp, Michael (11); Bolden, Philen (11); Hammaker, C. Atlee (1); Fischer, Daniel (1); Krauss, Ronald (11); Pour, Kenneth (10); Ryan, Frank (3); St. Clair, Daniel (19); Skinner, John (3); Twitty, Jeffrey (4); Vanderbush, Walter (6); Vercoe, John (6); Voyles, Curtis (15); Yuhas, Vincent (12).

PITTSBURGH—Bielecki, Michael (9); Camacho, Carlos (6); Clarke, Rick (4); Crispin, Ludgerio (4); Green, Christopher (9); DeLeon, Jose (11); Felt, William (2); Fiepke, Scott (8); Florey, Timothy (3); Guerra, Fernando (3); Huey, John (2); Jacobs, Daniel (1); Johnson, Michael (9); Kirby, Dennis (4); Leggatt, Richard (9); Maki, Gordon (2); Notarino, Anthony (1); Peralta, Sergio (15); Ray, Arthur (1); Rivera, Reinaldo (12); Styles, Lawrence (4); Williams, Donald (6).

TEXAS—Eason, W. Gregory (7); Fontenot, S. Ray (8); Fossas, E. Anthony (10); Gammage, Mark (3); Gilliam, Melvin (14); Hager, Timothy (8); Pettibone, Harry (13); Ricossa, Gordon (17); Roberts, Michael (24); Schmidt, David (7); Smith, D. Clay (16); Vasquez, Jerry (7).

GRAND SLAM HOME RUN—Sosa.

AWARDED FIRST BASE ON INTERFERENCE—Cooper (A. Rodriguez); Knoll (Garray); Mennemeier (Nunez); Schaefer (Garray).

CLUB FIELDING

Club	G.	PO.	A.	E.	DP.	PB.	Pct.	Club	G.	PO.	A.	E.	DP.	PB.	Pct.
Houston	52	1373	654	86	58	16	.959	Pittsburgh	52	1320	560	101	48	15	.949
Atlanta	54	1382	691	100	42	14	.954	Kan. City Blues	53	1306	591	116	51	19	.942
Kan. City Golds	52	1302	541	93	57	12	.952	Chicago NL	51	1346	627	148	56	21	.930
Texas	54	1434	646	105	52	20	.952								

Triple Plays—None.

INDIVIDUAL FIELDING

FIRST BASEMEN

*Throws lefthanded.

Player and Club	G.	PO.	A.	E.	DP.	Pct.	Player and Club	G.	PO.	A.	E.	DP.	Pct.
Donofrio, Texas	4	25	2	0	5	1.000	Strucher, Houston	29	263	24	4	30	.986
Salazar, Pittsburgh	1	11	1	0	1	1.000	Wotus, Pittsburgh	14	108	8	2	8	.983
Schaefer, Texas*	1	11	0	0	0	1.000	Made, Pittsburgh	36	253	10	5	29	.981
Gulaskey, Pittsburgh	1	7	1	0	0	1.000	Mennemeier, KC-Blues	30	244	16	7	26	.974
Johnson, Chicago NL	2	6	1	0	0	1.000	A. Martinez, Chi-NL*	43	307	17	9	31	.973
Childs, Texas	1	1	1	0	0	1.000	Wilson, Atlanta	16	155	12	5	6	.971
M. Rodriguez, Pitt	1	2	0	0	0	1.000	Grahek, KC-Golds*	7	29	3	1	4	.970
A. Rodriguez, Pittsburgh	1	1	0	0	0	1.000	C. Martinez, Chicago-NL	16	111	5	4	12	.967
WILLIAMS, Atlanta	40	376	26	3	33	.993	Wolff, Pittsburgh	4	26	2	1	2	.966
Snider, KC-Golds*	51	408	15	4	47	.991	Jones, Houston	7	62	3	4	11	.942
Atkinson, KC-Blues	23	187	12	2	15	.990	Ford, Pittsburgh	1	10	2	2	1	.857
Benjamin, Houston	20	168	7	2	10	.989	Snaith, Pittsburgh	1	1	0	1	0	.500
O'Brien, Texas*	50	465	44	7	40	.986							

SECOND BASEMEN

Player and Club	G.	PO.	A.	E.	DP.	Pct.	Player and Club	G.	PO.	A.	E.	DP.	Pct.
Black, Atlanta	3	4	9	0	0	1.000	Doran, Houston	44	107	144	11	33	.958
Tjader, Texas	2	4	5	0	0	1.000	Henriquez, Pittsburgh	30	80	77	8	16	.952
Townley, KC-Golds	2	4	4	0	0	1.000	Reedy, Pittsburgh	25	47	68	6	14	.950
A. Espinoza, Houston	3	5	3	0	2	1.000	Arroyo, KC-Golds	46	109	102	13	29	.942
Infante, KC-Blues	2	3	2	0	0	1.000	Wilson, Chicago-NL	36	104	75	11	19	.942
Baker, Texas	15	39	48	1	6	.989	Belmonte, Chicago-NL	25	67	55	8	22	.938
Luethy, KC-Golds	9	25	21	1	8	.979	Jansen, KC-Blues	13	26	19	3	9	.938
Goodman, Texas	17	48	45	3	13	.969	J. Ray, Houston	7	18	22	3	6	.930
Pocoroba, Atlanta	13	34	49	3	9	.965	Beaudoin, Texas	20	56	63	10	17	.922
AYALA, Atlanta	38	95	133	9	26	.962	Reasonover, Texas	1	1	2	2	0	.600
Patterson, KC-Blues	42	105	109	9	26	.960							

THIRD BASEMEN

Player and Club	G.	PO.	A.	E.	DP.	Pct.	Player and Club	G.	PO.	A.	E.	DP.	Pct.
A. Rodriguez, Pittsburgh	1	1	3	0	0	1.000	Atkinson, KC-Blues	21	23	40	9	5	.875
Salazar, Pittsburgh	2	1	3	0	1	1.000	Childs, Texas	7	3	11	2	3	.875
Gulaskey, Pittsburgh	1	3	0	0	0	1.000	Infante, KC-Blues	27	31	60	14	9	.867
Wotus, Pittsburgh	1	1	2	0	0	1.000	Wheeler, Pittsburgh	19	11	27	6	1	.864
A. Espinoza, Houston	2	0	3	0	0	1.000	Allen, Chicago-NL	27	24	71	16	7	.856
Goodman, Texas	1	2	0	0	1	1.000	Reasonover, Texas	19	10	31	7	7	.854
Neal, Atlanta	1	0	1	0	0	1.000	Tanzi, Texas	10	5	17	4	1	.846
DIKOS, Atlanta	52	57	144	13	8	.939	J. Ray, Houston	12	7	29	8	3	.818
Townley, KC-Golds	14	8	34	3	2	.933	Biafore, Chicago-NL	5	3	6	2	3	.818
Snaith, Pittsburgh	24	22	59	6	8	.931	Jansen, KC-Blues	8	5	8	3	0	.813
Baker, Texas	20	13	47	5	3	.923	Martinez, Pittsburgh	8	4	7	4	3	.733
De Aza, Houston	38	27	87	10	12	.919	Tjader, Texas	3	2	10	6	0	.667
Cooper, KC-Golds	39	44	92	15	10	.901	Beaudoin, Texas	2	2	0	1	0	.667
Knoll, Chicago-NL	6	1	8	1	1	.900	Pocoroba, Atlanta	3	2	1	2	0	.600
Stockstill, Chicago-NL	28	15	51	9	1	.880	Wolff, Pittsburgh	1	0	1	1	0	.500

SHORTSTOPS

Player and Club	G.	PO.	A.	E.	DP.	Pct.
Reedy, Pittsburgh	1	1	2	0	0	1.000
Bush, Texas	11	16	31	1	3	.979
A. Espinoza, Houston	6	13	21	1	5	.971
WHERRY, Houston	47	79	167	16	30	.939
Wotus, Pittsburgh	25	39	83	8	9	.938
Wellman, KC-Blues	46	79	159	20	25	.922
Baker, Texas	7	11	23	3	4	.919
Luethy, KC-Golds	42	74	126	18	27	.917
Bastien, Texas	39	75	135	20	22	.913
Biafore, Chicago-NL	35	66	144	21	23	.909

Player and Club	G.	PO.	A.	E.	DP.	Pct.
Jansen, KC-Blues	10	15	29	5	5	.898
Snaith, Pittsburgh	13	25	25	6	7	.893
Sosa, Atlanta	42	52	128	22	18	.891
Martinez, Pittsburgh	16	32	44	10	10	.884
Pocoroba, Atlanta	18	29	44	10	6	.880
Irvin, KC-Golds	15	10	31	6	7	.872
Owen, Chicago-NL	10	17	26	7	3	.860
Allen, Chicago-NL	4	9	14	4	3	.852
Belmonte, Chicago-NL	13	16	34	9	2	.847

OUTFIELDERS

Player and Club	G.	PO.	A.	E.	DP.	Pct.
Butler, Atlanta*	30	66	5	0	0	1.000
Reynolds, Texas	15	35	0	0	0	1.000
Knoll, Chicago-NL	17	24	1	0	0	1.000
Neal, Atlanta	6	14	0	0	0	1.000
Jones, Houston	10	14	0	0	0	1.000
Johnson, Chicago-NL	11	12	1	0	0	1.000
Robinson, Texas	6	5	0	0	0	1.000
Lucious, KC-Blues	3	3	1	0	0	1.000
McMath, Texas	3	3	1	0	0	1.000
Veith, Chicago-NL*	4	3	0	0	1	1.000
Scott, Texas	2	3	0	0	0	1.000
Jansen, KC-Blues	1	1	1	0	1	1.000
Biafore, Chicago-NL	1	1	0	0	0	1.000
Owens, Texas	1	1	0	0	0	1.000
Mork, Chicago-NL*	35	59	5	1	3	.985
Doak, KC-Golds	24	53	2	1	1	.982
JABALERA, Houston*..	48	99	6	2	2	.981
Arias, Pittsburgh	20	48	4	1	1	.981
Stafford, Texas	27	33	3	1	1	.973
Palmer, KC-Golds	44	116	3	4	1	.967
Wynne, KC-Blues*	46	108	9	4	1	.967
Ball, Texas	43	85	2	3	2	.967
Barnette, KC-Golds	20	28	1	1	0	.967
Austin, Chicago-NL	27	56	1	2	0	.966
Thomas, Houston	40	54	2	2	1	.966
McGehee, Pittsburgh*	44	107	0	4	0	.964
Luzon, Atlanta	53	121	10	5	1	.963

Player and Club	G.	PO.	A.	E.	DP.	Pct.
Vranesh, KC-Blues	39	69	6	3	1	.962
Schaefer, Texas*	38	69	0	3	0	.958
Felt, Pittsburgh	48	79	9	4	2	.957
Pederson, KC-Blues	22	45	0	2	0	.957
Lockett, Chicago-NL*	45	98	2	5	1	.952
De Sena, Houston	48	93	2	5	1	.950
Quezada, Atlanta	39	50	5	3	1	.948
Rodriguez, KC-Blues	34	62	10	4	1	.947
Jacoby, Atlanta	36	65	7	4	1	.947
C. Martinez, Chi-NL	23	28	4	2	0	.941
Brewer, KC-Blues*	46	72	5	5	2	.939
Townley, KC-Golds	30	57	2	4	2	.937
Gainey, Houston	11	13	1	1	0	.933
Cabellero, Pittsburgh	25	51	2	4	1	.930
Wilson, Atlanta	7	12	0	1	0	.923
M. Rodriguez, Pitt	21	33	2	3	1	.921
Rosa, KC-Blues*	29	43	3	4	0	.920
Smith, Chicago-NL	28	32	2	4	0	.895
Beaudoin, Texas	6	16	1	2	0	.895
Ashley, Houston	9	7	0	1	0	.875
Silverio, KC-Blues	5	13	0	2	0	.867
Childs, Texas	13	13	0	2	0	.867
Dixon, Pittsburgh	4	5	1	1	0	.857
Showell, Texas*	16	15	0	3	0	.833
Velasquez, Texas	3	3	0	1	0	.750
Romey, Texas	12	4	0	2	0	.667
Araujo, Chicago-NL*	1	0	0	1	0	.000

CATCHERS

Player and Club	G.	PO.	A.	E.	DP.	PB.	Pct.
Brito, Pittsburgh	4	20	6	0	1	1	1.000
Donofrio, Texas	20	101	14	1	5	10	.991
SCOTT, Texas	30	187	19	4	0	10	.981
Primante, Houston	36	219	10	5	3	9	.979
Williams, Houston	13	60	19	2	2	4	.975
A. Rodriguez, Pitt	34	158	24	5	4	11	.973
Whistler, Atlanta	27	86	18	3	0	5	.972
Jackson, KC-Blues	27	88	10	3	1	8	.970
Dewey, KC-Blues	22	83	13	3	2	3	.970
Triplett, Chicago-NL..	26	134	11	5	3	14	.967
Bazan, Chicago-NL	28	127	30	6	3	5	.963

Player and Club	G.	PO.	A.	E.	DP.	PB.	Pct.
Garray, KC-Golds	41	183	33	9	1	11	.960
Nunez, Atlanta	24	82	13	4	1	4	.960
Neufang, Texas	8	42	6	2	1	1	.960
Purdy, KC-Blues	19	59	10	3	1	8	.958
Guerrero, Atlanta	14	41	5	2	0	5	.958
Batter, KC-Golds	2	19	2	1	0	0	.955
Ford, Pittsburgh	17	81	12	5	1	3	.949
Porter, KC-Golds	16	52	3	3	1	1	.948
E. Espinoza, Hou	8	36	5	3	0	3	.932
Zebley, Texas	4	7	0	1	0	0	.875
Johnson, Chicago-NL.	11	18	3	5	0	2	.808

PITCHERS

Player and Club	G.	PO.	A.	E.	DP.	Pct.
BIELECKI, Pitt	9	16	13	0	0	1.000
Haley, Atlanta	9	7	10	0	0	1.000
Ricossa, Texas*	17	5	12	0	3	1.000
Fossas, Texas*	10	1	15	0	1	1.000
Brown, Houston	21	4	12	0	2	1.000
Williams, KC-Golds	10	5	10	0	1	1.000
Johnson, Pittsburgh	9	6	8	0	2	1.000
Perry, Houston*	9	5	9	0	1	1.000
Scheiwe, Chicago-NL	13	5	8	0	4	1.000
Welenc, Houston	9	4	8	0	2	1.000
Gilliam, Texas*	14	4	8	0	0	1.000
Mouse, 1 Hou-16 Atl	17	0	12	0	2	1.000
St. Clair, KC-Golds	19	0	11	0	1	1.000
Eason, Texas*	7	1	8	0	0	1.000
Kerdolff, Atlanta	7	2	7	0	0	1.000
Fiepke, Pittsburgh*	8	2	7	0	1	1.000

Player and Club	G.	PO.	A.	E.	DP.	Pct.
Schmidt, Texas	7	2	6	0	0	1.000
Rabun, Atlanta	10	1	6	0	1	1.000
Valdez, Atlanta*	10	1	6	0	0	1.000
Vanderbush, KC-Golds..	6	1	5	0	1	1.000
Green, Pittsburgh*	9	0	6	0	0	1.000
Weissmann, Chi-NL	12	4	2	0	0	1.000
McIntosh, Houston	4	0	5	0	1	1.000
Leggatt, Pittsburgh	9	2	3	0	0	1.000
Quealey, Houston	1	0	4	0	0	1.000
Biedenkapp, KC-Golds*	11	0	4	0	0	1.000
Felt, Pittsburgh	2	1	2	0	0	1.000
Maki, Pittsburgh	2	1	2	0	0	1.000
Clarke, Pittsburgh*	4	0	3	0	0	1.000
Bolden, KC-Golds	11	0	3	0	0	1.000
Albright, KC-Golds*	12	1	2	0	0	1.000
Smith, Texas	16	1	2	0	0	1.000

PITCHERS—Continued

Player and Club	G.	PO.	A.	E.	DP.	Pct.	Player and Club	G.	PO.	A.	E.	DP.	Pct.
Guerra, Pittsburgh*	3	0	2	0	0	1.000	Yan, Houston	9	3	5	1	0	.889
Petersen, Houston	3	0	2	0	0	1.000	DeLeon, Pittsburgh	11	3	5	1	0	.889
Ryan, KC-Golds	3	1	1	0	0	1.000	Boozer, Atlanta*	7	1	6	1	1	.875
Skinner, KC-Golds	3	0	2	0	0	1.000	Smith, KC-Blues	19	3	10	2	1	.867
W. Ray, Houston	8	0	2	0	0	1.000	Ruiz, Houston	12	3	3	1	0	.857
Hernandez, Houston	9	0	2	0	1	1.000	Canfield, KC-Blues*	14	2	4	1	0	.857
Driestadt, Atlanta	11	0	2	0	0	1.000	Matos, Atlanta	17	5	1	1	0	.857
Notarino, Pitt	1	0	1	0	0	1.000	Sanford, KC-Blues	12	1	10	2	1	.846
Ray, Pittsburgh	1	0	1	0	0	1.000	Trapani, Chicago-NL*	14	1	14	3	0	.833
Rice, Houston*	1	1	0	0	0	1.000	Styles, Pittsburgh	4	0	5	1	0	.833
Bonine, Houston	2	1	0	0	0	1.000	Krauss, KC-Golds*	11	0	5	1	0	.833
Huey, Pittsburgh	2	0	1	0	0	1.000	Lackey, KC-Blues*	14	1	4	1	0	.833
Gammage, Texas	3	0	1	0	0	1.000	Woodworth, KC-Blues	10	4	5	2	0	.818
Regalado, Houston	4	0	1	0	1	1.000	Begue, KC-Blues	3	1	3	1	0	.800
Lohuis, Houston	4	0	1	0	0	1.000	Kyles, Chicago-NL	7	0	4	1	0	.800
Camacho, Pittsburgh	6	0	1	0	0	1.000	Crout, Chicago-NL*	14	0	4	1	0	.800
Vercoe, KC-Golds*	6	1	0	0	0	1.000	Vila, KC-Blues	15	1	3	1	0	.800
Hager, Texas	8	0	1	0	0	1.000	Olsen, KC-Blues	16	1	3	1	0	.800
Cole, Chicago-NL	10	0	1	0	0	1.000	Gil, Chicago-NL	11	2	12	4	0	.778
Paris, Houston	10	5	12	1	1	.944	Hibbett, Atlanta*	6	3	6	3	1	.750
Timlin, KC-Blues	12	2	13	1	0	.938	Kirby, Pittsburgh	4	2	1	1	0	.750
Porter, KC-Blues	12	0	14	1	1	.933	Miglio, Chicago-NL*	13	0	5	2	0	.714
Yuhas, KC-Golds	12	2	11	1	1	.929	Laughton, KC-Blues	11	3	4	3	0	.700
Sellers, Atlanta	10	14	10	2	2	.923	Fontenot, Texas*	8	1	3	2	0	.667
Penate, Houston	10	5	7	1	0	.923	Williams, Pittsburgh*	6	0	2	1	0	.667
Nice, 2 Pitt-9 Atl*	11	2	8	1	1	.909	Pour, KC-Golds	10	1	1	1	0	.667
Pettibone, Texas	13	3	7	1	1	.909	Watson, Chicago-NL*	10	1	1	1	0	.667
Gorman, Chicago-NL*	14	2	8	1	1	.909	Rivera, Pittsburgh	12	0	3	3	1	.500
Vasquez, Texas	7	2	7	1	1	.900	Orzel, Texas*	9	0	2	2	0	.500
Rymer, Atlanta	8	2	7	1	1	.900	Ferguson, Atlanta*	6	0	1	1	0	.500
Peralta, Pittsburgh	15	2	7	1	1	.900	Graham, Houston*	6	0	1	1	0	.500
Voyles, KC-Golds	15	2	7	1	1	.900	Swaggerty, Chi-NL	12	0	2	3	0	.400
Roberts, Texas	24	3	14	2	1	.895	Smith, Houston	1	0	0	1	0	.000

The following players had no recorded accepted chances at the positions indicated; therefore, are not listed in the fielding averages for those particular positions: Bryan, p; Crispin, p; DePaula, p; Finch*, p; Fischer, p; Florey, p; Hammaker*, p; Hasbach, p; Jacobs, p; Robles, of; Ross, p; Twitty*, p. Burgin appeared as pinch-hitter and/or designated-hitter only.

CLUB PITCHING

Club	G.	CG.	ShO.	Sv.	IP.	H.	R.	ER.	HR.	BB.	Int. BB.	HB.	SO.	WP.	Bk.	ERA.
Houston	52	8	7	9	458	409	205	151	10	219	2	12	293	22	9	2.97
Kansas City Golds	52	6	8	11	434	255	189	13	229	7	20	226	33	6	3.92
Texas	54	3	4	17	478	472	271	209	12	245	1	13	338	38	6	3.94
Atlanta	54	7	3	11	461	474	280	215	9	286	9	8	185	30	11	4.20
Pittsburgh	52	6	4	6	440	419	288	208	21	293	4	21	238	29	5	4.25
Kansas City Blues	53	5	1	8	435	506	303	220	15	230	7	14	207	22	5	4.55
Chicago-NL	51	5	0	7	449	491	367	256	15	328	30	19	246	43	10	5.13

PITCHERS' RECORDS
(Leading Qualifiers for Earned-Run Average Leadership—43 or More Innings)
*Throws lefthanded.

Pitcher—Club	G.	GS.	CG.	ShO.	W.	L.	Sv.	Pct.	IP.	H.	R.	ER.	HR.	BB.	Int. BB.	HB.	SO.	WP.	ERA.
Roberts, Texas	24	0	0	0	5	1	11	.833	51	33	5	4	0	15	1	1	39	1	0.71
Trapani, Chicago-NL*	14	2	0	0	3	1	3	.750	49	38	20	10	1	23	1	3	29	1	1.84
Welenc, Houston	9	8	2	0	7	1	0	.875	58	45	16	12	0	25	0	1	51	2	1.86
Williams, KC-Golds	10	8	1	1	5	2	0	.714	58	41	16	14	2	24	1	1	33	0	2.17
Penate, Houston	10	10	2	1	5	2	0	.714	60	49	18	15	0	27	0	0	25	1	2.25
Bielecki, Pittsburgh	9	9	1	0	1	4	0	.200	51	48	21	13	1	21	0	0	35	1	2.29
Paris, Houston	10	10	2	2	6	2	0	.750	65	51	27	19	1	24	0	3	38	1	2.63
Yuhas, KC-Golds	12	7	1	1	5	1	1	.833	53	45	24	17	1	26	0	0	33	2	2.89
Fossas, Texas*	10	9	1	0	6	3	0	.667	60	54	28	20	2	26	0	3	49	2	3.00
Ricossa, Texas*	17	2	0	0	3	2	1	.600	53	55	22	20	0	21	0	1	30	2	3.40

Departmental Leaders: G—Roberts, 24; GS—Sanford, 12; CG—Hibbett, 3; ShO—Paris, 2; W—Welenc, 7; L—Gorman, Swaggerty, 6; Sv—Roberts, 11; Pct.—Vila, 1.000; IP—Sanford, 70; H—Sanford, 90; R—Pour, 58; ER—Pour, 45; HR—DeLeon, 7; BB—Gilliam, 51; IBB—Gorman, 6; HB—Weissmann, 8; SO—Welenc, 51; WP—DeLeon, Pour, D. C. Smith, 9.

(All Pitchers—Listed Alphabetically)

Pitcher–Club	G.	GS.	CG.	ShO.	W.	L.	Sv.	Pct.	IP.	H.	R.	ER.	HR.	BB.	Int. BB.	HB.	SO.	WP.	ERA.
Albright, KC-Golds*	12	0	0	0	1	1	1	.500	22	26	17	13	3	13	0	0	8	5	5.32
Begue, KC-Blues	3	3	0	0	0	1	0	.000	17	23	15	7	0	3	0	0	10	0	3.71
Biedenkapp, KC-Golds*	11	2	0	0	1	1	1	.500	33	38	23	16	0	15	1	1	13	2	4.36
Bielecki, Pittsburgh	9	9	1	0	1	4	0	.200	51	48	21	13	1	21	0	0	35	1	2.29
Bolden, KC-Golds	11	2	0	0	0	0	0	.000	23	29	20	16	2	19	1	1	8	3	6.26
Bonine, Houston	2	0	0	0	0	0	0	.000	4	5	4	3	1	1	0	1	1	0	6.75
Boozer, Atlanta*	7	0	0	0	2	1	0	.667	17	19	11	8	0	10	0	0	8	1	4.24
Brown, Houston	21	0	0	0	3	3	8	.500	42	38	16	11	0	14	0	3	39	1	2.36
Bryan, Houston	1	0	0	0	0	1	0	.000	⅓	0	0	0	0	0	0	0	0	0	.000
Camacho, Pittsburgh	6	1	0	0	0	0	0	.000	10	13	15	10	3	14	0	1	1	4	9.00
Canfield, KC-Blues*	14	4	0	0	0	4	1	.000	33	49	25	14	1	10	2	0	12	0	3.82
Clarke, Pittsburgh*	4	1	0	0	0	0	0	.000	12	13	9	7	1	6	0	1	4	0	5.25
Cole, Chicago-NL	10	0	0	0	0	1	0	.000	12	12	18	10	1	20	1	0	6	1	7.50
Crispin, Pittsburgh	4	0	0	0	0	0	0	.000	8	4	2	2	0	7	0	2	2	0	2.25
Crout, Chicago-NL*	14	1	1	0	4	2	1	.667	37	46	29	18	3	27	5	1	14	3	4.38
DeLeon, Pittsburgh	11	9	2	0	2	4	1	.333	59	76	47	42	7	38	1	1	33	9	6.41
DePaula, Houston	1	0	0	0	0	0	0	.000	½	2	4	4	0	2	0	0	1	0	108.00
Driestadt, Atlanta*	11	0	0	0	0	1	0	.000	19	20	13	13	0	18	1	2	5	1	6.16
Eason, Texas*	7	7	0	0	3	1	0	.750	32	37	24	17	0	22	0	1	14	0	4.78
W. Felt, Pittsburgh	2	2	0	0	0	0	0	.000	7	8	7	4	0	6	0	0	4	0	5.14
Ferguson, Atlanta*	6	4	0	0	0	1	0	.000	16	24	15	9	0	13	0	0*	8	0	5.06
Fiepke, Pittsburgh*	8	8	1	0	2	5	0	.286	42	27	20	16	0	34	0	2	31	1	3.43
Finch, Houston*	5	0	0	0	1	0	0	1.000	7	9	10	4	0	9	0	0	7	1	5.14
Fischer, KC-Golds	1	1	0	0	1	0	0	1.000	6	4	1	0	0	0	0	0	4	0	0.00
Florey, Pittsburgh	3	0	0	0	0	0	0	.000	6	6	3	1	0	5	0	0	4	1	1.50
Fontenot, Texas*	8	5	0	0	3	1	0	.750	31	28	20	14	1	12	0	0	42	5	4.06
Fossas, Texas*	10	9	1	0	6	3	0	.667	60	54	28	20	2	26	0	3	49	2	3.00
Gammage, Texas	3	2	0	0	0	1	0	.000	8	8	5	3	0	7	0	1	6	2	3.38
Gil, Chicago-NL	11	9	1	0	2	2	0	.500	58	66	41	24	2	25	3	2	47	5	3.72
Gilliam, Texas*	14	11	0	0	2	3	0	.400	64	56	40	38	4	51	0	1	49	4	5.34
Gorman, Chicago-NL*	14	7	0	0	6	1	0	.000	49	46	41	34	1	46	6	2	25	8	6.24
Graham, Houston*	6	0	0	0	1	0	0	.000	10	10	12	11	1	7	0	0	9	0	9.90
Green, Pittsburgh*	9	7	0	0	1	2	0	.333	32	28	28	22	2	40	0	1	31	3	6.19
Guerra, Pittsburgh	3	1	0	0	0	1	0	.000	4	11	15	15	1	9	0	0	2	0	33.75
Hager, Texas	8	1	0	0	1	2	0	.000	15	24	26	23	2	21	0	3	12	4	13.80
Haley, Atlanta	9	8	1	0	4	2	0	.667	54	59	33	22	4	21	1	0	18	3	3.67
Hammaker, KC-Golds*	1	1	0	0	1	0	0	1.000	5	3	1	1	1	1	0	0	6	0	1.80
Hasbach, KC-Blues	1	0	0	0	0	1	0	.000	3	2	3	2	0	3	0	0	2	2	6.00
Hernandez, Houston	9	0	0	0	2	0	0	1.000	14	17	6	4	0	10	0	0	10	3	2.57
Hibbett, Atlanta*	6	6	3	0	2	3	0	.400	40	44	21	16	1	16	1	1	24	1	3.60
Huey, Pittsburgh	2	1	0	0	0	1	0	1.000	5	1	0	0	0	3	0	1	6	2	0.00
Jacobs, Pittsburgh	1	0	0	0	0	1	0	1.000	4	1	0	0	0	5	0	0	2	0	0.00
Johnson, Pittsburgh	9	7	1	0	2	2	0	.500	53	45	26	24	2	28	0	4	23	3	4.08
Kerdolff, Atlanta	7	4	1	0	3	1	1	.750	32	34	15	9	1	5	0	1	22	2	2.53
Kirby, Pittsburgh	4	0	0	0	2	0	1	1.000	14	14	9	6	2	4	0	2	9	0	3.86
Krauss, KC-Golds*	11	10	0	0	6	3	0	.667	54	68	33	22	1	17	0	4	24	4	3.67
Kyles, Chicago-NL	7	3	0	0	1	4	0	.200	16	23	18	15	0	21	1	0	10	5	8.44
Lackey, KC-Blues*	14	1	0	0	0	1	1	.000	18	16	26	22	2	31	0	2	8	3	11.00
Laughton, KC-Blues	11	6	0	0	4	0	0	.000	42	49	39	27	3	29	0	4	18	2	5.79
Leggatt, Pittsburgh	9	0	0	0	3	3	0	.500	32	25	21	8	0	13	0	0	9	0	2.25
Lohuis, Houston	4	0	0	0	0	0	0	.000	6	7	2	2	0	3	0	0	1	0	3.00
Maki, Pittsburgh	2	0	0	0	1	1	0	.500	7	5	3	0	0	0	0	0	1	0	6.75
Matos, Atlanta	17	1	0	0	1	2	5	.333	39	33	18	10	0	21	1	0	17	1	2.31
McIntosh, Houston	4	1	0	0	0	0	0	.000	9	10	3	3	1	2	0	0	6	0	3.00
Miglio, Chicago-NL*	13	3	0	0	1	3	0	.250	41	34	30	24	1	34	1	0	21	4	5.27
Mouse, 1 Hou-16 Atl	17	0	0	0	3	3	1	.500	32	34	19	17	1	31	3	1	5	2	4.78
Nice, 2 Pitt-9 Atl*	11	7	0	0	2	3	1	.400	44	46	37	29	0	40	0	0	17	3	5.93
Notarino, Pittsburgh	1	1	0	0	0	0	0	.000	4	2	0	0	0	0	0	0	1	0	0.00
Olsen, KC-Blues	16	2	0	0	2	1	0	.667	32	39	14	12	0	9	0	0	11	1	3.38
Orzel, Texas*	9	0	0	0	1	0	0	1.000	20	17	11	8	0	15	0	0	14	5	3.60
Paris, Houston	10	10	2	2	6	2	0	.750	65	51	27	19	1	24	0	3	38	1	2.63
Penate, Houston	10	10	2	1	5	2	0	.714	60	49	18	15	0	27	0	0	25	1	2.25
Peralta, Pittsburgh	15	0	0	0	1	3	1	.250	27	31	11	10	0	8	2	0	10	1	3.33
Perry, Houston*	9	8	1	0	3	1	0	.750	49	55	21	20	1	16	0	0	24	3	3.67
Petersen, Houston	3	0	0	0	1	0	0	1.000	8	7	1	1	0	2	0	0	5	0	1.13
Pettibone, Texas	13	5	0	0	3	1	2	.750	47	57	29	19	1	15	0	1	26	1	3.64
Porter, KC-Blues	12	8	1	0	2	5	0	.286	48	68	45	37	2	25	1	0	28	7	6.94
Pour, KC-Golds	10	9	0	0	0	4	0	.000	39	52	58	45	2	49	0	5	14	9	10.38
Quealey, Houston	1	1	0	0	0	0	0	.000	5	1	0	0	0	1	0	0	7	0	0.00
Rabun, Atlanta	10	1	1	0	4	1	2	.800	32	29	15	12	0	17	0	0	20	5	3.38
Ray, Pittsburgh	1	0	0	0	0	0	0	.000	4	3	1	0	0	2	0	1	0	1	0.00
W. Ray, Houston	8	2	0	0	0	0	0	.000	18	9	5	3	1	20	0	0	16	1	1.50
Regalado, Houston	4	0	0	0	0	0	0	.000	7	3	0	0	0	6	0	0	3	1	0.00

Pitcher–Club	G.	GS.	CG.	ShO.	W.	L.	Sv.	Pct.	IP.	H.	R.	ER.	HR.	BB.	Int. BB.	HB.	SO.	WP.	ERA.
Rice, Houston*	1	0	0	0	0	0	0	.000	4	3	2	2	0	3	0	0	5	1	4.50
Ricossa, Texas*	17	2	0	3	2	1	.600	53	55	22	20	0	21	0	1	30	2	3.40
Rivera, Pittsburgh*	12	0	0	1	4	2	.200	24	29	18	13	2	18	0	2	14	1	4.88
Roberts, Texas	24	0	0	5	1	11	.833	51	33	5	4	0	15	1	1	39	1	0.71
Ross, Houston	2	1	0	1	0	0	1.000	7	5	3	3	0	1	0	1	2	0	3.86
Ruiz, Houston	12	1	0	1	4	0	.200	28	24	17	12	1	23	1	2	15	2	3.86
Ryan, KC-Golds	3	1	1	1	1	0	1.000	8	3	0	0	0	2	0	0	6	0	0.00
Rymer, Atlanta	8	5	0	0	2	2	.500	38	26	14	8	1	29	0	1	10	2	1.89
St. Clair, KC-Golds	19	0	0	0	2	4	5	.333	33	27	9	6	1	9	2	3	19	0	1.64
Sanford, KC-Blues	12	12	1	0	2	5	0	.286	70	90	49	36	0	26	2	3	31	2	4.63
Scheiwe, Chicago-NL	13	9	2	0	4	2	0	.667	59	63	42	33	1	39	3	2	31	2	5.03
Schmidt, Texas	7	6	0	0	2	2	0	.500	30	30	19	14	1	8	0	0	27	4	4.20
Sellers, Atlanta	10	10	0	0	1	4	0	.200	55	59	45	42	1	47	0	2	20	4	6.87
Skinner, KC-Golds	3	3	1	1	1	1	0	.500	15	15	11	6	0	11	0	1	11	3	3.60
Smith, Texas	16	0	0	0	3	3	1	.500	34	35	24	16	1	24	0	1	21	9	4.24
Smith, Houston	1	1	0	0	0	0	0	.000	5	2	2	1	0	2	0	0	6	0	1.80
Smith, KC-Blues	19	0	0	0	4	2	5	.667	32	24	14	7	0	31	1	2	32	2	1.97
Smith, Chicago-NL	1	0	0	0	1	0	0	.000	2	4	2	2	0	1	1	0	0	0	9.00
Styles, Pittsburgh	4	1	0	0	2	0	0	1.000	6	6	10	6	0	12	0	3	3	1	9.00
Swaggerty, Chicago-NL	12	6	0	0	1	6	0	.143	42	69	53	39	1	27	3	1	22	7	8.36
Timlin, KC-Blues	12	7	1	0	3	3	0	.500	50	59	29	23	1	24	0	2	20	0	4.14
Trapani, Chicago-NL*	14	2	0	0	3	1	3	.750	49	38	20	10	1	23	1	3	29	1	1.84
Twitty, KC-Golds*	4	0	0	0	1	0	1	.000	6	8	2	2	0	1	0	0	4	0	3.00
Valdez, Atlanta*	10	8	1	1	3	4	0	.429	49	56	26	21	0	22	2	0	12	2	3.86
Vanderbush, KC-Golds	6	4	2	0	2	2	0	.500	27	23	12	9	0	12	0	1	14	1	3.00
Vasquez, Texas	7	6	2	0	2	2	0	.500	33	38	18	13	0	8	0	0	9	1	3.55
Vercoe, KC-Golds*	6	0	0	0	2	0	0	1.000	10	5	1	1	0	7	0	0	8	1	0.90
Vila, KC-Blues	15	1	0	0	5	0	1	1.000	38	33	14	9	0	15	1	1	12	0	2.13
Voyles, KC-Golds	15	4	0	0	1	3	2	.250	43	52	27	21	0	23	2	3	21	3	4.40
Watson, Chicago-NL*	10	1	0	0	0	1	0	.000	20	34	27	20	2	20	2	0	7	1	9.00
Weissmann, Chicago-NL.	12	10	1	0	3	4	0	.429	64	56	46	27	2	45	3	8	34	6	3.80
Welenc, Houston	9	8	2	0	7	1	0	.875	58	45	16	12	0	25	0	1	51	2	1.86
Williams, Pittsburgh*	6	4	1	0	1	3	0	.250	28	18	18	6	0	17	1	0	12	1	1.93
Williams, KC-Golds	8	1	1	5	2	0	.714	58	41	16	14	2	24	1	1	33	0	2.17
Woodworth, KC-Blues	10	9	2	0	6	2	0	.750	52	54	30	24	6	24	0	0	23	3	4.15
Yan, Houston	9	9	1	0	2	5	0	.286	52	57	36	22	3	20	0	1	22	5	3.81
Yuhas, KC-Golds	12	7	1	1	5	1	.833	53	45	24	17	1	26	0	0	33	2	2.89

BALKS—Trapani, 5; Rymer, Sellers, Yan, 4 each; Green, Pettibone, 3 each; Albright, Gil, Rivera, Voyles, 2 each; Begue, Crout, Ferguson, Gilliam, Graham, Hernandez, Krauss, Kyles, Matos, Nice, Paris, Penate, Porter, Ricossa, Ruiz, D. C. Smith, Swaggerty, Timlin, Vila, Woodworth, Yuhas, 1 each.

COMBINATION SHUTOUTS—Nice-Mouse, Rymer-Nice, Atlanta; Paris-Petersen-Brown, Perry-Brown, Welenc-Brown, W. Ray-Hernandez-Brown, Houston; Woodworth-Olsen-Vila, Kansas City Blues; Wiliams-St. Clair 2, Krauss-Bolden-Vercoe, Krauss-St. Clair, Kansas City Golds; W. Felt-Jacobs-Huey, Fiepke-Nice-Green-Maki, Johnson-Peralta, Fiepke-Rivera, Pittsburgh; Ricossa-Pettibone, Eason-Smith, Gilliam-Smith-Roberts, Gammage-Orzel-Smith-Ricossa, Texas.

NO-HIT GAMES—None.

Argument Costs Daytona Beach Victory

Daytona Beach Manager Carlos Alfonso picked the wrong time to argue a call August 5 at St. Petersburg.

The Daytona club led 1-0 in the top of the sixth under gathering rain clouds. John Mizerock, who had driven across the run with a single, was forced at second on Mark Campbell's ground ball. The Cards' Skeeter Rivas threw late to first, but umpire Brian Cobb called Campbell out, too, ruling that Mizerock had interfered with Rivas' pivot.

The double play ended the inning for the Astros, but Alfonso argued with the ump for several minutes while storm clouds moved closer. And before the Cardinals could complete their turn at bat the rains poured down. The game was called with two out in the bottom half of the inning and the score reverted to what it had been at the end of the last complete inning—0-0.

Pioneer League

SUMMER CLASS A CLASSIFICATION

CHAMPIONSHIP WINNERS IN PREVIOUS YEARS

1939—Twin Falls* .... .581	1952—Pocatello .... .595	1962—Boise§ .... .565
1940—Salt Lake City .... .608	Idaho Falls (2nd)* ...... .573	Billings† .... .706
Ogden (4th)* .... .492	1953—Ogden .... .679	1963—Idaho Falls .... .702
1941—Boise .... .623	Salt Lake C. (4th)* ...... .527	Magic Valley† .... .643
Ogden (2nd)* .... .598	1954—Salt Lake City .... .595	1964—Treasure Valley .... .615
1942—Pocatello† .... .690	Great Falls (4th)* .... .530	1965—Treasure Valley .... .530
Boise .... .683	1955—Boise .... .588	1966—Ogden .... .591
1943-44-45—Did not operate.	Magic Valley (4th)* ...... .489	1967—Ogden .... .621
1946—Twin Falls‡ .... .585	1956—Boise .... .561	1968—Ogden .... .609
Salt Lake City† .... .585	1957—Salt Lake City .... .650	1969—Ogden .... .620
1947—Salt Lake City .... .618	Billings† .... .582	1970—Idaho Falls .... .629
Twin Falls† .... .600	1958—Great Falls .... .582	1971—Great Falls .... .643
1948—Pocatello .... .611	Boise† .... .615	1972—Billings .... .694
Twin Falls (2nd)* .... .595	1959—Boise .... .633	1973—Billings .... .629
1949—Twin Falls .... .624	Billings (2nd)* .... .523	1974—Idaho Falls .... .569
Pocatello (3rd)* .... .595	1960—Boise† .... .686	1975—Great Falls .... .577
1950—Pocatello .... .635	Idaho Falls .... .650	1976—Great Falls .... .577
Billings (3rd)* .... .571	1961—Boise .... .638	1977—Lethbridge .... .629
Great Falls (3rd)* .... .559	Great Falls* .... .571	1978—Billings x .... .735

*Won four-club playoff. †Won split-season playoff. ‡Ended first half in tie with Salt Lake City and won one-game playoff. §Ended first half in tie with Billings and Great Falls and won playoff. xBillings (first place) defeated Idaho Falls (second place) in First Place-Second Place playoff.

STANDING OF CLUBS AT CLOSE OF SEASON, AUGUST 31

NORTHERN DIVISION

Club	Leth.	Cal.	G.F.	M.H.	Hel.	Bil.	But.	I.F.	W.	L.	T.	Pct.	G.B.
Lethbridge (Dodgers)	..	4	5	9	5	2	5	8	38	30	0	.559	......
Calgary (Expos)	6	..	4	5	2	4	5	8	34	36	0	.486	5
Great Falls (Giants)	5	6	..	5	7	3	3	3	32	38	0	.457	7
Medicine Hat (Blue Jays)	1	5	5	..	2	3	7	4	27	42	0	.391	11½

SOUTHERN DIVISION

Club	Leth.	Cal.	G.F.	M.H.	Hel.	Bil.	But.	I.F.	W.	L.	T.	Pct.	G.B.
Helena** (Phillies)	4	8	3	8	..	8	5	7	43	26	0	.623	......
Billings (Reds)	8	6	7	7	2	..	5	8	43	26	0	.623	......
Butte (Brewers)	4	5	7	3	5	4	..	4	32	34	0	.485	9½
Idaho Falls (Angels)	2	2	7	5	3	2	4	..	25	42	0	.373	17

**Helena awarded first place on basis of having won season series from Billings.

Major league affiliations in parentheses.

Playoff—Lethbridge defeated Helena, two games to none.

Regular-Season Attendance—Billings, 59,880; Butte, 28,398; Calgary, 37,552; Great Falls, 54,842; Helena, 23,005; Idaho Falls, 34,905; Lethbridge, 20,656; Medicine Hat, 13,343. Total, 272,581. Playoff, 3,150. No all-star game.

Managers: Billings—Jim Hoff; Butte—Ken Richardson, Tom Gamboa; Calgary—Bob Bailey; Great Falls—Ernie Rodriguez; Helena—Rollie DeArmas; Idaho Falls—Reuben Rodriguez; Lethbridge—Gail Henley; Medicine Hat—Dennis Holmberg.

All-Star Team: 1B—Brock, Lethbridge; 2B—Paula, Medicine Hat; 3B—Perez, Calgary; SS—Manriques, Medicine Hat; OF—Darkis, Helena; Deer, Great Falls; Marin, Calgary; C—Kingsolver, Butte; P—Fiorillo, Billings; Henley, Lethbridge; Rodas, Lethbridge; Manager—Henley, Lethbridge.

(Compiled by William J. Weiss, League Statistician, San Mateo, Calif.)

CLUB BATTING

Club	G.	AB.	R.	OR.	H.	TB.	2B.	3B.	HR.	RBI.	SH.	SF.	BB.	Int. BB.	HP.	SO.	SB.	CS.	LOB.	Pct.
Lethbridge	68	2405	462	348	708	965	106	17	39	387	42	19	335	19	24	439	60	34	569	.294
Helena	69	2464	521	446	723	1014	101	23	48	434	12	14	345	17	24	572	88	38	548	.293
Butte	66	2297	477	430	649	1005	107	30	63	399	11	20	355	16	26	577	158	56	509	.283
Idaho Falls	67	2398	414	480	642	923	99	58	22	333	16	16	276	5	27	596	86	33	528	.268
Great Falls	70	2382	403	435	634	874	85	34	29	319	15	27	291	12	26	492	91	32	534	.266
Calgary	70	2384	383	474	616	931	107	17	58	329	16	15	282	2	33	558	91	35	529	.258
Medicine Hat	69	2377	388	512	611	854	88	28	33	318	13	19	277	8	33	547	42	21	524	.257
Billings	69	2300	360	283	584	770	77	20	23	302	38	19	315	10	28	548	97	25	522	.254

INDIVIDUAL BATTING
(Leading Qualifiers for Batting Championship—189 or More Plate Appearances)

*Bats lefthanded. †Switch-hitter.

Player and Club	G.	AB.	R.	H.	TB.	2B.	3B.	HR.	RBI.	SH.	SF.	BB.	HP.	SO.	SB.	CS.	Pct.
Bruno, Joseph, Helena*	68	291	78	112	138	12	4	2	48	3	2	48	0	18	32	7	.385
Wojcik, James, Great Falls*	60	212	48	78	99	8	5	1	35	2	3	45	0	31	12	5	.368
Hamric, Russell, Helena	59	243	51	87	104	9	4	0	40	1	3	30	1	25	13	9	.358
Brock, Gregory, Lethbridge*	66	247	61	88	158	18	2	16	77	0	4	54	0	26	7	3	.356
Schroeder, A. William, Butte	65	242	73	86	170	16	7	18	77	0	4	48	4	84	18	3	.355
Pellack, James, Calgary*	51	163	31	55	88	7	1	8	34	0	1	35	3	31	6	2	.337
Cruz, J. Luis, Calgary*	56	215	44	72	97	15	5	0	32	2	2	21	1	41	19	1	.335
Johnson, Rodney, Billings	63	214	49	70	85	10	1	1	37	1	3	42	2	35	27	10	.327
Su'a, Murphy, Lethbridge	62	275	56	88	117	13	2	4	53	4	2	12	2	35	3	3	.320
Pettis, Gary, Idaho Falls	50	198	39	63	102	10	10	3	26	1	0	17	4	53	15	5	.318
Guzman, Ruben, Billings	55	170	34	54	79	13	3	2	28	0	1	20	4	40	8	4	.318

Departmental Leaders: G—Perez, 70; AB—Bruno, 291; R—Bruno, 78; H—Bruno, 112; TB—Schroeder, 170; 2B—Maldonado, 20; 3B—Manriques, Pettis, 10; HR—Darkis, 20; RBI—Darkis, 83; SH—Silicani, Smith, 6; SF—Waugh, 5; BB—Brock, 54; HP—Acevedo, G. Johnson, J. Jones, 8; SO—Darkis, 109; SB—Perodin, 38; CS—Kingsolver, 10.

(All Players—Listed Alphabetically)

Player and Club	G.	AB.	R.	H.	TB.	2B.	3B.	HR.	RBI.	SH.	SF.	BB.	HP.	SO.	SB.	CS.	Pct.
Acevedo, Julio, Idaho Falls	50	163	32	41	59	7	4	1	17	2	1	23	8	40	3	4	.252
Aldridge, Eli, Idaho Falls*	50	167	34	52	62	4	3	0	12	2	2	19	2	45	14	4	.311
Alonzo, Raynomd, Butte*	45	163	43	50	66	10	3	0	18	0	1	29	2	26	37	4	.312
Anderson, Tracy, Helena	16	3	0	0	0	0	0	0	0	0	0	0	0	2	0	0	.000
Ayers, Jeffrey, Billings	4	13	1	2	4	0	1	0	1	0	0	0	0	5	0	0	.154
Barnett, David, Calgary†	26	57	10	13	17	4	0	0	9	1	2	8	0	15	0	2	.228
Beals, Scott, Billings	15	1	0	1	1	0	0	0	0	0	0	0	0	0	0	0	1.000
Biggus, Bengie, Butte	43	127	19	34	42	5	0	1	22	1	2	14	0	34	6	0	.268
Boddy, William, Billings	53	173	24	36	55	5	4	2	17	3	1	14	4	30	1	0	.208
Bolla, Anthony, Great Falls	24	18	1	1	1	0	0	0	0	0	0	4	0	9	0	1	.056
Box, Newton, Billings*	63	213	48	50	73	7	2	4	24	3	2	45	3	79	15	6	.235
Bradley, Otis, Lethbridge	56	161	21	41	58	10	2	1	23	2	1	15	1	24	2	1	.255
Breeden, Joseph, Calgary	26	39	5	10	16	0	0	2	5	0	0	4	0	10	0	0	.256
Brock, Gregory, Lethbridge*	66	247	61	88	158	18	2	16	77	0	4	54	0	26	7	3	.356
Brown, J. Christopher, Great Falls	47	171	24	46	72	5	3	5	30	0	3	10	1	47	3	0	.269
Bruno, Joseph, Helena*	68	291	78	112	138	12	4	2	48	3	2	48	0	18	32	7	.385
Buchanan, Robert, Billings*	17	39	3	8	8	0	0	0	2	0	0	0	1	8	1	0	.205
Buckley, Brian, Idaho Falls	13	4	0	0	0	0	0	0	0	0	0	0	0	2	0	0	.000
Bunn, Dale, Idaho Falls	24	34	2	3	3	0	0	0	1	1	0	3	0	19	2	0	.088
Burdi, Frank, Great Falls	57	209	31	62	80	6	3	2	32	2	4	15	4	24	0	0	.297
Castillo, Juan, Medicine Hat	34	77	13	15	23	2	0	2	6	0	0	14	2	44	4	1	.195
Cato, J. Keefe, Billings	12	14	0	1	1	0	0	0	2	1	0	3	0	7	0	0	.071
Celidonia, James, Idaho Falls*	52	167	27	41	60	12	2	1	29	0	0	20	0	41	3	1	.246
Chue, Jose, Great Falls	4	0	0	0	0	0	0	0	0	0	0	1	0	0	0	0	.000
Cleland, Russell, Great Falls	3	3	0	0	0	0	0	0	0	0	0	0	0	1	0	0	.000
Clevenger, Gary, Idaho Falls	22	30	3	5	5	0	0	0	3	0	0	0	0	16	2	0	.167
Cohron, Tracy, Calgary*	43	155	23	36	67	2	1	9	24	0	1	12	1	45	1	0	.232
Coker, Jeffrey, Calgary	67	227	30	52	79	12	0	5	35	0	3	40	1	51	6	3	.229
Collins, Timothy, Idaho Falls*	65	231	51	73	105	17	6	1	44	1	4	39	4	47	8	4	.316
Columna, Rolando, Medicine Hat*	32	76	17	15	21	4	1	0	7	0	0	16	1	19	2	2	.197
Concepcion, Jose, Medicine Hat	28	64	8	16	19	3	0	0	3	0	0	6	0	13	0	0	.250
Cruz, J. Luis, Calgary*	56	215	44	72	97	15	5	0	32	2	2	21	1	41	19	1	.335
Cuevas, Miguel, Helena	1	0	0	0	0	0	0	0	0	1	2	1	2	0	0	0	.000
Daniels, Stephen, Billings	22	7	2	0	0	0	0	0	0	1	0	0	0	6	0	0	.000
Darkis, William, Helena	69	272	55	73	153	10	5	20	83	0	1	40	6	109	1	2	.268
Deer, Robert, Great Falls	63	218	49	69	122	18	7	7	44	1	3	39	3	62	4	3	.317
DeJesus, Jorge, Butte*	28	36	3	10	11	1	0	0	8	0	0	4	1	11	0	0	.278
Dillard, Cordie, Great Falls†	33	95	17	28	39	4	2	1	11	1	2	13	1	19	0	0	.295
Dowless, Michael, Billings	14	19	5	3	4	1	0	0	1	2	1	3	0	9	0	0	.158
Eberly, Ricky, Medicine Hat*	63	210	32	58	78	7	2	3	46	0	3	43	2	26	0	0	.276
Ediger, Lance, Butte	49	136	27	33	35	2	0	0	11	1	0	10	0	40	23	6	.243
Ellenberg, K. Wayne, Helena	57	222	40	57	76	6	2	3	35	0	2	22	2	52	5	1	.257
Enos, David, Helena†	36	107	24	30	40	5	1	1	23	1	0	22	0	20	6	5	.280
Escalera, F. Javier, Calgary	48	129	14	32	37	5	0	0	9	0	2	9	2	19	3	3	.248
Estep, Perry, Billings*	18	34	4	8	12	1	0	1	5	0	0	7	0	17	2	0	.235
Feliz, Rodolfo, Billings	22	41	3	7	9	0	1	0	5	0	0	7	0	7	0	0	.171
Figueroa, Carlos, Calgary	16	1	1	0	0	0	0	0	0	0	0	0	0	0	0	0	.000
Fiorillo, Nicholas, Billings*	20	49	8	18	25	2	1	1	8	1	0	1	0	8	3	1	.367
Flannery, Kevin, Billings*	5	2	1	0	0	0	0	0	0	0	0	2	0	1	0	0	.000
Forbes, Kirk, Calgary	69	261	48	75	99	10	4	2	24	1	0	15	5	54	25	5	.287
Freeman, M. Todd, Butte	22	59	9	12	16	4	0	0	5	0	0	14	1	19	1	0	.203
Freeman, Preston, Idaho Falls	51	150	27	36	46	4	0	2	22	0	1	23	1	42	4	1	.240
Galarraga, Andres, Calgary	42	112	14	24	41	3	1	4	16	1	1	9	0	22	0	1	.214
Garrelts, Scott, Great Falls	11	19	0	4	5	1	0	0	2	0	0	1	0	7	0	0	.211

Player and Club	G.	AB.	R.	H.	TB.	2B.	3B.	HR.	RBI.	SH.	SF.	BB.	HP.	SO.	SB.	CS.	Pct.
Gilmartin, Daniel, Butte	48	130	13	24	34	3	2	1	9	5	1	11	1	43	0	0	.185
Guzman, Hector, Lethbridge	46	161	31	55	60	5	0	0	25	3	1	18	1	29	6	7	.342
Guzman, Ruben, Billings	55	170	34	54	79	13	3	2	28	0	1	20	4	40	8	4	.318
Hamric, Russell, Helena	59	243	51	87	104	9	4	0	40	1	3	30	1	25	13	9	.358
Hansen, Jon, Butte	60	227	64	71	136	17	3	14	45	0	2	46	2	44	8	3	.313
Hanson, Gregory, Idaho Falls	60	195	30	40	63	9	1	4	32	0	0	17	1	53	7	2	.205
Hanson, Michael, Helena	15	44	7	15	22	4	0	1	8	1	0	7	1	11	0	1	.341
Harrigan, David, Helena	44	179	33	43	71	11	1	5	31	0	1	15	5	54	3	0	.240
Harry, Whitney, Helena	50	190	39	44	62	3	0	5	29	1	1	24	1	66	1	4	.232
Henderson, Mark, Calgary	10	13	6	1	1	0	0	0	0	0	0	0	1	4	1	0	.077
Hernandez, Rafael, Medicine Hat	63	210	20	45	57	4	1	2	22	5	0	7	6	52	1	0	.214
Higgins, Mark, Butte	54	162	23	41	49	3	1	1	18	1	1	14	3	52	10	6	.253
Hinds, Kevin, Billings	56	175	26	36	55	7	3	2	26	2	3	36	7	35	9	3	.206
Houston, John, Lethbridge	35	116	19	32	50	4	1	4	19	1	0	16	4	21	3	0	.276
Hunter, Marion, Idaho Falls	64	272	44	78	102	10	7	0	34	3	0	21	1	47	13	4	.287
Javier, Ramon, Medicine Hat	22	41	3	4	5	1	0	0	3	1	1	7	0	19	1	0	.098
Johnson, George, Lethbridge*	47	144	38	45	55	4	0	2	15	0	0	33	8	14	5	4	.313
Johnson, Kevin, Great Falls	23	70	3	6	8	2	0	0	3	0	1	5	1	36	0	0	.086
Johnson, Rodney, Billings	63	214	49	70	85	10	1	1	37	3	2	43	2	27	10	5	.327
Jones, Jeffery, Billings	66	232	49	69	113	9	1	11	49	2	3	35	8	75	8	1	.297
Jones, Russell, Billings	61	198	38	57	78	5	2	4	36	3	0	37	3	50	10	2	.288
Keen, George, Calgary	11	27	3	7	9	2	0	0	2	0	0	1	0	4	0	0	.259
Kepshire, Kurt, Billings*	24	9	0	0	0	0	0	0	0	0	0	3	0	5	0	0	.000
Kibbe, Jay, Idaho Falls	1	1	0	0	0	0	0	0	0	0	0	0	0	0	0	0	.000
Kingsolver, Kurtis, Butte	52	186	41	51	88	10	3	7	42	0	1	32	1	65	15	10	.274
Koenigsfeld, Ronald, Butte	63	218	45	64	96	8	0	8	44	1	4	53	3	39	9	6	.294
Kopjo, Jeffrey, Lethbridge*	38	114	26	34	37	3	0	0	18	1	1	21	1	27	1	2	.298
Kutcher, Randy, Great Falls†	65	245	55	62	80	8	2	2	25	0	2	27	1	50	12	7	.253
Kwiecinski, Michael, Calgary	45	125	11	15	19	4	0	0	10	4	0	13	2	49	4	2	.120
Lamar, Daniel, Billings	34	107	7	18	20	2	0	0	7	4	1	7	0	16	3	1	.168
Levi, Stanley, Butte*	54	139	25	44	70	6	4	4	31	0	0	20	2	20	6	2	.317
Lindsey, Jon, Helena*	64	265	47	77	94	8	0	3	44	1	2	33	1	56	14	8	.291
Little, Ronald, Billings†	62	231	31	64	74	6	2	0	21	0	0	11	1	53	10	2	.277
Lorena, Joseph, Great Falls	38	93	9	23	26	1	1	0	16	1	2	20	2	17	0	0	.247
Maldonado, Candido, Lethbridge	59	234	42	70	111	20	3	5	33	5	3	18	1	56	4	2	.299
Malkin, John, Lethbridge	24	83	11	19	27	2	0	2	18	1	2	16	0	24	0	0	.229
Mann, Leo, Lethbridge	33	132	29	38	41	3	0	0	20	5	0	19	2	15	10	2	.288
Manriques, Fred, Medicine Hat	66	270	47	81	115	8	10	2	30	3	1	15	4	59	4	2	.300
Marin, Fernando, Calgary	69	260	50	65	143	19	1	19	52	0	1	43	5	88	4	5	.250
Martinson, Kenneth, Helena	46	183	33	55	75	9	1	3	26	2	0	19	1	31	1	3	.301
Masone, Anthony, Billings	7	23	1	5	5	0	0	0	2	0	1	2	0	6	0	0	.217
McClendon, Damion, Butte*	23	14	6	0	0	0	0	0	0	0	0	4	0	9	1	0	.000
McKay, Karl, Butte	58	235	45	67	95	13	3	3	25	0	3	22	1	62	21	9	.285
McNealy, Darryl, Great Falls*	36	95	16	19	22	1	1	0	7	3	2	16	2	22	2	3	.200
Meadows, Melvin, Lethbridge*.	8	18	2	2	2	0	0	0	0	0	0	2	1	6	0	0	.111
Miller, Darrell, Idaho Falls	60	205	35	55	87	10	2	6	34	0	4	28	3	62	5	1	.268
Miller, Mark, Billings	57	218	34	55	63	4	2	0	13	3	0	30	0	29	14	2	.252
Misuraca, Richard, Lethbridge	14	29	3	5	7	2	0	0	2	1	0	3	0	13	0	0	.172
Moncion, Hector, Medicine Hat*	56	191	36	43	52	5	2	0	17	2	4	23	3	17	8	6	.225
Monroig, Jorge, Great Falls	46	129	20	31	56	4	3	5	24	0	1	15	1	43	0	0	.240
Morillo, Rufino, Idaho Falls	48	147	19	30	45	1	7	0	10	3	0	9	1	35	6	2	.204
Moscat, Fernando, Medicine Hat	40	105	20	22	27	3	1	0	18	1	2	20	1	44	1	1	.210
Nate, Jeffery, Helena	24	67	17	16	20	2	1	0	5	1	1	6	2	15	2	0	.239
Nebrich, G. Peter, Idaho Falls	51	146	22	38	51	2	4	1	24	1	2	19	1	34	0	1	.260
O'Malley, Thomas, Great Falls*	42	119	13	29	40	6	1	1	20	1	1	21	0	14	0	1	.244
Pangborn, Mark, Idaho Falls	22	3	0	0	0	0	0	0	0	1	0	0	0	1	0	0	.000
Paula, Julio, Medicine Hat	56	226	41	65	89	8	2	4	30	1	1	26	1	56	10	3	.288
Pellack, James, Calgary*	51	163	31	55	88	7	1	8	34	0	1	35	3	31	6	2	.337
Pennachio, Frank, Idaho Falls	58	187	27	56	84	12	5	2	28	0	1	27	1	42	1	2	.299
Perez, David, Calgary	70	261	48	71	100	8	7	0	36	4	0	37	3	52	12	8	.272
Perodin, Ronald, Great Falls†	66	274	49	77	85	6	1	0	21	1	1	15	4	37	38	9	.281
Pettis, Gary, Idaho Falls†	50	198	39	63	102	10	10	3	26	1	0	17	4	53	15	5	.318
Pone, Vincent, Butte	41	131	13	32	43	1	2	2	20	1	1	21	4	33	6	4	.244
Porte, Carlos, Billings	5	5	0	0	0	0	0	0	0	0	0	0	0	0	0	0	.000
Purcell, Trent, Helena*	38	107	22	29	40	8	0	1	12	1	0	27	1	34	7	0	.271
Quinones, Rene, Calgary†	48	147	25	33	48	10	1	1	13	2	1	17	2	24	1	2	.224
Rathjen, Dennis, Great Falls	27	1	0	0	0	0	0	0	0	0	0	0	0	0	0	0	.000
Rich, Kean, Great Falls	34	84	16	21	31	5	1	1	12	0	0	14	2	23	0	0	.250
Robins, George, Butte	8	14	4	6	8	2	0	0	5	0	0	1	0	3	0	1	.429
Rodriguez, Marcos, Lethbridge	30	59	6	15	21	3	0	1	12	3	0	1	1	20	1	1	.254
Schrimsher, M. Keith, Billings	10	15	2	1	1	0	0	0	0	5	0	2	0	3	2	0	.067
Schroeder, A. William, Butte	65	242	73	86	170	16	7	18	77	0	4	48	4	84	18	3	.355
Shadid, James, Great Falls†	49	163	27	38	47	3	0	2	19	0	1	18	0	28	18	4	.233
Shepherd, Ronald, Medicine Hat	49	178	21	37	56	6	2	3	20	0	2	15	2	66	4	1	.208
Silicani, Robert, Lethbridge	49	173	30	47	57	6	2	0	13	6	1	26	0	35	4	1	.272

Player and Club	G.	AB.	R.	H.	TB.	2B.	3B.	HR.	RBI.	SH.	SF.	BB.	HP.	SO.	SB.	CS.	Pct.
Simon, Mark, Billings*	64	193	25	38	48	6	2	0	22	5	2	32	0	62	7	1	.197
Smith, Clay, Lethbridge*	57	221	30	64	85	10	1	3	35	6	1	26	0	30	1	1	.290
Sobbe, William, Lethbridge*	49	186	30	56	64	6	1	0	23	3	2	25	0	9	0	2	.301
Stone, Wayne, Idaho Falls	24	98	22	31	49	1	7	1	18	1	1	11	0	16	3	2	.316
Sua, Murphy, Lethbridge	62	275	56	88	117	13	2	4	53	4	2	12	2	35	3	3	.320
Sullivan, Michael J., Billings	4	13	1	4	6	0	1	0	1	0	0	0	0	2	0	0	.308
Sullivan, Michael T., Billings	8	4	0	1	1	0	0	0	0	1	0	0	0	2	0	0	.250
Szymarek, Paul, Great Falls	3	10	2	5	7	2	0	0	1	0	0	2	0	1	1	0	.500
Tirado, Julio, Billings*	31	74	6	15	19	2	1	0	8	0	0	6	2	20	0	0	.203
Turner, Phillip, Medicine Hat	69	269	39	72	92	8	3	2	37	0	0	35	3	36	2	2	.268
Valdez, Jose, Billings	6	9	1	4	4	0	0	0	1	0	0	0	0	2	0	0	.444
Warner, Harold, Helena*	39	131	32	35	53	4	1	4	32	0	0	23	1	38	1	2	.267
Waugh, Jimmy, Medicine Hat	57	227	43	72	115	14	1	9	36	5	5	21	4	42	5	2	.317
West, Timothy, Calgary	40	111	13	35	41	0	0	2	18	0	2	15	1	24	2	3	.315
Wetenkamp, Lee, Medicine Hat	66	233	48	66	105	15	3	6	43	0	0	29	4	54	0	1	.283
Wilkinson, William, Calgary	2	3	0	0	0	0	0	0	0	0	0	0	0	1	0	0	.000
Wojcik, James, Great Falls*	60	212	48	78	99	8	5	1	35	2	3	45	0	31	12	5	.368
Wyatt, Porter, Butte*	34	117	29	29	36	2	1	1	15	2	1	27	0	27	3	4	.248

The following pitchers had no plate appearances, primarily through the use of designated hitters, listed alphabetically by club, games in parentheses:

BILLINGS—Bangert, Gregory* (3); Myles, Rick* (3).

BUTTE—Beene, R. Andrew (5); Christison, Steven (12); Cicotte, Gregory (3); DeHart, Gregory (7); Donovan, Michael (14); Galloway, Frank (10); Grier, David (14); Matias, Luis (10); Maxson, J. Daniel (5); Meadows, Brian (14); Meyer, Randy (3); Morris, David (11); Thomas, David (1); Tkac, Joseph (15); Vasquez, Jesse (18); Walker, Alan (14); Walling, Ronald (4).

CALGARY—Blows, Louis* (14); Boger, Larry (11); Bradshaw, David* (14); Clarke, Ricky* (4); Colon, Luis (3); Fadhel, Antonio (13); Finch, Guy* (23); Nichols, Joey (6); Ruiz, Bobby* (2); St. Claire, Randy* (6); St. John, William* (8); Torres, Miguel (14); Vega, Randolph (5); White, Keith* (13); Winfield, Steven (25).

GREAT FALLS—Bricker, Craig (13); Felt, Jerald (3); Goodchild, Christopher (16); Hagemann, Timothy* (13); Hinrichs, Phillips G. (26); Maebe, Arthur R. (15); Sensenbrenner, David* (13); Stovall, Jerry (6); Thornton, David (3); Williams, Frank (14); Wing, Harry (3).

HELENA—Baller, Jay (13); Bennett, Herbert (7); Berenguer, Francisco (12); Conti, Adam (7); Dorin, Matthew (11); Dunnegan, Steven (16); Gums, Russell (27); Hutchinson, E. DeWayne (10); Lewis, P. David (21); Mitchell, David (16); Money, J. Kyle (9); Smith, LeRoy (5); Toyfair, Thomas (6); Warner, Fred* (27).

IDAHO FALLS—Adams, Larry (13); Brown, Curtis (12); Dugger, Lawrence (16); Duran, David (6); Hollier, Warren (1); Klein, Robert (15); Lindsey, Edward* (13); Pettit, Timothy (14); Saatzer, Michael* (12); Turpin, Dwight (13); Wysocki, Paul (8).

LETHBRIDGE—Borbon, Ernesto (9); Daniel, David* (13); Ewald, Robert (2); Johnson, Kent (13); Kellam, Wayne (12); Lindsey, Kenneth* (14); Madden, Morris* (13); Nelson, Rodney (16); Powers, Larry (11); Rodas, Richard* (13); Terry, Glenn* (12); White, Robert (10); Wilczewski, Francis (4).

MEDICINE HAT—Burger, Bradley* (8); Chavez, Cesar (12); Coughlin, Gregory* (7); Eichhorn, Mark† (16); Gambrell, P. Greg (14); Holton, Mark (11); Kiser, Orvin (24); Phillips, Junior (16); Rosenlund, William (8); Seiber, John (16); Senteney, Stephen (26); Soriano, Luis (18); Valdez, Silverio (12).

GRAND-SLAM HOME RUNS—Darkis 3; J. Hanson 2; Bradley, Breeden, Brown, Coker, Ellenberg, Harry, R. Jones, Levi, Malkin, Marin, 1 each.

AWARDED FIRST BASE ON INTERFERENCE—Perez 2 (Malkin 2); Bruno (Hernandez); J. Lindsey (Concepcion).

CLUB FIELDING

Club	G.	PO.	A.	E.	DP.	PB.	Pct.	Club	G.	PO.	A.	E.	DP.	PB.	Pct.
Calgary	70	1815	781	114	63	21	.958	Great Falls	70	1795	692	160	37	29	.940
Billings	69	1845	668	142	44	17	.947	Idaho Falls	67	1762	754	173	50	33	.936
Lethbridge	68	1809	760	154	59	30	.943	Medicine Hat	69	1791	794	179	59	35	.935
Helena	69	1809	711	156	50	33	.942	Butte	66	1724	724	184	59	17	.930

Triple Play—Medicine Hat.

INDIVIDUAL FIELDING

FIRST BASEMEN

Player and Club	G.	PO.	A.	E.	DP.	Pct.	Player and Club	G.	PO.	A.	E.	DP.	Pct.
Kingsolver, Butte	11	81	6	1	6	.989	R. Jones, Billings	52	372	18	12	29	.970
Lorenz, Great Falls	24	150	9	2	7	.988	Harry, Helena	30	247	7	8	18	.969
BROCK, Lethbridge	65	543	36	8	48	.986	Tirado, Billings*	23	110	9	4	6	.967
Galarraga, Calgary	26	181	11	3	18	.985	McNealy, Great Falls*	28	187	11	9	7	.957
Cohron, Calgary*	39	290	23	5	27	.984	Burdi, Great Falls	30	224	17	11	17	.956
Schroeder, Butte	24	192	13	4	19	.981	Nebrich, Idaho Falls	26	183	6	9	14	.955
Turner, Medicine Hat	67	627	34	14	51	.979	Escalera, Calgary	15	98	6	5	8	.954
Anderson, Helena	38	308	24	8	24	.976	Alonzo, Butte*	35	278	13	16	24	.948
Collins, Idaho Falls	42	333	18	9	23	.975							

FIRST BASEMEN—Continued

(Fewer Than Ten Games)

Player and Club	G.	PO.	A.	E.	DP.	Pct.
Pennachio, Idaho Falls ..	6	28	3	0	4	1.000
Kopjo, Lethbridge*	4	23	2	0	5	1.000
Eberly, Medicine Hat ..	1	7	2	0	0	1.000
Keen, Calgary	3	8	0	0	1	1.000
Coker, Calgary	1	5	0	0	2	1.000
West, Calgary	3	3	0	0	0	1.000
M. Miller, Billings	1	2	0	0	0	1.000
Clevenger, Idaho Falls ...	3	14	0	1	0	.933
Enos, Helena	3	13	0	1	0	.929
Wetenkamp, Med. Hat ..	1	9	1	1	2	.909
J. Jones, Billings	8	41	5	7	0	.868
D. Miller, Idaho Falls	2	8	0	2	1	.800

SECOND BASEMEN

Player and Club	G.	PO.	A.	E.	DP.	Pct.
Silicani, Lethbridge	40	91	123	8	34	.964
C. Smith, Lethbridge	25	61	45	4	16	.964
Pennachio, Idaho Falls ..	29	36	58	4	7	.959
HINDS, Billings	51	98	118	10	22	.956
Hamric, Helena	58	126	182	16	28	.951
Wojcik, Great Falls	43	94	126	13	19	.944
Forbes, Calgary	63	163	177	22	39	.939
Moscat, Medicine Hat ..	32	62	75	9	13	.938
Gilmartin, Butte	43	74	98	12	20	.935
Paula, Medicine Hat	44	101	145	18	33	.932
Enos, Helena	15	28	34	5	7	.925
Wyatt, Butte	19	46	46	8	12	.920
O'Malley, Great Falls	12	22	21	4	1	.915
M. Miller, Billings	25	33	51	8	9	.913
P. Freeman, Idaho Falls	50	114	108	23	22	.906
Ediger, Butte	22	39	42	14	11	.853

Triple Play—Paula.

(Fewer Than Ten Games)

Player and Club	G.	PO.	A.	E.	DP.	Pct.
Quinones, Calgary	6	11	9	0	5	1.000
Pettis, Idaho Falls	1	1	1	0	0	1.000
Stone, Idaho Falls	1	1	1	0	0	1.000
Perez, Calgary	1	0	2	0	0	1.000
Porte, Billings	1	1	0	0	0	1.000
Dillard, Great Falls	9	18	33	3	6	.944
Marin, Calgary	6	13	18	2	5	.939
Mann, Lethbridge	7	9	15	3	2	.889
Shadid, Great Falls	5	5	9	2	1	.875
K. Johnson, Great Falls	6	14	7	5	0	.808
Columna, Medicine Hat .	1	1	2	2	0	.600
Bunn, Idaho Falls	3	2	1	4	1	.429

THIRD BASEMEN

Player and Club	G.	PO.	A.	E.	DP.	Pct.
Enos, Helena	12	10	19	1	1	.967
PEREZ, Calgary	65	61	123	10	10	.948
Wetenkamp, Med. Hat ..	10	16	19	3	3	.921
R. Johnson, Billings	61	57	121	17	9	.913
J. C. Brown, Great Falls	36	31	77	11	6	.908
Shadid, Great Falls	28	26	55	9	5	.900
Sua, Lethbridge	62	54	133	23	10	.890
Stone, Idaho Falls	19	16	57	9	3	.890
Pettis, Idaho Falls	32	36	58	12	2	.887
Hunter, Idaho Falls	11	12	23	5	2	.875
Ellenberg, Helena	56	54	94	23	13	.865
T. Freeman, Butte	19	18	27	7	2	.865
Eberly, Medicine Hat	52	34	94	28	4	.821
Pone, Butte	41	31	44	21	2	.781
Lorenz, Great Falls	10	10	11	7	0	.750
Beals, Billings	10	3	10	6	1	.684

(Fewer Than Ten Games)

Player and Club	G.	PO.	A.	E.	DP.	Pct.
Feliz, Billings	5	2	8	0	0	1.000
Koenigsfeld, Butte	2	1	2	0	0	1.000
O'Malley, Great Falls	2	0	3	0	0	1.000
Misuraca, Lethbridge	3	1	1	0	0	1.000
J. Lindsey, Helena	1	0	1	0	0	1.000
Paula, Medicine Hat	9	8	14	1	0	.957
Galarraga, Calgary	6	2	10	1	1	.923
Pennachio, Idaho Falls ..	7	3	8	1	0	.917
M. Hanson, Helena	6	4	8	3	2	.800
Clevenger, Idaho Falls ...	3	0	4	1	0	.800
Ediger, Butte	6	7	3	3	0	.769
Gilmartin, Butte	5	1	5	2	0	.750
Silicani, Lethbridge	8	2	17	7	1	.731
Henderson, Calgary	3	1	4	2	1	.714
Wyatt, Butte	3	2	0	2	0	.500
Columna, Medicine Hat .	2	0	1	1	0	.500

SHORTSTOPS

Player and Club	G.	PO.	A.	E.	DP.	Pct.
Quinones, Calgary	43	51	88	7	18	.952
Feliz, Billings	11	8	12	1	3	.952
Mann, Lethbridge	28	43	90	9	17	.937
HUNTER, Idaho Falls ..	54	93	166	23	22	.918
Koenigsfeld, Butte	61	105	209	30	39	.913
Simon, Billings	61	94	124	23	16	.905
Manriques, Med Falls	65	103	208	37	36	.894
Kwiecinski, Calgary	33	35	82	14	14	.893
J. Lindsey, Helena	51	75	140	28	18	.885
Kutcher, Great Falls	55	79	109	29	7	.866
O'Malley, G Falls	10	17	8	4	2	.862
Beals, Billings	16	10	21	5	7	.861
H. Guzman, Leth	43	67	114	31	16	.854
Pettis, Idaho Falls	14	22	35	12	9	.826
Nate, Helena	19	21	30	16	4	.761

(Fewer Than Ten Games)

Player and Club	G.	PO.	A.	E.	DP.	Pct.
Perez, Calgary	6	9	16	0	1	1.000
Silicani, Leth	1	1	0	0	0	1.000
Castillo, Med Hat	1	0	1	0	0	1.000
Hamric, Helena	1	0	1	0	0	1.000
Shadid, Great Falls	4	8	10	1	3	.947
Paula, Med Hat	8	16	14	5	2	.857
Gilmartin, Butte	2	3	6	2	1	.818
K. Johnson, G Falls	6	8	16	6	2	.800
Enos, Helena	2	1	5	2	1	.750
Ediger, Butte	4	6	14	10	2	.667
Columna, Med Hat	1	0	0	1	0	.000

OUTFIELDERS

Player and Club	G.	PO.	A.	E.	DP.	Pct.
Cruz, Calgary*	40	62	4	0	2	1.000
R. Jones, Billings	13	18	2	0	0	1.000
Escalera, Calgary	17	8	0	0	0	1.000
R. Guzman, Billings	45	62	4	1	0	.985
Purcell, Helena	38	57	3	1	1	.984
DARKIS, Helena	69	98	5	2	1	.981
Waugh, Medicine Hat	27	34	3	1	0	.974
M. Miller, Billings	38	59	4	2	1	.969
J. Jones, Billings	58	83	5	3	1	.967
G. Hanson, Idaho F	50	67	7	3	2	.961
Bruno, Helena*	68	135	16	7	1	.956
Maldonado, Leth	59	81	5	4	0	.956
Perodin, Great Falls	65	122	6	6	0	.955
Deer, Great Falls	60	95	10	5	1	.955
Pellack, Calgary*	32	55	8	3	1	.955
Javier, Medicine Hat	19	19	1	1	0	.952
Rich, Great Falls	25	34	1	2	0	.946
Coker, Calgary	66	94	7	6	0	.944
Bradley, Lethbridge	62	96	9	7	1	.938
Hansen, Butte	59	85	6	6	2	.938
Monroig, Great Falls	38	53	6	4	1	.937
Levi, Butte*	47	36	5	3	1	.932
Aldridge, Idaho F*	43	51	3	4	0	.931
Collins, Idaho Falls	21	36	4	3	0	.930
Bunn, Idaho Falls	16	10	3	1	0	.929
H. Warner, Helena*	39	57	6	5	0	.926
Shepherd, Med Hat	49	92	5	8	0	.924
Rodriguez, Leth	30	22	2	2	0	.923
Little, Billings*	58	74	4	7	0	.918
Marin, Calgary	65	80	8	8	1	.917
Moncion, Med Hat*	50	69	7	7	0	.916
Wetenkamp, Med Hat	53	66	5	7	0	.910
Higgins, Butte	51	54	4	6	2	.906
McKay, Butte	57	83	9	10	3	.902
C. Smith, Leth	22	22	4	3	0	.897
Acevedo, Idaho Falls	48	63	3	8	0	.892
Morillo, Idaho Falls	47	62	4	8	1	.892
Estep, Billings*	13	15	1	2	1	.889
Kopjo, Lethbridge*	14	11	2	2	0	.867
G. Johnson, Leth	32	33	2	7	0	.833
Castillo, Med Hat	28	22	3	6	0	.806
Ediger, Butte	12	7	0	2	0	.778
McClendon, Butte*	12	3	0	1	0	.750

Triple Play—Wetenkamp.

(Fewer Than Ten Games)

Player and Club	G.	PO.	A.	E.	DP.	Pct.
Wojcik, Great Falls	5	11	1	0	1	1.000
Masone, Billings	7	7	0	0	0	1.000
Pennachio, Idaho F	9	4	3	0	0	1.000
Shadid, Great Falls	4	6	0	0	0	1.000
Szymarek, Great F	3	6	0	0	0	1.000
Barnett, Calgary	3	5	0	0	0	1.000
McNealy, Great Falls*	4	3	0	0	0	1.000
Robins, Butte	7	1	0	0	0	1.000
Valdez, Billings	3	1	0	0	0	1.000
Wilkinson, Calgary	2	1	0	0	0	1.000
Clevenger, Idaho F	3	0	1	0	0	1.000
Dillard, Great Falls	9	14	0	1	0	.933
K. Johnson, G Falls	9	9	0	1	0	.900
Meadows, Lethbridge	6	9	0	1	0	.900
Misuraca, Lethbridge	9	12	0	2	0	.857
Stone, Idaho Falls	5	4	0	1	0	.800
Eberly, Medicine Hat	3	3	1	1	0	.800
O'Malley, Great Falls	7	2	2	1	0	.800
Columna, Med Hat	4	3	0	1	0	.750
Galarraga, Calgary	1	3	0	1	0	.750
H. Guzman, Leth	2	2	1	1	0	.750
Wyatt, Butte	5	1	2	1	0	.750
West, Calgary	3	2	0	1	0	.667

CATCHERS

Player and Club	G.	PO.	A.	E.	DP.	PB.	Pct.
West, Calgary	26	152	14	2	0	5	.988
Celidonia, I Falls	31	202	31	3	2	17	.987
Concepcion, Med Hat	16	70	4	1	0	9	.987
Nebrich, Idaho Falls	10	65	6	1	1	3	.986
BOLLA, G Falls	53	356	27	6	4	22	.985
Schroeder, Butte	36	282	37	5	2	9	.985
Burdi, Great Falls	24	155	18	3	1	7	.983
Sobbe, Lethbridge	47	451	40	10	3	19	.980
Boddy, Billings	41	351	32	8	2	10	.980
Kingsolver, Butte	33	250	25	6	4	8	.979
Martinson, Helena	34	268	23	7	0	16	.977
Breeden, Calgary	50	336	51	10	1	9	.975
Harrigan, Helena	36	284	28	8	2	17	.975
Lamar, Helena	33	283	12	10	1	6	.967
Malkin, Lethbridge	21	151	26	6	0	11	.967
D. Miller, IF	30	246	40	10	3	12	.966
Hernandez, Med Hat	62	398	57	18	2	26	.962

(Fewer Than Ten Games)

Player and Club	G.	PO.	A.	E.	DP.	PB.	Pct.
Escalera, Calgary	4	9	0	0	0	3	1.000
De Jesus, Butte	2	4	0	0	0	0	1.000
Keen, Calgary	6	37	3	1	0	4	.976
M. J. Sullivan, Bil	4	28	2	3	0	1	.909
G. Hanson, IF	4	18	4	3	0	1	.880
Galarraga, Calgary	2	4	0	1	0	0	.800

PITCHERS

Player and Club	G.	PO.	A.	E.	DP.	Pct.
RODAS, Lethbridge*	13	3	23	0	0	1.000
C. Brown, Idaho F	12	5	13	0	2	1.000
Donovan, Butte	14	5	12	0	0	1.000
Schrimsher, Billings	10	3	13	0	0	1.000
Grier, Butte	14	6	9	0	0	1.000
Boger, Calgary	11	3	10	0	3	1.000
Kiser, Medicine Hat	24	0	12	0	0	1.000
Galloway, Butte	10	2	9	0	1	1.000
Bricker, Great Falls	13	3	6	0	0	1.000
Dugger, Idaho Falls	16	2	7	0	0	1.000
K. Johnson, Leth	13	3	5	0	0	1.000
Lewis, Helena	21	1	7	0	0	1.000
Winfield, Calgary	25	2	4	0	0	1.000
Soriano, Med Hat	18	2	3	0	0	1.000
Pangborn, Idaho Falls	18	1	3	0	0	1.000
K. White, Calgary*	13	1	3	0	0	1.000
Chavez, Med Hat	12	1	3	0	0	1.000
Ayers, Billings	16	0	4	0	1	1.000
Hagemann, G Falls*	13	0	4	0	0	1.000
Bradshaw, Calgary*	14	1	2	0	1	1.000
Adams, Idaho Falls	13	1	2	0	0	1.000
Clevenger, I Falls	10	1	2	0	0	1.000
Figueroa, Calgary	15	1	1	0	0	1.000
Valdez, Medicine Hat	12	1	1	0	0	1.000

PITCHERS—Continued

Player and Club	G.	PO.	A.	E.	DP.	Pct.
Vasquez, Butte	17	0	2	0	0	1.000
Hutchinson, Helena	10	1	0	0	0	1.000
Matias, Butte	10	1	0	0	0	1.000
Eichhorn, Med Hat	16	11	28	1	4	.975
Blows, Calgary*	14	5	28	1	2	.971
Mitchell, Helena	16	6	21	1	3	.964
K. Lindsey, Leth*	14	6	21	1	0	.964
Maebe, Great Falls	15	8	17	1	0	.962
Fadhel, Calgary	13	7	18	1	1	.962
Cato, Billings	11	7	15	1	2	.957
Christison, Butte	12	5	17	1	0	.957
E. Lindsey, I Falls*	13	1	17	1	1	.947
Torres, Calgary	14	7	25	2	0	.941
Klein, Idaho Falls	15	9	7	1	3	.941
Hinrichs, G Falls	26	3	11	1	0	.933
Baller, Helena	13	3	11	1	2	.933
Phillips, Med Hat	16	2	11	1	1	.929
Box, Billings*	19	0	13	1	0	.929
Biggus, Butte	15	4	8	1	1	.923
Kibbe, Idaho Falls	13	2	10	1	1	.923
Williams, G Falls	13	9	12	2	0	.913
Gambrell, Med Hat*	12	3	7	1	0	.909
Kepshire, Billings	24	2	8	1	1	.909
Seiber, Med Hat	16	6	12	2	1	.900
Daniel, Lethbridge	13	0	9	1	0	.900
Berenguer, Helena	12	0	9	1	0	.900
Buchanan, Billings*	14	7	17	3	1	.889
Madden, Lethbridge*	13	4	12	2	1	.889
Finch, Calgary*	22	3	5	1	0	.889
Gums, Helena	27	2	6	1	0	.889
Daniels, Billings	22	2	6	1	0	.889
Pettit, Idaho Falls	14	0	8	1	0	.889
Rathjen, Great Falls	27	5	17	3	3	.880
Turpin, Idaho Falls	13	2	5	1	1	.875
Senteney, Med Hat	26	1	6	1	0	.875
Walker, Butte*	14	0	7	1	0	.875
Dowless, Billings	12	3	9	2	1	.857
Morris, Butte	11	1	5	1	0	.857
Holton, Medicine Hat	11	0	6	1	0	.857
B. Meadows, Butte	14	4	18	4	0	.846
Fiorillo, Billings*	14	4	17	4	0	.840
Sensenbrenner, GF*	13	2	13	3	1	.833
Goodchild, G Falls	15	2	7	2	0	.818
Tkac, Butte*	15	0	9	2	0	.818
Buckley, Idaho Falls	11	5	12	4	0	.810
Powers, Lethbridge	11	3	4	2	0	.778
Dunnegan, Helena	16	1	9	3	2	.769
Saatzer, Idaho Falls	12	3	10	4	0	.765
F. Warner, Helena*	27	0	3	1	0	.750
R. White, Lethbridge*	10	0	3	1	0	.750
Kellam, Lethbridge	12	3	5	3	0	.727
Nelson, Lethbridge	16	1	5	3	1	.667
Vega, Calgary	15	2	2	2	0	.667
Dorin, Helena	11	3	2	3	0	.625
Terry, Lethbridge*	12	0	1	1	0	.500

(Fewer Than Ten Games)

Player and Club	G.	PO.	A.	E.	DP.	Pct.
St. John, Calgary*	8	3	6	0	1	1.000
L. Smith, Helena	5	3	3	0	0	1.000
Rosenlund, Med Hat	8	2	4	0	0	1.000
M. T. Sullivan, Bil	8	3	1	0	0	1.000
Maxson, Butte	5	2	2	0	0	1.000
Felt, Great Falls	3	1	3	0	0	1.000
Flannery, Billings	5	1	2	0	0	1.000
Borbon, Lethbridge*	9	0	3	0	1	1.000
Coughlin, Med Hat*	7	0	2	0	0	1.000
Bangert, Billings*	3	1	1	0	0	1.000
Conti, Helena	7	0	2	0	0	1.000
Cicotte, Butte	3	1	0	0	0	1.000
Wysocki, Idaho Falls	8	0	1	0	0	1.000
Duran, Idaho Falls	6	0	1	0	0	1.000
Clarke, Calgary*	4	0	1	0	0	1.000
Colon, Calgary	3	0	1	0	0	1.000
Ruiz, Calgary*	2	0	1	0	0	1.000
Cohron, Calgary*	1	0	1	0	0	1.000
Thomas, Butte	1	0	1	0	0	1.000
Garrelts, G Falls	8	2	7	1	0	.900
DeHart, Butte	7	2	6	1	1	.889
Money, Helena	9	2	3	1	0	.833
Burger, Med Hat	8	0	5	1	0	.833
Bennett, Helena	7	1	7	2	0	.800
St. Claire, Calgary	6	1	7	2	0	.800
Beene, Butte	5.	1	3	1	0	.800
Thornton, G Falls	3	1	3	2	0	.667
Ewald, Lethbridge*	2	1	1	1	0	.667
Nichols, Calgary	6	0	2	1	0	.667
Toyfair, Helena	6	0	2	1	0	.667
Wilczewski, Leth	4	0	1	1	0	.500

The following players do not have any recorded accepted chances at the positions indicated; therefore, are not listed in the fielding averages for those particular positions: Chue, p; Concepcion, of; De Jesus, of; Enos, of; Forbes, of; Henderson, of; Hollier, p; J. Jones, p; Keen, of; Kutcher, of; Meyer, p; Moscat, of; Myles, p; Simon, p; Stoval, p; Walling*, p; Wing, p.

CLUB PITCHING

Club	G.	CG.	ShO.	Sv.	IP.	H.	R.	ER.	HR.	BB.	Int. BB.	HB.	SO.	WP.	Bk.	ERA.
Billings	69	14	6	16	615	534	283	204	38	213	18	22	651	28	8	2.99
Lethbridge	68	21	5	6	603	579	348	250	34	271	5	23	590	55	10	3.73
Helena	69	8	3	12	603	652	446	318	54	355	5	32	552	62	8	4.75
Butte	66	11	2	8	575	657	430	304	26	296	11	25	530	60	5	4.76
Great Falls	70	14	1	16	598	672	435	331	37	293	8	28	484	44	7	4.98
Idaho Falls	67	10	1	3	587	688	480	356	37	327	9	35	521	70	4	5.46
Medicine Hat	69	7	1	15	597	698	512	363	47	326	10	29	473	63	7	5.47
Calgary	70	11	2	21	605	687	474	401	42	395	23	27	528	57	9	5.97

PITCHERS' RECORDS
(Leading Qualifiers for Earned-Run Average Leadership—56 or More Innings)

*Throws lefthanded.

Pitcher–Club	G.	GS.	CG.	ShO.	W.	L.	Sv.	Pct.	IP.	H.	R.	ER.	HR.	Int. BB.	BB.	HB.	SO.	WP.	ERA.
Rodas, Lethbridge*	13	13	11	2	12	0	0	1.000	113	81	22	14	3	18	0	4	148	3	1.12
Cato, Billings	11	11	6	0	9	1	0	.900	88	55	14	13	3	8	0	0	101	0	1.33
Fiorillo, Billings*	14	14	4	2	10	2	0	.833	99	73	29	22	1	45	2	6	114	13	2.00
Christison, Butte	12	10	2	0	5	3	0	.625	70	63	41	20	3	28	1	2	69	7	2.57
Madden, Lethbridge*	13	13	3	1	6	1	0	.857	83	62	44	27	5	45	0	4	106	9	2.93
Schrimsher, Billings	10	10	1	0	4	2	0	.667	64	59	26	21	2	17	1	4	65	3	2.95
Senteney, Medicine Hat	26	3	1	0	2	5	11	.286	64	51	29	22	1	29	1	0	79	4	3.09
Fadhel, Calgary	13	13	5	0	7	3	0	.700	97	81	41	34	2	46	1	2	98	5	3.15
Seiber, Medicine Hat	16	15	2	0	6	6	0	.500	92	101	58	33	7	39	0	0	73	11	3.23
Mitchell, Helena	16	10	1	0	5	3	1	.625	84	83	40	31	6	22	0	1	59	4	3.32

Departmental Leaders: G—Gums, Rathjen, Warner, 27; GS—Seiber, 15; CG—Rodas, 11; ShO—Blows, Fiorillo, Rodas, 2; W—Rodas, 12; L—Saatzer, Torres, Williams, 7; Sv—Winfield, 13; Pct.—Rodas, 1.000; IP—Rodas, 113; H—Torres, 121; R—Phillips, 69; ER—Torres, 58; HR—Baller, 9; BB—Dunnegan, 62; IBB—Five pitchers tied with 4 each; HP—Williams, 9; SO—Rodas, 148; WP—Holton, 16.

(All Pitchers—Listed Alphabetically)

Pitcher–Club	G.	GS.	CG.	ShO.	W.	L.	Sv.	Pct.	IP.	H.	R.	ER.	HR.	Int. BB.	BB.	HB.	SO.	WP.	ERA.
Adams, Idaho Falls	13	1	0	0	1	2	0	.333	22	42	29	25	2	12	0	1	15	1	10.23
Ayers, Billings	16	1	0	0	0	3	0	.000	23	29	26	19	6	20	2	2	18	3	7.43
Baller, Helena	13	13	3	1	5	6	0	.455	67	89	59	43	9	34	0	3	68	6	5.78
Bangert, Billings*	3	0	0	0	0	0	1	.500	3	5	4	2	0	3	0	1	4	1	6.00
Beene, Butte	5	5	0	0	0	2	0	.000	12	7	11	6	0	12	0	0	16	3	4.50
Bennett, Helena	7	5	0	0	1	3	0	.250	24	24	26	19	3	17	0	0	18	3	7.13
Berenguer, Helena	12	4	0	0	0	3	0	.000	38	73	56	41	5	21	0	3	19	3	9.71
Biggus, Butte	15	1	0	0	2	0	1	1.000	36	39	22	14	1	15	1	0	33	6	3.50
Blows, Calgary*	14	14	3	2	7	5	0	.583	94	104	51	37	4	42	3	2	85	6	3.54
Boger, Calgary	11	6	0	0	1	2	0	.333	34	45	31	28	3	27	1	4	21	2	7.41
Borbon, Lethbridge*	9	2	0	0	0	0	0	.000	23	26	15	12	3	14	0	1	22	2	4.70
Box, Billings*	19	2	0	0	2	4	0	.333	45	53	39	23	4	19	1	0	40	1	4.60
Bradshaw, Calgary*	14	0	0	0	3	1	0	.750	18	24	29	29	3	33	0	4	8	4	14.50
Bricker, Great Falls	13	1	0	0	2	2	2	.500	23	48	30	25	1	11	1	1	16	4	9.78
C. Brown, Idaho Falls	12	11	4	1	2	6	0	.250	72	86	49	37	3	13	0	3	47	2	4.63
Buchanan, Billings*	14	14	3	1	7	5	0	.583	91	82	42	34	6	25	2	3	80	1	3.36
Buckley, Idaho Falls	11	10	2	0	2	5	0	.286	72	68	43	30	4	49	0	5	79	11	3.75
Burger, Medicine Hat	8	3	0	0	1	3	0	.250	25	33	27	19	2	11	0	2	16	1	6.84
Cato, Billings	11	11	6	0	9	1	0	.900	88	55	14	13	3	8	0	0	101	0	1.33
Chavez, Medicine Hat	12	1	0	0	0	0	0	.000	20	25	25	21	2	13	0	0	14	4	9.45
Christison, Butte	12	10	2	0	5	3	0	.625	70	63	41	20	3	28	1	2	69	7	2.57
Chue, Great Falls	4	1	0	0	0	1	0	.000	9	12	6	4	0	2	1	0	9	0	4.00
Cicotte, Butte	3	1	0	0	0	0	0	.000	7	5	6	6	0	11	1	1	3	1	7.71
Clarke, Calgary*	4	1	0	0	1	0	0	1.000	17	16	15	9	0	17	2	1	9	5	4.76
Clevenger, Idaho Falls	1	1	0	0	0	1	0	.000	3	2	5	5	1	4	0	0	3	1	15.00
Cohron, Calgary*	3	0	0	0	0	0	0	.000	4	7	5	5	0	4	0	1	2	3	11.25
Colon, Calgary	7	0	0	0	1	0	0	1.000	19	27	13	13	3	9	0	0	13	5	6.16
Conti, Helena	7	0	0	0	0	0	0	.000	6	13	16	13	1	13	0	0	6	1	19.50
Coughlin, Medicine Hat*	7	0	0	0	0	0	0	.000	6	35	19	13	3	22	0	0	53	6	2.54
Daniel, Lethbridge	13	0	0	0	4	3	8	.571	46	35	19	13	3	22	0	0	53	6	2.54
Daniels, Billings	22	1	0	0	2	3	8	.400	52	37	19	12	2	12	4	3	74	0	2.08
DeHart, Butte	7	4	0	0	0	3	0	.000	17	24	25	19	3	14	0	3	13	1	10.06
Donovan, Butte	14	2	0	0	3	3	2	.500	53	42	25	23	2	25	3	0	57	5	3.91
Dorin, Helena	11	8	0	0	2	2	0	.500	40	53	33	28	4	27	0	1	30	0	6.30
Dowless, Billings	12	11	0	0	3	4	0	.429	62	66	41	24	4	22	0	3	54	1	3.48
Dugger, Idaho Falls	16	5	1	0	2	5	1	.286	47	44	36	28	1	39	1	6	69	8	5.36
Dunnegan, Helena	16	10	2	0	7	2	0	.778	89	79	52	38	7	62	3	5	95	10	3.84
Duran, Idaho Falls	6	0	0	0	1	2	1	.333	15	24	15	12	1	7	1	0	18	3	7.20
Eichhorn, Medicine Hat	16	14	3	1	7	6	0	.538	93	101	62	35	7	26	2	5	66	4	3.39
Ewald, Lethbridge*	2	2	0	0	1	1	0	.000	6	12	13	7	0	3	0	0	5	0	10.50
Fadhel, Calgary	13	13	5	0	7	3	0	.700	97	81	41	34	2	46	1	2	98	5	3.15
Felt, Great Falls	15	1	0	0	0	0	0	.000	20	26	29	26	1	31	4	2	21	7	11.70
Figueroa, Calgary	15	1	0	0	3	3	4	.500	43	50	37	31	3	25	3	0	45	3	6.49
Finch, Calgary*	22	1	0	0	0	1	0	.000	20	28	14	10	2	14	0	1	20	1	4.59
Fiorillo, Billings*	14	14	4	2	10	2	0	.833	99	73	29	22	1	45	2	6	114	13	2.00
Flannery, Billings	5	2	0	0	0	0	0	.000	16	17	11	7	0	5	3	0	13	1	5.06
Galloway, Butte	10	5	1	0	3	2	1	.600	48	51	23	17	0	12	0	2	52	1	3.19
Gambrell, Medicine Hat*	12	3	0	0	0	2	0	.000	37	43	45	37	2	34	2	1	31	5	5.84
Garrelts, Great Falls	8	8	0	0	1	4	0	.200	43	45	37	28	4	40	0	1	26	5	5.86
Goodchild, Great Falls	15	8	2	0	3	6	1	.333	79	85	60	45	3	33	1	3	57	5	5.13
Grier, Butte	14	12	3	1	6	4	0	.600	79	97	63	45	6	36	0	1	67	5	5.13
Gums, Helena	27	0	0	0	4	2	2	.667	53	48	35	16	4	28	1	4	60	6	2.72
Hagemann, Great Falls*	13	4	0	0	1	3	0	.250	26	27	23	19	2	30	0	2	29	3	6.58

Pitcher—Club	G	GS	CG	ShO	W	L	Sv	Pct.	IP	H	R	ER	HR	BB	Int. BB	HB	SO	WP	ERA
Hinrichs, Great Falls	26	2	0	0	1	1	7	.500	52	62	34	23	1	14	0	2	60	3	3.98
Hollier, Idaho Falls	1	0	0	0	0	0	0	.000	0	1	1	0	1	0	1	0	0	0	.....
Holton, Medicine Hat	11	10	0	0	1	0	0	.000											
Hutchinson, Helena	10	0	0	0	1	5	0	.167	46	62	53	40	5	41	1	2	25	16	7.83
K. Johnson, Lethbridge	13	9	1	1	4	0		1.000	21	24	24	11	1	26	0	1	20	11	4.71
J. Jones, Billings	1	0	0	0	4	4	0	.500	48	67	31	24	0	20	0	5	28	4	4.50
Kellam, Lethbridge	12	7	0	0	2	2	0	.500	0	1	0	0	3	0	0	2	0		0.00
Kepshire, Billings	24	1	0	0	2	2	0	.500	48	63	40	35	6	31	0	2	33	5	6.56
Kibbe, Idaho Falls	13	7	0	0	4	0	7	1.000	50	30	16	14	3	27	4	0	57	3	2.52
Kiser, Medicine Hat	24	0	0	0	3	5	2	.600	46	58	45	32	6	24	0	2	41	6	6.26
Klein, Idaho Falls	15	6	1	0	3	5	3	.500	44	40	27	15	2	31	1	3	37	2	3.07
Lewis, Helena	21	0	0	0	3	4	0	.429	58	73	45	39	4	25	1	1	48	5	6.05
E. Lindsey, Idaho Falls*	13	12	2	0	1	3	0	.500	26	37	26	22	2	24	0	4	26	4	7.62
K. Lindsey, Lethbridge*	14	11	3	0	4	5	0	.444	80	94	56	40	3	28	0	5	56	6	4.50
Madden, Lethbridge*	13	13	3	1	4	4	1	.500	87	73	47	34	2	28	0	1	77	9	3.52
Maebe, Great Falls	15	13	5	1	6	1	0	.857	83	62	44	27	5	45	0	4	106	9	2.93
Matias, Butte	10	0	0	0	6	5	0	.545	96	102	56	47	5	32	1	3	60	7	4.41
Maxson, Butte	5	1	0	0	3	0	0	.000	13	16	13	6	1	10	1	1	10	2	4.15
B. Meadows, Butte	14	13	5	1	3	0	0	1.000	14	18	9	6	0	7	0	1	9	0	3.86
Meyer, Butte	2	1	0	0	3	5	0	.375	90	113	61	44	3	35	4	3	75	9	4.40
Mitchell, Helena	16	10	1	0	5	3	1	.625	1	4	4	4	0	1	2	0	1	0	36.00
Money, Helena	9	8	0	0	4	1	0	.800	84	83	40	31	6	22	0	1	59	4	3.32
Morris, Butte	11	10	0	0	4	1	0	.400	42	38	24	18	4	23	0	3	37	1	3.86
Myles*	1	0	0	0	2	3	0	.400	47	77	57	41	1	35	0	4	36	10	7.85
Nelson, Lethbridge	16	0	0	0	0	0	0	.000	1	1	0	1	0	0	1	0		9.00
Nichols, Calgary	6	1	0	0	2	5	0	.286	25	30	27	19	4	14	4	3	15	4	6.84
Pangborn, Idaho Falls	18	0	0	0	2	0	0	.000	17	24	21	18	1	9	1	1	11	1	9.53
Pettit, Idaho Falls	14	1	0	0	1	0	0	1.000	31	45	34	29	3	26	1	2	32	5	8.42
Phillips, Medicine Hat	16	14	1	0	1	3	0	.250	31	30	22	11	1	19	1	3	29	8	3.19
Powers, Lethbridge	11	9	3	1	4	5	0	.444	88	103	69	57	7	39	2	7	69	8	5.83
Rathjen, Great Falls	27	0	0	0	2	4	0	.333	63	55	38	27	3	35	0	0	43	5	3.86
Rodas, Lethbridge*	13	13	11	2	12	6	0	.667	49	53	32	22	7	11	2	2	31	8	4.04
Rosenlund, Medicine Hat.	8	3	0	0	1	2	0	1.000	113	81	22	14	3	18	0	4	148	3	1.12
Ruiz, Calgary*	2	1	0	0	1	2	0	.333	18	18	21	12	0	17	1	7	2		6.00
Saatzer, Idaho Falls	12	12	0	0	0	1	0	.000	4	4	4	1	4	0		4			9.00
St. Claire, Calgary	6	6	0	0	1	7	0	.125	50	61	58	37	5	40	1	2	27	6	6.66
St. John, Calgary*	8	8	0	0	1	2	0	.333	33	30	22	16	5	15	0	0	17	2	4.36
Schrimsher, Billings	10	10	1	0	3	2	0	.600	39	48	44	29	5	36	1	0	42	7	6.69
Seiber, Medicine Hat	16	15	1	0	4	2	0	.667	64	59	26	21	2	17	1	4	65	3	2.95
Sensenbrenner, G Falls*	13	13	2	0	6	6	0	.500	92	101	58	33	7	39	0	0	73	11	3.23
Senteney, Medicine Hat	26	3	1	0	2	5	6	.455	78	104	58	48	6	31	0	2	69	2	5.54
Simon, Billings	1	0	0	0	0	0	0	.000	3	1	2	2	1	0	1		9		3.09
L. Smith, Helena	5	5	2	0	0	1	0	.000	1	1	0	0	0	0	0	0			0.00
Soriano, Medicine Hat	18	3	2	0	5	0	0	1.000	36	21	16	10	2	16	0	0	42	4	2.50
Stovall, Great Falls	6	2	0	0	0	1	0	.000	43	59	53	34	3	31	3	5	35	2	7.12
M. T. Sullivan, Billings	8	2	0	0	2	1	0	.500	22	20	14	9	0	10	0	0	15	1	3.68
Terry, Lethbridge*	12	0	0	0	2	2	0	.500	19	25	16	11	2	8	2	0	27	1	5.21
Thomas, Butte	1	0	0	0	2	4	1	.333	26	23	15	8	1	13	0	3	23	2	2.77
Thornton, Great Falls	3	0	0	0	1	0	0	1.000	4	1	1	0	0	0	0	1			3.00
Tkac, Butte*	15	1	0	0	1	2	0	.500	13	12	17	13	1	14	0	0	13	1	9.00
Torres, Calgary	14	14	3	0	6	7	0	.333	25	34	27	25	3	26	0	3	30	4	9.00
Toyfair, Helena	6	6	0	0	3	2	0	.462	92	121	65	58	3	44	3	2	59	5	5.67
Turpin, Idaho Falls	13	2	0	0	2	1	0	.600	27	36	26	17	4	15	0	4	21	3	5.67
Valdez, Medicine Hat	12	0	0	0	2	1	0	.667	32	30	19	16	4	15	1	2	31	3	4.50
Vasquez, Butte	17	0	0	0	1	1	0	.000	22	51	44	38	7	17	0	1	15	3	15.55
Vega, Calgary	15	2	0	0	1	2	1	.333	17	16	7	3	0	10	1	0	23	3	1.59
Walker, Butte*	14	0	0	0	2	3	0	.400	30	47	33	29	3	18	2	4	20	5	8.70
Walling, Butte*	4	0	0	0	4	2	3	.667	40	44	27	19	2	16	0	0	32	2	4.28
F. Warner, Helena*	27	0	0	0	0	0	0	.000	4	4	10	9	0	7	0	3	3	1	20.25
K. White, Calgary*	13	2	0	0	4	1	6	.800	37	20	16	11	0	31	1	3	44	2	2.68
R. White, Lethbridge*	10	2	0	0	1	2	0	.000	26	33	28	25	5	23	0	1	27	5	8.65
Wilczewski, Lethbridge	4	0	0	0	0	1	0	.000	30	44	30	24	4	23	1	0	34	3	7.20
Williams, Great Falls	13	13	5	0	6	7	0	.462	4	8	7	6	0	5	0	0	3		13.50
Winfield, Idaho Falls	25	0	0	0	4	5	1	.462	91	85	53	34	5	53	2	9	81	4	3.36
Wing, Great Falls	3	0	0	0	1	4	13	.200	44	36	23	21	2	21	3	3	62	0	4.30
Wysocki, Idaho Falls	8	0	0	0	0	0	0	.000	15	17	13	10	0	12	0	2	20	1	6.00

BALKS—Borbon, Eichhorn, Gums, Torres, 4 each; Buchanan, 3; Baller, Biggus, Box, Buckley, Goodchild, Johnson, Kellam, Rodas, Sensenbrenner, 2 each; Bennett, Berenguer, Blows, Bradshaw, Brown, Christison, Clarke, DeHart, Dowless, Figueroa, Fiorillo, Galloway, Gambrell, Garrelts, Hinrichs, Kepshire, Kiser, Phillips, Rathjen, Vega, Wysocki, 1 each.

COMBINATION SHUTOUTS—Dowless-Daniels, Fiorillo-Kepshire, Fiorillo-Kepshire-Bangert, Billings; Felt-Rathjen, Great Falls; Dunnegan-Warner, Money-Gums-Warner, Helena.

NO-HIT GAMES—None.

Index to Minor League Clubs, Cities

1980 NL East Clubs' Schedules...

1980	EAST					
	AT CHICAGO	**AT MONTREAL**	**AT NEW YORK**	**AT PHILADELPHIA**	**AT PITTSBURGH**	**AT ST. LOUIS**
CHICAGO		June 2*, 3* 4*, 5* / July 12* (Tn), **13** / Sept. 10*, 11*	April 10,11,12,**13** / Sept. 12*, 13, **14**	June 6*, 7* **8** / July 10*, 11* / Sept. 29* 30* / Oct. 1* 2*	April 14, 16* / Aug. 3*, 4-4, 5* **6** / Oct. 3*, **5**	April 28*, 29* 30 / Aug. 14*15*16*,**17** / Sept. 8*, 9*
MONTREAL	May 26, 27, 28 / Aug. 8, 9-9, **10** / Sept. 24, 25		April 15, 16 / July 3*, 4* (Tn), 5*, **6** / Sept. 16* 17*	April 11*12, **13** / June 24*, 25* 26* / Sept. 26*, 27, **28**	April 29* 30* / May 1 / Aug.15*16*,**17-17** / Sept. 22* 23*	May 30*, 31* / June 1 / Aug. 11*, 12* 13* / Sept. 19*, 20, **21**
NEW YORK	April 17, 19, **20** / June 24, 25-25, 26 / Sept. 22, 23	May 9, 10, **11-11** / Aug. 4*, 5* 6* / Sept. 9* (Tn)		April 21*, 22*, 23* / June 27* 28* (Tn), **29*** / Sept. 24*, 25*	May 30*, 31* / June **1** / Aug. 11*, 12* 13* / Sept. 19*, 20*, **21**	May 26, 27* 28 / Aug. 8*, 9* **10** / Oct. 3*, 4, **5**
PHILADELPHIA	May 30, 31 / June **1** / Aug. 11, 12, 13 / Sept. 19, 20, **21**	April 18, 19, **20** / June 30* / July 1* 2* / Oct. 3*, 4, **5**	April 29* 30* / May 1* / Aug. 14*15*16*, **17** / Sept. 10* 11*		June 2*, 3*, 4* / Aug. 8* 9, **10-10** / Sept. 16* 17*	April 15* 16 / July 3* (Tn), 4, 5* **6** / Sept. 22* 23*
PITTSBURGH	April 25, 26, **27** / Aug. 5, 6, 7 / Sept. 26, 27, **28**	April 21, 22, 23 / June 27* 28* **29** / Sept. 12*, 13, **14**	June 6*, 7, **8-8** / July 10, 11* / Sept. 29, 30 / Oct. 1	May 26* 27* 28* 29 / July 12*, **13**, 14* / Sept. 8* 9*		April 10,11*12,**13** / June 23*, 24* 25* / Sept. 10*, 11*
ST. LOUIS	April 22, 23 / June 27, 28-28, **29** / Sept. 15, 16, 17	June 6*, 7, **8-8** / July 10*, 11* / Sept. 29*, 30* / Oct. 1*	June 3*, 4*, 5* / July 12, **13-13** / Sept. 26*, 27, **28**	April 25* 26* **27** / Aug. 5* 6* 7* / Sept. 12*, 13*, **14**	April 17,18*19,**20** / June 30* / July 1* 2* / Sept. 24*, 25*	
ATLANTA	June 13, 14, **15** / Sept. 1, 2, 3	May 19, 20, 21 / Aug. 1*, 2*, **3**	May 23*, 24, **25** / July 28*, 29*, 30	May 5*, 6*, 7* / July 25*, 26*, **27**	May 2*, 3* **4** / Aug. 25*, 26*, 27*	June 16*, 17* / Aug. 28*, 29*, 30*, **31**
CINCINNATI	June 18, 19 / Sept. 5, 6-6, **7**	May 16, 17, **18** / July 28*, 29* 30*	May 5*, 6*, 7* / July 25* 26, **27**	May 19*, 20* 21* / Aug. 1*, 2* **3**	June 16*, 17* / Aug. 28*, 29*, 30, **31**	June 13*, 14*, **15** / Sept. 1, 2, 3*
HOUSTON	June 16, 17 / Aug. 28, 29, 30, **31**	May 5, 6, 7 / July 25* 26* **27**	May 20*, 21* 22* / Aug. 1*, 2* **3**	May 23*, 24*, **25** / July 28* 29* 30*	June 13*, 14*, **15** / Sept. 1-1, 3*	May 2*, 3* **4** / Aug. 25*, 26*, 27*
LOS ANGELES	May 23, 24, **25** / July 15, 16, 17	June 13*, 14*, **15** / Aug. 19*, 20* 21*	May 9*, 10*, 11* / Aug. 22*, 23, **24**	May 2*, 3, **4** / Aug. 25*, 26*, 27*	May 6*, 7* / July 18*, 19, **20-20**	May 9*, 10*, **11** / July 21*, 22*, 23*
SAN DIEGO	May 6, 7, 8 / July 18, 19, **20**	June 10*, 11* 12* / Aug. 22*, 23*, **24**	May 2*, 3, **4-4** / Aug. 26, 27*	June 13*, 14*, **15** / Aug. 19*, 20* 21	May 20*, 21* 22* / Aug. 1*, 2* **3**	May 23* 24* **25** / July 15*, 16*, 17*
SAN FRANCISCO	May 9, 10, **11** / July 21, 22, 23	May 2, 3, **4-4** / Aug. 25* 27*	June 13*, 14*, **15** / Aug. 19*, 20* 21	June 9*, 10*, 11* / Aug. 22*, 23*, 24*	May 23*, 24*, **25** / July 15*, 16*, 17*	May 5*, 6*, 7 / July 18*, 19*, **20**
1980	13 SUNDAYS / 0 NIGHT GAMES / 2 HOLIDAYS / (Memorial Day) (Labor Day)	13 SUNDAYS / 46 NIGHT GAMES / 2 HOLIDAYS / (Queen's Birthday) (Dominion Day)	13 SUNDAYS / 43 NIGHT GAMES / 1 HOLIDAY / (July 4)	13 SUNDAYS / 65 NIGHT GAMES / 1 HOLIDAY / (Memorial Day)	13 SUNDAYS / 54 NIGHT GAMES / 2 HOLIDAYS / (July 4) (Labor Day)	13 SUNDAYS / 57 NIGHT GAMES / 3 HOLIDAYS / (Memorial Day, July 4) (Labor Day)

* NIGHT GAME   (Tn) — Twi-night
NIGHT GAME: Any game starting after 5:00 p.m.
HEAVY BLACK FIGURES DENOTE SUNDAY

And Complete Slate in NL West

1980	WEST					
	AT ATLANTA	**AT CINCINNATI**	**AT HOUSTON**	**AT LOS ANGELES**	**AT SAN DIEGO**	**AT SAN FRANCISCO**
CHICAGO	June 20†, 21†, **22**† / Aug. 19†, 20†, 21*	May 2†, 3, **4-4** / Aug. 25†, 26*	June 10†, 11†, 12* / Aug. 22†, 23†, **24***	May 12†, 13†, 14* / July 25†, 26†, **27**	May 16†, 17†, **18** / July 28†, 29†, 30*	May 20†, 21* / Aug. 1†, 2, **3-3**
MONTREAL	April 25†, 26†, **27** / July 21†, 22†, 23*	May 23†, 24†, **25** / Sept. 15†, 16†, 17*	May 13†, 14* / July 18†, 19*(Tn), **20***	June 18†, 19* / Aug. 29†, 30†, **31-31**	June 20†, 21†, **22** / Sept. 1†, 2†, 3*	June 16†, 17* / Sept. 4, 5†, 6, **7**
NEW YORK	May 16†, 17†, **18** / July 15†, 16†, 17*	May 13†, 14 / July 18†(Tn), 19†, **20**	April 25†, 26†, **27** / July 21†, 22†, 23*	June 20†, 21†, **22** / Sept. 1, 2†, 3*	June 16†, 17* / Sept. 4†, 5†, 6†, **7**	June 18, 19 / Aug. 29†, 30, **31-31**
PHILADELPHIA	May 13†, 14* / July 18†, 19* (Tn), **20***	May 9†, 10, **11** / July 21†, 22†, 23*	May 16†, 17†, **18** / July 15†, 16†, 17*	June 16†, 17* / Sept. 4†, 5†, 6†, **7**	June 18†, 19 / Aug. 29†, 30*(Tn), **31**	June 20†, 21, **22** / Sept. 1, 2†, 3*
PITTSBURGH	June 18* (Tn), 19* / Sept. 5†, 6, **7**	June 10†, 11†, 12 / Aug. 22†, 23†, **24**	June 20†, 21†, **22**† / Aug. 19†, 20†, 21*	May 16†, 17†, **18** / July 28†, 29†, 30*	May 9†, 10†, **11** / July 22†, 23†, 24*	May 13†, 14, 15 / July 25†, 26, **27**
ST. LOUIS	June 9†, 10†, 11* / Aug. 22†, 23†, **24***	June 20†, 21, **22** / Aug. 18†, 19†, 20*	June 18†, 19* / Sept. 5†, 6* (Tn), **7***	May 19†, 20†, 21* / Aug. 1†, 2†, **3**	May 13†, 14†, 15* / July 25†, 26†, **27**	May 16†, 17, 18 / July 29†, 30, 31*
ATLANTA		April 9, 11†, 12, **13** / June 24†, 25* / Oct. 3†, 4, **5**	April 14†, 15* / July12†, **13**† (Tn), 14* / Sept. 30* / Oct. 1†, 2*	May 29†, 30†, 31* / June **1** / Aug. 11†, 12†, 13* / Sept. 22†, 23*	April 28†, 29†, 30* / May **1** / June 27†, 28†, **29** / Sept. 19†, 20*	June 2†, 3†, 4 / Aug. 14, 15†, 16, **17** / Sept. 17†, 18
CINCINNATI	April 17†, 18†, 19†, **20** / July 10†, 11* / Sept. 8†, 9†, 10*		April 21†, 22†, 23* / June 27†, 28†, **29** / Sept. 26†, 27, **28**	June 2†, 3†, 4* / Aug. 15†, 16, **17** / Sept. 19†, 20†, **21**	May 29†, 30†, 31* / June **1** / Aug. 11†, 12†, 13* / Sept. 24†, 25	April 25†, 26, **27** / June 30* / July 1†, 2†, 3 / Sept. 22†, 23*
HOUSTON	May 9†, 10†, **11** / June 30* / July 1†, 2†, 3* / Sept. 24†, 25*	April 29†, 30* / May 1* / July 4†, 5* (Tn), **6** / Sept. 17†, 18		April 17†, 18†, 19†, **20** / July 10†, 11* / Oct. 3†, 4, **5**	June 2†, 3†, 4* / Aug. 14, 15† **17-17** / Sept. 22†, 23	May 30†, 31 / June **1** / Aug. 11†, 12†, 13 / Sept. 19†, 20, **21**
LOS ANGELES	June 6†, 7†, **8*** / Aug. 4†, 5†, 6†, 7* / Sept. 15†, 16*	May 26-26, 27* / Aug. 8†, 9†, **10** / Sept. 12†, 13†, **14**	April 10†,11†12, **13** / June 23†, 24†, 25* / Sept. 9†, 10*		April 14†, 15†, 16* / July 12†, **13**†, 14 / Sept. 26†, 27†, **28**	April 29†, 30* / June 27†, 28, **29-29** / Sept. 30* / Oct. 1†, 2*
SAN DIEGO	April 22†, 23†, 24* / July 4†, 5†, **6** / Sept. 12†, 13†, **14**	June 6†, 7†, **8**, 9* / Aug. 4†, 5†, 6 / Sept. 30* / Oct. 1*	May 26†, 27†, 28* / Aug. 7†, 8†, 9†, **10** / Sept. 15†, 16*	April 25†, 26†, **27** / June 30* / July 1†, 2†, 3 / Sept. 17†, 18*		April 17, 18†, 19, **20** / July 10†, 11 / Oct. 3†, 4, **5**
SAN FRANCISCO	May 26†, 27†, 28* / Aug. 8†, 9†, **10** / Sept. 26†, 27†, **28**	April 14†, 15†, 16 / July 12†(Tn), **13,** 14* / Sept. 15, 16	June 6†, 7†, **8*** / Aug. 4†, 5†, 6* / Sept. 12†, 13†, **14***	April 21†, 22†, 23†, 24* / July 4†, 5†, **6** / Sept. 24†, 25	April 10†, 11†, 12†, **13** / June 24†, 25†, 26* / Sept. 9†, 10*	
1980	13 SUNDAYS / 72 NIGHT GAMES / 2 HOLIDAYS / (Memorial Day) / (Labor Day)	13 SUNDAYS / 53 NIGHT GAMES / 2 HOLIDAYS / (Memorial Day) / (Labor Day)	13 SUNDAYS / 73 NIGHT GAMES / 1 HOLIDAY / (Memorial Day)	13 SUNDAYS / 61 NIGHT GAMES / 2 HOLIDAYS / (July 4) / (Labor Day)	12 SUNDAYS / 62 NIGHT GAMES / 1 HOLIDAY / (Labor Day)	13 SUNDAYS / 38 NIGHT GAMES / 1 HOLIDAY / (Labor Day)

JULY 8—ALL STAR GAME AT LOS ANGELES
AUGUST 4—HALL OF FAME GAME AT COOPERSTOWN, NY (Pittsburgh vs. Chicago AL)

1980 AL East Game Schedules...

1980	EAST						
	AT MILWAUKEE	**AT DETROIT**	**AT CLEVELAND**	**AT TORONTO**	**AT BALTIMORE**	**AT NEW YORK**	**AT BOSTON**
SEATTLE............	May (26), 27*, 28* Sept. 19*, 20*, **21**	June 2*, 3*, 4* Aug. 1*, 2*, **3**	May 30*, 31* June 1 July 28*, 29*, 30*	May 13*, 14*, 15* July 25*, 26*, **27**	June 20*, 21*, **22** Sept. (1)*, 2*, 3*	June 16*, 17* Aug. 28*, 29*, 30*, **31**	June 18*, 19* Sept. 4*, 5*, 6, **7**
OAKLAND	June 30* July 1*, 2*, 3* Oct. 4, **5**	May 13*, 14* July 25*, 26*, **27-27**	June 2*, 3*, 4* Aug. 1*, 2*, **3**	May 16*, 17, **18** July 28*, 29*, 30*	June 18*, 19* Sept. 4*, 5*, 6*, **7**	June 20*, 21, **22** Sept. (1), 2*, 3*	June 16*, 17* Aug. 28*, 29*, 30*, **31**
CALIFORNIA	July (4), 5*, **6** Sept. 22*, 23*, 24*	May 30*, 31 June **1** July 25*, 26, **27-27**	May 13*, 14* July 25*, 26, **27-27**	June 2*, 3*, 4* July 1, 2, **3**	June 16*, 17* Aug. 28*, 29*, 30*, **31**	June 18*, 19* Sept. 4*, 5*, 6*, **7**	June 20*, 21, **22** Sept. (1)*, 2*, 3*
TEXAS	June 10*, 11*, 12 Sept. 5*, 6*, **7**	April 29, 30 Aug. 15*, 16, **17-17**	April 25*, 26, **27** Aug. 12*, 13*, 14*	June 13*, 14, **15** Aug. 25, 26, 27	July 12*, 13*, 14* July 18*, 19*, **20**	May 16*, 17*, **18** Aug. 4*, 5*, 6*	April 18, 19, **20** July 21*, 22*, 23*
KANSAS CITY	June 13*, 14, **15** Aug. 25*, 26*, 27*	April 18, 19, **20** Aug. 4*, 5*, 6*	June 9*, 10*, 11* Sept. 5*, 6*, **7**	April 28*, 29*, 30* Aug. 8*, 9*, **10**	April 15, 16*, 17* July 12*, **13**, 14*	May 12*, 13*, 14* July 18*, 19*, **20**	May 9*, 10, **11** July 15*, 16*, 17*
MINNESOTA	May 23*, 24*, **25** Sept. 16*, 17*, 18*	June 10*, 11*, 12* Sept. 5*, 6, **7**	June 13*, 14*, **15** Aug. 25*, 26*, 27*	June 16*, 17* Aug. 28, 29, 30, **31**	May 5*, 6*, 7* Aug. 1*, 2*, **3**	May 9*, 10*, **11** July 15*, 16*, 17*	May 12*, 13*, 14* July 18*, 19, **20**
CHICAGO	May 13*, 14*, 15 July 18*, 19*, **20**	June 13*, 14, **15** Sept. (1)*, 2*, 3*	June 16*, 17* Aug. 29*, 30*, **31-31**	June 18 TN, 19* Sept. 4*, 5*, **7**	April 18*, 19*, **20** Aug. 5*, 6*, 7*	April 25*, 26*, **27** Aug. 11*, 12*, 13*	April 21, 22, 23 Aug. 8*, 9, **10**
MILWAUKEE		June 16 TN, 17* Aug. 28*, 29*, 30*, **31**	April 29*, 30* Aug. 15*, 16, **17-17**	April 14, 16, 17 July 12, **13**, 14*	June 2*, 3*, 4* July 25*, 26*, **27**	April 18, 19, **20** July 21*, 22 TN, 23*	May 30*, 31 June **1** Aug. 4*, 5*, 6*, 7*
DETROIT	June 6*, 7*, **8** Aug. 18*, 19*, 20*		June 23*, 24*, **25** Sept. 12*, 13, **14-14**	June 27*, 28, **29** Sept. 29*, 30* Oct. 1*	May 22*, 23*, 24*, **25** Sept. 16*, 17*, 18*	May (26), 27*, 28* Oct. 2*, 3*, 4, **5**	April 14, 16, 17 July 12*, **13**, 14*
CLEVELAND	April 21*, 22*, 23* Aug. 8*, 9, **10-10**	June 30* July 1*, 2* Sept. 19*, 20, **21**		May 1*, 2*, 3, **4-4** July 10*, 11*	May (26)*, 27*, 28* Oct. 3*, 4*, **5**	June 27*, 28*, **29** Sept. 22*, 23*, 24*, 25*	May 23*, 24, **25** Sept. 16*, 17*, 18*
TORONTO	April 25*, 26, **27** Aug. 12 TN, 13*, 14	July 3*, (4)*, 5, **6** Sept. 22*, 23*, 24*	April 19, **20** Aug. 4*, 5*, 6*, 7*		June 24*, 25*, 26* Sept. 19*, 20*, **21**	May 30*, 31* June **1** Sept. 16*, 17*, 18*	May (26)*, 27*, 28* Oct. 2*, 3, 4, **5**
BALTIMORE	May 8*, 9*, 10, **11** July 15*, 16*, 17	May 16*, 17, **18** Sept. 8*, 9*, 10*	May 19*, 20 TN, 21* Sept. 26*, 27, **28**	June 30* July 1*, 2* Sept. 11*, 12*, 13, **14**		April 21*, 22*, 23* Aug. 8*, 9*, **10**	June 27*, 28, **29** Sept. 29*, 30* Oct. 1*
NEW YORK	May 6*, 7* July 31* Aug. 1*, 2*, **3**	May 19*, 20*, 21* Sept. 26*, 27, **28**	July 3*, (4), 5*, **6** Sept. 30* Oct. 1*	May 22*, 23*, 24, **25** Sept. 8*, 9*, 10*	April 28*, 29*, 30* Aug. 14*, 15*, 16*, **17**		June 30* July 1*, 2* Sept. 11*, 12*, 13, **14**
BOSTON............	April 10, 11*, 12, **13** July 10*, 11*	April 25, 26, **27** Aug. 11*, 12*, 13*, 14*	May 15*, 16*, 17, **18** Sept. 8*, 9*, 10*	May 19, 20*, 21* Sept. 26*, 27, **28**	July 3*, (4)*, 5, **6** Sept. 22*, 23*, 24*	June 23*, 24*, 25* Sept. 19*, 20, **21**	
1980	79 HOME DATES 54 NIGHTS	78 HOME DATES 51 NIGHTS	76 HOME DATES 55 NIGHTS	79 HOME DATES 47 NIGHTS	81 HOME DATES 66 NIGHTS	80 HOME DATES 61 NIGHTS	81 HOME DATES 48 NIGHTS

JULY 8—ALL STAR GAME AT LOS ANGELES
AUGUST 4—HALL OF FAME GAME AT COOPERSTOWN, NY (Pittsburgh vs. Chicago AL)

When and Where in AL West

1980	WEST						
	AT SEATTLE	**AT OAKLAND**	**AT CALIFORNIA**	**AT TEXAS**	**AT KANSAS CITY**	**AT MINNESOTA**	**AT CHICAGO**
SEATTLE............		April 14* 15* 16 Aug. 8* 9, **10-10**	May 1* 2* 3* **4** Aug. 4* 5* 6*	June 24* 25* 26* Oct. 3* 4* **5**	July 3* (4)* 5* **6** Sept. 30* Oct. 1* 2*	April 28, 29, 30 July 12* **13**, 14	May 16* 17* **18** Sept. 8* 9* 10
OAKLAND	April 21* 22* 23* Aug. 15* 16* **17**		April 28* 29* 30* July 12* **13**, 14*	May 30* 31* June **1*** Sept. 15* 16* 17* 18*	May 19* 20* 21* 22* Sept. 19* 20* **21**	April 25, 26, **27** Aug. 12* 13* 14	July (4), 5, **6-6** Sept. 30 Oct. 1, 2
CALIFORNIA	April 25* 26* **27** Aug. 12* 13* 14*	April 18* 19, **20-20** July 10 TN, 11*		May 19* 20* 21* 22* Sept. 19* 20* **21**	May 16* 17* **18** Sept. 16* 17* 18*	April 22, 23 Aug. 15* 16, **17-17**	June 30* July 1* 2* 3* Oct. 3* **4, 5**
TEXAS................	June 30* July 1* 2 Sept. 25* 26* 27* **28**	May 23* 24, **25** Sept. 8* 9, 10	May (26), 27* 28* Sept. 12* 13* **14**		June 16* 17* Aug. 28* 29* 30, **31**	July 3* (4)* 5, **6** Sept. 22* 23* 24*	June 2* 3* 4* July 25* 26 TN, **27**
KANSAS CITY	June 27* 28* **29** Sept. 22* 23* 24*	May (26), 27* 28 Sept. 12* 13, **14**	May 23* 24* **25** Sept. 8* 9* 10* 11*	June 5* 6* 7*, **8*** Aug. 18* 19* 20*		June 23* 24 TN, 25* Sept. 26* 27, **28**	May 6* 7* **8*** Aug. 1* 2* **3**
MINNESOTA	April 17* 18 TN, 19* **20** July 10* 11* .	April 10* 11* 12, **13** Aug. 4* 5* 6	April 14* 15* 16* Aug. 7* 8* 9* **10**	June 27* 28* **29*** Sept. 30* Oct. 1* 2*	June 30* July 1* 2* Oct. 3* 4* **5**		May 19* 20* 21* Sept. 12* 13* **14**
CHICAGO	May 23* 24* **25** Sept. 15* 16* 17* 18*	June 27* 28, **29** Sept. 23* 24* 25	June 24* 25* 26* Sept. 26* 27, **28**	May 9* 10* **11*** July 15* 16* 17*	May 30* 31* June **1** July 21* 22* 23* 24*	May (26)* 27* 28* **29** Sept. 19* 20* **21**	
MILWAUKEE	May 19* 20* 21* Sept. 12* 13* **14**	June 23* 24* 25 Sept. 26* 27, **28**	June 27* 28* **29** Sept. 29* 30* Oct. 1*	June 18* 19* Aug. 22 TN, 23* **24**	June 20* 21* **22** Sept. (1)* 3* 4*	May 16* 17, **18** Sept. 9* 10* 11	May 2* 3* **4**, 5* July 29* 30*
DETROIT	May 6* 7* **8*** July 18* 19* 20*	May 2* 3, **4-4** July 16* 17	May 9* 10* **11** July 21* 22* 23*	April 21* 22* 23* Aug. 8* 9* **10***	April 10* 11* 12, **13** July 10* 11*	June 18* 19 Aug. 21* 22* 23, **24**	June 20* 21, **22-22** Aug. 26* 27*
CLEVELAND	May 9* 10* **11** July 21* 22* 23*	May 5* 6* 7 . July 18* 19, **20**	April 11* 12* **13** July 15* 16* 17*	April 14* 15* 16* July 12* 13* **14***	June 18* 19* Aug. 21* 22* 23* **24**	June 20* 21, **22** Sept. (1)* 2* 3*	June 6* 7* **8** Aug. 18* 19* 20
TORONTO	April 9* 11* 12* **13** July 16* 17*	May 9, 10, **11** July 21* 22* 23	May 6* 7* **8*** July 18* 19* **20**	June 20* 21* **22*** Sept. (1)* 2* 3*	April 22* 23* **24** July 15* 16* **17**	June 5* 6* 7, **8** Aug. 19* 20*	June 10* 11* **11** Aug* 21* 22* 23* **24**
BALTIMORE	June 12* 13* 14* **15** Aug. 25* 26*	June 9* 10* 11 Aug. 22, 23, **24**	June 6* 7* **8** Aug. 19* 20* 21*	May 2* 3* **4*** Aug. 29* 30* 31*	April 25* 26, **27** Aug. 11* 12* 13*	May 30* 31 June **1** July 21* 22* 23*	April 10, 11, 12, **13** July 10* 11*
NEW YORK	June 6* 7* **8*** Aug. 19* 20* 21*	June 13 TN, 14, **15** Aug. 25* 26*	June 9, 10* 11* Aug. 22, 23, **24**	April 10* 11* 12, **13** July 10* 11*	June 2* 3* 4* July 25* 26* **27**	May 2* 3, **4** July 28* 29* 30*	April 14* 15* 16* July 12* **13**, 14*
BOSTON............	June 9* 10* 11* Aug. 22* 23* 24*	June 6* 7, **8** Aug. 19* 20* 21	June 12* 13* 14, **15** Aug. 25, 26*	May 5* 6* 7* Aug. 1* 2* **3**	May 2* 3* **4** July 29* 30* 31*	June 2* 3* 4* July 25* 26, **27**	April 28* 29* 30* Aug. 15* 16* **17**
1980	80 HOME DATES 71 NIGHTS	76 HOME DATES 40 NIGHTS	81 HOME DATES 62 NIGHTS	80 HOME DATES 75 NIGHTS	81 HOME DATES 65 NIGHTS	79 HOME DATES 45 NIGHTS	78 HOME DATES 54 NIGHTS

*—NIGHT GAME   TN—Twi-night   ( )—Holiday
HEAVY BLACK FIGURES DENOTE SUNDAY

Index to Contents

AMERICAN LEAGUE

NATIONAL LEAGUE

1979 Game Scores

1979 Game Scores

NATIONAL ASSOCIATION (MINOR LEAGUE) AVERAGES